Doug Pratt's

DVD-Video

Guide

Also By Douglas Pratt

Laser Video Disc Companion

Doug Pratt's DVD-Video Guide

More than 2,000 reviews of the best DVD-Videos

Douglas Pratt

With a Preface by James Monaco

New York   Sag Harbor
Harbor Electronic Publishing
2000

Library of Congress Catalogue Card Number: 99-066739

ISBN (paper): 0-9669744-4-1
ISBN (cloth): 0-9669744-5-X

First printing December 1999

Printed in the United States of America

CREDITS
Design Director: David Lindroth.

Editorial Assistance: Anne Sanow, Jill Meadows.

A NOTE ON THE TYPE

This edition of *Doug Pratt's DVD-Video Guide* is set in Adobe's release of Minion. Designed in 1990 by Robert Slimbach, Minion is one of the first purely digital faces—an Adobe Original. Slimbach was inspired by oldstyle typefaces of the late Renaissance, a period of highly readable designs. The display types are Gill Sans and Trade Gothic.

The book was set by UNET 2 Corporation and printed and bound by Sheridan Books at their Ann Arbor MI plant.

A NOTE ON THE COVER

A screen from the commentary track of the DVD release of *Ghostbusters*, courtesy of Columbia Pictures—a landmark for its creative use of the DVD-Video medium. Associate producer Joe Medjuck is on the left, producer-director Ivan Reitman is on the right, and screenwriter Harold Ramis is in the center. The disc was produced by Alita Holly. Morgan Holly served as technical director. Medjuck was a founder of Criterion, the company that set the model for laserdiscs—and hence DVDs—with their careful, extensively annotated productions; Morgan Holly and Alita Holly were both principals in Criterion.

WWW.DVDLaser.com

For

Loretta

Table of Contents

Preface

by James Monaco

A Short History of DVD

Introduced to the market in April 1997, DVD has exploded on the home-video scene. It has been the most rapidly accepted consumer electronics product ever, having been adopted almost three times more quickly by fans than the VCR. It's easy to see why: DVD offers exceptional picture and sound quality at a very reasonable price. But like all overnight successes, DVD had a lengthy prehistory. A lot of other technologies had to develop slowly and sometimes painfully before DVD could become such an 'instant' success.

Here's how it happened.

In the early seventies both Philips and Sony began working on the concept of encoding audio and video on plastic discs using a laser to first write, then read the information. The laser, invented in the early sixties, allows a light beam to be focused extremely narrowly so that it can write huge quantities of information on a receptive disc, and both companies saw great possibilities in this new recording technique. Philips and Sony, who were to collaborate on many electronics innovations in the 1980s and 1990s, took different paths at first. Sony concentrated on just capturing an audio signal. Meanwhile, Philips decided to apply the laser technology to video as well as audio. Because a video signal involves hundreds of times as much information as an audio signal you might think Philips had taken on a much more daunting challenge than Sony. But Sony had added an extra layer of technological complexity to their self-imposed task by deciding to digitize the original analog audio signal. As a result, it took them several years longer to bring their product to market.

Understanding the importance of software to the successful introduction of a new consumer-electronics technology, Philips formed a partnership with MCA (the corporate umbrella for Universal Pictures). The MCA-Philips Discovision system was announced for the 1975 Christmas selling season. But it wasn't ready in time. It didn't make it the next year either, or the next. Finally, in late 1978 Philips began test-marketing their system in Atlanta and Seattle. It was another year before the product was rolled out nationally.

Meanwhile, a surprising thing had happened. Sony had introduced their Beta videocassette technology to the consumer market in 1976 (the year after the Philips video disc was *supposed* to go on the market). No one had much expectation for videocassettes. After all, Sony's own reel-to-reel consumer videotape system had been on the market since 1970 and wasn't very successful, and Philips's audiocassette technology dated from 1963 and hadn't set the world on fire. Why should videocassettes do any better in the marketplace?

Well, they did.

By the time the video disc finally had a toe-hold in the marketplace consumers had become comfortable with the videocassette format. Hollywood had started releasing cassette versions of popular movies and cassette rental stores started springing up in neighborhoods across the country. No one had forecast this use of the medium. It just happened, because it made sense.

It didn't matter that the Philips laserdisc format (the Discovision brand name was soon dropped) offered twice the quality of videocassettes. It didn't matter that laserdiscs beat out competing physical-record videodisc technologies from RCA and Telefunken. It didn't matter that laserdiscs were easier to produce and longer-lasting than videotapes. The VCR was king, and would remain so for more than twenty years. The laserdisc was relegated to the status of film-buff format. Not until 1990, more than ten years after its introduction, did the installed base of laserdisc players reach one million (a goal DVD players achieved in less than two years).

Meanwhile, back at the Sony ranch, work on the audio laser record progressed even more slowly, thanks to the added challenge of digitization. However, when the Compact Disc (as it was unimaginatively named) was finally introduced in 1982, it quickly rose to dominance in the audio market. The extra work of digitization appeared to be worth the trouble. Consumers liked the clean sound and easy maintenance of the CD (even if audiophiles turned up their noses). By the end of the 1980s the CD was outselling the 105-year-old technology of vinyl records.

After the debut of the CD, Sony and Philips began to collaborate. They jointly introduced the CD-ROM in 1985. Since the audio CD was digital it could store any kind of information. The CD-ROM format attempted to utilize that technology for computer applications. The idea of producing multimedia on CD quickly took hold. If everything was digitized you could mix text, audio, video—whatever—on the same disc! But, as we noted earlier, the job of digitizing video was several hundred times more difficult than digitizing audio.

In 1989 the Voyager Company introduced its *CD Companion to Beethoven's 9th*, by Robert Winter, a landmark in multimedia (even though it didn't use any movie video). It's interesting to note that Voyager was an offshoot of Criterion, the company founded by Bob Stein, Aleen Stein, Joe Medjuck, and Roger Smith in the early 1980s, that was also responsible for the landmark laserdiscs *Citizen Kane* and *King Kong* (1984), which served as models for that medium—and hence for the next generation of DVDs.

In 1991 Apple Computer introduced the QuickTime architecture to serve as a basis for digital video and audio. Shortly after, movers and shakers in the industry started to think about the next generation of CD. Lasers with shorter wavelengths could write lots more information on the same polycarbonate disc that was used for old-fashioned audio CDs.[*] (By this time, thanks to Moore's Law, computer microprocessors were several magnitudes more powerful than they were in the days when audio CD was first introduced.)

Two camps soon developed: Sony/Philips proposed one standard for this advanced technology that was eventually to be named DVD; a group led by Toshiba and Time Warner proposed another standard—perhaps aware of the royalties that accrued to Sony every time a CD was sold. By the end of 1995 the two groups had compromised on the dual layer/double-sided DVD format we know today. The stage was set for the introduction of a new entertainment medium.

The first DVD players went on sale in April 1997, and the rest of the story you know. Within two years players were selling for less than $200, and thousands of feature films and other video products were available for purchase at price points less than $30, or for rental at your local video store or on the Web. DVD was established as the essential medium of audio-video product: an overnight success.

And it only took twenty years!

About Douglas Pratt

Douglas Pratt is uniquely qualified to write this book. He has been reviewing laserdiscs (and now DVDs) for seventeen years. As publisher, editor, and writer of the *DVD-Laser Disc Newsletter*—the insider's guide to the medium—he has established a reputation as the premier critic of films and other presentations on optical media.

Doug is far and away the most prolific film or media critics working today, logging between 1,200 and 1,500 reviews each year. (His entry in the annual *Media Review Digest* is always ten times longer than the listing for his nearest competitor.) There are very few writers indeed who have the vast experience necessary to produce an encyclopedia as comprehensive as the book you hold in your hands, and Doug is one of them.

It all started more than twenty years ago in the repertory houses of New York City where Doug—like most film critics of his generation—first discovered the joys of old movies, foreign cinema, and avant-garde film.

---

[*] It's worth noting that even though the DVD format stores from seven to 28 times as many bits and bytes as the old audio CD format that isn't nearly enough to record an hour or two of video. In order to do that, the raw signal has to be compressed as much as 100:1! The real heroes of the DVD revolution aren't the laser technicians but the practical mathematicians who figured out the 'codecs' that accomplish this feat.

Today, wherever you are, you have easy access to these movies through the Internet. If you hear about a new film you want to see you can probably buy or rent it (on video) within a few months of its theatrical release. But it wasn't that easy twenty years ago. Before video, if you didn't live near a repertory house or an art house it was impossible to see the obscure, the rare, the old. The best you could do was read about them.

At the time, Doug was working in the banking industry as a data communications specialist—but always with an eye to writing about his first love—film. He bought his first Laserdisc player in 1981 and immediately started collecting discs. After three years of frustration, trying to find out which discs were released and which were scheduled for release, he realized he had found his niche and started the *Laser Disc Newsletter* in 1984. The *Newsletter* quickly became the key information source for fans of the new medium, and Doug was launched on an odyssey of discovery.

As he notes in his online bio:

> Reviewing home video for a living is an incredibly satisfying vocation. Not only is it something I can do in my stocking feet and in the company of my family, but it has afforded me the opportunity to view the widest possible array of new and old motion pictures, musical programs, documentaries and other, uncategorizable programs. I consider the knowledge gained from exposure to these programs on a daily basis to be invaluable.

Here lies the key to Doug Pratt's unique position as a media critic. While film critics have been stuck for the last thirty years talking about an increasingly homogenous mix of Hollywood and independent product, Doug has been free to write about a wide range of artistic endeavor. From grand opera to sex, from historical essays to what we used to call travelogues, from classic cinema to the latest teenage blockbusters, Doug has seen it all these last seventeen years—and written about it all.

He is especially proud of the role the *DVD-Laser Disc Newsletter* has played in advancing the cause of film preservation. When the laserdisc medium was first introduced, distributors paid as little attention to the quality of the discs as they did to the quality of the VHS tapes that were bringing in so much unexpected cash. Pratt's newsletter was instrumental in convincing the studios that it was to their benefit to pay attention to production values. Gradually, more and more films were released in letterboxed versions, producers took care in the transfer process, and—following the lead of Criterion—released their discs with informative ancillary tracks. All of this prepared the model for the DVD-Video format that we know today. The newsletter also helped to bridge the gap between the studios and suspicious collectors, resulting in a richer film heritage for us all.

Finally, Doug Pratt brings to this wide-ranging critical purview a lot of common sense and a rare wit. You probably bought this book because you needed a good guide to DVD-Video product (and you got it), but I think you are going to be pleasantly surprised to discover that *Doug Pratt's DVD-Video Guide* is more than just a consumer handbook: it's also an amusing, insightful, and wide-ranging survey of our culture at the turn of the century.

Introduction

The New World of DVD

Some movies cost more than $100 million to produce and involve the efforts of more than two thousand people, and with a DVD you can take that finished product and place it in your jacket pocket. In fact, you can fit several of them in your pocket. You can put in action films, romances, science fiction movies, comedies, a TV miniseries or two, several operas, rock concerts and UFO documentaries, and still have room for your gloves. Yet from these 4-5/8-inch wide, 1 millimeter thick platters you can project a program with a picture and sound quality that rivals the projection in all but the finest first-run movie theaters—and even challenges those after they've played the same print for a couple weeks.

DVDs are awesome! The better the picture and sound are, the more your subconscious believes that what you are watching and listening to is reality, and so the more you are entertained. It is highly likely that at some point in your life you will watch a movie on some other medium and not be impressed with it, and then watch it later on DVD and be enraptured. With the improved quality there are more nuances for your brain to feed upon, there is more to enjoy.

The essence of a movie's picture and sound is interpreted as ones and zeroes and then compressed onto the DVD as microscopic pits to be read by a laser beam, a logical extension of the process that first takes reality and breaks it into 24 frames per second of grainy emulsions on film. The image is then reconstructed by digital and electronic sleights of hand, a process that is different only in style from the analog sleight of hand that video formats have traditionally employed.

A natural successor to the digitized Compact Disc (CD) and the analog Laser Video Disc (LD), the DVD was first taken to stand for 'Digital Video Disc,' then, when its functions were fully understood, 'Digital Versatile Disc,' but finally, for brevity's sake, standing for nothing whatsoever. Advancements in laser technology and imprinting have enabled a silver-sheen single-layer DVD to hold about 135 minutes of a movie with various audio tracks, and a gold-sheen dual-layer DVD can hold about twice that much. And that is just on one side—many DVDs have dual-sided programming.

The first DVDs appeared in stores in March of 1997. In just two years, the popularity of the format exploded faster than any home video medium had ever taken hold before. Scores of new titles are being gobbled up by consumers every month, while DVD players and DVD-ROM drives for personal computers are flying out the doors of electronics retailers. The ability of a PC to play a DVD has created a whole new entertainment dynamic—often giving junior a better audio-video system on his desktop than his parents have in the living room—and it insures that DVDs are in no way a passing fad but are instead an inevitable and assured step in the march of technology and consumer electronics. Indeed, with a properly endowed laptop PC or a miniature DVD player, you can now watch that $100 million dollar movie as you walk down the street.

As an outgrowth of the LD market, which was heavily collector-oriented, DVDs often contain more than just a film. Multiple audio track capabilities allow the movie to be played back in several different languages, and provide the opportunities for one or even several 'commentary' tracks, in which the filmmakers or interested bystanders talk about the production and inner workings of a movie as it unspools. Usually you can toggle between these tracks with the press of a button. Many programs can also be supported by optional subtitles, again a function that usually can be activated or deactivated at the press of a button. (In addition to subtitling, many DVDs also retain the traditional closed captioning, which requires a monitor selection or special de-captioning unit to activate.)

Because most movies run somewhere between 90 minutes and 2 hours, there can be room left on a DVD for documentaries about the film's production, 'outtakes,' bloopers, and other footage that, for whatever reason, did not make it into the original film. There are also trailers, music videos, production photos, drawings, essays and other supporting materials, all of which can enhance your appreciation and love of the film at hand. The picture quality on the best-looking DVDs is absolutely incredible. So detailed, so vivid and so smooth, your monitor looks more like a window than a screen. The picture, of course, can be compromised by the quality of the transfer and the effort that has gone into the compression process. If weak source material has been utilized, or if a movie is so old or so beyond Hollywood that it only exists as an iteration of weak source material, then there is nothing the DVD playback can do to make it look or sound any better than it is. There are times, as well, when video companies do not bend over backwards to use the finest source material available or follow through on the accuracy of its transition to video. The biggest problem with this is that once you've seen a really, really good-looking DVD, it is difficult to be patient with one that is less immaculate.

Some movies are shot with a wide, rectangular framing and others are shot with a squarish framing. Letterboxing, which includes black bands at the top and bottom of the screen, enables one to view each movie as it was originally intended to be viewed in the movie theater. Full screen or cropped framing allows the viewer to make full use of the video monitor. It makes great sense to us that both versions be issued on one DVD whenever possible, so that viewers can have a choice, or even an alternative. Some movies were shot in widescreen, period, and when they are shown on the monitor in full they are cropped. Others, however, are shot in full screen, either with the intention of being projected in the same manner or to be projected with the top and/or bottom of the image masked off. When these movies appear, it is often the letterboxed version that loses more picture information, and it is on a case-by-case basis that the quality of the direction and cinematography makes the letterboxed presentation a more valid or more satisfying presentation (because of balanced screen compositions) than the full screen version. When we identify an image as cropped, we mean it has been cropped. When we identify an image as being in 'full screen' format, we mean that a little may be missing off the sides, and that intentional masking may be missing from the top and bottom of the image, but that nothing major has been removed from the frame. When we refer to an image as being windowboxed, it means that all four edges of the frame are set apart from the edges of the viewing screen, though this may not be evident on all monitors.

In the early days of DVDs, data compression flaws were a widespread problem, but DVD producers gradually figured out the best methods for circumventing those errors. It didn't take long before digital artifacting—which could appear as smears, tiling, object displacement, movement ratcheting, or more obvious blotches—was brought under control, and now it is usually found only on the less expensive DVDs, where less care is taken with the mastering process. Even the most meticulous compression efforts, however, can sometimes be tripped up by older, unstable source material. When we refer to sampling rates in a review, we are referring to how much data compression has been executed. It is an art, not a science, and poorly applied high sampling rates can sometimes still have more artifacting than smartly applied lower sampling rates. As a rule of thumb, however, the higher the sampling rate, the purer the image.

A program encoded on a DVD platter should still be playable long after the last player on Earth breaks down, but discs must be properly handled. If you smudge them with fingerprints or other contaminants, the picture will lock, or break up into a checkerboard pattern, or simply won't play at all. Fortunately, cleaning the surface with a slightly damp cloth and then drying it well removes the smudges and enables the program to play through as if nothing had happened. We hate the cases DVDs come in, because they take up more than 15 times the space a DVD itself takes up, but it is important to keep the discs protected in something, because even minor scratches can cause digital gibberish to appear on the screen and prevent play.

There are three different audio formats that can appear on a DVD—the PCM format, which is a basic digital audio formula that allows for standard monophonic and stereophonic playback; the Dolby Digital format, which contains more data and routes independent audio signals to as many as five different positions (center, right forward, left forward, right rear and left rear), as well as a subwoofer signal (often referred to as '.1,' so that a fully loaded Dolby Digital track would offer '5.1' channels); and DTS, which functions like Dolby Digital but supposedly contains even more audio data. Although there is often a marked difference between a PCM mono track and a Dolby Digital mono track, there seems to be less of a variation between a PCM 2-channel track and a Dolby 2-channel, though from that point forward the more channels added to the Dolby track the more sophisticated it becomes—most of the time. The differences between Dolby Digital and DTS tracks, so far, have been slight.

Before DVDs came along, LDs offered the best video playback, but even the most meticulously produced LD can appear to be soft and unagressively colored when compared to even a modestly well-produced DVD. The audio, however, is another matter. The audio on an LD often has a fuller sound than the audio on a DVD, though there are exceptions. LDs rarely use Dolby Digital for monophonic playback, and a Dolby Digital mono DVD track is usually on par with a standard LD mono track. On contemporary films that have Dolby Digital 5.1 mixes but not elaborate sound editing, the audio on a well-made DVD is usually indistinguishable from the audio on an LD. This is even true of some of the bigger blockbuster efforts, but not of all of them, and not of older stereo audio tracks either, where LD tends to deliver a more complete sound.

And then there is DTS. Generally, DTS LDs have far and away the best sound of all—more detailed than either standard LDs or DTS DVDs—and fans generally concede that for the ultimate playback of a popular film, it would be ideal to synch up the picture from a DVD and the sound from a DTS LD.

Most enthusiasts, however, will find that the Dolby Digital tracks on the DVDs are terrific. With the best action movies or IMAX documentaries, the Dolby Digital 5.1 channel playback turns your viewing room into a thrill ride, sweeping you up in the aural detail and atmosphere of a location or an activity and not letting you go until it is over.

Whenever a new format is introduced, there are always a few bugs. Some first generation players were unable to play all DVDs, but those problems have since been eradicated. DVDs are more like computer programs than other home video programs in one respect—there are aspects of the playback that they control and you do not. We estimated once that with all the DVDs we review, we spend an entire day each year watching nothing but opening logos. Some DVDs allow you to Scan or Chapter Skip through them, but others force you to read the FBI warnings in foreign languages (some even have commercials) before they let you watch the show. And then there are menus. Well-designed menus are terrific if a DVD has a number of special features, but a menu can be annoying if all you want to do is watch the film. Some DVDs obligate you to activate the Dolby Digital encoding from a menu (you can't 'toggle') and many force you to start the film from a menu option instead of just spinning up and playing. Some menus are easy to use, with clearly delineated options and easy to follow pointers. Others are bizarrely obscure, where you practically have to guess what to press and hope you choose correctly. Still others, to attract puzzle seekers, have 'hidden' menu options, or make you take a test of some sort (usually trivia about the main program) before you are allowed to access an option. And as the menus have grown more sophisticated, they have also become even more annoying. Many include sounds or animated movements which, if you've left the menu on the screen while tending to something else, replay again and again in an annoying loop that can never be suppressed. These menus also tend to take a few seconds to 'load' and if you try to select options early, your player stops and you have to spin the DVD up and watch the FBI warnings all over again.

Because of the compression format, playback manipulation on DVDs is difficult (though not impossible) and, generally, moving forward is easier than moving backward. The most efficient function is the Chapter Search, which can rapidly and accurately get you to any generalized spot on a DVD, provided that the DVD has been intelligently chapter encoded. Still-frame playback is capable of producing an incredibly sharp, vivid image from a motion picture, provided one doesn't land on a still represented by the interlacing of two frames. Some players are much better than others at enabling the Scan function—which is probably the most useful function of all, next to Play and Pause—and technological enhancements have enabled the function on later machines to come closer to imitating the function on analog video formats, even during reverse playback.

DVDs also offer several other features: 'parental lock out' functions allow viewers to skip over the naughty sequences of properly encoded programs; 'alternate angle' functions allow viewers to choose between camera angles during a sequence if that sequence is encoded for that option; and anamorphic 16:9 playback options add extra capability for widescreen TVs. (If the DVD is encoded for it. Some of the first players defaulted automatically to 16:9 playback and reviewers in major video publications, not realizing the settings on their machines had to be manipulated, complained that the pictures on the DVDs 'looked squeezed.')

The DVD was conceived by its creators as a 'one format fits all' medium, intended not just for home video playback but also to replace CDs and CD-ROMs as audio and computer software delivery systems. Since the DVD holds a lot more data than a CD, DVD-ROM programs have also achieved popularity; and because it is all one medium, DVD-ROM functions can be integrated with DVD-videos, offering Web links, games and text-heavy items such as a copy of a movie's shooting script on the same DVD as the movie and its other special features. Other DVD producers, impatient with the slow development of audio DVDs, have used the Dolby Digital tracks on standard DVDs to offer a couple hours of music on one platter without video accompaniment. Since many consumers have their systems hooked up to some sort of hi-fi audio system, it is a logical move.

Lumivision (which has since been absorbed by SlingShot) and Warner Home Video released the first DVDs on the market, and within a year and a half all the major film and home video companies followed. LDs were inexpensive to master and expensive to replicate. Their production was controlled by a few major distributors and there was very little public domain material released. One company controlled almost all of the X-rated adult title output. DVDs, however, are expensive to master but inexpensive to replicate, and so there has been a wide proliferation of public domain programs, niche programming and adult programming. After two and a half years, however, there are still, understandably, many famous and popular movies that are not yet available on DVD—though, as we mentioned, more are being released every week.

Some DVDs are imbedded with a code that prevents them from being played in areas of the world except for the area, such as 'North America,' where the DVD has been sold. Others, however, have no such restrictive encoding. Since many DVDs are produced in Hong Kong in the American-compatible NTSC format, and since those programs are not restricted by region, there is a large market in America for Hong Kong imports, such as action films, fantasy films, kung fu movies and that sort of thing.

How To Use This Book

A number of the reviews in this book make use of the first person plural, because it is less grating on the inner ear than the first person singular, despite the obvious contradiction to the book's title. Consider it a paradox. The term 'Dolby Digital' in the reviews usually refers to a Dolby Digital 5.1 soundtrack, just as the term 'standard stereo track' refers to a DVD's 2-channel track and does not differentiate between Dolby Digital 2-channel and PCM stereo. While there is a desire to be as detailed as possible, the details should not overwhelm the primary focus—whether the audio playback is any good or not—and so are downplayed except when differentiation is required.

A comparison is offered to the LD version of the program only when it is deemed significantly unusual, the norm being that the image quality is superior on the DVD and the sound is equal or slightly inferior.

The catalog numbers listed next to the titles at the head of the reviews are precise. The company identifications are less so, because in these cutthroat times, the companies keep buying and selling parts of each other. As of this writing, Warner now has most of MGM's old titles, while MGM has the newer MGM titles and all of PolyGram. Artisan has Republic, SlingShot has Lumivision, and so on. Generally, we've tried to identify the company appearing on the label, particularly when the title has been subsequently reissued by the new parent company. In other instances, however, such as Buena Vista, we've tried to stick with the parent and ignore the subsidiaries. Some companies have licensed titles from other companies—Pioneer has some Artisan titles, Image has some Universal titles, Anchor Bay has some Buena Vista titles—and in these instances we've gone with the licensee since they are the ones putting out the DVD.

The title of a DVD is even less precise than its owner. Image conveniently places the exact title of its product in the small print on the back of the jacket, but the other companies are not so obliging, and when it comes to classical music programs this can be particularly vexing. We generally try to go by what is on the jacket spine (hence, **Dr. Strangelove**, not *Dr. Strangelove or How I Stopped Worrying and Learned to Love the*

Bomb), unless the jacket spine has left something out that appears in all other presentations of the title on the jacket and the platter. Some companies have started bundling titles originally released individually as boxed sets, and these we have ignored. Other boxed sets, however, have been released simultaneously with their individualized components, and these we have acknowledged.

The DVDs are listed alphabetically by their official titles, but these titles may be confusing sometimes. For example, the DVD title may differ from the title of the film or program on the disc. In addition, sometimes a disc is reviewed with a companion disc and therefore appears out of order. We've provided extensive cross-references throughout to help you find the title you are looking for. We've also included some references to people who are the subjects of discs. These entries are alphabetized by last name, but be sure to check first names, too—especially with musicians as, for example, Eric Clapton Unplugged   .

Titles that are reviewed in the book appear in boldface.

DVDLaser.com, the book's home on the web, offers other ways to search for titles, actors, subjects, directors, and more. We invite you to visit.

The purpose of this book is to offer in-depth reviews for a healthy selection of the DVDs currently on the market in America (as of August 1999). Most of the reviews originally appeared, in a slightly altered form, in *The DVD-Laser Disc Newsletter*, and logic would dictate that if you enjoy the book or find it useful, then you will find the *Newsletter* to be of great utility as well. A free copy of *The DVD-Laser Disc Newsletter* can be obtained by calling toll free (800) 551-4914, Faxing a request to (516) 594-9307, e-mailing a request to dpratt@DVDLaser.com, or writing the *Newsletter* at PO Box 420, East Rockaway NY 11518.

We hope the *DVD-Video Guide* will help you in your search for personal entertainment. The enjoyment of movies and other video programs is an emotional endeavor and subject to the mood of the viewer and the condition of the viewing. A film might make ideal viewing one day and be worse than picking gum off a shoe on another. What you want to do is collect a wide range of titles so that no matter how you are feeling, there will be movie or a UFO documentary to match it.

Acknowledgements

I am infinitely grateful to the patience and understanding granted by my wife, Loretta, and my children, Ryan, Nathan, Alby, and Lara, during the time that I spent working on this book. Thanks also to Steve Lippman, Penny Schwartz, and James Monaco for the help and support they provided, as well as to Bob Bedo, Fran Schaier, Stan Martin, and Larry Samele. Thanks as well to the many people within the home-video and DVD industries who have gone out of their way and beyond the call of their job descriptions to assist me in my efforts; and thanks to the many readers of my newsletter, who have been so kind and supportive to me over the years.

DP
East Rockaway NY
October 1999

The Greatest DVDs of All Time

THE 10 GREATEST DVDs

Armistead Maupin's More Tales of the City
Brazil (Criterion)
From the Earth to the Moon
La Bamba
Rambling Rose
The Red Shoes
Short Cinema Journal 1:2 Issue: Dreams
Starship Troopers
The Sweet Hereafter
Tomorrow Never Dies: Special Edition

10 MORE GREAT DVDs FOR THE SQUEAMISH

Apollo 13
Austin Powers: International Man of Mystery
Bull Durham
Contact
Das Boot
Ghostbusters
Grace of My Heart
My Fair Lady
You've Got Mail
Young Frankenstein

10 MORE GREAT DVDs FOR THE NOT-SO-SQUEAMISH

The Alien Legacy
Cube
Dark City
Enter the Dragon
The Evil Dead (Elite)
The Exorcist: Special Edition
Hard Boiled
Night of the Living Dead (Elite)
Platoon
The Thing

10 GREAT COMMENTARY TRACKS

Boogie Nights
El Mariachi/Desperado
Henry V
Jacob's Ladder
Rush Hour
Sophie's Choice
Thelma & Louise
This Is Spinal Tap
Vertigo
Walkabout

20 GREAT DVDs
WITH NO SIGNIFICANT SPECIAL FEATURES

Amadeus
Amarcord
Bonnie & Clyde
Bram Stoker's Dracula
Broken Arrow
A Bug's Life
The Die Hard Trilogy
Dune
The Ghost and the Darkness
Mouse Hunt
The Nightmare before Christmas
Oklahoma!
Picnic at Hanging Rock
Speed
Star Trek: First Contact
Terminator 2: Judgment Day
The Ten Commandments
The Truman Show
2001: A Space Odyssey
William Shakespeare's Romeo + Juliet

10 GREAT BLACK-AND-WHITE DVDs

Andrei Rublev
The Beatles: A Hard Day's Night
Casablanca
The Lady Vanishes
A Night to Remember
The Old Dark House
Psycho (original)
The Seven Samurai
Strangers on a Train
Who's Afraid of Virginia Woolf

10 GUILTY PLEASURES

The Avengers: Box 3
Bullitt
Con Air
Don Juan de Marco
The Good, The Bad and The Ugly
The Heroic Trio
Jeremiah Johnson
Kiss Me Monster
Tenebre
Tremors

10 GREAT MUSIC DVDs

Baaba Maal Live at the Royal Festival Hall
Beethoven: Symphony No.9.Op.125 "Choral"
The Doors Collection
The Judy Garland Show: Volume One
King Crimson: Deja Vroom
Parsifal
Rolling Stones Live at the Max
Rudolf Nureyev, Margot Fonteyn in Tchaikovsky's Swan Lake
Steve Vai: Alien Love Secrets
Turandot

10 GREAT MISCELLANEOUS DVDs

Africa: The Serengeti
Anima Mundi
Art and Jazz in Animation
Landmarks of Early Film
Lumière & Company
Man with a Movie Camera
Short Cinema Journal 1:3 Issue: Authority
Super Speedway
World's Greatest Animation
Yosemite Watersongs

10 AWFUL DVDs

Alf Bicknel's Personal Beatles Diary
The Boy in the Plastic Bubble
Chitty Chitty Bang Bang
The Lucy Show
Night of the Living Dead (all except Elite's)
President Clinton's Grand Jury Video August 17, 1998
Sports Bloopers Encyclopedia
The Titanic Expedition
"Two Women"
UFO and Paranormal Phenomena

10 X-RATED DVDs THAT OFFER MORE THAN JUST THE OLD IN-OUT IN-OUT

Bobby Sox
Boiling Point
Debbie Does Dallas: The Next Generation
Exposure
Janine: Extreme Close-Up
Kaitlyn Goes to Rio
Masseuse #3
The Mobster's Wife
Shock
Talk Dirty to Me 10

DVD-Video Guide

A

Abbott & Costello in the Foreign Legion (see **Bud Abbott & Lou Costello in the Foreign Legion**)

The Abbott & Costello TV Show Lou's Birthday / Getting a Job / Uncle Bozzo / Stolen Skates
(Shanachie, 402)
The Abbott & Costello TV Show Duck Dinner / Hillary's Birthday / Million Dollar Refund / Actor's Home
(Shanachie, 401)

The 1952–53 show came at the end of the comedy team's career (they look so old), and represents a looser format than their films (which weren't exactly tight), closer in spirit to a stage revue or a burlesque. Usually the episodes have more of a premise than a plot, giving the pair an excuse to run through that classic routine or that, though there are regular supporting characters, including the landlord, a bratty child (played by an adult) and the local beat cop.

Each black-and-white episode runs about 25 minutes and four appear in each collection, playing straight through with complete opening and closing credits (which were rather generic in those days). The source material looks super, with smooth, finely detailed contrasts and deep blacks. Damage or wear is sparse. The monophonic sound is fine and the programs are not captioned.

In *Lou's Birthday*, Costello attempts to celebrate his birthday end in disaster. Included are two terrific routines, one where everything Costello says is taken as an insult by the landlord and another where Costello attempts to order a cake from an Italian baker. In the most solidly plotted of the four episodes, *Stolen Skates*, gangsters try to retrieve diamonds from roller skates that have come into the possession of the heroes. There are some amusing twists and several clever routines including an auction bit (Costello always raising his hand involuntarily) and a funny sequence where Costello doesn't think the gangster threatening him is serious. Phyllis Coates appears as the gangster's moll, attempting to seduce Costello. The heroes end up in jail in *Uncle Bozzo*, with a killer who goes crazy whenever he hears 'O sole mio' and a crazy uncle who can't stop singing that very same song. There is a classic verbal routine in *Getting a Job* about 'loafing' in a bakery and 'kneading dough,' and another routine in which Costello is transporting a box of hats that are systematically destroyed by the people he meets. (Note that the chapter guide on the jacket has the episodes mixed up.)

They do the 'Who's on first' routine at the finale of *Actor's Home*, which also includes an amusing skit about an invisible baseball, and somebody playing a trick on Costello, replacing the ice cream he's selling with limburger cheese. There is a decent plot to *Million Dollar Refund*, when Costello is mistakenly given an IRS refund and his landlord thinks it is counterfeit. In *Duck Dinner*, Costello doesn't have the heart to kill the duck that is supposed to be the main course. They hire a hitman, but he doesn't have the heart to kill the duck, either. There's a routine in *Hillary's Birthday* in which Abbott bets Costello he can't stand on a handkerchief and hit him in the nose, and then puts the handkerchief in a doorway and shuts the door. Every time Costello tries to play the trick on

somebody, though, it doesn't work. The premise has the landlord forbidding them to play music, which puts a damper on their entertainment.

Above the Law (Warner, 11786)

Steven Seagal is a former CIA agent turned police detective who breaks open a plot by his former colleagues to traffic narcotics in Chicago. It was directed by Andrew Davis and has a fairly effective pace, with decent stunt sequences and stars-of-tomorrow such as Pam Grier (as his platonic partner) and Sharon Stone (as his patient but worried wife).

The film is letterboxed with an aspect ratio of about 1.8:1 on one side, with an accommodation for enhanced 16:9 playback, and is in full screen format on the other side. The letterboxing adds a bit of picture information to the sides of the image and masks off more from the bottom, though the framing on the letterboxed image is usually stronger. Colors are true and deep, with good detail and a sharp focus. The stereo surround sound is a little weak, but the Dolby Digital track is much stronger and more enjoyable. The musical score often uses an enjoyable ping-pong separation effect. The 99 minute 1988 film is also available in Spanish in mono and comes with optional English, French or Spanish subtitles, a decent cast-and-crew profile, very minor production notes and trailers for eight Seagal films.

Abraxas (Simitar, 7525)

Jesse Ventura stars as an alien cop who comes to earth to protect a child fathered by another alien several years earlier, while the villain wants to use the child for evil means. Set in a small town, the show has very limited special effects and equally limited performances outside of the central roles, but the narrative is competently constructed and Ventura is entertaining. The technical competence of the cinematography is impressive, and while the film usually looks like it had a low budget, the picture is almost always sharply focused and adequately colored, even during scenes involving difficult lighting situations—there is an opening sequence set at night in the snow near a river that is breathtaking

Colors are a little light and the image is a bit smeary in places, but the picture is reasonably sharp and the presentation is passable. The monophonic sound is dull. The 87 minute feature is not captioned.

Absolute Power (Warner, C2508)

Clint Eastwood directs and stars in a film about a burglar who secretly witnesses the President of the United States committing a murder. Gene Hackman portrays the president and his scenes are not well thought out, so the corruption that is at the core of the movie doesn't completely ring true. Everything else, however, is nicely executed, and if you can get past the starting gate with the film, you're in for the ride. It is a relaxed thriller with plenty of star power and enough suspense to keep the story moving, even on repeat viewings. Ed Harris, Scott Glenn and Judy Davis are also featured.

The film is presented on one side in letterboxed format, with an aspect ratio of about 2.35:1 and an accommodation for enhanced 16:9 playback, and in cropped format on the other side. The widescreen version looks super, with a crisp, flawless image, but the cropped version has a softer, grainier picture. The cropping is fairly useless anyway. The composition consistently feels cramped and looks unbalanced. Except for a couple of gunshots, the film's audio track rarely calls attention to itself, but the surround sound is reasonably smooth and the Dolby Digital track has energy and a nice atmosphere. Lennie Niehaus is credited with the musical score, but the best passages, particularly an extended chase piece, appear to have been composed by Eastwood himself. The 121 minute program is available with English, French or Spanish subtitles and is accompanied by a cast profile and a few production notes.

"About Last Night..." (Columbia TriStar, 07359)

Dating in the Eighties among adults young enough to still be enjoying the independence of their first apartments is the subject of the 1986 film, based upon a stageplay by David Mamet and featuring Demi Moore, Rob Lowe, James Belushi and Elizabeth Perkins. Belushi's lines no longer seem as subversively funny as when the movie first came out, and the film's emotional tensions no longer seem so vital, but it is fun to see the stars being so young (why isn't Lowe doing action films now?) and there are enough glimmers of humor to give viewers with a nostalgic affection for the film something to laugh at here and there. Edward Zwick directed.

The picture is letterboxed on one side, with an aspect ratio of about 1.85:1 and an accommodation for enhanced 16:9 playback, and is presented in full screen format on the other side. The image is a little soft and fleshtones are inconsistent, but hues are generally bright and the presentation is passable. The stereo surround soundtrack has a limited mix but no major flaws. There is also a French track and a Spanish track, and the 113 minute program can be supported by optional English, French or Spanish subtitles. Trailers for the movie and a couple other Moore films are included, as well.

Academy Award Winners: The First 50 Years (Image, DVD9827)

Ten 50 minute episodes from a patchwork documentary program chronicle a history of the Oscars using film trailers and a little other archive footage. The 1994 program looks at each year the Oscars were held up to 1977, generally profiling the winners and the competitors in the four principal categories of Picture, Actor, Actress and Director, though the coverage is inconsistent. For some years, they go into a lot of detail about a particular race or several particular races, and for other years they just tick off the winners and move on. The best episode is one devoted entirely to a single year—the year people say was the best one movies ever had, 1939—but that kind of spoils the rest of the collection because when the next episode starts rushing through things again, you're more aware of what it is being passed over.

At it's best, the program genuinely works its way through a 50-year history of the movies, making you more aware of significant turning points (such as *The Lost Weekend*) and general trends (war movies dominated the awards throughout the early Forties), as well as the politics behind the choices (a young friend of ours was shocked to learn that winners weren't always chosen on merit alone). At its worst, it is a haphazard look at the yearly winners, leaving out more than it includes, bending or misstating facts and focusing on distasteful gossip.

The trailers are mostly in poor condition—usually worse looking than the trailers that accompany movies on DVD—with very soft lines and bad contrasts. The trailer for **It's a Wonderful Life**, for example, is so deteriorated it almost looks solarized. There are no trailers in any of the 10 programs that look exceptional, though some for movies from the Fifties and Sixties are passable. There is a bland stereophonic musical score that is presented in Dolby Digital, though we preferred to run it through our monitor's sound system. Once in a while, the sound from the trailers is included, but the program usually uses just the images. The shows are not captioned and each platter is accompanied by a complete listing of the nominees and winners in the major categories.

Ace Ventura: Pet Detective (Warner, 23000)

The picture is cropped. The image adds nothing to the top and bottom of the screen in comparison to the movie's widescreen image and loses picture information (as well as a more balanced framing) from the sides. The picture is very sharp and colorful, bringing out textures and details in faces, objects and backgrounds. Contrary to the jacket notation, there is no Dolby Digital soundtrack. The regular stereo surround soundtrack is reasonably energetic. The 87 minute film is also supported by English, French or Spanish subtitles ("No, el tipo de los guantes de hule me trató con asombrosa delicadeza") and comes with the superbly conceived theatrical trailer (which is letterboxed), a cast and crew profile and some production notes.

The 1994 comedy is well made—the gags have a decent pace, the cast is fun and Jim Carrey, the star, varies what could easily be a one-note performance into a good, high-school-band's worth of voices and personalities; and there is even a very coherent and cute plot.

On another audio channel, director Jim Shadyac talks about working with Carrey and about putting the film together. He is very adept at explaining how the comedy in the film was achieved and has some interesting technical insights (the camera angles are often playful, to get the viewer into the spirit of the film). Despite the wealth of improvisation Carrey contributed, one can tell from his talk that Shadyac had a clear vision of what he wanted in every scene, and it was from that foundation that Carrey could extend himself wildly without toppling. In fact, Shadyac's advice for future filmmakers runs right along that line of thinking—you don't have to be a technical wizard to direct, you just have to have it clear in your mind what you want. From his descriptions of Carrey's improvisations, by the way, it is a shame the closing credit scroll wasn't turned over to the takes that didn't make the final cut.

Ace Ventura: When Nature Calls (Warner, 23500)

Which movie would you really be able to sit through for more than one viewing: *Out of Africa* or the Africa-based (well, most of it was shot in South Carolina, but it's close enough) **Ace Ventura When Nature Calls**? It is true that the ratio of humor per screen minute subsides in the second half of **Ace Ventura** without a proportional increase of plot, but the plot, about a search for a sacred white bat that has been stolen (guano is at the bottom of it all), is coherent and many of the gags are quite amusing. *Out of Africa*, on the other hand, isn't funny at all.

The presentation is in letterboxed format on one side, with an aspect ratio of about 2.35:1 and an accommodation for enhanced 16:9 playback, and in cropped format on the other. The cropping removes picture information from the sides and adds nothing to the top or bottom, but it isn't bad, since even the reaction shots to Jim Carrey's antics are usually near the center of the image. The picture has deep, rich colors. The stereo surround sound is reasonably strong and there is a Dolby Digital track that has a better bass, better detail and more active directional effects. The 94 minutes film is also available in French and Spanish without Dolby Digital and can be accompanied by English, French or Spanish subtitles ("Sabe Ud, la gingivitis es la causa número uno de las caries"). There is a small cast and crew profile section and some brief production notes, along with amusing trailers for both the 1995 movie and the original **Ace Ventura**.

Adam's Rib (MGM, 906610)

Spencer Tracy and Katharine Hepburn star in the 1949 feature, directed by George Cukor. This is the one where he is a district attorney and she is a defense lawyer. Their by-play about the role of women in society is mildly embarrassing, but Judy Holliday and Jean Hagen are marvelous in supporting roles and some sequences are highly amusing.

The black-and-white picture is very crisp, with deep blacks and detailed contrasts. Wear on the source material is minimal. There is one exceptionally noticeable instance of digital artifacting, during a left-to-right pan across the female 'witnesses' in the court-room, making the smooth camera movement appear irritatingly jerky. The monophonic sound is workable. The 101 minute program is also accompanied by a French language track and supported by English, French or Spanish subtitles. There is also a particularly creative original theatrical trailer, which is narrated by Pete Smith.

Addicted to Love (Warner, 15252)

Matthew Broderick and Meg Ryan star as a pair who meet in an abandoned building across from the apartment where their former mates are now shacking up. Comedies about excessive behavior can often become too excessive to be enjoyable, but this film seems to keep a careful balance between anxiety and sympathy, and the performers are engaging. The film is not perfect—near the end a character starts running around in a full body cast, which is a throwback from the comedies of thirty years ago—but it is a pleasant entertainment with a dark side, and you can't find that combination too often.

The 1997 film is presented in letterboxed format on one side, with an aspect ratio of about 1.85:1 and an accommodation for enhanced 16:9 playback, and in full screen on the other side. The letterboxed image adds some picture information to the sides and takes some off the top and bottom, but the framing is better balanced. The picture has stronger colors than the LD, but fleshtones are still a little pale and the image is still a bit grainy in places. The stereo surround sound is very weak, but there is a Dolby Digital soundtrack with much more power and dimensionality. The 99 minute film is also available in French in standard stereo and can be accompanied by English, French or Spanish subtitles. There is a decent cast-and-crew profile, some informative production notes and a theatrical trailer.

Adriana Lecouvreur (see Cilea's Adriana Lecouvreur: Teatro Alla Scala)

The Adventures of Baron Munchausen (Columbia TriStar, 76989)

Terry Gilliam's wildly fanciful 1988 comedy of tall tales has been released in letterboxed format only, with an aspect ratio of about 1.85:1 and an accommodation for enhanced 16:9 playback. Although blues are richer and, in some sequences, fleshtones are more realistic on the LD, in other sequences fleshtones on the LD are way too pink, while the reserved hues of the DVD are less disorienting and their detail more satisfying. The image is also substantially sharper, which helps as well. There is no Dolby Digital 5-channel track, but the standard stereo surround actually sounds a little stronger than the LD's stereo, with a nice dimensionality and a reasonable amount of power. The 127 minute program also has Spanish and Portuguese audio tracks, optional English, Spanish, Portuguese, Chinese, Korean and Thai subtitles ("Este es exactemente el tipo de cosa que nadie cree"), profiles of Gilliam and Eric Idle (but nothing on the film's star, John Neville), and a trailer.

The have-it-both-ways ending doesn't even seem to follow the illogical logic of the rest of the film, but getting there is great fun. The special effects are grand. The film is filled with fairly literal flights of fancy—men riding cannonballs, people falling off the moon and cushioned in their drop to earth by the hot air from a volcano—and the narrative keeps plodding along, if only to generate more fantasy.

The Adventures of Pinocchio (New Line, N4438)

As a young friend, who poked his head in for a moment while we were watching the film, commented, "Who wants to watch a movie about Pinocchio?" Martin Landau is the kindly puppet maker and Jonathan Taylor Thomas shows up at the very end—though he dominates much of the film's advertising—as the puppet fully transformed. Ultimately, we suppose, the story is just too familiar and too icky to be all that appealing. The film's special ef-

fects are plentiful but rarely awe-inspiring. Even the animated cricket seems more awkward than personable. Despite the special effects and other efforts to achieve a magical atmosphere, the 1966 film lacks the wit or the inspiration to sell the fantasy.

The 94 minute film is presented on one side in letterboxed format, with an aspect ratio of about 2.35:1 and no 16:9 playback, and in cropped format on the other side. The picture looks okay and is colorful, with accurate flesh and wood tones, though the cropped image is somewhat grainier. The stereo surround sound is okay, and the Dolby Digital track is good. The film's sound mix is not too elaborate, but has a reasonable amount of flourish at times. The film can be accompanied by English or Spanish subtitles and the DVD also features a cast profile, a trailer and 'making of' featurette, a couple minor 'interactive' games and trailers for three other New Line family films.

The Adventures of Priscilla, Queen of the Desert (PolyGram, 8006337132)

The genial tale of three drag queens traveling across the Australian outback in a broken-down bus, Terence Stamp is the best known member of the cast, playing the elder of the trio, who are on their way to a gig at a gambling resort in Alice Springs. All of the performers are fun, and their work is impressive, because drag queens rely on shadows to assist in their illusions and in most of this movie they are stuck in the bright desert sun. Stamp makes an especially strong impression, conveying the full weight his character's years and the practiced coyness he uses to keep at peace with the world. The film is an extreme example of placing characters out of their element, but extremity is what makes it so enjoyable. The musical sequences are also terrific.

The picture is presented in letterboxed format on one side, with an aspect ratio of about 2.35:1 and no 16:9 enhancement, and in cropped format on the other side. The image is reasonably sharp and the colors look okay, though the 1994 film doesn't always seem totally fresh. The film's budget is probably responsible for the slightly grainy night shots and the occasional compromised fleshtones, but we wonder if the source material used for the transfer is as close to original as it can be. Anyway, the flashy Oscar-winning costumes are uncompromised and the picture is in good enough condition to communicate the film's amusing pleasures. The cropping just cuts off interesting things and isn't good for much, so it is advisable to stick with the letterboxed side. The stereo sound is also presentable, though again, the film's budget may be preventing it from being as elaborate or as strong as it could have been. The 102 minute film has a French audio track, optional Spanish subtitles ("¿Este es un mojón de ABBA?") and English captioning. There is a cast profile section, along with a teaser trailer that is quite good and a standard trailer that probably didn't work as well because it doesn't focus as clearly on what the film is about.

Aelita, the Queen of Mars (Image, ID5665DSDVD)

The 1924 Russian silent is actually set in Moscow, though there are plenty of Martian scenes, featuring sets and costumes that certainly defy the notion of form following function. It is about the frustrations felt by an earnest engineer who is having trouble settling down with his wife. To escape, he builds a spaceship and flies to Mars. The spectacular Martian sequences are only the frosting, however, as the film is much more valuable as a daringly objective look at city life under socialization and communism. For example, the film presents negative but still sympathetic portraits of former aristocrats coping in the Soviet community, and depicts the black market as an unfortunate necessity. Superbly directed by Yakov Protazanov and featuring a compelling, magnetic performance in the lead role by Nikolai Tsereteli, the 111 minute film has a narrative flow and punch that remains fully accessible to today's viewers.

The black-and-white image is soft, as one would expect, but is in generally good condition for its age and source. Movement is mildly jerky, but tolerable. There is a gratifyingly subtle, monophonic piano score, based on themes by Sergei Prokofiev.

Aeon Flux (Sony, LVD49810)

Episodes from the captivating MTV animated series have been compiled on the two hour program. Set in a futuristic world at an impassable border between two states, the heroine is some sort of operative who often slips across on secret missions. The series is ideal for MTV because it works best as a channel surfing stop, where there is an assumption that there is more to the beginning and end of each episode than what one has caught. The episodes, however, are freestanding and often quite ambiguous, but they are also brilliant—exploring desires and other complicated emotions within a very imaginative and stimulating environment. Four longer episodes are presented, separated by short sequences that served as sort of the pilot for the series. The longer episodes include *Thanatophobia*, in which the heroine tries to assist a couple who were separated when one made it across the border and the other was injured trying (the injury is a broken spine, which has been replaced by an artificial segment that the character removes—and discards, replacing it with a fresh one—whenever she wishes to twist into a tight place. Bizarre.); *A Last Time for Everything*, in which the heroine is duplicated by the villainous corporate genius running the bad country across the border—at the end, it may be the heroine who has died and the duplicate who is carrying on her work; *The Purge*, in which the heroine investigates the implantation of skeletal controllers within various characters; and *Isthmus Crypticus*, in which the heroine tries to free two winged beings held and enamored by the villain. The picture looks terrific, though the image on the shorter sequences is a little soft in places. The stereo sound has no rear channel effects and there is no Dolby Digital or captioning.

Aerobisex Girls X-rated (Lipstik, 31112)

The all-female cast do have one exercise session, but mostly they just fool around with one another, in gatherings of larger and larger populations. The colors are dull and the image is blurry. The monophonic sound has a limited range and the program runs 83 minutes.

Aerosmith: The Making of Pump (Sony, CVD49064)

One of the best examples of the subgenre 'documentary about making a rock album,' the 110 minute program is a genuine documentary that really gets into the dynamics of the group and the creative process during all aspects of putting together what used to be called an LP. There are very few complete numbers performed. It is more snippets of music as the group painfully works their way toward satisfactory cuts of each song. Fans can get their music elsewhere and have an opportunity instead to see the band members free of artifice, while casual viewers will find the depth and detail with which the film depicts its subject to be fascinating.

The picture is usually of grainy documentary quality, but when the image is sharp and the colors are fresh, the DVD delivers them properly. There is both a stereo surround soundtrack and a menu-activated Dolby Digital track. The Dolby Digital track is better during the musical cuts, providing a wider dimensionality and better separations, but the regular stereo track is stronger during the (more numerous) conversation sequences, delivering the dialogue more clearly and loudly. The program is split in half and appears on two sides of the DVD. There is no captioning.

Affliction (Universal, 20588)

Nick Nolte stars, and James Coburn won an Oscar for his portrayal of Nolte's father, in Paul Schrader's 1998 portrait of a troubled sheriff in a small New England town. Based upon a novel by Russell Banks, the film's script holds too tightly to its literary origins and is narrated by a character who was devised entirely to serve the written word. His actual presence looks awkward. The conclusion is also somewhat oblique, though that is not really a flaw, just a disappointment that the film has to come, so soon, to an end. Shot in real snow, the film's atmosphere is meticulously executed and the characters are vividly conceived. There is a token mystery for the sheriff to investigate, which makes an ideal distraction from the story's real focus—a spellbinding exploration into the fatally defective personalities of the father and the son.

The picture is presented in letterboxed format only, with an aspect ratio of about 1.85:1 and no 16:9 enhancement. The letterbox framing is consistently elegant and involving. Except for a couple of Day-Glo hunting jackets and a few home movie-style flashbacks, there are no bright colors in the film (the hero's memories are brighter than his reality), but the image appears to be accurately transferred and is highly satisfying. The stereo surround sound is adequate (there is no 5-channel mix). The 115 minute program can be supported by optional English subtitles and comes with production notes, a cast profile section and a trailer.

Africa Screams (Master Movies, DVD5505); (Digital Disc Entertainment, 572)

The 1949 Bud Abbott and Lou Costello comedy contains dated depictions of African tribesman that some viewers may find offensive, though others may find that the humor exceeds the offense. In this one they go on a safari to look for treasure. The film runs 79 minutes.

The Master Movies black-and-white transfer looks terrific. The image is smooth, contrasts are nicely detailed and blacks are pure. Here and there the image weakens a bit, but it is never very much and it is never for very long. The monophonic sound is fine.

The Digital Disc Entertainment release is much weaker. The picture is often blurry, with poor contrasts, a few scratches and grain. Blacks and greys are not as pure. There is noticeable video artifacting at first, as well as distorted horizontal bands that pop up now and again, but after a little bit those problems subside. The monophonic sound is coherent.

Neither program is captioned.

Africa: The Serengeti (Lumivision, DVD0397); reissue (Lumivision, DVD2097)

James Earl Jones provides his authoritative-sounding narration to the IMAX documentary. Some IMAX documentaries are better than others, and this is one of the good ones. Not only are the images diverse and compelling, but the program, though only 40 minutes long, is well organized and informative, giving the viewer a viable survey of the types of life found in the Serengeti Plain. The picture quality is excellent, with the IMAX process providing an exceedingly crisp and vivid image at all times. The stereo surround sound track is elaborate and full bodied.

The program was reissued with 8 separate language tracks, all in Dolby Digital. The basic picture and sound quality are identical to the earlier release. In addition to Jones' English narration, the program is narrated by uncredited male speakers in Bavarian, Castilian, Catalan, French, Japanese, Korean and Mandarin.

After Dark, My Sweet (Pioneer, DVD68943)

Based upon a story by Jim Thompson, it is set in the Southwest and involves low life characters who participate in a kidnapping. The film is almost designed for multiple viewings, since it takes one or two run-throughs just to get the plot figured out. Jason Patric is an ex-boxer who may be crazy, Rachel Ward is a widow with a big house, and Bruce Dern is a schemer who could use a hair cut. Eventually they kidnap a little boy, but most of the story explores the three-way relationship and its inevitable downward spiral. As with much of Thompson's writing, the movie is not so much a thriller as it is a portrait of characters numbed by life. James Foley directed the 1990 feature.

The source material has some speckling. Fleshtones are a little dull and other hues are a little flat, but most of the movie is set in the bright sun and the full screen presentation is workable. The stereo surround sound has a limited dimensionality. There is no captioning.

Air America (Artisan, 60471)

Contrary to the film's own billing, Robert Downey, Jr. is the real star. Mel Gibson has more of a supporting role. The two portray pilots working for the CIA in Laos during the Vietnam era. The place is raft with corruption and the heroes cope with it for a while and then leave. That's it.

The picture is a bit dark, but colors are deep, fleshtones are accurate and the focus is smooth. The DVD is presented in letterboxed format, with an aspect ratio of about 2.35:1 and no 16:9 enhancement on one side and in cropped format on the other side, though cropping obscures a number of the film's pleasures. The stereo sound is somewhat muted. The 113 minute 1990 film can be accompanied by English or Spanish subtitles and comes with some production notes, a cast profile section and a theatrical trailer.

Air Bud (Buena Vista, 13681)

Although the dog doesn't really start playing basketball until the end, he does finally play in an official school game, a championship game no less, even though he clearly has no grade point average, so Air Bud is not for viewers who question such stretches of the imagination. The film is basically a boy-and-his-dog story, with a structure that is so close to E.T. in places that the filmmakers owe Melissa Matheson a few royalties. The dog is cute, but the movie is mostly for youngsters or very undemanding viewers.

The film is presented in full screen format only, adding a bit to the top and more to the bottom in comparison to the letterboxed versions, and taking only a hair off the sides. The image has deep fleshtones and rich, accurate hues. The stereo surround sound is a bit subdued, with a limited dimensionality. The 98 minute program can be accompanied by English subtitles. A theatrical trailer is also included that pretty much gives the whole movie away.

Air Force One (Columbia TriStar, 71885/9)

The movie is such a grand and superbly crafted, old-fashioned-but-high-tech cliffhanger that you are oblivious to everything but the characters and the action while it is unfolding. Harrison Ford stars as the American president, forced to act on his own when his airplane is hijacked by terrorists. His character is a war hero, but it is one of the film's many strengths that his fighting skills are a bit rusty and the hand-to-hand fights have an appealing sloppiness that makes them all the more exciting. The 125 minute film has a lot of ground to cover, and there are a couple plot points that probably ended up on the cutting room floor in the process, but the film has so many satisfying payoffs and heroic, don't-we-wish-Hollywood-shaped-the-world satisfactions that what little flaws there are, in the movie or on the disc, don't matter in the least.

The stereo surround sound is outstanding, especially the Dolby Digital track, which provides a constantly heightened atmosphere, with super-charged directional effects and a solid, intense dynamic range. The film's sound mix is superb and it puts the viewer in the middle of the movie. Even the dialogue levels vary subtly, depending upon how far the camera is from the character speaking. The standard stereo surround soundtrack has a little less detail than the Dolby Digital track but is basically just as entertaining.

The image is a little soft and the colors seem slightly muted. The picture is letterboxed on one side, with an aspect ratio of about 2.35:1 and an accommodation for enhanced 16:9 playback, and is in cropped format on the other side, though the cropped image isn't good for much. The 125 minute film is also available in French and Spanish and comes with optional English, French or Spanish subtitles ("Bájese de me avión").

The film's director, Wolfgang Petersen, provides a fairly good commentary, explaining how the various special effect shots were accomplished, talking about the contributions of almost all the major crew and cast members, and relating his experiences on previous films, particularly In the Line of Fire (for the Secret Service stuff) and Das Boot (for all those tracking shots down the cramped hallways), to its application in Air Force One. He acknowledges how some corners had to be cut for the sake of pacing (such as explaining that the phone Ford's character uses is a satellite phone, not a cell phone; also, why there is no real explanation of motivation for one of the main bad guys) and tells which parts of his version of the plane are based on fact and which are pure imagination. The only problem is, once again, the movie is so good there are times when you forget to listen to him because you get caught up, once more, in the action on the screen.

Airport (Universal, 0581029)
Airport 1975 (Universal, 0581010)
Airport '77 (Universal, 0581014)

The images on Airport 1975 and Airport '77 are letterboxed with an aspect ratio of about 2.35:1 and no 16:9 enhancement. The 1970 Airport is cropped, except the split-screen and cockpit sequences, which are semi-letterboxed, constantly reminding you that the rest of the film isn't. Generally, colors are a little light and the image has a mildly aged appearance. At the time, the film's stereo surround mix was quite enjoyable, but now it is fairly antique, with limited rear channel separations and little more than a generalized dimensionality. Airport 1975 looks super, with rich, vivid hues and a very crisp focus. The cinematography is blander in Airport '77 which has more of the Universal factory look to it than the others do, but the colors are solid and the image is sharp. The monophonic sound in both films has a modest range, but is workable, and both have small cast profile sections. All three films can be supported by English, French or Spanish subtitles ("Vous allez mourir pour rein si la bombe explose").

George Kennedy appears in all three films as the same character, even though the name of the airline he works for changes each time. Burt Lancaster, Dean Martin, Jean Seberg, Van Heflin and Jacqueline Bisset star in Airport, which runs 136 minutes, not the 91 listed on the jacket cover. Lancaster is the airport manager, dealing with a snowstorm and other problems, while Martin is the pilot of a plane and Heflin is a bomber. It is a shame that although the subsequent films retained the name, they all concentrated on the airplane problems and not problems in the airport itself, which can be just as interesting. Airport 1975, which runs 106 minutes, is refreshingly free of a villain. Charlton Heston is a pilot who has to be lowered into a hole in the cockpit of a damaged 747. Karen Black is a stewardess flying the plane. Fun stuff. James Stewart is featured in Airport '77, which runs 114 minutes, but he's just the airline owner and doesn't get involved in the disaster except to look worried. A high-strung Jack Lemmon is the pilot, with Brenda Vaccaro, Joseph Cotten, Lee Grant, Christopher Lee, etc. A bomber sends the plane into the water and divers have to rescue it before all the bubbles come out.

Alainis Morisette: Jagged Little Pill, Live (Warner, 384762)

An excellent concept live album that is intended to supplement and not replace the studio album, the 90 minute program combines live performances of the songs from Morissette's album at very different venues, so that a single performance will shift (usually at a proper point, such as a change from the chorus to the next verse) from a stadium-style performance to an intimate acoustical performance, to some moderate stage performance. The tone of the song shifts right along with the images. The concept works incredibly well, essentially taking the established song and showing it from several new angles at once—a cubist recording, as it were. Between the numbers there is the usual backstage and home movie material, and there isn't too much that is special about it, but it does reveal the many facets of Morissette, who looks like a cross between Geraldine Chaplin and a summer camp counselor. She's dressed up fancy for MTV performances, dressed loose for the big arena workout, and dressed funky for the simpler stuff. Rather than suggesting that you don't know which one she is, the program makes it clear that she's a combination of all those moods and styles.

There is no way of telling if the picture suffers from video artifacting, because there is already so much deliberate tiling and other digital effects in the concert sequences that any unplanned instances would probably not be recognized even by the program's editors. The stereo surround sound is okay and the Dolby Digital track is even better, with sharper tones and a stronger delivery. There are also English subtitles.

Alaska: Spirit of the Wild (SlingShot, 9837)

Charlton Heston narrates the IMAX documentary, which gives a brief climatic history of the area and then pokes around its wilderness for spectacular vistas of ice, trees and tundra. In some places the ice is so compact, it turns blue. Wildlife is also given a lot of attention, including bears, sea lions, whales, caribou, eagles and salmon. There is no organization to the segments really, but there is a great variety to the images, and the camera placements are often thrilling (the caribou stampede over it).

The picture quality is excellent, with a sharp focus and accurate hues. The film's 5.1 Dolby Digital audio mix is not as stimulating as the best IMAX efforts, but it is still worthwhile, with some decent bass sequences and fairly constant surround effects. The 40 minute program also has French, Spanish (Castilian), Swedish, Chinese (Mandarin), Japanese and German audio tracks, as well as a music and effects track, which is also in Dolby Digital. There are optional English subtitles, as well.

Alexander Nevsky (Image, ID4575CODVD)

Sergei Eisenstein's 1938 classic is about a Russian prince who organizes a line of defense to repel Teutonic interlopers. It is set in the thirteenth century but serves as a reminder that the Germans often enjoyed dropping in on their eastern neighbors. Not only is the cinematography compelling, but there is a battle scene which lasts a full half hour and is definitive in its execution.

The presentation is substantially inferior to a remastered home video version that came out in the mid-Nineties. The picture looks washed out, with weak contrasts obscuring details. The monophonic sound is scratchy and soft. The 108 minute film is in Russian with permanent white English subtitles.

Alf Bicknell's Personal Beatles Diary (Simitar, 7211)

Arisen from the woodwork, Alf Bicknell talks about the days in 1964 to 1966 when he used to drive the Beatles' limousine and get them sandwiches and things. The program is divided into two parts. The first runs about 50 minutes and combines Bicknell's reminiscences with visits to the locales where the Beatles used to hang, along with archive footage—much of it relatively fresh—and footage of present day Beatles memorabilia exhibits. Songs by the Beatles often wax by on the soundtrack and the program ends with several numbers from a Paul McCartney concert Bicknell attended in the Nineties.

The second part, which runs about 25 minutes (the DVD has no time encoding), is just Bicknell standing in different locations, telling a few more stories. The picture quality and monophonic sound are passable. Desperate Beatles fans should be pleased, but casual viewers will find the program more amusing—for the arcane moments in which Bicknell's life and the lives of the musicians intersected—than inspiring.

Alfred Hitchcock Collection (Madacy, DVD99004)
The Man Who Knew Too Much (Madacy, DVD990043)
Number 17 (Madacy, DVD990045)
Murder (Madacy, DVD990042)
Sabotage (Madacy, DVD990041)
Secret Agent (Madacy, DVD990044)

The films have been issued individually and as a boxed set. In addition to the movie, each program contains a different part of a Hitchcock biography and impressive filmography (it lists every movie he wrote intertitles for), as well as a clip that demonstrates Hitchcock's art in the movie at hand. Because the films are older

black-and-white productions with aged source material, there is occasional artifacting within the darker portions of the screen, though usually one doesn't notice it unless one is looking for it.

We've never seen a copy of the 1932 **Number 17** that wasn't battered and foggy, so we'd have to say that Madacy's presentation looks fairly decent. Scratches are constant and some sequences are hazy, but others are reasonably crisp. The same is true of the monophonic sound, which is heavily aged but coherent. The 83 minute film takes place mostly on a single, multi-story set, where dead bodies accumulate and the hero, like the viewer, tries to figure out what is going on, though there is a spectacular train crash sequence at the end. The film is deliberately abstract, about a group of strangers who converge upon a dilapidated townhouse for no apparent reason, though there is a dead body in the house, as well as a stolen diamond necklace. The most important parts of the plot are wrapped up by the end, but other pieces (such as where the corpse came from) remain unexplained. No matter. Hitchcock has a feast with technique and style, playing with shadows and elaborate camera movements. He also makes good use of the set, often peering over the balcony on one level to see what is going on in another. He approaches the mystery with a strong sense of humor, and the delight he takes in the plot's sudden incongruities is communicated directly to the viewer.

"Always make the audience suffer as much as possible," reads the Hitchcock quotation on the cover of the 1930 **Murder**, and that is usually an apt description of how the movie itself is presented. The picture tends to wobble and has its share of wear, though the presentation is workable and we've seen worse. The sound is also surprisingly clear, though old. The 92 minute mystery is not one of Hitchcock's strongest efforts, as the narrative does not unfold smoothly; but, like almost any Hitchcock production, it is still entertaining. Herbert Marshall stars in what is a basic murder mystery, involving a troupe of stage actors. Hitchcock uses elaborate camera movements and other inventive methods to convey visual information, and rarely seems chained to the recitation of the dialogue, even during a lengthy (and enjoyable) jury deliberation sequence. His integration of dialogue sequences with 'silent' footage shot at a circus is also inspired.

The 1936 **Man Who Knew Too Much** is about a man trying to retrieve his kidnapped child and prevent an assassination. The black-and-white picture has a soft, aged look, with plenty of scratches and other markings, and contrasts are a little weak in places, particularly during the night sequences. The sound is a little fragile, though it is cleaner and more coherent than it is on the older films. The film, which stars Leslie Banks and Peter Lorre, runs 74 minutes. Snobbish critics tend to prefer this 1934 version to Alfred Hitchcock's 1956 remake. In this one Hitchcock was still finding joy in the basics of filmmaking. There is a dissolve from St. Moritz to London at night that seems to say everything which needs to be said for the transition from tranquillity to bustle. The film has more action than its successor but less psychological elegance. Like several of his early thrillers, Hitchcock was forging a new type of entertainment and did not have the formula entirely worked out yet. Some of the scenes are wonderful, but others drag on, as if searching for a style as well as a conclusion. The movie's ending, a huge shootout, is quite spectacular, and set a precedent which would take other filmmakers decades to exceed.

For those who can keep track of such trivia, the 1936 **Sabotage** is based upon Joseph Conrad's book *The Secret Agent*, about a saboteur operating in London who is eventually betrayed by his wife after their son is killed by a bomb. **Secret Agent**, also from 1936, has nothing to do with Conrad's book and is one of Hitchcock's subtlest and finest films from the Thirties. The film is definitely an acquired taste, but the key to enjoying it is to disregard the title most emphatically and to remember that it is based upon a story by W. Somerset Maugham. In basic terms, although the plot is superficially about espionage, the movie is actually about sex. The hero and the heroine are teamed on a mission as husband and wife. After a while, they actually fall in love. Sounds like the material for a typical Hitchcock picture, but the manner in which it is presented discards the simple pleasures of watching the two (played by Madeleine Carroll and John Gielgud) bicker and gush. Instead, they act like real adults and sleep with other people, possibly even other sexes, until they get around to going with each other. As a suspense film, the movie, in which the hero has an innocent man murdered, is a disappointment. But as a drama about the ambiguities of adult relationships, about failure, and about compromise, it is a revelation, and one of Hitchcock's finest achievements.

Sabotage also takes a while to get used to, but it is a simpler and clearer morality play than **Secret Agent**. Hitchcock has a young boy killed in the course of the plot and the elaborate build-up to the death can leave one with ill feelings (these days the entire sequence would have been removed after previews). At its best, however, **Sabotage** is another demonstration of the art of conveying emotion through the combination of pictures and sound. Good and evil are clearly defined and the suspense when they clash, thanks to Hitchcock's techniques, is nerve-wracking.

On both programs, blacks are much rich and contrasts are effectively detailed, but the images are grainy and artifacting is noticeable. The monophonic sound is fairly weak **Sabotage**, which runs 76 minutes, but stronger on **Secret Agent**, which runs 86 minutes. On both, the age of the track is readily evident.

Alfred Hitchcock's Bon Voyage & Aventure Malgache
(Image, ID4190MLSDVD)

Shortly after Alfred Hitchcock moved to Hollywood and saw his career reach new heights of success, war broke out in Europe. Obviously reticent to abandon that success, he was nevertheless stung by British critics who suggested that he was ducking out of his responsibilities by staying in Hollywood as Hitler was threatening to overrun England. Many of his American films produced during the war years have strong patriotic themes, and in 1944 (albeit when Hitler was no longer dipping his big toe in the English channel), Hitchcock returned to Great Britain and directed two half-hour films in French, intended to boost the morale of those recently liberated from the Axis boot. It is these two 30 minute films that have been released on the DVD.

The first, *Bon Voyage*, feels like an abridged version of a feature length film and is very entertaining, about two escaped POWs who make contact with the French Resistance in order to return to England. The second, *Aventure Malgache*, has a more complete feel to it, but ends up being so ambiguous that it was never used for its intended purpose. Set in Madagascar, the narrative concerns the conflict between the leader of the resistance movement, whose goal is to smuggle able-bodied men off the island so they can go and fight in Europe, and the primary Vichy stooge, who also happens to be the hero's business rival. Told in flashback by actors before they are about to go out on the stage, the villain's fate is realistic, but not suited for the white hat/black hat atmosphere propaganda films require.

The black-and-white source material on both films is a bit soft and is visited fairly regularly by speckles, but the contrasts are rich and the presentations are workable. The image on both shorts has been slightly windowboxed on three sides. The monophonic sound is passable for the age of the films and permanent white English subtitles appear in support of the French dialogue.

Alice in Wonderland (Artisan, 91021)

A painfully bad miniseries adaptation that stops dead whenever it tries to move away from Lewis Carroll's original story, individual scenes seem to drag on redundantly, and there is no air of magic or wonder to hardly any of it. The 129 minute presentation (a full rendition of the 'three hour' broadcast) combines much of the title story with a helping of *Through the Looking Glass*. The narrative has also been given a linking device—the fantasy is caused by Alice's anxiety over performing at a dinner party—but something

very curious happens. The attempt to make 'sense' of Alice's adventures flattens them out and limits their possibilities—as pure nonsense, each interlude would be more stimulating.

Miranda Richardson is exquisite as the Queen of Hearts and Martin Short makes a viable Mad Hatter, though one still hears Ed Wynn whenever he opens his mouth. Others, such as Whoopi Goldberg and Ben Kingsley, are completely wasted. We gained just one insight from the production—while it has always been apparent that *The Walrus and the Carpenter* was about predators, this was the first time we realized that it has an undercurrent about child molestation.

The picture quality is excellent, with bright, sharp colors and accurate fleshtones. The stereo surround sound is reasonably good for a TV production, with a viable dimensionality and smooth tones. The program is adequately closed captioned and is accompanied by a home video trailer, a cast profile section, production notes, an essay on how Carroll created the story, and a selection of the book's original illustrations.

The Alien Legacy (Fox, 4110439)
Alien (Fox, 4110430)
Aliens (Fox, 4110431)
Alien³ (Fox, 4110432)
Alien Resurrection (Fox, 4110433)
The Alien Legacy (Fox)

All four THX presentations are available in a *20th Anniversary Edition* boxed set entitled **The Alien Legacy**. Additionally, if you follow the instructions on an inserted postcard, you can obtain a 68 minute program on another platter that is also entitled **The Alien Legacy**, has no catalogue number, and features a retrospective documentary about the first **Alien**.

The transfers on the first three films hold significant improvements over previous home video releases. All four are in letterboxed format only, with an accommodation for enhanced 16:9 playback. **Alien**, **Alien³** and **Alien Resurrection** have an aspect ratio of about 2.35:1. **Aliens** has an aspect ratio of about 1.85:1, masking a bit off the top and bottom and adding a little to the sides in comparison to full screen versions. All of the films except **Aliens** have an alternate French audio track in standard stereo and all four have optional English and Spanish subtitles, and original trailers. The documentary has optional English, French and Spanish subtitles.

Fleshtones are pinkish on the most recent **Alien** LD, and are paler, but more consistent on the DVD. Other colors are crisper and the presentation is free of grain. The Dolby Digital 5.1 channel sound is stronger than the standard stereo track, but the LD's Dolby Digital channel is better, with more energy and more detail. Listen to the eggs get excited when John Hurt's character first drops into their incubator.

The **Alien** DVD is loaded with special features. It contains extensive deleted scenes and outtakes that enhance the film's violence and elaborate upon the relationships between the characters. Included is the spine-tingling sequence depicting the fate of Tom Skerritt's character. There is also an extensive collection of the film's production artwork and photos, including many drawings by H.R. Giger, Ron Cobb, Jean 'Moebius' Giraud and Chris Foss, director Ridley Scott's thorough storyboards (Fox doubled his budget after seeing them), and advertising designs. There are also DVD-ROM materials, such as screen savers, and two additional audio tracks, one featuring Jerry Goldsmith's excellent musical score and the other featuring the audio playback without Goldsmith's music. The film itself runs 116 minutes.

Additionally, there is a commentary track by Scott, who has a superb grasp of the commentary format. He is very adept at explaining the reasoning behind his choices, the process behind various effects, and many basic but insightful filmmaking tips. It is best to listen to his commentary after watching the **Alien Legacy** documentary, which provides more of a background on how the film was created and who the various contributors were. (It does not get into the 'he said/she said' controversy over who was most responsible for the script, basically taking Dan O'Bannon at his word.) The combination of the commentary, the documentary and the other supplements supplies an excellent overview of how the film was conceived (it was sort of a sibling to the beachball sequence in **Dark Star**), and how enthusiasm for it snowballed, taking on more artistic quality at every turn.

The 1979 film has been imitated and ripped off so many times in the past 20 years it no longer conveys the nerve-numbing horror it did to its original audiences—even first-time viewers are now more jaded—but other aspects, such as the performances (Sigourney Weaver is terrific, but the others are wonderful too, including Yaphet Kotto, Harry Dean Stanton, Hurt, Ian Holm, etc.) and Scott's mature sense of style (he may not have discovered Giger, but he understood exactly how to employ him) have enabled the film's appeal to endure long past its gimmicky frights and pre-CGI special effects.

James Cameron's inspired 1986 follow-up, **Aliens**, has been issued as a *Special Edition*, running 154 minutes, some 17 minutes longer than the standard version. This is the first time that the **Special Edition** has appeared in Dolby Digital. In comparison to the most recent—and best looking—LD picture transfer, the DVD's picture is much improved. Fleshtones are too orange on the LD, and while the fleshtones look somewhat drained in comparison on the DVD, other colors are sharper, more stable and clearly more accurate. The grain that plagued previous presentations of the film has been eliminated. The Dolby Digital 5.1 channel sound has a slightly weaker ambience than the Dolby Digital sound on the LD, but it is fairly similar and reasonably effective—enhancing the thrills in a manner that the blander standard stereo surround soundtrack is unable to emulate.

Aliens also has some special features. There is an interview with Cameron, 'live' views of the various miniatures, tests of various special effects and lengthy still presentations of conceptual artwork and production photos. The extras may not be as exhaustive as they are on **Alien**, but they are still quite extensive and highly gratifying.

For those who are unfamiliar with the feature, the 'longer' **Aliens** adds more information about the colonists—including footage of their activities—and a few other odds and ends, notably some important information about Weaver's character and some cool-looking automatic guns that the heroes set up to stall the advance of the monsters. Where the first film is a horror movie, the second is more of an action feature, and if you aren't interested in the quality of the drama or the artistic blending the sequel makes with its predecessor, then you can comfortably skip the movie's first half hour and go right to chapter 7, where the heroine and the marines wake up and prepare to land on the planet. Weaver is joined by Michael Biehn, Bill Paxton, Paul Reiser and Lance Henriksen. Either way, it is an exciting, imaginative feature and ideal for DVD playback.

Alien³ should never be played after **Aliens**, for it is a real letdown in that context, but as a freestanding feature it is superbly directed and very entertaining, and seen in tandem with **Alien Resurrection**, it blows the latter away. Set on a 'prison planet,' Weaver's character is awakened from space travel hibernation, only to discover that one of the creatures has tagged along for the ride. She first has to convince the convicts there is a problem, and then find a method to destroy the monster without weapons. Directed by David Fincher, the setting is adeptly depicted, so you never see or comprehend more of it than what Weaver's character does. Fincher builds the excitement steadily, and provides a realistic mix of characters to sustain the 1992 film's believability.

The picture presentation is much improved over the LD. Not only are colors more accurate and more consistent, but the image is sharper and more stable. The LD had no Dolby Digital, so although the standard track is a little weaker than its LD counterpart, the Dolby Digital track is much stronger, with a better

dimensionality and sharper details. There are no elaborate supplementary features as there are on the first two DVDs, but there is a very good 20 minute or so (it isn't time encoded) 'making of' featurette, which includes interviews with the cast and crew, lots of behind-the-scenes looks at how the 115 minute film was staged and how the special effects were accomplished, and shots of Weaver getting her hair cut off. It can be supported by optional English or Spanish subtitles. There's also an ad for the tie-in video game.

The monster at the end is dopey looking (and if the alien mother can't lay eggs, where did the eggs come from?), but **Alien Resurrection** is an engaging variation on a continuing theme—not as spectacular as the seminal first two films or as tight as the third film, but atmospheric and fairly exciting. Weaver stars as a clone of her former self (another thing we dislike in this and many other science fiction movies—rapid maturation; there seems to be no scientific basis for it and wouldn't the story be much more interesting if the scientists had to wait a half-generation to see the results of their tinkering?), with Winona Ryder, Ron Perlman, Brad Dourif and others, all stuck on a spacecraft where the genetically altered but still quite deadly aliens (love that acid blood) have gotten loose. Weaver is terrific, presenting an altered version of her former self, and the film has enough effects and stimulating glimpses of the future to keep fans intrigued. Casual viewers may be a little less tolerant of the story's thematic permutations, but the basic special effects will be stimulating for almost everyone.

Hues are accurate and fleshtones look good. Because of its age, the 1997 film has the best sound mix in the series, and while the LD's Dolby Digital track has a little more punch, the DVD's Dolby Digital track is still highly pleasing, with lots of separation effects and an energetic dimensionality. The 108 minute feature is accompanied by a very brief 'making of' featurette that includes some cast interviews.

An All Dogs Christmas Carol (MGM, 907034)

The cartoon is strongly plotted, but the animation is unimaginative and cheap, the creators constantly ignore opportunities to instill scenes or shots with extraneous humor, and the series' awkward premise—the hero gets his orders from heaven—forces the characters to go through some tiresome sidetracking mechanics before getting on with the story at hand. Because there is a decent story—the heroes put on their own version of *A Christmas Carol* to change the heart of a bully, who then saves the holiday from a genuine villain—the 73 minute program is watchable, but it lacks artistry and most grownup viewers will look on it as a formula program with bland animation.

Colors are solid and crisp. The stereo surround sound has some distinctive separation effects and is adequate for the material. The film is also available in French and can be supported by English or French subtitles, as well as MGM's 'sing-along' song subtitling.

All Quiet on the Western Front (Universal, 20510)

Lewis Milestone's 1930 Oscar-winning drama is about a German soldier during World War I and how the war affects him and his companions. Told from the German perspective (though in English, with American actors), the film established a basic and oft-repeated war drama format, beginning with the sign-up, the boot camp, the horrors of war, the disillusionment, the acceptance and the final irony. The film runs 130 minutes, but the narrative shifts in subject often enough to never become tiresome. The performances are a bit archaic, but the action scenes are well executed and the film is a worthwhile classic.

The picture condition varies. Sometimes it is in excellent shape and other times it shows its age. The image often jiggles, with plenty of speckles and scratches. The picture is sharp, however, and blacks are deep. The monophonic sound is a little dulled. Much of the age-related background noise is suppressed, but so are the atmospheric details. The film can be supported by English, French or Spanish subtitles. There are production notes, a cast-and-director profile section and a reissue trailer. The trailer is interesting only in that it attempts to emphasize non-existent romantic sub-plots, to the point of showing a scene where a brother and sister embrace without delineating their relationship.

All the President's Men (Warner, 1018)

Scholars and other highbrows look down their noses at **All the President's Men**, but it is a captivating, forceful and important piece of cinema, as well as being a highly addictive entertainment. Robert Redford and Dustin Hoffman, both at the height of their popularity in 1976 when the film was produced, star as the two reporters who were most responsible for breaking open the Watergate case that led to president Richard Nixon's resignation. The film plays like an A+ TV docudrama and is best compared to a film such as Sergei Eisenstein's **October**, where historical accuracy and an enriched feel for the texture of the characters becomes a valid alternative to deeper psychological explorations.

The 139 minute film is presented in letterboxed format on one side and in full screen format on the other. The letterboxing has an aspect ratio of about 1.85:1 and can accommodate 16:9 enhanced playback. The full screen presentation loses a bit on the side but gains a lot on the bottom of the image. Nevertheless, the framing on the letterboxed version is excellent and it is the preferable presentation. The picture looks terrific, with bright, solid colors and deep fleshtones. In a direct comparison to the LD, however, the DVD colors look too dark, and whites and fleshtones are truer on the LD.

The monophonic sound is passable and the Dolby Digital mono track is fairly good. In addition to the film's remarkably intelligent cinematography and direction, creative and engrossing performances, humorous and incisive script, and amazingly detailed set designs, the movie also has outstanding sound editing. From the surprise opening power-of-the-press blast of a typewriter key onto a paper, to the whispered ambiguities of sounds just out of earshot, the soundtrack is constantly exploring and underscoring the film's themes, and the DVD's audio supports the sound effectively, even though its strongest effects are all kept to the mid-range. There is a decent cast and crew profile section, a few production notes, a brief blurb on 'Deep Throat' and a modest Watergate timeline. The film can be supported by English, French or Spanish subtitles ("¡Tengo una esposa y una familia y un perro y un gato!").

Because of the quality that went into the film's production, it is highly repeatable entertainment, and because the DVD replicates it so well, it is highly repeatable, too. Although Bob Woodward has never revealed who the mysterious "Deep Throat" character really is (is his pseudonym to be taken literally?), Hal Holbrook's interpretation in the film seems to be patterned after FBI Director L. Patrick Gray. He has the film's most important line, one that all those who see conspiracies behind every tree should listen to, carefully: "The truth is, these are not very bright guys, and things got out of hand." With a few exceptions, that is history, in a nutshell.

The Allman Brothers Band Live at Great Woods (Sony, EVD49146)

The 1991 concert program contains brief interview sequences between most of the numbers. The band members are true to their unslick selves and pretty much just sit or stand near one another and play. They seem to have matured as musicians, so even their best known hits, such as *Midnight Rider*, have a subtler complexity and a firmer sense of construction.

Although at the mercy of colored stage lights, the picture looks quite good, with accurate hues and reasonably sharp lines. The stereo surround sound is adequate, but the Dolby Digital track is much better, with greater detail at nearly every level and more energy. There are optional English subtitles and, contrary to a jacket listing, the program runs 55 minutes.

Alphaville (Criterion, ALP030)

Jean-Luc Godard's surreal film combines science fiction dialogue and sound effects with ordinary, contemporary (circa 1964) images. Shot in locations around Paris, with an eye for modernistic architecture and decor, the film pretends to have a science fiction plot, in which the hero, played by Eddie Constantine, matches wits with a master computer and assassinates a government mastermind. As with many of Godard's films, however, the plot is vague and delivered only by implication. One of the film's most striking concepts, presented both at the beginning and end, shows the hero's automobile traveling down a partially lit freeway at night, while the dialogue claims that he is in a spaceship, passing stars. The movie is flexible—you can believe he is in a spaceship, or you can believe he is in a car. Using this format and narrative outline, Godard fills **Alphaville**—which, as is indicated by the title, could also be said to be about the power of words—with philosophical discussions and catch-phrases about various aspects of modern life. The hero gets into fights and visits various locales, creating a consistently interesting visual stimulus to keep the viewer concentrating while the dialogue delivers loads of ideas, queries and opinions. Because the film is so rich in philosophical discussion, because the images are so intriguingly chosen and because the science fiction premise is such an automatic intellectual tickler, **Alphaville** is inherently repeatable.

The black-and-white image is quite grainy in places and there are some incidental scratches on the source material, but the presentation looks much nicer than the Criterion LD. Details are clearer, blacks are purer, the image is sharper and the picture is less hazy. The DVD is presented in full screen format, unmasking the top and bottom of the image. The monophonic sound is a little constricted, but viable. The 99 minute film is in French with optional English subtitles ("You know 'journalist' and 'justice' both begin with the same letter?").

Altered States (Warner, 11076)

Ken Russell's hyperkinetic science fiction tale is presented in letterboxed format on one side, with an aspect ratio of about 1.8:1 and an accommodation for enhanced 16:9 playback, and in full screen format on the other side. Except for the advantages of 16:9 enhancement, however, the full screen presentation is preferable. From the lettering that forms the film's title in the opening credits, to the rapid fire hallucination sequences and the elaborate special effects finale—not to mention the nudity—the full screen image gives more picture information than the letterboxing does. The letterboxing masks the top and bottom of the image and adds nothing to the sides.

The picture is free of grain, hues are sharp and fleshtones are accurate. There is a little softness here and there, and some age-related speckling, but on the whole, the image looks terrific. The stereo surround sound on the 1980 feature has some of the limitations inherent in an older mix and the bass, even on the Dolby Digital track, seems a bit reserved, but the audio's general dimensionality adds energy to the entertainment. The film is also available in French in standard stereo and can be supported by English or French subtitles ("On veut isoler les spécifiques responsables de la schizophrénie"). The 103 minute film is accompanied by a passable cast & crew profile section, a ridiculously brief essay about the film's themes that seems like kindergarten talk compared to the dialogue in the film, and two TV commercials that, sensibly, focus on the film's sexual content.

William Hurt stars as a brilliant Harvard professor who begins dabbling in hallucinogenic drugs that end up changing his physiology. No matter how hard they try, the scientists in the film can never convincingly explain why this is happening, but the film is a blast of intelligent blather, stimulating images and great sex. The movie's ending essentially dares you to point to the spot where reality ends and the metaphors begin. Along with its basic entertainment, the film also makes you think, and because of its pacing, it makes you think fast.

Always (Universal, 20556)

With every Steven Spielberg film comes a collection of astonishments. This 1981 feature, about a ghost who can't leave his girlfriend, is not one of Spielberg's best films. Richard Dreyfuss stars, as an aerial firefighter. His scenes with Holly Hunter are wonderful, but the other performers, including John Goodman, are tiresome, and even Audrey Hepburn, in one of her final screen appearances, seems out of place.

But as a DVD, **Always** is terrific. With a bright, rectangular picture, and a lively 4.1-channel Dolby Digital soundtrack, the flying footage is spectacular and the action scenes are gripping. The picture is in letterboxed format only, with an aspect ratio of about 1.85:1 and no 16:9 enhancement. Hues are carefully detailed and the image is crisp. The 4.1 Dolby Digital track (mono surround) has more flourish and punch than the standard track. The 123 minute feature has a French audio track in standard stereo, optional English subtitles, a small cast profile section, some production notes and a trailer.

Amadeus (Warner, 36218)

Amadeus is not true biography. You would barely have a sense that Mozart wrote more than a half-dozen operas. Its intention, and what it succeeds well at, is to be musical criticism. The sources of Mozart's inspiration and the power of his work are dissected in an entertaining manner. The movie provides a lively introduction to the music and life of Mozart. It also provides an adequate sampling of Mozart's music for those who feel like being entertained, but cannot settle on a single work for their entertainment. Milos Forman directed the Oscar-winning 1984 feature, which stars F. Murray Abraham and Tom Hulce.

The picture looks outstanding. Blacks are purer, fleshtones are richer and the image on the DVD is crisper. The 160 minute film is spread to both sides and is presented in letterboxed format, with an aspect ratio of about 2.35:1 and an accommodation for 16:9 enhanced playback. The stereo surround sound and Dolby Digital sound are fine. The music is grand, although the mix is not overly detailed. The Dolby Digital track is more embellished and forceful than the standard track. There is also a music-only audio track that is not in Dolby Digital. The film is available in French in standard stereo as well and comes with English, French or Spanish subtitles. There is a comprehensive cast-and-crew listing, extensive production notes and a theatrical trailer.

Amarcord (Criterion, AMA060)

Depicting life in a small Italian town during a year in the early Thirties, the film is one of Federico Fellini's finest accomplishments. Although he focuses much of his attention upon one family, he also moves about the town and captures vignettes involving many different and amusing characters. The effects of Fascism are a strong motif in the film but do not receive an undue emphasis. Some viewers may be put off by the attention the narrative pays to sexual activity, but the approach is fairly analytical, an examination of the odd things the libido makes people do, and the depictions are more teasing than explicit. As the seasons pass, the blend of humorous incidents, compelling images and intriguing characters, set to Fellini's circus-like atmosphere, creates a portrait of humanity that is rich and stimulating. The picture quality is immaculate and the beauty of the images is magnetic, drawing the viewer much deeper into the film and its joys than the standard revival house print could possibly manage. Every frame of the film is gorgeous and every frame, thanks to Fellini's eye, is a delight. The color transfer is captivatingly beautiful and crisp. The picture is letterboxed with an aspect ratio of about 1.85:1 and no 16:9 enhancement. The monophonic sound is also in excellent condition, delivering Nina Rota's musical score with a smooth freshness and the Italian dialogue with crispness. The 127 minute film, can be accessed in the original Italian or in a much less satisfying English dubbing, with or without white English subtitles. Contrary to a jacket notation, we could not locate a theatrical trailer.

The Amazing Feats of Young Hercules (UAV, 40088)

Cashing in on other cartoon features, the animated program is accompanied by a program entitled *Young Pocahontas*. The menu set-up will be confusing to youngsters, who will not be able to access the *Pocahontas* program without practice or adult intervention. In the **Hercules** program, the hero is given several tasks to perform by Zeus and learns to use his wit and his humanity while carrying out the commands. There are enough monsters and fantasy sequences to keep children interested, just as there are enough talking animals and battles in *Pocahontas* to hold their attention there (though not quite as effectively). Each show also has a couple of insipid songs. The animation is fairly basic. The artwork is bland, but the picture looks fairly nice, with crisp lines and vivid colors. The monophonic sound is passable..

Amazon Women on the Moon (Universal, ID4294USDVD)

The John Landis comedy anthology is in full screen format. The picture has bright hues, accurate fleshtones and is sharply focused. The monophonic sound is in passable condition. The 85 minute program is not captioned. The skits are erratic in quality, some seeming desperate for humor that is never generated and others, such as the Invisible Man sequence with Ed Begley, Jr., guaranteeing laughs to anyone watching for the first time.

Amber & Sharon Do Paris Part 1 X-rated (Lipstik, 31202)

The aged atmosphere and cheapness of the show enhance the program's eroticism, as the lack of slick production values gives it a sense of realism. The vague narrative is about two porn stars visiting Paris and talking shop with their French counterparts. The program runs 71 minutes and stars Amber Lynn and Sharon Mitchell.

America (see The Best of MusikLaden Live America)

America (Image, ID4726DSDVD)

D.W. Griffith's 1924 take on the American Revolution would have been a great film if it had been made in 1917, but by 1924 the language of cinema had become more sophisticated and Griffith was unable to keep up with advances in the medium he had, in an important way, helped to invent. Still, there are so darn few films around about the Revolutionary War that the movie fills a need, and it does so in an entertaining manner. Griffith's historical epics are always such a confusing mix of thoroughly researched accuracy and utter fabrication that you don't know what to believe and what not to, but his depiction of the fracas at Lexington and Concord has an air of authenticity to it and the stoic actor he picked to play George Washington looks exactly like a younger version of the guy on the dollar bill. The film blends a fictional story about a young Minuteman and the Tory lass he pines for with selected events from the Revolution. It builds to an appropriately exciting finale and has a nice scope, but stylistically it is somewhat archaic, a jumble of melodramatic moments and historical portraits come to life.

The presentation is slightly windowboxed and mildly tinted. Wear is never severe and movement is smooth. The image jiggles at times, but not to the point of distraction. There is a stereophonic organ and orchestra score that is best held to a modest volume. The program runs 140 minutes.

America by Rail (Simitar, 7401)

The 201 minute collection of train rides is a combination of two video cassette programs, one tracing a ride from Washington DC to San Fransisco, and the other traveling from San Diego to Seattle. In both programs there are also digressions along the way for local train jaunts (such as the Omaha Zoo Train and Seattle's Monorail), as well as brief travelogue portraits of the major stops. Most of the program, however, is just the scenery from the train as it chugs along—three-and-a-half hours across the backyards of America. If you don't get it, you don't get it, but enthusiasts will be ecstatic. The picture quality is very good throughout the program, with bright, crisp colors. The stereo surround sound is strong.

The American Bullfighter I & II (Simitar, 7354)

Two hours worth of footage exploring the world of rodeo clowns has apparently been included. The DVD is comprised of two 60 minute programs, *American Bullfighter II* and *Dances with Bulls*, which are accessed separately through the menu. However, we tried two copies of the DVD and both were defective—on each, the second program was inaccessible. Our review, therefore, concerns the first hour only. The picture quality is fine and the monophonic sound is passable. There is no captioning.

The rodeo clowns of the past backed into their profession, but today's rodeo clowns are not only fulfilling a life dream, they even compete in rodeo clown competitions, and there probably isn't a one of them who hasn't fractured almost every bone in his body. The program interviews clowns, provides profiles of the best known clowns, and tracks the changes that have gone on in the profession over the years. There are oodles of shots of the clowns getting mauled, tossed, stomped, bit, and otherwise maltreated, just as there are plenty of shots of the clowns deftly avoiding—or should we say, putting off until a later date—such damage. Everyone concedes that the clowns are the best part of the show, so even just an hour of them is quite appealing. Unemployment, however, looks safer to us.

American Graffiti (Universal, 20272)

The single-sided dual-layer program presents the 112 minute film and an excellent 78 minute retrospective documentary, along with a trailer, production notes and a cast profile section. The picture is letterboxed with an aspect ratio of about 2.35:1 and an accommodation for enhanced 16:9 processing. Blacks are purer than on the LD and there is a little less grain, but the two presentations are basically the same. The image looks slick when the lighting is good, but weaker during the toughest night or shadow sequences. The stereo surround sound is fine. The film is also available in French in mono and can be supported by English or Spanish subtitles ("¡Tu auto es más feo que yo!"). The documentary is supported by English, Spanish and French subtitles.

The documentary features interviews with George Lucas, Francis Coppola, all the main cast members and other significant crew personnel, and the program is filled with wonderful anecdotes and insights, as well as the film's Cinderella success story at the box office. Lucas talks about his inspirations for the film, such as his memories of cruising, which was a big thing in the Fifties but had faded away by the time the film was being made. There are some interesting screen tests (in the dance scene, Cindy Williams had her part down cold, while Ron Howard was still finding his), amusing tales about the cliques that developed on the set (Harrison Ford and Paul Le Mat were older than the others, and terrorized the younger performers), and genuinely informative segments about how the complex night cinematography was achieved on a very quick schedule and how Lucas directed the actors (he kept making them do a scene over until somebody made a mistake, and that would be the take he'd use). Lucas also tweaked the color in a couple places for the release, altering a twilight sky. As time grinds forward and the clock rocks on, the same thing happens to all nostalgic movies—they become nostalgic not only for the era they depict, but for the era in which they were produced, and the documentary, in which Lucas looks back on the days when he was still in essence a guerrilla filmmaker, evokes this benign double jeopardy superbly. Heck, a few years from now, we'll probably be nostalgic for the day we got the DVD (where were you in '98?).

American History X (New Line, N4739)

The story of the making of **American History X** would probably have made a really interesting DVD, what with the film's director, Tony Kaye, abandoning his first cut and trying out alternative versions until the film company finally took it away from him and said, 'Enough, already.' Three deleted scenes from the film are included on the DVD. Each fills in a bit more of the story, but each has the wrong tone and doesn't really match what got left in.

The 1998 film is structured with lengthy flashbacks so that what it is really about—which is one of the few trump cards the script has—isn't revealed until the last act. Concerning two brothers who are caught up in a neo-Nazi movement in Los Angeles, it is conceivable that the movie could become a cult favorite among those who would look past its op-ed speeches and moral conclusions to revel in its more incendiary passages. Much of the drama, however, is conversation, and very little is really raw enough to generate a compelling dynamic. The performances are okay—Edward Norton and Edward Furlong are the brothers—and the movie is more than just **Rumble Fish** with a topical backdrop, but it stops short of delivering any grand energy.

To help spot the flashbacks, the program is partially in black-and-white and partially in color. The colors are fresh and finely detailed, and contrasts in the black-and-white sequences are sharp. The presentation is in letterboxed format only, with an aspect ratio of about 1.85:1 and an accommodation for enhanced 16:9 playback. The film's audio mix is not elaborate, but there is a reasonably effective bass and a competent dimensionality. There seems to be very little difference between the standard stereo surround soundtrack and the Dolby Digital track. The 119 minute feature comes with optional English subtitles, a trailer, and a cast & crew profile section.

An American in Paris (MGM, 906273)

The incredibly colorful 1951 Vincente Minnelli musical, starring Gene Kelly, Leslie Caron and Oscar Levant, looks spectacular. The LD looks surprisingly washed out in comparison. There is some minor haloing around bright whites and faint over-saturation in other deep, deep hues, but generally the film's glorious chromatic splendors are replicated with marvelous precision.

The monophonic sound is a bit weak, but there is a Dolby Digital mono track that is reasonably strong. Some of the music comes across as a bit tinny, but that is the nature of the recording quality of the time. The 114 minute program also has a French audio track (most of the songs are in French, too), optional English and French subtitles ("J'ai du rythme/J'ai de la musique/J'ai ma chérie/Que demander de plus?"), and a trailer. The chapter encoding is pathetic, leaving you nowhere near the songs and not bothering to break up the final, multi-episode ballet. Although the film is set after WWII, it is actually evoking, in both story and music, a post-WWI tradition of expatriation. The narrative, a drawn out romance, is probably the film's weakest component, however, but it is sufficient for delivering the George Gershwin music, Kelly's dancing and Minnelli's kaleidoscopic art design. Although limited by the standards one might apply to ballet, Kelly's brilliance is in his adaptation of dance to the film medium. His dances always accept the confines of the screen, the requirements of a two-dimensional plane, and the need in popular film to entertain. It is not just the audacious nature of the final ballet sequence, where he really proved himself capable of using the medium to its fullest, but in the simpler moments, such as the opening apartment sequence when he prepares his flat for daytime by kicking drawers and moving props in an athletic smoothness, or when he first starts to shift from song to dance with Leslie Caron. The dialogue prelude and *Love Is Here to Stay* sequence, for example, is an excellent example of Kelly's quintessential American casualness (watch it separately, and your respect for the entire film may increase). There is hardly a serious ballet choreographer working today, in Paris and throughout the world, who hasn't been influenced by what Kelly brought to the screen.

American Pop (Columbia TriStar, 19599)

Ralph Bakshi's 1980 animated masterpiece follows a genetic talent for music through five generations while presenting a history of Twentieth Century pop culture in the United States. The narrative would seem superficial or shallow in a live action film, but with stylized animation it is a sufficient vehicle for exploring the emotional environment popular music created and how it mutated over the decades, and the focus can shift from one character to the next without alienating the viewer in a way that might happen if the characters were played by stars. It is a grown up film, exploring drug addiction, the horrors of war and the joys of sex, but most of all it is about man's unique spiritual bond with music, and the constancy of that bond regardless of changing styles or compromised moralities.

Columbia TriStar has preserved the film's original soundtrack, which includes cuts by The Doors, Jimi Hendrix, Dave Brubeck, Janis Joplin, Lynyrd Skynyrd and plenty of others. The stereo surround soundtrack is terrific, even though there is no further audio enhancement. The picture is presented on one side in letterboxed format, with an aspect ratio of about 1.85:1 and an accommodation for enhanced 16:9 playback, and in full screen format on the other side. The picture seems to lose much more on the top and the bottom in comparison to what it gains on the sides, so the full screen version is preferable. The source material has a few stray speckles, but the color transfer looks fine, with sharp, solid hues. The 97 minute film also has a Spanish language track, optional English, French and Spanish subtitles, and a trailer.

American Rampage (Simitar, 7405)

The dopey movie about a female cop, 'on loan from the vice squad,' investigating a drug war in Hollywood (apparently, the filmmakers didn't want to travel far to shoot on location). Troy Donahue has a couple scenes as the heroine's shrink and earns top billing on the jacket and a partial filmography as a result. The acting is awful, the action scenes are awful and the story is ridiculous, but some viewers may find the movie to be so stupid that they might be entertained by its inanities. The picture quality is also quite bad. The source material is battered and grainy, with faded colors and pale fleshtones. The monophonic sound is bland. The film runs 90 minutes and is not captioned.

American Steam / A Vanishing Era (Madacy, DVD99055)
American Steam / A Vanishing Era: Steam in the 50's & 60's (Madacy, DVD990551)
American Steam / A Vanishing Era: Twilight of Steam (Madacy, DVD990552)
American Steam / A Vanishing Era: Steam Giants across America (Madacy, DVD990553)

Like trains? Especially big oily, messy steam trains, which so evoke a more simpler time that they seem environmentally friendly regardless of how much black smoke chugs out of their engines as they rattle down the tracks? The three volumes, available individually and in a boxed set, run about 55 minutes each and contain a lot of color footage drawn from the Fifties, Sixties and afterward of steam engines on various runs. Narration opens each program, and identifies the trains throughout, but kind of steps back after the introduction to pretty much let the trains take their course. The shows don't tell you much about them, so you can't really use it to help identify one type of engine from another, but the variety of images and locales is highly appealing and although all three programs show nothing but trains, parked and in action, the images never seem redundant.

The picture quality is fine. Much of the footage is 16mm, yet it is very sharp, and colors are reasonably strong. Damage to the source material is surprisingly minimal. The sound effects have probably been added after the fact and really don't put you in the engine's cab, but the stereo sound is passable. The programs are not captioned. Each program is accompanied by a few text essays about trains and train-related trivia.

Steam Giants runs 54 minutes and depicts the largest engines, talking a little bit about where they operated and what they were used for. **Twilight of Steam** runs 55 minutes and is mostly about the trains that are kept in what is essentially a train preserve in Steamtown, near Scranton, Pennsylvania, taking a look not only at what they are like now, but also how they were used before they were taken out to pasture. **Steam in the 50's and 60's** runs 27 min-

utes and is just a general and engaging collection of footage of steam trains at work.

American Strays (Simitar, 7341)

A bargain basement Quentin Tarantino imitation, the film has several loosely connected stories, with a bag of money that threads together most of them (one, about two serial killers who meet, never links up with the others). Overwritten and overacted, the film could almost stand as a parody of Tarantino's writing if it wasn't so clear that the filmmakers were taking themselves seriously. There is dialogue containing sociological analysis of things like 8-track tapes, Francis Scott Key and Aerosmith. There are quirky tough guys who dance with sexy, macho women between bloodsports. There are two black characters, speaking the worst imitation black slang we've ever heard. Luke Perry, Eric Roberts, Jennifer Tilly and John Savage are featured in the cast, along with a number of other recognizable performers.

The image is reasonably solid and fleshtones look good. The Ultra-Stereo is inconsistent in dimensionality, but workable. The film runs 93 minutes and is accompanied by abridged cast filmographies. There is no captioning.

An American Werewolf in London (Artisan, 60453)

The outlandishly humorous 1981 John Landis movie stands up well to multiple viewings because Griffin Dunne's performance, Jenny Agutter's smile, and the peak-a-boo effect shots make the movie difficult to dislike. The picture is in letterboxed format only, with an aspect ratio of about 1.85:1 and no 16:9 enhancement. We prefer a full screen framing on the film, but the presentation is viable. Although some sequences retain a sort of refined grain, the image is solid, fleshtones are rich and other colors are deep. The stereo mix sounds a little awkward in places, with the music feeling distanced from the other sound effects, but most of the time the dimensionality is very effective, particularly on the Dolby Digital track. The 90 minute film is accompanied by a terrific theatrical teaser (blood flowing in water forms the shape of a wolf—and this in the days before CGI) and is captioned.

An American Werewolf in Paris (Buena Vista, 14376)

Tom Everett Scott plays the hero, one of three young Americans visiting France who come into contact with a pack of werewolves apparently plotting to take over the world. Julie Delpy also stars. The film has some humor (though not enough), lots of effects, some action and a few excitements, but it never explores the ambiance of its supposed locale and at times it feels like it is grinding out a story instead of running to keep up with one. If you're nuts about werewolf movies, the quantity of their appearances should be pleasing, but casual viewers will find little that is original. And everybody, by the way, will probably wonder how the hero can bungee jump off the pyramid-shaped Eiffel Tower and not crash into the girders below.

The image is letterboxed only, with an aspect ratio of about 1.85:1 and no 16:9 enhancement. The picture quality is okay, though the cinematography is rarely striking (there are some lovely night views of Paris) and the CGI effects, though abundant, have a nagging artificiality. The Dolby Digital track is a little harsher sounding than the standard track, but separations are also more distinctive. The 98 minute program also has a French language track in Dolby Digital, optional English subtitles, and a trailer.

America's Atomic Bomb Tests: Operation Tumbler Snapper (Image, ID4373DODVD)

The excellent and quite unnerving declassified military training film is about atomic bomb testing and appears to have been constructed in the early Fifties by the Defense Department. The audio track, however, appears to be a recent re-recording of the film's original narration. The ambiance is too clean for it to be from the Fifties, but the narration is too oblivious to irony and the morality of atomic testing to be contemporary. Anyway, the film succeeds on two levels—as a straightforward educational film about what is learned from atomic testing, and as an eerie look at how America tried to learn to love the bomb. The film does an excellent job at explaining the complex properties of a bomb blast (it has four parts—light, heat, radiation and a rapid, forceful modification of air pressure) and how each is measured. It also, with a completely straight face, shows military personnel visiting a nearby forest, cutting down trees, transporting them to the Nevada desert and planting them in concrete to measure the supposed effect of a bomb blast on forests. Each of these two aspects of the film is rewarding for a different reason, but combined they have the forceful artistic power of a fusion explosive. Unlike the sound, the picture quality shows its age, with fairly faded colors, but the wear is not bad enough to create a distraction. The show runs 47 minutes.

America's Greatest Roller Coaster Thrills in 3-D (Image, ID4383GHDVD)

America's Greatest Roller Coaster Thrills 2 (Image, ID4385GHDVD)

A dozen or so rollercoaster rides from around the country are profiled on the 85 minute **Thrills in 3-D**. The 3-D effect is something of a rip-off. The program uses the 'dark right eye' method to create artificial 3-D effects that only work when the camera is moving from right to left, something that is not consciously done in the program itself, so that the effects come and go haphazardly. The 3-D effects are a little more plentiful on 2, but the 3-D promo is still a rip-off and should not influence one's decision to obtain the program (one can get just as many thrills watching **Twister** while wearing the glasses that are included with the platter).

No matter, though, because even if you don't bother with the two pairs of glasses that come with the DVD, the show is a great treat for rollercoaster fans. The rides from nine different amusement parks are featured, Six Flags Magic Mountain, Six Flags over Texas, Cedar Point, Astroland in Coney Island, Paramount King's Island, Paramount's Great America, Busch Gardens Tampa, Busch Gardens Williamsburg and Kennywood. There is an overview of the park and each ride, which usually lasts around three minutes, is traveled twice, once from a variety of angles and once from the front seat. There is a reprise of the front seat rides at the end. The stereo sound is a mix of blandly enthusiastic music and unenhanced live recordings of the rides, along with a narration (the front seat shots go with the live sound only).

The 67 minute **Thrills 2**, another 3-D program, gives tours of another dozen or more amusement parks and rollercoasters. Again, you get a decent summary of the park's attractions and then a thorough ride on the coaster, usually in two passes, one from the outside and one from the front seat. Among the attractions are coasters at Great Escape in Lake George NY, Morey's Pier in Wildwood NJ, Paramount's King's Dominion in Doswell VA, the top of the Stratosphere Tower in Las Vegas, Kennywood in Pittsburgh, Busch Gardens in Williamsburg VA and Tampa FL, Cedar Point in Sandusky OH, Knoebels in Elysburg PA, Holiday World in Santa Claus IN, Worlds of Fun in Kansas City MO and Valleyfair in Scakopee MN. A mixture of older style and state-of-the-art rides, the program never seems redundant or tiresome, and even without the 3-D glasses, the you-are-there camera angles can really get you dipping, ducking and grabbing onto your seat.

Each ride is shot under different lighting conditions and the image quality varies from one to the next. One is even monochromatic. Most are crisp, however, with very fresh colors and a consistent focus no matter how speedy the turns become. The sound is stereophonic and features live recordings of the rides, but there is no surround activity and the audio isn't as involving as the images.

Amistad (DreamWorks, 84162)

We have a problem with one aspect of Steven Spielberg's surprising look at the horrors of slavery, but it is not enough to spoil what is generally a captivating and enlightening piece of entertainment. Set before the Civil War, the film concerns a legal battle over a group of Africans who took control of the ship that was transporting them into slavery. Under U.S. law, the only legitimate slaves were those who had been born into that status, and part of the film's drama comes from the quest to ascertain their point of origin. One of the really neat things about the film is how it slips history into the story—the dissemination of information is so archaic that the lawyers representing the Africans cannot even translate what their clients are saying or otherwise communicate with them; there are also loving glimpses of early Nineteenth Century technology—and it enriches your understanding not only of how society in the past functioned, but how the United States worked as it gradually overcame its growing pains. It all rings true until the finale, in which Anthony Hopkins, portraying the former president, John Quincy Adams, in an interpretation that raises Adams' heroic status tenfold, gives a very vague and unlikely speech (he talks of the Civil War as if it were an inevitability) before the Supreme Court. The scene ought to be the emotional climax, but that actually happens earlier, with a previous judge's decision, and while Hopkins' scene is necessary to the film's structure on paper, it drags the movie out and deflates it a bit. For the most part, however, the 1997 movie is thrilling and vital. Djimon Hounsou and Matthew McConaughey co-star, and both are super—an attribute we rarely apply when it comes to McConaughey.

The image is so crisp and rich that even in the darkest sequences, you can make out the details of the ebony fleshtones as precisely as Spielberg and cinematographer Janusz Kaminski intended. The 155 minute film is letterboxed with an aspect ratio of about 1.85:1 and an accommodation for enhanced 16:9 playback. The stereo surround sound is weaker than the Dolby Digital soundtrack, with less dimensionality and less detail. The film's audio is elaborately mixed—not only do the chains on the Africans clank continuously as a reminder of their presence, but the Nineteenth Century chairs creak, boots scuff and other environmental sounds steadily orient the viewer to the era—and the Dolby Digital track is great, though it could, perhaps, use a bit more power. The program is accompanied by optional English subtitles, a trailer, a cast-and-director profile section, production notes and an informative half hour promotional 'making of' documentary. The documentary is not captioned or subtitled.

Anaconda (Columbia TriStar, 81755/9)

Jon Voight looks like the snake that eventually eats him in the enjoyably trashy 1997 monster film. Jennifer Lopez, the always-reliable Ice Cube and Eric Stoltz co-star. The film, about a trip up the Amazon that takes a wrong turn, is fairly silly, but then so are most monster movies. Voight's performance is marvelous, and it sets a tone that communicates a message directly to the viewer—don't worry about the film's biological and behavioral inaccuracies, just have a good time. Of stronger concern are the special effects, a combination of computer graphics and animatronics that just aren't realistic or solid enough to sell the fantasy completely. Between the performances and the elaborate number of effects, however, there is plenty to keep a viewer engaged.

The picture is letterboxed on one side (how else do you film a very long snake?), with an aspect ratio of about 2.35:1 and an accommodation for enhanced 16:9 playback, and is in full screen format on the other side. The colors look okay, despite the complicated tropical lighting. The stereo surround sound and Dolby Digital sound are great, with all those rear channel jungle noises and everything. The 90 minute film also has French and Spanish language audio tracks, optional English, French or Spanish subtitles and a trailer.

Ancient Aliens (see **Odyssey: The Mind's Eye Presents Ancient Aliens**)

Ancient Secrets of the Bible / Shroud of Turin: Fraud or Evidence of Christ's Resurrection? (Direct Video, 21472)

Ancient Secrets of the Bible / The Battle of David & Goliath: Truth or Myth? (Direct Video, 21432)

Ancient Secrets of the Bible / Samson: Strongman Hero or Legend? (Direct Video, 21442)

Ancient Secrets of the Bible / The Fiery Furnace: Could Anyone Survive It? (Direct Video, 21492)

Ancient Secrets of the Bible / Walls of Jericho: Did They Tumble Down? (Direct Video, 21482)

Ancient Secrets of the Bible / Tower of Babel: Fact or Fiction? (Direct Video, 21452)

Ancient Secrets of the Bible / Noah's Ark: Fact or Fable? (Direct, 21422)

Ancient Secrets of the Bible / Noah's Ark: Was There a Worldwide Flood? (Direct, 21462)

Ancient Secrets of the Bible / Noah's Ark: What Happened to it? (Direct, 21512)

Ancient Secrets of the Bible / Moses' Red Sea Miracle: Did It Happen? (Direct, 21412)

Ancient Secrets of the Bible / Moses' Ten Commandments: Tablets from God? (Direct, 21522)

Ancient Secrets of the Bible / Ark of the Covenant: Lost or Hidden Away? (Direct, 21402)

Each episode, which runs around 30 minutes, explores the factual basis of a specific Bible story, padding whatever time there is left over with an enactment of the tale. Although the conclusion inevitably comes down on the side of the believers, there is at least time given to skeptics and alternative interpretations of the events, so one need not concur with the faithful to draw tidbits of knowledge out of the programs. The picture quality on each episode looks okay, with adequate fleshtones and reasonably sharp, unblemished images. The sound is fine and the shows are not captioned.

The historical enactments are held to a minimum on **Shroud of Turin: Fraud or Evidence of Christ's Resurrection?**. Although some statements are given as truth without support, the episode discusses everything from how the image could have been created, to the Shroud's provenance, to the controversy over radio carbon dating.

On the other end of the spectrum, there is **The Battle of David & Goliath: Truth or Myth** and **Samson: Strongman Hero or Legend?**. Both spend a lot of time dramatizing the stories, but scientists are also hauled out to discuss the possibilities that the feats described in the stories could have occurred, or that an alternate translation of the episodes was possible. For example, Samson is said to have defeated a thousand men single-handedly, but one scholar is pulled in to explain that the word interpreted as '1000,' could easily have meant '20 or 30.' The program also contains an excellent computer graphic sequence where it is demonstrated that a house with an architectural design from Samson's era could fairly easily be toppled when a bit of pressure is applied to the correct pillar. Some time is spent in **David & Goliath** arguing as to whether 'giants,' i.e., guys over nine feet tall, could exist, but there is also a reflection on the meaning of heroism and a discussion of military conflicts (would the armies have stood by while just two representatives fought?) and weaponry (that sling, which Palestinian teenagers still use against Israeli police).

Also combining an effective use of computer graphics with dramatization sequences is **The Fiery Furnace: Could Anyone Survive It?**, the story of three believers who emerged unharmed after being thrown in a kiln by King Nebuchadnezar. The dramatization scenes tell the story well and the computer graphic model explains how an ancient kiln worked and where there might have been 'cold

spots' in which the three could have survived the ordeal. **Walls of Jericho: Did They Tumble Down?** looks like a fairly elaborate production, with some crude but viable special effects showing the walls blasting away at the sounds of the trumpet. The military tactics of the siege are discussed, as is the possibility that earthquakes could have helped. It also appears that parts of Jericho were regularly collapsing anyway because of shoddy foundation work. The episode runs just 20 minutes. **Tower of Babel: Fact or Fiction** ignores or twists accepted linguistic science to prove some of its tenets, but it does get into the archeological search for the tower, debunks after some debate the possibility that the tower was used for UFO landings, and ends on a note of caution about Sadam Hussein (current landlord of the Tower's remains) and the end of the world.

Noah's Ark: Fact or Fable? gives an overview and includes the most extensive dramatization of the event, with authorities brought in to explain how every species of land animal could have been included (though, we took note, the explanation comes perilously close to justifying evolution) and where they might have been housed in the vessel. **Noah's Ark: Was There a Worldwide Flood?** goes into more detail about flood legends (they use the legend of Gilgamesh to 'prove' the story of Noah, but considering the order in which they were written, shouldn't the story of Noah 'prove' Gilgamesh?) and how the entire Earth could be covered with water, as well as the possibility that the 'rainbow' was actually a crescent eclipse at dawn. The best episode of the three, however, is **Noah's Ark: What Happened to it?**, about the attempts to locate the remains of the Ark on Mt. Ararat in eastern Turkey. Running a full 45 minutes, none of the footage involves a dramatization of Noah's story, although there are substantial and elaborate dramatizations of the various Ark sightings, with actual footage and staged footage rarely delineated. It would seem like the easiest task in the world in this day and age to prove conclusively whether something is there or not, but instead there are the usual tantalizing but unsubstantiated testimonials and blurry photos, which would never hold up to scientific scrutiny but make for an engaging 45 minutes of speculation and wonder.

The story of Moses is also covered in three separate programs. Several slightly varied theories are presented on how the Red Sea could have parted in **Moses' Red Sea Miracle: Did It Happen?** Our favorite was from an engineer with a modified 'wave' machine, which has red oil and a bump, to show how, if there was a strong enough wind, the liquid on the ridge of the bump would be sufficiently shallow for walking across. The problem was, on a proportional basis, it doesn't look shallow at all. Maybe he should have used a different color. There are also extensive dramatization sequences and, while the body of water standing in for the Red Sea looks substantially thinner, the special effects that show it parting are impressive—if this is what a cheap video can do, can you imagine a Cameron-esque production? **Moses' Ten Commandments: Tablets from God?** also contains extensive dramatization sequences and a few arguments over just exactly how many times the tablets got printed up. The most interesting segment, however, involves the suggestion that what is called Mt. Sinai in the *Bible* may actually have been a mountain in present day western Saudi Arabia. There is some overlap of coverage about the fate of the Ark of the Covenant, which is mentioned in **Ten Commandments** but explored in greater detail in **Ark of the Covenant: Lost or Hidden Away?** Both programs come to the conclusion that the Ark still exists, but is unfortunately buried beneath an Islamic shrine and unavailable to Biblical archeologists.

Ancient Secrets of the Kama Sutra X-rated (Vivid, UPC#0073214523); softcore (Vivid, UPC#0073214536)

Real elephants and camels are employed, but there's no need to call the ASPCA, because they're only watching. The program has a 'The Library Is Your Friend' type narrative, about a couple who are taken inside a book by a very amiable librarian to experience first-hand the imagination of a printed page. The costumes and make-up are an exaggerated faux-Hindu and are fairly entertaining. The narrative is broken down into briefer stories, witnessed by the couple, but most are little more than premises for the erotic activities.

The picture, from video tape source, looks good. Some darker shots are a little grainy, but in well-lit situations the image is crisp and fleshtones are rich. The sound is fine. The program runs 72 minutes and is accompanied by the usual Vivid interactive hardcore promotional sequences and multiple angles (including an orgy sequence where you can choose the couple you wish to view). Vivid has also issued a softcore version of the program, running 69 minutes and using more close-ups. It has a 'Cable DVD' sticker on the jacket and no promotion of the hardcore multiple angle feature, but otherwise the jackets are essentially identical. The picture and sound quality are the same on both programs.

Anderson Bruford Wakeman Howe: An Evening of Yes Music Plus (Image, ID4083GIDVD)

The one problem with the rock group Yes was that their songs always went on for too long, but that is not a problem on the 152 minute reunion concert. The maturity of the musicians brings an edge to their music that was previously missing, allowing their extended solos and instrumentals to elaborate upon their melodies without creating the dull, too perfect harmonies that made past recordings so bland. Shot in 1989 at Nassau Coliseum in New York, the musicians put on quite an energetic show and the concert's running time gives each performer a chance to show off his wares. All the major hits are covered, as well as material that was fresh at the time of the recording.

The stage is well lit for video and the colors are bright, but the picture is usually fuzzy or soft looking. The stereo sound is fine, with the concert recording providing an imprecise but workable audio fidelity. The concert is split to both sides of the DVD, but most of it appears on side one.

Anderson, Pamela (see Playboy: The Best of Pamela Anderson)

Andrei Rublev (Criterion, CC1550D)

Set in the first two decades of the Fifteenth Century in the countryside outside of Moscow, Andrei Tarkovsky's magnificent epic uses a historical figure, the Russian painter whose name supplies the movie's title, as a witness to events of cruelty and artistic epiphany. The narrative is a collection of about ten episodes, independent in plot but linked in character. There are many grand, epic-styled sequences, including a lengthy battle taking up much of the movie's middle, the casting and raising of an enormous silver bell (the movie's upbeat climax and also its clearest story), the Crucifixion, and a pagan orgy. From the movie's captivating opening, in which a character flies above his pursuers while grasping a diminishing bag of hot air, to the compelling color montage of Rublev's art at the end, each scene advances in an unexpected and sometimes baffling way from the one that preceded it. Even with the improved subtitling, it is not always easy to keep the characters straight or to understand why things are happening. The haunting imagery and the rich mixture of philosophical discussion and earthy activities give the film dense layers of meaning (so dense that Petric only seems to skim the surface in his comments) while the historical sweep of the narrative moves the film comfortably from the passions and tragedies of individual lives through the desires and legacies of artists, and on to the endurance and definition of a people and a civilization. **2001: A Space Odyssey** was produced around the same period of time and while the films have nothing in common except their vaguely episodic structures, they seem very much alike, especially in their ambitious search for God through the art and craft of filmmaking.

The 1966 feature is mostly in black and white—there is a brief color montage of Rublev's paintings at the conclusion—and is letterboxed with an aspect ratio of about 2.4:1 and no 16:9 enhance-ment. The film is presented on a single-sided dual-layer platter. Although, because of its production history, there are sequences with speckling and other minor wear, the sharpness of the picture is exhilarating, adding a freshness to the image and enhancing a viewer's concentration. The monophonic sound is adequate. The film is in Russian with optional English subtitles, and contains both nudity and graphic violence.

There is a sporadically applied commentary channel, by Vlada Petric, discussing both the film's production and its meanings. Criterion's copious chapter encoding and guide make these comments easy to locate. Additionally, there is an interview with Tarkovsky and a 'timeline' that covers the history of Russia, Rublev and Tarkovsky.

The Andromeda Strain (Image, ID4220USDVD)

Robert Wise's 1970 adaptation of Michael Crichton's sci-fi thriller really only works for one viewing, though the performances of the cast members make multiple viewings a feasibility. The exciting finale, in which the heroes must turn off a self-destruct device, is a classic piece of movie making. After that breathtaking first viewing, however, it becomes obvious that every plot step is a contrivance. The events leading up to the finale are about as exciting as the first part of Wise's *Star Trek: The Motion Picture*. Largely a depiction of an elaborate, six-story underground biological containment center, as the film's technological showcasing recedes in time so does its ability to hold a viewer's attention—though it is worth noting that after twenty years, the facility is still reasonably modernistic in appearance and functionality. By casting unknowns as the leads, Wise prevented the cast members from over-playing their parts—something the set was already doing—and it is enjoyable on subsequent viewings to listen to the actors tick off their theories and data reports (the characters are attempting to isolate the organism which decimated a small town).

The letterboxing has an aspect ratio of about 2.1:1 (definitely not the 2.35:1 listed on the jacket cover) and no 16:9 enhancement. There are a few minor wear marks on the source material, but the color transfer looks reasonably good, with bright hues and crisp fleshtones. The monophonic sound is fairly strong, with a Dolby Digital mono track that sounds a little smoother and brighter. The 131 minute feature is captioned.

The Andy Griffith Show (see The Best of the Andy Griffith Show)

Angel and the Badman (Master Movies, DVD5506)

John Wayne stars in the entertaining 1947 western, as a wounded gunfighter nursed back to health by a group of Quakers. Gail Russell, as a young Quaker girl, finds it impossible to pretend that she believes in passivity. Her natural inclination, which shows through her every expression, is to molest Wayne as soon as she gets him alone.

The presentation is nowhere near as good as the best looking LD, but if you don't have anything to compare it to, it looks fairly good. The image is clean, contrasts are passable and the picture is smooth. The monophonic sound is acceptable, and background noise is minimal. The film runs 100 minutes (not 79 as is listed on the jacket cover) and is accompanied by a decent cast-and-crew profile and optional Japanese subtitles.

Angel Heart (Artisan, 60457)

Mickey Rourke and Robert De Niro star in the 1987 demonic thriller, a potentially intriguing tale about a private detective hired by the Devil to find a man who reneged on his contract. The ending is legitimate, but the flashbacks that are supposed to prepare the viewer for the conclusion are overworked and ineptly presented. The movie has no soul, and its mechanics are creaky.

The colors are accurate and the image is sharp, a substantial improvement over previous home video versions. The picture has been letterboxed, with an aspect ratio of about 1.85:1 and an accommodation for enhanced 16:9 playback, adding nothing to the sides of the image and masking off picture information from the top and bottom in comparison to a full screen framing, though the letterbox framing is better balanced. The stereo surround is crisp, with nicely detailed tones. The 112 minute feature can be supported by Spanish subtitles ("Leía el tarot antes de aprender a leer") and English closed captioning. There is an 8 minute featurette, a theatrical trailer, production notes and a cast & crew profile section.

Angel Town (Sterling, 4075)

Oliver Gruner portrays a French college student—who also happens to be a martial arts champion—caught in a war for the barrio when he has trouble finding a room to rent in Los Angeles. The film overflows with stereotypes, as the hero has to find time between his studies to protect his meek landlord from neighborhood toughs. The plot is fairly dumb, but the fight scenes are passable and the situation gives Gruner leeway to do his thing in what would otherwise be an incongruous environment for him.

The full screen picture is somewhat hazy and is grainy in places, with bland colors. The stereo surround sound is adequate and the 106 minute program also has a Spanish language track and optional Spanish (but not English) subtitles, production notes, TV commercials and a trailer.

Anima Mundi (Simitar, 7313)

An outstanding half-hour Godfrey Reggio film with music by Philip Glass, the program is a step above the average natural wonders display, not only because many of the images are so unusual but because Reggio has combined them in some very artistic ways, releasing themes and emotions to swirl past the viewer like the debris in a rapidly flowing river. Although animal life is the primary subject, landscapes are also presented, from every corner of the earth. Among the more memorable passages are a sequence of incredibly magnified shots depicting different insects cleaning themselves, a number of interesting close-ups showing the faces and eyes of various animals and an underwater shot of a sea filled with manta rays. Glass's music is not one of his more innovative works, but it is one of his more accessible, providing enough of an edge to encourage a viewer's concentration. The sharply focused picture may have a little too much color, bringing more red to the image than it ought to, but overall the presentation is satisfying. The picture is letterboxed with an aspect ratio of about 1.85:1, without enhanced 16:9 playback. The stereo sound is very good.

Animal Crackers (Image, ID4272USDVD)

The master used for the Marx Bros. film is full of scratches and blurs, but the 1930 movie was made with the most minimal production values imaginable. What sometimes looks like a break in the film is actually bad editing to begin with. In transferring what was essentially a stage vehicle to the screen, the camera remains static throughout the whole movie and the volume levels go up and down as people move nearer to or further away from the mikes. Because of the presence of the Marx Bros., the condition of the movie is irrelevant. It is legitimately entertaining and only slightly more erratic than their best films. More stage-bound than their later efforts, this is the one where Groucho is an African explorer visiting a New York mansion. The monophonic sound is also a bit battered but coherent, and there is not much the Dolby Digital mono track can do to improve it. The 97 minute program is captioned.

Animal House (see National Lampoon's Animal House; National Lampoon's Animal House: Collector's Edition)

Animaland (Image, ID4393CEDVD)

David Hand, a Disney animator who worked on *Bambi* and *Snow White*, set off on his own and ended up in Europe producing cartoon shorts for a British film company. When the company signed a general distribution deal with one of the American film companies, the American company already had a cartoon unit and so those British cartoons fell out of the loop for about fifty years. Nine of the seven-and-a-half minute shorts are featured in the 69 minute program. The colors look terrific and the image is reasonably sharp, though there is some age-related softness here and there. The monophonic sound is okay. The cartoons have very little dialogue and rely mostly on music, sound effects and images. There is no captioning.

The cartoons seem like a mix between Hugh Harmon, Rudolf Isley and Chuck Jones. Depicting the adventures and troubles of various animals, they are never overly sweet and always have a lively pace. The artwork is very nice throughout, with strong characterizations and expressions, lots of detailed movement, and evocative settings. The best two, *The Ostrich* and *The House-Cat*, are also the most surreal. In *Ostrich*, the bird wanders into some desert ruins and is soon chasing after a female ostrich within some hieroglyphics that come to life. *The House-Cat* has a standard format, about a slightly wimpy cat who rises to the occasion when he has to impress a female, but the succession of images depicting the backyards and alleyways as perceived in the cat's imagination is unusual and stimulating. If the cartoons have a weakness, though, it is narrative. During a couple we found ourselves staring at them having no idea what was happening or why, as the animals chased and batted one another about. Most of the others are stretched out with little more than an introductory premise. Still, Hand's heritage is readily apparent and the clips are clearly from a classic and now gone forever age of animation, making each cel worth its weight and ink in delights.

Animation Greats! (Lumivision, DVD0497); (SlingShot, 9812)

One of the first three commercially released DVDs, The National Film Board of Canada cartoon collection includes the highly addictive *The Cat Came Back*, *The Lump*, *The Big Snit*, the **Joe's Apartment**-style tale, *Juke Bar*, *Getting Started*, *Get a Job*, *Black Fly* and *Special Delivery*. The colors are bright and sharp. The program runs 70 minutes and most of the cartoons are in stereo, with a strong bass.

The order of the cartoons has been altered on the SlingShot release, but the picture quality still looks as good as it did before and the sound is fine.

Animation Legend: Winsor McKay (SlingShot, DVD1397)

McKay, who began by drawing newspaper comic strips, was one of the first film animators, and the cartoons in the 100 minute collection are startling. Not only do they anticipate many different styles of cartoons that eventually developed, but they point to the possibility of 'adult' cartoons that, for some reason, were never explored further until recently. In addition, there is one cartoon that is so far ahead of its time the art of animation still has not caught up to it yet.

The collection opens with *Little Nemo*, from 1910, a live action short that frames a brief animation sequence in which McKay wins a bet by animating his cartoon strip. *How the Mosquito Operates*, from 1912, is a single gag cartoon, about a mosquito sucking so much blood from a sleeping victim that it explodes. It is drawn with simple ink lines, but it has such a sophisticated approach (you see the insect's needle jabbing the victim in close-up) that it is indistinguishable from the kind of independent short animated films being produced today. *Gertie the Dinosaur* from 1914 and *Gertie on Tour* from 1921 are more typical of the beginning cartoons, with what are essentially experiments in character movement, expression and humor, but the cartoons also represent a genuine attempt to bring 'life' to dinosaurs and explore, between the gags, how the creatures might have moved (and eaten—it becomes obvious as to why they went extinct, because they eat every tree in sight). *Flip's Circus* and *Bug Vaudeville*, both from 1921, are multiple gag shorts with simplistic art (*Bug Vaudeville* actually evokes the shadow plays that preceded cinema as an entertainment) and relatively sophisticated gags. *The Centaurs*, from 1921, is a promising but non-narrative (and fragmented) piece about a family of nude, half-human half-horse creatures, frolicking in the woods. Yes, it anticipates the *Pastoral Symphony* sequence of *Fantasia*, but it is done more realistically and actually suggests the more recent Japanese fantasy cartoons. The artwork on *The Pet* and *The Flying House*, both from 1921, will strike today's viewers as looking remarkably similar to *King of the Hill*. The narratives on both cartoons are also exceptional. In *Pet*, the hero dreams his wife's dog is getting bigger and bigger, while in *House* the hero dreams he has attached a propeller to his home and taken off. The mix of sophisticated, grown-up artwork and imaginative, fully realized fantasy in the two works is astonishing. But that is nothing compared to the collection's masterpiece, *The Sinking of the Lusitania*, from 1918. Can you imagine a cartoon about JFK's assassination, or Martin Luther King's, or what it was like in the cockpit of the Challenger? *Lusitania*, a depiction of the German torpedoing of an ocean liner that was perhaps the incident most responsible for drawing America into World War I, doesn't get quite that graphic, but (calling all you future animators) there has never been a cartoon like it (has there ever even been an animated depiction of the bombing of Pearl Harbor?) though the subject—real events—would seem to hold a wealth of possibilities. The closest animators have come to the genre is some of the Japanese (again) animation about the A-bomb going off, but even these tend to focus on character and not, directly, headline history.

The cartoons are all silent and are accompanied by unobtrusive musical scores. The source material is aged, but the essence of the cartoons are effectively communicated and all are fully window-boxed. The DVD comes with an extensive jacket insert essay, by John Canemaker, on McKay's background, the films, and how they were retrieved from obscurity.

Anne Murray's Classic Christmas (Fox Lorber, WHE73020)

In typical Christmas special fashion, Murray sings a couple of holiday songs with her family, a few more solo and a few with her guest stars on the 48 minute 1995 CBC TV special. She is a little stiff between numbers and tends, on the whole, to rush her songs a bit. The best number in the whole show is a fresh rendition of *God Rest Ye Merry Gentlemen* by the now hot singing group, Barenaked Ladies. Olympic skater Elvis Stojko performs a couple of captivating routines and Roch Voisine joins Murray for a few numbers as well. The picture looks fine, with fresh, sharp hues. The sound is monophonic, but smooth. A profile of Murray and a discography are also included.

Annie Hall (MGM, 906559)

At the time when **Annie Hall** was released theatrically, it was an important step for film comedies. Both Woody Allen and Mel Brooks had been making theme comedies—a funny western, a funny science fiction movie, etc.—and from that perspective Allen's **Annie Hall** truly seemed like a breakaway film, a comedy with emotional and analytical depth. In fact it was, though for all its cleverness it no longer seems like such a remarkable accomplishment. It is about adults who are incapable of maintaining long-term romantic relationships. In the case of the title character, she doesn't appear to be interested in more than going through the motions, a weakness that seems to be more a lack of sympathy on the part of the character's creator than a realistic and complete personality portrait. It is the side gags, which Allen gradually abandoned in his subsequent films, that give the movie its spirit, and the movie was successful because the gags were not the core of the film.

The image is crisp and fleshtones are accurate. Hues are not intense and the image has a very slight grain in places, but compared to the previous transfers it looks immaculate. The 1977 Oscar-winner is presented in letterboxed format on one side, with an aspect ratio of about 1.85:1 and no 16:9 enhancement, and in full screen format on the other side. The letterboxing adds a hair of picture information to the sides and takes off more from the top and bottom in comparison to the full screen release, but it has a more satisfying framing. Some dialogue seems strained, though on the whole the monophonic sound is workable. The film is also available in French and can be supported by English French or Spanish subtitles ("Je me drogulais à l'héroïne. Maintenant, je me drogue à la méthadone"). There are also two additional subtitling options that most DVD players will select automatically to provide the 'what they're thinking' subtitling during the balcony scene in support of the English or French dialogue tracks, but if the viewer shuts off the subtitles directly, the jokes are eliminated. A theatrical trailer has also been included.

Another Day in Paradise (Trimark, 7030D)

By now it is a fairly common premise—dope fiend heroes on a crime spree that inevitably unravels—and that is pretty much the plot of Larry Clark's, but Clark, who also directed **Kids**, brings a fresh point of view to the characters, the conflicts and the film's overriding morals, and it is sufficient to hold one's attention. You still have to be amenable to drug addict heroes who rob and kill, but Clark's manipulation of the genre can be quite satisfying. James Woods and Melanie Griffith star, with Vincent Kartheiser and Natasha Gregson Wagner as their protégés. All of the performers are terrific, but Woods has done this sort of thing before and it is Griffith who delivers one of the best performances of her career, shooting up in her neck, gunning down rival drug dealers, and getting excited when Wagner's character announces she is pregnant. It is a low budget movie with improvisations, makeshift scenes, and raw sex and violence, but the film's atmosphere and subject accommodates its style.

There is so much raw sex and violence that Trimark has released two versions of the film on one platter, the standard 101 minute cut of the film on one side and a 105 minute 'Director's Cut' on the other side. Except for historical purposes, however, who is going to want to watch the standard cut? It still has so many naughty activities that you're hardly going to want to show it to your family, and the Director's version is the one that legitimately fulfills Clark's vision, with sequences that significantly enhance one's understanding of the characters and their inner psychology—and for those of you who have absolutely no interest in psychology, well, you know, it's got more steam.

Both versions are letterboxed with an aspect ratio of about 1.66:1 and no 16:9 enhancement. This being a very low budget effort, the lighting is deliberately limited, and so colors are not always well defined and the image is not always in perfect focus. Once again, however, the presentation is workable and essentially contributes to the film's grungy atmosphere. The music and occasional surges of sound activity are stereophonic, and the DVD even has a Dolby Digital track, which has a more pronounced dimensionality and more energy. The music sounds great. Gunshots are deliberately realistic, delivering light firecracker-type 'pops' instead of the standard Hollywood kabooms. The standard version (but not the Director's Cut) can be supported by optional English, French or Spanish subtitles ("J'suis un toubib que te pique à l'héroïne"). Both are accompanied by a trailer, a music video by Clarence Carter (including sequences not involving Carter that didn't make it into the movie) and a cast profile section.

The Director's Cut also has a commentary track by Clark. Clark tends to let the film play and speaks intermittently, but what he has to say is interesting, about his fights with the MPAA, about his anti-Hollywood approach (he tries to deliberately break standard filmmaking rules) and about working with the cast. He only speaks obliquely about the fights he had with them and other problems during the shoot, but you still get a decent feel for his somewhat radical methods and can pretty much interpolate the rest, though the proof that he knew what he was doing is there on the screen.

Another 9 1/2 Weeks (Trimark, VM67720)

Mickey Rourke stars as a bossy guy who is despondent because the girl in **9 1/2 Weeks** that he used to boss around is gone. In the opening scene he looks out of his hotel window and sees a dead horse on the street below. Nobody is beating the horse, but the implication is there. So he flies to Paris, meets another girl who used to be friends with the first girl, and hangs out with her while she gets ready for a fashion show. He bosses her around a little bit, but it isn't as much fun, so he leaves. We never find out what happened with the horse. Although the erotic sequences are reasonably involving, the film is not focused on such interplay—it's mainly about the guy moping around Paris—and the only thing that is consistent in the movie is its inadvertent humor, which improves on multiple viewings, when you finally accept that this is all there is to it.

The picture looks okay. The fuzzy stuff—these kinds of movies always have fuzzy stuff—doesn't look too fuzzy and when the image is supposed to be sharp it is—all the better to wince at Rourke's close-ups. The picture is presented in full screen format but the framing is workable. Colors are reasonably bright and fleshtones are okay. The stereo surround sound is adequate. The 104 minute program has optional French and Spanish subtitles, and English captioning. There is also a trailer and a cast profile section.

Antarctica (Lumivision, DVD0297); (SlingShot, 9810)

One of the first three commercially released DVDs, the 40 minute IMAX program looks at different aspects of the southern continent, the most harrowing being when scientists don aqualungs and plunge beneath the ice. The image is quite nice and is sharply focused, but the colors look a little washed out. The stereo surround sound has a nice dimensionality.

The picture is much improved in SlingShot's reissue. Not only has the artifacting been corrected, but the image is sharper and colors are deeper. The audio mix has been modified, as well. The new Dolby Digital track is more refined, with better separations, though a few viewers may miss the overblown bass on the older track. The program is also available in French and Spanish in Dolby Digital and can be supported by English subtitles. Although the logo on the jacket suggests that the DVD contains PC-ROM functions, it offer nothing more than a promotional Web link.

Antz (DreamWorks, 84199)

The PG-rated computer animated feature has a great story and is quite witty. With Woody Allen, Sylvester Stallone, Gene Hackman and many others providing voices, it is a class act that is cleverly conceived and executed. The only problem is the animation, which is going to look very dated as the artform advances. The expense-capped artwork generates bland or repetitive textures, uninteresting lighting and dull backgrounds. Even the stiff faces of the characters get tired after a while, exoskeleton or no exoskeleton. The film is still worthwhile, but perhaps someday in the future they'll go back to their code and update the images.

The presentation is letterboxed, with an aspect ratio of about 1.85:1 and an accommodation for enhanced 16:9 playback. Generally the picture looks good, though it is hard to say if the softness in some hues comes from the source material or the transfer. At its best, the images are slick and vivid. There were times when we preferred the standard stereo surround sound to the Dolby Digital sound. While the Dolby Digital track is more meticulous at defining the separation effects, the standard track tends to throw more noises to the rear channel and create a stronger dimensionality. Like the artwork, the film's audio mix is not a regal effort, but it is adequate for the entertainment.

The 83 minute program is captioned and is accompanied by some amusing TV spots, a trailer that pretty much re-tells the whole story, a listing of the cast, a profile of the directors, a brief production essay, an excellent production featurette, an interesting piece on the development of the characters, and equally good breakdowns of the animation process that take selected scenes from the film and show how they look in each step.

There is also a commentary track by the two directors, Eric Darnell and Tim Johnson. They don't say anything about the film's race against *Bug's Life* and they don't give any sort of overview on how the movie was conceived (and they only mention Jeffrey Katzenberg's involvement once), but they do react to the individual scenes, explaining what got added earlier or later, what was changed and how things were modified as the production advanced. They talk about utilizing the specialties of computer animation (they claim 60,000 ants are depicted in one sequence), about working with the voice talent, about the details of individual scenes, and about ants (which really do drink aphids).

Anything Goes (see **Frank Sinatra His Life and Times The Singer /The Entertainer**)

Apollo 13 (Universal, 20153); DTS (Universal, 20461)

Future generations will look at Ron Howard's **Apollo 13** not only as a drama, but as a document of the earliest space flights, of how we managed to go all the way to the moon with primitive computers, slide rules and duct tape—it is more like the simplistic vision of Jules Verne than anyone at the time could have imagined. It is the film's methodical drama, however, that makes it so appealing—the cross-cutting between the astronauts in peril, their families, and the technicians on Earth trying to figure a way to keep the crippled spacecraft functioning.

The 140 minute film is presented in letterboxed format only, with an aspect ratio of about 2.35:1 and an accommodation for enhanced 16:9 playback. Although whites have a slightly pinkish cast, fleshtones richer and the image is sharp. The stereo surround sound is good, and the Dolby Digital track is a little stronger and more elaborately separated than the regular track. The film is also available in French and Spanish in Dolby Digital and comes with English or Spanish subtitles ("Hay un problema"). There is a brief production essay, a cast profile section and a terrific theatrical trailer.

A good hour-long documentary about the film's production is also included. The program combines interviews with the cast and crew, behind-the-scenes views, explanations of the special effect sequences and a healthy amount of archival footage from the actual incident. The documentary is in English only, with English, French or Spanish subtitling.

During the unspooling of the film itself, there are two commentary tracks. On one, Howard elaborates upon the material covered in the documentary, explaining how the film was conceived, the troubles he ran into while shooting it, and what it was like working with the cast and crew. In some ways, his talk is a bit superficial, never getting too technical or too reflective but, over the course of the two plus hours, he conveys a fairly thorough portrait of his experiences. He also shares a few tidbits of trivia that will delight movie fans, such as when he points out his homage to **American Graffiti**. We would have liked to have learned more about the pre-production process, specifically how the shots taken on the zero gravity airplane were planned and what changes he brought to the script. Nevertheless, the talk is reasonably informative and provides an entertaining way to revisit the film.

On the other channel, James and Marilyn Lovell, whose lives were the basis for two of the film's central characters, react to the film and reminisce about their experiences during the original flight. Interestingly, Marilyn Lovell becomes emotional only once, during a scene that we tend to see as superfluous, in which Tom Hank's character—her husband—dreams that he has landed on the moon. She also reveals that the impetus for the film's other (and also seemingly superfluous) dream sequence, a nightmare about a disaster in space, came from attending a screening of *Marooned* a couple months before the flight. We sympathize. James Lovell does most of the talking, however, and although you can tell that he has shared many of his stories many times in the past, he still has much to add, particularly when he gives rapid-fire descriptions of what the characters in the film are doing when they press various buttons and perform other astronaut functions that the movie otherwise leaves unexplained, for understandable reasons. Although the other special features are rewarding, it is probably the presence of the Lovells that makes the DVD an exceptional production. It is rare enough that one gets to compare a Hollywood depiction of a romance to the real thing, and rarer still that Hollywood turned out to be so accurate.

The DTS track is a touch louder than the Dolby Digital track on the standard release, but there are no significant embellishments and it is difficult to tell the two apart. The DTS LD, on the other hand, has more pronounced dimensionality and more energy. The frame transfer rate on the standard release swings wildly between the high range and the mid-to-low range, and while the transfer rate on the DTS DVD doesn't go quite as high, it stays more consistently in the upper range.

The Apostle (Universal, 20321)

Some of the best movies are about religion because the rules of religious practice can serve as a powerful magnification to a character's moral conflicts, and that is what happens with Robert Duvall's 1998 feature. Duvall wrote the script and used his own money to make the film, which is the movie's one real flaw—it runs 134 minutes and could stand to lose a half hour or so, although Duvall apparently cut it down quite a bit anyway and didn't want to lose any more of it. Duvall stars as well, portraying a preacher on the lam after he kills a man in a fit of rage. He wanders into a small Southern town and starts a church, reviving the community and his own soul as he rediscovers his roots and his true talents. The film makes a concentrated effort to observe the boisterous Sunday services of the Pentecostals objectively, and it is in the balance between the realism of its social exploration and the drama of the hero's personal failings that the film sustains its energy and rewarding insight.

The program is letterboxed with an aspect ratio of about 1.85:1, with no 16:9 enhancement, and has a deliberately rural color scheme, though the picture is effective detailed. The stereo surround sound is not elaborately mixed, but there is sufficient ambiance and dimensionality. The 134 minute program can be supported by English, French or Spanish subtitles. There is a brief but informative clip about the film's music, some production notes, a trailer, and a cast & crew profile section. Also included is a half hour documentary that works its way through the narrative, cutting to comments by Duvall and other members of the cast and crew. Since so much of the film is self-evident, there is little the documentary can add after telling the basic story of Duvall's financial risk. The background for Billy Bob Thornton's character is explained, though his motivations remain vague.

Duvall provides a running commentary as well, a few points of which are duplicated in the documentary. The commentary is okay. He spends some time explaining what is happening on the screen, but he also talks about how he conceived and staged the major scenes, about what has been left out, and tells about his fellow performers, with some (but less) information about the others in his crew.

Apt Pupil (Columbia TriStar, 22309)

Ian McKellen stars as a former Nazi and Brad Renfro is a typical American high school student with an unusual hobby. The film's moral compass acts, deliberately, as if it is in the center of a ring of dancing magnets, which will be alienating to those who expect films to have distinct heroes and villains. Even those who really get into it, though, may ultimately feel that it doesn't go far enough, or that it goes so far it gets ridiculous. Either way, it is more entertaining as a conflict of well-conceived personalities than as a story that is expected to go somewhere significant. David Schwimmer, incidentally, gives an outstanding supporting performance as a clueless guidance counselor. Bryan Singer directed.

The 1998 film is in letterboxed format on one side, with an aspect ratio 2.35:1 and an accommodation for enhanced 16:9 playback, and is in full screen format on the other side. The letterboxing adds very little to the sides and masks off picture information from the top and bottom. On the whole, we found the full screen image more suited to the conversational nature of the film, and the framing balances seem more appealing. The color transfer looks okay. The cinematography appears to be deliberately soft in some indoor sequences, but colors are bright and fleshtones are workable. The stereo surround sound has a basic, efficient mix, with decent directional effects. The Dolby Digital track is cleaner, and separation effects are better defined. The 112 minute program can be supported by optional English subtitles and is accompanied by a trailer, a 'making of' featurette and a cast-and-director profile section.

Arabian Nights (Image, ID4417WBDVD)

Shot in Africa and using local performers for most of the major roles, Pier Paolo Pasolini's 1974 feature is a superb blending of cultures, taking a few of the bawdy stories made famous by the Arabian Nights anthology and setting them in the gritty, spare environment where in all probability the tales originated. Although good and bad things happen to the characters within the narrative, the film has an essentially joyful (and realistically erotic—the film is rated 'NC-17') atmosphere.

The presentation is letterboxed with an aspect ratio of about 1.75:1 and no 16:9 enhancement. The image is soft and worn-looking, and colors are heavy on the brown tones. The monophonic sound is adequate and the 131 minute movie is in Italian with white English subtitles.

Arachnophobia (Buena Vista, 17098)

About a house infested with killer spiders, Jeff Daniels stars as the local physician who investigates the problem, with John Goodman giving a jokey performance as an ace exterminator. The plot is contrived and the finale is stretched out to squeeze every last scream possible from the situation, but the best jump cuts deliver what is expected from them and the more you dislike spiders, the more the film works in your favor.

The presentation is letterboxed with an aspect ratio of about 1.8:1 and no 16:9 enhancement. The color transfer looks fine, with sharp, bright hues and adequate fleshtones. The standard stereo surround sound is weaker than the Dolby Digital track, which has better defined separation effects and a little more power. The 110 minute program has optional English subtitles, a trailer and a surprisingly analytical 3 minute featurette—they seemed to be trying to sell the film from the perspective that they had learned, scientifically, how to make people scream.

Area 88—The Blue Skies of Betrayal (U.S. Manga, USMD1727)

The first episode in a terrific Japanese animation program about mercenary jet pilots working in the Middle East, the hero is a young commercial pilot who is tricked into signing a play-or-die mercenary contract by a secret rival and eventually becomes a top ace, hoping to earn enough money to fill his obligation and return to his sweetheart. The episode runs about 45 minutes, with end credits and previews extending the time to about an hour. The colors are bright and solid, and the source material is free of damage. That artwork is super. Although the desert country in which the story is set is fictitious, the time is the early Eighties and the program's creators are meticulous in their representation of established military hardware and aircraft. Animation allows the planes to perform stunts that are unlikely in real life, but buffs will appreciate the attention that is paid to realistic detail both inside and outside the cockpit. The action scenes are often quite exciting. The stereo surround sound is also very good. The program is available in English or in Japanese, with optional English subtitles. There are also menu options that bring up brief excerpts from the program.

Aretha Franklin—Live at Park West (Image, ID5502CADVD)

A wimpy audio recording steals some of the thunder from the otherwise promising concert show. Franklin builds up a sweat, but she pretty much stays in one position on the stage, holding the microphone with one hand and motioning with the other as she sings. The recording of her vocals lacks a strong presence, and there is little personality in her renditions. In general, her studio recordings are more engaging.

Franklin is well lit, so while those behind her look a little fuzzy at times, she remains sharply focused. Fleshtones are accurate. In addition to the weak vocals, the music does not have much dimensionality. There is no captioning.

Armageddon (Buena Vista, 15039); collector's (Buena Vista, 16720)

Even though the standard film runs 150 minutes, what we don't like about **Armageddon** is that it seems too short. The maddening blam blam blam zoom editing pushes the narrative along so quickly there's no opportunity to savor it, and it is clear that subplots have been trimmed or eliminated at every turn to encompass all the action scenes. The result is as dull as it is superficial, and while the film may have some showy special effects, they're not that unique and there isn't enough story power to make them worth the effort it takes to watch them. The summer blockbuster, about mining experts sent into space to blow up an earthbound asteroid, is letterboxed, has an aspect ratio of about 2.35:1 and no 16:9 enhancement. The picture looks fine. The image is sharp and colors are accurate most of the time. Here and there, a shot will look a little blander or grainier, but there are no shots in the movie that last for more than the blink of an eye anyway, so it really doesn't matter.

Since the movie is already so loud, you don't have to turn up the volume to appreciate the elaborately applied stereo surround sound and even busier Dolby Digital track. The Dolby Digital track on **Armageddon** has a little less body than its LD counterpart, and the standard track is noticeably weaker. It still delivers a lot of punch and is more detailed than the sound on regular movies but in a direct comparison, the tones are slightly hollow and directional effects don't have quite the same zing. There is a French language track in Dolby Digital and the program can be supported by English subtitles. The feature is accompanied by the Aerosmith music video, *I Don't Want to Miss a Thing*, a brief TV ad for the soundtrack album, a well made theatrical trailer and a jokier teaser.

The collector's edition runs 153 minutes, adding about 3 minutes of extra footage over the standard release, most of which involves a poignant scene between Bruce Willis' character and his father. The picture, letterboxing, frame transfer rate, standard stereo surround, Dolby Digital sound and subtitling are identical to the standard release, and the frame transfer rate are identical to the standard release. The film's sound mix is loud, but rarely inspired. Included in the supplementary section is a complete collection of TV commercials (including a sequence of commercials that counted down the days to the film's release), an exciting theatrical trailer and a theatrical teaser. The teaser has a better sound mix than any sequence in the film itself. There is no thrill to the sounds of **Armageddon**, only distractions to cover the film's utter lack of logic or believability, numbing the viewer into acceptance.

There is also a second platter in the collector's edition, which has no Dolby Digital sound or captioning, which contains the supplemental footage. Along with the trailers, there is an uninspired gag reel, a couple of deleted scenes that would have legitimately thrown off the movie's pace, extended presentations by the various people who worked on the film's special effects and art designs, and a segment on the Aerosmith music video, *I Don't Want to Miss a Thing*. The pieces about the special effects, which take up most of the supplement, are informative, and it is interesting to watch the components brought together, but the effects still don't work within the movie. The asteroid has all these bizarre colors and impossible scale problems that are there for the sake of the image and make no sense in reality. The shot of Paris getting blown up is super, and it's great to see how they put it together, but nobody mentions the follow-up shot within the film, which shows a much less decimated landscape. A popular science fiction movie can get away with one or two fibs, but **Armageddon** just loads them on.

During the film, on one audio track, director Michael Bay, producer Jerry Bruckheimer, Willis, and co-star Ben Affleck provide separate commentaries that have been edited together. Willis doesn't talk much, but Affleck has more to say about his performance, the production, and the film's incongruities. Bay and Bruckheimer tell a fairly complete story of the production and celebrate the movie's popularity. On the other track, cinematographer John Schwartzman provides a lot of informative technical information about the shoot, as well as some interesting anecdotes. Mixed with his talk are comments from two of the film's technical advisors, Dr. Joe Allen and Ivan Bekey, who debunk quite a bit of the film's premises ("This depiction of a nuclear weapon as being a tiny little thing that's going to be big enough to split something the size of Texas is ridiculous") and explain what science there is left in the movie.

Several of the speakers claim emphatically that their purpose was to make a 'summer blockbuster' and not **The Bicycle Thief** or something. They all cite *Raiders of the Lost Ark* as the film they wished to emulate and are amazed that the critics ganged up on them for not being more realistic, but **Raiders** was grounded in imaginative fantasy—its historical references were all tongue in cheek. **Armageddon** is like an **Apollo 13** that cheats, but what the heck, it was popular, and if the 14-year olds who loved it grow up, go to Congress, and increase NASA's budget, then it was all worthwhile.

Armistead Maupin's More Tales of the City (DVD International, DVDI0717)

A miniseries' worth of commentary and other supplementary materials have been added to the outstanding two-platter, six-episode *Prestige Collection* release. The DVD is an epic production that demonstrates how an already successful work of cinematic art can gain both depth and resonance when it is accompanied by intelligent and well-designed supplementary materials.

The first platter contains four episodes (each runs about an hour) and the second platter contains the final two episodes plus the supplement. There is more than four hours of commentary, some of it scene-specific, but it has been separately chapter encoded so you can avoid the dead spots (the chapter encoding and jacket guide are excellent—there are 145 chapters on the first platter—although the guide is printed in a difficult-to-read light orange on yellow). The DVD's worst flaw is that it has not been time encoded, making it impossible to mark a stopping place or even identify what chapter you're in with most players.

The picture quality looks fine. The image is a little soft in places, but most of the time it looks solid and colors are very fresh, with well-detailed fleshtones. There is a mildly stereophonic soundtrack, though dimensionality is limited to the musical score and ambient sounds. The cable program contains nudity and language that would earn it an R-rating, or perhaps something stronger, as a film.

One need not have watched the original miniseries to follow this sequel, which contains a few significant flashbacks but is essentially a freestanding work. Interweaving a half dozen stories (the editing often jumps from one to the next to the next), the program follows the romantic adventures (including a lengthy vacation cruise) of several residents in a small hillside apartment building in San Francisco. There are a couple wild coincidences and a couple more logical ones but, for the most part, Maupin's narrative skills are superb, using surprise revelations and behavioral imperatives to draw the viewer deeper and deeper into the dilemmas and joys of each character. Olympia Dukakis is top-billed, as the apartment's landlord and den mother.

Included with the final two episodes on the second platter, there are four fairly brief deleted scenes that would have moved the focus of the program too much away from its center but are still worth sampling. Each of these scenes also contains an optional introduction by Maupin in which he explains the significance of each sequence (one is very autobiographical) and why they were left out. Behind-the-scenes footage of the rehearsal and the shooting of four other sequences is included as well. While none contain a lightbulb moment where a performer suddenly gets a handle on his or her part, the sequences do provide insight on the unglamorous daily grind of making films. In another behind-the-scenes sequence, a roving camcorder explores the apartment building set (the set is somewhat disorienting within the film because budgetary restrictions prevent the filmmakers from establishing the location). There are also blueprints for the set, but without close-ups, this sequence seems rather useless. The original handwritten scripts for three scenes that were not part of Maupin's novels are presented, again with optional introductory comments by Maupin explaining why the scenes were necessary. There is also an interesting still collection of production photo collages and, for those who are under 25, a brief explanation of who Anita Bryant was.

The commentary is provided by Maupin, Dukakis and actresses Laura Linney and Barbara Garrick. The three actresses talk extensively about their characters and about how they approached their roles. They also talk about their experiences during the shoot and the performers they worked with, and Dukakis shares an interesting story about the research that she did for her role. Maupin takes up the bulk of the talk, however, for, as he says about the faithful miniseries adaptation, "I'm a rare commodity. I'm a writer who can't go around bitching about his work." Although the screenplay is credited to Nicholas Wright, Maupin was intimately involved with every step of the production and was on the set what sounds like every day while it was being shot. Needless to say, he is pleased and proud of the result. He goes into full detail about the inspirations for each character, how and why he drew from his own experiences in telling his stories, and some of the larger themes he wanted to convey (the theme of tolerance is obvious, but there is also a religious motif in the program that is less apparent). That a couple of the stories seem quite Hitchcockian turns out to have been deliberate. He talks as well about the details of the production (a Canadian sand pit was deftly used to stand in for the Nevada desert, with perspective turning smallish hills of sand into the impression of a distant mountain range) and about the performers. Much of the commentary during the fifth episode is about the vociferous reaction to the first *Tales of the City* miniseries and how that delayed the production of **More Tales**.

Armitage III: Poly-Matrix, The Movie (Pioneer, PIOA1370V)

The program combines four episode from a Japanese animated video program into a single 92 minute feature, without losing anything but credit sequences and recaps. Drawing inspiration from (in descending order) **Total Recall**, **Blade Runner** and **Tron**, the program is about a police detective who has recently transferred to Mars and his diminutive female android partner, as they investigate a series of android assassinations. As the episodes progress, more is revealed about the nature of the androids—the females can apparently bear children—and the two heroes become increasingly at odds with the establishment. The Martian setting, with its enormous, compact cities, is also explored, and the program has a satisfying amount of nudity and violence. The program is in English, with voices from Kiefer Sutherland, Elizabeth Berkley and others.

The animation is a bit stiff, but the artwork is stimulating. The colors are very bright and crisp. The program has been letterboxed with an aspect ratio of about 1.85:1 and no 16:9 enhancement, masking off (sometimes awkwardly) the original full screen images. The stereo surround sound is okay, and the Dolby Digital track

is super, with lots of extra directional effects and a deeper, more developed range. There is a brief profile of the writer and director. The program is available in English only and can be supported by English or Japanese subtitling.

Army of Darkness (Universal, 20322)

Sam Raimi's unique comedy horror adventure, about a contemporary store clerk who is thrust back in time to the middle ages where he must battle demons and unite a kingdom, is fresh and busy, with a fine sense of slapstick and a vigorous approach to horror and gore effects. The 1992 film looks a bit more piecemeal now, in these days of CGI, but the images are so creative you don't mind so much being able to spot the seams.

The program is letterboxed with an aspect ratio of about 1.7:1 and no 16:9 enhancement. In addition to the compromised special effects, the picture quality seems a little battered, with grain, minor speckling and slightly weak contrasts. The color quality is adequate and nicely detailed, though fleshtones are at times indistinct. The stereo sound is modest and is a little soft. The 91 minute program is also available in French and can be supported by English or Spanish subtitles. There is a trailer, some brief production notes, and a small cast and director profile section.

Around the World in 80 Days (Image, ID4803BFDVD)

Jules Verne fanatics will be somewhat perturbed at the embellishments given to 1989 miniseries starring Pierce Brosnan, but the basic narrative—about a Victorian era gentleman who wagers he can circumnavigate the globe in less than three months—is preserved, and it is highly dependable entertainment. Brosnan is ideal as the hero, and although Eric Idle, as his servant, and Peter Ustinov, as the detective who is trailing them, are not quite as perfectly cast, they have plenty of opportunity to work their charms. The scenes Ustinov and Idle share give the viewer a marvelous opportunity to watch two generations of British comedians pitting their skills against one another. The additions to the narrative—*Ragtime*-style appearances of historical personages, plus some TV-lite but still un-Verne-like sex—don't move the story forward, but are more stimulating than the travelogue-style sequences that bogged down portions of the 1959 feature film. Shot on location in several continents, the program is brisk and engaging, and the temptation to take it all in at a single sitting is quite strong.

The 280 minute program is comprised of three episodes, each having a complete set of opening and closing credits, and is presented on two sides. The colors look fresh, but the image is quite soft. The stereo sound is fairly nice, with some flourish and dimensionality. There is no captioning.

The Arrival (Artisan, 60446)

Playing like a well made TV show, with most of the special effects bunched up in one segment in the film's second half, **The Arrival** is not a blockbuster sci-fi action picture, but it is a reasonably entertaining and suspenseful feature about a scientist who uncovers a plot by aliens to cook the Earth and scorch out its human inhabitants. It is typical of the film's shortcomings that when you look at the show's star, Charlie Sheen, you do not automatically think, 'scientist,' but he provides a sympathetic protagonist that the viewer can follow and try to second guess.

The 1996 feature is presented in letterboxed format on one side and full screen format on the other. The letterboxing has an aspect ratio of about 1.85:1 and no 16:9 enhancement, adding nothing to the sides of the image and masking picture information off the top and the bottom in comparison to the full screen release. The framing on the letterboxed version looks good, but the full screen version is better for the film's special effect sequences. The picture is sharp and the colors are rich. The stereo surround is okay and the Dolby Digital mix gives the film a little more dimensionality. The film is also presented in French with Dolby Digital sound and can be accompanied by English, French or Spanish subtitles. A theatrical teaser and a theatrical trailer have been included with the 109 minute movie, letterboxed on the letterbox side and in full screen on the full screen side. There is also a modest cast profile section with a couple of production notes.

Art and Jazz in Animation (Image, ID4709LYDVD)

The single-sided dual-layer 245 minute collection of the films of John and Faith Hubley is so large that their own 71 minute compilation movie, *The Cosmic Eye*, takes up only a small part of the complete program. The pieces are not dated, but most were produced in the Fifties and Sixties. The animation is soft to begin with, and the picture often looks aged, with somewhat subdued colors. The monophonic sound is dated but workable, with a slightly brighter Dolby Digital mono track. Some of the cartoons have dialogue, which is not captioned. Most of the films are scored by jazz musicians, such as Dizzy Gillespie, Benny Carter and Quincy Jones, and pursuant to the DVD's title, the collection does provide a satisfying (and substantial) sampling of late Fifties jazz.

A theme also develops within the collection that is present but less obvious in shorter anthologies, of the interest the Hubleys had in physics and earth sciences. The cartoons teach viewers about geology, ecology, and relativity, as well as about the development of civilization. Even the 6 minute *Urbanissmo*, which is as close to frivolous as the pieces get, about a man having a conflict with a large, mobile city, has the inherent design of an educational toy.

Cosmic Eye includes clips from many Hubley cartoons, blended and framed by a conversation between several beings who are observing Earth, and depicting a variety of myths. Some of the cartoons also appear in their entirety in the collection, but others do not, so that the inclusion of the feature gives the whole anthology a stronger sense of completeness, at least in its presentation of the Hubleys' art. Other cartoons featured are the excellent 53 minute *Of Stars and Men*, which gives what is still a fairly decent summary of the nature of time and matter; the equally superb 25 minute *Dig*, about a young boy and a rock who learn about the Earth's geological history first hand; *The Hole*, which runs 15 minutes and is about two construction workers discussing the fate of the world; *The Hat*, which runs 18 minutes and is about two soldiers on opposite sides of a dotted-line border; the colorful *Voyage to the Next*, which seems to have been inspired by pre-Columbian art and myth while also looking at overpopulation and pollution; *The Tender Game*, a stick figure romance set to *Tenderly* that runs 6 minutes; *Eggs*, which runs 10 minutes and has two mythic figures, Death and an Earth Mother of some sort, exploring civilization and urban blight while sitting on bridges and riding around in a car; *Harlem Wednesday*, which runs 10 minutes and is a meditation on the paintings of Gregorio Prestopino, with no animation; *The Adventures of* *, which runs 10 minutes and is about the path from childhood through adulthood using cubist backgrounds and designs; and *Of Men and Demons*, which runs 10 minutes and depicts a group of evil beings attempting to upset a tranquil rural life with pollution and over-crowding.

Art of Fighting (Image, ID4413CTDVD)

Two young men with strong martial arts skills face off against a band of jewel thieves. Normally, a 45 minute Japanese animated cartoon can carry as much narrative as a standard two hour movie, but **Fighting** is simplistic and uninvolving. There is a complete story, a few inspired action sequences and a dabbling of humor, but the program, which feels like an episode of some kind, doesn't amount to much. The picture is passable. The show's colors are not intense, but the transfer looks accurate and the image is sharp. The monophonic sound is functional. The program is in English, with an alternate Japanese track, and can be supported by optional English subtitles.

The Art of Illusion (Simitar, 7335)

The pretty good 50 minute overview of the history of special effects in movies is subtitled *One Hundred Years of Hollywood Special Effects*. The program does a fairly decent job at touching on all types of effects, from pyrotechnics and puppetry to green screens and CGI. Behind-the-scenes footage and component breakdowns are presented for a number of films, including **King Kong**, *Things to Come*, **The Abyss**, **Demolition Man**, **Die Hard**, **Gremlins 2**, **Terminator 2**, **Total Recall**, a Paula Abdul Coca-Cola commercial and many others. The picture quality looks fine and the sound is decent. There is no captioning.

The Art of Nature (Image, ID4084CRDVD)

The 48 minute nature image program travels from the tops of mountains to beneath the surface of tropical waters, and makes extensive use of time lapse photography, making the show a little more varied than most. The title is taken from a popular photography book, but art in video and art in photography are two different things. While here and there a sequence may take on a profound resonance in its depiction of the fractal randomness of natural design, it does not build upon it with the kind of thematic variations implied by the weighty title. The image transfer looks sharp, with accurate colors. There is New Agey stereophonic musical score that is typical for such programs, one that fails to make a lasting impression. There is also a brief, overly poetic narration that has not been captioned.

Arthur (Warner, 22020)

Dudley Moore, Liza Minnelli and John Gielgud star in the romantic comedy about a wealthy inebriate. The 1981 feature is presented in full screen format, and the source material is free of wear that plagued earlier home video releases. Colors are bright and fleshtones look okay. The monophonic sound is weak. The 91 minute film is accompanied by a theatrical trailer that lets you relive the best gags. There is a small cast profile and production essay, and an intriguing but incomplete profile of the film's director, Steve Gordon, who passed away shortly after the film, his first feature, was released. A French language track is also available, as are English, French or Spanish subtitles ("¿Puedos tomar mi mano?" "Te dejaría sólo con una").

As Good As It Gets (Columbia TriStar, 21709)

Jack Nicholson portrays an emotionally challenged obsessive-compulsive writer whose acidity gives way to benevolence when he meets a pragmatic waitress, played by Helen Hunt. They both won Oscars. The film is intelligent and charming, with several emotional highs and lots of amusing, character-driven comedy.

The 1997 film is in letterboxed format on one side, with an aspect ratio of about 1.85:1 and an accommodation for enhanced 16:9 playback, and in cropped format on the other side. The cropping adds nothing to the top or the bottom in comparison to the letterboxed picture and takes away from the sides. The color transfer is excellent. Nicholson and Hunt appear to have entirely different complexions (maybe it's part of the age thing), but the image maintains the correct fleshtones on both without distortion. Other hues are crisp and precisely delineated, and darker sequences are stable. The stereo surround sound has an unremarkable mix, which is understandable for the film's narrative and orientation. When there should be atmospheric effects the rear channels kick in, but a lot of the movie is just talking, front and center, without embellishment. There is also a Dolby Digital track, but there is little difference between the two. The 139 minute film is also available in French and comes with English, Spanish or French subtitles ("Vous n'avez pas l'appétit aussi grand que le nez, hein?").

Nicholson, Hunt, co-star Greg Kinnear and director James L. Brooks provide a running commentary (with brief inserts from other production personnel on specific moments). It is a real treat to hear Nicholson laughing about his experiences making the film and how he worked to find his character. For those who haven't heard—although the film had a script, much of it was re-composed as they went along, so all four talk about the things that didn't work the first, second and third times they tried them. They often remark with excitement, in fact, at the rare shot that was achieved on one take. Hunt is a bit more introspective, talking about her character's motivations (she suggests, with some evidence, that her character is attracted to obsessive-compulsives), and Kinnear has fun ribbing Brooks on his initial misjudgments and errors. But you kind of sit through the whole thing waiting for each time Nicholson chimes in, even when he's just praising a piece of the movie—that's star power.

The talk gets a little sparser in the second half, but don't miss the final credits. Brooks asks Nicholson what he thinks of DVDs and Nicholson, reflecting upon digital recording and processing, replies, "What's better? You know we're sittin' here being remunerated for what is ultimately the cancer of film, which we claim to love above all else." Then, with perfect timing, Art Garfunkel's vocal on the film's soundtrack surges forward with, "Always look on the bright side of life."

As You Like It (Image, ID5666DSDVD)

Produced in Britain, the delightful 1936 interpretation of William Shakespeare's play features an unbelievably young and forcefully chinned Laurence Olivier. The black-and-white public domain film has a number of splices, but it looks much sharper and clearer than we've ever seen it before, and has fewer speckles as well. The monophonic sound, although rickety, is coherent enough that the dialogue is easy to follow—unusual for a pre-War British production. The film's charm is enhanced by the quality of the transfer—what had once seemed like a curiosity with unrealized potential is, thanks to transfer, a certifiable classic and one of the dozen or so great Shakespearean film adaptations.

A history of the movie is provided in a very lengthy and detailed background essay by Roy Hemming. Elisabeth Bergner stars with Olivier. Although the film abridges much of the text, the flavor and shape of the play, about a woman who disguises herself as a man to be near the one she loves, are retained. Beyond the acting, the highpoint of the film is its art direction. The set designs are heavenly, achieving both a British classicism and a near-Hollywood sense of magic. The woods become a character, and the hero's exuberant despoiling of the forest for the sake of proclaiming his love—he carves her name in all the trees—becomes a horrific reminder that the world may be a stage, but a closing notice is soon going to be posted if we don't clean up our act.

Ashes of Time (World Video, 1433)

We could never figure out what the heck was going on in this Hong Kong feature, and even the jacket copy emphasizes the film's deliberate obliqueness and disinterest in narrative. It has something to do with two sisters (twins?) and two hired assassins. There is some choreographed swordsmanship, but most of the film consists of obscure, sequential imagery, supported by a nonsensical voiceover narrative, and if it is some sort of grand artistic accomplishment, you need more context than we have acquired to appreciate its value.

The picture has variable letterboxing with an aspect ratio shifting between 1.85:1 and 2.2:1, and no 16:9 enhancement. The image is set on the upper edge of the screen, with permanent (and error-heavy) English subtitles appearing underneath in a kind of greyish band that suggests it is masking part of the picture off. The image is quite soft, with dull, hazy colors and bland fleshtones. Contrasts are weak and there are more than the usual number of digital artifacts. The monophonic sound, available in Cantonese and Mandarin, is adequate. The film runs 95 minutes and is accompanied by a trailer.

The Asphyx (Allday, DE110450)

Reminiscent of a Hammer-type production and set in the Nineteenth Century, the PG-rated film is about two men who discover a method of arresting death and staving it off indefinitely. The premise is a bit silly (they trap the spirit who comes to take away the soul) and much of the drama is conversational, but the film is adeptly executed and is reasonably involving. The cast features Robert Stephens and Robert Powell, who give first class performances. It also helps that the 99 minute film, which was directed by Peter Newbrook with cinematography by Freddie Francis, has a fairly elegant look. It has been letterboxed, with an aspect ratio of about 2.35:1 and no 16:9 enhancement. The colors are fairly rich and the movie is dressed in Victorian velvets that are reproduced with a reasonable accuracy and sharpness. The source material has a few stray speckles and there is an occasional jitter in background movement, but on the whole the presentation is nice. The monophonic sound has a little noise but is acceptable. Allday has also included filmographies for the cast and crew, an interesting production essay and a couple of ads clipped from a presskit. One final note. The film's pre-credit opening sequence appears to belong to another movie, but quick-witted viewers who haven't forgotten it will likely experience an 'Ah-ha!' moment about 45 minutes later. The rest will have to wait until the end.

Assassins (Warner, 13987)

Directed by Richard Donner, the implausible action feature stars Sylvester Stallone, Antonio Banderas and Julianne Moore. The action scenes are not spectacular and the premise is fairly silly, but so are hundreds of other movies. It doesn't take long to get over a natural aversion to the hero's profession—after all, he is trying to quit killing people, and his agency just won't let him go peacefully—so if you just sort of let the technical details of the plot breeze past you (watch Banderas type on his laptop with his right hand, never venturing anywhere near the left side of the keyboard even though a's and s's appear on the screen), then the film can be reasonably fun. Except for Moore, the less said about the performances the better.

The picture is in letterboxed format on one side, with an aspect ratio of about 1.85:1 and an accommodation for enhanced 16:9 playback, and in cropped format on the other side. The cropping adds nothing to the top or bottom of the screen and removes picture information from the side, so the letterboxed image is generally preferable, except for those gooey close-ups of the stars. The picture is a bit dark, but has it solid, accurate colors and a glossy sheen on many of the hues. The stereo surround sound has a few big moments and is competently put together, while the Dolby Digital track has substantially more bass and punch, and a lot more detail. The 133 minute film is also presented in French in regular stereo and comes with English, French or Spanish subtitles. There is a small cast and crew profile section.

The Assault (Image, ID4758DRDVD)

The jacket cover says that Jim Wynorski's film is reminiscent of **Die Hard**, but it sounds like somebody was picking titles out of a hat. The film is actually an evocation of *Rio Bravo* and **Assault on Precinct 13**, with a little non-supernatural **Night of the Living Dead** thrown in. Stacie Randall stars as a detective who brings a witness to a women's retreat for protection in an emergency. Villains then descend upon the place in droves and the women have to fight them off. Wynorski's sense of style stops at his checkbook, even when it comes to rudimentary continuity considerations, but the film is loaded with action scenes and supposedly helpless women wasting dozens of tough guys armed to the teeth, so what's not to like?

The picture is presented in full screen format, but that doesn't appear to be a problem. The image quality is at the mercy of the bargain basement lighting, but the transfer is likely an accurate representation of the source. The stereo surround sound is revved up in a crude, knock-em-over-the-head sort of way that fits right in with the spirit of the film and is worth amplifying if one can tolerate it. The 83 minute program is not captioned.

Assault of the Killer Bimbos (Full Moon, 8005)

With deliberately moronic humor and a deliberately insulting title, the film is amusing in a chauvinistic, dopey sort of way. The male characters are just as stupid and stereotyped as the female characters, so other than the orientation of the title the film seems to take potshots at everyone. The nominal story concerns two go-go dancers who are framed for a murder and must catch the real killer while they're on the run. It is a road movie in which none of the protagonists can read a map.

The image is reasonably sharp, but the cinematography is inexpensive and colors are somewhat flat, with inconsistent contrasts. The Ultra-Stereo surround sound is basic in design and dialogue is raspy in places. The 85 minute film is accompanied by trailers for **Bimbos** and four other Full Moon titles, along with the usual merchandising promotions.

Assault on Precinct 13 (Image, ID4161CKDVD)
John Carpenter's brisk and enjoyable thriller is about a siege by faceless bad guys on several cops, secretaries and prisoners trapped in an abandoned police station. The film's difficult and somewhat inexpensive cinematography has been transferred without a hitch. While viewers will note that an occasional fleshtone or hazy lighting effect is not as sharp looking as it might be on a larger budgeted effort, the focus is always crisp and it is clear that whenever possible the colors are precise. The image is letterboxed with an aspect ratio of about 2.35:1, without accommodation for 16:9 enhanced playback. The film was shot in Panavision and the letterboxing is necessary in practically every shot to convey the tensions Carpenter devised. The film's monaural soundtrack also sounds good and the 91 minute program (which always seems to run much faster than that) is not captioned. There is a trailer, too.

Carpenter provides a running commentary about the film. His talk is reasonably informative. He describes how the production logistics were achieved on the very limited budget and some of the influences—*Rio Bravo* being the most obvious—he drew from in creating the film. As he points out, the 1976 movie could probably not be made today, with its atmosphere of violence and anarchy, but while the film has a seemingly makeshift feel, it is evident from Carpenter's talk that there was a great deal of intelligence and talent behind it.

The Assignment (Columbia TriStar, 28359)
A well-made espionage film about a plot to defang 'Carlos the Jackal,' Aidan Quinn stars in a dual role, as Carlos and as an American naval officer whose facial similarity to the terrorist embroils him in an elaborate CIA plot. Donald Sutherland and Ben Kingsley are also featured. Although the outline of the story is a classic sort of escapist intrigue, and it was shot in several different locations around the world, the film retains a very human component, exploring the obsessions of the plotters and the emotional sacrifices the hero must undergo to accomplish his task.

The film is presented on one side in letterboxed format, with an aspect ratio of about 1.85:1 and an accommodation for enhanced 16:9 playback, and in full screen format on the other side. The colors are reasonably bright, but the image is a bit murky in places. Darker sequences, however, look stable. The stereo surround sound and Dolby Digital sound do not have the elaborate mix of a blockbuster action feature, but there is an efficient and reasonably enjoyable audio design that serves the movie well. The 119 minute film also has a French language track in standard stereo, optional English, French and Spanish subtitles, and a trailer.

Asteroid (Artisan, DVD60512)
The disaster miniseries has a running time of 120 minutes, which we believe is somewhere in the neighborhood of an hour less than the broadcast version. Except for a couple times where the characters jump too quickly from one situation to the next, however, you are not aware that anything is missing.

The program has been given a rather engaging stereo surround soundtrack with heightened rear channel activity that would be out of place in a sophisticated film but adds to the fun here. The image is a bit soft at times but, generally, the picture is on par with a typical television production, with unremarkable colors and ade-

quate fleshtones. The program is not captioned, and comes with a collection of asteroid trivia and a montage of production stills set to audio clips from the film.

Annabella Sciorra is the astronomer who is on hand whenever anybody wants to know something about asteroids, and Michael Biehn is a hands-on FEMA director. The first half the program is about various pebbles hitting America and the second half is the usual saved-from-a-collapsed-building stuff set in an obliterated Dallas.

At First Sight (MGM, 907447)
The first act is highly erotic, and it carries you along for a while, but pretty soon the film's soap opera cracks begin to show. The heroine, played by Mira Sorvino, is an architect, but when the blind hero, played by Val Kilmer, asks her to describe a building in front of them, she begins by saying it is dilapidated, goes on to mention the trees surrounding it, and never once says anything about the building's design. Later on, when the hero is getting his bandages off for the first time after an operation on his eyes, video cameras are there to record the event, with lights a-blazing, and the doctor removing the bandages doesn't seem bothered by it in the slightest.

The 1999 film is based on a true story, but it is filled with unlikelihoods and contrivances. Nathan Lane shows up for a while as a therapist, and that is fun, particularly his improvisations with Kilmer, but the movie never returns to the erotic potency it started out with, and none of its other emotions are anywhere near as affecting. They break up, they get back together, Kilmer's character grows up, etc., but the characters talk about their status abstractly and rarely show what they are feeling. Frankly, if the filmmakers had just repeated the massage scene from the beginning at the end, the film would work a lot better than it does.

The presentation is letterboxed on one side, with an aspect ratio of about 1.85:1 and an accommodation for enhanced 16:9 playback, and is in full screen format on the other side. The letterboxing masks a little picture information off the top of the image and adds some to the sides in comparison to the full screen image, but the framing on the full screen version looks cramped and the letterboxed presentation is more satisfying. The picture transfer looks fine, with sharp hues and accurate fleshtones. The stereo surround sound and Dolby Digital sound are okay, giving the musical score a nice dimensionality, although atmospheric effects are limited. The 129 minute feature also has a French language soundtrack in standard stereo, optional English and French subtitles and a trailer.

Atkins, Chet (see **Webb Pierce and Chet Atkins**)

The Atomic Submarine (Image, ID4428GODVD)
The 70 minute black-and-white production is about a sub chasing an underwater UFO around the North Pole. The stock footage and cheapo special effects are rough, but the controlled soundstage conversation scenes look fine, with a crisp focus, fairly detailed contrasts and only a few stray speckles. The monophonic sound is okay and the 1959 feature is accompanied by an enjoyable original theatrical trailer. There is no captioning.

Attila (see **Verdi's Atilla**)

At War with the Army (Digital Disc, 573)
The first Dean Martin and Jerry Lewis feature is an episodic service comedy with a few song numbers. The black-and-white source material looks fairly weak, with soft contrasts, a number of errant markings and an occasional wiggly image. The monophonic sound is also rough, but workable, and there is no captioning. The 1950 film runs 93 minutes. Martin is a sergeant and Lewis is private at an army base. The narrative is limited, but there is some romantic juggling, a few career advancements (and declines) and plenty of clowning, with a number of reasonably amusing sequences, particularly when Lewis dons a disguise in drag to sneak off the base.

Austin Powers: International Man of Mystery (New Line, N4577)

The spy spoof and spy spoof spoof, written by and starring Mike Myers and directed by Jay Roach, is a mess, with gags going nowhere and a half-baked narrative, but some of the jokes made us laugh harder than we have laughed in quite a long time, and we would never ask a movie for more than that rare pleasure. The film includes specific parodies of the early James Bond films and allusions to other highlights of the Sixties spy craze including *The Avengers*, the Matt Helm movies and *Casino Royale*. There are also toilet jokes and other forms of modern comedy that the spies of old, even the raunchiest, would never have stooped to. Myers plays both the hero and the villain, and it is in the latter role that he has the firmest grasp of what he is trying to accomplish. His hero—a Sixties spy brought out of a deep freeze in the Nineties—is an annoying mix of exaggerated imperfections, and you're almost sorry he wins.

Myers and Roach also provide commentary for the film. They have some interesting technical revelations, such as how a fairly complex nude scene was achieved in much less time than planned thanks to the use of multiple video monitors, so the performers could change their lines of sight and still make sure the naughty bits were covered. They also cite the many films that influenced the look of the movie, from the obvious (**A Hard Day's Night**, *Blow Up*) to the less obvious (*Sweet Charity*, *Sleeper*). As the scenes progress they reminisce about the shoot and talk about what they were trying to achieve, or how they changed an initial idea when something better came along. On the whole, however, there is less insight to the filmmaking process than other commentaries have provided, and Myers plays it straight throughout.

The movie's Carnaby Street production design is a dream come true in color, and the DVD is faithful to every ultra bright hue. The film is presented in letterboxed formation one side, with an aspect ratio of about 2:1 and an accommodation for enhanced 16:9 playback, and in full screen format on the other. The full screen version crops enough off the sides to look awkward and unmasks some picture information from the top to reveal a little bit more of the film's creative set designs here and there. The stereo surround sound and Dolby Digital sound are a little drab. The 90 minute program also has a standard stereo French language track and subtitles in English, French or Spanish ("Ils sont toujours après mes porte-bonheur"). The commentary track cannot be toggled.

There are a number of delightful supplementary features, the most significant being several sequences that were dropped before the film's final cut. It is easy to understand why a couple of the sequences were removed, because they would have stopped the film's pace completely, but that doesn't make them any less amusing and it is great the disc can include them, particularly a pair that show what happens to the family and friends of a nondescript evil henchman when he is killed. There are a couple of less developed endings, as well. The DVD has a cast profile section with extensive filmographies highlighted by clips from the stars' other New Line films, and an essay about Sixties spy movies, though the latter is of limited scope and contains a number of errors (they misspell Ann-Margret's name, among other things).

The Avengers (Warner, 15873)

With her strawberry blonde hair and her sly, knowing grins, we gush with satisfaction whenever the camera catches Uma Thurman. Her screen presence is magnetic, and of the film's many visual delights, she is its centerpiece and dynamo. With Ralph Fiennes and Sean Connery providing enjoyable supporting performances, the film is a grand, eccentric pleasure that is part nostalgia and part hip fashion, taken to its logical extremes.

Whoops! Isn't this the movie everybody said such mean things about and nobody went to see after the first week? Well, yes, but what were people expecting? We are far happier that somebody tried to make a movie out of **The Avengers** and came up short

than if nobody had ever tried at all. The film has a few serious faux pas (four letter words! why?), but it also has many exquisitely executed production and costume designs, a decent sense of humor, and an honest love of its source. And Thurman—in leather one moment and pink the next.

The picture is letterboxed on one side, with an aspect ratio of about 1.85:1 and an accommodation for enhanced 16:9 playback, and is presented in full screen on the other. The full screen image loses a bit on the sides in comparison to the letterboxed image and adds more picture information on the top and bottom. Both presentations have their charms, and it gives fans an excuse to watch the movie twice. The picture transfer looks terrific, with sharp, solid colors and rich fleshtones, and the CGI footage works much better on home video than it does in a theatrical exhibition. The stereo surround sound and Dolby Digital sound are adequate, with a number of engaging separation effects and other suitable noises, though the mix lacks the intensity of a confident hit. The standard track is not as forceful as the Dolby Digital track. The 89 minute film is also available in French and can be supported by English or French subtitles. There is a terrific theatrical trailer, a couple essays about the TV show and making the movie, and a cast-and-crew-and-cast-of-the-old-TV-show profile section.

The Avengers ' 67 Set 1 (A&E, AAE70014)
The Avengers ' 67 DVD Vol. 1 (A&E, AAE70018)
The Avengers ' 67 DVD Vol. 2 (A&E, AAE70019)
The Avengers ' 67 Set 2 (A&E, AAE70015)
The Avengers ' 67 DVD Vol. 3 (A&E, AAE70020)
The Avengers ' 67 DVD Vol. 4 (A&E, AAE70021)
The Avengers ' 67 SET 3 (A&E, AAE70016)
The Avengers ' 67 DVD Vol. 5 (A&E, AAE70022)
The Avengers ' 67 DVD Vol. 6 (A&E, AAE70023)
The Avengers ' 67 SET 4 (A&E, AAE70017)
The Avengers ' 67 DVD Vol. 7 (A&E, AAE70024)
The Avengers ' 67 DVD Vol. 8 (A&E, AAE70025)

Patrick Macnee and Diana Rigg star what most consider to be the pinnacle of the several manifestations the British TV series underwent during the course of its run. Loaded with eccentric characterizations, intensely styled wardrobes and imaginative decorations, the program is a definitive portrait of ultra-suavity and savoir faire in the Sixties. On the other hand, practically the first thing a young friend asked us was, "Is Steed an alcoholic?" That's the Nineties for you.

Rigg is shockingly young and given to bimbo-style karate chops, but the quality of her British-trained acting rescues her and the show in practically every scene she is in. Fight scenes aside, her line readings, movements, turns, mannerisms and dexterity are always precise and assured, and it is her physical proficiency that communicates to a viewer's subconscious that her presence is to be taken seriously. Her appearance is mesmerizing. The angles of her nose, her lips, her chin and her cheeks are more harmonically progressive and circular than a fugue, pulling a viewer into her dizzying beauty with a gravitational force. It is fortunate the program has editing, for that is the only way to break the trance of her presence, and if your finger wanders by accident to the still frame button you could find yourself glued to her smile for an entire afternoon. She has more smiles, by the way, than Eskimos have types of snow, and each one is substantially warmer.

Our heart doubled its rate of patter when first put our hands on the two boxed sets, each of which contains two DVDs that have also been issued as separate releases. Each platter holds three 50 minute episodes (the final one contains four), along with some delightful publicity stills for each episode. The episodes have fairly consistent monophonic soundtracks that are free of significant distortion, though the volume is set a touch lower than average. There is no captioning. We will discuss picture quality specifics below, but after a poor start in the first episode of **Vol. 1**, the transfers are generally very nice, with bright, solid hues and accurate fleshtones.

The source material has some damage and, even within the best looking episodes, there are passages where the focus or stability seems tentative, but such flaws are fleeting. Except for a ratcheting we noticed during a couple quick right-left pans, there seem to be no significant artifacting flaws.

Many of the episodes have the same format, in which what appears to be a supernatural occurrence at the beginning is found, by the end, to have an earthbound explanation, although some of the denouements are nearly as farfetched as the supernatural explanations would have been. Almost all the episodes are murder mysteries, and there are murders even in those that are not. At its best, the show combines Pinteresque dialogue with a surreal setting, spoofing the standard spy and detective films while beguiling the viewer in cleverness. When it doesn't work, the combination is just plain silly, but when the performances, pacing, humor and imaginative premise are fit together smartly, the result is singularly unique and enjoyable.

Of the episodes reviewed here, the first episode in **Vol. 1**, *From Venus with Love*, is probably the weakest, and may lead viewers to believe the show is more dated or contrived than later episodes prove to be. The heroes investigate what is apparently a UFO that is blasting astronomers and turning their corpses white in the process. The forced absurdities just seem to outweigh the wit. It may not help that the picture isn't all that good, either. Fleshtones are pale and colors, though well defined, are generally light, with some reels looking weaker than others. The companion episodes are a little stronger. In the classic *The Fear Merchants*, individuals are frightened to death when the villain develops an effective psychological profiling program to help businessmen get rid of the competition. There's also a fairly good action sequence where Macnee battles a bulldozer in a sandpit. A very typical episode, *Escape in Time*, stretches credibility slightly, but to enjoyable results. The heroes investigate a service that is sending criminals back in time to help them duck the law. To the show's credit, they never really attempt to hide the logical explanation, just finesse it. The picture on *Fear Merchants* is still a little faded and off-color here and there, but the picture on *Escape in Time* is very pleasing.

A&E has attempted to combine episodes with like themes in several of the collections. There are two bird-oriented episodes on **Vol. 2**, *The Bird Who Knew Too Much* and *The Winged Avenger*. With delightfully exaggerated owlishness, John Wood is featured in *The Bird Who Knew Too Much*, in which spies are using avian methods to obtain and communicate state secrets. People safely ensconced in upper story offices to which there are no ready accesses are clawed to death in *The Winged Avenger*. The mystery element is a little stronger—there are a couple suspects—and since comic books also play a role in the plot, there is a cute spoof of the *Batman* TV show in the finale. It is a good example of how the show can be playful without spoiling its mystique. Roy Kinnear is featured in the third episode in the collection, *The See-Through Man*, about obtaining a formula for invisibility. The picture on *Winged Avenger* is a little weak, while the colors on *See-Through Man* are quite strong.

An apparent ghost sighting leads to a plot that is both more real yet more farfetched, about an underground city, in *The Living Dead* on **Vol. 3**. The picture looks somewhat yellowed and fuzzy. Puns fly like fur in *The Hidden Tiger*, in which victims are apparently mauled by a large vicious cat, though no such animal appears to be present. Meow. The colors are stronger, but the image is grainy and contrasts are very weak. Charles Crichton directed *The Correct Way to Kill*, in which the heroes join forces with a pair of Russian agents to find out who has been murdering Russian spies. There is a lot of *Ninotchka*-style humor, and Crichton's assured hand allows the episode's pleasures to supersede its absurdities. Colors are a bit pale and fleshtones are a little greenish in spots.

The best episodes, however, have been saved for **Vol. 4**. Christopher Lee stars as an apparently indestructible scientist in *Never, Never Say Die*, although he reacts adversely to radios. Lee's performance brings a level of seriousness to the episode that counterbalances its inherent humor quite effectively. An episode that primarily features Macnee's character, *The Superlative Seven*, is an adaptation of *Ten Little Indians*, but with its own twists and turns. Not only are Donald Sutherland and Charlotte Rampling featured among the cast, but the set designs look like they are straight out of *Isle of the Dead*. An episode that primarily features Rigg's character, *Epic*, is somewhat more tiresome, in which she is kidnapped by a group of aging silent screen stars who want to make a snuff film. Conveniently, it is set in an abandoned movie studio. The epilogue, however, is priceless. There is an above-average amount of speckling on *Never, Never Say Die*, but the colors look great. *Superlative Seven* is also strong, and *Epic* is passable.

The picture quality is even better than usual on the opening episode in **Vol. 5**, *A Funny Thing Happened on the Way to the Station*. The colors are fabulous, fleshtones are rich and the picture is very crisp. About a group of assassins working on a train, the episode has a Hitchcockian wit and is quite entertaining. *Something Nasty in the Nursery* is a typical, well made **Avengers** episode, in which important government officials are having bouts of regressive memories, believing they are toddlers again, while they spill state secrets to the villains. As one would expect from the show, the toddler scenes are depicted with a youthful phantasmagoria. In the classic episode, *The Joker*, a villain searching for revenge traps Rigg's character in a remote mansion and starts playing mind games on her. Rigg's fans will find the constant close-ups and focus on her various poses and expressions to be highly gratifying.

Vol. 6 may be the best collection of all. Peter Cushing guest stars in one terrific episode, technically a sequel to an episode from an earlier season, entitled *Return of the Cybernauts*. Seeking revenge against the heroes, he romances Rigg's character while his robots kidnap important scientists. Later, he develops a mind-control device, turning Rigg's character into a zombie, which she enacts with great flair. In another marvelous episode, *Who's Who???*, two villains use a mind-swap machine to exchange places with the heroes, facilitating delightful performances by all and many amusements. Even the standard episode that fills out the collection, *Death's Door*, is reasonably intriguing. A sequential set of ministers tapped to head an important peace conference are frightened away by very precise premonitional dreams. Again, the dream sequences have a surrealistic flair, and the mystery is engaging. The colors on this episode are slightly yellowish, but very intense and pleasing.

There is a minor audio flaw on *The £50,000 Breakfast* on **Vol. 7**, creating an unnatural reverberation during some sound effects, but it is not a significant distraction. The episode is difficult to describe without giving away its ending, but it is about a reclusive millionaire, his nasty staff, and a ventriloquist who is found dead in a car accident with valuable diamonds in his stomach. A very engaging episode, the two heroes must participate in a road rally while solving riddles in *Dead Man's Treasure*, to locate some hidden government secrets. In the end, one of the heroes is trapped in a deadly driving simulator, while the other races to save her, and the editing cuts back and forth between the simulator and the real car. The heroes foil an elaborate extortion plot in *You Have Just Been Murdered*, in which millionaires are assaulted again and again by a would-be assassin who withdraws his threat at the last moment, unless they don't pay up. As a rule, the show never explains much anyway, but a lack of explanation as to how the assassin achieved some of his feats harms the narrative somewhat.

The colors are better than usual on the **Vol 8** episode, *The Positive-Negative Man*, in which the heroes investigate a villain who is murdering people with enormous electrical charges. The episode is both exciting and witty. The picture quality is somewhat weak on *Murdersville*, and there is an above-normal amount of scratches and speckling, as well. Rigg's character, traveling with a friend, winds up in a town where murders are a regular occurrence. Macnee appears at just the beginning, and then the end, to save the day. A delightful episode about a weapon that can shrink things and people, *Mission Highly Improbable* has some well executed special effects, a few props one will recognize from the other episodes and plenty of big-little jokes. Rigg's last episode, *The Forget-Me-Knot*, also introduces Linda Thorson, who would become Macnee's partner in the subsequent season. Within the episode, villains use a temporary amnesia dart to prevent the heroes from identifying a traitor in the organization. It is an engaging effort, but it is the epilog—Rigg's farewell—that is truly poignant, since it seems as much about what Rigg did for Macnee's career as it is for how her character helped his chase bad guys and right wrongs.

Aventure Malgache (see Alfred Hitchcock's Bon Voyage & Aventure Malgache)

Avia Guide to Home Theater (DMI, UPC#1438158672)

The program is exhaustive, beginning by telling you practically everything but how to push in the power button and then expanding, with menu options, into the complexities of adjusting video monitors and sound systems that are covered in **Video Essentials**. For specific adjustments, **Video Essentials** does a better job at systematically leading the viewer through the process, but as an introduction to home theater environments, the **Avia** program is stronger, and the information required for doing the adjustments is all there (colored filters are also included with the platter).

The **Avia** program is also easier to navigate. At the center is a 40 minute overview of home theater system components and environments. Although the narrator is an apologist for dull stereo mixes, insisting that dialogue should only come out of the center channel and surround effects should not distract one from the watching the screen, the presentation is generally well balanced, practical ("In the whole consumer electronics industry, there's no field more crowded with snake oil salesmen than signal connectors") and thorough. Between every major subject, a breakdown of topics appears on the screen, and there is time, before the program continues, to select detailed text embellishments on any of those topics if you desire. The program has Dolby Digital encoding and the picture, though not as intensely precise as **Video Essentials**, is sufficiently accurate for careful monitor adjustments. The program includes several clips from **Fly Away Home**. There is no captioning.

Awakenings (Columbia TriStar, 50565/9)

Robin Williams portrays a doctor who comes across a drug that, initially, brings a group of patients out of a decades-long catatonic state. Robert De Niro portrays the patient who is the first to take the drug, and his "awakening" is the highpoint of the 1990 film. The whole movie goes downhill after that. Although the subject clearly appeals to some viewers and, apparently, to critics, the film is rather dreary and unattractive. The acting is no great showcase, either, as both actors appear to have done just enough homework to get by in their parts and no more. You never really believe in their characters, only in their ability to get through a scene without overtly spoiling it.

Once in a while a minor speckle appears on the source material. Although the image is a little soft at times, fleshtones look strong and other hues seem fresh. The picture is letterboxed with an aspect ratio of about 1.85:1 and an accommodation for enhanced 16:9 playback. The stereo surround sound rarely draws attention to itself. The 120 minute program also has Spanish and French audio tracks, optional Spanish subtitles and English closed captioning.

Away All Boats (GoodTimes, 0581040)

Jeff Chandler is the hard-driving captain of an attack transport that carries amphibious troop landers in the 1956 WWII action feature. The film combines some decent action sequences with a basic military management drama, about getting the crew in shape and dealing with problems as they occur. The 114 minute feature is decently paced and is a typical but satisfying genre effort.

The VistaVision image is presented in full screen format and cropping appears to be minimal. There is some speckling around the reel-change points, and a little extra fading in a couple spots, but otherwise the picture, though not intense, is fairly colorful, with decent fleshtones. The focus is sharp and the presentation is satisfying. The monophonic sound is fine and the program can be supported by optional English, French or Spanish subtitles.

B

B.B. King Live in Africa (Pioneer, PA98585D)

The 48 minute concert, though brief, is fairly satisfying, as King plays a half dozen or so blues numbers, and the Dolby Digital track makes it a highly energized event, with more separation effects, more dimensionality and a stronger bass. The picture is clear, with mildly subdued colors and provides adequate coverage of the stage program. The live concert was held as part of the festivities surrounding the Muhammad Ali-George Forman battle in Zaire in 1974. The camera, which is responsible for some luscious close-ups, rarely leaves King out of view, and his backup band rarely does more than maintain the beat. The whole focus is on King and his guitar, and it is a rousing, dynamic session.

Baaba Maal Live at the Royal Festival Hall (Palm Pictures, PALMDVD30082)

The 70 minute concert, by the Senegalese singer, Maal, his band, and a number of guests, has a clear-as-glass picture, with crisp, exact colors, and is letterboxed with an aspect ratio of about 1.78:1 and no 16:9 enhancement. The standard stereo surround sound is excellent and the music surrounds the viewer with a vivid immediacy. Then there is a 5.1 channel Dolby Digital track with even clearer tones and more distinctive separations, and there is a DTS track that is even clearer still, with a better defined bass. The music is lively and the concert is captivating. There is a pleasing 4 minute montage of still photos, as well.

Additionally, Maal provides an excellent commentary on another audio track, as well as an additional 7 minute interview. Admittedly, we found his accent difficult to follow in places, but most of what he had to say was understandable. He talks about the roots of his music (he has large choruses backing him up—and many of his band members dance during the performance—because that is what it is like at the parties and village get-togethers where he first got started), about his collaborators, about the songs being performed, and he explains that he wanted to give Africa, which has gotten a lot of bad press in the past, a more positive image. He certainly succeeds.

Babe (Universal, 20013)

The amazing 1995 barnyard fantasy narrative cheats a bit by concluding with a traditionally reliable formula finish, the sporting competition, but no matter, the whole film is so much fun that the ending accomplishes precisely what it is supposed to do, wrapping the movie with the biggest emotional bow it can gather.

For those who haven't heard, the movie, which is as entertaining for adults as it is for children, is about a pig who wants to be a sheepdog. Within the film's world, the animals talk to each other in English, with impressive, natural moving lips, although humans are generally unaware of their collective intelligence. The farmhouse, with its tall thatched roof and multiple gables, looks like something out of a fairy story or snow globe, and the film, which is Australian, effectively transports the viewer to a delightful world where anything the filmmakers attempt seems utterly believable.

The film is presented in full screen format only. The colors are crisp and accurate throughout the presentation, and the stereo surround sound and Dolby Digital sound are super, with many delightful touches. The 92 minute program also has French and

Spanish language tracks in Dolby Digital, and optional English and Spanish subtitles.

Babe: Pig in the City (Universal, 20527)

Babe was so unique that duplicating its joys would almost be impossible and, as you've probably heard, the 1998 sequel does not achieve that goal. For one thing, the narrative is less organic. Separated from his human companion, the pig hero makes a new group of friends, and then saves them when they are taken to the pound—it is a substantially more common premise than his efforts in the first film to herd sheep. For another, it is skewed to an older audience, which turned out, quite logically, to be a marketing nightmare. The first film certainly had something of a rough and tumble atmosphere, and an acknowledgement of why people keep animals on a farm, but this one has a dog with wheels for hind legs, *Non Je Ne Regrette Rien* as a theme song, a menacing clown who accidentally sets the children's ward of a hospital on fire, and the extended anxieties of separation and defeat. One can also tell that the movie has been trimmed, for animal characters disappear without a trace or reappear looking substantially more bedraggled than when last seen. And yet, in its own right, **Babe Pig in the City**, though not the masterpiece some claim it to be, is a an enjoyable and humorous adventure. At its best, the special effects are terrific, the art direction is marvelous (the 'City' is an amalgam of every well-known metropolis, mashed together), and there are many funny moments, including the travails of the dog with wheels for hind legs. It is an enjoyable film but, in all likelihood, there are more people in the world who would like it than will ever see it.

The presentation defaults automatically to letterboxed format, with an aspect ratio of about 1.85:1 and an accommodation for enhanced 16:9 playback, but by accessing the Play function in the menu, you can choose to watch the film in full screen format. The letterboxing adds a little picture information to the sides and masks off some from the top and the bottom in comparison to the full screen image, but either seems workable. The color transfer looks super, adding to the magical tone of the sets and the characters. The stereo surround sound and Dolby Digital sound are okay, with plenty of separation effects and a reasonable amount of power. The 95 minute film (9 minutes of which are end credits) also has a French language soundtrack in standard stereo, optional English subtitles, production notes, a badly made trailer and a well made trailer, and a cast-and-director profile section. There is also a DVD-ROM 'Babe' screen saver.

Babel II: Perfect Collection (Image, ID4651SEDVD)

The Japanese cartoon starts promisingly, as a young boy discovers he has psychic abilities and is in fact the heir to an alien technology founded in the ancient Tower of Babel, which still exists, hidden in a desert. But after the first episode is concluded, the show dissolves into a sequences of redundant battles, so much so that the conclusion seems arbitrary. There's no gore or sex, either. The 111 minute presentation is made up of four episodes, each with opening and closing credit sequences. The picture is a bit worn-looking, with slightly pale colors in places. The 1994 program is presented in English in a mild stereo and is also available in Japanese in mono, with no subtitling options.

Backdraft (Universal, 20041)

The firefighter plot is insipid, but the action scenes and special effects work are just too spectacular to ignore. At its best, the 1991 film ignites with a flurry of cliffhanging moments as the heroes seem to be forever stepping out of frying pans and into something much worse.

The standard stereo surround sound and Dolby Digital mix may lack subtlety, but they are super when it comes to capturing the ambiance of a major blaze. The crackles, murmurs, and explo-

sions all get their due, and the impact of the stunt work is greatly enhanced by the emphasis the audio track creates.

The picture is in letterboxed format only, with an aspect ratio of about 2.35:1 and no 16:9 enhancement, masking off picture information from the top and bottom, and adding a bit to the sides in comparison to full screen versions. The color quality usually accommodates the complex fire scenes without a hitch and the image is sharp. The 132 minute program also has a French language track in standard stereo, optional English and Spanish subtitles, some production notes, and a cast-and-director profile section.

William Baldwin, Kurt Russell, Robert De Niro, and a few others star in the film, which was directed by Ron Howard. There are many subplots, including a few that could have withstood substantial trimming. The most interesting involves De Niro's character and his arson investigation. The least interesting involves Russell and Rebecca DeMornay analyzing their marital difficulties. Baldwin portrays everybody's little brother, just out of "the academy," who must learn how to anthropomorphize fire before he can fight it. The film's low point, however, is a jokey piece of symbolism in which images of a couple making love are inter-cut with shots of firemen entering a burning building. It made us want to throw a bucket of water on everybody.

Bad Boys (Artisan, 39004)

Not to be confused with the Will Smith and Martin Lawrence action feature, the 1983 feature is a superb drama about life in a juvenile detention center. Sean Penn stars. It is essentially a prison movie, with some slight variations, and it builds to an exciting climax in which the hero and his nemesis have an apocalyptic fight. The characters are given thorough and complex personalities and emotions, and the narrative effectively holds a viewer's interest in their fates. A very young Ally Sheedy co-stars, and there is an outstanding musical score, by Bill Conti.

The picture is letterboxed, with an aspect ratio of about 1.85:1 and an accommodation for enhanced 16:9 playback. The setting is deliberately drab, so the graininess and dull colors are not as detrimental as they might be on another film. There is enough instability in the contrasts, however, that an artifact ratcheting is noticeable at times. The stereo surround sound has a mild dimensionality and no significant flaws. The 104 minute program is not captioned.

Bad Boys (Columbia TriStar, 10715/9)

Every major plot turn defies logic and there are lots of minor contrivances, but the premise is marvelous and the film, directed by Michael Bay, is an enjoyable mix of comedy and action. Martin Lawrence and Will Smith are Miami vice cops, chasing after a large stash of drugs stolen from the evidence vault at their headquarters. What the 1995 film does really well is play up the conflicts in the private lives of the cops created by their job. Smith's character is wealthy—making the movie kind of a black *Burke's Law*—and single, while Lawrence's is a typical middle class family man, and the contrasts provide an endless potential for jibes and ironic situations. The action scenes are also terrific, and there is a final car chase where, for once, the characters are in genuinely fast cars.

The picture is presented in letterboxed format only, with an aspect ratio of about 1.85:1 and an accommodation for enhanced 16:9 playback. The framing often seems a bit too cramped on the top and bottom, however. The color transfer looks great and the picture is every bit as slick as all the other Don Simpson and Jerry Bruckheimer productions. There is nothing wrong with the stereo surround sound, but it doesn't have much energy. The dynamic range is never daring and the explosions don't shake anything. The Dolby Digital track, however, is a lot more energetic. The 119 minute program also has French and Spanish audio tracks in standard stereo, optional Spanish and Korean subtitles, and English closed captioning.

Bad Girls (see **Julie Strain's Bad Girls**)

Bad Girls 2: Stripsearch X-rated (Vivid, UPC#0073215556)

An enjoyable women's prison exercise, the plot isn't coherent and doesn't end interestingly, but the vignettes are amusing and well staged, and the erotic sequences are energetic. The picture quality is also very good, with sharp, strong colors and decent fleshtones. The sound is okay and there's even an attempt to supply background noises for the prison. The 69 minute program stars Lené, Debi Diamond, Kaitlyn Ashley, Isis Nile and Bionca. The DVD contains alternate angle sequences and elaborate hardcore interactive promotional features.

Bad Lieutenant (Artisan, 60476)

Harvey Keitel is a police detective who couldn't care less about solving crimes. Instead, he spends his time getting stoned on hard drugs and running up a six figure tab with his bookie. The NC-17-rated film uses graphic depictions of sex and violence to balance the hero's meandering slide, but the raunchy sequences seem gratuitous and without them the film seems empty and pointless.

The presentation is letterboxed with an aspect ratio of about 1.85:1 and an accommodation for enhanced 16:9 playback. The picture looks a bit grimy, but much of that is intentional. When the image is well lit, colors are sharp. When the image is darker, bright hues develop a pronounced haze. The stereo surround sound is a bit flat, but it still works up enough energy at times to be effective, and the flatness can seem thematic. The 96 minute program can be supported by optional Spanish subtitles and English captioning. There is a brief production essay and a small cast-and-crew profile section. Contrary to a notation on the jacket, there is no trailer.

Bad Wives X-rated (Vivid); softcore (Vivid, UPC#0073214552)

The 72 minute program has a fairly strong narrative, which has elements of humor, though it is generally serious in tone and even includes some special effects at the end. Two under-appreciated housewives meet a grocery clerk who has a devilish way about him, quite literally, as it turns out. The erotic sequences are somewhat limited, with so much attention being paid to the story, but multiple angles stretch things out a little. Shot on film, some sequences are underlit, but generally the colors look strong and the image is crisp, though there is some grain in places. The monophonic sound is passable. The DVD also contains elaborate hardcore interactive promotional features.

Like most of Vivid's softcore rehashes, the erotic sequences are still fairly elaborate. The picture and sound are identical to the hardcore version and the program actually runs longer, logging in at 80 minutes.

Badfinger Director's Cut (Pioneer, PA97578D)

The excellent documentary is about the Liverpool rock group that rose to fame under the nurturing wing of the Beatles (there were people who thought that the group was the Beatles, pretending not to be) and then sank when they shifted labels and their manager disappeared with all their money ("You'd better hurry cause it's not gonna last," etc.). The 88 minute program is called **Director's Cut** because it contains a standard sized hour-long documentary and then an addendum of interview sequences which are franker and less polished than the interviews in the regular documentary, but highly enlightening and entertaining, making the program much more worthwhile. Each of the group's biggest singles is heard in full, though little of their other music is heard. The documentary combines archive footage, interviews and narration to tell the band's fascinating story—two members eventually died—and the show is an excellent look not only at the group but at the brief heyday of Apple Records and the London music scene in the early Seventies. The picture looks fine and even ancient music videos look reasonably colorful and crisp. The stereo sound is okay. The older recordings are no match for today's super-engineered rock, but they are adequately presented and there is a Dolby

Digital track that sound crisper and better detailed. The program is not captioned.

Badlands (Warner, 16086)

Terence Malick's remarkable 1973 debut feature is in letterboxed format on one side, with an aspect ratio of about 1.75:1 and an accommodation for enhanced 16:9 playback, and is in full screen format on the other side. The full screen framing loses very little on the sides and adds picture information to the top and bottom in comparison to the letterboxed image. The full screen version is highly appealing, particularly if you watch the letterboxed version a couple times. The film is set in a dusty locale and fleshtones are a bit indistinct here and there, but overall the image is sharp and colors are carefully defined. It didn't need it, but the film's audio track has been remastered for stereo and is also available in 5.1 Dolby Digital. Fortunately, they haven't gone overboard. There are some dimensional atmospheric touches, but the music remains fairly centered and separation effects are never distracting. The Dolby Digital track sounds more precise than the standard track. The 95 minute program has optional English and French subtitles.

Martin Sheen and Sissy Spacek star as young lovers who kill several people (he actually does the killing, she just tags along) and then manage to elude the law for an extended period of time. There is nothing exceptional about the narrative, which has been done many times over, but Malick's approach is unique and artistically compelling. The heroes are barely aware of the world beyond their view, and the cinematography and editing continually reinforce their isolation. Both Sheen and Spacek bring a wonderful, dry humor to their performances, communicating far more with body language and facial expressions than with the scattered bits of dialogue they are given. Much of the film's impact is subliminal. The gorgeous cinematography and production design, the outstanding sound recording eccentric musical score, and the carefully measured performances can all easily disintegrate when the film does not look or sound as good as it is supposed to, and so the DVD pulls the curtain away from an American masterpiece.

Badman's River (Master Movies, DVD5528)

Lee Van Cleef, Gina Lollobrigida and James Mason star in an awkward attempt at mixing humor and action. The 1972 feature, set in revolution-era Mexico, where the heroes are trying to cash in some arms money, is cut in places like a silent comedy (Van Cleef even wears a Chaplinesque bowler), but clowning was never part of Van Cleef's limited repertoire and the jokey sequences are totally incongruous with the action. There are, however, lots of explosions, gun fights and chases, and they look so good fans may well be willing to tolerate the comedy to get to them.

The source material has a bit of wear, but such damage is isolated, and the colors look very nice. The picture is letterboxed with an aspect ratio of about 2.35:1 and an accommodation for enhanced 16:9 playback. The monophonic sound on both movies is less pristine, with some background noise, scratchy dialogue and a weak upper end, and is accompanied by optional Japanese subtitles (but no English captioning) and copious cast and director profiles. The copy we viewed started skipping at the end, without any apparent smudges on the platter.

Baker's Hawk (UAV, 40095)

Clint Walker and Burl Ives star in the 1976 family-oriented western. The narrative has two tiers. In one, a young boy helps Ives' character train a wounded hawk, while in the other the boy's father stands up against vigilantes who want scare off squatters, including Ives' character. The drama is competently presented and the stars are appealing. The source material looks somewhat worn and colors are a bit bland. Darker sequences have a tendency to smear. The monophonic sound is adequate. The film runs 98 minutes and is not captioned.

Ball of Fire (HBO, 90750)

Inspired by *Snow White*, Gary Cooper and Barbara Stanwyck star in the delightful story of a showgirl hiding from gangsters with a group of college professors. Written by Charles Brackett and Billy Wilder and directed by Howard Hawks, the 1941 feature is a wonderful blend of snappy dialogue and endearing characterizations, and we really can't imagine anyone disliking it.

With cinematography by Gregg Toland, some of the lighting effects in the black-and-white are breathtaking and many have a direct bearing on the plot. In the most memorable, the hero, played by Gary Cooper, falls in love with the heroine, played by Barbara Stanwyck, when she walks in front of a window and glows with a soft halo of sunlight. At one point, Cooper's character enters a dark room and begins talking, not realizing that Stanwyck is there. Indeed, all we see of her is the barest flicker of light around her eyes. Thanks to Toland, when it is said that Stanwyck's character looks attractive in the sunlight, it is not left to the imagination. The black-and-white picture is very sharp, with finely contrasts and pure blacks.

The basic monophonic sound is a little weak, but there's a Chace Surround Stereo track that gives the music a bit of dimensionality and the rest of the audio a little stronger presence. There are also French, Spanish, German and Italian mono tracks, and the 111 minute film can be supported by English, French or Spanish subtitles ("La palabra 'puss' en inglés vulgar significa 'cara.' Como por ejemplo, 'cara agria,' 'cara amargada.' 'Sugarpuss' implica una cierta dulzura en su apariencia"). A reasonably large cast & crew profile section is also featured.

The Band Live at The New Orleans Jazz Festival (Pioneer, PA98600D)

Contrary to a jacket notation that claims the program runs an hour and a half, the DVD runs 65 minutes. There are some interview sequences between a few of the numbers, but most of the show is given over to a concert by the aging but still effective rock group, who play their best known numbers with a competent freshness and intensity. The stage is well lit and the picture looks quite good, with crisp, accurate colors. The stereo surround sound and Dolby Digital utilize different directional allocations of the instruments and vocals, but both are fairly satisfying, with the Dolby Digital delivering slightly crisper tones. There is no captioning.

Bangkok X-rated (Vivid, UPC#0073214587)

The activities of a Thai brothel are depicted, though it is clear that the filmmakers never left the San Fernando Valley, and it is the cleanest Thai brothel any sailor ever wandered into. Anyway, there is a touch of the supernatural at the end, but the narrative doesn't amount to much. The erotic sequences are standard but reasonably energetic. The colors are bright, with decent fleshtones, and the image is sharp. The sound, including a musical score that tries to be Asian, is fine. The 67 minute program features Asia Carrera, Cumisha Amado and Jasmine Aloha. The DVD contains alternate angle sequences and elaborate hardcore interactive promotional features.

Barbarella: Queen of the Galaxy (Paramount, 068127)

Science fiction movies come in all shapes and sizes and one of the least respected is the burlesque, though, by its nature, it attracts as strong a cult following as it does derision. The Dino De Laurentiis production of Roger Vadim's funky 1968 feature has an elaborate Plexiglas-and-leather production design, bizarre costumes and a (PG-rated) sexual liberation atmosphere. Jane Fonda stars in the title role, traipsing about in see-through acrylic outfits and embodying, in a stage-like fashion, the adventures of a popular French adult comic book heroine. The film had a gaggle of scriptwriters, each seeming to go in a different direction and tone, and is peopled by even more young, statuesque and generally naked Europeans, who for the most part are treated as part of the decor. But while you may be attracted to burlesque because of the girls, it is

the clowns that keep you happy. Milo O'Shea, who doesn't appear until the side break, is in our opinion the film's savior, for it is his indulgently comical performance that has enabled us to continue enjoying the film after dozens of viewings. What? Dozens of viewings? Yes, we're afraid so, for after a while even the silliest looking sets take on a winsome sense of fantasy, Fonda was an alert actress even when she wasn't allowed to be one of quality, and just when things start to drag, O'Shea steps in and gets us giggling again.

The presentation is different from the letterboxed LD. Although it has an aspect ratio of about 2.5:1 and an accommodation for enhanced 16:9 playback, it is missing picture information on all four sides in comparison to the letterboxed LD image. The color transfer is stronger, with truer fleshtones and metallic tones (which look brownish on the LD). Like the LD, there are a few stray speckles and scratches, but the source material looks very nice overall. The image is sharp and free of grain. The monophonic sound is much blander than the LD's mono track and seems somewhat muffled. There is also a French mono track (it appears that Fonda does her own dubbing) and English closed captioning. The 98 minute program is accompanied by a lengthy theatrical trailer.

Barry Lyndon (Warner, 17366)

Stanley Kubrick's stately Eighteenth Century adventure based upon a novel by William Makepeace Thackeray runs 185 minutes, every second of which is stunningly photographed. Ryan O'Neal portrays an Irishman who travels to Europe in an army and stays on, to work his way up in society until his fortune takes a turn for the worse. The 1975 film can be as engrossing as a novel if the viewer is not alienated by the period atmosphere and deliberate pace. The critics who condemned the film as being akin to a coffee table book were wrong not in their metaphor, but in their assumption that it is a negative association. There are, however, many exceptional moments of human drama—something people rarely acknowledge in a work by Kubrick—and many memorable sequences, all of which are enhanced by Kubrick's finely honed and very dry humor. O'Neal's character makes an extreme and seemingly arbitrary personality shift shortly after the Intermission that takes some getting used to, and this may be the film's biggest joke of all.

The presentation is subject to some artifacting flaws, particularly a slight jitter in the backgrounds, and there are scattered speckles in the source material. The color transfer is excellent, however. The crisp image brings out fine detail and a clear view of the shifts in light and shade. The picture is letterboxed with an aspect ratio of about 1.58:1 and no 16:9 enhancement. The monophonic sound is okay. There is an alternate French audio track, optional English and French subtitles, production notes and a trailer.

The Base (Sterling, 7245)

The leader of an army platoon assigned to the border patrol in Southern California ends up becoming the drug kingpin of Los Angeles before the hero, working undercover, takes him down. Mark Dacascos is the hero and Tim Abell is the villain. The film begins promisingly but gets a little ridiculous towards the end, though the basic mix of action and drama is tolerable.

Presented in full screen format, the picture quality is workable, with reasonably sharp hues and adequate fleshtones. The stereo surround sound is functional but not elaborate. The 97 minute program can be supported by Spanish subtitles, but there is no English captioning. A trailer and a cast-and-crew profile section are included.

Additionally, the director, Mark Lester, provides a sporadic commentary track. He talks about the logistics of the shoot, about using quasi-military locations, and about the mistakes that were made during the filming. Once in a while he gets details about the film wrong while he is discussing the story, but maybe it has been a while since he made it. He also tends to offer backhanded praise at times, such as when he is discussing the skills of action star Dacascos: "Here I like the idea that Tim Abell could do the talking and Mark Dacascos could do the watching."

BASEketball (Universal, 20430)

The sports comedy, conceived by David Zucker and starring **South Park** creators Trey Parker and Matt Stone, had the potential of being outrageously funny, but it never builds that kind of momentum. There are moments of good humor, and some base, disgusting gags that pass these days for moments of good humor, but the narrative is s-l-o-w and there aren't enough jokes, good or raunchy, to fill the gaps. The two heroes are the founders and stars of a new sports league based upon a hoop-shooting game they devised. As the league becomes popular and money starts to move in, their loyalties are tested. In the relaxed atmosphere of home video the film might be a little easier to get through than it was in a theater, but if one is to really enjoy it, one's expectations had best be low.

The presentation is in letterboxed format with an aspect ratio of about 1.85:1 and an accommodation for enhanced 16:9 playback. The picture is solid and hues are bright. The stereo surround sound and Dolby Digital sound mix are functional—sometimes, with crowd sounds, noticeably so, as if the artificiality of the mix were deliberate—but rarely invigorating. The 104 minute film can be supported by English, French or Spanish subtitles. There is an uncredited music video, a good 'making of' featurette, a promising trailer, production notes and a cast-and-director profile section.

Basic Instinct (Artisan, 60443)

Unlike earlier home video versions, the picture is crisp, and while fleshtones may have a slightly orange tint, they still look accurate, as do the film's other colors. The picture is letterboxed on one side, with an aspect ratio of about 2.1:1 and no 16:9 enhancement, and is presented in cropped format on the other side. The 129 minute presentation is the standard 'R' rated version, not the really raunchy Director's Cut. The stereo surround sound is uninspired, but the Dolby Digital track better detailed and energetic. The film is also available in Spanish in standard stereo and comes with a DVS descriptive audio track, which can be fun for the sex scenes ("She slips a sharp, gleaming ice pick out from under the sheets and jams it into his neck"). The film can be supported by English, French or Spanish subtitles and comes with a decent sized cast and crew profile section, along with what was probably a red tag theatrical trailer. Michael Douglas and Sharon Stone star in the ludicrous, over-sexed and reasonably exciting 1992 thriller.

Basket Case (Image, ID4785BCDVD)

Made in 1981, the film was inexpensively produced but competently directed, achieving a level of humor and gore that enabled it to become a popular title on the midnight circuit. While the gore has long since been surpassed, the film remains an effective horror film that essentially delivers all that it promises. About a boy who has a thing he keeps in a basket that kills people, the budget is low but the number of makeup and model effects is satisfying and the inclusion of some stop motion sequences is particularly admirable. The actors are inexperienced, but never to the point where they fall out of character.

Cheap lighting prevents the colors from looking all that rich, and fleshtones vary in degrees of blandness from shot to shot, but the transfer is obviously quite nice, with a sharp focus and consistently stable hues. The monophonic sound seems to be a fairly cheap recording, with little ambiance and a flat musical score. The program is said to be the 'uncut' version and runs 90 minutes. There is no captioning.

Bataan (MGM, 907662)

Made in 1943 while the war still raged, it is an effective, surprisingly frank Alamo-esque action film about a platoon that helps their army retreat by preventing the Japanese from building a bridge. The enjoyable and stereotypical cast includes Robert Tay-

lor, George Murphy, Thomas Mitchell, Lloyd Nolan, Robert Walker and even Desi Arnaz. The characters speak disparagingly of persons of Japanese descent, but all's fair in war, right? Directed by Tay Garnett, the battle scenes are super, full of up close carnage and excitement, and the dramatic interludes, though formulaic, are well handled by the stars. The sets and special effects are lavish, but provide an effective balance to the focus on the heroes, particularly as their number begins to diminish.

The source material has some wear in places, but is in reasonably good condition, with adequate contrasts. The black-and-white image is sharp. The monophonic sound is okay, and there is an alternate French audio track as well. The 114 minute program can be supported by optional English and French subtitles, and is accompanied by an enjoyable trailer.

Batman (Warner, 12000)

The improvements to the picture on the Tim Burton film are fairly interesting. The image is darker than the LD—it is almost impossible to watch the movie in a well-lit room—but it is clearly more accurate. The LD looks too bright, as if intentional shadows had been compromised for the sake of the video presentation, and the balance of dark and light on the DVD feels much more accurate and more artistically satisfying. The colors and fleshtones are also more accurate and the image is crisper. The picture is presented in letterboxed format on one side and in full screen format on the other. The letterboxing has an aspect ratio of about 1.85:1 and an accommodation for enhanced 16:9 playback, adding some picture information to the sides of the image and masking off some from the bottom compared to the full screen image. The stereo surround sound and Dolby Digital sound are super. You can make out the lyrics to the Prince songs and feel the thunder as the Bat Plane rips across Gotham City's shopping concourse. It doesn't take long for Danny Elfman's woozy score to start vibrating inside you, either. The 126 minute film is also available in French in standard stereo, can be supported by English, French or Spanish subtitles, and comes with production notes and a cast & crew profile section. The incredible artistic detail that was part of the theatrical experience is compromised on a small screen, even with the fineness of the DVD's image, but other aspects of the movie improve, such as the presence of Kim Basinger. She no longer seems dwarfed by everything that is going on around her. Michael Keaton stars as the caped super hero and Jack Nicholson is his primary nemesis.

Batman and Robin (Warner, 16500)

A big, messy movie, jammed with superficial plot advancements (the film has to introduce and give quality time to six main characters) and overly cluttered art direction (compare the films to Tim Burton's movies, which had a specific vision—these just try to include everything), but the last act isn't as excruciating as the last act in **Batman Forever** and the film never really slows down, even for its token emotional sequences. Although there is nothing in **Batman and Robin** to match's Jim Carrey's with-it performance in the earlier movie, the cast is engaging and top-billed Arnold Schwarzenegger is more entertaining as the central villain than one might anticipate. George Clooney makes the best Batman—he's the first one to really look at home in the suit— but he is the weakest Bruce Wayne, less humanly flawed than Michael Keaton or Val Kilmer. Nevertheless, it is a fun movie with more than enough colors and sounds to make a terrific DVD.

The picture looks incredibly sharp, and every wild, day-glo color is crisp and pure. The stereo surround sound is okay and the Dolby Digital track is great. The 125 minute film is presented in full screen format on one side and in letterbox format on the other side, with an aspect ratio of about 1.9:1 and an accommodation for enhanced 16:9 playback. The letterboxing adds very little to the sides and masks off a lot of picture information from the top and bottom. Because the film is so busy, the action scenes are easier to follow on the full screen image and usually the dramatic sequences are also more satisfying. There are a few production notes and a small cast profile. The film is also available in French in Dolby Digital and comes with English, French or Spanish subtitles ("Je veux une voiture. Ça plaît aux filles").

Batman Forever (Warner, 15100)

Val Kilmer fills in as Batman this time out, with Jim Carrey and Tommy Lee Jones as the villains and Nicole Kidman and Chris O'Donnell as assistant good guys. The story takes a long time setting everything up and then comes to its conclusion fairly rapidly, but the action scenes are plentiful and well spaced out, the humor is engaging and Carrey is more fun than any of the heroes. In the name of art, the plot contains many contrasting dualities, giving the drama a workable psychological foundation. The show is so cluttered with production design, however, that it is sometimes difficult to see what is going on through the props. Still, the episode is worthy of its franchise and the DVD gives the film a terrific send-off. The picture, which is awash with colors, is crisp and bright in every scene, even during the darkest sequences. The 1995 movie is presented in letterboxed format on one side, with an aspect ratio of about 1.85:1 and an accommodation for enhanced 16:9 playback, and in full screen format on the other, adding some picture information to the sides and trimming some off the top and bottom in comparison to the full screen. The film's overly cluttered production design makes viewing each version at least once worthwhile, to soak up all the decorations, but on the whole, the letterbox framing is more appealing. The stereo surround sound is moderately energetic and the Dolby Digital track is much better, with many energized separation effects and lots of power coming from every angle. Dialog, however, gets lost in the noise from time to time. The 122 minute movie is also available in French in standard stereo and comes with English, French or Spanish subtitles. There is also a brief collection of cast profiles and production notes.

Batman Returns (Warner, 15000)

Easily the finest and most durable film in the series. Danny DeVito's spark loses a bit of its intensity and Michael Keaton seems to have been shortchanged by the script, but Michelle Pfeiffer just gets better and better. The action scenes are easier to follow on multiple viewings, and are less critical to the entertainment. Conversely, the film's moody atmosphere and intense design, which may have encouraged feelings of impatience during initial screenings, are far more accessible and inviting when their narrative context, a continuation of fairy tales by other means, is pre-established.

Added to these factors is the excellent transfer, which makes the film very easy to enjoy. Grainy in its theatrical presentation, the film not only avoids additional grain on DVD, it actually looks a little less grainy, without corrupting the filmmakers' intent. The colors are precise and every difficult lighting situation is handled with aplomb. The 126 minute film is presented on one side in full screen and on the other side letterboxed with an aspect ratio of about 1.85:1 and an accommodation for enhanced 16:9 playback. The full screen version adds some picture information to the bottom of the image but trims more off the sides, so the letterbox version is preferable, even though it does not quite present as wide a picture as the LD. The film's sound mix, however, is a little disappointing, since it tends to favor mass sound over individual noises. The stereo surround sound is weak, and although the Dolby Digital track has more distinctive directional effects, the dialogue channel is a remains subdued. The film is also available in French in standard stereo, and comes with English, French or Spanish subtitles. Production notes and cast information are also provided.

*batteries not included (Universal, 20520)

The somewhat misguided science fiction fairy tale is about miniature spaceships that help a group of tenants hold onto their condemned apartment building. The film has lots of special effects and plenty of good will, but the characters are predictable and the narrative has no special magic. Hume Cronyn and Jessica Tandy star.

The 1987 film is presented in letterboxed format, with an aspect ratio of about 1.85:1 and an accommodation for enhanced 16:9 playback. Colors are bright and fleshtones look okay, but the image is a bit soft and the deepest hues are a little fuzzy. There is a Dolby Digital track, which has more separations and a somewhat wider dimensionality than the standard track, though the mix isn't as aggressive as it would be if the film were produced today. The 107 minute program is also available in French in standard stereo and can be supported by English or Spanish subtitles. There is a production essay that talks about the location but says very little about the special effects, a short cast-and-director profile section and a trailer.

Battle Arena Toshinden (U.S. Manga, DUSM1630)

The hour-long Japanese animated program, presented in two parts with two sets of opening and closing credits, is a spin-off of a popular video game. The first part introduces all the characters and depicts a few minor skirmishes as they size one another up, and then the second part depicts a single elaborate battle against the bad guys. Fans will be satisfied with the action, but the show's artistic values are limited.

The supplement provides profiles of the characters. The supplemental features are time encoded, but the program itself is not. On a player that automatically displays subtitling, we could not suppress the English subtitling for the English dialogue, while on a player that doesn't automatically display subtitling, we could not activate subtitling for the English dialogue. The program is also available in Japanese, with and without English subtitling. The copy we viewed also displayed some bothersome manufacturing flaws. The picture quality has no significant problems and the stereo sound is bland but adequate.

The Battle of the Bulge: World War II's Deadliest Battle (Shanachie, 941)

The 90 minute documentary not only covers the battle's logistics, but explores such topics as the horrors and sacrifices of war. The film combines extensive archival footage (supported by subtle sound effects) with survivor interviews. It tells the full story of why the Allied commanders were caught off guard and why the Germans, or more specifically Adolf Hitler, chose such a suicidal strategy. There is the complete story behind the famous 'Nuts!' response to a German call for surrender, and probably more than you want to know about the grinding, tragic effort taken by the Allies to recapture the ground they'd lost after they stopped the German advance and rescued Bastogne. By focusing on the four-month battle, the documentary is able to provide specific reportage on the event and still explore it as a microcosm for the war as a whole. The picture quality looks fine. The audio is in decent shape and there is a stereophonic musical score.

Battlecade: Extreme Fighting (Image, ID5583FMDVD)
Battlecade: Extreme Fighting 2 (Image, ID5584FMDVD)

There is nothing phony about the no-holds-barred conflicts. Staged in a round ring, the programs depict fighters of different disciplines grappling with one another for extended time limits with limited rules. There is a lot of blood and some interesting match ups, but there is no tournament format, so the fighters, winners and losers, come and go without allowing the viewer to have much stake in their fates. The live commentary is awful. The commentators consistently make predictions that are then negated by the action in the ring, and twice they miss seeing the loser signaling to the referee to end the fight.

The first program is set in Wilmington, North Carolina and runs a solid 114 minutes. The second program runs 92 minutes and is set in Quebec, bookended by a rather amusing but longish documentary about the show's hapless promoters trying to find some place where they can stage their event, and it actually concludes with the promoters and fighters being marched off to jail.

The picture looks okay on both programs. There is a mild graininess, but the image is sharp and hues are bright. The monophonic sound on the first program is a little scratchy, and the stereo sound on the second program, though with a limited dimensionality, is smoother. The programs are not captioned.

The Battleship Potemkin (Image, ID4574CODVD)

The 1976 restoration of the 'pre-Stalin' cut of Sergei Eisenstein's 1925 black-and-white silent classic was constructed in Moscow in the mid-seventies. There is no mistaking the age of the source material, but the print is in fine shape and does not inhibit the film's pleasures. The monophonic orchestral musical score, by Dimitri Shostakovich, has faint scratches and other minor distortions, but is ideally suited to the film and adds to the drama. The film has wordy Russian intertitles that are translated with rapidly changing English subtitles.

One can understand why the film made Stalin so nervous, since it is about autocratic oppression in all forms. The film is full of beautifully photographed moments, from the sailors hanging in their hammocks in the beginning, to the battleship slicing the frame at the end. Eisenstein's staging, his sense of drama, his affection for humanity and his feeling for the texture of surfaces are steadfastly compelling. The film, about mutiny and revolution, is a grand accomplishment and contains examples of many very basic editing techniques. Although public domain versions are abundant in other home video media, this is the definitive version and the one that should be added to the Serious Movie Lover's library.

The Beach Boys: The Lost Concert (Image, ID5647SBDVD)

The 22 minute black-and-white set from 1964 was originally broadcast on closed circuit video to theaters. Only one of the band members looks like he's old enough to drink. Although brief, it is refreshing to seem them so young and enthusiastic. The live set lacks the nuances of a studio recording, the drums tend to drown everything else out in places, and their harmonies are haphazard, but the time machine glimpse of the group more than compensates.

They play nine numbers. The black-and-white picture is sharp, with crisp contrasts, and details are clear, though the video source lacks the texture that film would provide. The monophonic sound has a limited range and is subject to the recording shortcomings we detailed above, with a clipped high end, but it still seems fresh. There is no captioning. The program is accompanied by an extensive Beach Boys discography.

The Beach Boys - Nashville Sounds: The Making of Stars and Stripes (Image, ID4514ERDVD)

The hour-long program, about country stars recording Beach Boys tunes, has interview segments between each number, but most of the songs are heard in full. Most are performed in what looks like a staged recording studio performance, but there is also a music video and a genuine concert segment. None of the songs acquire an exceptional interpretation from the arrangements or the new singers, but none is ruined, either, and it is a chance to hear overly common tunes in a fresh way. Joining Brian Wilson and Mike Love are Colin Raye, Ricky van Shelton, T. Graham Brown, Jimmy Webb, Kathy Troccoli, Willie Nelson and others. Our favorite is Junior Brown bringing his rockabilly riffs to 409, but even he seems to take it a little too slow. The picture quality is adequate though there is some grain.

The stereo sound is surprisingly nice, with vivid, warm tones. The picture looks okay. The program is not captioned.

Bean: The Movie (PolyGram, 4400469132)

The film is an extension of the TV show (see **The Best Bits of Mr. Bean**). Rowan Atkinson portrays an inept museum employee sent to America to accompany the turnover of a rare painting to an American museum. The narrative, which seems a bit long at 91 minutes, inevitably breaks off into segments—Bean on an airplane (including a barf bag gag that comes from a TV skit), on an amusement park ride, in a hospital, cooking a turkey (which comes from another TV skit), etc.—and the story is virtually over well before the movie is. Peter MacNicol co-stars, coming up with a few amusing reactions to Atkinson's antics, and the film also has a few 'outsider's exaggerations' of what America is like.

The 1997 film is in full screen format on one side and in letterboxed format on the other side, with an aspect ratio of about 1.85:1 and no 16:9 enhancement. The letterboxing adds absolutely nothing to the sides and masks off picture information from the top and bottom in comparison to the full screen release. Since the movie is based upon a TV program, the full screen image tends to be more satisfying. The color quality looks very good, with vivid hues and accurate fleshtones. The stereo surround sound and Dolby Digital sound are energetically applied. Rear channel activity is limited, but the sound mix is reasonably aggressive and accommodates the film well. The film is also available in French in Dolby Digital and can be supported by English or Spanish subtitles. Also included are some very funny teasers and trailers (including one that parodies a black-and-white perfume commercial, with Bean wandering through it in color), a music video and a small cast & crew profile section.

Beast Cops (import, MSDVD03698)

There is a marvelous Fritz Lang moment in the Hong Kong crime film, when an older gangster, intent upon keeping the younger ones at bay, gives one young turk some Machiavellian suggestions. At the same time, the older gangster is drinking tea, and when he gets to the most devious part of his suggestion, he starts stirring the cup—stirring up trouble, as it were. Although there is a gory slaughter at the end and a few other furious action scenes, the film is primarily a character piece, about the relationships between a few cops and the young mobsters. Unlike some of the most flamboyant Hong Kong productions, it is more of an acquired taste, but one has to admit that few American gangster movies go into as much complex detail over the subtleties and stratified links between right and wrong.

The film can be presented in English, as well as Cantonese and Mandarin, and can be supported by optional English, traditional Chinese, Japanese, Thai, Mandarin, simplified Chinese, Korean, Spanish, and Bahasa Malaysian subtitles. The picture is letterboxed with an aspect ratio of about 1.85:1 and no 16:9 enhancement. The image is typical of a decent Hong Kong transfer. Fleshtones are a little dull but workable and colors are adequate but not intense. The source material is free of damage. The stereo surround sound and Dolby Digital sound have periodic surges of dimensionality but are best kept at a moderate volume. The 110 minute 1998 feature is accompanied by behind-the-scenes footage of co-directors Gordon Chan and Dante Lam and stars Michael Fitzgerald Wong, Anthony Wong, Roy Cheung and Kathy Chau, as well as trailers for four of Lam's and Chan's films.

Beastie Boys Sabotage (Pioneer, PA97574D)

The hour-long collection of music videos has a very good mixture of styles. There are a few foolish videos, where the band members run around with phony wigs and things, but since not all the videos are like that, even those efforts are tolerable. The best videos, such as a harrowing skateboarding piece set to *Time for Living*, are refreshing and unpretentious, expertly edited to color the music without detracting from it. Since many of the videos use makeshift cinematography, the picture is always a little grungy, but the transfer looks okay. The band's quick, hard rock sound also goes through a variety of tonal levels, some sounding like they were recorded on a cassette recorder and others knocking things over with the full power of a studio mix. The stereo surround sound, in its best moments, seems powerful and effectively detailed. There is no captioning.

The Beatles (see **Alf Bicknell's Personal Beatles Diary**)

The Beatles: A Hard Day's Night (MPI, DVD7082)

Like all the home video releases of **A Hard Day's Night**, the program opens with the ridiculous prologue number that you have to be fast on the draw to skip with the chapter controls so as to catch the film's true, the-world-is-forever-changed opening chords. The presentation has a solid black-and-white image with deep blacks and sharp lines. The stereo sound is less alive during the dialogue scenes, but during the songs it is wonderful, with a deep bass and smooth, clear tones. Turn it up, up, up. In addition to the 90 minute 1964 film, the DVD contains a theatrical trailer for a re-release, and two terrific newsreel clips, one about the group arriving in New York and the other showing the group receiving an entertainment award in Britain. Within the profile of the crew and supporting cast members, accessing Richard Lester's profile brings up a very good Sixties interview with him (when he was considered 'one of the four most influential directors working today') as well as the legendary (and rather blurry) *Running Standing Jumping Film*. Contrary to the jacket notation, there is no Dolby Digital track. The film is also available in French and Spanish in mono and can be accompanied by English, French or Spanish subtitles, although the songs are not subtitled.

The Beatles: The First U.S. Visit (MPI, DVD6218)

The black-and-white footage was shot in 1964 by the Maysles brothers, but was edited into its present form, which runs 80 minutes, in 1990. At its best, the non-music sequences feel like they've been pulled straight out of **A Hard Day's Night**. Although the group often acts up for the camera, they are so obvious about it that you can tell when they really let down their guard. There is also a tendency to look beyond the foreground, and to listen beyond the foreground, catching glimpses of the girls they've slipped into their rooms and the minor tensions that a road trip, even one as royal as this, can generate. There is also one concert clip, from their Washington DC gig, but the central appeal of the program is the recreation of the Beatles' three appearances on the *Ed Sullivan Show*.

The picture quality is excellent whenever possible. The stereo sound is even better. From the minor errors in microphone levels and the precise coordination between the music and the movements of the musicians, you can tell that the audio recording is legitimate. The audio is also "sensitive." Without the songs being spoiled, you still hear the vocals individually and the instruments separately. The performances may lack the steely power of the studio standards, but the minor flutters and occasional missteps are thoroughly welcome. For some, the recordings may even provide a revelation, a sudden intimacy with a song one has heard a thousand times before.

The program is accompanied by a collection of Beatles discographies and other trivia, and a brief background on the documentary. Navigating them, however, is difficult. It is supported by English, French or Spanish subtitles ("Elle t'aime, oui, oui, oui…").

The Beatles: The Magical Mystery Tour (Image, DVD1538)

Do you realize that kids today can get up and dance to a song that was a hit before their mother was born and *Your Mother Should Know* can be that song? When it first appeared on the art house circuit a decade after its creation, the 50-minute 1967 television film made by the Beatles, **Magical Mystery Tour**, seemed vital. Whether one was searching for further clues pointing to evidence of Paul's demise, or just relieved that there existed more footage of the foursome up to their Lesteresque antics, the film seemed like an important addition that the original British television audiences had stupidly misunderstood. Looking back upon it now, it is apparent that British television audiences were actually prescient. Since the advent of video compilations, even KISS's home movies are better organized than these.

Filmed under anarchic conditions, fleshtones often look washed out and the source material is erratic, though colors are reasonably strong and it is assumed most viewers know what they are getting into. The dialogue is a strained mono while the music is an enhanced stereo that sounds reasonably strong. There are two terrific newsreel clips, one from the opening of the Apple boutique on Baker Street and one about the Beatles visiting the Maharishi. Contrary to a jacket notation, the Dolby Digital track could not be activated and there is no French or Spanish track, although there are optional English, French or Spanish subtitles.

The Beatles: The Making of A Hard Day's Night (MPI, DVD7056)

None of the Beatles are interviewed, but the personnel behind the cameras reminisce about the enthusiasm and inspiration that created one of the most innovative and influential films ever concocted to cash in on a craze. The documentary gets its main points across fairly well—that the movie is one of the best musicals ever conceived, that it was constructed to seem more spontaneous than it actually was, and that it was pretty spontaneous anyway. It is not a documentary of intense scholarship and is not systematic in its analysis of the film's creation. Brief clips from the movie, for example, are used to punctuate statements made by the commentators, a gag that becomes tiresome fairly quickly but is continued throughout the program.

The entire 65 minute work seems to have been constructed as an excuse to present an uncovered outtake—a complete performance of *You Can't Do That* during the broadcast concert at the film's end. Nevertheless, fans will find that the program is a nice supplement to the film and viewers who haven't seen the movie in a while will find that it is a worthy appetizer.

The program is supported by English, French or Spanish subtitles and is accompanied by profiles of a couple cast members and the crew of **Hard Day's Night**. The image quality is okay, though footage from the film does not seem to be in pristine condition. The songs are presented in stereo but most of the commentary is monophonic and there is a bit of a volume level discrepancy between the music and the rest of the show. Since it's the Beatles, though, we didn't mind.

Beautiful X-rated (Vivid, UPC#0073214520)

A man about to be married to a wealthy woman meets a store clerk and falls in love. The erotic sequences are effective, but the narrative is fairly strong and takes up much of the 75 minute running time. Some of the performers are French and there are lengthy passages of French dialogue supported by yellow English subtitles. Shot on film, the picture is sharp but fleshtones are pinkish. The sound is fine. The DVD contains alternate angle sequences and elaborate hardcore interactive promotional features.

Beautiful Girls (Buena Vista, 16453)

If we have to sit through one more movie about some guy in his twenties who can't decide if he should marry his girlfriend we are going to gag. The 1996 feature has a large and attractive ensemble cast, including Timothy Hutton, Matt Dillon, Natalie Portman, Lauren Holly, Rosie O'Donnell, Mira Sorvino, Uma Thurman and others who also may become more famous someday. Hutton is the hero, returning from the big city to visit his little home town for a reunion and witnessing the various romantic dilemmas his friends are in as he tries to come to some sensible decisions about his own future. If you haven't seen too many of these movies before, or if you thrive on all the macho bonding and contrasting women-are-smarter-than-men witticisms, then you'll probably like it.

The presentation is in letterboxed format with an aspect ratio of about 1.85:1 and no 16:9 enhancement. Although the film has a sort of drab color scheme, the image transfer appears accurate and the picture is sharp and clear. The stereo surround sound lacks decent separation detail and a strong sense of presence. The 113 minute program can be supported by optional English subtitles.

Beauty and the Beast (Criterion, BEA120)

Jean Cocteau's 1946 film is a stunningly lyrical motion picture that anyone who is enamored of film and fantasy will want to have for their library. Cocteau was not just a film director. He was an artist who wrote stories and stage dramas, designed scenery for theater, and dabbled in every craft from plate design to wall hangings. Making movies gave him an opportunity to apply all of these skills on a single medium. Watching a film by Cocteau is like floating through a dream. The images soothe your anxieties and the narrative aggravates them. The differences between obsessive love and deep spiritual love are explored on a level that even children, at least those who are not scared to death by the faces in the walls and on the pots, will understand. Cocteau accomplished numerous special effects that have never been successfully imitated.

The black-and-white picture has been spruced up a bit. There are still plenty of scratches and other markings, as is to be expected, but the image is less grainy, blacks are deeper and the focus is a little sharper than on Criterion's LD. The monophonic audio track is noisier but brighter on the LD, even when compared to the DVD's Dolby Digital mono track, but the sound on the DVD is adequate, and the white English subtitles are optional. The film runs 93 minutes.

Additionally, the disc has been supplied with two extensive and thoughtful presentations on the film's structure and production background. One, a lengthy excerpt from a half hour introduction to the film, *Angel of Space and Time*, produced on a South Carolina public television program, *Cinematic Eye*, includes images of the Vermeer and Gustave Doré artworks that inspired Cocteau. The other, an alternate audio track lecture by Arthur Knight, provides a great many details about the film's production, drawn from Cocteau's diaries and other sources. Also provided is the short story/fairy tale, by Madame Leprince de Beaumont, upon which the film is based.

Beauty and the Beast: The Enchanted Christmas (Buena Vista, 15282)

Not the strongest made-for-video sequel Disney has produced, it is a formula holiday offering. Set mostly when the Beast was still the Beast, but when his relationship with Belle had warmed, there is a villain—an evil pipe organ—who tries to stir discontent and keep the two emotionally separated. There are action sequences (Beauty falls through the ice), a couple tolerable songs, plenty of cute gags and some wholesome messages about giving books as gifts, but the original movie is just too good to justify this sort of depreciation.

The color quality is excellent and the image is consistently crisp. The stereo surround sound is reasonably energetic and there is a Dolby Digital track that delivers greater dimensionality and more thrust without succumbing to overkill. There is a French language track, in standard stereo, and even the songs are done in French. The 71 minute program can also be supported by English subtitles.

Beavis and Butt-Head Do Christmas (Sony, LVD49807)

The 45 minute DVD contains two extended episodes—a parody of *A Christmas Carol* and a parody of **It's a Wonderful Life**—with two minor 'Letters to Santa Butt-Head' segments and holiday music videos by the Ramones, Run DMC and Buster Poindexter, with Beavis and Butt-Head voiceovers. The secondary segments are uninteresting. The two longer episodes are a mix of the usual irritating irreverence with a scattering of genuinely comical moments. It is not the strongest collection of Beavis and Butt-Head material released to home video, but fans should still be happy with it. A few passages that feature more than limited movement appear somewhat soft, but the colors are bright and the image is usually sharp, especially since movement in the cartoon is minimal. The stereo sound is okay, though audio details, like movement within the image, are limited. The program is not captioned.

Beavis and Butt-Head (see MTV's Beavis and Butt-Head: The Final Judgement)

Bed of Roses (New Line, N4784)

All the secrets in the plot are revealed almost right away and the characters seem a little artificial, but the 1996 film will still be appealing to those who enjoy romance for romance's sake. Christian Slater stars as a flower deliveryman who takes a fancy to a career woman, played by Mary Stuart Masterson. From a structural point of view, the final three quarters of the film are about Masterson's character overcoming her inhibitions and accepting the hero's love, but they make a pleasant couple and if you have the patience for it, the film's faithfulness to its genre is satisfying. An actress to watch for, Pamela Segall, stands out in a supporting role as Masterson's best friend.

The single-sided dual-layer program presents the letterboxed version on one layer, with an aspect ratio of about 1.85:1 and an accommodation for enhanced 16:9 playback, and in full screen version on the other layer. The color transfer is outstanding, with rich, deep, sharp hues and exact fleshtones. The standard stereo surround soundtrack doesn't have much to offer, but there is a 5.1 Dolby Digital track that is much better detailed and more invigorating. The 88 minute film can be supported by optional English subtitles and comes with a cast-and-director profile section, a trailer and a blurry Jonn Arden music video, 'Insensitive.'

The Bee Gees (see The Very Best of The Bee Gees Live! One for All)

Bee Gees: One Night Only (Image, ID5473ERDVD)

A 1997 'greatest hits' concert shot at the MGM Grand in Las Vegas, the concert goes on for 110 minutes, yet there isn't an even partially obscure song in the set, just one big hit after another. The group brings a matured edge to a couple of the numbers, but most vary only slightly from the standard studio recordings. The medium-sized stage is backed by a large screen and the video program moves between the band and the screen images effectively. The performers are well lit and the image is sharp, with accurate fleshtones. The Dolby Digital sound has a much greater range and more energy than the standard stereo surround soundtrack, with a strong dimensionality that is relatively unaffected by the live environment.

Beethoven: Symphony No. 9. Op. 125 "Choral" (Sony, SVD46364)

In most depictions of *Symphony No. 9*, the chorus stands in the back of the orchestra silent for the first three movements as the anticipation of their involvement builds. That is how a live performance works as well, but on the *Herbert von Karajan His Legacy for Home Video* rendition, Karajan, who was also involved in the conceptual direction of the video programs, keeps the images of the orchestra fragmented by close-ups, the only link being the cuts to his own image as he guides the music. Thus, the chorus, which is also shot in piecemeal and sometimes just at face level, enters as a surprise when the time comes, and their images add almost as much emotion to the work as do their voices.

The performance was recorded by the Berlin Philharmonic in 1983. The picture is markedly inferior to the LD. The image sharpness on the LD is identical to the DVD, but colors on the LD are much richer and fleshtones are more accurate. In a direct comparison, fleshtones on the DVD are pale and other hues are drained, turning the woodtones and brass on the LD to various shades of silver and grey on the DVD. The stereo sound is good, equal in quality to the LD, and the DVD's crisper Dolby Digital track is wonderful, adding just enough extra separation detail to widen the music without chopping it up. The 66 minute program comes with background essays, a profile of Karajan and subtitles for the choral sequences in English, French and German.

Beethoven's 2nd (Universal, 20270)

The film opens with a dog's POV, though in this kind of movie, it is inevitably in color. The dog finds a mate and puppies quickly follow, which the dog's family must then protect from the villains. Charles Grodin and Bonnie Hunt start, but it is Christopher Penn and especially Debi Mazar, as the bad guys, whose performances are entertaining enough to sustain an adult viewer. Mazar is Cruella DeVille, come to life.

The 1994 feature is in letterboxed format with an aspect ratio of about 1.85:1 and an accommodation for enhanced 16:9 playback. Fleshtones are uneven and pinkish, and the image is a little soft. The stereo surround sound is adequate but uneventful, and the 89 minute program is also available in French and Spanish and can be supported by English or Spanish subtitles. The DVD features a theatrical trailer, a cast profile section and some informative production notes—the filmmakers had to use 100 puppies to represent the 4 in the movie because they grow so fast.

Beetlejuice (Warner, 11785)

Danny Elfman's delightful music score has been isolated in Dolby Digital. The music also sounds great on the film's regular Dolby Digital track, which has some witty directional effects (usually during the netherworld sequences) and plenty of punch. The regular stereo surround soundtrack is somewhat blander, though curiously, the *Day-O* scene works better, because the singing seems less isolated from the rest of the soundtrack. The picture is presented in letterboxed format on one side, with an aspect ratio of about 1.85:1 and an accommodation for enhanced 16:9 playback, and in full screen format on the other. We tend to prefer the full screen format, which appears to add more than it subtracts, but either framing is effective. The colors are bright and the image is sharp. The 92 minute film is also available in French and Spanish in standard stereo surround sound, and comes with English, French or Spanish subtitles. There is an enjoyable theatrical trailer that replays the film's comical highlights and a small cast profile and production notes section. Tim Burton directed the witty 1988 ghost comedy, which stars Michael Keaton, Alec Baldwin, Geena Davis and Winona Ryder.

The Beguiled (Universal, 20238)

Don Siegel's 1970 Gothic melodrama stars Clint Eastwood, who portrays Union soldier recuperating in a girls' boarding school behind enemy lines. He plays on the emotions of each woman at the school to increase his chances for escape, but his lies are too effective and his makeshift plans backfire. Siegel has a great deal of fun with the material, shooting at crazy angles and making uninhibited use of memory flashbacks and voiceover thought streams. It is a measure of the film's entertainment that it contains one of the all-time great amputation scenes. Usually, amputations are about the worst dramatic choice a movie can make, and indeed, **The Beguiled** was not really a box office success, but Siegel milks the scene perfectly and it is a milestone in the visualization of castration fantasies.

The letterboxing has an aspect ratio of about 1.85:1 with an accommodation for enhanced 16:9 playback. The letterboxing masks picture information off the top and bottom of the screen in comparison to the full screen picture and adds a bit to the sides. The additional footage on the sides is most welcome, but we found the masking made the image feel a bit cramped at times. Hues are bright, sharp and effectively detailed. The colors are accurate and the image is smooth. The monophonic sound is fine. The 105 minute film is also available in French and can be supported by English or Spanish subtitles. There is an enjoyably misguided theatrical trailer, some informative production notes and a cast profile section.

Bela Lugosi Collection (SlingShot, DVD1597)

The double bill includes the 1946 color feature *Scared to Death* and the 1940 black-and-white film *The Devil Bat*. *Devil Bat* runs

69 minutes. *Scared to Death* runs 65 minutes and is accompanied by an enjoyable theatrical trailer. The monophonic sound on both films is adequate. *The Devil Bat* is a coherent tale about a jealous, bitter chemist (Lugosi) who bio-enhances a killer bat trained to attack anyone wearing a special scent the chemist has secretly incorporated in an aftershave formula. A nosy reporter eventually figures out what he is up to. Despite its silliness, the film adheres to its internal rules and what it lacks in real excitement it makes up for in feigned horror. In *Scared to Death*, which is narrated by a corpse, Lugosi is a mysterious stranger who arrives to taunt his cousin, a doctor, over a past injustice. Meanwhile, the doctor's son is being hassled by his loveless marriage and the son's wife is receiving mysterious death threats. It's a wild, silly, enjoyable film, and it is in scrumptiously bad color that has been meticulously transferred.

The monophonic sound on both films is tolerable and the program has not been captioned. *Devil Bat*, which is in black-and-white, is in fairly worn condition, with lots of scratches and similar markings, and soft contrasts. There are a number of scratches on *Scared to Death* and the picture's focus often seems tentative, but the Cinecolor colors are bright and the presentation is highly satisfying—after all, just exactly how often does one get to see Lugosi in color?

Belinda Carlisle: Runaway Live (Image, ID4397CADVD)

Stepping out in a white suit that looks more appropriate for a Sunday brunch than for a rock concert, Belinda Carlisle begins her 80 minute concert somewhat demurely, but she soon changes into a black cocktail outfit and starts to let loose. She performs about 16 songs and while the concert environment robs some of the color from her vocals, fans should be happy with the thorough and steady nature of the performance. There are a limited number of camera angles and there is a limited amount of activity on the stage, but the narrow focus channels attention back to Carlisle, turning what could have been a dull video into a compelling and attractive display of talent.

Carlisle is well lit (though the rest of the stage is often darker), so the picture is crisp and colors look good. The stereo sound is fine, though the concert recording tends to mute and blend tones. There is no captioning. A discography, covering both Carlisle's career on her own and her time with the Go-Go's, is also included.

Belle of the Nineties (Image, ID4280USDVD)

Mae West portrays an entertainer who is romanced by a crooked theater owner and an honest fighter, but it takes her a while to sort things out. Duke Ellington is featured for several musical numbers in the 1934 production, which was directed by Leo McCarey. The black-and-white picture is in fairly good condition, free of significant damage with reasonably detailed contrasts. The monophonic sound has some age-related noise, but is acceptable. The 73 minute program is adequately closed captioned.

The Bells of Cockaigne (see James Dean: The James Dean Story/The Bells of Cockaigne)

The Bells of St. Mary's (Artisan, 45506)

The 1945 sequel to *Going My Way* stars Bing Crosby and Ingrid Bergman. The narrative is nearly a duplicate of the first film. Crosby's priest character arrives with a secret mandate that he does not reveal to the staff. There are mixed-up kids who get straightened out, a marriage in need of counseling, and a stubborn staff member who is putty in the priest's hands. In **Bells**, the recipe may not be as fresh the second time around, but as holiday leftovers it still makes a fine meal.

The black-and-white picture is crisp, with finely detailed contrasts. Wear and speckling is minimal. The monophonic sound is clean and reasonably strong. The 126 minute feature has optional French and Spanish language tracks as well, along with English, French or Spanish subtitles and a trailer.

Belly (Artisan, 60738)

DMX, NAS and Taral Hicks star in the highly stylized 1998 feature, which was directed by Hype Williams. Ostensibly a black gangster film taken to the extreme, the film is as spellbinding as it is incoherent. The dialogue is so drenched in ebonics it takes several run-throughs to follow what the characters are saying (especially when they travel to Jamaica), and the editing and camera angles are so obscure it takes even longer to determine who is who and what they have done to one another. Yet it is this very obscurity that makes the film so mesmerizing, because it is as you work to decode it that you get drawn into its attitude and intensity. The narrative essentially follows the rise and fall of several friends who are dealing drugs, with the requisite shootouts, chases and betrayals. Each scene is shot at a challenging angle, with unusual, striking lighting effects. The performances are terrific and are very real. Then, at the end, a performer playing a preacher turns the film's morality upside down with a speech that is read with a halting amateurishness, and it is a brilliant touch, dividing the world into what is good—purity, simplicity, and directness—and what is bad—materialism, decoration and obfuscation.

The picture is letterboxed with an aspect ratio of about 1.85 and an accommodation for enhanced 16:9 playback. The director used a special process to enhance the contrasts and intensify colors and shades. Details are occasionally obscured, and some sequences that are pretty much lit in one color, such as blue or red, come off a little blurry, but the overall presentation is quite slick and vivid, and is highly satisfying. The stereo surround sound is also energized, and there is a Dolby Digital track with clearer separations and a stronger bass. The program has English closed captioning and is accompanied by production notes, a cast-and-director profile section, a trailer and a music video.

"Let me tell you guys it's hard to think clearly while you're trying to do this. As many movies as I saw in DVD and I've seen on laser disc where you have commentaries by the filmmaker, it's different when you have to do it," says Williams at one point on his commentary track. Still, he manages to keep talking, explaining what he was trying to achieve with the movie and the roadblocks that appeared here and there. He wanted to make the film three hours long—something we would have loved to have seen—but had to settle for 95 minutes. He complains about the SAG extras and the music his distribution company forced on him, but he's just being a perfectionist, because the extras look fine and the music is super. He also shares the discoveries he made about the filmmaking process. He explains that he originally didn't want to use close-ups but discovered that close-ups connect the viewer to the characters: "It's not always about the composition. Sometimes it's just about looking dead into the guy's face and feeling what he's feeling."

Beloved (Buena Vista, 17243)

Oprah Winfrey stars in Jonathan Demme's mystifying adaptation of the Tony Morrison story as the adult embodiment of a Nineteenth Century teen mother who kills her children to protect them from torture, only to have one come back a couple decades later as a very human-like ghost with a speech impediment and a craving for sugar. Danny Glover, Thandie Newton and Kimberly Elise co-star. Some scenes are fairly grotesque, but the film's real failure is that it falls into that rather refined category of film adaptations so faithful to its source they fail to establish an independent essence. Readers of Morrison's book may well be enchanted by its visualization—though not by Winfrey's uneven performance—but those who are unfamiliar with Morrison's story will be baffled by the film and will assume there is more that the filmmakers just haven't bothered to explain about the characters and their environment. There are also contrivances (a character carries around a well preserved newspaper clipping for twenty years just so he can share it with another character at a convenient moment) and vague, repetitive footage that longs to be trimmed. Somewhere

within it all there is a viable meditation on female empowerment and the unfairness of slavery, however, and the 1998 film's essential intelligence can be appealing.

The picture is letterboxed with an aspect ratio of about 1.85:1 and no 16:9 enhancement. The source material has some minor speckling, particularly at the beginning. Some flashback sequences are overly bathed in a yellow wash. The image is quite crisp, however, and for the most part colors are finely detailed, with rich fleshtones. The Dolby Digital soundtrack is much stronger than the standard track. The mix is elaborate and the music has a full dimensionality, adding to the film's arresting atmosphere. The 171 minute feature also has a French language audio track in Dolby Digital, optional English subtitles, a trailer, and a featurette trailer with a few interviews.

Beneath the 12-Mile Reef (SlingShot, DVD2297)

The first underwater adventure to be shot in Cinemascope has been letterboxed with an aspect ratio of about 2.55:1 and no 16:9 enhancement. About a group of Greek sponge fishermen in Florida who speak with Chico Marx accents, the story concerns their rivalries with a group of WASP sponge fishermen, with Robert Wagner and Terry Moore in a *Romeo and Juliet*-style relationship that eventually brings everyone together. Wagner is one of the Greeks. Although the DVD's value comes more from the film's historical significance, the movie can be mindlessly entertaining. The narrative has a number of implausibilities, however, particularly in its implication that sponge fishermen need only go out and do their job once a year to earn enough to support themselves. Our favorite implausibility in the movie, however, has nothing to do with sponge fishing or other underwater activities. It happens instead on dry land, when the young hero tells his new fiancee, "Wait till you taste my momma's cooking!" and she smiles eagerly in response.

Fleshtones are a bit light, contrasts are a little weak and hues are not always intense, but the colors are workable and the source material is free of significant wear. The film has an old stereo soundtrack, featuring a musical score by Bernard Herrmann, that has limited separation effects but is still fairly entertaining. The 102 minute feature is accompanied by an original theatrical trailer.

Benji (Image, ID4804BFDVD)

If you're the sort of person who sits up on his hind legs and barks every time he sees a dog biscuit, then you'll be excited to hear that the DVD has a fresh picture and sound transfer. Although the image is a little yellowish, with bland fleshtones, the picture is substantially sharper and substantially more colorful than the LD, and the full screen framing is also improved, with more picture information around he edges. The image is strong enough that it presents the film without distractions. The monophonic sound is also fresh and effectively detailed. The audio track is a pretty basic affair, but it is adequately presented. There is no captioning.

Joe Camp's 1973 movie is so awful it makes cats look exciting. The 86 minute film has about 15 minutes of plot, about a kidnapping, and the rest consists of shot after shot of Benji scampering down one avenue of McKinney, Texas and up another. The cast is mostly untalented and unknown, although the production did represent one of the last appearances of Edgar Buchanan, in a bit part, and Christopher Connelly is one of the kidnappers. The film is so dull, however, you can't even use it as a pacifier because the kids get bored too quickly.

Berlin, Symphony of a Great City / Opus 1 (Image, ID4673DSDVD)

Similar to **Man with a Movie Camera** except that it is a lot more relaxed, Walter Ruttmann's *Berlin, Symphony of a Great City* eschews character development, depicting the activity within a city during a 24 hour period. The film is broken into five acts, depicting the pre-dawn, morning, noon, afternoon and night activities on the street, in industries and at recreational areas. The editing is outstanding, not only conveying an organized sense of the images but doing so with purposeful shifts in rhythm. A definitive work, the 1927 film's artistry is so accomplished it is ideal for putting on Repeat Play as a background video at parties. It is also fascinating from an educational standpoint, as a look at how modern life functioned seventy years ago. It runs 62 minutes. The black-and-white picture looks fine, with no more than scattered markings and a mild grain. The stereo musical score is reasonably strong without becoming obtrusive.

The accompanying Ruttmann piece, *Opus 1*, is a 10 minute abstract 1922 short, in color. Ruttmann made markings directly onto the film, a series of rough geometric shapes that bounce around a lot and move to a Max Butting musical score that was re-recorded in 1993.

Berlioz, Hector (see **Hector Berlioz: Symphonie Fantastique Les Nuits d'Été**)

The Best Bits of Mr. Bean (PolyGram, 4405581512)

The 78 minute compilation is a collection of segments from the **Mr. Bean** TV series, with a linking device depicting Bean in an attic, reminiscing. While we would not necessarily rank the clips as the 'best' bits, they are all certainly amusing, and the attic interludes are also fairly funny. Among those featured are part of the segment where Bean gets a turkey stuck on his head, Bean struck with fear on a high dive, Bean in a dentist's chair playing with the instruments, packing a suitcase eccentrically, stuffing his car with purchases and then driving while sitting on the roof, unable to stay awake in church, trying to take a test, and primping himself while waiting in a reception line. Rowan Atkinson, of course, portrays Bean.

The image quality of the clips varies slightly, but the attic sequences are very crisp and smooth, with bright colors, and other segments are okay (like many British TV shows, the indoor sequences appear to have been shot on tape and are more vivid than the outdoor sequences, which were shot on film). The sound features a stereophonic laughtrack that we preferred to suppress and the program, which has limited dialogue, is adequately closed captioned. Also included are a half dozen marvelous teasers and trailers for **Bean The Movie**.

The Best of MusikLaden: Live America (Pioneer, PA98602D)

Running a brisk 45 minutes, the program depicts the band America (you know—"Oz never gave nothing to the Tin Man...," etc.) playing through eleven numbers in a relaxed studio environment, without an audience. Between each number, the band pauses for a few minutes and engages in some small talk as they prepare for the next number. Firstly, the recording is incredibly vivid, particularly on the Dolby Digital track, though even the standard stereo track sounds terrific. The set would never be mistaken for a contemporary recording—there is some weakness on the upper end and a bit of noise in the background—but it sounds very fresh and immediate. Secondly, the show is an excellent record of the band hard at work. We have no idea what they are practicing or playing for, but the seriousness with which they approach the songs—as opposed to the rote playing they have done on other live videos—is highly gratifying, and will coax even casual viewers into observing their technique and musical abilities with an unanticipated level of concentration—at least, that's what it did to us. The picture is aged, but sharp, and although fleshtones have little yellow ghosts and there are other age-related drawbacks, the studio is brightly lit and the image is sufficiently detailed to support the music. The program is not captioned.

The Best of MusikLaden: Live Volume 1 (Pioneer, PA98601D)

The hour-long collection contains numbers from nearly a dozen classic rock bands, including Deep Purple, Jethro Tull, Joe

Walsh, Johnny Winter, Santana, Procol Harum, Badfinger, Alice Cooper, Free, Nazareth and Humble Pie. Each plays a song in front of or within an active rear projected or blue screen psychedelic design. There are some good close-ups of the rock stars in their prime, but the cluttered images distract a viewer from appreciating the techniques of the musicians and the program is mostly a nostalgia piece. Most of the recordings appear to be synched to the images and are original, as opposed to the standard studio recordings of the numbers, but the audio quality is muted and not even Dolby Digital encoding can bring much life to the sound. Enthusiastic fans will still be pleased by the program, but casual viewers will not be all that excited about it. The program is not captioned.

The Best of MusikLaden: T-Rex / Roxy Music (Pioneer, PA98603D)

The DVD contains two sub-half hour programs from the early Seventies, one depicting each band. The T-Rex program, which runs 18 minutes, appears to be older. Despite the inherent sharpness of the DVD playback, the colors are bland and the image is soft. The band performs five numbers, superimposed upon typical psychedelic lights and artwork. This would be okay, but the show's sound is very fuzzy and the Dolby Digital encoding doesn't help it, it just makes the fuzziness more aggressive.

The Roxy Music set, which runs 29 minutes, has somewhat stronger production values. The picture is still soft, but it isn't degraded by overlaid video art and the colors look fresher. The band performs six numbers in a variety of live venues, sometimes wearing grotesquely padded outfits, which will see the group through car crashes without harm but do not add to either the excitement or the poetry of their performances. The stereo sound is stronger and the Dolby Digital brings an additional clarity to the playback, but such audio fidelity just magnifies the music's shortcomings.

The Best of The Andy Griffith Show (UAV, 40094)

It may not be the greatest TV show in the world but it is a classic, and an excellent example, in Griffith, of what a talented actor can do with a role that is shaped specifically for his personality and capabilities. The show's theme music has been removed from the three public domain episodes, though you do get a whiff of it as a background cue in one sequence. The episodes run 23 minutes each and are presented sequentially with the closing credit sequences intact. The black-and-white picture has a faint video smear to it at times, and if you look closely you can see a lot of artifacting in the supposedly solid backgrounds, but the source material is in fairly good condition—there are only a few, isolated sections that are scratched or otherwise mildly damaged—and the picture basically looks no different than what one is likely to see on broadcast TV. The monophonic sound is adequate and there is no captioning. The episodes come from the winter and spring of 1963. In the first, identified as *Episode #93*, a pack of friendly dogs invades the jailhouse house just as a state inspector is due to arrive. In the second episode, which is the best of the group, identified as *Episode #80*, an ex-convict that the sheriff once arrested has announced his intention to visit, and the sheriff's friends panic, attempting to protect him from the supposed threat. In the finale, identified as *Episode #87*, a medicine man comes to town and sells an elixir that turns out to be 80% alcohol. He also romances the sheriff's aunt. In all the episodes, it is Griffith's aw-shucks attitude, contrasted to Don Knotts' nervousness, that creates the comedy but, on another level, Griffith's accent and ease are sending a timeless, subliminal sense of peace and nostalgia to the viewer, making life in America feel both safe and comforting.

The Best of the Blues Brothers (UAV, 40091)

Keeping score of cheap marketing tricks? UAV has plastered the jacket with a critic quote and advertisement tag line from the **Blues Brothers** movie, though the actual hour long program is entirely different. A compilation of performances from *Saturday Night Live* and from the recording of a stage concert, the show is actually quite good, with Dan Aykroyd, both as himself and in character, undergoing a make-believe interview but speaking truthfully about creating the band, joining *Saturday Night Live*, experiencing the arc of the band's success, and even about John Belushi's death. The mantra—but it has always been a legitimate mantra—is that Aykroyd and Belushi were not so great as musicians, but they were talented performers and their efforts brought the real musicians in their band well-deserved fame and fortune. The performance sequences are enjoyable, the interview is interesting, and the whole compilation works better than one might expect it to. In addition, UAV has included a half hour instructional video about playing a blues harmonica that will make you want to run to a music store and buy one of your own along with a pair of dark glasses. The colors on the **Blues Brothers** program look very good. The concert sequence is underlit, but when the source material is in good shape, the presentation is as well. The image is a little soft, but workable. The stereo sound is passable and the program is not captioned.

The Best of The Wonder Years (LaserLight, 82001)
The Christmas Wonder Years (LaserLight, 82002)

No television show fills us so simultaneously with joy and anxiety as **The Wonder Years**. Capturing with absolute perfection the adolescent years of a certain subset of suburban Baby Boomers, the program explored all the ins and outs of growing up in the Sixties. The plots were often little more than situations, though they were executed with the sort of surprising and witty turns that are apt to happen in real life. The show gave us anxiety because the hero, played by Fred Savage, is a normal person and subject to the flaws and mistakes and tragedies big and small that befall normal persons, but just as often he succeeds, and regardless of the emotional highs and lows the show gets all the details so right.

Best of the Wonder Years contains three episodes from the TV series, a 'highlights' program that conveniently replayed the show's major turning points and the most significant events in the hero's love life, combined with a few of the show's funniest scenes, followed by the program's two-part finale (the hero takes off for a vacation resort where his girlfriend is working for the summer), of which the highlights show serves as an ideal prelude. Hence, the 71 minute program works quite well as a freestanding coming-of-age comedy that will delight newcomers as much as it will warm the hearts of fans. The concluding burst of fireworks in the last shot of the final episode brought us to tears.

Two 41 minute episodes with a holiday theme are combined on **The Christmas Wonder Years**. In both, the hero worries about what to get his girlfriend, while his family undergoes a minor crisis, particularly in the second episode, in which the hero's father has quit his job to start a new company, only to have the loan fall through.

Each episode is presented with complete opening and closing credits. The picture is often grainy or hazy. Colors are reasonably strong in well-lit scenes, but murkier in darker sequences. We wish it could look better than it does, but it is not a complete disaster. Some of the music has a faint dimensionality, but almost all of the sound, including the music, is centered. The bass is a bit distorted in places, but generally the audio is acceptable. The program is not captioned. **Best** is time encoded, but **Christmas** is not.

The Best One Ever (PolyGram, 4400464432)

A 20 minute NFL game film about the 1998 Super Bowl (Denver beat Green Bay) has been decked out with several enhancements. The film summarizes each quarter, looking at the major plays in the sort of grandiose fashion one expects from NFL programming. Much of the camera work and the audio are superior to a standard game broadcast. The telephoto close-ups of the players in action are vivid and the Dolby Digital sound is super, particularly when the fireworks go off before and after the game. Still, 20 minutes isn't much of a movie. You're also forced to sit through a

commercial (for RCA TVs) before the show starts. Anyway, there are segments of the film where multiple angles are available, segments where one can choose alternate narration, catching snippets of a play-by-play biased toward either team, and segments where one can activate additional text information about the game, not that these bon mots ever amount to much. Some of these options are better served, however, by a separate menu function that allows the viewer to select a specific play and watch it from a choice of angles with a choice of audio tracks. There are also a few text options, providing biographical sketches of five people—the two coaches, the two quarterbacks and the MVP—and listings of team rosters, records, and previous Super Bowl scores. Although the closed captioning logo appears on the jacket, we could not activate any captioning or subtitling format. The narration is also available in Spanish.

Betrayed by Innocence (Simitar, 7280)

Barry Bostwick stars in a TV movie about a commercial filmmaker who has an affair with a film student in a moment of weakness and is then arrested when it turns out that she is under age and her father, played by Paul Sorvino, is a vice cop. Since it is a TV film, the emphasis is not on the eroticism (though there is a bit) but on the confrontations between the characters, and much of the film's latter half is taken up with the hero's trial. The film is fairly predictable and some of the acting is pretty bad, but like most TV movies, the temptation to keep watching is strong. The color transfer is good, with fresh, crisp hues. There is some tiling, however, in darker sequences, and the lighting is erratic, causing some shots to look washed out and other to come across a bit hazy. The monophonic sound is flat and the music sounds a little warped at times. The 1986 film runs 94 minutes, is not captioned, and is accompanied by partial filmographies of Bostwick and Sorvino.

The Betsy (Warner, 864)

Harold Robbins' novel was so bad you could hear the fractured cadence of Robbins' dictaphone dictation in the transcribed prose. The 1978 motion picture adaptation isn't much better, but it has a tantalizing cast, and the lesser known actor who portrayed the hero and shared top billing with the likes of Laurence Olivier, Robert Duvall and Katharine Ross has now come into his own—Tommy Lee Jones. Jones is terrific, and you can see Olivier perk up when they share a scene.

The film is part of a dying movie genre—the trashy novel adaptation—about rich and powerful people in some industry trying to get one up on one another or get into one another's boudoir. It is a genre that has been absconded by the miniseries format, to which, except for restrictions on nudity, it is more appropriately suited. Jones portrays an injured racing car driver who is hired by the semi-retired chairman of a large automobile company to spearhead the design and introduction of a new car, keeping the project secret as long as possible from the company's president. There is also a flashback to the Thirties that is intercut with the contemporary narrative. The story has a sort of boilerplate feel to it (the hero romances the president's mistress, but really has his eye on the chairman's great-granddaughter), and it doesn't explore the ins-and-outs of making automobiles as carefully as it could have, but the cast is fun and there is enough of a plot to keep a glamour-struck viewer smiling and attentive.

There is still some deliberate blurring in places, but for the most part, colors look sharp and fleshtones are viable. The source material has some minor speckling and hues are not intense, but the presentation does not impede the entertainment, such as it is. The picture is presented in full screen format only, losing almost nothing on the sides and gaining picture information on the top and bottom in comparison to letterboxed presentations. The monophonic sound is somewhat weak and lacks subtlety. The 125 minute program also has a French mono track and is adequately closed captioned.

A Better Tomorrow (import, MSDVD00698)
A Better Tomorrow II (import, MSDVD00998)
Both John Woo movies are in Cantonese and Mandarin with optional English, traditional Chinese, simplified Chinese, Japanese, Korean, Malaysian Bohasa, Indonesian Bohasa, and Thai subtitles. The English subtitles are littered with errors, but remain coherent.

The first film, from 1986, is a tolerable gangster drama about a young police officer and two former gangsters who cannot escape their fates, but Woo's penchant for sentimentality is especially thick, and the long, lyrical pauses where the characters regret what has happened to them in the past can easily feel monotonous. Chow Yun-Fat, Ti Lung and Leslie Cheung star.

Woo's 1988 sequel is a sillier film (Fat's character, dead at the end of the first movie, is suddenly given an identical twin for the second), but it is less lethargic and there is a spectacular Woo-style bloodbath at the conclusion.

Both presentations are letterboxed with an aspect ratio of about 1.85:1 and no 16:9 enhancement, and the picture quality on both isn't bad. The image on the first film, which runs 95 minutes, is smooth with no more than scattered wear. Colors are viable and fleshtones, though bland, are consistent. The same is true of **II**, which runs 104 minutes and has slightly cleaner source material. The sound on both films is a gas. On both the standard stereo surround soundtrack and the Dolby Digital soundtrack of both DVDs, the music and gunfire have clearly been enhanced after the fact, but the result, particularly on the Dolby Digital track, is a flurry of very specific directional effects that would distract a viewer from a better film but enhance these movies in all the right ways. Each movie is accompanied by a number of video trailers.

Betty Page: Pin Up Queen (Cult Epics, DVD0001)
Betty Page: Bondage Queen (Cult Epics, DVD0002)
The first part of the 93 minute **Pin Up Queen** contains some marvelous sequences from a couple old color burlesque films, but the bulk of the program is taken up by silent black-and-white footage of Page dancing about in lingerie. The clips from the 35mm burlesque films *Striporama*, *Varietease* and *Teaserama* show Page bopping around in lingerie and tassels, gradually working her way down to a modest bikini. The sense of what the complete films are like can be garnered from trailers for two of the movies, which have also been included, and they essentially have the same program mix that a normal burlesque house would have had a decade or so earlier. The first black-and-white section contains excerpts from two documentaries that showcased the 16mm bondage films of a Fifties mail order pornographer, Irving Klaw. Voiceover narration from the documentaries provides an interesting biography of Page and details about the nature of the clips being viewed. The final segment is the least satisfying. It features clips from 8mm movies, also shot by Klaw, of Page 'dancing' in skimpy outfits. A lame instrumental musical score has been added after the fact.

There is essentially no nudity. None of the source materials are in all that great a condition, but it is assumed the viewer will tolerate most of it as part of the collection's nostalgic appeal. The color sequences look the best. They are tattered and blurry and the colors are faded at times, but there are shots where the colors are still quite bright and the 35mm source provides a reasonably solid image. The bondage sequences are also somewhat ragged and grainy, but again their condition seems to add to their illicit appeal. The 8mm dances, though, look awful, and the horribly blurry picture combined with the monotony of the subject matter makes the section difficult to get through. The soundtracks to the color films are monophonic, but the other segments have modestly stereophonic musical scores that seem adequate to their task.

The black-and-white source material on **Bondage Queen** is stronger. It is still loaded with speckles and scratches, and always looks fairly worn but, in most of the footage, details are discernible and there is a sense of focus. The 112 minute program is a combination of two more retrospective films featuring Klaw's mail-order one-reel movies, with Page appearing in about half the footage. The programs have an occasional voiceover narration that gives some background on Klaw and the models, though after a while it falls into play-by-play introductions of the sequences. The women remain clothed, albeit in their underwear. There is a frisky nostalgia to the pieces. Some viewers will find them titillating just as others will find them tedious. In addition to the elaborate roping and shackling sequences, there are fetish-oriented dressing sequences, and in addition to the narration, there is an unobtrusive musical score.

Neither program is captioned.

Beyond The Mind's Eye (Simitar, 7322)
Set to a varied but subdued stereo score by Jan Hammer, ranging from electronic music to acoustic guitar, the program is a seamless blending of two dozen or so computer animated works. Excerpts from **Lawnmower Man** pop up, but they are abstract enough to fit well with the other pieces. Some sequences have a narrative, such as an insect chase that turns out to be occurring on a small bio-dome in outer space. Others are just exercises in imagination expansion, bringing a topography to Pablo Picasso's self-portrait or exploring the intricacies of gear movements.

The picture quality is very good, with solid, crisp hues, and the stereo sound, a mostly electronic musical score, is fine. In addition to the main program there is a music video set to a reprise of the first sequence.

The Bicycle Thief (Image, ID4572CODVD)
Vittorio De Sica's 1948 classic about poverty and desperation has an ending that makes you want to throw your shoe at your television set. It wouldn't be **The Bicycle Thief** if it didn't have scratches and splices, but the black-and-white picture looks fairly sharp and smooth. The 89 minute program can be accessed in Italian, with or without unobtrusive white English subtitles, or dubbed in English without the subtitles. There is also a profile of De Sica and a good English language trailer, apparently from the early Seventies, that is loaded with quotes from important film personages.

About a man searching for his stolen bicycle, the film can encourage positive emotions (disgust with the ending, though endemic even on multiple viewings, is only fleeting) for two reasons. The first is simple. The filmmakers, in telling the tale of a man who loses his chance to earn a living when his bicycle is stolen, never lose sight of the real story, the man's relationship with his young son. That is a universal plot construction which can transcend historical modifications. The other reason for the film's artistic success is more complicated. The hero's dilemma is contrived—there must be a dozen options for him if he would just get his act together—but you can't help thinking as you watch the film that while this exact set of circumstances may not be true, there must be dozens of situations which are almost as similar—of adults trying their hardest but failing to cure their poverty or save their families. The movie is not an allegory and it is not even a parable, but it exposes the viewer to the emotions of despair and puts one in touch, if only momentarily, with the heartache of the world.

Big Bad Mama (New Horizons, NH00136)
One of the most erotic sequences ever made for motion pictures is the love scene between Angie Dickinson and William Shatner in **Big Bad Mama**. Not. Dickinson's a babe, and she has extensive nude scenes with both Shatner and with Tom Skerritt, but Shatner has hairy legs and doesn't know whether he should be licking her breasts or pleading with Scotty to beam him up. The film is a **Bonnie & Clyde** rip-off with a generally illogical plot, but sex and gore in the 1974 feature is plentiful and the cast is good for a few yucks.

The picture tends to be grainy and colors are a little flat, with dull fleshtones and minor evidence of wear in places. The monophonic sound is adequate. The film runs 83 minutes. There is also an interview with the producer, Roger Corman, which is very interesting ("I would say that somewhere in the neighborhood of 35–40% of our income from the whole United States came from drive-ins").

The Big Chill (Columbia TriStar, 02632)

Lawrence Kasdan's film is presented as a *15th Anniversary Collector's Edition*, with a few special features, including some deleted scenes, though not with the famous Kevin Costner segment. The 1983 comedy, about a group of college friends who reunite for a funeral and let their emotional laundry out over the ensuing weekend, tapped into a psychic shift within a generation that suddenly found itself, like the characters, growing older and less idealistic. Despite the high powered cast, which includes Glenn Close, William Hurt, Jeff Goldblum, Kevin Kline, Tom Berenger and others, some viewers may find the characters uninteresting and the comedy sporadic, but others will be more forgiving, and will find an enthusiasm for the film's cultural discoveries.

The picture is letterboxed with an aspect ratio of about 1.85:1 and an accommodation for enhanced 16:9 playback. Colors are a little dull and cold, and fleshtones are bland, but the image is nicely detailed and hues are clearly defined. It is mostly the film's famous pop musical score that is stereophonic, with a moderate dimensionality and few separation effects. The 106 minute film has an alternate French and Spanish audio tracks, optional English, French and Spanish subtitles and a trailer.

There is an excellent, hour-long retrospective documentary, with Kasdan and many members of the cast and crew talking about how the film was put together (they had extra rehearsal time so they could become a cohesive group) and sharing anecdotes about the production. All the actresses wanted Mary Kay Place's role (as the lawyer who wants a baby) and all express the doubts they originally had about Kasdan's most outrageous plot turn, in which Close's character arranges for her husband to be the father's baby. Even the female screenwriter who collaborated with Kasdan on the script, Barbara Benedek, expressed discomfort with the concept when Kasdan first proposed it. Based upon the film's popularity, all of them at least pretend now to approve of the idea, but it is a blatant male fantasy that cheapens the film's believability and they should have stuck to their original instincts, regardless of the box office returns.

There are also about 10 minutes of deleted scenes (they're not time encoded), most removed for pace, though many contain amusing lines and situations that are worth seeing once you are familiar with the film.

The Big Lebowski (PolyGram, 4400565392)

Joel and Ethan Coen's 1998 feature almost seems like self-parody. It has a funny, eclectic humor, but the narrative is more abstract than the narratives in the Coens' best films, and it is less vital. Jeff Bridges stars as a bum you can almost smell, who gets drawn into a kidnapping scheme, with John Goodman as his better manicured but crazier friend. There is a dream sequence staged as a Hollywood musical number and similar delights, but the characters with bizarre European accents, iron lung patients and other forced eccentricities call attention to themselves in too great abundance. It's amusing, but artificial.

The single-sided dual-layer presentation features a full screen version on one layer and a letterboxed version on the other. The letterboxing has an aspect ratio 1.77:1 and an accommodation for enhanced 16:9 playback. The colors seem a little light at times and the image is a bit grainy here and there, but for the most part it looks okay, particularly when the lighting is set to intensify the presence of characters and objects. The film has what is perhaps the most peripatetic pop score ever conceived and gathered for a feature production and it sounds terrific on the stereo surround sound and Dolby Digital soundtracks. The Dolby Digital delivers more surround detail with the sound effects and keeps the music properly centered, while the standard track bleeds the music to the

rear a bit too much. The 117 minute program can be supported by optional French and Spanish subtitles or English closed captioning and is accompanied by a trailer, a comprehensive 25 minute 'making of' documentary, also captioned, and a cast & crew profile section.

Big Night (Columbia TriStar, 81019)

Two Italian immigrants running a restaurant in New Jersey put together one last fancy meal for their friends before going out of business. The film is an independent production that received a lot of raves, but it is badly over-hyped and does not amount to much. The characters are quaint, but the story is predictable and largely uneventful, and the food sequences are not exceptional.

The 1996 feature is presented in letterboxed format only, with an aspect ratio of about 1.85:1 and an accommodation for enhanced 16:9 playback. The picture is a bit soft and the brightest colors are a little hazy. The stereo surround sound is reasonably good, particularly the Italian Fifties pop music score. The 109 minute program also has an Italian audio track, optional English and Spanish subtitles, and a trailer.

The Big Red One (Warner, 939)

Sam Fuller's WWII film, from 1980, is a shorthand history of the European war, as seen through the eyes of a single squad. Because of the production problems, the opening sequence in North Africa is static and confused, but thereafter the film is excellent, a knowing and sober collection of vignettes about battle and camaraderie, culminating in a concentration camp sequence that essentially proves the madness of the fighting and lives lost in battle were utterly justified. Lee Marvin and Mark Hamill star, with Robert Carradine doing a marvelous turn as Fuller's alter-ego.

The film is in letterboxed format on one side, with an aspect ratio of about 1.85:1 and an accommodation for enhanced 16:9 playback, and in full screen format on the other side. The letterboxing adds a bit to the side in comparison to the full screen image and masks off picture information from the top and the bottom, though generally the framing is more appealing. Colors are a little bright and the image is sharp. The film's financing problems leaves the image grainy and somewhat faded in places, but on the whole the presentation looks good, with reasonably accurate fleshtones and bright hues. Although directional effects are limited, the stereo enhances the sound's dimensionality and the film's emotional impact. The 113 minute feature can be supported by English or French subtitles.

Big Wars (Image, ID4410CTDVD)

Not only is the sex and violence terrific, but **Big Wars** is an excellent animated science fiction adventure, with stimulating ideas and plenty of action. Set on Mars, well into the future, the 71 minute narrative is about the beginnings of an armed conflict between humans and an alien race known as 'The Gods.' The film incorporates intriguing religious symbolism in the references and depictions of the aliens, but never allows the embellishment to overwhelm the story, which is about the captain of a powerful new battleship and the efforts by alien spies to subvert his assignment.

The picture is letterboxed with an aspect ratio of about 1.85:1 and no 16:9 enhancement. Movement in some passages is fairly limited, but the animation is functional and the picture looks fairly good, with bright, sharp, solid hues. The stereo sound is also fairly decent, and the film is available in both English and Japanese, with optional English subtitles.

The Bikini Car Wash Company (Simitar, 4005)

The narrative ends about 20 minutes before the 1990 film does, while the conclusion is padded out with images of the cast in various states of undress hopping about to music. The plot is trifling to begin with, about a car wash establishment that is successful when a group of women decide to work there in the alltogether. The 81 minute film is primarily an excuse for displays of toplessness, accentuated by vague stabs at burlesque comedy. The opening credit sequence, incidentally, sets a new standard for bad computer animation with a mishmash of simplistic images that look like they were composed on a Commodore 64. The full screen picture is occasionally crisp but just as easily given over to blur and grain. The colors are reasonably fresh. The stereo audio track has an unimaginative mix and a limited range.

Billy Jack (Warner, 1040)

The super hero we would most like to see get run over by a truck, Tom Laughlin's Billy Jack, was introduced to an unsuspecting populace in the 1971 movie of the same name. The movie was made in the days when many people in America thought they conquer the world economy by teaching their children street theater instead of arithmetic, or when they didn't know they were suppose to be conquering anything. What they did know was that they had to stop beating up Indians, and those two topics—beating up Indians and teaching children how to perform street theater—are what **Billy Jack** is about. But since a movie about teaching children street theater and saying it isn't nice to beat up Indians would be uninteresting, Laughlin made the hero somebody who could care less about street theater but supports it in principle and who beats up anybody that even thinks about beating up Indians, and all they have to do is think about it and he mystically appears, smirking.

A film where you root for the bad guys even when they are hitting young pregnant teenagers, **Billy Jack** also features a PG-rated rape that is two frames away from **I Spit On Your Grave**; a stuffed doll that gets thrown through a window, only to be replaced with a real person by the creaky magic of film editing once it/he lands; a marvelously staged town meeting that pre-dates C-Span by nearly two decades yet evokes it precisely; and an insipid Indian who gets 1) flour poured over him, 2) his leg broken, 3) hit really hard in the stomach, and 4) shot four times in the head—a role which Herbert Lom could have done wonders with. Apparently the video technicians working on the DVD were at peace with their totems and at one with the spirit of film transfers, for the colors look quite good and the monaural sound is fine. The 114 minute program has English captioning.

There are a few scratches and splices, but the film is in remarkably good condition for a low-budget feature which actually earned its place in the cinema history books because of its innovative marketing strategy—the people who made **Billy Jack** had to rent all the theaters themselves to show the movie, but it was the Age of Aquarius and everybody came, more likely for the rapes and beatings than for the progressive education lectures, but that's the way the world works.

Billy Joel Greatest Hits Volume III The Video (Sony, CVD50162)

We Didn't Start the Fire, *The Downeaster "Alexa,"* *Hey Girl* and a dozen other videos are collected on the 80 minute program. About half are conceptual videos and the other half are concert or performance clips given a nominal music video structure. Joel introduces each number and discusses the inspirations that led him to write or perform each tune.

The source material looks reasonably fresh and the colors are usually solid and bright, though there is some variance from one clip to the next. The stereo sound is okay and there is a Dolby Digital track, though it doesn't add much more to the audio quality. The DVD also comes with optional English lyrics (which can help you break down *We Didn't Start the Fire* if the visual clues in the video aren't enough), a Joel biography and discography.

Billy Madison (Universal, 20461)

A film that goes beyond dumb, deep into the realm of the utterly stupid, Adam Sandler stars as the irresponsible heir to a hotel company who is forced to revisit grade school and high school for a few weeks to prove his competence. The1995 film defies even its own internal logic, the story really makes no sense, the characters

shift personalities at will, and the humor is innocuous or insulting, depending upon a viewer's sensitivities. Except for an unusually forthright bisexual undercurrent, the film has no artistic merit and is equally lacking in intelligence, wit and style.

The picture is letterboxed with an aspect ratio of about 1.85:1 and an accommodation for enhanced 16:9 playback. The image is bright and sharp, with accurate fleshtones. The stereo surround sound is okay, and there is a Dolby Digital track as well, though isolated rear channel effects are limited. The Dolby Digital mix has a slightly wider dimensionality, but the two tracks are fairly similar overall. The 90 minute film is also available in French and Spanish in standard stereo and can be supported by English or Spanish subtitles ("¡Soy el hombre más inteligente del mundo!"). There are some production notes, a cast and director profile section and a theatrical trailer.

Billy's Hollywood Screen Kiss (Trimark, VM6900D)

A gay-oriented romantic comedy, the low budget film was shot in Cinemascope and visually it is very pleasing, with bright, bold colors and uncroppable widescreen framings. The presentation is letterboxed, with an aspect ratio of about 2.35:1 and no 16:9 enhancement, and the image is sharp, so the film looks gorgeous. The stereo sound is also fairly nice, with some decent separation effects and well-rounded tones. The 92 minute program can be supported by French or Spanish subtitles, or English closed captioning, although the latter has a number of encoding flaws. There is also a trailer and soundtrack promo.

The film itself seems a bit too bubbly and is basically one more movie about a young man trying to find romance, albeit in a milieu that is a little out of the ordinary, though less so than it might have been a few years ago. The movie's director, Tommy O'Haver, provides a commentary track and talks about the films that inspired him, how the cast was chosen, how various objects and songs wound up in the movie and the logistics of low budget filmmaking. He is earnest, sounding very insightful at times about the process of filmmaking and at other times seeming as naive as his hero. Some viewers, however, will find that his commentary is a more rewarding accompaniment to the film's images than the movie's dialogue.

Bird on a Wire (Universal, 20318)

There is not a moment in the Mel Gibson and Goldie Hawn chase drama that is at all believable and Hawn's characterization is an embarrassment to her gender, but that magic thing called star appeal makes the 1990 movie inherently watchable and even repeatable.

The picture is letterboxed with an aspect ratio of about 1.85:1 (not 2.35:1 as is claimed on the jacket) and no 16:9 enhancement. The colors are reasonably bright and, in some scenes, the picture is sharp, but when the lighting is less controlled, strong colors tend to dominate weaker colors and the image becomes hazier. The stereo surround sound is adequate, and is reasonably energetic in the action scenes. The film is also available in French and can be supported by English or Spanish subtitles. There are some production notes (although set in the Midwest, the film was shot—at times, quite noticeably—in British Columbia), a cast profile section and a theatrical trailer.

The Birdcage (MGM, 906035)

Mike Nichols' fabulously successful 1996 Anglicization of *La Cage Aux Folles* has so many funny one-liners and other humorous situations that the movie can generate laughter after even a dozen viewings. Like *La Cage Aux Folles*, it seems easier to just pretend like the heroes are from another planet or something instead of falling into the trap of suggesting they are endorsing gay stereotypes, but it is hard to believe that even those given over to anger at the images of the heroes mincing about will not succumb to chuckles at some point in the film. Why can't all movies have this many good jokes? Robin Williams and Nathan Lane star as a gay couple who try to hide their persuasion from their future in-laws. Gene Hackman and Dianne Wiest are also featured, with Hank Azaria, who is so funny portraying a Guatemalan houseboy even your couch and coffee table will be laughing.

The image is very crisply detailed and the colors are rich. The program is presented letterboxed on one side, with an aspect ratio of about 1.85:1 and an accommodation for enhanced 16:9 playback, and is in full screen on the other side, with the letterboxing trimming picture information off the top and bottom of the image and adding nothing to the sides. The film's title refers to a nightclub, run by the heroes, that showcases female impersonators, so not only is the picture full of crisp razzle dazzle, the sound is also in high gear, with lots of punch and wide separations. For some reason, the theatrical trailer MGM/UA has included with the 119 minute film is presented only on the full screen side and not on the letterboxed side. The stereo surround sound is a bit subdued, but the Dolby Digital track is strong, with deep tones. The film is also provided with French and Spanish stereo soundtracks and has subtitling in English, French and Spanish.

The Birth of a Nation (Image, ID4674DSDVD)
The film directed by Griffith that raised motion pictures to a new level of artistic achievement runs 187 minutes and is accompanied by an interesting 24 minute retrospective documentary. Well after its original theatrical release, Griffith continued to tinker with the editing of certain scenes ('modernizing' it), so there is no real definitive version, but Image's presentation is viable. The picture, though tinted, is bright and well detailed, and is a substantial improvement over Image's LD (Aug. 94), which is much darker and hazier, with poorer tints and less detail. Movement is natural, and while the image jiggles in some sequences, it is steady during most of the film and artifacting is minimal. The source material on the 1915 production has an expected amount of wear, but the damage is never obtrusive. There is a pleasant and modest stereophonic musical score. The documentary uses fascinating, rarely seen footage to show the film's antecedents (Griffith himself directed 11 Civil War one-reelers), outtakes and behind-the-scenes shots to tell how **Birth of a Nation** was created.

The movie is about the creation of the Ku Klux Klan, so it has its drawbacks, but its eyewitness stagings of Civil War battles and the assassination of Abraham Lincoln are remarkable, and its dramatic structure brought together ideas about storytelling with film that still form the basis of most moviemaking today.

The Bishop's Wife (HBO, 90658)
An angel comes to Earth to give a troubled bishop guidance but spends most of the time putting the make on the guy's wife. The 1947 film is accompanied by an outstanding original theatrical trailer showing the movie's three stars, Cary Grant, David Niven and Loretta Young, on the lot at the Goldwyn Studios. The movie itself is an acquired taste. Since it has touches of fantasy and an enjoyable supporting cast, not to mention Gregg Toland's superb cinematography, some viewers have a natural attraction to it, but the narrative makes less sense the closer one analyzes it and other than the fact that everyone is smiling at the end, it is difficult to say how their problems have been solved. The whole thing relies a bit too much on faith.

The black-and-white image looks terrific, with a consistently sharp focus and a minimum of damage. Contrasts are carefully detailed, and blacks are pure. The 109 minute feature can be accompanied by either the standard monophonic soundtrack or an artificial stereo soundtrack that enhances the musical score. The monophonic track, however, is less disorienting. There are also French, Spanish and Italian soundtracks, in mono, as well as optional English, French or Spanish subtitles.

Black Dog (Universal, 20391)
You probably read nothing but negative reviews for **Black Dog** (if you read any at all) and the film is not exactly in the same dramatic league as **Portrait of a Lady**—heck, it is doubtful even the French will be writing about it 20 years from now—but the 1998 movie is a bit of a throwback to the trucker action movies of the Seventies, and for its genre it is well executed and reasonably entertaining. Patrick Swayze stars as a former driver who has lost his license and is so desperate for work that he accepts a job hauling contraband from Atlanta to New Jersey, only to discover that both hijackers and the FBI are on his tail. The action scenes and stunt sequences are rousing, and the film has just enough plot to justify all the crashes. It's a perfect drive-in movie for an era when there aren't drive-in movies anymore. Randy Travis and Meat Loaf co-star.

The image is letterboxed with an aspect ratio of about 2.35:1 and an accommodation for enhanced 16:9 playback. Colors are sharp and fleshtones are accurate, and the image looks very nice. The stereo surround sound has about half the punch the Dolby Digital track has, but the Dolby Digital track is super, with plenty of directional effects and a solid punch. The 89 minute film is also available in Spanish and French in standard stereo and comes with English or Spanish subtitles. There is a Rhett Akins music video, *Drivin My Life Away* (good song, lousy video), a theatrical trailer, some production notes and a cast-and-director profile section.

Black Mask (import, DVD015)
Jet Li stars in the terrific super-hero style Hong Kong action film, portraying the former member of a group of super-assassins who were neurologically altered so that they do not feel pain. Dressed up like a cross between Kato and the Green Hornet, he helps the police foil the group, which is trying to take over the drug business by massacring all the other drug dealers in the city. Although it is a bit confusing at first, everything is eventually clarified and the battles are outstanding (the bad guys have guns that shoot through wood, metal and everything else), while the relationship between Li's apparently shy alter-ego and a young woman provides effective comic relief.

The picture is letterboxed with an aspect ratio of about 1.7:1 and no 16:9 enhancement. The image is fairly sharp. Colors are a little drained and darker scenes are fairly murky, but that is run-of-the-mill for a Hong Kong production and for the most part the image quality does not interfere with the fabulous stunts and action scenes. The mildly stereophonic audio is presented in both Cantonese and Mandarin (the latter is a bit louder, but less well mixed), supported by permanent Chinese and English subtitles (which are free of the usual translation flaws). The film runs 98 minutes.

Black Orpheus (Criterion, BLA070)
The fabulously colorful musical fable is set in the Rio de Janeiro carnival. The 107 minute presentation runs 4 minutes longer than the LD, and while the LD looked plenty colorful, the enhanced sharpness and improved contrasts of the DVD make it look even more spectacularly chromatic. The full screen image has a very slight windowboxing and a hair more picture information on the sides than the LD had. The source material has a couple scattered speckles, but they do not matter in the least. The monophonic sound is also stronger and cleaner, with smooth, crisp tones. The film is in Brazilian Portuguese and can be supported by optional English subtitles. There is also a workable English-dubbed track, though it doesn't seem quite appropriate, and there is a terrific trailer, in French, that is narrated by a talking guitar.

The additional footage appears to have been removed on earlier versions for pacing, and adds a number of nice little touches to the story, strengthening the twines of fate that bring the two lovers together. Marcel Camus directed the 1960 classic, a re-telling of the tragic Orpheus and Eurydice romance set within the impoverished but happy-looking slums on the hills around Rio, with music by Antonio Carlos Jobim and Luis Bonfa. Miserly critics condemn the film for, what? being too perfect?, but its joyful imagery, captivating music and time-tested interpretation of love and grief is glorious moviemaking and essential home video.

The Black Pirate (Kino, K112DVD)

The two-strip color silent film spectacle from Douglas Fairbanks is not really one of Fairbanks' best, but the color gimmick gives the movie the boost it needs to really sweep away the viewer. A classic pirate movie, most of the action takes place in a harbor, where Fairbanks, pretending to be with the pirates, tries to save a captured princess from their evil plans. Donald Crisp and Billie Dove co-star. At its weakest, the two-strip Technicolor process makes the film look like it has been given a two-tone tint, but in the best passages, blacks are a solid black (the pirate flag looks cool), whites are reasonably white and there is some semblance of wood, flesh and variety in the intensity of the fabrics and decorations. There is even red blood when the pirates stab their victims. The addition of color energizes the film's atmosphere, so that despite the static setting, Fairbanks' wild stunts are highly involving (the black-and-white version tended to leave a viewer distanced from the hero's actions), giving the fairly basic story a greater sense of vitality.

The stereo musical score is based on orchestrations written specifically for the film in 1926 and provides an upbeat accompaniment to the feature without overwhelming the action. On another track, historian Rudy Behlmer provides commentary, talking about the production, biographies of the cast and crew, the color process, the music and even such things as a history of sword fighting in movies (the fencers must exaggerate their movements) and a history of pirate films. After the 90 minute movie is completed, 19 minutes of outtakes and behind-the-scenes footage are presented, also narrated by Behlmer, and it is really quite a treat to see what went on in making the film—at one point Fairbanks becomes quite annoyed at the way a swordfight is going.

Black Rain (Image, ID4305FLDVD); (Paramount, 32227)

The threat of nuclear war may have subsided for the moment, but the horrible poison of atomic weapons has not been eradicated, it has only been put back on the shelf. Shohei Imamura's **Black Rain**—not to be confused with the graceless title of the Ridley Scott film—is about the lives of residents in the outskirts of Hiroshima during the decade that followed World War II and the detonation of the Atomic Bomb. It is shocking that it took forty years to produce a film like this—Alain Resnais' *Hiroshima, Mon Amour* was groundbreaking but lacked an immediate point-of-view—and more so when one considers all of the fantasies, such as *On the Beach*, *Testament*, or *The Day After*, that were produced in America during that time. In the context of **Black Rain**, those films seem as much a form of denial as they were earnest attempts to sound alarms.

Large scale tragedies can sometimes appear to be nothing more than an accelerated part of the normal life/death process, and it is only when the tragedies are humanized that the robbery time committed upon those who are stricken can be comprehended on a larger scale. **Black Rain** focuses on a family suffering from various states of radiation poisoning and in particular on a young woman whose plans for marriage are constantly undercut by the health of those around her. It is worth noting that the American nuclear war films are partially soap operas, with the gimmick of the Bomb providing enough of a distraction that the mundane nature of the subplots becomes excusable. Those familiar with the best Japanese domestic dramas, however, recognize that they are closer to poetic family portraits than to emotional melodramas, and it is the beauty of the subplots in **Black Rain**—that the story would still be compelling even if the characters weren't dying of radiation sickness as they tried to live it—which gives the film its real power. The more it contrasts to the nuclear war fantasies, the more moving and horrifying it becomes.

The film was shot in black-and-white so that sequences depicting the explosion and its immediate aftermath would remain believable. The black-and-white image is soft, mildly grainy and looks a bit washed out, though some of these attributes seem to be a deliberate part of the cinematography—deep blacks and sharp, glossy shines would not blend with the message Imamura wants to convey—and not a fault of the transfer. The image is letterboxed with an aspect ratio of about 1.85:1 and no 16:9 enhancement. There seem to be no solid blacks, just sort of grainy greys, though the images are often compelling. The monophonic sound is in adequate condition, with minimal background noise, as is the Dolby Digital mono track, which seems to be on par with the standard track. The 123 minute film is in Japanese and is supported by very annoying large yellow English subtitles, which subvert the beauty of the black-and-white montage.

Black Rain (Paramount, 32227)

Ridley Scott's 1989 feature has rightfully been accused of pandering to "Remember Pearl Harbor" sentiments, but it is first and foremost an action film, the sort which works well on DVD, and it is difficult to remain righteous towards it once the plot starts hopping. Michael Douglas stars as a tainted American cop who loses a prisoner he's transporting to Japan. The views of Osaka, which make the city look more futuristic than L.A. in **Blade Runner**, are as captivating as they are falsely represented. There is also one wonderful scene that stops the movie dead, however, in which Andy Garcia, playing Douglas' partner, gets up in a crowded nightclub and starts singing *What'd I Say*. It seems to be Scott's little message to the viewer to stop being so uptight and just enjoy what is going on.

The Super-35 picture is in letterboxed format only, with an aspect ratio of about 2.35:1 and no 16:9 enhancement. The film is filled with moody colors, Scott's over-enthusiastic smoke machines, and a dozen other slick visual effects that can easily be spoiled on the journey from film to video, and Paramount often allows too much grain to slip into the mix. Hues are weak and the transfer often hampers the dynamism of Scott's imagery. The stereo surround sound and Dolby Digital sound are also somewhat lackluster. The 125 minute program also has a French stereo track, English captioning and a trailer.

Black Sabbath (Pioneer, PA99615D)

The 20 minute running time printed on the back of the jacket on *The Best of MusikLaden* offering is wishful thinking, since the program only runs 18 minutes and a couple seconds. Still, three of the four numbers featured represent the essence of the group, *Black Sabbath*, *Paranoid* and *Iron Man*, while the fourth, *Blue Suede Shoes*, gives one a chance to compare them to others (they're not as sharp as Ten Years After). The performances of the first three numbers are very similar to the album cuts. The band is framed by superimposed video art and the picture is workable. The musicians are reasonably clear and fleshtones have a little life. The Dolby Digital sound is super, providing a much more distinctive and dimensional bass than the duller standard track. The program is not captioned.

The Black Stallion (MGM, 906269)

The first time we saw **The Black Stallion** tears came to our eyes during the opening sequence because it was so beautifully conceived and executed. Now, when we watch the movie, the tears flow practically non-stop from beginning to end, for the same reason. The only drawback the film has is its unusual narrative structure, consisting of three or even four separate and resolute emotional units, but that is not a problem on multiple viewings, since the shifts in locale and subject can be anticipated. Directed by Carroll Ballard and photographed by Caleb Deschanel, the movie has grown in stature since its release in 1979, at least in our eyes, and seems to be one of the finest, most heartfelt creations of pure cinema to have been conceived in the sound era. Its beauty and its emotion are so closely entwined that every image in the film takes on a multitude of meanings and yet, since events in the movie are seen through the eyes of a child, it is also starkly simple and direct, so simple that it cannot be improved upon.

The film is presented in dual layer format with the full screen version on one layer and the letterboxed version on the other. The letterboxing has an aspect ratio of about 1.85:1 and has no 16:9 enhancement, adding just a little to the sides and masking off more from the top and the bottom of the image, but the cinematography is so exquisitely composed that the intended framing of the letterboxed version is preferable. The color transfer is questionable, with overly pinkish washes creating slightly unnatural fleshtones and impure whites. The problem, however, is a minor one of taste, for the hues remain within an acceptable range, the image is free of grain and the presentation looks lovely. The two-channel stereo sound, which is not available in Dolby Digital, lacks a decent bass and is unimpressive. The 117 minute DVD also has monophonic French and Spanish audio tracks, with English, French or Spanish subtitles, and is accompanied by a nice theatrical trailer.

The Black Tulip (Simitar, 7203)

The 1989 Australian cartoon program, released as *Good Housekeeping Kids* title and loosely based upon a novel by Alexander Dumas, runs 50 minutes. The colors are bright and the picture is sharp, though the animation is jerky and the focus is inconsistent. The monophonic sound is fine and the program is not captioned. There are vague similarities to *Cinderella* in the story of a young man who is mistakenly imprisoned and is rescued by two mice (like we said, the Dumas connections are loose indeed). A sorcerer needs the hero's tulip to achieve absolute power. The animation is stilted and the plot is fairly basic, but there is enough action to keep viewers who were attracted enough to the programs to begin with interested.

Blade (New Line, N4709)

Wesley Snipes is a vampire hunter who blows the fiends away with hollow tip silver bullets (filled with garlic), silver stakes, and a silver sword. Being part vampire himself, he's super strong and the fight scenes are gloriously cool (as the vampires disintegrate, their skeletons are the last to dissolve). The story is simple, but effective (the bad guys are young vampires who want to farm humans for blood instead of tolerating their society), the performances are appealing (Kris Kristofferson, with long hair, portrays Snipes' sidekick), and the film's production designs are captivating.

The picture is letterboxed with an aspect ratio of about 2.35:1 and an accommodation for enhanced 16:9 playback. Regardless of how dark the image becomes, the picture remains stable and colors remain solid, with glossy hues and accurate fleshtones. The stereo surround sound and the more distinctive Dolby Digital sound do not have the full thrust of a larger budgeted Hollywood production, but otherwise they are still worth amplifying to the max, with plenty of separation effects and a firm knowledge in the design that the film is intended to be played in a dimensional environment.

The 120 minute feature is in English only, and can be supported by English subtitles. There is a feature-length commentary track that features Snipes, co-star Stephen Dorff, screenwriter David Goyer, cinematographer Theo Van De Sande, production designer Kirk M. Pretruccelli and co-producer Peter Frankfurt. Recorded separately and mixed to create a seamless narrative, they provide a lot of satisfying technical details about the shoot, as well as how they gradually found an effective tone and atmosphere for the film. Snipes explains where his stunts leave off and the stuntman steps in, and De Sande speaks extensively about how the film's various shots and effects were achieved. Over the closing credits the speakers talk with some ambiguity about the director, Stephen Norrington, though their comments are generally positive. Snipes also promises a sequel. On another audio channel, Mark Isham's musical score is isolated in standard stereo, with Isham speaking between the cuts (and over music that isn't his). His talk is excellent, describing the creative process and how he chose the sounds and melodies to match what Norrington wanted for the film. He also

talks about the music that has influenced him, from classical to pop; working with the sound effects department so they don't impinge upon his sonic territories; what he gained playing for Van Morrison for six years; composing on a computer; and the problems of supplanting a temp score.

Additionally, there are four featurettes, each running 15–20 minutes. One takes a look at the discarded special effects created for the film's initial and less effective ending and another provides a background and overview of the film's production design. Another goes into the history of comic books and the comic book production code, including a lengthy interview with Stan Lee, while another provides a thorough history of vampires (the experts interviewed for this piece are quite entertaining). There is also the usual cast & crew profile section, an exciting trailer, a modest collection of production drawings and a text summary of the vampire clans appearing in the story and their symbols.

And that's just the video stuff. There is also DVD-ROM encoding that includes the complete, printable, original screenplay (which has elaborate descriptions and is somewhat different from the completed film—it's an enjoyable read), access to a large **Blade** posting site, access to all sorts of New Line promotional materials, an adaptation of the film as a self-advancing 'foto-novel,' and minor text summaries of the film's promotion at a comic book convention.

Blade Runner: The Director's Cut (Warner, 12682)

When you are introduced to an adult character in the beginning of a movie you naturally presume the character has had a full life leading up to the first moment you see him, but what if that wasn't the case? That is the premise suggested by Ridley Scott's **Director's Cut** version of the 1982 feature, in which the first shot of Harrison Ford's character, unbeknownst to him, is his first 'day on the job,' hunting down other androids. It is a popular concept in science fiction writing to create a world full of well-known people, revealing eventually that the people are manufactured and that the creators have been deliberate in their choices. One gets the feeling that the few humans left on Earth in **Blade Runner**, such as M. Emmett Walsh's character, are doing just that, putting on elaborate detective games to pit smart good guys against powerful bad guys and then sitting back to see what will happen, like a living movie. Without the obtrusive narration of the original release, the **Director's Cut** magnifies the many hints and allusions to this effect. "A new life awaits you," drones a public address advertisement early on, and later there are numerous references to Ford's character "earning his manhood." Ultimately, however, Scott's presentation remains ambiguous to the true nature of the hero's DNA, and viewers searching for answers, rather than for a more powerful and more stimulating mood, are likely to be disappointed. What is important to remember is that this is home video, and that long after the answers become irrelevant, the movie's atmosphere can continue to have an impact in repeat viewings and can continue to keep your own mind in a state of speculation and reflection. The images may be two dimensional, but the ideas they germinate are not. The film ignites a philosophical self-examination strong enough to support the dense special effects and intense actions sequences. After all, characters in movies really don't have pasts, and really do enter into existence in the first shot they appear.

The crisp detail delivered by the DVD is exhilarating. To see the credits from the LD scroll up with hazy, blurred letters, and then to bring up the DVD and see those same letters as crisp as they would appear on a printed page was thrilling, particularly since the special effects that follow undergo the same level of improvement. The details are outstanding, and you can read background messages that in the past looked incoherent. There are some digital artifacts, particularly as the camera moves over the huge, intricately lit model of the pyramid, but when the camera stops moving, the details sharpen up and look incredible. Colors and fleshtones are more accurate. The stereo surround sound is fine, but there is no Dolby

Digital track. The program is windowboxed on one side, with an aspect ratio of about 2.35:1 and an accommodation for enhanced 16:9 playback, and is cropped on the other side, with the cropped version giving the viewer an opportunity to see even more detail in some of the special effects. Parts of the movie are conceptually grainy and on the blown up cropped image, the grain is distinctive, but manageable. The digital artifacts seem more plentiful, but it is difficult to differentiate them from the natural distortion created by the cropping. The film runs 117 minutes, comes with a cast profile section and can be supported by English, French or Spanish subtitles ("He visto cosas que los humanos ni se imaginan. Naves de ataque incendiándose cerca del hombre de Orión").

Blazing Saddles (Warner, 1001)

Mel Brooks's 1974 comedy western is presented on one side in letterboxed format and in cropped format on the other side. The letterboxing, which has an aspect ratio of about 2.35:1and an accommodation for enhanced 16:9 playback, is a vast improvement over the cropped version. You get more gags with the letterboxing. The color transfer is very rich, with sharp hues and accurate fleshtones. The monophonic sound is fine and the 93 minute film is also available in French and Spanish, with English, French and Spanish subtitles. There is a reasonably good cast profile section and a less helpful set of production notes, along with an original theatrical trailer that seems primitive in comparison to today's comedy trailers.

Brooks speaks for an hour on one of the audio channels. His commentary is not tied to an unspooling of the film, though it does play over it. He talks about all aspects of the production, about how he wanted to hire Dan Dailey for Gene Wilder's part and how he actually did hire Gig Young, only to have Young collapse during the first day of shooting. His manner of speaking would probably not translate well to a written text, so the talk is appropriate for the medium. Brooks is engaging and, at least in general terms, tells you everything you probably wanted to know about the film. He does include some practical filmmaking advice (always use two cameras, always film a close-up of something in each scene for the editor to use in an emergency) and shares what seems to be a very common Hollywood story about the reticent executives who didn't think the film would be popular or that the film should include what ended up being some of its funniest sequences.

Blind Spot X-rated (Vivid, UPC#0073214538)

There doesn't seem to be much of a plot, since it is made up mostly of erotic sequences, but the ending is very clever and justifies what has preceded it. Most of the story is set at a strange mansion where erotic dancers mingle with the guests. A man becomes infatuated with one dancer and she seems to like him, too, but he can't get her to leave the place. The reason is a surprise. Shot on film, the image is somewhat grainy and the colors are light, with bland fleshtones. The monophonic sound is a little strained but passable. The program runs 72 minutes and stars Lené, Lady Rose, Sierra, Laurie Lameron and Rasha Romana. The DVD contains alternate angle sequences and elaborate hardcore interactive promotional features.

Blithe Spirit (Image, ID45426JFDVD)

In Noel Coward and David Lean's ethereal confection about ghosts, Rex Harrison stars as an author who finds himself in a romantic jam with his second wife when his first returns from the Great Beyond to haunt him. Constance Cummings and Kay Hammond co-star, with Margaret Rutherford as a batty medium. The dialogue is ultra-breezy and the characters are beautifully formed. The 1945 film uses lighting effects and makeup to convey the ghost, and for those of you interested in arcane facts, Coward wrote the play (which has a weaker third act than the film) at the same resort where they shot The Prisoner.

Both the picture and the sound are inconsistent. On some reels, the colors look faded and, on others, fleshtones seem overly yellow. The colors are strong enough to hint at how nice the film once looked, but are unable to sustain that condition. The monophonic sound loses its upper end in places and has plenty of age-related noise, though the precious dialogue is never affected. The 96 minute program is not captioned.

Blondage X-rated (Vivid, UPC#0073214533)

A few backstage interludes are combined with vivid videotape footage from a fancy topless dancing establishment. Some of the sequences appear to be shot live, though it is difficult to say how much of the audience has been salted with paid performers. Although there are several hardcore sequences, there is also a lot of what is essentially softcore footage of the women dancing. The image is extremely sharp, with accurate fleshtones and bright hues. The sound is fine and the program runs 73 minutes. The DVD contains alternate angle sequences and elaborate hardcore interactive promotional features.

Blonde Justice X-rated (Vivid, UPC#0073214484)

A topless dancer is receiving threatening mail, so a female police detective goes undercover to investigate. The erotic sequences are reasonably energetic and the narrative is relatively satisfying—not only do they catch the suspect at the end, but there is some character growth along the way. The picture quality is passable, with reasonably sharp contrasts and bright hues. The sound is fine. The 75 minute program contains alternate angle sequences and elaborate hardcore interactive promotional features.

Blood for Dracula (Criterion, CC1547D)

Paul Morrissey's ultra-campy, ultra-gory 1974 horror spoof was shot back-to-back with **Flesh for Frankenstein** in Europe. The 103 minute **Dracula**, which, like **Frankenstein**, features Udo Kier and Joe Dallesandro, is blatantly comical. Kier is a dying Count Dracula, who visits Italy in search of virgins ('wirgins,' as his assistant continually calls them) to revive him, only to find Dallesandro's character spoiling the goods (whenever Dracula drinks a non-virgin's blood, he vomits it up—if the film has done its job, you're in the right frame of mind and the vomiting scenes are as funny as they are gross). The performances seem off-kilter—the four sisters in the remote mansion that Dracula visits each have a distinctively different accent—but that quickly becomes part of the fun, with plenty of over-the-top gore and sex.

Dracula is letterboxed with an aspect ratio of about 1.94:1 and no 16:9 enhancement. Colors are fresh and darker sequences are stable, with pure blacks and detailed contrasts. The monophonic sound is strong and distortion is minimal. There is no captioning.

The film is accompanied by a montage of production stills (set to a flourishing stereophonic rendition of its musical score) and by an audio commentary track from Morrissey, Kier and film historian Maurice Yacowar. Morrissey has some interesting things to say on the commentary track, notably about the differences between reality and artificiality in films. He praises Italian cinematographers, whom he claims are less concerned with locating a 'natural light source' in a room and are more interested in simply making the stars look captivating. Less convincing is his argument about suppressing 'sincerity' in his cast's performances, which certainly heightens the comical effects he is striving for but does not seem practical outside of specific dramatic situations. Kier provides personal reminiscences about working on the film and about his career in general. Yacowar's comments are off-putting at first, as if he were trying to read too much into the movie, but most of what he has to say is valid. Yacowar essentially proves the unstated argument that Morrissey knew exactly what he was doing, even though the strengths of the film are in its slapdash tone and seemingly free-for-all activities.

The Bloodsucker Leads the Dance (Image, ID4612SADVD)

The dubbed and ludicrously titled 1975 production was directed by Alfredo Rizzo. Supposedly set in Ireland, a group of female performers is invited to a remote castle by a count who has become smitten with one of them. After a lot of romping about in the nude, the women are systematically decapitated. It's great fun, for male and female misogynists alike, and there are several plot twists at the end, though they actually pass through the best ending as a red herring to arrive at a weaker one.

The 89 minute *Redemption* program is preceded by a pointless 8 minute intro. The picture is letterboxed with an aspect ratio of about 1.75:1 and no 16:9 enhancement. The colors are light and yellowish, and the image has a lot of minor speckling, but the presentation is tolerable when one takes the source into account. The dubbing is awful, but that's part of the fun, and the music is fairly compelling, a classic Seventies Italian score. The monophonic sound has a limited range, but is workable. The program has no captioning and is accompanied by an Italian trailer that seems to have some spicier sex sequences than the film itself.

Blown Away (MGM, 906259)

We hate mad bomber movies that depend upon the hero choosing between the red wire and the green wire for excitement, because the choice is arbitrary (as a young friend of ours pointedly inquired, "What do you do if a bomb has all green wires?"), and as overworked as the editing and dialogue scripting become, there's no underlying motivation for what happens. It is merely the whim of the filmmakers. **Speed** largely and wisely avoided such predicaments, but there is a little too much of it in **Blown Away**. Jeff Bridges and Tommy Lee Jones star in the somewhat absurd film, with Forest Whitaker featured in an important supporting role. Much has been made about the ineptitude of the performers' accents, and with good cause. It appears that there were one or two weeks of filming where Bridges, who also didn't bother to get a haircut, really tried to sound like he was from Boston, where the film is set, and the rest of the time he just says words any old way. Jones, on the other hand, as an IRA dropout, tries too hard all the time, but the net result is the same—distraction and embarrassment. After 30 minutes or so of fooling around, Whitaker appears and the film's entertainment improves. It never becomes believable and never shakes the impression that the filmmakers are controlling the fates of the characters, but the action, the explosions and what charisma the stars have left are enough to satisfy those attracted to the premise or the genre.

The 121 minute film is presented on one side in letterboxed format, with an aspect ratio of about 2.35:1 and an accommodation for enhanced 16:9 playback, and in full screen format on the other. The picture has rich colors. Fleshtones are deep and the image looks crisp and smooth. The regular stereo surround sound is bland, but the Dolby Digital track delivers the punch the film requires. There is also a French Dolby Digital track and a Spanish track in standard stereo, along with English, French or Spanish subtitling. A shameless theatrical trailer, which rips off the marketing for **Die Hard**, has also been included.

Blue Angels 50th Anniversary Edition (Simitar, 7359)

Two excellent 45 minute documentaries are combined on one DVD. The title program, narrated by John Travolta, provides a complete history of the flying team, including how the group was created, the various planes they used as technology advanced and how their role has changed over the years. There are also informative sequences depicting how they prepare for air shows, how they train and practice, and plenty of footage of their actual stunts, from every angle. By providing so much background information, the program is much more satisfying and stimulating than the straight air show video programs of the group.

The second documentary, *Ace Factor*, is also fascinating. Narrated by Monte Markham, the program explores the history of air combat and how pilots have trained through the years to prepare for dogfights. Although the emphasis is on the U.S. military, there is also substantial discussion about training in other countries—particularly those the U.S. is likely to meet in an air fight. Both programs contain a wealth of archival footage (there are even clips from the old *Blue Angels* TV show—Blue Angels officials are rather embarrassed by it, but we recall loving the program in our youth), which is in various states of quality, and fresh new footage, which looks fine, of the jets in action. The sound is not elaborately mixed, but is adequately presented. There is no captioning.

Blue Angels Rolling in the Sky (Pioneer, PSID97002)

An ideal demonstration program for those who like to treat their guests to flyovers (it helps if your rear speakers have good woofers) and other zippy sound effects. The 50 minute program depicts the synchronized American flying team from every angle, including ground preparations, aerobatic flying set to music, flying accompanied only to real sounds, cameras in the ground, cameras on the planes and cameras on other planes nearby. The picture is outstanding, with crisp, ultra-vivid colors. There is a terrific stereo surround soundtrack and a really terrific Dolby Digital track, which has much stronger directional energy and greater detail.

Blue Öyster Cult Live 1976 (Image, ID4400CADVD)

If you like your Öysters raw, check it out. The band wasn't the greatest, and their live concert reflects this, but a spirit of fun pervades the 86 minute show with its hokey light-and-smoke effects, badly illuminated picture and coherent but terrible, dropout-infested audio recording. Anyone with a nostalgia for the band or their quasi-heavy metal milieu will probably enjoy the show thoroughly. The picture is somewhat on the hazy side and the monophonic sound is best held to a modest volume. The program is not captioned.

Blues Brothers (see **The Best of the Blues Brothers**)

The Blues Brothers (Universal, 20299)

Expanded to 148 minutes and accompanied by an excellent hour-long retrospective documentary, **The Blues Brothers**, a cult musical comedy film with a still-growing reputation, has been given first class treatment. Among other things, the 1980 John Landis film is dedicated to excess, and so an expanded running time seems wholly appropriate. The additional 18 minutes of footage adds a bit to the narrative (although the narrative, if anything, needed trimming), more to the musical numbers (which is always welcome) and many irrelevant but pleasing gags. Since the film is a celebration of too much everything anyway, the longer version is more entertaining and appropriate than the standard version. Dan Aykroyd and John Belushi star in the musical comedy about two musicians trying to put together a band to earn money for an orphanage while staying one step, or tire squeal, ahead of the law.

The film is letterboxed with an aspect ratio of about 1.85:1 and an accommodation for enhanced 16:9 playback. Although there is still some softness, the picture is reasonably sharp. The colors look terrific. The stereo surround and Dolby Digital sound are fairly strong. The Dolby Digital track, in particular, has nice separation effects and plenty of power during the musical numbers. The film can be supported by English, French or Spanish subtitles ("Estamos en una misión de Dios"), but the documentary is only supported by English captioning. There is also a trailer, publicity photos, some production notes and a cast profile section.

The documentary gives the complete history of the Blues Brothers band and discusses the legitimate contribution it made to popular culture, essentially reviving a genre that was being stamped into oblivion by disco music. Landis, for example, tells about the fight he had with Cab Calloway to have *Minnie the Moocher* performed in the traditional style instead of the style that was current in 1980. The story of the film's creation is also given full coverage (Aykroyd's original script was 340 pages long) and some of the major production sequences are discussed in detail. Among the many interesting tidbits: Aretha Franklin and several other performers in the cast had difficulty lip synching, because they were used to doing a song differently every time they sang it; the cars were really going 100 MPH down the streets of Chicago; they really did drop a car from a helicopter (you get to see what it looked like after it hit) but they had to do tests for the FAA first; they found an unused mall to stage the mall destruction sequence, and the security guards they hired to keep an eye on the rented goods in the mall were caught stealing the goods; and D. Day in **Animal House** (the biker) is based on Aykroyd.

Blues Brothers 2000 (Universal, 20281)

Those who liked **The Blues Brothers** because it was a comedy will probably not like **Blues Brothers 2000** all that much, but those who liked **The Blues Brothers** because it was a musical will take delight in the sequel, which is unabashedly more of a musical than even the first film. The plot is limited—there is some kind of cross-country chase, with police in pursuit, to reach a 'battle of the bands' gig—but the collection of rock and blues musicians showing up for cameo performances is enough to fill a dozen all-star concerts. The songs sound marvelous, the choreography is contagious and there are enough gags and car crashes to carry the viewer from one song number to the next. Directed by John Landis, the film stars Dan Aykroyd and John Goodman.

The picture is letterboxed with an aspect ratio of about 1.85:1 and an accommodation for enhanced 16:9 playback. The color transfer is excellent, and the bright, smooth hues add to the impact of the music. The stereo surround sound is grand and the Dolby Digital track is even better, with more separation details and fuller tones. The 123 minute film is also available in French in Dolby Digital and comes with English or Spanish subtitles, along with some production notes and a cast & crew profile section. There is also a 24 minute promotional documentary about the movie, a trailer, and a few production photos. Among other things, the documentary pretends to explain how the biggest car crash sequence was done, but it really doesn't.

Blues Masters (Image, ID5305CADVD)

A terrific collection of clips from a 1966 Canadian TV special, Muddy Waters, Otis Spann, Mable Hillery, Sonny Terry, Brownie McGhee, Sunnyland Slim and Willie Dixon are featured on the 47 minute program, which is hosted by Colin James. The black-and-white picture looks good, with crisp lines and rich contrasts, and the monophonic sound is fairly vivid. The music is outstanding, and the TV format provides a wealth of close-ups on the musicians, which brings a further emotional amplification to their songs.

Boarding School Lesbos X-rated (Lipstik, 31182)

The 72 minute effort supposedly depicts the activities at night in an all-girl school, and features one performer who is substantially overweight. The program features older-looking images with grain, ghosting, aged colors, and substantial video smearing in places, as well as monophonic sound that is often distorted on the upper end and subject to sporadic dropouts. Narrative development is limited and the erotic staging has a somewhat dated feel.

Bobby Sox X-rated (Vivid)

The film runs 107 minutes and is a better-than-average hardcore feature, with a developed narrative (set in a small town, it is about a guy who gets jealous when his girlfriend befriends a drunken, has-been actor) and freshly conceived erotic sequences, including an extended bondage sequence and cross-dressing scenes. The picture, too, is better looking than most adult programs shot on film, as opposed to videotape, but fleshtones are pinkish, other colors are a little bland and the image is grainy in places. The monophonic sound is weakly recorded and dullish.

The DVD was the first adult program to feature alternate angle options, something that became quite common shortly thereafter.

They occur during some of the erotic scenes, and are cued by a logo that appears on the picture. The toggle is fairly instantaneous, so it is easy to jump through as many alternate angles as are offered without losing continuity. There is no organization to the choices—angle 2, for example, does not show a consistent point-of-view from one sequence to the next—and erotic sequences in X-rated programs are by nature under-edited to begin with, so who really needs more footage?

The program was also the first to feature Vivid's extensive interactive hardcore promotional features.

Body Armor (Simitar, 7429)

Matt McColm stars as a private something-or-other investigating the disappearance of a virologist. Ron Perlman is the villain, developing viruses and their antidotes simultaneously, giving the world one for free and then making a profit selling the other. In the film's second half, McColm is infected with a new prototype and has a certain amount of time to crash Perlman's pad and cure himself. The story is an adequate backdrop for the gunfights, car crashes and other activities this sort of movie can be depended upon to deliver.

The color transfer is fine, the image is sharp and fleshtones look okay. Gunshots are wimpy on the Ultra-Stereo surround soundtrack and separation effects are limited. The 95 minute program is accompanied by brief filmographies of Matt McColm and Carol Alt, and is not captioned.

Body Heat (Warner, 20005)

The birth of the modern erotic thriller, the most ubiquitous video genre there is, can pretty much be traced to Lawrence Kasdan's 1981 **Body Heat**. Sure, it wasn't the first time that lovers got together in a movie to kill someone, but it was the first significant film where yuppie baby boomers mixed sweaty sex with murder. It was the ultimate in instant gratification fantasies. While the film wasn't a huge hit, it has endured. It struck a chord, making stars out of its two featured players, William Hurt and Kathleen Turner, and rapidly spawning more imitations and variations than any movie since **Nosferatu**.

The film is letterboxed on one side, with an aspect ratio of about 1.85:1 and an accommodation for enhanced 16:9 playback, and in cropped format on the other side. The cropping is workable but the letterboxed framing is preferable. The film has a sultry atmosphere and was shot with a lot of hazes—a major sequence is even set in a dense fog. The picture is sharp, however, and the colors are rich. It does a good job taming the film's deliberate haze and conveying the humidity without smearing the image. The stereo sound is somewhat flat, but the Dolby Digital audio track has an enveloping dimensionality and a little more power, though rear channel activity is limited. The 113 minute film is also available in French in mono and comes with English, French or Spanish subtitles. There is a cast and crew listing, a few production notes about the 1981 film's financing, and a terrific, steamy, dialog-less trailer.

Body Strokes (Simitar, R-rated, 7448); (Simitar unrated, 7471)

An artist having trouble with his wife hires two nude models, who reminisce about their love lives in erotic flashbacks while he paints. The drama is subdued, but if one is seeking out the softcore romance genre then the film seems to meet the requirements, and it has a better female point of view than most. The picture is somewhat soft, but hues are reasonably fresh. The sound is a little strained and dialogue is a bit distorted at times. The program is not captioned. Although there are differences in the jacket art, the only way to identify the unrated DVDs is to read the fine print on the back or to check the running times—the R-rated versions run around 80 minutes and the unrated versions run about 90 minutes. The image quality is the same on the two releases. Why anyone would consciously buy the R-rated versions, however, is beyond us, not because we look down on prudes but because the movies are about sex in the first place, so in for a penny, in for a pound.

The Bodyguard (Warner, 12591)

Kevin Costner, whose no-nonsense performance prevents the movie from ever seeming too ridiculous, stars as an ex-Secret Service agent hired to protect a singing star, played with a studied limitation by Whitney Houston. Extended by musical numbers and a relaxed narrative, the film goes on for 130 minutes, but it has just enough excitement, just enough glamour and just enough humor, intentional and unintentional, to beguile most fans.

The DVD is in full screen format only, adding a little bit of picture information to the bottom of the screen, but cropping a lot more off the side. The screen composition is such that the cropping is rarely noticeable. The hues are strong, but the film has a soft, blandly colored look. The standard stereo surround sound is also dull, but the Dolby Digital track is sharper, more powerful, more detailed and more dimensional, and it sounds terrific. The 130 minute film is also presented in French without Dolby Digital and is available with English, Spanish or French subtitles. There is a modest cast profile section and a paragraph or two about the 1992 film's production that basically says the movie was originally conceived for Steve McQueen, which explains Kevin Costner's haircut.

The Bodyguard from Beijing (World Video, WVDVD1427)

Forget about Kevin Costner and Whitney Houston (or, for those of you who remember the Eighties, Don Johnson and Sheena Easton) and check out Jet Li and Christy Chung in **Bodyguard from Beijing**. Li, who has the same haircut as Costner but wears it to his advantage, portrays an elite Communist bodyguard hired to protect the girlfriend of an important Hong Kong businessman who works with the Red Chinese. The story is utterly predictable, but the action scenes are creative and Li exudes excitement every time the camera turns to him—there is no wonder at all why Chung's character is willing to dump all her riches to be in his arms.

The picture is letterboxed with an aspect ratio of about 1.8:1 and no 16:9 enhancement. The letterboxed image is set high on the screen so that permanent and somewhat large white English subtitles can appear beneath it, in the black band. The 95 minute film is available in either Cantonese (the preferred track) or Mandarin, and is monophonic with minor range distortions. The picture is in passable condition. Colors are subdued, there is a bit of wear around some reel-change points, and darker sequences are a bit greenish. Fleshtones are also bland, but the presentation seems about average for a Hong Kong production.

Boiling Point X-rated (Vivid, UPC#0073214602)

Every erotic sequence is justified by the narrative. A drifter gets a job at a ranch and discovers that the rancher's daughter is very unhappy about her upcoming marriage. Not only is there a real plot, but the dialogue has a believable feel and the performers work hard at the acting aspects of their roles. The picture is a bit grainy and colors are a little dull. The monophonic sound is okay. Dyanna Lauren, Kaitlyn Ashley, Tera Heart, Rebecca Bardoux, Debi Diamond and Lana Sands are featured. The program runs 76 minutes, but the LD ran 86 minutes. The DVD also contains alternate angle sequences and elaborate hardcore interactive promotional features.

Bolton, Michael (see **Merry Christmas from Vienna: Plácido Domingo /Ying Huang /Michael Bolton**)

Bonanza (Madacy, DVD99047)
Bonanza: Desert Justice (Madacy, DVD990471)

Bonanza: Badge without Honor (Madacy, DVD990472)
Bonanza: The Last Viking (Madacy, DVD990473)
Bonanza: The Blood Line (Madacy, DVD990474)
Bonanza: The Silent Thunder (Madacy, DVD990475)

Madacy has released a box set of five episodes from the venerable western television series. The episodes are also available individually. The show's opening and closing theme song has been replaced by a godawful electric guitar thing, probably because of rights conflicts, though the theme does percolate through the scoring within the episodes. The picture quality is generally sharp, though colors are subdued and the source material has occasional scratches and similar-type flaws. The monophonic sound is very harsh, with a limited range, though the dialogue is coherent. Each episode runs about 50 minutes and is accompanied by a minor trivia game and brief notes about the series that often have nothing to do with the episode at hand. The episodes are not captioned.

The Baby Boom generation was in all likelihood the last generation to be inundated with Westerns to a point that it is in our blood. The pre-technological setting was an ideal one for removing the complications and distractions from drama or action (or even comedy, though less often—and let's not forget the singing cowboys), but it is that very lack of technology that prevents westerns from being as widely popular today. There was a time when such programs dominated the top-ten Nielsens, and that time is rapidly becoming as distant as the Old West itself. **Bonanza** is set on a ranch at the north of Lake Tahoe and depicts the adventures of the rancher, played by Lorne Greene, and his three grown sons, played by Michael Landon, Pernell Roberts and the steer-sized Dan Blocker. The show was oriented toward drama instead of action, though there is inevitably a fight or two of some sort during the course of an episode. The four stars essentially had equal standing within the show, which was able to vary its appeal by focusing substantially on one character or another in various episodes.

Claude Akins portrays a sheriff in **Desert Justice** who arrives at the ranch one day to arrest a hired hand. He's rough with his prisoner, however, so Roberts' character accompanies them to prevent his friend from being harmed before he stands trial, and during the journey the true nature of the relationship between the sheriff and his prisoner is revealed.

Dan Duryea (who talks like Jon Lovitz) portrays a marshal in **Badge without Honor**, arriving in town to take a friend of the heroes back for a trial. Similarities to the previous episode end there, however, since it turns out Duryea's character is also a hired assassin. The drama is fairly effective and the conclusion is exciting.

Neville Brand portrays an errant relative who suffers a conflict of interest when the bandits he leads raid a ranch and kidnap one of the heroes in **The Last Viking**. Although the situation is unlikely, the episode is fairly entertaining. Landon and Blocker, who aren't seen too much in the first two episodes, get more screen time. Greene's character shoots a man in self-defense in **The Blood Line** and must then cope with the man's understandably distraught teenage son. Jan Sterling is featured, and Greene has a terrific shoot-out with Lee Van Cleef near the end.

It is best to view all these episodes first to appreciate how much better the episode directed by Robert Altman, **The Silent Thunder**, is. Stella Stevens portrays a deaf girl who lives in a isolated cabin with her father, a trapper. This is the only episode in the group to highlight Landon (Greene appears briefly, the others not at all), who teaches her rudimentary sign language, and Albert Salmi is on hand as a grisly villain, pawing Stevens whenever he gets within an arm's length of her. The episode is loaded with sexual tension, pathos and other pleasures. There is a psychological precision that is completely missing from the other episodes, and there are experiments (Altman shows one sequence from Stevens' point-of-view, i.e., without sound) and creative uses of the screen's frame. Indeed, film students could probably learn a lot of basic, intelligent cinematic storytelling by analyzing the episode on a shot-by-shot basis. The colors on the episode are a little faded, but damage is minimal.

Bonnie and Clyde (Warner, 14423); reissue (Warner, 17274)

The 1967 Arthur Penn film, starring Warren Beatty, Faye Dunaway and Gene Hackman, is a classic work. It does an exceptional job at conning the viewer into rooting for evil people (it never seems cynical about it) and is equally accomplished at instilling with the viewer the emotions of historical accuracy—not just showing the past but enabling the viewer to feel the Texas countryside during the Depression. At the time of its release it broke new ground with the intensity of its violence, but unlike most previous or subsequent gangster features, the protagonists are emotionally affected by the pain and death they are causing. On every technical level **Bonnie and Clyde** is brilliantly constructed, and at its heart it suggests that even amoral criminals are susceptible to the mysteries and frustrations of love, a challenging premise that a less sensitive motion picture could never have communicated.

Warner's first release of the title (one of the first DVD releases) was in full screen format only, but the subsequent release is in letterboxed format on one side with an aspect ratio of about 1.85:1 and an accommodation for enhanced 16:9 playback, and is in full screen format on the other side. The picture transfers are identical and look gorgeous, with rich fleshtones, deep, solid hues and a crisp focus. Except for a stray speckle or two, the presentations are immaculate. The data transfer rate is a couple notches higher on the reissue, toning down some jerkiness in movement here and there, but basically it is impossible to tell the full screen versions apart. It is the letterboxed version, however, that is the legitimate presentation of the film. Masking off a touch of picture information from the bottom and adding a lot more on the sides, the letterbox framing consistently adds to the drama and pulls the viewer into the entertainment.

The film runs 112 minutes. On both, the monophonic sound is offered in English and French, and can be supported by English, French or Spanish subtitles ("'Sal était d'une beauté peu ordinaire, mais aux traits durs….' 'Elle louchait, avait un bec de lièvre et aucune dent'"). Both have production notes, a cast & crew profile section, and a theatrical trailer.

Bon Voyage (see Alfred Hitchcock's Bon Voyage & Aventure Malgache)

The Boogey Man / The Devonsville Terror (Anchor Bay, DV10664)

Two cheap horror films from the early Eighties directed by Ulli Lobbel and starring Suzanna Love are combined on the double bill. Both films are letterboxed, with an aspect ratio of about 1.85:1 and no 16:9 enhancement, though here and there the matting seems somewhat tight, obscuring one or two effects. Generally, the picture transfers looks okay. When the image is well lit, colors have a mild flatness, but are solid, and fleshtones are bland but workable. In darker sequences, the image is murkier, but not overly distorted. The monophonic sound is tinny and mildly distorted on the upper end. There is no captioning. *Boogey Man* is accompanied by two TV commercials.

Each film appears on a separate side of the platter. The opening of the 83 minute *Boogey Man*, from 1980, steals from **Halloween**, but soon the film is off on its own and is essentially about a haunted mirror that causes gruesome deaths. The most memorable: the heads of two teenagers are skewered in such a way that it appears they are kissing one another. The 82 minute *Devonsville Terror*, from 1983, has inserts featuring Donald Pleasance supposedly removing worms from his arm and is about three present day women, working in a small rural town, who are accused of being witches. Although neither narrative is developed sufficiently, both

films offer a few minor thrills and enough plot turns to keep fans attentive.

Boogeyman III (see **Return of the Boogeyman**)

Boogie Boy (Sterling, 7095)

An often promising but ultimately sappy drama about low lifes pondering their fate in a deserted desert motel, Mark Dacascos portrays a punk rock drummer fresh out of prison who looks up his former cellmate and immediately gets roped into a broken drug deal. He high tails it out of town with his friend to beat the heat, but then pauses too long to recover before moving on. Peopled among the supporting players are Emily Lloyd, Traci Lords (in a small, but captivating performance as a horror actress junkie) and Joan Jett, and there are times when the film is fairly rewarding—at one point, it looks like it might become a musical, which would be cool, and the final fight is terrific—but, despite the apparent realism of the characters, it is too drenched in romantic melodrama to reach for something higher and ends up becoming much more predictable than it had seemed at first.

The picture is presented in full screen format and is a bit grainy, with dull colors though, considering the movie's subject, a glossier image might not capture its mood as well. There were also scattered incidences of noticeable digital artifacting. The stereo sound is adequate but not finely detailed and the 103 minute film can be supported by Spanish subtitles. There is a letterboxed trailer and a cast & crew profile section.

Boogie Nights (New Line, N4650)

Great movies come in all shapes and sizes. Director Paul Thomas Anderson coaxes a superb performance from Julianne Moore and several of her fellow ensemble players in his epic about making pornographic films in the late Seventies and early Eighties. By nature a satire, the film must nevertheless be taken seriously. Viewers approaching it thinking, 'Seventies + porn business = camp,' will be disappointed, because it is a serious comedy, rich in irony but modest when it comes to cheap sensationalism. Based upon real characters and blending what are likely genuine anecdotes with a fictional narrative organization, the film achieves on a technical level what its subject achieves on a visceral level, a seemingly endless succession of multiple cinematic joys. The camera, for example, doesn't move to the beat of the music on the soundtrack—it follows the melody instead, bobbing and weaving through conversations and characters with the confidence of a disco queen. The editing is also exquisite—watch for what would normally be a cliché, a cork popping out of a bottle, come just far enough after a discussion of ejaculation to provide resonance instead of punctuation.

Moore, as the den mother porn star who takes the hero, an overly endowed teenager played by Mark Wahlberg, under her wing, gives a captivating, flawlessly detailed and genuinely touching performance, completely obliterating the barrier a viewer would normally place between the image of a porn star icon and the concept of a real human being somewhat unknowingly taken prisoner by her lifestyle. Burt Reynolds, as the director of the porn movies, is on his best behavior, delivering a consistently understated performance that lets out just enough of his star persona to tentpole the multiple storylines and extended chronological setting. And then there are the supporting performers, who make up the soul of the film and provide various levels of comic and dramatic relief (often simultaneously, such as with William H. Macy's sad sack character married to a nymphomaniac who won't go near him). **Boogie Nights** isn't perfect—the narrative probably unwinds a little too much in the last act—but it is a compelling showcase of entertaining talent, so much so that, like the hero, it is substantially over endowed.

The 155 minute film is presented on a single-sided dual-layer platter in letterboxed format with an aspect ratio of about 2.35:1 and an accommodation for enhanced 16:9 playback. The picture is a bit darker and loses a little detail to the shadows, but it is in reasonably good condition, with bright, solid hues. Dialog and pretty much everything tends to bleed to the rear channels on the standard track, so the Dolby Digital track is preferred. There are rarely much in the way of directional sound effects, but there is a near-constant musical score, a tag team effort that switches invisibly between pop hits and original instrumentals by Michael Penn. It is on the Dolby Digital track that the music moves far enough away from the dialogue to slip the viewer into the milieu. The film is available in French in Dolby Digital and comes with English, French or Spanish subtitles. There is an elaborate cast & crew profile that includes amusing and informative backstory profiles of each character, including imaginary filmographies. There is also an itemization of the primary pop songs on the soundtrack, including a direct access to each song.

Anderson's provides a straightforward commentary in which he explains what he was doing and how he was doing it. He provides background information, insight on camera angle choices and an analysis of the contributions of his fellow filmmakers. He explores the difference between pornography on film, which at least had a kinship to genuine filmmaking, and pornography on video tape, which can be an assembly line process where the end result is designed to be re-edited, i.e., scanned, by the viewer (a process taken even further with DVD multiple angle programs). He also gives the best universal piece of advice we have heard yet on filmmaking—to wit, make a movie that you yourself will enjoy sitting back and watching.

There is a reasonably lengthy collection of outtakes in the supplement, though they have less substance or scope than we had anticipated (what Anderson claims was one of his favorite sequences, a car crash intercut with a domestic violence incident, hasn't been included), and there are no significant erotic sequences. There is also a Penn music video, directed by Anderson during a pause in the **Boogie Nights** post production process, that depicts the singer rocking down what appears to be an endless corridor. Anderson provides commentary over the outtakes (pointing out, during one extended improvisational sequence, that, "The shortest time on a movie set is the stuff between 'Action' and 'Cut.'") and the video.

Booty Call (Columbia TriStar, 94959)

Booty Call is probably not going to find its way into the curriculum of any kind of Cinema or Black Studies program any time soon, and it is loaded with the kind of racially biased humor that white comedians get raked over the coals for suggesting—heck, it even opens with the hero playing dice, which was a staple for keeping black characters in their place in films during the Thirties—but it is a satisfying little comedy that does everything wrong for the right reasons and gets away with it.

Jamie Foxx and Tommy Davidson star with Vivica A. Fox and Tamala Jones as two friends on a double date whose attempts to consummate their evening are consistently interrupted, particularly by the need to obtain prophylactics. The film is brief, running just 79 minutes, and the comedy situations are varied enough that the show never becomes tiresome or redundant, despite the continued frustrations the heroes face. Even the apparent immaturity of the heroes and of the film's subject matter is redeemed by the comical adeptness of the performers and the overriding respect-the-one-you're-with moral.

The picture is presented on one side in letterboxed format, with an aspect ratio of about 1.85:1 and an accommodation for enhanced 16:9 playback, and in full screen format on the other side. The picture quality is okay, though colors seem a little light at times and the image is mildly grainy here and there. The stereo surround sound is adequate and the Dolby Digital track is a little sharper. There is also a French audio track and a Spanish audio track in standard stereo, along with English, French and Spanish subtitles ("'Trois mots sur ta coiffure: Fa-bu-leux!' 'J'ai trois mots pour toi: Dégage, Yoko Ono'") and a trailer.

Bordello of Blood (see Tales from the Crypt Presents Bordello of Blood)

Born in East L.A. (GoodTimes, 0581009)

An American of Hispanic descent leaves his wallet home one day and is deported to Mexico. Directed by Cheech Marin and starring Paul Rodriguez with mucho cameo appearances, the 1987 comedy is not intensely humorous, but it is pleasingly witty and has a strong political moral. The ending is perfect.

The picture is slightly cropped, but only a handful of shots appear harmed by it. The image is extremely sharp, and the colors look perfect. The music on the monophonic presentation is stronger than similar efforts in many stereophonic programs. The 85 minute program has optional English, French or Spanish subtitles.

Finally, it is worth noting the intriguing value of one scene in which Cheech attempts to teach *Twist and Shout* to a group of Mexican musicians and they insist that it is *La Bamba*. There is a lot of valuable musical criticism available solely through the medium of film comedy, if you stop to think about it, and this is one of the clearest examples of how effortlessly complex ideas can be communicated when humor is the mode of communication.

Born on the Fourth of July (Universal, 20208)

A movie like Oliver Stone's **Platoon** is entertaining because it pushes you to a certain level of emotional intensity and never lets up. Stone's **Born on the Fourth of July**, however, is a biographical drama (about Vietnam veteran/activist Ron Kovic) and the emotions are more scattered. Except for the single viewing to satisfy one's curiosity, it is difficult to think of the movie as entertainment. The film is intent upon rubbing a viewer's nose in the unseemly aspects of war, veterans' hospitals, and paraplegia. It is efficiently educational and artistic, but its rewards are minimal. To top things off, the star, Tom Cruise, gives a sporadic and mostly pedestrian performance. He transcends the material in only a handful of scenes and is bound by it most everywhere else. In marked contrast, Willem Dafoe appears all too briefly in one segment and is so fully captivating that you wish the story would follow his character instead of Cruise's.

Contrary to a notation on the jacket cover, the letterboxing has an aspect ratio of about 2.35:1, with no 16:9 enhancement. The picture is very crisp, but Stone gives a number of scenes a strong orange or brownish tint, which tends to overpower the image in those sequences. The stereo sound is passable, but the Dolby Digital track has better defined tones and purer separations, which is ideal for Stone's elaborate layering of pop music and other environmental noises. The dual-layer 145 minute program is also available in French in standard stereo and comes with English or Spanish subtitles, as well as a trailer, informative production notes and a cast profile section.

The Borrowers (PolyGram, 4400551252)

The wonderful 1997 fantasy film with terrific special effects is a delight on several levels, presenting a city that is an odd mix of present technology and past designs, and it moves seamlessly between depicting the standard human inhabitants and the fingertall protagonists who also live there. The narrative is a standard concoction—a villain, played by John Goodman, has stolen a will and wants to tear down the house where the heroes, big and small, live—but it is filled with intriguing visions of life on a shorter scale and the creative joy of having the two worlds intersect. On a technical level, the narrative takes several big leaps to keep things moving and defies its internal logic at a couple more junctures for the same reason, but the fantasy is so well executed and so potent that few viewers will be put off by its shortcuts. It almost doesn't deserve to be pigeonholed as a family film, since its action, comedy and visual panorama are as sophisticated as they are universally engaging.

The dual-sided, dual layer program is letterboxed on one layer, with an aspect ratio of about 1.85:1 and an accommodation for enhanced 16:9 playback, and is in full screen format on the other layer. The picture quality is okay. As part of the film's unusual non-era specific design, the color scheme has a kind of antique, yellowish pall, which often compromises fleshtones. We got the feeling that here and there contrasts were a little weak, reducing detail in the darker areas of the screen, but overall the image is crisp and the colors are sharp. The stereo surround sound is okay, but it is the enhanced directional capabilities of the Dolby Digital track that really underscore the film's actions effectively and enhance the entertainment. The 86 minute program also has a French language track in Dolby Digital, a Spanish track in standard stereo, English closed captioning, a terrific 22 minute 'making of' documentary that is also captioned, a couple trailers and a cast profile section.

Bottle Rocket (Columbia TriStar, 11629)

A somewhat contrived comedy about three young men in their twenties who go on an inept crime spree, it is rescued about halfway through when it turns into a sweet romance between one of the young men and a motel maid, the latter played with exquisite charm by Lumi Cavazos. Floating on the good feelings generated by the romance, the contrivances become less troublesome and the 1996 movie achieves the insubordinate comical tone it wants desperately to convey.

The single-sided dual-layer program is presented in letterboxed format on one layer, with an aspect ratio of about 1.85:1 and an accommodation for enhanced 16:9 playback, and in full screen format on the other layer. The cinematographer experimented a bit with color schemes for the film's three movements. The transfer appears to replicate this fairly well, though the image also seems a bit too soft at times. The stereo surround sound is passable. The 91 minute program also has a Spanish language track and optional English and Spanish subtitles.

Bound (Artisan, 46298)

A mob money thriller that uses lesbianism to provide a fresh twist on a dependable plot, Jennifer Tilly and Gina Gershon star as lovers who cook up a scheme to lift two million dollars from the mob, only to see their plan take a few unanticipated turns. The 1996 film is sexy and stylish, but most important of all, the narrative and characters keep the viewer involved in every scene. Much of the action may take place in one apartment, but you really feel like the film is taking you for an enjoyable ride.

The picture is in letterboxed format only, with an aspect ratio of about 1.85:1 and no 16:9 enhancement. The color transfer is okay. Fleshtones are a little too smooth, but hues are rich and contrasts are adequately detailed. The stereo surround sound doesn't have an elaborate mix, but it has its moments. There is also a Dolby Digital track, but the two are fairly similar. There is one tense sequence, however, where a bass heartbeat dominates the soundtrack, and here the Dolby Digital is able to pack more punch than the regular soundtrack. The 109 minute program also has a French language track in standard stereo, optional English and Spanish subtitles, and a trailer.

There is a commentary track, as well, with directors Andy and Larry Wachowski, actor Joe Pantoliano, editor Zach Staenberg and advisor Susie Bright. The talk is highly informative, decoding a lot of the film's lesbian symbolism for the uninitiated and discussing the reasoning behind various shots and actions, along with enjoyable anecdotes about the production. It begins to sag about halfway through, but then Tilly and Gershon show up and enliven the final third. It is especially amusing to hear the three actors joke about beating one another up and who fouled up what take.

The Boxer (Universal, 20240); DTS (Universal, 20467)

Included with Jim Sheridan's highly intelligent exploration of the troubles in Northern Ireland are two commentary channels, one by Sheridan and one by producer Arthur Lappin, along with a half hour documentary about making the film, cast profiles and production details, a trailer, and an astonishing 15 minutes of de-

leted footage. Daniel Day-Lewis stars as the title character, attempting to ply his trade during a very tense Belfast cease-fire. Emily Watson co-stars. The film is very involving and fresh, mixing in perfectly measured amounts a love story, a sports story and a detailed but fully accessible political analysis. Yet, as perfect as it seems, most of the footage revealed in the collection of deleted scenes would have made the film even better. Lost in the opening, for example, is a wonderful 4 minute sequence where a man who has been in prison for 14 years tries to walk home, discovering he cannot take the familiar routes because they have all been barricaded. Almost all of the footage enhances the backstory and tells the viewer more about the characters, without slowing things down and without seeming at all superfluous.

The film has been letterboxed, with an aspect ratio of about 1.85:1 and an accommodation for enhanced 16:9 playback. The picture transfer is excellent, with a consistently sharp focus and detailed colors. The stereo surround sound is good and the Dolby Digital track is even better, with a strong dimensionality, crisp separation effects and plenty of power. The film is also available in French and can be supported by English or Spanish subtitles. We found ourselves leaving the English subtitles on, to help navigate the Irish accents.

It is best to listen to Lappin's talk first, as he gives a basic history of the production, of the Irish troubles and an explanation of what is going on in the film. He also talks about Sheridan's working methods, though his comments become a bit sporadic after the first half hour. Sheridan's talk is more esoteric, rarely getting into production details, but we enjoyed it quite a bit anyway, because he has a lot to say about what inspired the film (it was based on true incidents and his own childhood in Northern Ireland), about other subjects (he suggests that the Spanish Civil War was the beginning of the end for communism) and his many memories of growing up amid the strife.

The DTS audio track is stronger than the standard DVD's Dolby Digital track, and tones are sharper, but the differences are slight and the delivery of the Dolby Digital track seems sufficient for the drama. The picture, however, is also improved. The frame transfer rate on the standard release stays in the upper mid range, while the transfer rate on the DTS release is in the low upper range, eliminating some scattered artifacting flaws. Fleshtones also look a little richer and better detailed. The picture is letterboxed, with an aspect ratio of about 1.85:1 (not 1.66:1, as is suggested on the jacket cover) and an accommodation for enhanced 16:9 playback. There are no supplemental features and no captioning.

A Boy and His Dog (Lumivision, DVD1197); (SlingShot, 9816)

The 1975 production was conceived and directed by the character actor L.Q. Jones, who speaks on a commentary track with prompting by film critic Charles Champlin and a few additional statements by the cinematographer, John Morrill. Jones has a folksy demeanor and is very pleasant to listen to. He explains why he approached the movie in the way that he did, tells the story of the film's production and analyzes why the film is so effective. The commentary is informative and enjoyable.

Parts of the movie take some getting used to, but it is a witty and intelligent work that accomplishes a great deal on what is obviously limited resources (the energized action scenes can also be seen as having been inspired by one of the directors Jones often worked for, Sam Peckinpah). Set on a desert landscape some time after a nuclear holocaust, the film is about a young man, played by Don Johnson, who has a telepathic bond with a dog, the latter basically being the smarter of the two. He helps the dog find food and the dog helps him sniff out women. The final third of the movie has an unusual shift in tone that can throw some viewers off, but on subsequent screenings the segment makes a great deal more sense than it seems at first. The film, and its memorable ending in particular, can be construed as misogynistic but, as Jones points out in the commentary, that is only a gut reaction. In reality, the hero and his mutt have no use for anybody, except each other.

The picture, which is letterboxed with an aspect ratio of about 2.35:1 and no 16:9 enhancement, is a bit battered. Scratches and even a few more prominent markings appear periodically throughout the presentation. Darker scenes are grainy and sometimes the hues are a little pale, but the image quality is stronger than previous efforts and the colors are reasonably accurate. The monophonic sound is also a little harsh, but workable, and is not captioned. Two trailers are also included with the 90 minute feature.

SlingShot's reissue is a full replication of Lumivision's DVD with an identical transfer, except that a Web access and SlingShot's logos have been added.

The Boy in the Plastic Bubble (D-Vision, DVD1001)

The picture quality is horrible. The colors are so faded that fleshtones are indistinguishable in hue from the clothing the characters are wearing. The image is fuzzy and almost monochromatic. The scratchy monophonic sound is hardly better and the music sounds hopelessly warped. John Travolta stars in the famous TV film, directed by Randal Kleiser, about a boy who grows up without an immune system. The film's verisimilitude is dubious, but it makes an engaging star vehicle for the young Travolta. The 1976 program runs 93 minutes, though reference sources list its correct running time at 100 minutes. It may just be time compressed. The program is not captioned.

Boyfriends and Girlfriends (Fox Lorber, FLV5100)

Eric Rohmer's delightful 1987 entry in his *Comedies & Proverbs* series (it is actually called *L'Ami de Mon Amie*, or "The Friends of My Friends"—as in "the friends of my friends are my friends") appears to be slightly time compressed. The program runs 98 minutes, while most versions runs 102 minutes. The colors are somewhat light, and weak contrasts create a mild grain in places. The presentation is in full screen format, though the framing looks okay. The monophonic sound is adequate and the program is supported by permanent white English subtitles.

Until a key moment near the end, the movie takes place in a world without cars. It is set in a campus-like mall and planned community called Cergy Pontoise, which is a healthy train ride outside of Paris. Although there are cars in the distance and the characters refer to their own autos at times, Rohmer appears to deliberately avoid street scenes. The characters are seen on the mall, in their homes, or at a park surrounding a lake. He creates an atmosphere that almost has a fairy tale feeling to it. The narrative concerns two young women who are in the process of settling into relationships. Rohmer asks a lot from his cast, placing them in very awkward situations and having them stutter and shift uneasily as they would in true social situations. The acting is at times off-putting, but, once the narrative gets going, the performances gather a real strength in conveying the emotions of the characters to the viewer. The film is a romance, and although it is very much like real life, it has an odd setting and a happy ending, making it a wonderful escape from the kind of real life most viewers are burdened with.

Boys on the Side (Warner, 13570)

Herbert Ross' 1995 feature is partly a female buddy movie and partly a drama about AIDS. Whoopi Goldberg, Mary-Louise Parker and Drew Barrymore star in the tale about three women who travel across the country, ending up in Tucson. One of them has the disease, the other two have other problems, and all three pitch in to meddle in each other's lives. There is little in the way of dramatic conflict, but the balance between humor and more serious emotions is well handled and after a slow start the characters and the film begin to grow on the viewer.

The 117 minute film is presented on one side in letterboxed format, with an aspect ratio of about 2.35:1 and an accommodation for enhanced 16:9 playback, and in full screen format on the other

side. The full screen image loses a little bit of picture information on the side and adds a substantial amount to the top and bottom in comparison to the letterboxed image, but we preferred the framing on the letterboxed version. Darker scenes remain a bit murky, but on the whole, the color transfer looks okay, especially in daylight sequences, and the image is sharp. The stereo surround sound is good. The dialogue is clear and there is a decent dimensionality to the music and atmospheric effects. There is also a French stereo soundtrack and the film can be supported by English or French subtitles.

Bram Stoker's Dracula (Columbia TriStar, 51419)

Anyone who has been in love for more than a couple of weeks can understand the appeal of romantic vampire films, specifically the attraction of taking passion to a higher spiritual and corporeal plane than reality is capable of providing. That appeal is captured in a grand theatrical style in Francis Coppola's superbly staged and vigorously executed 1992 production. The film, reminiscent more than anything else of John Boorman's *Excalibur*, is a culmination of the exploration in stage effects and sleights-of-hand that Coppola began in *One from the Heart*. Keanu Reeves, Winona Ryder, Anthony Hopkins and Gary Oldman star in the lavish, hypnotically compelling fantasy.

The picture is presented on one side in letterboxed format, with an aspect ratio of about 1.85:1 and an accommodation for enhanced 16:9 playback, and in cropped format on the other side. There is a bit of picture information added to the bottom of the image on the cropped version, but important imagery is often truncated from the side. The color transfer looks great. As well produced as they were, the LD versions could not handle the film's deepest and most illuminated hues, while the DVD maintains an essential sharpness regardless of how extensive the cinemtography's lighting and multiple exposure tricks become. The stereo surround sound is functional, but the Dolby Digital track is much better, with nicely detailed surround separations, a more energetic dimensionality and purer, sharper tones. The 130 minute program also has French and Spanish audio tracks in standard stereo, optional Spanish and Korean subtitles, and English closed captioning.

Although the character does pop up from time to time on the stage, it is film that has kept Dracula alive, and that is what Coppola is acknowledging with his visual trickery and expressionistic effects while, at the same time, he himself is contributing significantly to Dracula's immortality. Dealing as it does with a subject that is eternally entertaining, the film is a glorious melding of images, passions and excitements, and is ideal DVD fare.

Bram Stoker's The Mummy (Simitar, 7432)

A moderately entertaining tale of possession and greed, Louis Gossett, Jr. is top billed, but he just has a brief, showy part. Eric Lutes and Amy Locane star, attempting to determine why an important archeologist, the father of Locane's character, has fallen into a coma. The story is somewhat nonsensical, but the film manages to sustain a reasonably elegant atmosphere, while murders or other supernatural events occur with a dependable regularity. The picture is reasonably glossy and colors are smooth. The stereo surround sound is basic but dimensional, and there is a Dolby Digital track, though the two sound fairly similar with the Dolby Digital adding, at the most, slightly sharper separation effects. The 100 minute program is not captioned.

Bram Stoker's Shadowbuilder (Sterling, 7045)

A passable horror feature that takes advantage of the ever-lowering price of CGI effects has been issued with a really cool 3-D jacket cover. Set in the present day, the film is about a devil figure who can only survive in shadows—he breaks apart whenever he's confronted by direct light—and is trying to take the soul of a very special child. A 'black ops' priest (part of a secret Roman Catholic Church unit), played by Michael Rooker, rushes to save the boy.

Most of the action takes place in a small town that succumbs to barbarianism after the demon arrives. The special effects look fine and the narrative is reasonably interesting. The image is presented in full screen. The picture has a low budget look to it, with bland fleshtones and light hues, but the stereo surround sound isn't bad and a few effects, usually involving the demon, are fairly exhilarating. The 101 minute film can be supported by Spanish subtitles and is accompanied by a cast profile and a really good trailer. There is also a commentary channel by director Jamie Dixon, who explains how many of the scenes were staged and how the special effects were accomplished, but he also spends a lot of time just doing a play-by-play.

Branded to Kill (Criterion, BRA090)

The incomprehensible and totally compelling 1967 Seijun Suzuki film is in black and white, but it is otherwise exhilarating. The plot, about an assassin-for-hire, played by Shishido Joe, who has been targeted for elimination, is impossible to understand on the first viewing and irrelevant on subsequent viewings. The film's set pieces, however, are mesmerizing. He launches a balloon and times its ascent so he can kill somebody in a high-rise and then jump out the window to escape without hurting himself. For another victim, he unscrews the pipe beneath a sink, waits for the victim to wash his hands (or in this case, an eyeball—don't ask), shoots through the pipe and then screws it back. In an extended sequence near the end, he has a lengthy psych-out session with the killer who is supposed to eliminate him, as the two walk arm-in-arm and sleep in the same bed to keep an eye on one another in a glorious parody of the drawn out showdowns of yesteryear. The film also has rampant nudity and bizarre evocations (which may or may not be deliberate) of *The Passion of Joan of Arc*. The 91 minute feature is letterboxed with an aspect ratio of about 2.25:1 and no 16:9 enhancement. Contrasts are reasonably well detailed and the image is sharp, with minimal wear. The monophonic sound is a little noisy but workable. The film is in Japanese with optional English subtitles and includes an interview with Suzuki and a neat montage of Japanese movie posters.

Brassed Off (Buena Vista, 17252)

The very sweet movie is about a group of British coal miners facing permanent layoffs, and their dedication to participating in a brass band competition. The characters are wonderful and the film combines their stories with a strong political message against the closings of the mines (inadvertently, however, the film also supports the argument for closing them, by suggesting, basically, that they be kept open purely for sentimental reasons). The **Rocky**-like finale is made all the more spirited because of the number of characters involved that the viewer has grown close to during the course of the story. The music sounds great, too. Pete Postlethwaite (as the band leader), Tara Fitzgerald and Ewan McGregor (the romantic leads) star.

The film is letterboxed with an aspect ratio of about 1.85:1 and no 16:9 enhancement, though the top and bottom of the image look a bit tight at times. The colors are bright and the image is sharp. The stereo surround sound is adequate and the 101 minute film is effectively closed captioned, including an attempt to evoke the dialect with phonetic spelling.

The Brave One (Lumivision, DVD1697)

Except for a mild bluish tint in some of the darker parts of the screen, the Technicolor transfer is gorgeous, and there doesn't appear to be a single scratch or spot on the entire film. Shot in Cinemascope (Jack Cardiff was the cinematographer), the image is letterboxed with an aspect ratio of about 2.5:1 and no 16:9 enhancement. The rectangular compositions are outstanding. At one point a character runs across the screen, beginning at the bottom left as a small dot and ending on the right with his body arriving at the full height of the picture. The film was produced in stereo, and the DVD's restored stereo sound is also highly impressive. The mu-

sic has a fine dimensionality, giving the film an air of importance that nicely counterpoints the simplicity of the plot. The score, by Victor Young, has been isolated with the sound effects on another track. The 100 minute program is not closed captioned and is followed by an effective original theatrical trailer.

This is the film that earned blacklisted Dalton Trumbo a screenplay Oscar under a pen name. Directed by Irving Rapper, the shell of the plot tells the story of a young boy who raises a motherless calf and later tries to save the animal when it is sold for the bullfights. The 1956 film, however, is also a light-handed examination of property rights and other class-conflict issues. The action and sentimentality have an appeal that crosses all ages, and if the messages slip past at the same time, you're hardly going to want to drive a sword into them.

Brazil (Criterion, BRA100); (Universal, 20168)

Criterion's DVD is a massive and totally captivating three-platter exploration of Terry Gilliam's dark bureaucratic fantasy-comedy. The first platter contains the 142 minute 'European theatrical release cut' of the 1985 film, which also appears on the Universal DVD, with an identical picture and sound transfer, but without special features. The third platter features what Universal Pictures would have done with the film if they had gotten their way, a 97 minute cut, known as the 'Love Conquers All' version with a happy ending, that does show up occasionally on television. Gilliam provides commentary during the unspooling of the 142 minute version and journalist David Morgan provides audio commentary during the 97 minute version.

The middle platter contains a wealth of supplementary features, including a 30 minute 'making of' documentary that was shot during the film's production but has such an objective, non-commercial point-of-view you wouldn't believe it was made in 1985 if the filmmakers weren't sitting in the middle of the sets as they talked (it apparently won some awards); an outstanding 60 minute documentary, put together by film reporter Jack Mathews, about the conflict that developed between Gilliam and Universal after the film was in the can; and shorter interviews with screenwriters Tom Stoppard and Charles McKeown, production designer Norman Garwood, costume designer James Acheson and composer Michael Kamen, each coordinated with appropriate still frame material or other materials that relate to their specific contributions; and elaborate storyboards, exhaustive still photos, a comprehensive look at how the special effects were accomplished, and other odds and ends we've undoubtedly neglected to mention. Yet regardless of how complex and elaborate the mix of stills and motion footage becomes, the middle platter remains blissfully simple to navigate, and we hope every budding DVD producer in the future lines up to obtain a copy and see how it should be done. The menus are clearly delineated, the selections are easily identifiable, and the material is intuitively organized.

Although the picture quality on the main feature is identical to the Universal release, the frame transfer rate is a little higher, staying in midrange on the Universal version and favoring the upper-midrange on the Criterion version. The picture is letterboxed with an aspect ratio of about 1.85:1 and no 16:9 enhancement. The color transfer is excellent, with crisp hues and accurate fleshtones. The opening shot of a silver blue sky, framed by clouds, is startling in its purity and gem-like luster. The movie's images may be wildly varied in subject and tone, but the picture transfer is consistent and solid from beginning to end. The stereo surround sound, also identical to the Universal version and maintains a pleasing dimensionality. This version of the film can be supported by optional English subtitles. The picture quality on the 97 minute version is not as sharp, looking a bit hazier at times, with slightly more washed out colors.

The 142 minute version is letterboxed with an aspect ratio of about 1.85:1 and no 16:9 enhancement, while the 97 minute version is presented in full screen, as it appears on broadcast television. A comparison reveals that nothing is added to the sides of the picture and picture information has been masked off the top and bottom of the letterboxed version. In the behind-the-scenes shots of the editing room and elsewhere, however, it is clearly demonstrated that the movie was composed with the 1.85:1 masking in mind. While the production design is such that the full screen image delivers small but enjoyable details masked off in the letterboxed version, the framing is better balanced on the letterboxed version and the emotional impact of its images is stronger.

The stereo surround sound on the 142 minute version is in fine shape. Although the mix lacks the power of more recent productions, the ambiance it conveys is satisfying. Again, the stereo on the 97 minute version is less impressive. The mix seems more oriented to the center and is less forceful. The 142 minute version has optional English subtitles, while the 97 minute version and the documentaries are not subtitled.

Jonathan Pryce stars as a bureaucrat, living in a sort of nightmare alternate universe filled with impractical technology, who begins to challenge the system after he catches sight of the 'girl of his dreams.' The dreams, which punctuate the action, contain an even more fantastic series of images and situations. Robert De Niro and Michael Palin co-star, with Katherine Helmond, Bob Hoskins and Kim Greist. The 142 minute cut plays more smoothly than the 131 minute cut represented by the eventual U.S. theatrical release. There are no major thematic differences between the two, but the rhythm of the longer version has a clear design to it, while scenes where footage has been removed tend to feel more abrupt and alienating. Since the film's subject matter—oppression, torture, hopelessness—is in such a delicate balance with the whimsies that hold a viewer's sympathies to it, anything that corrodes its emotional precision harms it significantly. One of the advantages of DVD is that if you really make the commitment to work your way through all of its features—it took us two days—you'll come out of it appreciating the film greatly, regardless to how you felt about it when you went in.

The 97 minute version is also worth viewing, though you have to clear your mind of the legitimate version before taking it on. It isn't just a trimmed down feature. The editors at Universal had access to the dailies and, in a number of sequences, used alternate cuts or footage that never appeared in Gilliam's versions to give the movie an entirely different, optimistic tone. What they hoped to do was cash in on the film's fantastic designs. Although the dream sequences are gone, most of the major set pieces remain, and the movie has been given a ridiculous happy ending. There is one critical transition near the conclusion that fails because, since it was never his intention, Gilliam did not film an appropriate get-the-characters-from-here-to-there sequence, so it is highly doubtful that Universal's cut would have done more or even equal business in comparison to Gilliam's version, but the lengths to which they went in trying are amazing. Morgan's commentary, which does have moderate gaps here and there, identifies the principal differences and explains in impressive detail how these changes affect the movie's tone. We were disappointed, however, that Morgan fails to point out one significant blemish in the movie's final shot, leftover from the 131 minute film, of the torture platform jutting into the heavenly sky—a hint, perhaps, that not everything is as happy as it looks.

The detail Criterion goes into covering the film's production history is also incredible. Within the still frames, there are pictures of everything from the forms and cheques used as props in the movie to the usual collection of publicity and production photos. Every aspect of the movie's production is covered in detail—but, and we can't emphasize this enough, a detail that never overstays its welcome. Because the movie's budget was limited—relatively speaking—the filmmakers used real locations instead of soundstage sets for most of the production. How these locations were dressed and altered is explained, and stills detailing the development of the production designs and costumes are provided. With a

combination of motion clips, still photos, drawings and text, the special effects are broken down and explained. A text summary and a storyboard for each of the movie's dream sequences are also provided, including several that did not make the final cut.

Through extensive paraphrasing, the five major screenplay drafts are described, detailing the contributions each made to the final film and how each varied from the next. Although this sequence of still frames takes a couple of hours to read, it is much more stimulating than a simple re-creation of the original screenplay and gives the viewer a decent understanding of the process of creative development undergone for the film.

Acheson narrates the costume sequence, talking about the wardrobes being depicted in montage. Kamen's sequence is more of a talking head interview, but his stories of how Gilliam persuaded him to work on the score (even though he had to link it to the song the movie was named for) are wonderful and the technical detail he provides about the music is enlightening.

The 'making of' documentary works best as an introduction to the still frames and these other production sequences, giving the viewer a close look at the personalities contributing to the film and providing an overview to the different production components. Palin's interview is especially funny. Gilliam's audio commentary, which rarely feels redundant in relation to the rest of the DVD's supplement, emphasizes the day-to-day production challenges and the contributions of his collaborators. At one point he provides a very reflective and sensitive analysis of how preview screenings should and should not be used by a filmmaker, pointing out that it is easier for a movie company to browbeat a vulnerable director than to market a complex film. Although he has 142 minutes to speak he sometimes has to talk very fast to get in everything he wants to say about a specific sequence before it is over.

If you take two lines that are extending at just slightly different angles, they eventually spread far apart from one another, and that is basically what happened between Gilliam and the head of Universal, Sid Sheinberg. We recommend saving Mathew's documentary about the fight over the movie's release for the very end, because, next to the movie itself, it is the best part of the DVD. The documentary covers both sides of the argument objectively and crosscuts between the two sides a lot, giving the viewer a chance to see both the flaws and the strengths of each side.

Sheinberg loved the movie. As he points out, if he hadn't liked it, he wouldn't have gone to so much trouble to try and make it marketable. **Brazil**, however, was simply too abstract to be reconstructed by anybody except the original artist, and so Sheinberg was in way over his head as soon as he started trying. Gilliam, on the other hand, likely feeling the stress of a long and arduous shoot, stopped trying to work within the system and declared war on Universal, directing his volleys (through the press) directly at Sheinberg. Everybody seems to deny it, but the publicity from this war probably enabled the movie to earn more money on its initial theatrical release (and turn a small profit) than it would have under any other conceivable set of circumstances. The irony here is not lost on the participants. By indulging in a self-destructive rebellion against the corporation, Gilliam was substantially duplicating the actions of his film's hero. And although Sheinberg claims there is no parallel because a corporation is not like a government ('Now who's being naive, Kay?' to quote from another famous movie), his good intentions turned into misguided actions as absurd as any in the film. But Gilliam was wrong to try and personalize it, picking on Sheinberg when the real problem was that he had made a movie Universal could not sell.

Brazil is not a simple film, and its production history was not a straightforward affair, but Criterion's exhaustive DVD not only details every aspect of how it came into being, but thoroughly explores every attribute of its artistry. In the beginning, Gilliam hammered out his ideas and brought together the personnel he needed to turn his fantasy into a film. Fearing a marketing nightmare but loving what Gilliam had accomplished, Universal tried to take it away from him and, at the very least, generated a lot of free publicity by failing to do so. Those who already admire the film will be overwhelmed by the wealth of insight and revelation Criterion has brought to it, and those who dislike or are indifferent to the film need only study the DVD to undergo a complete change of heart, learning not only about the extent to which film can replicate the imagination, but how art can survive and thrive in a world of commerce. At last, and thanks to the DVD, the movie has a true happy ending.

Universal's version is accompanied by a theatrical trailer, a brief production note section and a good cast profile section. The film can also be supported by English, French or Spanish subtitles ("Qui a réparé vos conduits?").

Breakdown (Paramount, 334547)

There are two things that can go wrong with a disappearing wife plot. The solution to the mystery can be ridiculous ('she had cholera') or the ending can go flaccid (Roman Polanski's **Frantic**). **Breakdown**, starring Kurt Russell, avoids both those problems. The solution to the mystery is utterly logical and believable, and the finale is marvelous, an ideal splurge of action and excitement to compound and relieve the tension that has preceded it. The film is a wonderful suspense thriller with a high repeat potential and it makes a great DVD.

The picture is letterboxed with an aspect ratio of about 2.35:1 and no 16:9 enhancement. The image is very sharp and colors are bright (the film is set on highways in the Southwest). Fleshtones are accurate and thoroughly detailed. The stereo surround sound is fairly good and there is a Dolby Digital track that is very good, with greater rear channel activity and more punch. The 93 minute film is also available in French in standard stereo and can be supported by English or Spanish subtitles. A well-designed theatrical trailer is also included.

Breaker Morant (Fox Lorber, FLV5002)

Bruce Beresford's 1979 adaptation of a stage drama is based upon a true occurrence. Jack Thompson, Edward Woodward and Bryan Brown star in the courtroom drama, with action flashbacks, about a group of Australian soldiers in the Boer War who are court-marshaled, for executing POWs, as a face-saving measure for the British high command (ever notice how Australians always get the bum end of the deal in war movies?).

The image transfer looks very good. The film naturally has a dusty brown color scheme, but fleshtones are accurate and other hues are crisp. The presentation is letterboxed with an aspect ratio of about 1.85:1 and no 16:9 enhancement. The monophonic sound is fine. The 107 minute film is accompanied by a small cast and crew profile, and a theatrical trailer.

The Breakfast Club (Universal, 20210)

Emilio Estevez, Anthony Michael Hall, Judd Nelson, Molly Ringwald and Ally Sheedy star in John Hughes' single-set stageplay-like drama, about five high school kids enduring a Saturday detention. They get to know one another and break down the presupposed stereotypes each has of the others. None of it is all that inspiring, but a certain age group responded to it and that age group is now definitely old enough to have purchased their first DVD players and to have gone in search of nostalgic programming.

The picture quality is fine, with solid hues and accurate fleshtones. The image is letterboxed, with an aspect ratio of about 1.85:1 and no 16:9 enhancement. The monophonic sound lacks the energy a stereo mix would have but is reasonably strong and delivers the pop music score with confidence. The 92 minute film is also available in Spanish or French and comes with English or Spanish subtitles. There are some interesting production notes and a cast profile, so you can find out how each performer's career went downhill afterward, but we could not figure out how to access the Hughes profile.

Bride of Chucky (Universal, 20521)

Hong Kong veteran Ronny Yu directed the fourth installment in the 'killer doll' horror series. There is a very Asian setting near the end, a graveyard amid reeds in a wintry wind, and the film is a nice shift in gears from the standard Chucky movies. The narrative has been trimmed a little for pacing, but if you get past the basic, silly-as-all-get-out premise of serial murderers being reincarnated in malevolent-looking dolls, the film can be enjoyable. Jennifer Tilly stars as one of the murderer's former girlfriends, who resuscitates the villain after his final supposedly be-all-and-end-all demise in the previous film. To say more would spoil things but eventually there are two dolls for twice the fun. Yu bring energy and a strong sense of humor to the production, without skimping on the gore.

The DVD has an entire toy chest of extra features. There are two commentary tracks, a very good 'making of' featurette that shows how many of the special effects were achieved, an interesting 'diary' by Tilly about shooting the film, which originally appeared in Premiere magazine, and a concise summary of the previous Chucky films. Tilly's diary, which appears handwritten in a legible script, can also be printed through a DVD-ROM QuickTime utility. The picture is letterboxed, with an aspect ratio of about 1.85:1 and an accommodation for enhanced 16:9 playback. The image transfer is excellent, with bright, clearly defined colors and a crisp details in even the darkest sequences. The stereo surround sound and Dolby Digital sound are not as elaborate as a larger budgeted production, but they offer many engaging moments. The Dolby Digital track is a little smoother and a little better detailed than the standard track, although the two are fairly similar. The 89 minute film is also available in French in standard stereo and can be supported by English or Spanish subtitles ("'¿Tienes una goma?' '¿Que si tengo una goma?' 'Sí.' 'Tiffany.' '¿Qué?' '¡Mirame! ¡oy de goma!'"). On one of the commentary channels, Yu talks about the production and how certain effects were achieved, though he runs out of steam after the first half hour or so, making only intermittent comments beyond that point. The second channel, with Tilly, Brad Dourif (who voices Chucky) and screenwriter-producer Don Mancini in a group talk, is a lot more satisfying. They say plenty about how various sequences were shot, share many amusing anecdotes about the shoot, and have a great time reacting to the film.

The Bride with White Hair (Tai Seng, 45224)
The Bride with White Hair 2 (Tai Seng, 45234)

A rousingly bloody romance set in feudal China, with wild martial arts sequences and touches of the supernatural, **Bride with White Hair** is based upon a popular legend. The 92 minute film has mild *Romeo & Juliet* overtones and is about two kung-fu masters in rival clans who fall in love. The fight scenes are great—the heroine has a whip that cuts people in half—and the narrative is sufficient to keep the viewer involved and alert. Concluding on sort of an emotional cliffhanger, the hero and heroine are separated at the end of the first film, and the heroine turns bitter. The film's stylized images and unusual camera angles are highly pleasing, making the film enjoyable even during the rare instances where the action slows down. In the sequel, her minions are busy killing all the hero's relatives, trying to end his bloodline, and it is up to a couple of nephews to stop her. **2** appears to have had a smaller budget. The fight scenes are less elaborately staged and there are fewer of them. Although the gore is reasonably widespread, the actual glimpses of action are brief and the continuity is weak. Still, for those who can't stand seeing the story stop in the first film without an emotional closure, **The Bride with White Hair 2**, which runs 80 minutes, should satiate. Both movies were produced in 1993 and star Brigitte Lin Ching Hsia and Leslie Cheung.

The first movie is letterboxed with an aspect ratio of about 2.35:1 and the second with an aspect ratio of about 1.85:1. Neither have 16:9 enhancement. The color transfers look fairly good. The image on both movies is a bit soft, especially where intense hues are involved, but colors are generally bright and nicely detailed, and fleshtones are passable. On both, there is an occasional stray scratch, but never enough damage to create a distraction. The Dolby Digital monophonic sound on the films has some slight distortion at the upper end but is in adequate condition for the presentation. The films are presented in English, Cantonese and Mandarin, and can be supported by optional English subtitles. Each is accompanied by original trailers and trailers for other Tai Seng products, and each has a decent cast & crew profile section.

The first movie is accompanied by a 12-minute 'making of' featurette. Director Ronny Yu's provides commentary on **Bride with White Hair**, but it becomes sporadic after the first quarter of an hour. He has a number of interesting things to say, however, about low budget Hong Kong filmmaking, such as how he staged a battle using just four horses, and the intentions of the imagery, such how the sequence where he has a character bouncing around the room was inspired by a pinball machine.

The Bridge of San Luis Rey (Image, ID365FWDVD)

Based upon the novel by Thornton Wilder, the story is about a young singer in colonial Peru who attracts the romantic attentions of the Viceroy, putting her relationship with a young sailor in jeopardy. The film retains some of the fable-like qualities of Wilder's writing, but it lacks the depth of introspection that would give it a true philosophical bite, and it remains little more than a partial, linear interpretation of Wilder's work and fairly light entertainment. Louis Calhern, Akim Tamiroff and Lynn Bari are featured in the 1944 production.

The image remains a bit soft and blacks are not deep, but the presentation is still quite satisfying, particularly in comparison to how the film has looked in the past. The source material has a few stray markings, but is fairly clean overall, and contrasts are nicely detailed. The monophonic sound is a bit scratchy, but workable. The 108 minute program is not captioned.

A Bridge Too Far (MGM, 906757)

The 1977 feature, awkwardly peppered with stars, tells the story of an Allied surge into The Netherlands during World War II that fell short of its ultimate goal. Clunkily directed by Richard Attenborough, the film is overloaded with stars, including Sean Connery, Robert Redford, James Caan, Ryan O'Neal, Laurence Olivier, Dirk Bogarde, Anthony Hopkins, Michael Caine and Gene Hackman, to name a few. Within the 176 minute running time there are a number of pleasing sequences and plenty of good gunfights, but the film, like the campaign it depicts, never coalesces.

The letterboxing has an aspect ratio of about 2.35:1, with an accommodation for enhanced 16:9 playback. Although there is substantial speckling on the source material throughout much of the film and colors are a little soft, hues and fleshtones are reasonably accurate. The stereo surround sound does not have the sort of mix it would receive these days, but there is some dimensionality and some good booms. The film is also available in French in mono and can be supported by English or French subtitles ("Vous le savez, j'ai toujours pensé qu'on essayait d'alle un pont trop loin"). There is also a trailer.

The Bridges of Madison County (Warner, 13772)

Clint Eastwood and Meryl Streep star in the slow moving story of a farmer's wife who has a three-night stand with a visiting photographer. The film is intelligent and explores the meanings of romantic attraction in a consistently believable fashion, but for the most part it left us cold. Eastwood directed the 135 minute drama, as well.

Colors and fleshtones are rich, and the image is sharp and clear. The image is presented in full screen format, adding picture information to the top and bottom, and taking very little off the sides in comparison to letterboxed picture on the weaker looking LD. By and large, we like the look of the full screen framing better. The

stereo surround sound and Dolby Digital mix are rarely interesting, and the film is presented French in standard stereo.

Brigadoon (MGM, 906560)

The film was made with Ansco color instead of the more reliable Technicolor, and there is just so much which can be done with it. Since costumes and art direction seem to constitute one half of the appeal of a Vincente Minnelli film, even the best transfer will seem dry and sleepy. Having logged that consideration, let us say that the color transfer is lovely, and that the color scheme of the movie, in its own way, is haunting. Hues are reasonably strong and the image is reasonably sharp. The 108 minute film is presented in letterboxed format only, with an aspect ratio of about 2.35:1 and no 16:9 enhancement. The stereo sound is has a forceful presence and an engaging dimensionality. The 108 minute program can be accompanied by English, French or Spanish subtitles ("Et je vais l'épouser/Ma chère petite Jeanne").

Gene Kelly, Van Johnson and Cyd Charisse star in the Lerner & Loewe musical, directed by Vincente Minnelli, about a magical Scottish town. We like **Brigadoon**. It is not a great movie, but it is a nice one. However, whenever we sit through it, we can't stop our mind from wandering, and imagining a comedy skit, "Brigadoon II: The Following Week," where a succession of crazier and crazier characters wander into the village as each day progresses.

A Bright Shining Lie (HBO, 91220)

One of the best books we ever read about Vietnam, written by Neil Sheehan, was turned into a cable film written and directed by Terry George. A biography of Lt. Colonel John Paul Vann, who was, off and on, involved in the war from 1962 until he was killed in a helicopter crash in 1972 (he became, through a very unusual appointment, a 'civilian' two-star general), the reason we admired it so much is that Vann saw everything first hand, from the horror and confusion of the battlefield to the political strategies in the Oval Office, and he understood what he was seeing. The moral quagmire of the war also reflected the moral quagmire of his personal life, but the 118 minute film is unable to do more than touch the surface of this concept.

The film is very different from almost all other Vietnam movies. There are terrific action scenes, with enough gore and explosions to please genre fans, but there is also a deft, sober look at the political complexity of America's involvement with the South Vietnamese, with a clear concept of what strategies worked, at least in the short term, and what did not. It's an involving film and we wish it had been a miniseries instead, because whenever it jumps over a segment of time, summarizing events or incidents with brief conversations, we felt a letdown. But the movie is also a disappointment because the star, Bill Paxton, sleepwalks through his role as Vann. He says his lines flatly and without expression, exuding none of the charisma or energy a person in Vann's position would have to utilize to succeed. It's like he's slumming in cable, and his apathy takes the shine off of what could have been an important and memorable historical drama.

The picture quality looks quite good. Fleshtones are accurate, other hues are bright and the image is sharp. The stereo surround sound has a cable quality mix, but in the heat of battle, it is still fairly rousing. There is an alternate Spanish audio track, optional English and Spanish subtitles, a decent 4 minute 'making of' featurette, and a cast & crew profile section.

Brighton Beach Memoirs (Image, ID4295USDVD)

Blythe Danner and Judith Ivey star in the 1986 nostalgia comedy about family interactions and independence set in Brooklyn in the Thirties. Neil Simon's mildly autobiographical story is a predictable mixture of memory and cliché, but it is well intentioned and contains a witty collection of one-liners.

As is indicated by the windowboxed title sequence, the rest of the program is slightly cropped, and it is enough to make the image framing seem awkward and distracting. The color transfer looks good, with accurate fleshtones, bright hues and a sharp focus. The monophonic sound is okay, and there is a Dolby Digital mono track that is even cleaner and better detailed. Although there is no indication on the jacket cover, the 110 minute program is closed captioned with some paraphrasing.

Broadway at the Hollywood Bowl (see Jerry Herman's Broadway at the Hollywood Bowl)

Broken Arrow (Fox, 4110420)

John Travolta stars in John Woo's spectacular rollercoaster of a film as the villain, an Air Force pilot who has hijacked a pair of atomic weapons, and Christian Slater is the hero, the co-pilot who has enough wits and stamina to keep fudging the villain's plans. There is even a major female character, played by Samantha Mathis, who assists Slater's character and provides a minor emotional dimension to the action. It is the action, however, that makes the movie such a great disc. Like an old-fashioned serial, the film, reminiscent of **Speed** and the Indiana Jones movies, comes up with one cliffhanger after another. Woo's gifted hand, with his impenetrable but successful formula of mixing film speeds, combined with his you-are-there camera angles, prevents any of these sequences from seeming at all routine or seeming like anything short of pulse-pounding popcorn ecstasy.

The DVD has such a good looking picture and such fabulous sound that there are probably only a handful of theaters in the world where the movie looked and sounded better than it will on your own audio-video system. The colors are consistently sharp no matter how complex the lighting becomes and fleshtones are flawless. The image is letterboxed with an aspect ratio of about 2.4:1 and an accommodation for enhanced 16:9 playback.

The film's sound mix packs a lot of punch and the sound is still quite enjoyable, particularly the highly detailed Dolby Digital track. The film is also available in French in standard stereo and can be supported by English or Spanish subtitles. A trailer has also been included with the 108 minute feature.

Broken Blossoms (Image, ID4720DSDVD)

D.W. Griffith's 1918 effort is about an Asian immigrant in London and a street urchin. Lillian Gish is the urchin. The 1918 film is less elaborate than many of Griffith's efforts and is a bit of an emotional downer (with non-PC references to the Asian character, too), but Griffith's masterful staging and sense of pace pull the viewer through the action effectively. The film is easier to take on subsequent viewings, when you are better prepared for its downward spiral. For Griffith, the film is reasonably subdued, using only a half dozen sets and no subplots.

The image is not windowboxed. The picture is heavily tinted in places, but the tinting seems to add to the film's emotions while helping to disguise the more obvious wear marks. Details are still reasonably sharp. The monophonic musical score, which has a kind of Salvation Army Band sound to it at times, is adequate. The film runs 89 minutes.

A Bronx Tale (HBO, 90954)

In Robert De Niro's maiden directoral effort, De Niro also stars as the father of a boy who grows up in the Bronx during the Sixties. The boy befriends a mob chieftain, creating an obvious dichotomy being presented between the hardworking father and the slick mobster. The film's screenplay was based upon a stageplay and both were written by Chazz Palminteri, who also has the movie's juiciest role as the mobster. Ending in a funeral parlor where the characters explain the plot by taking turns talking to a corpse about life, the 1993 drama has some nice nostalgic touches and a good feel for neighborhood dynamics, but it is an aimless and unenlightening work and the further one is from the Bronx, spiritually, the less interested in it one will be.

The picture is in letterboxed format only, with an aspect ratio of about 1.85:1 and no 16:9 enhancement. It adds nothing to the sides and masks picture information off the top and bottom in comparison to full screen versions. Although the framing looks nice in some sequences, there are just as many where it looks cramped and, generally, we prefer the standard version. Fleshtones are a bit dull in places and contrasts are somewhat limited, but hues are accurate in well lit sequences and the focus is reasonably sharp. There is some mild artifacting in darker sequences, however. The stereo surround sound and Dolby Digital sound are competently mixed. The 122 minute feature also has a French language track in standard stereo, a Spanish track in mono, optional English, French and Spanish subtitles, a trailer, TV commercials and a 6 minute 'making of' featurette, showing De Niro behind the camera.

Bruckner: Symphony No. 8 (Image, ID5434CLDVD)

Anton Bruckner's sweeping *Symphony No. 8* is performed by a pastiche of the world's greatest orchestras. Pieced together with representatives from many orchestras around the world, The 'World Philharmonic Orchestra,' conducted by Carlo Maria Giulini, performs in Stockholm at a charity concert. The orchestra seems to improve on its cohesion and precision as the work advances, and the Third and Fourth movements are superbly executed.

The program runs 95 minutes, including several opening speeches. The picture is somewhat soft and the direction is not very creative, but the visual presentation is functional. The PCM stereo is fairly sharp and conveys the orchestra's range effectively.

Brute Force (Image, ID5745MKDVD)

Burt Lancaster stars in Jules Dassin's 1947 Universal-International prison drama. The cast includes Charles Bickford, Howard Duff and Whit Bissell (the first screen appearances for the latter two) as convicts festering inside a corrupt penitentiary, with Hume Cronyn in the film's most memorable role, as a sadistic and power-hungry assistant warden. Although newer prison films have superseded the movie in terms of realism and thematic depth, the drama remains a gripping and potently nihilistic tale of incarceration.

The black-and-white picture transfer is very good, looking sharp most of the time with solid blacks and very little damage. The image is crisp and there are no more than a handful of scattered speckles. Contrasts are nicely detailed. The monophonic sound is okay. The 96 minute program is not captioned. A 4 minute montage of still photos and pressbook materials has also been included, presented in montage to a reprise of Miklos Rozsa's energetic musical score. There are also a few comprehensive filmographies.

Bubblegum Crisis (AnimEigo, BCDV101)

Acknowledging the proliferation of DVD drives installed in personal computers, the Japanese animation series has been released on three platters in what looks like a computer software box jacket. The DVDs contain no specific ROM material, however, just the show's six episodes (most of which run about 40 minutes or so) and some music videos. The seminal series is about a group of female vigilantes who battle cyborg robots in a futuristic metropolis. The animation is often stiff, and artistically the show is a little dated—the nudity and gore are also fairly calm—but the episodic narrative is reasonably intelligent, the basic concept—women in super hero suits on motorcycles kicking butt—is still very appealing, and the 1987 program essentially set a trend that many others would follow.

The episodes are presented in both English and Japanese, with optional English or French subtitles. The English and Japanese audio tracks are quite different from one another, with different music and sound effects. The stereo sound is adequate, with a reasonable amount of power and some separation effects. The earliest episodes look a bit worn on the DVD, with weak colors and soft edges, but later episodes are fresher and sharper in appearance. Colors are generally accurate, but lack intensity.

The first platter features *Episode 1, Tinsel City*, which runs about 40 minutes, and *Episode 2, Born to Kill* and *Episode 3, Blow Up*, each of which run about 25 minutes. The episodes have a vaguely progressive narrative and so it is best to see them in order. The women, who all have normal day jobs, dress in fancy armored suits at night and battle bionic robots who are tearing up the city and driving the police nuts. Within each episode the villains attempt to achieve a specific goal and are defeated by the heroines, though always at a cost. The show has a moderately sophisticated political viewpoint, depicting the ability of a multi-national corporation to exceed the grasp of a local government. It is essentially a comic book with movement, however, and the editing sometimes does not seem to have progressed beyond the storyboards, forcing the viewer to infer many of the details within an action scene. The show's soundtrack is supported by an engaging Japanese rock score that blasts away when the characters are not blasting each other.

The second platter features a three 40 minute episodes: *Episode 4, Revenge Road, Episode 5, Moonlight Rambler* and *Episode 6, Red Eyes*. The narratives are fast paced and dense, and plot points are sometimes explained in flashback long after the pertinence of their utility has subsided. If you stick with it, everything eventually makes sense, but it takes some patience to see it through. In this context, *Revenge Road* is the most accessible episode, about a young man who is driving around in a souped-up car and bashing hoodlums in revenge for the harm they did to his girlfriend. In the other two episodes, which form a two-part narrative, the heroines battle illegal super-robots that have been developed by a mega-corporation. In the first part, two mysterious women crash land in a space shuttle, and the heroines find themselves in the middle of a secret but intense search by some very powerful forces. In the adeptly escalated second part, the heroines are suddenly the only obstacles standing in the way of an all-powerful being bent upon world dominance.

The third platter contains two complete 45 minute episodes, *Episode 7, Double Vision* and *Episode 8, Scoop Chase*, and two collections of music videos derived from the series. In *Vision*, a spider-like robot is used to abduct a scientist. The heroes must determine whether they should support or stand against the robot's activities. A visiting rock star is also linked to the activities of the robot. Provided one is familiar with the previous episodes, the entry is highly satisfying and ties up several emotional loose ends. In *Chase*, a renegade scientist attempts to measure the limitations of the heroes' special fighting suits in order to construct robots that will destroy them. At the same time, a young photographer attempting to uncover the heroes' secret identities coincidentally befriends one of them. In both episodes, the action scenes are a bit easier to follow than in earlier entries, while the narratives, somewhat less ambitious than the previous tales, are more accessible. Some of the videos feature clips from various episodes, some feature the Japanese girl rock groups who recorded the songs used in the program, performing live, and some have mildly altered series footage and token original art.

Buck Privates (Image, ID4267USDVD)
Buck Privates Come Home (Image, ID4285USDVD)

The classic Bud Abbott and Lou Costello service comedy was produced in 1941, on the eve of WWII, and also features the Andrew Sisters, who introduced that unusually enduring hit, *The Boogie Woogie Bugle Boy*. The black-and-white picture is not as vivid as the best looking transfers, and the source material has some scattered wear, but there are no significant flaws. Blacks are reasonably deep. The monophonic sound has a limited range but is reasonably free of overt wear. The 84 minute film is not captioned.

The post-War sequel, in which the two attempt to adopt a war orphan, has a consistently smooth and crisp black-and-white image. The monophonic sound is workable, and is captioned. The 1947 77 minute feature culminates in an elaborate automobile race.

Bud Abbott & Lou Costello in the Foreign Legion
(Universal, ID4298USDVD)

It's fun in the faux desert on the 1950 feature, a typical but enjoyable Abbott & Costello effort, with the comedians searching Algeria for a star wrestler and getting mixed up with Arabian spies. There is a classic mirage sequence, a cute bit about a fish with false teeth and plenty of other amusements.

The black-and-white source material is in good condition and the image is reasonably smooth, with sharp contrasts. The monophonic sound is okay. The 79 minute program is not closed captioned.

Buffet Froid (Fox Lorber, FLV5031)

Bertrand Blier's very abstract murder comedy is letterboxed with an aspect ratio of about 1.7:1 and no 16:9 enhancement. The colors are bright and the image is sharp, with pale but accurate fleshtones, though pure whites have a slightly yellowish tone. The monophonic sound is crisp and is free of significant distortion. The 95 minute film is in French with optional yellow English subtitles.

Structured like a dream, with a constantly changing sense of immediacy, the film dryly embraces various murder thriller clichés as the three central characters, played by Gérard Depardieu, Bernard Blier and Jean Carmet, find themselves embroiled in a variety of conflicts. Some viewers will find the artificial narrative and performances too alienating, but because of its enigmatic story, the film does have a strong repeat potential and is ideal home video fare.

A Bug's Life (Buena Vista, 16698)

The outstanding computer animation feature has been issued as a single-sided dual-layer program, with a letterboxed presentation on one layer and a full screen presentation on the other, the full screen version having been digitally altered to improve its composition and framing. Don't get too excited though. The picture still looks cramped, and the emotional flow of the images is not as smooth. The bird, for example, is too big to fit properly in the full screen version, so it isn't as realistic or as involving as it is on the letterboxed version. About the only advantage to the full screen version is that it fills your monitor with the exquisite picture.

Do get excited over the sticker on the jacket that claims **Bug's Life** is the "World's First DVD Created Directly From The Digital Source." The image quality is breathtaking, and the backgrounds have a photo-realistic vividness that is astounding. Every color is exact and solid, creating incredibly real perspectives and textures. The letterboxing has an aspect ratio of about 2.35:1 and no 16:9 enhancement.

The film's narrative, an uncredited adaptation of **Seven Samurai**, only with klutzes, is inspired, and the characters are amusing. The stereo surround sound is okay and the Dolby Digital track has a stronger dimensionality and more thrust. The film's sound mix is not intense, but there is a decent amount of detail and flourish. The 95 minute feature can be supported by English subtitles. There is a trailer, and the film's original end credit sequence is replayed, along with an alternate end sequence, released after the initial one became so popular, that contains a different set of gags.

Bull Durham (Image, ID40780RDVD)

The first two-thirds are fantastic and although by the time of the seventh-inning stretch the story is basically finished, the mop up operation doesn't stop the movie from being a winner. It is rare that a film about baseball actually plays as baseball literature or the best color commentary, and rarer still that it can do so and still appeal to a wide audience. **Durham** is amazingly innovative, with a gutsy, voice-over stream-of-consciousness that not only tells one what the players are thinking on the mound or at the plate, but really, accurately sounds like the voice in one's head during such moments. The non-sex parts of the plot use the standard coach-takes-raw-talent-and-grows-while-processing-it genre, but disguises it by changing the coach into just another player. As for the sex, well everyone knows you're suppose to think about baseball…and **Bull Durham** is home video that was designed with rainouts in mind.

Even in the DVD format, where badly transferred movies look okay and the best transfers look fantastic, **Bull Durham** is exceptional. The image is so solid, so detailed and so vivid it is unnerving, and indeed if the DVD has any flaw it is that it looks too good—we were so busy marveling at the incredible texture and realness of each camera angle we sometimes neglected to pay total attention to the drama. The picture is letterboxed with an aspect ratio of about 1.85:1 and an accommodation for enhanced 16:9 playback. The stereo surround sound is adequate. The 1988 film's sound mix is functional, but it does not have an elaborate energy, and so what is missing on the DVD's audio is not critical to the movie's entertainment and is more than outweighed by the advantages of the image. There is also a commentary track featuring the director, Ron Shelton, who talks about making the film, about baseball, about working with the cast and about aspects of the story that are not readily evident on the screen. He also has some strong opinions about the nature of popular film and readily identifies and analyzes the technical mistakes he made. The 108 minute program can be supported by English subtitles and is accompanied by filmographies for the cast and for Shelton. Kevin Costner, Susan Sarandon and Tim Robbins star.

Bulletproof (Universal, 20276)

Damon Wayans is a cop and Adam Sandler is a crook-turned-mob-witness who has become the target of assassins. The two, however, have a shared past and must get over their animosities if they are to survive. Most viewers would probably be able to live without some of Sandler's baser humor and all the gay jokes, and the plot is fairly simple, but the two comedians have a strong, easy confidence in front of the camera, the action scenes are executed with wit and the film is good fun if you like this sort of thing.

The picture has bright, sharp colors and accurate fleshtones. The image is letterboxed with an aspect ratio of about 2.35:1, with an accommodation for enhanced 16:9 playback. The stereo surround sound is bland, but the Dolby Digital track is stronger although, like the standard track, rear channel effects are limited. The 85 minute 1998 film is also available in French in standard stereo and comes with English or Spanish subtitles, along with some production notes, a cast profile section and a theatrical trailer.

Bullets Over Broadway (Buena Vista, 16789)

The colors are incredible on Woody Allen's 1994 comedy. Carlo DiPalma's outstanding cinematography is unlike anything that has been accomplished before, giving every scene in the Jazz Age period film the look of an old painted photograph. It probably comes across as a mess on video cassette, but the DVD replication is perfect (in the very last scene, there is an inexcusable hole in the image, but you only see it for a flash) and the effect is enchanting.

Allen's script, written with Douglas McGrath, is also outstanding, about the problems besetting a young playwright when a gangster invests in his play. The film's humor is generated by its characters, and it builds gradually as they interact and their true natures are revealed. The image is letterboxed, with an aspect ratio of about 1.85:1 and no 16:9 enhancement, and the framing is as perfect as the colors. Allen's typical mono-sounding stereo soundtrack is fine and the 99 minute film has optional English subtitles.

Bullitt (Warner, 1029)

Bullitt takes place over a Mother's Day weekend. We first saw the movie during adolescence and responded to it more fanatically than we ever had to any other film, though it was not until 15 years later and a passing knowledge of Freud that we discovered why. The action scenes are spectacular—the movie won an Oscar for editing—but it is the relationship Bullitt (Steve McQueen) maintains between the father figure (Robert Vaughn, who actually threatens to castrate him at one point) and the mother figure (Jac-

queline Bisset) that clearly cements a young viewer's identification with the rebellious hero. Bisset, portraying Bullitt's girlfriend, is so safely sequestered from the other men in the film that she never shares a scene with anyone but McQueen.

The picture is presented in letterboxed format on one side, with an aspect ratio of about 1.66:1 and an accommodation for 16:9 enhanced playback, and in full screen format on the other side. The letterboxing adds a bit to the sides and takes off picture information from the bottom in comparison the full screen version, but the framing is stronger. In some shots, fleshtones have a slight purplishness, and the cinematography is purposefully stark, but there are other shots where the fleshtones look perfect and the image is so finely hewn that every crease in McQueen's face is clearly etched upon the screen. Movement in some minor sequences has a slightly jerky feel but, if artifacting and compression are at work, it is a fleeting anomaly. On the whole, the presentation is sharp and vivid, a near-precise replication of how the film looked when it was first released to theaters.

Warner remastered the sound for stereo some time ago. The stereo enhances the vividness of the sound effects and every instrument performing Lalo Schifrin's score. There are only a few separations—sirens crossing from left to right and that sort of thing—but the whole movie has a heightened thrust which it never had before, even in theaters. This is most effective in the great car chase sequence, and one quickly realizes that another reason why the chase has never been equaled lies in the sounds being used for the car engines, points of friction, and aerodynamics. Much of what the director, Peter Yates, is trying to pass off as linear sequencing is actually the same take from three different cameras (watch for the green VW). The chase provides a free-flying thrill, a feeling that movies, like dreams, can do anything.

The 113 minute film is also available in mono in French and Spanish, and comes with English, French or Spanish subtitles ("'Il faut accepter les compromises…' 'Foutaises!'"). There is a theatrical trailer, a decent cast-and-crew profile, and some interesting production notes—the film was shot entirely on location in San Francisco, striving for realism in each location and setting (real doctors, for example, were cast as doctors in the hospital scenes). Also featured is a wonderful 'making of' featurette—which has an excellent picture transfer—that often uses alternate camera angles for its film clips and provides substantial behind-the-scenes footage of McQueen working on his stunts. "The things we did on the streets with automobiles, I don't think will be done for a long time," says McQueen at one point, not realizing that he was in fact starting a trend, though no movie car chase before or since has ever had such a deliberately languorous, foreplay-like build up before the first screeching wheel.

Bulworth (Fox, 4110396)

Warren Beatty, who also directed, portrays a senator who has a nervous breakdown in the final days of his re-election campaign. Rather than being scandalized by his bizarre pronouncements and behavior, however, the media and public embrace the inherent populism in his stream-of-consciousness jabbering, particularly after he starts patterning his speech on rap schematizations. There are hints of faeries and other vaguely supernatural touches, and the narrative is about as confused as the hero's spiel, but it is an invigorating, funny movie in which you really never know what is going to happen next (for example, although the ending is readily projected, the film is so unpredictable that we could never be sure that was what was going to happen until it did).

Once the hip-hop music kicks in, the bass on the stereo surround sound and Dolby Digital channels takes charge, with the Dolby Digital offering slightly clearer separations. There are many throwaway gags buried in the background dialogue, and these, too, are a bit easier to pick up on the Dolby Digital track. The 108 minute 1998 feature can be supported by English or Spanish subtitles ("Hay momentos en que un negro/Tiene que arriesgarse y pelear/Por lo que cree/La verdad hay que predicar").

The picture is letterboxed with an aspect ratio of about 1.85:1 and no 16:9 enhancement. The image is sharp and glossy most of the time, with bright, shiny hues, but there are sequences where it appears the cinematography has a deliberate makeshift look and, in these segments, the image is appropriately compromised.

The 'Burbs (Universal, 20528)

Tom Hanks stars with Bruce Dern, Carrie Fisher and Rick Ducommun in the 1989 Joe Dante comedy. Ostensibly about a group of neighbors who think the unfriendly people living in the mysterious house next door are murderers burying bodies in the cellar, the three actors play their roles as if they hadn't entirely grown up, and the film's subtlest humor comes from the mischievous-little-boyness each exhibits when he gets excited about something. Hanks, in particular, gets the tone just right, reminding one that kids never do really grow up completely. Like much of Dante's work, the film is rather bizarre in a number of ways and has a tone that some viewers will find tiresome, but the narrative has a satisfactory ending and the satire is clever, if belabored in spots.

Universal has included an alternate ending on the DVD that is interesting and more pointedly satirical, but less coherent. The picture on the film is letterboxed with an aspect ratio of about 1.85 and an accommodation for enhanced 16:9 playback. The cinematography is well lit, and colors are rich and sharp. The stereo surround sound has a number of enjoyable separation effects, and Jerry Goldsmith's humorous musical score is particularly well served by its dimensionality. The 102 minute program also has a French soundtrack and can be supported by English subtitles. There are some production notes, a cast-and-director profile section and a trailer.

Burglar (Warner, 11705)

Coming precariously close to being duplicated by **Absolute Power**, Whoopi Goldberg is a thief who witnesses a murder while rifling an apartment. Lesley Ann Warren, who gives a super performance, co-stars in the enjoyable comedy thriller, which has chases, funny comedy routines (Goldberg using different personalities), a whodunit and everything a viewer needs to pass the time. Some of Goldberg's antics can seem tiresome but, on the whole, the film is fairly enjoyable. John Goodman and Bob Goldthwait are also featured.

The presentation is in full screen format only. The picture transfer does not look all that fresh. Colors are reasonably bright, but the image is soft and often looks a bit fuzzy—it doesn't help that much of it is set in a thick San Francisco fog—with weak contrasts and indistinct fleshtones. The stereo surround sound is sporadically energetic. The 102 minute program also has a French track in mono and is adequately closed captioned.

Butter Me Up X-rated (Lipstik, 31192)

A bunch of people fooling around in a house eventually make use of a common dairy product, and that's about all the narrative there is. The picture is somewhat grainy and colors are bland. The monophonic sound is also dullish. The show runs 73 minutes.

C

Cabaret (Warner, 785)

Liza Minnelli watchers will be fascinated by the 20 minute retrospective documentary accompanying **Cabaret**. Not only does the present day Minnelli appear, rough voiced and with a hint of weary melancholy, reminiscing about making the film, but there are camera tests and screen tests that were shot for the film before production began and in those she looks astoundingly youthful, like a half a decade younger than she does in the film itself. The documentary is not very well organized (they never tell you where the film was shot or discuss things like the cinematography and editing) but it is enjoyable, with lots of rehearsal footage and tests, and appropriate memories by the surviving filmmakers. Additionally, there is a 'making of' featurette that was shot when the film was, in 1972, telling a bit more about the location work. There is also what appears to be an original theatrical trailer, which gives the film the subtitle, 'Goodbye Berlin.' Bob Fosse directed the breakthrough 1972 musical, set in Germany during the rise of the Nazis. The 124 minute film is presented in letterboxed format with an aspect ratio of about 1.85:1 and no 16:9 enhancement. Blacks are pure and the image is free of grain, but hues are flat and fleshtones look a bit too pinkish. The stereo sound provides a modest enhancement to the musical score. The film can be supported by English (which translates the German), French or Spanish subtitles ("'Ce n'était pas une fleur d'innocence. Elle gagnait sa vie à la sueur de son corps'"), and is accompanied by a decent cast & crew profile section and a few worthwhile production notes.

In addition to the documentary and featurette, there are outtakes from the documentary. The outtakes are arranged so that the viewer has to access each one separately, but they are worth the trouble, offering up anecdotes and insights that didn't conform to the format of the documentary. Joel Grey, for example, talks about the moment of catharsis he felt, as a Jew, when he first landed in Germany to shoot the film. Minnelli and Michael York describe Fosse's working methods, and one of the producers, Martin Baum, tells how the film was rescued in a month-long give-and-take brainstorming session after an initial disastrous director's cut.

The Cabinet of Dr. Caligari (Image, ID4099DSDVD)

The source material comes from a generation very close to the original, but when it was created, an error in sprocket alignment created a frame line superimposed upon the image. Most presentations of **Caligari** overcome this flaw with masking, slicing off the top of the image in the process, so even though a line runs through it at times, the presentation is a great improvement. The picture is also windowboxed. The black-and-white image is tinted, and although the age of the 1919 German classic is readily evident, blurred passages and speckles are subdued in most sequences.

For those unfamiliar with the film, it is set in an abstract world of Expressionist design, with severely angled corners, crooked lines and objects highlighted by decorative stripes. Ostensibly about a carnival performer who commands a zombie to murder people, the film is framed by a clever plot device that turns one's assumptions about the narrative upside down. It is an entertaining work and because of the sets and appropriately exaggerated performances it can be enjoyed even by today's sophisticated viewers. Whether those viewers will tolerate the distracting black bar is another matter but, if you look at all the picture information above the black bar as having been revealed for the first time in many years, it is easier to appreciate.

The 72 minute film is accompanied by a mildly stereophonic musical score that is quite good—a kind of modernist chamber music suite—and has commentary by scholar Mike Budd (he also wrote the music) on an alternate audio channel. Budd talks about the production and about the film's artistry. There is also a brief but highly satisfying supplement, featuring still frame photos of the theater where **Caligari** first opened and original pressbook publicity materials for the film, along with tantalizing excerpts from director Robert Wiene's intriguing follow-up feature, *Genuine*, which sustained the innovative set designs and abstract character interplay made famous by the first film.

The Cable Guy (Columbia TriStar, 82429)

If you watch the sort of junk we have to sit through sometimes, **The Cable Guy** doesn't seem so bad. The 1996 film is definitely not for children and Jim Carrey playing a villain is coasting compared to the effort he has to make to be a convincing hero, but the film is loaded with humorous pop cultural references and Carrey is always doing something interesting, even if he has given himself over to the dark side of the force. The film contains parodies of many films (Eric Roberts has a marvelous cameo portraying twins in an ad for a TV movie), but seems to use *Cape Fear* as a primary structural model. Matthew Broderick is the hero, stalked and bullied by a madman posing as a cable TV installer. Since the narrative sends the hero's life into a long steady dive, the film is a turn-off on an emotional level, but if it is approached with an unbiased mind and a bit of patience, it has its share of comical rewards.

The picture is presented on one side in letterboxed format, with an aspect ratio of about 2.35:1 and an accommodation for enhanced 16:9 playback, and in full screen format on the other side. The letterboxing adds picture information onto the sides of the image and masks picture information from the top and bottom in comparison to the full screen image, but the letterbox framing is more effective. The image looks a little soft in spots, but colors are fresh and, overall, the presentation is workable. The stereo surround sound is okay and the Dolby Digital track is excellent, with many realistic separation effects and lots of power. The 96 minute program also has French and Spanish tracks in standard stereo, optional Spanish and Korean subtitles, and English closed captioning.

Caddyshack (Warner, 2005)

The 1980 anarchic golfing comedy is also presented in full screen format. The framing is slightly different on the two presentations, but it is doubtful that letterboxing would affect the film one way or the other. The colors are reasonably strong and the image is fairly sharp. The Dolby Digital monophonic soundtrack has more power and more detail than the standard mono track. The 99 minute film is accompanied by a theatrical trailer that pretty much catches every highlight, as well as a modest cast profile section. The film is also available in French and has English, French or Spanish subtitles. The movie is about class rivalries at a golf and country club, and the filmmakers were inspired enough to pit Rodney Dangerfield against Ted Knight. The plot has a sufficient number of supporting characters and goings on that it never bogs down. Even the mechanical gopher, which looked cheap and ridiculous on a big theatrical screen, works better on the TV.

Call of the Wild (D*Vision, DVD1005)

Ken Annakin's adaptation stars Charlton Heston. The 1972 film does a tolerable job at transcribing some of the essentials of Jack London's novel into a workable film, and it is a relatively pleasing outdoor adventure drama, though by no means a definitive interpretation of London's work. The picture is slightly cropped. The colors are bright, but the image often looks smeary, with poor contrasts. The monophonic sound has a weak dynamic range and is a bit scratchy. The 100 minute film was shot in Scandinavia and has an international cast, so the actors who are dubbed often sound a bit out of synch.

Camelot (Warner, 12238)

It is the individual, "brief, shining moments," if you will, that make **Camelot** appealing. At three hours and with an ending that halts the show immediately before the big battle is supposed to start, the film can seem lengthy and pointless to casual viewers, yet the legend of King Arthur contains so many interesting parables and concepts (Merlin lives backwards in time) that the musical's creators, Alan Jay Lerner and Frederick Loewe, and the filmmakers scoop up a great many ideas to scatter throughout the program. Both **Camelot** and **The King and I**, for example, explore the concept of "law" from a kingly, egocentric viewpoint, but in **King and I** the discussion is used only to embellish character and move the plot along, whereas in **Camelot**, beyond the narrative function, the intention is to really make a viewer think about the sociological purpose of law. You might even wish to argue that the slower passages of **Camelot** were placed there deliberately so that a viewer could have had time to ponder its lessons. Richard Harris stars in the 1967 musical, directed by Joshua Logan and featuring a consummate performance by Vanessa Redgrave as Guenivere.

The picture is letterboxed with an aspect ratio of about 2.35:1, with an accommodation for enhanced 16:9 playback. The image is very crisp and the colors look quite fresh and finely detailed. The DVD has a Dolby Digital track, but it is indistinguishable from the standard track, both of which are wimpier and hollower than the old LD's stereo surround soundtrack, and none of which have the separations or dimensionality of the movie's own original multitrack audio mix. Since even the DVD's sound is stereophonic and in pitch, most viewers will probably accept it and be pleased by the production as a whole.

The 180 minute feature is presented in single-sided dual-layer format and can be supported by English, French or Spanish subtitles ("Bref, il n'y a pas/De plus bel endroit/Où l'on peut vivre tout heureux/Qu'ici a Camaalot"). There is an extensive cast & crew profile, a few skimpy production notes (though there is a thumbnail summary of who King Arthur really was), five theatrical trailers, a standard 8 minute 'making of' featurette and a more entertaining 30 minute featurette that incorporated footage from the film's premiere and also has its own commercials, for **Camelot**-inspired nighties.

Campus Vamp (see Nothing Sacred)

The Candidate (Warner, 14577)

It is a measure of how brilliantly accurate Michael Ritchie's superb 1972 satire depicts the American political scene that years after it was produced it still seems topical and unexaggerated. The ideal test is to pick up an article about the current American political races—any article, any race—and read it immediately after watching the film. You will not feel like you have missed a beat.

The 110 minute film is presented in full screen format only, but much of the film is about television and the squarish framing seems appropriate. The colors are bright and sharp, and fleshtones are rich. The monophonic sound is a bit dull, but the Dolby Digital mono track is much stronger. There is a small cast and crew profile section, a few brief production notes and a comprehensive theatrical trailer. The movie is also available with English, French or Spanish subtitles.

Robert Redford stars as a somewhat reluctant senatorial candidate who is cajoled into presenting a winning image by his handlers. Once in a while the film, to fulfill its comical intentions, will accentuate a gag or point-of-view that might have more compellingly been allowed to pass without emphasis, but that is the closest the movie comes to a flaw. Redford's performance is marvelous, allowing the viewer to feel the pulse through the entire ordeal while those around him remain oblivious to it. At first he is flattered by the attention, but then he is frustrated by the realities which reshape his intentions. When he finally becomes desperate enough to embrace the cynicism surrounding him, the viewer is tricked into being pleased that the hero has sold his soul. It is something which happens to the public in the real world of American politics not every four years, but every day.

Candy Factory (DaViD, D0576)

Shot on videotape, the picture is quite vivid, with bright colors and crisp edges. When the lighting is good, fleshtones are perfect and when the lighting is slightly off, fleshtones are a little reddish. There is some mild artifacting around the edges at times, but it is rarely noticeable. The monophonic sound is fine. The narrative, about a candy company run by females, is halfhearted, and the erotic sequences are fairly standard. Shayla LaVeaux, Alexis DeVell, Kaylan Nicole, Debi Diamond, Keisha, Tammi Ann and Angela Summers are featured in the 80 minute program.

Cani Arrabbiati (see **Rabid Dogs**)

Cannonball Adderley Sextet (see **Jazz Scene USA: Cannonball Adderley Sextet / Teddy Edwards Sextet**)

The Canterbury Tales (Image, ID4416WBDVD)

Pier Paolo Pasolini's 1972 anthology film was shot in England, using mostly British actors (including Hugh Griffith), and it conveys the mud and rot of Medieval times as only a low budget movie can. It is not as charming as Pasolini's other literary adaptations, **The Decameron** and **Arabian Nights**, but is of the same ilk, reveling almost as much in the grime, earthiness and lack of conveniences in the past as it does the literary spirit. Fans will definitely want to complete the trilogy, and almost anybody with an interest with English literature's rude beginnings will want to see *The Miller's Tale* acted out, particularly if they could never wade through the spelling to read it.

The image is letterboxed with an aspect ratio of about 1.8:1 and no 16:9 enhancement. All things considered, the color transfer is reasonably good. The film's hues are as earthy as its subject, but the image is sharp and changes in shading are well defined. Fleshtones are pale but workable. The source material has some wear, but is not in bad shape. The monophonic sound is weak, but the Dolby Digital track is more effective. The 111 minute film's English dialogue is usually coherent and the audio track is free of overt distortion. There is no captioning.

Canyon Dreams (Simitar, 7324)

Tangerine Dream supplies the music for the 40 minute natural images program. Depicting various scenic views of the Grand Canyon and Colorado River, the show includes a whitewater rafting sequence as well as helicopter fly-overs and canyon floor explorations. The image is fairly grainy, especially away from the center viewpoint, and the colors are nice, but slightly on the dull side. The stereo sound is passable.

Capricorn One (Artisan, 60475)

Forget the movie—Jerry Goldsmith's musical score has been remastered in stereo surround sound and Dolby Digital, and it sounds fantastic. The music is a typical thriller score, but it is rendered with an intensity and sweep that only Goldsmith can create. The orchestration is filled with aural leaps and breakneck turns and having it in surround sound is like going from a two-dimensional video game to a three-dimensional game. Every cue is filled with glorious excitement.

The dopey 1978 production, written and directed by Peter Hyams, not only has a distasteful premise—the U.S. government fakes a Mars flight and then tries to kill the astronauts—but is loaded with one ludicrous illogical plot development after another. Its only redeeming values are Hyams' talent for staging action scenes regardless of whether they make any sense or not; a winning performance by Brenda Vaccaro, as the wife of one of the astronauts, that makes what could have been the film's slowest scenes the most compelling sequences in the drama; and Goldsmith's score. James Brolin and Elliott Gould star.

The letterboxing has an aspect ratio of about 2.35:1 and no 16:9 enhancement. Fleshtones look a bit too pinkish. Blacks are pure, but details are darkened out, but the image is sharp and has deep colors. The 123 minute film is closed captioned and is accompanied by optional Spanish subtitles, some production notes, a cast profile (yep, they mention O.J.'s problems, and even make the incorrect claim that he was found 'guilty' in the civil trial), and two theatrical trailers.

Career Opportunities (Universal, 20418)

The John Hughes scripted film, directed by Bryan Gordon, is kind of a reworking of **The Breakfast Club**. Frank Whaley and Jennifer Connelly star as a geeky guy and a rich, pretty girl who get locked into a huge store one night together. They play with all the appliances and get to know one another. There are also some burglars, to give the final act some momentum, but the core of the film is the conversational romance, and given the exaggerated stereotyping of the hero and heroine, it isn't all that compelling.

The picture is letterboxed with an aspect ratio of about 2.4:1 and no 16:9 enhancement. The image is very sharp, and colors are bright and accurate. The stereo surround sound is passable and the 83 minute 1991 feature can be supported by English, French or Spanish subtitles. There is a fairly good production essay about shooting the film at nights in a busy Target store and a small cast-and-director profile section. Contrary to jacket notations there is no theatrical trailer.

Carlito's Way (Universal, 20222)

The 1993 film is a redundancy and only those who have played Brian De Palma's other films so much they've memorized the dialogue are going to be interested. Al Pacino portrays a reformed gangster trying to break away from his earlier lifestyle. Needless to say, he goes at it the wrong way.

The 145 minute feature is presented on a single-sided dual-layer platter in letterboxed format, with an aspect ratio of about 2.35:1 and no 16:9 enhancement. The picture transfer is the same, although the DVD brings a naturally enhanced sharpness to the presentation. The stereo surround is fair, but the Dolby Digital has more dimensionality and a stronger bass. The film is also available in French in standard stereo and comes with English or Spanish subtitles ("Un favor te mata más rápido que una bala"). There are some background production notes, a cast profile section and a trailer.

Carnal Instincts X-rated (Metro, UPC#5135312716)

There is a genuine narrative in the 80 minute program. Nikki Tyler stars as a stripper who cons two men into helping her rip off her boss. The erotic sequences are stretched out a little, but the story makes up for it. Shot on film, the image is fuzzy, with bland fleshtones and subdued hues. The sound is okay.

Carnival of Souls (Trimark, VM69310)

Not the classic low budget 1962 black-and-white horror feature, the release is a new color remake that for all its improved production values and enhanced narrative is nowhere near as good as the original. Produced by Wes Craven and directed by Adam Grossman, the film has the same premise as the original—it's pretty much like **Jacob's Ladder**—only more characters have been added, including a crazed killer who is out to get the heroine. Yet the film has sacrificed the original film's two strongest assets, its stark black-and-white cinematography and its very simple, almost allegorical plot. Like the original, the new film has startling images of ghosts and other horrors, and an effective dripping water motif, but the metaphysical symbolism—typified most strongly in the first film by a carnival that sat at the end of an isolated, abandoned pier; the viewer has no sense of place whatsoever for the location of the carnival in the remake—is lost, and so, unlike the first movie, the remake has no soul.

The picture is letterboxed with an aspect ratio of about 1.85:1 and an accommodation for enhanced 16:9 playback. Colors are bright and the image is solid, losing very little in the darker sequences. The stereo surround sound is also reasonably effective, with a number of well-chosen separation effects. The 86 minute program is supported by English, French or Spanish subtitles and comes with a trailer.

Carolina Skeletons (Image, ID5588FMDVD)

Louis Gossett, Jr. portrays a soldier on leave in the early Sixties who returns home to the deep South and starts investigating a 30 year old crime. The 1992 telefilm is set in the Sixties, so that race relations can have an impact on the drama. Lacking a sense of style that would make the mystery more involving, the film still succeeds through the appeal of the performers—Bruce Dern co-stars and no, he didn't do it—and its evocation of the locale.

The picture is fairly hazy, even after the flashback sequences are over, with dull hues and pale fleshtones. The stereo sound has a limited dimensionality but is nice for a TV production. The 93 minute program is not captioned.

Carousel (Fox, 4110868)

The 1956 musical, which stars Gordon MacRae and Shirley Jones, was directed by Henry King. Emotionally, **Carousel** isn't really about adults—it's about what teenagers think being an adult will be like, which is one of the reasons why the show has been so popular with summer stock companies and the like. When the hero, in the beginning, is in heaven and looking back over his life, he's actually looking at it about as far forward as a teenager might be able to see, and the melodrama that ensues is just the sort of generalized love and tragedy a teenager might imagine adulthood involves.

Although that LD looked terrific in comparison to previous efforts, it looks washed out, with pale fleshtones, compared to the smooth, solid hues on the DVD. The picture is in letterboxed format only, with an aspect ratio of about 2.55:1 and no 16:9 enhancement. The standard stereo surround sound is passable, and the Dolby Digital track has clearer, smoother details and brighter sounds. The 128 minute program has optional English and Spanish subtitles ("Puedes divertirte con un hijo/Pero debes ser un padre para tu hija"), a cast & crew profile section, production notes and terrific Movietone footage of the film's opening.

Carpenters, The (see **Close to You: Remembering The Carpenters**)

Carrie (MGM, 907057)

Brian DePalma's 1976 breakthrough horror feature is letterboxed with an aspect ratio of about 1.85:1 and no 16:9 enhancement. The picture looks very hazy, with somewhat fresh but quite fuzzy colors. The film's sound has been remixed for stereo and it is highly enjoyable. It is mostly Pino Donnagio's musical score that has been given a full dimensionality, but it never breaks away from the film or distracts the viewer from the drama. Most of the film's audio remains up front and in the center, but when an effect does pop up in the back, it is at an ideal moment. The soundtrack has a strong presence and enhances the film's theatricality. Fans, however, will be less pleased with the disc's Dolby Digital track, which is a wimpier, less detailed, less dimensional echo of the standard track. A friend was concerned about the speed-up of the sound in the tuxedo shopping sequence, but that has always been part of the film. The 98 minute program is also available in French in mono and can be supported by English or French subtitles ("Carrie White brûle en enfer!"). There is a theatrical trailer, as well. The film, about a teenage girl whose telekinetic powers are wired directly to her unstable emotions, is as memorable for its evocation of high school relationships as it is for its special effects. Sissy Spacek stars, with Piper Laurie, Amy Irving, William Katt, Nancy Allen and John Travolta.

Cartoon Crazys (Fox Lorber, WHE73002)

The 100 minute collection of cartoons from the Thirties and Forties has been spruced up with paintbox colors and Dolby Digital sound effects. A dozen shorts are featured, along with previews of future collections and a 'before' and 'after' demonstration of the cleaning up the cartoons have undergone. The color quality doesn't look bad. The image retains an antique appearance and edges are always a bit soft. Hues are bright but not outlandish. The sound is another matter. The stereo processing has made the dialogue very echoey, as if you were listening to the cartoons in a huge, empty theater. The music has also been amplified and some sound effects have been modified or added. If you aren't a purist, then the surround sound can be enjoyable, but it can also seem

harsh and overblown, like too much dynamite was used. There is also a Dolby Digital track where the enhancements are more distinctive, and, depending upon your attitude, more disconcerting. The cartoons are consistently tight on all four sides, too, often trimming heads on the top of the screen.

Included are eight *Looney Tunes*—the classic *Falling Hare* (Bugs Bunny battles gremlins on a bomber), the classic anthology *Corny Concerto* (three stories set to classical music with Bugs, Elmer Fudd and Porky Pig), the WWII-themed *Daffy the Commando*, *Yankee Doodle Daffy* with Porky Pig as a talent agent and Daffy desperate for a gig, *Tale of Two Kitties* (the cats modeled after Abbott and Costello chase a Tweetie-like bird), *Crowing Pains* (Foghorne Leghorne tries to convince a chicken hawk that Sylvester is a fowl), *Fresh Hare* with Bugs and Elmer (as a Mountie) and *Have You Got Any Castles* (book covers come alive)—a Gabby cartoon (*Gabby Goes Fishing*), a Felix the Cat cartoon set underwater (*Neptune Nonsense*), Tex Avery's *Robin Hood Makes Good*, and a Toonerville Trolley short, *Trolley Ahoy*. The chapter listing on the back of the jacket places one cartoon incorrectly, but it throws off the number scheme for all of them.

Cartoon Crazys Christmas (Fox Lorber, WHE73017)

The anthology contains a baker's dozen of older public domain cartoon shorts with a Christmas or wintertime theme. The source material on the cartoons vary, though they often look a little worn down even when they have apparently undergone restoration. Some of the transfers have kind of a wavy, video copy look to them, as well, and the edges often seem tight. On the whole, however, the presentation is workable, and the best looking cartoons (notably the incredibly dimensional pre-multi-plane effort, *Hawaiian Birds Christmas*) are enthralling. The sound has been souped up for Dolby Digital and stereo surround playback, though the effect can be distracting. Fox Lorber has provided superb supporting materials for each cartoon, including a full synopsis and production history.

Included are the Fleischers' *Rudolf The Red-Nosed Reindeer*, *A Waif's Christmas Welcome* (an RKO Rainbow Parade effort with a standard narrative about a mischief-maker who gets an innocent child—brought in from the snow, no less—in trouble), *Fresh Hair* with Bugs Bunny, *The Christmas Circus* with Ginger Nut the squirrel (a parrot tries to sneak into an animal circus being held—well, sort of in the snow, though it looks like a real circus when you get inside; the circus acts take up most of the show), *The Pup's Christmas* featuring Hector the dog (who tries to stop three puppies from messing up the Christmas decorations), *Private Eye Popeye* (the link to Christmas is obscure, though he does chase the bad guy up a mountain and into some snow at one point), *Santa's Surprise* (a nice cartoon in which the elves play Santa for Santa), *Snow Foolin'* (a pastiche of wintertime situations with animals, including a *Jingle Bells* sing-along), the Fleischers' *Christmas Comes but Once a Year* (Grampy helps some orphans celebrate Christmas by creating inventive toys out of junk), *The Gingerbread Man* (again, the holiday link is tenuous, but the cartoon, about a young girl who dreams of visiting a land of anthropomorphic deserts, is imaginative), *The Shanty Where Santy Claus Lives* in black and white (Santa hires a young homeless child to help him in the toy shop; one of the dolls turns into Kate Smith and the tree catches on fire), and *Christmas Night* with The Little King, also in black and white.

Cartoon Crazys Goes to War (Fox Lorber, WHE73018)

The collection contains animated shorts produced during the WWII era. Some of the cartoons contain the barest references to the war, while others—the most intriguing in the collection—are propaganda efforts created to bolster support for the war. Included are *Bugs Bunny Bond Rally* (a good War Bonds commercial); *Daffy the Commando*; *Falling Hare* in which Bugs Bunny battles gremlins; the Superman-as-terrorist *Eleventh Hour* and another Superman piece, *Jungle Drums* (it is in the context of an anthology such as this that the remarkably adult tone of the Fleischer Bros. Superman cartoons is especially impressive); *Ding Dog Daddy*, about a dog that falls in love with a statue (the war connection comes at the end, when the statue is turned into scrap metal); *Jurky Turkey* (a turkey trying to avoid hungry Pilgrims, with wartime overtones); *Tale of Two Kitties* with Tweety and the cats fashioned after Abbott & Costello, again with references to blackouts, air raids, etc.; *Fifth Column Mouse* with Sylvester in a strongly allegorical story about mice who attempt to 'appease' a cat; *Fony Fables*, which re-tells a number of fairly tales and fables with wartime references; three black-and-white Private Snafu cartoons, the oft-anthologized *Snafuperman*, *Booby Traps* and *Spies*; an invigorating black-and-white Daffy Duck scrap metal service commercial, *Scrap Happy Daffy*, and a fascinating re-election promotion for Roosevelt funded by unions and animated by Chuck Jones, *Hell Bent for Election*. Additionally, there is a color clip featuring an effectively animated battle map of a bombing run, and some terrific still photos of wartime cartoon artwork. There are also trailers for other **Cartoon Crazys** programs.

As with the other **Cartoon Crazys** titles, each cartoon is also provided with elaborate and highly gratifying background information, and each is available in several audio formats, from subdued, virtual-monophonic playback to a wildly artificial but engaging directional stereo. The source material is often a bit worn-looking, with solid but not overly rich colors. The black-and-white pieces are even a bit more bedraggled. The collection is not captioned.

Cartoons That Time Forgot: From the Van Beuren Studio (Image, ID4681DSDVD)

Two home video programs, *The Van Beuren Rainbow Parade* and *The Odd and the Outrageous*, are combined on the single-sided, dual-layer 156 minute program. Most of the 21 cartoons are in Technicolor, produced under the Rainbow Parade banner, and those that are in black-and-white have been chosen for their exceptional artistry. Overall the collection is very strong.

The monophonic sound is a little scratchy on some of the older black-and-white shorts but reasonably good on most of the color efforts. The cartoons that contain dialogue have not been captioned. The shorts include scattered instances of negative Black and ethnic stereotyping. Not every short is taken from luscious source material. One or two look a little faded and there are plenty of scratches spread around the collection. Most of the cartoons, though, do look gorgeous, and the effect of seeing them succeed one another is almost psychedelic.

Created primarily in the mid-Thirties, a number of the cartoons take their characters from comic strips, including "Toonerville Trolley" shorts, several color Felix the Cat efforts, and even an episode of The Little King. More interesting is a character created especially for the screen, Molly Moo-Cow, who is seen in several adventures saving various characters—Robinson Crusoe, butterflies, a papoose—while remaining very cow-like in appearance and movement. Other notable selections include *It's a Greek Life*, about a Centaur cobbler who gets carried away with Mercury's shoes, *Wot a Night*, a good haunted house piece, *Candy Town*, about a fanciful trip to the moon, *Cupid Gets His Man* featuring cupids dressed as Mounties trying to nail a character based on W.C. Fields, and *In a Cartoon Studio*, a humorous imagining of the animation process.

Casablanca (MGM, 906261)

The 1943 classic looks and sounds so good that it will rekindle the film's pleasures for those who have burned themselves out memorizing dialogue or humming *As Time Goes By*. The clarity of the presentation brings out the background details in the elaborate nightclub scenes, enriching the locale's atmosphere and heightening a viewer's concentration. Often with a movie which has been subject to numerous repeated screenings, a viewer will see the film so many times that a poor presentation will leave an uneasy and dissatisfied feeling. The flaws of the presentation will subcon-

sciously be mistaken for flaws within the movie itself. If that has happened to you lately with **Casablanca**, it is time to watch the DVD and rediscover how much fun the film can be.

At the point where Rick first comes running over to Sam to tell him to stop playing that song and then sees Ilsa, there's what appears to be a splice or a watermark that disrupts the dramatic rhythm of the moment, but otherwise, the presentation is lovely. There are a couple other markings on the source material, though none is as inconveniently placed and, markings aside, the black-and-white image is gorgeous. Contrasts are vivid, blacks are rich and the focus is very sharp. Lines that are fuzzy and contrasts that are hazy on the best LD versions look absolutely crisp and exact on the DVD and whites, such as Humphrey Bogart's dinner jacket, are pure and stunning.

The monophonic sound is fine. The 103 minute film is also available in French and can be supported by English or French subtitles ("Je suis venu prendre les eaux." "Les eaux? Lesquelles? On est en plein désert!" "J'ai été mal renseigné"). There is a 36 minute retrospective documentary about the film, entitled *You Must Remember This*. Narrated by Lauren Bacall, the program steps through the film's narrative line, using different points to talk about the production history and the personalities involved with the project. There are interviews with surviving personnel and film historians, and a substantial amount of replayed footage. The documentary gives a basic overview of how the film came into being and celebrates the many components which have made the film so eternally popular. There is also an original trailer (not a re-release) as well as trailers for eight other Bogart films.

The beautifully edited, marvelously scripted, wittily acted film is always enjoyable to hear and see. There are many different reasons for this, but one is its feeling of oasis and respite. The war is very much a part of the plot, but it is happening somewhere else. Watching **Casablanca**, one feels the same escape from the pressures of life which the characters, most of them waiting to go elsewhere, are experiencing. The ending pulls one gently back into reality, concluding with a bittersweet ambiguity which becomes amplified only after the television is switched off.

Casino (Universal, 20159)

Martin Scorsese's glitzy look at corruption in Las Vegas was shot in the Super-35 format and has been letterboxed with an aspect ratio of about 2.35:1, with an accommodation for enhanced 16:9 playback. While there is a sequence here and there where we would like to have seen the full frame, such as Saul Bass' opening credits, for most of the footage the rectangular framing is outstanding and adds considerably to the film's dramatic and artistic impact. The 179 minute feature is presented on one side in dual layer format and has a gorgeous picture transfer. The image is crisp, colors are vivid and fleshtones are accurate. The stereo surround sound does not have an elaborate mix and is fairly monophonic in design, and even the Dolby Digital track is a little subdued. The film is also available in French in Dolby Digital and in Spanish in standard stereo, and comes with English or Spanish subtitles. There is a passable production notes segment, a decent cast profile section and a nice theatrical trailer.

The 1995 film is terrific, exploring through one set of characters the dynamics of Las Vegas pretty much from the point where *The Godfather, Part II* left off to the present day. At the heart of the movie, however, is its true saving grace, an absolutely smashing, star performance by Sharon Stone. Robert DeNiro and Joe Pesci also star, but their efforts are essentially retreads of what they've done before, and in Pesci's case it is often accompanied by a staccato line delivery that borders on rote recitation. Stone, on the other hand, is a fluid, captivating presence who keeps her character believable no matter how many emotional and physical changes she goes through. She brings a liveliness that is sufficient justification for the movie's political and economic portrait of the casino industry, enabling the film to entertain on a scope that is far greater and more enduring than most films can muster.

Casper the Friendly Ghost (Digital Disc Entertainment, 501)

The collection contains four cartoon shorts and runs about 30 minutes. Originally produced by Paramount's animation unit in the Thirties and Forties, the cartoons were not handled by the Fleischers but clearly exhibit their influence. The collection contains four prime cartoons: the very first Casper cartoon, *Casper the Friendly Ghost*, in which he befriends a human family and saves them from their creditors; *A Hunting We Will Go*, in which he befriends a duck and saves it from hunters; *There's Good Boos Tonight*, which has an identical narrative to *Hunting*, except that he befriends a fox; and the best cartoon in the group, *Boo Moon*, in which he travels to the moon and befriends a miniature kingdom being attacked by aliens. The internal logic of the cartoons leaves much to be desired (Casper is sleeping with the duck when it starts to rain. He tries to cover the duck, but the rain goes right through him. He picks up the nest, puts it on his head—it stays—and holds the duck in his arms—so is he corporeal or ethereal?), but the animation is good, the concept has clearly had staying power and the collection is quite enjoyable. The colors in **Casper** are also faded, but at least hues are still discernible. The source material looks worn, with soft edges and regular visitations of scratches. The monophonic sound is noisy—with a noticeable hum in a couple places—but coherent. There is no captioning.

Castle Freak (Full Moon, 8002)

Stuart Gordon directed the film, which stars Jeffrey Combs, the same combination that did **Re-Animator**, though **Freak** lacks the humor that made **Re-Animator**'s gore so engaging. The 95 minute film is identified as the 'Director's Cut' and contains images of cannibalism (a woman's breast is eaten) that are not for the squeamish. The movie, about a dysfunctional American family that moves into an Italian castle the father has inherited, only to discover that 'something' is living in the cellar, is a passable genre effort but, despite the gore effects, there is nothing special about it. There are enough action and genre components to hold one's attention, but it is not particularly exciting, and the monster's full body makeup sequences aren't all that convincing.

The picture is presented in full screen format and has bright, sharp colors. The stereo surround sound has some nice energy, giving Richard Band's engaging music a good articulation and a strong bass. A 'making of' and promotional *VideoZone* featurette are included, as well. In one segment, Combs himself laments that the movie and the atmosphere on the set are not as jovial as **Re-Animator** was, and for what is supposed to be a promotional effort, that is fairly strong criticism.

Casual Sex? (Image, ID4299USDVD)

At the time of its 1988 theatrical release, the film was a sort of breakthrough comedy about what boors men can be. The heroine, played by Lea Thompson, speaks directly to the camera about her sexuality, and a pre-nasty Andrew Dice Clay is one of her main foils. Specifically about two friends who vacation at a singles health resort (Victoria Jackson co-stars), the film's humor doesn't seem as vital now, though some of its insights and amusements will remain relevant as long as men and women intermingle. The film is presented in full screen. The color quality looks decent and the image is reasonably sharp. The musical score is stereophonic, though little else is, and the 87 minute program is not captioned.

The Cat and the Canary (Image, ID4387DSDVD)

The murder mystery that plays so well you barely realize it is a silent film. Except for nitpickers well versed in probate law, viewers will be fully wrapped up in the classic 1927 crime drama, based upon a stageplay, about heirs gathered in a haunted house twenty years after the death of a wealthy man for the reading of his will. The house has lots of secret passages, a madman has escaped from a nearby lunatic asylum, and there are suspects and victims in every room and hallway. There is also a good deal of comedy, with the hero coming apart at the seams at each fright, real or imagined.

The film is judiciously tinted (indoor scenes are brown, outdoor scenes are slightly bluish, and there are a couple of strong red tints slipped in at appropriate moments for effect) and is in reasonably nice shape for its age. The image is soft and minor markings are fairly constant, but the wear is not severe enough to impinge upon the entertainment. Movement is smooth and natural. The unelaborate musical score, based upon the music and sound effects originally conceived for the film, was recorded in stereo this year. Some passages are creative but other passages are bland and repetitive. The sound effects are appropriately subdued, designed more to touch on your subconscious as you view the images. Stereo dimensionality is limited and it is best to keep the audio at a modest volume.

The 81 minute film is accompanied by a 20 minute silent Harold Lloyd short, *Haunted Spooks*, about a newlywed couple who are being discouraged from staying in a mansion. The narrative has a rushed conclusion, but the comedy sequences are carefully executed and the film is an enjoyable epilogue to the main feature. There are negative stereotypes of black characters in the Lloyd short, but in moderate compensation they save the day at the end. The black-and-white presentation is not tinted. The source material looks good, with less wear than **Canary**, and the outdoor sequences are especially crisp. The music is stereophonic and is reasonably fun.

Cat on a Hot Tin Roof (MGM, 906617)

Paul Newman, Elizabeth Taylor and Burl Ives star in the watered down 1958 adaptation of the Tennessee Williams play, though it is worth noting that as the characters move from one scene in the house to the next, they seem to advance 'deeper' into the house while their conversations became more frank and revealing. Richard Brooks directed.

Although it looks a bit worn in places, the picture is fresh, colorful and crisp. The film is presented on one side, in letterboxed format with an aspect ratio of about 1.85:1 and an accommodation for enhanced 16:9 playback, and in cropped format on the other side. The monophonic sound is strong and the Dolby Digital mono audio track is even stronger. The 108 minute film is also available in French and comes with English, French or Spanish subtitles ("Tu ne trouves pas que ça pue la dissimulation, Brick?"). A theatrical trailer is also included.

Cat on a Hot Tin Roof (Image, ID4375DODVD)

The captivating rendition of the Tennessee Williams' play stars Tommy Lee Jones, Jessica Lange, Rip Torn and Kim Stanley. The 1984 American Playhouse production is highly satisfying as a preservation of a stage interpretation of the piece, as opposed to a film adaptation. All of the action takes place in Brick and Maggie's upstairs bedroom, and the performances retain a sense of broadness better suited to the stage than the screen (though in this context, most welcome). Best of all, the show stays very close to Williams' original text, so the weaving river of conversations and revelations that is at the heart of the piece's entertainment is adeptly delivered. The poetic rhythm of Williams' dialogue is mesmerizing, yet the characters are utterly real and believable, so that their gradual efforts to uncover what is on one another's' minds remains compelling no matter how many times you share their company.

The 144 minute production tends to have a soft and even blurry image, but the dual-layer DVD's transfer rate stays consistently at the highest levels and fleshtones are a reasonably deep and colors are fairly rich. The monophonic sound is strong and the program is not captioned.

Cat People (Image, ID4221USDVD)

The stereo surround sound is fabulous on the 1982 remake. The music has a strong presence, the separation effects are grand, and when the deep feline growls roar out of your sound system, every animal within five miles will scurry for cover. The letterboxing has an aspect ratio of about 1.85:1 and no 16:9 enhancement, and presents a confidently balanced image. The picture is a bit hazy at times, but the colors are rich and, except for scenes involving very strong lighting effects, the presentation is highly satisfying. The 119 minute film has been closed captioned. Director Paul Schrader walks a fine line, delivering contemporary mayhem while retaining the spirit of the source. Nastassia Kinski and Annette O'Toole star in the film, which is suitably mystical and reasonably exciting, especially after an initial viewing establishes the story's rules for the viewer. The DVD's powerful audio track enhances the entertainment considerably.

Cats (PolyGram, 4400479952)

The long-running hit musical has derived much of its popularity from audience interaction, as the cast members, dressed in feline form, roam the auditorium between numbers, rubbing up against the knees of patrons and otherwise delighting the young at heart. The Andrew Lloyd Webber musical itself, however, is a little on the sleepy side, and the video recording, which isolates singers and otherwise pares down a viewer's sensory inputs from the show, is even duller.

A couple numbers have been dropped, though the video still runs a full 120 minutes. At its best, the program captures much of the show's dancing, which combines athletic gymnastics with creative mime and costuming. The songs sound very fresh—more immediate than the cast albums (it's been recorded with a larger orchestra)—and the cast includes such heavyweights as Elaine Paige and the John Mills, so there is nothing rote about how they present themselves. The musical itself, derived from an entertaining cycle of poems by T.S. Eliot, has a limited narrative—no more than a linking device, really—to present the different cats (a train cat, an old cat, a sneaky cat, etc.) as individual numbers. With the focus that editing and image isolation brings to a video program, however, each number seems to go on for several reprises too many, inducing the viewer to catnap or, at the very least, start fiddling with a ball of yarn.

The picture is letterboxed with an aspect ratio of about 1.81:1 and no 16:9 enhancement. Although the show's lighting is often meant to evoke night, with strong blue washes and other colored intensities, the image is very sharp and differences in shadings are clearly and accurately defined. The image is consistently crisp and appealing. The stereo surround sound has a nice dimensionality, and the Dolby Digital track is even better, with clearer separations and more detail. The 120 minute program is accompanied by a good, lengthy 'making of' featurette that looks back to the show's original London opening as well as the shooting of the video. Both the show and the featurette are adequately closed captioned.

Caught Up (Artisan, 60470)

A deliberate contemporary evocation of film noir with a black cast, at times the film goes overboard with its performances and its dialogue ("Nobody was waitin' for me but a dude named 'Destiny'"), but at other times the repartee between the characters is fresh and witty, and the story is appropriately tangled. Bokeem Woodbine is a paroled con who meets a femme fatale with a stolen diamond, played by Cynda Williams. Although one is initially put off by some of the film's artifices, it is eventually more inviting to enjoy what the filmmakers are reaching for than to condemn them for coming up short.

The dual-layer program is presented on one layer in letterboxed format, with an aspect ratio of about 1.85:1 and an accommodation for enhanced 16:9 playback, and in full screen format on the other layer. The letterboxing adds a sliver to the sides of the image and masks off picture information from the top and bottom. Either framing seems to work well. The picture transfer looks very good, with bright, clear hues and accurate fleshtones. The stereo surround sound is a bit dull, but the Dolby Digital track is strong,

with better defined separations. The film can be supported English closed captioning or Spanish subtitles. The director, Darrin Scott, cinematographer, Tom Callaway, and star, Bokeem Woodbine, provide a running commentary. Scott places an emphasis on play-by-play reporting, but the three do go into detail on how the scenes were set up and what went into their craft, and they also offer up a few anecdotes here and there. Additionally, there is a theatrical trailer (which tries to sell the film as a supernatural thriller, something it isn't), a TV commercial, a radio commercial and two cool music videos, from Snoop Doggy Dog and Killah Priest.

In one of the DVD's best features, five significant scenes from the film are presented, each represented by several 'pages' that show about six storyboards at a time, with the final footage represented by those six storyboards playing in a continuous loop in the upper corner of the page. Besides being able to advance through the storyboards and simultaneously see how closely they were followed (Scott used them as a guide, not a bible), each page is also linked to a camera set-up diagram that specifies the camera placement for each planned shot. The links between the proposed approach and the final footage create a valuable tool for film students wishing to learn how a movie is made, or for anybody who is curious about the creative process.

Cause of Death (Simitar, 7307)

The convoluted but uninspired thriller is about a couple who get drawn into a drug rip-off scheme by a relative. The erotic sequences aren't bad and there is plenty of action, but the story turns out to be less elaborate than it seems at first and doesn't really amount to much. The picture quality is pretty good, with accurate fleshtones and a sharp focus, and the stereo sound is reasonably strong. The film runs 86 minutes and is not captioned.

Celine Dion: The Colour of My Love Concert (Sony, BVD50136)

The French-Canadian singer performs a pre-Titanic 67 minute concert in Quebec. Part of her act seems stuck in the Eighties and the farther she gets from her roots the less appealing she becomes, but her voice has a rare strength and when her songs are produced properly, the vocals are magnetic. The stage show is busy and at times looks more like a revue (the headset mike she uses for dancing, at least, is a model of discretion), but she remains at the center of attention throughout the program. Clive Griffin joins her for When I Fall in Love and Peabo Bryson is on hand for Beauty and the Beast. The picture has pale fleshtones and a somewhat hazy image. The stereo sound is strong, with the Dolby Digital mix providing more distinctive separations and a greater dimensionality. The DVD comes with optional English or French subtitles, though neither appear over the one French language song she sings. There is also a brief discography.

Celtic Tides (Putumayo, PUTU1417)

A Canadian film about Celtic music in Ireland, Scotland and on Cape Breton Island in Canada, it isn't a very well made documentary. Even general viewers will cringe at some of the non-scholarly statements ("[Celts are remembered as] fierce, naked warriors with long blond hair who displayed the severed heads of their enemies over their doorways") included within the narration, and the focus jumps from subject to subject without much sense of organization. The music never lasts long enough to let the viewer savor it. But the only real problem these drawbacks create is that the documentary requires more than a single viewing to absorb the information it wants to impart.

Included among the many interviews are The Chieftains, Clannad, Altan, The Rankin Family, Natalie MacMaster, Ashley MacIsaac, Old Blind Dogs, Mary Black, Seamus Egan, Dougie MacLean and Matt Malloy. Concert sequences are unevenly lit and the image is a little grainy, but colors are reasonably fresh and clear, and fleshtones look fine when the lighting allows. The stereo sound is okay and the program is not captioned. There is no time encoding.

Centennial Gala (see The Metropolitan Opera: Centennial Gala)

A Century of Science Fiction (Passport, DVD2217)

Using trailers and 'making of' featurettes, the moderately entertaining genre overview is narrated by Christopher Lee. The narration of is rarely informative, but it does provide a sense of organization to the parade of clips, which include scenes from films from the mid-Nineties, such as *Independence Day* and **The Island of Dr. Moreau**. The show is fairly enjoyable when it focuses on lesser known films, for many reasons—the commentary is fresher because the films have not been as thoroughly analyzed elsewhere, the clips are less likely to seem familiar and, as an almost consistent corollary to their being less famous, they are more amusing and hokey. The abundance of special effects and fantasy images is highly gratifying. The picture quality varies but is often overly soft and faded. The monophonic sound is scratchy and there is a lack of crispness in the tone. The 96 minute program is not captioned.

The Chamber (Universal, 20268)

Chris O'Donnell and Gene Hackman star with Faye Dunaway in the adaptation of one of John Grisham's legal novels. The story, about a young lawyer handling the last appeals of his grandfather, who is on death row, has enough little surprises and mysteries to stay interesting, and the stars milk it for all they've got. It probably didn't seem like much on the big screen, for although it was shot in widescreen, its tensions are intimate. On video, the stars take over and it doesn't hurt that the pace is leisurely.

The letterboxing has an aspect ratio of about 2.35:1 and an accommodation for enhanced 16:9 playback. The color transfer is exceptionally good, looking consistently crisp and richly colored from beginning to end. The stereo surround sound has a couple of showy moments and some subtle background effects, which is about all one can ask with this sort of drama. The stereo surround sound is a bit weak, but the Dolby Digital track provides a slightly enhanced dimensionality. Neither track delivers the dialogue all that well, however, as it remains overly soft and a bit bassy. The 113 minute film is also available in French and Spanish in standard stereo and comes with English or Spanish subtitles. There are some production notes, a cast profile section and a theatrical trailer that makes the film appear more active than it turned out to be.

Chances Are (Columbia TriStar, 70159)

A marvelously romantic comedy that uses reincarnation to fuel its narrative drive, it manipulates the fantasy elements nicely, with no more unreal occurrences than necessary to score its points. The performances, particularly from Cybill Shepherd and Robert Downey, Jr., also lend credibility to the sequence of events. The 1989 romance is intoxicating and the humor is a pleasant bonus. Share the disc with someone you wish to seduce.

The picture is letterboxed on one side, with an aspect ratio of about 1.85:1 and an accommodation for enhanced 16:9 playback, and is in full screen format on the other side. The color transfer looks fine. The stereo surround sound does not have an elaborate mix. The 108 minute program also has French and Spanish language tracks, optional English, French or Spanish subtitles and a trailer.

Changing Habits (Simitar, 7449)

In order to save money, a young artist feigns destitution and gets a room in a hostel run by a nunnery. At the same time, she grows up enough to work out the emotional demons that haunted her childhood and have prevented her from forming meaningful relationships. Moira Kelly stars, with Eileen Brennan delivering a choice performance of the Mother Superior and Christopher Lloyd as the heroine's estranged father. The film works its way through

the heroine's maturation effectively and presents an adequate emotional drama with enough dabs of humor to keep things from seeming too depressingly much like real life.

Colors are bright and the focus is fairly sharp. The stereo sound mix is a somewhat standard effort. The DVD also features partial filmographies of the film's stars, Moira Kelly and Christopher Lloyd, and is not captioned.

Chapin, Harry (see Soundstage Series: An Evening With... Harry Chapin)

Chaplin (Artisan, 60483)

Those who have developed a passion for Charles Chaplin through the study of film or the exposure of home video will find much that is pleasing in Richard Attenborough's biographical **Chaplin**, but we cannot imagine who, other than that somewhat limited number still carrying the torch for the Little Tramp, would be interested in the movie. Film biographies are often like kittens. In the depiction of the subject's early years they are delightful, but they inevitably turn into staid cats. The early part of the program, showing Chaplin's introduction to the motion picture art form and his rapid mastery of its potential, is a good enough story to enchant most anyone. But the later events in his life, and the details surrounding the production of his longer films, are more esoteric, and however interestingly the movie presents them, only dedicated fans will get a kick out of it. Robert Downey, Jr. gives a seamless performance in the title role, allowing the filmmakers to use clips from Chaplin's movies without disrupting the continuity even slightly. A number of other stars, including Dan Aykroyd and Kevin Kline, are employed to embody famous figures from Chaplin's era.

The 135 minute program is presented in dual-layer format and is letterboxed with an aspect ratio of about 1.76:1 and no 16:9 enhancement. The colors are good and grain is minimal. The stereo surround sound rarely calls attention to itself. The film can be supported by Spanish subtitles or English closed captioning. There is a theatrical trailer (with a picture that looks even sharper), an 8-minute featurette, a 6-minute featurette, a large cast & crew profile section and brief essays about the production, Chaplin, his films and the silent era.

The Chaplin Mutuals Volume 1 (Image, ID4100DSDVD)
The Chaplin Mutuals Volume 2 (Image, ID4101DSDVD)
The Chaplin Mutuals Volume 3 (Image, ID4163DSDVD)

The three volumes feature beautiful transfers of the twelve silent two-reel comedies Charles Chaplin made for the Mutual Film Company during 1916 and 1917. The films, each running a little over 20 minutes, represent a turning point in Chaplin's art, as he progressed from pure slapstick to films with stronger dramatic story lines. Each short is windowboxed. The black-and-white pictures are aged, with a few scratches and things, but compared to what was previously available they are terrific, with a crisp focus, rich contrasts, and a stable image. The musical scores are nice stereophonic orchestrations by Michael Mortilla that serve the programs well without drowning them. For some reason the volume on **Volume 1** is turned up way high and has to be played back with limited amplification., while the other two are set at normal levels. The films are gathered in an apparent random order. **Volume 1** features *The Immigrant* (just off the boat, Chaplin's character has trouble in a restaurant, but meets a girl), *The Adventurer* (Chaplin's character is an escaped convict eluding police on a wealthy estate), *The Cure* (an inebriate in a spa) and *Easy Street* (a rookie cop takes care of some street toughs). **Volume 2** features *The Count* (a tailor pretends to be an aristocrat at a fancy party), *The Vagabond* (a Chaplinesque tale in which the hero, somewhat destitute, rescues a girl from an abusive relationship), *The Fireman* (a slapstick involving a fire brigade), and *Behind the Screen* (a comedy about a film studio). **Volume 3** features the most repeatable short, *One A.M.*, in which an inebriate battles a room full of wild decorations, along with *The Pawn Shop* (Chaplin is a clerk in a second hand store), *The Floorwalker* (Chaplin's character works in a department store) and *The Rink* (after some waiter gags, Chaplin's character puts on skates for a balletic roller skating sequence and chase).

Charade (UAV, 40098); (Front Row, 3507)

Audrey Hepburn and Cary Grant star in the 1963 public domain film, directed by Stanley Donen, which also features Walter Matthau, James Coburn and George Kennedy. A supreme example of form successfully exceeding content, the story makes almost no sense but the stars are so luminous it never matters. Hepburn is at her most radiant and her chemistry with Grant is pure movie star magic.

The film is so wonderful that many fans will probably want to have the DVD, even though the transfer leaves much to be desired. Barely on par with a poor looking broadcast presentation and probably not much better than the video cassette versions we keep seeing in pharmacy bargain bins, the colors change from tolerable to faded, the image is grainy, background features are unstable and the source material has scratches and a splice or two. The image is also slightly cropped. The sound, which appears to have undergone a mild stereo processing, is somewhat noisy, but the music isn't badly distorted and the dialogue is only raspy if you turn the volume up too high. UAV has included a nice theatrical trailer, which is even letterboxed. Contrary to a jacket notation, however, there appears to be no profile of Grant offered on the menu, and although the jacket cover lists the running time at 93 minutes the movie appears to actually run the full 113 it is supposed to run.

Front Row's transfer looks exactly the same as near as we can tell. Fleshtones are pale, contrasts are weak and the image is often grainy. The monophonic sound is distorted on both the upper and lower ends. Front Row includes a laughably brief 'biography' section for the cast.

Chariots of Fire (Warner, 20004)

The 1981 Oscar-winning drama, about several runners on Britain's 1924 Olympic team, is beautifully, even perfectly, understated. The narrative brings up one historical insight, how the disintegration of true "amateurism" was linked directly to the gentrification of competitions, but it is primarily a celebration of inconsequentiality. The film implies that anyone who sticks to his principles, and strives to do the best he can, achieves the glory that a winning athlete achieves, even if the world is not applauding. Few fact-based films have ever seemed to come so close to the "truth" without resorting to transcript dialogue or hand-held cinematography.

The full screen framing is generally acceptable, but there are occasions when the image seems cramped on the sides. The color transfer has deep, rich colors and a sharp focus, but there are a few stray speckles and other marks of wear. The stereo surround sound is quite strong and effectively detailed. The program also comes with English, French or Spanish subtitles. There is an extensive cast profile and a few production notes, the latter suggesting that the idea for the film originated with producer David Puttnam, but that its brilliantly understated mood was the conception of the director, Hugh Hudson. A theatrical trailer heaped in critic quotations also accompanies the 124 minute feature.

Charles Mingus: Triumph of the Underdog (Shanachie, 6315)

Using interviews and performance clips, the 78 minute 1997 program makes a strong case for ranking Mingus among the preeminent Twentieth Century American composers. It traces his development as a musician while also covering the stormy ups and downs of his personal life. Although the emphasis is on reporting, there is a decent amount of music in the documentary as well, and the filmmakers are never in a hurry to rush or interrupt a concert sequence. The archive material is in varied condition, but the pic-

ture quality is decent and the stereo sound is good. The program is not captioned.

Charlotte Church: Voice of an Angel (Sony, SVD61770)

The amazing 14-year old soprano, Charlotte Church, performs in a 45 minute concert with the London Symphony Orchestra. Her voice is remarkably mature and the recital has a unique calming effect that is enhanced by the clarity of the DVD's image and the purity of its standard stereo surround soundtrack and its more dimensional 5.1 Dolby Digital track (the DVD is not captioned). But knowing a good thing when they have one, Sony is not selling the music alone. Accompanying the concert is an additional 20 minute profile of Church, who is as personable (she introduces her stuffed animals to the audience at the start of the concert) as her voice is lovely. A great effort is expended within the documentary to demonstrate that her ambition is genuinely her ambition and not some pushy adult's, and that her success has not changed her basic, good-natured fourteenness. The little red guy with the horns and a tail on our left shoulder was rubbing his hands and whispering how much he couldn't wait for her to get a little older and discover the pains of adulthood, but the guy dressed in white with the wings and a halo on our right shoulder told him to shut up and pointed out that the DVD has preserved both Church's vocals and her personality in a state of innocent purity until the end of time.

Chasey Saves the World X-rated (Vivid, UPC#0073214577)

Aliens have turned the locals in a remote town to zombies, and the only way to free a person is to have sex with them. The thing is, if a person isn't a zombie and climaxes during sex, they're turned into one. The set-up works so well that it is disappointing the filmmakers couldn't spend a little more money and take it further. The picture is inconsistent, with some sequences looking bright and crisp, but others looking a bit more drained, with weak contrasts. Fleshtones are passable. The monophonic soundtrack has an enjoyable alien score that pops up here and there. The 70 minute program features Chasey Lain, Missy, Jill Kelly and Amber Woods. The DVD contains alternate angle sequences and elaborate hardcore interactive promotional features.

Chasin' Pink X-rated (Vivid, UPC#0073214550)

An amusing takeoff on *Cops* with an all-female cast, the heroine is a uniformed policewoman in a patrol car who has various encounters as she goes about her business. The erotic sequences are fresh and the premise is effective. Some sequences are rather grainy and others are somewhat pale, with bland fleshtones throughout. The monophonic sound is adequate. Chasey Lain, Tia Bella, Coral Sands, Asia Carrera, Meka, Chawnee and Felecia are featured in the 68 minute program. The DVD contains alternate angle sequences and elaborate hardcore interactive promotional features.

Chick Corea Pat Metheny Lee Konitz: Woodstock Jazz Festival (Pioneer, PA98596D)

An intimate, open-air hour-long concert, the stage is effectively miked and the instruments are spread nicely across the front of the room on the Dolby Digital playback. The rear channels have little more than echoes and incidental atmosphere, and the standard stereo track does not provide definitions as pure as the Dolby Digital track but, at its best, the separations on the Dolby Digital track add greatly to the dynamics of the music. Colors are a little light, but the picture looks okay and retains its stability after the sun sets.

The number of spotlighted performers greatly exceeds those promoted on the jacket. Featured musicians include Howard Johnson, Marilyn Crispell, Baikida Carroll, Julius Hemphill, Attilio Zanchi, Ed Blackwell, Karl Berger, Aiyb Dieng, Nana Vasconceles, Dewey Redman and Collin Walcott, along with the title artists and the additional artists identified on the jacket cover, Anthony Braxton, Jack DeJohnette, and Miroslav Vitous. The music is equally diverse, and our favorite segment features an engaging collection of folk instruments. There are also a couple backstage interview segments, but they do not upset the flow of the show.

Child's Play 2 (Universal, 20522)

Directed by John Lafia, an evil doll attempts to transfer his soul to a young boy, while the boy is unable to convince the grownups around him that the doll is animate and wicked. Lafia keeps him popping out of the left when you're looking at the right and that sort of thing, and while the narrative is rather straightforward, it delivers the thrills and incidental humor expected from it. Jenny Agutter and Gerrit Graham are the boy's foster parents.

The picture is letterboxed, with an aspect ratio of about 1.85:1 and an accommodation for enhanced 16:9 playback. The image looks terrific, with very bright, solid, basic colors and a crisp focus. The stereo surround sound doesn't have many directional effects, but the dimensionality is sufficient for enhancing the excitement. The 84 minute program also has an optional French audio track, optional English or Spanish subtitles, production notes, a cast-and-director profile section, and the engaging trailer.

Children Shouldn't Play with Dead Things (VCI, DVD8208)

Essentially a two-part film, the first half is one long tease, where a group of would-be actors play gags on one another in a graveyard and talk a lot with the sort of arch phrasing that would-be actors are apt to employ. In the second half, however, an incantation or whatever causes the dead to rise out of their graves and stalk the heroes with a hunger only the dead are apt to employ.

The presentation runs 87 minutes, a couple minutes longer than most previous home video versions of the 1972 feature. Since the low budget feature has rather murky cinematography to begin with, the image looks overly dark, with very bland fleshtones, but details seem about as clear as they're going to get, and hues are reasonably bright. The picture is letterboxed with an aspect ratio of about 1.78:1 and no 16:9 enhancement. The monophonic sound seems adequate. There is also a trailer, a collection of lobby cards and profiles of the director, Bob Clark, and the star, Alan Ormsby.

Chinese Box (Trimark, VM68590)

An overly symbolic romance set in the final days of the British rule of Hong Kong, Jeremy Irons stars as a British national who is in love with a local girl, the mistress of a Chinese businessman. The film opens on New Year's Day, 1997, and Irons' character learns from a doctor that he has six months to live. Get it? (Britain turned the city over on July 1.) Every character is so prominently representative of a political concept that the story becomes less important than its meanings, and the result is a lifeless exercise in playacting. The Hong Kong location photography, however, is quite appealing, particularly as it is delivered by the gorgeous picture transfer. Wayne Wang directed the film, which co-stars Gong Li.

The picture transfer is gorgeous. The image is letterboxed with an aspect ratio of about 1.85:1 and no 16:9 enhancement. The colors are very smooth, sharp and glossy, and fleshtones are rich and finely detailed. The stereo surround sound is also quite nice, with strong dimensional effects and lots of power. The 99 minute film comes with a trailer, optional French and Spanish subtitles and English closed captioning.

The Chinese Connection (GoodTimes, 0581004); (Digital Multimedia, 00133)

You have to read the fine print on the jacket to notice it, but the picture on the GoodTimes presentation is fully letterboxed, with an aspect ratio of about 2.3:1 and an accommodation for enhanced 16:9 playback. The 1972 production, starring Bruce Lee, is a typical concoction about a student seeking revenge for the murder of his teacher, but with Lee's fabulous fighting and charisma it is an engaging feature. The film is virulently anti-Japanese, but gives Lee a good opportunity to show a variety of emotions and is generally a

satisfying mix of threats and fights. The narrative, however, is also a classic example of a screenplay that has been written into a corner, concluding with a freeze frame after all else fails. The source material has its share of scratches and other markings, and the image is soft at times, with bright colors appearing to exceed their boundaries, but hues are reasonably fresh and fleshtones are acceptable. The monophonic sound is somewhat distorted but workable, just as the English dubbing is awkward but functional. The film runs 106 minutes.

Digital Multimedia Limited has also released a copy of the film, without a 'The' in the title, but it is cropped, with smeary colors and an even weaker dubbed mono soundtrack.

Chino (D*Vision, DVD1008)

Charles Bronson stars with Jill Ireland in a really bad 1973 John Sturges western. Bronson portrays a horse rancher who has some trouble with a rich landowner because he likes the guy's sister. There is nothing else to the 92 minute movie, except lyrical, unhurried shots of horse ranching, and the story ends in a fizzle.

The picture quality is poor. The transfer rate rarely rises above low settings, and the image is constantly smeary, with strong artifacting. The source material is in bad condition, with scratches, faded colors and whatever else could go wrong. The only thing that doesn't seem to be much of a problem is the cropping. The monophonic audio is so hissy it sounds like a punctured tire. There is no captioning.

Chitty Chitty Bang Bang (MGM, 907032)

The 1968 Super-Panavision film has been released in cropped format only (some shots look like they might be squeezed, as well), in fear perhaps that parents will not want to expose their children to such grown-up concepts as letterboxing. The image is so distorted by the cropping that the nice picture transfer is negated, though, for the record, colors are fairly bright and the image is crisp. The stereo surround sound and Dolby Digital sound, unaffected by the scissoring of the picture, are super, with strong directional effects and an aggressive dimensionality. The 145 minute film can also be accessed in French in standard stereo and comes with English or French subtitles, along with a 'sing-along' option that subtitles the songs only with advancing chromatic changes coordinated to the lyrics, karaoke-style. A partially letterboxed trailer is included as well. Dick Van Dyke stars in the musical about a flying car.

Chloe in the Afternoon (Fox Lorber, FLV5018)

Eric Rohmer's 1971 feature is about a lawyer who almost slips into an affair with an old friend. The film builds its emotional structure gradually, dissecting a mid-life crisis in careful detail, but that in turn makes the ending all the more powerful, because by the time it arrives you can see not only the future of each character, but their alternative futures if they were to make different choices. There is also an ambiguity about the hero's wife at the end that leaves one thinking Rohmer at least toyed with the idea, for a while, of telling the story again from her point of view.

The film is presented in full screen format (cropping is minimal or non-existent) and the color has a mildly aged appearance. Hues are reasonably bright, but the image is soft and worn-looking in places, and fleshtones are a little pale. The monophonic sound is workable but bland. The film is in French and is supported by white English subtitles. Since the movie is often dominated by conversation or voiceover narration, the subtitles run pretty heavy here and there, and we sometimes suspect that this has enhanced the standing of the film with English speaking audiences. To give just one example, there is a scene with the hero and a shop girl. If you ignore the subtitles and just watch the performance of the actress playing the shop girl, she seems self-conscious and halting in her responses, but if you try to keep up with the subtitles, you never notice her shortcomings. The running time clocks in at 93 minutes instead of the standard 98, though it may just be a mild compression error coming from a PAL master. There is also a Rohmer filmography.

A Christmas Carol (Roan, 8201)

The classic 1951 British production, starring Alastair Sim, appears on one side of the DVD in black and white and on the other side colorized. Both sides begin with an introduction from Patrick Macnee (who has a small role in the film—he looks very young in the movie, but sounds the same), and both include Max Fleischer's *Rudolf, The Red Nosed Reindeer* cartoon, along with some production notes that are well written, but difficult to read.

The black-and-white source material is by no means pristine, but it looks decent enough—clearer and brighter, in fact, than the prints that usually get shown on TV—with minimal wear and reasonably detailed contrasts. Most of the time the image is quite sharp. What we were most aware of on the colorized version, besides the dark or grey mouth interiors, was the lack of a strong red, which, in a Christmas movie, is something of a drawback. Since the film has an air of antiquity that extends beyond its production date to the era it depicts, the colored-postcard hues can be appealing if one is amenable to the process, but we found ourselves feeling more attentive to the black-and-white version, which distracted us less from the emotions of the characters.

The monophonic sound seems about ten years older than it is, and is somewhat noisy, with lots of distortion on the upper end. The 86 minute program is not captioned.

We found ourselves fascinated by the film's structure. Despite its brisk running time, it squeezes in a lot of material, largely by focusing on plot and on Scrooge's story, with the rest of the milieu making little more than a token appearance. By the time the 20 minute mark rolls around, Marley's ghost has already visited Scrooge, and the next half hour is devoted to Scrooge's past. Tiny Tim appears in only a couple of scenes. The ending may seem a bit rushed, but the filmmakers are banking upon the viewer readily filling in the emotional gaps. It is a rich, no-nonsense adaptation that can dependably be pulled out Christmas after Christmas, and be taken out for a few Fourth of July viewings, as well.

A Christmas Story (MGM, 906558)

Based on the writings of Jean Sheppard and set in the snowy days approaching a Forties Christmas, all viewers will respond to the movie's mixture of dreamy nostalgia and outrageous pranks. There is a department store Santa scene that must be the ultimate of its kind. Some of the humor is subtle, such as the grotesque meals the mother is forever preparing, and will only catch your attention after several viewings.

The picture transfer on the riotously funny 1983 Bob Clark film is substantially improved over previous home video releases. Colors are much deeper and more accurate, and fleshtones look warmer. The 98 minute film is presented in full screen format only, but the letterboxing would just mask off the top and the bottom of the image without adding anything to the sides. The sound is full and nicely detailed, and the DVD also has a Dolby Digital mono track that is even stronger. The film is accompanied by a very humorous theatrical trailer, French and Spanish soundtracks, and English, French or Spanish subtitling ("Asegúrate de tomar tu chocolate Ovamultina").

Christmas Vacation (see National Lampoon's Christmas Vacation)

The Christmas Wonder Years (see The Best of The Wonder Years)

Chronos (Simitar, 7323)

Making extensive use of time-lapse photography, the 40 minute image music program looks at major artifacts of Western civilization, stretching from the Pyramids at Giza to Grand Central Station. Often examining architecture under the sped up illumination

of a day's light, the production shifts from one major era to the next in a visual meditation on art and the passage of time. Set to a soothing electronic score by Michael Sterns, the subjects under view change often enough to keep a viewer attentive, climaxing with a frantic intermingling of lightening fast trips through Los Angeles, Venice and Paris that can leave one breathless. Colors are accurate and the image is sharp, even during left-right pans. The stereo surround sound is okay. The chapter access menu works, but it has been left blank, so you have no idea what the content is of the chapter you are accessing.

Chuck Berry Rock & Roll Music (Pioneer, PA98595D)

A terrific pre-*Ding-Aling* 46 minute outdoor Chuck Berry concert, the film's title card identifies it as D.A. Pennebaker's *Keep on Rockin' Part Three Chuck Berry*. The stereo has been spruced up to great effect, with distinctive tones and engaging separation effects that sound even more rousing on the Dolby Digital track. Since the film is set outdoors during the day, the image is clear and colors are bright, even though the source material is a little aged. Berry runs through a dozen rock 'n' roll classics in his 1969 Toronto gig with an energetic freshness that would later subside when his popularity resurged. It was sort of the last chance to see him young, but fortunately it has been preserved, smashingly well.

Chushingura (Image, ID4570EWDVD)

Revival houses have traditionally had a problem with the compelling 1962 Japanese classic, for patrons attended expecting to see samurai action scenes and were instead treated to more than two-and-a-half hours of complex political maneuvering before the swordplay got underway. Yet many patrons were nevertheless won over by the film's artistry and epic drama. Insulted by an elderly lord, the leader of a clan loses his temper and assaults the old man. For his action, the clan leader is forced to kill himself. The remaining members of his clan then plot, with great secrecy, a revenge attack on the lord, which they eventually carry out. The film tells the story, which is based upon a true historical incident, but it also uses the characters and their predicaments to explore many aspects of human life and society. The film's visual beauty and variety of characters provide additional stimulation.

The 207 minute feature appears on a single-sided dual-layer platter. The presentation is letterboxed with an aspect ratio of about 2.25:1. Hues are a little flat, but are crisply detailed and solid, with accurate fleshtones. The source material has a few scattered markings, but is in reasonably good shape. The monophonic sound is adequate for the film's era, but has a limited ambiance. The film is in Japanese with permanent white English subtitles that appear beneath the letterboxed image.

Toshiro Mifune heads the cast of early Sixties Japanese stars. There are still a few moments in the film where the narrative seems to advance too quickly and one has difficulty keeping track of where characters have gone, but for the film's scope it is effectively paced and viewers will have the real sense of having experienced an epic story by the time it is over—and when that fight does finally come, it is a thrill.

Cilea's Adriana Lecouvreur: Teatro Alla Scala (Image, ID4362PUDVD)

One of Mirella Freni's finest roles, the staging is grand but spare and the video direction is competent. The four act, 154 minute program is presented on a single-sided dual-layer DVD, and is sung in Italian with English subtitles. The colors look good and fleshtones are accurate. The image is a little unstable in darker areas of the screen but center stage looks fine. The stereo sound has very little dimensionality, but the music is adequately delivered and Freni's arias are unhindered. The viable story concerns liaisons between several noblemen and actresses. Peter Dvorsky, Fiorenza Cossotto and Ivo Vinco are also featured and all sing admirably, though it is primarily Freni whose vocals grip one's attention.

City of Angels (Warner, 16320)

An honorable simplification of the German classic, *Wings of Desire*, Meg Ryan is an L.A. heart surgeon whose life is compacting under stress and Nicolas Cage is an angel who becomes smitten with her when he arrives to take away one of her patients. You could go through the movie scene-by-scene and make a case for the fantasy elements being entirely a figment of the surgeon's imagination, but it is more inviting to accept the film literally and to be drawn through its ciphers of metaphysical longing. The sorrowful-looking Cage (who doesn't blink) seems perfect for his part and Ryan's established screen persona is an adequate foil, even if she doesn't appear quite ground down enough to be a genuine doctor. The film is an intellectual romance that will grasp firmly onto the loyalties of some viewers and completely mystify others, but its highest moments of style, in the depiction of angels inhabiting our spaces, are bound to linger in the imagination of even the most stringent anti-romantics.

The 114 minute film is presented on one side, with special features appearing on the other side. The picture is letterboxed. with an aspect ratio of about 2.35:1 and an accommodation for enhanced 16:9 playback. The colors are bright and solid, and the image is sharp, bringing greater power to the cinematography's otherworldly lighting. The stereo surround sound is a bit weak and even the Dolby Digital track is adequate but a bit dull. The film is also available in French in standard stereo and can be accompanied by English or French subtitles.

On the side with the special features, there is a half hour 'making of' documentary, about fifteen minutes of deleted footage and two music videos. None of the supplement is captioned. Both the film and the deleted scenes are also supported by commentary from director Brad Silberling. The documentary and Silberling's commentary complement each other nicely. Silberling talks at great length about what he wanted to accomplish, about working with the cast and crew, and, in informative terms, about the meanings of the movie and of individual scenes. There are times, however, when he fails to go into specific details, such as how he coaxed Cage onto a girder atop a tall building for a shot, but the documentary covers that sequence (Cage made Silberling go up there, too) and other such items thoroughly. Silberling also talks about his problems with the preview process (he makes a convincing case that some movies have a delayed reaction appeal) and about showing the film to *Wings of Desire* director Wim Wenders—for those who were baffled by *Wings of Desire*, incidentally, City of Angels can function as a 'key' to understanding it.

With the exception perhaps of an extended operating sequence, the deleted footage deserved to be removed, though it will still be of interest to the movie's fans. Most of it involves further incidents of Cage's character haunting Ryan without revealing himself. In the movie's commentary Silberling speaks of one scene that had to be re-shot after production had wrapped because of errors (discovered in the preview process—there are two sides to every coin), but it would have been interesting to have the erroneous version included in the supplement. The music videos include *Iris* by the Goo Goo Dolls, which uses a lot of footage from the film, and *If God Will Send His Angels* by U2, which uses very little.

There is a second feature commentary by producer Charles Rovin and writer Dana Stevens, another feature audio track with the isolated musical score (which is often captivating) in standard stereo with scattered comments between cues by composer Gabriel Yared (the talk would have been better served as a straight essay), a 10 minute explanation of how the special effects were accomplished, quickie VH1 interviews with Alanis Morissette and Peter Gabriel and trailers for other Warner romances.

Rovin is the husband of producer Dawn Steel, who initialized the project and who passed away before its completion. Silberling's commentary is fine, but it is the Rovin and Stevens commentary track that really lets you see the passion that went into the film's conception. They talk about Steel's vision, about the enthusiastic support Wenders gave to the project, about a key contribution to the development from Johnny Depp, and the many other changes they struggled to achieve in the script.

They also lament the critics who called City of Angels a 'Hollywoodization' of *Wings of Desire*, claiming that they thought they had made the least Hollywood-like movie they'd ever worked on. That may be the case, but they are still Hollywood filmmakers and that is the movie's orientation, however well it succeeds. It isn't so much what they say, however, as it is the immediacy and naturalness of their conversation that makes their commentary track so worthwhile. One of the many themes in *Wings of Desire* that City of Angels could not address is the chasm between filmmakers and their characters. During the course of their talk, Rovin and Stevens speak of several instances where the mystery of creativity exceeded the conscious intentions of those working on the film by enhancing the psychology of a character or the philosophy and attitude of a scene. It is only with the DVD that you hear from so many of the participants and can really begin to visualize how the ghost of Dawn Steel and the other angels of creation whispered in the ears of the filmmakers and moved their hearts in the right direction.

City on Fire (import, 5061)

Most film fans are aware that Quentin Tarantino lifted the basic concept of **Reservoir Dogs** from the last act of this Hong Kong crime thriller. Chow Yun-Fat stars in the 1993 film as an undercover cop working so deeply that most of the police bureaucracy think he is no more than a crooked informer. The story is primarily about his tribulations as he tries to balance the pressures of his situation with what is left of his private life and self-respect, and it concludes with the busted jewel robbery that Tarantino expanded upon. The film is very well made and competently draws the viewer through the narrative. It isn't just another Hong Kong crime film—its one of the definitive movies of the genre.

And for Hong Kong home video standards, the DVD is in very good condition. Colors are a little pale in places but are well detailed, fleshtones are decent and wear on the source material is limited. Compared to Hollywood DVDs, the image is a little soft, but compared to the usual Hong Kong production, the picture is sharp. The image is letterboxed with an aspect ratio of about 1.9:1 and no 16:9 enhancement. The film's stereo surround soundtrack is also available in Dolby Digital. The standard stereo track is smooth, with modest dimensionality. The Dolby Digital track is more piercing, but has wider, more pronounced separations. It also has analog-style noise during quieter moments, but we're not complaining. The film is in Cantonese and Mandarin (both in Dolby Digital) and is supported by optional subtitling in English (though sometimes rather awkwardly—"Go to the hell," a girl tells her boyfriend), traditional Chinese, simplified Chinese, Japanese, Indonesian, Malaysian, Thai, Korean and Vietnamese. There are also star profiles available in most of those languages, including English, and a bunch of trailers. Danny Lee co-stars in the 100 minute film, which was directed by Ringo Lam.

Claire's Knee (Fox Lorber, FLV5019)

Eric Rohmer's 1972 feature is set in Switzerland. The hero has a different sort of mid-life catharsis, becoming infatuated with a teenage girl. He attempts to resolve his desire by channeling his impulses to a seemingly acceptable act—touching her knee—but the film's humor and elegance comes from showing, again in gradual and meticulous detail—that his impulses and focus are almost as reprehensible as they would have been had he actually wanted to molest her.

The film is presented in full screen format (cropping is minimal or non-existent) and the color has a mildly aged appearance. Hues are reasonably bright, but the image is soft and worn-looking in places, and fleshtones are a little pale. The monophonic sound is bland. The film is in French and is supported by white English subtitles. Since the movie is often dominated by conversation or voiceover narration, the subtitles run pretty heavy here and there.

The running time on **Claire's Knee** clocks in at 101 minutes, which is somewhat less than the standard 106 minute running time, but we assume the DVD's master comes from a PAL source or is otherwise slightly compressed. The program is accompanied by a Rohmer filmography.

Class of Nuke 'Em High (Troma, DVD9200)

A jokey 1986 burlesque of slime and gore about a high school infected by nuclear waste, the picture quality is strong when one takes the film's limited budget into account. When the cinematography is in focus, so is the DVD, and colors are generally quite bright. The sound is workable, as well. The program is not captioned.

The film's co-director and Troma's CEO, Lloyd Kaufman, provides a decent running commentary. He talks about how the film was made on a restricted budget, where it was shot, who some of the secondary performers were, how some of the actors were directed, and once in a while he throws in a gag or two about the artistic value of his creation. He also explains how some performers, finding more gainful employment, would just not show up anymore for the shoot, so their characters simply disappear halfway through the film. More importantly, he points out that the film has thrived on home video and suggests that its popularity can be linked directly to the enthusiasm of those who made it.

About a half dozen excess scenes have been included in the supplement. Although they were clearly dropped to pick up the film's pace and don't add much to one's understanding of the film's deeper meanings, fans will likely appreciate their presence. Additionally, there is a brief explanation of one of the film's special effects by its creator, an enjoyable interview with a couple who met as performers in the movie and are now married, a weakly scripted and cheaply shot group tomfoolery sequence meant to promote Troma products, a brief nude modeling sequence thrown into the supplement for the heck of it, a dozen-and-a-half color stills, and trailers for five Troma features.

Classic Views Vol. 1 No. 2: Bryn Terfel (Image, ID4448CWDVD)

Frankly, they ought to be giving away the **Classic Views** *The Classical Music and Opera Video Magazine* video for free. The program, which contains short segments on various classical music subjects, is highly informative and fairly entertaining, but many of the segments are also virtual commercials (and the segments are often separated by real commercials), so that as you sit through the video you begin to compile a mental list of all the CDs and videos you're going to buy when the show is over. The program runs 94 minutes and contains eight segments, an interview with Terfel about his career, violinist Dmitry Sitkovetsky talking about the *Goldberg Variations*, Bobby McFerrin dipping his toes in classical performances, two segments that are almost pure marketing, with critics Martin Bernheimer and William Livingstone discussing opera on video and recent CD releases respectively, a more scholarly and satisfying discussion of modern 12-tone music by John Adams, an informative promotional segment on the restored *Alexander Nevsky* and an animated clip from *Opera Imaginaire*. The pieces regularly mix music and talk, so the program may not function well as a music entertainment, but the interviews are stimulating and enlightening.

Classical Fireworks (Platinum, 2311)

There are no pyrotechnics, just animals. The 72 minute program features passages from seven well known classical music pieces, including *The Ride of the Valkyries*, a piece of Beethoven's *Fifth Symphony*, Bach's *Fugue in D Minor*, Tchaikovsky's *Piano Concerto No. 1* (complete), a piece of Mozart's *Symphony No. 40*, the finale of *Scheherazade* and Offenbach's *Overture to Orpheus*, popularly known as the *Can Can*. Each public domain recording is by a different ensemble, ranging from the San Diego Philharmonic under Lalo Schifrin to the Royal Philharmonic under Norman Sat-

tler. The performances are rather generic, but have been enhanced with Dolby Digital sound (which must be activated from the Audio control on one's remote). Although the recordings vary a bit in quality, the Dolby Digital tends to deliver more active and better defined separations. African wildlife footage accompanies all the pieces. The image quality is often very good.

Classical Visions (Madacy, DVD99051)
Classical Visions: The Magic of Vienna (Madacy, DVD990511)
Classical Visions: Spring Flowers (Madacy, DVD9905112)
Classical Visions: Autumn Dream (Madacy, DVD9905113)

There are no shots of an orchestra in any of the programs, which are offered individually and as a box set. **Magic of Vienna** features images of Vienna intercut with shots of a formally dressed couple waltzing in various locales. Most of the pieces are performed by the Vienna Opera Orchestra under Carl Michalski, with Peter Falk conducting one number and another performed by the London Symphony Orchestra under Alfred Scholz. The performances are legitimate and tend to be a bit more aggressive than the standard generic renditions of the pieces, which include *The Blue Danube*, *Emperor Waltz*, *Voices of Spring*, the overture to *Die Fledermaus* and *The Gypsy Baron*.

Beethoven's *Spring Sonata*, *Moonlight Sonata*, *Piano Concerto No. 2 in B flat major* and *Adante Favori in F major* are performed to images of flowers and other nature views on the 48 minute **Spring Flowers**. The piano pieces are played by Peter Schmalfuss, Josef Bulva, and Friedmann Rieger. Violinist Nora Chastain accompanies Rieger on **Spring Sonata**, but there is nothing exceptional or even noteworthy about any of the workmanlike performances.

There is a major typographical error on the back of the **Autumn Dreams** jacket. Although the detail listings are correct, the heading claims the program is **Spring Flowers**. Anyway, the 61 minute presentation is set to rather fascinating people-less autumnal images of the Ukraine. If they aren't dripping in radioactivity, there are some terrific potential movie locations in the wild but calm landscapes. There are also lots of close-ups of fallen leaves and those kinds of things. Most of the concertos are performed by the Slovak Philharmonic Orchestra. Schmalfuss and Bulva return on the piano, along with Marian Pivka and Ida Cemicka. The performances have a bit more personality than the Beethoven program and, of the three DVDs, this is probably the strongest. The picture quality on all three programs looks fine, with crisp, bright hues. The stereo sound is not elaborately separated and some of the pieces on **Spring Flowers** and **Autumn Dreams** are mixed with environmental sounds. The recordings of the orchestral works tend to be stronger and cleaner than the recordings of the piano pieces but, on the whole, the audio quality is acceptable. Each DVD contains a composer time line, brief essays about musical instruments and a trivia section.

Clean and Sober (Warner, 11824)

The film is a comedy. Not the kind you laugh at, but a comedy nonetheless. It is about a man who enters a detoxification program to hide from the police and—punchline—detoxifies in spite of himself. It is good to know that Michael Keaton, who stars, can include restraint among his many fine talents. One shudders to think what many other actors would have done with the part. Even his vomiting scene is subdued. He knows that he's going to be on the screen a lot and that he doesn't have to exhaust himself to make an impression. It is because he treats the part so soberly that he is able to play up the irony of his character's situation, thereby saving the movie from going off the deep end.

The picture is presented in full screen format. There is some grain, fleshtones are bland and hues are not vivid, but the image is workable. There is a mildly stereophonic soundtrack with a modest dimensionality. The 124 minute program is adequately closed captioned.

Clear and Present Danger (Paramount, 324637)

The advantage to big budget adaptations of popular novels is that they usually have some substance to them. **Clear and Present Danger**, based upon the book by Tom Clancy, has an action scene here and there, but its primary appeal is in its political and high-tech dialogue, as delivered by Harrison Ford and the rest of the cast. It may not have great philosophical content, but at least you have to concentrate to keep track of what is going on. The 1994 feature is in letterboxed format, with an aspect ratio of about 2.35:1 and no 16:9 enhancement. The picture is sharp and colors are nicely detailed. The 1994 film's audio mix is sort of linear, offering one effect after another instead of piling them up on top of each other, but it is still a strong effort that is worth amplifying and the DVD delivers it effectively. The standard stereo track is okay and the Dolby Digital track is sharper and stronger. The 141 minute film is also available in French in standard stereo and can be supported by English or Spanish subtitles. A theatrical trailer is also included.

Harrison Ford portrays Clancy's hands-on CIA executive hero, Jack Ryan. In this episode, another government agency instigates an illegal military operation against the Columbian drug lords and Ford's character must set things straight before he is blamed for the mess it will cause. As is often the case, Ford moves through the part with a seemingly minimum effort, but keeps his grip on the viewer by parceling out emotion at just the right intervals. Although repeat viewings may be limited, the movie is fairly involving and delivers everything fans will expect from it.

Cleopatra Jones (Warner, 11275)

Tamara Dobson is a statuesque government agent marked for death by a drug mob being run by Shelley Winters. Shot in widescreen and presented in letterboxed format, with an aspect ratio of about 2.35:1 and an accommodation for enhanced 16:9 playback, the 1973 film is a fairly classy attempt to present a black female action hero. Dressed in flashy outfits by Giorgio di Sant' Angelo, Dobson keeps a cool composure and kicks the daylights out of every nemesis. The action scenes are stretched out a bit and the story isn't all that creative, but the production looks slick and there is a strong nostalgic appeal, along with a few amusingly awkward inter-racial insults. The color transfer is super, with crisp, bright, smooth hues and rich fleshtones. The monophonic sound is so strong is seems stereophonic in places. There is a French audio track as well, and English captioning.

Clerks (Buena Vista, 17365)

Kevin Smith's debut effort is a black-and-white comedy about a convenience store clerk and a video store clerk who talk with a marvelous, earthy wit about love and other subjects as oddballs come and go from their stores. There is also a narrative, of sorts, as the hero argues with his new girlfriend and yearns for his former one.

The transfer is probably as good as it is going to get. The filmmakers readily admit that budget limitations forced them to use damaged film on occasion and employ other cost cutting measures that can impact the quality of the image. However, since the 1994 film also has a sort of anti-establishment air, the grainy image and occasional soft focus shot can seem artistically appropriate, in the spirit of rebellion against the status quo and that sort of thing. The same is true of the stereo surround sound, though it was beefed up a bit right before the movie's theatrical release and is generally acceptable. The picture is letterboxed with an aspect ratio of about 1.85:1 and no 16:9 enhancement. The 92 minute program can be supported by optional English subtitles.

A number of members from the film's crew are on hand for an alternate audio commentary, although Smith does most of the talking and is better miked than the others. Unless it is some kind of joke, one of the cast members apparently spends the entire time zonked out at Smith's feet, rising up once in a while to make some completely incoherent statement and then falling back into his ine-briated coma. Everybody appears to find this funny, though if they are really his friends they ought to be rolling him into a clinic as soon as possible. Smith's description of the film's production is moderately informative, giving the viewer an idea of how the movie was conceived and how individual scenes were executed. He tends to digress and is not thorough in his reporting, but by the end of the talk you have a general idea of what went on behind the camera.

There is also deleted footage. It is usually material that slowed down the pace of the film and deserved to be excised. One sequence, however, presents the film's original ending, which is more expected but more devastating than the ending that has been used. We would like to have heard from Smith as to why he decided to change it, but coming as it does at the end of the extra footage segment, the viewer could well end up remembering it as the way the movie concludes. Also featured are a theatrical trailer and a music video, the latter shot in color by Smith on the **Clerks** location, imitating a scene from the film.

The Client (Warner, 13233)

A young boy privy to information about a murder very smartly hires a lawyer before talking to an aggressive D.A. in the entertaining thriller. Susan Sarandon is the lawyer and Tommy Lee Jones is the D.A. Yet another hit based upon a John Grisham tale, the Joel Schumacher film generates as much excitement from arched eyebrows as it does from chases through empty hospital corridors, but it has dilemmas and moral conflicts that you can really sink your teeth into. The cast is wonderful and the narrative gives them plenty to work with.

The picture is in letterboxed format on one side, with an aspect ratio of about 2.35:1 and an accommodation for enhanced 16:9 playback, and in cropped format on the other side. The cropping is workable, since the film contains a lot of talking heads, but the most dramatic sequences are much more pleasing in widescreen. There is no obvious effort to create a balanced rectangular image. Rather, the film seems to let the viewer in on a larger slice of the world, giving the characters a more detailed context than could be achieved with a square image. On a large theatrical screen, the design pulls the viewer into the film, and even on a small screen the effect is subtle but impressive, making up for the script's heavy reliance on conversation by forcing the viewer to spend more time absorbing each shot. The image is a bit under-colored and there is a mild haze in some shots that goes beyond the deliberately soft cinematography. The stereo surround sound is weak and sounds a little hollow, though since the best parts of the movie are conversations and not sound effects, it doesn't hamper the entertainment. The 121 minute 1994 film can be supported by English, French or Spanish subtitles. There is a passable cast-and-crew profile, a couple of production notes and a nice theatrical trailer.

Cliffhanger (Columbia TriStar, 52239)

Renny Harlin's somewhat violent film, which stars Sylvester Stallone and John Lithgow, about an innocent mountain rescue team battling a stranded group of cutthroat treasury hijackers, is ideal for viewing in winter time, when movies set in the wind-whipped snow are the most congruous with one's viewing atmosphere. The show has so much inventive action, adept characterization, and dramatic flair, however, that it will be spellbinding in any season, and such repeat potential that viewers may well end up watching it the year around. One need only look at the movie's opening scene to see how thorough Harlin's skills as a popular filmmaker are. Although Michelle Joyner's performance, as the climber whose buckle breaks in mid-air, is nerve-wrackingly precise and an outstanding piece of work, it is Harlin's step-by-step conception of the scene, and his coordination of all the performances, that makes the sequence so harrowing and devastating. Because the performances and narrative are so much fun, the stunts are so thrilling and the scenery is so spectacular (one aspect of the film that most critics ignored), **Cliffhanger** is highly enjoyable and open to many repeat viewings, making it ideal DVD entertainment.

The 1993 thriller is presented in letterboxed format on one side, with an aspect ratio of about 2.35:1 and an accommodation for enhanced 16:9 playback, and in cropped format on the other side. There is one long shot in the mountain climbing thriller where one group is walking across the top of a cliff face and two other people are directly below them, edging across a ledge on the same cliff. Even with a thirty foot screen you could barely see the two on the ledge, and on the letterboxed version it is doubtful you would spot them if you didn't know where to look, but they are there and the power of the film's grip holds no matter how small your screen is. The color transfer on both versions is perfect, and although the cropped version is a blown up rendition of the letterboxed presentation, no grain is added to the enlarged image. We would recommend the standard version only to viewers who are adamantly opposed to letterboxing, however, since the scanning and cropping add nothing to the drama and are restrictive at times to the action. In the sequence involving an explosion on a suspension bridge, for example, you only see the hero on the bridge when it explodes on the letterboxed version. On the cropped version, it looks like the filmmakers are cheating the stunt with editing. Nevertheless, the drawbacks on the cropped version are minor and both versions deliver enough excitement to leave a viewer weak in the knees.

The stereo surround sound is okay and the Dolby Digital track is befitting of the film's budget, though sound effects generally take a supporting role to the film's visuals. The 115 minute program also has French and Spanish tracks in standard stereo and can be supported by optional Spanish subtitles or English closed captioning.

Clinton, President (see **President Clinton's Grand Jury Video: August 17, 1998**)

Clive Barker's Salomé & The Forbidden (Image, ID4606SADVD

Destined to be unloaded by successions of collectors for years hence, two very uncommercial experimental/beginning films by Clive Barker have been combined on the *Redemption* program. Both films are silent 8mm black-and-white pieces, accompanied by an electronic stereo score composed for the home video release. The source material for both films is raunchy and bedraggled, though while *Forbidden* the condition of the image works in favor of the film's themes. Although the DVD has a 78 minute running time, the first 8 minutes are given over to Redemption's tiresome gore & nudity prologue. *Salomé*, shot in 1973, runs 18 minutes and *Forbidden*, shot between 1975 and 1978, runs 36 minutes, followed by a 16 minute interview with Barker and his collaborators. *Salomé*, however, is even more of a waste of time than Redemption's prologue. Horrendously grainy and blurry, most of the film consists of vague shots of a young woman intercut with a couple other vague shots of a guy with a beard. Eventually, there is an image of someone descending a ladder and a couple other activities, but one can no more discern the story of *Salomé* from these proceedings than one can discern a logic to either the staging or the editing. *The Forbidden* is a much stronger work and may induce at least a few fans to hold onto their copies after an initial viewing. Deftly using negative processing to obscure the images, the film (cleverly) includes a depiction of a man's skin being peeled off him, as well as other suggestively violent activities, in keeping with the sort material Barker would go on to revel in with his later works. There is also a substantial amount of male and female nudity. The film has no narrative, but it comes close to achieving a rhythm of dark desires and fears. The interviews provide a thorough explanation as to what the filmmakers were trying to accomplish and how the movies were made.

Clockers (Universal, 20016)

Spike Lee oozes style from every filmmaking pore. He's had a couple of misfires, but every movie he makes is a masterful exercise in technique if nothing else. **Clockers**, one of his best films, is a police procedural about an inner city murder investigation, and Lee shoots it like a documentary or a surveillance film. There are none of the fancy, sweeping crane shots he's used elsewhere. Instead it is all rough and immediate, so even when scenes are elaborately blocked they look like they are pieced together from scraps of film shot in a hurry. That he can let go of one style and grab another when the drama calls for it is what makes him such an exciting director. It is his flexibility that will enable his career to survive the varied subject matter he tackles.

Clockers is adapted from a novel by Richard Price and has a more convoluted plot than an original screenplay would have. It is gritty and raw in places, exploring the psychologies of small time drug dealers and layabouts as the investigating detective, played by Harvey Keitel, tries to stir up the status quo to find out what really happened. John Turturro, Mekhi Phifer, Delroy Lindo, and Isaiah Washington are also featured.

The Dolby Digital track has a brighter, more dimensional presence than the standard track, adding to the film's involving atmosphere. The movie has a colorful but cluttered and occasionally grimy urban look, and the DVD appears to deliver it accurately. The image is letterboxed with an aspect ratio of about 1.85:1 and an accommodation for enhanced 16:9 playback. The 129 minute program is available in French in Dolby Digital and can be supported by English or Spanish subtitles. There are some informative production notes, a cast-and-director profile section and an artistically compelling trailer.

A Clockwork Orange (Warner, 17367)

Malcolm McDowell is a punk sent to prison for murder who is then allowed to undergo a mind control regimen to go free, subsequently becoming a political pawn between liberals and law-and-order enthusiasts. Throughout the 1971 film, Stanley Kubrick uses very narrow set designs, reinforcing the representation of the hero as a personification of Libido—no wonder he is irrepressible. One might say that many people like the film for the wrong reason—responding directly to its violence and sex without acknowledging the lessons it wants to impart—but the film's abstract inserts, its political, psychological and cultural satire (making fun, for example, of the ubiquity of Beethoven's *9th Symphony*), and its loveless eroticism make it a celebration of wrong reasons. Those who condemn it and those who praise it can be equally embarrassed when they try to detail their arguments, because the film continually negates the values it pretends to espouse. The lingo may be different, but it is a gangsta movie, without a constituency.

The wear on the source material is not enough to spoil the film—you probably won't even notice most of them if you don't look for them (they're mainly in the second half)—but it is difficult to believe that Kubrick would have allowed such a print to be exhibited in even one theater, let alone be disseminated on home video, were video, were he cognizant of the flaws (example—44:17). Otherwise, the film's colors look accurate. Fleshtones are purposely pale and other hues also look deliberately light or washed out (there are often lights shining directly into the camera, another Kubrick touch), but the replication appears accurate and, occasional speckles aside, is highly pleasing, particularly in the sharpness of its detail. The picture is letterboxed with an aspect ratio of about 1.55:1 and no 16:9 enhancement. The monophonic sound is weak, but the Dolby Digital mono sound is stronger. The 137 minute program has an optional French language track, optional English or French subtitles ("Mais assez parlé. Les actes sont plus éloquents que. Aux actes, à présent"), and an exactly 1 minute long trailer that discourages blinking.

Close to You: Remembering the Carpenters (MPI, DVD7278)

A fine documentary about Karen Carpenter's rise to fame, brother Richard Carpenter appears to have been extensively involved in the production and it is the interviews with him that provide the show's structural narration. The program does not dig too deeply into their private lives, but it does provide an authoritative summary of how their career advanced, to the accompaniment of many rare and pleasing film and performance clips. Other notable personalities, including Herb Alpert, Petula Clark, Paul Williams and the members of the Carpenter's backup band, also speak in talking head clips. None of the songs are played fully from beginning to end without interruption, but there are other programs and media that provide that service. You do get a lot of music during the course of the show, and the songs are so familiar that they will continue playing in your head for hours afterwards, anyway.

The documentary runs 73 minutes and is accompanied by an additional 12 minutes of clips, featuring commercials, videos and news footage. There are an additional two Japanese soft drink commercials and a montage of publicity photos, set to recordings, that run another 12 minutes or so. Also, there is a superb discography section, the most complete we have yet seen on DVD, itemizing the singles (with their jacket covers) and the albums (with their song listings), as well as miscellaneous recording errata. The contemporary interviews look fine, with accurate fleshtones and stable colors. The archival material varies in quality, but most of it looks reasonably nice and some of the 'mod' Seventies sets in the clips are great fun. The stereo sound is fine, though again it varies with the nature of the recordings. The program (but not the song lyrics) are supported by English, French or Spanish subtitles.

Cloud 9 X-rated (Vivid, UPC# 0073215558)

The vague narrative about ghosts helping a guy with his relationship, through his and his partner's dreams, has little to offer. The erotic sequences are bland and colors are a bit light and hazy. The sound is passable. The 67 minute program stars Racquel Darrian ("Her first feature since June of 1994," hails the jacket cover), Felecia and Barbara Doll. The DVD contains alternate angle sequences and elaborate hardcore interactive promotional features.

Cobra (Warner, 11594)

"Well this movie didn't get the Oscar," proclaims director George P. Cosmatos facetiously on a commentary track accompanying the 1986 action feature. The 87 minute Sylvester Stallone film has been released in letterboxed format on one side, with an aspect ratio of about 1.85:1 and an accommodation for enhanced 16:9 playback, and in full screen format on the other side. The letterboxing adds nothing to the sides and loses picture information on the top and bottom compared to the full screen framing, and we preferred the latter, which doesn't look as cramped. The image is rarely grainy, hues are deep and fleshtones are accurate. The cinematography still leaves some sequences overly lit, but when the film is glossy and crisp, the DVD presentation is as well. The stereo surround sound has a pronounced bass and an accomplished range, and the DVD has a Dolby Digital track that is even better, with more separation details and a greater dimensionality.

Stallone stars with Brigitte Nielsen in the story of a cop trying to protect a witness from a motorcycle gang. The film is also available in French in standard stereo and in Spanish in mono, and can be accompanied by English, French or Spanish subtitles ("Eres una enfermedad y yo soy el remedio"). There is a modest cast profile section, some decent production notes, seven Stallone trailers, including one for Over the Top, and a fairly comprehensive 8 minute 'making of' featurette. Cosmatos is laid back and in good humor, but he doesn't have much to say and mostly provides a play-by-play account of what is evident on the screen. He does go into a bit of detail about the locations, about what he wanted to shoot but couldn't, and about the scenes he might have trimmed if he were to recut the film today, but even when he breaks off to provide his au-

tobiography he doesn't do much more than reel off the other films he's made and who starred in them.

The Cocoanuts (Image, ID4279USDVD)

Critics tend to dismiss the first Marx Bros. film in favor of their later, more accomplished and cinematic efforts, yet the film is actually less awkward than their second feature, **Animal Crackers**, and has always been one of our favorites. Although based upon a stageplay, the 1929 Paramount feature, in which Groucho is running a failing Florida resort and jewel thieves are trying to hide a hot necklace, has some elaborate musical sequences and a better mixture of camera angles than **Crackers** does. It also has funnier jokes, and more of them. Some reels look fairly sharp, with crisp contrasts and manageable damage, but a few reels are weaker, with much softer contrasts and a more aged, worn appearance. The monophonic sound is wobbly and noisy, but that is to be expected and the distortions are manageable. The 93 minute program is not closed captioned.

Cold Eyes of Fear (Image, ID4611SADVD)

The *Redemption* feature comes from 1970 and was directed by Enzo G. Castellari, a.k.a. Enzo Girolami, under the title, *Gli Occhi Freddi Della Paura*, and has also been known as *Desperate Moments*. A lawyer and a woman he's picked up in a bar are held hostage in an apartment by two gunmen. The motive of the villains is unclear at first, and the narrative has several fairly good twists before things get sorted out. The 91 minute film is set in London and is in English, although some of the cast speak their lines phonetically. There is a gratuitous nude scene at the very beginning and brief glimpses of gore, but generally the film is rather tame. The strength of the story and Castellari's hip visuals (well supported by an Ennio Morricone jazz score), however, make the movie legitimately entertaining (and repeatable), enabling it to overcome any drawbacks its international production and exploitational trappings might suggest. Fernando Rey has a supporting role. Colors are reasonably fresh and fleshtones look nice. The image is fairly sharp and the source material has no more than scattered damage. The picture is letterboxed with an aspect ratio of about 1.8:1 and no 16:9 enhancement. The monophonic audio, which is not captioned, suffers from the sort of scratches one associates with a well-used optical track, but is in tolerable condition. Like all Redemption titles, the program opens with a lengthy and tiresome video prologue containing a lot of nudity. There is also an enjoyable trailer.

Cold Sweat (D*Vision, DVD1006)

Charles Bronson stars with an unlikely action film companion, Liv Ullman. Set on the French Riviera, the 1971 film was directed by Terence Young and co-stars James Mason and Jill Ireland. The plot is a standard template, with Bronson's character, settled and with a family, forced to defend himself when hooligans from his past reappear, but there always seems to be something happening, even if some of the car chases and gun fights do get stretched out a bit.

The picture quality is very poor. The image is cropped and colors are weak, changing tone from one reel to the next. The source material has wear marks and other damage, and the image is also beset by video transfer flaws and heavy artifacting. The monophonic sound is tinny. The film runs 94 minutes.

The Color Purple (Warner, 11534)

The color purple is the color of bruises, the color of passion, and the color of the sort of prose Steven Spielberg is often accused of creating on film. The first time we saw the movie we thought it was the ultimate emotional roller coaster ride, but those feeling have not lasted through multiple viewings. We haven't tired of the film, however, since its subtler charms—the humor, the photography, the performances—grow in stature as the deliberate heart tuggings diminish. Based upon the novel by Alice Walker, Whoopi

Goldberg stars in the 1985 drama about a young woman in the South whose life is almost destroyed by the men around her before she is barely old enough to start enjoying it. Those who thrive on Spielberg's suspense and fantasy efforts may have found **Purple** to be a little too prissy, but there is an adolescent spirit that the movie speaks in a voice as clear as the snakes and bugs of the Indiana Jones pictures. **The Color Purple** manipulates the emotions of familial happiness and self-discovery in the same way that *Jaws* manipulates fear and *Close Encounters* manipulates wonder. It is the purity of those emotions that drives some people crazy and others back to the film again and again.

The crisp accuracy of the DVD format is stunning. The purple flowers burst forth, and thereafter every image in the film looks richly detailed, be it in the bright sun, like the opening, or in the shadows. The 147 minute movie is spread to two sides and is letterboxed, with an aspect ratio of about 1.85:1 and an accommodation for enhanced 16:9 playback. The stereo surround sound is weak, but the Dolby Digital track is stronger, with a more detail. There is also a French audio track, in standard stereo, and English, French or Spanish subtitles, along with a small cast profile and some press kit production notes. Two trailers are also included, one that is a black-and-white montage of still photos and a re-release trailer.

Come and Get It (HBO, 90660)

Frances Farmer's magnetic presence can be seen in its full bloom in the Edna Ferber generational tale about the Wisconsin logging industry. Farmer actually has two roles, playing both a prostitute and her daughter. It is in the former role, in scenes directed by Howard Hawks, that she truly shines, giving the kind of throaty, eye-to-eye with the men performance that Hawks was renown for eliciting from a handful of actresses. The 1936 film was directed in part by Hawks and in part by William Wyler, and film fans will have no trouble spotting who did what. Because of the nature of the narrative, one part taking place some twenty years and in a much rougher environment than the other, the shift in directoral styles is not a bad thing, though the first part of the movie holds so much promise one longs to know what Hawks would have done with the rest of it (there is also some outstanding logging footage that was shot by a third director). Edward Arnold stars as the logging baron who goes through a middle age crisis when he meets the daughter of an old flame. Joel McCrea and Walter Brennan also appear. Thanks to the thick plotting Ferber provides, the film is highly engaging, and Arnold's performance, like Farmer's, is beautifully crafted.

The black-and-white picture transfer looks quite good, getting the most out of Gregg Toland's often gripping cinematography. The source material is fairly clean and contrasts are crisp, with rich, smooth blacks. The sound is available in both mono, which sounds a little subdued, and remastered stereo, which is a little brighter without being ridiculous. The 99 minute film also has Italian and German mono audio tracks, optional English, French and Spanish subtitles, a cast & crew profile section and an original trailer.

Coming to America (Paramount, 321577)

A gem in the careers of both Eddie Murphy and John Landis (and costume designer Deborah Nadoolman), the 1988 feature is a wonderful and very amusing romantic comedy, about an African prince who moves to Queens to find a woman, unaware of his nobility, that can love him. In addition to his broader comical antics, Murphy does magical things with the cadence of his voice, and it is probably because he nailed his performance so perfectly in this film that he went on to attempt several more (and less successful) romances. The film features a number of other black actors who have gone on to bigger things, including Samuel L. Jackson and Eriq La Salle, and if James Earl Jones has ever been funnier (as Murphy's father, the King), we don't remember it.

The picture is letterboxed with an aspect ratio of about 1.85:1 and an accommodation for enhanced 16:9 playback. Hues are solid and unblemished, and the picture is sharp. There are rarely any exceptionally intense hues, but the presentation looks fine. We tended to prefer the standard stereo surround soundtrack to the Dolby Digital track. The standard track routed more effects to the rear channel, and while the tones on the Dolby Digital track are somewhat more refined, the tones on the standard track are more rambunctious. The 114 minute program is adequately closed captioned and is accompanied by an amusing trailer. Oh, and in addition to everything else, the movie is also about what a wonderful, egalitarian place America is.

Commando (Fox, 4110424)

Arnold Schwarzenegger stars in the 1985 film, about a former special forces officer whose daughter is kidnapped. The humorous exaggerations of Schwarzenegger's strength make for some inspired touches, never getting too outrageous. The film establishes its premise quickly and doesn't slow down, so it is easy to let all the holes in the plot just breeze by (Rae Dawn Chong's character, for example, knows what sort of gasoline old seaplanes use because she's taking flying lessons). For those who enjoy high body counts and a bit of humor with their violence, it is ideal entertainment.

The picture is presented in letterboxed format only, with an aspect ratio of about 1.85:1 and no 16:9 enhancement. The picture looks fine, with bright, crisp hues and accurate fleshtones. There is no 5.1 Dolby Digital track, but the standard stereo surround sound is reasonably boisterous, with an adequate dimensionality. There is also a French audio track, optional English and Spanish subtitles and a trailer.

The Complete Uncensored Private SNAFU: Cartoons from World War II (Image, ID5533BKDVD)

A 130 minute collection, the black-and-white cartoons are severely windowboxed, often trimming picture information from all four sides of the image, but the source material is in fairly good condition, with sharp, clear lines and solid contrasts. There is some scattered wear, but it seems minor. The monophonic sound is fine and the program is not captioned. The director of each cartoon (many were by Chuck Jones, Friz Freleng, Bob Clampett, etc.) has been identified with a superimposed credit. The cartoons were produced in 1943, 1944 and 1945. The collection is said to include every SNAFU cartoon that was created, including one that was never released to the Armed Services, and the DVD's comprehensiveness is an attractive asset.

Although there are understandably caricatured depictions of the Germans and the Japanese, the cartoons were intended not so much as propaganda, but as instructional entertainment, demonstrating how not to camouflage, look for booby traps, let slip secrets and that sort of thing. There is some enjoyable nudity and lots of bawdy gags, and they can still boost morale, even though the war has long since ended.

Computer Animation Celebration (see **Odyssey: The Mind's Eye Presents Computer Animation Celebration**)

Computer Animation Classics (see **Odyssey: The Mind's Eye Presents Computer Animation Classics**)

Computer Animation Showcase (see **Odyssey: The Mind's Eye Presents Computer Animation Showcase**)

Con Air (Buena Vista, 13860)

Critics have always had trouble defining the more visceral thrillers and they often resort to calling them comedies, even films such as *North by Northwest* and **Psycho**, because there is no other real way to convey the release of tension such films facilitate. **Con Air** is more deliberately a comedy, and that is the essence of its appeal. It's premise—the airplane full of America's worst criminals—is ticklishly absurd, but a natural, exaggerated step in the progression of high rise buildings, destroyers and other locales where such action movies have been set. The cast plays wonderfully to expectations, because many of the actors—John Malkovich, Steve Buscemi, Ving Rhames—already seem to have criminal personalities; they have just steered into entertainment instead of lawbreaking. The film's finale could have been better than it is, blowing what could have been a spectacularly absurd punchline—the destruction of a Las Vegas landmark—but the film is a great deal of fun and the critics who continue to put it down are taking life and the movies too seriously.

The 1987 summer blockbuster is in letterboxed format only, with an aspect ratio of about 2.35:1 and no 16:9 enhancement. The picture has sharp, glossy colors and decent looking fleshtones. The stereo surround sound is marvelous, full of directional effects and oomphs, and there is a Dolby Digital track with even better dimensional and directional effects. Accompanied by a pair of theatrical trailers, the 115 minute film is also available in French and comes with English or Spanish subtitles ("Guarda el conejito en la caja"). Nicolas Cage stars.

The Con Artists (Simitar, 7250)

An enjoyable 1978 Italian production that was clearly influenced by **The Sting**, Anthony Quinn and Andriano Celentano star as a pair of confidence men who pull several scams on some mobsters. The scams are clever and the film is a pleasant mixture of comedy and crime. The 86 minute film is dubbed, but that is to be expected. The picture looks somewhat worn and lines are soft, but colors are reasonably deep and fleshtones are more pale in some sequences than in others. The image is a bit tight, but does not appear to be cropped too badly. The monophonic sound is tolerable and is not captioned.

Conan the Barbarian (Universal, 20156)

The 1981 production stars Arnold Schwarzenegger as the muscular warrior thief who tangles with a sorcerer in a non-technological era. The film has its pleasures, not the least of which is Sandahl Bergman (cast for her physique instead of her face, her close-ups are gloriously real and far more satisfying than the other actresses in the film, all of whom conform to the standard movie producer concepts of beauty), but it is also overblown and undernourished, spending a great deal of time on just a few linear incidents.

The presentation is letterboxed with an aspect ratio of about 2.2:1 and no 16:9 enhancement. The picture is crisp and colors are strong, with accurate fleshtones and stability in the darker sequences. The monophonic sound has a good bass and a decent range. The 129 minute program is also available in Spanish and French and can be accompanied by English, French or Spanish subtitles ("Ce qui en nous tue pas nous rend plus forte"). There is a decent cast profile section, some good production notes and a theatrical trailer.

Conan the Destroyer (Universal, 20172)

No bothersome quotations from Friedrich Nietzsche open the title cards **Conan the Destroyer**, a less taxing and in many ways more enjoyable sequel to **Conan the Barbarian**. The first film had a number of fine sequences, but it also seemed over-produced and leaden. The second has little in the way of memorable moments, but it is an efficient and enjoyable adventure with a fun cast, including Arnold Schwarzenegger and Grace Jones, some decent fights, and a steady, forward moving narrative.

The 1984 feature is in letterboxed format with an aspect ratio of about 2.35:1 and no 16:9 enhancement. Colors are crisp and fleshtones are accurate. In some scenes, the lighting is a little hokey, but outdoor sequences look super and well-lit indoor scenes look fine. The monophonic sound is passable and the 101 minute program can also be accessed in French or supported by English subtitles. There is a theatrical trailer, some production notes and a decent cast profile section.

Concert at Saint-Severin (Image, ID5027GCDVD)

Giovanni Pergolese's *Stabat Mater* and Wolfgang Mozart's *Coronation Mass* are performed. Staged inside the Saint-Severin cathedral by the Versailles Soloists and conducted by Mernard Le Monnier, with featured singers Antoine Garcin, Delphine Haidan, Sophie Fournier and Daniel Galvez Vallejo, the editing cuts between close-ups of the singers, the orchestra and occasional pans across the decorations and architecture of the cathedral.

The performances are competent and the PCM stereo isn't bad. It has a nice dimensionality and is free of distortion. The acoustics of the cathedral tend to amplify the echoes of louder sounds and not of softer ones, but the effect just gives the concert a slightly unique flavor. The picture is letterboxed with an aspect ratio of about 1.78:1 and an accommodation for enhanced 16:9 playback. The picture is crisp, with accurate fleshtones and rich colors. There is no captioning.

Condorman (Anchor Bay, DV10823)

A 1981 Walt Disney espionage comedy that does not do a bad job evoking **The Spy Who Loved Me**, young children will be unmoved by the film, but older children will enjoy it, as will adults looking for some mindless fun. The narrative is farfetched, but the story moves so quickly it is easy just to take each situation as it comes and not question how one thing led to the next.

Michael Crawford stars as a comic book artist enlisted by a friend, played by James Hampton, to help a Russian agent, played by Barbara Carrera, defect. Oliver Reed is the villain. The film was shot in Europe, and the locations add legitimacy to the film's atmosphere. The hero makes use of a number of gadgets, there are lots of chases, fights and explosions—the film was rated PG—and the humor rarely degenerates into the standard, broad Disney style.

The picture is presented on one side in letterboxed format, with an aspect ratio of about 2.35:1 and no 16:9 enhancement, and in cropped format on the other side. In addition to losing picture information on the cropped side, the blown up cropped image magnifies flaws within the source material that are less noticeable on the letterboxed image. The letterboxed presentation looks quite nice. There is some speckling, but it is rarely obtrusive. Colors are not intense, but they are passable and fleshtones seem okay. The image does become a little grainy in darker sequences, but it is never pronounced enough to cause a significant problem.

There is a rudimentary stereo soundtrack, giving a modest dimensionality to the music and a handful of separation effects. The 90 minute program has no captioning.

Confidentially Yours (Fox Lorber, FLV5072)

Our favorite François Truffaut movie, it is a basic but delightfully executed romantic comedy. Fanny Ardant is a secretary who tries to clear her boss, played by Jean-Louis Trintignant, of a multiple murder charge. The narrative has a suitably mysterious atmosphere, enhanced by Truffaut's mild displacement of space and time, and a lively pace. The performers are marvelous. Truffaut's other works may have stronger artistic resonance and more spiritual depth, but few are as effervescent or as flawless.

The 1983 black-and-white feature (Truffaut's last) is letterboxed, with an aspect ratio of about 1.66:1 and no 16:9 enhancement. Nestor Almendros' cinematography looks meticulously crisp and smooth. The monophonic sound is strong. The 110 minute film is in French, with permanent English subtitles. The program is accompanied by trailers for a number of Truffaut films.

The Conqueror (GoodTimes, 0581039)

The landscape is obviously not Mongolia and the dialogue was obviously not written with the cadence of John Wayne's speech in the writer's ear, but some movies are so, so bad that you can't resist watching them and **Conqueror** is a prime example of the-more-inept-the-better entertainment. Directed by the actor, Dick Powell, Wayne stars as Genghis Khan—yes, you're reading this correctly—

with the stupid little mustache and everything, in the story of how the chieftain consolidated his power and won the heart of a Tartar princess, played, as if she were lounging by the Beverly Hills Hotel pool, by Susan Hayward. Wayne's line readings are so incredibly bad you really wonder what was going on. He proclaims, "Let's hear no more of this. I have made great conquests. I shall need your wisdom hence forth" in an unmodulated monotone (except for 'need,' which he bumps a little higher), looking off as if this was the first time he'd read the cue cards and he'd forgotten his glasses. Sixth graders genuinely give better performances in school plays.

The 1955 film is bad in other ways, as well. For narrative momentum, the good guys escape being captured by the bad guys, run around a lot, and then get captured again. One character is apparently identified as a villain, although he helps the hero overthrow his boss. Things get so twisted around that Wayne's character thanks him for the help, and then has him killed. And, worst of all, in case you haven't heard, it turned out later that they filmed the movie near an atomic test site, so everybody—Wayne, Powell, Hayward, Agnes Moorehead and others—eventually got cancer and died.

They have, however, left this legacy of gloriously bad art for future generations to ponder. The Cinemascope picture has been letterboxed, with an aspect ratio of about 2.35:1 and no 16:9 enhancement. For the most part, the color transfer looks great. Fleshtones are reasonably accurate, and while all that sagebrush-strewn, radioactive Gobi Desert dust makes things a bit brownish, the colors are crisp and fairly bright. The only drawback is an occasional displacement artifacting flaw.

Even better than the image quality, however, is the wonderful stereophonic sound. Since you know it is an older movie, you really don't expect much from it, but the highly dimensional Victor Young musical score and viable dimensional atmospheric effects give the playback a real sense of old-fashioned movie grandeur. What the DVD reveals is that the fancier the movie looks and sounds, the more gloriously silly it becomes. The 111 minute program has optional English, French and Spanish subtitles.

Conspiracy: The Trial of the Chicago 8 (Simitar, 7284)

The combination documentary and docudrama from 1987 recreates, from court transcripts and other sources, the events of the 'Yippie' trial in which Abbie Hoffman, Bobby Seale, Tom Hayden and others were accused of conspiring to instigate a riot during the 1968 Democratic convention in Chicago. Several well-known actors appear, including Robert Loggia (as William Kunstler), Elliott Gould, Peter Boyle and Martin Sheen (in a very brief part). The dynamically designed film also has video clips of the actual defendants appearing in corners of the image from time to time and commenting upon the proceedings, as well as newsreel footage of the events discussed at the trial. It is the trial itself, however, that is the most entertaining part of the 117 minute program. The prosecution's absurdly flimsy case, the judge's incredible but apparently blind bias against the defense, and the defense's maddening lack of discipline and propensity for digression, combine to create a circus that may have set American justice back a few centuries but make for wonderful courtroom acrobatics. A sense that the details are fairly close to the truth most of the time also contributes to the show's inherent fascination. Colors are bland, contrasts are weak and digital tiling is readily and almost constantly apparent in the darker portions of the screen. The monophonic sound is passable and gossipy biographies of the four stars have also been included. There is no captioning.

Conspiracy Theory (Warner, 15091)

Do you like conspiracies? Here's one. All the pre-publicity and even a lot of the reviews said that **Conspiracy Theory** was about a slightly crazy, paranoid conspiracy enthusiast and cab driver, played by Mel Gibson, who publishes a newsletter about his wacky ideas and stirs up a hornet's nest when one of those ideas turns out to be on the mark. Julia Roberts is the sensible government attor-

ney whom he involves. Well, it just isn't true. That was probably the idea originally, but it got morphed a lot in the process of becoming a big budget, star-bound action picture, and only fragments of that original concept are left. He does publish a newsletter, because one plot turn still requires it, but there are no theories in the publication that anyone pays attention to (except in a gag) and the real narrative, which is best left as a surprise for the viewer, goes off on an entirely different tangent. At its best, the movie is quite similar to **Twelve Monkeys**, but it is also reminiscent of I Love Trouble, mistakenly compromising its intelligence and rawness in a bid for a broader appeal, which is what happens when the marketers start conspiring against the artists. The film can still be enjoyed—the stars don't create much sexual tension, but there is a strong Platonic sympathy between them—but you have to sit back and let it flow by, because if you start analyzing any piece of it too closely, you'll see what a contrivance it all is.

The 135 minute program is presented on one side in letterboxed format, with an aspect ratio of about 2.35:1 and an accommodation for 16:9 enhanced playback, and in cropped format on the other side. The cropping is workable except during the heat of the action scenes and the two-shots of the stars, but the letterboxed picture is generally more satisfying. The picture looks super, with crisp, accurate colors (even on the blown-up cropped image), and pure blacks. The standard stereo surround soundtrack is weaker than the Dolby Digital track, with less power and detail. The Dolby Digital track, however, is fairly decent, with effective directional embellishments. The film is also available in French in standard stereo and comes with English, French or Spanish subtitles. There is a small cast profile section and a few production notes.

Contact (Warner, 15041)

A full seven mindboggling hours of commentary—and that's not counting the 40 minutes of commentary in the supplement—accompany the 150 minute (well, 140 minute, there's a good 10 minutes of closing credits) 1997 feature. The film has three commentary tracks, one by the director, Robert Zemeckis and co-producer (with Zemeckis), Steve Starkey; one by the film's star, Jodie Foster; and one by special effects supervisors Ken Ralston and Stephen Rosenbaum.

The big budget science fiction adaptation of Carl Sagan's novel was sort of the darling of the intellectual crowd, because it was about ideas and not killing large bugs. Well, we know we're stepping on a lot of toes, but the film is lightweight entertainment and we'd rather watch people killing large bugs. **Contact**, in which radio astronomers receive plans for interstellar space travel, is a blatant rehash of the 30-year old **2001: A Space Odyssey** with less imagination and lousier special effects. The opening sequence, which has been praised to the hilt, is a worn over cliché that looks no different from the opening credit sequence of Star Trek: The Next Generation. In fear of recouping its costs, the film treads so softly on its theism-atheism-agnosticism argument—the central idea it is exploring—that it fails to stir the slightest bit of passion for any side or opinion. At key points throughout the movie the narrative is illogical or ridiculous—the heroine (Foster) doesn't know her recording device ran for 18 hours; the heroine doesn't know they built a second huge launching device; the president's 'spiritual advisor' appears to be part of his national security cabinet; they pick a man so clearly past his physical prime he is probably nearing retirement to be the first to ride an untested interstellar vehicle—and, as badly as we wanted to like the movie, it just disappointed us at every turn.

The movie is presented in dual layer on one side of the DVD and is in letterboxed format only, with an aspect ratio of about 2.35:1 and an accommodation for enhanced 16:9 playback. The color transfer is excellent and the image is sharp. Fleshtones are deep and other colors are rich. We did notice a bit of artifacting early on in some of the more detailed shots, but it was minor and for most of the movie we were unaware of any distortion. The stereo surround sound is adequate but restrained. The Dolby Digital track, however, is super, with rear channel separations, clear definitions and lots of power. The film is also presented in French in standard stereo and can be accompanied by English, French or Spanish subtitles. There are two trailers (we couldn't tell what they were marketing differently, although the second one seems a bit more excitable), a decent cast and crew profile and some production notes. As we mentioned, there are also about 40 minutes worth of special effect breakdown sequences, where each of the components for a special effects shot is presented in both preliminary and final stages while voiceover narration by the various effects personnel explains how the sequence was put together.

Zemeckis and Starkey take a while to get warmed up, talking in general terms at first and jumping around to cover scattered details, but they eventually get deeper into why certain approaches were taken—such as the reasons behind using complicated effects to achieve special camera angles in the place of simpler, less interesting angles at key dramatic moments—and explain what they wanted to achieve thematically. Ralston and Rosenbaum leave some gaps during longer dialogue sequences, but they talk most of the time, explaining the components that went into each shot (even in non-fantasy shots, they had to fiddle with the weather and things) and giving sort of an alternate, 'outsider's' view of Zemeckis' working methods. Foster's commentary is the least interesting of the three. She has a few anecdotes about the shoot, talks a bit too much about what is happening to her character on screen and says very little about her craft, except the extreme necessity of knowing how to hit your three dimensional marks in a special effects-heavy film like this. Starstruck viewers will still find her talk worthwhile, because Foster goes the distance, but the substance of her comments is limited. Nevertheless, the combination of all three commentary tracks gives the viewer a much deeper sense of how the film was created than any one of the three, even Zemeckis and Starkey's effort, can deliver singularly.

Control X-rated (Vivid, UPC#0073214155)

With the exception of the erotic sequences, the dialogue sounds suspiciously like verbatim recreations of genuine Hollywood anecdotes. The film, reminiscent of *Swimming with the Sharks*, is about an assistant to a film producer who works her way to the top by not sleeping with him (at least for a while). The deal making and assistant brow beating scenes are quite witty and, if it isn't all true, it seems very much like it could be. Fleshtones tend to be a bit pinkish, but otherwise the image is reasonably strong, though once in a while a shot or scene will look substantially weaker. The monophonic sound is a little sloppy, but passable. The 75 minute program contains alternate angle sequences and elaborate hardcore interactive promotional features.

Cool Hand Luke (Warner, 11037)

Paul Newman stars in the 1967 feature as a convict sentenced in the deep South to a road gang, where his irrepressible non-conformity eventually gets the better of him. The 127 minute film is presented in letterboxed format on one side, with an aspect ratio of about 2.35:1 and an accommodation for enhanced 16:9 playback, and in cropped image on the other. There are many sequences in which the wider image improves the play of the drama, from scenes involving groups of characters to the carefully composed closeups. In Jo Van Fleet's one scene, for example, her frailty and toughness are both emphasized to a much greater degree when the viewer can see the complete image of how she is set up in the back of a pickup truck. And then there is the film's closing dissolve, from one Crucifixion image to another, that is obliterated when the sides are trimmed. The picture is sharp and colors are rich. The monophonic sound is somewhat weak. The DVD also has Spanish and French language tracks and comes with English, French or Spanish subtitling ("Le mal vient du manque de communication"). There is a letterboxed theatrical trailer, a modest cast profile section and some interesting production notes about filming the

movie near Stockton, California (and you thought it was shot in the South, right?).

Cop and a Half (Universal, 20511)

A precocious young boy witnesses a murder and then drives the police detective assigned to protect him to distraction. Burt Reynolds stars, with Ray Sharkey as the killer. The film itself is about half made, with underdeveloped comical situations and makeshift plot advancements. Coupled with Reynolds' lackadaisical performance and the young child actor's hopeless hamming, parts of the movie can be excruciating. Some viewers will be comforted by the 1993 film's unthreatening predictability and occasionally energetic action sequences, but it is best approached with limited expectations.

The picture is letterboxed with an aspect ratio of about 1.85:1 and an accommodation for enhanced 16:9 playback. Colors are reasonably bright and fleshtones are workable, but the image is often fairly blurry, particularly during the film's first half. The stereo surround sound has a limited mix and uninteresting separation effects. The 93 minute film is also available in French and Spanish, and can be supported by English or Spanish subtitles. There is a trailer, a featurette (including shots of the movie's director, former TV star Henry Winkler), and the usual production essay and cast profile section.

Cop Land (Buena Vista, 14257)

Sylvester Stallone portrays the slow-witted police chief of a small community across the river from New York City. The town is supposed to have a population of only a thousand or so, but looks like it has about ten times that number. Ray Liotta, Harvey Keitel and Robert DeNiro also star in the tale of corrupt New York City cops who live in the community and attempt to hide their crimes there. Specifically, the story is about a cop who fakes his death after an accidental shooting of a suspect. Although the other cops hide him at first, they soon turn on him to cover their own involvement. The film has star power to spare, but the story never makes much sense and isn't believable even when it does. There is also a fairly bloody shoot-out at the end, which lowers its potential as a date movie.

The presentation is letterboxed with an aspect ratio of about 1.85:1 and no 16:9 enhancement. The color transfer looks very good, with crisp, accurate hues in all lighting conditions, and blacks are pure. Although the Dolby Digital track is a little loud, the Dolby Digital and stereo surround soundtracks are about equal in quality, with limited rear channel effects but a reasonably nice dimensionality. Near the end, when the hero is deafened by a gunshot, the audio takes on his point-of-view and imitates the loud annoying buzz that would occur in such a situation. As an innovative sound effect it is admirable, but, aurally, it is not pretty. The 105 minute feature is also available in French and comes with a theatrical trailer and optional English subtitles.

Copycat (Warner, 14168)

Sigourney Weaver and Holly Hunter star in the film, and they get the guy in the end with no last minute help from male detectives or anything like that. Hunter is the cop, tracking down the murderer whose pattern turns out to be an imitation of famous previous serial killers. Weaver is a serial killer expert who had a bad experience with one once and is now a neurotic mess, succumbing to a severe panic attack whenever she tries to leave her apartment. It is so much fun watching the two actresses do their thing that the absurdities of the plot don't matter. There is enough mystery to keep the show moving and enough star power to make you wish that it would never come to an end.

The director, Jon Amiel, provides a commentary track, but he doesn't really have much to say. He generally provides a play-by-play account of what is depicted on the screen, occasionally explaining why he chose certain camera angles or noting when something interesting happened on the set, such as the point where a female stuntperson broke her nose. He does go a bit into the difference between suspense and surprise, and how long, unedited takes can be more exciting than montage in certain situations, but that level of insight is limited.

The presentation is letterboxed on one side, with an aspect ratio of about 2.35:1 and an accommodation for enhanced 16:9 playback, and in cropped format on the other side. The cropped version is pointless. The picture has a crisp focus and detailed hues. The stereo surround sound is pretty good, but the DVD also has a Dolby Digital track with sharper, better defined sounds that create a more dimensional and exciting viewing environment. The film is also available in French in standard stereo and comes with English, French or Spanish subtitles. There are some brief production notes, a cast & crew profile section and a theatrical trailer.

Corridors of Blood (Universal, ID4431GODVD)

Not a horror film per se, though it was sold as one ("A N-E-R-V-O-R-A-M-A Shocker!," says the trailer), Boris Karloff also stars as a Nineteenth Century doctor working to develop a surgical anesthesia and falling into a kind of Jekyll-and-Hyde existence under the influence of the drugs he is experimenting upon. He remains innocent, however, as thugs around him kill for money and take advantage of his impaired reason to generate phony death certificates. The 1958 film has a fairly nice looking black-and-white picture, with sharp contrasts and deep blacks. The monophonic sound is passable and the 87 minute film is accompanied by the theatrical trailer quoted above.

The Corsican Brothers (Simitar, 7202)

Twin brothers are captured by an evil sorcerer, who needs their amulets to achieve absolute power. The 1989 Australian cartoon program, released with the title *Good Housekeeping Kids* and loosely based upon the Alexander Dumas novel, runs 50 minutes. The animation is stilted and the plot is fairly basic, but there is enough action to keep some viewers interested. The colors are bright and the picture is sharp, though the image goes in and out of focus in places and the animation is jerky. The monophonic sound is okay and the program is not captioned.

Così Fan Tutti (see Mozart's Così Fan Tutti: Teatro Alla Scala)

Cousin Bette (Fox, 4110449)

An enjoyable period film about a spinster taking revenge upon those she believes have slighted her, Jessica Lange stars in the title role, with Elisabeth Shue, Bob Hoskins and others. Based upon a story by Honoré de Balzac and set in mid-Nineteenth Century France, the narrative is quite appealing, particularly if you like to see the bad guys win. Despising the family that employs her, Lange's character begins lying, forging and otherwise confounding the truth to pit those around her against one another. Along with Balzac's assured narrative, the stars' engaging performances and the movie's succulent decor, there are a number of captivating erotic sequences to blend with the film's psychological explorations and its glorification of devious behavior.

The picture is letterboxed with an aspect ratio of about 2.35:1 and no 16:9 enhancement. The color transfer looks super, with finely detailed hues and accurate fleshtones. The stereo surround sound has a functional mix and a reasonable amount of energy. The film has some sequences set in a musical theater and uses some very interesting original songs that, in a just world, would attract the attention of Oscar. The 110 minute film can be supported by English or Spanish subtitles and is accompanied by a trailer that tries to sell the film as a madcap comedy, although in reality it is somewhat more urbane.

The Coven X-rated (Vivid, UPC#0073214584)

Something about a woman who has visions, including a few where she is participating in pagan rituals, there are a lot of erotic sequences. The program, which has mostly voiceover narration of a poetic, New Age nature, is weird enough to be effective, but it doesn't really amount to much. Shot on videotape, the picture is in reasonably good shape, although a number of scenes are lit partially by firelight, creating a mild grain and somewhat bland fleshtones. The sound is strong and the 70 minute program features Janine, Brittany O'Connell, Laurie Cameron, Tianna Taylor, Krystal Lynn and Nikki Shane. The DVD contains alternate angle sequences and elaborate hardcore interactive promotional features.

The Cowboy Way (Universal, 20446)

The humorous 1994 action film, about New Mexican wranglers who mix it up with bad guys in New York City, stars Woody Harrelson and Kiefer Sutherland Harrelson's performance, as the dumber of the two, is very funny, and although the narrative has its share of illogical coincidences, each sequence has a souped-up intensity that keeps the viewer involved and charmed.

It is letterboxed with an aspect ratio of about 1.85:1 and an accommodation for enhanced 16:9 playback. Colors look deep and are nicely detailed, with a smooth image, crisp lines and decent fleshtones. The stereo surround sound is light, but the Dolby Digital track exceeds the standard track in separation detail and clarity. The 107 minute film is also available in French in Dolby Digital and in Spanish in standard stereo, and can be supported by English or Spanish subtitles. There are some production notes, a cast and director profile section and a theatrical trailer.

The Cowboys (Warner, 15183)

John Wayne is a rancher who is forced to hire a group of adolescents to assist him on a cattle drive. The film has its drawbacks—Wayne's character berates one of the kids who has a stuttering problem and the problem is immediately cured—but the cinematography is compelling, especially when letterboxed, and the romance of the range, combined with the action and the narrative (a group of bad guys, led by Bruce Dern, threaten the drive), make the movie appealing entertainment.

John Williams' musical score has been remastered in Dolby Digital. The standard stereo surround sound is somewhat weak, but the Dolby Digital encoding is okay. It is only the music that is stereophonic—the dialogue and effects are centered—and dimensionality and dynamic range are limited, but the stereo does imbue the music with a touch of flourish, raising the film's sense of importance.

The presentation is letterboxed with an aspect ratio of about 2.35:1 and an accommodation for enhanced 16:9 playback. The picture is quite pale and brownish, although hues are a little deeper and the image is sharper. The DVD also contains 13 Wayne trailers, however, and the trailer for **The Cowboys** has much stronger colors than the feature. The 135 minute film is also available in French in mono and can be supported by English or French subtitles. There is an elaborate cast & crew profile section, essays on westerns and cowboys, and a good 9 minute 'making of' featurette about training the child actors for the rigors of a cattle drive and acting with the Duke.

Crackdown (Digital Versatile, DVD103)

The two heroes go about murdering drug dealers in cold blood. Hey, why not. The film is pretty bad. Set and shot in Southeast Asia, the cinematographer has apparently never heard of 'lighting,' just as the performers have never heard of 'acting.' The action scenes don't have enough coverage to generate any thrills and the drama (people's lives being harmed by drugs; the heroes working their way through the network) is poorly executed.

The picture is dark and dreary, though the transfer doesn't seem to have done any more harm to the already lousy looking image. The monophonic sound has shrill surges of volume but is otherwise a cheap mix and who knows what language it was originally shot in. At least the picture is so dark most of the time you don't see the lips of the performers moving anyway. The 93 minute program is not chapter encoded or captioned.

The Craft (Columbia, 82415/82416)

About four (Catholic) high school girls who dabble in the supernatural, the script is perfectly paced, spending plenty of time on the simple, daydream-type stuff and then upping the ante for the big finale. Because there are four heroines, each with a distinctive personality, the drama need only mix and match the realistic insecurities of each of the girls to create a complex emotional narrative that is sufficient to justify the fantasy. The film is youthful in the best sense of the word, exuberant and unsullied, and it has strong repeat potential.

It is presented in letterboxed format only, with an aspect ratio of about 1.85:1 and an accommodation for enhanced 16:9 playback. The colors are crisp and bright, with accurate fleshtones. The stereo surround sound is fair, but the Dolby Digital track has a lot more power and the mix is enjoyably detailed. The 101 minute feature is also available in Spanish and French in regular stereo, comes with Spanish or Korean subtitles and English closed captioning. Fairuza Balk stars with Robin Tunney.

Crash (New Line, N4681)

J.G. Ballard is primarily a science fiction writer, and David Cronenberg's film, adapted from Ballard's novel about people who obtain erotic pleasure from car crashes, is, ever so slightly, a science fiction film. The characters in a standard pornographic softcore film act in a fictional manner, forming liaisons after unrealistically speedy emotional interactions. What **Crash** adds is an oddball scientific explanation for the pornographic interludes, a suggestion that the characters are somehow transformed by the flaws in the technology that governs their lives and it is erotic desire that is leaking from those flaws. There are obvious symbolic overtones about the price of progress and what technology has done to humanity, and there is enough material to see the story as an allegory about unprotected sex, as well. For Cronenberg, it is also another opportunity to dress the world in his strange, inside-out organic artifices, and some viewers will respond automatically to the eccentricity of his vision.

The film, which features James Spader, Elias Koteas, Holly Hunter and Deborah Kara Unger, has an extremely potent curiosity factor, and some of the driving scenes are startling. Having established its premise, however, exploring the various ways that a person could become fascinated with car crashes, the narrative has nowhere else to go. The film is too small to explore its society on a larger scale (there are delicious hints at the beginning of an organized underground movement, but these are never followed up) and the characters remain so long out of context (Hunter all but disappears in the second half of the film) that their actions and couplings become absurd instead of abstract. Ultimately, **Crash** is aimless, dull and infantile—an insult to anyone who has ever lost a loved one in an automobile accident.

Both the NC-17 and R-rated cuts are presented for optional playback. Why anybody would want to watch the R-rated version is beyond us (is this the one you're supposed to show to your kids?) unless it is just to get the film over with quicker. The NC-17 presentation runs 100 minutes and the R-rated version, which is taken from the same film but programmatically jumps over the naughty bits, runs 90 minutes.

The picture is letterboxed with an aspect ratio of about 1.75:1 and an accommodation for enhanced 16:9 playback. The image quality is an improvement over the Criterion Collection LD release, with a sharper focus and pinker, more accurate fleshtones (the LD was accompanied by extensive supplementary features not available on the DVD). Generally, the image looks okay, with bright, reasonably sharp hues, although there is a mild softness in some lighting situations. The stereo surround sound is reasonably strong and has a generalized dimensionality, although there aren't many distinctive separation effects. The program is also available in French in stereo and can be supported by English, French or

Spanish subtitles. The 1996 film is accompanied by a red tag theatrical trailer and a modest cast & crew profile section.

Crash: Impact II (Digital Disc, 502)

An 80 minute compilation of race car and cycle crashes, it shows everything from Formula One racers to drag racers, stock racers, dirt bikes, etc. Each crack up is replayed two or more times at different angles and speeds. There are some horrific incidents, particularly when subsequent vehicles travel over the former drivers of the incapacitated vehicles, and there are some that seem hardly worth including (aren't dirt bikes expected to upend themselves a few times?). The footage is in passable condition and the sound is fine.

Cream (see **Fresh Live Cream**)

Cream On X-rated (Vivid, UPC#0073214519)

A book editor is instructed by her boss to begin a line of erotica, bringing her into contact with some unusual authors. The performances and the editing have an accelerated comical manner that add to the program's entertainment. Shot on videotape, the picture looks good, with rich fleshtones and sharp focus. The sound is okay. The program runs 72 minutes. The DVD contains alternate angle sequences and elaborate hardcore interactive promotional features.

Creator (Trimark, 7038D)

The central narrative of Ivan Passer's 1985 comedy is about two couples falling in love—one represented by Peter O'Toole and Mariel Hemingway, and the other by Vincent Spano and Virginia Madsen. O'Toole is a brilliant research scientist and Spano is his graduate assistant. That is all one really needs to know, because the mechanics of the plot are less important than the characters and the performances. We found ourselves replaying a number of individual scenes several times over, and were so happy with them that we really didn't care how the movie started or ended. There is a wonderful beach house seduction scene involving Spano and Madsen, a terrific turn by O'Toole as he goes before a grant committee to get his funding renewed, and a hysterical put-down rendered by Hemingway when another professor comes on to her. Those scenes, and a few others, are what the movie is really about, and where its pleasures are to be had.

After a letterboxed credit sequence, the picture is presented in full screen and is slightly cropped, though the framing never feels tight. Fleshtones are a little light, but hues generally look fresh, speckling is minimal and the image is sharp. The monophonic sound is okay and the 107 minute program can be supported by English, French or Spanish subtitles. There is a cast profile section and a trailer.

Creepers (see **Phenomena**)

Crime Broker (Simitar, 7317)

Jacqueline Bisset is an Australian judge (a 'magistrate') who plots heists on the side, Thomas Crown-style, anonymously hiring the rabble that passes by her on the docket to carry out the jobs. Things become complicated, however, when a Japanese criminologist, played by Masaya Kato, arrives in town and quickly surmises what is going on. The plot has several twists and turns, not all of them readily believable, but Bisset gets to stretch herself and the 93 minute film is an enjoyable entry in the caper genre. Colors are fairly bright and the image is reasonably sharp, although fleshtones seem a little soft or pinkish at times. The stereo sound is passable and is not captioned.

Crimes and Misdemeanors (Image, ID40800RDVD)

Looking back now, it appears that Woody Allen's 1989 **Crimes and Misdemeanors** was still part of his Eighties artistic slump, though he was gradually working his way out of it. The film has some very nice touches and a number of stimulating ideas, but a lot of it is obvious and not strongly acted. The dialogue often comes out sounding like written dialogue and not spoken thought. Martin Landau stars as an eye doctor who arranges for the murder of his mistress, while Allen, in a parallel narrative, is a documentary filmmaker shooting a piece on a successful brother-in-law he cannot stand. Anjelica Huston, Alan Alda, Mia Farrow and Sam Waterston are also featured. Looking back now, too, after Allen's well-publicized troubles, there are aspects to the film that are downright creepy, including the lack of fortitude in Farrow's character, the amoral view of the murder and a seemingly unrelated subplot in which Allen's character escorts a very young niece about town.

The colors have strong pinkish tones and fleshtones are too red. The mono-like 'stereo' sound is adequate. The 104 minute program has no special features but is closed captioned.

Crimes of Passion (Anchor Bay, DV10333)

Ken Russell can often be counted on to test the limits of silliness in adult films and you'll probably end up giggling at **Crimes of Passion** instead of getting turned on by it, especially if you watch it more than once. The chief laugh generator is Tony Perkins, a street preacher who eyes the heroine with lust and fondles a razor-edged vibrator that he picked up God knows where. The heroine, played by Kathleen Turner, is not any more serious. By day she works as a clothing designer and by night she dons a blond wig and turns tricks in a cheap hotel room for honorariums and thrills. No pimps, venereal diseases, sleep, or other aspects of the real world intrude on this fantasy playland.

The presentation is letterboxed with an aspect ratio of about 1.85:1 and no 16:9 enhancement. On the whole, fleshtones and other hues are a bit restrained, but the image presentation is workable. Contrasts are smooth and the image is sharp. The stereo sound has a limited dimensionality. Separation effects are minimal and tones sound a bit clipped at times. This is the 107 minute 'unrated' version of the film, with 6 extra minutes of slobbering lust that did not appear in the original 1984 theatrical version.

Crimson Tide (Buena Vista, 13679)

Gene Hackman is the captain of a nuclear submarine and Denzel Washington is his first mate. When the commands to launch their nuclear missiles are garbled, due to extenuating circumstances, the two have a disagreement over the interpretation of both the commands and their receptive duties as officers on the ship. The argument is taken one or two steps beyond what would probably happen in real life, but no more than that, so the movie becomes a tense nuclear drama with several good action scenes, but never gets too out-of-hand in its fictionalization. Hackman's character, in particular, could easily be portrayed as a Queeg-type, but he isn't, he's just being a bit too pragmatic for his circumstances. Directed by Tony Scott, the 1995 film has a slick style and terrific production values, but it is also effective at communicating the emotions of hierarchical conflicts. After the movie is over, you walk away feeling like you have total command over your domain, whatever that domain may be. The image is sharp, which is nice, but the picture is somewhat dark, with slightly purplish fleshtones. The picture is letterboxed with an aspect ratio of about 2.35:1 and no 16:9 enhancement. The stereo surround sound is good and the Dolby Digital sound is terrific. The 116 minutes program is also available in French in standard stereo and comes with English or Spanish subtitles.

Crimson Wolf (Image, ID4652SEDVD)

There's lots of hot and heavy sex and gore in the Japanese animation release, so the somewhat incoherent plot doesn't interfere with the entertainment. The 60 minute program is primarily about three young fighters, who share a common mark on their bodies and who avoid assassination attempts to stand against a big evil something-or-rather. The creators are intelligent enough to position the show as a political metaphor for repression in Communist China, but that doesn't make the plot any more understandable

and you just sort of end up going with the flow and waiting for the next burst of blood or nude grappling. The artwork is nicely conceived and the picture transfer looks good, with bright, solid colors and a sharp focus. The program is in stereo, with a very modest mix, and has English and Japanese audio tracks but no subtitles.

Crooklyn (Universal, 20515)

Spike Lee's 1994 feature was mistakenly promoted as a happy comedy. In fact a major character dies towards the end and the tone of the movie is closer to nostalgic ambiguity. The narrative—about a family living in Brooklyn—is sufficiently involved to keep a viewer caring about the characters. The movie is also on the money at capturing the dynamics of family life. Alfre Woodard and Delroy Lindo star as the mother and father. It is Lee's exploration of style, however, that makes the film truly exciting. He breaks rules, and although not all of his experiments work—there is an extended sequence in the middle of the film that is presented 'squeezed,' as a representation of the heroine's discomfort with her surroundings, but it goes on too long to remain effective—the ones that do, especially the increased volume levels on the musical score, are fabulous, adding texture and depth to the drama with bold strokes.

The film is a near musical, as the audio track is loaded with pop classics and other well-chosen orchestral surges, and the DVD has been given an excellent Dolby Digital track, which accentuates the dimensionality of the separations and also enables the music to play loud without drowning out the dialogue. The picture is letterboxed with an aspect ratio of about 1.85:1 and an accommodation for enhanced 16:9 processing. The color transfer looks fine. Fleshtones are nicely detailed and other hues are bright. The 114 minute program is also available in French in Dolby Digital and can be supported by English or Spanish subtitles. There are some informative production notes and a cast-and-director profile section.

The Crow (Buena Vista, 13677)
The Crow: City of Angels (Buena Vista, 13678)

Brandon Lee stars as a ghost who comes back from the dead to massacre those responsible for doing him in. Hearing the premise, one would think that there wouldn't be much to the movie—the bad guys can't kill him because he's already dead, etc.—but the 1994 film is a stylistic virtuosity, an opera of violence and dark emotions. The film is outstanding, too, as an adaptation of a comic book so effectively realized that you can feel the rhythm of advancing panels not only in the film's cinematography and editing, but in the movie's emotions. The film makes extensive use of models and other visual effects to achieve a precisely controlled mood and atmosphere. The DVD not only presents it accurately, it provides an ideal format for the film, encouraging the multiple playback that such an emotionally-composed work is designed for, and fulfilling the designed capabilities of a viewer's audio-video hardware components as well.

The 1996 sequel in no way touches the quality or impact of the first film, but if you approach it on a lower plane of entertainment, it isn't bad. Reiterating the plot of the first movie, with some slight modifications, Vincent Perez stars as the innocent victim of a drug gang execution who comes back from the dead to waste his killers. The film has the same dark, comic book atmosphere that the first movie had, and the same surreal urban nightscape, but the dialogue is not as searching, the action scenes are not as thrilling and the transitions are not as stylish. It's a wimpier, cheaper version of the first movie, but it is briskly paced and exotically staged, and if you can avoid comparing it to its predecessor, it has an intriguing concept and an entertaining setting.

The stereo surround sound on both is noticeably weak, but both have Dolby Digital tracks that are fully invigorating, with terrific separation effects and a hard-driving bass. From the sheer purity of the breaking glass to the loud, powerful and deep-seeded rock score, the massive, elaborate and piercing audio track of **The Crow** has been delivered with perfection on the Dolby track. The sound is outstanding, but it is the sound mix, its design, that makes the presentation so exceptional, because not only do the sound effects pack a wallop, they are meticulously integrated with the film's narrative. The sequel doesn't deliver quite the same impact.

Both DVDs are letterboxed, with an aspect ratio of about 1.85:1 and no 16:9 enhancement. The color transfers on both movies manage superbly the difficult task of conveying distinctive hues within dark surroundings. The images are sharp, clear and enhance the thrills of each film. **Crow** has a French language track in standard stereo and can be accompanied by English subtitles. **Crow City of Angles** can be accompanied by English or Spanish subtitles. **The Crow** runs 93 minutes and **Crow: City of Angles** is a 'Director's Cut' that runs 101 minutes.

Crumb (Columbia TriStar, 10699)

An accomplished and critically lauded 1995 documentary about the underground comic book artist, R. Crumb, the 119 minute film is too long by a good 20 minutes and uses the excuse, as Crumb does himself, of presenting offensive material as satire so that viewers can revel in it without feeling guilty. As a documentary, it is not that great of a logistical accomplishment. The filmmakers simply followed Crumb around for a while, and interviewed members of his family and a few associates. The film works, though, because Crumb is an interesting character and the dysfunctional family he grew up in left a wealth of psychological scars, creating an involving narrative. If Crumb's comics had seemed abstract or imaginative before one viewed the film, by the end they seem like an utterly logical mode of expression for the artist to release his demons and form the semblance of an emotional détente with the world.

The presentation is letterboxed with an aspect ratio of about 1.66:1. The colors are bright and sharp. There is some grain from time to time, in tougher lighting situations, but overall the picture looks fine. Technically, the sound is stereophonic, but since it is mostly conversations, with musical accompaniment here and there from Crumb's collection of old 78rpm records, there is not much in the way of separations. The program has optional English subtitles.

Cry Freedom (Universal, 20516)

Denzel Washington plays Steve Biko in Richard Attenborough's stodgy presentation of the South African racial conflicts, but he has third billing, after Kevin Kline, starring as a journalist who wakes up one morning to discover that 1) the sun is rising in the East, and 2) the apartheid government of South Africa is mistreating blacks, and Penelope Wilton, who plays the journalist's can't-you-just-get-another-profession wife.

The 1987 film had for what is in its day an excellent stereo surround mix, and it still sound terrific on the DVD, even though there is no 5-channel expansion. Tones are forceful and separation effects are distinctive. The picture is letterboxed with an aspect ratio of 2.35:1 and no 16:9 enhancement. The picture quality looks very good, with sharp accurate colors. We did, however, detect occasional artifacting instabilities in the backgrounds here and there, and some ratcheting in moments of quick movement. The 159 minute program is also available in French and can be supported by English or Spanish subtitles. There are production notes, although they include a whopping typo ("South Africa achieved majority rule under President Nelson Mandela in 1984"), a small cast-and-director profile section and a trailer that emphasizes Washington's part.

The Crying Game (Artisan, 60463)

Stephen Rea is an IRA gunmen who, out of remorse, looks up the sweetheart of a former captive, falling into a romance until his past catches up with him The dual-layer single-sided DVD presents the 1992 film in both letterboxed format and cropped format. The letterboxing has an aspect ratio of about 2.35:1 and no

16:9 enhancement. Since most of the film is built around intimate dramatics—after an opening sequence, a half hour of the movie takes place on one set, an abandoned greenhouse—those who are not enamored with letterboxing may find that the enclosed nature of the cropping still delivers a valid rendition of the film, and the movie's most notorious sequence is probably more effective in the cropped presentation, since nobody watching the movie in a theater is looking at the sides of the screen at that point anyway. It is the letterboxing, however, that is best suited for multiple viewings of the film, for as the impact of the narrative recedes, it is the personalities of the characters and the strength of the images that remain. The movie's opening credit sequence, letterboxed on both versions, contains a lyrical blend of phallic imagery, and in shot after shot the characters are set off against their environment by the widescreen framing, creating what in essence is more breathing room for the viewer.

The stereo surround sound is a bit light the drawback does not affect the drama and the audio quality is adequate. The 112 minute program is closed captioned and is accompanied by a fascinating theatrical trailer, a modest cast-and-director profile section and a few production notes. There is apparently closed captioning as well.

Cube (Trimark, VM6914D)

An honest-to-goodness modern allegory, the highly intriguing film is part **Twilight Zone** and part video game. A group of people awaken in large square rooms with doors on every side. Behind some doors are deadly traps and behind others are simply more rooms in different colors. Each door, however, is numbered, and when they break the code they discern a pattern to their predicament. Within the tension of avoiding the gore-inducing traps and working out their personality conflicts, however, they also speak about why they have been placed in the rooms—the meaning of it all—and their perfectly measured comments are at once a solution to part of the mystery and an on-the-money description of Man's metaphysical circumstance in the modern world. The film manages to remain intriguing and even exciting for its full 90 minute running time, and is refreshingly clever from start to finish.

The picture is letterboxed with an aspect ratio of about 1.85:1 and no 16:9 enhancement. The color transfer looks fine, with stable hues and passable fleshtones. The Ultra-Stereo surround sound is very good. As the characters go about their business, they periodically hear loud noises banging behind the walls of the rooms—noises that are eventually explained—and these sounds maintain an effective detachment from the immediate sounds of the room and from the musical score. The film can be supported by French or Spanish subtitles, and there is English closed captioning.

On a second audio channel, the director, Vincenzo Natali, star David Hewlitt, and co-writer, Andre Bijelic, talk about creating the movie on a very low budget, their experiences during the shoot and the film's subsequent successes. They term the film 'an action movie that takes place on a single set' (actually it was two sets, one a complete six-sided cube and one of just three sides), talk about the various challenges they were confronted with when doors didn't work or when problems and situations arose that they hadn't anticipated, and they point out the special effects that make the movie work and that were done for them gratis by hungry Canadian special effects houses wanting to make a name for themselves. They also discover a realization as they are speaking, that in one sense the film is about the purity of technology and the impurity of Man. The three are comfortable talking together and rarely interrupt one another, and they have a lot of fun reminiscing about the stress of making a movie, so it is an informative and engaging track.

The DVD also includes three minutes of deleted scenes from the film (as the filmmakers explain, the more they took out during the editing, by way of explanation and narrative enhancement, the stronger the film became); an excellent collection of production sketches, with close-ups, that show how the Cube set was designed; some storyboards with scene comparisons (the boards tend to be grosser than what was actually shot); and a trailer.

Custer of the West (Simitar, 7230)

An episodic western from 1969, Robert Shaw stars as the title character, with Jeffrey Hunter, Mary Ure, Ty Hardin and others. The film was a widescreen production and contains several thrill ride sequences, so the presentation is severely compromised by the cropping. The 140 minute film is spread to two sides. The colors are a little bland and fleshtones are dull, with mild smearing in the darker sequences. The monophonic sound is weak and scratchy, requiring extra amplification. The film is not captioned and is accompanied by profiles and filmographies for Shaw, Hardin and Hunter, though a film listed as one of Hunter's credits was produced about a decade after he died. There is also a brief collection of documentary clips about the life of Custer. The movie covers the major events in Custer's life after the Civil War, and while it is never very accurate it does strive to evoke a sense of the times. It tends to be more anti-Indian than a lot of Custer movies are, but Shaw brings some energy to his performance and enough money was spent on the production to make parts of it fairly entertaining for fans of westerns.

Cutthroat Island (Warner. 60447)

We still don't understand why more people don't like **Cut-Throat Island**, but perhaps the DVD, which houses both the letterboxed and the cropped version of the 118 minute feature (one on each side), will attract more fans. The drama is shallow and superficial, but there is a coherent, forward-moving plot, enjoyable characters, numerous, elaborately staged action scenes and wall-to-wall sound. What's not to like? The film never slows down, leaping from one set of perils to the next. Geena Davis and Matthew Modine star, with Frank Langella as the villain. It is a Seventeenth Century pirate movie—did we mention the breezy anachronistic dialog?—about the search for buried treasure.

The letterboxed version, which has an aspect ratio of about 2.35:1 and no 16:9 enhancement, is preferable to the cropped version, which obscures too much of the action. The picture on the letterboxed image looks great, with sharp, accurate colors, but the cropped image is a little soft. The stereo surround sound is passable, but the film has a rousing Dolby Digital mix that is more active and more enjoyable. The film is also available in French, without Dolby Digital, and comes with English, French or Spanish subtitles. There is a slightly letterboxed teaser that sells the film superbly and a full screen trailer (on both sides) that loses the edge the teaser establishes. There is also a nice cast and crew profile. The 'Production Notes,' however, consist of a single, badly composed sentence that we shall repeat in its entirety, missing commas and all, for your amusement: "**Cutthroat Island** was shot in Malta, a small island south of Sicily in the Mediterranean Film Studios, which houses some of the largest water tanks in the world."

Cyber Tracker (Sterling, 4050)

Don "The Dragon" Wilson stars in the 1994 action film, with a few nice futuristic touches, about corruption in a computer controlled legal system that uses robot executioners to dispense justice. Richard Norton is also featured, as Wilson's primary rival. Although the movie has a few too many (and redundant) car crashes, some of the high-tech imagery is quite intriguing and the pace rarely slows down.

The full screen picture is foggy with indistinct colors and the stereo sound has a limited dimensionality. The 91 minute program comes with a trailer and is not captioned.

Cyberlin (see Seasons: A Journey Through Vivaldi—Cyberlin)

Cybernator (Simitar, 7252)

The acting is awful and the filmmakers often shoot in the dark so they don't have to dress their sets, but the story isn't bad and the DVD is tolerable if you're partial to cheapie made-for-video sci-fi action films. A cop is investigating the assassinations of several politicians by androids. When he starts to dig too deeply, however, he gets pulled off the case, and investigating on his own, he makes a shocking discovery about his past (can you guess, can you guess?). The androids look like the Cenobites in **Hellraiser** (the movie tends to steal from all over the place) and the laser flashes coming out of the guns look like they've been hand painted, but even though the performers couldn't read their lines believably if their lives depended upon it, we've seen worse. The colors are reasonably bright but the picture is very grainy and video artifacting is also fairly evident in some sequences. The stereo sound is active and forceful, but the sound recording is so weak and distorted that the energy in the audio track doesn't help it. The program runs 85 minutes.

Cyberscape (Sony, LVD49925)

A poor computer animation program, the surreal images tend to take a single idea and try to squeeze as many angles or variations on it as can be conceived. The settings often look like pointless video games, and the images, at their best, appear inspired by the works of René Magritte, though again they take an initial idea and work it to death. The music isn't much better, often set to a frantic rhythm that distances a viewer from the images instead of creating bonds. The picture quality looks fine, with sharp, vivid colors, and the stereo sound is okay. The program runs 45 minutes.

Cyborg (MGM, 906561)

The 1989 Jean-Claude Van Damme post-apocalypse action film is in dual layer format, with the letterboxed presentation on one layer and the full screen version on the other. The letterboxing has an aspect ratio of about 1.85:1 and no 16:9 enhancement, adding nothing to the sides of the image and trimming off the top and bottom in comparison to the full screen release. The full screen framing is a bit more enjoyable, but either works. The color transfer looks terrific, with deep, rich fleshtones and bright, crisp hues. The stereo sound has a basic, lots-of-loud-noises kind of mix. The 86 minute film is also available in French in mono and comes with English, French or Spanish subtitles. There is a theatrical trailer, too.

D

D.O.A. (Master Movies, DVD5509)

We've seen worse presentations of the film noir classic. The black-and-white image on the Master Movies version is somewhat soft, but it is smooth and the source material is generally free of wear. The only distracting flaw appears to be an unusual artifacting anomaly, causing ghost-like waves to emanate from darker objects in a few scenes. The monophonic sound is somewhat scratchy and sheer, and is best kept at a moderate volume. The 82 minute presentation is not captioned.

The 1950 movie stars Edmond O'Brien, filling his role in such a way that you constantly picture what it would have been like if Bogart were playing the part. For those unfamiliar with the classics, this is the movie where a man is subjected to a fatal dose of radiation poisoning and compulsively searches for his murderer before he succumbs to its delayed effects. The pace, the plot twists, and the frantic search for "truth" are lively fun, and the film manages to be metaphysical—why do we die?—without imposing a philosophy.

Da Last Don (see Master P MP: Da Last Don—The Movie)

Damage (New Line, N4668)

Louis Malle's all-too-serious **Damage** is most reminiscent of *Meet Pamela*, the ersatz film-within-a-film being produced in François Truffaut's moviemaking comedy, *Day for Night*. About a man whose affair with his son's fiancee meets with a tragic end, **Damage** is a low key film about high strung characters so implausible in its unfolding that a viewer's initial reaction will be to laugh at every plot turn. Jeremy Irons and Juliette Binoche star, and their lovemaking scenes remind one of crash dummies in facing seats undergoing a series of tests without safety belts. Attracted like magnets to a refrigerator door, they quickly start sleeping with one another, an act of passion that, of course, can only end in death.

Anyway, the 1992 feature has been released in both its unrated format, which runs 111 minutes, and its R-rated format, which is a minute shorter. The picture is letterboxed with an aspect ratio of about 1.66:1 and an accommodation for enhanced 16:9 playback. The letterboxing has more picture information on all four sides than the LD, and the picture is sharper, with more accurate colors. The image is still a little hazy at times, but some of that is conceptual and hues are nicely detailed, with accurate fleshtones. The stereo surround sound is highlighted by a legitimately pleasing musical score from Zbigniew Preisner, though otherwise the audio mix is of limited interest. The film can be supported by English, French or Spanish subtitles. There is a 15 minute interview with Malle and a theatrical trailer.

Dances with Wolves (Image, ID4710ORDVD); DTS (Image, ID5159ORDVD)

Kevin Costner's performance captures the subdued articulation of his character so perfectly it is likely many viewers will mistake the monotone narration for an inability on Costner's part to emote. His direction is inspired as well, finding ways to keep the film interesting despite its length and somewhat bare plot. Its sense of reverence may be tiresome, but the movie conveys the culture that pre-existed the European settlement of America in a highly memorable and persuasive manner. **Dances with Wolves** is an effective romance (about a cavalry officer whose contact with an Indian tribe and a woman who can interpret their talk causes him to change his basic allegiance) and an action adventure film with a number of fine stunt sequences. It is also, however, a linguistic delight. The utilization of the true Lakota tongue to demonstrate that sophisticated concepts were conveyed in its employment is a glorious stroke. Like all language, it communicates a subconscious structure beneath the dialogue, speaking plainly but silently to the viewer that it has a right to exist.

This is the standard 181 minute version of the film, and it is presented in single-sided dual-layer format. It is letterboxed with an aspect ratio of about 2.35:1 and an accommodation for enhanced 16:9 playback. The color transfer is improved over previous home video efforts, with brighter, deeper colors and a sharper focus. There are some shots where fleshtones look a touch orange, but on the whole the film's lovely vistas are greatly enhance and, overall, it is highly satisfying. Hues are rich and intricately detailed. The stereo surround sound is weak, but the Dolby Digital track has more flourish and crisper definitions. The film can be supported by optional English subtitles and is accompanied by filmographies for some of the cast and crew, though we spotted at least one error.

Costner also provides a commentary, with producer Jim Wilson. They reminisce about the shoot, discuss Costner's approach to many of the scenes, share anecdotes and talk about working with the other performers (the Native American actors were apprehensive at first, but apparently became gung ho after they witnessed Costner's commitment to realism). "The differences between men

is not great," is one of the 1990 film's primary themes, suggests Costner. While the film conforms to the rules of that difficult subgenre where white males experience the tribulations of a minority group, it is Costner's careful veracity in his depiction of Native American life that makes the movie so appealing, and is clearly what the performers were responding to.

The DTS audio track is vastly better than the Dolby Digital track on the standard DVD release. Separation details are much clearer, the bass is better defined, the dimensionality is stronger and the audio track on the DTS DVD just has more energy, bringing a greater sense of epic adventure to the film. The 181 minute feature is presented on two platters. The first is a dual-layer platter and holds about two hours of the film, while the second is a single layer and holds the final hour. The film is letterboxed with an aspect ratio of about 2.35:1 and an accommodation for enhanced 16:9 playback. We could detect no significant difference in the picture quality between the standard DVD and the DTS DVD, but the sampling rate on the DTS version is about 75% higher, so there are bound to be minute improvements that will be discernible on larger screens. The color transfer is very good, with bright, deep hues and a crisp focus. Once in a while fleshtones seem a little too orange, but that is more a question of preference than distortion and the flow of the entertainment is never affected. The DVD also has a standard stereo surround soundtrack and the commentary track. Costner is cut off in the middle of a statement with the platter break. There is English captioning.

Dangerous X-rated (Vivid, UPC#0073214521)

A wild young woman encourages her friends to have fun in unusual places, such as on some railroad tracks. The narrative is skimpy (the final scene is well staged, however), but the erotic sequences are energetic and inventive. In a profession founded upon uninhibited activities, the film's star, Taylor, brings an exceptional sense of hyper-devil-may-care to her craft. The picture, from a videotape source, is excellent, with crisp, accurate hues, and the sound is fine. The 70 minute program also features Ruby and Chloe. The DVD contains alternate angle sequences and elaborate hardcore interactive promotional features.

Dangerous Beauty (Warner, 14775)

Some people shy away from costume dramas, but they're missing out. It is true that the American actors seem a bit incongruous with the film's 16th Century Venetian setting, but the story is so entertaining and sexy a viewer is inclined to give it liberal license. Catherine McCormack stars as a young middle class woman who turns to a life of elegant prostitution when she is unable to marry the man she loves. The film explores the details of Venetian society and politics from an appealing perspective (according to the movie, the only educated women in Venice were prostitutes—wives were expected to remain ignorant of the world beyond the next canal) and manages to include a compelling romance along with the fascinating details of what it took to be Venice's number one—how shall we put it?—Venus.

Fleshtones are accurate, contrasts are effectively detailed, hues are strong and the picture is crisp. The image is letterboxed with an aspect ratio of about 2.38:1 and an accommodation for enhanced 16:9 playback on one side, and in full screen format on the other side. The letterboxing adds no more than a sliver to the sides of the image and masks considerable picture information off the bottom of the screen in comparison to the full screen image. Although the widescreen picture composition is better balanced, a viewer may well want to watch the full screen version, perhaps on the second or third viewing, for the enhanced period detail it provides and the increased intimacy it creates in the closer shots.

The stereo surround sound and Dolby Digital sound are adequate. The 112 minute film is also available in French in Dolby Digital and can be supported by English, Spanish or French subtitles. There is an elaborate cast & crew profile section and a nice trailer, but a sadly brief production essay misses the opportunity to

draw parallels between the film's heroine and the genuine historical figure upon whom her character is based.

Dangerous Game X-rated (Vivid, UPC#0073215529)

Shot on film, the colors are faded and fleshtones are bland. The
image is also a little dull, but the narrative, about filmmakers
whose love lives are distracting them from shooting a movie, is appealing, and most of the erotic sequences of have a strong emotional context. The monophonic sound is as weak-willed as the
picture and is distorted on the upper end. The 73 minute program
features Jenteal, Melissa Hill, Mona Demoan, and Krista Maze.
The DVD also contains alternate angle sequences and elaborate
hardcore interactive promotional features.

Dangerous Liaisons (Warner, 11872)

We get tongue-tied trying to repeat the plot to friends. It is a period costume drama about sneaky aristocrats who have nothing
better to do than compromise virtue and indulge in intrigues. The
he-does-this-to-her-because-she-wanted-the-other-one-to-em-
barrass-him stuff becomes so confusing so quickly you need to talk
in color codes to keep everyone straight. It is better just to see the
drama for yourself and absorb as much as you can. The film, starring Glenn Close and John Malkovich, is marvelously entertaining.
Few characters in drama are more enjoyable to watch than wily degenerates trying to get one up on each other. The script has been
honed by endless adaptations and onstage tryouts. The film is
beautifully directed by Stephen Frears with static screen compositions serving only to bundle and charge the energy of the characters within.

Fleshtones are accurate, other colors are deep and the image is
crisp. The letterboxing has an aspect ratio of about 1.85:1 and an
accommodation for enhanced 16:9 playback. The 120 minute film
is also presented on the other side of the DVD in cropped format,
which has a workable framing, but is less elegant. The stereo surround sound is clean but somewhat muted. Although the standard
stereo track has more rear channel activity, the forcefulness and
detail of the Dolby Digital track are highly pleasing. The 1988 film
is available in French in regular stereo and comes with English,
French or Spanish subtitles. There is also a decent sized cast and
crew listing and a few production notes.

Dante's Peak (Universal, 20149/20065); DTS (Universal, 20450)

Pierce Brosnan stars as a volcano expert and Linda Hamilton is
the mayor of a small town nestled a little too closely to a percolating pimple of pumice. The heroes dodge flying boulders, drive
across fiery lava flows, take a metal boat across an acid lake (not a
good idea), get buried in a collapsing tunnel, dodge the eruption's
shock waves, evade floods and mud slides, keep their balance during earthquakes and basically leap from one thrilling situation to
the next. With a dog, too.

The 109 minute film is letterboxed, with an aspect ratio of
about 2.35:1 and an accommodation for enhanced 16:9 playback.
Colors are sharp, fleshtones are deep and even the dark and ashy
scenes are clear and crisp. The stereo surround sound is a little
weak, but there is a Dolby Digital track with stronger separation
effects and more power. The film is also available in French and
Spanish in standard stereo and comes with English, French or
Spanish subtitles. There is an hour-long 'making of' documentary,
a commentary track by director Roger Donaldson and production
designer Dennis Washington, a CD-style music soundtrack which
plays on an alternate audio channel over the documentary, storyboard sequences, production design sketches, publicity and advertising materials, and even the entire shooting script. Even the
documentary has the subtitle options, and there is a theatrical
trailer, a brief cast profile, and some standard production notes as
well. The script and photo section is a bit difficult to find—you
have to go through the chapter selection on the documentary. The
documentary and isolated musical score are not in Dolby Digital.

The documentary shows how the film was conceived and developed, what shooting it was like, and how many of the impressive
special effects (so impressive that you don't realize they are special
effects) were achieved. Donaldson, was a geology enthusiast long
before he became a filmmaker. He and Washington are blissfully
oblivious to the movie's plot on the commentary track, but tend to
keep their insights on a fairly superficial level, reacting to what is
happening on the screen by commenting as quickly as possible on
whatever was the most interesting aspect of shooting that scene.
They don't go into too much detail about the other personnel
working on the film (Donaldson acknowledges them at the end,
however) and say nothing about the 'race' the movie was having
with another volcano film. Fans will still find the talk worthwhile,
particularly Donaldson's descriptions of working in the small Ida-
ho town they used for most of their location footage and the pan-
demonium during the big destruction scenes, but revelations
about the filmmaking process are limited. He tells you how a stunt
was accomplished, but rarely reflects upon why he chose one way
to shoot something over an alternative.

The film appears by itself on the DTS DVD, in English only,
with no captioning or supplementary features. There is a standard
stereo track as well as the DTS track, but there is no way to toggle
between them. The picture looks identical to the standard release
and is letterboxed, with an aspect ratio of about 2.35:1 and an accommodation for enhanced 16:9 playback.

The DTS track seems a little sharper than the Dolby Digital
track on the older DVD. When we upped the volume past sensible
levels, the DTS track seemed less prone to distortion. The bass response, however, seemed to be the same on both DVDs. Separation effects are identical, and most of the time we could detect no
differences whatsoever between the two tracks. The bass on the
DTS LD, however, is much better defined, the audio track has
more detail and there is more thrust in the mid range.

Dario Argento's World of Horror (Synapse, SFD0002)

A survey of Argento's films up to the mid-Eighties, the 71
minute program contains a healthy selection of excerpts as well as
revealing behind-the-scenes footage and analysis. The narration
and some of the film clips are in English, but many of the interviews are in Italian with English subtitles. The color quality is
workable, but the source material is still fairly battered and worn,
so there is only so much that can be done with it. The picture is
tolerable if one takes its source into account. Colors are fairly
strong in places and the image isn't too soft. The monophonic
sound also has some wear, but is acceptable. There also an Argento
filmography, and the program is not captioned.

Dark City (New Line, N4657)

A fascinating, cerebral science fiction film that is loaded with
eye-popping special effects, the film takes a whole viewing to figure
out what is happening (though ultimately, the narrative is fairly
straightforward). Its design is so meticulous and integrated with its
purpose, however, that it makes great home video, offering up new
revelations and new understandings with each subsequent viewing. Set in a claustrophobic metropolis that mutates every night at
midnight as aliens conduct experiments on the unsuspecting populace, the hero, played by Rufus Sewell, is the one person who has
seen through the ruse and not gone crazy. We do not subscribe as
heartily to the film's epistemological and metaphysical themes as
do the filmmakers or the movie's strongest proponents, but it is a
fresh and entertaining work of legitimate science fiction and it
could well end up becoming the classic some folks think it is.

The 101 minute film is presented on one side in letterboxed format with an aspect ratio of about 2.35:1 and an accommodation
for enhanced 16:9 playback, and in cropped format on the other
side. On shots not involving the special effects, the letterboxed version masks off a substantial amount of picture information from
the bottom of the screen and adds only a little to the sides in comparison to the cropped version, but on shots with special effects,

the letterboxing loses nothing on the top or bottom and adds a considerable amount to the sides of the image. The image is deliberately dark, but the transfer appears accurate and is quite pleasing. The stereo surround sound creates a strong ambiance and smooth tones, and the Dolby Digital track has a better organized, more specific separation mix. The film is also available in French in Dolby Digital and can be supported by English or French subtitles. In addition to a pair of commentary tracks, is a cast & crew profile section, production notes that mostly echo what was said in the commentary, a couple design sketches and a theatrical trailer. The DVD also contains a very negative but on-the-money review by H.G. Wells of Fritz Lang's **Metropolis**, from which some of the imagery of **Dark City** was derived. Wells complains, rightly, that the science behind the film's designs is mistaken and out of date, the irony being, of course, that we now look at the entire era in which it was produced as quaintly out of date, something the visionary Wells seemed to foresee in his frustration over the film's simplicities.

On one audio track, there is a collective commentary by the director, Alex Proyas, writers Lem Dobbs and David S. Goyer, the production designer, Patrick Tatopoulos and cinematographer Dariusz Wolski. Surprisingly, they do not talk very much about the special effects and we wish we could hear more about how they brought the whole film in on such a modest budget and shooting schedule. They do talk a lot about the film's conception and the meanings of the story. They go into the designs and the different allusions intended by an object or a shot, and they offer up a little bit about working with the cast. On the whole the talk is informative, but selective.

On another track, there is a very good critical commentary of the film by Roger Ebert. Ebert's talk is no fly by night whim. He spent three days once with a film class analyzing **Dark City** shot by shot and knows the movie inside out. His talk is very worthwhile, not only explaining the film's basic concepts and pointing out its intricate details (such as a hidden Biblical quote) but, in the finest critical tradition, using the film to provide mini lessons on movies, literature and other topics.

Dark Planet (Simitar, 7461)

The special effects are cheap looking, but the story isn't bad. Michael York stars as the commander of a space ship containing a mixed crew of two warring groups, who have declared an uneasy truce in order to explore a space warp. The characters are nicely conceived and, as long as the action stays inside the ship (there are betrayals to the truce), the 1996 film is engaging. The picture is a bit hazy, with soft colors and slightly bland, pinkish fleshtones. The stereo sound is a little noisy and often lacks dimensionality. The 96 minute full screen presentation is captioned.

Dark Secrets (Simitar R-rated, 7447); (Simitar unrated, 7468)

A softcore erotic film with unusually elaborate S&M sequences, Monique Parent stars as a reporter who goes undercover to investigate the dealings of a wealthy financier, but ends up dating him instead. The pair make several visits to a strange underground nightclub where anything goes. The narrative is irrelevant, however, since the point of the film is its detailed erotic sequences, at least on the unrated version, including some on-camera shots of actual body piercing. A number of the actresses look like they just stepped out of a Russ Meyer film. The picture is often grainy or smeary and colors are sometimes off, creating orange fleshtones and other distortions. The audio track is reasonably energetic with an occasional distortion. A filmography of the star, Julie Strain, is also included, and the program is not captioned. The unrated version runs about 90 minutes and the R-rated version runs about 80 minutes.

Dark Star (Roan, 8205)

Both the 68 minute *Special Edition* cut and the 83 minute standard cut are presented. The 1974 feature was originally produced

as a film school movie by Dan O'Bannon and John Carpenter. When a distributor picked it up for release, they filmed some extraneous material to bring the running time up to a normal parameter. The *Special Edition* version is indeed the more entertaining of the two. The outer space comedy essentially has three parts—the setting of the mood and detailing of the boredom experienced by the spaceship crew, a lengthy interlude in which one of the crew members tries to subdue an alien that has more than a subtle resemblance to a beachball with feet, and problems with an armed bomb that will not disengage. These three components are not only better integrated on the shorter version, they are less tiresome, and so the film's comical ideas have a stronger and more focused impact. There are plenty of fans, however, who prefer having the longer version simply because it is longer.

This was a student film, so the cinematography is not slick and the production values are not glossy. Bright colors tend to blur, fleshtones are pale, contrasts are washy and other hues are very light. Nevertheless, it would be difficult to find a presentation stronger than the version released on DVD, and fans should be happy with the job Roan has done. The picture is letterboxed with an aspect ratio of about 1.85:1 and no 16:9 enhancement.

The film's audio track has been remastered for Dolby Digital sound, but we found the overindulgent separations rather annoying and preferred to run the audio through our monitor's speakers, in which case it works quite well, providing an adequate dynamic range and clear dialogue track. There is no captioning. A trailer, profiles and very thorough filmographies for O'Bannon and Carpenter have also been included.

Dark Victory (MGM, 906679)

The classic terminal illness movie, in which Bette Davis' character has one of those Hollywood diseases that renders its victims both eloquent and graceful right up to the final fatal moment. We all should die so well. Humphrey Bogart (with an Irish accent) and Ronald Reagan (not very convincing as a playboy inebriate) have supporting roles.

The 1939 feature has deep, well-pronounced contrasts and well-textural detail. The monophonic sound is weak, but the Dolby Digital mono track brings out more detail. The noise inherent in the older recordings is also more pronounced, but management of the volume controls can keep such natural discrepancies in check. The 106 minute films comes with English, French or Spanish subtitles ("C'est notre victoire sur la nuit") and is accompanied by a trailer.

Dark Waters (Image, ID5367FEDVD)

Merle Oberon is the heroine in the passable 1944 gothic thriller, set in a mansion in a Louisiana swamp. She portrays a young woman recovering from a recent accident who, to convalesce, visits relatives she has never met before. Soon she is hearing noises in the night and finds herself threatened by an ever-increasing set of dangers. Unusually seedy performances by Thomas Mitchell and Elisha Cook, Jr. give the film a nice touch of spice. Franchot Tone is also featured. Directed by Andre de Toth, some sequences are superbly executed while other appear to have been done on the cheap, and the shadow of the sound boom even makes a lengthy appearance at one point.

The black-and-white picture is in fairly decent shape, particularly when compared to previous home video presentations. There are some scratches and speckles, and contrasts are a bit weak in places, but the image is often sharp and smooth, with rich blacks. The monophonic sound is somewhat scratchy, and the 90 minute program is not captioned.

Darkman (Universal, 20179)

Sam Raimi's 1990 feature would make a great double bill with **The Crow**. Although **Darkman** has more instances of humor, both movies are about heroes with supernatural strength seeking revenge, and both have a dark atmosphere and fatalistic tone. The action sequences are breathless, the dramatic interludes are tight, and Raimi's talent extends far beyond just knowing how to dangle a stunt man from a helicopter—the shot of the heroine waltzing with the bad guy at a dance is one of the most memorable in the whole film. Liam Neeson stars, with Frances McDormand

The presentation is letterboxed, with an aspect ratio of about 1.85:1 and an accommodation for enhanced 16:9 playback, creating a nice-looking balance. The picture has finely detailed hues and a sharp focus. The stereo surround soundtrack, replete with a Danny Elfman score, is high powered and free of distortion. The 96 minute film is also available in French and comes with English or Spanish subtitles, and is accompanied by a few production notes, cast profiles and a terrific theatrical trailer.

Darkman II: The Return of Durant (Universal, 20323)

Although the villain is seen riding in a helicopter that crashes into a wall and explodes at the end of **Darkman**, he's back in the made-for-video sequel. Larry Drake reprises his role as the bad guy. The film is not as invigorating as the first movie, but if you watch it separately with no more than a dim memory of the original's flair, then it can be passable entertainment. Drake, incidentally, gets to spend a lot time being the hero, since the good guy uses the bad guy's 'face.' Arnold Vosloo co-stars.

The image is a little hazy, fleshtones are dull and blacks are not pure. The stereo surround sound is somewhat weak, but the show's sound mix isn't very elaborate anyway, so you aren't missing much in the way of subtle detail. The 92 minute program is also available in French and Spanish and can be supported by English or Spanish subtitles. There are production notes, a cast-and-director profile section and a trailer promoting the show's video release.

Das Boot - Director's Cut (Columbia TriStar, 22215/9)

The deliberately sudden cuts between calm and chaos remain in the 209 minute 1997 **Director's Cut** version of the German epic. An hour of footage, mostly character enhancement, has been added to the 1981 movie, which previously ran 149 minutes, yet it still seems to just breeze by as the film's basic structure remains—the WWII U-boat goes out on a mission, waits a long time before finding anything, gets chased but eventually escapes, receives another mission (requiring that it pass Gibraltar), almost gets destroyed and finally pulls into port, only to have disaster strike. There are more dinner table shots, more sequences where sailors share photographs, more stumbling in the hallways and many more sorts of details like that, but the set pieces remain the same and the design of the cutting, where, like in real life, disaster strikes without warning, remains intact. The extra footage isn't padding. The film is richer and by the end you feel you know the characters much more deeply, but the movie's excitements are never compromised or stalled.

The film is presented in letterbox format only, with an aspect ratio of about 1.85:1 and an accommodation for enhanced 16:9 playback, and is split to two sides. Colors are very strong and details are clearer. The stereo surround sound is passable, and the Dolby Digital track is significantly stronger, delivering a much greater bass, more separation details and a more compelling ambiance. What's more, the DVD format allows the viewer to play the film in German or in English in Dolby Digital with or without English subtitles. The film also has a Spanish language track in standard stereo and can be accompanied by Spanish or French subtitles.

On top of all that, there is a brief but rewarding 'making of' featurette that gives the viewer a picture of how many of the film's effect sequences were staged, and a commentary featuring the director, Wolfgang Petersen, the star, Jürgen Prochnow and the producer of the **Director's Cut**, Ortwin Freyemuth. The filmmakers discuss all aspects of the production, its history (at one point John Sturges was going to make the film with Robert Redford), trivia (Steven Spielberg borrowed the boat for *Raiders of the Lost Ark* and broke it) and legacy (the film helped Germany come to

terms with its past). They talk extensively about the restoration effort, how the elements were restored, why scenes were added and how the long version and the short version were simultaneously conceived during the original shooting. There are also many more details, about the history of the real boat and its crew, about the young actors working in the film, about the blend of models, real boats and soundstage inserts, and many other fascinating insights on how the film was created. Petersen also likens film direction to being the captain of a submarine, and then has a healthy laugh about it.

Das Lied Von Der Erde (see **Gustav Mahler: Das Lied Von Der Erde/Kindertotenlieder**)

Daughters of Darkness (Anchor Bay, DV10494)

The 1971 Belgian film about female vampires is reminiscent of *The Hunger*, to which it was likely a major influence. Shot in English (with live sound, there is no lip synching), the film is about a young newlywed who discovers on her honeymoon that she may have entered into an abusive marriage. The two are staying at an oceanside hotel off season and there is but one other couple in residence, a mysterious pair of elegant women who seem to have designs upon their marital union. Like *The Hunger*, **Daughters of Darkness** is wealthier in style than it is in substance, but there is enough of a plot to make repeat viewings appealing. The director, Harry Kümel, dresses the central predator, Delphine Seyrig, like Marlene Dietrich and poses her as Josef Von Sternberg did or Gustav Klimt might have, but the evocations are subtle and the film is a unique blend of sex, emotional conflict and supernatural mystery. Although there is a scattering of minor speckles here and there, the source material is in excellent condition and the color quality is wonderful, with deep, smooth hues and accurate fleshtones. The source material is in good condition, with no more than incidental wear. The image is letterboxed with an aspect ratio of about 1.66:1 and no 16:9 enhancement. The monophonic sound is fine and there is no captioning.

The film's male lead, John Karlen (he is also a *Dark Shadows* veteran), provides a conversational commentary, prompted by David Del Valle. They discuss the production, the personalities of the cast and crew (Karlen had a fistfight with Kümel near the end of shooting), interpretations of the film and other related matters. They have some pretty good laughs as well, and provide an adequate overview and background for viewers who have found the movie itself to be intriguing.

Dave (Warner, 12962)

The 1993 charming political and romantic comedy is about a lookalike double who steps in when the President of the United States becomes ill. Kevin Kline, Sigourney Weaver and Frank Langella star, with a number of other fine performers popping up at appropriate moments. Directed by Ivan Reitman, the film follows a near-perfect emotional path, so that its unlikely premise is always less important than the dilemmas of the characters and the very funny comical abilities of the performers. The film's unsung special effects, seamlessly placing the characters in buildings the actors couldn't possibly visit, are also commendable.

The colors are deep and crisp, with accurate fleshtones. The picture is letterboxed on one side, with an aspect ratio of about 1.85:1 and an accommodation for enhanced 16:9 playback, and is in full screen format on the other side. The letterboxing adds a bit to the sides and masks off a bit from the top and a lot from the bottom in comparison to the full screen release, but generally the framing is a little more elegant. The stereo surround sound is workable, particularly since the film's audio design is not critical to the entertainment. The 110 minute movie is also available in French or Spanish and comes with English, French or Spanish subtitles ("Tu ne pouvais pas en crever comme tout le monde?"). There are a few production notes, a cast & crew profile, a well made trailer and an interesting 6 minute 'making of' featurette.

Dave Grusin Presents West Side Story (N2K, N2KD10021)

An hour-long jazz interpretation of the music from **West Side Story,** various artists tackle the different songs from the show, including Grusin, Bill Evans, Jonathan Butler (singing *Maria*), Michael Brecker, Gloria Estefan (singing *Tonight*), and Jon Secada. Each number is an individual music video. One is a concept video (a bunch of people running around the streets of Manhattan), a couple present montages of photos from the movie and stage productions, and the rest are of the artists performing, interspersed with shots of quivering sound lines that appear a little too often for our liking. The album is pleasant and the picture quality is fine. The stereo surround sound is excellent, with smooth, warm tones, and there is a menu-activated Dolby Digital track with more dimensionality (it moves the focus from the front to the center of the viewing room) and even brighter tones. There is also a brief 'making of' segment interviewing some of the artists. There is no captioning.

Dawn of the Dead (Anchor Bay, DV10325)

George Romero's 1978 zombie epic, a masterpiece of horror and gore, has a deliberately makeshift look, but the colors in the transfer are strong and the image is sharp. The same goes for the monophonic sound, which has a somewhat flat ambiance but is clearer and sharper than any of the film's earlier home video iterations. Anchor Bay presents the 137 minute *Director's Cut* (not the 142 minute version) on two sides, accompanied by a pair of theatrical trailers. On the copy we viewed, what was identified as side one turned out to be side two and vice-versa, and you practically need a microscope to read the side identification in the first place. The more often we see the film the more brilliant it seems. Since it contains oodles of grotesque makeup and mutilation effects, some viewers will understandably not have the patience for it. However, it may be the best merger of a daydream and a nightmare anyone has ever achieved, and viewers who tolerate or live for grotesque thrills should not pass it by. The movie's most daring aspect is not its special effects but its length. It deliberately takes its excruciating time showing the process the characters must go through to protect themselves (the movie is about four people who attempt to hold out in a shopping mall after zombies begin to take over the world—the events are communicated in a low-key style that adds considerably to the viewer's acceptance of the narrative). It is an elaborate satire on middle-class life and shopping habits, it is a thriller, and it is a low-budget spectacle. Most importantly, however, the running time allows the movie to not only play the nightmare through, it gives the viewer a full chance to soak up the daydream (having the run of the mall) as well.

Dawn Rider (see **The John Wayne Collection**)

Day of the Dead (Anchor Bay, DV10602)

Lacking the sense of inspired innovation that marked the first two George Romero **Dead** films, the 1985 production is not as brilliant as its siblings, but not every movie can break new ground. The film does have improved makeup and a viable narrative (how about a TV series, anyone?), enough to support the many engaging gore effects. The underground bunker setting has a strong daydream quality, there is an easy humor to much of the carnage and the action scenes are fairly exciting. Characterizations are weak, but the film is efficiently executed and most viewers are just happy to revisit Romero's zombie-infested universe.

The presentation is in letterboxed format with an aspect ratio of about 1.85:1 and no 16:9 enhancement. The film was shot grainy and that's how it looks except when the lighting is especially bright. The colors are reasonably fresh, however, and are adequately detailed. Contrasts and fleshtones are accurate. The stereo sound has a mild dimensionality but is basically monophonic in design. Like the grain in the image, the dialogue recording has its limitations, but the audio presentation is passable. The program is not closed captioned. The 102 minute film appears on side one, with a brief but effective trailer and 20 minutes of behind-the-scenes footage on side two. The behind-the-scenes material, which includes an impromptu interview with Tom Savini, is fairly rewarding, showing how the extras were rounded up, how some of the makeup was applied, and how a couple of the stunts and effects gags were executed.

The Day of the Jackal (Universal, 20261)

What makes **The Day of the Jackal** such great home video is that it is so repeatable. Whether you've never seen it or seen it a dozen times, you know Charles DeGaulle doesn't get assassinated (people still know that, right?), so the pleasure comes in watching the step-by-step account of the detectives working to prevent the assassination. It isn't just Frederick Forsyth's deft plotting which makes the movie work so well, however. The director, Fred Zinnemann, did an exquisite job bringing the kind of elegance and precision that the story needs to hold a viewer's attention. The whole movie has a French feel to it, a classy and continental demeanor which locks the viewer into the film's world much in the way a safety bar does on a roller coaster. The picture looks quite nice. It has been letterboxed with an aspect ratio of about 1.8:1 and no 16:9 enhancement. The colors are fresh, hues are solid and even minor speckling is limited. The monophonic sound is okay. The 143 minute program is presented in dual-layer format and is supported by English, Spanish or French subtitles. An enjoyable theatrical trailer is also included, along with some brief production notes. Edward Fox and Michel Lonsdale star.

Daylight (Universal, 20267); DTS (Universal, 20452)

It can be embarrassing watching a collector's edition of a really bad movie when the filmmakers seem oblivious to their artistic bankruptcy. Rob Cohen, the director of **Daylight**, was once caught in a serious hotel fire, and approached the big budget disaster film with a knowledge of the emotional dynamics created in a disaster situation. It didn't seem to help, though. The film, about people trapped in a collapsed tunnel who are saved by an emergency expert played by Sylvester Stallone, is a silly, ridiculous contrivance with elaborate but uninteresting special effects. Whatever spiritual enlightenment Cohen obtained from his own experience remains internalized and has not been transferred to the screen.

The only advantage to the movie is it's fully energized sound mix, which is passable on the standard stereo surround soundtrack but fabulous on the Dolby Digital track. The picture is letterboxed, with an aspect ratio of about 1.85:1 and an accommodation for enhanced 16:9 playback. The picture is also in excellent condition, with a sharp focus and accurate hues in even the most difficult lighting situations. The 115 minute film is also available in French and Spanish in Dolby Digital and comes with English or Spanish subtitles. Along with Cohen's commentary track, there is a decent 'making of' documentary, trailers, a music video, production stills and drawings, a cast-and-director profile section and a production essay. The documentary is also captioned.

Knowing more about how the movie was made didn't help us like it any better. Cohen's superlatives, on the disc's alternate audio track and in the 'making of' documentary, about his crew and their accomplishments, are oblivious to the film's shortcomings, and his overly polite praises kind of make you squirm. The stills include conceptual drawings, storyboards of key sequences, some publicity photos, an interesting collection of unused advertising artwork, and publicity essays about the production and the crew. Cohen's talk during the movie has some useful insights on how a few filmmaking challenges were overcome, but he also spends a lot of time explaining the plot and putting a positive spin on his accomplishment. The documentary is a more generalized portrait of the film's production. The construction of the 'tunnel' set is especially interesting, an elongated replica of the Holland Tunnel that was built on a movie lot in Rome.

The DTS presentation is letterboxed like the standard release, but there are no other special features and there is no captioning.

There is a standard stereo track in addition to the DTS track. In comparison to the Dolby Digital track on the standard DVD, the DTS track has slightly sharper definitions and a slightly stronger bass, but it is nowhere near as good as the DTS LD, which has clearer tones and an even more powerful kick. The picture quality is identical. The frame transfer rate on the standard DVD was already quite high, so while the transfer rate on the DTS DVD is even higher, it is not enough to make a noticeable difference.

Days of Jesse James (see Roy Rogers Collection 1)

Dazed and Confused (Universal, 20277)

A superbly textured teenage comedy that draws its humor from the social fabric of high school instead of from manufactured stunts; even when it dwells upon clichés, they are realistic clichés. The 1993 film is set upon the afternoon, evening and night of the last day of school (in 1976), as the various characters, whether they like it or not, choose their next steps in life. Loosely structured, the narrative follows the kids around with enough forward motion to keep the viewer hooked, but it is free of the pushy theatrics that bog down most teen comedies. The film was directed by Richard Linklater and it is composed and acted in such a way that on multiple viewings there is a tendency to fall deeper and deeper into the setting, because the peripheral characters have just as much realism and just as many intriguing idiosyncrasies as the central characters.

The picture is letterboxed with an aspect ratio of about 1.85:1 and no 16:9 enhancement. The color quality is good, with bright, crisp hues and accurate fleshtones. The stereo surround sound is dull, though its presentation of the film's rock music score is adequate. The 103 minute program is also available in French and comes with English or Spanish subtitles, along with essays about the film and about Linklater.

Dead Man Walking (PolyGram, 8006382432)

A broccoli movie—one that is supposedly good for you but isn't much fun—**Dead Man Walking** provides a superb exploration into the arguments for and against capital punishment. Although it uses a standard dramatic format by providing a naive protagonist who learns about something along with the viewer, the film is intelligent enough to skip over the clichés and get right to the heart of the emotional conflict—the anger and remorse of the victims' families versus the innocent suffering of the criminal's family and the humanity, such as it is, of the criminal. The problem with the movie is that, except for criminals' families and a few activists here and there, nobody cares about the welfare of Death Row inmates— let's face it, even baby seals deserve more concern and protection.

Based upon a true story, Susan Sarandon is a nun who gets roped into providing spiritual support for a convicted murderer and rapist, played by Sean Penn. She also visits the families of the victims. Both actors give fine performances, making the movie watchable, and the film's heavily researched depiction of the Death Row process has an appealing sense of accuracy. There isn't any more to the movie than that, however, and while the filmmakers create tension from the methodical countdown to the execution, the movie is restrained by the spirit of the truth from manipulating it. Tim Robbins directed.

The picture is a bit too dark, losing too much detail in shadows. Often, in such situations, the darkness is intentional, with the lighter image having been lightened specifically for the video release and not an accurate representation of the intended cinematography, but here the darkness seems to go too far. Fleshtones are a little too pinkish, as well, but, overall, the problems are minor and the picture is acceptable. The image is presented in letterboxed format on one side, with an aspect ratio of about 1.85:1 and no 16:9 enhancement, and in cropped format on the other side. The cropped version adds a little bit of picture information to the bottom of the screen in comparison to the letterboxed version (the shots of TV monitors are more satisfying) but loses a lot more picture information from the side in comparison to the letterboxed image. The stereo surround sound is acceptable. The film is mostly talking, anyway.

There is also a Spanish audio track and, on another channel, a running commentary from Robbins. There are minor gaps throughout his talk where dialogue from the film kicks in. Robbins gives a reasonably good overview of the production. He doesn't go into detail on a consistent basis (for example, he never talks about the apparent thoroughness and accuracy of Penn's accent and how it was achieved), but he does manage to explain his strategies for the most important scenes. He also provides background information and discusses the logistics of the shoot. Like the film, he manages to let the viewer know where his sympathies lie in regards to the capital punishment argument, but remains objective in discussing its pros and cons. The 122 minute program can be supported by English, French or Spanish subtitles, and the DVD also has brief profiles and filmographies of Robbins, Sarandon and Penn, along with a good theatrical trailer that seems to deliberately tell you how the story is going to turn out, so you can focus your attention on other things.

Dead Poets Society (Buena Vista, 15092)

We stopped caring about Peter Weir's **Dead Poets Society** when the boy committed suicide. Here is a movie in which the central figurehead, an English teacher portrayed by Robin Williams, admonishes his students to avoid cliché and seek out the path not taken by others, and all the while the script is following every cliché available. Williams stars as an English teacher who enhances the lives several boarding school students, though it is the coming-of-age problems of the kids that take up most of the drama.

The standard 129 minute version of the film is letterboxed with an aspect ratio of about 1.85:1 and no 16:9 enhancement. Fleshtones are a bit indistinct in places, but the picture is reasonably sharp and other hues are bright. The stereo surround sound and Dolby Digital sound are okay, though the movie's sound mix is not all that elaborate and the high end is a little harsh in places. The 1989 film is also available in French in Dolby Digital and can be supported by English subtitles.

Dead Presidents (Buena Vista, 14258)

The experiences of black Vietnam veterans have never been the subject of a mainstream Hollywood film before, and so the sophomore effort from The Hughes Brothers tries to break new ground. Inspired by a true story, the hero becomes a criminal when his life falls apart after he returns from the war. The directors avoid the standard Vietnam vet clichés, but they never get under the surface of their characters, and sections of the film could end up seeming as campy someday as the blaxploitation movies that inspired the film's style. The Vietnam sequence is terrific, and the holdup in the finale (the film, curiously, was sold as a heist movie) is worth waiting for, but the drama surrounding these sequences is slow and unfocused, as if the filmmakers never really figured out how to get from A to B. Larenz Tate and Keith David star, with Chris Tucker.

The picture looks very nice, with deep hues and stability in some very complicated lighting situations. The image is letterboxed with an aspect ratio of about 2.3:1 and no 16:9 enhancement. The stereo surround sound is bland, but the Dolby Digital track provides a strong dimensionality and a pronounced bass. The 119 minute film is also available in French and comes with English or Spanish subtitles.

Dead Ringers (Anchor Bay, DV10329); (Criterion, CC1541D)

We don't like the 1988 David Cronenberg film, an interesting but meandering tale about twin gynecologists, played by Jeremy Irons, who go crazy, but we still feel Criterion's DVD is an excellent accomplishment, delivering a pristine transfer of the movie, a constantly informative audio commentary and other worthwhile supplementary materials.

The colors on Anchor Bay's version are a little dark. The image is smooth, but contrasts are inconsistently detailed. Criterion's version is better, with a much sharper picture and better contrast detail. The 115 minute film is letterboxed with an aspect ratio of about 1.66:1 and no 16:9 enhancement on both presentations. The stereo sound is okay, though the mix is nothing special and there is a little noise in the recording here and there. There is no captioning on either DVD. Anchor Bay's jacket claims that a theatrical trailer has been included, but we could not locate it.

A still photo segment on the weird medical instruments depicted in the movie has been included on the Criterion program, along with a look at how the special effects were achieved, an electronic press kit and an alternate design for the opening sequence.

Cronenberg, Irons, cinematographer Peter Suschitzky, editor Ronald Sanders and production designer Carol Spier discuss all aspects of the film's history and production on the commentary track of the Criterion DVD, going into particular detail over how the 'twinning' effects were achieved. Perhaps the most fascinating commentary of all is Irons' explanation of how he approached the two very similar characters he was playing, giving each a different 'point of energy.' He also makes one off-hand statement that seems to encapsulate some aspects of the film perfectly: "When I started making noises about perhaps I'd better go see gynecologists and go to operating theaters [Cronenberg] said, 'No, no, no. All doctors do it their own way. You just do it your own way and people will believe you.' I did no research at all."

Dead-Alive (Trimark, VM6841D)

Peter Jackson's elaborately grotesque 1992 film, shot in New Zealand (it was Jackson's first commercial effort), is deliberately comical, and the grosser it gets the funnier it gets. The film also features stop motion animation effects and takes its narrative on several different vectors, so that along with accumulating more blood and spewing innards than your average block of slaughterhouses, it shifts in subject matter often enough to prevent the splatter sequences from ever seeming redundant or tiresome. In the end, the hero turns a lawn mower on the ghouls approaching him and just grinds them all down to hamburger.

The picture is tolerable. The image is a little soft and darker sequences are a bit grainy, but hues are reasonably bright and fleshtones are workable. The image is letterboxed, with an aspect ratio of about 1.85:1 and an accommodation for enhanced 16:9 playback, though the framing seems a bit tight at times. The stereo sound has a limited mix and little dimensionality. The 97 minute program can be supported by English closed captioning, as well as French or Spanish subtitles ("A plus tard Nénuphar!"), and there is a trailer.

Death Becomes Her (Universal, 20143/20049)

The campy Robert Zemeckis special effects comedy features Goldie Hawn and Meryl Streep as bickering rivals who, through a magical potion, continue to function after murdering one another. The film is generally more pleasing to the *Mommie Dearest* crowd than the *Who Framed Roger Rabbit* masses, but Hawn and Streep, along with the spectacular morphing effects, make the show difficult to resist. Bruce Willis also appears.

The special effect sequences were shot in a partial widescreen and the non-special effect sequences were shot full frame, so the full screen image on the DVD is not cropped during regular scenes, but it is cropped during the fantasy sequences. The image is a bit bland, with pale fleshtones and a faintly grainy background at times. The stereo surround sound seems adequate. There is a cast profile and a good 'making of' featurette that shows how some of the special effects were accomplished. The 1992 103 minute film is also available in French and Spanish, and can be accompanied by English or Spanish subtitling. Zemeckis, in the DVD's production notes, describes the film as "**Night of the Living Dead** as if it were written by Noel Coward."

Death Race 2000 (New Horizons, NH00144); (Digital Multimedia, DML00243)

A grey satire about a cross-country road race in a totalitarian U.S., in which the contestants score points for running people down, the film stars David Carradine, but is today more recognized as one of Sylvester Stallone's first major films, in which he plays the principal villain. The 1975 film, directed by Paul Bartel, runs a spare 78 minutes and features a lot of repetitive long shots of cars running down empty roads. The humor is as exaggerated as the violence but, surprisingly, there are elements of a workable political drama mixed into the plot.

Both are presented in full screen format. The colors on the New Horizons release are a touch brighter than the Digital Multimedia version, but the New Horizons presentation is substantially sharper. In general, the colors are a little drab and fleshtones are bland, with a touch of wear here and there, though the New Horizons version, at least, is workable. The monophonic sound is actually brighter and more satisfying on the Digital Multimedia release, and is somewhat muted on the New Horizons version. Neither version is captioned. The New Horizons version is accompanied by an interview with producer Roger Corman.

Debbie Does Dallas: The Next Generation X-rated (Vivid, UPC#0073214501); softcore (Vivid, UPC#0073214537)
Debbie Does Dallas '99 X-rated (Vivid, UPC#0073215571)

The mother of a cheerleading candidate acts underhandedly against her daughter's competition to help assure her a slot on the squad. The age difference in the actresses is believable and the erotic sequences are fresh. The color quality is reasonably strong, though some sequences have slight, momentary instabilities. The sound is promoted as stereophonic, but if there is any dimensionality, it is limited to the musical score. Nevertheless, the ambiance is solid. The 75 minute program contains alternate angle sequences and elaborate hardcore interactive promotional features.

Even though the camera angles have been changed on the softcore version, the mechanics of the performers' positions are of a hardcore and not a softcore design. It also runs 75 minutes and has the same picture and sound quality, but no alternate angle options.

Less inspired than **Next Generation**, in **'99** the cheerleaders have to earn a lot of money, so they bet on one team and wear out the other. Not the first time that plot has been used in an erotic film, and not the last. The program also seems consciously designed to accommodate a softcore version as well as the hardcore version, and the erotic sequences are rarely creative. The picture is grainy and colors are bland. The monophonic sound is okay. The 74 minute program features Lexus, Lovette, Raina and Stephanie Swift. The DVD contains alternate angle sequences and elaborate hardcore interactive promotional features.

The Decameron (Image, ID4419WSDVD)

Perhaps the best of Pier Paolo Pasolini's classic literature anthology films, wisps of romanticism are strung through its tales of dirty tricks and lascivious scheming. Discarding the novel's framing device, the only things linking the stories together are the suggestions of a common location—most of the characters appear to live in or visit the same filthy little marketplace—and an inconclusive piece about a painter working on a church fresco which is cut and spread through the film's latter half. The painter's final words are an artistic lament which appear to echo Pasolini's own feelings about his work. Nevertheless, the tales are often amusing and the film is not only accessible, but as entertaining when viewed piecemeal as when viewed in one sitting.

The disc is letterboxed with an aspect ratio of about 1.75:1 and no 16:9 enhancement. The colors look surprisingly good considering how miserable the source material appears otherwise. Scenes involving darkness often look grainy and blurred, but when the lighting is decent the fleshtones look presentable and the skies are a real blue. There are, however, many scratches and splices, and some segments of the 1970 film appear far more deteriorated than others. The monophonic sound is adequate, but it does fall out of synch from time to time. The 111 minute program is in Italian with permanent white English subtitles.

Deception X-rated (Vivid, UPC#0073215506)

A woman sets her boyfriend up with another friend, only to see the two fall in love. The character development is fairly satisfying and the erotic sequences are well executed. The picture is somewhat soft and fleshtones are a bit pinkish, with mildly bland colors. The monophonic sound is okay. Lené, Alexis Dane and Neena are feature in the 72 minute program. The DVD also contains alternate angle sequences and elaborate hardcore interactive promotional features.

Deconstructing Harry (New Line, N4653)

Woody Allen's film is about an author's bad marriages, with liberal clips from enactments of his stories, where the people in his life reappear in slightly modified forms. The film is rather frank about men's desires, which will cause some people to find the characters unappealing, but the humor is sophisticated and thoughtful, and the film's fantasy sequences and story excerpts give it a liveliness that Allen's straighter comedy-dramas have lacked. Allen also stars with a large cast that includes Kirstie Alley, Bob Balaban, Judy Davis and Demi Moore.

The picture is letterboxed on one side, with an aspect ratio of about 1.85:1 and an accommodation for enhanced 16:9 playback, and is in full screen format on the other side. The letterboxing adds picture information to the sides of the image and takes just a little off the bottom, providing a more satisfying framing. The colors are crisp and the image looks very good, with accurate fleshtones. Allen's audio tracks tend to be monophonic in design even when they are technically stereophonic. The stereo surround sound is reasonably clear. The 95 minute program can also be accessed in French and can be accompanied by English, French or Spanish subtitles ("Ils vont m'honorer, et je suis une tache"). There is an extensive cast profile section, as well.

Dee Snider's Strangeland (Artisan, 60498)

The truly sick movie—but then, there are plenty of people around who adore truly sick movies—is about a psychotic who kidnaps teenaged girls and tortures them **Hellraiser**-style. Snider wrote the script, and it could have used some polishing. Many opportunities for excitement are wasted, and dramatic transitions are needlessly awkward. The basic concept, however, is solid. If you are expecting a frivolity by the Heavy Metal singer who used to look like a ungroomed poodle, you will be greatly mistaken, because this is a movie that revels in the 'Sloth' and 'Gluttony' sequences from **Seven**. The prosthetic effects ring the bell on the gross-out scale, particularly on the DVD, which presents an 'unrated' cut of the film instead of the understandably tamer R-rated version released to theaters. The narrative follows a detective, played by Kevin Gage, who has to rescue his own daughter from the villain, played by Snider. The story has a basic **Dirty Harry** structure (the villain is caught by the hero, then released) and there is enough reality-based horror to thrill fans, but the film is also cheap and sloppy, coasting on its makes-A Man Called Horse-look-like-a-children's-party thrills.

The picture is letterboxed, with an aspect ratio of about 1.85:1 and an accommodation for enhanced 16:9 playback. The picture looks inexpensive. The transfer is okay, but the lighting is bland and the image compositions are dull. When the lighting is good, the image is solid and colors are smooth. Snider talked all his Heavy Metal pals into contributing to the musical score, so it is reasonably energetic. There is no five-channel track, but the standard stereo surround sound has smooth tones and a nice bass. Rear channel effects are adequate but not overly detailed. The 91 minute program is closed captioned and is accompanied by more than 15 minutes of music videos.

Snider also provides a commentary track. "We brought in a criminal psychiatrist who read the script and said I'd created a perfect schizophrenic sexual sadist. [He] wanted to know what books I'd read, and I hadn't [read any]. He didn't want to see me much after that." He doesn't go into too many filmmaking details but, as a practiced performer, he knows how to talk for an hour and a half and keep the listener entertained.

The Deep (Columbia TriStar, 01689)

Peter Yates' terrific 1977 underwater adventure film is available on one side in letterboxed format, with an aspect ratio of about 2.35:1 and an accommodation for enhanced 16:9 playback, and in cropped format on the other side, though it is the letterboxed version that enhances the movie's sense of adventure and realism. The picture looks great. The underwater scenes barely have any grain at all, and the above water sequences are limited only by the occasional blandness of mid-Seventies cinematography. Fleshtones are bright and colors are effectively defined. The stereo surround sound is more atmospheric than directional, and is marred by über-producer Peter Guber's need to cross-promote a disco soundtrack, but its best moments are exceptionally edited, and transport the viewer to the ocean depths as surely as the images. The 126 minute film also has a French soundtrack and can be supported by English, French, Spanish, Portuguese, Chinese, Korean and Thai subtitles.

Yates' accomplishments can be broken down into three categories. He is a good action director, and moves the above-water sequences along at a decent pace. He is experienced, and was therefore capable of pulling off the complex underwater scenes, the details of which are thoroughly described on the back of the disc jacket. Finally, he coaxed winning performances from the cast members. There is just enough understated tension in the relationship of the couple, played by Nick Nolte and Jacqueline Bisset, so that their adventures are believable—they are not bland, background-less movie heroes, and their reactions and resources fit with their characters. Better still is Robert Shaw. Previously assigned to character roles, he gets to play himself in **The Deep** and he does so with such taciturn charm that you hang on his every sly grin.

Deep Impact (Paramount, 330827)

We know a bunch of twelve-year old boys who hate **Deep Impact** because the movie is 121 minutes long and the comet-hitting-the-earth part only lasts 3 minutes. Our favorite section, however, is the first half hour, where the young reporter tracks down the biggest story of her life, and the movie is reminiscent of *The Day After* with its death-hanging-over-us personal dramas, though there are a few more special effect scenes than just the comet splashdown. The film was made smartly and, for its size and subject, fairly cheaply. It may not have the thrills of the other sci-fi blockbusters, but there is enough plot and human interaction to give it some substance and repeatability, and enough effects to tide over everybody but the twelve-year olds. Téa Leoni stars with Robert Duvall, Elijah Wood and Morgan Freeman.

The picture is letterboxed with an aspect ratio of about 2.35:1 and no 16:9 enhancement. The image is sharp, hues are rich and fleshtones are accurate. The film has an exhaustive stereo surround mix that make full use of one's audio system. The Dolby Digital track has plenty of power and clear rear channel definitions. There is a French language track in standard stereo and the film can be supported by English closed captions. The 121 minute program is accompanied by a fairly good teaser and a theatrical trailer that gives away too many of the movie's little surprises.

Deep Rising (Buena Vista, 14911)

If you've already watched all your other special effects action movies so many times that you're bored with them, then you may want to pick up **Deep Rising**, about thieves battling a monster in a cruise ship, but there is nothing overly original or clever about it.

Because of the CGI effects, the film seems most reminiscent of **Anaconda**, but you can take your pick as to what it is ripping off—the jacket cover even tries to relate it to *Titanic*, but that's stretching things considerably, **Speed 2** being a more appropriate analogy. Treat Williams stars, with Framke Janssen and Anthony Heald among the characters who survive somewhat longer than the majority. There are plenty of gunshots, explosions and icky-looking creatures, but it doesn't take long to realize that there isn't anything else.

The picture is letterboxed with an aspect ratio of about 2.35:1 and no 16:9 enhancement. Darker sequences are stable fleshtones look fine and the picture quality is okay. The stereo surround sound and Dolby Digital sound are loud and busy, but there are incongruities, particularly with the ambiance behind the dialogue, which changes from echo to no echo with an apparent randomness. The Dolby Digital track has more specific directional effects than the generalized standard surround soundtrack can manage and is the more entertaining of the two. The 106 minute film can also be accessed in French in standard stereo and can be supported by optional English subtitles. There is a pretty good theatrical trailer, too ("Women and children first. You're next").

The Deer Hunter (Universal, 20177)

The 1978 Oscar-winner is in letterboxed format with an aspect ratio of about 2.35:1 and no 16:9 enhancement. The colors are fairly strong but the image is a little soft and contrasts are not extensively detailed. The film's working class milieu seems to accommodate whatever drawbacks the image quality may have, however, and on the whole the picture presentation is satisfying. The stereo sound, on the other hand, is very dull, and amplification brings distortion to the audio's limited range. The 183 minute film, presented on a single side of a dual-layer platter, can be supported by English, French or Spanish subtitles ("Tu es trop belle pour être vraie") and comes with a production essay, a cast & director profile, and a lengthy critic quote trailer.

Despite a groundbreaking segment on the war in Vietnam, the film is about blue collar life in the Northeastern United States, and about a part of America that stretches from James Fenimore Cooper to the death throes of the steel industry. At the time it was made, Vietnam looked like a viable political parallel to the Northeast's economic decay and America's suicidal decline, but although that is no longer the case, the film's artistry is sustained, particularly when the transfer is as nice as it is on the DVD.

Demolition Man (Warner, 12985)

Sylvester Stallone, Wesley Snipes and Sandra Bullock star in the 1993 futuristic action picture, with comical overtones, about a cop from the present day who is awakened several decades hence, where violence and all other social ills have apparently been eliminated. The 115 minute film is presented on one side in letterboxed format, with an aspect ratio of about 2.35:1, and in cropped format on the other side. The cropped version loses a lot of the expensive set decorations but gives you juicier closeups of the stars. The picture has vivid, glossy colors and crisp fleshtones. The Dolby Digital track is livelier and sharper than the regular stereo mix, with better defined separations. There is a commentary track, too. Producer Joel Silver speaks for a little bit at the beginning, but most of the commentary is taken up by the director, Marco Brambilla, who does quite a good job at providing a background on the production, sharing anecdotes about the shoot and explaining why various choices were made, such as his desire to include as much of the expensive sets as he possibly could in his dialogue scenes. He doesn't go into too much detail about why Lori Petty was dropped from the role that then went to Bullock, but at least he mentions the incident. The film also comes with a monophonic Spanish soundtrack and can be supported by English, French or Spanish subtitles. There is a theatrical trailer that is presented in full screen on the cropped side and slightly letterboxed on the letterboxed side, along with a modest cast and crew profile section. The trailer

contains footage shot especially for it and takes a particularly long time trying to explain the plot.

The Demolitionist (Simitar, 7431)

An enjoyable comic book-style action film reminiscent of **Robocop**, Nicole Eggert stars as a cop killed in the line of duty who is resurrected, with nano-machines replacing her blood. She is given an indestructible suit, along with carte blanche to clean up the city. The first half hour could use substantial trimming and the film's limited budget inhibits the action scenes a little, but the basic concept is highly appealing and, after a bit of a rough start, the program delivers. The action scenes are great fun and the heroine's psychic pain over her condition gives the drama some decent substance.

The program is presented in full screen format, and some shots look a little tight on the edges. The picture quality is compromised a bit by the budget and some sequences look soft or hazy, with fuzzy reds, but the filmmakers have been ambitious in giving the film a consistent comic book tone and the DVD conveys the bright, glossy colors and darker mood admirably. The stereo surround sound is also limited to a certain extent, but is still worth raising the volume for and delivers the basic punch the movie requires, and there is a Dolby Digital track that is somewhat stronger. The 93 minute program is not closed captioned. There is a nice little 5 minute 'making of' documentary—not a standard marketing effort but a specific overview narrated by the director, Robert Kurtzman—that shows the initial production designs, the creation of the heroine's body armor, the creation of other props and effects, storyboards for several sequences, including one that had to be dropped, and a trailer.

Demon Knight (see Tales from the Crypt Presents Demon Knight)

Demons (Anchor Bay, DV10728)
Demons 2 (Anchor Bay, DV10729)

Lamberto Bava's two non-stop zombie movies are derivative of George Romero's films, but still fun. **Demons** is set in a movie theater, where the patrons are trapped and gradually turned into monsters as they run around the building, trying to get out. **Demons 2** is set in an apartment building and has pretty much the same premise (there is a common theme in both films, associating the horrors with watching movies—in **2** on a TV), though there is also a **Gremlins**-type ogre causing trouble and obvious allusions to **Videodrome**. Both films are so overloaded with gore effects that you could cut out half of them and still get an NC-17 rating. The DVDs, however, are not rated at all and are Bava's approved versions of the films. **Demons**, from 1985, runs 88 minutes. **Demons 2**, from 1986, runs 91 minutes.

Both movies are letterboxed with an aspect ratio of about 1.66:1 and no 16:9 enhancement, and it is surprising how much the slight addition of picture information to the sides improves the play of the films over cropped versions. Both picture transfers look terrific. In both cases, colors are vivid, blacks are purer, fleshtones are rich and contrasts are well defined. The images are smooth, and while they are not as sharp looking as a Hollywood movie would be, the presentations are still highly satisfying and a significant improvement over earlier home video efforts.

The films have been issued in stereo, as well, and have Dolby Digital tracks. Directional effects are limited, but the enhanced dimensionality of the screams and the musical scores is energizing. There doesn't seem to be too much of a difference between the standard tracks and the Dolby Digital tracks. The films were shot in English, although some performers are dubbed, and the programs are not captioned.

Both movies are accompanied by somewhat unsophisticated trailers and cast & crew profile sections, and both have commentary channels featuring Bava, speaking partially in English and partially in Italian, make-up and special effects creator, Sergio Stivaletti, and Loris Curci, who translates the Italian and prompts Bava with questions. Alas, they don't talk too much about the special effects on either track. Here and there they'll mention how something was done, but not with any consistency. Bava talks about the films that influenced him, about his collaborators, and a bit about how the movies were shot, but he's also a little coy ("Who locked them into the theater?" "I don't remember") and some time is spent talking about the obvious ("There's a lot of blood spurting out from everywhere"). Nevertheless, it is the transfers that make the programs worth obtaining, and the commentary tracks are simply welcome extras. **Demons** is also accompanied by a nice 2 minute film clip about the movie's model effects.

The Dentist (Trimark, VM6886D)
The Dentist 2: Brace Up (Trimark, VM7010D)
Some so-called horror films take a premise and just grind away at it, trusting that a sufficient number of people in the world are demented enough to get off on the blood. Such is the case with **The Dentist**, which delivers precisely what it promises, though without much finesse. Corbin Bernsen is the title character, who goes crazy in the simple, unrelenting narrative and starts torturing his family, friends and patients. There are lots of gory in-the-mouth close-ups, showing teeth being destroyed, needles being jammed into the gums and other graphic indignities, but…What's that? You're dropping the book right now and running to the phone to order your copy? Oh well, we tried.

The 1996 film is letterboxed with an aspect ratio of about 1.85:1 and an accommodation for enhanced 16:9 playback. The color transfer looks fine and the image is sharp. The stereo surround sound is okay, though the mix is fairly basic. The 93 minute program has optional French and Spanish subtitles, English closed captioning, a cast profile section and a trailer.

Enough people must have responded to it, because there is also a sequel. In that the film is able to expand on characters and situations from the first feature, the sequel is a little stronger, and in the last scene it finally achieves the blend of comical severity and grotesque imagery we had been hoping for, but the premise is the same—Bernsen's character escapes incarceration and moves to a small town, where he takes over the local practice and starts wreaking havoc again—and so are the movie's grossest moments, finale excepted.

Again, the picture is letterboxed, with an aspect ratio of about 1.85:1 and an accommodation for enhanced 16:9 playback. The color transfer looks fine, with sharp, accurate fleshtones and bright hues. The stereo surround sound is actually a little stronger than it is in the first feature, with more pronounced separations and a more aggressive mix. The 98 minute program can be supported by optional English, French or Spanish subtitles and is accompanied by a trailer.

Desert Trail (see Young Duke Series: The Fugitive)

Desert Visions (Simitar, 7325)
The 50 minute natural image program visits several National Parks in the American Southwest, depicting different aspects of desert topography in various segments, to music composed by David Lanz and Paul Speer. There is also a cave sequence. The picture looks a little too red at times, and there seems to be some mild artifacting, particularly in the cactus sequence. The image is sharp most of the time, but there is a little ghosting here and there that appears to come from the source material. The stereo sound is passable.

Desperado (see El Mariachi Desperado)

Desperate Measures (Columbia TriStar, 21759)
The very ridiculous story is about a cop who arranges to have a vicious killer donate bone marrow, only to have the killer escape and run loose in the supposedly secure hospital building. It gets even more ridiculous, because it is the cop's son the killer was do-

nating the marrow to, and so the cop feels compelled to help the killer, or at least prevent the other police from shooting him dead on sight. Andy Garcia, as the good guy, and Michael Keaton, as the bad guy, star. If you are tolerant of the illogical or are from another planet and unfamiliar with how the police and hospitals function on Earth, then you may enjoy it, for within its make-believe world it is reasonably exciting, with enjoyable performances and lots of tense action. For most viewers, however, the premise and its corollaries will be an insurmountable blockade to the entertainment.

The film is presented in letterboxed format on one sides, with an aspect ratio of about 1.85:1 and an accommodation for enhanced 16:9 playback, and in full screen format on the other side. The picture quality is passable, with the hospital lighting dampening fleshtones in some sequences. The image is usually crisp and bright hues are glossy. The stereo surround sound is adequately mixed, with a constantly involving ambiance and a decent bass. The Dolby Digital track is reasonably similar, but provides slightly better defined separations. The 100 minute program also has French and Spanish tracks in standard stereo, optional English, French or Spanish subtitles, and a trailer.

Desperate Moments (see Cold Eyes of Fear)

The Devil Bat (see The Bela Lugosi Collection)

Devil in a Blue Dress (Columbia TriStar, 51349)
Denzel Washington is an unemployed machinist in post-War L.A. who is hired as a gumshoe in the terrific Forties detective thriller. The 1995 film has the format of a classic detective story—the private eye looking for the missing dame—except that most of the characters are black and the relationship between races is integral to the narrative. The movie lacks the historical or political resonance of *Chinatown*, but it is in the same vein and would make a worthy companion piece in a double bill. It also has some wonderful secondary moral conflicts (the hero has an affair with his friend's girl; one of the good guys is a nearly psychopathic murderer) that enrich the central drama considerably.

The picture is presented on one side in letterboxed format, with an aspect ratio of about 1.85:1 and an accommodation for enhanced 16:9 playback, and in full screen format on the other side. The letterboxing, which has a nicer framing, adds a little to the sides of the image and masks picture information off the bottom in comparison to the full screen release. The picture transfer looks super, with crisp, solid colors and carefully detailed contrasts. The standard stereo surround soundtrack is bland, but the Dolby Digital track is much livelier, with more detail, more complex separations and more energy. The 101 minute feature is also available in Spanish and Portuguese and can be supported by English, Spanish or Portuguese subtitles ("Mijavam na minha cabeça e diziam que era chuva"). There are trailers for this movie and a couple others.

The film's director, Carl Franklin, provides a commentary. He talks a lot about the changes made from Walter Mosley's book, about black culture and society in Los Angeles in the late Forties, about the personnel who worked on the film and a little bit about the production. He supplies some of the backstory and explains a little more of the mystery than what is readily apparent on the screen. He also has some very interesting things to say about the Los Angeles music scene during that era and how it shifted from swing to a virtual rock 'n' roll. On the whole, though, his talk is adequate, but not elaborate. Also included on the DVD is some interesting footage from Don Cheadle's screen test, in which it was discovered that the character fit perfectly the first time he tried him on.

Devil's Advocate (Warner, 15090); revised (Warner, 16172)
There are all sorts of problems with Devil movies—mostly having to do with the all-powerful nature of the protagonist (what can you do besides beat him in the occasional fiddling contest?)—but **Devil's Advocate** manages to avoid the usual pitfalls. The ending is

particularly well handled, and that is probably why everybody got on board with the project to begin with. Keanu Reeves is a hotshot lawyer, brought to New York to join an important law firm. Al Pacino is his new boss, who seems to be well connected. Directed by Taylor Hackford, the movie's focus is on ethics and the genuine tests of good and evil within the human heart. There are special effects and an abundance of softcore eroticism, but this isn't a Sunday School lesson, it's an expensive motion picture, so they have to include some temptations to hold onto a viewer's attention span. The film succeeds in the details and coasts pleasurably along on standard dramatics until it absolutely has to switch over to fantasy to keep moving forward. The picture is presented in letterboxed format only on the single-sided, dual-layer DVD, with an aspect ratio of about 2.35:1 and an accommodation for 16:9 enhanced playback. The image quality is outstanding, with crisp, meticulously detailed colors. The stereo surround sound and Dolby Digital sound are also very good. The 144 minute film is also available in French and can be supported by English, French or Spanish subtitles.

The film is accompanied by deleted scenes and a director's commentary, along with the usual cast & crew profile, trailer, TV spots and brief essays (including a short history of Satan). Hackford has an interesting approach. Although his talk would technically fall into what we call the 'play-by-play' category, he includes in his descriptions of what is happening on the screen what was probably the entire back story he had worked up with the actors, so in listening to his talk you get extensive, new details about the characters and their motivations. He also manages to speak a bit about how the most interesting sequences were staged, and throws in one very cryptic negative comment about his producer, Arnold Kopelson. There are about a half hour of deleted scenes, which are also accompanied by Hackford's commentary. In fact, we could not suppress Hackford's commentary on those sequences, to hear just the dialogue, so either it can't be done or doing it is very complicated. It is a shame, too, for although Hackford's commentary over the scenes is valuable (among other things, he talks extensively about how he works with his editor), the scenes include a couple of significant dialogue sequences where hearing each line and how it was delivered would be enlightening. You get the gist of it, but not the totality. The DVD's time coding is also bizarre, though it doesn't appear to affect playback.

Warner's revised release of the film has just one change. In the party scene early on, the frieze in Pacino's office is altered with CGI to eliminate the human figures, although they still appear on the frieze during the office scenes at the film's end. In addition to the different catalogue number, the revised version says '*Special Edition*' on the jacket spine, while the original version does not. Both say '*Special Edition*' on the front jacket cover.

Devil's Nightmare (Image ID4684SADVD)

The *Redemption* release is a 1971 production directed by Jean Brismee under the title *La Terrifcante Notte Del Demonio*, about a group of tourists trapped in a castle overnight with a succubus. There are brief glimpses of breasts, an appealing lesbian scene and some modest gore. The film has a dream-like quality that some viewers will respond to, the narrative has a well-formulated conclusion and fans of Italian exploitation features are likely to be excited, but general viewers may find the film a bit ponderous, with dated thrills and limited elaborations.

The source material is aged, but we don't doubt that it is the best available. The jacket copy is quite excited about the restoration of the lesbian scene. Without the tiresome 8 minute *Redemption* intro, the film runs 93 minutes and is letterboxed with an aspect ratio of about 1.6:1 and no 16:9 enhancement. The contrasts and hues are markedly light and fleshtones are bland, with minor wear in evidence during some sequences. Although grain is present in darker scenes, the focus is reasonably sharp. The monophonic sound, which is not captioned, is dubbed in English and is

very scratchy in places, with hiss and upper range limitations. There is also an enjoyable trailer.

The Devil's Own (Columbia TriStar, 82469)

The dreamboat casting of two major stars does little to awaken a slow paced and unremarkable 1997 thriller. Brad Pitt stars as an Irish terrorist living incognito in the house of an American cop, played by Harrison Ford, while he puts together an arms deal. The film was directed by Alan J. Pakula, who, frankly, blows the assignment. The stars never come alive and the film never becomes exciting, wandering to its conclusion like a drunk stumbling home one night from his pub. There are brief moments where the movie seems to live up to its promise, where Ford and Pitt really interact and where the pace of the narrative quickens promisingly, but these moments are never sustained and one gets the impression they are more accidental achievements than calculated pleasures. Because the stars are so big, viewers will stare at the film and think they've been entertained, but many more are going to feel restless, wishing the movie would get on with whatever it's supposed to be about.

The picture is presented on one side in letterboxed format with an aspect ratio of about 2.35:1 and an accommodation for enhanced 16:9 playback, and is in cropped format on the other side. The letterboxing is essential to catch all the times Ford and Pitt appear together, but Pakula and cinematographer Gordon Willis stick to formula setups and never really make as much use of the widescreen format as they could have. The picture is dark and colors are deliberately drab, but the transfer appears accurate. The stereo surround sound and Dolby Digital sound are flaccid and never contribute to the entertainment. The 111 minute program also has French and Spanish language audio tracks, optional English, French and Spanish subtitles, and a trailer.

The Devil's Rain (VCI, DVD8204)

The 1975 wax makeup extravaganza is primarily about a group of people, made of paraffin and led by a goat, who melt when their oracle is smashed. The film is pointless, and never achieved the status publicity over the extensive makeup effects for the final meltdown hoped to inspire. It is too disjointed and boring to sustain one's attention until the finale.

Colors are bright and sharp, and fleshtones are rich. The picture is in letterboxed format, with an aspect ratio of about 2.35:1 and no 16:9 enhancement (including the opening credit sequence, which wasn't letterboxed on the LD). The source material has a few stray speckles, but is otherwise in gorgeous condition. The monophonic sound is adequate and there is no captioning. There is a trailer and a very brief still section.

One of the film's few enjoyable aspects is the collection of bad actors it has assembled. There is John Travolta, with a single line of dialogue, whose entrance as one of the paraffin people is typically confused—if he's a zombie, why are his reflexes so quick when he fights? There is William Shatner, who begins to deteriorate, with those mid-sentence pauses, an hour before he is even turned into paraffin. And there is Eddie Albert, who never gets turned to paraffin at all, but who reads his lines with the urgency of someone going over a grocery list (our favorite part is his offhanded declaration, "These're, these're written in blood, these signatures"). Ernest Borgnine plays the goat. We suppose the publicity people never really had a chance, since they were trying to convince potential viewers that it was a big deal to make Borgnine look ugly and potential viewers quickly wrote it off as Hollywood's easiest makeup trick.

The Devonsville Terror (see The Boogey Man/The Devonsville Terror)

Diabolique (Criterion, DIA050)

Simone Signoret, Vera Clouzot and Paul Meurisse star in the 1954 H.G. Clouzot classic about a disappearing corpse, pitting a stern headmaster of a private school against his wife and his mistress in a deadly triangle. The story has been re-made so many times that one can watch the original and still be surprised by which plot turns are employed and which are not. It is the performances, however, which make the film so repeatably enjoyable. Supported by Clouzot's faultless visual intensity, the nervousness of the actresses can be contagious no matter how often one is exposed to them.

The black-and-white picture on the DVD is greatly improved over Criterion's LD. Although the presentation still looks a little worn, the blacks and whites are brighter, the image is sharper, and contrasts are better defined. The monophonic sound is clean, but a bit dull. The 116 minute feature is in French and can be supported by optional English subtitles.

Diana: The People's Princess (Pacific Digital, UPC#4440550001)

"Diana was more than a princess, she was a demi-goddess," intones the narrator of the somewhat hyperbolic 50 minute program. The commemorative documentary spends about a third of its time on everything up to her divorce, a third on her life after her divorce ("Diana, named after the goddess of hunting, became the most hunted woman of modern times"), and a third on the aftermath of her death. There is an enormous resource of film and video clips to draw from, so fans will likely be pleased with the many shots of the princess performing her official duties, promoting charities, and trying to show her kids a good time. Although it varies from clip to clip, the picture quality is fine and when the source material looks fresh, the image does as well. The stereo sound is passable and is not captioned. The DVD also features textual biographical profiles of the Royal Family.

Diddley, Bo (see 30th Anniversary of Rock 'N' Roll All-Star Jam with Bo Diddley)

Die Hard Trilogy (Fox, 4110414)
Die Hard (Fox, 4110399)
Die Hard 2 (Fox, 4110412)
Die Hard with a Vengeance (Fox, 4110417)

The three **Die Hard** movies have been released individually and as a box set with a slightly lower price. If you want one, you want 'em all, right? All three have Dolby Digital soundtracks that offer more separation effects and more thrust than the standard stereo surround soundtracks. All three films are letterboxed with an aspect ratio of about 2.35:1 and no 16:9 enhancement. All three are accompanied by trailers for all three movies, a small collection of publicity stills for the featured film, a cast profile section and a 'making of' featurette. The trailer for **Die Hard** includes a witty dialogue exchange between Bruce Willis and Alan Rickman that did not make the film's final cut. All three are also available in French in standard stereo and can be supported by English or Spanish subtitles ("Dijo Simón el simplón al hombre con los bizcochuelos, 'Dame tus bizcochuelos o te romperé la cabeza'"). Bruce Willis stars in the series, taking out bad guys in a tall office building in the first movie, at an airport in the second, and trying to stop a robbery of the Federal Reserve Bank in Manhattan in the third.

Colors on the first **Die Hard** may have a slight pinkish tint in places, but the image is crisp and very sharply detailed, bringing out subtle shifts in hue. Although the 1988 feature was the first in the series, the sound mix is still quite engaging, with lots of directional noises and bass-heavy gunfire. The featurette accompanying the 132 minute film is terrific, showing many behind-the-scenes activities and interviews with a lot of personnel (Rickman says he's not playing a villain, just a person who's made 'certain choices').

The picture on **Die Hard 2** is sharp, the darker sequences are free of grain, and colors are strong. The 1990 feature runs 124 minutes. There aren't as many behind-the-scenes shots in the featurette as there were in the first, though there is one interesting clip

of Willis getting mad at a makeup person, and there are plenty of on-set interviews.

The picture on **Die Hard with a Vengeance** may be the sharpest of them all. Colors are accurate, and the image is so crisp the quality of the picture adds to the film's excitement. The Dolby Digital track sounds great, but it doesn't quite provide the earth-shattering shake it is capable of, and separation details are average. The featurette is a little brief, but gives the viewer a taste of what the production was like. The 1995 feature runs 131 minutes.

Die Winterreise (Image, ID5654CLDVD)

A 68 minute Nineteenth Century music video directed by Peter Weigl, the program cuts between shots of Brigitte Fassbaender singing the Franz Schubert song cycle (to the unseen klavier, performed by Wolfram Rieger), and the adventures and fantasies of passengers aboard a coach, including a sick young girl who eventually dies. Fassbaender is dressed in a habit and appears vaguely spiritual. Included among the Czech actors performing the narrative is Lucie Gibodová, who has the most incredibly delicate brown eyes and is, next to Fassbaender, the soul of the program. Since there is no dialogue, the performers tend to overplay their expressions and poses, but the film is an ideal conceptualization of Schubert's work and an enlightening accomplishment.

The presentation contributes greatly to the program's appeal. Although there are a couple scattered speckles, the color transfer is crisp and the image is finely detailed. The presentation is letterboxed, with an aspect ratio of about 1.66:1 and no 16:9 enhancement. The stereo sound is strong and clear, and the program can be supported by optional yellow English subtitles.

Dinosaurs and Other Amazing Creatures (Simitar, 7244)

The program, from the British Museum of Natural History, combines regular 2-D segments with brief right-left camera movement 3-D segments. It comes with a single pair of glasses, but you can order more if you happen to have some British £'s sitting around. The DVD actually combines two programs, both of which are quite good, though only the second has really worthwhile 3-D segments.

The first part is a 56 minute tour of the museum's dinosaur exhibits. The narration, posed as a fantasy figure explaining things to a young boy, presents worthwhile information about the various dinosaurs and how they lived, while the graphics combine traditional paintings, computer graphic animation, genuine fossils, and models cast from fossils. It is mostly the computer graphic material that is rendered in 3-D, but the segments pose no challenge to the *Jurassic Park* animators and the 3-D doesn't offer much enhancement. Nevertheless, as a straight documentary program, the show is both entertaining and informative if you are at all fascinated by those extinct thunder lizards.

The second program, about reptiles and bugs, runs 37 minutes. Two naturalists sit at a counter facing the camera and introduce various creatures—snakes, cockroaches, spiders, etc.—to the viewer, about a half dozen at a time. Each introduction segment is then followed by 3-D views of the animals in a controlled but more natural-looking environment. There is nothing in the 3-D segments that is going to make you cringe or duck, but the 3-D effects offer an enhanced sense of structure and texture, and they help keep things interesting. The naturalists are laid back and talk as if they are sitting in a room, chatting with you. Although we would have liked a little more information about each creature's feeding habits—which, in each case, would explain why the animal is shaped the way it is—the show is reasonably informative and entertaining. The stereo sound on the shows is fine and the picture quality is very good, with bright, crisp and fresh-looking hues. Kids may have difficulty negotiating Simitar's menu pattern to reach the second program, which is not readily accessible.

Dirty Dancing (Artisan, 60444)

Patrick Swayze and Jennifer Grey star in the coming-of-age story of a teenage girl vacationing in the Catskills. It is about the sin of mixing with another social class and how every once in a while a special relationship can develop from a rendezvous. The cast has a great time, because the roles they play are archetypical but believable. They can fulfill romantic and filial fantasies (and Jerry Orbach's embodiment of the girl's father is just as appealing as Swayze's embodiment of her lover) without stepping out of character.

The picture on the entertaining 1987 romantic musical is a little soft, but not to the point where it could become a flaw. Fleshtones look accurate and other colors are effectively detailed. The picture is presented in letterboxed format on one side, with an aspect ratio of about 1.85:1 and no 16:9 enhancement, and is in full screen format on the other side. We prefer the framing on the letterboxed version, but either is workable. The film's soundtrack underwent a stereo remaster for an anniversary theatrical reissue. The standard stereo track is bland, but the Dolby Digital track is okay. The separation mix is not elaborate, but it is sufficient to bring the viewer nearer to the characters. The film is also available in French in standard stereo and in Spanish in mono with English, French or Spanish subtitles ("'¿Cómo llamus a tu amante?' 'Ven aqui, amante'"). There is a decent cast and crew profile section and some interesting production notes about how the original shoot was plagued with accidents. Trailers for the original release and the reissue have also been included.

The Dirty Dozen (MGM, 906563)

Directed by Robert Aldrich, the 150 minute WWII adventure film has a large cast ranging from such forgotten icons as Trini Lopez and Clint Walker to the more lasting presences of Lee Marvin, Ernest Borgnine, Charles Bronson, Jim Brown, John Cassavetes, George Kennedy, Telly Savalas, and Donald Sutherland. Marvin, in the central role as the officer assigned to take twelve men condemned to death and turn them into a crack commando squad, is flamboyant and effective. Borgnine, Cassavetes, Kennedy, and Savalas overplay their parts while Bronson and Brown underplay theirs. Sutherland, in a small role, adds some flair without chewing up the screen.

The letterboxing has an aspect ratio of about 1.85:1 and no 16:9 enhancement, but there is more picture information on the sides and on the bottom in comparison to previous letterboxed home video releases. The color transfer is also spruced up. Hues are deeper and the image is significantly sharper. The only thing we have a problem with is the fleshtones, which look a little pinkish. The sound is also better, with cleaner, stronger tones. The film has a very modest stereo mix, but most of the audio stays in the front and center. The 1967 feature is presented in dual-layer format and can be accompanied by English, French or Spanish subtitles ("¡Estás haciendo un hoyo sin fondo de vicios de este lugar!"). There is a standard theatrical trailer and an entertaining 9 minute 'making of' featurette, showing the cast having a good time in 'swinging' London.

The witty film also has strong elements of satirical comedy. It is deliberately cast with non-comical actors to make the irony of its premise—convicted murderers are assigned to kill the enemy during wartime—more palatable. The script is indistinguishable in structure from the likes of **Private Benjamin** or *Stripes*, spending more time on training and the "war game" sequence than on the heroic finale. The camera angles, unveiled by the letterboxing, are also comical, and are superbly composed. If the camera is not aiming through a floor or a ceiling, it is jammed sideways into the faces of two cast members, so that the angles of their jaws are as humorous to the viewer as they are threatening to one another. The comedy is so tenuous that any compromise in the presentation turns the movie into just another reliable, rainy afternoon war picture.

As a comedy, however, the film tackles many subjects, from authority and rebellion to ethnicity (in most war films, the members of the squad have different social backgrounds, here they have different methods of homicide) and human relationships. By keeping things deadpan, Aldrich, can get in a great number of satirical jibes without offending the oblivious.

Dirty Harry (Warner, 1019)

The colors are not perfect, but the presentation is reasonably nice. The sky is blue, but concrete is not an exact grey and fleshtones are overly pinkish. The film is presented on one side in letterboxed format, with an aspect ratio of about 2.35:1 and an accommodation for enhanced 16:9 playback, and in an awkwardly cropped format on the other side. The bass seems muted on the stereo surround soundtrack but the Dolby Digital track is brighter and cleaner. The 103 minute film is also available in French and Spanish, without Dolby Digital, and comes with English, French or Spanish subtitling ("Je sais ce que tu penses. 'Il a tiré 6 coups ou 5?' A dire vrai, j'étais s'excité, je ne sais plus très bien"), a good original theatrical trailer, a decent cast and crew profile and some production notes.

Clint Eastwood stars in Don Siegel's breakthrough 1971 San Francisco detective thriller, about a cat and mouse game with a serial killer. We must also add that we are starting to enjoy Andy Robinson's performance, as the slimy villain, more and more with each viewing, particularly the eerie pitch to his screams.

Dirty Rotten Scoundrels (Image, ID40850RDVD)

The pairing of Steve Martin and Michael Caine as two con artists attempting to one up each other on the French Riviera is an inspired mixture of urbanity and cynical humor. Frank Oz directed the 1988 feature.

The picture is letterboxed with an aspect ratio of about 1.85:1 and no 16:9 enhancement. The image is bright, with crisp solid hues. The stereo surround sound brings dimensionality to the musical score but keeps most everything else up front and center. The 110 minute film is captioned.

Disclosure (Warner, 13575)

Sex sells, and so it is sex that runs down the spine of **Disclosure**, but the film is actually about office politics, and while the sex is integral to the plot, it also turns out to be much less important than it initially seems. The real enjoyment of the film is its fictionalization of the backbiting and promotion scrambling almost everybody who works in a multiple-employee environment encounters. The film is unusual in one respect—it is an exciting yet bloodless thriller. The only things that get killed are computer files, and fortunately, the hero has a backup. Michael Douglas stars with Demi Moore in the Barry Levinson film, based upon a Michael Crichton novel and set in Seattle.

The letterboxed version of the 129 minute film, which has an aspect ratio of about 2.35:1 and an accommodation for enhanced 16:9 playback, appears on one side of the DVD, and the cropped version appears on the other side. The widescreen images are pretty and tastefully composed, but the cropped image rarely loses anything of importance and brings you closer to the characters, with many wonderful face-filling-the-screen close-ups. Just as the intimate view of the characters can increase your emotional ties to them, so does the slightly off kilter framing leave you a bit more tense and unsure of what is going to happen next. The colors are deep, fleshtones are rich and the picture is sharp, revealing a great deal of texture and other detail. The stereo surround soundtrack is bland, but the Dolby Digital track is good. The mix is not elaborate, but the sounds are sharp and full. The film is also available in French, without Dolby Digital, and comes with English, French and Spanish subtitles. There is a too small cast profile and a brief production essay.

Disturbing Behavior (MGM, 907432)

James Marsden, Katie Holmes and Nick Stahl star in the tale of high school students who suddenly become unusually square, forsaking their former friends. The narrative is completely illogical and there aren't many thrills, but the performances are enjoyable and it is easy to get hooked into it.

Surprise! The narrative actually is logical and there is some emotional depth to the drama, making its excitements more compelling, but the scenes that make it thus were all sliced out—lobotomized like the teenagers in the movie—before the film's release, including a stronger and tighter ending. The director, David Nutter, speaks no more than cryptically about why these cuts were made on a commentary track, but he is clearly on the viewer's side, wishing that the scenes had been left in (including his favorite scene, where the hero and the heroine make love for the first time—what marketing genius thought the movie didn't need that sequence?). Fortunately, a number of these scenes have been included on the DVD. They don't solve all the movie's problems, but they contribute much more than they could possibly take away and it is ridiculous that somebody made Nutter take them out. Nutter also speaks generally about shooting the film, working with the actors and the Vancouver locations. He also explains story points that may be evident to him from working on the script but are not immediately evident to the viewer, with or without the deleted scenes.

The picture is presented in letterboxed format on one side, with an aspect ratio of about 1.85:1 and an accommodation for enhanced 16:9 playback, and is in full screen format on the other side. The letterboxing adds a tiny bit of picture information to the sides and masks picture information off the top and bottom. Either version seems workable. The color transfer is okay, though fleshtones are a little indistinct at times. The stereo surround sound has some engaging separation effects and is adequate for the production, and the Dolby Digital track doesn't really add much more to the mix. The 84 minute film is also available in French in Dolby Digital and can be supported by English or French subtitles. There are no subtitles for the deleted scenes. A music video from The Flys and a trailer are also included.

Diva (Fox Lorber, FLV5000)

For those of you who have never been there before, one of the primary methods of transportation in New York City is the subway, an underground rail train that runs from one station to another, uptown and downtown. The tunnels the trains run through are old and enclosed and when one is standing on a station platform and a train passes, it is extremely noisy. In most stations, people waiting for the trains pay no attention to the noise at all, but there is one station where you can always see several people covering their ears when the trains go by—the 66th Street subway station that serves Lincoln Center, where the ballet, opera and symphony halls are located. The station isn't any noisier than the other stations, but the stop attracts more people with sensitive ears. Where is this leading? Well, the monophonic sound on Diva is muted and its musical passages are often distorted before they get anywhere near the high notes. Even dialogue passages lose their upper end at times. In the context of the film being a lower budget European production, this isn't all that surprising. The old LD had a brighter and fresher sound, which we prefer, but it was also noisier and had its share of upper range dropouts. If the movie were The Toxic Avenger or I Spit on Your Grave or something, those obtaining the DVD probably wouldn't get too upset over it, but Diva attracts more consumers with sensitive ears, and, by and large, they find the DVD presentation to be unacceptable.

Although there is no time encoding, the running time appears to be slightly compressed, coming closer to 117 minutes than the jacket cover's stated 123. The picture is letterboxed with an aspect ratio of about 1.66:1 without accommodation for 16:9 enhanced playback. The colors look quite nice, with workable fleshtones and bright, solid hues. The 1981 film is French with optional English

subtitles. Contrary to a notation on the jacket cover, there are no 'Production Notes,' just a credit list.

The director of Diva, Jean-Jacques Beineix, never made another movie that was even half as good as the 1981 film. The plot, about two audio tapes that different villains want to retrieve from a young mailman for different reasons, is just complex enough to keep the story exciting and vital. The film's images and its sounds are beautifully styled, yet they are paced with a hip rhythm that keeps a viewer alert and open to any sort of artistic indulgence. One of the tapes is a recording of an opera singer's recital, and the singer's emotional dilemmas, though not central to the story, are blended perfectly with the rest of the narrative, as are a number of other disparate components. In the end, one of the heroes disposes of the bad guy not with a shoot out, but by moving a dim light about two feet out of position in the total darkness, making Diva the only Zen action movie ever produced west of Asia that got the concept right. Now, if only somebody could get it right on DVD...

Divas Live (see VH1: Divas Live)

Divine Madness (Warner, 20001)

The widescreen image compositions on the Bette Midler concert film, directed by Michael Ritchie, are outstanding. The balance and design of each shot are surprisingly compelling, and it adds a great deal of class to the show, even though class is something Midler appears to be deliberately forsaking. Midler takes long rests between her numbers, filling the time with bawdy stories and pregnant pauses. In some ways the program does function as its stated desire, to be the ultimate Midler extravaganza, but the constant wheeling in and out of every outfit and prop she's ever used becomes too archival. It's fun, but it seems at times that, except for the camera compositions, too much energy is being misapplied.

The 1980 program is in letterboxed format only, with an aspect ratio of about 2.35:1 and no 16:9 enhancement. The picture is often grainy, but the presentation keeps control of the grain. The color transfer is very good, with bright, well-defined hues, and while there are halos and background blurs, the image still seems very crisp, as if the distortion was part of the design. The stereo surround sound is less impressive, and never achieves a penetrating resonance. As is detailed on the jacket cover, the 95 minute program leaves out two numbers that appeared in the theatrical release. The program is closed captioned with some paraphrasing.

Doc Hollywood (Warner, 12222)

Michael J. Fox stars in a typical Fox role, a young surgeon waylaid in a small town while driving to California who eventually becomes hooked on the friendships he forms there. The image compositions, particularly during the middle act, deliberately evoke the paintings of Norman Rockwell. The colors are flat, but solid, and shadows are diminished, creating a sequential tableaux of would-be Saturday Evening Post covers. The picture is presented in full screen format. The stereo sound is adequate, with some decent surround effects, and the 104 minute film is closed captioned with a lot of paraphrasing.

Document of the Dead: The Special Edition (Synapse, SFD0001)

Directed by splatter filmmaker Roy Frumkes, the documentary, about George Romero shooting Dawn of the Dead, doesn't just go behind the scenes, it also analyzes how a low budget movie is made, with segments on pre and post production, marketing, and how the filmmakers took over a shopping mall every night for a couple months without disturbing the shoppers. There are also segments on several of Romero's other movies, an elaborate segment on the shooting of Two Evil Eyes, Romero's commercials and extensive, insightful interviews with Romero and with Tom Savini. Additionally, the DVD contains another terrific 28 minutes of footage, from both the Dead and Eyes shoots, that didn't make it into the 84 minute film. It is highly informative, including footage on the financing of the films and the plight of independent filmmakers. There is also an excellent commentary track by Frumkes on how the documentary was put together, on filmmaking in general and on other captivating topics, and a Frumkes filmography. The picture is grungy looking but tolerable, and the monophonic sound is fine. The program is not captioned.

Dodsworth (HBO, 90659)

William Wyler's 1936 adaptation of a Sinclair Lewis novel features one of the finest motion picture screen performances ever recorded. It is a very grown-up movie, about a retired industrialist, played by Walter Huston, who discovers during an extended trip to Europe that his wife no longer loves him. Huston's character is obviously a talented and successful man, yet clearly naive about the ways of the world outside of where he has lived and worked. As the film progresses, you see him confronted by situations new to him, and you see him analyze and master those situations—sometimes by making mistakes at first, sometimes by applying his knowledge instinctively—as he would tackle a business problem or as he has clearly dealt with any conflict in his life up to that point. Huston's voice, his body language, his attitude and his command of the screen convey every impulse passing through his character's head. It is this understanding that makes his patience for his wife's indiscretions so moving, and since the relationships depicted are so complex, they remain fresh to contemporary viewers.

The source material has some scattered speckling, particularly around the reel-change points, but the black-and-white image is otherwise very smooth, with finely detailed contrasts and deep blacks. The monophonic sound is a little wobbly in places, but there is a remastered stereo track that brings a bit more stability to the dialogue without imposing a frivolous dimensionality. The 101 minute film has French, Italian and German audio tracks in mono, optional English, French and Spanish subtitles, a cast & crew profile section.

Dog Day Afternoon (Warner, 1024)

Al Pacino and John Cazale star in the popular hostage drama. The 1975 feature is in full screen format on one side, and is in letterboxed format on the other, with an aspect ratio of about 1.85:1 and an accommodation for enhanced 16:9 playback. The letterboxing adds a bit of picture information to the sides and masks off picture from the top and bottom in comparison to the full screen image, but the framing is much more satisfying and adds to the film's tension. The picture is sharp, but hues are somewhat faded and bland. The monophonic sound is bland, but the Dolby Digital mono track is stronger. The film is fairly dialog-heavy, with very few sound effects or music cues, and the delivery is passable. The 124 minute film can be accompanied by English, French or Spanish subtitles. There is a small cast-and-crew profile section but, contrary to the jacket notation, there are no production notes.

Dolores Claiborne (Warner, C2548)

Free of the campy histrionics that made *Misery* such a big hit, **Dolores Claiborne**, based upon another Stephen King novel, is a sensible, character-driven murder drama. While the film may lack components that would make it attractive to the box office, it is a well-told tale enhanced by the thorough performances of the leading cast members and the vivid New England coast atmosphere. Kathy Bates, Jennifer Jason Leigh and Christopher Plummer star in the 1995 feature directed by Taylor Hackford, about a woman reconciling with her daughter as flashbacks reveal their troubled past.

The color transfer is excellent, with bright, smooth hues and precise details, and its intense accuracy pulls one deeper into the drama. The picture is letterboxed, with an aspect ratio of about 2.35:1 and an accommodation for enhanced 16:9 playback. The stereo surround sound is identical to the LD. The film's audio mix is competent but not elaborate, and the DVD delivers it efficiently. The film is also available in French and can be supported by En-

glish or French subtitles ("Etre une garce, c'est parfois la seule issue, pour une femme"). There is a cast & crew profile section and a brief step-by-step explanation of how the solar eclipse sequence was put together.

Hackford also provides a fairly good commentary track. He goes into elaborate detail discussing the contributions of his crew, and while he tends to dole out the superlatives too liberally, thereby decreasing their value, the viewer is made very aware by the evidence upon the screen just how talented the wigmakers and hand makeup people and cinematographer and set decorator, and so on, are. He explains the story from his perspective, but it is an effective tour of the drama, enhancing one's understanding of the characters instead of simply—as other directors sometimes do—anticipating the action. He also provides plenty of anecdotes about the shoot and why, for financial or artistic reasons, he shot certain scenes in certain ways. He alludes to some alternate footage in his talk, but the footage has not been included on the DVD.

Domination Nation X-rated (Vivid, UPC#0073214547)

A moderately creative sci-fi narrative, the story is set in a future where men die if they engage in too much erotic activity. The world is controlled by women, until a female scientist figures out a cure. The erotic sequences are energetic and there are even some crude special effects. Colors are somewhat pale, fleshtones are bland and the image is often grainy. The sound is flat, distorting the upper end. The 71 minute program features Christy Canyon, Sindee Coxx, Cherokee, Krista Maze, and Julie Rage. The DVD contains alternate angle sequences and elaborate hardcore interactive promotional features.

Domingo, Plácido (see **Merry Christmas from Vienna: Plácido Domingo / Ying Huang / Michael Bolton**)

Don Giovanni (see **Mozart's Don Giovanni: Teatro Alla Scala**)

Don Juan De Marco (New Line, N4636)

Rapidly growing in popularity as a cult title, the wonderful 1995 romantic comedy is about a young man who thinks he is Don Juan and the psychiatrist who becomes apprehensive about curing him. Johnny Depp and Marlon Brando star, and if the film's marvelous humor and palpable romantic spirit were not enough, the film will stand forever as proof that Brando did not entirely waste his later years as an actor on tomfoolery. For those who are in awe of his talent, it is spellbinding to see him relax in a part that is relatively free of eccentricities, and he doesn't coast with it, he really does act and draw the most that he can out of the comedy. The film's one problem is that the plot, by necessity, must come to a conclusion, clearing up the mystery of the patient's background and resolving conflicts, but that is a small price to pay for the delight most of the film has to offer.

The standard stereo surround soundtrack is okay and there is a reasonably bright and detailed Dolby Digital track. The picture is presented on one side in letterboxed format, with an aspect ratio of about 1.85:1 and no 16:9 enhancement, and in full screen format on the other side. The letterboxing adds nothing to the sides of the image and masks off picture information from the top and bottom in comparison to the full screen image. In general, the letterbox framing is pleasing, but there are instances where the open image is more satisfying. The colors are sharp, but fleshtones are somewhat pinkish, though they remain within an acceptable range. The 97 minute film can also be accessed in French in standard stereo and can be played back with just the musical score—which is often running over dialogue when Juan is giving his spiel—in regular stereo. There are optional English, French or Spanish subtitles, a profile and filmography for Depp, Brando and Faye Dunaway, including accessible clips from a couple of the other New Line movies Depp and Brando have appeared in, 'domestic' and 'international' theatrical trailers, with the 'domestic' selling the movie much better, and a Bryan Adams music video in which everybody wears Don Juan masks.

Don't Be a Menace to South Central while Drinking Your Juice in the Hood (Buena Vista, 15863)

A direct take-off on the films of John Singleton and the Hughes Brothers, the movie also gets its bite by taking a satirical jab at real life in South Central L.A., with gags about drive-by shootings, cheap liquor and other aspects of low income living. Shawn and Marlon Wayans star.

The picture is letterboxed with an aspect ratio of about 1.85:1 and no 16:9 enhancement. The color transfer looks solid, with bright hues and accurate fleshtones. The stereo surround sound is okay, with a number of directional effects and plenty of power, and the 89 minute program can be supported by English subtitles.

Don't Do It! (Image, ID5591FMDVD)

A bad movie about relationships among young people, set in a single evening, the film follows the conversations of three separate couples who, we gradually come to understand, have been paired in other combinations in the past. They then happen to all meet at a restaurant. There is also a subplot about two guys driving around somewhat aimlessly. The conversations have nothing new to offer and the film has 'sophomore movie script' written all over it. Of the couples, only Sheryl Lee and Esai Morales keep the viewer interested. Heather Graham, James Marshall, James LeGros and Alexis Arquette are also featured.

The picture is reasonably sharp and colors are adequate, with workable fleshtones. The stereo sound is functional and the 88 minute program is not closed captioned.

Don't Touch the White Woman! (Image, ID4777SIDVD)

Shot in Paris, mostly in an excavated construction site, the performers in Marco Ferreri's 1973 film are dressed as cowboys and Indians, and enact a garbled version of Custer's last stand. Meanwhile, the rest of Paris goes on as normal. There is a top-heavy cast, including Marcello Mastroianni as Custer (with black hair), Catherine Deneuve, Michel Piccoli, Philippe Noiret, Ugo Tognazzi and others, but their play-acting never achieves the level of satire that could sell their tomfoolery. The messages about Caucasian expansion and economic oppression in America have been heard many times before and hold no fresh insight. While some people may very well find the movie eccentric enough to seem brilliant (for the final battle, the locale switches to a larger quarry and includes some excessive gore effects), most will find it so ghastly stupid that they'll be lucky to get beyond the first fifteen minutes.

The picture is slightly cropped, obscuring business on the sides of the screen at times. The colors are a little faded and contrasts are somewhat limited, but for a low budget foreign production, the picture looks fresh enough. The monophonic sound is muted and the 110 minute feature is in French, with yellow English subtitles that sometimes obscure significant aspects of the images.

Donnie Brasco (Columbia TriStar, 82515/9)

Al Pacino portrays a low level hood who befriends an undercover FBI agent, played by Johnny Depp. The situation creates a naturally strong narrative, but the film's real appeal is the tour it gives of gangsterland—the codes, the lingo, the schemes—letting the viewer soak up the environment without the fear of getting rubbed out. Pacino is terrific. Depp seems like a double for Ray Liotta, but that really isn't his fault. There are a couple of loose ends at the conclusion, including $300,000 that seems to disappear into thin air, but the film is so good you really don't want it to end at all. You just want to keep on watching as these guys go to work every day and do their twisted things.

The film is presented in letterboxed format on one side, with an aspect ratio of about 2.35:1 and an accommodation for enhanced 16:9 playback, and in full screen format on the other side. The letterboxing adds some picture information to the sides and masks some off the top and bottom in comparison to the full screen format. There are shots where the top looks too tight, but there are other shots where the sides are cramped, so either version has mild disadvantages. The color transfer is very good and the image is crisp. The stereo surround sound is also fairly nice, with music and atmospheric effects filling the rear channel, and the Dolby Digital track is even stronger. The 127 minute 1997 feature also has a French language track in standard stereo, optional English, French or Spanish subtitles, and a trailer.

Doomed to Die (see **Mr. Wong Collection**)

The Doors (Artisan, 60451)

All film musical biographies reflect the tastes not of their subjects but of the society in which the films themselves were produced. At its best, **The Doors** celebrates the rock group's music with an inner precision, shifting not only images to the beat, but subjects to the music's melodic changes. To that effect, the movie fits right in with the music bio genre. After all, it is well known that in Hollywood musical biographies, so long as the filmmakers get the music right, they can lie all they want about the musician. However, Morrison, as depicted by Val Kilmer, is so zonked from beginning to end that it is a wonder he ever produced any song lyrics at all, let alone vocalized them. The film probably gives a very accurate description of Morrison taking his pants off during a Miami concert, but the real mystery in the movie is how he ever got them on in the first place. It is myth-making in reverse, searching not for the heroic soul of the unfortunate artist, but robbing his soul and replacing it with an empty shell.

The colors are strong and the image is crisp. There are many scenes in the film that are set in difficult lighting situations and there is a soft haze to some of the colors in some of these sequences, but overall the presentation is admirable. The 141 minute film is presented on one side in letterboxed format only, in an aspect ratio of about 2.35:1 and no 16:9 enhancement. The stereo surround is okay and there is a Dolby Digital track with a much stronger bass and clearer separations. The film can be accompanied by English, French or Spanish subtitles ("No queda nada que hacer excepto escapar, escapar, escapar…") and comes with a cast and crew profile, production notes that include access-ready references to the film, a teaser trailer and a standard trailer.

The Doors Collection (Universal, 20542)

It could be argued, as the members of the band do in the tantalizing DVD collection, that The Doors was the greatest American rock band of the late Sixties. There are several other bands that could make the same claim, but The Doors, with their often sophisticated lyrics and un-imitated, glass-on-the-guitar-strings sound, combined with Jim Morrison's sublime, soul-spilling vocals, were unarguably one of the greatest, and their reputation has continued to grow, surviving even the pelting Oliver Stone gave them in his awful biographical film.

The multiple anthology package presents about four hours of Doors music and trivia on a single-sided dual-layer platter. The main program is a combination of three previously separate home video releases, *The Doors: Dance on Fire* (a collection of primitive—but prescient—music videos), *The Doors: Live at the Hollywood Bowl* (a live performance) and *The Doors: Soft Parade* (a documentary about the group, with music clips). Musical overlap between the three programs is minimal.

The older footage is somewhat worn and soft looking, while footage shot specifically for the collection is very bright and sharp. Generally, the presentation is highly satisfying. The stereo sound has not undergone any sort of electronic sweetening, leaving dimensionality and separation effects to a minimum. The collection has optional English subtitles, for those of you who ever wondered about a particular lyric (Ah-ha! It's 'A thousand girls, a thousand thrills!') or feel like singing along. The programs are also supported by an informative commentary track, featuring the three band members who are still kicking around, Ray Manzarek, John Densmore and Robby Krieger, and sound engineer Bruce Botnik.

Dance on Fire, which was produced right around the time that a biography about Morrison rekindled an interest in the group, is a collection of music videos, some produced by the Doors as promotional films in the Sixties and others produced in the early Eighties when the collection was first released. Ray Manzarek, the Doors keyboardist, went to film school at UCLA and retained an interest in the medium that the band's renewed popularity allowed him to exercise. One of the videos he created—the one that has been replaced on the DVD by the 'director's cut'—*L.A. Woman*, is a highly pleasing and elaborate work that does justice to the epic single it is illustrating. Several others are nearly as good. *Hollywood Bowl* is a straight concert film, giving the viewer a taste of what The Doors were like on stage, where Morrison was unquestionably in his element. *Soft Parade* is a bit of a documentary, combining Sixties interviews with music and concert clips. It was, as Manzarek explains on the commentary track, an alternative to Stone's idiotic depiction of Morrison, showing the writer-singer to be sober (at least on occasion), thoughtful, and in full possession of his faculties even during the twilight of his career.

John Densmore, the Doors drummer, put together a stage monologue about his experiences with the group and excerpts from it are presented. Most of it is hysterical, particularly Densmore's marvelous description of how Morrison first introduced *The End* to the other members of the band. Two of Manzarek's student films from UCLA have been included. They are typical student works, though reasonably sophisticated from a technical standpoint. Both have a somewhat earnest and fatalistic view of male/female relationships, and in the context of the DVD package their inclusion seems fully appropriate. Robby Krueger, the Doors guitarist, is featured in another segment, performing an instrumental variation based upon the classic Doors number, *The End*. There is also a presentation by Kerry Humphreys, a fan among fans, of Doors memorabilia.

Led by Manzarek, who seems to be the disc's guiding creative force, the band members reminisce about their experiences, as depicted in the videos and concert clips, on the commentary track. Some of their statements are very amusing, such as the reasons why they didn't go to Woodstock and how one band member ended up on a nationally televised performance clip with a black eye. Other commentary is more reflective, describing how the group used improvisation to develop some of their classic numbers and how they found their distinct sound. Manzarek also takes the time to identify almost every piece of footage when it appears—which usually sparks the memories of the others—and he explains, quite lucidly, what he was attempting to accomplish thematically in the videos. Botnick, contributing to the commentary on the *Hollywood Bowl* program, provides a fascinating description of the elaborate methods used to coax great live recordings out of madly disorganized concerts. Because the commentary is reactive to the program material it does not present a comprehensive history of the group or a complete profile, but it is assumed that the viewer will obtain that elsewhere and, as a supplement to a basic knowledge about The Doors, it is a terrific and rich gathering of materials about the band, opening, as it were, many portals for exploring and celebrating the group's accomplishments.

The Doors: Live in Europe 1968 (Image, ID4304ERDVD)

The black-and-white footage of the group, and the lead singer, Jim Morrison, performing seductively raw versions of their hit songs before small audiences in places like Amsterdam, is grainy and smeary, yet never to a point of distraction, adding more to the realness of the performances than it takes away through distortion. The sound is monophonic but vivid. The 58 minute program has some interview sequences, but the dozen or so songs are played in full and the show is a fervent glimpse of a fiery talent that couldn't get much higher. The program is not captioned.

The Doors: The Doors Are Open (Pioneer, PA98593D)

The hour-long black-and-white film depicts a 1968 London concert, intercut with political images from the times. We could discern little difference between the standard stereo track and the Dolby Digital track. The audio is muted, but fans are sure to appreciate its rawness and the variations the performances offer to the standard studio recordings of the numbers. There are some separation effects and the sound's limitations do not obscure the instruments, vocals or melodies, they just get flattened out some. There are also some terrific close-ups of Jim Morrison and a few snippets of interviews where he seems looped, but coherent. The image is mildly smeary and grainy, but workable, and details are adequate. Seven numbers, most of them extended with jams, are performed during the course of the hour. There is no captioning.

Dose Hermanos: Shadows of the Invisible Man (Pioneer, PA99608D)

An excellent combination of abstract video art and avant garde music, the images are nothing more than manipulated patterns and colors, but their mutations are linked directly to the rhythm of the music, and so the visuals become more closely tied to the audio than in most programs of this nature. The music, mostly keyboard improvisations, is so effectively reinforced by the visuals that one might even count them as an accompanying instrument, transmitting at the least, a silent beat, and perhaps, in the shifting hues, a tonal emphasis as well.

The picture looks great and the sound is quite good. The standard stereo track has a strong immediacy, and there is a Dolby Digital track with more detailed separation effects that consciously work all four corners of one's listening area. There is also a brief introduction by composer Bob Bralove and text essays about the music and the images.

Do the Right Thing (Universal, 20242)

Spike Lee's riveting entertainment is about a very hot day in a fairly poor neighborhood, and it ends with violence. It is peopled, however, with a dozen vibrant characters, and the camera spends much of the time cruising up and down the street during the course of the day, peeking in on them. The shifts in style are radical but elegant, so that Lee's asides, when characters seem to be speaking more to the camera than to each other, work like musical bridges to facilitate a disguised quickening in the dramatic tempo. Lee also demonstrates an adoration for language, something which few filmmakers have been interested in since the days of radio. His subject material, essentially the life and culture of African-Americans, is a turn-off for many viewers, so much of a turn-off that these viewers will refuse to accept what the film has to teach about the realities of contemporary life. Since the narrative is partially about that refusal, in another context, those who feel uncomfortable watching **Do the Right Thing** are inevitably reacting to their own emotional reflections.

The color transfer, which has heavy orange washes, is sharp, with finely detailed contrasts. The stereo sound is fresh, though it lacks muscle in places. The picture is letterboxed with an aspect ratio of about 1.66:1 and no 16:9 enhancement. The 1989 feature is also available in French and can be accompanied by English or Spanish subtitles ("¿Por qué no hay hermanos ahi?"). There are some production notes, a decent cast profile section and a theatrical trailer.

There is such virtuosity in Lee's direction that the film's dramatic impact on an initial viewing is overwhelming. The movie remains highly admirable on subsequent viewings, but a few minor reservations start to bubble to the surface. Lee stars as well, with Danny Aiello, John Turturro, Rosie Perez, Ossie Davis, Ruby Dee and a number of others. The motivations for Aiello's character, who finally snaps, are not made as clear as they ought to have been. He is supposedly working in front of a hot pizza oven on a very hot day without air conditioning, yet he never seems particularly irritable until he blows up. Additionally, Lee's most gimmicky shots, which seem clever and inspired at first, call too much attention to his authorship, instead of to the drama, on subsequent viewings. **Do the Right Thing** remains a brilliant, thoughtful work, with marvelous touches of humor, but Roger Ebert's claim in the jacket essay, that it is one of "the best-directed, best-made films of our time," overstates its value.

Double Dragon (GoodTimes, 0581032)
The juvenile sci-fi martial arts film is entertaining if you accept its limitations. Based upon a syndicated cartoon series, the film is set in a post-earthquake 'New Angeles,' with the dual heroes trying to stop the bad guy (Robert Patrick) from obtaining both parts of a magical pendant. There are many futuristic cityscape views in the background, many humorous touches that depict life in the next century, inexpensive but astutely applied special effects (the bad guy turns into a shadow creature that slithers across the floor), plenty of engaging action sequences and the heroes are attractive.

The picture is in letterboxed format only, with an aspect ratio of about 1.85:1. The picture transfer looks okay. Some sequences are a bit too dark, especially near the beginning, but the colors are stable and once the action picks up none of the errors are noticeable. The stereo surround sound is reasonably forceful and gets the job done. The 96 minute program has optional English, French and Spanish subtitles.

Double Indemnity (Image, ID4222USDVD)
Billy Wilder's 1944 noir classic stars Barbara Stanwyck, Fred MacMurray and Edward G. Robinson. The movie is a marvelously involving concoction, since the hero, played by MacMurray, seems just normal and dumb enough to become involved in a murder.

The black-and-white image is very crisp and contrasts are nicely detailed, but greys tend to be grainy and the source material has some minor wear that shows up regularly. The monophonic sound is adequate and there is a Dolby Digital mono track of equal quality. The 107 minute is closed captioned.

Double Team (Columbia TriStar, 83239)
We must admit that Tsui Hark's 1997 action feature, starring Jean-Claude Van Damme, Dennis Rodman and Mickey Rourke, is first movie we have ever seen that was inspired, in part, by the television show *The Prisoner*, but except for that lengthy digression, the movie is a straightforward effort where Van Damme's character, with the unexplained help of Rodman, races to stop Rourke from hurting his wife. Most of the plot turns are ludicrous and the constant action scenes are outrageous exaggerations, but if you look at the movie as a Hong Kong action film in European clothing (it was shot in France), then its excesses become more excusable—not to be taken seriously, but to be enjoyed for its flamboyant indulgences. Seen in that perspective, Rodman fits right in.

The picture is letterboxed on one side, with an aspect ratio of about 2.35:1 and an accommodation for enhanced 16:9 playback, and is in cropped format on the other side. The color transfer is excellent, with crisp, sharp hues, and the quality of the image also enhances the entertainment. The stereo surround sound and Dolby Digital sound are good, with plenty of rear channel effects and boisterous moments. The 93 minute program also has French and Spanish audio tracks, optional English, French or Spanish subtitling, and a trailer.

Dr. Giggles (GoodTimes, 0581024)
So gruesome that some fans are bound to love it, the film mixes medical horrors with a constant stream of wisecracks about doctors and doctoring as the villain, a psychotic MD played by Larry Drake, works his way through town one evening, performing unnecessary operations on the local teenagers.

The movie has plenty of gore, but the premise is discomforting without being fun and the fright sequences have a dull inevitability to them. The film is presented in full screen format and the image is reasonably solid. There is some grain from the cinematography

in a few of the darker sequences, but the transfer looks sharp, blacks are pure and other colors are accurate. The stereo surround sound is a little garish but passable and the 95 minute program can be supported by English, French or Spanish subtitles ("Todavía no estoy atendiendo a pacientes. Pero puedo hacer una excepción") and is accompanied by a brief production essay.

Dr. Hugo (see **Eve's Bayou**)

Dr. Jekyll and Mr. Hyde (Image, ID4667DSDVD)
John Barrymore stars as the title character(s) in the 1920 silent production, creating a viable dichotomy between the dashing doctor and his horrible alter-ego. Along with the dependable story and Barrymore's captivating performance, there are some gruesome murders and other basic delights.

The windowboxed source material is heavily marked with scratches and speckles, and is tinted, obscuring some detail, although other home video versions are even more heavily damaged and have thicker tinting. The 79 minute feature is accompanied by a monophonic Carter organ score. There is also an interesting 5 minute excerpt from a 1911 rendition of the Robert Louis Stevenson story, enough to show an effectively staged Jekyll-to-Hyde metamorphosis.

Dr. No (MGM, 906724)
The first movie in the James Bond series is presented in dual-layer format, letterboxed on one layer, with an aspect ratio of about 1.8:1 and an accommodation for enhanced 16:9 playback, and presented in full screen format on the other layer. The letter-boxing adds a bit to the sides and trims a bit off the top and bottom in comparison to full screen versions. Hues on the 1962 feature still seem a bit light at times, but are substantially brighter and deeper than on previous efforts. The image is crisp and should please fans considerably. The monophonic sound is bland, but adequate. The film is also available in French and Spanish and comes with English, French or Spanish subtitles ("Écoutez-moi, vous deux. Ça n'existe pas, les dragons. Ce que vous avez vu ressemblait à un dragon peut-être"). The 110 minute film is accompanied by an original theatrical trailer, a 2 minute James Bond 'Greatest Moments Montage' (as if), an essay on the history of the martini, and background trivia about the film.

The film would be less tolerable if it were not the first episode in what is now the most extensive action and adventure saga motion pictures have produced. Sean Connery's accent still has a heavy Scottish brogue, and his acting is too leery to be suave or worldly. He drinks heavily, smokes like crazy, and practically rapes every woman he meets. Worst of all, he treats the impossibly stereotyped black fisherman and part-time CIA operative, played by John Kitzmiller, as a second-class being. At one point he tells Kitzmiller to "fetch my shoes," as he himself goes traipsing into the woods with Ursula Andress. There are at least three shots in the film where you can see the camera crew, and unnatural light reflections are present in almost every scene. What made **Dr. No** spellbinding when it was first released, however, and what makes it still entertaining a number of decades later, is the pacing. The new wave editing of the late sixties was still generally unknown, but the style of the Bond films presaged its coming into fashion. **Dr. No** is a movie that refuses to slow down, and that is, perhaps, why you don't notice the reflections of the camera crew until you've watched the film a hundred times.

Dr. Seuss' How the Grinch Stole Christmas! & Horton Hears a Who! (MGM, 906722)
We wish we could pull Chuck Jones out from behind a pillar and ask his opinion about the transfer of the cartoon double bill. The solidity and crispness of the colors are excellent. Hues are smooth and bright. But, are the colors right? The Grinch, who is an envious green on the jacket cover, is a yellow with no more than a hint of grey-olive on the DVD. The picture looks so terrific, most

viewers won't mind, but purists may have a qualm or two. *Horton Hears a Who* also has strong, brighter colors, with hues that are less suspect. The monophonic sound is a little muffled, but clean, and the dialogue is fully coherent. The 50 minute program is also available in Spanish and comes with English or Spanish subtitles. The cartoons must be selected separately and through several menu steps, which will make it difficult for little ones to access by themselves. The DVD also contains a half dozen or so preliminary sketches, profiles of Jones, Seuss and a couple others, and a simple but entertaining *Grinch* game (it gives you multiple choice answers to questions about *Grinch* and if you get one wrong, you have to start over).

Dr. Strangelove (Columbia TriStar, 01729)
Dr. Strangelove or: How I Learned to Stop Worrying and Love the Bomb (Columbia TriStar, 04093)

Stanley Kubrick's 1963 black comedy about nuclear warfare has a variable aspect ratio that shifts, sometimes from shot to shot, between being presented in full screen format and being presented with a mild letterboxing band. There is no 16:9 enhancement for the letterboxed sequences. The black-and-white picture transfer looks terrific. There are a few errant speckles here and there, but contrasts very crisp and finely detailed, and blacks are pure. The monophonic sound is fine. The 93 minute program also has Spanish and French language tracks, optional Spanish subtitles ("¡Caballeros, no pueden pelearse aquí! ¡Esta es la Sala de Guerra!"), and English closed captioning.

Peter Sellers has three parts and is joined by George C. Scott, Sterling Hayden and others in the inspired classic, one that still seems relevant even though the specific threats it depicts no longer loom quite as large. In addition to its obvious slapstick, the Kubrick employs a near constant stream of sexual imagery and allusions to accentuate the boys-will-be-boys world of the Pentagon and its Russian equivalent. Long after the most obvious comical one-liners and visual gags are committed to memory, however, the film remains highly repeatable entertainment, not only because of the calculated suspense which keeps the narrative moving briskly, but in Sellers' remarkable triple character performance. Of all Adlai Stevenson's many accomplishments, it is sadly ironic that he will probably be most remembered for Sellers' interpretation of what his presidency might have been like. In the days when the government was producing films telling school children to pull their jackets over their heads if an atomic bomb goes off down the street, Stevenson's unassuming pragmaticism was ripe for ridicule.

Dr. Strangelove or: How I Learned to Stop Worrying and Love the Bomb is identical to Columbia's earlier **Dr. Strangelove**; in fact, the platter for the later release, identical to the old, retains the shorter title, although the jacket art has squeezed in the longer title.

Dracula (see Bram Stoker's Dracula)

Dracula (Image, ID4377USDVD)

Sometimes movie directors get carried away. Working on the letterboxed version of the 1979 feature, John Badham had the colors in the film drained away deliberately. The effect is striking in many sequences, giving the film the near black-and-white design of the stageplay upon which it was based, but it is artistically questionable (must the outdoor scenes during the day, where Dracula is nowhere around, also look so pale?) and if one is not prepared for it, it can seem unappealing. Nevertheless, the picture is crisp, and the best sequences look unusual and haunting, but fans who just want to kick back and enjoy a good Dracula movie may well feel frustrated by its relentless pallor. Frank Langella stars. The presentation is letterboxed with an aspect ratio of about 2.35:1 and no 16:9 enhancement. The film has an older stereo surround soundtrack with an indiscriminate dimensionality, though it does provide the audio with an extra sense of flourish. The 109 minute

film is apparently closed captioned, and is identified as the 'home video' version, with some musical rescoring.

Dracula: Prince of Darkness (Anchor Bay, DV10502)

The 1966 Hammer production, directed by Terence Fisher, stars Christopher Lee in the title role and is letterboxed with an aspect ratio of about 2.35:1 and no 16:9 enhancement. After a lengthy prelim (Lee doesn't appear in the film until the 50 minute mark and he has no dialogue at all, just a number of engaging growls and hisses), he terrorizes some travelers who have accidentally stopped at his castle. Hues are dull but fleshtones are workable and the image is relatively free of haze. The monophonic sound is okay and the program is not captioned. The 90 minute 'uncut' film is also available in French and comes with some 'behind the scenes' home movies, a couple trailers and a jovial commentary featuring Lee and co-stars Barbara Shelley, Francis Mathews and Susan Farmer. There is also a 25 minute *World of Hammer* episode that covers Hammer Dracula movies, though it still didn't help teach us how to tell them all apart. On the commentary track, Lee talks a bit about his career and shares some insights on the art of playing Dracula and acting in general. All four reminisce about the shoot, discussing Fisher's laissez-faire directoral style, the fun of working at Hammer, and sharing anecdotes about their fellow performers.

Dragnet (Universal, 20392)

Dan Aykroyd does his Jack Webb parody throughout the film, but the movie couldn't get past being a *Saturday Night Live* skit if it weren't for Tom Hanks, as Aykroyd's more relaxed partner, bringing a genuinely well timed comical performance to the supporting role. Aykroyd creates the mood, but it is Hanks who sells it.

The picture has been letterboxed, with an aspect ratio of about 1.85:1 and an accommodation for enhanced 16:9 playback, masking picture information off the top and bottom and adding a bit to the sides in comparison to full screen versions. The image is soft in places, but the colors are bright and fleshtones are fine. The stereo sound is a little muffled, but there are some viable separation effects. The 106 minute film is also available in Spanish and French and can be supported by English or Spanish subtitles ("Los hechos, señora"). There are some good production notes, a cast and director section, and a trailer.

Dragon: The Bruce Lee Story (Universal, 20224)

The engaging dramatic biography celebrates Lee's spirit using a rough outline of his career as a narrative guide. To its credit, the film never ventures far from the standard martial arts genre format, though it is more slickly produced than most. Lee's relationship with his wife, upon whose book the film is based, pads the action and stretches the running time to a full two hours, but that is an entirely permissible embellishment and the filmmakers come up with plenty of situations for the hero to leap about and crunch bones between the romance and financial struggles. There is also a fascinating dream subplot that leads eerily toward the tragic death of Brandon Lee although the film itself was shot before the accident occurred.

The color transfer is okay and there is a scratch on the image at the 35:49 mark. The presentation is letterboxed with an aspect ratio of about 2.35:1 and no 16:9 enhancement. The stereo surround sound is a bit weak, but the Dolby Digital track is better, with crisp definitions and a decent bass during the dream sequences. There is a 6 minute 'making of' featurette, two lengthy and interesting behind-the-scenes segments that did not make it into the featurette, a laudatory introduction by Lee's wife, Linda Lee Cadwell, a montage of Lee photos that are also collected in still file, a couple of trailers, storyboards of the dream sequences, publicity materials, a cast profile section and some decent production notes. Of particular interest are star Jason Scott Lee's elaborate screen test and an interesting interview with Bruce Lee himself, conducted during the early days of his acting career when he was best known for a few TV appearances and as Hollywood's hottest martial arts trainer.

The entertaining 1994 biopic is also available in French and comes with English or Spanish subtitles.

The director, Rob Cohen, also provides a commentary track. Pulling away the curtains on the production does nothing to diminish admiration for what the movie accomplished and can actually increase one's respect for the film. Cohen apparently came up with most of the concept in his head, discovering only after he had mapped everything out that the script's mystical aspects were genuinely reflected in Lee's own beliefs. The casting of Jason Scott Lee was also fortuitous. Not only is he a competent emotional actor, but he mastered the physical demands of the part with surprising aplomb. The fascinating screen test is more of a demonstration film, designed not so much to show that the actor could handle the part but for Cohen to prove to the film company that he could deliver the subject.

As Cohen explains on his commentary, the purpose of a movie biography is to capture the spirit of the truth in an entertaining manner, something his movie achieves brilliantly. Even on the audio track, Cohen speaks only in generalized terms about the details of Lee's life, though he does explain the reasoning behind the film's biggest fictionalizations (such as, in the commentary's most amusing passage, how Lee really hurt his back). Cohen uses the talk to explain how the film's major sequences were achieved (to beat a Hong Kong monsoon, the industrious crew built a huge tent over an entire outdoor set) and to go over what he feels were the significant aspects of Lee's career. The interview with Lee, which closes out the disc, brings the whole project into perspective. Lee talks about his philosophy and about the promise of his performance artistry and how the two seemingly diverse concepts can converge without corruption. That, too, is what Cohen's film achieves.

Dragon Fist (Simitar, 7258)

Jackie Chan, who also directed, is a kung-fu student who seeks to restore his clan's honor after his master is killed in a duel. His emotions, however, allow him to be manipulated by the real villains, who pretend to assist him for their own gain. The stunts are creative and the story is workable. The 1979 program is cropped, with bland colors and lots of wear. The 77 minute program (the film originally ran 93 minutes) is presented in English on one track and Cantonese on another. The monophonic sound is always fairly rough, with warped or muffled music, and the Cantonese track doesn't sound all that much better. They also use the theme music to *The Sand Pebbles* over and over. The film is not captioned.

Dragonball Z: The Movie Dead Zone (Pioneer, PIDA1336V)

The 45 minute Japanese cartoon takes place far in the future, but has an ecological setting. The hero is a child with an important hat, who is kidnapped by an evil sorcerer. Most of the program depicts a battle with the sorcerer and his henchmen against the child's family and protectors, making the show one long bout of typical fight sequences, mixed with a few humorous gags here and there. The DVD, however, also contains lengthy clips, identified as 'deleted TV scenes,' but functioning as complete, miniature episodes, that depict the series in a much stronger light. In one, the hero loses his hat to a tiger and then falls into a river. In the other, the best one, the hero wanders into a cave, where he finds an ancient robot. Unlike the main program, these sequences have compelling narratives and make imaginative use of character. The audio can be accessed in English or Japanese. There is a thorough profile of each character appearing in the film, with reference links to the program, and English subtitling with either the loose standard translation or a more thorough transcription of the English dubbing. The picture on the show itself is excellent, with sharp, vivid colors and an impressive multi-plane effect in places. The stereo surround sound is fine.

Dragonheart (Universal, 20161)
Dragonheart DTS (Universal, 20463)

About a dragon and a burnt-out knight who team up to fight a bad king (the 1996 film is set in 996—get it?), the movie's ending is obvious from the moment the characters are introduced, and so the film must labor to keep the viewer interested without the advantage of narrative surprise. It succeeds, on DVD at least, because the dragon, elaborately voiced by Sean Connery, is superbly animated and appears totally integrated with the live action. Dennis Quaid is somewhat bland as the hero and David Thewlis is typecast as the evil king, though portions of his performance are still fairly enjoyable. Julie Christie is also featured.

The picture is letterboxed, with an aspect ratio of about 2.35:1 and an accommodation for enhanced 16:9 playback. The color quality is fine and the image is sharp, even in darker sequences. The stereo surround sound is fairly weak, but the Dolby Digital track is okay. The sound mix has a few engaging moments and is suitable for a special effects laden adventure. The 103 minute program can also be accompanied by French or Spanish dialogue, in standard stereo, and comes with English or Spanish subtitles. There is a brief production essay, a cast & crew profile, a bevy of commercials and trailers, a couple of interesting deleted scenes, and a still archive with production drawings, storyboards, behind-the-scenes photos and marketing artwork. There is also a good retrospective documentary and a commentary by the director, Rob Cohen.

Within the documentary are two minor but interesting non-effect scenes that were dropped from the film before it opened. The documentary shows the various steps that were required to achieve these effects, and provides plenty of 'before and after' examples. Cohen's superb commentary track elaborates upon what is shown in the documentary, as well as discussing the aspects of the production that had nothing to do with special effects, such as how the production logistics were managed. He also provides a historical background about dragons and things, and essentially answers every question you might have about how and why the movie was made. He seems oblivious to the film's narrative weakness and believes strongly in the story's fantasy and its morals.

The DTS track is indistinguishable from the Dolby Digital track on the standard release, while the DTS LD has more separation detail and stronger, better-defined tones. The frame transfer rate on the standard release swings wildly between the high and midrange, while the transfer rate on the DTS release holds more consistently in the upper end. The DTS presentation is letterboxed in the same manner as the standard release, but it has no supplementary features and no captioning.

Dragons of the Orient (Tai Seng, 34494)

A travelogue-style documentary about martial arts in China, much of it is presented in the context of a fictional female reporter and her companion, a stunt man, visiting the Shaolin Temple, but they also look at other sites around China, and the narration at times steps away from them to go off on its own. There are many impressive sequences that actually seem closer to dance than to fighting, as well as a couple segments that could easily show up on *Guinness World Records*, such as the man who pulls a small truck full of people from a cord attached to a needle that has been passed through the skin of his arm, and another who climbs about six stories of a sheer brick wall. There are also home movies of Jet Li when he was a child.

The scenery itself is often quite lovely, and the many images of people practicing fighting techniques and exercises can be fascinating, but the film's pace is not smooth and viewers who are not totally into it may become impatient. It doesn't help that the film is very awkwardly dubbed in English, and the monophonic sound is mildly distorted on the upper end. The picture has such a mix of source materials that it ranges from being reasonably sharp and colorful to totally blurry and faded, though most of the footage is passable. Most of the show is mildly letterboxed, but that, too, varies from one sequence to the next, and the letterboxing completely disappears in some segments. The 88 minute program is not captioned and is accompanied by 20 minutes of trailers for other Li movies.

Dreams of Gold (Simitar, 7278)

Cliff Robertson as salvage expert Mel Fisher and Loretta Swit as his wife in the docudrama about the discovery of the Atocha treasure ship. There was a tragedy involved with the search, and that incident, along with Fisher's elaborate wrangling for financing and keeping the government out of his hair, provide enough narrative to see the 1986 TV movie through its 87 minute running time. The picture quality is passable but not overly bright and the monophonic sound is functional. Partial filmographies of Robertson and Swit are also included, and the program is not captioned.

Driving Miss Daisy (Warner, 11931)

A lot of people are upset because it isn't letterboxed, but we don't see what the big deal is. The full screen image adds picture information to the top and bottom and loses just a hair from the sides compared to the film's letterboxed presentation. We see nothing wrong with the framing on the full screen version and can't get too excited over the lack of a letterboxed version, though we suppose it is the principle of the thing that has most consumers up in arms. Anyway, it appears that Warner has remastered the film, because the colors are substantially deeper and richer on the DVD than they were on the hazy looking LD. The presentation retains the conceptual gauziness that was part of the cinematography's design, but the effect is under control and colors are rich, with accurate fleshtones. The stereo surround sound is bland, but the three channel Dolby Digital surround track on the DVD has a fuller and better detailed presence. On the whole, however, the mix is limited. The 99 minute film is available in English or French (the dubbing is very good) and has English, French or Spanish subtitles. There is also a theatrical trailer and a few cast profiles.

The film, though somewhat trifling, is pleasant and engaging. About the relationship between an elderly woman and her black chauffeur in the South after World War II, the filmmakers wisely avoid any obvious commentary that would undercut the film's reasonably light mood. The tension inherent in the situation—not only the dramatic situation, but in the cast members acting out their roles—is plain enough that it needs no further attention drawn to it to be effective or to support the superficial aspects of the plot. Like the characters themselves, the film is much wiser than it first appears. Morgan Freeman and Jessica Tandy star.

Drop Squad (Universal, 20517)

An uneven but daring abstract satire about black resentments toward assimilation, the narrative has two parts. In one, a black advertising executive is kidnapped by a group dedicated to 'de-programming' black people who have become too accepting of white peoples' values and habits. Intercut with this are flashbacks in which we see the executive, whose commercials are exaggerated examples of stereotype marketing, learning how to succeed by placating his white clients and bosses. The film means to stimulate thought and argument—the kidnappers also have conflicts among themselves about their methods—but there is little in the way of narrative tension and the film feels like a jumble of promising ideas that failed to gel. Eriq LaSalle stars.

The picture is letterboxed, with an aspect ratio of about 1.85:1 and an accommodation for enhanced 16:9 playback. Colors are a touch light and there's a bit of haze here and there, but the image looks reasonably good, with sharp lines and accurate fleshtones. The stereo surround sound has a decent dimensionality and the 88 minute program can be supported by English, French or Spanish subtitles. Contrary to a listing on the jacket, there appears to be no featurette, but there is a trailer. There is also a decent production essay and a cast-and-director profile section.

Duck Soup (Image, ID4223USDVD)

The 1933 film, ostensibly about political intrigues in a make-believe country, is considered to be the Marx Bros. comedy team's most abstract and intellectually satisfying work. The black-and-white picture is smooth and crisp, but wear on the source material is readily evident. The monophonic sound is dull, but the Dolby Digital mono track is reasonably clear. The brisk 68 minute film, in which Groucho is the dictator of a country that goes to war, is closed captioned.

Duel in the Sun (Anchor Bay, DV10656)

The linchpin of Martin Scorsese's *Personal Journey through American Movies* was a 1946 western he saw as a child in which the adults acted strangely toward one another, biting and scratching one moment, embracing and kissing the next, and then shooting each other after that: King Vidor's **Duel in the Sun**. As a drama, it is fairly ridiculous, but as a motion picture, it is glorious, using the western backdrop and Grand Master cinematography to balance the excess of emotion among the characters. Indeed, we envied a young friend who watched the film with us and was as transfixed as Scorsese must have been by the contradictory and animalistic desires it depicts. If anything, the film begs to be turned into an opera, and that is certainly how you have to approach it if you're going to enjoy it legitimately and not just laugh it away.

Lionel Barrymore is a rancher patriarch, with Gregory Peck as the rambunctious son that he likes and Joseph Cotten as the conscientious son that he doesn't. Into this mix appears Jennifer Jones, with dark bronzing makeup and eyes that could ignite a wet match at twenty paces. There are a couple nicely staged action scenes, including one that has an unusual number of extras, but the film is primarily a romance, with the raw frontier environment matching the raw passions of the characters.

The master looks terrific. There are one or two scratches and, in a couple spots, the three-strip Technicolor isn't lined up right, giving everybody tiny green halos, but mostly the image is luscious, with deep, rich fleshtones, breathtaking vistas and finely detailed interiors. The image was shot in full screen format and that is how it is presented, with the compositions reminiscent of an IMAX film. The trouble comes in the DVD frame transfer rate, which is wildly erratic, causing momentary blurs or shifts in what ought to be solid textures or backgrounds. The transfer rate swings from 2 to 8. When it is high, the picture looks fine, but when it is low, the compromises are all-too-visible. Since it is inconsistent, there are plenty of sequences that look perfectly fine, but when the distractions do pop up, it is extra frustrating because you know it could be better. The monophonic sound is adequate. The 129 minute film is not closed captioned.

Dumb Luck in Vegas (Simitar, 7214)

A cheaply produced comedy thriller about four friends from New Jersey who become mixed up with mobsters in Las Vegas. Joey Travolta stars in the film, which has a promising script (one of the heroes is blamed for a murder he didn't commit, and the others have to clear him), but is staged in a very juvenile manner that few viewers will have the patience for. Although the image is reasonably sharp, the cinematography is bland and fleshtones are indistinct. The stereo sound on the 96 minute program is flat and dull.

Dune (Universal, 20184)

Although it has several years of special effects advancements behind it, David Lynch's 1984 adaptation does not look the least bit dated, and with the DVD's picture and sound transfers, the film is an outstanding piece of sci-fi entertainment. The color transfer is excellent, with accurate fleshtones and a crisp, clean image that hides all but the most awkward matte lines. The letterboxing has an aspect ratio of about 2.42:1 and no 16:9 enhancement, and a widescreen presentation is essential for conveying the film's scope and grandeur. The Dolby Digital soundtrack was a great surprise, carrying a stronger bass, more separation detail and a greater mass of sound than the standard stereo surround soundtrack. The audio is thrilling and it almost never lets up, so that we found ourselves looking forward to even the worst passages of Toto's musical score, because of the extra kick the notes added to the already deafening glory of noise. The movie is also available in French in standard stereo and can be accompanied by English or Spanish subtitles ("Soy la shadout mapes, el ama de llaves"). Apparently fit onto a single layer, the 137 minute film is accompanied by a theatrical trailer, a paltry cast profile section and some interesting production notes.

The film rushes through the story much too quickly (the movie's first 40 minutes cover the first 40 or so pages of Frank Herbert's novel, leaving the remaining 97 minutes to cover the other 460 pages), but images (watch the shadow of the hunter-seeker cross the hero's bed like a snake) and sounds are so dazzling that the inevitable shortcuts in the plot become irrelevant. Extra footage would be nice, but it isn't necessary. With the DVD, 'as is' is good enough.

Dvorak: Symphony No. 9 "From the New World" (Sony, SVD48421)

The image on the *Herbert von Karajan His Legacy for Home Video Series* is extremely crisp and vivid, with deep colors and accurate fleshtones. The standard stereo track is strong, so there isn't improvement on the Dolby Digital track, though it is a bit deeper and clearer. Shot in February 1985 with the Vienna Philharmonic, Karajan's rendition of *New World Symphony*, which runs 43 minutes, has sustained passages of insightful organization and thrilling execution, though he tends to embrace Dvorak's Beethoven quotations a little too enthusiastically, throwing off the balance of the work in the Third Movement. Visually, the presentation is superbly executed, giving the viewer a stimulating variety of images, without detracting from the soul of the composition.

E

The Eagles: Hell Freezes Over (Image, ID5529EADVD); DTS (Image, ID5479EADVD)

The 99 minute 'greatest hits' concert has been released in two different packages, a standard jacket and a jacket promoting the DVD's DTS track, but if you break open the wrappers, pull out the platters, drop them on the floor by accident and pick them up again, it will not matter which platter you return to which jacket. It's the same DVD. There is no Dolby Digital track, however, so your choices are the DTS track or the standard PCM track, and you have to select which one you want when you first spin up the platter—there is no menu or audio selection to move between the two after you get started. The DVD's DTS track sounds better detailed than the DVD's standard track. The audio mix is fairly nice, including the audience but keeping them at bay, and finding the right balance between the instruments and the vocals. The picture is fine.

The band plays their best-known songs in the 1994 reunion concert, though their orchestrations sometimes get a bit schmaltzy. The program opens with a ten minute documentary of sorts, depicting the preparations and the reflections of the band members, but no interruptions occur during the concert itself on the 99 minute program. The five musicians, most of whom have gone on to successful solo careers, sit on a row of stools in front of a large backup band and sing their best known hits. The performance lacks the excitement that other bands have brought to their reunions, but then some critics will likely point out that the Eagles rarely had that much fire in their hearts to begin with. In any case, fans should be pleased to see the group reunited and happy that the singers remember the words as well as everybody else does.

Earth Girls are Easy (Artisan, 60480)

Although Jim Carrey's presence has spurred a renewed interest in the home video release, he has a secondary role and is rarely the center of attention. Geena Davis stars as a Valley girl, with Jeff Goldblum (her eventual romantic interest), Carrey and Damon Wayans as three aliens who crash their spaceship in her swimming pool. They act a bit Morky, get into some trouble and have some fun. There is a little humor to the 1988 film, and several elaborate musical numbers (probably the best part of the film), but it's pretty silly and the gags don't have a strong momentum.

The picture is letterboxed with an aspect ratio of about 2.35:1 and an accommodation for enhanced 16:9 playback. The image looks reasonably fresh and there are lots of bright colors. The stereo surround sound is not elaborate, and it is mostly the music that has dimensionality. The 99 minute program can be supported by optional Spanish subtitles and is closed captioned in English with some paraphrasing. There are also a number of supplementary features, including a cast-and-director profile section, some production notes, outtakes that give one a better chance to see Carrey in action, a costume test that shows Goldblum doing a dance, a complete run of the faux soap opera playing on a TV during a scene, a behind-the-scenes look at the hairdresser's set being prepared, karaoke renditions of the film's musical numbers, and a really bizarre dream sequence. We could not locate the theatrical trailer promised on the jacket cover, however.

Earth, Wind & Fire Live in Japan (Pioneer, PA98582D)

The band delivers an energetic 88 minute mix of funk and dance music before an enthusiastic audience in the 1990 production. The picture quality is very good, with sharp, accurate and well-lit hues. The stereo surround sound is also terrific, with lots of power, a clear definition of tone and a strong dimensionality. We actually preferred it to the Dolby Digital track, which sends more sounds to the back, but with less purpose, though on the whole either track is pleasing.

Earthlight (Mill Reef, DVDI0813)
Earthlight Special Edition (DVD International, DVDI0815)

An image music program created exclusively for DVD, it contains 80 minutes of NASA-supplied video footage of the Earth as seen from the Space Shuttle (there is one segment depicting the Mir, but for the rest, the camera points at Earth), set to an unobtrusive and pleasant musical score by Ryan Shore. The picture quality is very good. The stereo surround sound is a bit bland, but the Dolby Digital surround soundtrack is excellent, with a strong bass and crisp dimensional effects. What sets the program apart is its innovative use of the DVD format. It is divided into 28 chapters and, through the menu, offers subsets of the complete program, so that with one click you can watch just the sequences depicting oceans, deserts, etc. There is also a menu selection for various levels of continuous play. By toggling on the Subtitle function, you can access map locations to tell you what you are looking at (the map locations are available in English, French, Spanish, German, Italian, Japanese, Russian and Korean) and what direction the camera is heading. You can also access a map that shows the actual path of each sequence. Additionally, there are production credits containing information about how the program was created and a profile of Shore. The DVD is also designed for play on DVD-ROM systems and offers extra material in that format, including NASA still photos and screensavers.

Special Edition contains everything the first DVD had, plus a full Dolby Digital rendition of the shuttle Atlantis taking off, and a collection of still photos. The language option has been expanded to a dozen languages, including Arabic, Hebrew and Klingon. **Special Edition** also has an expanded DVD-ROM section, now 'optimized for Windows 95 and 98,' and adding twelve languages to the Earth view screensaver.

Earthquake (Universal, 0581027)

The 1974 film stars Charlton Heston, Ava Gardner and a half dozen others of moderate stature. The movie is dopey but people watch it anyway, dumbfounded at the silly shake-the-camera effects and the ridiculous melodramatic subplots. (There is no plot, only subplots.) It is the film's subject itself that has enabled it to endure as entertainment. The dramatics are bland, the special effects are scattered and the action scenes are brief, but the concept is a knockout and the film sustains repeated viewings not just for its spectacle but for the possibility that, like the characters in the movie who are watching a movie themselves when the Big One hits, it could happen at any time.

Fleshtones are a little bland, but hues are well defined and the image looks fairly slick. The picture is letterboxed with an aspect ratio of about 2.35:1 and no 16:9 enhancement. There is a mild stereophonic soundtrack, and while there's no Sensurround encoding, the bass still shakes pretty good when it's supposed to. The 123 minute program can be supported by English, Spanish or French subtitles.

Earthscapes (Simitar, 7326)

There is some artifacting, including one quite jittery left-to-right camera pan, but the backgrounds are solid and the colors are reasonably bright. The 37 minute natural images program looks at different landscapes from the American West, including Monument Valley, the Rockies and flowering meadows, with a varied collection of musical artists providing the relaxing score. The stereo sound is passable.

Eat My Dust (New Horizons, NH00157)

A key film in the career of Ron Howard, the 1975 production, directed by Charles Griffith, was an enormously popular drive-in feature and allowed Howard to pressure producer Roger Corman into making the follow-up film his first directing gig. Howard portrays the son of a cop in a small town who steals a championship stock car and takes the local law enforcement officials, including his father, on a daylong joyride. Character motivation and other niceties are somewhat incoherent, but the performers are appealing and there is near-constant driving action, including a number of effective shots taken with the camera mounted on the hood of a speeding car.

The source material has a couple scratches and some other minor wear. Fleshtones are a bit bland, but other hues are bright. The monophonic sound is passable and the film runs 88 minutes. There is no captioning, but the film is accompanied by a Corman interview.

Ebony Ivory & Jade (Anchor Bay, DV10821)

Lacking elegance or coherence, the 1976 film is set in Hong Kong, though the movie was actually shot in the Philippines and looks it. Several American female athletes, including the three heroines, are kidnapped. They stage various escape attempts, have a lot of fights with the bad guys, and get rescued in the nick of time. Colleen Camp, Rosanne Katon and Sylvia Anderson are featured. Some of the fights are good. Camp isn't all that athletic (her performance in the 100 meter race is very amusing), but the others are. Individual scenes, however, are poorly staged and the story's logic is vague.

The picture is presented in full screen format and appears a little tight on the sides at times. The color transfer is fine, with fresh hues and workable fleshtones, but the film's own production has a low budget, slapdash look to it and the image is a bit soft at times. The monophonic sound is flat and bland. The 80 minute program is not captioned.

Ed McBain's 87th Precinct (Simitar, 7595)

Ed McBain's crime novel *Lightning* provides the source for the entertaining cop film. The crimes are a little farfetched, but the story moves with McBain's deft confidence, and the characters are substantially more detailed than the usual home video crime movie types. Randy Quaid is badly miscast as McBain's hero, Steve Carella, but it is not enough to put a damper on the basic pleasures the procedural thriller—about a serial killer who is murdering female athletes—has to offer. Bruce Paltrow directed the 1995 program. The picture is somewhat grainy and colors are bland, with pale, pinkish fleshtones. The stereo surround sound has a limited dimensionality and a weak high end. The 96 minute program is not captioned.

The Eiger Sanction (Universal, 20442)

Clint Eastwood's jokey 1975 espionage thriller with bad stereotypes and terrific climbing sequences is letterboxed with an aspect ratio of about 2.35:1 and no 16:9 enhancement. The image is very sharp and colors are usually bright, though some sequences look a little yellowish. There is some minor speckling throughout the presentation, as well. The monophonic sound has age-related limitations and is a little rough at times. The 129 minute program can be supported by English, French or Spanish subtitles and is accompanied by production notes, a cast profile section and an enjoyable theatrical trailer.

8Man After: Perfect Collection (Image, ID4650SEDVD)

The Japanese animated variation on Robocop is about a superhero android disguised as a private detective. There isn't any sex, but there's plenty of gore and a good science fiction story about the tug between the android's programmed reactions and the emotional memories of the human whose body he now inhabits. Presumably, the 104 minute program is derived from individual episodes in a made-for-video program, but it plays seamlessly and it is impossible to tell where one episode concludes and the next starts. The picture looks fine, with sharp, crisp colors, and the stereo sound is okay. The 1993 program is in English with no subtitling or other language options.

El Mariachi / Desperado (Columbia TriStar, 01969)
Desperado (Columbia TriStar, 11659)

Robert Rodriguez is a wizard not only at creating dazzling action films, but also at creating them cheaply. His first movie, *El Mariachi*, is already a Hollywood legend, shot on a budget of several hundred dollars, transferred from tape to film for several thousand and then sold to Columbia TriStar for several hundred thousand. His gloriously smooth sequel, **Desperado**, was shot within the studio system but still for a very modest amount of money, so that it could reach its specialized audience—those of us who love seeing people getting shot and blown up—and still turn a profit, something the more bloated action features often fail to achieve. Each film appears on a separate side and is accompanied by a Rodriguez audio commentaries. **Desperado** was also released separately, without the commentary.

It appears that the picture transfer for **Desperado** is the same on both DVDs, and the frame transfer rates seem to be identical. Both presentations are letterboxed, with an aspect ratio of about 1.85:1 and an accommodation for enhanced 16:9 playback. The film derives much of its emotional impact from Rodriguez's stylistic dexterity, so the glossy hues and crisp details on the DVD contribute considerably to a viewer's response to the action. The stereo surround sound is weak and less focused than the Dolby Digital track. The bass could use a little more power on the Dolby Digital track, but separations are strong and details are crisp. The soundtrack album to **Desperado** is the best collection of music we have ever come across for driving down dark roads in the middle of the night, and the DVD's audio sustains that level of enchantment. The freestanding **Desperado** has optional Spanish and French soundtracks in standard stereo and can be supported by English closed captioning and Spanish or Korean subtitles. The **Desperado** of the double bill is also available in Spanish and Portuguese in standard stereo and can be supported by English, Spanish or Portuguese subtitles.

The picture on **El Mariachi** is windowboxed, with an aspect ratio of about 1.75:1 and an accommodation for enhanced 16:9 playback. It still looks somewhat soft and inexpensive, but the presentation is not alienating. Colors are true and the image is sharp. The film was shot in Spanish and is presented in Spanish in stereo. The stereo brings some dimensionality to the music and the film's atmosphere, but little in the way of specific directional effects. Unlike the LD, there is no English dubbed track, although there are Portuguese and French audio tracks, the latter in stereo. There is, of course, optional English subtitling, as well as optional Spanish and Portuguese subtitling.

Both films take place in Mexico. **El Mariachi** is a fun little movie about a musician, played by Carlos Gallardo, who is mistaken for a hitman because both have arrived in town with the same black guitar case, one carrying a guitar and the other a portable armory. Technically, **Desperado** is a sequel, in which the hero, now played by Antonio Banderas and fully armed himself, seeks revenge against the criminal class that caused so much trouble in the first film, but the tone is entirely different and the narrative is almost irrelevant to the film's lyrical depiction of warring machismo. Both films also have appealing romantic interludes, and **Desperado** co-stars Salma Hayek.

Included with **El Mariachi** is Rodriguez's student film, *Bedhead*. The short is an amusing comedy, with a practiced action film look, about a young girl who wreaks havoc upon her annoying brother after an accident gives her psychokinetic powers. The featurette is in English, with a decent looking picture and a solid monaural audio track.

Each side also contains a 10 minute sequences by Rodriguez in which he discusses an aspect of each film's production. On **Desperado**, he demonstrates his use of 'video storyboarding' as a shortcut to standard storyboarding and rehearsals. On **El Mariachi**, he demonstrates exactly how the footage he shot became the footage he used in his film (basically, he would change angles and distances during the same take, so when he cut the movie together, it looked like it had been shot with more cameras than it was). These sequences dovetail perfectly with Rodriguez's commentary tracks because, on both films, he uses most of his talk to share with the viewer everything he has learned about cost-effective filmmaking.

Without so much as a hint of bragging, Rodriguez spends much of his talk on **Desperado** explaining how he brought the film in so cheaply—using the same stunt men over and over, rushing through 60 to 70 camera setups a day and throwing members of his production crew in front of the camera when he needed to fill a scene. He explains that he initially used most of the soundtrack music on his temp tracks, intending to change it later on, but ended up liking it so much that he kept it. He also explains why the movie's recording of the music is more elaborate than the album recording. On **El Mariachi** he explains how he put together the film for less than the price of a new compact car. One of his tricks was to find a cooperative town and use a mix of town officials and his own relatives in the cast. His main trick, however, was to edit the film in his head. The pace is often so brisk that you don't notice, until he points it out, how often actors who appear to be in the same scene are never in the same shot.

His comments will be of biblical value to film students, but general audiences will also appreciate the underdog spirit of his project and feel the enthusiasm of his success. It ought to be required listening for film company stockholders, as well.

Electric Blue Sex Model File #1 (Image, ID4563JPDVD)
Electric Blue Sex Model File #2 (Image, ID4564JPDVD)
Electric Blue Sex Model File #3 (Image, ID4565JPDVD)
Electric Blue Sex Model File #4 (Image, ID4566JPDVD)
Electric Blue Wobbling Whoppers (Image, ID4567JPDVD)
Electric Blue Presents Boobmania (Image, ID4568JPDVD)

Each program in the British series runs about 55 minutes and has a decent looking picture with a sharp focus and well-detailed fleshtones. The programs are not captioned and feature topless models who pose for the video camera, sometimes accompanied by quasi-erotic voiceovers (with British accents, supposedly from the models on view).

A dozen models are profiled on **1**. Each does a topless shoot for a female photographer who claims she likes to dress in lingerie like the models do when she is shooting, to get in the mood or something. Anyway, the voiceover speeches by the models as they pose often lasts for most of each segment and pretty much every model claims to love her work and that sort of thing.

2 is a continuation of the first program, featuring more models who talk about how much they just love being sex objects while posing for a topless photographer who is supposedly taking their picture. There are a half dozen models and the program runs about 48 minutes.

3 has more voiceover sequences, while **4** has more of what one might term 'exotic' or, at least, non-Anglo Saxon models. Both programs have mild stereophonic musical scores with some dimensional ambiance.

"Beautiful Giant Breasts" is one of the more printable phrases that appears on the cover of **Wobbling Whoppers** and **Presents Boobmania**. Both programs feature exceptionally enlarged models. The models in **Wobbling Whoppers** are slicker, but many viewers may be attracted to the more natural appearing models on **Boobmania**, one having a discernible mustache and another whose amplified measurements do not cease at the bust line. Both programs are monophonic.

The Electric Horseman (Image, ID4276USDVD)

Robert Redford portrays an ex-rodeo star who kidnaps a valuable race horse in Las Vegas to set him free in the foothills of the Rockies, and Jane Fonda is a reporter who invites herself along. Directed by Sydney Pollack, the 1979 comedy adventure is pleasing despite its clunky design because Redford and Fonda are too relaxed to let the film's flaws and simplicities interfere with their charms.

Although the jacket cover claims that the presentation is the 'Home Video version' with 'some music rescored,' the opening Willie Nelson song, *My Heroes Have Always Been Cowboys*, which was replaced by an instrumental on the LD, has been restored on the DVD. The picture is letterboxed with an aspect ratio of about 2.35:1 with no 16:9 enhancement. It is a bit dark, with slightly purplish fleshtones and a mild grain in some sequences. Overall, however, the presentation isn't bad. Music cues aside, the monophonic sound is somewhat subdued, but there is a Dolby Digital mono track that is brighter.

Electric Light Orchestra: "Out of the Blue" Tour: Live at Wembley / Discovery (Image, D4562ERDVD)

A 63 minute concert program is combined with a 39 minute music video collection. The 1978 concert typifies the gutless, flavorless that music idiom companies attempted to impose upon pop in the late Seventies, and is an unexciting melodic mush masquerading as rock. The stage show accompanying the music, an energetic array of light and smoke effects, was elaborate in its day, but also looks rather tame now and seems to be more intent upon distracting listeners from the music than enhancing it. The videos, though primitive even by mid-Eighties standards, are livelier than the concert program and are more satisfying. The videos include *Shine a Little Love, Confusion, Need Her Love, Diary of Horace*

Wimp, Last Train to London, Midnight Blue, On the Run, Wishing and *Don't Bring Me Down.*

The picture on the concert is quite hazy, with somewhat faded hues, and the concert light show tends to exaggerate the distortion, though when the stage lighting accommodates, the picture is reasonably sharp. The image on the videos is sharper and hues are stronger. Directional effects are limited on the stereo soundtrack, and again the videos are a little more satisfying than the concert recordings.

Elephant Parts (DVD International, DVDI0714)

The ground breaking 1981 home video program, a mixture of a few music sequences and a lot of black-out comedy skits, created by former Monkee and son of the White-Out inventor, Michael Nesmith, has now been resurrected for DVD as a *17 1/2th Anniversary Edition.* The 62 minute program is said to include a little footage that wasn't in previous releases.

The image is often rather soft, but colors are bright and the stereo sound is fine. The program is not captioned. Nesmith also provides a commentary, sort of. It is essentially 62 minutes of utter gibberish, unrelated to the images on the screen, and while the first ten minutes or so can seem amusing, once you figure out that he isn't planning to shift gears, it becomes monotonous. There is a Nesmith discography with scattered song snippets, difficult-to-read reviews of the original **Elephant Parts** release, promotional stills, and a lengthy Nesmith biography. We were happy to discover, by the way, that many of the skits are still funny.

Elizabeth (PolyGram, 4400582732)

Shekhar Kapur's story of how England's Queen Elizabeth I secured her reign is told with great modern flair. Some plot points are a little confusing (because it is based on reality, several characters have the same name), but the film brings home the concept that court intrigue in Sixteenth Century England is just like political intrigue today, except that it was more ruthless. Kapur adeptly mixes radical camera angles and editing techniques with classic costume and set designs to root the film in the past but open it to the present. Cate Blanchett seems ideally cast in the title role, gradually warming up to the duplicity and conniving that surround her. She wasn't England's first queen, but she was the first to assert herself, and the conflict between achieving this goal and maintaining a viable love life has intrigued gossips for ages. What the film suggests, based upon ample evidence, is that after instinctively avoiding an early betrothal, she discovered the only way she could rule was as a single woman, 'married to England.'

The picture quality is excellent. The film's costumes and set designs are highly intricate and colorful, and the DVD delivers them flawlessly. The picture is letterboxed with an aspect ratio of about 1.85:1 and an accommodation for enhanced 16:9 playback. The stereo surround sound and Dolby Digital sound are fine, though specific separation effects are limited. The 124 minute program has optional French and Spanish subtitles, English captioning, a modest collection of still photos, a cast-and-director profile section, a cool teaser and a pretty good trailer, and two 'making of' documentaries, one standard version that mixes interviews with behind-the-scenes footage and clips from the film, and one longer version that only mixes scenes from the film with cast interviews.

Additionally, Kapur provides a commentary track, talking about making the film, the history that the narrative is founded upon, and what is going on with the characters. He doesn't go too deeply into how he staged the film (he mentions only in passing that some scenes involve two different locations and three soundstage sets without detailing the where and when; he also points out that a sequence depicting people being burned at the stake was real, without explaining how nobody got singed), but he does explain why he chose his camera angles, what he wanted from the performances, and why he interpreted history in the manner that he does (e.g., although common wisdom says that people at court

danced formally, it is far more likely that they got very drunk and just boogied till dawn).

Elmo Saves Christmas (Sony, LVD49940)

The cast and puppets of *Sesame Street* appear on the hour-long episode. It has a cute narrative, in which Elmo wishes that Christmas would happen every day and then discovers what a disaster that would be if the wish came true. At first, everyone really enjoys it, but after a while everybody gets worn out and wants to get on with their regular lives, plus there's nothing on the television but **It's a Wonderful Life** day in and day out. Charles Durning portrays Santa. The picture looks okay, with reasonably solid colors and bright reds, and the stereo sound is adequate. The program is not captioned.

Elmopalooza! (Sony, LVD49441)

A busy and enjoyable *Sesame Street* compilation program, there is a linking narrative concerning a concert program the *Sesame Street* characters are trying to put on, but the bulk of the 45 minute show is a collection of nine music videos, featuring artists such as En Vogue, Gloria Estefan, Fugees, Rosie O'Donnell, Jimmy Buffett, Kenny Loggins and others doing Sesame Street-style gag numbers (*I Want a Monster to Be My Friend, Caribbean Amphibian,* etc.) with the characters.

The picture quality looks excellent, with crisp, vivid colors and rich fleshtones, though the image is a little softer in a couple of the music clips. The same goes for the stereo surround sound and better defined Dolby Digital sound, which have elaborate separation effects and lots of power during the interludes, but are a little less dynamic during the musical numbers. The program can be supported by English, French or Spanish subtitles, but only the interlude dialogue is translated, not the songs, though the DVD also has English closed captioning that covers everything. There are cast profile-style summaries of each character, as well.

Elvis: That's the Way It Is (MGM, 906612)

A program for fans only, the disc's color transfer and letterboxing may stimulate the interest of a slightly larger viewership. A documentary about Elvis Presley's 1970 Las Vegas appearance, the film mixes concert footage with typical backstage moments and fan profiles, with the backstage material seeming trivial and the concert often being interrupted for the insertions. Presley's song choices are also weak—he does *Sweet Caroline, Bridge Over Troubled Waters,* and some of his more classic tunes orchestrated to match—and although he appears to be having a good time, music doesn't seem to be a priority.

The documentary was shot in Panavision, and the film is presented on one side in letterboxed format, with an aspect ratio of about 2.35:1 and an accommodation for enhanced 16:9 playback, and in cropped format on the other side, but it is the widescreen version that gives the show an aura of importance. The documentary image is not as well lit or sharp as a soundstage production. The colors are reasonably bright, but the image is soft or even fuzzy, particularly on the cropped picture. The sound is in a modest two-channel stereo for the concert sequences, but it doesn't have much body. The 109 minute program can be supported by English, French or Spanish subtitles ("Amame teirnamente ámame de verdad") and is accompanied by a trailer.

Elvis: The Complete Story (Passport, DVD2221)

The archive footage is drawn mostly from trailers to Elvis Presley's films. There is some super footage from an old Frank Sinatra TV show of Presley and Sinatra performing a duet, but that is one of the few genuinely rare sequences. The voiceover narration tracks Presley's film career and pays scant attention to his singing career except when the two intersect. There is also an actor reading Presley's own words in an Elvis voice that takes some getting used to. If one disregards what has not been covered, however, the narration is fairly insightful and delivers an interesting perspective on Presley's rise and fall. The picture quality varies depending upon the archive footage. Colors are reasonably bright much of the time, but the image is never too crisp. The voices often sound a little fuzzy on the monophonic audio track. A jacket notation claims that the program runs two hours, but it actually clocks in at 93 minutes. The program is not captioned.

Emma (Buena Vista, 15862)

Gwyneth Paltrow stars in the Jane Austen story that also served as the basis for *Clueless*, about a young would-be matchmaker. The film is a little less organic than the other Austen adaptations, but that serves its slightly enhanced comedic charms, with characters acting in a vaguely exaggerated manner to embellish the humor of their actions. Still, when it does finally come time for romance, it is as effective and heartwarming as any.

The picture is letterboxed with an aspect ratio of about 1.85:1 and no 16:9 enhancement. The colors are bright and smooth. The darkest scenes may lose a little too much detail in the shadows but, otherwise, details are exact and the presentation is satisfying. Surround effects are limited but the stereo surround sound is fine. The 121 minute program can be supported by English subtitles and is accompanied by a faded, full screen trailer.

Emmanuelle 2 (Fox Lorber, FLV5032)

A movie from the days when softcore pornography could still pretend to be artistic, it is also known as *Emmanuelle: The Joys of a Woman*, and is in surprisingly good condition. It is letterboxed with an aspect ratio of about 2.35:1 and no 16:9 enhancement. The picture transfer is okay. Colors are reasonably fresh and while some sequences are overly soft, others look quite crisp. In letterboxed format the cinematography is often quite striking, enhancing either the humor or the eroticism of many of the scenes, depending upon your orientation. And the 92 minute movie is available in its original French language soundtrack, as well as the much weaker English dubbed soundtrack, with optional English subtitles. There is also a luscious Francis Lai musical score. Sylvia Kristel stars in the 1977 release, shot mostly in Hong Kong, about a married couple experimenting with an open lifestyle, and the DVD also contains a Kristel profile and filmography.

The Engelbert Humperdinck Spectacular (Image, ID5508CIDVD)

Humperdinck takes his Las Vegas show to London's Albert Hall. Humperdinck has a mechanical voice, a workhorse set of pipes that can achieve just enough melody to legitimize the output as singing while grinding it out night after night amid all those overly painted chorus girls. He does a selection of Nat King Cole tunes that would make the Mona Lisa weep, but when he gets into the sappier stuff, like *Help Me Make It Through the Night* and *I Just Called to Say I Love You*, he shames no one. The stereo mix is not elaborate and dimensionality is limited. The picture is a little hazy in places, but workable. The program runs 59 minutes, but don't be fooled by the 25 chapters, most of the songs amount to a few phrases in a medley.

The English Patient (Buena Vista, 14175)

Not only does the 1996 Oscar-winning romance place the passions of its characters against exotic historical backdrops and not only does it create an intense and challenging moral ambiguity around its heroes, but it is filled with spellbinding details. The movie's asides, its throwaway inserts and casual, filler dialogue are rich with intrigue and knowledge. As much as it is a dense and detailed story, however, it is also a symphony of images and emotions. Nothing happens, for example, in the film's final montage, yet the movie can't really end until the montage is finished, as if, visually, each of the film's motifs had to be wrapped up.

Yet there is nothing austere about the movie, either. It makes a terrific DVD, with explosions, airplane crashes, deafening windstorms and all sorts of visual and audio delights. The 162 minute

film is presented on one side in dual-layer format and has been letterboxed with an aspect ratio of about 1.85:1 and no 16:9 enhancement. The color transfer is excellent, and the film's many challenging lighting effects are presented with confidence. The stereo surround sound is also superb, with a steady dimensional atmosphere and a powerful impact at appropriate moments. The Dolby Digital track is even richer, with a more detailed mix and slightly stronger surround separations. The film can be accompanied by English or Spanish subtitles.

Enter the Dragon (Warner, 15921)

Bruce Lee portrays an undercover agent in the martial arts classic. To celebrate the film's 25th Anniversary, it was spruced up with a sparkling new picture transfer and remixed stereo surround musical score. The image is much sharper and the colors are much brighter than previous home video releases. Fleshtones that look yellowish are now crisp and accurate. The film runs 102 minutes, some 3 minutes longer than the standard 99 minute version, adding a few talky sequences that enrich the film's philosophical content but were deemed too lethargic when the movie was first released.

The film is letterboxed with an aspect ratio of about 2.35:1 and an accommodation for enhanced 16:9 playback. The stereo surround sound is great fun. There is a pounding bass and lots of dimensionality, with the Dolby Digital mix providing clearer separations and better defined tones than the standard mix. Contrary to an indication on the jacket cover, the film is presented in English only, but can be supported by English, French or Spanish subtitles.

The musical score is isolated on one track in Dolby Digital and the film's producer, Paul Heller, provides a sporadic commentary on another track. Heller doesn't have too much to say, but he does reminisce about the production and how it came into being, talks about how some scenes were set up (such as the mirror room shoot; also, they used an old tennis club for the tournament scenes, and if you look close you can see the lines in the ground) and about working with Lee.

The film is presented on one side of the platter. On the other side, there is an excellent 20 minute interview with Lee where he discusses his martial arts philosophies. There is also extended interview footage with Lee's widow, Linda Lee Caldwell, who talks more about what Lee was like behind the scenes. Her clips, however are broken into annoying segments that have to be accessed individually. There is an entertaining 8 minute 'making of' featurette that was shot in tandem with the film, some home movies of Lee working out in his backyard, a bunch of trailers and TV commercials, a decent cast & crew profile section, production notes, and essays on Hong Kong martial arts films and on Jackie Chan who, like Sammo Hung, had a small part in the film.

Eraser (Warner, 14202)

Arnold Schwarzenegger is a good government agent protecting a witness, played by Vanessa Williams, from bad government agents, who use fancy futuristic guns while trying to kill her. James Caan and James Coburn are also featured. They chase around all over the place, with lots of explosions and other high-priced stunts and effects. There isn't any more to it than that, but the show is a maximum energy ride and should please viewers searching for a bit of loud relaxation.

The presentation is presented in letterboxed format on one side, with an aspect ratio of about 2.35:1 and an accommodation for enhanced 16:9 playback, and is cropped on the other side, though we had almost no use for the cropped version, which takes away too much from the action scenes and gave us close ups of actors we really didn't want to look at all that closely. The picture quality looks terrific, with glossy colors and crisp fleshtones even in the darker scenes. The stereo surround sound and Dolby Digital sound are also of summer blockbuster quality, with plenty of punch. The 115 minute film is also available in French in Dolby Digital. There is also an original theatrical trailer.

Eric Burdon and the New Animals (Pioneer, PA99604D)

Older rock groups tend to reunite, do a concert of greatest hits numbers and then reap the home video residuals, and this is one such effort. The live 100 minute program was staged in October 1998 at the Coach House. Burdon has lots of energy, but his voice lacks the memorably plaintive tone it had in his youth, and in fact it pretty much lacks any tone whatsoever. Still, it can be enjoyable to hear the group (no Alan Price) play their old hits, such as *When I Was Young*, *Sky Pilot*, *House of the Rising Sun*, *Monterrey*, *Don't Let Me Be Misunderstood*, as well as Burdon's *Spill the Wine* and Sixties Brit rock classics *Paint It Black* and *It's My Life*. The standard stereo surround soundtrack is adequate, but the Dolby Digital track has substantially more dimensionality and is more engaging. The picture looks fine and the performers are well lit. There are informative interview clips with Burdon between some of the numbers, and these clips have been given a separate on-screen chapter guide.

Eric Clapton Unplugged (Warner, 238311)

Playing acoustical guitar with just a few sporadic backup musicians, Clapton performs 14 numbers in the intimate setting, and the crisp, perfectly colored image brings the viewer practically into his lap. The 70 minute program is Dolby Digital encoded, but since the concert is uncomplicated, the mix on the two tracks is fairly similar. The strength of the Dolby Digital track over the standard stereo track, however, is startling, with the Dolby Digital delivering a much brighter and better-detailed sound. In addition to optional English subtitles, there are a couple still frames where the members of the backup band are identified.

Erotic Dancer World Championship (Vivid, UPC#00732155539)

Eleven contenders are featured in the 85 minute program, originally broadcast on cable. Each contestant performs an elaborate costume dance and striptease, but only one knows the real secret to attracting men—she pours beer all over herself.

The picture looks fine, with decent fleshtones and crisp hues. The stereo surround sound is loud and garish, with dimensional catcalls. There is no captioning and the DVD contains extensive interactive softcore promotional features.

Escape from L.A. (see John Carpenter's Escape from L.A.)

Eternal Evil (Simitar, 7303)

Eternal Evil lasts 85 minutes. It opens with a viewer-point-of-view astral projection, but it was raining the day the filmmakers leased the helicopter, so this is the first astral projection in the history of the cosmos to have water streaks. After that, the movie gets better. Two souls extend their life on earth by transferring from one body to another. The film centers on their attempt to take over the body of the hero, a commercial director. For a cheap supernatural thriller, the film isn't bad. The murders are reasonably gruesome and the pacing is moderately suspenseful.

The colors are murky and the picture is blurry. The monophonic sound is scratchy and has a limited range, and dialogue is raspy. The film runs 85 minutes and is not captioned. A partial filmography for Karen Black, who has a small part, is also included.

Eurythmics: Sweet Dreams (the video album) (Image, ID4702LYDVD)

Much of the 62 minute classic Eighties music video compilation program is taken up by live performances and has a mildly aged look to it. Colors are a little pale and the image is somewhat grainy. The stereo sound is also a bit weak-willed. Although some of the group's music is bland and the concert performances are unpolished, the videos are entertaining and the lead singer, Annie Lennox, generates a compelling mystique in the live sequences. The group's biggest hit, the title tune, is played twice, once live and once with the music video beneath the closing credits.

Eva Braun (Simitar, 7207)

Even the staunchest feminists would have to concede that Braun's only claim to posterity is having slept with Adolf Hitler while he was trying to take over the world. Somebody gave her a 16mm camera when she was 19, however, so she did scholars and WWII fanatics a big favor by recording hours of Hitler's leisure time for posterity. It is these home movies that make up the bulk of the 87 minute DVD. Female and male speakers periodically read from Braun's diary and other sources, which is mixed with an occasional 'Nero fiddled while Rome burned' commentary, all accompanied by a mildly stereophonic musical score. The music is a mix of accordion tunes, folk melodies and bland orchestral pieces, but it often drowns out the voiceover, particularly some of the women's voices. There are also sporadic sound effects that are meant to evoke events and not tied to specific images on the screen. There are long passages, however, of just movies and music.

The footage varies in quality. Some of the color sequences look quite fresh. Others are more faded, and the black-and-white footage often looks blurry and worn. All have the roughness one would expect from amateur films—Leni Reifenstahl, Braun wasn't—and it is impossible to tell where flaws like smears, jitters and hazes have been added to the images. It could be anywhere from existing on the original source material to the transfer to the digital artifacts of the DVD playback. Overall, the images look like typical home movies and it is best to watch them sitting back aways from the screen. There is one transfer-related flaw, where the image freezes for a few moments.

The program comes with very little documentation and the figures in the films are rarely identified. It is even difficult to tell which one is Braun until you really get into it. The footage is mostly of vacation idylls—Hitler didn't exactly take Braun to meetings with him—and there is a lot just of Braun's family, while Hitler was off fighting a war or something. There is also a lot of swimming footage—including images of naked children romping in the water—and very little where Hitler is not dressed like he was about to speak at a rally. You do find yourself staring at him, wondering how such a pathetic looking person could have done so much harm, but the overall utility of the program is questionable. Watching it more than once would be like watching anybody's home movies more than once except your own.

Event Horizon (Paramount, 334827)

There are so many worthy science fiction stories waiting to be filmed that we have to bow our heads and sigh when we see so much money wasted on a clunker like **Event Horizon**. Yes, it has a few scientific and futuristic ideas to set its premise, and it has a basic narrative, about an evil force inhabiting an otherwise lifeless space cruiser, but nothing about it is original and the elaborate special effects just bring attention to the film's paucity of intellectual stimulation. Laurence Fishburne, Sam Neill and Kathleen Quinlan star as the leaders of the rescue crew sent to see what the matter is with the drifting ship. The 1997 movie isn't fun and the director, Paul Anderson, can't do more than grind the formula through its routines. Roger Corman's trainees do this kind of thing much better with much smaller budgets.

The picture is in letterboxed format only, with an aspect ratio of about 2.35:1 and no 16:9 enhancement. The picture quality looks decent, with complicated shades of darkness clearly defined. Fleshtones are accurate and other hues are crisp. The stereo surround sound is adequate and the Dolby Digital track is smoother, with better-detailed separations. The 97 minute feature also has a French audio track, optional English and Spanish subtitles, and a trailer.

Ever After: A Cinderella Story (Fox, 4110381)

As perfect a retelling of the tale of Cinderella as anyone could hope for, it is a wonderfully-directed costume romance about a young girl, who toils as a servant in her step-mother's house, until she meets a prince of the realm. Unlike the best-known versions of the story, the heroine and her prince get together a number of times and build up a firmly loving relationship before the forces of wickedness separate them. Also, one of the step-sisters is sympathetic. The film is brisk, engagingly performed and is just familiar enough to keep a viewer intrigued without becoming predictable. Drew Barrymore and Anjelica Huston star.

The presentation is letterboxed with an aspect ratio of about 2.35:1 and no 16:9 enhancement. The color transfer looks terrific, with rich, deep forest greens and excellent fleshtones. The stereo surround sound and Dolby Digital sound have a comforting dimensionality and well-defined separation effects. The Dolby Digital track is more forceful than the standard track. The 100 minute feature is also available in French in standard stereo and can be supported by English or Spanish subtitles ("Mi padre era experto con la espada y me enseñó"). There is also a thrilling theatrical trailer.

Eve's Bayou (Trimark, 6741D)

Samuel L. Jackson stars as a philandering doctor in the Gothic family drama. Seen through a child's eyes, but with enough adult goings on to earn an 'R' rating, the film explores family tensions and life in a thriving black community on the Louisiana delta. There are touches of mysticism and voodoo, but the film does not really qualify as a thriller, though that is how the jacket cover categorizes it. It is more of a memory story that mixes anecdotes and other incidental occurrences to depict a very tragic summer in the life of the heroine. Elegantly composed and executed, the film is definitely worth seeing once, though multiple viewings are questionable.

The picture transfer looks gorgeous, with bright, crisp hues and accurate fleshtones. The image is letterboxed with an aspect ratio of about 1.75:1 and an accommodation for enhanced 16:9 playback. The letterbox framing looks much better balanced and more satisfying than the full screen theatrical trailer that appears in the DVD's supplement. The stereo surround sound is fine and the Dolby Digital sound is very rich, with a smooth dimensionality and solid details. The film can be supported by French or Spanish subtitles and by English closed captioning.

In addition to the trailer, there is a featurette promo for the soundtrack album and a very good 20 minute short film, *Dr. Hugo*, by the movie's director, Kasi Lemmons. The short, which was a warm-up for the feature, has nearly the same picture quality as the feature and duplicates a scene that was carried over to **Eve's Bayou**, though without its short story-style conclusion, about a philandering doctor who visits a not so sick patient.

During both the movie and the short, Lemmons, cinematographer Amy Vincent and editor Terilyn Shropshire provide commentary. Producer Caldecot Chubb also speaks on the short's commentary track. The commentary on the film is mostly reactive and abundant with superlatives as each speaker praises the work of the others and the cast. They do provide some informative bits, explain how certain shots were achieved and tell how the set-ups in some sequences were dictated by the budget. We were disappointed that Lemmons did not go into more detail about the gestation of her script (she touches on it a little at the very end), but she does talk about working with the cast and what she wanted to achieve in specific sequences. The commentary on the short is more specific, explaining why it was made and what happened during the production.

The Evil Dead (Anchor Bay, DV10667E); collector's (Elite, EE7265)

Films about demonic possession are the most unnerving because the evil force is immaterial and can easily slip into a viewer's nightmares. **The Evil Dead** is the scariest movie we've ever seen, so much so that the film's sequel had to be a comedy—there was no other way to turn. About a group of college kids, staying in a cabin in the woods, who unleash evil powers that turn almost all of them into hoary demons, the film's internal logic is tight enough to make the narrative work and the pace is relentless, never giving one the chance to stop and remember that it is only a movie.

The low budget production has always looked grainy and has always had weak colors, even during its initial theatrical run, and it is doubtful that the image could look better than it does on the DVDs, which have identical transfers. Brightly lit hues are usually solid and fleshtones are well detailed. The picture is presented in full screen format. The 1982 film's audio track has been remastered for stereo, adding more excitement to many of the sequences. In addition to the standard stereo track, Elite's presentation has a remastered Dolby Digital track that is a lot more fun, with more dimensionality and clearer details. The 85 minute film is not captioned on either DVD and is accompanied on Anchor Bay's release by a theatrical trailer. Anchor Bay's platter art is available in five variations.

Elite's presentation has two commentary tracks. On one, director Sam Raimi and producer Robert Tapert reminisce about the shoot. They don't go into too much detail about the special effects, and say even less about how the story was developed, but they do have interesting anecdotes about securing funding, shooting on 16mm with a skeleton crew, what the cast was like behind the scenes, and about how audiences first reacted to the film, which achieved a level of terror that has really never been surpassed. There are stretches, however, where they get to watching the movie and forget to talk. On the other track, one of the stars, Bruce Campbell, shares his memories of the production, with a lot more flair. His vocal inflections bring delight even to the passages where he is merely reporting upon what is happening on the screen. He provides a lot more details about how things were shot and what was going on during the shoot. You need to hear the other track to get a little background, but Campbell's is the talk that entertains.

Also included on Elite's DVD are a very gory trailer, some production stills and 18 minutes of behind-the-scenes shots (actually, 'raw footage'—takes where you can see the crew as well as the actors). Along with Campbell's detailed explanations, the footage gives one a clear idea of how some of the special effects were accomplished and what it was like on the set.

Evil Dead 2: Dead by Dawn (Anchor Bay, DV10504)

Having exhausted the possibilities of serious horror with the first **Evil Dead**, the creators of the film, led by director Sam Raimi, turned to comedy for its 1987 follow-up, To be sure, the film is rampant with grotesque horror effects but, unlike the unnerving first film, you're supposed to laugh at what is essentially gory slapstick, and it is the film's sense of humor that makes it worth revisiting. Set once again in an isolated cabin infected by evil spirits, the heroes do a surprisingly good job, all things considered, at staving off the inevitable for most of the film's 84 minute running time. Assuming one is not averse to severed limbs, gushing blood and pop-eyed demons, the film is an enjoyable and witty concoction.

The picture is letterboxed with an aspect ratio of about 1.85:1 with no 16:9 enhancement. Blacks are pure and the image is sharp, with reasonably deep hues and nice details. The monophonic sound works fine. A theatrical trailer is also included with the 85 minute feature. There is no captioning.

Evil Ed (Image, ID4656APDVD)

If you haven't seen the jacket cover, it shows a full sized man's head being split in two with an axe as blood and brains splash out of the cleft. The program is a spoof on splatter films that tries to be the ultimate splatter movie at the same time, but offers no emotional foundation to support its multitude of splatter effects. A Swedish production, the lip movements match the English dialogue, but the voices don't always match the characters. The film is about a movie editor who is working in the 'splatter and gore de-partment' of a large film company. He goes nuts being exposed to all the bloody movies and initiates a rampage of his own. The ef-fects are plentiful, but the movie isn't even much fun, really. It is just filmmakers seeing how high they can raise the stakes and for-getting to play the game in the process.

The picture is passable, with adequate fleshtones and a manage-able haze. The presentation is letterboxed, but the aspect ratio ap-pears to be closer to 1.5:1 than to the 1.66:1 indicated on the jacket cover, and there is no 16:9 enhancement. The stereo sound hasn't much to offer and the 86 minute program is not closed captioned.

Evita (Buena Vista, 13849)

The all-singing musical about the wife of the former Argentine president and dictator, Juan Perón, had confounded Hollywood for a long time when director Alan Parker finally worked up enough courage to go through with it, and he cast Madonna, who was probably the best bet for a worldwide box office return, in the title role. Madonna's lip synching skills are superb—it is what she does for a living—and perhaps she was the best actress available for the part if that was a major requirement. Alas, if only some-body else had done her singing. Her performance, both vocally and dramatically, is sincere and earnest, but she never nails the part. Something must be wrong. Here is a person many people consider to be the sexiest woman in the world, and we couldn't take our eyes off Jonathan Pryce.

Pryce, as Perón, is the film's saving grace. His performance is a tribute to the art of the possible, proving that the musical could work as a movie if the right players had been chosen and the right director had guided them. He is the DVD's saving grace as well, be-cause if you don't want to watch the whole movie again, you at least want to play his big scenes over and over. Antonio Banderas also appears in a role that is a leftover stage device, but in the trans-fer to film his presence and authority are compromised. His vocals aren't that much stronger than Madonna's and he never achieves an ounce of Pryce's charisma.

The real blame, however, lies with Parker. Parker deliberately avoids using closeups in the film (there is one sequence, where ex-treme closeups of Madonna's lips and eyes are used in a montage, and it comes across badly because it is so severe in comparison to the previous medium length shots). The movie is about a woman who achieved leadership by disdaining aloofness and Parker insists on keeping her at an arm's length or more. Banderas should also be in your face and tapping you on the chest, but instead he's usually hidden in the crowd or slinking around the edges. The film isn't shot like a musical at all. There is virtually no choreography (al-though every line of dialogue is sung, Parker insisted that the rest of the film be 'realistic') and the music seems amputated without dancing. The orchestration goes through a wild range of styles, but it rarely sounds Latin enough and is often besieged by amplified electronic instruments with a Seventies beat that makes the music sound plain awful. After the movie came out, we suddenly started seeing articles that call Andrew Lloyd Webber the world's worst fa-mous composer, when he really isn't—he just doesn't know how to play the music he writes, and Evita crystallized an awareness of this flaw.

The 135 minute 1997 feature has been released in letterboxed format only, with an aspect ratio of about 2.35:1 and no 16:9 en-hancement. The picture is okay. Colors are rich and contrasts are effectively rendered.

The standard stereo surround soundtrack lets the entire musical score and vocals bleed into the back channels, whereas the Dolby Digital track has virtually nothing sent to the rear. The film is can be accompanied by English or Spanish subtitles ("¡Atrás, Buenos Aires!").

Excess Baggage (Columbia TriStar, 82305/9)

The uneven 1997 comedy is about a young rich girl staging her own kidnapping to get her father's attention, and a young car thief who interrupts her plans. Alicia Silverstone and Benicio Del Toro star and both need more direction than they receive. Del Toro of-ten falls back on unconvincing mannerisms and Silverstone occa-sionally breaks the spell of her character to appear lost or unmotivated. The narrative is also weakly constructed and ends up fudging on several plot points, but the film can be fun if you aren't too demanding.

The presentation appears on one side in letterboxed format, with an aspect ratio of about 1.85:1 and an accommodation for en-hanced 16:9 playback, and in full screen format on the other side. The color transfer looks fine and fleshtones are good. The stereo surround sound and Dolby Digital sound are not too elaborate, but work reasonably well. The 101 minute program also has French and Spanish audio tracks in standard stereo, optional En-glish, French and Spanish subtitles, and an interesting trailer.

Executioners (Tai Seng, 44614)

Nominally a sequel to the Hong Kong action feature, **Heroic Trio**, **Executioners** carries over the same three heroines, but places them in a very different situation. Set after some sort of nuclear di-saster, the women must find a source of fresh water for their city and prevent a military coup. Not only is the film's tone different, but the action scenes are less fantastic. Fans will find satisfaction enough in the personalities of the three heroines and the regularity of the fight sequences, but if one is planning a double bill it would be best to watch the films in reverse order. Michelle Yeoh stars with Anita Mui and Maggie Cheung in the 100 minute feature.

The film is letterboxed with an aspect ratio of about 1.75:1 and no 16:9 enhancement. The image is fairly soft, but the colors are workable. The film itself uses monochromatic lighting for a num-ber of scenes, making things blue and white or brown and white, etc., but the image is always sharp and stable, and no matter how challenging the colors become the disc delivers them accurately. Damage is also minimal. There are three audio tracks, in Manda-rin, Cantonese and English, and optional English subtitles. The English dialogue is fairly easy to follow. There are slight variations with the subtitling, particularly in the names of the characters, which the dubbing has Anglicized. The film is accompanied by trailers and cast profiles.

Executive Decision (Warner 14211)

Kurt Russell stars as an intelligence consultant, called in on a hi-jacking case, who eventually finds himself leading a group of com-mandos inside the airliner in mid-air. For the most part it follows the current high-concept action formula correctly, but with a few well chosen, unexpected twists, and is a highly entertaining, DVD-friendly production. Steven Seagal co-stars.

The 133 minute thriller is letterboxed format on one side, with an aspect ratio of about 2.35:1 and an accommodation for en-hanced 16:9 playback, and in cropped format on the other. The colors are strong, the picture is crisp and colors are solid. The film has a number of darker sequences, set in airplane attics and things like that, and these sequences have a somewhat bland coloring, but on the whole the presentation looks slick. The cropped image is mildly grainy. Because the 1997 film has many intense intimate moments, the cropped presentation cannot be written off out of hand, but the weaker picture compromises its appeal. The Dolby Digital mix is preferable to the standard mix, providing a more blustery, big movie atmosphere. There is a small cast profile sec-tion and a couple paragraphs of production notes, and there are English, French or Spanish subtitles.

The Exorcist (Warner, 1007)
The Exorcist: Special Edition (Warner, 16176)

The tale of demonic possession remains a remarkable accom-plishment, a schlock movie premise which was given a big budget and major studio Hollywood treatment, and regurgitated every bit of class and polish that was put into it. Some of the performances have always been problematic and some of the movie's pacing now seems dated, but it is still an exciting and unnerving drama. Of all the horror film subjects, demonic possession seems the most nightmarishly palpable because it lacks a physical antagonist—it's the hardest to shake when you wake up, because who's to say the danger has left? The film tapped directly into these fears, using language that would still give the **South Park** kids pause and hoary special effects tricks that would be difficult to duplicate even in the age of CGI, while retaining the red carpet production values one associates with the grandest studio films.

The original, standard release is in cropped format on one side and letterboxed on the other, with the 1.85:1 letterboxing providing a bit more picture information on the sides and less on the top and bottom than the cropped version. The letterboxing has an accommodation for enhanced 16:9 playback. The image framing on the letterboxing, however, is much better balanced and nicer to look at, making the 1973 horror film even more exciting than it already is. Curiously, the audio is in standard stereo only on the letterboxed side, but has a 5-channel Dolby Digital track on the full screen side, with the Dolby Digital mix providing more detail and energy to the audio track. The DVD has English, French and Spanish subtitles and a few production notes. There is also a theatrical trailer, if you can call it that—it is just the still image that is used in all the advertising, accompanied by voiceover teaser copy that doesn't sound original.

The standard release is superseded by the *Special Edition 25th Anniversary* release, which features a remastered presentation of the film with a remastered Dolby Digital soundtrack, and all the supplementary features you could ever hope for. The picture is in letterboxed only, with an aspect ratio of about 1.85:1 and an accommodation for enhanced 16:9 playback. The letterboxing has a bit more picture information on the sides of the image in comparison to the letterboxing on the earlier release. The color transfers on the two DVDs are very different, yet both seem valid, although there are, ultimately, fewer flaws on the new transfer. The older version has starker colors and is brighter, with purer whites. The newer version has darker contrasts and warmer, softer colors. In some sequences, such as the dream montage, the older version is more colorful and more rewarding, but usually the shadows on the newer version are preferable to the overlit image on the older version, and fleshtones—at least during indoor sequences—are richer.

With its new mix, the stereo surround sound and Dolby Digital sound have more dimensionality and a stronger ambiance. While there is something to be said for the harsh focus of the film's original audio track, the embellishments provided by contemporary audio playback are highly rewarding. The program is also available in French in mono (with Jeanne Moreau voicing the Mercedes McCambridge lines) and can be supported by English or French subtitles ("Vous n'êtes pas ma mère").

The 122 minute film is presented on one side, opening with a mildly annoying introduction by director William Friedkin (this is the sort of film that one does not wish to be distracted from, even in the first frame). The film has two separate commentary tracks, one by Friedkin and one by author and screenwriter William Peter Blatty. Friedkin talks about the shoot (Pazuzu got shipped to the wrong country!), about the fights he had casting the film, and about the film's themes. Instead of getting into how the effects in the end were achieved, however, he sort of falls into a play-by-play description of the film's final act. He also gives you the address of the house and the stairs, if you're ever visiting Georgetown. Blatty talks for about an hour, describing the circumstances that led up to his writing of the novel and his initial hassles selling the film to Hollywood. He talks extensively about his belief in the factual basis for the film and about the disagreements he had over the movie's ending. After his talk is over, about 12 minutes of the original recordings of Linda Blair and McCambridge reciting the dialogue during the possession sequences are played, McCambridge making Yoko Ono sound like Doris Day.

On side two of the *Special Edition*, there is a 75 minute retrospective documentary that contains a number of interesting segments, including a **Casablanca** ending that isn't all that good (although Blatty is broken hearted that it wasn't included); a very good 'explanation' of what is happening that occurs while the two priests are resting on the staircase, and a terrific piece where Linda Blair's character descends a staircase while bent over backwards (it wasn't included because they couldn't get the scene's emotional transition right—as they are sitting for the interview, they suddenly figure out how it should have been done); Blair's screen test; and behind-the-scenes footage of how the makeup and effects tricks were staged. There are interviews with all the main cast members (although, in one of the documentary's few shortcomings, little is said about Lee J. Cobb), a discussion of the real case upon which Blatty based his book, a look at the locations and how they appear today, and many other interesting pieces of trivia. The documentary runs longer than abridged version that appeared on other home video media. Also included on the side is a complete version of the unused ending, a 3 minute montage of production sketches, further interview clips with Friedkin and Blatty (some of what they say is duplicated on the commentary track), TV commercials (including a marvelous 'audience reaction' clip in which a young woman appears to have undergone a very satisfying experience watching the film), and several trailers, including one for *Exorcist II* and one very startling black-and-white strobe piece.

Exposed TV's Lifeguard Babes (Simitar, 7233)

About a half dozen models wiggle around in a standing position in various states of undress at the beach and, between wiggles, brag about having been hired as extras on *Baywatch*, a dubious career goal at best. Movement is smooth, and the colors are good. The program runs an hour. The sound is adequate and is not captioned.

Exposure X-rated (Vivid, UPC#0073215551)

Fleshtones are rich, hues are bright and the image is sharp. The narrative is also very effective, a spin-off of **Disclosure**, about an advertising executive saddled with an evil female boss, and the erotic sequences are energetic. The sound is passable, though there is some buffeting in one sequence and extraneous background noise in another. The 70 minute program features Celeste, Jenna Jameson, Anna Malle and Rebecca Bardoux. The DVD contains alternate angle sequences and elaborate hardcore interactive promotional features.

Extreme Sex X-rated (Vivid, UPC#0073214496)

A couple returns to their favorite restaurant on their anniversary, unaware that the place has been sold and turned into an S&M dungeon. There are about a half dozen erotic sequences, each exploring a different fetish and, as a result, the program content is at least a little different from the standard Vivid release. The picture quality looks fine, with generally accurate colors and a sharp focus. The sound is okay. The 75 minute program contains alternate angle sequences and elaborate hardcore interactive promotional features.

The Eye of the Serpent (Simitar, 7309)

A leather and sword concoction from 1992, the indoor sequences are shot with dark backgrounds to avoid the need to dress the sets, but there are a lot of outdoor scenes that were shot in the woods somewhere to make up for it. The hero gets caught in a battle between two sisters and falls in love with the daughter of the less evil of the two, though all the women have the hots for him. The film's one redeeming aspect is that its numerous fight scenes are astutely edited, and from the foundation of entertainment these sequences provide, the softcore sex, silly conversations and S&M battle gear are supported in all their engaging dumbness. The picture on the 85 minute program is soft looking and fleshtones are a little dull. We couldn't tell if the sound was stereo or mono, but it is a fairly basic mix either way, with a limited dynamic range. Three is no captioning.

F

Face/Off (Paramount, 154957)

John Travolta and Nicolas Cage star as the good guy and the bad guy, switching roles after the first act in an unlikely but fully workable sci-fi plot turn that changes the movie into *Freaky Friday* on speed. John Woo directed the film, and where one is normally a bit impatient with Woo's dramatic scenes, anxious for another action sequence to start up, here it is the action sequences that seem in the way. Both Travolta and Cage have a grand time, and they communicate the concept of the switch so well that every aspect of it is loaded with feeling and imagination. The term, 'mindless action film,' is commonly appropriate for a summer blockbuster, where expensive explosions mean more than the plot being used to detonate them, but **Face/Off** is an action film that thrives on thought without shortchanging the gunplay.

The picture on the DVD is presented in letterboxed format, with an aspect ratio of about 2.35:1 and an accommodation for enhanced 16:9 playback. The image is super crisp and hues are deep. The stereo surround sound is bland, but the menu-activated Dolby Digital track is closer in quality and delivers the film's outstanding audio mix effectively. The 140 minute feature is also available in French in standard stereo and can be supported by English or Spanish subtitles. There is a terrific theatrical teaser, sporting a sequence shot expressly for it with John Travolta.

Faces (Pioneer, PSE99100)

Overly laudatory jacket copy claims the 1968 John Cassavetes classic is one of "two or three supreme masterworks in all of American film." Hardly. The second half is very good, however, and while the first half comes across as an indulgent mess in need of substantial trimming, that was basically how Cassavetes made all his films and viewers are sort of required to take the chaff with the grain.

John Marley—you know, the guy who wakes up with the horse head in *The Godfather*—stars as an executive who, in classic 'middle age crisis' form, decides to leave his wife, played by Lynn Carlin, because he has become infatuated with a good time girl/prostitute, played by Gena Rowlands. To assuage her anguish, Carlin's character also has an affair, and then tries to commit suicide. It is the second half of the movie, which cuts back and forth between the romantic adventures of the husband and the wife, that imparts a legitimate emotional power, perhaps because the narrative actually has a goal. The first half is spent establishing the characters, but it is aimless and contrived. The performers talk unconvincingly about nothing, shift moods for no discernible reason and interact without really seeing one another.

The focus in every decade since the invention of television has been on the young, since they are the ones marketers want so desperately to reach. One thing that **Faces** accomplishes quite well is its portrait of middle aged adults in the Sixties—shy or embarrassed when it came to the sexual revolution, intimidated by the lack of automatic power that accompanied their elevated but matured status and frustrated that the young were getting all the attention. At its best, the film is about spiritual impotency, for it is with that theme that the 1968 feature becomes a portrait and not just a product of its times.

The black-and-white picture is presented in full screen format and the framing looks fine. The image is very grainy and accompanied by a number of scratches and other damage, but one of the film's legacies is that it was shot very inexpensively—even by guerrilla filmmaking Sixties standards—and so the wear and the strain

are part of the art. It should be noted that the grain is extremely crisp and contrasts are superbly detailed (even when the movie itself is almost completely washed out), so it is doubtful one has ever come across a copy of the film that looks quite as good. The monophonic sound is okay, too. The 130 minute program is not captioned.

Fahrenheit 451 (Universal, ID4231USDVD)

The letterboxing has an aspect ratio of about 1.85:1 and no 16:9 enhancement, adding picture information to the sides of the image in comparison to the cropped presentations and losing nothing on the top or bottom. The colors are bright and the image is solid. Virtually every shot (Nicolas Roeg did the cinematography) is stunning for both its composition and its clarity. The monophonic sound is a bit weak, but the Dolby Digital mono track strong and clean, presenting Bernard Herrmann's score, the dialogue and sound effects with an engaging immediacy. The audio slips out of synch during one brief, jerky shot about three quarters of the way into the film, but the anomaly also occurs on the LD and is either a flaw in the source material or a deliberate manipulation on the part of the filmmakers. The 112 minute feature is closed captioned.

The best DVDs bring a fresh perspective and enhanced appreciation to the films they represent and **Fahrenheit 451** is an excellent example of how this is so. We had the opportunity to re-read Ray Bradbury's novel upon which the 1966 film is based and we were shocked to discover how poorly written it was. The prose is awkward, scenes advance clumsily, the characters are blandly conceived and important concepts (such as how everyone learned to read in the first place) are not explained. Like most people, we were probably so taken by the novel's ideas in our adolescence that the mechanics of the writing didn't matter.

François Truffaut's film is, in this regard, quite the opposite. It is an exquisite exercise in cinematic technique, and to this effect the new DVD is outstanding, because it magnifies the film's strongest assets, leaving the viewer transfixed by every scene. The film's central idea, on the other hand, is rather silly. Bradbury wrote the book in part as a reaction to what the Nazis had done in Germany and to contemporary totalitarianism, but on a literal level the concept—firemen burning books; people memorizing books to preserve them—is rather ridiculous. The purity of the DVD, however, brings out the film's subtexts. The sensory input is so vivid that you become aware of every nuance and detail, and Truffaut had retained enough allusions to an alternate interpretation—that this entire world is the hero's delusion (the most obvious clue is the casting of Julie Christie in a dual role as the two female leads)—to prevent an alert viewer from dismissing the film's premise out of hand.

Fair Game (Warner, 14072)

William Baldwin co-stars with Cindy Crawford (his girlfriend in the movie's first scene is Salma Hayek—some guys have all the luck) as a cop protecting a witness from hell-bent assassins—the 1995 movie is based upon the same story that inspired the Sylvester Stallone feature **Cobra**. Crawford's acting has been highly criticized, but that is primarily people picking on her because she's beautiful. To be sure, she has a very limited range, but her performance is not distracting the way a really bad performance can be, and the camera loves her. Once the action starts, who cares?

The picture is presented in full screen format, losing a tidbit from the sides and adding picture information to the top and bottom in comparison to letterboxed presentations. The framing is adequate. Overall, the picture is sharp. While there is still a bit of haze in places, the colors are reasonably strong and the image appealing. The stereo surround sound is strong, and there is a Dolby Digital track that even better, with clearer tones, better detail and a more encompassing dimensionality. The 91 minute feature also has a French soundtrack in standard stereo and is effectively closed captioned.

Fallen (Warner, T6434)

In **Fallen**, there is one memorable scene where the hero, a police detective played by Denzel Washington, realizes that the villain, an unseen evil spirit, is passing from person to person in his office by touch, and he follows the being out to the street entirely by observing the changes in the people the being is passing through. But how can you fight invisible evil? You can't, and that is ultimately the problem with **Fallen**, which is a fairly routine exercise in supernatural thrillers. For mindless entertainment it has enough going on to stay interesting, but it only addresses deeper issues peripherally and the premise is too confined by its own logic to give the hero much of a chance. John Goodman and Donald Sutherland co-star.

The 1998 film is presented on one side in letterboxed format, with an aspect ratio of about 2.35:1 and an accommodation for enhanced 16:9 playback, and on the other side in cropped format. The cropped image is workable, but the widescreen image is preferable. The picture quality is very good, with consistently stable colors in all lighting conditions and a crisp focus. The stereo surround sound is okay, and the Dolby Digital track is more enjoyable, with better defined separations and more energy. The 125 minute program is also available in French in standard stereo and can be accompanied by English, French or Spanish subtitles. There is a cast & crew profile section, a skimpy production notes section, and a theatrical trailer.

There is also a pretty good commentary track by director Gregory Hoblit, writer Nicholas Kazan and producer Charles Roven. They talk in detail about the production, the problems they encountered (Sutherland didn't like having the writer on the set, and he didn't want squibs going off on his forehead), and what they were trying to achieve. The sense we get from the whole thing, however, is that those who were reading the script for the first time and had no idea what to expect were far more engaged by the story than those who have been bombarded with its marketing.

Falling in Love Again (Simitar, 7355)

The two-tiered story shows a married couple going through a mid-life crisis while their memories flash back to when they first met as teenagers. Elliott Gould and Susannah York portray the couple in the 1981 film, with Michelle Pfeiffer (billed as her introductory role) giving a flawless performance as York's younger self—they don't seem like two different actresses. The film itself is a mix of mildly amusing nostalgia and predictable drama, but Pfeiffer makes it fairly worthwhile. The colors look a little aged and the image is rather soft. The monophonic sound is a bit strained but coherent, and there is a Michel Legrand musical score. The film is not captioned.

The Fan (Columbia TriStar, 82475/9)

A star vehicle that will entertain the undemanding viewer—though by the end the plot gets fairly silly—it stars Robert De Niro and Wesley Snipes. De Niro plays his typical psycho assassin part and Snipes is a baseball star who is the object of his murderous obsession. Directed by Tony Scott, the 1996 film is slick-looking and energetically paced, and while no one will mistake it for art, the first half is promising, with clearly drawn characters and well-defined dilemmas. The necessity of raising the dramatic tension to big budget proportions, however, sends the film down a fairly loony path (the villain demands the hero hit a home run for him), and the plot spends more time working itself out of a corner than being interesting.

The picture is presented on one side in letterboxed format, with aspect ratio of about 2.35:1 and an accommodation for enhanced 16:9 playback, and is in cropped format on the other side. The colors are crisp and solid, and the glossy image looks terrific. The stereo surround sound and Dolby Digital sound have plenty of power, though the separation mix isn't all that interesting. The 116 minute program also has French and Spanish language tracks and optional English and Spanish subtitles.

Fantastic Planet (Anchor Bay, DV10702)

The superb 1973 animated feature by René Laloux is set on another world, where humans are small and kept as pets by large blue-skinned creatures. The hero is one such pet, who gets a hold of his master's learning machine and eventually leads a rebellion. The final act of the 78 minute film is somewhat rushed—political problems forced the movie's production to be moved from Czechoslovakia to France—but it doesn't compromise the story. The film's images are phantasmagorical. As the hero wanders across the planet's landscape, there are many creatures and plants that interact with strange ecologies, sometimes contributing directly to the narrative and sometimes just passing as an incidental piece of imagination.

The presentation letterboxed with an aspect ratio of about 1.66:1 and no 16:9 enhancement. The colors look terrific and the image is sharp. There are monophonic audio tracks in both French and English, but unfortunately, they are accompanied by permanent English subtitles. The sound is stronger on the French track and a little fuzzy overall, but the English track is workable.

In addition to the main feature, three Laloux animated shorts have also been included. The best, *Les Escargots (The Snails)* from 1965, is an 11 minute effort about gigantic snails that attack mankind. The other two are more esoteric and dark, with very simple animation. *Les Dents Du Singe (Monkey's Teeth)* from 1960, uses painted images with clear brush strokes to evoke nightmarish images of dentistry, with people, as teeth, being plucked from life, while a dark monkey hovers in the background. It runs 14 minutes. Equally weird, *Les Temps Morts (Dead Times)* from 1964, uses mostly camera pans across pen and ink drawings, though there is some block figure movement in places. The ten minute short is a rumination on the human propensity for death. All three are in French with English subtitling, although dialogue is sparse.

Fantasy Lane X-rated (Vivid, UPC#0073214573)

A guy doesn't believe this girl has a French boyfriend, because every time they're supposed to meet something gets messed up and they miss each other. That's all the plot there is, but the performers are attractive and the erotic sequences are well staged. The picture looks okay. Colors are not intense, but they are reasonably strong and the image is only a bit soft. The monophonic sound has a lot of buffeting and is best held to a modest volume. The 71 minute program features Leslie Glass, Chloe and Ruby. The DVD also contains alternate angle sequences and elaborate hardcore interactive promotional features.

Far and Away (Universal, 20212)

There aren't enough subplots to make **Far and Away** an epic, but it is an enjoyable historical adventure with a larger sweep than most films can afford. Directed by Ron Howard, the movie stars Tom Cruise with his Ryan O'Neal-style Irish accent, and Nicole Kidman, who is at times quite delightful. Set a century ago, the film has three sections, one in Ireland, one in Boston and one in Oklahoma. The plot moves forward patiently from one learning experience to the next, though with less zest than the characters deserve. Thanks to the good nature of the filmmakers, however, it is easier to like the movie for what it is than to disdain it for what it is not.

The presentation is letterboxed, with an aspect ratio of about 2.38:1 and an accommodation for enhanced 16:9 playback. The cinematography holds down the colors until the heroes reach the West. Contrasts seem a little subdued in places and, even in the final segment, some shots are duller than others, but on the whole the image presentation is workable. The stereo surround sound is a little flatter than the Dolby Digital sound, but the mix seems about the same. There is a decent amount of rear channel activity, but it is not elaborately detailed. The 140 minute film is also available in French and Spanish in standard surround and comes with English or Spanish subtitles. There is a good production essay, a brief cast profile section and a theatrical trailer.

Fargo (PolyGram, 8006386932)

The off-beat crime film from Joel and Ethan Coen seems to capture with perfection the rhythms and inanities of real life, managing almost magically to bend them into a coherent crime drama. To some viewers, the film will seem hysterically funny, and to others it will seem weird and pointless. The humor comes from what the filmmakers choose to emphasize and how that contrasts with the relative seriousness of the subject. The Muzak in restaurant sequences, for example, is always just a bit too prominent on the soundtrack, drawing attention to its artlessness and the absurdity of its presence as a replacement for a genuine film score.

William H. Macy stars as a car salesman whose embezzlements are about to catch up to him. He arranges his wife's kidnapping to put a squeeze on his father-in-law, but the inept kidnappers leave a trail of blood in the wake of the abduction. It is up to a very pregnant small town sheriff, played by Oscar-winner Frances McDormand, to piece things together and stop the criminals. Set in early winter in Minnesota and North Dakota, the characters speak with strong north-midwestern (Scandinavian-based) accents and the landscape has a desolate, half-civilized feel, even when the action moves to a larger city. The focus on realistic details—the kind of details, like the effects of the sheriff's pregnancy, that have no direct bearing on the plot but provide the essence of the film's atmosphere—gives **Fargo** its humor and a potential for extensive repeat viewings.

The picture is presented in cropped format on one side and letterboxed, with an aspect ratio of about 1.85:1 and no 16:9 enhancement, on the other. The letterboxing masks a very small amount of picture off the top and bottom, but adds substantially to the sides in comparison to the cropped version. On both, textures are incredibly vivid and colors are rich. The stereo surround sound is passable. The 98 minute program comes with English, Spanish or French subtitles, along with a cast profile section. There are also theatrical trailers for **Fargo** and several other PolyGram releases.

The Fatal Hour (see **Mr. Wong Collection**)

Fatal Pursuit (Image, ID4759DRDVD)

Somebody named L.P. Brown gives an absolutely awful performance as the hero. Shannon Whirry is an insurance agent attempting to recover some stolen diamonds in New Orleans and Brown is the local investigator assigned to assist her. His line readings are so flat and so halting they stop the movie dead, and it is only his equally awkward mannerisms and pathetic fighting skills that save the film, since they are so bad they provide a constant humor. There is enough narrative to keep the 103 minute feature grinding forward. Our favorite moment; a character speaks French to Brown and Brown replies in such a way that it is clear he doesn't know a word of the language, yet he then turns to Whirry and provides a perfect translation of what was just said. Malcolm McDowell is the bad guy.

The picture is soft, with some weak contrasts and dull fleshtones, though other hues are reasonably bright. The stereo sound has a very limited dimensionality and a weak upper end. The 103 minute program is not captioned.

Father of the Bride (Buena Vista, 16322)

Although we laughed and cried through much of the 1991 remake, we still found it to be both nasty and unfeeling in comparison to the Vincente Minnelli classic upon which it is based. The differences in the two films seem to highlight the reasons why older Hollywood films are so special and so seemingly unreclaimable. Where the older film played delicately on the emotional bonds that held the family together, and characterized the father's misgivings with little more than a stuttering "harrumph," the newer film is abrasive and literal. The star, Steve Martin, is reasonably successful in his verbal and physical slapstick, and he carries his success into

the emotions of the story's conclusion smoothly, but the humor, and indeed the entire movie, is no longer virginal.

The picture transfer is a substantial improvement over the picture on the LD. The LD was quite grainy with pinkish colors. The image on the DVD is free of grain and looks smooth, with pure whites, bright hues and accurate fleshtones. The picture is letterboxed, with an aspect ratio of about 1.85:1 and no 16:9 enhancement, adding a smidgen to the sides of the image and masking off a little from the top and bottom compared to the letterboxed LD, which had a 1.75:1 aspect ratio. The framing looks a bit tight during close-ups, but is otherwise presentable. The stereo surround sound is adequate. The 105 minute film also has a French audio track and can be supported by optional English subtitles. There is a theatrical trailer, as well.

Father's Day (Warner, 15386)

Robin Williams and Billy Crystal are teamed in the flaccid box office failure. Based on a French film that was quite humorous, the movie has enough sequences of individual clowning to make a viewing or two worth one's while, but the movie seems to take as many wrong turns (the farther it moves away from its source) as right ones. Williams and Crystal portray strangers informed by a woman that they may be the father of a teenage boy who has run away from home. They get roped into tracking him down, learning about friendship and responsibility themselves in the process. The film tries to get a lot of mileage out of having the pair mistaken for pederasts, and also spends an undue amount of time with a secondary character, who is trapped in a portable outhouse. Williams and Crystal improvise like crazy when they're given the chance, but even those scenes have a kind of contrived, stagey feel. The film is benign and tries hard to be liked, so fans of the stars, at least, won't be turned off by it, but it is a secondary effort with little beyond the dream casting to make it unique.

The program is in letterboxed format on one side, with an aspect ratio of about 2.35:1 and an accommodation for enhanced 16:9 playback, and in cropped format on the other side. The cropped presentation, often cutting into the body language of at least one of the stars, is useless. The color transfer looks great, with crisp hues and accurate fleshtones. The stereo surround sound and Dolby Digital sound are dull, though the film's sound mix is not important enough for it to matter. The 99 minute program is accompanied by English, French or Spanish subtitles, along with a decent cast profile section and a couple of production notes. There is also a theatrical trailer, which is presented in cropped format on the cropped side and slightly letterboxed on the letterboxed side, that doesn't even use the film's best gags to try and sell the movie.

Fawcett, Farrah (see **Playboy: Farrah Fawcett: All of Me**)

Fear (Universal, 20393)

William Peterson stars as a concerned father who doesn't like his daughter's new boyfriend, played by Mark Wahlberg. Up to a point, the film is thoughtful, and you could almost put the program on Pause in a couple places and lead a lively discussion about what the father should or should not do. After all, almost everybody is going to lose their virginity at some point. The boyfriend, however, turns out to be an even worse psycho than the father could have imagined, and the film throws logic, emotional validity and any pretense of seriousness out the window (and, in the end, the boyfriend, also) in a vain attempt to generate some marketable thrills.

The picture is letterboxed with an aspect ratio of about 2.35:1 and an accommodation for enhanced 16:9 playback. The colors are strong and the image looks good, with accurate fleshtones and crisp, glossy hues. The stereo surround sound is dull and although the Dolby Digital track is reasonably energetic, not even it can equal the impact of the LD's standard track, which was exceptionally good. The 97 minute program is also available in French in standard stereo and can be supported by English or Spanish subtitles. There are some production notes, a cast and director profile section and a theatrical trailer.

The Fear (Simitar, 7316)

A group of college students spending the weekend at a house in the woods—a common situation in this sort of film—are terrorized by a large wooden statue. Apparently, they forgot to bring matches. The 96 minute film isn't bad for its genre. There is one fairly good scare and a general atmosphere of uneasiness. The picture presentation is passable, with reasonably bright, solid colors and workable fleshtones. The Ultra-Stereo sound is unsophisticated but adequate, and is not captioned.

Fear and Loathing in Las Vegas (Universal, 20339)

Based on the writing of Hunter S. Thompson, the film, directed by Terry Gilliam, is almost painful to watch unless one's mind is numbed by drugs beforehand. Set in 1971, the narrative follows Thompson on a reporting assignment in Vegas that was largely distracted by his chemical indulgences. Johnny Depp's interpretation of Thompson seems very mechanical, and while Depp may have based his performance on the time he spent with the real Thompson, he doesn't convey the voice Thompson achieved on the written page. Many of the finest passages in Thompson's writing are repeated on the voiceover narration, including a lyrical elegy to the end of San Francisco's counter-cultural dawn, but Depp's mannerisms are so clowningly stiff he's less real than a Doonesbury drawing. And because Thompson wrote in the first person, there is a sense in his writing that even though he's digesting all those drugs he's still smarter than you, but with the outside perspective that comes in a film adaptation, you see how ridiculous he looks and his words carry less weight. What Gilliam should have done was take more liberties with the source and play up his own forte, the hallucinations (which are actually, after a promising start, rather scant), but the film deteriorates into comically postured rantings and ravings, and one feels neither fear nor loathing watching them, only apathy.

There are a collection of deleted scenes, but the only thing they get you thinking is how much more of the movie should have been trimmed. Generally, the scenes depict slightly more sober moments, but they remain within the spirit of the film. There is also a black-and-white segment that is left unexplained but appears to be a prologue of some sort, parodying old-fashioned government information films. There is an optimistic 'making of' featurette, along with the standard production essay, a very short cast and director profile section, and a trailer, all exclusive to the DVD.

The picture is letterboxed with an aspect ratio of about 2.3:1 and an accommodation for enhanced 16:9 playback. Some of the creatively lit casino interiors are a little grainy, but generally the colors are solid and bright, and fleshtones are accurate. The image is sharp and colors are well detailed. The picture looks very crisp. The stereo surround sound is slightly subdued but workable. The 119 minute film can be supported by English, Spanish or French subtitles ("El circo/casino es donde todo el mundo pasaría los sábados si hubieran ganado los nazis").

Fearless (Warner, 12986)

The picture on Peter Weir's enigmatic 1993 feature is in cropped format, losing picture information on the sides in comparison to the 1.85:1 letterboxed LD and adding nothing to the top or bottom. The film's emotions are delicately nuanced and any interference with the Weir's vision—such as cropping, duh—upsets the balance of the drama. Jeff Bridges and Rosie Perez are survivors of an airliner crash who have trouble coping with their grief. Some viewers will be unable to get past the concept of random tragedy, but those who can open themselves to the film's emotional explorations will find the drama to be exceedingly moving, though more so when you can see the whole picture.

Other than the cropping, the image transfer looks okay. Fleshtones are adequate, other hues are reasonably bright and the image

is sharp. The stereo surround sound is solid and some of the separation effects are rather eerie. The 122 minute program has a alternate French audio track and English captioning.

Fearless Hyena (Simitar, 7237)

The comedy sequences are satisfying and the fight choreography is impressive. In fact, the 96 minute film, which was directed by Jackie Chan, who also stars, has no more than a nominal plot (the hero must train before seeking vengeance after his grandfather is killed, having attracted the killers when he shows off his initial fighting skills to earn money), with each fight scene going on much longer than would be necessary for the narrative, leading the viewer to surmise, rather quickly, that it is the choreography and not the story that is the purpose of the film. Some sequences, however, are quite humorous, and Chan does one fight in drag. Though it is milked for all it is worth, the fight choreography is consistently elaborate and inventive.

The film is presented in English on one track and Cantonese on another. The dubbing is Australian, however, which seems especially disorienting. The monophonic sound is always fairly rough, with warped or muffled music, and the Cantonese track doesn't sound all that much better. The picture is cropped. The source material is relatively free of damage and the color transfer is passable on the 1979 production. The program is not captioned.

Fearless Hyena II (Simitar, 7238)

The first 40 minutes of the 1983 Jackie Chan film, directed by Chan Chuen, make almost no sense at all. While it is possible that the 94 minute film has been trimmed from a longer running time, it is more likely that budgetary restrictions dictated its confused structure. Nevertheless, the individual sequences are creative and a story does finally materialize, coalescing the seemingly disconnected elements into a coherent conclusion. Chan portrays the son of a man being sought by two nasty bad guys, who are also after the man's brother and are intent upon wiping out his clan. Chan's character and his cousin are the younger generation—seemingly frivolous but ready to pick up the slack when the villains finally locate them. Despite the cropping, which adds to the confusion, the movie is fairly entertaining and the fight scenes are creative.

The presentation is cropped, but the colors are reasonably strong. The film is awkwardly dubbed in English on one channel and presented in the original Cantonese on another, without subtitles. It is accompanied by a brief interview with Chan, as well as a Chan profile and filmography.

Felicity Lott in Recital (Image, ID5037GCDVD)

A genuine chamber in a French castle is the setting for the vocal and chamber orchestra concert. Lott only appears for the first 20 minutes of the 86 minute program, singing five songs by Maurice Jaubert and one song by Ernst Chasson, accompanied by The Paris Kammerensemble conducted by Armin Jordan. The ensemble then performs Richard Wagner's *Siegfried Idyll* and Johannes Brahms' *Serenade No. 1*.

The picture quality is excellent. The image is letterboxed with an aspect ratio of about 1.75:1 and no 16:9 enhancement. Colors are bright and precise, and the image is crisp. The stereo sound is fine, although dimensionality is limited.

The setting is marvelous, and the camera is free to get as intimate with the musicians as it pleases. Lott's vocal performance is steady and assured, and Jordan's guidance of the orchestra is adept.

Felix! (SlingShot, DVD1297)

The artwork is simple and the program will mostly be of interest to collectors, but the cartoons are often witty and imaginative. Four cartoons are silent—the earliest, *Feline Follies*, was made in 1918—accompanied by an unobtrusive contemporary piano soundtrack. Three others, produced in 1928 and 1930, have original monaural soundtracks that are moderately scratchy but acceptable. The black-and-white cartoons have a few markings on them but are in generally good condition. There is also a brief silent documentary segment, *Otto Messmer at Work*, showing how animated drawings are produced. Those who are interested in the history of film animation will find the collection includes valuable examples of the development of cartoon humor. *Follies*, the oldest cartoon, contains many inter-titles, while several others use balloon dialogue. It is not until the sound cartoons, in fact, that the animation on the disc is freed from the necessity of dialogue. From the very beginning, however, the cartoons achieve their strongest humor on the strength of characterization, and even as this is supplemented later on by elaborate fantasy gags, it is the impish enthusiasm of the feline hero that draws the viewer into the adventures.

Felix the Cat (see Presenting Felix the Cat)

Fetishes (Simitar, 7412)

A surprisingly good 1996 documentary about an S&M bordello, by Nick Broomfield, is loaded with titillating sequences, but it also filled with plain, clear psychological explorations of both the clients and the women who dominate them. Broomfield even visits the apartments where the women live, to peel away their facades. The 87 minute program has a gratifying, straightforward structure. Broomfield basically talked his way into hanging out in the place for several weeks, and then got not only the women but the clients to open up in interviews, explaining why their activities appeal to them and the practical details involved in their activities.

The picture is somewhat grainy and washed out, but that is from the documentary cinematography. Colors are adequate and the image presentation is workable, although because of the grain, digital artifacting is a bit more prevalent than usual. The monophonic sound is okay and the program is not captioned.

A Few Good Men (Columbia TriStar, 27895/9)

The 138 minute program has been squeezed onto one side in letterboxed format, with an aspect ratio of about 2.4:1 and an accommodation for enhanced 16:9 playback, and in full screen format on the other side. Since much of the film is conversation, however, artifacting appears to be minimal.

Tom Cruise, Jack Nicholson and Demi Moore star in the highly enjoyable military courtroom drama, along with a number of other accomplished performers. Ideally executed, the title is rich in the sort of dramatic turns and revelations that a viewer can watch over and over, making the disc a strong candidate for extensive repeat viewing.

The picture transfer looks fine. Fleshtones are not always distinct, and some solid colors contain a mild instability, but for the most part the image is bright and crisp. The stereo surround sound is fine, although the mix has no unique moments. The program also comes with French and Spanish audio tracks, optional Spanish and Korean subtitles, and English closed captioning.

Fiddler on the Roof (MGM, 906728)

The letterboxing has an aspect ratio of about 2.35:1, with an accommodation for enhanced 16:9 playback. The color transfer is excellent, though it must be remembered that the movie, for all its widescreen glory, does try to evoke the grimy realities of a poor Russian farm community. The standard stereo soundtrack is dull, while the Dolby Digital track has greater separation detail and more power. The 179 minute film can be supported by English, French or Spanish subtitles ("Il y aurait un long escalier juste pour monter/Et un plus long pour descendre/Et un autre ne menant nulle part, juste pour épater") and comes with a theatrical trailer. There is an interwoven commentary track by director Norman Jewison and the star, Topol, in which they talk, separately, about the production, the other cast & crew members, and what they wanted to accomplish with the film. They talk about their backgrounds, about putting the production together and about various technical aspects to the shoot, such as how the cast was induced to

move in rhythm to the music even during minor shots. They talk about the other cast members, and about the film's subject and background. Jewison explains why he didn't hire Zero Mostel (his stage performance was geared more for comedy and Jewison didn't want that for the movie), which shots were specifically inspired by the paintings of Marc Chagall and how the film was able to expand upon the stage version. One sequence he points to somewhat proudly, a shot of the Cossacks getting ready to raid the village during the wedding, is justified by suggesting that it adds realism to the proceedings, preparing the viewer for the forthcoming disaster. What Jewison fails to recognize, however, is that by doing so he takes away the intimation that the Cossack attack might be a punishment from above incurred when the women and men began to dance together.

The film is a magnificent accomplishment. A sometimes bittersweet but uplifting celebration of Jewish culture, the film extends beyond a specific ethnic appeal to explore the universal bonds and conflicts between parents and their children, and how the sometimes immutable laws of tradition are used to manage that eternal relationship. How we wish, though, that we could watch **Fiddler on the Roof** as one reads Hebrew, from back to front, beginning with the drawn-out sadness of the conclusion and working up to the best songs—which all come in the first half—and then climaxing with the spine-tingling, heart-pounding opening montage. A break with tradition, to be sure, but in Hollywood musicals even pogroms should have happy endings.

The Field (Pioneer, DVD68965)

An almost unrecognizable Richard Harris earned an Oscar nomination for his portrayal of an elderly farmer who wants to obtain a parcel of land at any cost. The 1991 film offers a rather dreary look at poverty and bitterness in rural Ireland, and while the narrative has a number of limitations, the film's sociological portrait is involving. The similarities to the much happier **Quiet Man**, incidentally, are too numerous to seem coincidental (both involve haggling over farmland). Jim Sheridan directed, and Tom Berenger co-stars, as the American. The picture is presented in full screen format and is fairly grainy, with subdued colors and pale fleshtones. The music and sound effects have a mild dimensionality, but the film's stereo mix is limited. The dialogue is sometimes difficult to make out, even when Berenger is speaking, and to make matters worse, the 113 minute program is not captioned.

Fierce Creatures (Universal, 20144)

We were excited during the opening credits. The color quality was a marked improvement over the LD, with more accurate fleshtones and deeper hues, and the standard stereo surround sound was about equal to the LD's audio track, with a Dolby Digital track that came across even a little stronger. But, as soon as the credits were over, the letterboxed image disappeared and the film filled up the whole TV screen, losing nearly half of its widescreen image. What good is a comedy if you can't see the reaction and background business, especially with the zoo financial takeover story in **Fierce Creatures**, which is filled with secondary characters and animals cavorting humorously beyond the center of the screen's attention?

For the record, the 94 minute program also has French and Spanish language tracks in standard stereo, optional English or Spanish subtitles, a decent cast-and-directors profile section, production notes that include an explanation as to why the film had two directors, and a theatrical trailer. Jamie Lee Curtis, Kevin Kline and Monty Python alumni star. The film is dedicated to both Gerald Durrell and Peter Cook, and is an ideal blend of their two spirits. The animals are adorable, the comedy is ribald but clean, and the performers are all wonderful clowns who seem to be having a great time fooling around with the creatures and with each other, when you can see them.

5th Day of Peace (Simitar, 7236)

A 1972 Italian-Yugoslavian co-production with an international cast, Richard Johnson, Franco Nero and Bud Spencer are featured in the film about a Canadian officer coping with German POWs at the end of WWII. The Germans accuse two of their number of being deserters, and the Allied officers must decide if they should allow the Germans to execute the pair. The music is by Ennio Morricone.

The transfer is extremely weak. The film was not shot in widecreen, but cropping still makes everything seem tight. The colors are drained and the image has a cloudy, smeary appearance. Video skips and large rectangular irregularities are also common place. Since the 102 minute film has an international cast, there is no language that it could be presented in without dubbing. The lip movements match the English dialogue in some sequences, but not others. The monophonic sound is muffled and there is a bad buzz at the 40:49 mark.

The Fifth Element (Columbia TriStar, 82409)

Luc Besson's dopey sci-fi spectacle is deliberately comical and perhaps, to its credit, never takes itself too seriously, which is just as well since the seen-it-on-Star-Trek-a-dozen-times plot, about some big thing heading towards Earth, doesn't amount to much. Bruce Willis is a cab driver who has to retrieve several important bricks before the thing gets here in order to save the planet. The more complicated and empty the plot becomes, the more Besson starts adding comedy, particularly a clownish black transvestite-like TV reporter, played by Chris Tucker, to leaven the mood. The special effect sequences, though, have 'demo' written all over them. They are fabulously cluttered with movement and imagination. The film also has plenty of gunfights to satisfy one's sound system, particularly since the Dolby Digital soundtrack is as satisfying as its crisp letterboxed image.

The 1997 film is presented in letterboxed format on one side, with an aspect ratio of about 2.35:1 and an accommodation for enhanced 16:9 playback, and in cropped format on the other side. The letterboxing adds a lot of picture information to the sides and masks off a little bit from the top and bottom in comparison to the cropped version, though exact trade off appears to change from one shot to the next. The color transfer is terrific and the focus is very sharp, so you can make out the tiny details that the special effects people labored so hard to include (one advantage to the cropped version—though the sides are missing, the details are enlarged).

The Dolby Digital track is much better than the standard stereo surround soundtrack—the low frequency opening, for example, is more complex and penetrating on the Dolby Digital track—but even the standard stereo track has some great separation effects, great dimensionality, and rock 'em sock 'em explosions. The 127 minute program also has a Spanish language track in standard stereo, and optional English and Spanish subtitles.

Film-Fest DV, Issue 1: Sundance (Broadcast, 8123700012)

Holding, with alternate audio tracks, well over 130 minutes of material, the DVD is a collection of trailers, clips, shorts, interviews and roving camera portraits from the 1999 Sundance Festival.

The picture quality varies from one segment to the next but looks fine over all. The sound is pretty much centered stereo and is functional, but not a focus of the program. There is no captioning, but there are DVD-ROM Web links. Navigating parts of the menu is a little challenging, but you eventually figure it out. The roving camera stuff lets you get a feel for the atmosphere of the Festival and its hangers on.

A clip from The Blair Witch Project clip includes interviews with the filmmakers, who explain how they made the film on such a small budget and talk about how excited they are that it was picked up as a major theatrical release. Other promotional features that had us salivating included a letterboxed trailer for a French film

called Train de Vie, about Jews during WWII who disguise themselves as Germans and hijack a train for Palestine, and four clips from a German punk crime thriller, Run Lola Run, each of which is a mini-movie itself. There is also a 'making of' featurette for Ravenous, an American film about cannibalism in the Old West that has supernatural overtones, and clips from Three Seasons, a film about a Vietnamese girl who discovers she has an American father, played by Harvey Keitel.

Each short that is presented is accompanied by a commentary track by its director. The best ones include 10 Seconds (a very well told tale about the institutionalization of vengeance—a family is given ten seconds to kill the man who murdered their son/brother), Whacked! (people are dropping dead on the streets of New York—why?) and the impressively computer animated Bingo. Others include a one-gag short, Culture; Bubblepac, about a dead body wrapped in plastic; a classic-styled short, The Clock, about a clock tower chime that is bothering the seniors in a nursing home; and An Incident Near Falaise, which we didn't care much for, about a child who has a vision of a WWII battle. The best of the commentaries—the director of Whacked!, Rolf Gibbs, spends two audio tracks discussing his own background and explaining almost shot for shot how his amusing piece was created.

As for the interviews, Robert Redford defends the popularity of Sundance, Robert Altman discusses the difference between working on big budget movies (for the rent) and working on smaller films (for the soul), Laura Dern talks about making short films and her acting in her latest feature, Sheryl Crow talks about dipping her toe in films, Eric Stoltz talks about his Ayn Rand movie, Illeana Douglas and Steve Zahn talk about the Sundance scene, Stewart Copeland talks about scoring films, and Tim Roth, Guy Pearce, Robert Carlyle and Antonia Bird promote their most recent efforts.

Final Analysis (Warner, 12243)

Richard Gere portrays a curiously uninquisitive psychiatrist, but we suppose if Gere's character were actually as bright as his credentials suggest he would not fall so easily for a heroine with murderous inclinations. Provided one finds the cast, including Kim Basinger and Uma Thurman, to be appealing, the movie is a highly enjoyable psychological thriller. It can't stand up to close examination and the romantic angle is weak, but the script has a sufficient number of twists, courtroom antics, and cliffhanging thrills to kill a couple of hours effectively.

The 1992 program is presented in full screen format only, adding picture information to the bottom of the image and taking some off the sides in comparison to letterboxed versions, though we find the letterbox framing to look more balanced and satisfying. Fleshtones are strong, and the image is clean and sharp. There is a mild haze in less strongly lit sequences, but it doesn't dissolve into a total blur, and strongly lit sequences are sharp. The stereo surround sound is fine, and the 125 minute program also has a French stereo soundtrack. The program is adequately closed captioned.

Final Justice (Digital Versatile, DVD106)

John Don Baker is a Texas lawman who ends up in Malta chasing after the Mafiosi who murdered his partner. The 1984 film is fairly predictable, but it maintains a manageable pace despite the cheap production values and halting, phonetically spoken dialogue. There is also one sequence in which the villain accosts a young lady, in a shower with clear doors, which will find favor with fans of such misogynistic activities. The picture is soft with pale fleshtones, weak contrasts and bland hues, and the monophonic sound has a limited range. The 90 minute program is not captioned.

Fire Down Below (Warner, 14914)

The eco-hero who strikes fear in the heart of every polluting industrialist and sighs of pity in the heart of every fashion designer, Steven Seagal, takes his act to the backwoods of Kentucky. Seagal is an EPA agent who wants the locals to help him nail some toxic waste dumpers, even though they're bringing bucks into the community economy. So what if all the kids are sick and their hair is falling out, you know. The film follows a predictable formula and Seagal's character rarely so much as musses up his heavily greased hair as he dispatches villains left and right. For those who long for the gallant heroes of old—forget about it. Seagal's character visits a woman's house after having been invited over for dinner. She ushers him in and he goes right to the dining table to sit down, without lifting a finger or even offering to help her bring in the food. Harry Dean Stanton (in an intriguingly good performance), Marg Helgenberger, Levon Helm and Kris Kristofferson co-star.

The fight scenes look sped up, but they look that way on the LD too, so we assume that the director simply blew his camera set-ups and they're trying to make up for it with optical work in the editing. The picture is colorful and solid-looking, but fleshtones are pale and yellowish, and the image is rarely smooth. The picture is letterboxed on one side, with an aspect ratio of about 1.85:1 and an accommodation for enhanced 16:9 playback, and in full screen format on the other side. The letterboxing takes some picture information off the bottom, but also adds some to the sides and has a better balanced framing. The stereo surround sound is somewhat weak, but the Dolby Digital track is strong. The film is also available in French in regular stereo and comes with English, French or Spanish subtitles. There is a decent cast-and-crew profile, a couple of production notes and trailers for eight Seagal films.

Firehouse (Simitar, 7396)
A 1986 burlesque derivative of the **Police Academy** movies, we love the Dalmatian in the jacket art, pulling down the nubile firefighter's pants, but the movie itself is less inspired. In response to a problematic hiring mandate, a group of female firefighters are assigned to the worst fire company, in a neighborhood that is secretly being arsoned to clear the way for an apartment development. The boyfriend of one of the females is arranging the arson, etc. There is plenty of gratuitous nudity and some rather forced humor, but if the formula pleases you, the film is tolerable entertainment.

The picture is rather grainy and colors are somewhat pale, with bland fleshtones. The sound is nominally in stereo but remains centered and is a little fuzzy. The 90 minute program is not captioned.

Firestarter (Image, ID4274USDVD)
Drew Barrymore stars as a little girl who has the power to ignite fires with her mind. The government wants her, so she and her father, played by David Keith, are on the run. George C. Scott—wearing this bizarre eye patch in some scenes, but, for reasons left unexplained, not in others—and Martin Sheen are among the villains, and Louise Fletcher and Art Carney are included among the good guys. Carney's performance, in a relatively small part, is particularly impressive.

The 1984 feature is letterboxed with an aspect ratio of about 2.35:1 and no 16:9 enhancement. The picture is a little dark, losing details in the shadows, though colors are generally acceptable. The monophonic sound is dull, but the Dolby Digital mono track is okay. The 115 minute program is not captioned.

First Blood (Artisan, 60465)
An audio commentary is delivered by David Morell, the author of the novel upon which the 96 minute film is based. Although he was not directly involved in the production, he was emotionally involved with it and has many interesting things to say about the film. As he explains, the movie changed the face of the action genre, one of the first to deliver what was essentially non-stop action after the initial 15 minute set-up. He speaks insightfully about Sylvester Stallone's career and how much the film stood as a breakthrough for the actor. He admits being inspired by *Lonely Are the Brave* (to say the least—Kirk Douglas was originally cast in Richard Crenna's role, but dropped out at the last moment) and talks

amusingly about the anachronism that occurred between the ten years in which the novel was written, when only some men had long hair, and when the movie was made, when every guy had long hair. 'Rambo' was apparently named after the poet, Rimbaud, cross-referenced with a brand of apples, and Morell confirms that the film's original ending did indeed kill off the hero, but test audiences couldn't stand for it. Some of what he has to say is an analysis of the action, but from his perspective it remains worth listening to, particularly in how a person he made up in his own head entered the consciousness of the entire world as deeply as Sherlock Holmes, Tarzan and James Bond.

The 1982 feature is letterboxed with an aspect ratio of about 2.4:1 and an accommodation for enhanced 16:9 playback. The image is solid, fleshtones are realistic and colors are reasonably strong. The stereo surround sound has a modest dimensionality, and there is no Dolby Digital track. The film can be supported by English closed captioning or Spanish subtitles and is accompanied by a trailer, a featurette that is little more than a glorified trailer, 'spoken' production notes supported by text, an extensive cast & crew profile section, and a multiple choice 'trivia' game.

The First Deadly Sin (Warner, 11368)
Frank Sinatra's last film is also one of his most embarrassing. Based upon a Lawrence Sanders novel where you already know the characters, it has two distinct plot strands. In one, a police detective, portrayed by Sinatra, uncovers the pattern of a serial killer, who is perforating his victims with a small pick axe. In the second, the detective spends time in a hospital with his wife, played by Faye Dunaway, during her final days. The serial killer story is dry and exploitative, but the performances are fun and the pace is involving. The dying wife story, on the other hand, is roll-your-eyes awful, with Sinatra reading to her about bunny rabbits, trying to start a fight with the doctor who removed her kidney, and generally looking at Dunaway as if she represented his future in motion pictures.

The 1980 feature is in full screen format only (the tops and bottoms of shots are often kind of empty). Colors are bright, the image is reasonably solid and fleshtones are decent. The monophonic sound has a limited range and dull tones. The 112 minute program is adequately closed captioned.

The First Emperor of China (Lumivision, DVD0597); reissue (SlingShot, 9809)
An IMAX film with a cast of thousands, it is a dramatic re-creation of the efforts undergone by Qin Shihuang to unite China in the Third Century BC. Sweeping battles and palace intrigue are presented in the crisp, finely detailed IMAX format, with elaborately directional stereo surround sound. The story is narrated by Christopher Plummer with incidental Chinese dialogue left untranslated. The program runs 42 minutes. Because it is a family-oriented IMAX show, however, there is a frustrating tendency for the film to cut away right as things look like they are going to get gory. The most disappointing—a traitor has his arms and legs tied to four horses, but just as the whips fly and the horses take off in opposite directions, the view shifts to the cheering crowd.

The picture on the Lumivision version is noticeably sharper than the picture on the SlingShot version, though without a comparison the new version looks fine and colors are bright. The Lumivision DVD, however, had only a 2-channel Dolby Digital track, so the 5-channel Dolby Digital track on the SlingShot release is more satisfying, with a greater dimensionality. It enhances the program's entertainment far more than the softness in the image takes away from it. The sound is also available in French, Spanish, Indonesian, Japanese, Korean and Mandarin in Dolby Digital and can be supported by English subtitles. Although the logo on the jacket suggests that the DVD contain PC-ROM functions, it offers nothing more than a promotional Web link.

First Knight (Columbia TriStar, 71175/9)

Don't be completely put off by the bad word-of-mouth surrounding the 1995 feature. It is a very engaging action film, mixed together with a very out-of-touch and deadeningly chaste love story. Remember Richard Gere in *King David*? Well, he puts across the same sort of impression here, playing Lancelot to Sean Connery's Arthur and Julia Ormond's Guinevere. The film was directed by Jerry Zucker, who used to make fun of movies like this. Anyway, like we said, the action scenes are pretty good and there are a lot of them, it is just that the movie grinds to a screeching halt between each one. That, however, is why God invented the Scan button. On DVD you can push the lovers along, while reveling in the grand sword fights and Gere's heroics.

The presentation looks terrific. It is letterboxed on one side, with an aspect ratio of about 1.85:1 and an accommodation for enhanced 16:9 playback, and in full screen format on the other side. In spite of all the dark forest scenes, the picture is clear and colors are sharp. The stereo surround sound and Dolby Digital sound are suitably elaborate. The 133 minute program also has French and Spanish audio tracks in standard stereo, optional Spanish and Korean subtitles, and English closed captioning.

First Man into Space (Image, ID4429GODVD)

Marshall Thompson stars in the black-and-white 1958 feature, about an astronaut exposed to an extra-terrestrial virus that turns him into a gooky monster. The stock footage and cheapo special effects are rough, but the controlled soundstage conversation scenes look fine, with a crisp focus, fairly detailed contrasts and only a few stray speckles. The monophonic sound is okay and the 76 minute film is accompanied by enjoyable original theatrical trailers. There is no captioning.

The First 9 1/2 Weeks (Sterling, 7085)

Although it is set in the present day, it is supposedly the story of how the guy in the other **9 1/2 Weeks** movies got to be so bossy. Basically, he's a broker who goes down to New Orleans to visit a wealthy client. He falls for the client's wife, discovers she is being abused and 'rescues' her, and then undergoes all sorts of indignities, only to discover, well, we won't reveal the ending though it is pretty obvious and pretty much as ridiculous as the ending of **The Game** is. Paul Mercurio is the hero and Malcolm McDowell is the villain. It isn't really like the other **9 1/2 Weeks** movies, though some of the erotic sequences involve a mild psychological pitch and toss. Even then, the film's love scenes are very dull, and the rest of the narrative is pretty silly.

The picture is unappealing, with slightly brownish hues, dull fleshtones and blurs whenever the setting turns to evening. The stereo sound is uninteresting. There is no English captioning, but the 99 minute program does have Spanish subtitles, along with a trailer and some production notes.

The First Wives Club (Paramount, 326127)

The story is a mess and the plotting has a very makeshift feel to it, but who can resist the premise and star power of the 1996 hit? Goldie Hawn, Bette Midler and Diane Keaton star as three middle-aged divorcees who take financial revenge upon their ex-husbands. Even giving the film the leeway that comedies deserve there are aspects to the characters and the logic of events that seem weakly conceived. Still, it is so much fun watching the three actresses do their thing, and so satisfying to have their characters achieve their goals, that such details are much less important than just waiting for the next time two or three of them are in a shot together.

The presentation is letterboxed with an aspect ratio of about 1.85:1 and no 16:9 enhancement. Colors are bright and nicely detailed. It is a tribute to the cinematography that the image is not as hazy as it often is when three actresses of such stature are in front of the camera. The image is blandly lit at times, but the presentation is sharp and fleshtones are accurate. There isn't much to the stereo surround sound and menu-activated Dolby Digital audio

mixes, but the audio quality is adequate. The 102 minute film can be supported by English or Spanish subtitles ("¡No se de jen llevar, llévense todo!") and is accompanied by a trailer that makes no more sense than the movie does (there also appears to be some footage in it that didn't make the final cut), but sells the film well anyway.

A Fish Called Wanda (MGM, 906266)

The very amusing ensemble caper comedy is in letterboxed format on one side, with an aspect ratio of about 1.85:1 and no 16:9 enhancement, and in full screen format on the other side. We tend to prefer the full screen framing, though either is workable. The letterboxing masks picture information off the top and the bottom of the image and even a little from one side, while adding more to the other side. The image is so sharp and effectively detailed that it doesn't matter if the hues look a little flat in places. The monophonic sound is fine and the 108 minute film is also available in French, with optional English or French subtitles. A trailer is also included.

About jewel thieves hiding and haggling over their loot, Jamie Lee Curtis and Kevin Kline star with John Cleese and Michael Palin in the 1988 feature. You need the chain reaction of a large audience to get the most out of the film the first time you see it, but that is no reason not to buy the DVD and invite a lot of friends over. The dishonor-among-thieves comedy is suitable for multiple viewings because most of the humor comes from the performances of the stars instead of from witty one-liners. On multiple viewings, a few discrepancies start to materialize. The heroine puts a special key into a locket and later the hero's wife accidentally comes across the locket, believing it to be a gift from her husband. There is then a lengthy set of business as they go about trying to get the locket back, but the wife, though she is quite taken by the gift she thinks her husband has given her, never opens it up. One other complaint about the film—they worked on the movie for four years and yet they couldn't design a shot to show the guy flattened in the wet cement?

Fishing with John (Criterion, FIS060)

We laughed and laughed and laughed at the six episodes of an inspired half-hour send up of *American Sportsman* from 1992. John Lurie (the tall guy with the hat in *Stranger Than Paradise*, he is also a member of The Lounge Lizards) directed and stars in the episodes, in which he takes his famous friends, such as Matt Dillon, Tom Waits and Dennis Hopper, to various places around the world to go fishing. The joke is that they don't really know what they are doing—not in an obvious slapstick way, but in a subtler, kind of too-stoned-to-get-it-right way. There is a throwback-style voiceover narration ("There are fish in the water, but when they are not hungry, there is no way to catch them"), as well as idle chatter as they wait, often indefinitely, for the fish to bite (we learn, for example, that Dillon was born around the time that *Gunsmoke* was popular on the TV). In the funniest episode, Lurie goes ice fishing with Willem Dafoe, but things don't go too well ("The situation is growing serious. John and Willem have consumed only melted snow since their supply of cheese crackers ran out, two days ago"). We've been telling the ending to everybody we meet, but it is too funny to tell you.

The episodes appear on one single-sided dual-layer platter. The picture and sound quality are superb. The image, shot by unacknowledged camera operators, is vividly colorful and sharp, and looks very clear. The stereo surround sound has some great directional effects and a wonderful dimensionality, and there is an eccentric but highly compelling musical score, as well. There is no captioning and the program is not time encoded, although it returns to the menu after each episode. Also included is a Lounge Lizards music video, shot on Sardinia. Lurie provides a running commentary for all six episodes, talking about what really happened during each shoot (Waits wouldn't speak to him for two years after it was over) and sharing other anecdotes about his life and career (he was in *The Last Temptation of Christ* and talks a lot about that shoot, too). You have to reactivate the commentary for each episode.

Fist of the North Star (Image, ID4661SEDVD)

Gushers of blood decorate the decent post-apocalypse Japanese martial arts cartoon. Set in a post-apocalyptic world that appears to have been lifted mostly from **The Road Warrior**, the hero once got beat up by the bad guy but is now much stronger and has returned to set things straight. There are other bad guys to contend with first, and there is a mute child carrying a bag of seeds with dreams of re-foresting the Earth. The premise is basic and oft-used, but the show has an impressive scope, the characters are well formed, and the pacing is good, mixing the gore and the plot in ideal amounts of thrills.

The 109 minute show is dubbed in English without captioning, and the story has a few gaps in it, but it is hard to tell if the program has been modified as part of its Americanization. The animation is stilted and bland at times, but there are some striking images and the fights are reasonably exciting. Bright colors are a little over-saturated and some sequences are a little aged, but the image is workable. The stereo sound is generally centered, but adequate.

Five Corners (UAV, 40096)

Jodie Foster (in her first important film after she got out of college), Tim Robbins and John Turturro are featured in the 1987 production. Written by John Patrick Shanley (before **Moonstruck**) and directed by Tony Bill, the film weaves together the stories of about a dozen characters living in a neighborhood in the Bronx in 1964. Foster's character works in a pet shop. Robbins´ is a convert to non-violence and planning to join the civil rights demonstrations in the South. The film is an odd mix of styles, careening from avert-your-eyes violence to lyrical romantic comedy, and it would be easy to laugh off the action in the end as going over the top, particularly as Turturro, a would-be rapist and cop killer, carries Foster across the rooftops King Kong-style. Robbins tries to stop him by hugging him.

We could barely synch up the DVD with the LD because the 93 minute program is time compressed or something. The monophonic sound has such a different pitch it almost seems like the voices and music are an alternative track. Then there's the color transfer. Indoor scenes on the DVD have a general orange wash that makes fleshtones a little pink, but it makes everything else pinker, too. Outdoor scenes have brighter and purer hues but the image is so grainy that it is hard on the eyes. The presentation is also cropped.

Flash Gordon (Universal, ID4630USDVD)

Released initially with a faulty soundtrack, the DVD was subsequently released with a correct stereo surround audio track. The difference is immediately noticeable. On the bad version, the sound stays in the front, while on the revised version, there are full surround effects. The UPC number on the jacket for the faulty DVD is 14381-42732 and the UPC number on the jacket for the good DVD is 14381-46302. There is no way to differentiate the platters themselves, however, without playing them.

The image is letterboxed with an aspect ratio of about 2.35:1 and no 16:9 enhancement. The color transfer is fantastic. Watching it is like swimming in an ocean of sequins. The DVD does more than simply deliver the film with perfection, it takes what was theatrically a limp fantasy exercise, and turns it into a gloriously colorful evocation of the old Flash Gordon serials, surely what the filmmakers first envisioned when the project was conceived. Delivered without cropping; with precise, intense hues that never falter. The campy performances are steadily entertaining and, most importantly, the cheap special effects are spellbinding from beginning to end, a triumph of decoration over design. To be sure, the film still has too few sustained action sequences and an IQ in the medi-

um two digits, but every set, costume, and screen pixel is so eye-popping that it never matters. It's all glitter and flash, and it's awesome. The 1980 Dino De Laurentiis production, starring Max Von Sydow, Timothy Dalton, Topol, and Sam J. Jones, runs 111 minutes and is not captioned.

Fleetwood Mac (see The Original Fleetwood Mac: The Early Years)

Flesh (Image, ID4731PYDVD)

Produced by Andy Warhol and directed by Paul Morrissey, the 1968 film depicts a day in the life of a young hustler, who wakes up in his girlfriend's pad, goes out to turn a few tricks and do some nude modeling, and then returns to crash. There are many jump cuts and other jerky camera movements, combined with long, pointless shots of Joe Dallesandro standing around, but you can see Morrissey start to get a good handle on the concept of characters and interesting conversation as the 89 minute film advances. It remains more compelling from an academic standpoint, as a representation of Morrissey's artistic beginnings, than as pure entertainment, but it also establishes a tone that Morrissey's later movies play off of.

The film is presented in full screen format. The source material on has incidental damage and other evidence of wear, but colors are surprisingly rich and there is no more grain or fuzzy blurring than what the original cinematography brought to the source. The monophonic sound is passable There is no captioning.

Flesh for Frankenstein (Criterion, CC1546D)

Paul Morrissey's ultra-campy, ultra-gory horror spoofs, the 1973 **Flesh for Frankenstein**, was shot back-to-back in Europe with **Blood for Dracula**. Udo Kier and Van Vooren are, apparently, an incestuous brother and sister (with two children who seem to be developing the same relationship amongst themselves). Kier is also a mad scientist, trying to create an artificial man and woman out of spare and freshly obtained body parts. Joe Dallesandro is a servant who upsets their plans.

Originally produced in 3-D, is presented in 2-D and is letterboxed with an aspect ratio of about 2.43:1 and no 16:9 enhancement. The colors are vivid and the image is crisp. Forests are properly green and brown, and fleshtones are realistically pale. The monophonic sound is mildly scratchy and has a limited range. The 95 minute film is not closed captioned. There is also a montage of production stills (set to a flourishing stereophonic rendition of the musical score) and by an audio commentary track from Morrissey, Kier and film historian Maurice Yacowar. Morrissey has interesting things to say about the production of each film and discusses his approach to moviemaking intelligently. Kier provides personal reminiscences about working on the film and about his career in general, including a fascinating story, about what happened in his hospital room the day he was born. Yacowar's comments are fairly academic, but are informative and balanced by the other two commentaries. The 3-D effects, even when presented in 2-D, are marvelous, especially the memorable finale when Kier is punctured through the back by a long stake that pops one of his internal organs right into the face of the viewer (none of the commentators appear sure as to exactly which organ it is, as the item is variously identified as a stomach, a liver and a pair of kidneys). First time viewers may find parts of the film to be slow moving and may view the performances as inept, but the movie has enough nudity, simulated intercourse and severed limbs (the film was one of Carlo Rambaldi's pre-Hollywood breakthroughs) to hold anyone's attention, and once you get on their wavelength, the performers get funnier and funnier (and so does the gore, and so, even, does the sex). As Yacowar studiously details on the commentary track, there is an artistic method to the film as well, themes (such as the male/female pairs) that hold the movie together as tightly as the stitches around the monster's neck.

Fletch (Universal, 20285)

In the DVD's production notes, novelist Gregory McDonald bubbles excitedly about how Chevy Chase was the perfect choice to embody his fictional character and you can imagine, if the publicist writing the blurb wasn't just making the whole thing up, McDonald speaking through clenched teeth and rising to strangle Chase the instant the actor's back is turned. The mystery thriller has a catchy plot—the hero is hired to assist in a man's suicide, but a little digging quickly reveals that the man has no reason to die and every reason to disappear—but the film's heaviest Chase-isms, such as his fumbling disguises and pratfalls—not to mention dream sequences—distance the viewer from the real entertainment of the narrative.

The picture is letterboxed, with an aspect ratio of about 1.85:1 and an accommodation for enhanced 16:9 playback. The picture is a little soft, but colors are bright and the image is workable. The stereo surround sound has a fairly basic mix, with an overbearing musical score. Accompanied by a theatrical trailer, the 98 minute film is also available in French and comes with English or Spanish subtitles ("¿Me presta su toalla un momento? Mi auto le pegó a un búfalo de agua").

A Flight to Dreams: Ju-52 Junkers (Pioneer, PSI99213D)
A Flight to Dreams: Seaplanes G-73T Turbo Mallard (Pioneer, PSI99215D)

Shot in Switzerland, the 53 minute **JU-52 Junkers** has a typical format, in which the camera explores every angle of the German propeller transport plane, on the ground and in the air, to a stereophonic musical score and to environmental sounds with no score. Except for incidental conversation in some of the cockpit sequences, there is no narration or dialogue, but the directional effects and clarity of the airplane sounds are excellent.

We liked **G-73T Turbo Mallard** even better. Shot in 1992, the 55 minute program depicts a working passenger propeller seaplane that travels from Key West to Paradise Island in the Bahamas, with a stop over in Miami/Ft. Lauderdale. You get to watch the plane take off over the pilot's shoulder, and land with water splashing onto the camera lens. Again, they cover the craft from every angle, and get in some good views of its landing areas as well. Except for a couple brief musical sequences, the sound is all 'live' and the stereo surround sound is fantastic. Radio and cockpit sounds come from the front, but when the pilot makes his announcements to the passengers, it comes from the rear. The engine noises are vivid and highly directional, and if you close your eyes, you'll think you're really in the plane. The color quality on both programs is terrific.

The Flintstones (Universal, 20274); (DTS) (Universal, 20562)

The director, Brian Levant, was one of the dozens of writers who contributed to the film's screenplay, but he never says a single word about the narrative in his breathless commentary, spending most of his time speaking as fast as he can to identify the film's many inspired decorations and special effects. He also talks about working with the cast and about the production, and he reports that Prince Charles laughed hardest at the pterodactyl droppings gag during the London premiere. The most informative aspects of his talk, however, are repeated in the 43 minute documentary about the making of the film, which has a lot of behind-the-scenes footage and interviews. There is also a split screen comparison of the opening theme song sequence, a modest collection of production drawings (we would have liked to have seen more), a decent collection of still photos, a cast-and-director profile section with some related trailers, production notes that pretty much reiterate everything that was in the documentary and Levant's talk, a B-52s music video of the show's theme song, a standard trailer and an engaging sing-along teaser.

The 1994 film is letterboxed, with an aspect ratio of about 1.85 and an accommodation for enhanced 16:9 playback. The color transfer is terrific, with consistently bright, sharp hues and rich fleshtones. The stereo surround sound is somewhat ungainly, but it has a reasonable amount of energy, and the Dolby Digital track has better-defined separations and less bleeding to the rear channel, improving the impact of the mix a little. The 90 minute film is also available in French and can be supported by English or Spanish subtitles. Interestingly, according to the documentary, Levant gathered a number of comedy writers in a room, as he used to do while making TV sitcoms, to work out the story—but from the look and sound of it, they got distracted by all the gags they kept dreaming up.

John Goodman, Rick Moranis, Elizabeth Perkins and Rosie O'Donnell star. The drama often seems embarrassing, a demonstration that you cannot adapt a cartoon's emotions directly, you have to expand them to the more complex responses real performers are capable of communicating. The filmmakers should have gone back to the true source—*The Honeymooners*—to measure the balance between domestic conflict and pathos (there's not a moment in the film where you really believe that Wilma loves Fred), but instead they created something shrill and dumb, and then spent oodles of money on set designs and special effects to hide it.

The picture on the DTS version, which has no special features, is identical to the *Collector's Edition* release and is letterboxed, with an aspect ratio of about 1.85:1 and an accommodation for enhanced 16:9 playback. The frame transfer rate appears identical, and there is no closed captioning. The DTS audio is stronger and sharper than the Dolby Digital track on the *Collector's Edition* DVD, but the differences are not elaborate and rarely add to the entertainment.

Flirting with Disaster (Buena Vista, 17250)

Ben Stiller stars in a very funny, very adult comedy about a man searching for his birth parents, with Patricia Arquette and Téa Leoni. Alan Alda, Mary Tyler Moore, George Segal, Lily Tomlin and others also pop up in amusing supporting parts. (Although Moore got quite a bit of press for her performance, she's not really all that good. It's just that her part is written so well that she gets the laughs anyway.) As the hero travels across the country, what initially seemed like a simple trip is complicated by a number of misunderstandings, turning the film into a contemporary road picture that explores modern culture amid its witty dialogue, unique characters and ribald slapstick.

The picture is letterboxed with an aspect ratio of about 1.85:1 and no 16:9 enhancement. The image is fairly sharp and colors look fine, with workable fleshtones. There is no 5-channel Dolby Digital encoding, though since the film is mostly conversation, the stereo surround sound is adequate. The 92 minute program can be supported by optional English subtitles.

Floundering (Simitar, 7338)

Living up to its title all too well it is an aimless, socially concerned comedy drama about a young man, played by James LeGros, who doesn't know what to do. About anything. He wanders around, bumps into characters played by the likes of Steve Buscemi, John Cusack and Ethan Hawke, eventually hooks up with a girl for a while, and even assassinates a police chief, but the 1992 movie is top-heavy with voiceover narration, too deliberate to be artistic and too artsy to be entertaining. The picture is soft and the colors are very pale. The Ultra-Stereo sound has a limited dimensionality. The 97 minute film is not captioned.

Fly Away Home (Columbia TriStar, 82436/82439)

Directed by Carroll Ballard, Anna Paquin and Jeff Daniels star in the story of a young girl living in Canada who raises some geese and then teaches them to fly south for the winter. It is sort of a cross between *Born Free*, **The Black Stallion** and **Chitty Chitty Bang Bang** but, in the hands of the naturalist-auteur Ballard, every scene is tightly composed and the story has the right mix of intellectual interest and emotional satisfaction.

The presentation is in full screen format only. We tend to prefer the framing on the movie's letterboxed image, but you really don't lose too much on the full screen version and it seems acceptable. The picture looks good, with bright, reasonably sharp colors. The standard stereo surround soundtrack is bland, but the menu-activated Dolby Digital track is good, with strong rear channel activity. The 107 minute 1996 film also has a Spanish language option (without Dolby Digital) and comes with English, French or Spanish subtitles.

Fools Rush In (Columbia TriStar, 94949)

Matthew Perry and Salma Hayek star in the pleasant 1997 romance. A one night stand leads to a pregnancy and an impulsive marriage, which the pair then have to reconcile with more rational morning after feelings. Some of the conflicts seem contrived, but for the most part the film has star power and tells a very basic story with a fresh sense of discovery. The film is set in Las Vegas.

The picture is presented on one side in letterboxed format, with an aspect ratio of about 1.85:1 and an accommodation for enhanced 16:9 playback, and is in full screen format on the other side. The colors are fine and fleshtones look good. The image is reasonably sharp. The stereo surround sound and Dolby Digital sound are passable, but the mix is limited beyond the musical score. The 109 minute program also has French and Spanish language tracks, in mono, optional English, French and Spanish subtitles, and a trailer.

For a Few Dollars More (MGM, 906271)

The letterboxing has an aspect ratio of about 2.35:1 and no 16:9 enhancement. The colors on the 1965 Sergio Leone-Clint Eastwood feature are fresher and more accurate than any previous home video versions, and the image is better detailed. The film has a sort of dusty look, of course, but the sky is a deep blue and fleshtones are accurate. Even the monophonic sound is less harsh and a little cleaner. The 131 minute film is also available in French and can be supported by English, French and Spanish subtitles ("Toi à l'extérieur et moi à l'intérieur"). There is a wonderful original, original trailer, back when Leone was still calling himself 'Bob Robertson,' and a jacket insert with extensive production notes. Lee Van Cleef co-stars in the intuitively artistic western, about bounty hunters becoming involved in a bank robbery.

For Love of a Child (Simitar, 7272)

Religious overtones permeate the TV movie about the emotional conflicts between neighbors that arise when the child of one drowns in the other's swimming pool. The subject is clearly a potent one for exploring moral and emotional issues, and the screenplay covers most of the bases, while very lightly touching upon the need for atheistic penance and forgiveness, and the ambiguous role of God in tragedies. It seems to balance its essay question components and its narrative components with a practiced efficiency, and there should probably be more such programs available than there are, though they obviously fill a niche and will not be of interest to everyone.

The colors are a little bland and the image is slightly blurry. The monophonic sound is dull but workable. The 93 minute program is accompanied by a partial filmography for its star, Michael Tucker, and is not captioned.

For Love of Ivy (Anchor Bay, DV10834)

1967 was a big year for Sidney Poitier. He had three large box office successes, including a film that went on to win the Oscar for Best Picture, but then, as sometimes happens with such careers, he started to appear in bombs. The first was a movie with an appeal pretty much limited to the **How Stella Got Her Groove Back** crowd. It is not that the film is outrageously bad or anything, it is just that it is limited dramatically in a manner that the previous films were not. Poitier's star appeal, though potent enough to keep the film in circulation, was not enough to compensate for its shortcomings. Still, the film is a gas, particularly now that thirty odd years have passed since it was made.

Poitier is the owner of a trucking firm that runs legitimate jobs during the day, but turns one rig into a roving casino at night (the film's art direction is one of its few genuinely admirable components). Abbey Lincoln is a live-in maid for an upper middle class family that includes Carroll O'Connor, as the father, and Beau Bridges, as the long-hair-and-sideburns-and-Nehru-collar-wearing son. When Lincoln's character gives her notice, because she wants to pursue a different career, Bridges blackmails Poitier into romancing her so that she'll change her mind about leaving. Naturally, they fall in love for real, and most of the movie depicts their drawn-out path to romance. This was the first or virtually the first mainstream Hollywood movie about black characters who act like Ginger Rogers and Fred Astaire off the dance floor, and as such, it is woefully bland and almost timid. But as an aged cultural landmark, it is fascinating and funky. The dialogue and character interaction regarding race are self-conscious, but achingly liberal. The colors are all Sixties pop, we already mentioned the art direction, and Poitier looks so great in a tux you wish they'd signed him up to play James Bond. The film was inconsequential in its day, but it is a nostalgic treasure now.

The picture quality contributes greatly to the film's appeal. All those right-on colors are fabulously bright and fresh looking, and the image is very sharp. The source material does have some scattered damage, but it is not enough to interrupt the flow of the drama. If you get too close to the screen, you can see a number of displacement artifacting effects, but if you remain at a sensible distance, compression flaws are rarely noticeable. The picture is presented on one side in letterboxed format, with an aspect ratio of about 1.85:1 and no 16:9 enhancement, and in full screen format on the other side. The letterboxed image adds nothing to the sides and masks off picture information from the top and bottom in comparison to the full screen version, and we tended to prefer the framing on the latter. The monophonic sound is fine, and the 101 minute program is not captioned.

For Richer or Poorer (Universal, 20265)

Tim Allen and Kirstie Alley star as a married couple from Manhattan who hide from the IRS by staying with the Amish in Pennsylvania. Angry at each other, their marriage strengthens during their quasi-cultural confinement and their problems dissipate. The film, designed as a comedy, is not very compelling. Even if one allows for a relaxation of logic there are story points that don't make much sense. The narrative really isn't all that funny, either, since good taste prevents the filmmakers from lampooning the Amish, so attempts are made to generate humor from farm gags and other base subject matter, which register an immediate incongruity with the nobility of the supporting characters. At its best, the film tries for the emotions of a feel-good sitcom, but at 116 minutes it can't manage the pace. Besides, any film that casts both Michael Lerner and Wayne Knight in similar but unrelated roles has not been planned out with a full clarity of thought.

The picture is presented in letterboxed format with an aspect ratio of about 2.35:1 and an accommodation for enhanced 16:9 playback. The color quality isn't very good, with slightly dull fleshtones and subdued hues. The stereo surround sound is okay, and the Dolby Digital track presents a more satisfying dimensionality. The 1998 program is also available in French in standard stereo and can be accompanied by English or Spanish subtitles.

For the Love of Benji (Image, ID4805BFDVD)

Benji the dog scampers around Athens. There is a brief plot—an international intrigue—and endless, endless shots of the dog poking about town. The picture looks very clean and sharp, with slightly bland but adequate hues. The monophonic sound is okay and since much of the music has a Greek twang to it, the soundtrack is pleasant. The 1977 program runs 84 minutes. There is no captioning.

For Whom the Bell Tolls (Universal, 20423)

In typical burn-your-assets fashion, the original road show presentation was trimmed for standard theatrical release and then trimmed even more for reissues. The trims were tossed away, and so the film, in addition to its few other flaws, has always seemed choppy and superficial. Now, however, some of those trims have been restored, and the movie is greatly improved as a result. The 1943 Paramount film originally ran 170 minutes and was eventually cut down to 130 minutes, which is the version usually shown on TV. The DVD presentation runs about 156 minutes, a copy of the initial standard theatrical release. While the narrative still jumps forward in a couple places, the movie is a far more rewarding experience than it has been in the past. Curiously, although the DVD's jacket cover promotes a 'photo montage,' which appeared during the Overture and Entr'acte on the LD, the Overture on the DVD plays to blank screen and the photo montage is nowhere to be found. There is, however, a still photo collection, lobby card collection and theatrical trailer, along with production notes and a cast-and-director profile section. The picture has rich colors, deep fleshtones and pure blacks. The image is not as vivid as it is on other Technicolor productions from the era, and the picture is a little soft, but the presentation looks solid and is often very satisfying. The monophonic sound is a little light, but remains within an acceptable range and age-related noise is limited. The film can be supported by English, French or Spanish subtitles.

Based upon a once highly respected novel by Ernest Hemingway, Gary Cooper and Ingrid Bergman star in the story of Republican guerrillas in the Spanish Civil War who are biding their time in a mountain hideout until they are scheduled to blow up a bridge. What the restored cuts reveal is that the movie, which was directed by Sam Wood, made a serious attempt at being faithful to Hemingway's attentions. In other words, the digressions, flashbacks and character interactions are far more important than whether or not the bridge is blown up on time, and it was the digressions and flashbacks that were the first to go when the film was trimmed. Cooper, said to be Hemingway's choice in the part, is still very awkward and somewhat unconvincing, but as the film progresses and the details mount up, he blends in better, again something the shorter version never allowed him to do.

The Forbidden (see Clive Barker's Salomé & The Forbidden)

Forbidden Planet (MGM, 906565)

The transfer is inferior to the best LD release, with less accurate colors, paler fleshtones and a softer image. The DVD is presented in letterboxed format on one side, with an aspect ratio of about 2.35:1 and an accommodation for enhanced 16:9 playback, and in cropped format on the other side, the cropping being detrimental to the film's lovely art direction and to the most important action sequences. The picture quality on the cropped version is just as bad as the picture quality on the letterboxed version, and looks even softer because of the blown up image.

The stereo sound has muted and occasionally muffled tones. There is a monophonic French audio track, but contrary to the jacket notations, there is no Spanish track. There are English, French or Spanish subtitles ("Les monstres de l'Id"), and the enjoyable trailer is presented in letterboxed format on both sides. The film runs 98 minutes and stars Leslie Nielsen, Walter Pidgeon and Anne Francis.

The movie epitomizes all that was right and wrong with science fiction films before the art of special motion picture effects had advanced to the point of adult believability. (Only ten years separate **Forbidden Planet** from **2001: A Space Odyssey**, but the difference seems as great as the lifetimes it took to go from Kitty Hawk to Apollo.) In the "wrong" category, the film's ambiance is sound-stage-bound, the repartee among the crew on the spacecraft is vaudevillian, and more time is spent trying to amaze the audience than trying to tell the story. But, in the "right" category, MGM

contributed its art and costume design muscle to create the ultimate fifties science fiction trip. Since the moviemakers couldn't disguise the artifice, they did the next best thing. They made the critical effects sequences so creative and awe-inspiring that the imagination is captivated whether or not a viewer believes in what comes before or after. Finally, the screenwriters had the inspiration to use one of William Shakespeare's most ambivalent and thought-provoking plays, *The Tempest*, as their source material. The ending avoids becoming a dime-store Freudian interpretation of Shakespeare's work because of the scope of the fantasy. The Calibanish "Id" monster is not the result of a father's lust for his daughter, it is the unleashed fury of an entire, dead civilization, one that wanted immortality and got eternal damnation instead.

Forever and a Day (Image, ID4533JFDVD)

The brilliantly designed, one-of-a-kind film manages to create legitimate speaking parts for six dozen famous actors and actresses. The 1943 production, designed to boost British morale during the War, explores the experiences of a family through several generations. Also written and directed by teams of talented screenwriters and directors, the 106 minute film is remarkably coherent and engaging, and, of course, the steady parade of stars doing their thing (Buster Keaton as an inept plumber; Eric Blore as a smarmy butler, Charlie Ruggles as a concerned father, Claude Rains as a villainous suitor, and so on, and so on) is an utter delight.

The black-and-white source material is somewhat worn down, with numerous scratches and other markings. The image is reasonably sharp most of the time and contrasts are fairly well defined, even when parts of the picture appear grainy. The film's condition tends to reinforce its wartime origins and does not present an insurmountable detriment to the entertainment. The monophonic sound is adequate and the film is not captioned.

Forever Young (Warner, 12571)

Mel Gibson is a test pilot, involved in an early cryogenics experiment, who is frozen in 1939 and is accidentally awakened by a pair of kids in 1992. Taking heart in the film's title, the kids play a major part, and the film is rated "PG," but since the movie is also a romance, segments of the story may be alienating to one or another age group. Because of the fantasy elements and Gibson's star appeal, the film is worth viewing once, and it does push all the right emotional buttons, but some viewers will probably want to let a century or so go by before watching it again. Jamie Lee Curtis also stars.

The picture is presented in full screen format only, losing a significant amount of picture information from the sides and adding a bit to the top and bottom in comparison to the film's widescreen framing. The colors are strong and the image is nicely detailed. The stereo surround sound isn't bad and the film has a few sequences where its audio track is particularly effective. The 102 minute film is also available in French and Spanish, and comes with English, French or Spanish subtitles. There is a decent sized cast profile and production notes section, and a theatrical trailer.

Forever Young X-rated (Vivid, UPC#0073214593)

A workable adaptation of *Seconds*, not only is the basic concept of the narrative followed, but they even use the nihilist ending. The picture is reasonably sharp, with workable colors, and the sound is fairly aggressive. The 70 minute program features Asia, Tina Tyler, Brook Waters and Valeria. The DVD contains alternate angle sequences and elaborate hardcore interactive promotional features.

The 47 Ronin: Parts 1 and 2 (Image, ID4541JFDVD)

Kenji Mizoguchi's taxing 222 minute examination of samurai ethics has been issued on a single-sided dual-layer platter. The film is filled with seemingly endless and seemingly redundant conversation, as characters say the same things over and over (though always with slight variations). Based upon the famous and often-filmed story about a group of samurai who avenge the forced suicide of their master, the massacre that is the climax of most versions (such as **Chushingura**) happens off stage. Although it was created as two separate movies, made in 1941 and 1942, it plays as one methodical narrative. Viewers who are fascinated by the subtleties of Japanese manners and decorum will find it interesting, and those who admire finely composed camera angles will have plenty of time to absorb the intricacies of each shot. Those who are looking for swordplay, zippy dramatics or something that defies the inevitable, however, had best look elsewhere.

The black-and-white picture is worn and aged. There are scratches, splices, speckles, blurs, weak contrasts and other flaws, though few films produced in Japan during the War look much better. The monophonic sound is also heavy with wear, and there are passages where the Japanese dialogue is probably unintelligible, though the optional English subtitles are always clear.

The 400 Blows (Criterion, FOU060); (Fox Lorber, FLV5078)

François Truffaut's film is an intimate look at the maturation of a young Parisian delinquent. The picture and sound have been cleaned up a little in comparison to Criterion's LD release. Scratches and more severe markings that were present on the LD have been eliminated. The image also has an increased sharpness and blacks are purer. Black-and-white images convey the texture of the boy's surroundings—the stone walls, chain fences, and cramped apartments, and the vivid images on the DVD increase a viewer's involvement with the hero and his environment.

The presentation is letterboxed, with an aspect ratio of about 2.35:1 and no 16:9 enhancement. The monophonic sound is clean. The film is in French and the English subtitles can be toggled on and off. In addition to the film's chapter encoding, the English commentary track, by Brian Stonehill, has its own chapter encoding with a separate access menu. Stonehill presents a breathless interpretation of the film's meanings and autobiographical underpinnings, incorporating translated excerpts of the interviews. Though sometimes stating the obvious, Stonehill gives fascinating interpretations to important sequences, particularly as he draws parallels between the hero's newfound freedom and Truffaut's "New Wave" filmmaking style and also provides worthwhile translation enhancements to the disc's English subtitles. On another commentary track, there is an interview with Truffaut collaborators Robert Lachenay and Marcel Moussy on another commentary track, which is mostly in French. There is also a French theatrical trailer. The 1959 film runs 94 minutes.

The picture and film sound transfer on the Fox Lorber presentation are identical to Criterion's version, with optional English subtitles. Fox Lorber came up with their own commentary, however, by film critic Glenn Kenny. Although not as detailed as Criterion's commentary, Kenny does provide a fair overview of the film's production, Truffaut's background and the story of the French New Wave. He has less to say about the other production personnel behind the camera, and he gets the 'auteur theory' exactly wrong, but for the most part the talk is informative, and he reads a number of excerpts of writings on film by Truffaut and his contemporaries. Fox Lorber's presentation is also accompanied by a number of Truffaut trailers.

The Four Musketeers (see The Three Musketeers)

Four Rooms (Buena Vista, 16786)

The four-part omnibus comedy is about odd goings-on in a hotel. The first two stories, one directed by Allison Anders about witches, and one directed by Alexandre Rockwell, about a couple playing psychological games on one another, are rather taxing, particularly if a viewer is not prepared for their lack of focus and weak pacing, but the second two, directed by Robert Rodriguez and Quentin Tarantino respectively, are fairly amusing. The Rodriguez piece is about a pair of wicked children who terrorize a bell hop babysitting them, and Tarantino's effort is a perfectly timed piece, deliberately evoking the old Alfred Hitchcock TV episode,

about a bet involving a cigarette lighter and a finger. Featured within the cast are Tim Roth, Madonna, Antonio Banderas, Jennifer Beals, Marisa Tomei and Lili Taylor.

The image is letterboxed with an aspect ratio of about 1.85:1 and no 16:9 enhancement. The color quality is good, with bright, shiny hues. The focus is crisp and fleshtones are accurate. The stereo surround sound has an appealing dimensionality. The 98 minute program can be supported by optional English subtitles.

The Four Seasons (see Vivaldi: The Four Seasons; Seasons: A Journey through Vivaldi —Cyberlin)

Four Weddings and a Funeral (PolyGram, 8006317692)

The charming 1993 British romantic comedy starring Andie MacDowell and Hugh Grant is both amusing and thoughtful, and is an efficiently conceived piece of entertainment that sustains its charms for its full 117 minutes. MacDowell is a talent-challenged actress and you can hear the change in tone on what sounds like substantial re-looping. Additionally, the hero has a brother with whom he appears to be very close, yet in order for a key scene at the end to be staged properly, the brother is not in the groom's wedding party. Such flaws, however, are as inconsequential as grains of rice beneath the wheels of a limousine, and the film is too slick and too solid to be impeded.

The presentation is in letterboxed format on one side, with an aspect ratio of about 1.8:1 and no 16:9 enhancement, and in full screen format on the other side. The letterboxing masks a little off the top and bottom of the full screen version and adds a little more to the sides. The letterboxed framing is definitely preferable, as there is enough missing on the edges of the full screen version to lose character reactions and compositional balance in many sequences. The picture looks super, with sharp, solid details and deep, strong colors. The stereo surround sound is reasonably smooth. The 117 minute film is accompanied by a theatrical trailer that sells the film superbly, as well as a nice music video, *Love Is All Around*, performed by an unidentified band. There is a small cast profile section and subtitles in English, French or Spanish.

Francesca da Rimini (see The Metropolitan Opera: Francesca da Rimini)

Francesco (Simitar, 7378)

Mickey Rourke stars as St. Francis of Assisi. The 1989 film, directed by Liliana Cavani and co-starring Helena Bonham Carter, tells the story of St. Francis in flashback as his followers discuss and record their memories of his life. The film follows a tradition of low budget Italian period films that evoke history with grime and tight camera angles, which don't have to show much dress or decor, but do pay close attention to the minor details of life in the past. Rourke's performance isn't bad, and the film's exploration of the Saint's philosophy (giving everything to the poor) and its downside (he's dirty and has sores all over—*Brother Sun, Sister Moon* this isn't) is stimulating.

The presentation is slightly cropped. The film's look is deliberately muddy to begin with, but the colors do not look fresh and there is often smearing or tiling in darker sequences. The stereophonic sound has a limited dimensionality and range. The lip movements of the central characters match the English dialogue, but some of the peripheral players are dubbed. The 118 minute film is accompanied by a partial Rourke filmography and is not captioned.

Frank Capra's American Dream (see The Matinee Idol)

Frank Sinatra /A Man and His Music (Warner Reprise, 332012)

Frank Sinatra / Sinatra in Concert at Royal Festival Hall (Warner Reprise, 382052)

Frank Sinatra / A Man and His Music + Ella + Jobim

(Warner Reprise, 382022)
Frank Sinatra / Ol' Blue Eyes Is Back (Warner Reprise, 382032),
Frank Sinatra / Sinatra: The Main Event (Warner Reprise, 382062)
Frank Sinatra / Francis Albert Sinatra Does His Thing (Warner, Reprise, 382092)

Sinatra's legendary voice is delivered with an incredible clarity and smoothness, while the video performances personalize his artistry. The older programs are a little more worn looking than the newer ones. In all, there is some grain and occasional ghosting, but well lit hues are bright and fleshtones are workable. The programs can be supported by optional English subtitles. On most of the programs, numerics on the jacket chapter listings do not coincide with the encoded chapters.

If we had to recommend just one of the six, it would probably be **A Man and His Music + Ella + Jobim**. Not only are there the added pleasures of Ella Fitzgerald and Antonio Carlos Jobim, giving the program a satisfying variety of musical genres, but Sinatra performs what may be the best rendition of *Ol' Man River* he ever recorded—it is even more articulated and emotionally accurate than his exquisite Reprise studio recording. Four of the programs, including **+ Ella + Jobim**, use the standard TV music special format, shot in front of a studio or make-believe audience with simple abstract sets, plenty of songs and amusing banter to bridge each sequence.

What was the first in this series of specials, **A Man and His Music**, is also quite good, though the program material is confined to his most ubiquitous standards and there is less exploration in his phrasing. The show's purpose, however, seems to be to introduce Sinatra to the Sixties TV viewership, and from that perspective it is an excellent accomplishment, basically defining that phase of Sinatra's career. Okay, okay, you have to get both this one and **+ Ella + Jobim**.

With **Ol' Blue Eyes Is Back**, Sinatra, who had just come out of his 'retirement,' was reinventing himself, giving up the energy his stamina could no longer maintain for more segmented phrasings that allowed his voice to explore each song deeply without strain. He had entered the autumn of his years, but found a manner of singing that could stave off winter indefinitely. The program includes some of his standards (you can compare *I've Got You Under My Skin* and *I Get a Kick out of You* with his renditions on **Man and His Music** to see his strategic adjustments) and he has an extended and enjoyable sequence with Gene Kelly. Okay, okay, you have to get this one also.

Although musically he never lost his footing, Sinatra was thrown for a loop by the upheaval in popular music formats that occurred in the Sixties and **Francis Albert Sinatra Does His Thing** is an example of how he attempted to tread the water of the times. He is joined by Diahann Carroll and by The Fifth Dimension, and tries very hard to seem hip. Still, the musical selection has fewer repetitions from the other programs and features *Lost in the Stars*, *Baubles Bangles and Beads*, and *Angle Eyes*.

The two concert programs are less satisfying than the studio programs. The highlight of **Concert at Royal Festival Hall**, is an introduction by Princess Grace. As for Sinatra, his concentration seems off a little, and most of the songs he performs are the songs he performs everywhere else, better.

You don't have to be a feminist to fidget uneasily at the number of times Sinatra uses the words "chick" and "broad" in song lyrics, replacing lyricists' more respectful appellations. It is one of the reasons some people find it difficult to acknowledge the brilliance of his talent. This comes to the forefront in the 1974 concert in Madison Square Garden on **The Main Event**. As a musical performance, the program has little to offer—the acoustics of the hall were not designed for intimate crooning—but the **Event**, produced by Roone Aldredge, is a fascinating near-disaster. Sinatra is testy and misses a number of cues. The crowd is only partially respectful and

an occasional cat-call can clearly be heard. The cameras often cut to members of the audience as he is singing, and when he begins his rampant lyric substitutions, you can catch more than one fan wincing at the changes. Thus, as he ends the set with *My Way*, the song takes on a new irony, and a hint of desperation.

Frank Sinatra / His Life and Times (Madacy, DVD99005)
Frank Sinatra / His Life and Times: The Singer / The Entertainer (Madacy, DVD990053)
Frank Sinatra / His Life and Times: The Early Years / The Radio Days (Madacy, DVD990051)
Frank Sinatra / His Life and Times: The Hollywood Years / The Television Era (Madacy, DVD990052)
Frank Sinatra / His Life and Times: The Friendships / The Rat Pack (Madacy, DVD990054)
Frank Sinatra / His Life and Times: The Humor / The Memorable Moments (Madacy, DVD90055)

DVDs don't get more serendipitous than this: Ethel Merman as Reno Sweeney, with Frank Sinatra and Bert Lahr, starring in a kinescoped recording of a live TV performance of *Anything Goes*, which, running about 50 minutes, is just half of **The Singer / The Entertainer**. The other half? Another TV special, this one in color, featuring Sinatra, Judy Garland and Dean Martin. They sing duets, trios, the works, and Garland performs a thrilling medley of Al Jolson tunes. As for *Anything Goes*, it is so precious fans will be afraid to blink while it is on. The black-and-white image has its share of impurities, and there is noticeable tiling on top of it, but the image is always sharp and the presentation looks super, particularly since, before the DVD spun up, we hadn't even known such a program existed. The picture on the Garland and Martin segment is fairly soft and the hues are faded, but again the power of the images supersedes such minor drawbacks. The monophonic sound on both pieces is also decent.

Madacy has released five Sinatra programs individually and collected in a box set. Each combines two programs that run around 50 minutes apiece and each DVD also contains a biographical segment with different sorts of discographies, filmographies and other material. There is some overlap and some new material in each DVD supplement. Each program opens with a five minute or so voiceover that summarizes different aspects of Sinatra's biography and career, usually in glowing terms (the voiceover also drowns out the opening minutes of *Anything Goes*, but it is done by the time Merman makes her entrance).

Not every program, however, is as strong as the two featured on **The Singer / The Entertainer**. After a quick montage of snapshots depicting Sinatra growing up and a couple clips from his big band days, **The Early Years** presents excerpts from a TV special that shows Sinatra performing with Bing Crosby, Louis Armstrong and Peggy Lee. The companion program, **The Radio Days**, is nothing but a recording of a radio broadcast played over a montage of rarely interesting archive photos. **The Hollywood Years** features a collection of original trailers, covering everything from *The Kissing Bandit* to *Dirty Dingus Magee*, including a 'making of' featurette for *The Detective*. The picture quality is often horrible and the trailers are rarely presented in their entirety. Its companion, **The Television Era**, presents another kinescoped TV special, from the late Fifties and, along with an extended segment with Elvis Presley, its most interesting component is the presence of Nancy Sinatra, in a fascinating pre-*Boots* get up that makes her look like Julie London or something. Sinatra interviews Eleanor Roosevelt in a TV clip on **The Friendships**, but most of the program is taken up by a promotional documentary depicting a world-wide charity tour. There are several concert sequences intercut with shots of Sinatra visiting various children's hospitals and such, but the picture quality is quite weak and the image is almost colorless. The picture and sound quality are both very strained on **The Rat Pack**, but fans will appreciate the program anyway, because it is a straightforward record of a Vegas nightclub routine performed by Sinatra, Martin and Sammy Davis, Jr. in the late Fifties or early Sixties and is more interesting for the horsing around they do than for the music, which is distorted and fuzzy on the soundtrack anyway. **The Humor** features two extended clips from *The Tonight Show*. The first is especially good, where Sinatra is interviewed by Johnny Carson and then assaulted by Don Rickles. In the second, Sinatra himself is a guest host, with George Burns as a guest, but none of the other evening's guests are shown. The color transfer is passable. The final program, **The Memorable Moments**, is simply a compilation of highlights from the other programs.

Frankenstein (see **Mary Shelley's Frankenstein**)

Frankenstein (Universal, 20325)

The black-and-white picture transfer is gorgeous. Although the image on the 1931 feature has some age-related softness, the image is much sharper than the previously definitive LD edition. Blacks are richer, and contrasts are more vivid. In fact, a blasphemous line of dialogue that was still missing in the 'Restored' LD version has been reinstated. The standard mono track is duller than the LD. There is also a Dolby Digital track that seems a little flat, though it is cleaner and is stronger than the standard track. The 71 minute program can be supported by optional English or French subtitles ("Et ici, le cerveau anormal du criminel typique"). Boris Karloff, Colin Clive and Mae Clarke star in the still enjoyable film, directed by James Whale.

The movie is accompanied by a number of supplementary materials. There is a 45 minute retrospective documentary, a 10 minute montage of stills and ad materials set to music and dialogue, a jokey 10 minute short from 1932, trailers from 1938 and 1951, production notes, a cast-and-director profile section (including what looks like a complete list of the 140 or so films Karloff was in) and a commentary track by film historian and commentary track veteran Rudy Behlmer. The *Universal Brevity* comedy short, using footage from Frankenstein, Nosferatu and some original material, has a Pete Smith-type narrative full of bad puns ("He better keep away from the casket or he'll be coughin'") and other amusements.

Universal makes great DVDs, but they also have some the worst menu designs on the market and the menu for **Frankenstein** does nothing to alter this reputation. Specifically, the menu selection for the documentary, which is called *The Frankenstein Files*, opens on an audio option screen (with no 'Play' option) and it took us a good 20 minutes to figure out that this screen represented the audio options for the documentary and not for the feature film.

Still, the documentary is worth the effort, going into the history of the film with interesting still photos of previous stage versions and preliminary makeup designs. There are clips from all the sequels, though while Universal takes pains to point out the availability of these titles on home video, they don't bother with rudimentary documentary-type information such as the date of each film. Between the documentary and the production notes, though, most of the film's production story is covered quite thoroughly. Behlmer, who is in the documentary, repeating some of what he says on the commentary track, adds a lot of anecdotes and interesting digressions on the latter, but he doesn't talk as much about Whale's technique as we would have liked and doesn't really have too much to say about the film at hand. He does provide a good summary of the stage productions of the work that occurred during the hundred years between the publication of the novel and the making of the film, and he is also well versed in the changes the script went through during its development and some of the interesting curiosities from earlier scripts that survive in the final film.

Frantic (Warner, 11787)

Four-fifths of a terrific thriller, Roman Polanski's 1988 feature is wonderful until the last act, where suddenly one character defies logic not once but twice in order to keep the plot moving, and the finale turns into a ludicrous ballet of convenient deaths. It is less disorienting on multiple viewings, and the rest of the movie—Harrison Ford is a tourist in Paris whose wife disappears—is so entertaining that for most of the 120 minute running time the viewer is enthralled with excitement, but the conclusion can leave one with a feeling akin to interrupted sex. Memories of its pleasures evaporate.

And about four-fifths of the picture is on view in the cropped DVD. You don't lose vital information with the cropping (the end credit scroll reveals the film's true 1.85:1 framing) but you do lose emotional resonances when characters are partially trimmed on the edges of the screen and background detail is obscured. The film is in clear need of a remastering effort in any case. The picture is way too grainy and colors are light, with bland fleshtones. The stereo surround sound is better. Although the mix is somewhat dated and separation effects are erratic, tones are well defined and the gunshots in the conclusion are super. The film is closed captioned with minor paraphrasing.

Free Willy (Warner, 18000)

The 1993 boy and his whale tale is letterboxed on one side, with an aspect ratio of about 2.35:1 and an accommodation for enhanced 16:9 playback, and is presented in cropped format on the other side. The cropped version works fine, even though you lose some of the whale. Fleshtones are pinkish, but the picture quality is fairly good, with deep hues. The stereo surround sound is okay, and the Dolby Digital track has more power and more dimensionality (though rear channel effects are more pronounced on the standard track). The 112 minute film is also available in French and Spanish in standard stereo and comes with English, French or Spanish subtitles, trailers for all three Willy films (the trailer for the first film tells the entire movie, but somehow still managed to draw customers), a cast and crew profile and extensive production notes.

Fresh Live Cream (Image, ID5505CADVD)

The retrospective documentary combines interviews with the band members from the early Nineties and old performance footage from the late Sixties. The 73 minute program moves chronologically, tracing the separate histories of the three band members, Ginger Baker, Jack Bruce and Eric Clapton, and how they formed what they believed at the time to be the 'cream' of the British rock and blues bands. Most of the song clips are played in full and the show provides an excellent overview of the classic British blues rock band, along with contemplating the impact the band had on its era. The most significant aspect to the program, however, is that the three musicians are still in full command of their intellects and can reflect upon their past experiences with insight. As one points out, even on evenings when they knew their performances stunk, they were met with incredible adulation.

The concert clips usually play in full and present the group's best known numbers. There are a few TV spots and the like, but most of the footage comes from stage shows and features extreme close-ups of the group's faces. The Nineties footage looks okay and the older footage can be appreciated for its historic value. Some of it looks super, while some of it looks fairly battered. Even at its grainiest, however, artifacting does not appear to be a problem. Technically, the sound is stereophonic, but most of the music is mono. Still, it sounds good, even when it is compromised by makeshift live recordings. The program is not captioned.

The Freshman (Columbia TriStar, 90299)

Despite a somewhat sophomoric opening, the 1990 feature is a delightfully clever comedy that revels in American cultural absurdities. Matthew Broderick is a college student who is employed for a special task by a gangster, played with great delight by Marlon Brando. In that the director, Andrew Bergman, is drawing humor from exaggerations, some viewers may be uncomfortable with the story before the denouement lays everything out, but we found ourselves laughing at things—such as the offhand reference to the nickname of Brando's character, "Jimmy the Toucan"—in a way that we have not laughed for a long time. Indeed there is joy simply in the thought of seeing Brando in a college dormroom, one of the film's many incongruities that a viewer, beforehand, would have supposed could never be viewed in a natural lifetime. Bert Parks also indulges in astute self-parody, and there are several good gags about film criticism and scholarship. The movie has stretches that are significantly weaker than its best moments, but with comedies this is usually excusable.

The picture is presented in letterboxed format on one side, with an aspect ratio of about 1.85:1 and an accommodation for enhanced 16:9 playback, and is in full screen format on the other side. Colors are consistently solid and fleshtones look sharp. There is a stereo surround soundtrack is reasonably entertaining. The 102 minute program also has French and Spanish language soundtracks, optional English, French or Spanish subtitling, and a trailer.

Friday (New Line, N46680)

A comedy about life in South Central Los Angeles, Ice Cube and Chris Taylor star as two unemployed youths who are witness to or involved in a number of incidents during a supposedly typical neighborhood day. The acting is often broad and grating, but there are also a few amusing gags and the tone of the film can grow on you as the day progresses. Some of the film's thunder was stolen by the more blatantly parodistic **Don't Be a Menace…**, but it is still a funny concoction with enjoyable characters and a touch of insight, and it has developed a strong following. John Witherspoon is also featured.

The picture is letterboxed with an aspect ratio of about 1.85:1 and an accommodation for enhanced 16:9 playback. The low budget film has a deliberately drab color scheme, and is a little grainy and reddish. The picture is very sharp, though, and colors are adequately delineated. The stereo surround sound is passable, though the bass could use a little more color. The 91 minute feature can be supported by English, French or Spanish subtitles and is accompanied by a cast & crew profile section, a green tag and a red tag trailer, music videos by Ice Cube and Dr. Dre, and several funny deleted or alternate (longer) take sequences. There is also a 20 minute interview with the director, F. Gary Gray, and another interview that is almost as long with the producer, Patricia Charbonnet. Charbonnet explains that she wanted to create a 'cult' hit and talks about bringing the personnel together. Gray shot the film on the block where he grew up, and talks about working with the cast and the limited budget (it was so tight, they literally couldn't afford to laugh at Tucker's improvisations).

Fried Green Tomatoes (Universal, 20244)

Director Jon Avnet calls **Fried Green Tomatoes** a 'fable' on the commentary track, pointing out that Fannie Flagg's novel, upon which the film is based, follows a rich tradition in Southern literature of 'larger than life' storytelling. The 1991 film is a lovely, delicate mixture of comedy and drama—episodes in the lives of two women being retold long after the fact—and it works because it teeters on exaggeration—and the humor instilled by exaggeration—without succumbing. Mary Stuart Masterson and Mary-Louise Parker star, with Jessica Tandy and Kathy Bates in the framing narrative.

The film presented on DVD runs 137 minutes, some 7 minutes longer than the standard theatrical release. There is one sequence near the end, where Tandy and Bates attend a gospel concert, that stops the movie dead when it ought to be getting on with the finale, but it is easy to see why Avnet included it, because the music is so good. Most of what has been added, however, is simply amplifications of character, filling in bits of details that don't movie the story forward, but give it a stronger foundation.

The picture is letterboxed, with an aspect ratio of about 1.85:1 and an accommodation for enhanced 16:9 playback. The image transfer is great, with bright, crisp hues and accurate fleshtones. The film's stereo soundtrack does not have an elaborate mix, but is

adequately delivered. The movie can be supported by English, French or Spanish subtitles. Avnet provides some insights to the drama on his commentary, and shares stories about the production, but there is a 65 minute documentary, also included, that does a better job at explaining how the movie came together. Some of what Avnet says on the commentary track is word-for-word what he says in the documentary, and he also provides a lot of play-by-play. Other supplementary features include excerpts from the script that feature Avnet's notes, a very good and extensive montage of production photos, posters (many varieties—it is hard to tell if they were all used, or if they were proposed and abandoned), a collection of recipes (printable on DVD-ROM) including the making of 'fried green tomatoes,' an optional isolation of the film's musical score (in stereo) during the documentary, cast and director profiles and a theatrical trailer.

Friend of the Family (Image, ID5593FMDVD)

A pointless softcore erotic film about a dysfunctional family that is brought together by a free-spirited houseguest, the 1995 effort has value only for its unintentional humor, and even that doesn't amount to much. The bad acting (and casting—the 'teenage' daughter looks older than her 'father'), awful dialogue ("I love my filmmaking. It's all I ever think about") and silly plot (the father thinks the oldest son is going to law school when in reality he's going to film school; in this, there is supposed dramatic conflict) are good for some chuckles, but that is about it. Fleshtones are pinkish and contrasts are washy, with bland hues. The stereo sound is uneventful and the 102 minute program is not captioned.

Friend of the Family II (Image, ID5594FMDVD)

The Hand That Rocked the Cradle is the inspiration for the better than average erotic thriller from 1996. Shauna O'Brien stars, but the film is no relation to the first **Friend of the Family**. A distracted businessman has a one-night stand that leads to a brief affair. When he breaks it off, she goes cuckoo and gets a job as nanny to his child. He can't say anything, or she'll tell his wife what happened. The erotic sequences are suitably steamy and for a while the narrative has a strong momentum. The ending is a bit of a fizzle, but not enough to leave you feeling cheated.

The picture is sharp, with bright colors but bland fleshtones. The stereo sound is modest, but reasonably dimensional. The 90 minute program is not captioned.

The Frighteners (Universal, 20286)

Peter Jackson ran to his native New Zealand to shoot his first big budget Hollywood production (which is set in America), but it didn't help. The Wellington locations are one of the 1996 film's most attractive features, but the script is loaded with moments that could zap a viewer with dizzying scares, and Jackson just doesn't deliver. The special effects are bland and the camera angles rarely generate thrills. The pre-credit gag, for example, ought to conclude with a specter lunging straight at the viewer. Instead, it dives under a rug and you barely see it. Michael J. Fox stars as a psychic who is fighting the ghost of a mass murderer while being blamed for the ghost's new victims. The premise has strong comical overtones and could have been a *Ghostbusters* with bite. Instead, it is a *Casper* with milk toast.

The presentation is letterboxed with an aspect ratio of about 2.35:1 and an accommodation for enhanced 16:9 playback. The colors are fine (the film's color scheme is often subdued) and the image is sharp. The stereo surround sound is weak, but the Dolby Digital soundtrack packs a decent punch. The 110 minute film is also available in French and comes with English or Spanish subtitles. There is a production essay, cast & crew profile and a theatrical trailer.

From Dusk till Dawn (Buena Vista, 14373)

George Clooney and Quentin Tarantino star in the 1998 film, with Harvey Keitel and Juliette Lewis. Tarantino also wrote the script. The film has a great deal of violence and is for dedicated genre fans only, but it is ideal DVD material, with the action scenes begging for multiple replays. Clooney and Tarantino portray bank robbers who pick the wrong Mexican bar to while away the night. The script alone would make it a worthy genre exercise, but Rodriguez's hands-on direction (his name is listed almost a half dozen times on the end credit scroll in the different technical categories) hot-wires the film's energy, while the casting is overloaded with star power—even Tarantino is a delight, in his own way.

The image is letterboxed with an aspect ratio of about 1.85:1 and no 16:9 enhancement. The film had a modest budget and the lighting is not meticulous, so some sequences are more colorful than others, but the image is consistently sharp and fleshtones are okay. The stereo surround sound and Dolby Digital sound also seem on par with the LD, providing a lively energy at appropriate moments. The 108 minute program can be supported by English or Spanish subtitles. There are also two enjoyable trailers ("Vampires. No Interviews").

From Russia with Love (MGM, 906725)

The James Bond film is presented in dual layer format, letterboxed with an aspect ratio of about 1.75:1 on one layer, with accommodation for enhanced 16:9 playback, and slightly format on the other layer. Fleshtones are rich, blacks are solid and other colors are bright. The monophonic sound is fairly bland. The 115 minute film is also available in French and Spanish and comes with English, French or Spanish subtitles. It is accompanied by a theatrical trailer, some informative production notes, an uninspired montage of action sequences from the pre-Pierce Brosnan Bond films, and elaborate but uninteresting reference functions that pull up key sequences from the films. The end title sequence has the 'James Bond will return' message that earlier video presentations were missing, but there is still a bad splice that suggests not all of the dialogue has been restored. Sean Connery stars in the 1963 feature, about stealing a Russian code machine.

From the Earth to the Moon (HBO, 99363)

Comprised of twelve 55 minute episodes, a dramatization of America's Apollo moon landing program, the show has been issued on three single-sided dual-layer platters, with a fourth platter containing supplementary features. The picture quality is excellent, with smooth, crisp colors and a dependable stability regardless of the complicated imagery, special effects or lighting. Rear channel effects are limited, but there is a strong dimensionality and crisper detail on the Dolby Digital track than on the standard stereo track, and for a cable television production, the sound is quite satisfying The program is also available in Spanish in mono and can be supported by English, French or Spanish subtitles ("C'est un petit pas pour l'homme…un bond géant pour l'humanité").

In tone and attitude, the miniseries is essentially a sequel to **Apollo 13**, and if it is the brainchild of Hanks, Ron Howard is clearly its godfather. The special effects are outstanding, not just for their realism, but for their application—there is, for example, an utterly arresting shot, supposedly from the moon's surface, of Apollo 8 silently crossing the lunar night sky. The combination of the sophisticated effects work with the rapidly paced, historically accurate head shot dramatics that the best TV docudramas do so well creates a day's worth (or week's worth, depending upon your viewing habits) of engrossing and moving entertainment. The series is inconsistent. Many of the twelve episodes have different directors, different writers, and different crews—even different music composers, the cast (featuring a great number of character actors and secondary stars, including Ted Levine, Lane Smith, Cary Elwes, Clint Howard, etc.) is the show's only consistency—but the weaker episodes are irrelevant to the overall effect the program has when seen in a single or closely spaced viewing. The tragedies and the triumphs, the anecdotes and the revelations, the humor and the excitement are enthralling, and it is very easy to lose yourself in

the series and to end up, at the very least, watching more episodes at one time than you originally intended.

Because each episode is so different, however, it is worthwhile to make some brief notations upon them. Hanks directed the opener, *Can We Do This?*, about the Mercury and Gemini programs and everything that led up to Apollo. It assumes a familiarity with **The Right Stuff** and the standard documentaries, yet it manages to provide a comprehensive (if all too brief) overview that is fresh and original. The show's depiction of the first American space walk does not coincide with what we have read about the incident and appears to gloss over both the manner in which it was conceived and the way it was executed, but that sort of dramatic license rarely infringes upon the accuracy of the drama. *Apollo One*, directed by David Frankel, is a complete and free-standing story about the fatal fire and the investigation that followed. Lili Fini Zanuck directed *We Have Cleared the Tower*, about getting the program underway after Apollo One. Much of the episode is seen through the eyes of a 'documentary' crew, but the device is too distancing and while there are a few sequences that are fairly involving, much of the episode is a bore. The same cultural advancements that brought the engineering knowledge needed to reach the moon brought an information explosion and associated social turmoil created by the availability of that information. This phenomenon is depicted quite effectively in *1968*, a year that was marked by assassinations and demonstrations, and yet ended with man's first full escape from the grasp of the Earth, the Apollo 8 mission. It was as if the whole human race (including Hanks and Howard) were going through its adolescence. The episode was directed by Frankel.

One of the best episodes in the series, *Spider*, directed by Graham Yost, opens the second platter. About the development of the Lunar Excursion Module, the narrative jumps back in time to trace the story of how the method for landing on the moon was developed (i.e., what parts stay with the orbiter and what parts go down to the surface), and the seven years of intense design and testing undergone by the Grumman Corporation to deliver the vehicle. The next episode, *Mare Tranquilitatis*, the central episode of the whole series, depicts the first moon landing. Directed by Frank Marshall, the episode is competently executed and tells the inside story of the crew's efforts to execute their assignment, but it remains a bit distanced from the personalities of the astronauts and never gets as deeply into the technical aspects of the landing as some viewers may want. The second moon landing is depicted in *That's All There Is*, also directed by Marshall, and the filmmakers do everything in their power to differentiate it from the previous episode. The narrative jumps back and forth in time in a seemingly random pattern and the personalities of the astronauts (a more lighthearted bunch than the first crew) are given a greater emphasis. It is annoying, but at least it doesn't seem as redundant as the flight itself. The Apollo 13 story is told in *We Interrupt This Program* from the perspective of the press—again, the filmmakers were trying to find some angle that hadn't been used before—with a secondary theme being the generational shift between old journalism and new journalism. Directed by Frankel, it seems the most fictionalized of the episodes and never builds up the tension of the flight as greatly as other depictions of it have, but as a portrait of NASA's relationship with the press and what that meant to NASA's existence, it may be the most insightful episode in the series.

The two episodes that open the third platter, *For Miles & Miles*, directed by Gary Fleder, and *Galileo Was Right*, directed by David Carson, are outstanding. *Miles & Miles* jumps back in time again to catch up on what happened to Alan Shepard after his fifteen minute Mercury flight, which was depicted in the first episode. Since Shepard was the commander of Apollo 14, the episode is able to depict the details of the mission and still retain a strong character drama. *Galileo* was the only episode in the series that brought tears to our eyes. Because of budget cuts the later Apollo missions were condensed and the astronauts were forced into a crash course on geology and scientific method to execute previously unplanned assignments. Fortunately, they found an instructor who did not just provide them with the knowledge they required, but instilled within them the desire to learn. Not only does the episode depict the Apollo 15 mission succinctly while doing an exceptional job at exploring the personalities of all three astronauts (usually just one or two are profiled in detail), but it is a heartwarming tribute to the priceless value of teachers everywhere. Sally Field directed *The Original Wives Club*, about the Apollo 16 mission (briefly) and the astronaut wives. You could probably make a whole miniseries about the wives, and the one problem with the episode is that you need to watch it a couple times to figure out who everyone is. In attempting to cover so much, the episode jumps around a lot, but it has a number of emotional climaxes and is a welcome shift in tone from the other episodes. The finale, *Le Voyage dans la Lune*, cuts between a depiction of Georges Méliès filming his famous 1906 silent film and the very successful, though sadly conclusive, Apollo 17 excursion.

And then there is the platter devoted to supplementary materials. It contains a longish, generalized 'making of' featurette, which emphasizes the film's cast, and an all-too short 'making of' featurette, which looks at how the outstanding special effects were achieved (and the incredible art direction—the simple re-creation of the lunar landscapes for the moonwalk sequences is amazing; on the whole, the show's special effects are as good, in an effect-to-narrative-quality ratio, as anything that appeared in the movies this year), along with a collection of a dozen TV commercials, an up-to-date interactive 'tour' of the solar system, a less interesting profile of three '3D' models, a poorly conceived summary of the specific Apollo flight mission directives, a decent timeline that emphasizes the Apollo missions while putting them in a wider context, and the text to John F. Kennedy's go-for-the-moon speech. The platter also contains DVD-ROM materials that require, among other things, 100 megabytes of hard drive. Most of those megs are for things like Netscape, however. There are also extensive hooks to Sprint's EarthLink site (we're still trying to delete them all), while material contained within the ROM itself includes a longer text version of the Kennedy speech, text profiles of a dozen famous astronomers, text summaries of a half dozen future unmanned space probes, text descriptions of deep space phenomena such as black holes, and QuickTime views of a moonscape and lander interior.

From the Journals of Jean Seberg (Image, ID5107WBDVD)

An irritating profile of the film actress Jean Seberg, it is filled with admittedly intelligent insights about movies and society, but it also takes off on tangents and digressions using Kevin Bacon. Game-type links to relate Seberg's work to that of Jane Fonda and Vanessa Redgrave. Mary Beth Hurt narrates, kind of pretending to be Seberg, though there is no real 'Journal,' just heavy academic and political analysis applied to aspects of Seberg's life and career. Surprisingly, Seberg's nightmarish harassment by the FBI, though mentioned, is not extensively explored, and her involvement with the Black Panthers is kind of glossed over. There is a fascinating overview of how directors cast the stars that they marry, an interesting look at the 'jinx' that follows actresses who play Joan of Arc in films, and gossip about Seberg's fling with Clint Eastwood during *Paint Your Wagon*. It appears that Otto Preminger deliberately burned her during the shooting of *Joan*, and had Life Magazine standing by to capture the moment, and there is a thorough analysis of Seberg's presence in *Breathless*, which Jean-Luc Godard claimed was an extension of her character from *Bonjour Tristesse*. But the filmmakers also get a bit silly, placing Barbra Streisand's face on Seberg's body when speculating on how things would have turned out if Streisand had been cast as Joan, and bringing out arcane 'facts' (Josh Logan directed Fonda in her first film and Seberg in her last film) that have nothing to do with anything and cheapen the film's legitimate insights.

The film clips vary in quality, but are rarely strong, and some are even misapplied—a cropped image from *Klute* is used to suggest that a monologue by Jane Fonda has been shot with direct allusions to Carl Theodor Dreyer's *The Passion of Joan of Arc*. The monophonic sound is adequate and the 96 minute program is not captioned.

The Front Page GoodTimes, 0581020)

Billy Wilder's adaptation of the classic media frenzy comedy is in cropped format only. Characters often speak into empty space and comical double takes are lost in the area beyond the edge of the screen. Curiously, Wilder keeps the story's cynicism to a minimum. He and I.A.L. Diamond updated the well known play for their 1974 release, adding saucier dialogue and a few other frills. Although they muffed the third act, the film, which stars Jack Lemmon and Walter Matthau, is good, lighthearted entertainment, or would be if you could see its sides.

Along with being cropped, the picture also looks fuzzy in a blown-up sort of way. The accuracy of the colors can compensate if one stands far enough away from one's monitor to lose the grain. The monophonic sound is fine. The 105 minute program has optional English, French and Spanish subtitles.

The Fugitive (Warner, 21000)

The picture transfer is gorgeous. Fleshtones are always accurate, the image is always crisp and the colors are so glossy that the aerial views of Chicago look three dimensional. The DVD is letterboxed on one side, with an aspect ratio of about 1.85:1 and no 16:9 enhancement, and presented in full screen format on the other. The letterboxing adds some minor picture information to the sides of the image and masks off more from the top and bottom compared to the full screen picture, though either seems to work. The regular stereo surround sound is passable, but the Dolby Digital track has a lot more going on and comes much closer to the theatrical experience. The 131 minute film is accompanied by biographical sketches of the cast. The film is also available in French in standard stereo and can be accompanied by English, French or Spanish subtitles.

The film, which stars Harrison Ford and Tommy Lee Jones, works terrifically well on DVD, perhaps even better than it does on a large theatrical screen. The film's pace, its showy action scenes, crisp dialogue and certified star power are spellbinding from beginning to end. We would caution only that under repeat viewings aspects to the plot may start to seem a bit illogical—How did the villain expect to get away with the murder to begin with? Where does the hero get the end date he uses in his search criteria when he enters the computer database? If the police interviewed the one-armed man at the time of the original investigation, why wasn't the hero aware of it and given access to the guy's picture? A movie does not have the luxury of a TV series to investigate the psychology of the characters in any sort of elaborate manner, and the film is smashingly good at giving out just enough personality so that the viewer feels what is going on inside the hero's head (and he also saves a child). Barry Morse's interpretation of the pursuer, Philip Gerard, on the TV show, however, was a gripping portrayal of a man conscious of his obsession with his job, so conscious that he is wracked with guilt every time he abandons his family to chase after a lead. Jones' character, Samuel Gerard (what's wrong, doesn't Jones look like a "Phil?") has no outside life in the movie and no obsession. That is, perhaps, why Jones' Oscar-winning performance is so admired, because he took a characterization that was written purely on the surface (until the film's last line, which turns the movie into sort of a "Sleepless in Chicago"), keeps it on the surface, and through the force of his own presence and leash-like diction, binds the viewer to him.

Full Metal Jacket (Warner, 17371)

Many of Stanley Kubrick's films are segmented into smaller whole narratives and one of the most distinctive examples of this is his Vietnam movie, **Full Metal Jacket**. The boot camp drama that takes up the 116 minute film's first 40 or so minutes is a freestanding and unnerving portrait of soldiers pushed to the edge. Kubrick's mastery of technique so powerful that he is able to enter one of the most repetitive extended situations in movies—the training of recruits—giving it a fresh viewpoint and an incredible sense of immediacy. His camera floats about chest high and always makes you believe you are in the barracks with the soldiers instead of on the outside looking in. The subsequent Vietnam sequence is more abstract and less deeply involving, but that is a calculated reflection upon the nature of the War, and the action scenes hold a viewer's attention to the end, while the film's complicated moral and psychological explorations unfold. It is easier now to follow the characters, incidentally, than it was when the 1987 film first came out, because many of the actors have gone on to become stars, including Matthew Modine, Adam Baldwin and Vincent D'Onofrio. R. Lee Ermy, of course, gives a definitive performance as the drill sergeant.

The presentation is not letterboxed, which is not how it appeared in theaters, though it is doubtful much is missing from the sides. The source material also contains some speckling, including white dots on the supposedly solid black end credit scroll. Fleshtones appear accurate, the lighting is always stable and the image is very crisp. The monophonic sound is fine. There is an alternate French audio track, optional English or French subtitles and a trailer.

Funny Farm (Warner, 11809)

Chevy Chase and Madolyn Smith try their hand at a premise that is older than movies—city folks moving to the country—in George Roy Hill's 1988 comedy. Hill's talents were on the wane, but it is a formula effort with some decent amusements, and the story improves as it goes along.

The picture is presented in full screen format. Darker sequences are a little soft, but generally hues are bright and the image is crisp, with passable fleshtones. Dimensional effects are limited, but the stereo is very clear and Elmer Bernstein's musical score is robust. There is also a French stereo track, and the 101 minute program has English captioning.

Funny Games (Fox Lorber, FLV5055)

A sadistic Austrian thriller with a metaphysical twist at the end, most of the film is a straightforward tale about two nicely dressed punks who terrorize a well-to-do family in a large but isolated vacation house. Directed by Michael Haneke, the film is allows the unrelentingly mean villains to get away with everything, including murder, and then, after the viewer is thoroughly numbed by the pain and torture of the sympathetic characters, Haneke has the villain start winking at the camera and changing the sequence of events. He's clearly making a movie about fantasizing serial crimes, but the balance of the film's emotions is not changed by such sleight-of-hand excuses. The conclusion opens a great many intriguing ideas and encourages philosophical contemplation, but the rest of the movie is still nasty and distasteful.

The picture is letterboxed with an aspect ratio of about 1.75:1 and no 16:9 enhancement. The picture is sharp and well lit, with strong colors. Even scenes set in semi-darkness are clear, with well-defined shadings. The stereo surround sound is also fairly good, with a decent dimensionality and a reasonable amount of power, though most of the film is just dialogue and incidental sound effects. The 103 minute program is in German with permanent English subtitles. A trailer and some filmographies are also included.

G

G.I. Jane (Buena Vista, 14250)

Demi Moore stars as the world's first female SEALs trainee. The plot doesn't make much sense—if Anne Bancroft's character expected her to fail, why wasn't that the criteria she used to choose her?—but the film manages to whip up enough gung ho emotion that if you don't question orders and just get swept along with it, it can be fairly entertaining. Directed by Ridley Scott, the film has a familiar structure, depicting the rigors of training and the apparent inability of the trainees to coalesce, followed by a for real situation where they rise to the occasion. The bottom line is we need a new, loud, military action movie every month or so to make up for all the Henry James adaptations that keep appearing, and **G.I. Jane** fits that bill just fine.

The picture is fairly dark, losing too much details to the shadows. Otherwise, it is passable, with an abundance of artistic grain and blue-grey color tones. The stereo surround sound has a slightly more pronounced bass but slightly less developed upper end. The Dolby Digital track is more energized. There is a French language track in Dolby Digital. The 125 minute film can be supported by English or Spanish subtitles ("Su presencia nos vuelve a todos vulnerables") and is accompanied by a theatrical trailer.

A Gala Christmas in Vienna (Sony, SVD60759)

The stage is gussied up like a department store Santa corner, and the songs are much more likely to be popular standards and less likely to be obscure 'traditional' hymns. Plácido Domingo is joined by Sarah Brightman, Helmut Lotti and Riccardo Cocciante, with the Vienna Symphony Orchestra and a children's chorus, conducted by Steven Mercurio.

The picture is excellent, with very sharp, stable colors and accurate fleshtones. The stereo surround sound and menu-activated Dolby Digital sound are also superb, with smooth, undistorted tones and a strong dimensionality. The 73 minute program is accompanied by performer profiles and a background essay, presented in several languages including English.

Gallipoli (Paramount, 015047)

Peter Weir's international hit also brought a vastly increased stardom Mel Gibson's way. The last 20 minutes are about battle, and the film concludes with the famous World War I slaughter, but most of the 111 minute feature depicts the adventures of two young men who eventually enlist and travel halfway around the world to participate in a war they do not understand in the least.

Because the real life events it depicts are so senseless and so tragic, we really don't care much for the film, but others admire it and Paramount has done a fine job bringing it to DVD. It is in letterboxed format only, with an aspect ratio of about 2.35:1 and an accommodation for enhanced 16:9 playback. The color transfer is excellent, with sharp, accurate hues and good looking fleshtones. The 1981 feature has a stereo surround sound mix, but it isn't all that active, providing little more than a generalized dimensionality for the musical score and some of the battle sequences. There is also a 5.1 Dolby Digital track, but it doesn't add much to the mix, either. There is a French audio track in mono, optional French subtitles, English closed captioning and a trailer, as well as a very good 7 minute or so interview with Weir, who talks about many facets of the film's creation and execution.

The Game (PolyGram, 4400478352)

Michael Douglas stars as a very rich guy who gets what in essence is an epic street performance for his birthday. He is sent on an undefined mission by his brother and soon finds reality slipping away from him at every turn. We found it clever that one of the game's rules turns out to be a need to collect keys, since that usually seems to be what a player has to accumulate in the typical computer or video game that the film, in its best moments, starts to imitate. David Fincher directed, and it is his sense of style and rhythm that saves the movie from seeming ridiculous or artificially manipulative. However, we read in a number of places that after the film was over a viewer was going to want to watch it again right away, while we found that once was quite enough to take everything in.

The 1987 film is in full screen format on one side and in letterboxed format on the other, with an aspect ratio of about 2.35:1 and no 16:9 accommodation. The letterboxing masks picture information off the top and bottom of the image and adds picture information to the sides in comparison to the full screen release, but we found the letterbox framing to be more satisfying. The 128 minute film has many darker sequences, but the image is generally slick and glossy. The stereo surround sound and Dolby Digital soundtracks are good. The dialogue often has a souped-up resonance or echo and other sounds are precisely defined and elaborately compiled, with the Dolby Digital track delivering a slightly fuller sound than the standard track. The film is also available in French and can be accompanied by English or Spanish subtitles. There is a teaser (which doesn't work very well), a standard theatrical trailer (which works a bit better) and a small cast profile section.

Ganja & Hess (Allday, 98040001)

The 1973 film about black vampires was made by an African-American director on a very cramped budget. The film's budget is so constrained that dialogue is often presented in voiceover while the characters' faces are kept offscreen.

Having read and listened to the DVD's supplementary materials, we have a moderate amount of respect for the film and the writer-director, Bill Gunn. The dialogue is intelligent, some of the images are striking and the story is clearly exploring more than just a vampire myth and its metaphors, as it ponders links between African and western culture. On the other hand, the narrative is not immediately accessible (a story eventually materializes, in which the vampire falls for the wife of one of his victims), and some scenes tend to drag on about seemingly nothing. When this is combined with the movie's very low budget production values, it is easy to see how some viewers would regard it as an incoherent mess. At its best, it evokes guerrilla films such as *The Harder They Come*, but that may just be wishful thinking on our part.

The picture is letterboxed, with an aspect ratio of about 1.85:1 and an accommodation for enhanced 16:9 playback. Shot in Super-16, the film is naturally grainy and soft-looking, particularly since the cinematography is rarely lit with much elaboration. The colors do look reasonably bright and we have no doubt that this is the best possible transfer that could be eked out of the only available source material. The monophonic sound is equally battered, but coherent much of the time. The film runs 110 minutes (it has been circulated theatrically with a shorter cut under the title, *Blood Couple*) and is accompanied by a comprehensive Tim Lucas essay that originally appeared in third issue of Video Watchdog, and a handful of stills.

On one audio track, producer Chiz Schultz, cinematographer James Hinton, actress Marlene Clark and composer Sam Waymon provide a very good commentary, reminiscing about the shoot with great humor, providing insightful technical details (use only hard lenses, not zooms, with super-16) and discussing how, for its time, the film was truly innovative (Hinton had to fight to allow the fleshtones of the performers to vary realistically). The best story, however, is about the time the Teamsters tried to close down the production, until they learned it was an all-black shoot and decided they wanted nothing to do with it. Sometimes bigotry can be put to good use.

The Gate to the Mind's Eye (Simitar, 7321)

Set to music by Thomas Dolby, the 50 minute program is a compilation of computer animated images and shorts that consistently spark the imagination, from an amusement ride-like trip through the portals of a futuristic city to the animation of Leonardo Da Vinci's drawings and Egyptian hieroglyphics. Several of the segments have science fiction themes, zipping about moon bases or futuristic cityscapes, but there is also a chorus of dancing chrome penguins and several abstract pieces that do no more than shift in shape and color, though usually in unexpected and remarkable ways. The colors are deep and sharp, and movement is smooth. Hues are bright and the image is crisp. The stereo surround sound is also sharp and is nicely detailed.

Gattaca (Columbia TriStar, 82649)

A very rare type of movie, an intelligent, grown up science fiction film, Ethan Hawke stars as an elite technician who is trying to hide his true identity and humble beginnings in a world where random genetic testing and identification are an everyday occurrence. Although the film uses modernistic architecture and has a minimum of special effects, it is consistently suspenseful and rich with ideas about the future of mankind. The narrative is easy to follow, and yet it has enough detail and depth to support the film's imagination. Uma Thurman co-stars.

The film is presented in letterboxed format on one side, with an aspect ratio of about 2.35:1 and an accommodation for enhanced 16:9 playback, and in cropped format on the other side, although the cropping destroys the film's meticulously chosen imagery (if you were to take the filmmakers' philosophy to heart, however, then the cropped picture is preferable to the letterboxed picture). The cinematography uses difficult colored lighting at times, but the image remains sharp and stable in all situations. The film's sound mix has a kind of austere ambiance, but directional and atmospheric details are carefully applied. The standard stereo track sounds fine, but the Dolby Digital track is slightly sharper, with clearer details. The 106 minute film is also available in French and Spanish, and comes with English, French or Spanish subtitles. The DVD has several extras, including a theatrical trailer, a somewhat longer 'making of' promotional piece, a few nice publicity photos and several deleted scenes, including a blooper segment. The deleted scenes do not belong in the film, but they do give the viewer a better rounded understanding of what the filmmakers were trying to put across, particularly an intriguing text epilogue about the supposed need for genetic imperfection.

The Gauntlet (Warner, 11083)

Clint Eastwood is a slow-witted cop who has to transport a mob witness from Vegas to Phoenix with assassins lurking at every turn. The 1977 film is an adequate exercise, but it is somewhat far-fetched and Eastwood's character is not all that appealing—to the point, in fact, where his personality is incongruous with the film's smooth jazz musical score.

The 111 minute film is presented in letterboxed format only, with an aspect ratio of about 2.35:1 and an accommodation for enhanced 16:9 playback. The colors look fine, with accurate fleshtones, though it is possible that more intensity could be squeezed out of them. The image is sharp. The stereo sound is a bit weak, but the Dolby Digital track has clearer definitions. The program also has a French mono track and can be supported by English or French subtitles. There is a cast & crew profile section and a trailer.

The General (Columbia TriStar, 03726)

John Boorman's 1998 drama about an Irish crime boss was shown in theaters in black and white, and so Columbia TriStar has opted to present the film in black and white on one side, and with 'desaturated color' on the other. Both presentations are letterboxed, with an aspect ratio of about 2.35:1 and an accommodation for enhanced 16:9 playback. We can't really say that if we had watched the color version first we would have been able to sit through the black-and-white version, and we could detect no com-pelling reason for the film to be in black and white except that it enhances the tabloid elements of the narrative, but taken as it was intended, the black-and-white presentation is valid. Contrasts are consistently striking, and blacks are deep and glossy. The image is spotless and crisp. The very drained color version (only yellows seem vivid) is so blandly hued that it is not a strong alternative, and is simply a balm for those who can't countenance the black and white.

Brendan Gleeson gives a very memorable performance as the ti-tle character, covering his face whenever he's in public so people can't get a good look at him. Except that he routinely breaks the law, he's like any other blue-collar worker or, more closely, like a union leader of some sort. The first half of the film has a series of very clever capers—and a fair amount of humor—so that as the fortunes of the hero turn downward in the film's second half, you don't mind going along for the fall. Based upon a true story, the film might be mistaken for another IRA picture—which turns some people off—but it has very little to do with that and is prima-rily a crime movie, with rich characters and a stimulating conflict between the murky worlds of the morally right and the morally wrong.

On the copy we viewed, the label side that said the film was in black and white contained the color version, and vice versa. The stereo sound includes a nice, vaguely jazzy musical score by Richie Buckley, but dimensionality is fairly basic. The 124 minute film has optional English, French or Spanish subtitles, and a cast-and-di-rector profile section.

George Balanchine's The Nutcracker (Warner, 13000)

The New York City Ballet version features Macaulay Culkin, who, according to the informative cast and crew profile, was no stranger to the piece, having appeared on stage in a production by the American Ballet Theatre before he became famous. The film is a fairly straightforward, elegant, and perhaps a bit too refined pre-sentation of the famous holiday ballet. Darci Kistler, Damian Woetzel, Kyra Nichols and Bart Robinson Cook are among the fea-tured dancers in the 1993 film, which was directed by Emile Ar-dolino. The 93 minute program is in letterboxed format on one side, with an aspect ratio of about 1.85:1 and an accommodation for 16:9 enhanced playback, and is in full screen format on the oth-er side. The letterboxing adds a bit to the sides and presents a very satisfying rectangular composition, though there are shots where being able to see the unmasked top and bottom of the image is preferable. The color transfer has rich, crisp, vivid colors, tapestry-like textures and warm fleshtones. The music is a bit too smooth, but the stereo surround sound is adequate. There is some voiceover narration explaining the story, and it is also available in French and Spanish, and can be supported by English, French or Spanish subtitles. Along with the cast and crew list, there is a brief history of the ballet and a brief but pertinent background on the production. A theatrical trailer is also included.

George Clinton: The Mothership Connection (Pioneer, PA98599D)

We can't find a date saying when it was shot, but in style the concert is pure Seventies funk. Clinton's hair, a blow-dried afro so massive it is a wonder he could get through doorways, should go to the Smithsonian, and his outfits could make the color blind detect hue. The music, however, is lively, and when he is not dabbling precariously in New Age razzle-dazzle or spewing out the filthiest lyrics this side of Prince, his band displays a mastery of intricately rhythmic cacophony that has not, like other aspects of his act, lost its edge with the advance of time. There is also an a cappella se-quence that is both the show's most tingling moment and proof that Clinton, for all his flash, has a firm grasp on the basics.

The picture ranges from somewhat soft to way blurry, but that has not been a drawback with the *Concert Film* programs, which are to be valued for the rarity of footage they contain. The stereo

surround sound is fine, and the Dolby Digital sound is excellent, with lots of punch and plenty of isolating clarity that can help dis-cerning listeners deconstruct Clinton's music and perhaps some of the cultural expressions it was representing.

George of the Jungle (Buena Vista, 13213)

Based upon one of those rare cartoons that had as many jokes for grownups as it had for kids, **George of the Jungle** makes an un-even transition to the big screen, but it is too darned good natured and amusing to find fault with. The film tries, with voiceover nar-ration and exaggerated cartoon-like effects, to pay homage to its source, a Tarzan parody, but it also gets caught up in its own reali-ty, such as the romance between George, played by a buff Brendan Fraser, and his Jane, played by Leslie Mann. On a technical level, the parts don't always blend well, but on a practical level it hardly matters, because rather than being a serious movie that gets too silly, it is a silly movie with occasional, harmless infestations of se-riousness.

The 1997 film is presented in full screen format only, losing a smidgen off the sides and adding a lot more to the top and bottom of the image in comparison to a letterboxed presentation. The pic-ture has bright, crisp colors and accurate fleshtones. The stereo surround sounds little dull, but the Dolby Digital track is brighter, with decent separations and plenty of bass. The 92 minute pro-gram also comes in French and Spanish, has optional English sub-titles and is accompanied by a very funny theatrical trailer.

Geronimo (Columbia TriStar, 58709)

The story of Geronimo has a basic dramatic problem in that he does not die or engage in any sort of final, blazing fight—instead he surrenders peacefully, which is not how western action pictures are supposed to close. The filmmakers try to solve this problem by inserting a contrived saloon gunfight as near to the end as they possibly can, but it is clear that the absence of more activity leaves a viewer feeling a bit restless as the movie winds down. Artistically, the 1993 Walter Hill film has significant things to say about the concentration camp internment and genocide that the American government committed against its indigenous peoples, but this message never consumes the entertainment. The film's first two thirds have more than enough excitement to fill most movies, and with the disc's sound and picture the program is fully captivating. Jason Patric and Matt Damon star as Union officers charged first with acting as liaison to the Indian warrior and, later, as consult-ants in the quest for his capture. Robert Duvall and Gene Hack-man weigh in as older generation military figures, but each is given a well-rounded personality and their scenes provide an ideal re-spite from the action—it is after both characters are eliminated that the movie suddenly has nowhere to go.

The picture and sound are outstanding. The Dolby Digital track has a sheer, highly detailed punch that enhances almost every se-quence, and the picture is flawless and crisp. The standard stereo soundtrack is also in good condition. The Panavision image is let-terboxed on one side, with an aspect ratio of about 2.35:1 and an accommodation for enhanced 16:9 playback, and is in cropped format on the other side. The 115 minute program also has a French language track in standard stereo, optional English and French subtitles and a trailer.

Get Shorty (MGM, 906036)

A marvelous concoction about a loan shark enforcer who comes to Hollywood and discovers he has the ideal skills to be an effective movie producer, John Travolta heads an inspired cast that includes Gene Hackman, Rene Russo, Danny DeVito, Dennis Fari-na and an uncredited Bette Midler. The script has an elegant per-fection to its structure that is matched by its witty dialogue and insightful digs at the nature of the film industry.

The presentation is letterboxed on one side, with an aspect ratio of about 1.85:1 and an accommodation for enhanced 16:9 play-back, and in full screen on the other side. Either version presents a workable framing. The color are bright and sharp, and the image looks great. The standard stereo surround soundtrack on the DVD is weaker than the soundtrack on the LD, but the Dolby Digital track seems to be comparable. The problem here is that the standard stereo surround soundtrack on the LD has more power than the Dolby Digital track, so that even though the Dolby Digital track is a bit more dimensional, the LD's regular stereo surround soundtrack remains the more preferable of the three. The 105 minute film is accompanied by a theatrical trailer. It has French and Spanish audio tracks and French, Spanish and English subtitles.

The Getaway (Warner, 11122)
Sam Peckinpah's 1972 adaptation of Jim Thompson's story, with the star-powered casting of Steve McQueen and Ali MacGraw, has been letterboxed on one side, with an aspect ratio of about 2.35:1 and an accommodation for enhanced 16:9 playback, and is in cropped format on the other side, which gives you gorgeous close-ups of the stars but is otherwise useless. The cropped image also looks a bit grainy, although colors are vivid. The monophonic sound is flat and the Dolby Digital mono soundtrack has a bit more power, though it still isn't as fully detailed. The 123 minute film is also available in French and comes with English, French or Spanish subtitles, a cast and crew profile, a couple of production notes (MacGraw had never driven a car before) and a theatrical trailer.

The story, about an ex-con who robs a bank in Texas and then attempts to cross the border into Mexico, has some problems in character motivation and logic, but the filmmakers and stars are a potent bunch, making the movie's flaws easy to dismiss. Even MacGraw, who could not transmit a believable emotion with her facial muscles if her life depended upon it, is redeemed by her well-publicized romance with McQueen, which took place during the movie's production and gives the film's love scenes an air of glamorous abandonment. Peckinpah's technique is so exquisite that the stars can do very silly things, like hiding in a trash compactor, and still look sexy as all get out. The music is by Quincy Jones with passages performed by Toots Thielemans.

The Getaway (Universal, 20269)
Roger Donaldson's entertaining 1994 remake of the Jim Thompson crime thriller stars Alec Baldwin and Kim Basinger, and is presented in letterboxed format with an aspect ratio of about 2.35:1 and no 16:9 enhancement. The color transfer is excellent, with crisp hues and accurate fleshtones. The stereo surround sound is good, but the DVD has a wonderful Dolby Digital track, with an enhanced thrust and greater dimensional detail. The 116 minute film—the 'unrated' version—is also available in French in standard stereo and can be supported by English or Spanish subtitles. There are some pretty good production notes discussing the relationship between the film and the earlier Sam Peckinpah version, a cast profile section and an interesting theatrical trailer.

The film itself is highly entertaining. Even though Donaldson tries, he does not have the stylistic mastery of Peckinpah, but very few filmmakers do. There is a satisfying tightening of the narrative, which was the earlier film's weakest component, and then there are the advances in eroticism, which help perk up the film between car chases and gun battles. The performances are enjoyable, the action is logical and exciting, and the pace is brisk.

The Ghost and the Darkness (Paramount, 323507)
The Oscar-winning audio track has been replicated with full intensity. Based on a true story, the film is about a railroad construction crew in Africa being terrorized by a pair of lions. Val Kilmer stars, with Michael Douglas in a smaller but showier part. The film's soundtrack is outstanding, not just when the lion is clearing his throat—although those sounds will send chills down your spine—but, like all great audio tracks, even during most innocuous scenes—people standing in a library talking to set up the story—the separation effects and layers of sound are mesmerizing. The bass is super, and the separation effects are constant and wonderful, with the Dolby Digital track providing an even stronger sense of presence.

The DVD is letterboxed with an aspect ratio of about 2.35:1 with no 16:9 enhancement. The colors are rich and precise, and the image is finely detailed. It looks super. The 109 minute film is also available in French and Spanish in standard stereo and can be supported by English or Spanish subtitles. There is a theatrical trailer, as well.

Ghost Stories: A Paranormal Insight (Madacy, DVD99052)
Ghost Stories 1 (Madacy, DVD990521)
Ghost Stories 2 (Madacy, DVD990522)
Ghost Stories 3 (Madacy, DVD990523)
Patrick Macnee narrates three episodes from an hour-long (43 minutes without commercials) TV series about 'real ghosts,' which are collected in the box set and are also available as individual releases. Each episode is itself constructed of freestanding shorter pieces, with titles and by-lines. The color quality is workable, although pictures of ghosts are by nature blurry to the point of illegibility. Much of the show is grainy, and littered with visible artifacting. The stereo sound has a general dimensional ambience and is adequate. The programs are not captioned. Each DVD also contains minor essays about some of the subjects covered in the program and a 'trivia' game. The chapter encoding is generally co-ordinated with the short pieces, though the beginning marker of each chapter often occurs a couple minutes be for the one piece gives way to the next.

Macnee runs through a history of the seamier aspects of British royalty in the opening piece on **1**, about the Tower of London. From there they go to Mexico where a ghostly bride is reported to be wandering about a mansion, and to England again, where another lovelorn barmaid apparently hails travelers after having died from a broken heart. If there's one thing we learned from **Poltergeist**, it is never, ever to build houses over graveyards, but that is apparently what happened in a town in Texas, where the wascally spirits started playing with appliances they were probably denied from using in life. In Mokelumne Hill, California, the proprietor of a hotel from the Gold Rush days still putters about, picking up after guests or something. Back to Texas again, where ghosts of children from a bus accident—or a downgrade, depending upon your level of gullibility—push cars onto and off of railroad tracks at a particular crossing near San Antonio, leaving their fingerprints on the bumpers. At least they don't offer to sell lemonade at the same time.

Remember the Alamo? Apparently the spirits haven't forgotten the place, according to the first story in **2**, though they seem to prefer a nearby arena, perhaps because the popcorn and hot dogs are better. In Palos Verdes, California, kids lucky enough to live in one nice suburban home have an extra set of friends to play with the back yard, friends that will never steal their toys, while in Rawlings, Wyoming, the prison may have been shut down, but nobody told the dead inmates it was time to leave. The ghost of a little girl, acting like no other child we are aware of, keeps trying to go to school in Gorman, California, while some antique enthusiasts living 'near the desert' have discovered that the original owners of the objects they have acquired are not quite ready to give them up. A hotel in California constructed over a mine shaft plays host to a reunion of dead miners periodically, although they tend to get rambunctious and set the place on fire, again and again.

An Indian maiden haunts an Arizona canyon according to **3**, visiting campers and admonishing them not to feed the dead bears. In Rensselaer, Indiana, site of 'one of the greatest unexplained mysteries of the century,' a light appears in a farmer's field when you blink your car lights to 'call' it, while a little way up the highway, in Chicago, there is a cemetery that is apparently as busy as O'Hare when it comes to booking trips into the afterlife. Having had her career suppressed during her life, Marion Davies is apparently still putting on shows in a house now owned by an artist, whose dogs have become her biggest fans. There is also a couple profiles of people who 'investigate' ghosts, and another about 'channeling.'

Ghost Story (Image, ID4228USDVD)

Four venerable motion picture stars, Fred Astaire, Melvyn Douglas, Douglas Fairbanks, Jr. and John Houseman, are featured in the 1981 thriller. As horror movies go, it doesn't amount to much, but the casting gives the film an enduring appeal. Astaire's dramatic performance is poor—either his training in lighter movies left him unprepared for this sort of thing or his age impeded his emotional dexterity—but even that doesn't matter. You hang on both the image and the words of each actor, knowing how rare and finite those words and images are, and the silly supernatural plot—about a murder victim who finally decides to avenge her death—is just an excuse to bring them together.

The picture looks okay, with consistent fleshtones and reasonably bright hues. The image is letterboxed with an aspect ratio of about 1.85:1 and no 16:9 enhancement. The monophonic sound is fairly bland, but there is a Dolby Digital mono track that is acceptable. The 111 minute film is captioned.

Ghostbusters (Columbia TriStar, 04139)

The classic 1984 special effects comedy is letterboxed with an aspect ratio of about 2.35:1 and an accommodation for enhanced 16:9 playback. The picture is free of grain, with decent fleshtones and bright, nicely detailed hues. The standard stereo surround sound is a little weak, but clean, and the film has been given a 5.1 channel Dolby Digital mix that is more dimensional and better detailed. The audio doesn't have quite the punch that a newer movie's audio would provide, but its best moments add to the fun. The 107 minute feature, starring Dan Aykroyd, Bill Murray and Sigourney Weaver, can be supported by English subtitles.

In addition to the movie, which is plenty funny if you haven't seen it in a while, the DVD is loaded with extras. There is a commentary track with director Ivan Reitman, co-screenwriter and star Harold Ramis, and associate producer Joe Medjuck. They laugh at the film while talking about the atmosphere on the set and how the film's various imaginative sequences were conceived and executed. One option allows you to see the three in silhouette at the bottom of the screen, **Mystery Science Theater** style, while they talk, though the utility of this option is limited (and you have to de-activate the enhanced 16:9 playback). More promisingly, a subtitling option brings up notations about the film's various sequences as they appear.

There is a decent collection of deleted scenes, most of which contain amusing gags that would have slowed down the pace of the narrative. There is a nice 10 minute behind-the-scenes 'making of' featurette from when the film was originally produced, another 10 minute retrospective featurette that includes reminiscences from some of the cast and the director, and an informative 15 minute retrospective featurette on the movie's special effects. Three major special effect sequences are replayed with a multiple angle option, so you can toggle between a preliminary version of the shot and the final version. Three more scenes are presented in split screen with storyboards, and there are more storyboards for about a dozen sequences that weren't shot. An excellent collection of production photos and drawings (including early versions of the **Ghostbusters** logo, which look quite Casper-ish) are also featured. There is a lot of menu overlapping for these features, which is convenient, but also a bit confusing.

The only input we can add to what everyone already knows about the movie is to point out the emphasis of the linkage between the ghosts and food. The script, by stars Aykroyd and Ramis, zeros in on an association between the phantoms and junk food and won't let go of it. The movie suggests that demons are waiting for you in refrigerators and pantry shelves everywhere.

Ghostbusters 2 (Columbia TriStar, 50169)

About a possessed painting kidnapping a baby, 1989 the sequel isn't very funny on the first viewing, and holds even fewer surprises on subsequent viewings. It has enough special effects and basic gags to get by, but is not an inspired follow-up to the original and has the feel of filmmakers cashing in. The picture is presented on one side in letterboxed format, with an aspect ratio of about 2.35:1 and an accommodation for enhanced 16:9 playback, and is in cropped format on the other side, adding nothing to the top or bottom of the image and losing a lot of picture information on the sides (Harold Ramis complains on the **Ghostbusters** commentary track that he is forever getting dropped off by the cropping).

The image is sharp and colors are strong. Fleshtones look accurate and other hues are bright. Darker sequences are free of distortion. The Dolby Digital track is a great, with more distinctive separation effects and more power than the standard track. There are alternate Spanish and Portuguese audio tracks in standard stereo, optional English, Spanish, Portuguese, Cantonese, Mandarin, Korean and Thai subtitles, a cast-and-director profile section, and several trailers.

Among the film's main disappointments we would highlight the shift and short changing in the personalities of the minor characters, particularly those portrayed by Annie Potts and Rick Moranis. The biggest disappointment, however, comes right near the beginning of the film and seems to epitomize exactly what is wrong with it. In the first movie, one of the best lines was Sigourney Weaver's analysis of Bill Murray's character, "You don't seem like a scientist. You're more like a game show host." In the opening of the new movie, he is a talk show host. It is supposed to show how low his character has stooped, but it only shows how low the writers, two of the movie's stars, were willing to bend to steal from the first film.

Gigi (MGM, 907482)

Vincente Minnelli directed the Alan Jay Lerner and Frederick Loewe musical, which somehow managed to garner a number of Oscars in 1958, more out of sentiment than merit. Leslie Caron stars as a young French girl being schooled in the ways of love in the slow moving feature. Louis Jourdan, who has a major part, not only looks ill-at-ease, he transmits the feeling to the viewer. Maurice Chevalier's pedophilial opening number is less unnerving when excerpted as a clip. The final twenty minutes of the turn-of-the-century Parisian romance are enjoyable, and Chevalier redeems himself with I'm Glad I'm Not Young Anymore, but the other musical numbers are too few and the gorgeous sets aren't utilized effectively.

Even with all the colorful DVDs on the market, however, **Gigi** could very well be the most stunningly colorful of all. Fleshtones are perfect, other hues are exact and crisp, and Minnelli's use of color was almost unparalleled. The DVD serves him well.

The picture has been letterboxed on one side, with an aspect ratio of about 2.3:1 and an accommodation for enhanced 16:9 playback, and is in cropped format on the other side if anybody cares. The LD's Dolby Digital track had four channels, while the DVD's Dolby Digital track only has the three front channels. Since there is virtually no surround activity on the LD anyway, it really doesn't matter, though the mix seems slightly different and we tended to prefer the dimensionality and presence delivered by the LD's Dolby Digital track. In any case, the DVD's Dolby Digital track is grander than its standard stereo track (even though the standard track allows rear channel bleeding) and is an adequate presentation of the film's audio track. There is also a French track, in two-channel Dolby Digital, with French songs (Maurice Chevalier does his own singing). The 116 minute program has optional English and French subtitles, and a trailer.

The Gingerbread Man (PolyGram, 4400850492)

Kenneth Branagh is a successful lawyer led down a primrose path to murder in Robert Altman's 1998 rendition of a John Grisham script. The plot has more in common with a cable thriller than with the typical big budget Grisham adaptation, but that is to its advantage, not its disadvantage. The lawyer and courtroom details are still exhilarating and the story doesn't get lost in its own self-importance the way most of Grisham's stories do. Altman's direction is wonderful, giving the film a heady, paranoid atmosphere and maintaining a kind of unspecified point-of-view that leaves the viewer in the center of the mystery with very little to grab onto except the hero's frustrations. The performances are super, the setting (Savannah) and cinematography are compelling, and the film's sound design, in typical Altman fashion, is complex and gratifying. Even Altman, however, admits on the disc's commentary channel that the film is best suited for only a couple of viewings, because once the story's secrets are revealed it has little else to offer an audience. Oh—did we mention?—much of the movie is set during a hurricane.

The presentation is letterboxed on one side, with an aspect ratio of about 1.85:1 and an accommodation for enhanced 16:9 playback, and is in full screen format on the other side, but there is a commentary by Altman that appears on the letterboxed side only. The colors are deliberately subdued (making, for example, the hero's bright red car stand out amid many duller-looking vehicles), but the image is crisp and darker sequences are stable. The stereo surround sound is super and the Dolby Digital track is even better, with more detail and a stronger dimensionality. The 114 minute program has optional French and Spanish subtitling, English captioning and a trailer.

Altman delivers the commentary, in a kind of piecemeal fashion with some moderate gaps. He spends most of his time providing a play-by-play analysis of what is happening on the screen. He does verify that the film's many ambiguous red herrings are deliberate and provides a little more background information on the characters and their motivations. Here and there, however, he speaks about his approach to his craft, and since it is Altman talking, every filmmaking tidbit is valuable (he mostly kind of stands back and lets the artists under him do their thing) and worth wading through the rest of his easy going patter to retrieve.

Girls: Wet & Wild in 3D (Simitar, 7245)

Three volumes of a topless modeling program entitled *British Starbirds: Leather, Lace & Lingerie* have been issued in one 80 minute DVD. The show features about 20 segments, each depicting a nude or topless model stretching or otherwise gallivanting for the camera. Some sequences are shot on film and are a bit soft, with moderately bright hues and occasional instances of tiling, which create odd looking shadows on flesh away from the center of attention. Other sequences have been shot on a rotating platform on video, creating the appearance of a right-left camera movement that is designed to present the illusion of 3-D when viewed through glasses with a darkened left eye. A pair of glasses in enclosed with the DVD. The video images are very crisp, with bright hues, and any video artifacting is obscured when one is concentrating on using the glasses. Generally, the more cluttered the set, the better the effect works. Sometimes it barely works at all, but other times it is reasonably good, though the models usually retain a two dimensional appearance and it is only the decorations that take on a sense of depth. The music has an annoying beat, but is never distorted.

The Girls of Scores (Image, ID5089SHDVD)

Seven young ladies employed in New York City as lap dancers are profiled. Each talks a little about herself and is then depicted in various topless (or briefly bottomless) modeling sessions, some surreptitiously shot on the streets of the city and others just pretending to have been shot that way. Each model claims to love being a lap dancer and to know Howard Stern. The picture is a bit soft, but colors are passable and the stereophonic musical score is adequate. There is no captioning.

A Girl's Own Story (see **Short Cinema Journal 1:2 Issue: Dreams**)

Gleaming the Cube (Pioneer, DVD5275)

In the viable 1989 action thriller that is a little padded with skateboard stunts, a bleach-blond Christian Slater stars as the young skateboarder who witnesses a murder and then has as much trouble convincing the police he saw something as he does avoiding the hitmen who come after him. The picture is presented in full screen format. Colors a little light, contrasts lack a bit of detail and fleshtones are bland. The stereo surround sound is reasonably dimensional and serviceable. The 105 minute program is not captioned and is accompanied by a trailer, a 5 minute 'making of' featurette ("Skateboarding is used as a metaphor for the story," explains director Graeme Clifford), a cast profile section, and 1 minute of behind-the-scenes footage showing the skateboard stuntmen trying to top one another.

Gli Occhi Freddi Della Paura (see **Cold Eyes of Fear**)

The Glimmer Man (Warner, 14479)

Once a promising action star, Steven Seagal sank quickly into an unusually severe form of self-parody, and there seems to be no retrieving him. He plays this Buddhist former-CIA-assassin police detective whose serial killer case becomes directly related to his old job. In another astounding coincidence, his ex-wife is one of the killer's victims, and so he then becomes a suspect. It's the Buddhist thing, though, that is really bizarre. He walks around like a 1968 fashion model, fingering his worry beads and kidding his partner, Keenen Ivory Wayans, about the properties of holistic medicines and other New Age mantras. If somebody else had been cast in the role, it might have been amusing, but since everybody knows that Seagal is into this stuff anyway, his performance seems more like a product endorsement. On the other hand, he's been putting on weight, and his martial arts abilities have diminished, but no one seems willing to tell him that. So, the plot is dumb, the star is a joke, and the film's action scenes are rarely convincing, but **The Glimmer Man** is still an entertaining work. There is enough action that the bad camera angles and weak fight choreography are unimportant, and the story is complicated enough that some people may not even notice how ludicrous it is. For all its faults, we still had a good time watching it and most dedicated action movie fans will probably feel the same way.

The 1996 film is presented in letterboxed format on one side, with an aspect ratio of about 1.85:1 and an accommodation for enhanced 16:9 playback, and in full screen on the other side. The letterboxed version adds a bit to the sides but masks off a lot of picture information from the bottom of the image and, since the film is hardly what one would consider artistic, the full screen version is better for following the fights and other action sequences. The colors are strong and the image is sharp. The regular surround soundtrack is okay and the Dolby Digital track is stronger. The action scenes are reasonably boisterous and the Dolby Digital track gives them more kick. The 92 minute feature is accompanied by a theatrical trailer, letterboxed on the letterboxed side and in full screen on the full screen side, that contains some material designed specifically for the promo, which again looks better when it isn't letterboxed. There is a modest cast profile and production note section. The film is presented in French, also with Dolby Digital, and can be accompanied by English, French or Spanish subtitles.

Gloria Estefan / Don't Stop! (Sony, EVD50178)

The anthology opens with the very sexy dance video, *Oye*, and features a mix of a dozen concert videos and conceptual pieces (including the colorful and Fellini-esque *tres deseos*). The jacket claims there are also interview segments between the numbers, but these sequences are actually very short, rapid montages of backstage and road footage. Very bright hues are a little fuzzy, but otherwise the image is sharp and colors are accurate. The stereo surround sound and Dolby Digital sound are both highly energized, with the Dolby Digital playback offering slightly more detailed separation effects. The 70 minute program can be supported by subtitles, which provide English lyrics for the English language songs and Spanish lyrics for the Spanish songs. There is also an Estefan disc-and-videography, and a promotional trailer for all of Estefan's video collections.

Gloria Estefan / Everlasting Gloria! (Sony, EVD50128)

The 89 minute program contains fifteen Gloria Estefan music videos and two extended versions, with Estefan providing brief introductions to each. A couple of the videos are Christmas oriented. *Silent Night* is a particularly striking piece, well suited to Estefan's moving vocals, but every offering on the disc is terrific, from the brightly animated *Live for Loving You* to the nostalgic *Hold Me, Thrill Me, Kiss Me*, not to mention the amusing *Everlasting Love*, which features a gaggle of Gloria Estefan imitators, as she herself was too pregnant to participate.

The picture looks fine, with even the oldest videos appearing sharp and richly colored. The Dolby Digital sound has a much stronger bass and a deeper resonance than the standard stereo track, which isn't nearly as moving when you compare the two directly. There are optional lyrics (English for the English songs and Spanish for the Spanish songs), and an Estefan discography. The videos are super, and the collection provides an excellent overview of Estefan's music, as well.

Gloria Estefan / Live in Miami: The Evolution Tour (Sony, EVD50149)

The 120 minute concert has been released on two sides. The color quality is fine and the image is sharp. The two hour concert was shot in the Miami Arena and it gets pretty smoky, but the DVD keeps everything in focus and doesn't let the smoke get in the way. The stereo surround sound is good, and there is a Dolby Digital track that is super, with lots of power and great dimensional effects, putting the viewer in the middle of the concert. The program can also be accompanied by subtitles that give lyrics for the English language songs in English and the Spanish songs in Spanish.

Glory (Columbia TriStar, 70825/9)

What a terrific movie **Glory** is—it not only has exciting battle scenes and a drama to support the action, it also has historical consequence. The drama, about a black regiment fighting in the Civil War, is flawed in the way that it avoids complexity in characterizations and conflicts, but it has so many lofty goals that most viewers will be quick to excuse these shortcomings. If, in the script, the characters are sketchily conceived, on screen they are divinely embodied by the wonderful cast. The motivation behind each character's activity may not be clear, but it is readily apparent that each has a soul, and there is a feeling of gratitude in being able to spend time with the group. This feeling extends to Matthew Broderick as well, whose ungainly top billing carries an oddly accurate and positive resonance to his character.

The picture is presented on one side in letterboxed format, with an aspect ratio of about 1.85:1 and an accommodation for enhanced 16:9 playback, and in full screen format on the other side. The 1989 film's cinematography is beautiful, and the image is crisp, with accurate fleshtones. The stereo surround sound and Dolby Digital sound are good, especially during the battle scenes, but the filmmakers tend to cheat with voiceover narrative to avoid recreating the sounds of the regiment's camp. James Horner's score is sometimes both too low-key and too lofty. The 117 minute program also has French and Spanish language tracks in standard stereo, optional English, French and Spanish subtitles, and a trailer.

God of Gamblers (import, DVD139)
God of Gamblers Return (import, DVD176)

If you want cool, and we mean ultimate, absolute *cool*, check out Chow Yun-Fat in the **God of Gamblers** features. Both films have pretty much the same lengthy running time and the same narrative structure, in which Yun-Fat's character is super-cool at the beginning and end of the film, but becomes involved in an extended and markedly comical middle section—taking up much of each movie—where he lets that persona go. Both films probably work better this way than if he were to remain in character for an entire narrative—relentless cool tends to melt—but it is those sequences at the start and conclusion of each movie, in which Yun-Fat's character has a total mastery over every game of chance he encounters and every gun he grabs, that make the shows worth obtaining, even with the compromised image transfers sported by the DVDs.

God of Gamblers is in the poorest shape of the two. The program has not been letterboxed, and while very little is missing from the sides of the image, the lack of letterboxing pulls the English subtitles down to the very edge of the screen, and will make them disappear entirely on some monitors, depending upon how one's overscan is set. We found it coherent on our monitor, but unless a viewer has a guaranteed view of the complete video image, it will be gamble as to how much will appear. **God of Gamblers Return** is letterboxed with an aspect ratio of about 1.75:1 and does not have the subtitle problem. Some colors on both films are bright, but fleshtones are dull with darker sequences and shadows sporting smeared contrasts that encourage digital artifacting, particularly in the first installment. The source material on both also has scattered scratches and other markings. The films are available in Mandarin or Cantonese, with permanent Chinese and English subtitles. The monophonic sound is adequate. Both films are accompanied by trailers.

In the first film, which runs 126 minutes, the hero gets hit on the head, loses his memory and reverts to the personality of a child—a risky story turn that succeeds because Yun-Fat's performance manages the comical aspect of the situation while retaining an essential believability. In **Return**, which runs 124 minutes, the hero is stranded in mainland China and links up with several low-life characters who help him escape, the situation providing an opportunity for the filmmakers to make fun of the Red Chinese establishment and officialry. Although the comical aspects may be an acquired taste, they are in synch with the hero's exaggerated proficiency at the gaming tables. The problem is that every part of your consciousness want to take the gambling exaggerations literally, so you can daydream not just about winning, but about winning with flair.

Gods and Monsters (Universal, 20584)

The story of James Whale, the director of *Frankenstein* and many other fine works, is told in the 1998 production. There isn't, however, all that much of a story. Mimicking ever so slightly *Sunset Boulevard*, the focus of the film is on Whale's final days and his infatuation with a straight gardener, played by Brendan Fraser, that turns out to be something far more complicated than plain lust. Ian McKellen plays Whale. There are flashbacks to other parts of Whale's life, and these are the fun parts of the film, but a good percentage of the movie is given over to the stageplay-like encounters between McKellen and Fraser, and these sequences, though competently directed and acted, don't amount to much. It is ever so gradually revealed why Whale retired early, what his interests are, and why he's going through a crisis, but there is no urgency to finding the answer to any of these questions, and no enlightening resonance when the answers are learned.

It is interesting to hear the director, Bill Condon, speak on the alternate audio track. The film was made for a very small amount of money and it was a smart production, for it ended up earning an Oscar for McKellen and a tidy profit, but Condon remains perplexed as to why, after he finished the film, he had so much trouble finding a distributor. It seems clear to us that the distributors, failing to recognize the film's competence and earnings potential based on investment, were responding to its inconsequentiality.

Condon is an enthusiastic DVD collector and couldn't wait to have his turn at the commentary mike. He tells the full story of his struggles to get the movie made, while describing how many of the scenes were shot and why he made the choices he made. He also describes scenes left out of the film. The talk is thorough and informative, but it is also supplemented by a very good half hour documentary, which goes into more detail about the real James Whale (with clips from a number of his films) and provides interviews with the cast and production crew. There are also production notes, a cast profile section and a trailer.

The 106 minute film is in letterboxed format only, with an aspect ratio of about 2.35:1 and an accommodation for enhanced 16:9 playback. Condon says that he wanted to use the Super-35 widescreen framing to evoke the Fifties, which is when the film is set, instead of the Thirties, which is when Whale was in his prime. That's fine, but the widescreen compositions are never as dynamic as such compositions were in the past. While his argument is sound in theory, in practice it is less convincing, as is his counter-argument that using a squarish frame would be too expected (so what, if he did it well).

The picture quality looks fine, with solid, accurate fleshtones and bright hues. The stereo surround sound gives the music an adequate dimensionality, but the film, by design, does not have an elaborate soundtrack. The film and the documentary can be supported by optional English subtitles.

The Godson (Sterling, 7065)

A shotgun comedy that hits a bullseye once in a while, the film parodies a number of gangster and action features, from *The Godfather* on down. Kevin Hamilton McDonald stars as the inept son of a retiring mobster who tries to step in and run the family business when his older brother is untimely dispatched. Dom DeLuise co-stars with an amusing Brando imitation, and Rodney Dangerfield shows up too, though his inserts look like they were shot in a day or so.

The picture quality is fine, with solid, fresh-looking hues, and the stereo surround sound is passable. The 100 minute program can be supported by Spanish subtitles ("¡Hey, Don King! Parece que viste a mi esposa desnuda.") and is accompanied by a trailer and a cast profile section.

Godzilla (Columbia TriStar, 23129)

The creatively inert Americanization of **Godzilla** is no better than a Fifties monster movie, but its special effects budget is so elaborate that there is an unresolved conflict between the film's expensive visual tone and its bankrupt dramatics, confusing a viewer's expectations. After one viewing, Matthew Broderick's performance is almost unwatchable and the scenes between the special effect shots seem longer and longer. But even the special effects aren't edited with a decent sense of excitement (except at the end) and one gets the impression that had it been storyboarded better, the film could have been shorter and more thrilling than it is.

The image is letterboxed with an aspect ratio of about 2.35:1 and an accommodation for enhanced 16:9 playback. Despite the movie's ridiculous non-stop rainstorm, the color transfer is excellent in all lighting conditions, and fleshtones are accurate. The Dolby Digital sound is better sculpted than the standard stereo surround sound, but both are very loud and very busy, with lots of separations effects, lots of thundering, dish-rattling bass, and lots and lots of other noises. It isn't pretty, but it's there. The 139 minute film can be supported by English subtitles.

There is a commentary track by the special effects supervisors. Considering the number of effects in the film, the commentary is a little disappointing. It is mostly anecdotal, and the speakers spend a lot of time just identifying which effects house did which shot. At times they go into worthwhile detail, but not with a dependable consistency. There are also three teaser trailers, original Japanese trailers for *Godzilla vs. King Ghidora/Godzilla vs. Mothra*, a brief

but informative 'making of' featurette, a handful of publicity photos and 'before and after' special effects photos, and cast-and-crew profiles. The opening part of the menu navigation is enjoyable (a foot stomps out your choice) but when you get into the details of the special features, it is less easy to move around.

Godzilla: King of the Monsters (Simitar, 7473)

The granddaddy of them all, with Raymond Burr commenting breathlessly on the monster's advances, is presented in letterboxed format on one side, with an aspect ratio of about 1.7:1 and non 16:9 enhancement, and in full screen format on the other side. The letterboxing adds a smidgen to the sides but masks off more from the top and bottom compared to the full screen image. A marvelous Dolby Digital soundtrack accompanies the full screen image, which is the version presented on side one. Accompanying the letterboxed presentation on side two is a 20 minute 'documentary' about movie monsters, drawn from very bad looking trailers. As awful as it appears, however, it is still a hoot.

The black-and-white picture has plenty of marks and scratches, but it looks cleaner and sharper than earlier home video releases. Much of the original Japanese dialogue is retained in the 1956 79 minute feature, which uses Burr's voiceover narration to explain what is happening. The standard track presents the standard monophonic sound, while the menu-activated Dolby Digital track provides occasional rear channel enhancements, periodic bursts of dimensionality, and wonderful sub-woofer thumps whenever the big guy lumbers through. Sure, the artificial mix would seem like a travesty if one looked upon the movies as art, but few viewers are likely to make such a delineation. There is no captioning. The DVD is accompanied by five home video trailers for five Godzilla films, a text-based 'trivia' game about the feature, and a general 2 minute montage of photos and artwork, and DVD-ROM features, such as screen savers. It is impossible to tell from the label or the jacket which side is letterboxed and which is cropped.

Godzilla Versus Monster Zero (Simitar, 7447)

Nick Adams stars with a Japanese cast in the 1969 93 minute feature, about an attempted alien takeover that is thwarted by Godzilla, Rodan and some quick-thinking human scientists. The letterboxing, which has an aspect ratio of about 2.35:1 and no 16:9 enhancement, is essential for taking in the fantasy images, entertaining set designs, and the battles between the two monsters and the three-headed Ghidra, who is controlled by the aliens. The color transfer looks great. Fleshtones do vary (there are times when Adams looks pink and his Japanese compatriots look yellow) and there is some minor wear on the source material, but the models and other imaginative designs look lovely, and the general impression one gets from the colors and the images is satisfying. The cropped image is much softer, but the colors are still quite bright. The letterboxed image, incidentally, also displays more picture information on the top of the screen than the cropped image. The Dolby Digital sound mix (available only on the letterboxed side) is also super, and the program can make a great sub-woofer demonstration piece. The film is dubbed in English, with no captioning. The film is accompanied by five home video trailers for five Godzilla films, a text-based 'trivia' game about the feature, a general 2 minute montage of photos and artwork, and DVD-ROM features, such as screen savers. It is impossible to tell from the label or the jacket which side is letterboxed and which is cropped.

Godzilla Versus Mothra (Simitar, 7474)

Perhaps the best of all the old Godzilla sequels, this is the one with the giant egg and the two tiny twin girls. It runs 88 minutes. The colors are solid, but a touch dull, and fleshtones look overly pinkish. Still, the presentation, which has an aspect ratio of about 2.35:1 and no 16:9 enhancement, isn't bad. The stereo on the Dolby Digital track is a little erratic, even dropping severely out of phase at one point. The music never seems loud enough and the thumps aren't as plentiful as on a couple of the other Godzilla programs. The cropped side also has Dolby Digital encoding, and there is no captioning. The film is accompanied by five home video trailers for five Godzilla films, a text-based 'trivia' game about each feature, a general 2 minute montage of photos and artwork, and DVD-ROM features, such as screen savers. It is impossible to tell from the label or the jacket which side is letterboxed and which is cropped.

Godzilla Vs. King Ghidorah: Godzilla and Mothra: The Battle for Earth (Columbia TriStar, 03132)

With improved technology and umpteen films experience behind them, the Japanese Godzilla remakes from the early Nineties represented on the double bill are, at least for their genre, quite well made and entertaining. Viewers who don't relate to Godzilla are not going to be impressed, but fans will appreciate the improved special effects, more intelligent narratives and better cinematic style choices (more dynamic camera angles) featured in both films.

The movies are great fun, and the DVD would have been as well except that both movies have been cropped (from 1.85:1), left in mono and are dubbed into English with no other options except English closed captioning. *Ghidorah* runs 103 minutes. The plot involves villains from the future attempting to mess with their past by eliminating the big lizard and substituting his three-headed nemesis. It's a pretty wild movie, but it is well paced and something interesting is always happening. *Mothra*, which runs 102 minutes, maintains the spirit of the original Mothra movie. There is a strong ecological theme, and the miniature singsong twins are back to tell people what Mothra wants. This time, there is a 'bad' Mothra, too, as well as a good one. The film is a little less energetic than *Ghidorah* and is best watched first if one is planning to take on the whole double bill in an afternoon, but it is still highly enjoyable.

Each movie appears on a separate side. The color transfer on both movies looks real good, with bright, sharp hues, accurate fleshtones and a clean image. Although the mono playback is a drag, the sound is clear, with smooth tones. Both sides contain original letterboxed Japanese trailers for the two movies, supported by English subtitles.

Godzilla's Revenge (Simitar, 7475)

The picture transfer looks fairly nice. It is letterboxed with an aspect ratio of about 2.35:1 and no 16:9 enhancement. The colors are strong and crisp, although darker scenes have a mild green shading and some murkiness. The cropped side is occasionally squeezed, and the blown up image magnifies a few more flaws.

The 1969 film, however, is strictly for little ones and is about a young boy who uses his Godzilla fantasies to become more assertive in the real world and save himself from some bank robbers. The monsters, including Godzilla's son, who talks, only appear in dream sequences. The film is dubbed in English. The standard track presents the standard monophonic sound, while the menu-activated Dolby Digital track provides occasional rear channel enhancements, some dimensionality, and wonderful thumps whenever Godzilla appears. There is no captioning. The movie is accompanied by five home video trailers for five Godzilla films, a text-based 'trivia' game about the feature, and a general 2 minute montage of photos and artwork. There are also DVD-ROM features, such as screen savers. It is impossible to tell from the label or the jacket which side is letterboxed and which is cropped.

Going Overboard (Trimark, VM7017D)

When a star becomes really successful, the public is inundated with every scrap of celluloid he ever worked on as he learned his craft, and such is the case with this Adam Sandler vehicle. It makes **Billy Madison** seem like *Citizen Kane*. Sandler is a waiter aboard a cruise ship who wants to become the ship's resident standup comic and gets a chance when it appears the first comic has fallen overboard. Or, at least, that's what you wish it was about. In reality, the

film is a pastiche of silly clowning that barely forms a coherent narrative. (Burt Young plays 'Manuel Noriega,' who watches the action on a video cassette and then sends terrorists to kill a woman on the ship—the terrorists decide they want to be standup comics, too, and by then you're screaming and willing to release every political prisoner in the country). The movie's pace is deadly, and while Sandler may be appealing for 5 minutes or so at a time, even he gets tiresome after a while, straining for limp laughs at every turn—and he's the most talented member of the cast. The jokes are mad unfunny, and the childishness of the characters begins to grate almost immediately, continuing for 97 long minutes.

The colors are little light and the full screen image is grainy in places, though the picture quality seems in keeping with the film's artistic content. The stereo sound has a limited range with very little dimensionality, but is functional. There are optional English, French and Spanish subtitles ("Je suis sorti avec une fille qui avait tout ce dont un homme rêve. De la moustache, du poil sous les bras, des sourcils fournis") and a trailer.

The Gold Rush (Digital Disc Entertainment, 510)

This is the silent, 1925 version of Chaplin's classic, with a monophonic musical score that clearly comes from the source material print (the left side of the image is clipped). Unfortunately, the presentation is not appealing. Contrasts are so weak that facial expressions disappear at moderate distances, and you can't even see Chaplin's nose in straight-on close-ups. There are also a lot of scratches and other damage, and the image is usually fuzzy. The DVD gives you the general idea of what the 78 minute film (not 114 minutes as is mistakenly listed on the jacket) is like, but it isn't half as funny as a good-looking presentation would be.

GoldenEye (MGM, 906035)

There is some artifacting, but the picture looks super, with crisp, vivid colors that are sharp and glossy, and the quality of the image adds to the excitement. The 1995 movie, which restored the James Bond franchise to the luster of its greatest productions, is exciting and funny, yet it never succumbs to the clowning that even some of the later Sean Connery Bond pictures fell into, and the drama has a few moments that are as psychologically deep as any James Bond movie ever got. Pierce Brosnan is outstanding as Bond, and the rest of the movie lives up to his presence, as does the DVD.

The 130 minute film is presented on one side in letterboxed format, with an aspect ratio of about 2.35:1 and an accommodation for enhanced 16:9 playback, and in cropped format on the other side. We found the cropped version to be duller and less involving, despite the to die for full screen close-ups of Brosnan it creates. The cropped image also seems to have even more pronounced video artifacts. The program is presented in stereo in Spanish and in French, along with the English soundtrack. The film's stereo mix is the best ever for a Bond movie. The stereo surround sound is great, though the Dolby Digital track is even better, with more entertaining details. From the chill-inducing opening chords—a fresh orchestration—during the signature gun barrel iris shot, to the elaborate, earth-shaking explosions in the finale, the audio is tremendous and contributes a great deal to placing the viewer in the middle of the action and the glamour. There is an original theatrical trailer, which is super, but it looks oddly squeezed. The film comes with English, French and Spanish subtitling, too.

Goldfinger (MGM, 906726)

The James Bond film is presented in dual layer format, letterboxed with an aspect ratio of about 1.75:1 on one layer, with accommodation for enhanced 16:9 playback, and slightly cropped on the other layer. Blacks are pure, fleshtones look terrific and other colors are crisp, though here and there the age of the image can be seen in a slight background grain. The monophonic sound is weaker and somewhat indistinctive. The credit sequence in **Goldfinger**, which is in stereo on LD releases, remains in mono on the

DVD. The film is also available in French and Spanish, and comes with English, French or Spanish subtitles ("'¿Espera que hable?' 'No, espero que muera'"). The 110 minute film is accompanied by a theatrical trailer, some informative production notes and elaborate but uninteresting reference functions that pull up key sequences from the films. There is also has an engaging two minute black-and-white promo featurette, emphasizing Harold Sakata and Honor Blackman.

The 1964 feature stars Sean Connery as James Bond, preventing a gold nutcase from destroying Ft. Knox. There are times when we watch the film that we feel it is horribly dated, and other times when it is quite entertaining, but the quality of the DVD's picture can make it seem like you are watching it for the first time.

Gone with the Wind (MGM, 906311)

You know those glossy movie stills you see in picture books where the colors are vivid, the fleshtones are porcelain and the image seems to look better than any movie ever made? That's how good the DVD looks, from beginning to end. The only problems on the DVD are an above average tendency toward digital artifacting, particularly a faint smearing in the darker portions of the screen, and a loss of some minor textural detail in the shadows due to the contrast levels. The sound, which can be accessed in Dolby Digital or in the original mono track, has a mild stereophonic dimensionality and is much cleaner than earlier audio tracks have been. Because of its age, the soundtrack on the 1939 film still has a limited range and a generalized dullness, but viewers are likely to be fully tolerant of such age-related limitations. The 233 minute film has been split to two sides, with the side break occurring at the Intermission point. On the first side, it is accompanied by a trailer, while side two has some 'trivia' questions. The film can be supported by English or French subtitles ("'Si vous partez…que deviendrai-je?' 'Franchement ma chère, je m'en moque'").

The appeal of **Gone with the Wind** rests with the conniving, selfish personalities of Scarlett O'Hara and Rhett Butler. Tragedy breezes by in the best novel-into-film manner, and the Civil War, while it is genuinely felt, barely intrudes upon the proceedings (and the racism inherent in any story glorifying the South's efforts during these times is soft-pedaled so well that even today there are only a few embarrassing moments). What you are treated to instead is Vivien Leigh's Scarlett and her performance is so involving that you want her to succeed in every scheme she concocts. Poor Leslie Howard and Olivia de Havilland must portray Ashley Wilkes and Melanie Hamilton and no matter how convincing they are, Ashley and Melanie are too naive to earn admiration. Making Melanie a little snooty and Ashley a little lecherous would have enlivened the ménage and made them more realistic. No one wants Melanie to be happy, anyway.

Good Luck (Simitar, 7427)

An enjoyable film with big marketing problems, according to the production profile that comes on the DVD, the 1996 film has also gone under a couple of other titles, *Guys Like Us* and *The Ox and the Eye*, and it is the sort of movie that is difficult to sell no matter how good it may actually be. Vincent D'Onofrio stars as a former professional football player who was blinded in a game accident and Gregory Hines is a paraplegic who convinces him that the two can enter a white water rafting contest. The film is lighthearted but not ridiculous and the performers are terrific. Nevertheless, as soon as you start talking about blindness and paraplegia, viewers start running in the other direction, not knowing what they're missing.

The picture quality looks fine, with bright, sharp colors and accurate fleshtones. The stereo surround sound is adequate. The 95 minute program is accompanied by a Hines filmography and is not captioned.

Good Morning, Vietnam (Buena Vista, 15279)

The movie never falters from its goal, which is to put the comedy of Robin Williams into a believable context. There are no distractions and no mushy subplots—just a romance where the hero never gets to first base (he's too busy pitching) and the lessons/meanings/horrors of Vietnam, done lightly but sufficiently. Unlike the war, we wished the movie would never end.

The Dolby Digital sound is particularly impressive, bringing a nice variation between the centered dialogue and the surround pop hits. The picture is letterboxed with an aspect ratio of about 1.85:1 and no 16:9 enhancement. The image looks fine, with bright, crisp hues and accurate fleshtones. The 121 minute feature is also available in French in standard stereo (with French opening credits on an alternate angle!) and can be supported by English subtitles.

The Good, The Bad and The Ugly (MGM, 906729)

Sergio Leone's classic 1966 Civil War epic is accompanied by the legendary 14 minutes of deleted scenes. The scenes were originally included in the film's initial Italian theatrical release, and are presented separately in a supplementary section on the DVD, along with a couple production essays and the theatrical trailer that gets the characters wrong.

Clint Eastwood, Lee Van Cleef and Eli Wallach star in the 162 minute feature, about a quest for buried gold that takes the protagonists across a landscape of war. The more often we watch the movie, the more we love Wallach's performance, particularly the way he keeps crossing himself every time there is violence. Eastwood and Van Cleef remain locked in their archetypes, and are bearable because the film is so beautifully photographed that you're too busy taking in the view to notice the deficiencies in their parts. Wallach, however, saves the movie, ingratiating himself to the viewer as successfully as he fails to ingratiate those around him in the film. He makes the film worth savoring.

The movie appears on one side of a dual-layer platter in letterboxed format only, with an aspect ratio of about 2.35:1 and an accommodation for enhanced 16:9 playback. Fleshtones have a slightly olive cast, but the picture transfer has excellent detail (you can see grains in wood that appears uniform on other home video versions) and generally accurate hues. The monophonic sound is weak and even the Dolby Digital mono track is not all that bright. The film is also available in French and Spanish and comes with English, French or Spanish subtitles ("¡Cuando tengas que disparar, dispara! ¡No hables!").

The deleted scenes are presented in Italian with English subtitles, and each is bookended by a bit of the regular film so you can tell where it was supposed to have gone. The first scene would be quite helpful to new viewers, giving an explanation to the back story that one otherwise has to figure out through multiple viewings. A couple of the other scenes make Eastwood's character seem slightly more vulnerable, but on the whole the film didn't need the footage and it was wisely dropped from the theatrical release—nevertheless, we're still ecstatic to finally have a chance to see it.

Good Will Hunting (Buena Vista, 16422); collector's (Buena Vista, 14888)

The Oscar-winning story is about a mathematical genius and the psychotherapist who helps him get on track with his life. Matt Damon and Robin Williams star, with Minnie Driver. Directed by Gus Van Sant, chunks of the movie seem very bogus, but it is great storytelling anyway, and the momentum of the narrative will carry most viewers past the film's weaker suppositions. We couldn't help thinking about Jack Nicholson's character in *Five Easy Pieces*, however—how much truer his demons and failings seemed to be, and how much more maturely that film reflected the social psyche of its era. These days, it appears that every rebel just wants to be hugged.

The film is letterboxed with an aspect ratio of about 1.85:1 and no 16:9 enhancement. The cinematography has an inconsistent look, with some sequences seeming less chromatically intense than others. The stereo surround sound and Dolby Digital sound are a little weak, but generally it is the film's story and not its production values, that viewers will respond to. The 126 minute film can be supported by English captioning. It is accompanied by a trailer and a music video (*Miss Misery*).

The *Collector's Series* version features the picture and sound transfer, with several extras. There are eleven deleted scenes (about 20 minutes worth), though they don't offer any great revelations about the film. There is an extended St. Patrick's Day parade scene, shot several months before the rest of the film, that was originally intended to serve as the credit sequence. There are a few sequences that expand upon the relationships between characters, but a few others that would have put the movie off track if they had been included. The DVD's supplement also contains a brief 'making of' featurette, a trailer, more than a dozen TV commercials, the montage they used at the Oscars (whatever happened to showing a good scene?), the music video and some behind-the-scenes footage of several outdoor location shoots.

The film and the outtakes are supported by a commentary track featuring Van Sant, Damon and Affleck. They talk mostly about the characters and what is going on in the story, though with more depth than the usual play-by-play. They also provide a background on the production, the hassles they went through to get the movie made, and the impact it has had on their lives. They don't talk as much about the technical aspects of the shoot or the crew except for their fellow cast members (including Williams' working methods). The story of how the film was made—two childhood friends end up winning Oscars and everything—is a good one, and so the commentary enhances the value of the DVD even if it isn't thorough in its approach to the film's creation.

GoodFellas (Warner, 12039)

Martin Scorsese's excellent 146 minute 1990 feature, about mobsters planning an airport robbery, has been released on two sides in letterboxed format, with an aspect ratio of about 1.85:1 and no 16:9 enhancement. There are also two theatrical trailers that are presented in full screen format, and a quick comparison demonstrates how better balanced and more satisfying the letterboxing is in every shot. The picture transfer looks very good, with sharp colors and accurate fleshtones. The stereo surround sound is bland, but the Dolby Digital track is better detailed and a bit more powerful. The usual cast backgrounds and modest production notes are provided, along with a list of the film's awards. The audio track is also available in French in standard stereo. We've finally figured out, by the way, what's wrong with Scorsese—he's trying to be John Ford in a business that only wants Howard Hawks these days.

Gorillas in the Mist: The Adventure of Dian Fossey (Universal, 20421)

We don't care too much for the 1988 Michael Apted film with Sigourney Weaver as Fossey, because the narrative lacks complexity and it just seems like there's nothing to the movie but clever shots of her and the gorillas. The DVD, however, is outstanding. The picture is crisp, colors are vivid and the Dolby Digital surround is all encompassing. The 130 minute feature is letterboxed with an aspect ratio of about 1.85:1 and an accommodation for enhanced 16:9 playback. The image is very sharp and hues are exact, with accurate fleshtones. Even the darkest jungle night scenes are clear, with distinctive variations in shading. The stereo surround sound is terrific, but the Dolby Digital track has more precise separation definitions and more energy. Even when characters are only sitting around talking—which they do quite a bit—the jungle sounds creep in from all corners and transport your viewing room to the tropics. Just turn up the heat and you're set (okay, these are mountain gorillas—so turn down the heat). There is a French language track in standard stereo surround sound, and optional English subtitles. There is an excellent 'making of' featurette, with footage of the real Fossey and a behind-the-scenes look at Weaver's harrowing interaction with the gorillas, narrated by Jason Robards, as well as a trailer, production notes and a cast-and-director profile section.

The Gospel According to St. Matthew (Image, ID5108WBDVD)

Pier Paolo Pasolini turned to the countryside to create what is arguably his finest achievement, pastoral rendition of the *New Testament*'s *Book of Matthew*. The 1964 film is exactly the opposite from what was at the time the standard Italian biblical epic. It is not just that Pasolini hired performers with genuinely bad teeth. His depiction of the life of Jesus Christ has an uncanny rhythm, washing familiar events and words over the viewer and then drawing away to expose the material's underlying purposes. The 137 minute film is brisk for its subject matter, yet it never feels rushed or abridged. Shot in Italy, the locations look convincingly Middle Eastern, conveying a real sense of a time when the population of the world was much smaller and technology was far more limited. Pasolini instills the tale with some minor echoes of Marxist thought, but in placing Christ on the side of change, he also attempts to reconcile religion and atheism, his creation of the film being proof that the two concepts are not mutually exclusive. He tells the story with a divine economy, using faces, a few familiar quotations, and an instinctive feeling for the passages that best deserve visualization. Most of all, however, and in opposition to all other versions beyond the most rudimentary elementary school Christmas pageants, he conveys with sincerity the humility of the film's source and teaches this humility as a gospel of filmmaking.

The black-and-white picture is crisp, and has intricate contrasts in brightly lit sequences. There are a number of splices and some stray scratches, but the tone of the film accommodates a little wear. The image also jiggles a bit. The presentation is letterboxed with an aspect ratio of about 1.75:1 and no 16:9 enhancement. The film is in Italian with permanent white English subtitles, and the monophonic sound is adequate.

Grace of My Heart (Universal, 20438)

Depicting the eventful life of a Carole King-like songwriter-singer from the late Fifties to the early Seventies, the film has a few flaws, but none of them are important. What is important are the marvelous, original 'sounds-like' pop tunes and the incredible good will generated by the star, Illeana Douglas, as she takes her character from youthful enthusiasm to bittersweet wisdom. The movie is a joy, full of original 'sounds like' songs and knowing insights on the music industry and the trials of being a career woman. John Turturro, Eric Stoltz, Patsy Kensit and Matt Dillon are also featured in the 1996 production.

The picture and sound transfers are outstanding. The image is in letterboxed format only, with an aspect ratio of about 1.85:1 and an accommodation for enhanced 16:9 playback. Colors are bright and fleshtones are accurate in all lighting conditions. The image is very crisp. One of the film's delights is its depiction of the shifting tastes in decor and fashion during the Sixties, and every hue has a perfect intensity.

Where the music on the standard stereo track bleeds to the rear channel on every song, the Dolby Digital track is far more accurate, keeping the music up front when appropriate and applying dimensional effects only when the scene calls for it. The Dolby Digital track is sharper as well, so that all effects and tones are more distinctive, creating a finer audio tapestry than the standard stereo track can achieve. There is also a French audio track (with English songs) in standard stereo and optional English subtitles.

Along with the usual cast-and-director profile section, production notes and trailer, there are four excellent supplementary features, a 41 minute documentary, a commentary track by the director, Allison Anders, 32 minutes of deleted scenes, and a collection of e-mails Anders wrote a friend during the editing (the e-mails can also be printed with a DVD-ROM function).

The commentary and the documentary go hand in hand. You see Anders in the documentary, to round out your understanding of her character, but you also get to see and hear from many of the other individuals who contributed to the film in front of and behind the camera. In addition to providing a comprehensive description of the production logistics and the creative process, including the contributions of her collaborators, Anders talks on the commentary track about the music business during the era being depicted and about the references in the narrative to her own life and experiences. On the documentary, the film's creation is explored from a broader perspective, including a breakdown of the construction and purpose of each major song.

The deleted scenes include the complete performances of several songs heard only in snippets in the movie, as well as several superbly acted sequences that waylaid the narrative too much. It is the e-mails, however, that stunned us. They contain a devastating analysis of establishment Hollywood editors, who are more apt to try to please the company that hired them than to accommodate the director in charge of the film. Fortunately, Anders obtained the collaboration of one of the finest, independently-minded editors working today, Thelma Schoonmaker, and her descriptions of how Schoonmaker pulled her material together is almost mystical. Anders also shares a compelling insight on the problems artists face not just in Hollywood but where ever they have to make a living from their art: "The people who ask you to compromise are guys who are negotiators by nature—executives, producers, financiers. They always hold back. That's the way they do business—they lowball money, resources, etc. So they assume that we, directors, think the same way, but in fact we are the opposite. While they promise less than their capabilities and withhold, we actually promise more than our capabilities—so by the time they force us to compromise, we are already stretched as far as we can stretch." Somehow, though, the process creates DVDs as brilliant and satisfying as **Grace of My Heart**.

The Graduate (PolyGram, 4400842552)

The classic 1967 Mike Nichols comedy has never looked as good as it does on DVD. The picture is free of grain and lines are solid, with fresh, accurate fleshtones and rich hues. The source material has a scattered speckle or two, but the presentation is pretty much immaculate and freshens the humor and the emotions of what, in its more battered forms, had seemed like a tired classic. The picture is letterboxed with an aspect ratio of about 2.35:1 and no 16:9 enhancement. The sound is available in both the original mono track and the remastered stereo track that brings a little more dimensionality to the music. Either one is workable. The 106 minute film can be supported by English closed captioning, as well as French or Spanish subtitles ("Vous essayez de me séduire").

A 25 minute retrospective documentary and further comments by Dustin Hoffman that run an additional 20 minutes are also included. Katharine Ross, Buck Henry, and Calder Willingham are interviewed in the documentary. Their stories and comments are marvelous, and Hoffman's extended talk is outstanding, going into details on acting techniques and the events leading up to the role that changed his life forever.

Grambling's White Tiger (Simitar, 7275)

The story of the first white player on a previously all-black college football team, Bruce Jenner stars, with Harry Belafonte as the coach and LeVar Burton as one of the few teammates to befriend him. The director wisely uses Jenner's awkwardness as an actor to reflect upon the character's discomfort, and the film has a solid docudrama construction that makes it compellingly watchable as the team goes through its season. The reverse-prejudice situations are thought provoking and not overdone.

The picture quality on the 1981 TV film is fairly good, with fresh-looking colors and a sharp focus. The monophonic sound is passable. The program runs 96 minutes and is accompanied by filmographies for Belafonte, Burton and Jenner, though there are a few errors, including the misspelling of Burton's name and the laughable suggestion that *Can't Stop the Music* was a documentary. There is no captioning.

Grand Canyon: The Hidden Secrets (SlingShot, DVD9804)

The Grand Canyon and IMAX were made for each other and the only challenge is to keep such a program interesting for a full 40 minutes, something that is handled with aplomb. The film provides a history of human interaction with the canyon, including reenactments of early explorations. The camera is placed on promontories to soak up the view, and on helicopters to buzz the canyons. They even strap the old IMAX camera to a raft and send it down the Colorado River as if it were Meryl Streep or something. The images are incredibly crisp and finely detailed, regardless of how close or far away objects are, and you don't need a huge, huge screen to appreciate the beauty and the thrill of what the camera was able to capture.

The picture looks super, with sharp, accurate hues. The Dolby Digital soundtrack also adds to the fun, with elaborately separated environmental sounds and music—and even the narration has an unusually impressive timbre. The standard stereo surround soundtrack is also excellent, though it isn't quite as dimensional or as exquisite as the Dolby Digital track. The narration is also available in French, Spanish, German, Swedish, Japanese, Korean and Mandarin, all in Dolby Digital. The film is accompanied by an interesting 20 minute 'making of' featurette (not 10 minutes as is indicated on the jacket cover) that shows the director at work and how many of the most amazing shots were accomplished. The DVD is closed captioned in English, but the captioning is littered with typos. There is no time encoding.

Grateful Dead: Ticket to New Year's (Monterey, 319872)

There are many Grateful Dead concerts floating around, but this is one of the better ones, with varied camera angles, lots of close-ups, a good mix of songs and a little fooling around to break up the flow of the music. Shot in Oakland in 1987, the 145 minute program has been released on a single-sided dual-layer DVD There is an amusing Intermission sequence that features interviews and tomfoolery among the band members, with Jerry Garcia seeming particularly animated and vivacious. The picture is a bit soft in places and colors are a little subdued, but the image looks good on the whole. The stereo sound is also reasonably strong, though the concert recording has natural limitations in dimensionality and clarity. The song lyrics are supported by optional English subtitles, and the DVD includes interesting profiles of the band members and a 'Dead Quiz.'

Gravesend (PolyGram, 4400555072WR01)

Four youths drive around Brooklyn trying to dispose of a body in the trunk of their car. It isn't a very good movie, but if one takes into account that the movie's writer-director, Salvatore Stabile, was still a teenager when he started putting it together (and 22 when he finished it), it is an admirable effort. Shot on a very low four-figure budget in color and black-and-white, the footage is constantly grainy, with weak contrasts, soft lines, dull hues and bland fleshtones, and there is a lot of smearing on the DVD image. The sound is also a low budget affair with environmental noises intruding on the dialogue, but the audio is adequate. The film runs 85 minutes and is captioned.

The Great Battles of World War II (Madacy, DVD99061)
The Great Battles of World War II / The Battle of Britain (Madacy, DVD990612)
The Great Battles of World War II / Battle of Russia (Madacy, DVD990613)
The Great Battles of World War II / D-Day: Battle for the Beach (Madacy, DVD990611)

If you have the **World War II** box set, beware of obtaining the **Great Battles of the World War II** box. Two of the DVDs contained in the box (the three are also available as separate releases) are duplications of the **Battle of Britain** and **Battle of Russia** films appearing in the **World War II** box, with the same quality picture transfers. Each runs about 50 minutes. The programs are accompanied by brief essays about historical personages, aircraft and medals from the War.

D-Day: Battle for the Beach has very little to do with D-Day per se and is actually a film entitled *The True Glory*, co-produced by the American and British war departments, that depicts everything that happened on the Western Front (not Italy) from the invasion of Normandy to the liberation of the concentration camps and the fall of Berlin. Like the others, it is a well-made film, conveying nuances of emphasis that were fresh in the minds of those who fought the war. And, like the others, the source material is a little worse for wear.

The Great Barrier Reef (SlingShot, DVD9835)

The 40 minute IMAX program examines a great variety lots of fascinating sea life with the vivid, reach-out-and-touch-them immediacy of the IMAX format. There are the obligatory depictions of Great Barrier Reef scientists at work, to keep the narrative moving, and the viewer will pick up plenty of informative fish trivia, but the main appeal of the program is the chance it provides to visit the exotic world beneath the waves on the coast of Australia, without getting wet.

The picture quality is outstanding, particularly for a difficult-to-light underwater program. Colors are vivid and the image is crisp, even in the shadows. The 5.1 Dolby Digital sends air bubbles gurgling all around you and has a nice blend of music and water sounds, all with a bit more crispness than the standard stereo surround soundtrack. There is an alternate Japanese language track, also in Dolby Digital, and optional English subtitles.

The Great Escape (MGM, 906680)

The colors might be able to use a little sprucing up, but the image quality is fairly sharp. The single-sided dual-layer presentation of the 172 minute film is letterboxed with an aspect ratio of about 2.7:1 and no 16:9 enhancement. The monophonic sound is slightly subdued. The film is also available in French and comes with English, French or Spanish subtitles ("Il y a un angle morte au milieu"). There is a very faded theatrical trailer and an outstanding 24 minute retrospective documentary. The documentary contains marvelous interviews with many of the surviving cast and crew members, and mixes tales of shooting the film with the real experiences of the airman upon whose lives the film was based. Steve McQueen, James Garner and Richard Attenborough star in the terrific 1963 WWII POW classic.

Great Expectations (Criterion, GRE270)

David Lean's 1946 film is a marvel of condensation, capturing the essence of the Dickens story and seeming to leave nothing of value out, save for the too brief appearances of several minor characters. Being Dickens, of course, the story, about a young blacksmith apprentice who is turned into a gentleman by a mysterious benefactor, is catchy as all get out and remains highly involving even for those who are familiar with its every twist and turn. A youthful John Mills stars, along with the equally youthful Alec Guinness and Jean Simmons. High among the movie's attractions, however, is its rich imagery, something that seems to go beyond even Dickens' powers of description. Not only, for example, is Miss Havisham's banquet room filled with cobwebs and not only is she dressed in her decrepit wedding gown, she is also made to look like a spider in the center of the webs around her, manipulating the youngsters who are caught in her designs. There are also the poles that hang like gallows at the film's opening, along the road to the graveyard. The film is filled with such subtle delights, and it is this richness that has made it an eternal classic, one that is on par with the novel upon which it is based.

The image has pure blacks and a sharp focus, but the source material has some wear and soft contrasts in places. There is also a tendency for the backgrounds to momentarily succumb to digital artifacting, The Dolby Digital monophonic sound is somewhat muted but audio noise is also suppressed. The 118 minute program can be supported by optional English subtitles and is accompanied by an original theatrical trailer.

The Great Outdoors (Universal, 20228)

The lack of urban amenities is the subject of the 1988 comedy. The inability of Dan Aykroyd to create a realistic personality that can mesh with the other performers inhibits a viewer's acceptance of the material. The scenes involving John Candy in which Aykroyd is not present have potential, but when Aykroyd appears, emotional involvement with the characters disappears.

The presentation is letterboxed with an aspect ratio of about 1.85:1 with no 16:9 enhancement. The color quality is okay, with bright hues and accurate fleshtones. Darker scenes are a touch grainy, but generally the picture looks fine. The stereo sound has a limited dimensionality and separation effects are usually reserved for the musical score. The 91 minute program is also available in French and comes with English or Spanish subtitles ("Mantén el ojo en el mur ciélago"). There are some brief production notes (it was filmed at the same lake used in *Leave Her to Heaven*), a brief cast profile section and two trailers on one menu selection, the second being more creative than the first.

The Great Rupert (Image, ID5506ALDVD)

The title character in George Pal's 1950 Jimmy Durante vehicle is a squirrel, often animated in stop motion. It takes the cash the landlord of Durante's character is hiding in his wall and drops it onto Durante's family, who think the cash is coming from Heaven. Fortunately, their daughter and the landlord's son have a thing going, so the money stays in the family. The special effect sequences are of minor importance, however, as the focus of the film is on the human comedies, which are schmaltzy but enjoyable. Durante, though a memorable personality, appeared in very few movies, and despite the animation, the program is most worth having for his presence.

The black-and-white source material is a little uneven, looking reasonably sharp in some sequences and soft, with minor wear, in others. There is some displacement artifacting during the most damaged sequences. The monophonic sound is fine and the 88 minute program is not captioned.

The Great Train Robbery (see **Landmarks of Early Film**)

The Great Train Robbery (MGM, 907149)

"What was really so shocking about The Great Train Robbery was that it suggested, to the sober thinker, that the elimination of crime might not be an inevitable consequence of forward-marching progress." So wrote Michael Crichton in an essay taken from the novel he adapted as a screenplay and subsequently directed. The 1978 production, about the first time a major robbery was committed aboard a moving train, stars Sean Connery, Donald Sutherland and Lesley-Anne Down. From a structural point of view, almost half of the movie is about the obtaining of copies of four keys, which the heroes then use on the strongbox in the train, and as a caper film it is somewhat flaccid. As an exploration of the Victorian Era, however, it is a rewarding experience. Crichton takes great pains not only to replicate period details, but to draw meaning from them. Provided a viewer doesn't approach the film with misguided expectations (it has just enough crime to keep the plot moving), the movie's star power and atmosphere can be quite entertaining.

The presentation is letterboxed, with an aspect ratio of about 1.85:1 and no 16:9 enhancement. Geoffrey Unsworth's cinematography is deliberately hazy and, although the effect is intentional, it makes the picture look hopelessly blurry at times. If you can tolerate that, however, the colors are fresh and the image appears to be accurate. The stereo surround sound has a fairly good mix for a 1978 feature and there is a Dolby Digital track with better defined detail and more power. The 111 minute film is also available in French in mono and comes with English, French or Spanish subtitles, along with a theatrical trailer (which calls the film 'The First Great Train Robbery').

Crichton (he pronounces his name 'cry-ton') also provides audio commentary, and his talk is as fascinating as his writing. He covers the production of the film in fairly superficial terms, discussing how and where certain scenes were shot. His manner of direction is apparently to let his film crew do their job and to stay out of their way, unless his opinion is required. He has some very nice things to say about Unsworth, and he explains how he was able to bring the film in on a relatively low budget. Where his talk excels, however, is in his digressions into the lessons Victorian society provides for contemporary times. He covers everything from how criminals earned their living and what brothels were really like in those days, to how cities smelled and what life was like without cellular phones. This is the sort of thing that shows Crichton at his best, remarking upon some historical or scientific detail in the film and then using it to elaborate upon different insights concerning how we live now and how we got here.

The Great Trans-American Train Ride (Simitar, 7227)

The *Doug Jones Travelog* is an enjoyably anachronistic travel film, with images and information from the Nineties but a style and narrative format that is stuck firmly in the Fifties. The 90 minute program depicts the Amtrak journey from New York City to Los Angeles, with digressions at each stop, such as Philadelphia, Chicago, Omaha, Denver, etc., to provide the tourist highlights of the city being visited. The program also gives a brief profile of each train (the trip involves several connections and different types of locomotives) and should delight train lovers, travelogue fanatics and those looking for a little contemporary camp. There is also an eight minute bonus sequence of scenic train rides in Washington State and Texas. The picture has a moderately worn look and there is substantial video artifacting, with a lot of tiling and smearing effects. The monophonic sound is passable.

The Great Waldo Pepper GoodTimes, 0581015)

George Roy Hill's 1975 feature is fairly daring, not only because of the life-threatening stunts, but because of the bleak and uninspiring content of the plot. The film's most dramatic moment is an honest-to-goodness soliloquy, where a character describes, in evocative detail, a dogfight which took place over France in World War I. The story takes place after the war is over and is about barnstorming pilots trying to make a living by showing off. Robert Redford, who stars, never stays in a situation long enough to make a strong impression, and the film is one of his weaker efforts.

The presentation is badly cropped, which spoils much of the film's impact. The colors are somewhat faded and the image is dull, with a bland monophonic audio track. The 108 minute program has optional English, French and Spanish subtitles.

The Greatest Places (SlingShot, DVD9833)

Seeming like a collection of IMAX audition also-rans, the 40 minute program contains seven separate sequences, about Madagascar, Tibet, Greenland, the Namib Desert, the Amazon River, Iguazu Falls, and the inland Okavango Delta. Some, such as the Madagascar sequence, long for expansion, but others, such as the Greenland sequence, seem to present pretty much everything there is to display about the subject. The best sequences make good use of format's Dolby Digital 5.1 channel sound, with an earth-shaking bass (those Tibetan horns) and elaborate separation effects (the jungle sequences).

The picture looks terrific throughout, and while the standard stereo surround sound is not as dimensionally detailed as the Dolby Digital sound, it is adequate. The program is accompanied by a

decent collection of still photos and has alternate French and German audio tracks, as well as a music-and-effects track and an English track that includes imagery descriptions for the blind, all of which are in Dolby Digital. There are also optional English subtitles.

Greedy (Universal, 20429)

In the informative production notes on the DVD, screenwriter Lowell Ganz admits to having been inspired by Charles Dickens' *Martin Chuzzlewitt*, "Fortunately, Dickens isn't alive to ask any questions." The amusing 1994 feature, directed by Jonathan Lynn and starring Michael J. Fox and Kirk Douglas, is presented in letterboxed format with an aspect ratio of about 1.85:1 and an accommodation for enhanced 16:9 playback. The image is a little soft in places, but colors are bright and the presentation is workable. The stereo surround sound is not elaborately mixed, but there are a few separation effects that add to the film's atmosphere, particularly on the Dolby Digital track. The 103 minute program is also available in French in Dolby Digital and can be supported by English or Spanish subtitles. There is a very good trailer and a cast profile section. Douglas stars as a wily millionaire being pestered by his heirs and Fox is the one grandson who is supposedly above it all.

The Green Berets (Warner, 1002)

John Wayne's one-of-a-kind 1968 Vietnam film is presented on two sides in letterboxed format, with an aspect ratio of about 2.35:1 and no 16:9 enhancement. The color transfer looks super, with bright, crisp hues and rich fleshtones. The monophonic sound has decent strength and a rich bass. The 142 minute film is also available in French and Spanish, and comes with English, French or Spanish subtitles. There is a decent cast and crew profile section, a couple of production notes, several trailers, and a 'making of' featurette with lots of behind-the-scenes footage.

With its super battle scenes and simple-minded dramatics, the movie is easy entertainment. Enough time is passed that its earnest preaching should no longer overshadow its real pleasures. The film was an opportunity to see Wayne in a fresh venue, and for many fans that alone is reason enough for obtaining the disc.

Green Legend Ran (Pioneer, PIDA1131V)

Broken into three episodes, the 140 minute program tells a coherent and fairly interesting tale about the remaining human inhabitants of Earth and their conflict with the planet's mysterious, plant-like rulers. Reminiscent of Frank Herbert's *Dune* books, the animated adventure is a good mixture of character, action and imagination, and the artwork is satisfying.

The colors are sharp and solid, and the stereo sound is fine, though dimensionality is limited. The audio is available in English or Japanese and can be supported by two subtitling options, a literal transcription of the English dubbing or a looser translation of the Japanese track. A brief interview with the film's creator is included at the show's end, along with a music video.

Gremlins (Warner, 11388)

Joe Dante's 1984 fright comedy, about little furry toys that turn vicious, is set during Christmas, though we doubt few viewers put it on as an annual holiday tradition. The film is as loaded with cultural references as it is with nasty creatures, however, and its depth of detail and other business is ideal for multiple viewing.

The Dolby Digital track is everything you could want in a **Gremlins** soundtrack. It is more energetic and better detailed than the bland standard stereo soundtrack, with loads of directional effects and split rear channel effects, all with plenty of power. The 106 minute film is presented in letterboxed format on one side, with an aspect ratio of about 1.75:1 and an accommodation for enhanced 16:9 playback, and in full screen format on the other side. The letterboxing masks off picture information from the top and bottom of the image and adds a little to the sides. We tend to prefer the full screen image. The color transfer looks great, with crisp hues and accurate fleshtones. The film is also available in French and Spanish without Dolby Digital and can be supported by English, French or Spanish subtitles. There is a decent cast profile section, some brief production notes and three trailers, a standard trailer, a very funny re-release trailer and a trailer for the sequel.

Gridlock'd (PolyGram, 4400549672)

A comically staged tale about two drug addicts trying to hustle their way into a detox program, Tupac Shakur and Tim Roth star. The 1997 film tends to exaggerate the bureaucratic problems the heroes run into—the apathetic social workers and vicious Emergency Room receptionists seem overplayed—and some viewers may dismiss the whole project because of this, but others will enjoy the film's audacity and its accepting view of life on the streets. Both Roth and Shakur are highly entertaining and there is always an aspect to being stoned that can seem quite funny no matter how deadly serious the rest of the world becomes.

The picture is presented on one side in letterboxed format, with an aspect ratio of about 1.85:1 and an accommodation for enhanced 16:9 playback, and is in full screen format on the other side. The color transfer looks okay. The setting is fairly grungy, but bright hues are solid and fleshtones are passable. The stereo surround sound has a workable mix and is adequately delivered. The 91 minute program also has a French language soundtrack, optional Spanish subtitles, English captioning, a cast profile section and a trailer.

Grim (Image, ID4657APDVD)

Don't be fooled by the succulent jacket cover. The film is a cheap, awful mess and is not the least bit satisfying as a horror film or as anything else. About a group of homeowners exploring a cave wherein lives a hulking beast, the narrative makes no sense, the gore is inept and the special effects are nonsensical. Since most of the movie takes place underground, the image is dark and grainy and colors look drained. The monophonic sound is as cheap as the rest of the film and the 86 minute program is not closed captioned.

Gross Pointe Blank (Buena Vista, 14259)

A professional hit man attends his high school reunion and rekindles a lost love in the marvelous romantic comedy thriller. John Cusack stars with Minnie Driver and Dan Aykroyd in the surprisingly intelligent tale. Every plot turn and every line of dialogue seem very carefully chosen, but the result is that the film never strikes a wrong note. Its preposterous premise plays out steadily, as a dark but believable comedy, and each plot turn is an unanticipated but logical surprise. The film is really about Cusack's character gradually opening his heart, so he wins you over at first by being a smooth pro at the top of his game, and then holds onto you by revealing more and more of his soul as the film progresses. The presentation is letterboxed with an aspect ratio 1.85:1 and no 16:9 enhancement. The picture is sharp and colors are accurate. The Dolby Digital track providing slightly better defined separations than the standard stereo surround soundtrack. The 107 minute film is also available in French in standard stereo and can be supported by English or Spanish subtitles. A terrific theatrical trailer has been included, too.

Ground Control (Trimark, VM70140)

We're surprised they haven't made more air traffic control movies, because is it is such a great way to create tension on a single set using occasional inserts of a screen speckled with green lines and numbers. **Ground Control** has no dynamic camera moves or other tension-inducing film tricks, and the situations don't ring entirely true even if you know nothing about the air traffic control business, but the basic situation is so easily tension-inducing that the film glues your eyeballs to the screen anyway. Kiefer Sutherland stars as a burnt-out controller who is talked back in to doing some grunt work on a busy holiday night by his former boss. Storms hit,

things really start cooking and he has to overcome his psychological blocks to save the day. Like we said, it is all mostly in one set and takes place during one long night. Regardless of its dubious realism, it is good enough to make you switch to taking the train.

The picture is okay. Fleshtones are a bit orange in some places and other colors are a little bland, but the image quality is reasonably sharp and the presentation is adequate. There is an Ultra-Stereo surround soundtrack, but separation effects are limited. The 89 minute program has optional English, French and Spanish subtitles, cast filmographies, and a trailer. Kelly McGillis, Bruce McGill and Henry Winkler are also featured.

Groundhog Day (Columbia TriStar, 52295/9)

Bill Murray stars in the very clever and captivating fantasy about a man who keeps waking up to find his day starting over again. Andie MacDowell is the romantic interest he seemingly cannot win no matter how many fresh starts he is given. Stylistically the film is notable for presenting what can seem like multiple takes in succession to represent the hero's experiences on advancing days. The film's core philosophical flaw is that the hero eventually achieves his redemption through the accumulated knowledge he has achieved during his repeated failures to pass on to the next day, instead of through only the increased understanding that he can achieve fulfillment by helping others. It is a minor point, however, since the gist of the message is still conveyed and the film, as it stands, is a fresh and satisfying comical daydream.

The 1993 film is letterboxed on one side, with an aspect ratio of about 1.85:1 and an accommodation for enhanced 16:9 playback, and is in full screen format on the other side. The color transfer is fine and the picture looks solid. The stereo surround sound is okay although the mix is not elaborate. The 101 minute program also has French and Spanish audio tracks, optional English, French and Spanish subtitles, and a trailer.

Grumman F6F Hellcat (Program Power, UPC#4017898012)

Also identified as *Roaring Glory Vol. 1*, it opens with a half-hour look at how the WWII fighter plane operates. The narrator pilot first gives a tour of the plane's outside, explaining its specific design innovations and how the various parts functioned. He then gets into the cockpit, explaining the instrument panel and how to start the plane. Subsequently, he takes off for a flight, still talking over the radio as he shows how the plane maneuvers. Aspects of the takeoff and flight are supported by multiple angle functions. In the second half hour, archival footage is combined with staged black-and-white footage to dramatize the reminiscences of a WWII pilot. Additionally, there is a terrific 20 minute War Department training film about flying the Hellcat, as well as an interview with a former WWII pilot, who reminisces, and still photos from both then and now. The picture quality is passable and the sound is fine. The program is not captioned.

Grumpy Old Men (Warner, 13050)
Grumpier Old Men (Warner, 14191)

The 1993 geriatric comedy is about two cantankerous neighbors, played by Jack Lemmon and Walter Matthau, and a vivacious widow, played by Ann-Margret, who moves in across the street. The film has a predictable mixture of slapstick, illness and death jokes, and affection masked in bitterness, but the direction is calm and the stars bring out the best in the material, breezing by the rest.

The program is presented in cropped format only, trimming a little off the sides and adding more to the top and bottom of the image in comparison the movie's letterboxed framing. The 104 minute film is not one where the exact framing of the image is critical to the entertainment, but some fans are likely to be frustrated by the lack of a letterboxing option. The colors are nice and the image is sharp. The stereo surround sound is adequate. The DVD also has French and Spanish language tracks and English, French or Spanish subtitling. A theatrical trailer has been included, along with a cast profile and production notes about filming in Minnesota.

The 1995 sequel, with Sophia Loren joining Lemmon, Matthau and Ann-Margret, has also been issued in full screen format only, adding picture information to the top and bottom of the image and taking some off the sides in comparison to the letterboxed version. The colors look dark, the image is crisp and fleshtones are a bit pinkish, but workable. The stereo surround sound has a detailed resonance, and there is a Dolby Digital track that is even more active, stronger and more dimensional. The 101 minute film is also available in French in Dolby Digital and in Spanish in standard stereo, and comes with English, French or Spanish subtitles. There is a decent cast and crew profile, some minor production notes and amusing trailers for both the film and its predecessor.

The romance between Matthau and Loren is not the least bit convincing, and the sparring between Matthau and Lemmon, which made the first film so amusing, seems more forced and contrived, but the movie fills a niche created by its predecessor. It is fresh, it has an appealing cast, and there just aren't that many movies like it being made any more.

Daryl Hannah and Burgess Meredith are also featured in both films.

Guarding Tess (Columbia TriStar, 78709)

Shirley MacLaine is an aging, widowed former First Lady and Nicolas Cage is a beleaguered Secret Service agent stuck with her and dreaming of more glamorous assignments. The film delivers precisely what it promises, and the stars fulfill their roles with a delightful predictability.

The color transfer looks super. The detail in MacLaine's lipstick, for example, conveys the full texture along every rolling crease in her mouth. The film is letterboxed on one side, with an aspect ratio of about 1.85:1 and an accommodation for enhanced 16:9 playback, and is in full screen format on the other side. The stereo surround sound is good. The 96 minute program also has French and Spanish audio tracks, optional English, French and Spanish subtitling, and a trailer.

Guilty By Suspicion (Warner, 12053)

An interesting flaw develops in **Guilty By Suspicion**, and it is hard to tell if it was anticipated by the filmmakers or whether it is an accident that they were forced to cover up. Robert De Niro portrays a successful film director during the fifties whose career comes to a screeching halt when he balks at cooperating with HUAC. The film's flaw is that blacklisting is the best thing that ever happened to his character as a human being. It turns him away from his obsession with filmmaking, forces him to communicate emotionally with his family, and sifts his true friends from the phony ones. Hence, a movie that is supposed to be about the evils of blacklisting is consistently the most fascinating (except for one sequence depicting the director at work, which is the only time the movie really come alive) when it is showing the upside of the tragedy. The film might have even succeeded if the filmmakers had gone all the way with this concept instead of trying to suppress it. Everybody knows that blacklisting was bad—it is like saying that Communism is bad—and as it stands the film's best intentions are noble and boring. Annette Benning and George Wendt co-star.

Although the movie uses hazes and such to evoke its Fifties setting, the picture is sharp. Fleshtones are passable and other hues are reasonably fresh. The stereo surround sound is not elaborately mixed, but it is adequately presented and the 105 minute feature is effectively closed captioned.

Guncrazy (Sterling, 4030)

Drew Barrymore gives a superb performance as a teenage girl who marries a paroled convict, the two forced into a crime and murder spree by circumstance, prejudice and their own ineptitude. The film, directed by Tamra Davis, is very good, always keeping the viewer on an emotional edge and yet maintaining a sufficient dis-

tance and humor to prevent the plot's more severe turns from becoming too depressing. James LeGros co-stars.

The full screen picture is sharp, but the hues have a mild paleness at times and fleshtones are a bit light. Some darker scenes look a little grainy. The Ultra-Stereo surround sound is super, so well defined that viewers will probably notice the gunshots are given a different sound when LeGros pulls the trigger than when Barrymore pulls it. The 97 minute film has not been captioned.

The Gunfighter (Sterling, 7175)

Christopher Coppola, nephew of Francis Ford (who has lent his name as executive producer) and brother of Nicolas Cage, has written and directed a wonderful updating of Hopalong Cassidy. Sterling is apparently so petrified of associating with the classic TV (and 'B' movie) cowboy that they only call him 'Cassidy' on the jacket cover, and don't name him at all in the trailer. Coppola, however, shows no such reserve. The film has modern violence and realistic emotional relationships, but the hero, played by Chris Lybert, still looks like he's so clean dirt falls off him without washing, and he has an intuitive relationship with his horse that is far more intimate than the connections he makes with the heroine. And boy, can he shoot—he knocks the buttons off the bad guy's vest. The story—cattle rustlers kidnap the heroine to set a trap for the hero—is sufficiently interesting to hold one's attention for the 95 minute running time, although there is a rather pointless prologue and epilogue, featuring Martin Sheen and Robert Carradine, apparently to boost the show's marquee appeal.

The picture is letterboxed with an aspect ratio of about 2.35:1 and no 16:9 enhancement. Some darker sequences are a bit grainy, with murky colors, and fleshtones are bland, but the image is workable, particularly in the daylight sequences. The stereo surround sound kind of goes overboard at times (fistfights sound like dueling jackhammers), but it is lively, delivering in energy what it loses in finesse. The program is not captioned and is accompanied by a cast-and-director profile.

Gunshy (Sterling, 7235)

William Peterson is a writer gone to seed and Michael Wincott is an Atlantic City loan shark collector who befriends him in the somewhat pretentious drama. Diane Lane has the Ingrid Bergman/Lena Olin part, if you get our meaning, or theirs—they even splurged to have a clip from **Casablanca** playing on the TV when Peterson and Lane first meet. Wincott asks Peterson to teach him about books, and Peterson asks Wincott to show him the darker side of life. There is one reasonably inspired plot turn and the filmmakers try very hard to make the movie seem classy, but it doesn't amount to a hill of beans, and if you roll your eyes as much as we did when Peterson and Wincott start reading *Moby Dick* together, you'll get dizzy.

The picture is presented in full screen format. Fleshtones are a bit indistinct, but the color transfer is adequate and the image is reasonably sharp. The musical score, including some Miles Davis tunes, has a nice dimensionality, and the stereo surround sound is passable. The menus take an annoyingly long time to hand control over to the viewer. The 101 minute program can be supported by optional Spanish subtitling, but there is no English captioning. There is a cast-and-crew profile section and a trailer.

Additionally, there is a commentary track by the director, Jeff Celentano and the writer, Larry Gross. They are both blissfully unaware of their film's artistic shortcomings and speak with great enthusiasm about the performances (though we would have to agree that Peterson, with his matinee idol looks, deserves to be a much bigger star, regardless of his acting abilities), the script and other aspects of the production. They detail the logistics of the shoot (most of it was done in L.A., subbing for Atlantic City, but you don't notice the palm trees until they point them out), the difficulties they encountered working from a limited budget (get the shots as quick as possible and move on) and other reasonably informative insights.

Guns That Won the West (Simitar, 7219)

The 80 minute program provides a concise history of America's western expansion, from Lewis & Clark until World War I, and traces the development of firearms during that time, noting how symbiotic advances in gun making were with the opening of the west (many gun manufacturers made a home in St. Louis). In addition to history, the film shows how the guns work, how people really carried and fired them, and allows you to see by process how and why the technological advances in design made the guns more effective. The film also touches on the famous personalities of the West and the guns they used.

The documentary is a bit unsophisticated—there is wind buffeting when some of the demonstration narrators are talking out doors, and some are so nervous they flub their lines—but that only makes the show's accomplishments more admirable. It is loaded with educational material, providing genuine insight on everything from American history and gunsmith technology to wild west dramas and action films. It is well organized, briskly delivered, and so highly stimulating that even viewers who are not enthusiasts for the period or the material will find it entertaining. The picture quality looks fine and, buffeting aside, the stereo sound is good.

Gustav Mahler: Das Lied Von Der Erde / Kindertotenlieder (Image, ID5039GCDVD)

An outstanding rendition of Gustav Mahler's sublime *Das Lied Von Der Erde* is presented as almost an avant garde opera. The male and female singers, Hélène Jossoud and Vincent de Rooster, portray Mahler and his wife, mourning the death of their child, on the sparsely decorated stage. The visual dramatization of the enigmatic song cycle increases its emotional impact significantly. Shot at a different venue, *Kindertotenlieder* is presented as a straightforward recital. Although the performance by soloist Claire Brua is quite good and the video is deftly edited, it is a soft letdown after the intellectual stimulation *Das Lied Von Der Erde* creates. Indeed, the video draws much of the dramatic power it has from its juxtaposition with the other work. *Das Lied Von Der Erde* is performed by the Bass Normandy Orchestral Ensemble and conducted by Dominique Debart. *Kindertotenlieder* is performed by the Atelier Lyrique et Symphonique du Centre, conducted by Amaury du Closel. On both, the PCM stereo sound is very good, with pure, strong tones and minimal distortion. The songs are in German and can be supported by optional English subtitles. Both programs are letterboxed, with an aspect ratio of about 1.78:1 and an accommodation for enhanced 16:9 playback. On both, the image quality is excellent, with crisp, smooth colors and accurate fleshtones. The combined program runs 98 minutes.

H

Hackers (MGM, 907169)

The 1995 teen-oriented computer thriller depicts a subculture of teenagers who can access virtually any computer system at will. Doing so, one kid comes across an embezzling scheme and soon the whole gang is being framed for some very nasty things by the embezzler. The cast is attractive and energetic, the computer stuff is absurd but stimulating and things do get exciting here and there. The premise is unlikely, and it is already getting kind of a stale taste to it.

The picture is letterboxed with an aspect ratio of about 2.35:1 and an accommodation for enhanced 16:9 playback. The colors are bright and the image is sharp. The stereo surround sound is a bit bland, but there is a much stronger Dolby Digital track, with clearer separations and a stronger bass. The 105 minute film is also available in French in standard stereo and can be supported by En-

glish, French or Spanish subtitles. There is a theatrical trailer, as well.

Hair (MGM, 907641)

Only a foreigner such as Milos Forman could have misunderstood the depth with which **Hair** was considered part of another era when he took on the task in 1979 of interpreting the stage show on film, a good five years after its popularity had subsided. How fortunate, too, that he went ahead with it, for the film is wonderful, and it was only that five year gap which prevented **Hair** from becoming a box office hit. The script pulls together a pleasant enough story about a young man's visit to New York two days before he is inducted in the Army, and the music takes care of the rest. Forman's humanistic style and the free-spirited Twyla Tharp choreography turn the movie into a friendly, two hour dance. John Savage, Treat Williams, Beverly D'Angelo, Annie Golden and others are featured.

The film is presented in letterboxed format on one side, with an aspect ratio of about 1.85:1 and no 16:9 enhancement, and in full screen format on the other side. Fleshtones are warm, colors are bright and crisp, and the image is sharp, giving the film a great shot of vitality.

The standard stereo surround sound is a little dull, but the Dolby Digital mix is energetic and better detailed. It is not elaborately dimensional, but it does bring the film's soundtrack up to par. The 121 minute feature also has a French audio track in mono (with English songs), optional English and French subtitles ("Les Blacks sont délicieux/L'amour à saveur de chocolat...."), a trailer, and a wonderful collection of 36 different poster designs, which demonstrates how desperately they tried to sell the movie to an uncaring populace.

Half a Loaf of Kung Fu! (Simitar, 7259)

The 96 minute 1977 comedy has too much juvenile and culturally oriented humor to sit well with western viewers. Jackie Chan portrays a martial arts novice whose skills improve when he assists a group of travelers transporting a valuable package that is being sought by rival clans. The comedy includes sped up film speed sequences, flatulence gags and other simplistic efforts at humor, and the fight choreography is rarely inventive, even when Chan is pretending to be inept. The picture is cropped. The source material has a few tears and other damage marks, and the image is a little soft, but the colors are reasonably bright and fleshtones look good. The film is presented in English on one track and Cantonese on another. The monophonic sound is always fairly rough, with warped or muffled music, and the Cantonese track doesn't sound all that much better. The program is not captioned.

Half-Baked (Universal, 20246)

An awful, awful, awful comedy about selling and smoking marijuana, the acting is atrociously juvenile, the film unashamedly promotes drugs, the plot (the heroes rob a 'medicinal purposes' hospital stash and sell it to raise bail for a friend) is dumb, parts of the film deliberately allude to the old Batman TV series, many of the 'jokes' are painfully forced attempts at weak humor, and stereotypes run rampant. So here's our question: Why were we laughing so much? Yep, almost as if the fumes from the film were escaping through the screen, we found ourselves giggling or outright ha-ha-ing at many of the gags, and the worse the movie got the more we enjoyed it.

The picture is letterboxed with an aspect ratio of about 1.85:1 and an accommodation for enhanced 16:9 playback. The colors are very bright and the image is crisp. The stereo surround sound and Dolby Digital sound aren't all that elaborate, but they're passable. The 83 minute film can be supported by English, French or Spanish subtitles and is accompanied by production notes, a cast profile section and a red-tag theatrical trailer that systematically tells the entire plot. Over the years people have often asked us to rate movies with grades or numerics, but **Half-Baked** is a perfect example of why we can't. It's a horrible movie that isn't funny most of the time but is funny in places, so much so that we look forward to watching it again someday.

Hall & Oates (Pioneer, PA99610D)

Only hardcore fans will be interested in the *Best of MusikLaden Live* offering. On the positive side, the 45 minute program provides a clear view of the performers and a number of their biggest hits are included in the set. On the downside, the live environment flattens their already harmonically challenged vocals and the instruments have a tinny, clipped sound, giving the recording a garage tape ambience. Not even Dolby Digital encoding can rescue it. Colors are also dull, with pale fleshtones and background grain. The program is not captioned.

Halloween (Anchor Bay, DV10324)

John Carpenter's 1978 atmospheric horror classic is about teenage babysitters being stalked by relentless killer. The film has been letterboxed on one side, with an aspect ratio of about 2.35:1 and no 16:9 enhanced playback, and is presented in cropped format on the other side. The darker sequences are a little grainy and the image is soft, even in brightly lit scenes. We don't know why anyone would want to watch the blown up cropped image, since it wrecks the movie, but for the record, the enlarged picture tends to make the fuzziness of the image even more apparent. The monophonic sound has a reasonably strong bass but a bit of scratchiness on the upper end. The 96 minutes program is accompanied by a theatrical trailer.

Halloween II (GoodTimes, 0581022)

Except for a weakness in contrasts in the darker scenes, allowing the shadows to obscure details and variations in shadings, the letterboxed image looks terrific. Colors are bright, all the cars have showroom shines to them, fleshtones are accurate and the blood is a deep, gorgeous red. The picture is also free of grain. The presentation is letterboxed with an aspect ratio of about 2.35:1 and no 16:9 enhancement, the first time the film has been issued on home video in its original widescreen format.

The film has a fairly basic stereo mix, with little dimensionality, and the musical score is a harsher orchestration of John Carpenter's compositions from the first film. The sound quality is acceptable but not elaborate. The 93 minute program can be accompanied by English, French or Spanish subtitles ("Si ce type qui brûlait dans la voiture n'était pas Myers, beaucoup d'autres jeunes vont se faire massacrer ce soir"). There are also a few production notes.

Jamie Lee Curtis and Donald Pleasance pick up their roles in the second movie from where the first left off, though most of the stalking and slashing is set in the world's least busy hospital. Rick Rosenthal directed the 1981 feature.

Halloween III: Season of the Witch (GoodTimes, 0581023)

An interesting failure, it forgoes the plot of its predecessors, but retains the style that was established in the original feature. John Carpenter's music from the first movie is re-used and given moderate variations, and his sweeping handheld camera moves and accentuated shock cuts are also employed. And, of course, the movie takes place at the end of an October. It starts out promisingly, as the hero uncovers a lamian plot undertaken by a sinister corporation using an army of androids, but the narrative tries to do too many things and so there is no real ending, just a kind of 'let's stop here' moment. If you see the movie a bunch of times or are very stoned, then the ending won't matter as much as the creepy atmosphere and incidental excitements, but it is a wonder the film ever got past the script stage. Tom Atkins stars in the 98 minute feature, which was directed by Tommy Lee Wallace.

The 1982 feature is in letterboxed format with an aspect ratio of about 2.35:1 and no 16:9 enhancement. The picture is in very good shape. Colors look fresh and are reasonably crisp, and fleshtones

are decent. The monophonic sound is okay and the film can be supported by English, French or Spanish subtitles.

Hamburger Hill (Artisan, 60495)

John Irvin's 1987 **Hamburger Hill** was clearly given the go ahead because of the success of **Platoon**, and because of **Platoon** it has, as an also ran, never really received the respect it deserves. Like **Platoon**, however, it is, clearly, a very personal work, which gets to the heart of how completely out of control America's involvement in Vietnam became. It spends a brief time establishing characters, but once that is over, it focuses on the chaotic and costly efforts of a squad to take the hill. American helicopters fly over and start shooting American soldiers, the rains become so torrential that the squad could not make it up the hill even if nobody was shooting at them, and death is random and pervasive. It is a devastatingly powerful feature, and should be required viewing for all politicians.

The picture is letterboxed, with an aspect ratio of about 1.85:1 and an accommodation for enhanced 16:9 playback. Letterboxing loses nothing on the top or bottom and adds picture information to the sides in comparison to cropped versions. The film's hues are mildly subdued on purpose, but the picture transfer looks excellent, with clearly defined colors and shadings, and accurate fleshtones. The image is solid and darker sequences are free of distortion. The stereo surround sound is bland, but the 5.1 Dolby Digital channel is much stronger, with more separation effects, better definitions and a clearer mid-range. There is an outstanding musical score, by Philip Glass. The 110 minute program is not captioned and is accompanied by a trailer.

The Hand That Rocks the Cradle (Buena Vista, 15283)

The well-written and quite clever thriller is about an Iago-like nanny out for revenge against an unsuspecting young mother. The psychological terror story is a good home video title, because the logic of the narrative is so tight that repeat viewings are highly inviting, provided one can stand the suspense. Annabella Sciorra and Rebecca De Mornay star in the 1992 production, directed by the now highly respected Curtis Hanson.

The picture is noticeably sharper, but the colors are conceptually soft and fleshtones are a little light. The image is letterboxed with an aspect ratio of about 1.82:1 and no 16:9 enhancement. The stereo surround sound is effective when it comes to making things exciting. The 110 minute program is also available in French and can be supported by English subtitles. There is a very good theatrical trailer that gives you the concept without giving away the plot.

Hang 'Em High (MGM, 906730)

Clint Eastwood's first 'American-made' western, directed by Ted Post, has held up well over the years. When released initially, it was an artistic letdown from Eastwood's 'spaghetti' work, but in retrospect it is a lot more valid as a western and as a drama than most of the Eastwood films which followed. More than just a revenge thriller, the film is about the politics of law enforcement and the consequences of justice. It helps, too, that the film was made in a leery, late sixties visual style, with cameras pushing in on faces and cuts which seem timed to upset a viewer's internal rhythms. Dominic Frontiere's music is also terrific. Again, a letdown after Ennio Morricone's efforts in the Sergio Leone films, the score is wonderfully gaudy and abrupt. For all of its deliberateness—and it is a great score to play at an increased volume—it is not tiresome, and sets the tabloid mood which the whole movie is attempting to convey.

The 1968 feature is presented in letterboxed format on one side, with an aspect ratio of about 1.8:1 and an accommodation pre-enhanced 16:9 playback, and in full screen format on the other side. The letterboxing adds nothing to the sides of the image while removing picture information from the top and bottom, and we find the framing on the full screen version to be more satisfying. The colors are passable, though in general the film has a kind of dusty tone. As with past home video releases, odd reverberations that pop up on the soundtrack from time to time, and, in general, the monophonic sound is a bit weak. The 115 minute film is also available in French and is accompanied by English, French and Spanish subtitles ("Pendez-le!"). There is also an original theatrical trailer.

Happiness (Trimark, VM70230)

Todd Solondz' 1998 feature is a film you cannot recommend to people unless you know them really well. It is a movie that, once seen, is never forgotten. At once outrageously absurd and utterly real, the film will stimulate the finest intellectual provocations in some people and will totally nauseate others. Running 139 minutes, it follows the lives of three sisters and a handful of their acquaintances, advancing through the various stories to contrast and build emotions like themes in a concerto. Several of the tales are about the basest types of human behavior, conducted by people who are unable to place a psychic retaining wall around their erotic fantasies. The film's most controversial character, the husband of one of the sisters, sodomizes his young son's friends. He knows he's doing wrong and he eventually gets caught, but the mere fact that he isn't depicted as a sweaty fiend or as one of the bad guys in Con Air is unnerving. It makes you start to look differently at the people standing around you, particularly the ones who are recommending you watch **Happiness**.

The movie's cinematography is outstanding and the transfer is excellent. Colors, be they the soft pastels of some of the apartments or the unnaturally vivid greens of park lawns, are delivered with a precision that enhances the impact of almost every scene. Fleshtones are finely detailed, as well. The transfer rate appears low, however, generating distracting artifact flaws. Although not as meticulous as the cinematography, the stereo surround sound is good, often providing an ironic ambiance to the action. The program has optional English and French subtitles, and is accompanied by a red tag theatrical trailer.

Happy Gilmore (Universal, 20151)

Adam Sandler portrays a novice golf player with an exceptionally powerful drive who worms his way onto the pro circuit and attracts fans with his antics. The film is no great work of art, but the humor is consistent (playing in a celebrity match, he is teamed with Bob Barker and they get into a fist fight) and the narrative is strong enough to hold everything together.

The colors are very bright and the image is crisp. The improvements to the colors almost outweigh the disadvantage of the film having been released in full screen format only, losing a bit on the sides and adding picture information to the top and bottom in comparison to letterboxed versions of the film. About half the time, the full screen framing is better for taking in the film's physical comedy, but just as often the cropping on the sides upsets the image framing a bit. The stereo surround sound is a little weak, but the Dolby Digital track is good, delivering better defined and separated tones. The 92 minute film is also available in French in standard stereo and in Spanish in mono and comes with English and Spanish subtitles. There is also an enjoyable theatrical trailer (with some footage that doesn't appear in the film), a lengthy production essay and a cast profile section.

Hard Boiled (Criterion, CC1516D)

John Woo's 1992 action spectacle is about two cops, one undercover and one ostracized by his department, who are working to break a gun smuggling ring. The film has some fairly serious themes, but it is the big stunt sequences that it so addicting. Especially memorable are the opening sequence, a gunfight set in a crowded restaurant where bodies go flying and bullets go bursting in a wild yet lyrical frenzy, and the half hour finale, set in a hospital where, at one point, the hero helps to evacuate the maternity ward amid flying bullets and explosive fires. To make one other point of praise—where, in American films, the hero's superior is often depicted as impotent or foolish, here he happens to be several steps

ahead and they clash only when it comes to the somewhat sloppy methods the hero employs in executing his duties. Chow Yun-fat and Tony Leung star.

The film is a thrill and so is the DVD. The picture looks super. Naturally, the colors aren't as rich as they would be in a Hollywood production, but the transfer is fine and the quality of the image never detracts from the flow of the drama. There are scratches and other marks, and a mild softness, but colors are bright and reasonably fresh. The picture is letterboxed with an aspect ratio of about 1.93:1, with no 16:9 enhancement. The monophonic sound is workable. The 126 minute film can be accessed in Cantonese or in English, with optional English subtitles. Also included is an essay on **Hard Boiled** by David Chute, a 'guide' to Hong Kong crime films, a summary and wonderful collection of trailers for Woo's Hong Kong features (our favorite is one for a Cantonese musical), and Woo's student film, *Accidental* (the black-and-white Super-8 film is pretty bad, but worth taking a look at if you want to see how master artists get started). There is also an audio commentary that provides a focused discussion about Woo's filmmaking and the meanings of **Hard Boiled**. Appearing are Woo, producer Terence Chong, American director Roger Avery, who is working on a film with Woo, and film critic David Kehr. Kehr provides just enough insight to orient the viewer to the film's themes without stating the obvious. Woo, Chong and Avery provide different viewpoints, giving the listener a well-rounded view of Woo's working methods (though there continue to be cryptic references to his temper on the set) and increasing an understanding of what, besides great gun battles, the film is accomplishing.

A Hard Day's Night (see The Beatles: A Hard Day's Night)

Hard Rain (Paramount, 332137)

Set in the middle of a flood, the 1998 crime thriller is an enjoyable if predictable action feature. Christian Slater is the hero, an armored car driver whose truck has drowned, and Morgan Freeman is the villain scheming to retrieve its contents. Mini Driver and Randy Quaid are also featured. There are jet ski chases, an ever-rising water line that gradually envelops a town, and a few basic twists to keep things interesting.

The picture is in letterboxed format only, with an aspect ratio of about 2.35:1 and no 16:9 enhancement. The film has a number of visual effects that seem well blended on the video screen. The movie is set at night and in the rain, but the picture is sharp and colors are accurate. The stereo surround sound is okay. The mix lacks detail, but the basic water-all-around-you effects are there and, with all the action, pretty much any additional sound adds to the fun. There is also a Dolby Digital track, but it, too, reflects the film's competent but unelaborate audio design, and bass effects are limited. The 98 minute program also has a French audio track in standard stereo, optional English and Spanish subtitles and a trailer.

Hard Target (Universal, 20230)

Even in its emasculated, R-rated form, John Woo's 1993 film, with Jean-Claude Van Damme, makes a dandy DVD. The elaborate shoot-out and motorcycle chase is an ideal demonstration sequence that rivals the motorcycle sequence in **Terminator 2**. Van Damme stars as an ex-GI who helps to crack a murder-for-pleasure ring in New Orleans. The real star of the film, however, is behind the camera, for although the film is certainly one of Van Damme's best efforts, it is Woo's imaginative stunts and his astonishing mix of camera angles and speeds that make the film much more than simply another mindless action picture.

It is letterboxed with an aspect ratio of about 1.85:1 and an accommodation for enhanced 16:9 playback. Colors are glossy and fleshtones are rich. The Dolby Digital is much more invigorating than the standard stereo track. The 97 minute film is also available in French in standard stereo and comes with English or Spanish subtitles, along with some carefully worded production notes, a cast profile section and a high-charged theatrical trailer.

Hard to Kill (Warner, 11914)

Steven Seagal is a cop who has been in a coma for seven years and reawakens with evidence that will put a large conspiracy of bad guys and politicians behind bars. Kelly LeBrock co-stars. The story may be farfetched, but it makes an enjoyable premise and the action scenes are good fun.

The film is letterboxed with an aspect ratio of about 1.8:1 on one side, with an accommodation for enhanced 16:9 playback, and is in full screen format on the other side. The letterboxing adds a bit of picture information to the sides of the image and masks off more from the bottom, though the framing on the letterboxed image is usually stronger. Colors are true and deep, with good detail and a sharp focus. The regular stereo surround sound is a little weak, but the Dolby Digital track has a very strong bass, good separation effects and lots of energy. The 96 minute 1990 film is available in French in regular stereo and Spanish in mono, and comes with optional English, French or Spanish subtitles, a decent cast-and-crew profile, very minor production notes and trailers for eight Seagal films.

Hard Vice (Simitar, 7315)

The jacket claims that the movie is rated 'R,' but Simitar's more reliable 'Film Facts' section lists the title as being 'PG-13,' and that is pretty much how the subdued violence and sex plays in it. Sam Jones (remember **Flash Gordon**?) and Shannon Tweed star as cops investigating the ritual murder of a hooker's clientele. The narrative is rather straightforward and uninteresting, but the performances are good enough to keep undemanding fans attentive. The picture is bland, with dull fleshtones, and the stereo sound is a bit flat. The film runs 86 minutes and is not captioned.

The Hard Way (Universal, 20434)

Michael J. Fox stars with James Woods in the action comedy, but the film, directed by John Badham, is a mixed bag where for the most part the good outweighs the bad. Fox is a famous movie star researching his next role and Woods is a New York cop forced to babysit him while a serial killer runs loose around the city. The tone of the film is inconsistent (and unrealistic), and the script prevents the stars from making their characters believable, but there are scenes and sections where the premise and the performances work quite well, and these sequences are so entertaining that most viewers will be happy to overlook the film's shortcomings.

The 1991 feature is presented in letterboxed format with an aspect ratio of about 2.35:1 and an accommodation for enhanced 16:9 playback. Fleshtones are pinkish and other hues are indistinct, with soft contrasts. The stereo surround sound is passable. The 111 minute film is also available in French and can be supported by English or Spanish subtitles. The movie comes with a 'making of' featurette (that has better colors), a standard trailer, a music video by LL Cool J, production notes, and a cast-and-director profile.

Harry Connick Jr.: The New York Big Band Concert (Sony, CVD49168)

If Harry Connick, Jr. didn't exist, it would be necessary to invent him. Seemingly the only active male vocalist outside of some small piano bar to keep the torch lit for the classic songs of the Thirties and Forties, his only problem is that he doesn't always play it straight. He's at his best when he's singing the old standards with his smooth, focused vocals, in a perfect imitation of the singers from a previous generation, but there are times when he can't suppress a smirk or a knowing wink, like he's in on some satirical joke, mocking the past, and it spoils the mood. Such moments, however, are minimal on the night club-style **Big Band Concert** program, where he is for the most part well behaved, accompanied by a tal-

ented collection of musicians and performing a pleasing array of songs from the past and from more recent times.

The image is dreamily soft, but clear. Connick is well lit, while the audience, though they can be heard, remains in the dark. Colors look fine. The stereo surround sound is fine and there is a 5.1 Dolby Digital track that has better detailed separations, which can be real fun during the busiest passages. The hour-long program can be supported by optional English subtitles and is accompanied by a Connick bio and discography.

The Haunted Strangler (Image, ID4430GODVD)

Boris Karloff portrays an author investigating a series of murders committed twenty years earlier, hoping to prove that the man executed for the crimes was innocent. We don't want to give away the main plot twist—the trailer has no compunctions about that, however—but Karloff does get a chance to stretch his acting abilities and genre fans should be pleased, despite a somewhat drawn out and convoluted finale.

The black-and-white picture has a few markings here and there, but the image is quite crisp, with excellent contrast detail and smooth, deep blacks. The monophonic sound is fine and the 80 minute 1957 film is accompanied by the aforementioned engaging original theatrical trailer.

Havana (Universal, 20414)

Sydney Pollack's flaccid 1990 **Casablanca** imitation runs 145 minutes, but there is barely enough plot for a movie half that length. Robert Redford is the sticks-his-head-out-for-nobody gambler who falls head over heels for the most beautiful woman on the boat (Lena Olin) sailing for Havana, right before the revolution. Raul Julia is the Victor Lazlo of Cuba.

Everything looks so slick and handsome you want the movie to work, but it is just never convincing, stalling the drama at points where things ought to be accelerating. Olin strongly resembles one of Redford's greatest screen partners (no, not Paul Newman), Natalie Wood, but the two fail to generate the same sort of chemistry. Whether he isn't connecting with her or she isn't connecting with him, they seem to be making poses, not love, and when they are subsequently split asunder, it's no big deal. He has more fire with two actresses playing the pickups his character has a romp with in the beginning of the film.

The picture looks super. Colors are vibrant and fleshtones are rich. The image is letterboxed with an aspect ratio of about 1.85:1 and no 16:9 enhancement. The stereo surround sound is very good, and the film also has a really nice Dolby Digital track, with better-defined separations and sharper tones. The film is also available in French in standard stereo (but not Spanish, contrary to the jacket cover) and can be supported by English or Spanish subtitles. There are some good production notes (they shot the movie is Santa Domingo), a small cast-and-director profile section and a longish but unsuccessful trailer.

Hawaii X-rated (Vivid, UPC#0073214484)

The image, from a videotape source, is very sharp, fleshtones are accurate and colors, to excuse the adjective, are vivid. The sound is also fairly good. The 73 minute program was shot on location in the Aloha State and has a workable narrative, about a pair of topless dancers from California who have been booked into a new club. There are plenty of outdoor sequences, though the erotic scenes are rarely creative. Watch the tide change between the medium shots and the long shots. The program contains alternate angle sequences and elaborate hardcore interactive promotional features.

He Got Game (Buena Vista, 15281)

Spike Lee's excellent drama is about a convict who is given a furlough in exchange for trying to talk his son into signing with the state university basketball team. The stereo surround sound and particularly the Dolby Digital sound are slightly weaker than the sound on the LD release. Although the difference amounts to minor compromises in detail and definition, the film's audio track is so well mixed that the DVD's shortcomings can affect one's emotional responses to the film. The picture is a little smoother than the LD, but the film has a deliberately urban look and the advantages of a slightly better picture don't add to the drama the way the better sound does. The image is letterboxed with an aspect ratio of about 1.85:1 and no 16:9 enhancement. The 136 minute film can be supported by optional English subtitles and is accompanied by a theatrical trailer. The film's emotional drama outweighs its political conscience to a greater degree than in Lee's best works, but it does function as a loving ode to basketball, which for some viewers will be more than enough compensation.

Head Over Heels X-rated (Vivid, UPC#0073214542)

The narrative, about a shoe store clerk who gets fired, has a stronger than average emotional premise, foot fetishes and some innovative scenes, including a sequence that is presented in black-and-white and meant to imitate The Andrew Sisters. The picture quality varies a bit (often on purpose) but is in acceptable condition and the sound is fine. The 71 minute program features Janine, Laura Palmer and Christi Lake. The DVD contains alternate angle sequences and elaborate hardcore interactive promotional features.

Head to Head X-rated (Vivid, UPC#0073214588)

There isn't much of a narrative, about the female management of a tavern, but the erotic sequences are very well done, including a scene inspired by the story of Pyramus and Thisbe. The colors are strong, but the picture is quite grainy. The sound is okay, but you can hear the film crew shouting instructions to the performers in one spot. Janine, Alexis Christian, Madlyn Knight and Chelsea Blue star in the 71 minute program. The DVD contains alternate angle sequences and elaborate hardcore interactive promotional features.

Hearst Castle: Building the Dream (SlingShot, DVD9842)

It wasn't produced in IMAX, but the 70mm production is the same sort of program. Running 40 minutes, it is a narrated re-enactment of William Randolph Hearst's life and the construction of his home at San Simeon, including, for example, extended views of European tourist sites that Hearst visited as a young boy. There is also a period re-creation of a typical party at the castle—suitable for family viewing, of course. The length of the program is just about right for covering the history and display of the subject.

We have no idea if the full screen presentation is cropped or not, since the image compositions always look well balanced. The picture is sharp and colors are accurate, though we did detect some very minor artifacting effects in a couple places. There are very few environmental sounds, but the music is adequately dimensional and has a reasonable flourish, with the Dolby Digital track providing a bit more energy than the standard track. The program can be supported by optional English subtitles.

The Heartbreak Kid (Anchor Bay, DV10408)

The film is unpredictable only in that it is so predictable you can't believe the plot would actually move in the ways that it does. A man meets a woman, marries her, meets another woman on his honeymoon, divorces the first and marries the second. He even matures from the experience. Had the filmmakers reversed the situation a little, to have Cybill Shepherd portray Charles Grodin's first wife, and to have him discover that there is more to love than good looks and athletic ability, it might have had a lasting moral. But with Shepherd portraying the second wife, the viewer is left anticipating what will happen on the second honeymoon. The script doesn't even mention that there is a second honeymoon.

The 1972 Elaine May film is presented in full screen format. The colors are very drained, with extremely pale fleshtones, and the

presentation is bland at best. The monophonic sound is a little aged but workable. The 106 minute program is not captioned.

Hearts and Souls (Universal, 20433)

A wonderful *Topper*-like fantasy about four ghosts haunting a young man, Robert Downey, Jr. is the Topper character and, with great flair, must imitate his fellow cast members when they alternately 'take possession' of his character's body. Charles Grodin, Alfre Woodard, Tom Sizemore, and Kyra Sedgwick are the ghosts. Elisabeth Shue also stars in the 1993 Ron Underwood film.

The picture is in letterboxed format only, with an aspect ratio of about 2.35:1 and an accommodation for enhanced 16:9 playback. The color transfer looks fine, with a smooth, sharp image and accurate hues. The comedy does not have an abundance of audio effects. There are some nice musical passages enhanced by the power and detail of the Dolby Digital track (B.B. King appears in one terrific sequence), and a few surges in surround activity, but generally the audio is subservient to the narrative, the performances, the humor and the video effects. The 103 minute feature also has a French language track, optional English or Spanish subtitles, a cast-and-director profile section and some production notes.

Heat (Image, ID4730PYDVD)

Sylvia Miles stars as wealthy matron who takes a liking to a young stud, played by Joe Dallesandro, until her daughter, awash in filial resentment, stirs up trouble. The eccentricities of the characters are highly comical and, from the acting to the camera work, the production values on the 1972 feature are somewhat improved over director Paul Morrissey's earlier efforts.

The 100 minutes film is presented in full screen format. The source material on has incidental damage and other evidence of wear, but colors are surprisingly rich and there is no more grain or fuzzy blurring than what the original cinematography brought to the source. John Cale did the music, and the monophonic sound is passable. There is no captioning.

Heathers (Anchor Bay, DV10672)

In the best black comedy tradition, Winona Ryder and Christian Slater star as high school students who start killing the most popular kids in their class. The surprise twist in the script is that it turns out to be logical after a viewer is convinced the story has gone wacko. The dialogue is exquisite, the film's tone has just the right level of seriousness to keep things in perspective and, as we mentioned in our previous review, this is one of the few high school movies that can be fully enjoyed by people who normally despise high school movies.

The picture looks super. The colors are sharp and vivid, and the image is smooth. The picture is letterboxed with an aspect ratio of about 1.85:1 and no 16:9 enhancement, and the framing is very well balanced. The monophonic sound is also very strong. The 105 minute film is accompanied by a trailer and an 11 minute featurette. There is no captioning.

Hector Berlioz: Symphonie Fantastique Les Nuits d'Été (Image, ID5023GCDVD)

An excellent 86 minute introduction to the works of the Romantic French composer, Hector Berlioz, is presented by the Montpelier Philharmonic Orchestra conducted by Cyril Diederich, with vocals, on *Nuits d'Été*, by Françoise Pollet. *Nuits d'Été* is presented first, inter-cutting shots of the orchestra with a wide variety of nature shots. The camera remains on the orchestra for *Symphonie Fantastique*, but the editing is very good, capturing the essence of the instrumentation without bouncing too abruptly from one image to the next. Pollet's personality tends to dominate *Nuits d'Été*, but her singing is competent. The orchestra's performance of both works is studious and involving.

Hues are light and fleshtones are pale in the orchestra sequences, but generally the picture looks fine (the nature images are quite colorful), the image is crisp, and the stereo surround sound, though not intensely immediate, is acceptable. Although we wiped off our platter really good, we couldn't get rid of a blip in chapter 11, around 82:45 mark, so the flaw may be in the transfer.

Hellbound Hellraiser II (Anchor Bay, DV10331)

The picture is sharp and blacks are pure. The colors are also strong. Fleshtones are a little too pinkish at times but workable. The picture retains some intrusions of grain, but the distortion is minimal. The image has been letterboxed with an aspect ratio of about 1.85:1 and no 16:9 enhancement. The stereo sound is dull, but the 1994 film does not have an elaborate mix and the presentation seems adequate if one pushes the volume a little. The 108 minute feature is a lethargically paced and uninspired sequel, except for the final third of the film, which takes place in an effects laden, labyrinthine inferno. The pace of the editing is excruciatingly slow and padded with superfluous footage. Ashley Laurence, one of the few survivors from the first film, stars.

Hellfighters (Universal, 20512)

John Wayne and Jim Hutton star as oil fire cappers who encounter motivational difficulties after Hutton's character marries the daughter of Wayne's character, played by Katharine Ross. Except for a scattered speckle or two, the 1968 feature looks flawless, with a crisp focus, bright, solid hues and lovely fleshtones. The picture is letterboxed with an aspect ratio of about 2.6:1 and no 16:9 enhancement. The combination of the widescreen cinematography and captivating image quality can get the viewer past more than one of the film's artificial domestic squabbles. The 122 minute movie looks so good that it can thrive on star power and a handful of major action sequences. There is also a nice stereo surround soundtrack. Separation effects are generalized, but the music is dimensional and atmospheric effects are fairly constant on the rear channel. Not only is the picture on the DVD crisper than the LD, but the sound is also substantially stronger. The film is also available in Spanish in mono and can be supported by English, French or Spanish subtitles. There is a good production essay that explains how the massive oil fires were achieved (they burned a lot kerosene) and a passable cast profile section. Contrary to the jacket listing, however, there is no trailer.

Hello Norma Jeane X-rated (Video Team New Entertainment, NE005)

The picture, from a videotape source, is in excellent condition, with crisp hues and smooth, realistic fleshtones. The monophonic sound is passable, but the dialogue is poorly recorded at times and remains a bit under emphasized. The narrative is nonsensical, about a blonde, beauty-marked actress who gains power in the adult film business by tricking some producers with fake amnesia, but it is sufficient to keep things moving and the erotic sequences are effectively staged. Norma Jeane, Chayse Manhattan, Summer Cummings, Tami Ann, and Skye Blue are featured in the 75 minute program.

Hellraiser (Anchor Bay, DV10330)

Hellraiser is not just another horror movie, it is the horror movie you long for. It has everything. Sex, romance, gore, special effects, gruesome looking things (there is creature that is half human, half scorpion), first-rate storyboarding and editing, irony (the biggest scream comes from the inopportune appearance of a statue of Jesus), a coherent, even clever plot with a beginning, middle and satisfactory ending, and stereo sound. Andrew Robinson and Claire Higgins star.

The 1987 feature has been letterboxed with an aspect ratio of about 1.85:1 and no 16:9 enhancement. Blacks are pure and fleshtones are natural. The picture still looks a little ragged compared to a larger budgeted production, and hues remain subdued, but the smoothness of the darker areas in the image can be a significant factor in drawing the viewer into the film. Dimensional effects are limited and the background is a little noisy at times, but the di-

mensionality of the mix is pleasing. The innovative 118 minute program is not captioned.1987 erotic horror film stars. An enjoyable theatrical trailer and several TV spots have also been included.

Help! with the Beatles (MPI, DVD7081)

The new color transfer totally blows away every previous home video release of the film. The colors are smooth, bright and lucid. It is the ideal showcase for the film's toy-like designs and vivid decorations. The stereo sound seems smoothed over, but is perfectly acceptable. The 90 minute 1965 film is accompanied by fascinating newsreels, depicting the group's reception of an award, and their arrival in Britain after a concert tour. There is also silent footage from behind-the-scenes of the premiere, along with a montage of still photos that unspool to radio ads and radio interview responses. A Richard Lester interview and his *Running Standing Jumping Film*, which also appeared in **Hard Day's Night**, are repeated. Contrary to the jacket notation, there is no Dolby Digital track. The film is available in French and Spanish in mono, and can be supported by English, French or Spanish subtitles ("Hé Bea-atle"), although the songs are not subtitled.

Henry & June (Universal, 20518)

Philip Kaufman's 1990 erotic literary adventure was notable for ushering in the largely failed 'NC-17' rating, and is an episodic but generally captivating depiction of the relationship between the writers, Henry Miller and Anaïs Nin, and their respective partners. Fred Ward, Uma Thurman and Maria de Medeiros, who pretty much steals the picture, star, with an interesting early appearance by Kevin Spacey in a major supporting role. The sex scenes, though numerous, rarely move beyond suggestion. As one character appropriately points out, there is more obscenity in war.

The DVD is also captivating because the picture transfer is so nice. Colors are exact and the image is smooth, removing all impediments between the carefully shaded cinematography and the eye. The image is so lovely that those who may have had a problem with the film's pacing before will have no problem now, and will become wrapped up in its passions. The presentation is letterboxed with an aspect ratio of about 1.75:1 and no 16:9 enhancement. The stereo surround sound does not have elaborate separation effects, but there is a subtle dimensionality that plays upon your subconscious. The 137 minute program also a French stereo soundtrack, optional English and French subtitles, and a dandy red tag trailer for the R-rated version.

Henry: Portrait of a Serial Killer (MPI, DVD7382)

The concept may be difficult to imagine, but the movie is a low key film about a psychopathic murderer. Being low key, it builds up emotions without providing a release for them, and memories of the movie can linger for days afterward. Ostracized by the Ratings system, probably for a scene in which a child is murdered in front of his mother, the movie is not exploitatively violent but it can be unnerving. It is a wonderfully acted film, depicting the relationship between the title character, a temporary roommate, and the roommate's sister. The movie's emotions are perfectly balanced but realistic and, under the cover of a seemingly bland domestic drama, the film whispers to the dark side of a viewer's psyche.

Director John McNaughton sits for a half hour interview on the DVD, talking about how he got into film, and how conceived and shot the stunningly violent 1990 film that kickstarted his movie career. The audio in the segment is out of synch, but it is still a valuable introduction to McNaughton and an inspired tale about how to break into the movies. He also talks about his luck in finding Michael Rooker to play the lead.

Contrary to the jacket cover, the film runs 86 minutes. The film is presented in full screen format. Shot on a low budget, the film's colors remain somewhat compromised, though they look reasonably fresh and fleshtones are tolerable. Because of the film's subject matter, it's supposed to look a little dank anyway. The image is less grainy, and better detailed than the LD, but it is also prone to some displacement artifacting. The musical score has a reasonably aggressive stereo mix, though not much else is dimensional. The film can be supported by English, French or Spanish subtitles. In addition to the McNaughton interview, there are trailers, filmographies and some brief production notes.

Henry V (Criterion, HEN030)

Opening on a supposed production of the play during Shakespeare's time, Laurence Olivier's captivating adaptation of William Shakespeare's play gradually shifts from the confines of the Globe Theatre to the outdoors for the climactic and quite spectacular battle sequence, and then with equal cunning it slowly returns to the original setting during the anti-climactic romance that takes up the final act. The play-within-a-play gimmick allows Olivier to finesse what is normally a tedious explication of the history leading into the play's events in one of the opening scenes, by turning it into marvelous slapstick, just as his discarding of the gimmick allows him the freedom to make full use of the capabilities of cinema when the action in the play's center demands it. As is well known, the staging also emphasizes the play's patriotic aspects, which was obviously a motivation for producing it in Britain in 1944 (although it is about a leader who invades another country under a pretense of historical imperative, it is also about England landing a foothold in France), but the movie has transcended this context and remains a brilliant exercise in the flexibility of motion picture entertainment, embracing one of the most memorable and inspiring dramas ever to employ the English language. Olivier also stars in the title role.

The picture transfer looks terrific. The colors are splendid and finely detailed, and wear on the source material is minimal. The monophonic sound is a little soft, but there is no compromise in the purity of the tones and the delivery is effective. The 137 minute full screen presentation is not captioned.

The film is accompanied by an excellent commentary track from Bruce Eder, in which he supplies everything from an in-depth analysis of the play and its historical basis, to an analysis of its innovations as a film (he suggests it was the first movie to genuinely succeed at doing Shakespeare), to a complete background on all the major cast members and filmmakers, to a surprisingly detailed breakdown of how the movie was shot, and on to a breathless 500-year history of the succession of the British crown, from William the Conqueror to Queen Elizabeth I. There is also a selection of illustrations from the *Book of Hours* (a collection of limited perspective illustrations that Olivier clearly used as inspiration for several settings), a handful of really good production photos, a chronology of Britain's kings that pales in comparison to Eder's summary, and a trailer.

Her Alibi (Warner, 11835)

Tom Selleck is a mystery writer who falls for a woman who may or may not be a murderess. Except for the wonderful musical score from Georges Delerue and a perfectly timed performance from William Daniels, there isn't much to like The 1989 feature was directed by Bruce Beresford, who usually can be relied upon to inject a dark undercurrent, but none is forthcoming. Instead the film turns nearly to slapstick, and the hero's brushes with danger never feel threatening. However, the romantic touches are handled well, and every time the movie really starts to slow down, Daniels appears with a brilliantly delivered remark or wince. The picture is presented in full screen format, but the framing usually looks well balanced. Colors are sharp and the image is reasonably fresh. The stereo surround sound doesn't have much to offer, except Delerue's music. The 94 minute program is closed captioned with some paraphrasing.

Hercules and Xena: The Animated Movie—The Battle for Mount Olympus (Universal, 20160)

The narrative is decent and good material for a cartoon, with Hercules and his companions fighting against the legendary Titans, but the animation is often stylized (there are also a couple of horrible songs) and sketchy. While it may be a valid artistic approach—evoking the art of ancient Greece and the like—it just looks quick and cheap, leaving the viewer less involved with the action. Other than the quality of the animation, the picture transfer and delivery looks fine. The stereo sound has limited separation effects. Kevin Sorbo and Lucy Lawless provide voices. The 80 minute film is also available in stereo in French or Spanish, and can be accompanied by English, Spanish or French subtitles. Profiles of the performers providing the voice talent are also included. And is that really the image of an electrical outlet on the wall at around the 51 minute mark?

Hercules / The Legendary Journeys: The Amazon Women and The Lost Kingdom (Universal, 20254)

Lucy Lawless appears in *Amazon Women*, though in a supporting role and not as Xena. Both 1994 TV films, which star Kevin Sorbo, feature Anthony Quinn as Zeus, and both have the engaging CGI special effects, enthusiastic action sequences and imaginative plots that make the TV series, which is produced in part by Sam Raimi, so entertaining. In *Amazon Women*, Hercules battles a giant snake monster that grows back two heads whenever one is cut off, and then helps to bring peace between an independent group of warrior women and the pathetic society of male farmers they occasionally raid for pleasure. In *Lost Kingdom*, he is swallowed by a huge serpent, which he subsequently defeats by breaking through its stomach, climbing up to its heart, and physically instigating a cardiac arrest. He then helps a young woman lead her people back to a fortress city that had been overrun by evil beings. Although there is some minor grain in a few of the darker sequences, the picture quality is generally pretty good, with bright, stable hues, reasonably accurate fleshtones and a sharp focus. The stereo surround sound is also admirable for a TV production, with a fairly constant dimensionality. The programs can be accompanied by English, French or Spanish subtitles, and the DVD also offers brief biographical portraits of Sorbo and Quinn.

Hercules / The Legendary Journeys: The Xena Trilogy—The Warrior Princess / The Gauntlet / Unchained Heart (Universal, 20256)

Only one of the three episodes contains the sort of special video effects that makes the Sam Raimi produced series so enticing, but the three episodes also form the pilot for the equally engaging **Hercules** spin-off, *Xena The Warrior Princess* and therefore represent an intersection of appeal. Kevin Sorbo is Hercules and Lucy Lawless, still finding her way a bit with her character, is Xena. Each of the three episodes is freestanding, but there are narrative links so that watching all three at once is an enjoyable adventure. In *Warrior Princess*, Xena is a villain who seduces Hercules' best friend, hoping to eliminate both of them. In *Gauntlet*, she turns from being villainous to joining with the heroes when her bloodthirsty second-in-command stages a mutiny. In *Unchained Heart*, the villain from *Gauntlet* acquires a monster from the gods and the heroes must defeat them both. The picture looks terrific—so crisp that the seams show in some of the computer-generated effects, but no matter—with crisp hues and rich fleshtones. The stereo sound is adequate but a bit dull, with little more than the music getting much dimensionality. Each episode is presented in its entirety, with complete opening and closing credits, and the programs can be supported by English, Spanish of French subtitles ("On est des guerriers, pas des barbares"). There are also brief profiles of Sorbo and Lawless.

The Heroic Trio (Tai Seng, 30294)

Epitomizing everything that we love about lighthearted Hong Kong action films, **The Heroic Trio** is a wonderful movie about three super-women battling a super-demon who is stealing babies from a maternity ward. The narrative is coherent, the elaborate fantasy action scenes are marvelous and the ending, which takes its cues from **The Terminator**, is resolute. The characters are also great fun—one of the heroines is married to a police detective who is unaware of her secret identity—and there is as much humor as there is gore. Anita Mui, Maggie Cheung and Michelle Yeoh star.

The film is offered in English, Mandarin or Cantonese, with or without English subtitling. The presentation is letterboxed, with an aspect ratio of about 1.85:1 and no 16:9 enhancement, although colors look a bit deeper and fleshtones are a bit more accurate. The monophonic sound is muted, but there is a Dolby Digital mono track, for all three languages, that has much more energy. The 87 minute film is also accompanied by trailers for Tai Seng product and by a small but thorough cast and director profile. in the film, about three women with modest super powers who fight a demonic force.

Hidden Hawaii (SlingShot, DVD9807)

The 35 minute Imax program takes a look not only at the less accessible topography of the island chain, but at the plants and animals that have found a niche in those environments. The image composition is designed for big, big screens and includes many precision-detailed vistas that make an effective transition from IMAX to DVD. The picture is sharp and colors are accurate. The stereo surround sound and Dolby Digital sound have a deliberate dimensionality, but there are not many sequences where it is worth much, as it is mostly the flourishing musical scores and a few incidental location noises that show up on the surround channels. The program is also in Spanish, Danish, Japanese and Mandarin, all in Dolby Digital, and is subtitled in English.

High and Low (Criterion, HIG050)

Toshiro Mifune is a manufacturing executive who loses everything when he is forced to pay a ransom to kidnappers in Akira Kurosawa's superb 1963 crime thriller. The film, based upon an Ed McBain novel, is an outstanding procedural with vivid characters and a steadfast logic that pushes the viewer through the tense narrative like a pressure valve. Mifune, who has little to do other than fret and chafe, cuts such a realistically dynamic figure that despite the elaborate widescreen image compositions you can't take your eyes off him.

The movie is beautifully constructed. The first hour is almost like a stageplay and takes place on a single set with a limited number of characters. Then, as the hero's stature deteriorates, the movie opens up in a way which would be impossible to recreate on a stage. That is the key to the film's power—Kurosawa has taken McBain's novel (*King's Ransom*) and filmed it as if he were doing another one of his Shakespeare adaptations. Shakespeare used to do the same thing himself.

The picture is letterboxed with an aspect ratio of about 2.35:1 and no 16:9 enhancement. The source material is in reasonably good shape, with no more than a stray speckle or two. The black-and-white image is sharp and blacks are rich, with nicely detailed contrast. The monophonic sound is a little lighter than the LD's sound, but there is a Dolby Digital mono track that is stronger and a bit less noisy, though distortion on the upper end remains. The 143 minute film is in Japanese with optional English subtitles that appear beneath the letterboxed image.

The High Crusade (Pioneer, DVD0310)

The funny Pythonesque comedy is about inept Fourteenth Century knights who are taken to another planet in a spaceship and defeat a group of even stupider aliens. Rick Overton stars with John Rhys-Davies in the 1997 feature, which was produced by Roland Emmerich and has some fairly decent special effects. Some of the comedy is desperate, and many viewers will think the film is dopey as all get out, but it has a vaudeville-like charm to it. There are some inspired gags (an elevator in the alien ship has alien elevator music) and amusing verbal by-play ("Je t'adore." "Okay." The character turns and shuts the door.).

The picture is letterboxed, with an aspect ratio of about 2.5:1 and no 16:9 enhancement. The color transfer is strong, even during scenes bathed in yellow candlelight, and the image is sharp. Separation effects are moderate, but the stereo surround sound has a strong atmospheric dimensionality. There is no captioning.

High Lonesome: The Story of Bluegrass Music (Shanachie, 604)

The retrospective documentary on Bluegrass band leader Bill Monroe branches out from Monroe's career to provide an overview of the genre's development. The 95 minute program contains lots of archive footage, interviews with Monroe and other musicians (and fans—there is a lot of delightful footage of two guys standing in a field, recalling what they enjoyed listening to on the radio), and plenty of musical passages to trace the development of a style of music that is described at one point as 'folk music on overdrive.' The reminiscences also include a lot about what life was like in rural Kentucky during most of this century and the gradual changes that took place over the years. Monroe, whose band featured, at one time or another, many bluegrass stars, including Flatt & Scruggs, managed to mature and change with the format to remain at or near the top of popularity from the days when the music was played live in the living room for an evening's entertainment, to concerts, radio, records and television performances.

The archive footage varies in quality from one shot to the next, but the transfer looks excellent and the picture is consistently sharp. When the colors in the source material are fresh, the image is superb. The sound is also in good shape. The jacket says it is in stereo. The audio remains somewhat centered, but tones are smooth and there is a mild sense of dimensionality to it that is unhindered by the age of some of the recordings. There is no captioning.

High Noon (Artisan, 43486)

Watching **High Noon**, a viewer becomes keenly aware of Gary Cooper's features and how vividly the history and the feelings of the hero are expressed in the dried creases of his countenance. The 1952 western is due for a pendulum swing. Long the butt of serious critical consideration, the film nevertheless continues to stand tall on repeated viewings, and it's minimalist construction is worth a hard look. The movie has many basic elements, but the questions it asks about violence, marriage, masculinity, etc., are complex, and it never provides clear answers. The viewer is both entertained and provoked to think.

The print is beautiful, but, like the hero of the film, the picture has a few scars and scratches. Contrasts are rich, however, and the image is pleasing. The monophonic sound is a little strained, but workable, and there are also optional French and Spanish language tracks, as well as optional English, French or Spanish subtitles. The film's magnificently exciting trailer is included (it always makes us want to see the movie again), along with an excellent featurette about *The Making of High Noon*, created and hosted by Leonard Maltin. Both producer Stanley Kramer and director Fred Zinnemann are interviewed, along with Lloyd Bridges and the children of several other artists who participated in the film's production. Maltin explores the film's locations, the psychology of the times in which it was made, and the history behind each major component of the film. There is also a wonderful interview clip with Cooper in which he explains with his beautiful succinctness the essential appeal of the western genre, "The western picture tells stories of the pioneer period. The pioneers braved the elements and we are brought close to the pioneer people by seeing the western picture. We realize our country was, and is, full of people who believe in America."

High Plains Drifter (Universal, 20152)

Clint Eastwood's 1973 western has been letterboxed, with an aspect ratio of about 2.35:1 and no 16:9 enhancement. The picture has crisp, bright colors, accurate fleshtones and complete stability in Eastwood's obsessively darker sequences. The monophonic sound is in acceptable condition. The 106 minute program is also available in Spanish and French and can be accompanied by English or Spanish subtitles ("¡Pero el pueblo va a parecer el infierno!"). There is a nice collection of production notes and a brief cast profile, along with an original theatrical trailer.

The film itself is a somewhat rude manipulation of Eastwood's image, but those who are not offended are inevitably entertained by the slightly supernatural tale of revenge that a mysterious stranger commits upon an isolated mining town. The film is simplistic, but we can testify to its mindless repeatability, and it offers further proof that with a star such as Eastwood a film's artistic components can be lax without upsetting its appeal.

High School High (Columbia TriStar, 82489)

Jon Lovitz stars in a funny take off on *Blackboard Jungle*-type inner city high school films. The production mixes parody and slapstick with a narrative that is sufficiently developed to keep the 86 minute film moving smoothly.

The picture is letterboxed on one side, with an aspect ratio of about 1.85:1 and an accommodation for enhanced 16:9 playback, is in full screen format on the other side. The color transfer is sharp, with accurate fleshtones. The stereo surround sound and Dolby Digital sound are smooth and efficient. The 1996 feature also has French and Spanish language soundtracks, optional English, French and Spanish subtitles, and a trailer.

Highlander: 10th Anniversary Director's Cut (Artisan, 45895)

Christopher Lambert stars as an immortal who must eliminate several rivals during contemporary times as the film intercuts this story with an explanation of his past in Fifteenth Century Scotland. Sean Connery also appears, though as a Spaniard rather than a Scot. Stylishly directed by Russell Mulcahy, the film has a stimulating narrative and some terrific action scenes. As is detailed in several fascinating memos in the supplement, however, the movie does not take its premise far enough, as Mulcahy shied away from the emotional depth of the original script to give the movie a more shallow pizzazz.

The 1986 film runs 116 minutes and is the 'European' version, which is about 6 minutes longer than the U.S. version. The changes are for the better—the most notable of which is a sequence set during World War II that explains the background of one of the characters—though as is detailed in the supplement, the film itself could probably have used a little more dramatic meat.

In any case, the picture transfer is very good when one takes into account the movie's previous iterations on home video. Earlier versions were grainy and drained of color, so the DVD presentation, while not as slick as the fanciest Hollywood blockbusters, has rich, solid hues and accurate fleshtones. The presentation is letterboxed, with an aspect ratio of about 1.85:1 (not 2.35:1 as is claimed on the jacket cover) and no 16:9 enhancement. The picture loses nothing on the top and bottom of the image and gains important information on the sides in comparison to the older cropped versions of the film.

The stereo surround sound mix has been juiced up a little in comparison to the original theatrical mix, but the improvements are welcome. The massive explosions that occur when a character wins a fight are quite stupendous, and Queen's musical score has an attentive bite. Certain dialogue scenes retain a scratchiness that was present on earlier versions, but when the talking stops the movie rocks. The Dolby Digital audio track doesn't pack quite as hard a punch in places, but has a more stimulating dimensionality with better detailed and isolated separation effects. There are optional English and Spanish subtitles, and a trailer.

The DVD also has an excellent supplementary section that explores many aspects of the film's creation and iconography, but it is poorly organized and may be difficult or even impossible to navigate on some players. Basically, it is a replication of the supplement that appeared on LD—a format that allows unhindered still frame manipulation—and it has been moved over to DVD without an accommodation for the limitations of DVD still frame playback. You can see most of it if you select the menu, and then activate the Still function really quickly, but working through it is tedious and it is almost impossible to jump around the supplement with much accuracy or control.

The supplement contains memos about the script's development and the film's reception (including a bevy of short-sighted negative reviews), and a hefty collection of appealing production stills. Included among the stills are shots from three scenes that were filmed but did not make the final cut, along with the script for each of these three scenes. Some of the memos present script 'revisions,' though in several cases it would be of more use to the viewer to find out what it was that was being revised. As the filmmakers read the script and saw the rough cut of the movie began to critique it in memos, however, the memos, preserved on the DVD, present a fairly unique 'self-criticism' that explores the movie's weaknesses as well as its strengths. Mulcahy and the film's producers, Peter S. Davis and William Panzer, speak on a commentary channel during the running of the film, skimming over these weaknesses and focusing, instead, upon an informative history of the production that is often useful for its insights to the filmmaking process.

Although the movie's sequels negated the initial film's concepts, the real point of **Highlander** is that a man who has had first-hand training in 500 years of history and has been given an open window onto the minds of every living person is, at the end of the film, about to start a benign intervention into the course of human affairs. The concept has very strong religious overtones and these, quite sensibly, were downplayed, but Mulcahy's elimination of the hero's anecdotal experiences and of the details in his romance with the heroine (the scenes didn't work, according to the commentary) robs the viewer of the intellectual impact the ending ought to have. Under Mulcahy's hand, the film is visceral as all get out, but in the process he compromised the real promise of what was a fairly daring movie script, giving the film a compelling style but withholding what might have been a substantive and enlightening drama.

Highlander: The Final Dimension (Buena Vista, 14374)

Less ambitious than the first sequel, the 1995 film is more like the TV series, pitting the immortal hero, played by Christopher Lambert, against another immortal, played by Mario Van Peebles, who sort of appears out of the woodwork after being buried for a couple centuries. The narrative is overly contrived, but the basic premise remains entertaining.

The 99 minute 'Director's Cut' has been letterboxed with an aspect ratio of about 2.35:1 and no 16:9 enhancement. The picture looks fairly nice, with a sharp focus and accurate fleshtones. Some of the more evocatively lit sequences are a little blurry, but that is probably intentional. The stereo surround sound has an effective dimensionality and a decent punch when called upon. The film can be supported by English subtitles and is accompanied by a trailer.

Highlander 2: Renegade Version (Artisan, 45900)

It turns out that **Highlander 2** was a victim of hyper-inflation. Seeking fresh and unique locations, the filmmakers chose to shoot the 1992 film in Argentina, only to drown in the country's economic troubles. As director Russell Mulcahy explains on the commentary track, "Every morning when I used to get up for breakfast before going off to the shoot, the price of orange juice would change. So, by the price of orange juice going up every day, I knew how many pages we would have to tear out of the script that day." When the budget ran out of juice, the movie was taken away from the filmmakers and substantially re-arranged. Sent to theaters, it died.

Thanks to the popularity of the TV show and the enduring appeal of the first film, however, the filmmakers were finally given a renewed opportunity to present the sequel pretty much in the way they intended. Using previously unused footage and a few new shots made especially for the restoration, the **Renegade Version** runs 110 minutes where the original theatrical release ran 90. Scenes were also substantially re-arranged. The revision is imperfect—there are scenes missing that would explain how characters get from here to there and similar transitional gaps—but it is less insulting to a viewer's intelligence than the theatrical version was and truer to the spirit of the first film. Fans should be very pleased and, despite the gaps, even casual viewers will have a good time. A jacket insert details the changes.

The picture transfer is excellent. There is no degradation in the added footage. Colors are crisp and glossy, and the image is sharp, though artifacting is evident in some darker sequences. The letterboxing has an aspect ratio of about 2.35:1 and no 16:9 enhancement. The stereo surround sound is quite energetic, and the Dolby Digital track is even more boisterous. There are optional English and Spanish subtitles, an 18 minute retrospective documentary about the film and its restoration, and a nice still file collection of production drawings, costume designs, cast profiles and publicity photos. Like Highlander, the still section was designed for LD and is awkward or (on some players) impossible to navigate on DVD. The documentary is not captioned.

In the commentary track, Mulcahy and producers Bill Panzer and Peter Davis discuss the production and the changes they made for the revised cut. They are less than forthcoming about a lot of the problems on the original shoot, and their reticence lowers the value of the disc as a work of scholarship. They do share interesting details about how certain scenes were achieved, but they also pause a lot as scenes unfold, and they talk very little, except in obscure terms, about how and when the film was taken out of their hands. It is also unclear, in both the documentary and the commentary, exactly how much new material was shot specifically for this version.

Hill Number One (see James Dean: Hill Number One/I Am a Fool)

The Hindenberg (Universal, 20413)

Robert Wise's bloated 1975 disaster film depicting fictionalized characters aboard the ill-fated dirigible was so poorly conceived from a dramatic standpoint that the famous newsreel clip of the airship collapsing in flames is more moving and exciting. Still, for a pre-CGI effects film there are some striking model shots and other minor pleasures—the film's stereo surround sound mix, for example, was exceptionally good for its day and is still highly pleasing.

The film is in letterboxed format with an aspect ratio of about 2.2:1 and no 16:9 enhancement. Because of production problems, many shots look very grainy, but the color transfer is nice and the best parts of it convey the modest thrills that Wise did manage to elicit from the material. The stereo surround soundtrack, however, does not live up to its original theatrical impact. If you turn the volume way, way up you can get hints of it, but the dialogue levels are too low, the music is too loud, there doesn't seem to be enough bass, and sound effects aren't as actively distributed as they were in the theater. The picture quality is excellent, with crisp, rich colors and accurate fleshtones. The 127 minute program can be supported by English, French or Spanish subtitles ("¡Se incendió y está cayendo y se estrella!") and is accompanied by a good production essay and a cast-and-director profile section. George C. Scott and Anne Bancroft star.

His Bitter Pill (see The Toll Booth/His Bitter Pill)

Hitman (import, DVD126)

One of the best of Jet Li's contemporary action films, the story is witty and the action scenes are outstanding (including a harrowing fight inside an elevator shaft). Li portrays kind of a bumpkin soldier, though adept at martial arts, who signs up to earn a huge amount of cash as part of a 'put a price on the head of my murderer' legacy left by a wealthy man who was assassinated. The story is easy to follow (not always the case with tightly budgeted Hong Kong features) and maintains a brisk pace, yet allows some room for character development and humor. It's a cool movie, and a must for anybody attempting to gather a representative collection of the best Hong Kong productions.

Some sequences appear overly yellowed and others look a little drained, but for a Hong Kong production, the transfer is generally in tolerable shape. In well-lit scenes, hues are bright and fleshtones are workable. The picture is letterboxed with an aspect ratio of about 1.85:1 and no 16:9 enhancement.

The dialogue can be accessed in Cantonese or Mandarin and can be supported by optional English or Chinese subtitles. The sound is in stereo and Dolby Digital, but the mix is limited, with little more than the music surging into dimensionality from time to time. There is also a trailer.

The Holcroft Covenant (MGM, 907499)

John Frankenheimer provides a commentary track on his 1985 adaptation of the Robert Ludlum story. Like a number of Ludlum adaptations, the narrative is spellbinding the first time you watch the movie and utterly ludicrous on subsequent viewings. Michael Caine, in the heat of the 'the bees are coming!' period in his career, doesn't help matters playing the hero, but the film has terrific European locations and it has Frankenheimer's assured handling of the action scenes, no matter how silly their narrative basis becomes.

The picture is letterboxed with an aspect ratio of about 1.85:1 and no 16:9 enhancement. The letterboxing adds nothing to the sides and trims picture information off the top and bottom in comparison to full screen presentations. Fleshtones are a little bland, but hues are reasonably bright and the image is solid. The colors are reasonably strong, and the image is sharp and clear. The monophonic sound is adequate. The 112 minute program is also available in French and can be supported by English or French subtitles. There is a trailer, too.

Frankenheimer's talk is very sporadic and he has little to say about making the film. Michael Caine was an emergency replacement at the very last minute, and Frankenheimer praises his skills, particularly the final shot in which a tear is seen rolling down his cheek—he did it on all four takes. Frankenheimer has some good advise—use good actors for long speeches to keep the dialogue interesting—and talks a bit about the performers and the production, but he is also given over to superlatives and he seems oblivious to the film's problems, large or small.

The Hollywood Ten (see Salt Of The Earth)

Holy Man (Buena Vista, 16536)

Jeff Goldblum stars as a programming director for a home shopping network in danger of losing his job until he meets a saint-like drifter who ends up in front of the camera, energizing the ratings and sales. Eddie Murphy is top billed, but has what is in essence the 'guest star' part, as the drifter. The story is very simple, and while some of Murphy's aphorisms ("The only time you are ever alive, really, is when you're connecting") are worthwhile, the 1998 film is not sufficiently stimulating or funny to make much of an impression. Besides, in terms of screen time, it's Goldblum's film, not Murphy's. Kelly Preston is also featured.

As much as we love the concept of widescreen movies, the technique is not always appropriate to the program content, and that is certainly the case with **Holy Man**, which is about TV and gains nothing by defying its video sequences to spread its characters across its framing. The DVD is appropriately letterboxed, however, with an aspect ratio of about 2.35:1 and no 16:9 enhancement. The color transfer looks good, with bright, sharp hues and reasonably accurate fleshtones. The Dolby Digital sound is okay, with a fairly dimensional musical score and reasonably strong sound effects, and the standard stereo track, though not as forceful, is passable. The 114 minute program can be supported by optional English subtitles.

Home Alone 3 (Fox, 4109065)

Although it has been geared a little more directly for youngsters than the first two films and although it could use better comedians playing the bad guys, once **Home Alone 3** gets into the middle of its story it is fully entertaining. There's a new kid, a new family and a more artificial plot—bad guys looking for a computer chip—but a more sensible excuse for the boy being home—he's sick, and his parents have to work—and no restrictions whatsoever when it comes to the boy setting up booby traps in his house. After the preliminaries, the slapstick takes over and it is difficult to resist.

The presentation is in letterboxed format, with an aspect ratio of about 1.85:1 and no 16:9 enhancement. The colors are bright and the image is sharp, though some darker scenes have a mild softness. The stereo surround sound and Dolby Digital sound are decent, with simple but well applied effects during the stunt sequences. The 102 minute program is also available in French and Spanish in standard stereo and can be supported by English subtitles. There is a viable cast profile section and a good trailer.

Home Fries (Warner, 15169)

The very charming romantic comedy has a plot that is best kept secret. What we can say is that Drew Barrymore is a very pregnant fast food cashier and Luke Wilson is an Army reserve pilot who falls for her. It isn't that straightforward, however, as there are a couple of well-placed coincidences and a lot of marvelous, logical links between the characters. Catherine O'Hara and Jake Busey are both quite amusing as Wilson's mother and brother, and Shelley Duvall makes a rare appearance, as Barrymore's mother. There's even a murder—well, sort of—and a couple other life-threatening situations to maintain the film's vitality.

The picture is presented on one side in letterboxed format, with an aspect ratio of about 1.85:1 and an accommodation for enhanced 16:9 playback, and in full screen format on the other side. The letterboxing adds nothing to the sides and masks picture information off the top and bottom in comparison to the full screen presentation, and we tended to find the full screen framing more pleasing. Shot in a small Texas town, the film is a bit dusty looking on purpose, with light hues. Fleshtones are okay and other colors are workable. The stereo surround sound and Dolby Digital sound do not have extensive mixes, but the audio delivers the goods when it is supposed to. The 95 minute program is also available in French in Dolby Digital and can be supported by English or French subtitles. There is a cast-and-director profile section and a trailer that effectively extracts the love story from the film without revealing the plot twists.

Homegrown (Columbia TriStar, 25329)

A delightful and unassuming comedy, the richness of **Homegrown** sort of sneaks up on you. Three pot-heads who tend to an enormous marijuana crop see their boss gunned down. They bury him and decide to harvest and sell the weed for themselves. But who shot their boss? They take stabs at trying to figure it out as they get further into the business, but once again not everything is what it seems. In one of the 1998 film's funniest sequences, they start trying to piece together an explanation for the mystery, but they're stoned and their theories just get more convoluted and more convoluted—becoming, and we believe on purpose, a satire of the explanations behind the plots in standard murder mysteries.

The performances are super—Billy Bob Thornton stars with Hank Azaria, Kelly Lynch, Jon Bon Jovi and John Lithgow—and along with being a terrific crime thriller, the production proves there's still life in movies about marijuana, regardless of how far behind us the Sixties and Seventies have receded.

The picture is letterboxed on one side, with an aspect ratio of about 1.85:1 and an accommodation for enhanced 16:9 playback, and is in full screen format on the other side. The color transfer is workable. The stereo surround sound and Dolby Digital sound are not elaborately mixed, but the best musical passages have a nice dimensionality and there are some well-chosen separation effects. The 102 minute feature also has French and Spanish language tracks, optional English, French or Spanish subtitles and a trailer.

Homeward Bound: The Incredible Journey (Buena Vista, 13079)

The remake of *The Incredible Journey* features entirely new footage to retell the story of two dogs and a cat crossing the wilderness to find their family, supported not by a single folksy narrator but by voices for the three animals, *Look Who's Talking* style. Don Ameche voices the elderly dog and Sally Field the cat, with Michael J. Fox dominating the film as the frisky younger dog. Unable to torture animals with the latitude that older filmmakers and foreign filmmakers enjoy, the nature scenes lack a sense of gripping adventure, but humor is in strong supply and the story's love-your-pet emotions are impossible to foul up.

The 1993 film is presented in full screen format only, but the image loses only a hair from the sides and adds picture information to the top and bottom compared to the film's letterboxed version, creating a more complete framing. The colors look pinkish and the image is dark, but reasonably sharp. The stereo surround sound is fairly strong,. The 84 minute film comes with French and Spanish language tracks, and with optional English subtitling. There is also an interesting theatrical trailer that avoids showing the animals talking.

Hommage à Noir (RykoDisk, PALMDVD30092)

The 47 minute montage of black-and-white images of Africa is set to a fairly intense musical score. The film's artistry is outstanding. While we could discern no specific thematic progression to the images—which include many individual faces as well as tribal group shots, masks, scattered shots of wildlife, and random depictions of everyday life—there appears to be a religious motif to the film, and almost every shot is so compelling the viewer is likely to impose his own meanings to what passes by.

The picture transfer is excellent, with precise contrasts and a crisp focus. The presentation is letterboxed, with an aspect ratio of about 1.66:1 and no 16:9 enhancement. The standard stereo surround sound has exceptional energy and a full range, and the Dolby Digital track provides even crisper tones and better detail. There is also a very brief interview with the movie's director, Ralf Schmerberg, and a well-conceived 'gallery' of stills from the film.

Hoodlum (MGM, 906995)

Our favorite anachronism in **Hoodlum**, a gangster drama about fights over the numbers racket in Harlem in the Thirties, was when two characters sit in front of an old gramophone listening to an opera and José Careras came blasting out of our sound system in full stereo. Laurence Fishburne, Tim Roth and Andy Garcia star as famous gangsters from the period. Roth uses the 'F' word like it was 1969 or something and there are other faulty historical touches—former presidential candidate Thomas Dewey also gets a bum rap—but if you like shoot 'em ups in period decor with Machiavellian scheming then you should enjoy the film.

Hues are deliberately subdued to evoke a nostalgic setting. The 130 minute film is presented on one side in letterboxed format, with an aspect ratio of about 1.85:1 and an accommodation for enhanced 16:9 playback, and in full screen format on the other side. The letterboxing adds only a sliver to the sides of the image and removes picture information from the top and bottom of the full screen presentation, and we often found the full screen more to our liking. The Dolby Digital mix conveys a more immediate presence than the standard stereo surround soundtrack. The nightclub music, with a more appropriate stereophonic presence than gramophone records, sounds terrific and the gunshots have a tremendous punch. The film is also available in French in standard stereo and comes with English, French or Spanish subtitles. The theatrical trailer included on the LD is also featured.

Hooper (Warner, 16881)
Having sort of run out of stunt ideas for movies, Hal Needham and Burt Reynolds made this 1978 film about a stunt man. It didn't have much of a plot, but it did have ideal situations for stunts, though the format is such that even though they are perfectly integrated with what narrative there is, the revealed artifice prevents the stunts from being all that thrilling. While it has some moderately amusing moments, as well as quite a few moments which are less so, it is hard to imagine watching the movie more than once in a great while. The in-jokes are too self-congratulatory to have any sting, and the other humor is too belabored to seem fresh. Sally Field and Jan-Michael Vincent co-star.

The picture is presented in full screen format. The image is sharp, with reasonably bright colors and workable fleshtones, though contrasts are a little weak in places. The monophonic sound is substantially muted, but the Dolby Digital mono track is somewhat louder. The 99 minute program is captioned in English.

Hoosiers (Artisan, 60452)
The compelling, enjoyable yarn is about a high school basketball team of limited manpower whipped into a championship unit by a gung ho coach, played by Gene Hackman. Like the coach's own game plan, the 1986 movie doesn't let you peak too soon.

The image on the DVD is sharp and the color transfer is okay, but fleshtones look a bit pinkish and shadowed areas lack detail. The picture is letterboxed only, with an aspect ratio of about 1.85:1 and no 16:9 enhancement. The stereo surround sound has limited separation effects but is reasonably effective, particularly during the frenzy of the big games. The 114 minute film is closed captioned in English and is accompanied by a good theatrical trailer.

Hope Floats (Fox, 4109063)
Sandra Bullock stars as a divorcee who returns to her hometown and her mother's house to raise her daughter and figure out what to do with her life. The film meanders along, coming up with a very strong and well-performed scene, hibernating for a while and then coming up with another one. On the whole, not much happens, but the emotional exchanges will be sufficient entertainment for many viewers. Harry Connick, Jr. and Gena Rowlands co-star in the feature, which was directed by Forest Whitaker.

The picture is letterboxed with an aspect ratio of about 1.85:1 and no 16:9 enhancement. The picture quality looks fine, with accurate fleshtones and sharp, fresh colors. The stereo surround sound and Dolby Digital sound are not elaborate, but there are some very nice moments, such as a sequence when Connick attempts to keep Bullock quiet while fishing. The 114 minute film is also available in French in standard stereo and comes with English or Spanish subtitles. There is a cast-and-director profile section and a trailer that plays up the film's comical moments.

Horror Express (Simitar, 7225)
Christopher Lee and Peter Cushing star in a wonderful 1972 adaptation of *The Thing from Another World* that is set on a train crossing China and Russia in the early part of the century. The 86 minute film has terrific gore effects, great plot twists and marvelous performances, all paced by captivating shots of the train rushing across the snowbound tundra. Unfortunately, the transfer is pathetic. The film appears to be cropped, though most of the time the framing is functional. The image is drained of color and flesh-

tones are anemic. Although the picture has the sharpness inherent in a DVD presentation, lines and distinctive borders between objects often have a slightly smeared appearance. The monophonic sound is fairly painful, with a completely distorted upper end and a hazy mid-range. The thing is, even with all these problems, we still had a great time watching the movie. The movie is accompanied by a brief summary of the film along with profiles and abbreviated filmographies of Lee, Cushing and Telly Savalas, who appears in the film's second half. The program is not captioned.

Horror Hotel (Elite, EE0819)
The 1960 British horror film was originally titled *City of the Dead* but is known in America as **Horror Hotel**. Set in New England, with the cast working desperately to affect American accents, the film is about a student who walks into a witches' coven while doing research on the subject, and about her friends who then come searching for her. The cinematography and art direction are marvelously stylized—the dry ice works overtime—and the film is sufficiently creepy to keep a viewer involved as the story unfolds, leading up to an exciting and quite satisfying conclusion.

Blacks are deep and the image is sharp, but there is some noticeable digital artifacting here and there. Contrasts are a little weak in places, losing details and textures on faces, but the picture on the inexpensive production is generally in very good shape and adds to the film's appeal. The image is letterboxed, with an aspect ratio of about 1.8:1 with no 16:9 enhancement. The monophonic sound is a little softer than the LD but acceptable, though dialogue seems a bit raspy at times. The 76 minute program is accompanied by a theatrical trailer and is not closed captioned.

Horse Feathers (Image, ID4289USDVD)
The black-and-white image is quite clean on the 1932 Paramount Marx Bros. feature. It looks fairly smooth and sharp. Some sequences still have noticeable wear and a bit of jiggling, but on the whole the image is quite satisfying. The monophonic sound is also sharp, though age-related noise remains. The 67 minute program is not closed captioned. This is the one where Groucho runs a college, ending in a wacky football match.

The Horse Whisperer (Buena Vista, 15640)
Robert Redford's lengthy but generally engaging soap drama asks us to believe that a magazine editor (played by Kristen Scott Thomas) and her crippled daughter drive a trailer containing a very skittish horse all the way from Connecticut to Montana effortlessly and, had they just stuck some stamps on its rear end and mailed it, the movie would not have been less believable. Once they get there, though, and Redford shows up in front of the camera as the animal expert who can cure the horse (as well as mending the psyches of the two females), the film becomes dreamily romantic and pastoral.

For some reason, the film's first 33 minutes are windowboxed, while the rest of the movie is letterboxed with an aspect ratio of about 2.35:1. There is no accommodation for enhanced 16:9 playback. The picture is a bit soft, with halos emanating from bright white objects. The stereo surround sound and Dolby Digital sound are adequate, though the film's sound mix is rarely dynamic. The film can also be accessed in French in Dolby Digital and is supported by optional English subtitles. The 169 minute feature is accompanied by a reasonably good (and much brisker) theatrical trailer.

Horton Hears a Who! (see Dr. Seuss' How the Grinch Stole Christmas! & Horton Hears a Who!)

Hot Blooded (Image, ID4760DRDVD)
A college student driving home for the holidays gives a ride to a hooker in trouble and soon finds his life falling apart. Kari Wuhrer stars, with Burt Young giving a surprisingly affecting performance as a trucker who pesters them for much of the film. The narrative quickly turns into utter nonsense—nobody does anything emo-

tionally or rationally logical—but the erotic sequences are potent (even though Wuhrer keeps her clothes on) and the action scenes aren't bad.

Fleshtones are bland and the image is a little grainy, but the picture presentation is viable for the genre and the stereo surround sound is adequate. The 86 minute program is not captioned.

Hotel Lesbos X-rated (Lipstik, 31162)

The dialogue is horrendously dubbed (like two different voices for the same character in places). The program features older-looking images with grain, ghosting, aged colors, and substantial video smearing in places. Narrative development is limited and the erotic staging has a somewhat dated feel. The 72 minute show is about an aspiring model and the comings and goings in a hotel for women. Dominique St. Clair, Prisca, Candy, Chantal Trobert, Melissa Bonsardo and Isabelle Lagrande are featured.

Housesitter (Universal, 20319)

Steve Martin and Goldie Hawn star in the wonderful romantic comedy, which also features an on-the-money performance by Dana Delany as the 'other woman.' The 1992 production is letterboxed with an aspect ratio of about 1.85:1 with an accommodation for enhanced 16:9 playback. The colors are bright and the image is sharp, with decent fleshtones. The stereo surround sound is passable, although again the film's audio mix is not elaborate. The 102 minute movie is also available in French and comes with English or Spanish subtitles, as well as a cast & crew profile, some production notes and a theatrical trailer.

Martin is an architect and Hawn is a waitress who, through a series of circumstances, pretends to be his wife so he can make Delany's character jealous. The casting, however, is a clear indication of what actually happens. The script becomes precarious here and there, but never goes over the precipice. Martin and Hawn each have some marvelous moments, delivering comedy, reacting each other's comedy and shifting into genuine romance with deceptively easy finesse.

How Stella Got Her Groove Back (Fox, 4109660)

Angela Bassett is a well-off fortyish broker who takes a vacation in Jamaica and meets a well-off young man half her age. The 1998 film's appeal does not expand far beyond its central constituency. There are a couple scenes that are fairly sexy, but the dramatic conflicts are limited and the characters are too goody-goody to sustain much interest. The title explains the movie, and there isn't any more to it than that.

The presentation looks terrific, however. Colors are bright and sharply defined, and fleshtones are nicely detailed. The picture is letterboxed, with an aspect ratio of about 1.85:1 and no 16:9 enhancement. The stereo surround sound has quite a bit of power, and not just when the music is switched on. Sound effects have a heightened dimensionality, and the dialogue is crisp. The standard track is so good that the Dolby Digital track doesn't really have much to add. The 124 minute feature can be supported by optional English or Spanish subtitles, and is accompanied by a cast & crew profile section and a trailer.

How the Grinch Stole Christmas! (see Dr. Seuss' How the Grinch Stole Christmas! & Horton Hears a Who!)

How the West Was Won (MGM, 906292)

The star-studded Cinerama epic is presented in dual-layer format, and is letterboxed with an aspect ratio of about 2.35:1 and no 16:9 enhancement. The picture appears to be the same as the LD release, with the panel edges of the Cinerama image readily evident much of the time. The color transfer looks very nice, with bright hues and decent fleshtones. The image is sharp and wear is minimal. Perfectionists complain that it isn't good enough, but until everybody has curved living rooms with wall-sized screens and three projectors, it will have to do. The sound could probably use some sprucing up. The basic stereo surround soundtrack is enjoy-

able, but the film's original seven-track stereo separations have not been preserved and there is no Dolby Digital encoding. The 150 minute film can also be presented in French and comes with English, French or Spanish subtitles ("Venez avec moi/Je sais un pays/Où nous bâtirons, notre maison/Dans le prairie"). There is a nice general release trailer, emphasizing the film's cast, and a terrific 15 minute retrospective featurette, partially about Cinerama and partially showing a behind-the-scenes look at some of the movie's stunt sequences.

There are people who insist that movies, and DVDs for that matter, are supposed to be Art, and we wonder what these people do for relaxation. **How the West Was Won** is art all right, folk art. The technology that was used to create it was aiming not for a high ideal, but for a mass entertainment. With as many directors as it has panels and four times as many stars, it is a conglomeration of talent with no individual's imprint looming larger than another. In telling a generational story that codifies the growth of the American West in a collection of movie action sequences, the film's limitations are readily apparent. The vignettes are precisely what the filmmakers intended them to be, however, enough of a story to provide a mild commentary on the path of generational growth, while stringing along the thrills. It has one grandstanding moment after another, and when you become attuned to them you can get excited just seeing the shot of the St. Louis street, because looming in the center is a large show palace and you just know the next cut will be to a widescreen dance number. What the movie is really saying is that our forefathers fought to expand and settle America so that we could sit back and enjoy movies like this, and we certainly do not intend to let them down.

How to be a Player (PolyGram, 4400559552)

The 1997 film plays like a male fantasy movie, but it is presented as if the characters are actually from this planet and that this is what day-to-day life is like for the hero, successfully smooth talking every woman he meets and juggling a dozen or so dates at a time. The film is supposed to be a comedy, but the hero is rarely placed in jeopardy, so it never becomes very funny. Instead, it is just a don't-you-wish Casanova tale that the star, Bill Bellamy, can show his grandsons someday.

The single-sided dual-layer presentation is letterboxed on one layer, with an aspect ratio of about 1.85:1 and an accommodation for enhanced 16:9 playback, and is in full screen format on the other layer. The color transfer looks fine, with bright, solid hues. The stereo surround sound is okay, but the Dolby Digital track is better, with a stronger, more defined bass and more elaborate separation effects. The 93 minute program also has optional English or French subtitles, a cast profile section and a trailer.

How To Make an American Quilt (Universal, 20018)

A film that is made up of short stories, stitched together as is implied by its title, the stories have indistinct structures and emphasize character over narrative. The huge cast is headed by Winona Ryder and features Anne Bancroft, Ellen Burstyn, Kate Nelligan, Alfre Woodard and numerous others. Ryder is a graduate student, about to be married, who spends the summer with her aunts in a kind of Golden Girls household and is eventually treated to the recollection of each woman's greatest romance. Some segments are stronger than others and it gets better as it goes along, though on the whole the movie seems a bit laid back, and its concluding moral, about the value of love, is somewhat unconvincing.

The picture is letterboxed with an aspect ratio of about 1.78:1 and no 16:9 enhancement. The image is sharp and colors, though a touch drab, look accurate. The stereo surround sound and Dolby Digital sound are fairly pleasing, with a nice dimensionality. The 117 minute program is also available in French in Dolby Digital and in Spanish is standard stereo, and can be supported by English or Spanish subtitles. There are some extensive production notes and a decent cast-and-director profile section, but we could not locate the trailer promised on the jacket cover.

Howards End (Columbia TriStar, 26779)

Anthony Hopkins and Emma Thompson star in what eventually becomes a tale about a woman betrothed to a wealthy widower who is often uncharitable in his associations with others. Based on E.M. Forster's novel, there are also a number of subplots, concerning the families of both characters. The film succeeds by maintaining its dramatic integrity while presenting conversation in an uncannily realistic manner.

The performances are both energetic and meticulous, and the film's period setting provides an impetus for transporting the viewer more deeply into its world. To this end, the DVD's production values also enhance the film's impact. The picture transfer looks super and the stereo surround soundtrack is outstanding. The image is in letterboxed format only, with an aspect ratio of about 2.3:1 and an accommodation for enhanced 16:9 playback. The fleshtones are accurate and the film's softly lit sequences always look stable. The stereo surround sound is consistently forceful and the separations are constantly active, with many satisfying sound effects. The 143 minute film has optional English and French subtitles and a couple trailers.

Hubley, John and Faith (see Art and Jazz in Animation)

Hudson Hawk (Columbia TriStar, 70599)

Badly marketed and woefully misunderstood, **Hudson Hawk** was sold as a **Die Hard**-type caper film with a smattering of humor, but it is actually a very funny, sophisticated *Moonlighting*-type comedy, and its deliberate humor grows on you the more often you see it. Giving it the attention it deserves, Columbia TriStar has released the 1991 feature in single-sided dual-layer format, letterboxed on one layer with an aspect ratio of about 1.85:1 and an accommodation for enhanced 16:9 playback, and in full screen format on the other layer. Willis and Danny Aiello are professional thieves who get strong-armed into robbing several ultra-secure museums, as several interest groups battle for the items they have lifted. Sandra Bernhard, Andie MacDowell and James Coburn also appear. There are some terrific slapstick sequences (Willis tosses a box of hypodermic needles at a bad guy and moments later the bad guy is chasing him with the needles still hanging from his face), some marvelously absurd humor (for precision timing during one of their heists, Willis and Aiello sing *Swinging on a Star*), and some just plain funny performances (Bernhard; even MacDowell generates decent laughs as a nun who falls for Willis). There are those who resent movie stars, and they will likely see the whole exercise as some sort of in-joke ego trip, but for those who have no preconceptions, the film is a wild, brisk, different and very amusing send up of action film expectations.

The picture transfer looks super. The image is sharp and colors are crisply defined, with nicely detailed fleshtones. The letterboxing masks picture information off the bottom of the image and a little off the top, adding a little to the sides in comparison to the full screen image, but either seems workable. There is no 5-channel Dolby track, but the standard stereo surround sound is great, with plenty of dimensionality, separation effects and strength. The 100 minute program also has a French language track, optional English or French subtitles ("Ou préférais-tu être un mulet"), and trailers for other Columbia Bruce Willis movies, but not for **Hudson Hawk**.

There is also a commentary channel, from the film's beleaguered director, Michael Lehmann. He talks about all the gags (he was also making deliberate film flubs, such as showing the same view out of both sides of a car, but people just thought he was making errors) and speaks emphatically of the film's comic intentions. He talks about the film's tribulations (an actress dropped out because of back problems, and MacDowell came in after shooting started to replace her), the ridiculous gossip (paparazzi took photos of Willis and MacDowell kissing within an outdoor scene of the film, and then distributed the pictures as if they had been taken surreptitiously of a hot and heavy affair), and about the actual production (it was the first film to digitally remove safety wires). "I hope that in retrospect people can look at the film and enjoy it as it was intended to be enjoyed," says Lehmann at the conclusion. Hear, hear.

The Hudsucker Proxy (Warner, 13166)

The 1994 film by Joel and Ethan Coen, with the collaboration of Sam Raimi, is a highly appealing and very funny original work, but it seems that there was just no way, short of giving out free tickets, the film's backers could describe its pleasures well enough to get audiences to see it. The film begins as a cross between *The Producers* and **Brazil**, with a touch of *Mr. Deeds Goes to Town* thrown in, but is ultimately so unique and fresh it can't even be compared to the Coens' other movies, or Raimi's. Tim Robbins stars as a dupe voted in as president of a corporation so the board of directors can depress the stock price, with Paul Newman as the board's mastermind and Jennifer Jason Leigh as a snoopy reporter. Shot with a great deal of effects and model work, the soundstage sets are highly stylized and the movie is magical to look at. The film's sense of humor, however, is always right up front, often making fun of the movie itself or mocking the densely clichéd actions of the characters. The film that it really reminded us the most of, then, was **The Wizard of Oz**, since, like **Oz**, the filmmakers take a somewhat sappy story, set it in a world entirely of their own invention and then keep distracting the viewer with new sleights-of-hand, liberating the viewer from the stresses of the real world in the process.

The presentation is in letterboxed format on one side and in full screen format on the other side. The letterboxing has an aspect ratio of about 1.85:1 and an accommodation for enhanced 16:9 playback, masking picture information off the top and bottom and adding some to the sides in comparison to the full screen version Colors have a soft, pastel sheen and are carefully delineated. The image is smooth and solid. One sequence is done entirely with black and white and fleshtones, and if the fleshtones were off it would spoil the whole effect, but it looks perfect and is fully captivating. The stereo surround sound has a general dimensionality and a nice flourish. There is a French audio track as well, and optional English and French subtitles. Carter Burwell is listed as the film's music composer, but the haunting primary theme is Aram Khachaturian's anti-capitalist music from the ballet, *Spartacus*.

Humanoids from the Deep (New Horizons, NH00200)

An adeptly executed 1980 horror thriller, Doug McClure, Vic Morrow and Ann Turkel star in a *Creature from the Black Lagoon*-style tale about monsters terrorizing a fishing village in Northern California. The 79 minute film has lots of good cat-jumps-through-the-window screams, some terrific grotesque effects, many fun, hokey effects, some marvelous nude scenes, excellent Fort Bragg CA location work, a decent James Horner musical score, and a plot that is sufficient to bind it all together.

The picture is somewhat blurry but colors are reasonably bright and fleshtones are tolerable. The monophonic sound has some strength and never sounds too distorted. The program is not captioned, but there is a trailer, a good interview with producer Roger Corman about the film, and a cast profile section.

The Hunchback of Notre Dame (Warner, T2058)

Charles Laughton stars in the exciting 1939 classic with amazing set designs. The black-and-white image looks incredibly rich and smooth. The vivid image enhances the film's entertainment. The monophonic sound is fair and the Dolby Digital mono track is a little stronger. The 117 minute feature is also available in Spanish and comes with English, French or Spanish subtitles. There is a 12 minute retrospective documentary, along with a theatrical trailer, a good cast profile section and some interesting production notes. Maureen O'Hara co-stars in the film, which was directed by William Dieterle.

The Hunt for Red October (Paramount, 320207)

The picture is sharper than the LD, with better detail. Colors are crisp, even with the difficult submarine interior lighting, and flesh-tones look great. We noticed a minor artifacting flaw in a couple of whip pans, but otherwise the image is flawless. The presentation is letterboxed with an aspect ratio of about 2.25:1. The film's sound mix is wonderful, putting you right in the middle of the submarine, the aircraft carrier, the helicopter and everywhere else the film takes you. There are many separation effects and plenty of thrust on all channels. The film is also available in French in standard stereo and can be supported by English or Spanish subtitles. The 135 minute film is accompanied by a theatrical trailer on the single-sided dual-layer platter.

Those who labor at white-collar occupations will have a special affection for **The Hunt for Red October**, a movie about a man who makes such a sharp impression during a briefing to senior officials at a crisis meeting that 40 hours later he is on a Russian submarine helping the captain sneak the craft past the Soviet navy. Oh, the movie has torpedo fights and similar pieces of excitement, but nothing quite matches the high it achieves showing people sitting in chairs and doing their jobs well. The film stars Alec Baldwin, who is super, and Sean Connery, who gets the job done but is less appealing, and contains a terrific team of supporting actors. Our favorite is Joss Ackland, as the Soviet ambassador who squirms in his seat as he lies to the national security advisor. John McTiernan's direction is also inspired, achieving a pace that is steady but un-rushed, pulling the viewer further into the story with every pulse. The film, which is a bright adaptation of a novel that had seemed impossible to coerce into a theatrical time frame, is a terrific adventure with limited violence and a good sense of realism.

The Hunted (Universal, 20443)

A genuine samurai film set in modern day Japan, Christopher Lambert stars in the film and John Lone is the bad guy, but the narrative avoids the usual cultural clashes and concentrates on the action. Lambert's character sees the face of a ninja boss, and soon every ninja around is out to murder him, with only the police and a couple of good ninjas to help protect him. The story advances the action effectively, and the film makes fine use of its Tokyo locations, including an elaborate massacre aboard a bullet train. Shot in Japan (supplemented by studio work in Vancouver), it is an elegant action feature, with exciting fight scenes (Lambert's character is no super hero—he has to learn how to fight to protect himself) and classy locations. Joan Chen is also featured.

The picture is sumptuous. Colors are deep, vivid and slick. The image is letterboxed, with an aspect ratio of about 1.85:1 and an accommodation for enhanced 16:9 playback. The stereo surround sound and Dolby Digital sound are also super. Rear channel effects are modest, but the front channel separations are distinctive and add considerably to the film's rapture. The 111 minute program is also available in French in standard stereo and can be supported by English or Spanish subtitles. There is an informative production essay about the problems of shooting a movie in Japan, a small cast-and-director profile section and a trailer.

Hush (Columbia TriStar, 02356)

Okay, so there's been evil babysitters, evil tenants, evil cops, evil neighbors—it is only natural then that there should be an evil mother-in-law movie. Jessica Lange is the villain and Gwyneth Paltrow is the heroine, pregnant and at the mercy of her husband's mother. Lange's character wants a grandchild very badly but is not necessarily interested in the baggage that comes with one. At its best, the film evokes *Rosemary's Baby* and the performances of the two stars are delicious. The story is pretty silly and, structurally, some of it looks like it has been rather awkwardly pieced together in a cutting room (they appear to try to soften Lange's character), but it has a subject everyone can relate to and that will probably be enough to carry most viewers past the film's weaknesses. If it isn't

camp now, it will be in a few years. Johnathon Schaech is the husband.

The film is presented on one side in letterboxed format and on the other side in full screen format. The letterboxing has an aspect ratio of about 1.85:1 and an accommodation for enhanced 16:9 playback. Some of the lighting is inconsistent, but on the whole the colors look bright and fleshtones are accurate. The stereo surround sound is passable, with a few choice sound effects, though generally the mix is not elaborate. The Dolby Digital track is a bit sharper. The 96 minute film also has a French language track in standard stereo, optional English or French subtitles, and a trailer.

I

I Am a Fool (see James Dean: Hill Number One/I Am a Fool)

I Know What You Did Last Summer (Columbia TriStar, 23929)

It doesn't have the repeat potential or wit of **Scream**, but **I Know What You Did Last Summer** is a fully enjoyable and well-crafted thriller, with an attractive cast, plenty of scares, and a narrative that, like **Scream**, is as concerned about the psychological state of the heroes as it is about finding the killer. The film lives up to its promises, and you can't ask any more of it than that. It's a perfect drive-in movie, but it is also great home video.

The film's cinematography is often quite impressive, with eerie lighting effects and lovely widescreen vistas (the movie is set by the sea, supposedly in North Carolina, but with California cliffs), and the image transfer is excellent. The picture is letterboxed on one side with an aspect ratio of about 2.35:1 and an accommodation for enhanced 16:9 playback, and is in cropped format on the other side. The cropping delivers a few gooey close-ups of the film's nubile stars but is otherwise not good for much. The picture quality is excellent, with bright, sharp hues and accurate fleshtones. Colors are consistently crisp and vivid, and remain so in all lighting conditions (including the unlikely well-lit underwater night scenes).

The stereo surround sound and Dolby Digital sound also contribute to the fun, with plenty of directional effects and carefully applied crescendos, though the standard track is a bit weaker. The Dolby Digital track has a little better control over the range and tone of specific sounds, but the rawness of the standard track is just as effective at delivering the thrills. The 101 minute program is also available in French in standard stereo and can be supported by English, French or Spanish subtitles ("'Sé Lo Que Hicieron El Verano Pasado'"). A trailer is included, as well.

The director, Jim Gillespie, provides a commentary, with prompting from others. He has a good memory and basically reports upon what happened during the shooting of each scene—what the conditions were, how much trouble they had (the cast members got roughed up a bit) or why they staged a shot the way they did. He also talks a bit about his working methods (he doesn't rehearse much) and the complexity of keeping the clothing on each of the four heroes from clashing with the others.

I Like To Play Games (Simitar, R-rated, 7423); (Simitar unrated, 7466)

A softcore erotic feature that essentially delivers what it promises, it is about a young advertising executive who becomes involved with a woman from the office. A psychological cipher to him, the woman leads him on by insisting that they act out a different fantasy on each date, with the emotional stakes rising steadily the more they become involved with one another. It is neither a thriller nor a romance really, but the narrative is reasonably witty and the performances are competent enough to keep the viewer interested in the fates of the characters. The erotic sequences are fairly elaborate in the 90 minute unrated version, but less involved in the 80 minute R-rated version.

The colors are bright, but fleshtones are pinkish at times. Some sequences are a little grainy, but others, even darkly lit scenes, look crisp. The sound is a bit flat and is mildly distorted on the upper end. A filmography of the star, Lisa Boyle, is also included and the program is not captioned.

I Spit on Your Grave (Elite, EE7749)

The film, which has an acknowledged cult following, gives off more bad karma than good in its unadulterated depiction of a gang rape and the subsequent murders of the perpetrators. It is letterboxed with an aspect ratio of about 1.85:1 and no 16:9 enhancement, masking picture information off the top and bottom of the frame in comparison to the full screen versions, including imagery of a sexual nature, and adding a smidgen to the sides. The film still looks like the cheap, makeshift exploitation feature it is, but hues are bright and accurate, and the picture is reasonably clean and solid. Fleshtones are a bit light, but workable. The monophonic sound seams somewhat muted. There is no time encoding but the jacket cover lists the running time at 100 minutes, and the program is accompanied by a trailer.

I Spy (Image, ID5021BRDVD)

The first TV drama to pair a black actor and a white actor as heroes, the show stars Bill Cosby and Robert Culp. With extensive location photography, Culp's character travels the world as a tennis pro, with Cosby as his what? Lover? It's never clear, but the two actually work for the government, fighting communism and that sort of thing.

Two 50 minute episodes, circa 1968, are combined on the release. Neither episode is very good. A young but still towering Richard Kiel is one of the guest stars in the first episode, *A Few Miles West of Nowhere*, in which the two heroes investigate a town's reluctance to accept a nuclear power plant in their neighborhood, and find a group of right wing fanatics trying to keep the plant out of town (Barry Commoner was obviously not involved with the script). The heroes get beat up a lot, but eventually save a little girl from a well, proving to the townspeople that they are good guys and the right wing fanatic is the bad guy. The plant should be up and running in no time.

In the second episode, *The Trouble with Temple*, which is set in Spain, they meet an Errol Flynn-type actor, played by Jack Cassidy, who is selling NATO secrets. Cosby's character gets captured and drugged, while Culp's character convinces the actor's bimbo girlfriend (we're not speaking pejoratively—she's supposed to be an airhead, for plot purposes) that she should stop living a life of luxury dressed like a sexpot and finish her high school education so she can become a history teacher. She likes the idea, and eventually moves back to Ohio.

On both episodes, the colors are fairly nice, with reasonably bright hues and accurate fleshtones, and the image is reasonably sharp as well, with minimal wear. The monophonic sound is a bit scratchy, but tolerable. There is no captioning.

I Still Know What You Did Last Summer (Columbia TriStar, 39789)

The final shot of **I Know What You Did Last Summer** is explained in one quick, throwaway line near the beginning, and if you blink your ears, you'll miss it. The best slasher thrillers, like **Scream** and the first **I Know What You Did**, combine their thrills with decent psychological explorations of their heroes. By the end of the movies, you're not only awash in sweat from fear, but you understand the moral flaws and emotional vulnerabilities of the protagonists and antagonists. **I Still Know What You Did Last Summer** isn't as good as that, but it is good enough to be fun. The heroes win a trip to an island resort, but when they get there, the other guests have left and the staff start turning up as corpses. The filmmakers use the same made-ya-jump gimmicks more than

once, and the premise is pretty farfetched, but what the heck, there's plenty of blood and the heroines, Jennifer Love Hewitt and Brandy, are cute when they're scared.

The 1998 film is in letterboxed format on one side, with an aspect ratio of about 2.35:1 and an accommodation for enhanced 16:9 playback, and in cropped format on the other side. We found the letterboxed version to be more satisfying, particularly during the frantically edited chase sequences. The color transfer looks okay. The film's darker sequences are actually stronger than the few scenes set in the bright sunlight, the latter producing somewhat bland fleshtones, though it is more likely a limitation of the cinematography than of the transfer. On the whole, hues look crisp and shades are clearly delineated. The stereo surround sound and Dolby Digital sound are shamelessly employed to enhance the frights, but that is to be expected, with the Dolby Digital track supplying a more aggressive dimensionality. The 100 minute program can be supported by English subtitles. There is a brief but appealing 'making of' featurette, a couple trailers and, for those of you who can't get enough of her, a Jennifer Love Hewitt music video.

I Vespri Siciliani (see Verdi's I Vespri Siciliani)

Ike & Tina Turner (Pioneer, PA99611D)

Tina Turner always seems to be full of energy, but she looks like she's got even more energy than usual in the *Best of MusikLaden Live* offering. She also has a body suit that seems to leave nothing to the imagination. The picture on the 30 minute program is heavy with video effects, which limit contrasts and remove details, but when the effects subside, the picture looks okay. The colors aren't fresh, but details are reasonably good and fleshtones are workable. The stereo surround sound is great, with a strong dimensionality and plenty of thrust, and the Dolby Digital track is even better. They seem to sing a lot of reverse cross-over numbers, including *Get Back*, *Honky Tonk Woman* and (from later, without Ike) *Acid Queen*. In any case, the set is very enjoyable. The program is not captioned.

I'm No Angel (Image, ID4230USDVD)

In one of Mae West's most lasting hits, she plays a sideshow and circus performer who eventually sues Cary Grant's character for breach of promise. It is also the film in which she says, "Beulah, peel me a grape," an unaccountably funny line that pretty much sums up the film's makeshift plot and leisurely charms.

Blacks are pure and the image is sharp, but the black-and-white picture on the classic 1933 feature looks its age, with grain, scratches and other markings, though the presentation is tolerable. The monophonic sound is subdued, but there is a Dolby Digital mono track that is clearer and more forceful. Like the picture, the sound is a bit on the worn side, but workable. The 88 minute program is supported by English closed captions.

I'm Your Man (DVD International, DVDI0715)

A theme park-type program from 1973, an audience in a theater watching the film would 'vote' on the narrative at various choice points, so that, theoretically, every time one attended a screening, one would see a different movie. Basically, there is about 45 minutes of footage and a single run through lasts from 10 to 15 minutes. About a woman who arranges to turn evidence of corruption over to the police at a party, the viewer can follow the story of the woman (Colleen Quinn), the villain (Mark Metcalf) or an innocent bystander (Kevin M. Seal), as the adventures of the three continually intersect. Instead of the audience voting, the viewer uses the DVD controls to choose the story paths. The film has some real humor—Metcalf is particularly competent in this regard—but not much excitement or intrigue, and on home video the sense of community the film promoted, which was part of its appeal, is gone. Because of its limited budget, some story concepts were dropped, leaving a monotonous opening for one of the characters and a 'try again' message at another point.

The picture and sound are both great. An important introduction, however, which not only explains how the movie works, but gives the viewer profiles of the three protagonists, has been allocated to a supplementary section instead of opening the film. Cleverly, the film's own initial segment is designed to 'teach' viewers through practice how to 'vote,' giving them the opportunity to sort of channel surf between the three characters for a while before the real story choices are presented. On a couple of our DVD machines, however, this sequence would freeze on the first choice point and not allow further movement, though it worked fine on other players. We discovered that a linear progression of the storyline being viewed could be activated by pressing the Chapter Skip function, but to access the other characters one would have to go back to the start, and many viewers, unable to randomly hit keys until they find one that works, will assume the DVD is defective. After the opening sequence is completed, then the choice functions worked properly on all players, although determining which choice is highlighted on the screen can still be difficult.

Accompanying the program itself is a nice collection of supplements about the whole system, and trailers for two other movies that were made for theaters. There is a bloopers segment, a 'making of' promo piece, a look at how the movie was conceived and designed, storyboards for some proposed scenes to be added in a possible expansion of the film (which we could not exit), and a commentary track—yes, to hear the entire commentary you have to navigate through every plot thread. The commentary, from director Bob Bejan, is more generalized than the text supplement at explaining how the film was put together, but there are numerous anecdotes about how he shot the movie on a shoestring budget (that was apparently burning at the other end) and he takes delight at the way the way it came out.

Image of an Assassination: A New Look at the Zapruder Film (MPI, DVD7282)

The 88 minute program tells the story of a 22 second strip of film depicting the 1963 murder of John F. Kennedy. The film itself has appeared in movies in the past, notably in **JFK** and its predecessor, *Executive Action*. The most interesting part of the documentary is the step-by-step retelling of what happened to the footage after Zapruder shot it—the rush around Dallas to find a company that could process it, the quick deal cut with Life Magazine and the eventual effort to archive the original copies. Less compelling for casual viewers is the level of detail given over to the restoration process—how each individual strip of film is captured on a computer and enhanced through computer imaging.

The program concludes with a half dozen replays of the film—it is shown in standard frame at standard speed and slow motion, in full frame, including the sprocket holes (which were punched into the image on the Super-8 film) at standard speed and slow motion, and then at two levels of closeups in slow motion.

The transfer quality is good, though the quality of the image on the original film, for all its restoration, is not significantly improved over what appeared in the feature films we cite above. The sound is fine and the narration is supported by English, Spanish, French and German subtitles ("Eine Zwischenmeldung aus Dallas, offensichtlich offiziell, Präsident Kennedy starb um 13 Uhr Central Standard Time, 14 Uhr Eastern Standard Time, vor ungefähr 38 Minuten"). There are also brief text profiles of Zapruder and his family.

Immortal Combat (Simitar, 7314)

Roddy Piper and Sonny Chiba portray cops who take a leave of absence and visit the Caribbean to investigate the murder of an undercover policewoman. They infiltrate a fiendish drug company that is also holding martial arts contests—well, none of it makes much sense, but the fight scenes are pretty good—especially Chiba's—and the story keeps moving, even if it doesn't go anywhere much. The cinematography has an inexpensive look, but the picture transfer is passable and fleshtones are reasonably deep. The

sound has a rudimentary stereo mix and is inelegant but functional. The program runs 109 minutes and is not captioned.

The Impossible Voyage (see **Landmarks of Early Film Volume 2: The Magic of Méliès**)

Improvisations (see **Olivier Messiaen: Quartet for the End of Time/Improvisations**)

Impulse (Anchor Bay, DV10608)

A movie that plays like a bad *X-Files* episode, Meg Tilly stars as a dancer who returns to her hometown when her mother attempts suicide, only to find that the whole place is going crazy. Must be something in the water, or the milk, more precisely. It isn't just that the premise is hokey, the film has a poor dramatic structure, so that what surprises there are get telescoped too far in advance, and the ending is pretty much a cop out. Tim Matheson and Hume Cronyn co-star.

The 1984 film is presented in full screen format. Colors are a little light and fleshtones are bland. Contrary to a notation on the jacket cover, the sound is monophonic, and the mix is of limited interest. The 93 minute feature is not captioned.

In & Out (Paramount, 329877)

The popular comedy about confused sexual identity is letter-boxed with an aspect ratio of about 1.85:1 and an accommodation for enhanced 16:9 playback. The film's color scheme tends toward pastels and tans, so hues are rarely vivid and fleshtones are subdued, but the image presentation is adequate and the picture is solid. The film's audio mix is nothing special. The 92 minute film is also available in French in standard stereo and comes with English or Spanish subtitles ("¿Todo el mundo es gay?"—to which one might answer, 'Todo, too,' perhaps?), as well as a theatrical trailer.

The final act of **In & Out** is moderately uplifting, but the film is probably best seen in a theater, where the laughter of an audience can pull a viewer through the film's most bothersome contrivances. Some viewers will find it well timed and humorous, but others are likely to stare at it dumbfounded, wondering how such embarrassments could possibly be considered funny. Kevin Kline plays a high school English teacher who is identified, apparently without proof, as gay by a former student during the Oscar ceremonies, impacting not only his status within his community, but his forthcoming marriage as well. For a movie that appears to be concerned with accepting people for what they are, the film creates hopelessly bland and unfair stereotypes of everybody from high school kids to supermodels. For the most jaded viewers, however, the film may become a comical gem, because it gets worse and worse on multiple viewings, to the point where its ridiculousness becomes surreptitiously amusing in ways its deliberate humor could never hope to equal.

In Dreams (DreamWorks, 84665)

Neil Jordan is no hack and **In Dreams,** though wrongheaded, is no *Eyes of Laura Mars* rip-off. Parts of it, in fact, are thrilling, even gut wrenching, and the performance of Annette Bening in the lead role is sublime. Bening is a mother who has visions, mostly of what a killer who has abducted a little girl is seeing. She soon learns that some of these visions involve her own daughter and, when she is unable to prevent them from coming true, she attempts suicide in a sequence so spellbinding there is a tendency to stop breathing or blinking until it is concluded. And yet, here we have the same old gimmicks found in so many other lousy supernatural thrillers—dead children, psychic visions, a wacko killer, embodied by Robert Downey, Jr. with a wig, who sings a catchy tune (*Don't Sit under the Apple Tree*) as he goes about his terror, etc. The ending is unable to transcend the genre conventions and so the movie is no metaphysical masterpiece, but it is so compellingly executed that if you can stomach its premise (children in harm's way is not an easy entertainment), the excitement as it goes along more than compensates for the inevitably compromised wrap up. Aidan Quinn and Stephen Rea co-star.

The 1999 film is letterboxed with an aspect ratio of about 1.85:1 and an accommodation for enhanced 16:9 playback. The picture quality is very good. The many dark and underwater sequences are sharp and carefully detailed. Fleshtones are accurate and blood is a deep, solid red. The stereo surround sound and Dolby Digital sound are fine. The mix is fairly direct, but it underscores the best scenes effectively without getting in the way. The 100 minute program has optional English subtitles, production notes, a cast & crew profile section and a trailer.

In Love and War (New Line, N4785)

Film academics speak in elevated tones of 'pure cinema,' the ability of a motion picture director to tell a story entirely with images, but then film academics have never had to trouble themselves with the movies of Richard Attenborough, a director whose films are burdened with such redundant dialogue the stories are told through the images by default. Attenborough's 1997 romantic adventure is such a bland film you could watch it in a foreign language and understand perfectly what was happening. Chris O'Donnell stars as the young Ernest Hemingway, wounded during a WWI battle and nursed back to health by a Red Cross volunteer, played with a perky detachment by Sandra Bullock.

The 113 minute film is presented on a single-sided dual layer platter, in letterboxed format on one layer, with an aspect ratio of about 2.35:1 and an accommodation for enhanced 16:9 playback, and in cropped format on the other layer. Some shots are conceptually soft, but the presentation is generally crisp and colors look good, with accurate fleshtones. The stereo surround sound is fairly good and the Dolby Digital track is excellent, with a number of effective separation and back channel effects and a strong, pronounced bass, though the movie also has many passages where the characters are talking and nothing else is going on. There are optional English subtitles, profiles of Attenborough, O'Donnell and Bullock, and a trailer. Romances are about anticipation, but every emotional turn in the film is so projected, and is enacted with such a duplication of efforts, that you're tired of the couple and tired of their affair long before it starts.

In the Company of Men (Columbia TriStar, 26019)

Okay, so we hope the main character burns in Hell, and the film is the intellectual equivalent of I Spit on Your Grave, but it is also made clear, by the end, that the main character is a complete emotional psycho (albeit a very successful one) who is as rotten to the men around him as he is to the women. Aaron Eckhart and Matt Malloy star as two business executives who compete for the affections of a hearing impaired temp, played by Stacy Edwards, fully intending to drop her once the contest is over. The film's staging is almost no different from a play, but the director, Neil LaBute, stirs up some very powerful feelings with his concoction, although it is an arguable point as to whether he has the right to do so.

The film is presented in letterboxed format on one side, with an aspect ratio of about 1.85:1 and an accommodation for enhanced 16:9 playback, and in full screen format on the other side. The framing on the letterboxed image masks picture information off the top and bottom of the image in comparison to the full screen image, but creates a much more compelling image composition. The image is a little soft and contrasts seem a bit weak in places, with inconsistent colors, but for a super-low budget production, the image looks decent and the transfer is probably fairly good. Although the film is mostly talking, there is Robert Bly-style drumming between scenes, which sounds great on the stereo surround soundtrack. The film can be supported by English, Spanish or French subtitles and is accompanied by a red tag theatrical trailer.

There are also two commentary tracks, one basically from the crew, including LaBute, and one from the cast, though Eckhart appears on both. Between the two tracks, the film and its production history are thoroughly broken down. The crew commentary track tends to have a bit more technical information, while the cast track is more anecdotal, but both provide plenty of insight on how the film was shot—on its restricted budget—and both have amusing reminiscences. They also talk a lot about the critical and popular reactions to the film, as practically everyone who worked on it has some story about a viewer who has misunderstood the movie's intentions. The cast track drops out at one point for a couple minutes.

In the Line of Fire (Columbia TriStar, 52315/52319)

Beautifully directed and perfectly edited, the 1993 film, in which Clint Eastwood portrays an aging Secret Service agent and John Malkovich counters as a devious, would-be assassin, is an outstanding dramatic thriller. The picture is incredibly smooth and sharp. Colors are rich and precisely detailed. For artistic reasons, some of the film's sequences contain a mild emphasis of haze or grain, an allusion to the public record and an attempt to soften the ten-year age difference between Eastwood and the character he is playing, but the disc so clearly captures the film's glossiest moments that viewers will readily take the rest of it in stride.

Except for one momentary image jitter, we could detect no digital artifacts whatsoever. The presentation is letterboxed, with an aspect ratio of about 2.35:1 and an accommodation for enhanced 16:9 playback. The sound mix is also grand, with many well-chosen atmospheric and directional effects. Details are clearly defined and the bass is strong. The Dolby Digital track is a lot better than the standard track, with more active separations, a more aggressive mid-range and a stronger bass. The 127 minute film is available in English and French (the Dolby Digital is in English only) and comes with Spanish or Korean subtitles and English closed captioning. Ennio Morricone's music, incidentally, is superb, an ideal distillation of his favorite motifs that creates a classic mystery thriller score. Everything about In the Line of Fire, in fact, is classic in design. It has a captivating pace; a flawed, realistic and accessible hero; a marvelous and even surprising romance; and an elegant style that makes the most innocuous filler sequence as spellbinding as the major action sequences. Most important of all, it is a drama. While there are many engaging action scenes and equally enjoyable sequences about the deciphering of clues, In the Line of Fire is also about growing old and coming to terms with anxiety, and while the filmmakers wisely keep these themes in the background they make sure viewers are cognizant of them, so that the movie enriches the psyche while it entertains.

In the Name of the Father (Universal, 20248)

Based upon a true story, Daniel Day-Lewis stars as a young man from Northern Ireland living in London who is falsely arrested as a terrorist and ends up spending a number of years in jail, along with his poor father, who is incarcerated solely because of the trumped up charges brought against his son. The 133 minute movie, which falls into three fairly delineated parts, was directed by Jim Sheridan. The first part depicts the troubles in Northern Ireland and the steps leading to the hero's arrest, but it is also a nostalgic look at the free spirited life young people could have in London in the early Seventies. The section is directed very well and has action, romance, humor and even a sense adventure. The second section depicts the hero's stay in prison, and it unfolds pretty much like most prison movies, showing the power struggles and indignities of prison life. Although it opens in tragedy, the final part is a rousing courtroom drama, culminating in the exhilaration of the hero's exoneration. The hero's relationship with his father is the film's emotional core, and to some extent its weakest component (he tends to blurt out the resentments he's held inside toward his father, an overly dramatic device that Lewis has difficulty doing in a convincing way). Hovering beyond the narrative are the movie's political lessons: that the transgressions in justice imposed upon the hero were not simply a result of an ill-considered law or panicky administration, but the inevitable result of an unjust policy that had been festering for many years.

The 1993 film's color scheme seems deliberately drained, and fleshtones are greyish, but the picture transfer is good, with sharp, distinctive colors. The picture is letterboxed, with an aspect ratio of about 1.9:1 and an accommodation for enhanced 16:9 playback. The stereo surround sound is a little weak, but the film's sound mix is not elaborate anyway and the audio presentation is adequate. The film is also available in French and comes with English or Spanish subtitles.

In the Navy (Image, ID4296USDVD)

Although it has a terrific cast, including Dick Powell, the Andrew Sisters and Shemp Howard, the 1941 feature is one of the weaker Bud Abbott and Lou Costello service comedies. The black-and-white picture is in reasonably good shape, with smooth contrasts and very few speckles. The monophonic sound is clear and the 85 minute program is adequately closed captioned. Among the gags are a money counting mix-up and a screwy long division problem that proves 28 divided by 7 is 13. The straight narrative, in which Powell is a famous personality who has signed up and wants to duck a reporter, generally makes no sense.

In the Realm of the Senses (Fox Lorber, FLV5037)

The Japanese erotic drama is time-compressed. The jacket declares the film's running time of 104 minutes but it clocks in at 97 minutes. The compression distorts the monophonic sound if the volume is raised, but if it is kept to a modest level and you aren't familiar with Japanese voices or music, you don't really notice the flaw. The slight cropping is often noticeable, particularly in close-ups. Colors, however, are reasonably nice, and fleshtones are rich. The film is in Japanese and is supported by optional white English subtitles. There are filmographies for the director and star. The 1976 film, mostly about two people hanging out in a room, can get tedious after a while, despite its artistically graphic sexuality.

Incident at Oglala (Pioneer, DVD69013)

Two FBI agents who had followed a suspicious pick-up truck onto an Indian reservation were killed in a gun battle in the mid-Seventies. While the incident might have seemed cut-and-dried at first, it turns out that the residents who did the shooting were in fear of their lives from strangers participating in a widespread campaign of intimidation and homicide. And, apparently, the man who actually killed the FBI agents was never identified by the authorities. Three other men, however, were brought to trial, and after the first two were found innocent—very quickly—by a jury, the third, Leonard Peltier, was found guilty in a different venue under a judge overly sympathetic to the prosecution.

Directed by Michael Apted, the 1991 documentary, which is narrated by Robert Redford, jumps into the middle of things rather awkwardly, though once it establishes the situation and systematically runs through the story of the trials, it becomes much easier to follow. Visual reenactments amount to the depiction of how the automobiles turned and where they parked. There are many interviews, with all the sides involved in the controversy, and some archive footage. The story has a strong emotional foundation and is very interesting, but we also found it interesting to look at how Apted organized the material, choosing to let the story play out instead of letting the viewer know what to expect in advance.

The picture quality varies from one piece of footage to the next, but the best looking sequences would indicate that the transfer is competent. There was some severe displacement artifacting in one scene, but otherwise the image looked fairly stable. The sound, which is essentially monophonic, is fine, and the 90 minute program has not been captioned.

Incognito (Warner, 14538)

Jason Patric stars in the John Badham thriller as a master art forger who gets talked into doing a Rembrandt by a pair of unsavory art dealers. He does it so well the dealers get greedy. The film has a sort of old-fashioned air to it, structurally, and the narrative

strains believability, but it is also reasonably involving if you just take what happens at face value. The ins and outs of the forgery business are quite intriguing, and it is worth noting that despite the screenplay's shortcomings, Patric gives an accomplished, movie star performance.

There is a fascinating audio commentary track by Badham, screenwriter Jordan Katz and composer John Ottman. Remaining absolutely cordial, as if they were unaware of a conflict, they talk about how they disagreed over the way certain scenes should have played out, and about details in the story. If you listened to as many commentary channels as we have, you would know that this is not a normal occurrence. Once in a while there's maybe one or two brief sequences in a movie that some filmmaker would have liked to have done differently, but here there are conflicts about the beginning, the middle and the end, and they talk about them as if it were a curiosity and not an indication that the movie was in trouble long before it got to a screening room. They also talk about the normal stuff, setting up the shots and working with the actors, but there is an odd lack of depth to their descriptions of this part of the process, again something that is more noticeable when you're listening to a dozen such tracks every month.

The DVD's most rewarding supplement, however, consists of interviews with Rod Steiger, Irène Jacob, and artist James Gemmill. Steiger's comments alone are worth the price of the DVD as he talks about the craft of acting, how his career got started and what's wrong with the state of the world today. Jacob also has valuable insights on intuitive performances and about working with Patric. Gemmill's talk is fascinating. He discusses not only the techniques used to forge paintings, but the atmosphere that fosters the forgeries, as well as describing in detail what he had to do for the movie.

The picture is letterboxed with an aspect ratio of about 2.35:1 and no 16:9 enhancement. The color quality looks very nice, though fleshtones are a bit bland in some darker sequence. The stereo surround sound is passable, and there is a Dolby Digital track, with more detailed separation effects. The 108 minute film is also available in French in Dolby Digital and can be supported by English, French or Spanish subtitles. There is a cast-and-director profile section, a small collection of publicity photos, a soundtrack promo section and press kit-style production notes.

Indigo Girls: Watershed—10 Years of Underground Video (Sony, EVD49195)

A collection of music videos from the feminist folk rock group, each cut is separated by a somewhat lengthy interview sequence. Many are just concert performance clips, but the 66 minute program is still highly satisfying, creating a pleasant blend of avant garde attitudes and earthy sensibilities.

We have no idea how good the picture transfer is, because most of the footage is deliberately homegrown, but seeing as there are times when the image is sharp and colors are accurate, we assume that the show looks the way it is supposed to look. The stereo surround sound is fine and the Dolby Digital track is very good, with better detail and more energy. There are optional English subtitles, and in addition to the main program there is a 10 minute video overview of the band's career, and a text discography.

The Inheritance (Simitar, 7235)

We love a good joke, and here's one on Simitar. They have released the 1978 Dominique Sanda vehicle with a running time of 102 minutes, yet they have earnestly included a small 'Film Facts' section on the DVD where, among other things, the film's official running time is listed, as 121 minutes. This would explain why the narrative takes sudden leaps and otherwise seems confused and incomplete. The presentation is also cropped and the source material is a little ragged. The colors are bright but not fresh and the image is mildly smeared in places. The soundtrack is dubbed and Ennio Morricone's musical score (his name is misspelled in the credits) sounds a bit wobbly. Anthony Quinn co-stars. The film represents the peak of Sanda's much too brief career as a screen star, earning her a Cannes acting award for her role as a young schemer who sleeps her way through a family to get to the wealthy patriarch. Set in Italy in the mid-Nineteenth Century, the costumes and sets are fairly appealing, but unless you are a Sanda fanatic, the condition of the DVD is too detrimental to the entertainment.

Innocent Blood (Warner, 12570)

In John Landis' amusing 1992 vampire thriller, Anne Parillaud stars as a creature of the night who only feeds on wise guys, even though she doesn't like garlic. When one of her feedings is interrupted and her victim becomes like her, she enlists the help of a cop to put the now all-powerful mobster away. Anthony LaPaglia and Robert Loggia co-star. The film starts out with terrific momentum and never really lets up, blending the right amounts of humor, excitement and romance.

The image is presented in full screen format only, adding picture information to the top and bottom in comparison to the letterboxed presentations and losing a little from the sides. While it would be best to have both versions available on DVD, we tend to prefer the full screen image and never found the slight cropping to interfere with the entertainment. The image could probably be more vivid and crisp than it is, but the presentation seems fine, with accurate fleshtones and bright, solid hues. The stereo surround sound adds a nice dimensionality to many scenes. The 112 minute program also has a French stereo soundtrack and is adequately closed captioned.

Inseminoid (Elite, EE4674)

A 1982 British **Alien** rip-off, also known as *Horror Planet*, the film has some gooey gore effects but few other thrills. A female member of an expedition to an archeological site on a faraway planet is impregnated by a local lothario. She then sets about killing the other members of her party. The acting is really bad (but British bad, not American bad—they are earnest where American actors would just look lost), which can be amusing, and the high-tech equipment is pretty phony looking. The film goes through the motions properly, however, so fans will probably find it worth passing the time.

The picture is letterboxed with an aspect ratio of about 2.35:1 and no 16:9 enhancement. The source material has some wear, but the color transfer looks pretty good, with bright hues and accurate fleshtones. The monophonic sound is a bit fuzzy, but workable, and the 92 minute program is not captioned. The film is accompanied by a trailer in fairly bad condition.

Interactive Personal Trainer (Simitar, 7403)

Kickboxer Madusa Miceli hosts the workout, which emphasizes boxing stances in a vigorous aerobics workout. It is presented in the usual fashion, with Miceli performing in front of the camera and shouting out instructions to the viewer. The picture quality is fine, the sound is okay and the program is not captioned. Simitar's menu layout is outstanding, making it appear as if the program has been designed specifically for DVD. The workout runs 42 minutes, but you can choose intermediate or beginner sequences that run about 10 and 20 minutes less, respectively, taking the longer workout and, through the DVD's own programmed encoding, trimming out routines to shorten the sequence. You can also access workouts for specific sections of the body on an individual basis. As an epilogue on a separate menu access, there is a section on dieting that shows the viewer how to make simple healthy meals for breakfast, lunch and dinner, including a still frame access for the menus to each meal.

Interview with a Milkman X-rated (Vivid, UPC#0073215554)

The 76 minute program has the semblance of a story, humor, and a milk motif. An elderly milkman reminisces about how much fun he used to have with his customers. The picture is grainy, but colors are passable and the monophonic sound is okay. The 76 minute program features Madelyn Knight, Laura Palmer, Kum

Kummings and Sindee Coxx. The DVD contains alternate angle sequences and elaborate hardcore interactive promotional features.

Interview with a Vampire (Warner, 13176)

Great on atmosphere and ideas, but weaker when it comes to diction and narrative coherence, the 1994 feature is just exotic enough to be appealing and justify its expense. With all the whispering, and not to mention them trying to talk with exaggerated incisors, Brad Pitt, Tom Cruise and Antonio Banderas have difficulty delivering their dialogue clearly, but if you like how they look in the costumes, you really don't care. Most vampire movies, incidentally, deal with a single incident in time, so it cannot be discounted that the film tries to look at the hero's experiences across two centuries. It is a fresh viewpoint.

Some of the darker scenes were shot with a pronounced grain, but generally the color transfer looks scrumptious. The film ranges in time from the late Eighteenth Century to the present, and it is a challenge for the cinematographer, Philippe Rousselot, to find a style that is consistent with all the film's eras. It helps that most of the movie is set at night, and the result is luxurious and shadowy, which is replicated beautifully on the disc. There are a few more noticeable artifacts than usual, the most common being a split-second smear when the camera moves on a stationary light source, but these flaws never accumulate enough to create any real sort of distraction. The 123 minute film is presented in full screen on one side and letterboxed, with an aspect ratio of about 1.85:1 and an accommodation for enhanced 16:9 playback, on the other. The letterboxing trims picture information off the top and bottom of the image but adds a nice amount to the sides. The framing is more elegant on the letterboxed version, but we found the full screen version to be reasonably satisfying. Since Cruise and Pitt talk in tiny whisper voices through most of the film, and you can barely hear what they say. For the most part, the film's sound mix is weak, and the surround effects are rarely interesting, though the separations in the musical score are fairly nice. The Dolby Digital track is brighter and stronger than the standard stereo surround soundtrack. The DVD has French and Spanish language tracks in standard stereo and has English, French or Spanish subtitling. There is a cast list and brief production notes, but no theatrical trailer.

Into the Woods (Image, ID3951MBDVD)

The Stephen Sondheim and James Lapine videotaped stage show merges many familiar fables into a single, inter-woven narrative. Officially a musical, the show's songs fall somewhere between traditional operatic lyric and recitative. It's true brilliance is not in its music but in its lyrics, which dash through the English language tripping delightfully over the same coincidences the characters themselves are experiencing. The first act is wonderful—a cheerful, humorous blending of fairytales that can appeal to both children and adults, and had the show's creators left it at that, it would probably have been playing Broadway to this day. The second act, however, is plain awful. The jokes stop, the songs become boring and the narrative downshifts. It attempts to be artistic and meaningful, by changing the happy endings that concluded the first act into realistic, ambiguous and downright depressing epilogs, and however philosophically correct such embellishments might be, it is an intellectually snotty thing to pull on a viewer whose goodwill had already been courted and won. The original Broadway cast is featured in the production, including Bernadette Peters and Joanna Gleason.

Act One is on one side and Act Two is on the other, which is convenient, because you can just skip the second side altogether. The image is not as vivid as the crispest picture transfers but is never significantly distorted. The videotape production of a live performance is not lit for video, and although the colors are strong and sharp, once in a while portions of the screen look softer and characters take on brief ghosting effects. The stereo sound lacks the purity of the studio soundtrack recording but is an adequate rendering of a live event. There are no special features or captioning.

Invaders from Mars (Anchor Bay, DV10328)

Instead of going for modern sci-fi horror shocks, Toby Hooper's inspired remake consciously attempts to evoke the unsettling atmosphere of the original Fifties classic, about a young boy who discovers that the souls of his parents and many of his friends have been absconded by aliens that have landed in the back lot. The slightly unrealistic camera angles and elaborate rectangular image compositions achieve a kind of surreal tension that flavors the film from beginning to end. Rated 'PG,' the movie has few overt sequences of terror, but its consistency of tone fully compensates, creating a work that is at once nostalgic and modern, eerie and humorous. Karen Black, Timothy Bottoms and Louise Fletcher are among the adult stars featured.

The picture is letterboxed with an aspect ratio of about 2.35:1 and no 16:9 enhancement. Fleshtones are a little pinkish and the image is a bit soft in places, but the colors are strong and the presentation is adequate. There is a modest stereo soundtrack. The 102 minute film is accompanied by a theatrical trailer and is not captioned.

Invasion of the Body Snatchers (MGM, 906274)

The original black-and-white film was set in a small town, and it seemed like there might be safety in escaping to a big city. Philip Kaufman's 1978 update, however, is set in a big city (San Francisco), and the only safety there might be is a small town too insignificant for the invaders to bother with. The heroes, however, never make it that far. Donald Sutherland, Brooke Adams, Veronica Cartwright and Jeff Goldblum star. We find that there is not enough logic in the actions or capabilities of the pod people (some seem to be quite lucid while others are robotic) to sustain the film's drama, but as a mindless reworking of a horror classic it is sufficiently entertaining. Surprisingly, a triple bill with the original film and the later Abel Ferrara remake would probably work well.

Kaufman's movie is in letterboxed format on one side, with an aspect ratio of about 1.85:1 and no 16:9 enhancement, and in cropped format on the other side. The letterboxing loses nothing on the top and bottom of the image, and adds significant picture information to the sides. The image on the DVD is smooth and colors are generally acceptable, though fleshtones are a little pinkish. The stereo sound is workable. The mix has only sporadic separation effects, but when the dimensionality does kick in it is quite effective. Accompanied by a theatrical trailer, the 117 minute movie is available in monophonic French as well, and comes with English, French or Spanish subtitles ("Vous serez les prochains! Les voilà! Ils sort déjà là! Ils arrivent!"). There is also a commentary track by Kaufman. He spends some of the time pointing out the obvious, but he does have some interesting things to say about the production (particularly concerning the camera angles he used to give the world a skewed look, and the special effects), about his cast and crew, and about his career ("There is no future in science fiction," a movie executive told him shortly before Star Wars came out).

Invisible Strangler (Simitar, 7304)

A criminal, who has spent so long in solitary confinement he has learned how to make himself invisible, slips out of jail to murder the women that testified against him. The 1981 feature—the heroes are in leisure suits—is so bad it can be entertaining, particularly when the actresses, who apparently have not been trained in mime, must pretend they are being choked to death. Robert Foxworth stars in the 82 minute program, with Elke Sommer. Sue Lyon and Stefanie Powers also appear. The picture is soft and sometimes hazy, but colors are passable. The source material also has its share of wear. The monophonic sound is fairly noisy and scratchy. The program is accompanied by filmographies for Fox-

worth, Sommer and Powers, with decent biographical profiles provided on a jacket insert. There is no captioning.

Iria Zeiram: The Animation (Image, ID4407CTDVD)

An excellent six-part Japanese animated cartoon, each episode runs about 25 minutes, but the single-sided dual-layer presentation combines three home video releases of two episodes each, so there are three sets of opening and closing credits during the course of the program. The artwork is imaginative and the show has a lot of neat gadgets, often evoking a parasol motif.

The heroine is a bounty hunter whose brother is killed by an apparently unstoppable being. When the being lands on her home planet and begins destroying everything in sight, she takes it personal. The narrative has a strong political undertone (the powers that be want to use the being as a controllable weapon), and the plot is elaborate without succumbing to confusion. Additionally, the characters are well conceived, and although movement in the animation is limited, the action scenes are so effectively staged you don't notice it.

The picture looks fine, with sharp, accurate colors. The monophonic sound is passable. The program is available in English or in Japanese and can be supported by optional English subtitles that provide an alternate translation to the dubbing.

Irma Vep (Fox Lorber, FLV5015)

An enjoyable French film about moviemaking, Hong Kong action star Maggie Cheung portrays herself, so to speak, hired by a mentally unstable director, played by Jean-Pierre Léaud, to be the lead in an adaptation of a silent film about jewel thieves. As Léaud's character sinks into a depression, however, the shoot becomes more chaotic. Directed by Olivier Assayas, one wishes the film itself could have been a little better organized and succinct. There are often large leaps in the narrative and plot points left dangling. Still, it is a pleasant concoction with a knowing humor.

The presentation is letterboxed with an aspect ratio of about 1.66:1, with no 16:9 enhancement. The color transfer looks okay, though the lighting is generally a low budget effort and the image is a little grainy at times. The stereo sound is passable and the 96 minute film is in a mixture of English and French with optional English subtitles. There is a small cast profile section and a trailer that uses too many clips from Cheung's Heroic Trio to sell Vep's less energetic activities.

The Island at the Top of the World (Buena Vista, DV10825)

Walt Disney's 1974 Jules Verne-ish adventure was directed by Robert Stevenson. David Hartman, who, as an action hero, has the screen presence of a wet sponge, and Donald Sinden star. They portray adventurers traveling into the Arctic in a fanciful dirigible and discovering a lost colony of Vikings, who give them a great deal of trouble for a while. In a questionable marketing move, an intriguing portion of the dialogue is performed in ancient Norse, not always with translation. Disney's unconvincing but highly enjoyable special effects and the tale's briskness make the production entertaining, but the simplified drama and the untalented cast place a limit on what it can accomplish.

It is presented on one side in letterboxed format, with an aspect ratio of about 1.66:1 and no 16:9 enhancement, and in cropped format on the other side. Fleshtones are rich (though a little pinkish), colors are fairly accurate and the image is sharp, which adds to the escapist atmosphere of the entertainment. The monophonic sound is okay and the program is not captioned.

The Island of Dr. Moreau (New Line, N4444)

The death of Marlon Brando's character is one of three significant scenes that have been enhanced with 4 minutes of extra footage on the Unrated Director's Cut of the 1996 John Frankenheimer film. Each of the three sequences, which appear in the 100 minute film's second half, contains violence that probably compromised the film's PG-13 rating, but each sequence also advances the narrative and gives the story a little more depth—something it desperately needs. The demise of Brando, however, is the high point, with the animal creatures feasting on him and ripping him apart. It is a much more fitting end to someone of his stature than the standard theatrical cut, which just showed the creatures starting to gang up on him.

The film doesn't hold back on makeup effects the way the earlier adaptations of the H.G. Wells story did, and the fantasy aspects of it are pleasing. Brando, doing an imitation of Charles Laughton on dope, is attractive as the title character because in real life he's almost as weird and it shows through his performance. Val Kilmer and David Thewlis are also featured. The film's dramatic structure is off. The screenwriters also miss opportunities to spit out some scientific dialogue and give the fantasy an air of high tech action—all they would have to have done was to paw through a couple old Scientific Americans to get the phrases right. Unless it's a badly told joke, which it might be, Brando's character, clearly a geneticist, is said to have won a Nobel Prize for having invented Velcro—we didn't know the Nobel prizes had a Fabrics category. The special effects are elaborate and the atmosphere is exotic, so the film can even hold up to a few repeat viewings, but the source novel is rich in philosophical contemplation and moral horror and the script can't deliver more than the basics. The picture has pure blacks and sharp, bright colors. The film is presented in letterboxed format on one side, with an aspect ratio of about 2.35:1 and an accommodation for enhanced 16:9 playback, and in full screen format on the other side, with more picture information on the top and bottom of the image and just a little missing from the sides. As can be seen in the five minute 'making of' featurette that appears with two trailers in the supplementary section, the film was composed for the widescreen image, but the full screen picture isn't bad and viewers who dislike letterboxing in principle should be pleased with it. The trailers are slightly letterboxed on the letterbox side and in full screen on the full screen side. The stereo surround sound isn't as impressive, but the Dolby Digital track is super, with lots of directional animal noises and other powerful effects. The film is also available in French in standard stereo and can be accompanied by English, French or Spanish subtitles. There is a cast profile section that contains clips from other New Line films featuring the movie's stars.

The Isle of Wight Festival (see Message to Love the Isle of Wight Festival —The Movie)

It Could Happen To You (Columbia TriStar, 50862)

Poor Rosie Perez has the thankless job of playing the evil wife in the 1994 romantic lottery winner comedy. The part accentuates her ethnicity and a desire by her character to move beyond her station, which stands in contrast to the altruistic, squeaky goodness of the two heroes, played by Nicolas Cage and Bridget Fonda. Cage, verging at times upon a Jimmy Stewart impersonation, portrays a beat cop who offers to share the winnings of his lottery ticket with a waitress in lieu of a tip. The ticket is a winner and he follows through on his promise, to the chagrin of his wife, who eventually takes the two to court. The film presses all the right buttons, but some viewers will feel that it presses a few too many wrong ones as well.

The film is presented on one side in letterboxed format, with an aspect ratio of about 1.85:1 and an accommodation for enhanced 16:9 playback, and is in full screen format on the other side. The picture looks quite good, with excellent color detail and a sharp focus. Some shots are a little hazy, but that seems to be conceptual. The stereo surround sound and Dolby Digital sound are fine. The 101 minute program also has French and Spanish language tracks, optional English, French, or Spanish subtitles and a trailer.

It's a Wonderful Life (Artisan, 42071)

A perennial motion picture classic that can serve as a model in the shaping of one's values, **It's a Wonderful Life** teaches many les-

sons—the value of friendship, the way to be rid an enemy by discounting the enemy's potency—and it can even serve, in this harried, modern world, as an anchored reminder of the precious value of one's own existence. The joy that is shared at the movie's conclusion easily escapes the confines of a screen to embrace every viewer. **It's a Wonderful Life** has created its own community and, across the years, as people have seen it and felt it, life itself has become a bit more special. Frank Capra directed Jimmy Stewart in the 1946 feature.

The black-and-white full screen transfer has been given elaborate attention. After the opening credits, it is relatively spotless, with crisply defined contrasts and smooth, pure greys and blacks. There is some noticeable artifacting, however, in the darker areas of the screen. The monophonic sound is good, with clear, sharp tones and limited background noise. The 129 minute movie also has French and Spanish audio channels, and optional English, French and Spanish subtitles. On the other side of the platter, there is a trailer and two retrospective documentaries, a 22 minute program hosted by Tom Bosley and a 14 minute program hosted by Frank Capra, Jr. Both seem to cover the same material, a superficial overview of the film crew and the magic they created. Neither is captioned.

Ivan the Terrible Part I (Image, ID4577CODVD)
Ivan the Terrible Part II (Image, ID4578CODVD)

Although it is conceivable that a collector would obtain one of Sergei Eisenstein's magnificent final films from the Forties and not the other, it is unlikely. Both are legitimate classics of world cinema and both are entertaining. The sound is integrated, yet in no way diminishes the impact of the visual composition. Sergei Prokofiev's score is in grand harmony with the film's emotional impact. And the acting, although melodramatic, is well suited for the drama. The emotions of the characters are believable, or, in the case of the actor portraying a man who realizes he made the right decision in the nick of time, priceless. Eisenstein planned and storyboarded the films for several years before going into production. The image compositions have a binding force, locking a viewer's gaze to the screen.

Part I is a patriotic portrayal of the consolidation efforts by the ruler who first united Russia. It is straightforward and upbeat, as Ivan directs battle efforts and begins cleansing his court of aristocrats. The picture transfer looks fine for a war-era non-American black-and-white film. The image is nicely detailed and wear is manageable.

Part II was the inspiration for *Godfather Part II*, not only in title, but in the use of a sequel to present scenes from earlier as well as later events, and as an opportunity to explore established characters. The patriotism subsides in **Part II**, replaced by the paranoia of maintaining a power base (needless to say, Stalin was not as happy with it as he was with **Part I**). Both the picture and the sound are in passable condition. The film is in black-and-white, but has an extended (and well-preserved) color sequence. The image is sharp and blacks are pure.

The films are in Russian with permanent English subtitles. The monophonic sound is a little weak, but that just helps suppress the audio noise. **Part I** runs 99 minutes and **Part II** runs 85 minutes.

J

Jack Frost (Simitar, 7422)

A deliberately jokey gore thriller with a tacky special effects, the 1997 movie is sort of a holiday cheer alternative (the musical score makes ironic use of seasonal tunes). Through a carefully explained series of scientific accidents, the spirit of a serial killer is transferred to a snowman, who then goes upon a rampage of revenge. It is deliberately dumb, with enough blood to satisfy viewers who don't consider dumb to be a drawback.

The presentation is letterboxed with an aspect ratio of about 1.85:1 and no 16:9 enhancement. The color transfer looks fine. The stereo surround sound and Dolby Digital sound are rarely lively, but workable. The 89 minute program is not captioned.

The Jackal (Universal, 20262)

Bruce Willis, Richard Gere and Sidney Poitier star in the exciting action adventure film. It draws its inspiration from the 1973 thriller **The Day of the Jackal**, but it is a very different movie, with more of an emphasis upon character relationships and elaborate action sequences. Willis is the villain, an assassin who has apparently been hired to murder somebody important, and Poitier is the FBI agent trying to piece together the scheme and track down the killer. In a fresh plot turn that was not part of the earlier film, Gere is a former IRA assassin hired by Poitier's character to assist in the investigation. The performances and the interaction of the stars are enjoyable, and the film has a number of slick, boisterous action sequences to punctuate its intellectual thrills.

The 125 minute film is presented in dual-layer format and has been letterboxed with an aspect ratio of about 2.35:1 and an accommodation for enhanced 16:9 playback. The image is smooth, fleshtones are accurate and other hues are bright. The stereo surround sound is passable and the Dolby Digital track is super, with a strong bass, a carefully measured dimensionality and plenty of invigorating separation effects. The film is also available in French in regular stereo and can be supported by English, French or Spanish subtitles. Additionally, there is a 20 minute documentary, another 20 minutes of outtakes, a trailer and a modest collection of production stills. There is also a very brief production essay and a cast profile section. The 20 minute documentary is made up primarily of interviews conducted during the filming, with the cast, the director and other crew members discussing their concepts and hopes for the film. The outtakes consist primarily of two lengthy sequences that were dropped from the movie for time considerations, including one that duplicates a sequence in the older film. It is great to see the scenes, but it is clear, since the film's continuity was unaffected by their removal, that they didn't have to be in the film. There is also an 'alternate' ending that has some minor differences from the finalized ending, with Gere given more heroic actions in the latter.

The director, Michael Caton-Jones, also provides a commentary during the unspooling of the film, and it is a good one. He consistently explains why things were done in the manner they were done, offers up many esoteric pieces of filmmaking advice, and goes into good detail about the production and contributing personnel. To give just a few examples—he talks about how he had to compensate for the difference in height between Gere and Poitier; about Gere's beard in the beginning of the film and why it had to go once the studio saw the rushes; about shooting scenes where a dozen people sit around a table talking (and how to get them from a standing to a sitting position without it appearing choreographed); about using a desk lamp for intimacy in a well-lit room; about why cinematographers hate the color orange except in a sunset; about what viewers do and don't notice in a scene; about 'flipping' an image during the editing to create a continuity where none had been shot; and about how the film was pieced together from a wide variety of locations.

Jackie Chan: My Story (import, MSDVD03798)

An excellent profile of Chan, the documentary includes extensive interviews with him. Shot around the time he was making **Mr. Nice Guy**, the program was recorded in both Chinese and in English (he shot the interviews twice, once in each language), and that is how it is presented, the 72 minute Chinese version on one side and the 74 minute English version on the other. The show is loaded with terrific clips, including a summary of his major films and best stunts, an identification of his biggest accidents, an expla-

nation of his various techniques, a fascinating contrast between the American version of *The Protector* and the fight scenes he re-staged for the Asian market, and clips from his earliest movies as a child and as an extra and stunt man in Bruce Lee's movies. Both sides can be supported by subtitles in English, traditional Chinese, simplified Chinese, Japanese, Korean, Bahasa Malaysian, Bahasa Indonesian and Thai ("Sekalipun Jackie tak lagi membuat film seni tangan ke tangan, kaki ke kaki dan adegan baku hantam de filmnya tak henti-hentinya membuat standar baru untuk industri film"). Included on the DVD with the film are essays in English on how the movie was made, Chan's biography, a look at his 'ten best movies' (not the ten we'd pick), an excellent collection of still photos from throughout his life and career, and a trailer.

Jackie Chan: My Stunts (import, MSDVD04898)

The terrific documentary, directed by Jackie Chan, is about how he stages his stunts in his films. Like **Jackie Chan: My Story**, the program was shot simultaneously in Chinese and in English, with the Chinese version, which runs 97 minutes, appearing on one side and the English version, which runs 94 minutes, appearing on the other. Film students will pay particular attention to the tricks of the trade that Chan reveals (the grunting the characters do during their fights are actually instructions to move forward, duck, and that sort of thing), but even casual viewers will find the material fascinating. There is extensive behind-the-scenes footage from **Who Am I?** and **Rush Hour**, a concise explanation of how the different kinds of stunts, such as fights, falls, chases, etc., are staged, and a look at how Chan and his stuntmen train and plan their stunts.

The picture quality is excellent. Some of the film clips are a bit old, but the fresh material is bright, with crisp, smooth colors. The English track, which has a stereophonic musical score, can be supported by optional English, Spanish traditional Chinese, simplified Chinese, Japanese, Vietnamese, Bahasa Malaysian and Thai subtitles. The Chinese version can be supported by English subtitles, too.

Jackie Chan's Who Am I? (Columbia TriStar, 02717)

Chan, who also directed, stars as a CIA operative who loses his memory. Everybody is trying to kill him and he doesn't know why. Shot in South Africa and The Netherlands, the stunts are super (he slides down the slightly angled side of a thirty-story skyscraper—just watching him do it made our heart jump out of our mouth), the narrative is adequately constructed and decently paced, and there is plenty of humor mixed with the thrills. Unlike many American Chan releases, the 108 minute program doesn't appear to be missing any footage, either.

The film is presented on one side in letterboxed format, with an aspect ratio of about 2.35:1 and an accommodation for enhanced 16:9 playback, and is in cropped format on the other side, though practical uses for the cropped image are limited. The color transfer looks super, with bright, crisp hues and accurate fleshtones, and the film itself looks sleek and glossy. Although there is some dubbing, even among the English-speaking characters, at least part of the film appears to have been shot in English. The stereo surround soundtrack is fine and the Dolby Digital track is great, with many easy-to-spot separation effects and plenty of energy. The film is also available in French in standard stereo and can be supported by English or French subtitles ("Je suis peut-être amnésique, mais je ne suis pas stupide!"). There is a post-**Rush Hour** trailer, as well.

Jacob's Ladder (Artisan, 60458)

The 1990 Adrian Lyne film, an acknowledged adaptation of *Occurrence at Owl Creek Bridge*, about a Vietnam vet, played by Tim Robbins, who is having flashbacks and seeing demons, can seem intriguing, but if the viewer is not mesmerized by the concept, then the film can seem contrived or tiresome. The supplementary features, however, bring a complexity and depth to the drama that may not be as accessible if one has only viewed the film.

The picture is letterboxed with an aspect ratio of about 1.82:1, with an accommodation for enhanced 16:9 playback. The image is a little soft and colors are a bit dull, though fleshtones seem a little truer. The stereo surround sound and Dolby Digital sound are rather subdued. The 116 minute film can be supported by Spanish subtitles and English closed captioning. There is a trailer and a rather unnerving TV commercial, three significant deleted scenes, along with a cast profile section and some production notes.

Lyne provides a reasonably good running commentary. He does state the obvious at times, but he also explains what he was trying to achieve, why he made certain choices and what it was like working with his crew. He delves into the film's meanings, and talks about coming to terms with death and other metaphysical quandaries. There is also a half hour documentary that shows a lot of behind-the-scenes footage, explains how some of the major effect sequences were accomplished, and provides a further elaboration on the themes broached by Lyne. The most important part of the supplement, however, is the 15 minute collection of three deleted scenes. The scenes were dropped to tighten the film's running time, but each also adds to the complexity of the story, so that removing all three dumbed the movie down considerably. The scenes don't solve the mystery of the character's state, but each adds more enigmas, filling in the bigger picture, even if it is only with more riddles.

Jade (Paramount, 329867)

Both bad screenwriter Joe Eszterhas and bad since the mid-Seventies movie director William Friedkin have an adolescent fascination with pornography that they keep itching to slip into a major feature film and they come pretty close to doing so in **Jade**. David Caruso stars as an assistant district attorney investigating the murder of a rich man who hired women to place his friends and associates in compromising poses for hidden cameras. Linda Fiorentino and Chazz Palminteri are also featured. Littered with sex paraphernalia, the film seems to live for how much it can get away with showing or implying ('strong scenes of aberrant sexuality' is how the ratings tag puts it), and the more sex stuff the filmmakers try to include the less legitimate the movie seems. That said, however, **Jade** is still fairly enjoyable. It has a very slick look to it, some great action scenes, including a San Francisco car chase that makes **Bullitt** look like a Sunday stroll, and a plot that, while it may be ludicrous, conforms sufficiently to the requirements of a mystery to pull the viewer along.

The picture is presented in full screen only, but the framing is viable. The color transfer is fine, with sharp, accurate hues. The stereo surround sound and Dolby Digital sound are very good, with strong, clear separations and a powerful punch. The 94 minute program has English captioning and a trailer.

Jailhouse Rock (MGM, 906611)

The 1957 Elvis Presley musical is presented on one side in letterboxed format, with an aspect ratio of about 2.35:1 and an accommodation for enhanced 16:9 playback, and in cropped format on the other side. The picture has a soft focus, dark contrasts and impure whites (the LD looks better). The source material also has a number of scratches and other minor markings. The monophonic sound is also a bit weak, but the soundtrack seems functional. The cropped image has the same flaws as the letterboxed image, with the scratches and softness looking somewhat more noticeable than on the letterboxed image. Neither presentation is a disaster, but it is not the best that could be done with the film. The 96 minutes program is also available in French or Spanish dialogue (the singing remains in English), and come with English, French or Spanish subtitles ("Le directeur donnait une fête dans la prison du comté…"), as well as a trailer. The more Presley films one sees, the more respect one has for the movie's coherency, about an ex-con trying to make a start as a singer.

Jamaica Inn (Kino, K105)

Although it is often considered to be one of Alfred Hitchcock's worst films, we have always found **Jamaica Inn** to be both charming and entertaining. The 1939 period thriller, based upon a Daphne Du Maurier story, is about pirates in Cornwall who shift or suppress warning lights during storms and then raid the shipwrecked boats. Maureen O'Hara is a young visitor to the Inn, unaware that her aunt, who runs the Inn, is married to one of the pirates, and Charles Laughton is a local lord or something and the secret pirate boss. The sets and black-and-white cinematography are striking and the star performances are delightful. It was O'Hara's first screen role, but she is in full command of the spunky, self-reliant personality she brought to most of her subsequent characters. The narrative is rather simple, with a lot of sneaking around (one of Hitchcock's best staging devices in the film, and it is used several times, is to have two sets of characters in view, with one unaware of the other's presence), but there is sufficient activity to keep a viewer interested and entertained. Frankly we can't understand why the people who don't like it don't like it except perhaps that they want to pigeonhole Hitchcock into one kind of movie, the contemporary thriller, and then, curiously, claim he was the world's greatest film director, even though, to their minds, he only made one kind of movie well. Anyway, it is a fun film and proof that Hitchcock could be quite versatile when he wanted to.

The source material is regularly visited by speckles and, around the reel change points, the damage gets a bit heavier, but on the whole, the image is fairly nice, with well-defined contrasts and a crisp focus. The presentation is substantially windowboxed and the monophonic sound has some age-related noise and range limitations. The 98 minute program is not captioned.

James Brown: Body Heat (Pioneer, PA98594D)

A concert from the highpoint of Brown's big resurgence during the disco era, the 1979 performance, captured in Monterey, is not slick or overly choreographed, and Brown retains an earthy attitude that gave him an edge over most of his competition in those days. The highpoint of the hour concert: A stunningly unexpected rendition of *Georgia on My Mind* that moves through a full range of approaches and that he seems to pull himself inside-out to complete.

The source material is smeary, badly colored and weakly detailed, and the transfer can't do much with it, though the camera stays close enough that you can make out the details of Brown's face most of the time. The stereo surround sound is good and the Dolby Digital sound is better, with stronger, more precise details and more power. There is no captioning.

James Dean: Hill Number One / I Am a Fool (LaserLight, 82014)
James Dean: The James Dean Story / The Bells of Cockaigne (LaserLight, 82013)

Two of James Dean's black-and-white television appearances from the early Fifties, *I Am a Fool* and *The Bells of Cockaigne*, provide valuable looks at the young actor developing his craft. *I Am a Fool* is a 25 minute teleplay by Sherwood Anderson with Dean, Natalie Wood and Eddie Albert as Dean's older self, reminiscing about his one, lost chance at love. Dean's manner is evocative of Dennis Hopper. He gives a kind of sloppy, overindulgent performance, but it is fascinating to see him in the raw. The story is simple and direct, and even in these sophisticated times it pulls at your emotions because of its directness.

Dean's performance is more sophisticated in *Bells of Cockaigne*. He plays a warehouse worker, trying to make ends meet and support his family, who enters into a poker game on payday. Gene Lockhart stars, as a fellow worker who takes pity on him. The 1953 half-hour episode (not an hour as the jacket claims), from the *Armstrong Circle Theater* and replete with commercials for Armstrong tile, is a trifle of a drama that would be utterly forgotten were it not for Dean's presence. His performance, however, is very detailed and affecting, a giant leap over what he did in *I Am a Fool*, and it sparks your imagination for how his other performances might have been had he not died.

Dean has a small role with a handful of lines in the *Family Theater* ensemble religious program, *Hill Number One*. Essentially a dramatization of the three days between Christ's death and His resurrection, Dean is the disciple, John. Of course, your eyes are riveted to him, but he is still finding his way and not using the camera to any advantage. He functions more as an extra than anything else. As for the hour-long drama, it seems to be talking to the converted, but it does play like a low budget Biblical epic and is sporadically entertaining. Roddy McDowall, Michael Ansara and a few other familiar performers are also buried in the cast.

The James Dean Story is an excellent retrospective documentary on Dean's life and brief career, produced by Robert Altman in 1957. The 80 minute feature contains many photos and interviews, along with a couple rare clips, while attempting to evoke Dean's life and times in a somewhat artistic manner.

Hill Number One was shot on film. The image is a bit grainy, and there is lots of wear, but details are reasonably clear and contrasts are well defined. *I Am a Fool* appears to be a kinescope of a kinescope, depicting a re-broadcast of the *General Electric Theater* program after Dean's death, with an introduction by Ronald Reagan. The image is soft, the darker portions of the screen are smeary, contrasts are limited and again there is a lot of wear, but Dean's expressions are clear and the presentation is viable. The image on *Bells of Cockaigne*, another kinescope, is smeary but workable. The black-and-white picture on *James Dean Story* is reasonably sharp, but contrasts are weak, losing detail in shadows, and there is a lot of displacement artifacting.

On both DVDs, the monophonic sound is noisy but coherent (the music on *James Dean Story* also quivers), and the programs can be supported by Spanish, Japanese and Chinese subtitles ("La familia que ora unida permanece unida"), although there is no English captioning. A letterboxed trailer for *East of Eden* has also been included on **Hill Number One / I Am a Fool** and a trailer for *Rebel without a Cause* is on **James Dean Story / Bells of Cockaigne**.

Jammin' with the Blues Greats (Image, ID4706LYDVD)

British blues enthusiasts join the stage with their idols in the 90 minute 1982 concert, performed in New Jersey at the Capitol Theater. John Mayall and his Bluesbreakers mix with Etta James, Albert King, Sippie Wallace, Buddy Guy and Junior Wells. The show is an enjoyable blend of classic and adapted styles, with the personalities of the performers contributing almost as much as their musicianship to the concert's pleasures. The cameras are close to the performers and catch them responding to one another effectively. The colors are a little dull, the image is a bit soft and the murky lighting creates some faint background artifacting, but the performers are lit well enough that their expressions and fingering are always easy to make out. The stereo sound has a limited dimensionality and has not been mixed to place your viewing room in the center of the stage, but it has an adequate range.

Janet Jackson: The Velvet Rope Tour Live in Concert (Image, ID5518ERDVD)

Janet Jackson puts on a Madonna-style spectacle concert in Madison Square Garden on the 121 minute program. Backed by a huge screen that was probably the only way most concert attendees were able to see her, Jackson performs a series of elaborate song-and-dance numbers, with many costume changes. It's an impressive act and should segue well into a Las Vegas revue should she ever decide to go that route. The music is just about the least of it, and you really wonder sometimes if she's actually singing or just lip-synching the numbers, particularly when you can hear her vocals while her lips aren't moving. The sound is more cacophonous than a studio recording but, on the other hand, compared to Madonna's concerts, it's lyric opera.

The picture looks fine. By necessity, Jackson is well lit so she will show up on that screen. Some of the crowd shots are a little grainy, but who cares, right? The Dolby Digital soundtrack is good. As we imply, the vocals are a little drowned out by the environment, but they're coherent, and the instruments are adequately separated. The standard stereo track, however, is substantially less energetic, with fewer separations and duller tones. The program is not captioned. The chapter encoding doesn't break up the medleys.

Janine & Vince Neil: Hardcore & Uncensored X-rated (Vivid, UPC#0073214592)

Celebrating that anything-you-can-do-I-can-do-better world of rock musician oneupsmanship, the program is both more professional and more spontaneous than the **Pamela & Tommy Lee** fiasco. Neil is a member of Motley Crue, for those of you who are too young to follow the old heavy metal groups. This being a video tape recording, there is one sequence on the 57 minute program that runs uninterrupted for more than a half hour, where Neil and Janine are joined by a third woman who seems much too friendly to be Neil's mother-in-law. The eroticism is effectively executed and Neil's stamina is enviable. While the colors are weak and the recording goes in and out of focus as the bodies rock back and forth, the presentation is viable. The sound is fine.

Janine: Extreme Close-Up X-rated (Vivid, UPC#0073215510)

The 'documentary' program provides an exceptionally strong emotional context for its erotic sequences. It features interviews with the actress, who talks about how much she enjoys performing, etc. It doesn't matter if she's telling the truth or not when she says she has a 'dream job.' What is important is that she is totally convincing when she says it, as is her 'initiation' of another actress in what is apparently the latter's first lesbian experience.

Colors are flat and the image is grainy at times, with some sequences looking stronger and sharper than others. The conversations aren't always well miked, but the dialogue is always coherent. The program runs 72 minutes and co-stars Jill Kelly, Chelsea Blue, Holly Mason and Tatiana. The DVD also contains alternate angle sequences and elaborate hardcore interactive promotional features.

Jason and the Argonauts (Columbia TriStar, 00259)

The 1963 production is often considered to be Ray Harryhausen's finest effort because of the inventiveness of the special effects, their strong integration with the narrative and the narrative's relative fidelity to Greek legends.

Although there is room for improvement, the picture is smoother, better detailed and much more solid than any previous home video release of the title. For the most part, the colors are more accurate as well. Many scenes that probably should be taking place at night look like they are taking place at sunset instead, but the colors look so rich in these sequences that real day-for-night processing looks murky and alienating in comparison. Fleshtones on the DVD look somewhat orange, and fleshtones on the Columbia TriStar LD are much closer to true fleshtones. Many other hues (but not all) have a cleaner, truer look on the LD. The picture on the DVD, however, still seems classier and better, because it is so sharp and because the colors that have been used are so deep.

The picture on the DVD is letterboxed on one side, with an aspect ratio of about 1.85:1 and an accommodation for enhanced 16:9 playback, and is in full screen format on the other side. Interestingly, while the letterboxing adds a lot of picture information to the sides and takes almost nothing off the top and bottom in comparison to the Columbia LD, the LD turns out to be cropped on all four sides, because the letterboxing masks much more off the bottom in comparison to the full screen DVD image and adds very little to the sides. The monophonic sound on the DVD is much nicer than the LD, which sounds muted in comparison. The 104 minute program also has (weaker) French and Spanish language tracks, optional English, French or Spanish subtitles, a trailer, and a brief conversation between Harryhausen and John Landis.

Jazz Scene USA: Cannonball Adderley Sextet / Teddy Edwards Sextet (Shanachie, 6310)

The collection features two episodes from an excellent 1962 TV music program, **Jazz Scene USA**. Each episode runs about 25 minutes and features the identified artist, with introductions and brief conversation between the numbers by Oscar Brown, Jr. The programs provide a terrific glimpse of early Sixties jazz (you'll probably recognize Adderley's rendition of *Work Song*—dut dit da dut dit da dut dit da dah). Additionally, while Adderley's keyboardist is white, everybody else in both episodes is black, an exceedingly rare occurrence in the early Sixties, presenting an impressive, positive view of black culture.

The black-and-white picture looks super. Lines are sharp, contrasts are carefully detailed, and the source material is free of distortion or wear. The image is often vivid. The monophonic sound is also great, and comparable to most recordings from that era. The shows are not captioned.

The Jazz Singer (Artisan, 33334)

The dopey 1980 Neil Diamond vehicle directed by Richard Fleischer is a remake of the mother of all motion picture musicals. Except for Catlin Adams, however, who gives a solid, affecting performance as the hero's first wife—like the only tree not being blown over in a windstorm of stupidity—the acting is awful, and it is made worse by the utterly unlikely sequence of events that makes up the plot. Laurence Olivier, in tightly-wound self-conscious pieces, portrays Diamond's father, a cantor who rejects his son's career choice—famous pop star—because it goes against the family tradition. The film leaps diagonally from one unlikelihood to the next, and the actors stand around pretending as if this sort of thing happens every day. The film's opening montage, set to Diamond's song about immigration, is the film's highpoint, and it is all downhill after that.

The presentation is in letterboxed format only, with an aspect ratio of about 1.8:1 and no 16:9 enhancement. The picture is fairly blurry, with slightly bland hues and dull fleshtones. The stereo sound brings an adequate dimensionality and energy to the music, but doesn't offer much else. The 115 minute feature (not 111 minutes as the jacket suggests) is adequately closed captioned. The chapter encoding and jacket guide are good, and the menu offers a separate chapter access to the songs.

Jefferson Starship: The Definitive Concert (Image, ID4707LYDVD)

An old Jefferson Starship concert with lame inserts about an outer space pirate radio station, the 63 minute program features hits from various stages in the group's career, sung without much flavor (and without Marty Balin) and with rote instrumentals. There is a general softness to the picture, but the stage is fairly well lit, so facial expressions and fingering are usually clear. The sound is vaguely stereophonic, but there is little dimensionality.

Jenteal: Extreme Close-Up X-rated (Vivid, UPC#0073215517)

A number of hardcore performers are interviewed on the documentary program. They talk about their 'first times,' what they like to do at home and even get into weightier matters, such as a convincing differentiation between what they do and prostitution. The interviews are intercut with hardcore erotic sequences that appear to have been shot expressly for the program. It is not important that what they are saying is true or not, what is important is that they appear to be believably sincere.

The picture is a little murky, but the erotic sequences are better lit and colors are reasonably bright. The monophonic sound is okay. The program runs 71 minutes and features Jenteal, Mila, Leanna Heart, and Lexi Eriksson. The DVD also contains alternate

angle sequences and elaborate hardcore interactive promotional features.

Jeremiah Johnson (Warner, 11061)

A highly repeatable adventure film about solitude and survival, Robert Redford stars as a Nineteenth Century mountain man etching out a life for himself in the Rockies. The film has a kind of symmetrical structure as he meets various characters and interacts with them, pretty much one at a time, and then meets them again later on. He does take on a family of sorts at one point, giving the movie an emotional core, but what remains most compelling about the film—and what can survive multiple viewings the best—is the sense the film achieves of depicting one human being alone in the woods making a life for himself. It is a good movie to watch without company. The color transfer is beautiful, with bright, crisp hues and accurate fleshtones. The 1972 film is presented in letterboxed format on one side and in cropped format on the other, but that is a waste of time, since it was shot in widescreen and requires the presence of the wilderness around the hero to convey its deepest meanings. The highly gratifying letterboxing has an aspect ratio of about 2.35:1 and an accommodation for enhanced 16:9 playback. The letterboxing can also accommodate 16:9 enhanced playback. The music has been remastered for stereo surround and Dolby Digital surround. The dialogue and sound effects remain up front, but the dimensionality of the music doesn't hurt and adds to the film's sense of grandeur. The Dolby Digital track has a stronger presence than the standard track. The movie is also available in French in mono and can be accompanied by English, French or Spanish subtitles. There is a small cast and crew profile and some brief production notes, along with a good trailer and an entertaining 'making of' featurette. The 116 minute film also has an Overture and Intermission.

The Jerk (Universal, 20214)

Carl Reiner directed Steve Martin in the 1979 rags-to-riches-to-rags comedy, Martin's debut as a leading actor, showcasing Martin's once eccentric brand of humor. The picture is dark, with pinkish fleshtones, though the effect too severe and many sequences look okay. The 94 minute film is presented in full screen format, and the monophonic sound is passable. There is also a French language track, and the show can be supported by English or French subtitles ("¡Llegó la guía de telefono nueva! ¡Llegó la guía de telefono nueva!"). There is a good production notes section, a cast profile section and an ambitious theatrical trailer.

Jerry Herman's Broadway at the Hollywood Bowl (Universal, VDV5852)

A 116 minute all-star concert, Leslie Uggams, Lorna Luft and Lee Roy Reams perform most of the numbers, backed by the Los Angeles Philharmonic, but Carol Channing, Rita Moreno, Bea Arthur, Michael Feinstein and George Hearn also sing, while the likes of Liza Minnelli, Paul McCartney and Angela Lansbury appear in taped inserts to salute Herman. The songs come from such shows as *Hello Dolly*, *Mack and Mabel*, *Mame*, and *La Cage Aux Folles*. The best segment is a medley of variations on the title tune to *Hello, Dolly*, but there are a number of less well known songs—particularly several from *Mack and Mabel*—that gain life from their exposure and only a few that fail to strike a spark. Although there is some slight artifacting around the edges, the picture is brightly lit and colors are crisp. The stereo mix is not elaborate, but the recording is fairly good, imparting the live atmosphere without losing the immediacy of the singers.

Jerry Lee Lewis: The Story of Rock and Roll (Pioneer, PA98590D)

Although there is a segment on Lewis' disastrous British tour, the 52 minute collection of performance clips is mostly music rather than biography, depicting Lewis at all the stages in his life as he rocks and rolls. A single concert program would probably communicate his talent and energy a little more effectively, but the clips are terrific, the music sounds great and the changes that occur as he ages are fascinating.

Some of the footage is in black and white, and some is in color with various levels of brightness. The stereo sound is wonderful and the DVD also has a Dolby Digital track, though we tended to prefer the hardness and directness of the standard track. A biography of Lewis that runs a few paragraphs is also included. There is no captioning.

Jerry Maguire (Columbia TriStar, 82535/82539)

An intelligent romantic comedy, Tom Cruise portrays a sports agent who has lost all his clients but one and has to rebuild both his professional life and his personal life. All 138 minutes and 43 seconds of the movie are fit onto one layer of one side of the DVD, though we could detect no significant artifacting in what is essentially a movie of people standing and talking, albeit quite charmingly. The film is letterboxed with an aspect ratio of about 1.85:1 and an accommodation for enhanced 16:9 playback. The colors strong and the image is sharp. The Dolby Digital track is stronger and more detailed than the standard stereo track. The film's audio mix is energetic and smooth, and the pop songs that show up in the musical score sound marvelous. The program is also available in French or Spanish (without Dolby Digital) and comes only with Spanish subtitles ("¡Muéstrame el dinero!"), though there is apparently English closed captioning.

Jerry Springer Show: Too Hot for TV! 2000 (Realbiz, 6514)

In all the honest-to-goodness fights that we have seen, there is one common ingredient that is completely missing from the supposed fights on the stage of the *Jerry Springer Show*—blood. The only time you do see blood is when a character—excuse us, guest—accidentally stumbles or something. There is no blood and very little coherency on **Jerry Springer Show: Too Hot for TV! 2000**, also known as *Welcome to the Hellenium!*. Taken from Springer's daily talk show, where guests share secrets on the air to alarmed friends and loved ones, the program presents footage that children arriving home from school in time for the show on TV would be psychically harmed if they saw, at least in theory. Instead of presenting complete segments from the show, however, parts of segments are reeled off without much organization, and different pieces of one segment can appear in a half dozen places. There are some amusing moments in the reactions of the guests to discovered infidelities and that sort of thing, particularly when the guests have exceptionally regional accents, but without context the clips don't mean much and are less interesting than the slower building sequences in the actual TV show. There is plenty of cussing, hair pulling, suggestive dialogue and flashes of nudity, but it gets stale fairly quickly. The program runs about 45 minutes, but is accompanied by a 20 minute addendum that borders on softcore pornography as it depicts the antics of lap dancers and that sort of thing.

The picture is passable, though color quality and fleshtone intensity varies from one clip to the next. The 'stereo' sound is generally centered. There is no captioning. The program also features a 4 minute interview with Springer in which he talks about how the show evolved.

Jesus Christ Superstar (Universal, 20524)

Norman Jewison's energized 1973 adaptation of Andrew Lloyd Webber's musical seems to get better and better with each passing year. Webber's music runs out of steam after the first half hour, but Jewison has staged the film so creatively that by then the viewer is totally wrapped up in the premise and more than willing to ride it through to the end. Shot in the Israeli desert, the film depicts a street performance of the musical that gets interrupted by military maneuvers, but is seemingly even more affected by the passions of the characters the cast members are representing. Because the mu-

sical deals with a subject that everybody has a heartfelt opinion upon, its approach may irritate some, but in addition to presenting a viable take on the story of Christ, the film genuinely captures the noblest aspects of the Sixties counter-culture, drawing a pointed and moving parallel between this nobility and the finer aspects of Christian values. With the help of Webber's music, Jewison uses every pre-MTV editing trick he can come up with, creating a zippy, energetic intensity that is solidified by the depth of the film's subject. People tend to put the Sixties down, particularly now since its representatives are running everything, but the film captures the ideal, evoking what was best about the era and what is best about humankind.

The film is in letterboxed format with an aspect ratio of about 2.35:1 and no 16:9 enhancement. The letterboxing is essential for conveying the full power of Jewison's design. The color transfer looks terrific. Shot in the desert, the film is supposed to look dusty and a bit makeshift, but fleshtones are accurate, bright hues, when they do appear, look super, and the image is very crisp. The source material is speckled in places, but is free of significant wear, and darker sequences have a touch of natural grain.

The stereo sound is a bit more aged. The music still sounds terrific, but its aural limitations are readily apparent, and even dimensionality is tentative. Fortunately, the 107 minute film's format accommodates these drawbacks effectively. There is a four-track Dolby Digital channel as well as the standard stereo track. Definitions are a little better detailed, though the two are basically interchangeable. The film's dialogue is entirely sung, and the DVD has a stereophonic French language track in addition to its English tracks. There's no listing of whose voices are employed, but it sounds terrific and makes it worth watching the movie at least a dozen times more. There is also English and Spanish subtitling ("Jesucristo superestrella. ¿Crees que eres, Lo que dicen que eres?"), along with production notes, a cast-and-director profile section and a trailer.

Jezebel (MGM, 906679)

The 1938 film is an enjoyable vehicle for Bette Davis, as her character must pass through some extensive emotional and moral changes, all of which happen right before the viewer's eyes. It is set in the South before the Civil War and co-stars Henry Fonda. Davis won an Oscar for her portrayal of a headstrong Southern belle who muffs her romantic life and then has to backtrack and expose herself to humiliation and disease to reclaim it. Fun stuff. The picture on the 103 minute presentation is very sharp, and details, such as facial creases, are clearly visible.

The monophonic sound is okay and the Dolby Digital mono track is even stronger. The noise inherent in the older recordings is also more pronounced, but management of the volume controls can keep such natural discrepancies in check. The film is also available in Spanish and comes with English, French or Spanish subtitles. A re-release trailer is included, as well.

JFK (Warner, 12614)

You don't have to believe in witches to get excited when Toto escapes, and you don't have to believe Oliver Stone's manipulation of the evidence in the John F. Kennedy assassination to enjoy his thrilling depiction of its aftermath. Not only is the film a highly involving mystery story with genuine thematic resonance, it is also history in the making—not truth, but the molding of the truth so that it will endure the tests of time. In the same way that all historians bend the facts to fit their personality, so has Stone created a work which really shakes things up. If his specific charges are wrong, his generalized condemnations—that those in power seem to think they are above the law, and that the country's economic base will not voluntarily unhinge itself—are not only valid, but can be applied to a much wider variety of topics than just Kennedy's assassination, such as environmental issues and social discontent. He accomplishes his goals through some very clever editing that makes it difficult to tell where reality leaves off and fiction begins, casting prominent stars in bit parts to suggest legitimacy, and presenting Kevin Costner as the hero, a tenacious New Orleans District Attorney trying to follow up leads that point to high places. Stone and Costner achieve an ideal balance, making the hero just bland enough so that his story does not supersede the big picture, but tightening the emotional tension as the investigation progresses to turn what could have been as dull as acted-out transcripts into a gripping detective story.

The 206 minute *Special Edition Director's Cut* is spread to two sides in letterboxed format. After a full screen opening montage, the image is letterboxed with an aspect ratio of about 2.35:1 and no 16:9 enhancement. The film has a mix of image styles, some of which are deliberately grainy, but it is clear that the transfer is excellent. Digital artifacts, however, are also a little more prevalent than usual, especially in the background during the jiggled camera movements. The stereo surround sound has not been remixed for 5-channel Dolby, so neither the 3-channel Dolby Digital track nor the standard stereo surround soundtrack have much color or power. The film is accompanied by English, French or Spanish subtitles and comes with a brief cast profile.

The excellent jacket chapter guide makes note of scenes that were not in the theatrical release. The additional sequences are primarily limited to a few additional subjects that were dropped from the center of the film, some dealing with minor activities of the conspirators and others dealing with the increasing antagonism directed at the hero. The most memorable is an apparently narrow escape from some kind of undefined setup in an airport restroom. The film's brilliant dramatic construction is unaffected one way or the other by the additions. Several of the sequences are flamboyant and add some flavor to the proceedings, but it is easy enough to understand why they were dropped from the theatrical release.

Jimi Hendrix Live at the Isle of Wight 1970 (Image, ID4394CADVD)

It isn't a concert we would recommend to introduce Jimi Hendrix to an uninitiated viewer, but fans will be happy with the fresh material on the 55 minute program. Hendrix gives a somewhat modest performance—it's as if he wasn't stoned enough—and the camera angles rarely capture his fingering or convey the excitement of his performance. In addition to his standard numbers, he plays *Sgt. Pepper* and *God Save the Queen*. On the whole, the set is great, but he has shown a more dynamic presence and given riskier performances on other programs. The glimpses of the festival, incidentally, are fascinating.

The picture is grainy and the colors have that Sixties rock concert blandness, but the transfer appears to have squeezed as much out of the source material as can be had. The image is also invaded by vertical scratches at times. The stereo sound is nothing great, but it has some dimensionality to it. There is no captioning.

Jingle All the Way (Fox, 4109066)

Arnold Schwarzenegger stars in a role that seems to have been designed for a Chevy Chase type. The part has been modified to include gags that make use of Schwarzenegger's physique, but his performance as a distracted but concerned father (who tries to find a popular toy for his son the day before Christmas) is totally unconvincing, and his attempts at comic pratfalls are woeful. The film is rescued by a strong third act, but getting there is torture. Sinbad, playing his principal nemesis in the rush for the toy, also seems miscast.

The picture is letterboxed with an aspect ratio of about 1.85:1 and no 16:9 enhancement. The color transfer is excellent and the image is very sharp. The stereo surround sound and menu-activated Dolby Digital sound are also in good shape, and the 1996 film does have a few scattered directional effects that are worth pumping up. The 85 minute program is also available in French (but not Spanish as is suggested on the jacket cover) in standard stereo and can be supported by English or Spanish subtitles. There is a trailer and brief profiles of three cast members.

Joe Cocker Live: Across from Midnight Tour (Image, ID4624ERDVD)

Performing beneath an elaborately decorated and impressive looking arch, Joe Cocker delivers an equally decorative and impressive performance. Shot in Berlin in 1997, the 86 minute concert features all of Cocker's hits and other classic tunes. His performance is both fresh and precise, with the live environment bringing just enough of an edge to prevent the music from seeming overly pure. It also helps that the picture and sound are in such good condition. The image is very sharp and colors are vivid, taking the world's most famous air guitarist out of Berlin and placing him in the center of your living room. The stereo sound is finely detailed and effectively mixed, so that the live atmosphere adds to the flavor of the sound instead of suppressing it. By the way, not only has Cocker not appeared to have aged in the thirty years since Woodstock, he actually looks a bit younger.

Joe Kidd (Universal, 20288)

Clint Eastwood also stars in John Sturges' 1972 feature, from a script by Elmore Leonard. The film is in letterboxed format with an aspect ratio of about 2.35:1 and no 16:9 enhancement. The picture quality is excellent. The color quality is excellent, with bright hues, rich fleshtones, and a very crisp, precise and highly satisfying image. The monophonic sound is a little soft, but adequate, and the film is also available in French and Spanish, with English or Spanish subtitles ("Quiero ver a un hombre llamado Joe Kidd"). There are some good production notes that talk about problems in the 1972 film's creation, a cast and director profile, and a theatrical trailer that knew how to sell Eastwood. Robert Duvall, with wonderful diction, portrays the villain in the 89 minute feature. Character logic is rampantly inconsistent, but the film, about a hunt for a Spanish-American leader who is protesting land development, still has a way of growing on you, thanks to the performances, Sturges' mastery of the western genre and Leonard's feel for political conflict.

Joe's Apartment (Warner, 14042)

We don't know why **Joe's Apartment** wasn't a hit because it is a very funny movie, about cockroaches and the poor slob they live with. The roaches think, talk, sing, dance, surf the sewers and perform a complete Busby Berkeley-style production number, including a swimming sequence in a dirty toilet bowl. The special effects are marvelous. The plot isn't much more complicated than a half hour TV show (and the 80 minute movie isn't much longer), but the dialogue is fairly witty and the timing is super.

The program is presented in full screen format only, clipping a little bit of picture information off the sides of the screen but revealing more on the top and bottom in comparison to letterboxed versions, but due to the nature of the film, you miss effects either way. The color transfer is very good, with solid hues and sharp contrasts. Although there is no Dolby Digital encoding, the stereo surround soundtrack is great, with funny directional dialogue popping up from so many places you'll think you're own viewing room has become infested. The 80 minute 1996 film also has a French stereo track and is closed captioned.

John Carpenter's Escape From L.A. (Paramount, 332497)

John Carpenter's 1996 rehash of the witty *Escape from New York*, **Escape from L.A.**, is presented in letterboxed format only, with an aspect ratio of about 2.35:1 and no 16:9 enhancement. We wonder if the technicians doing the image transfer could not have finessed the special effects sequences a little bit better, since foreground and background rarely blend smoothly (you might make a case that they're not supposed to, that the film is such a put-on the effects are deliberately hokey, but that would be self-defeating), but otherwise the picture looks great. The stereo surround sound is suitably boisterous and busy, and the Dolby Digital track is even more boisterous. The 101 minute program also has a French audio track in standard stereo, optional English and Spanish subtitles, and a trailer. Where the first film had a sense of discovery and inventiveness to it, **L.A.** offers nothing new. The scenery and special effects are more elaborate, but they are often unconvincing. Still, the movie is more fluid than, say, **Judge Dredd**, and it has a coherent if illogical plot, along with a number of amusing one-liners. Kurt Russell reprises his role from the first film, and many fans will see the opportunity of viewing Russell in action and character is reason enough for obtaining the film and watching it a bunch of times.

John Carpenter's Prince of Darkness (Image, ID4275USDVD)

Carpenter's 1987 film is an undergraduate mixture of physics and metaphysics that postulates Christ was an alien from outer space. It contains conceptual elements from many of Carpenter's other films, as well as his experienced command of mood and tension. The ending cops out by not finding a true science fiction resolution, but Carpenter has never been strong on endings anyway. He usually prefers an unnerving sleight of hand over a definitive show stopper. The film has some stimulating ideas and several good jumps, but it is best not analyzed too closely.

The letterboxing has an aspect ratio of about 2.35:1, with an accommodation for enhanced 16:9 playback. The letterboxing enhances the excitement in a number of sequences and gives the film a smoother, more determined feel in comparison to cropped versions. The color transfer looks very good, with accurate fleshtones, reasonably bright hues and a sharp focus. The film is technically in stereo, but dimensional effects are mostly non-existent. The music, Carpenter's never ending electronic duh-da, gets to you after a while, but that is what it is supposed to do. The 101 minute program is not captioned.

John Carpenter's Vampires (Columbia TriStar, 03064)

A terrific kickbutt action film, James Woods stars with Daniel Baldwin and the scintillating Sheryl Lee in a fairly basic and efficient story about people who hunt vampires for a living. The film is set in the Southwest and has the feel of a modern western. Woods, playing a good guy for once, spits out his nasty lines with marvelous comical flair, and the action scenes are so invigorating you wish they'd throw away the plot and just spend the whole movie raiding vampire nests. Yet the story isn't bad either, and since the film combines so many pleasing elements, those who are attracted to it in the first place are likely to play it many times over.

The film is presented on one side in letterboxed format, with an aspect ratio of about 2.35:1 and an accommodation for enhanced 16:9 playback, and in cropped format on the other side. The cropping is awkward and not worth watching. The picture is terrific, with a sharp focus and accurate fleshtones. The film has a dusty, brownish look at times, but hues are always as bright as is allowed, and the image is solid. The stereo surround sound is okay and the Dolby Digital track, which has a more pronounced dimensionality, is super. Carpenter's musical score envelops you and gets you in a perfect mood for wasting vampires. The 108 minute program is also available in French in standard stereo and can be supported by English or French subtitles ("D'abord, ils sont pas romantiques. C'est pas une bande de pédée s qui se baladent en tenue de soirée et séduisent tout le monde à vue avec des accents européens de merde"). There is an exciting trailer but, contrary to a jacket notation, we could not locate a 'photo gallery.' Carpenter provides a commentary track, describing the action and filling in production details. Carpenter tends to do better when he has someone else with him but, on the other hand, he has done quite a few commentary tracks now and is fairly adept at covering all the bases. Hence, even though he does spend an inordinate amount of time describing the obvious, it usually leads into more enlightened topics. He doesn't say enough, however, about how the special effects were achieved.

John Denver: A Portrait (Monterey, 326712)

The only problem with the 60 minute collection of John Denver music videos is that music videos didn't become a popular format until after Denver had written most of biggest hits, so there are only a couple well-known songs in the collection and the rest are second rate folk numbers with lyrics that tend to encourage literal visuals. Denver introduces each clip and talks a little about his life and philosophy, as well as about the song being presented. Colors are reasonably bright, but the image on the Denver introductions is soft, with hazy fleshtones, and the clips—mostly from the late Eighties—look a bit worn. The stereo sound is fine and we will refrain from commenting on Denver's ability to articulate notes on a scale. The songs are supported by optional English subtitles and the program is accompanied by a Denver profile.

John Grisham's The Rainmaker (Paramount, 335037)

If you didn't see the credits you would be hard-pressed to tell that it was a Francis Ford Coppola film. There's nothing in the movie, about a young lawyer taking on the world's evilest insurance company in his first case, that is particularly Coppola-esque (no cross-cutting to a cow being butchered or something, as hero tears the defense's case to shreds). Matt Damon stars, with Danny DeVito as his sidekick, Jon Voight as the insurance company's attorney and Claire Danes as his girlfriend. Mary Kay Place is almost unrecognizable in an intriguing performance as the client. The cast is great and there is plenty of story to keep the movie interesting, but it all seems somewhat contrived.

The 1997 feature is in letterboxed format, with an aspect ratio of about 2.35:1 and no 16:9 enhancement. The film's colors are subdued. The image is sharp and bright, but hues are somewhat bland overall. The stereo surround sound is a little weak, but the Dolby Digital track is reasonably strong. The film's musical score has some nice separation effects, but otherwise the film is mostly just conversation. The 135 minute program is also available in French in standard stereo and can be supported by English or Spanish subtitles.

John Lennon: Sweet Toronto (Pioneer, PA98584D)

The 1969 concert recording is fairly crude and raw, but the mix is effectively engineered and the audio presentation is lively. The picture is grainy and aged, but colors are reasonably bright and when the grain subsides the image is sharp. The program runs 56 minutes and appears on a single side. Lennon, with a heavy beard, is on stage with Bo Diddley, Jerry Lee Lewis, Chuck Berry, Eric Clapton and others performing an enjoyable set of rock 'n' roll classics, such as *Blue Suede Shoes* and *Money*. Of note as well are the two Yoko Ono numbers, which no longer sound out of place. Lennon has a full, washed, unclipped beard and very long hair, as was the style of the time, but for fans the material will seem fresh and vital. Considering the age of the footage, the quality of the color film is amazing, and the program is superbly edited. The sound is nominally in stereo although most of it seems to stay in the center and there is a certain amount of hiss. The standard stereo surround sound is a little dull, but the Dolby Digital track is stronger. The program is not captioned.

The John Wayne Collection (Madacy, DVD99003)
The John Wayne Collection / Vol. 1: Man from Utah / Sagebrush Trail (Madacy, DVD990031)
The John Wayne Collection / Vol. 2: Riders of Destiny / The Star Packer (Madacy, DVD990032)
The John Wayne Collection /Vol. 3: Dawn Rider / Trail Beyond (Madacy, DVD990033)
The John Wayne Collection / Vol. 4: Lawless Frontier / Randy Rides Alone (Madacy, DVD990034)
The John Wayne Collection / Vol. 5: Winds of the Wasteland / Lucky Texan (Madacy, DVD9900335)

Ten of the (approximately) hour-long westerns John Wayne made in the early Thirties have been issued in a box set and as five separate, paired releases. Most were produced by a company called Lone Star Productions, though one, *Winds of the Wasteland*, was a Republic Pictures feature and is a little more sophisticated. By and large, the picture transfers are really bad, but a couple of the films are tolerably presented. Madacy tends to pair a good one with a bad one, however. All are accompanied by biographies of filmmakers who have nothing to do with the movies on hand, a Wayne filmography with different segments appearing on each DVD and trivia questions. The chapter encoding is okay, but the chapter search is very poor, landing the viewer in the middle of the chapter rather than at its beginning, and none of the programs are time encoded. The monophonic sound is also weak and noisy, but is usually manageable. There is no captioning. *Sagebrush Trail* and *Randy Rides Alone* also appear to have revised musical scores, though the audio is consistent in tone with the older audio tracks on the other films.

In many of the films, Wayne is an undercover lawman pretending to be a drifter, who investigates corruption and brings the guilty to justice. While the plot follows a general and reliable template, the stunts are often invigorating and unique, with elaborate chases, falls and fights. The acting is often at near-amateur level, though in such company Wayne towers as a competent professional. His youthful vigor and comfort with the cowboy mystique add greatly to the appeal of the films, particularly when the picture quality is not a total strain.

A step above the others, the 1936 Republic film *Winds of the Wasteland* on **Vol. 5**, is, dramatically, the best in the group and the image transfer, though battered and soft, is tolerable. Wayne plays a former Pony Express rider who is duped into investing his savings in a stagecoach line that runs to a ghost town. Slowly but surely, however, his efforts bring the town alive, and he then attempts to cap his success by participating in a race to win a mail contract. The picture quality on the companion film, the 1934 *Lucky Texan*, is an abomination, a smeary, blurry mess that makes enjoying the film, which is also one of the better efforts, very taxing. Wayne's character teams up with an elderly friend of his father's and the two discover gold. As they work their claim in secret, a corrupt assessor attempts to locate their strike and kill the old man.

The two films on **Vol. 3** are quite good. In both, Wayne befriends another character but inadvertently steals that character's girl. In the 1935 *Dawn Rider*, he has to find his father's killer, who happens to be the brother of the girl. The picture is blurred and smeary, and the sound is quite scratchy. Noah Beery Junior and Senior co-star with Wayne in the 1934 *Trail Beyond*, which is set in Canada. Wayne's character helps the proprietor of a trading post protect his interests against a group of bad guys who also want to steal Wayne's treasure map. At one point, a stuntman misses a leap, but they keep rolling the camera as he gets back on his horse and tries again. The villain, by the way, has a very bad French accent.

In the 1933 *Riders of Destiny* on **Vol. 2**, which has a really awful picture transfer, a land baron is monopolizing water rights and Wayne's character helps the owner of one of the few non-monopolized wells protect his property. The picture is relatively stronger on the 1934 *Star Packer*, though contrasts are light and there is a lot of speckling. Wayne's character, with an Indian sidekick, is investigating corruption in a town where the main villain hides his identity, giving out orders through a phony wall safe.

The narrative in the 1935 *Lawless Frontier*, on **Vol. 4**, is a little more convoluted than the others, about a villain with a bad Mexican accent who is terrorizing an elderly homesteader and his young daughter. The picture is very poor again, looking smeary and wiggly, with details disappearing in any sort of shadow. The picture quality is more confident on the 1934 *Randy Rides Alone*, in which Wayne's character goes undercover and joins an outlaw band to help a young woman protect her cashbox. The image is reasonably crisp and overt damage is modest.

In the 1934 *Man from Utah*, on **Vol. 1**, Wayne enters a rodeo to identify the individuals attempting to fix the contest and in the 1933 *Sagebrush Trail* he befriends the man who really committed the murder he has been accused of. The image quality on both is weak but workable, with *Sagebrush Trail* looks somewhat smeary.

Johnny Mnemonic (Columbia TriStar, 73471)

We've sat through so many cheap cyber thrillers that when a mainline effort comes along it seems like a revelation. **Johnny Mnemonic** is probably the dopey little action movie everybody says it is but we found its details to be intelligent, its stars engaging, its visuals stimulating and its script satisfying. Based upon a story by William Gibson, the original cyber thriller conceptualist, Keanu Reeves stars as a courier carrying an unstable wad of information in his head, which must be uploaded within a certain amount of time or he will die. The information is also critical to solving the social imbalances within the society where he resides, and the bad guys don't want it to get out. The film moves quickly and the dialogue is heady enough to make you concentrate on what is happening. The film's vision of the future is thorough and often very imaginative. We feel it is unfortunate, however, that the movie has been constrained by the ratings standard, for there are several important moments where it is clear that exceptionally violent images are required to give the narrative an emotional release. At each point, there is a very quick cut and only a hint of gore.

The picture is presented on one side in letterboxed format, with an aspect ratio of about 1.85:1 and an accommodation for enhanced 16:9 playback, and is in full screen format on the other side. The color transfer is fine, no matter how dark or oddly lit the set (most of the film takes place in a typical futuristic wasteland at night). The stereo surround sound is dull, but the Dolby Digital track is fairly rousing. The 98 minute program also has French and Spanish soundtracks in standard stereo, and optional English and French subtitles.

Joni Mitchell: Painting with Words and Music (Image, ID5515ERDVD)

Joni Mitchell gives a concert in what looks like the furniture section of a department store. Apparently, it was meant to make the studio audience feel comfortable, and if the environment didn't relax them, then Mitchell's music certainly does. There is a wonderful dimensionality to her recording, especially on the Dolby Digital track, and tones are smooth and strong. The analog track has a more generalized mix, but it is still pleasing.

Mitchell sings numbers from many points in her career on the 98 minute program, and she also pauses quite a bit to tell stories about her life. Keyed by the luscious immediacy of the recording, her singing sounds lively and unfettered. The stage illumination is darkish, giving a haze to everything not in the key light, but the picture looks fine. There is no captioning, but there is a discography and filmography for Mitchell.

Journey to the Far Side of the Sun (Image, ID42197USDVD)

Produced by Gerry Anderson and directed by Robert Parrish, the 1969 film combines live actors with the special effect model work that was Anderson's specialty. It is about the discovery of another planet which orbits the sun at a point directly opposite the Earth, and has one marvelous plot turn. Anyone with a passing familiarity of the film will know what that plot turn is, but if you don't, we recommend watching the film as blind to its content as possible. The movie has a downbeat ending, which probably cost it substantially at the box office, and the filmmakers sometimes resort to using their puppet camera tricks, such as closeup zooms, on human actors, but fans of Anderson's work and those who enjoy a good tall tale should be pleased. Roy Thinnes stars.

The picture is letterboxed with an aspect ratio of about 1.87:1 and no 16:9 enhancement. The colors look super, and the image is crisp and spotless. The monophonic sound is okay and the 101 program can be supported by English subtitles.

Judge Dredd (Buena Vista, 14899)

Sylvester Stallone stars in the adaptation of a comic book, portraying a successful cop in a deteriorating city of the future who is framed by the ruling powers to facilitate the installation of a dictatorship. The film is filled with futuristic landscapes, and has plenty of gun battles and explosions. The supporting cast is ritzy, even in many of the bit parts. It is all so relentlessly superficial—even the jokes are superficial—however, that you never feel emotionally involved with the characters. The film will make a viable double bill with **Demolition Man**, and it isn't boring so it has some use, but intense multiple viewings are unlikely, since the more often you watch it the dumber it seems.

The colors are bright and fleshtones are accurate and the image is sharp, providing an ideal showcase for the many special effects. The presentation is letterboxed with an aspect ratio of about 2.35:1 and no 16:9 enhancement. The stereo surround sound and Dolby Digital sound are fine. There isn't much in the way of subtle sound effects, but for jacking up the amplifier and letting it rip, the title is appropriate software. The 96 minute film is also available in French in Dolby Digital and can be supported by English subtitles. An energetic theatrical trailer is also included.

Judgment Night (GoodTimes, 0581005)

Four men from suburbia take a wrong exit one night and find themselves stranded in an urban wasteland, being chased by violent killers in the xenophobic thriller. The 1993 film is careful to avoid making it a racial thing—most of the bad guys are white and one of the good guys is black—but the "stay out of the inner city if you know what is good for you" message still comes through loud and clear. The heroes are boorish, so most of the film is rather unappealing. The climactic confrontation in the finale is exciting, but it is not unique enough to compensate for the mundane events leading up to it. Emilio Estevez stars.

The picture is in letterboxed format only, with an aspect ratio of about 1.8:1 and no 16:9 enhancement. The color transfer is passable. The stereo surround sound has little to offer that is out of the ordinary. The 109 minute program has optional French or Spanish subtitles, English captioning and some production notes.

The Judy Garland Show Volume One (Pioneer, PA99613D)

Two episodes from the 1963 CBS TV series are featured. The black-and-white picture quality is outstanding. There is not a single smear or speckle in either show, and even the outtakes look better than most preserved TV broadcasts. The close-ups of Garland are incredibly vivid, conveying the full texture of her complexion and every minute subtlety and crease in her expressions.

The episodes are numbered based upon the order of shooting rather than the order of broadcast. In the two episodes featured, #1 and #3, Garland is joined by Mickey Rooney and a 17-year old Liza Minnelli respectively. Hence, in both, she is very at ease with the banter between the numbers and enthusiastic during the duets. To modulate the rhythm in both programs, Jerry Van Dyke appears as a series regular, doing comedy bits and interacting with some of the secondary guest stars (Van Dyke does a very funny lip synch routine to a sped up version of *The Legend of the Lone Ranger* in #3). With the outtakes (numbers and skits that had to be cut to make the show's time slot), each episode runs a bit over an hour.

As the jacket essay suggests, Garland was not in a career ebb because her motion pictures had fallen off, but was, instead, at a career high as a concert entertainer and recording artist, the TV show capturing her at the height of her maturity as a vocalist. Included among the many songs are Garland's renditions of *Old Man River* (an abridged version with some articulation flaws but still brilliantly delivered), *I Believe in You, As Long As He Needs Me*, and in a duet with Minnelli, *The Best Is Yet to Come*. In Dolby Digital. The original mono track is offered as one option, but the audio has also been spruced up in stereo, bringing an amazing depth to the instrumental accompaniment, as well as an improved clarity to the vocals and an enjoyment created by the widening of the sound field. The show is not captioned.

Julie Strain's Bad Girls (Simitar, 7232)

A collection of two hour-long nude dancing programs, *Julie Strain's Bodacious Friends* and *Julie Strain's Bodacious Friends "D"*-

lightful, features about a half dozen models who wiggle around in a standing position in various states of undress and, between wiggles, talk about how much fun it is to have large breasts. Each sequence is separated by a brief segment with Strain. The color quality is okay, but the program has severe artifacting and movement often has the ratchety appearance of a personal computer video. The sound is adequate and is not captioned.

Jumanji (Columbia TriStar, 11745/9)

The 1995 film—a fantasy about children forced to play a board game that creates real, havoc-raising animals—may be lacking in emotional breadth, but it conforms to its own rules beautifully and its simple narrative force, created by the necessity of finishing the game before the animals will go away, is enough, when combined with the great special effects, to keep a viewer fully attentive. It also helps that Robin Williams stars in a featured role, as a man who has been trapped inside the game for a very long time and is finally freed. The humor of his delivery and body language is precisely the sort of balance the drama requires to prevent the entertainment from seeming too serious or too absurd.

The color transfer looks very good, with accurate fleshtones and a sharp focus. The picture is letterboxed with an aspect ratio of about 1.85:1 and an accommodation for enhanced 16:9 playback. The stereo surround sound and Dolby Digital are super, particularly the way the bass kicks in whenever the animals come around. The 104 minute film is also available in French or Spanish (the Dolby Digital is English only), and comes with Spanish or Korean subtitles and English closed captioning.

Jungle Fever (Universal, 20428)

One of Spike Lee's very best movies, Wesley Snipes, Samuel L. Jackson (in one of his most amazing performances), and Annabella Sciorra star in the multi-pathed tale that is partially about an interracial romance and partly about a family coping with a drug addict. The movie is astoundingly visualized, from one of the most original opening credit sequences we've seen in a long while, to shots of people walking without walking, and to poking around the lives of the characters with a rhythm that is at once free-floating and meticulously paced. The movie is also acted with gusto, turning Lee's argumentative dialogue into thoughts so natural to the characters their conversations often seem completely improvised. The film has some wonderful moments of humor, as well as some absolutely spine-tingling drama, and it tends to hold up better on multiple viewings than Lee's other films do.

The picture is letterboxed, with an aspect ratio of about 1.85:1 and an accommodation for enhanced 16:9 playback. It has slightly subdued, yellowed colors. The presentation is fairly soft, with hazes around the most illuminated objects. The stereo surround sound lacks crispness, but it is sturdy, with well-rounded tones and there is a pleasingly forceful dimensionality. The 132 minute program is also available in French and Spanish, and can be supported by English, French or Spanish subtitles ("Vous avez tous les deux la fièvre de la jungle"). There is a good 8 minute featurette, a trailer, a cast-and-director profile section and some minor production notes.

Jungleground (Image, ID5600FMDVD)

The premise is a bit absurd. The film is set in a lawless (but somehow still economically viable) area of a city, where gangs roam about, engaging in rituals. The hero, a cop, is caught and given a certain time limit to get out while he is chased by a hunting team. That said, though, the film is a passable action exercise. The explosions are good and the narrative never slows down or gets sidetracked. Roddy Piper stars.

The picture looks fine. Fleshtones are a little bland, but other hues are well defined and the image is sharp. The stereo surround sound is passable and the 87 minute program is not captioned.

Junior (Universal, 20338)

One of the most monumentally bad films ever conceived, **Junior** still has a lot going for it. Because of its big budget, the dialogue is dependably witty (the last line especially so) and the plot has plenty of clever, logical turns. Arnold Schwarzenegger gives what is easily the most complex and delicate performance he has ever turned in, and the supporting players, Danny DeVito, Emma Thompson and Pamela Reed, are also in top form. But the movie's concept—a man gets pregnant and carries the child to term—no matter how logical and how earnestly it is presented, just makes your skin crawl. Almost every funny line in the movie is followed by an eye-rolling detail, meant to reinforce the pregnancy concept, that is as alienating or more alienating than the line was funny. From Thompson's questionable representation of women as hopeless klutzes to Schwarzenegger's equally questionable pregnancy-causes-prissiness personality shift, the 1994 film is a monstrously bad idea that should never have left the test tube.

The program is letterboxed with an aspect ratio of about 1.85:1 and an accommodation for enhanced 16:9 playback. Colors are solid and fleshtones are accurate, though the image is a little soft in places. The musical score is quite effective in Dolby Digital encoding, bringing a strong dimensionality to those passages, but otherwise the audio is fairly centered and uninteresting. The standard stereo track is fine. The 110 minute film is also available in French and Spanish, and can be supported by English or Spanish subtitles. There is a theatrical trailer and a 'making of' featurette, along with production notes and a cast-and-director profile section.

Junior Bonner (Anchor Bay, DV10730)

Steve McQueen is an aging rodeo star who passes some time with his family when the rodeo arrives at his hometown. There are some wonderful performances in the 1972 Sam Peckinpah film, from McQueen, Robert Preston (who plays his father), Ida Lupino (his mother), and Joe Don Baker, who may never have been better as he is playing the brother who stayed home and did good to McQueen's Prodigal Son. In theaters, the 1972 film was excruciating, since it unfolds slowly and nothing much happens (McQueen's character doesn't even catch up to Preston until about the movie's halfway point). Plus, while the performances are great, the dialogue is very cliched and the dramatic conflicts are simple and unsurprising. Peckinpah seems to make no effort to smarten things up, or to bring much realism to the narrative's contrivances. On home video, however, the movie is not as alienating. Since it is easier to accommodate the film's pace from the comfort of one's home, the appeal of the stars, the rodeo milieu and Peckinpah's occasional stylistic coups override the dramatic simplicities, aimless plot, and the ubiquitous barroom brawl.

It helps, as well, that Anchor Bay has done such a lovely job delivering the film to DVD. It is presented on one side in letterboxed format, with an aspect ratio of about 2.35:1 and no 16:9 enhancement, and is in cropped format on the other side, although except for the close-ups of the stars, the severe cropping isn't good for much. The film's opening uses split-screen segments and has a lot of optical work, but once that is over, the colors look very fresh and fleshtones are nicely detailed. There are some very minor artifacting flaws, creating a slight jerkiness in a couple shots, but otherwise the presentation is smooth. The monophonic sound is very strong and has a near-stereo ambiance. The 110 minute program is not captioned.

The Juror (Columbia TriStar, 11609)

Demi Moore is the juror in the trial of a mobster. She is terrorized by a hit man, played by Alec Baldwin, not only to throw the verdict, but to sway all of her fellow jurors to an acquittal. Once the trial is over, she plots her revenge. If one can accept the plot's exaggerations, then one can have a good time with the performers and the suspense. If one is not so tolerant, however, it would be best to skip the concoction and hope that Hollywood has exhausted the concept for a while.

The 1996 feature is presented on one side in letterboxed format, with an aspect ratio of about 2.35:1 and an accommodation for enhanced 16:9 playback, and in cropped format on the other side. Parts of the movie are rather dark (Gordon Willis was dropped as the cinematographer about halfway through the film) and monochromatic, but the image seems reasonably sharp and colors look accurate. The stereo surround sound is okay and the Dolby Digital track is a little brighter. The 118 minute program also has French and Spanish soundtracks in standard stereo, optional English, French and Spanish subtitles, and a trailer.

Just Cause (Warner, 13623)

There are a couple of minor plot points that don't make sense—one character who is in prison is missing a significant portion of his anatomy and yet the authorities don't seem to know about it—but it is an entertaining thriller, highlighted by engaging performances from Laurence Fishburne as a tough Florida sheriff and Sean Connery as a somewhat befuddled law professor researching the evidence against a client on death row. Casting Connery as the hero beguiles the viewer into thinking that his character is infallible, an ideal set-up for the clever turns that occur in the film's second half. The 1995 film begins as an intellectual puzzler and ends with a clichéd fight in an alligator-infested swamp, but the movie's appeal is sustained with each shift in tone because of the cast and the general Sun Belt thriller atmosphere.

The picture is in letterboxed format only, with an aspect ratio of about 2.35:1 and an accommodation for enhanced 16:9 playback. The color transfer is excellent, with crisp hues and accurate fleshtones, even in darker sequences. The stereo surround sound helps a couple of good shock cuts and is generally sharp. The 102 minute program also has a French stereo track and optional English and French subtitles.

K

K-9 (Universal, 20585)

Jim Belushi is a cop hounding a drug kingpin with the assistance of his police dog partner. The film's humor and formula action sequences compensate sufficiently for its plot contrivances (the dog's motivations are wildly inconsistent from scene to scene—we guess he couldn't complain to the director), and the 1989 movie is the sort that gives mindless entertainment a good name.

The picture is letterboxed with an aspect ratio of about 1.85:1 and an accommodation for enhanced 16:9 playback. The colors are bright and smooth, and fleshtones look good. The stereo surround sound has a limited dimensionality and uninteresting mix. The 102 minute program also has a French audio track in stereo, optional English subtitles, a cast-and-director profile section, production notes and a trailer.

Kaitlyn Goes to Rio X-rated (DaViD, D8031)

The program has no real narrative, just a few excursions around Brazil, where the American heroines mix with the locals, and an above average cinematography that brings some flair to the otherwise commonly staged erotic sequences. But the program is worth considering because it also has a reasonably intelligent director commentary by Stuart Canterbury.

Canterbury tells the story of the production, but he also goes into interesting details about the adult film industry. He talks extensively about AIDS testing, the threats of censorship, why the same few male actors appear in all the films, how actresses who are rebelling against a strict upbringing have a tendency to run hot and cold on the set, and he also talks about his career—how he used initial jobs in the industry to pay for his film school training and then felt too established to switch to the mainstream (has anyone ever taken a poll looking at how many people have backed into their careers?). And then there's the actress who won't work with him anymore because the airline lost her luggage, as if it was his fault.

The picture looks sharp and colors are reasonably good. The sound is okay. The program runs 75 minutes and features Kaitlyn Ashley, Kia, Channone, Andrea, Natielli, Simone and Victoria.

Kalifornia (PolyGram, 4400432992)

The 1993 thriller has a lucky cast of stars who were mostly unknown when the film was shot. David Duchovny, Brad Pitt, Juliette Lewis and Michelle Forbes are featured in the film, about a writer researching serial killers who doesn't realize he's picked one up on a cross-country trip. The picture quality is good, with sharp colors and pure blacks. The program is presented in letterboxed format on one side, with an aspect ratio of about 2.35:1 and no 16:9 enhancement, and in full screen format on the other side. The letterboxing adds nothing to the sides of the image in comparison to the full screen format and masks picture information off the top and bottom. Although the letterboxed framing is how the filmmakers intended the movie to be seen, the full screen version is worth taking a look at. The stereo surround sound is workable, with a strong bass and plenty of separation effects. The film is available in French as well and comes with Spanish subtitles and English closed captioning. An introductory menu offers either the 118 minute 'unrated' or the 117 minute 'R-rated' cut of the film, and even has an 'Are you sure?' confirmation before continuing. There is also a theatrical trailer, which pretty much tells you the whole film, along with a brief 'making of' featurette, and profiles of the four stars and the director, Dominic Sena.

Karaoke — The Ladies of Country (Pioneer, PDKCD201)
Karaoke — The Hits Made Popular by Neil Diamond (Pioneer, PDKND001)
Karaoke — Classic Rock Vol. 1 (Pioneer, PDKCR501)
Karaoke — Rock/Pop Hits (Pioneer, PDKRP401)
Karaoke — Standard Classics (Pioneer, PDKST301)
Pioneer Karaoke Library Vol. 1 (Pioneer, PDL001)

The songs are menu driven and the music numbers do not play sequentially—after each tune the program returns to the menu for your next pick. Menus are offered in both alphabetical order by song and by artist, with a secondary option of selecting only the chorus segment of each song. The songs themselves are presented on one audio channel with just instrumental and background vocals, so you can sing along, and on another channel with the lyrics being sung, so you can toggle back and forth if you want to hear how the number is supposed to be performed. The DVDs also have Dolby Digital tracks, but unless we're doing something wrong, we really didn't understand the Dolby Digital mix, because on the instrumental-only track, the singer still comes through loud and clear on the rear channels (if you have the rear channels suppressed, then you would get just the instrumental part). We were quite happy with the standard audio track, however, and the quality of the stereo playback seems just fine. The picture quality is also decent, usually with sharp, accurate colors. A few of the videos accompanying the songs look a little grainy or faded, but most are fresh. Except for a slight jerkiness in some right-to-left pans, we were unaware of any artifacting.

The videos themselves are surprisingly elaborate—proof, we suppose, of how big a business karaoke is. Most depict generic couples, happy in one another's company, cavorting with nature or otherwise having a good time. Others show them doing things separately with intercutting to imply that they are thinking about one another. But many of the videos have abstract or surreal elements and some of them are even more creative, or just different—there is one that consists entirely of buffalo grazing in a meadow. The unseen singers often attempt to imitate the best known renditions of the songs, as does the instrumentation. Hence, if you're not too picky, the programs can work even without the sing-along compo-

nent. On the other hand, we want to know when Pioneer is going to invent a shower unit.

The Ladies of Country features *Blue* (the video emphasizes that hue), *You Win My Love*, *Let's Go to Vegas*, *Cleopatra Queen of Denial* (the best video in the group), *A Thousand Times a Day*, *Fancy*, *Ring on Her Finger Time on Her Hands*, *That's What I Like about You*, *It's Lonely Out There*, *Take Me As I Am*, *Let That Pony Run*, and *Blame It On Your Heart*. The songs have a very gender-specific female orientation, but that shouldn't stop gentlemen from jumping in once they've had a drink or two—after all, even if you can't relate directly to *Fancy* ("Then Mama spent every last penny we had to buy me a dancin' dress…"), you can pretend.

Brief biographical details about Neil Diamond are included on a menu selection with the songs on **The Hits Made Popular by Neil Diamond**. *America* has a suitably sociological video, there is no alcohol in *Cracklin' Rosie*, and otherwise the cuts are fairly generic. Also included are *Song Sung Blue*, *Sweet Caroline*, *Holly Holy*, *Forever in Blue Jeans*, *Hello Again*, *Love on the Rocks* (boulders and ice cubes), *Play Me*, *Solitary Man* and *Kentucky Woman*.

A couple of the videos on **Classic Rock Vol. 1** are kind of far out, but the collection has no real thematic cohesiveness. Included are *Whenever I Call You Friend*, *Ride Like the Wind*, *Reelin' in the Years*, *Come Monday*, *Tragedy*, *Please Come to Boston*, *What You Won't Do for Love*, *Fanny*, *Lightning Strikes*, *Day after Day*, *25 or 6 to 4* and the especially karaoke-friendly *An Old Fashioned Love Song*.

The most interesting videos are collected on **Rock/Pop Hits**, including the buffalo thing, which is set to *It's Good to Be King*, and a suitably hip, high-tech montage set to the partial rap number, *Funky Cold Medina*. Other numbers include the updated rock orchestration of *Red Red Wine*, *With or Without You*, *Her Comes the Rain Again*, *White Wedding*, *Rosanna*, *Don't You*, *Even Better Than the Real Things*, *Modern Love*, *Drive* and *Look Away*.

Since **Standard Classics** contains the most ubiquitous pop classics, however, it is probably the collection most viewers will want to sing-along with. After all, who has not pictured themselves in a tuxedo at a fancy bar, crooning the theme to *Mondo Cane* to attractive patrons of their sexual orientation? In addition to *More*, the collection includes such shower classics as *Cheek to Cheek*, *There's No Business Like Show Business*, *Mona Lisa* (shot at a Renaissance Fair in black and white except for a dwarf running around in red—the concoction kept reminding us of *Don't Look Now* and distracting us from the song), *Everybody Loves Somebody*, *I Can't Stop Loving You*, *My Favorite Things*, *On the Sunny Side of the Street*, and *Too Young*. Included as well is the holiday classic, *I'll Be Home for Christmas*, and the spiritual *Amazing Grace*, which has the most impressive and sober video. Also offered in the collection is a number designed for 'two microphones,' *Me and My Shadow*.

A catch-all collection, **Pioneer Karaoke Library Vol. 1** includes more than two dozen numbers, all selections from the other collections, including several Neil Diamond songs, songs from *Grease*, *I Will Survive*, *For All We Know*, *The Tide Is High*, *Please Come to Boston* and others.

Kathy Smith Kickboxing Workout (Sony, LVD51570)

It is a hallmark of the Information Age that people no longer do one thing at a time. They do two or three things at once, instead. Hence, we have a program that is like the most popular exercise programs these days, combining a daily workout with lessons on self-defense. The DVD is expertly designed, presenting three workouts with a host of audio options and a number of supplemental guides.

There are two long workouts, a basic 45 minute kickboxing workout and a 55 minute advanced kickboxing workout, and a short but intense 12 minute Tai Chi workout. There is also an option to select specific segments from the workouts. Smith is joined by martial arts expert Keith Cooke, and if it is all confusing, you can go back to the menu and select an 8 minute segment in which

Smith and Cooke teach you the specific moves—with two angle options.

The picture quality is fine. The audio allows you to select just the music, just Smith, a combination of the music and Smith, or Spanish prompting with or without the music. A 10 minute conversation between Smith and Cooke is also featured, in which they talk about martial arts philosophies and how mental development is as important as physical development. Smith is amusingly self-conscious in this sequence and thinks you have to 'rewind' DVDs, but everything Cooke has to say is worthwhile. There are also profiles of Smith and Cooke and ads with clips for other Smith videos.

Kenny Loggins Outside: From the Redwoods (Sony, CVD49176)

Performing underneath a bunch of very tall trees, Kenny Loggins gives an 80 minute concert of hits from his solo career and his days with Jim Messina. Loggins has a large backup band, but the orchestrations remain fairly low key, in keeping with the peaceful forest glade atmosphere that the setting, despite the concert paraphernalia, imparts. The picture looks good, with accurate fleshtones and crisp colors in all lighting situations. The stereo surround sound is a little bland, with an indistinct mix, but the menu-activated Dolby Digital sound is super. Rear channel activity is limited, but tones are well defined and the dimensionality is considerably enhanced. Optional English subtitles are also available.

Kept Husbands (see **Pre-Code Hollywood: The Risqué Years #1**)

Kids (Trimark, LDVM6311D)

We continue to read negative commentary about the 1995 film, but it seems to us that the writers are confusing the movie—which is well made and, in some ways, profound—with the characters, who are mostly contemptible little snots. Rather than restricting its viewing, they ought to be showing **Kids** to every fourteen year old girl in America. To be sure, the film is a mild exaggeration, packing more incidents into its sunrise-to-sunrise narrative structure than would likely occur in real life, but the individual scenes are all highly believable and more than a little frightening. The villainous protagonist is an adolescent boy who has found a talent and a hobby in the seduction of young virginal females. The rest of the time he hangs out with his incoherent friends and talks about his exploits. The film isn't all that entertaining, but it does provide a sort of creepy, voyeuristic nostalgia and then shatters it—early on—with the realities of AIDS, creating a dramatic immediacy and giving the aimless characters an ulterior fate

The picture transfer is very good, with accurate fleshtones and crisp contrasts. The movie is presented in letterboxed format on one side, with an aspect ratio of about 1.85:1 and no 16:9 enhancement, and in full screen format on the other side. Either version seems workable, but we tended to prefer the framing on the letterboxed version, which draws a viewer's eyes more readily to the emotional center of the screen. The stereo surround sound is okay, though the audio has a sort of makeshift ambiance and it is really only the occasional pop song in the musical score that contains much energy. The 102 minute program has optional English subtitles.

Kika (Image, ID41890CDVSD)

Pedro Almodóvar's amusing 1994 black comedy, about rape and murder, has such a confident sense of style he can incorporate subjects and images that in most movies would be alienating, without losing his grasp on the viewer. The rape sequence, for example, is handled so dryly and goes on for so long that you stop feeling offended by it after a while, yet it never becomes so absurd that you cease to take it seriously. The same is true of one of the central characters, a TV journalist who walks through much of the film with a camera attached to her head. It looks silly and it is silly, but Almodóvar presents it so naturally that, while it is giggle-in-

ducing, it never seems out of place in the film's world. Peter Coyote, who is dubbed in Spanish, is one of the featured players, an author living with his stepson and the stepson's girlfriend (with whom the author is also having an affair). At first, the film draws its comedy from the amorous adventures of the enjoyably quirky characters and their interference in one another's lives, but gradually the stakes are raised, so that the humor becomes darker and the actions of the characters more critical and meaningful.

The letterboxing has an aspect ratio of about 1.85:1 and no 16:9 enhancement. Hues look somewhat washed out, though the production design is often so intensely colorful that it hardly matters. Fleshtones are a bit pinkish but adequate. The stereo sound comes off just a little too muted, and separation effects are limited. The 114 minute film is in Spanish with permanent but soft white English subtitles.

Kill and Kill Again (Digital Versatile, DVD104)

A film that lives up to its acronym, the giggle-inducing martial arts feature, shot in South Africa, stars James Ryan, who is hired by the daughter of a scientist to retrieve her kidnapped father. "My father has been working for several years on a project to extract fuel from potatoes," she explains. "One year's crop could provide enough gasoline to drive every car in the world, to the moon." "You mean to tell me the good doctor was kidnapped because of potatoes," Ryan asks, placing his hands on his hips. "During his research, my father accidentally discovered there was a by-product," she replies, picking at a flower. "An incredible new mind-control drug that enables whoever administers it to bend people to his will." The bad guy, who plans to take over the world by putting the drug in the water supply (hey, wait a minute, won't that make everyone beholden to plumbers?), has the phoniest beard we've ever seen that isn't supposed to be a phony beard, so rather than cowering in terror, there is a tendency to laugh uproariously at his every close-up. The fight scenes are pathetic. Ryan may be versed in the art of hand-to-hand combat, but the extras they have him taking on know absolutely nothing and just sort of wave their arms a bit before falling over. There's more, but we don't want to spoil all the fun.

The cinematography is either poorly composed or cropped, or both, and the colors are worn-looking, with yellowed fleshtones. The stereo surround sound is best held to a modest volume and the 100 minute program is not captioned.

The Killer (Criterion, CC1515D)

The Killer is *City Lights* for an era of urban chaos and director John Woo is the Charlie Chaplin of violent death. The film is more than just a shoot-out with a high body count. It opens with the line, "Do you believe in God?" and remains focused throughout on the souls of the characters and their quests for absolution. Chow Yun-Fat stars as the hit man who accidentally blinds a nightclub singer and then tries to watch over her as the police close in on him. The story has melodramatic tones that might be laughable if performed in English, including high minded buddy talk and the blind girl, who needs an operation to regain her sight, but under Woo's exquisite mastery of the language of film such excesses are operatically excusable. The movie also has a few basic flaws delineating the minor characters and orienting the action, but things happen so fast there isn't time to become too confused.

The film retains the slightly battered look most Hong Kong productions are saddled with, but there are fewer speckles and the colors are richer than on Criterion's LD. Fleshtones that appear yellow on the LD are more realistic and natural on the DVD. The picture is letterboxed with an aspect ratio of about 1.85:1 and no 16:9 enhancement. The monophonic has an adequate dynamic range, though it is limited by Hollywood standards. The 1989 100 minute film is presented in Cantonese with optional English subtitles. There are deleted scenes that were used to pad the running time in some foreign releases of the film, a trailer, and a commentary track by Woo and production executive Terence Chang. Woo and Chang talk about the movie's production and a few related subjects. Chang provides specific production details while Woo talks about his goals in the major sequences and the influences he has responded to as a filmmaker. There is no mention made of the musical score or other background technical details of that nature, but Woo does explain at times why he chose certain camera angles or editing styles. Because of his thick accent and a softness in the recording, it is sometimes difficult to understand every word, but most of Woo's comments are accessible.

The Killer Elite (MGM, 907443)

Sam Peckinpah's 1975 spy thriller is about a black ops agent seeking revenge against his crooked partner. James Caan and Robert Duvall star. The action scenes are terrific and the drama is involving, though we kick the wall every time we think about how the film had to be trimmed down to earn its 'PG' rating.

The picture is letterboxed with an aspect ratio of about 2.35:1 and no 16:9 enhancement. The image is sharper than the hazy LD and hues are a little brighter, but fleshtones are still pale and darker sequences are fairly grainy. The monophonic sound is rather flat, but adequate. The 123 minute feature can be supported by English or French subtitles and is accompanied by a trailer.

The Killer Inside Me (Simitar, 7296)

Burt Kennedy directed the 1975 adaptation of a Jim Thompson crime novel, which is presented in a cropped format. James Keach stars as a police detective in a Montana town who is gradually losing his grip on reality. Scandal and corruption surround him, so when he does finally go nuts it looks for a while like nobody will notice. Susan Tyrell co-stars. It would be easy to write the film off as being a fairly silly concoction, but Thompson's plotting, Kennedy's sure hand and Keach's gutsy performance hold a viewer's attention effectively, and the film remains more appealing for what it does have to offer in atmosphere and intrigue than what it can't deliver in logic and common sense.

Along with the cropping, the colors are a little aged and darker sequences are smeary. The monophonic sound has a limited range but remains workable. The 99 minute program is accompanied by a partial filmography for Keach and is not captioned.

The Killer Meteors (Simitar, 7254)

Jackie Chan just has a small part as a primary villain, but his name is plastered all over the jacket anyway, and Simitar includes the same five minute interview they've run in all their Chan DVDs. The film is hopelessly cropped. The colors are very nice, especially in the film's second half, and the image is reasonably sharp and free of damage. The film is a fairly good martial arts tale, about a kung fu expert hired to assassinate the wife of a dying man. The plot has a number of turns but is fairly easy to follow. The fights are creative and the other stunts are energetic. The monophonic sound, badly dubbed, is in English on one track and Cantonese on the other. Contrary to the time listing on the jacket cover, the film runs 103 minutes and is not captioned.

Killer Twisters! and Lethal Lightning Super Storms (UAV, 40090)

Two *Nova* programs have been combined and given a tabloid title. The hour long episodes from the PBS science program are actually entitled *Tornado!* and *Lightning!.* Both have essentially the same format. *Tornado!* spends a lot of time with tornado scientists (Bill Paxton and Helen Hunt, they're not), explaining what would happen if they actually caught up to a tornado, which they never do, showing the footage from the past when they did catch up to a few, explaining the science, as it was known in the early Nineties, of how a tornado works, and profiling a town that was destroyed by a tornado.

The 1995 *Lightning!* spends a lot of time with lightning scientists, who have an easier time gathering data, explains the science of how lightning works, at least as it was known in 1995, and pro-

files a school athletic tragedy where several participants were struck during a sudden storm. *Lightning!* is the better of the two shows because you don't see as many programs on the subject, there are more facts to work with and the visuals are more numerous, but both are reliable and informative. The picture transfer on both programs is passable, combining grainy documentary location footage with solid, well-lit interviews. *Tornado!* is monophonic and is closed captioned. *Lightning!* has a nice stereo soundtrack, but is not captioned.

Killer Volcanoes and Deadly Peaks (UAV, 40084)

For those of you who aren't getting enough magma in your viewing diets, two episodes of the Discovery Channel series, *The World of Volcanoes*, have been combined onto one DVD. Each 45 minute 'hour' program, shot by Katia and Maurice Kraft, looks at active and inactive volcanoes around the world, including spectacular shots of lava flows and ash eruptions. Both programs have a voiceover narrator who explains what is going on in the images, and both include drawings and models that further illustrate the metamorphic processes on view. Among the highlights are underwater footage of lava flowing into the sea, footage of a town in Iceland being swallowed, scenes of two scientists taking a rubber raft out on a lake so acidic that their metal instruments do not survive their tests, and shots of scientists in hard-hats ducking chunks of molten rock that are splashing down around them. On a few right-to-left pans, the image wobbles, perhaps with video artifacting caused by the DVD transfer. The 16mm footage varies in quality but has the color, sharpness and constitution of a typical educational film. It isn't IMAX, but it is sufficient for conveying the drama and beauty of the Earth's bleeding. The monophonic sound is drab and the occasional classical music piece that is inserted between the passages of narration comes out muted.

Killer's Kiss (MGM, 907707)

Stanley Kubrick's earliest available commercial film, from 1955, runs 67 minutes. The narrative, about a boxer's involvement with a dance girl and the murder their relationship causes, is sufficient to move the story forward, though it is in the captivating black-and-white cinematography and the execution of individual scenes that the film achieves its real power. The film's qualities are best represented in the acting abilities of the film's cast. They read the dialogue awkwardly, but have such interesting faces and mannerisms that it hardly matters. Shot on a shoestring budget, Kubrick consistently overcomes his production limitations with imaginative images (there is a startling dream sequence, done in negative, that foreshadows the narrow hallway effects he uses in the other films) and an alertness to what can and cannot be accomplished in each sequence. There is also a mature attitude toward sexuality that never wavered throughout his career.

The source material has a few marks on it, and as a low budget thriller that might have been forgotten if Kubrick hadn't been behind it, the picture is not always pristine, but it is consistently clear and is sometimes strikingly detailed. The monophonic sound has a viable compromise between clarity and hiss. The program can be supported by optional English or French subtitles.

The Killing (MGM, 907706)

Stanley Kubrick's 1956 feature, about a botched robbery, is very similar in format to John Huston's *The Asphalt Jungle* and dozens of subsequent films, notably **Reservoir Dogs**. The voiceover narration was later skewered by Woody Allen in **Take the Money and Run**. Sterling Hayden stars as the mastermind of a race track heist, which is undone by greed and lust. It is a taut, well-executed thriller, with a number of subtle stylistic innovations and a cleverly shuffled chronology. The film also shares some remarkable similarities with the events surrounding the Kennedy Assassination, though what this means we're not sure (were the conspirators familiar with the film?).

The black-and-white picture is presented in full screen format and looks very sharp, with rich blacks and well-defined contrasts. The monophonic sound is fine. The 89 minute program has optional English and French subtitles and a cool trailer.

The Killing Jar (Simitar, 7302)

A man 'witnesses' a serial killing, but under hypnosis it starts to appear that he did a little more than just look, which understandably disturbs his new bride. There are the usual collection of red herrings, and the Dolby Digital encoding provides several nice enhancements, making the 1996 movie a little more fun than the usual psycho-killer thriller. Our favorite—the hero throws a rock over the camera and after an appropriate delay you hear thump behind you on the rear left. The regular stereo surround soundtrack has a little more power up front, but the separations on the Dolby Digital track make that mix the more appealing of the two. The presentation is letterboxed with an aspect ratio of about 1.85:1 and no 16:9 enhancement. The picture looks okay, with minimal grain and reasonably accurate fleshtones. The 101 minute program is not captioned.

The Killing Man (Simitar, 7339)

A cheap but workable action thriller, Jeff Wincott stars as a former mob assassin recruited by the shadowy government agency that is trying to control a special formula. Michael Ironsides is also featured. This is the sort of film where limited lighting is used to hide the lack of set dressings, and the whole thing appears to have been shot on some kind of campus somewhere, but after a long preliminary sequence of events to establish the characters, the hero falls in love with his target and rebels against his new bosses, enlivening the narrative by providing an emotional hook to the action.

The picture quality is tolerable, although fleshtones are pale and other hues are subdued. The Ultra-Stereo sound is very wimpy and monophonic in spirit. The film runs 100 minutes and is not captioned.

The Killing of a Chinese Bookie (Pioneer, PSE99102)

Ben Gazzara is the owner of a topless nightclub in John Cassavetes' 1978 feature. Owing a lot of money from gambling debts, he is allowed to tear up his markers in exchange for assassinating a mobster. The plot has a typical thriller premise, but Cassavetes' dramatic style has a deadening pace, and the peripheral performers look lost in their parts. Yet, if you have patience for the film, then the premise delivers, and the drawbacks simply enhance the film's eccentricity.

The picture is presented in full screen format, and the color transfer looks terrific, with bright hues and accurate, nicely detailed fleshtones. The film's lighting has minor inconsistencies, but the flaws are not significant enough to distract from the entertainment. The monophonic sound is set a little low, but can be amplified without distortion. The 109 minute program is not captioned.

Kindergarten Cop (Universal, 20145/20046)

Arnold Schwarzenegger portrays a cop who goes undercover as a kindergarten teacher to protect one of the children. The film is presented in full screen format only. Fleshtones have a purplish hue at times, other fleshtones look pinkish here and there, and the colors are not intense. The image is also a little soft. The stereo surround sound is adequate but rarely elaborate. The 111 minute 1990 film is also available in French and comes with English or Spanish subtitles. There are some worthwhile production notes, explaining how the kids were handled, as well as a cast profile and a good theatrical trailer. The film is peppered with a fine supporting cast, including the resourceful Pamela Reed as Schwarzenegger's partner, and Linda Hunt as the no-nonsense principal. The movie could probably have been more efficiently and humorously designed, but it is funny enough and entertaining enough to get by.

Kindertotenlieder (see Gustav Mahler: Das Lied Von Der Erde/Kindertotenlieder)

The King and I (Fox, 4110826)

The picture is in letterboxed format only, with an aspect ratio of about 2.55:1 and no 16:9 enhancement. The colors are outstanding, and the splendor and sharpness of the image enhances the pace and grandeur of the 1956 musical considerably. Yul Brynner and Deborah Kerr portray the title characters.

In comparison to the standard track, the Dolby Digital track is rousing, with a strong dimensionality, but it still has a limited range and lacks energy. There is also a flaw, a kind of pre-echo, primarily of Brynner's voice, that can be distracting if you've got your volume jacked up. The 144 minute program, which includes Overture, Entr'acte and Exit Music, also has a French language audio track (with English songs), optional English and Spanish subtitles, a cast & crew profile section, production notes, two Movietone clips, a trailer and two fairly useless options, a 'sing-along' that isn't (the lyrics are printed in a jacket insert) and a trivia quiz.

King Crimson: Deja Vrooom (Discipline Global, DGM9810)

The concert program contains more than two hours of music (it's not time encoded) and many interactive features. Our favorite: you can play one song, 21st Century Schizoid Man, by mixing it yourself with a combination of vocalists, solo instrumentals and rhythm sections from the band's various iterations across time. In other words, you can choose the group's 1996 rhythm section, Robert Fripp, Tony Levin, Trey Gunn, etc., and combine their work with Greg Lake's vocals from 1969. The concert by the esoteric fusion rock band is split to two sides (one number, listed in the chapter guide as appearing at the end of side one, actually opens side two). It is not well lit and the image, though smooth, is almost always blurry, with fresh but hazy colors. Bundled with the DVD in a separate slip jacket is a Discipline sampler CD featuring more than 70 minutes of cuts, many from Fripp and King Crimson.

The DVD's menu format is just about the most frustrating concoction we've come across in DVD menus. The choices flash one at a time and then disappear, and there is no logic to their progression in relation to one's controller arrows. If you follows the instructions that come on the jacket insert closely, you can eventually master it, but, like appreciating the band's music, you have to work at it. This is especially true of the menu options that activate the DVD's Dolby Digital and DTS audio tracks, which are very difficult to locate or access. The standard stereo surround soundtrack is plenty loud, but a bit garish, and both the Dolby Digital and DTS tracks have better defined separations and a better balance. The group's music is ideally served by a 5.1 mix, because the independence of the individual performers is as critical to their art as is their cooperative harmonics. The DTS track has slightly clearer detail than the Dolby Digital track, but the differences are minor. Several concert numbers are presented with a choice of multiple angles, so you can see the work of a particular musician highlighted. One number also uses multiple audio choices to give the viewer power over the audio mix, allowing the viewer to choose which musicians appear on the center channel and which are relegated to the surround channels.

Each side is accompanied by several other supplementary segments, as well. There are lengthy essays by Fripp about the band and its music, as well as tirades about financial underhandedness in the music business and about rock critics. There are a few silent 'home movies' of the band on tour and a couple other minor options. Additionally, in DVD-ROM supported by Acrobat Reader 3.0, there is an expansion of Fripp's musings, gathered together with letters, memos and other documents to give you a fairly complete history of the band as both an artistic and a business entity.

Getting back to the concert however, despite the fuzzy picture (which, considering the rest of the production, could well be conceptual), the music is both stimulating and contemplative. Initially we felt the music was the antithesis of the DVD's cluttered design, but once we licked the ins and outs of the menu, it seemed like the presentation enhanced one's appreciation of the music's complexity.

King of the Cowboys (see **Roy Rogers Collection 1**)

Kingpin (MGM, 906275)

Woody Harrelson stars as a former bowling whiz kid who has been on the rocks for a couple decades after his arm was mangled by a group of disgruntled hustle victims. Randy Quaid is an Amish bowler that Harrelson decides to manage with hopes of scoring on a winner-take-all purse in Reno. Bill Murray is the villain and Vanessa Angel is the romantic interest. The film makes fun of Amish people and people with prosthetics, and much of the humor is rather base, but the narrative has steady forward motion and the comedy is varied enough that you're bound to find something to laugh at along the way.

The 117 minute feature is 4 minutes longer than the standard 113 minute version. Some of the footage was taken out to quicken the film's pace, but some was removed to appease the MPAA, although the DVD's jacket rather adamantly underscores the fact that the program has retained its 'R' rating. The everything-they-touch-with-their-soiled-hands-turns-to-money Farrelly brothers, Peter and Bobby, who directed, provide a commentary channel. The brothers spend a lot of the commentary pointing out the friends and acquaintances who have walk-ons as extras, but they do explain their basic concepts (they didn't go to film school, which may be one reason why their work seems so fresh), talk about working with the performers (and letting Murray adlib like crazy), and share some anecdotes about the shoot.

The demented 1996 feature is presented on one side in letterboxed format, with an aspect ratio of about 2.35:1 and an accommodation for enhanced 16:9 playback, and in full screen format on the other side. The Super-35 letterboxing adds some picture information to the sides, but masks off picture information on the bottom in comparison to the full screen version. The letterboxing framing is better balanced, however, and tends to focus the viewer more effectively to the comedy of a scene. Colors are sharp and the fleshtones are accurate. The stereo surround sound and Dolby Digital sound are fine, though the film's audio mix is not elaborate. The program can be supported by optional English and French subtitles, and comes with a trailer.

The Kinks (see **Ray Davies: Return to Waterloo/Come Dancing with the Kinks**)

Kiss Me Monster (Anchor Bay, DV10600)

A nearly incomprehensible but iconographically engaging 1970 European trash spy movie, the continuity is very flakey, and it leaps so bizarrely from one shot to the next that you just give up after a while expecting it to make sense. There is one wonderful sequence where the heroines—two jet-setting IQ-challenged strippers who apparently solve crimes or something—discover that a windmill is a large combination lock, and there are dead bodies aplenty, but the best way to watch the movie (they are hired to obtain some kind of secret formula) is to just kind of sit back and ogle at it, reminiscing about the days of bouffants, miniskirts and small convertible sports cars. Multiple viewings are a definite possibility.

The picture is letterboxed with an aspect ratio of about 1.66:1. The color quality changes from one shot to the next, with hues ranging from good to bedraggled. Fleshtones also vary, though some shots look great, and there are a number of scratches, but when you take the nature of the film into account, the flaws don't seem important. The film was originally an Italian production and has been dubbed into English, the speakers pausing unnaturally at times to try and match the lip movements. You gotta love it. The monophonic sound, like the picture, is nothing great, but func-

tional. The film runs 78 minutes and is accompanied by a dull trailer.

Kiss of the Vampire (Image, ID4286USDVD)

The picture on the enjoyable 1962 Hammer Production is letterboxed with an aspect ratio of about 1.85:1 and no 16:9 enhancement. Although some sequences show a slight grain, the colors are terrific and the image is generally sharp. The monophonic sound is okay and the 88 minute program is adequately captioned. For those of you who can't remember one Hammer vampire movie from another, this one has no significant stars and is about a honeymooning couple who chance upon a castle. Eventually they are invited to a costume party, where the wife is kidnapped. The vampires are finally destroyed by a flock of bats (on strings), called forth with an incantation (or grips with shaky hands). The ending is a hoot and the film is a competent entry in the vampire genre.

Kiss the Girls (Paramount, 331887)

The serial killer thriller attempts to capitalize on **Seven** by casting Morgan Freeman as the psychologist-detective hero. We don't want to give away the plot, except to say that *Jennifer 8* is more logical and **Seven** is more profound. The film is very exciting in spots—next to Freeman and co-star Ashley Judd, that's probably its greatest asset—and while the mystery is cooking it smells good, but the resolution is a half-baked movie contrivance—not distasteful, but flavorless. With a film like **Scream**, you can go back and watch it a second time, seeing things from a different perspective. We tried that with **Kiss the Girls** but found nothing had changed.

The presentation is letterboxed with an aspect ratio of about 2.35:1 and an accommodation for enhanced 16:9 playback. The colors are well defined and the image is sharp, even in darker sequences. The stereo surround sound is a little light, but the Dolby Digital track has some dimensionality and power when the drama calls for it. The 117 minute program is also available in French in Dolby Digital and can be supported by English or Spanish subtitles. There is also a theatrical trailer that gives away most of the plot.

Kissing a Fool (Universal, 20320)

A romantic comedy about two guys in love with the same woman, David Schwimmer stars as a Chicago sportscaster and Jason Lee is his best friend, an author, with Mili Avital as the object of their affections. Schwimmer's timing, as well as that of Bonnie Hunt in a secondary role, generates a sustained humor, so that the somewhat embarrassing mechanics of the plot—the two guys are using one another to test the woman's love—don't grind that badly. There are better romantic comedies available, but romantic comedies are like kisses—we can never get enough.

The presentation is in letterboxed format, with an aspect ratio of about 1.85:1 and an accommodation for enhanced 16:9 playback. The letterboxing is substantially different from the letterboxing on the LD, masking picture information off the top and bottom, and cropping more off the sides, to deliver a slightly blown up image in comparison to the LD's image. The picture transfer, however, is less hazy, with slightly deeper hues. The stereo surround sound is a bit weak, but the Dolby Digital encoding is stronger. The film's stereo mix, however, is not all that interesting. The 92 minute program can be supported by English, Spanish or French subtitles and comes with a trailer, a couple production notes and a cast-and-director profile section.

Kitaro World Tour 1990 Kojiki: A Story in Concert (Pioneer, PA99609D)

The camera stays pretty close to the Japanese electronic jazz group's primary keyboardist, and the video direction, perhaps, does not present the performance in quite as dramatic a manner as it could be presented (or as it is presented in spots), but the Dolby Digital sound is super, with clear, hyped up tones coming at you from every side. The 55 minute *Kojiki* suite, inspired by a Japanese creation myth, is a rousing composition, with more variety and energy than the Kitaro programs we've seen in the past. (There are a lot of drums and a violinist, in addition to the keyboards.)

The picture is somewhat grainy, and colors are a little bland. The Dolby Digital track is super, but even the standard stereo surround soundtrack sounds terrific.

Klondike Annie (Image, ID4283USDVD)

The 1936 film has a slightly stronger narrative than other Mae West Paramount films, perhaps because the Production Code was firmly in place by the time it was made. West is a saloon singer who disguises herself as an evangelist and travels to Nome, Alaska to duck out on a murder rap (it was self-defense) in San Francisco. The story ends abruptly and it is better behaved than her best movies, but any time West is in front of the camera there is enjoyment to be had, and **Klondike Annie** is no exception.

The picture is sharp and blacks look true. Contrasts are nicely detailed, though there is some wear on the source material. The monophonic sound is a little weak, but not to the point where distortion sets in. The 76 minute program is adequately closed captioned.

Knebworth (see Live! At Knebworth)

Knock Off (Columbia TriStar, 25889)

The Tsui Hark feature, starring Jean-Claude Van Damme, is a pure action movie and very much a Hong Kong-type film, about explosive buttons that have been slipped onto imitation designer shirts and jeans (hence the title). The plot teeters on incoherence and the characters are little more than faces with bodies attached, but the energetic movie must contain at least a dozen stylistic innovations or experiments, and it is an exhilarating look at how movies could be made. Remember, for example, split screens? The Sixties experiment in multiple viewpoints never quite caught on, though it seemed ideal for filling a viewer's head with information quickly and keeping the pace up, particularly in the expository sequences of an action film. Here, Hark brings the technique up-to-date, isolating a close up of an activity in a small square within the larger image, like a computer screen window. But that isn't the only fresh trick. The camera zooms in and out of the tiniest holes, ratchets or freeze-frames in the middle of the action (are the look of films already being influenced by DVD playback?) and drops 50, 60 feet down the side of a building, straight for the street. Jumping from near-microscopic to full sized images, the movie advances from one scene to the next by slamming into each new setting, the way an action scene ought to and the way Van Damme approaches each villain.

The picture is letterboxed on one side, with an aspect ratio of about 2.35:1 and an accommodation for enhanced 16:9 playback, and in full screen format on the other side. The full screen image loses just a smidgen on the side in comparison to the letterboxed image and adds substantial amounts of picture information to the top and the bottom. The movie is confusing enough as it is, so anything that makes it easier to follow is advantageous and we tend to prefer the full screen framing. The film has both the look and sound of a Hong Kong production, though the picture quality is less compromised. The image is cluttered but solid, with decent hues and viable fleshtones. The stereo surround sound and menu-activated Dolby Digital sound are more problematic. The dialogue channel is coherent, but it doesn't have much strength and the whole audio balance seems off. The gunshots and explosions lack resonance, as well, though if you jack up the volume, it can be as engaging as any action feature. Rear channel separations tend to be more distinctive on the Dolby Digital track. The 91 minute program can be supported by English subtitles and is accompanied by a small publicity still section, and trailers for the film and for a couple other Van Damme features.

Kobe's Tie X-rated (Vivid, UPC#0073215530)

A couple meet at a masquerade party but don't exchange identities. Then, when the man tries to find the woman later on, her roommate pretends she's his dreamgirl. The story is fairly basic and the erotic sequences are a little stretched out, but the program is competently put together. The picture looks okay, with bright hues and a sharp focus. The monophonic sound is fine. Kobe Tai, Brooke Ashley, Julia Ann, Maya and Dakoto are featured in the 74 minute program. The DVD also contains alternate angle sequences and elaborate hardcore interactive promotional features.

Kolchak (see The Night Stalker /The Night Strangler)

Konitz, Lee (see Chick Corea Pat Metheny Lee Konitz: Woodstock Jazz Festival)

Kool & the Gang (Pioneer, PA99612D)

Since the show was shot in Germany, an all-white audience can be seen trying fitfully to boogie, though that doesn't stop the popular Seventies dance group from delivering a terrific performance on the nostalgic *The Best of MusikLaden Live* offering. The 45 minute program is an ideal live performance, free of the slickness imposed by a studio recording, but still fully melodic. It is delivered in a setting that is still sufficiently confined to bring out the details in the contributions by the individual performers, and every camera angle captures two or three of them doing something interesting.

Colors are reasonably bright, but fleshtones are a little bland and there is some video smearing, more apparently a flaw of the original taping than of the DVD transfer. The stereo surround sound is clear and nicely defined. The bass is subdued, but it helps you hear everything else better. There is a Dolby Digital track with somewhat clearer tones. The program is not captioned.

Krakatoa: East of Java two versions (Simitar, 7224)

The wonderfully cheesy 1969 adventure film was released initially with a rather drastic flaw. It was supposed to be letterboxed, but due to an error in the formatting, it was presented squeezed. Simitar then reissued it, letterboxed with an aspect ratio of about 2.6:1, but with no accommodation for enhanced 16:9 playback. Sometimes you just can't win. Anyway, the first version was issued in Simitar's old packaging format, a jewel case inside a cardboard box, while the corrected version appears in the standard slipcase jacket. Both have the same catalogue number and the only way to tell the platters apart without playing them is that the inner ring on the good version is white, while the inner ring on the old version is clear.

The source material is a little bedraggled in places, but fans will recognize that this is not a standard studio-financed production and who knows where the negatives are. There are numerous scratches and other speckles, and even a few splices. For the most part, the colors are decent. Dark areas of the screen lack detail, the image is a little soft and contrasts are weak in places, but hues are fairly bright and fleshtones are workable. Segments that are free of distortion or wear look terrific.

The sound is mildly stereophonic and is best not played at too great a volume. The upper end sounds quite fuzzy and there is also a lot of noise on the track. The program is not captioned. The film runs 105 minutes, which is its standard length, though it was trimmed from its initial road show running time.

Maximilian Schell, Brian Keith, Sal Mineo, Diane Baker and Rossano Brazzi head the cast. They are on a boat, searching for some valuable pearls in a sunken cabinet, and happen to be in the neighborhood when the big one blows. The onboard dramatic conflicts are serviceable, the stars are competent (Mineo is especially good as Brazzi's son), and the special effects—not the silly miniature volcanoes, but the substantially more realistic tsunami—are great fun.

Kull the Conqueror (Universal, 20154)

It's good to see that they still make Saturday afternoon movies because we were afraid it had become a lost art. All you need for **Kull The Conqueror** is some rain and some popcorn and you'll have a great time. Kevin Sorbo stars in the title role, based upon a Robert E. Howard character, who must defeat an evil sorceress to free his kingdom from enslavement. The music, by Joel Goldsmith, epitomizes how foolproof the movie's design can be. There is a typical orchestral score, with plenty of flourish, but whenever the sword fighting gets real hot and heavy, this absolutely awful electric guitar riff kicks in—and darn if it doesn't get your heart racing a little faster each time you hear it. The special effects are utterly adequate, there are muscles galore and there is plenty of scheming and betrayal to keep you worried about the plot and the hero's fate. And just when things look like they might become complacent, Harvey Fierstein pops up, in pelts.

The picture is in letterboxed format, with an aspect ratio of about 2.35:1 and an accommodation for enhanced 16:9 playback. The picture is sharp and well detailed, but fleshtones are a little pinkish. The stereo surround sound is fair, but the Dolby Digital track is stronger, and the film's audio mix is enjoyable. The 96 minute program is also available in French in standard stereo and can be accompanied by English or Spanish subtitles. There is a theatrical trailer that mistakenly emphasizes the film's humor (it just doesn't catch the movie's spirit properly), along with extensive production notes and a decent cast profile section.

Kundun (Buena Vista, 14890)

One of Martin Scorsese's periodic forays away from the crime genre, the excellent biographical drama, about the life of Tibet's Dalai Lama up to the point where he was forced to go into exile, is the first Scorsese film to have an unambiguously moral hero. The 1997 film, which is as precisely measured and designed as a sand painting, gives a concise history of Tibet in the 20th Century and an overview of the Dalai Lama's maturation, the loss of his country occurring at almost the exact point where a normal man would begin to regret the loss of his youth. The film has its gangsters in the vulturous Chinese, and there is a wonderful, Fellini-esque depiction of Chairman Mao. Running 135 minutes, the drama is essentially in two even parts, the first half being about the education of the Dalai Lama and the second half being about the Chinese invasion. Backed by an aggressive Philip Glass score and visually arresting, classically styled montage interludes from cinematographer Roger Deakins and editor Thelma Schoonmaker, Scorsese uses narrative to tell the history and uses artistry to communicate the philosophies of the Dalai Lama and of Buddhism. The film's lessons are wrapped in such elegant and engrossing packages, however, that some viewers may feel discouraged from taking the effort to unbundle its wisdoms. We also felt that **Kundun** would make an excellent double bill with **The Last Emperor**, one film being about a man, born and educated to lead, following his destiny, and the other being about a leader by birth who went astray of his education.

The picture is letterboxed with an aspect ratio of about 2.35:1 and no 16:9 enhancement. Colors are precise, fleshtones are accurate and details are crisp, even in challenging lighting conditions. The stereo surround sound is good and the Dolby Digital sound is super, with crisp details, intelligent separation effects and unambiguous strength. The program can be supported by optional English subtitles and is accompanied by a theatrical trailer that does its best to sell the film.

L

L.A. Confidential (Warner, 14913)

An exquisite mystery thriller about corruption and gangsterism in Los Angeles in the early Fifties, the film has three heroes, who can't stand each other, but their inherent morality eventually brings them together. One of the joys of the film, however, is watching them each uncover overlapping parts of the puzzle, none aware of what the others have learned. There are contrivances in the film, particularly in regard to Kim Basinger's character, but so much about the movie is so ideally realized that its accomplishments vastly outweigh its flaws. Russell Crowe, Guy Pearce and Kevin Spacey star.

An 18 minute 'making of' featurette, an interactive 'tour' of the Los Angeles locations and architecture used in the film, and a further 8 minute examination of the photographs director Curtis Hansen gathered to inspire his collaborators accompany the 1997 feature. The pieces provide enlightening background information about the film and about the artists contributing to it. There is also the standard cast & crew profile section, an amusing overview of 1953 prices, and a look at the real historical figures upon which some of the characters in the film are based.

The colors are deep and smooth, and are soft, such as Basinger's lipstick, only when the image requires a variation. The picture looks super, with crisp, consistently vivid colors and rich fleshtones. The image has been letterboxed, with an aspect ratio of about 2.35:1 and an accommodation for enhanced 16:9 playback. The stereo surround sound is terrific and the Dolby Digital sound is even better. Jerry Goldsmith's music is perfectly measured, and it has been gloriously mixed, with different pieces of it weighing in from every speaker, again like parts of a puzzle. For those who want greater thrills, check out the climactic siege on the motel room in Dolby Digital—you'll think those footsteps are outside your own viewing room, about to bust in. Additionally, the DVD has a music-only track, which is also in Dolby Digital, bringing out not only Goldsmith's outstanding score, but the many period pop songs Hansen used to set the mood. The 138 minute film also comes in French in Dolby Digital and can be supported by English, French or Spanish subtitles. A collection of trailers and TV commercials can be accessed, as well.

L.A. Story (Artisan, 60478)

The pixilated Steve Martin comedy opens with an amusing takeoff on *La Dolce Vita*, depicting a helicopter transporting a large hotdog and bun, a gag that sets the tone for the entire film, a mixture of witty intelligence and harmless silliness. The film is a romance, sprinkled with mildly absurd gags about L.A. lifestyles (the hero has to get his credit approved at a German bank in order to secure a reservation at a posh restaurant) and some well-placed touches of fantasy.

The picture is letterboxed with an aspect ratio of about 1.85:1 and no 16:9 enhancement. The image has a mild softness, and colors are reasonably bright and fleshtones are workable. The stereo surround sound has a sporadic dimensionality and scattered separation effects. The film can be supported by Spanish subtitles ("Conocí a gente inteligente aquí en Los Angeles") or English closed captioning. The 98 minute 1991 feature is accompanied by a trailer that doesn't sell the film too well, a 6 minute featurette that includes more footage from the film than behind the scenes, two 'hidden' sound bites, from the Martin and director Mick Jackson, talking about the film, cast & crew profiles, and production notes that claim, though we don't see it, that Martin based his script on *Midsummer Nights' Dream*.

La Bamba (Columbia TriStar, 08549)

What can you say about a movie and a DVD that are so good the 'making of' featurettes bring tears to your eyes? Luis Valdez' breakthrough 1987 musical biography about the brief, shining life of the Hispanic-American rock 'n' roll singer, Ritchie Valens, has been released with an outstanding collection of extras. Written and directed by the legendary Hispanic-American dramatist, Luis Valdez, after being conceived and nurtured by Valdez' brother, Daniel, and veteran filmmaker, Taylor Hackford, if you didn't already love the movie, which is as much about the pain and strength of families and a testament to the very best of the American spirit as it is about rock 'n' roll, then surely you will by the time the DVD is over. Lou Diamond Phillips stars as Valens, with Esai Morales as his brother, Rosana DeSoto as his mother and Elizabeth Peña as his sister-in-law.

The film is presented in letterboxed format only, with an aspect ratio of about 1.85:1 and an accommodation for enhanced 16:9 playback. The letterboxing adds some picture information to the sides of the image and masks picture information off the top and the bottom in comparison to full screen versions, but the letterbox framing is better balanced and pulls you instinctively toward the heart of each shot. The color transfer is excellent. The film was a tightly budgeted effort, and there is some grain in the darker scenes, but the image is very sharp, with finely detailed hues.

The standard stereo surround sound is strong and fresh. Most viewers will probably prefer it to the 5-channel Dolby Digital track, though the Dolby Digital track does offer an interesting perspective on the film. On the standard track, environmental sounds and music fill the rear channels as one expects them to, but on the Dolby Digital track, the rear channels are nearly silent, usually offering little more than a subtle underscore to what is happening in front. The result evokes the monophonic sound of the era the film is depicting, while retaining the sophistication of a contemporary recording.

The 108 minute film also has a 4-channel Spanish language soundtrack and optional English, Spanish, Portuguese, Chinese, Korean, and Thai subtitles (as a scene in the film explains, Valens' professional name used a 't' in Ritchie, while his original nickname did not—the DVD's jacket copy and menu copy use the original spelling, while the subtitling and closed captioning applies the personal and professional spelling during their appropriate moments). The DVD's only flaw: the cast profile section is paltry.

There are three featurettes—a generalized overview that includes an interview with the 'real' Donna; one that emphasizes the movie's music; and one that emphasizes the movie's close ties to Valens' family, with shots of his mother (she passed away shortly after the film premiered) hanging out with DeSoto, shots of his brother hanging out with Morales (the similarities are uncanny), and archival photos of Valens himself. In blending the brilliantly edited footage from the film with an affirmation of truth in the film's essence, each featurette brings the viewer to a moment of emotional epiphany.

There are also two terrific music videos. One is a complete rendition of Howard Huntberry's performance as Jackie Wilson singing *Lonely Teardrops* (within the film, it is chopped up, understandably, by scenes with Phillips); and the other is the beautifully measured rendition of the title song, combining the footage of Phillips performing it with joyously energetic footage of the number's true performers, Los Lobos. Even the movie's trailer, which is also included on the DVD, is a masterpiece—it has the guts to tell the film's ending, and yet still sells the movie as something so exciting you'll want to see it and feel it no matter where it leads.

In addition to those features, there are two commentary tracks, one by Hackford and Daniel Valdez, and one by Luis Valdez, Phillips, Morales and Executive Producer Stuart Benjamin. We recommend that you listen to the Hackford and Daniel Valdez talk before the Luis Valdez & Co. talk (it is also best to watch the featurettes af-

ter having been steeped in the information provided by the commentaries). Hackford, who has contributed to audio commentaries before, provides a clear chronology of how the film was conceived and executed. Both speak descriptively about the atmosphere during the film's creation and about the film's meanings.

The Benjamin, Morales, Phillips and Luis Valdez talk is much more laid back and anecdotal (when Phillips first went to the audition, his agent mistakenly told him he was trying out for a part in a biography of Frankie Valli; the 'lemon tree' that Trini Lopez made famous is in the Valens' backyard). They do talk about the production, but not in an organized fashion, and spend a lot of time pointing out the mistakes and identifying the many members of the cast who came from their own or Valens' families. Like Valens, Phillips was an unknown talent whose popularity rocketed because of a single youthful role (one of the producers told him, 'We're giving you the keys to the candy store. Don't rot your teeth'). Phillips also shares the DVD's most touching moment outside of the film itself—a moment so moving that it not only legitimizes the otherwise lackadaisical commentary track, but would make the DVD worth obtaining even if it had no other extras but Diamond's one recollection. Visiting the set, Valens' mother approached Diamond, who was dressed in character. She embraced him, and started sobbing, asking why he'd left them.

Film buffs may be aware that Hackford has been involved in a number of Hispanic-themed films. As he explains, he grew up in a mixed neighborhood, and considers Hispanic-American culture to be a central point of reference for how he looks at the world. Daniel and Luis are brothers, and parallels within the script about Valens' relationship with his brother gave the film much of its power because it came from their hearts, and because Luis Valdez is so much a master of metaphoric symbolism he understands that the film is also about the stormy sibling relationship between the Chicano and American cultures. Although the DVD comes out a decade after the film itself was produced, it is a legitimate capstone to the movie's artistry, offering testimonials not only to how Hispanic folk art has seeped into the general culture, but how the success of **La Bamba**—the movie, like the song before it—opened the sluice gates and irrigated the fruits of assimilation.

La Bohème (see **The Metropolitan Opera: La Bohème**)

La Cosa Nostra Mafia / An Exposé (Madacy, DVD99002)
La Cosa Nostra Mafia / An Exposé: Vol. 1 (Madacy, DVD990021)
La Cosa Nostra Mafia / An Exposé: Vol. 2 (Madacy, DVD990022)
La Cosa Nostra Mafia / An Exposé: Vol. 3 (Madacy, DVD990023)
La Cosa Nostra Mafia / An Exposé: Vol. 4 (Madacy, DVD990024)
La Cosa Nostra Mafia / An Exposé: Vol. 5 (Madacy, DVD990025)

The ten-part history of 'organized crime' in America is available as a box set and five separate releases. Each of the five contains two 45 minute episodes, along with a bit of background information on the mobsters and their families in a supplement. The picture looks very fresh and crisp during contemporary interviews and the archive footage is passable. The sound is okay and the programs are not captioned.

The documentary is not especially well organized, but it covers a lot of material that is bound to be of interest to many viewers. **Vol. 1** features *Coming to America* and *Al Capone*, charting the rise of gangsterism during the early part of the Twentieth Century and how it crystallized during Prohibition. There is some good footage of Bonnie & Clyde's corpses (the police used bullets that went through the car and both bodies) and a coherent explanation of the St. Valentine's Day Massacre. **Vol. 2**, *Valachi Luciano Genovese* and *Hollywood*, explains the power struggles that followed Capone's demise and discusses the substantial influence the Mob has apparently had on Hollywood and vice versa. **Vol. 3**, *Vegas* and *Hoffa*, goes into detail about the creation of Las Vegas (the character Joe Pesci portrayed in **Casino** is almost indistinguishable from the real individual the character was representing), the Cuban revolution and the corruption within the Teamster's union. **Vol. 4**, *Kennedy Connection* and *Gallo Columbo Bonanno*, completes the material covered in *Hoffa* and then goes on to explore the power struggles during the Seventies and Eighties, while *Gotti*, on **Vol. 5**, *Gotti* and *Resume*, shows how the government's anti-racketeering efforts finally began to make headway and break up the influence and control the Mob has supposedly maintained over the years. *Resume* is a compilation program featuring highlights from the other nine episodes.

La Donna del Lago (see Rossini's La Donna del Lago)

La Fanciulla Del West (see Puccini's La Fanciulla Del West)

La Femme Nikita (Pioneer, LDVM5471D)
The French spy thriller is letterboxed has an aspect ratio of about 2.35:1 and no 16:9 enhancement. The colors are a little dark, creating a glossy, rich image in most shots, but making things look a little too dark in a few others. The image is sharp. The French soundtrack is in Dolby Digital, while the English soundtrack, which has less flourish, is in standard stereo only. The Dolby Digital sound, with its multi-genre music score and elaborate action effect sequences, has the energy and dimension needed to support the images and the narrative. The film is available with or without English subtitling and English closed captioning, but to activate some of the language options, such as English with English subtitles, you have to use both the menu and your machine's audio toggle. The 1991 feature, about a young woman, arrested for killing a cop, who is recruited by the government as an assassin, was directed with great style by Luc Besson and runs 117 minutes.

La Jetée (see Short Cinema Journal 1:2 Issue: Dreams)

La Toya Jackson's Interactive Exotic Club Tour: A Hawaiian Fantasy (Vivid, UPC#0073214614)
The collection of topless modeling & dancing sequences is hosted by a fully clothed La Toya Jackson. The program, which originated on cable, runs 45 minutes, but is combined with Vivid's extensive promotional supplements, and visits a topless nightclub on Oahu. Several of the employees are shown both at work and visiting remote parts of the island for a sort of busman's holiday. The supplements include a 13 minute 'making of' featurette, extended clips, clips from other programs and a still photo section. The picture on the feature program is fairly blurry, though colors are reasonably bright. The stereo sound is okay, but somewhat reserved.

La Toya Jackson's Interactive Exotic Club Tour: Hot Texas Nights (Vivid, UPC#0073214580)
The 37 minute program, part of a softcore cable series, visits an establishment called Fantasy Ranch and features standard topless dance sequences, shot in a live environment and introduced by a fully clothed Jackson. The picture is rather fuzzy and colors are okay. The monophonic musical score is reasonably loud, but the dialogue has no upper end.

La Traviata (Universal, 20326)
Teresa Stratas, Plácido Domingo and Cornell MacNeill star in Franco Zeffirelli's smart 1982 adaptation of Giuseppe Verdi's operatic rendering of *Camille*, to which Zeffirelli applies his usual opulence with great flair. With the luxury of pre-recording, Stratas' singing is outstanding. It may lack a bit of color, but her vocals slide up and down the scale with a solid and compelling intensity. Her demeanor is, on the other hand, suitably frail. Domingo's singing is also highly attractive, with an energetic efficiency that is well suited for his screen performance.

The picture is letterboxed with an aspect ratio of about 1.8:1 and an accommodation for enhanced 16:9 playback. The letterboxing adds a little to the sides in comparison to full screen versions and masks more off the top and bottom. Sometimes the masking seems a little tight, but generally, the framing is workable. Because the narrative is told in flashback or something, the cinematography is deliberately hazy, and the haze is occasionally so dominating it draws a viewer's attention away from the images beneath it. Still, the picture is sharper than previous efforts and colors are more accurate. Fleshtones look good.

The stereo surround sound has no directional effects, just a total bleed of the music and the vocals to the rear channel. The audio is reasonably clean and has an adequate dynamic range. The 115 minute film is in Italian and is supported by optional English subtitles that read like captions, identifying sounds as well as translating the lyrics. There are also optional French subtitles, a production essay, a cast-and-director profile section and a trailer that pretty much tries to hide the fact that the film is an opera.

Lady in White (Elite, EE5240)
Lukas Haas stars in the film as a young boy who has a run-in with a serial killer and meets the ghost of the killer's first victim. It is a nostalgic piece, set in 1962 and clearly drawn from the formative years of the film's director, Frank LaLoggia (he even uses a story he wrote in the third grade, quite effectively, for a classroom scene), who named Haas' character, 'Frankie.' The 1988 film has a number of highly evocative scenes and a couple of real good scares, but the narrative is also overly elaborate and is not logical, even on its own terms.

The presentation, a 'Director's Cut,' runs 119 minutes, adding about 6 minutes to the standard theatrical release, mostly scenes of character development that do not do much to advance the plot. The colors are rich and the picture is fairly blurry, a fault, apparently, of the low budget production (the filmmakers sold 'shares' in the movie as a penny stock and had to check with their brokerage house every day to see how much money they had to work with). The picture is letterboxed with an aspect ratio of about 1.85:1, without an accommodation for 16:9 playback. Letterboxing adds nothing to the sides of the image in comparison to a full screen version and masks off picture information from the top and bottom, but the framing looks fine.

The stereo surround sound is more difficult to judge. Some sequences have been re-mixed and enhanced for the presentation, though the original soundtrack is brighter and sharper. The Dolby Digital track seems even less powerful than the standard stereo track. The bass is more pronounced on the regular track, and it is only on rare occasions that the Dolby Digital mix exhibits more distinct separations and improved detail. There is no captioning.

Accompanying the film are theatrical, TV and radio ads, followed by a promo reel that was used to lure investors, in which LaLoggia essentially created a miniature version of the film previous to shooting the feature. There are several deleted scenes that LaLoggia chose not to include in the *Director's Cut*, largely because they throw off the pace or don't entirely fit with the surrounding emotions, though the sequences do add even more to the characters. An hour's worth of director LaLoggia's musical score, broken into three 20 minute suites and presented to a montage of production stills in standard stereo.

LaLoggia also provides a commentary track, talking about his experiences during the film's production and a few related subjects. His best stories are about the way the film has touched others, be it the citizens of the small New York town where the movie was shot, who started screaming with excitement when they first learned what the filmmakers were up to, the girls on the train who were frightened by the actress playing the title character the day after a cable screening, or the girl LaLoggia had a crush on in grade school and hadn't seen since, who called him up after she unknowingly took her niece to the film and had the surprise of her life (he named most of his characters after real people and replicated real situations for the non-thriller, non-fantasy sequences). He has less to say about the technical aspects of the shoot, though he does explain how he had to make do on a very limited effects budget and talks in general terms about how to bring in a film with major performers (Alex Rocco, Len Cariou and Katherine Helmond are also featured) on no money, a few good ideas and lots of stomach knots.

The Lady Vanishes (Criterion, LAD120)

Margaret Lockwood and Michael Redgrave star in the 1938 Alfred Hitchcock thriller, which runs 97 minutes and is set mostly on a train. The black-and-white picture is much cleaner and sharper than Criterion's LD. There is still an age-related softness in some sequences, but the image is spotless, contrasts are nicely detailed and blacks are smooth. The standard monophonic sound is clean but subdued, and the Dolby Digital mono track is sharper, without the noise. There is a commentary track from film historian Bruce Eder, who provides a typically thorough talk, discussing the background and career of each performer and much of the crew, providing a history of the production and branching off into a discussion of train films, missing people movies and other digressions. He also analyzes why the movie works as an entertainment (with the new transfer, we had a great deal more patience for the opening act, where much groundwork is laid but little of substance occurs) and points out some of Hitchcock's subtler touches (watch for the waiter with the champagne bottle and the two strategically placed breads).

Ladyhawke (Warner, 11464)

The 1985 she's-a-bird-by-day-and-he's-a-dog-at-night romantic fantasy action costume film stars Rutger Hauer, Michelle Pfeiffer and Matthew Broderick. It has been released in letterboxed format on one side, with an aspect ratio of about 2.35:1 and no 16:9 enhancement, and cropped on the other side. The cropping makes things confusing and isn't worth much. The color transfer is reasonably strong, though minor speckles on the source material still show up here and there. The stereo surround sound is not elaborate, but the Dolby Digital track is much better, with smoother and more detailed tones, particularly on the lower end of the register. The 121 minute film is also available in French in standard stereo and in Spanish in mono and can be accompanied by English, French or Spanish subtitles. There is an extensive cast profile and some good production notes, particularly concerning all the European castles where the film was shot. A flaccid trailer has also been included.

The Land Before Time (Universal, 20278)

Fortunately, the 1988 animated feature only runs an hour (with an endless final credit scroll). Part of its narrative was excised before its theatrical release (the picture books have the complete plot), probably for the better. About young dinosaurs who have to help one another on a journey when they are accidentally abandoned by their elders, the story isn't all that interesting, the artwork isn't all that inspiring and any similarity to real dinosaurs seems totally coincidental. Oh, and for who knows what reason, the hero of the series looks like Ronald Reagan.

Colors are reasonably sharp and adequately defined. The film is presented in full screen format. The stereo surround sound is fairly basic, but it has a nice dimensionality and a fair amount of power in spots. The film is also available in French and Spanish, and can be supported by optional English subtitles.

The Landlady (Trimark, VM6897)

A typical psycho thriller, Talia Shire (in a somewhat campy performance) gets the hots for one of her tenants and kills his girlfriend, as well as anybody else who gets in her way.

The 1997 feature is in full screen format, though the framing looks fine. Hues are a bit subdued, but the image presentation is

adequate and fleshtones look okay. The musical score has a pleasant dimensionality and the stereo surround soundtrack is fine. The 98 minute program has optional French and Spanish subtitles, English closed captioning, a cast profile section and a trailer.

Landmarks of Early Film (Image, ID4103DSDVD)

The outstanding 117 minute program is a compilation of motion pictures from the beginning years of cinema. The collection not only provides the viewer with complete renditions of the basic masterpieces cited in most reference works—A Trip to the Moon, The Great Train Robbery, Edison's The Kiss—it conveys a true sense of how the motion picture format developed during its first two decades of existence, beginning with Eadweard Muybridge's sequential photo studies, moving on to Thomas Edison's original single-subject productions, the French Lumière brothers and their famous single shot documentary portraits (including the first film 'gag'—a gardener's hose stops running and then sprays him in his face when he examines it—the sequence is fascinating for how its timing runs against modern anticipations) and American documentary footage depicting, among other things, San Francisco immediately after the 1906 earthquake, the lower Manhattan skyline as seen from the harbor in 1903 and the only footage we are aware of depicting William McKinley in action. Longer pieces created shortly after the Turn of the Century include a fanciful colored ballet entitled The Golden Beetle, a comedy short consisting of sequential portraits entitled The Whole Dam Family and the Dam Dog, an early French slapstick piece about policemen chasing a dog entitled The Policemen's Little Run, a Max Linder short entitled Troubles of a Grasswidower, an intriguing Roman epic, Nero, Or the Fall of Rome, Windsor McKay and His Animated Pictures, a good D.W. Griffith short, The Girl and Her Trust, and one of the first Keystone Cop concoctions, Bangville Police, featuring Mabel Normand.

The quality of the source material is excellent. Trip to the Moon, for example, is accompanied by a voiceover narration that was intended to be read to the audience as the film was unspooling. The hand-painted explosions on Great Train Robbery are vivid and the colors in Golden Beetle are almost unbelievable. The audio track is a mixture of calm, contemporary stereo underscoring and earlier monophonic music that is a bit scratchier, but passable.

The collection demonstrates the different cinematic experiments and shows how the language of modern film can be seen developing as the programs advance. It is also valuable as a time machine-type glimpse of the past. More so than when the films stand individually and more so than films made later on, you really get the feeling, watching the movies contained on the DVD, that you are looking at a window onto the past. Although every person depicted in the collection is dead, their lives and even their youthfulness are not only preserved but conveyed to and felt by the viewer. You also get the sense that while technology has changed, styles have changed and manners have changed, the earth—in yards and creek beds and rolling hills—remains exactly the same. If you want to see the future, just look at the ground or in a garden, because it will still be like that, somewhere, 100 years from now.

Landmarks of Early Film Volume 2: The Magic of Méliès (Image, ID4668DSDVD)

Fourteen shorts by the great French experimenter in fantastic cinema, George Méliès, are presented. along with a 20 minute overview of Méliès' life and career. Méliès' best known film, A Trip to the Moon, was featured on the first Landmarks of Early Film collection and is not repeated here.

The 101 minute program opens with the 20 minute biographical sketch of the filmmaker's life, which is followed by a complete presentation of his extravagant, 20 minute fantasy, The Impossible Voyage, depicting a trip around the world through all the elements. The print is hand-colored.

All of the shorts in the collection are incredibly sharp-looking. There is damage at times to the source material that results in scratches and splices, but otherwise the black-and-white images are crisply focused and often look surprisingly vivid.

In *The Untamable Whiskers*, a man draws a picture of a beard, which then appears on his face. More pictures are followed by more changes. In *The Cook in Trouble*, set in a kitchen, imps frustrate a cook, stealing food, leaping out of pots and otherwise causing trouble. Similarly, a devil enchants the objects within an alchemist's laboratory in *The Mysterious Retort*. In *Tchin-Chao: The Chinese Conjurer*, *The Enchanted Sedan Chair* and *The Wonderful Living Fan*, inanimate objects are changed into beautiful women by conjurers. In *The Mermaid*, a man fills up a fish tank, obtaining the fish from his hat, and concludes by dropping a mermaid into the container. The figures within large playing cards come to life in *The Living Playing Cards* and, similarly, the images on a wall of posters come to life in *The Hilarious Posters*. *The Scheming Gambler's Paradise* eschews editing and double exposure tricks for straight stage gags, depicting a gambling parlor that is quickly turned into a clothing store during a raid. An anthropomorphic moon passes across an equally human-like sun, their expressions changing as their images cross in *The Eclipse (The Courtship of The Sun and Moon)*. An amusing, speculative depiction of video projection is provided in *Long Distance Wireless Photography*, in which the images appear to reveal the true nature of the person being shot. Approaching the form of a standard slapstick farce, *Good Glue Sticks* is about a glue peddler who uses his wares to frustrate a pair of cops.

Along with *The Impossible Voyage*, the best short is probably *The Black Imp*. Similar to *The Cook in Trouble* and *The Mysterious Retort* but less complex and more refined, the piece is about an imp who bedevils a man by moving around furniture in the man's bedroom. The work anticipates Norman McLaren's *A Chairy Tale* and achieves a genuine rhythm of comedy, a consistent pace Méliès rarely achieved.

Throughout the works, the set decorations are marvelously cluttered. With modifications, some of the shorts could easily have been performed on the stage, though most rely on the ability to manipulate the images on film to achieve their most fanciful tricks. Despite the promise shown in some of the later shorts, such as *Good Glue Sticks*, Méliès was apparently unable to advance his art to the next plateau and audiences moved on to more sophisticated cinematic entertainment, but the essence of the gimmicks and gags that he explored, evidently with some thoroughness, are responsible for virtually all the top box office hits of today.

Lap Dancing (Image, ID5602FMDVD)

A naive actress is encouraged to take a job at a strip joint, where she can learn to better get in touch with her inner, sensual self, and perhaps land roles very much like the one the actress who is playing her has landed. The erotic sequences are very drawn out and the dramatic passages are limited, but one does come across some choice pieces of dialogue ("Angie, you're a beautiful woman, but you're trying to get by on your good looks. You still haven't used what's inside. Acting sexy isn't pretending to be sexy, it's being sexy") and enough ludicrous situations (she falls in love with a blind guy who can always recognize her from a distance) to prevent the show from being a complete waste of time.

The picture is very soft, with orangey fleshtones and dull hues. The dialogue recording is distorted and irritating, but the stereo sound is reasonably strong. The 90 minute 1995 program is not captioned. The chapter encoding and jacket guide are limited.

Last Action Hero (Columbia TriStar, 27935/9)

Arnold Schwarzenegger stars in the clever 1993 action movie fantasy, about a young boy who enters the world of his movie hero, and then has the hero join him in the real world. The film lacks a profound ending, but much of it is legitimately inventive and high-

ly pleasing in a breathless, introspective manner. For those who care, the film's artistic examination of itself is inspired comedy, and for those who don't, the explosions and crashes and wild fights are spectacular, with the stereo surround sound and Dolby Digital sound amplifying the thrill of the moment from every conceivable direction.

The picture is presented on one side in letterboxed format, with an aspect ratio of about 2.35:1 and an accommodation for enhanced 16:9 playback, and is in full screen format on the other side. The scenes shot outdoors in the Los Angeles sun look bright and crisp, but indoor scenes and night scenes are a little weaker. The 131 minute program also has French and Spanish language soundtracks, optional Spanish or Korean subtitling and English captioning.

The Last Boy Scout (Warner, 12217)

Opening on a football player who is being pressured by bookies to 'win' a game, and then shifting to a phone conversation in which the person making the call acts, not very long afterwards, as if he had no idea the person he had just spoken to was actually in town, **The Last Boy Scout** requires a total abandonment of reason to be enjoyed. Bruce Willis portrays a private detective who teams up with a former football star, played by Damon Wayans, to investigate a pair of murders. The plot is absurd, but the performers take the material seriously, so it is possible to pretend that the story makes sense.

The DVD is letterboxed on one side, with an aspect ratio of about 2.35:1 and an accommodation for enhanced 16:9 playback, and is in cropped format on the other side. The cropping is severe, however, and not worth watching. The colors are deep and the image is glossy and slick, but the picture is grainy in places, perhaps by concept. The standard stereo surround soundtrack is bland. The Dolby Digital track has a stronger dimensionality and a stronger bass. The film is available in French in standard stereo and comes with English, French or Spanish subtitles ("Así me quedo con tus pantalones de $600"). There is a decent cast & crew profile, some production notes and a theatrical trailer, along with trailers for other Warner action features.

The Last Days of Disco (PolyGram, 4400582672)

Taking place in a make-believe discotheque where people can actually hear themselves talk, Whit Stillman's 1998 effort is something of a misfire. Usually, Stillman's very witty films are peopled with intelligent, realistic characters whose conversations were rich with ideas, insight and irony. In **Disco**, you can barely tell some of the characters apart, and much of what they say and do seems like a parody of Stillman's earlier works.

Set in the mid-Eighties, the movie is about a group of Yuppies who go out dancing practically every night and gradually pair off. Generally, the characters are unappealing, their dilemmas are irritating and their fates are inconsequential. The disco itself, supposedly the 'hottest' spot in the New York, looks like it would barely past the muster in Toledo. Chloë Sevigny, who plays the heroine, however, comes away from the movie smelling like a rose.

The picture is presented on one side in letterboxed format, with an aspect ratio of about 1.8:1 and an accommodation for enhanced 16:9 playback, and in full screen format on the other side. The color transfer looks fine and the image is reasonably sharp, but contrasts are a little weak and once in a while some details get lost in the shadows. A steady stream of K-Tel disco classics runs across the surround channels, though the music is oddly lifeless. Otherwise, the stereo surround sound is not very elaborate and the Dolby Digital track isn't all that much of an improvement. The 113 minute program can be supported by optional French subtitles or English closed captioning, and is accompanied by a short cast-and-director profile section and a trailer.

The Last Don (see Mario Puzo's The Last Don)

The Last Don II (see Mario Puzo's The Last Don II)

The Last Emperor (Artisan, 60496)

The 164 minute version of Bernardo Bertolucci's epic, which played theatrically in America, did not deserve to win the Oscar for Best Picture of 1987. It was a bloated, incoherent indulgence, all style and no substance. With the substance returned, however, to the 218 minute version that was Bertolucci's genuine cut of the film, released as a single-sided dual-layer DVD, the movie most emphatically deserves every honor that was accorded it and then some. The film doesn't just make more sense, it has had its depth of understanding restored. Depicting the collapse of the Chinese aristocracy and the rise of communism before and after World War II, the film explores both sweeping political shifts and minute personality flaws, showing the collapse of one culture and the rise of another from its rubble. So many details about the politics surrounding the hero, so much simple artistry in the rhythm of cuts, so much of the cinematography and the music and the art direction and all those other things that won Oscars in their partiality have been restored that maybe they deserve double Oscars for their completeness. In any case, the movie is much easier to follow now, and it is a far more satisfying and enlightening experience. John Lone stars in the title role, with Peter O'Toole (in a much-expanded part) and Joan Chen.

A number of friends have reservations about Artisan's presentation but we don't really share their concerns. The picture quality is certainly better than either home video efforts. Fleshtones are more accurate and other hues are sharper and better detailed. Contrasts are a little weak. The image is dark and loses detail in under-lit sequences, and it is probable that stronger hues could be coaxed out of the source material. As is pointed out in the jacket essay, the color schemes of some sequences have also been modified deliberately by Bertolucci and cinematographer Vittorio Storaro to reflect the hero's moods, but the presentation is viable. The picture is very crisp and well-lit scenes are opulent. The presentation is letterboxed with an aspect ratio of about 2.35:1 and no 16:9 enhancement.

The audio track isn't great. There is dimensionality to the music and the general ambience, but separation effects are limited and tones are somewhat fuzzy. Among many other things, the musical score is greatly enhanced by the longer presentation. The viewer has more time to become familiar with melody and instrumental motifs and how these passages are coordinated with the drama. In a direct comparison of the short and long versions, the removal of individual shots plays havoc with the score. The program is adequately closed captioned. A home video trailer, a cast & crew profile section and some production notes are also included.

The Last Flight of Noah's Ark (Anchor Bay, DV10831)

Elliott Gould is a pilot, Geneviève Bujold is a missionary transporting farm animals to a Pacific Island and Rick Schroder is a stowaway in Walt Disney's 1980 feature. They crash on a different island, meet two Japanese WWII soldiers, and transform the plane into a boat to sail home. Except that the opening credits don't appear until 17 minutes into the 97 minute film, it is a formula effort, mixing safe thrills and pleasantries, and is fairly harmless entertainment.

The picture is presented on one side in letterboxed format with an aspect ratio of about 1.85:1 and no 16:9 enhancement, and in full screen format on the other side. The letterboxing doesn't add much to the sides and masks picture information off the top and bottom, but either version is workable. The color transfer looks fine. Fleshtones are reasonably accurate and other hues are bright. The image is fairly sharp most of the time and darker scenes are stable. There are a few scattered speckles. The monophonic sound is adequate and the program is not captioned.

The Last Game (Simitar, 7209)

A hearing-impaired teenage girl on a championship basketball team is in the last game before the final, yet she doesn't seem to know how to play and her team loses. Her brother gives her a bunch of tips that week and she is the star of the final game. Meanwhile, her father, who is supposed to be 44 but looks 20 to 30 years older, has a heart attack and an out-of-body experience, watching her win the game before going back to the E.R. and recovering. If you can tolerate the obvious, then the 70 minute drama is watchable, but if you're looking for intellectual stimulation, turn elsewhere.

The picture looks incredibly nice. The colors are bright and the image is consistently sharp. The sound is erratic, though that is the fault of the film's limited budget and not the DVD's transfer. In any case, the audio often has a phony ambiance—and watch for the joy riding teenage boys 'rocking' to the insipid musical score. There is no chapter encoding or captioning.

The Last Metro (Fox Lorber, FLV5074)

François Truffaut's 1980 film, about a Parisian theatrical troupe putting on a production during the Nazi occupation, is beautifully constructed, so that an equal amount of time seems to be devoted to the pre-rehearsal, rehearsal, and production phases of the play. The film is intentionally nostalgic, balancing that nostalgia effectively against the serious threat posed by the Nazis, but it also creates a stimulating set of interwoven dichotomies about the fixed and the mutable, about the theater and the acting profession, and about marriage and love. Catherine Deneuve and Gerard Depardieu star.

Nestor Almendros' cinematography is deliberately strained, with often yellowish colors, but fleshtones are a little too indistinct at times. The image is quite sharp and the source material is reasonably free of wear. The 131 minute presentation is letterboxed with an aspect ratio of about 1.6:1 and no 16:9 enhancement. The monophonic sound is reasonably nice and the French dialogue is supported by permanent English subtitles. Chapter encoding is paltry. The program is accompanied by trailers for a number of Truffaut films.

Last Man Standing (New Line, N4507)

Edited to within an inch of coherence and then covered up with an insipid voiceover narration like duct tape, in an attempt to piece everything together, Walter Hill's mystifyingly lousy gangster remake of Yojimbo is a misconceived realization of what we would have thought would be a can't miss idea. We admit to enjoying the DVD more than we enjoyed the film in the theater, largely because the picture isn't as grainy and the stereo surround sound is terrific. The movie is still dopey, though, there's no getting around it. Bruce Willis stars as an itinerant gunman who wanders into an almost empty Texas town (during Prohibition) where two gangs are holed up. He proceeds to play one against the other, hoping to make a little profit by hiring out his violent skills to both sides. The gunfights aren't all that well staged, but if you turn the volume up they sound great, and the pictures just sort of follow the sound. The seemingly easy logic that made both Yojimbo and it's first classic remake, A Fistful of Dollars, witty and exciting films is either ignored or discarded. Few characters have any kind of believable motivation; the dynamic of the town's layout is ignored, as is its economic vitality; and what were once essential components of the plot—a father & son, stolen goods, and a moving corpse—have been abandoned or substantially downplayed. All that is left is the posing and the tough talk. It may look pretty good when it's backed up with Ry Cooder's score, but it is not enough foundation for a full-length drama.

The colors are more like brown-and-white than like color, though on the DVD they are more orange-like than the LD, where they are more grey-like. It is probably a matter of choice as to which version is preferable, but the DVD hues seem instinctively stronger. Either way, the picture still looks a bit soft and dusty. The

1997 film is presented on one side in letterboxed format with an aspect ratio of about 2.35:1 and an accommodation for 16:9 enhanced playback, and in full screen format on the other side. The framing looks better on the widescreen image but some viewers may not mind the full screen version, which adds substantial picture information to the top and bottom of the screen and takes a little bit off the sides. The stereo surround sound is adequate, but the Dolby Digital track has a stronger bass and a more forceful presence. The 101 minute program is also available in French without Dolby Digital and comes with English, French or Spanish subtitles. There is a cast and crew profile, including clips of Willis' cameo appearances in **The Player** and *National Lampoon's Loaded Weapon 1*, and a theatrical trailer.

The Last Starfighter (Universal, 20519)

Some of the computer animation is so primitive it looks like an interim step in the process, but the basic Arthurian story and the performances have allowed the enjoyable science fiction adventure to endure. Lance Guest stars as a young boy who breaks a record on a video game machine in a trailer park and soon finds himself inducted in a space war against aliens who want to conquer the galaxy. Robert Preston is divine as his recruiter and Dan O'Herlihy is his alien co-pilot.

The 1984 film was one of the first to use computer animation in the place of model effects, and much of the *Collector's Edition* is taken up by the story of how filmmakers sort of made things up as they went along to work out the process. There is a terrific half-hour retrospective documentary that covers all their trials and tribulations (model effects people kept trying to get them to drop the animation), and also includes some terrific behind-the-scenes footage of Preston. There is also a commentary channel, by the director, Nick Castle, and the production designer, Ron Cobb. Although not as focused as the documentary, they also talk about the breakthrough effects work and what they wanted to achieve in various scenes (some material proved so popular in test screenings that they went back and shot more of it).

There is also has a lengthy collection of production stills. Fortunately, you can step through them, because if you let them unfold as a montage, they run for more than two hours. The stills are super. There's shots from scenes that didn't make the final cut, behind-the-scenes looks at the makeup applications and props, extensive portraits of all the characters and aliens, an exhaustive look at Preston's car and the other space ships, designs, drawings, a look at the whole computer animation process, toys, posters and lots of other stuff.

The film's image is letterboxed with an aspect ratio of about 2.35:1 and an accommodation for enhanced 16:9 playback. The picture has smooth, spotless lines, bright colors and solid backgrounds in the darker sequences. Fleshtones are bland, however, or even reddish at times. Some of the blending of the effects and the live footage does not match up well, either, and the presentation is not as slick as a newer film would be. The sound is presented in 5.1 Dolby Digital, but we could detect almost no difference between that track and the standard track. The film's audio has periodic separation effects and a generally dimensional musical score. The 101 minute program also has optional English and French subtitles.

Last Tango in Paris (MGM, 906570)

Marlon Brando stars with Maria Schneider in Bernard Bertolucci's 1972 film, about a recently widowed American and a young Parisian who have an extended **9 1/2 Weeks**-type affair while retaining a mutual anonymity. While the movie's basic theme remains the predatory relationship between youth and age and between men and women, the film's actual eroticism is less compelling than its emotional explorations. Because Bertolucci's visual sense is so dynamic, the film is engrossing and lyrical, especially on DVD.

The image is letterboxed with an aspect ratio of about 1.85:1 and an accommodation for enhanced 16:9 playback. The source material has a few scattered speckles, but the wear is never strong enough to create a distraction. The colors are strong and the image is very sharp. It looks as fresh as Maria Schneider's complexion, and it gives the film an invigorated life.

The monophonic sound is fine, although the recording has some budgetary limitations that leave it sounding a bit tinny and noisy in places. The 129 minute film is in a mix of English and French with optional English or French subtitles covering all the dialogue. When the subtitles are deactivated on the menu, there are still English subtitles for the French dialogue. A trailer is also included.

The Last Time I Saw Paris (Madacy, DVD99028)

An MGM title that accidentally slipped into the public domain, the source material is not all that fresh, but it is passable until something better comes along. The monophonic sound is actually much stronger than the sound on the MGM LD. The slightly soft picture has a lot of thin scratches and weak contrasts, with olive or pale fleshtones, but other hues are relatively bright and the presentation is sufficient to make Elizabeth Taylor ravishing, not that it is a difficult thing to do. There is also a wavy artifacting effect that pops up in places.

Loosely adapted from F. Scott Fitzgerald, the 1954 drama, directed by Richard Brooks, remains interesting for what of Fitzgerald it retains. Van Johnson and Taylor are a married couple living in Paris, often suffering from the sense of depression that lurks beneath high living. Taylor is wonderful and although Johnson is a drag, he conforms with the requirements of his character. Restricted by the conventions of its era, the film still conveys a sense of maturity and bitterness that can be gratifying when it is set against the regular Hollywood romantic conventions.

Last Year at Marienbad (Fox Lorber, FLV5061)

A classic in the category of cinema as object d'art, Alain Resnais' 1961 classic is a totally pointless movie that is ideal for running on Repeat Play all day long. The black-and-white feature is beautifully photographed, and the DVD has a super transfer, so it is a perfect way to make your television look interesting when it is not otherwise engaged.

The film has a plot, sort of, and appears to be a memory within a memory, about a guy recalling how he tried to convince a girl at this fancy hotel that they'd met at the same hotel the year before and had a little fling. There are a few other characters, and there are also other people, standing about like mannequins, or moving as one imagines mannequins would move if they could. This mannequin-ness seems most associated with the memories of the earlier year, but some of it drifts into the later memories as well. Much of the dialogue is voiceover and is in French, which is supported by optional English subtitles. We wish, however, that the white subtitles had been placed beneath the image in the letterboxing band rather than over the image.

The film also explores the architecture and decor of the palatial hotel, and these sequences are so exquisitely rendered by Resnais' floating cameras that they are more stimulating than the obscure and dry character interaction. Our favorite shot: check out minute 42. Resnais is cheating, using cutouts or something, because the people standing in the grand hotel gardens have shadows, and the shrubs do not.

The picture is in letterboxed format only, with an aspect ratio of about 2.35:1 and no 16:9 enhancement. Contrasts are finely detailed, the image is sharp, blacks are rich, and the presentation appears free of any noticeable artifacting. The monophonic sound is adequate and the 94 minute program is accompanied by filmographies for Resnais and some members of the cast.

Lawless Frontier (see **The John Wayne Collection**)

The Lawnmower Man (New Line, N4092)

The standard 108 minute theatrical cut is accompanied by about 26 minutes of the extra footage in a supplement (the 'Director's Cut' home video release runs 141 minutes), along with some storyboard comparison, behind-the-scenes footage and a trailer. The movie itself is presented on one side in letterboxed format only, with an aspect ratio of about 1.85:1 and an accommodation for enhanced 16:9 playback). The supplement is presented on the flip side. New Line has also managed to squeeze in most of a commentary track by director Brett Leonard and co-screenwriter Gimel Everett, although the track was originally recorded to go with the longer cut. There is no commentary over the supplementary scenes. The track has been sped up, so there are times when the correlation between the talk and the screen action is negated. The commentary is fairly good. They describe the groundbreaking process they went through to prove that computer graphics would look decent on a big screen and could be delivered for a modest price. No mention is made of Stephen King's disfavor with their production, but they do mention how they built the narrative up from an eleven page short story that, in effect, comprised a single, throwaway sequence in the film. They provide nice profiles of the cast members and some of the crew, and discuss the logistical problems they encountered. It is an informative talk that improves an appreciation of the film and of the filmmaking process.

The color quality looks terrific, with sharp, accurate hues and pure blacks. The stereo surround sound is good, and the Dolby Digital track has a much better bass and a more accomplished dimensionality. The 1992 film can be accompanied by English or Spanish subtitles and also features profiles and filmographies of its two stars, Pierce Brosnan and Jeff Fahey, including clips from three other Brosnan films in the New Line library.

The DVD increases our respect for what the film accomplished, but it didn't really help us like the movie any better. We're afraid we cannot be as generous as Leonard and Everett are when it comes to assessing the performances of the cast because, except for Pierce Brosnan, the performers tend to have trouble conveying the simplicities of the script convincingly (it is as much the script's fault as it is theirs). The narrative, about a slow-witted man who become all powerful with the help of a few drugs and a virtual reality program, seemed to be a cliché even when the movie first appeared, and the film's technical breakthroughs mean very little to the entertainment.

Le Scomunicate di S. Valentino (see the **Sinful Nuns of Saint Valentine**)

A League of Their Own (Columbia TriStar, 51229)

From Jon Lovitz's hysterical appearance during the film's opening minutes, to the show's teary finale, Penny Marshall's 1992 movie about women's professional baseball the movie is a joy. Geena Davis is amazingly agile as the league's star player, and Tom Hanks is suitably ignoble as the team's sullen coach. Using a sibling rivalry and the effects of World War II as its primary dramatic devises, the film combines humor, historical trivia, and the thrill of baseball to create a fully entertaining, fictional tale of the league's first year.

The picture is presented in full screen format, with an aspect ratio of about 2.35:1 and an accommodation for enhanced 16:9 playback. The fleshtones look reasonably accurate and the colors are usually sharp. The stereo surround sound is efficient, but has no remarkable features. The 127 minute film also has French and Spanish audio tracks, optional Spanish and Korean subtitles ("¿Prometieron escribirle a las vacas?"), and English closed captioning.

Lean On Me (Warner, 11875)

Based upon a true story, Morgan Freeman gives a terrific performance as a disciplinarian principal who whips an inner city high school into shape. The script is an unenviable attempt to take real life and mold it into a movie and it only half succeeds, but Freeman takes it the rest of the way. Freeman's character is flawed, so wrapped up in the imposition of discipline at the school that he can't release the choke hold once he's achieved order. It is easy to play a hero who comes out swinging and righting wrongs, but it takes a lot more gumption to portray a hero whose flaws are insurmountable and to make it not matter.

The 1989 film is presented in full screen format but the framing looks fine. Colors are bright and the image is clear. The picture looks sharp and fleshtones are accurate. The stereo surround sound is a little soft and it has a flat upper end, creating a mild distortion in some of the louder dialogue sequences. The 109 minute program is closed captioned with some paraphrasing.

Leave It to Beaver (Universal, 20150)

We offer up an appreciation of **Leave It to Beaver** only because we doubt too many others will bother trying. True, the film, based upon a popular Fifties TV show that still pops up in syndication now and then, is a fairly lackadaisical affair, but then so was the series itself, which essentially dealt with the kind of adventures and troubles a typical American boy and his older brother could get into in the days when innocent behavior among young people in broadcast television was virtually mandated. The film, set in the Nineties, has a number of teasing references to the Fifties. At one point, for example, the characters run through a parking lot that is filled with shiny old automobiles. And, although the hero gets a computer for his birthday and has a recent model mountain bike, and although he lives in an integrated community, the film has an overpoweringly homogenous atmosphere that harks directly to the idealized suburban images promoted by American advertisers in the early days of TV. On the other hand, fathers in the TV shows of the Fifties were gods, and today they are butts, with the film opting for today's model. The character of Eddie Haskel was at his prime when he was seventeen, but for other reasons the film has to make him twelve, which doesn't work as well. Adding several segments of blatant slapstick to assure a basic level of appeal, the film draws its inconsequential plot from several episodes of the TV series, notably what was perhaps the most memorable sequence of the entire run, when the young hero is talked into climbing up and into a billboard-sized coffee cup. Few watching the movie, adults or children, will fully fathom the references and allusions it is built upon, but it is a harmless little family film that kids may enjoy more than they're willing to admit (it shows twelve-year olds kissing). For those old enough to recall the apparent securities of the past, it offers a glimmer of happy nostalgia and the vague daydream-like hope that such security is still attainable, somewhere in the American suburbs.

The picture is presented in full screen format only, though the TV-oriented film probably deserves that kind of framing. The colors are deep and bright, and the image is crisp. The regular stereo surround soundtrack is fairly weak, but the Dolby Digital track is passable. The 88 minute film is also available in French and Spanish without Dolby Digital and can be accompanied by English or Spanish subtitles ("Ward. Me preocupa Beaver"). There is also an informative production essay, a good cast-and-director profile section and a theatrical trailer.

Leaving Las Vegas (MGM, 906997)

Ah! A movie about alcoholism that has no pious AA meetings, no gritty lectures on the evils of addiction and characters who appear to be enjoying their decent into Hell, stopping on the way, as it were, to take in the scenery. **Leaving Las Vegas**, with Oscar-winner Nicolas Cage and Elisabeth Shue, is a grandly enjoyable film, one that puts glitter and gloss on manic depression, infuses suicide with humor and gives glamour to the lives of the hopelessly destitute. Directed by Mike Figgis, it has many adeptly balanced self-contradictions. The hero is completely impotent, yet the movie's sexual content is one of its primary assets. The narrative is a romance, about two people who find one another too late to be together, but they would have had nothing to do with each other if they'd met any earlier. Once in a while the drama becomes so superficially absurd that you could laugh at it, but such moments are fleeting and are usually drowned out by Cage's party animal performance. There were three significant films about Las Vegas released in 1995, and if the stupendously dopey *Showgirls* could be said to represent the flesh and the analytically historical **Casino** could be said to represent the mind, then it is **Leaving Las Vegas** that evokes the city's soul—rotting, but having a great time.

The regular stereo surround soundtrack is okay and the Dolby Digital track gives the film's jazz score a warmer, more enveloping presence. The color transfer is in good condition, with some graininess inherent in the 16mm source material and slightly faded fleshtones, but plenty of gloss when it comes to the neon signs and brightly lit sequences. The dual layer DVD presents the film in letterboxed format on one layer, with an aspect ratio of about 1.66:1 and an accommodation for enhanced 16:9 playback, and in cropped format on the other. The letterboxed version is preferable, adding substantially to the sides of the image and masking just a little off the bottom in comparison to the cropped version. The 1995 feature comes with a theatrical trailer and English, French or Spanish subtitles ("Vine aquí a morir tomando"). The film is identified as the 'unrated' version and runs 112 minutes.

Lee, Bruce (see **Dragon: The Bruce Lee Story**)

Lee, Tommy (see **Pam & Tommy Lee: Hardcore & Uncensored**)

Legal Eagles (Image, ID4287USDVD)

You can't beat the star casting of Robert Redford, Debra Winger and Daryl Hannah. It is enough to make the contrived murder mystery, about paintings and an insurance scam, feel witty and exciting, not to mention sexy and glamorous. The letterboxing has an aspect ratio of about 2.2:1 with no 16:9 enhancement. The colors look okay and the picture is usually crisp, but some passages are overly fuzzy and there are occasional minor anomalies. The stereo surround sound is still enjoyable. The 116 minute program is adequately closed captioned.

The Legend of Mulan (Digital Versatile, DVD101)

The 45 minute animated program is no Disney cartoon. The animation is very stiff and movement is limited. The artwork isn't all that hot, either, and although the show is designed for youngsters, the dialogue contains a couple of phrases we wouldn't use in this magazine. The narrative is about a female warrior who saves her land from an evil warlord after she undergoes a consciousness-raising journey. It's watchable, but repeat potential is limited.

The PCM track appears to be monophonic. The DTS track is vastly superior to the two-channel Dolby Digital stereo track, but that is like comparing apples and oranges. As for the DTS audio, it is not intricately detailed. There is a reasonable amount of surround activity, although surround separations are limited, and there is an active but not carefully defined bass. On the whole, the sound is a little more sophisticated than what one would expect for such a program, and the midrange has a nice solidity, but it comes nowhere near the sort of big budget sound mixes that DTS shows off so well.

There is no captioning. The picture quality looks fine, with reasonably sharp hues. The DVD also contains DVD-ROM material, including an apparent CD playback of the score (which has reasonably strong and satisfying Chinese motifs), a picture book that can be printed out, screen savers, a simple color book program, a child's jigsaw puzzle game, a more challenging collection of concentration-type games, and a couple other minor features.

The Legend of the 7 Golden Vampires (Anchor Bay, DV10560)

The original 89 minute version of **The Legend of the 7 Golden Vampires** has been combined with an abridged 75 minute version that was titled *The 7 Brothers Meet Dracula*. *Brothers* is the version most Americans who saw the 1974 film will be familiar with, but beyond a curiosity about how the minds functioned in the box office exploiters who tried to trim it down, *Brothers* is pointless. It is **Legend** that is the fun movie, an energetic blend of a Peter-Cushing-as-Van-Helsing vampire thriller and a kung fu action film. You can't analyze the plot or much else of the program too closely, but if you just kick your feet back and take it as it comes, it is a brisk and entertaining production.

Each film appears on one side of the DVD, with a trailer. The picture on both films is letterboxed with an aspect ratio of about 2.35:1 and no 16:9 enhancement. On the whole, both movies look good. There are scattered wear marks and mild inconsistencies from one reel to the next, but colors are solid and nicely detailed. There is stability in the brightest hues and a mild paleness in the softer hues. Fleshtones are also a little light. **Legend** tends to look fresher than *Brothers*. The monophonic sound is a bit battered but workable on both movies. The films are not captioned. On one of the audio channels, Cushing narrates what is apparently a 45 minute audio retelling of the film. It is a nice extra, but its practical uses are limited, though the accompanying musical score, by James Bernard, is more elaborately orchestrated than the music in the film.

Legends of the Fall (Columbia TriStar, 78725/78726)

Resurrecting not one but two seemingly lost film genres, the adaptation of a magazine story (longer than a short story, shorter than a novella) and the family saga drama (heretofore absconded by the miniseries format), **Legends** is as entertaining for its uniqueness as it is for its grand passion and time-spanning narrative. The story of three brothers and the woman they all love, the film is set in Montana during WWI and the Roaring Twenties, but its scope is such that it spans from the battlefields of France to the South Seas. The sometimes irritating Brad Pitt is anything but that here, portraying the dashing, free-willed middle brother, with Aidan Quinn as the more staid, older brother and Henry Thomas as the virtuous younger brother. Julia Ormond and Anthony Hopkins are also featured. The 1995 film is great storytelling, entertaining the viewer at each turn and providing a sense of completeness by the end, at the same time evoking the twilight of America's pioneer era.

The 133 minute film is presented in letterboxed format with an aspect ratio of about 1.85:1 and an accommodation for enhanced 16:9 playback. The Oscar-winning cinematography has undergone a perfect transfer, with a crisp focus and consistently accurate and gorgeous hues. The stereo surround sound is subdued, but the Dolby Digital track is very good, with sharp details and consistent strength. The film also comes with French and Spanish soundtracks in standard stereo and Spanish and Korean subtitles, along with English closed captioning.

Legionnaire (Sterling, 7145)

Set in the Twenties, Jean-Claude Van Damme is a boxer who is supposed to throw a fight but doesn't, and then signs up for the French Foreign Legion to do a lot of male bonding and shoot a few indigenous Moroccans. Those who are attracted to a movie such as **Knock Off** because it has lots of action will be squirming in their seats through most of **Legionnaire**. There is the boxing match at the beginning and a couple battles in the final third, but most of it suffers from Legionnaire's disease—cliched characters who are hiding from the world, a tough commandant to whip them into shape, comrades succumbing to moisture deprivation, and sand as far as the eye can see.

The picture is letterboxed with an aspect ratio of about 2.35:1 and no 16:9 enhancement. The picture looks spotless and hues are reasonably strong, although fleshtones have a conceptual yellowish tint in some interiors. The stereo surround sound does not have an elaborate mix, but it delivers functional responses during the action sequences. The 99 minute feature can be supported by Spanish subtitles, but there are no English subtitles or captioning.

There is an audio commentary track by the film's screenwriter and producer, Sheldon Lettich, who gives background information, explains how the story was developed, and talks in general but informed terms about the production. There are passages where he does little more than describe what is happening on the screen, but there are other times where what he has to say is more interesting than the movie itself, such as his story about the Israeli soldier. The Israeli joined the Legion to hunt down two former German soldiers who had also enlisted, and who had murdered the Israeli's family during World War II. He also describes a sequel set in Indo-China, though that's an unlikely bet now, isn't it? As for the production, his most interesting revelation is about the construction of a fort. Instead of creating a phony Hollywood-style fort, the producers were able to save about 90% of that cost by having Moroccan builders construct a fort in the traditional manner, with mud bricks, the way the real forts were made. It made the explosions more believable, as well.

There are also a couple trailers that never got a chance to be used, a decent cast & crew profile section, production photos, some interviews with the filmmakers, and a decent thumbnail history of the French Foreign Legion, including an interview with an historian and a documentary look at the Legion's activities in Desert Storm and other recent conflicts. On DVD-ROM you can scroll through the film's original screenplay, which contains a number of minor differences from the completed film—most of them even more clichéd—and a more elaborate ending.

Lené: Best Friends X-rated (Vivid, UPC#0073214516)

A man and a woman who are good friends have trouble maintaining relationships with others but don't realize that they were meant for each other. The narrative is minimal but sufficient for establishing the erotic sequences, a couple of which are somewhat more engaging than most. The picture, from a videotape source, is excellent, with bright, crisp hues and accurate, properly lit fleshtones. The sound is passable. The program runs 70 minutes and features Lené, Julie Rage, Jocklyn Lick and Monique. The DVD contains alternate angle sequences and elaborate hardcore interactive promotional features.

Leprechaun (Trimark, VM6840)

About a green imp who wants his gold back, the 1993 feature is kind of a monster movie for kids—though the gore is R-rated—featuring Warwick Davis and, delivering a viable performance, Jennifer Aniston.

It is presented in full screen format but could probably have used a little masking. The image is fairly vivid, with bright, sharp hues and accurate fleshtones. The stereo surround sound is forceful in spots, but the separation mix is limited. There are optional French and Spanish subtitles, English closed captioning, and a trailer that tries to hide what the leprechaun looks like.

Les Misérables (Columbia TriStar, 23999)

One of the nice things about a book as large as Victor Hugo's Les Misérables is that no two movies adapted from it are ever very much alike. Most have the best known scenes, but each one draws from different sections of the book and condenses different ideas and characters, so you could probably collect them all, watch them all day long and not get bored. The 1998 feature was directed by Bille August with Liam Neeson, Geoffrey Rush, Uma Thurman and Claire Danes. It is fairly enjoyable, with Neeson coming across effectively as a heroic moralist and Rush as the obsessed, morally deluded lawman. The romance that forms the movie's final act seems a bit rushed, but that would be a minor complaint. The film was shot in Czechoslovakia, so it is able to get out on the streets a

lot without losing its period setting, and the crowd scenes are really quite impressive.

The presentation is letterboxed format only, with an aspect ratio of about 2.35:1 and an accommodation for enhanced 16:9 playback. The color transfer looks fine. Although some of the settings are gritty, the picture is sharp and hues are accurate. The battle scenes and other big moments make a strong impression on the Dolby Digital track, as well as on the standard stereo surround soundtrack, though apart from these moments the movie's sound mix is a bit sedate. The 134 minute program also has a French soundtrack, optional English or French subtitles, and a trailer.

Leslie Nielsen's Stupid Little Golf Program (Fox Lorber, WHE73006)

Shot in Banff, some of the uneven made-for-video comedy program is quite funny ("You are not playing against an opponent. You are not playing against the course. You are playing against [the ball]") but a lot of it is desperately unfunny, so you have to be in the mood to tolerate the bogeys. The picture, from a video tape source, is fairly bright, but a little soft, with bland fleshtones. The stereo sound is crisp but not elaborately mixed. The program is accompanied by an elaborate and informative profile of Nielsen (Jean Hersholt was his uncle), and is not captioned.

Lethal Weapon (Warner, 11709)

The script is just another improbable action thriller, with a complicated and illogical plot about evil drug runners. The action scenes, however, have a crisp and furious impact; the director, Richard Donner, always supplies exactly enough information so that you know what is going on, but never any more than that, so you don't have time to think about it. Visually, the film is pleasing, not because of any fancy camera angles but because, even when there is no action, the director keeps showing you things. The casting was also an inspiration. Danny Glover is perfect as a hero—straight, bland, and tough. It is a relief seeing him on the screen in the place of the many flamboyant personalities which Hollywood would normally place in a role like that. Mel Gibson fulfills all the requirements for flamboyancy, yet his character remains subsidiary to Glover's. Lethal Weapon becomes more addictive with every viewing—the performances are so good that the film doesn't fall apart in multiple screenings, while the buzz created by the stunts and gunfire just gets harder and harder to resist.

The 1987 film is presented in full screen on one side and letterboxed, with an aspect ratio of about 1.85:1 and an accommodation for enhanced 16:9 playback, on the other. The letterboxing masks a bit off the top and bottom but adds enough picture information to the sides of the image to make it the preferable version. The colors are sharp, and the picture is clear and shiny. There are some noticeable artifacts in one or two of the action scenes, but they are fleeting. The stereo surround sound and Dolby Digital sound are outstanding, turning every car engine into a directional roar and every explosion into a hyper-blast. An interesting theatrical trailer for the film, with early Seventies graphics, is included, appearing in full screen on the full screen side and letterboxed on the letterboxed side. The 110 minute film is available in French in standard stereo and can be accompanied by English, French or Spanish subtitles.

Lethal Weapon 2 (Warner, 11876)

Mel Gibson and Danny Glover reprise their roles as L.A. cops in the one about the South African drug dealers. The regular stereo surround soundtrack is somewhat weak, but the power and separation activity on the Dolby Digital track is super. In the past we have found stretches of the 1989 film to become tiresome in multiple viewings, but the Dolby Digital track sharpened our attention span and increased the entertainment substantially. The picture is in cropped format on one side and is letterboxed on the other, with an aspect ratio of about 2.35:1 and an accommodation for enhanced 16:9 playback. The colors are crisp and the image is polished. The cropping provides a few to die for close-ups of Patsy Kensit and Gibson, but otherwise is of little use, obscuring much of the action and even dampening some of the comedy sequences. The 114 minute film is available in French without Dolby Digital and can be supported by English, French or Spanish subtitles ("¡Me encanta este trabajo!"). There is an extensive cast and crew profile, a featurette depicting the filming of the truck chase and the helicopter attack, and a theatrical trailer (full screen on the cropped side and slightly letterboxed on the letterboxed side), though Warner sadly neglected to include the memorable teaser trailer, which focused solely on the explosive toilet sequence. Joe Pesci is also featured.

Lethal Weapon 3 (Warner, 12475)

The least demanding entry in the series makes a great put-your-feet-up-and-relax DVD. The story is more drawn out and episodic, but the creative, high-charged action scenes, the terrific character-generated humor, and the orienting touches of serious drama create a breezy, attentive entertainment. Both Mel Gibson and Danny Glover seem, if anything, to be more comfortable in their roles, and the series keeps on adding clever supporting players to boost its energies. Viewers, incidentally, should make sure they keep the disc on through the final credits.

The presentation is letterboxed on one side, with an aspect ratio of about 2.35:1 and an accommodation for 16:9 enhanced playback, and in cropped format on the other side. The colors are strong and the image is sharp. The blown up cropped image looks somewhat more grainy. The stereo surround sound is dull, but the Dolby Digital track that is substantially stronger, with greater dimensionality and thrust. The 118 minute 1992 film is available in French in regular stereo and comes with English, French and Spanish subtitles ("Lune, lunaire, lunatiques"). There are also two well-made theatrical trailers, a decent cast-and-crew profile and a couple of pertinent production notes.

Lethal Weapon IV (Warner, 16075)

Okay. Okay. Okay. It's a fun movie. There's plenty of humor, there's lots of action sequences and, until the bad guy dies 20 minutes before the end, there's less pace-destroying character development than the previous films were burdened with. Plus, there's Jet Li, whose athletic martial arts skills raise the quality of the fight scenes considerably. Mel Gibson and Danny Glover repeat their roles as L.A. detectives, Joe Pesci has kind of turned into their abused sidekick, Rene Russo is back as Gibson's love interest and least-convincing-detective-in-the-world Chris Rock is also on hand for some fast humor as Glover's son-in-law. There is enough of a plot to keep them busy.

The 1998 film is letterboxed, with an aspect ratio of about 2.35:1 and an accommodation for enhanced 16:9 playback. The picture is glossy and crisp, with accurate fleshtones. The stereo surround sound is great, and the Dolby Digital track has all the activity and thrust one expects from it. The film is also available in French in Dolby Digital and can be supported by English or French subtitles. The 127 minute film appears on one side, along with a commentary track from director Richard Donner, who is accompanied by occasional contributions from producers J. Mills Goodloe and Goeff Johns. Donner talks about the incredible six month schedule he had to take the film from its first shot to its theatrical release. He also speaks about the series as a whole, talks a lot about his own career (including an interesting explanation as to why he made *Superman*), and goes into pertinent details about the shoot and the crew.

On the other side, there is a half hour of bloopers, behind-the-scenes and deleted scenes from all four films, including the original opening and ending to the first feature; an ending to the second feature where Patsy Kensit lives; and a breakdown of the demolition explosion in *III*. The reel captures the essence of the camaraderie among the filmmakers, which non-fans will decry as the essence of the series' failing, but to heck with them. There is about 5 minutes of additional deleted scenes from each movie. Most of it deserved to go, but there's an excellent scene dropped from first film where Gibson's character takes out a sniper in a school building. There is a collection of 2-3 minute interviews with each of the cast members from **IV** (including Li, who explains that he had to learn how to scowl because this is his first role as a villain) as well as Donner and producer Ron Silver. Following that is 10 more minutes of behind-the-scenes footage from **IV**, showing how the action scenes were staged, and trailers for all four movies.

Leviathan (MGM, 907044)

The **Alien**-style 'monster in an underwater mining station' thriller is in letterboxed format with an aspect ratio of about 2.35:1 and an accommodation for enhanced 16:9 playback. Fleshtones look good and the image is exceptionally crisp. The stereo surround sound is okay, but it is a bit dull. The 98 minute feature is also available in French and can be supported by English or French subtitles. There is a theatrical trailer, as well. Peter Weller, Richard Crenna, Amanda Pays and Ernie Hudson star in the 1989 effort.

Liar Liar (Universal, 20146/20051)

Jim Carrey stars in the wonderful comedy hit, about a lawyer who is forced to tell nothing but the truth for 24 hours after his little boy makes a birthday wish. The 1997 film is in full screen format only, losing nothing on the sides in comparison to a letterboxed presentation and adding picture information to the top and bottom of the image. Most of the time, however, that picture information is superfluous and even distracting. The colors are deep and rich, and the image is sharp. The stereo surround sound is somewhat weak, but the Dolby Digital track is reasonably strong, though the film's audio mix is not elaborate. The film is also available in regular stereo in Spanish and French and comes with English or Spanish subtitles ("Porque tiene tremenda pechuga"). There is a decent-sized press kit production essay and a modest cast-and-crew profile section, along with the film's highly successful theatrical trailer.

Life of Brian (see Monty Python's Life of Brian)

Light Sleeper (Pioneer, DVD69006)

Willem Dafoe is a former junkie running drugs to Manhattan's night spots for a society dealer, played with some flair by Susan Sarandon. Dafoe's character has no long term goals but events, including the murder of someone close to him, force him to take stock and decide upon a life path. Paul Schrader, who also wrote the script, has the character keep a journal so we can hear his thoughts, and drops in other obnoxiously symbolic or philosophical touches—Manhattan is having a garbage strike, Dafoe's apartment has no furnishings except a mattress although the kitchen has an abundance of cooking utensils—but the essential parts of the movie are fascinating, and the dramatic developments are sufficient to hold one's attention. The film also establishes a lasting mood, not of decadence or existential insomnia but of a class in its twilight, fragmented almost like a civilization would be, the successful parts mutating into new forms and the unsuccessful parts falling by the wayside.

The picture is in full screen format and is fairly grainy, with dreary, underdeveloped colors. Fleshtones are bland and other hues are brownish. The stereo soundtrack seems very centered, but tones are well rounded. The 103 minute feature is not captioned.

Lightning! (see Killer Twisters! and Lethal Lightning Super Storms)

Lindbergh: The Shocking, Turbulent Life of America's Lone Eagle (Shanachie, 950)

An excellent hour-long biography of Charles Lindbergh, the 1990 PBS *American Experience* episode provides a succinct overview of Lindbergh's life and its many complexities. There are interviews (his elderly wife still gets choked up discussing the kidnapping), archival clips (including recordings of anti-Semitic speeches he made before World War II) and photos from all segments of his life. The picture quality is fine. Background music is stereophonic and the audio is clear. The program is not captioned.

Lion of the Desert (Anchor Bay, DV10483)

Depicting Arab resistance to the Italian invasion of Libya before WWII, the film has plenty of grand battles and interesting executions of strategy. Anthony Quinn delivers a strong and appealing performance as the elderly resistance leader, and Oliver Reed is suitably evil as the ruthless Fascist general who systematically defeats the rebels. Standard reference books list the film's running time at 162 minutes but, although the DVD is not time encoded (which is a real drag, considering its length—on most players you won't be able to use the Last Memory function), it apparently runs 200 minutes or thereabouts. For theatrical play, the film could certainly stand to lose an hour, but in the easygoing confines of home video, the expansion is welcome.

The film is spread to two sides, with the majority of the movie appearing on side one. The presentation is letterboxed with an aspect ratio of about 2.4:1 and no 16:9 enhancement. The picture quality looks pretty good. Fleshtones are generally accurate and colors are reasonably fresh. Once in a while a reel will seem a little more worn or faded, but not to the point of distraction. There is an elaborate stereophonic musical score by Maurice Jarre that achieves a fairly nice dimensionality. There are also a few directional effects during the battle scenes, though nothing that is too industrious. The film is not closed captioned and is accompanied by a montage of publicity stills, trailer, commercials and an excellent 'making of' featurette (again, it is not time encoded, but it seems to run about a half hour), which goes into the film's historical background and the many problems confronting those who try to make a film in the desert.

Lionheart (Universal, 20388)

Jean-Claude Van Damme is an AWOL French Foreign Legionnaire who participates in no-rules fight contests, held by rich people, so he can earn money and help his widowed sister-in-law. All this would be tolerable for fans, but the formulaic story gets written into a corner and so the filmmakers are forced to impose an arbitrarily happy ending, reinforcing the pointlessness of the narrative and the action.

The picture is presented in full screen format, but little or nothing appears to be missing from the sides. The colors are okay, but the picture is a bit soft and grainy in places. The stereo surround sound is passable and the 105 minute program can be supported by English, French or Spanish subtitles. There are some production notes, a cast-and-director profile section (though most of the production notes are also given over to profiling Van Damme and the director, Sheldon Lettich), and a misleading trailer that suggests the 1990 film will be a revenge thriller.

Liquid Television (see Wet Shorts: The Best of Liquid Television)

Little Buddha (Buena Vista, 17375)

If somebody dressed like a Buddhist monk came up to us at a school playground and asked what our son's date of birth was, we'd be dialing 911 faster than you can say 'court injunction,' but it is the central conceit of Bernardo Bertolucci's 1994 feature that the boy's parents are receptive to the monks and their stories of reincarnation. If a viewer can make it past that one hurdle—and frankly, we couldn't—then the rest of the film falls into place very effectively. The movie is actually a combination of two films intercut together. One tells the story of the American boy, who is eventually coaxed into visiting Katmandu and meeting a couple of Asian kids with whom he is apparently going to become lifelong friends. His parents are portrayed rather vacantly by Bridget Fonda

and Chris Isaak. The other is the actual story of Siddhartha, set in ancient India, with Keanu Reeves as the Prince who goes searching for enlightenment, and it is the Reeves segment that gives the movie its pizzazz and phantasmagoria, preventing it from failing completely. It is to Bertolucci's credit that the movie never becomes tiresomely reverential the way Conrad Rooks' 1973 adaptation of the Herman Hesse novel did, but in breaking the film in two, neither part is around long enough to build a valid emotional momentum, and the drama remains sketchy.

The larger the screen one views **Little Buddha** upon the better, thanks to Bertolucci's breathtaking images and the gorgeous cinematography of Vittorio Storaro. The picture is letterboxed with an aspect ratio of about 2.1:1 and no 16:9 enhancement. Although the colors become very intense or glowing at times, the transfer renders them accurately, and always presents a sharp image, no matter how much haze Storaro employs. The stereo surround sound is also effective, particularly Ryuichi Sakamoto's musical score, which leaps in at appropriate moments. The 123 minute program can be supported by optional English subtitles.

The Litttle Foxes (HBO, 90754)

A crafty play by Lillian Hellman that has one attention-getting scene, where a woman lets her husband die, which makes the whole drama worth sitting through, was turned into an equally crafty 1941 movie by William Wyler. The play's tested dramatic momentum and Wyler's expert staging are a terrific combination, particularly with Bette Davis as the villainous and witchy heroine, a role model for anybody who wants to get ahead in the world.

The black-and-white picture is outstanding. The image is exceedingly clear, with crisp, precise details in every shot. The monophonic sound is okay, but there is an alternate stereo-enhanced track that has a little more body to it. There are also mono tracks in French, Spanish (poorly recorded), Italian and German, as well as optional English, French and Spanish subtitles, a cast profile section and a trailer.

A Little Princess (Warner, 19100)

We had to drag not only our children but our spouse practically kicking and screaming to the couch and tie them down in order to get them to watch **A Little Princess**, but in less than a minute they were so firmly in the grip of the film's phantasmagoria that we could loosen our bonds without incident. Each shot is succulently composed and often breathtakingly staged. Each dramatic incident is smartly conceived, building upon character and advancing the narrative while providing its own independent entertainment to keep the viewer alert and interested at all times. Based upon a novel by Frances Hodgson Burnett that is best known as the basis for the Shirley Temple film with a similar title, the 1995 movie was directed by Alfonso Cuarón, and is a model of controlled beauty and instinctive passion. It is exciting, hallucinogenic, funny, tear-inducing, intelligent and therapeutic, and if we could tie you down and make you watch it, we would.

The film is letterboxed on one side, with an aspect ratio of about 1.85:1 and an accommodation for 16:9 enhanced playback, and in full screen format on the other side, with more picture information added to the top and the bottom of the image and some taken away from the sides. The cinematography is outstanding and the letterboxed framing is preferred, but the full screen images pose no real problems. The colors are a little dark and fleshtones are a bit pink, but on the whole the picture looks terrific. The stereo surround sound is satisfying, with plenty of energy and separation effects, and the Dolby Digital track has even more flourish. The 102 minute program also has a French Dolby Digital track and a Spanish track in standard stereo. It can be supported by English, French or Spanish subtitles, and is accompanied by cast and crew profiles, brief production notes and a couple trailers.

The Little Princess (SlingShot, DVD1897); (D-Vision, DVD1003); (Madacy, DVD99009); (Master Movies, DVD5512)

One of Shirley Temple's most enduring vehicles, the film is simplistic and the ending is weakly edited, but nothing seems to interfere with Temple's appeal. She portrays the daughter of an English officer who must stay at a boarding school when her father leaves to fight overseas, finding herself at the mercy of the school's headmistress when her father is reported MIA. Since the film spells out so clearly what is going to happen before it happens, the editing need not be adept to convey the film's emotions to the viewer, and the young star's perkiness is a sufficient crowd pleaser. Whenever the filmmakers are in doubt about a scene, they just cut to her smile and everything is fixed.

The Technicolor source material on SlingShot's release is regularly visited by minor markings, but the hues, though not intense, are lovely, fleshtones look fine and the image is sharp. The monophonic sound is adequate, with an expected amount of age-related noise and hiss. The 91 minute film is accompanied by two bonuses, a wonderful, full color original theatrical trailer and a black-and-white service announcement, featuring Temple, for supporting the Red Cross.

From a standpoint of color intensity, D-Vision's version may even be a little stronger than SlingShot's, but SlingShot's image is cleaner and much better detailed, with clearer, better defined textures. The monophonic sound is also a bit less noisy. Madacy's version has slightly weaker colors and noticeably paler fleshtones. The framing is much tighter than the SlingShot version and the image is not as smooth. The sound is louder, but noisier and more distorted.

The Master Movies version comes the closest to equaling the quality of the SlingShot version. Fleshtones are slightly more pale, other hues are slightly lighter, and the framing cuts some picture off the bottom, but wear is minimal and the presentation would seem identical to SlingShot's if you didn't compare them directly. The sound is also equal in level and quality to the sound on SlingShot's version.

There is no captioning on any of the DVD.

The Little Rascals (Universal, 20034)

Although the DVD is letterboxed, with an aspect ratio of about 1.85:1 and an accommodation for enhanced 16:9 playback, the letterboxed LD has more picture information on both sides of the image as well as the top, and the DVD looks cropped in comparison. The colors on the DVD are stronger, however, and the picture is sharper and less inclined toward haze. The stereo surround sound is a little brighter on the LD, but the DVD has a Dolby Digital 5.0 track with better-defined separations and plenty of power. The 83 minute program is also available in French and Spanish and can be supported by English or Spanish subtitles ("La madera no la regalan"). There is a cast-and-director profile section, production notes and an inspired trailer. The live action remake of the classic Little Rascals routines is tolerable children's entertainment. The child actors are in part imitating the best known performers in the old series instead of fully utilizing their own personalities, so the movie has few if any natural moments, but once it gets under way and you accept the format it can be appealing. Kids, at least, will enjoy it.

Little Richard: Keep on Rockin' (Pioneer, PA98591D)

The running time for is nowhere to be found on the jacket cover, the reason probably being that the concert only runs 28 minutes. Shot in Toronto in 1969, Richard is less flamboyant than usual and maybe a little less energetic (sometimes he seems to sing in shorthand, like he's skipping over the parts he thinks everybody already knows), so the program is pretty much for die hard fans only. The stereo and Dolby Digital mixes don't help the sound all that much (Richard's vocal levels are very inconsistent) and the picture is blurry and smeary, with minimal detail. There is no captioning.

Little Shop of Horrors (Master Movies, DVD5513)

The legend goes that, after three days of rehearsal, Roger Corman shot the1960 film in two days. The movie is a deliberate put-on—a jokey comedy about a man-eating plant that finds just the right tone to accommodate its cheap production budget and hokey premise. The black-and-white source material looks pretty nice and is free of significant wear. Contrasts are decent and blacks are smooth. The image is a little soft, but for a Public Domain title, it is in great shape. The monophonic sound is a little harsh but passable, and the movie is accompanied by some good profiles of the cast and crew. The 79 minute program also has optional Japanese subtitles but no English captioning.

Little Shop of Horrors (Warner, 11702)

No sooner had the DVD appeared in the stores than it was withdrawn, because of a conflict regarding the supplementary features that does not portend to it being reissued anytime soon. Nevertheless, there are still a few floating around and certainly some eager collectors were able to purchase legitimate copies before they got swept back up and swallowed by the Time Warner conglomerate. Anyway, it is a DVD worth obtaining for the joy of the film, the pizzazz of the transfer and the enlightenment of the extra features.

The 1986 musical is presented in letterboxed format only, with an aspect ratio of about 1.85:1 and an accommodation for enhanced 16:9 playback. Colors are bright and vivid, melding perfectly with the musical's deliberately simplified songs. Fleshtones look accurate and the image is crisp. The stereo surround sound is adequate, but there is a Dolby Digital track that is much stronger, with a more pronounced bass and more energy up and down the range. The 94 minute film is also available in French in standard stereo (with French lyrics) and in Spanish in mono (with English lyrics) and comes with English, French or Spanish subtitles ("Tout à coup, Seymour…"). There is a 'music only' audio track during the film, a good cast and crew profile section and some decent production notes. The film is presented on one side.

On the flip side, there are about 42 minutes of supplementary footage, including TV commercials, trailers, a documentary, and an 8-minute gag reel. Also included is a sequence that runs a bit over 20 minutes, in black and white, depicting the film's original ending, which gets a bit carried away with itself and was shot down in the preview process, probably for the better although the special effects are spectacular. After killing off the hero and the heroine (who get married and 'live happily ever after' in the standard film, albeit with another plant growing in their garden), the plant multiplies and grows huge, eventually trashing the streets of New York like a Godzilla movie. Even in black and white, it is a spectacular sequence that fans will not want to miss, and one can imagine the money that went down the drain when the filmmakers realized it had to be dropped.

The film's director, Frank Oz, also provides a commentary track, over both the film and the 'original ending' segment. Oz's talk is quite good, consistently explaining how and why various shots were staged, talking about the performers, and discussing his approach to the material (he emphasized master shots to retain the show's stage-like atmosphere; everything was shot indoors on a huge soundstage anyway, so it was sort of like putting it on in an extra big theater). He still seems to be in partial denial over the inappropriateness of the first ending, but that just shows how much his heart is still in the film.

Little Witches (Image, ID4658APDVD)

A few distinctively muscled construction workers unearth a hidden chamber at a girls' Catholic boarding school and in no time at all the heroines are standing around a large stone pot, naked, calling up the Horned One. The program is predictable but proves how reliable and fun the witching genre can be, at least if you are at all interested in the corruption of innocent teenagers. The colors on the DVD are bright, fleshtones are reasonably consistent and the image is sharp most of the time. The stereo sound has a tinny, low budget hollowness to it, but the audio seems adequate for the material. The 91 minute program is not closed captioned.

Little Women (Columbia TriStar, 01025/9)

Very quietly and with scant notice, the language of film has matured over the decades. It is usually the most discernible when a classic story that has been made into a film in the past is remade again, and this is quite clearly the case with Gillian Armstrong's terrific 1994 adaptation of Louisa May Alcott's **Little Women**. The confidence and sophistication of Armstrong's version, compared to the two best known previous film adaptations, is in itself compelling. The acting is more natural and thorough. The set designs are more believable and accurately detailed. The dramatic rhythm of the narrative is smoother, and because the filmmakers have focused their resources better, they are able to squeeze more narrative, more emotion and more meaning into a feature length running time.

The film is not exactly appropriate for the sweltering days of summer, unless you want to cool off by the power of suggestion. Much of it is set in winter and around Christmases, and it is best viewed when one's own environment can be coordinated with such an atmosphere. Nevertheless, it is a highly pleasurable experience. Winona Ryder is greatly appealing as the heroine, the one of four sisters who has literary ambitions and eventually records the experiences of her family and acquaintances in the mid-Nineteenth Century.

The film is presented on one side in letterboxed format, with an aspect ratio of about 1.85:1 and an accommodation for enhanced 16:9 playback, and is in full screen format on the other side. The image quality is good, although some darker sequences are a bit too soft and fleshtones are a bit flat at times. The stereo surround sound and Dolby Digital sound are efficient, though never flamboyant. The 118 minute program also has French and Spanish language tracks in standard stereo, optional Spanish subtitles and English closed captioning.

The Littlest Horse Thieves (Anchor Bay, DV10830)

Great motion picture music comes in all shapes and sizes, but rarely is it as unexpected as Ron Goodwin's brass band score in the 1977 Walt Disney feature. The film is a typically solid effort by Disney's British unit, directed by Charles Jarrott and featuring Alastair Sim in one of his final roles. It is set in a Yorkshire mining town a little before World War I, when ponies were still being used to drag the coal bins back and forth through the mines. The mine is losing money, and so the manager decides to replace the horses with machinery. His own daughter, and the sons of one of the miners, collude to save the horses from the slaughterhouse. The film is smartly constructed and while it seems, from a marketing angle, to be a good two decades out of date, it is, from an entertainment angle, a well made drama that adults and older children can enjoy with equal pleasure.

Now brass bands are the ALL CAPS of the musical world, but they are also practically indigenous to England and particularly to Yorkshire coal mining towns. Because it is a Disney movie, the music can be a little playful, and Goodwin does a superb job at modulating the enthusiasm of the score to suit the emotional level of the scene. But what makes the score exceptional is that along with adeptly defining the film's emotions—thereby bringing you to tears even more quickly during a scene than you might if there had been no music—it also resonates upon the film's locale. When a film is set in Mexico and uses guitar music, then that effect is no big deal, because the guitar is quite adaptable, but in using a brass band to evoke the society involved in the drama while at the same time while still accommodating the film's subtlest shifts in mood and atmosphere is a remarkable accomplishment. And when the band finally appears in person during the film's joyful conclusion, it is yet another added thrill.

The film is presented in letterboxed format on one side, with an aspect ratio of about 1.85:1 and no 16:9 enhancement, and is in

full screen format on the other, trimming some picture information off the sides and adding a little to the bottom. Either framing seems workable. The color transfer is nice. Hues are a little light in places and there is a bit of grain in some sequences, but the image is crisp and colors are clearly defined, even in the dark mine scenes. The monophonic sound is good and the music has a near-stereo ambience. The 104 minute program is not captioned.

Live! at Knebworth (Image, ID3950CADVD)

Three concerts have been combined onto one 194 minute program, featuring highlights from a 1990 all-star benefit concert in Britain for the marvelous Nordoff-Robbins Music Therapy Centre ("Helping the retarded kids reach out and touch the world," as Paul McCartney rather inelegantly puts it). Held outdoors in front of about 120,000 people, the featured artists include McCartney, Eric Clapton, Tears for Fears, Cliff Richard, Phil Collins and Genesis, Dire Straits, Status Quo, Elton John and Robert Plant. Each performs about three or four numbers. Musically, the performances are nothing great, and the concert's acoustics are limited, but the show's star power is potent (some of the musicians wander into one another's sets) and fans will enjoy the show's energy and scope.

The image looks terrific during the day sequences and is passable for the night sets. During the course of the lengthy concert there are shots here and there where digital artifacting is noticeable, particularly if a musician turns quickly or a camera pan moves rapidly, but such instances are brief. The concert's acoustics lack subtlety, but the stereo sound is strong and reasonably detailed. The DVD has no special features and no captioning. Paul McCartney, Eric Clapton, Robert Plant, Genesis, Pink Floyd, Tears for Fears, Cliff Richard and Elton John are among the performers at the 1990 event.

Live Sex Shows of Paris X-rated (Lipstik, 31152)

Live Sex Shows of Paris is just what it says it is, bored stage performers videotaped in hardcore erotic activities in front of an audience. The 65 minute program is interesting for its realism, but has little else to commend. Colors are very drab and the image is a little smeary, though it has been lit well enough to prevent severe distortion. The monophonic sound is incidental and of limited quality.

Lo frate 'nnamorato (see Pergolesi's Lo frate 'nnamorato)

Lock Up (Artisan, 60469)

The script, about a mad warden, played by Donald Sutherland, who persecutes the hero, played by Sylvester Stallone, is farfetched. Stallone's character has no personality, and the action scenes are poorly edited (though other sequences are not). The movie is not an embarrassment, it is just boring and unbelievable.

The 1989 feature is presented in letterboxed format only, with an aspect ratio of about 1.85:1 and an accommodation for enhanced 16:9 playback. Since the movie is set in a prison, the color scheme is intentionally dour, with institutional greys and anemic fleshtones. The color transfer appears reasonably accurate. The source material has a few stray markings—notably a vertical black line that runs through the image around the 76 minute mark—but generally the condition is passable. The stereo sound is adequate but unremarkable. The 115 minute feature can be supported by English or Spanish subtitles and comes with a theatrical trailer, a 7 minute 'making of' featurette, a 3 minute 'making of' featurette, production notes and a cast & crew profile section.

Logan's Run (MGM, 907029)

Michael York and Jenny Agutter star in the 1976 film, about a society where everyone who turns 30 is eliminated. They decide they don't like that, so they run away and are chased. It's bad science fiction, but as a movie spectacle with attractive stars, futuristic decor and plenty of action sequences, it can be appealing.

The letterboxing has an aspect ratio of about 2.4:1, and an accommodation for enhanced 16:9 playback. The picture is sharp and colors are deep. The 1976 film has bright, kind of pastel hues and they have been well preserved. The stereo surround sound is somewhat weak, but the track is preferable to the less aggressive Dolby Digital track. In a couple of showy places, the rear channel effects on the Dolby Digital track are more pronounced, but generally there are more separation effects on the standard track, and the standard track delivers a bigger, brighter and busier aural entertainment most of the time. The 119 minute film is also available in mono and can be supported by English or French subtitles ("Nommer un chat est chose malaisée/Fort loin du jeu du société. Je ne suis point fou à lier/Mais il faut qu'un chat soit trois fois nommé"). There is also a trailer and a promotional featurette.

York, director Michael Anderson and costume designer Bill Thomas provide a commentary. Anderson, who also directed *Around the World in 80 Days* (and talks a bit about that film, as well), provides a generalized reminiscence about the production. There are times when he describes a scene at hand and adds nothing to it, but most of the time he is able to talk about what he was trying to achieve, some of the problems he encountered, and how well he thinks his crew succeeded. York is a more enthusiastic speaker, perhaps by profession, and does a better job at humanizing his experiences on the production, sharing his memories of how various sequences were achieved, and sharing profiles of his fellow filmmakers. Thomas speaks specifically about some of the costume designs and the compromises he had to make to accommodate the large cast of extras.

Lola Montes (Fox Lorber, FLV5050)

Martine Carol stars in the Max Ophüls' 1955 costume drama, about the notorious European courtesan and her romances. The 110 minute feature begins and ends in a circus, with the heroine cashing in on her notoriety and the publicized affairs she has had with composers and kings. Her life is then depicted in a series of flashbacks integrated with the circus showcase. The cast, including Peter Ustinov (as the circus ringmaster) and Oscar Werner (as a young student), is appealing. Carol, who looks and acts more like a spinsterish Deborah Kerr than a royal seductress, suppresses all displays of emotion to short bursts and follows with long stretches of guarded determination. If the flashback scenes are approached as pieces of memory, then the fact that she is too old to depict herself as a child or that she accepts much of what happens to her without expression becomes understandable. Some say it is brilliant.

The colors are dull, with soft edges. Fleshtones are bland and there are hazes around the brightest hues. The letterboxing on the Cinemascope image has an aspect ratio of about 2.27:1 and no 16:9 enhancement. Permanent English subtitles for the French dialogue appearing beneath the image in the letterboxing band. The monophonic sound has a weak high end, causing the music to warble or go scratchy. There are some minor text supplements, and watch for the reflection of the camera at 59:46.

Lolita (Warner, 65004)

Stanley Kubrick's 1962 comedy uses Vladimir Nabokov's novel as its framework, but it does not pursue the novel's agenda and is best appreciated if indulged without a context. James Mason stars as a college professor who becomes infatuated with his landlady's teen daughter and eventually runs off with her. Parts of the film withstand a great many multiple viewings and continue to be quite humorous, but the deterioration of the hero's fortunes in the drawn out second half can also begin to feel trying. The viewer can tire of the hero's possessiveness as quickly as the heroine does, but when the film's blatantly comical aspects are blended with an awareness of Kubrick's drier humor, it is enough to see one through the hero's lapses in judgment. Best of all, there is Peter Sellers, who becomes sort of a White Rabbit. Kubrick seizes upon the film's paranoia, allowing the viewer, through the eyes of the he-

ro, to have glimpses of what seems like another movie taking place in the same space, in which Sellers is also pursuing the girl.

The DVD is letterboxed with an aspect ratio of about 1.66:1 and no 16:9 enhancement. The picture is sharp, blacks are rich and whites are bright, creating a slick, compelling image. The monophonic sound is a bit weak, but the Dolby Digital mono track is satisfying. The 153 minute feature has an alternate French language track, optional English and French subtitles and a trailer.

The Lonely Guy (Universal, 20422)

Steve Martin stars in Arthur Hiller's 1983 comedy about a single man looking for romance in New York City. Charles Grodin and Judith Ivey co-star in the exaggerated satire, which can seem either amusing or painfully stupid depending upon one's view of Martin and the form of the comedy. Regardless of the movie's broad humor, the narrative is stretched out awkwardly to reach its 91 minute running time and by then you get the joke.

The picture is letterboxed—the first time it has appeared that way on home video—with an aspect ratio of about 1.85:1 and no 16:9 enhancement. Fleshtones are somewhat pale and other colors are a bit light, but the image is reasonably sharp and hues are solid. The monophonic sound is adequate and the film can be supported by English, French or Spanish subtitles. There are some production notes, a cast-and-director profile section, and a theatrical trailer.

The Long Good Friday (Criterion, CC1544D)

A mobster is about to close a billion dollar real estate development deal when he wakes up one morning to discover that someone is making hits on his organization. He spends the day trying to hold the deal together and figure out who is behind the hits. Bob Hoskins stars the impressive and entertaining 1979 British production. Helen Mirren gives an outstanding performance as Hoskin's main squeeze, and Pierce Brosnan pops up in a small role as an assassin. The mystery plot is engagingly methodical, but it also provides a backdrop to other things, and the film is in many ways reminiscent of *The Godfather, Part II*, suggesting, ever so satirically, that all big league capitalists are essentially gangsters. Hoskins gives an inspired, memorable performance that allows you to see not only who his character is, but where he came from.

The picture on the LD is quite hazy compared to the crisp-looking DVD, which has nicely detailed hues and accurate fleshtones. Darker sequences are still a little soft, but on the whole the image is very satisfying. The presentation is letterboxed with an aspect ratio of about 1.77:1 and no 16:9 enhancement. The monophonic sound is fine. There is no captioning. The 114 minute program is accompanied by American and British trailers.

The Long Kiss Goodnight (New Line, N4446)

Cutthroat Island got bad reviews and did lousy box office, but it was a fun movie and made a great DVD. The team responsible for **Cutthroat**, director Renny Harlin and star Geena Davis, then collaborated on **The Long Kiss Goodnight**, which got surprisingly good reviews, didn't do all that much better at the box office and isn't as much fun, though the elements are there to make the DVD appealing to some viewers. To keep the movie moving, editing has trimmed down so much of the plot that the narrative is too confusing to follow—you just have to accept the action and eventually the semblance of a coherent story materializes. It is about a hit woman who has had amnesia but snaps out of it just in time to foil a nasty government plot. Samuel L. Jackson co-stars and, while the motivation of his character is never fully explained, he becomes kind of Davis' sidekick as the film progresses. Some of the dialogue is witty, but just as much of it is overworked, artificial-sounding or simply in bad taste. The film lives for its action scenes, and several are spectacular, but without a plot to back them up they aren't as inspiring as the stuff Harlin has come up with elsewhere.

The 1996 film is presented on one side in letterboxed format, with an aspect ratio of about 2.35:1 and an accommodation for enhanced 16:9 playback, and in full screen format on the other. The letterboxing adds just a little bit to the sides of the image while losing a little on the top and a whole lot on the bottom in comparison to the full screen image. Because the sides aren't substantially trimmed and so much is added, we preferred watching the full screen side. The stunt sequences are clearer and the dramatic scenes have a stronger presence. The colors are always crisp and the image is smooth. Although there is a lot of movement, artifacts are rarely a problem. The stereo has a pleasing dimensionality and plenty of power when called upon. There is a theatrical trailer—which plays better than the film—that is letterboxed on the letterbox side and presented in full screen on the full screen side. There is also elaborate coverage of the principal cast members. The 120 minute film is available French as well, in standard stereo, and is accompanied by English, French or Spanish subtitles.

The Long Knives (Simitar, 7212)

The documentary is about the U.S. Cavalry's campaigns against the Indians of the Northern Plains. Although informative, it is not much of a movie, and most of it would be more efficiently presented as text. As the narrator explains what happened in the different battles, photographs and drawings—often repeated—are intermingled with clips from old black-and-white westerns that contain vague similarities to the actions the narrator is describing. There are no maps and no comprehensive summary of events, but viewers interested in the subject are likely to be pleased by the individual battles that are described and the other anecdotes that are shared, such as the story about the band of about three dozen soldier who held off several thousand attackers because of a newly developed repeating rifle the attackers were not prepared to face. The film clips and the pans across the still photos are often in a mildly worn or rough condition, so it is difficult to say if video artifacts contribute to the distortion of the image. The stereo sound is adequate. The film runs 88 minutes, but the final eight is a montage of the photos (many already seen several times) set to music without narration.

The Long Shadow (Simitar, 7298)

Acclaimed cinematographer Vilmos Zsigmond directed the 1992 feature, which was shot in Israel and stars Michael York and Liv Ullman. York has a dual role. He portrays a famous stage actor and, in video clips, the actor's father, who has passed away after a long estrangement from his family. Learning of his death, the actor visits his grave in Israel and discovers not only that his father had become a famous archeologist, but that the circumstances surrounding his abandonment of his family were far more complicated than he'd believed. Eventually he finds himself acquiescing to portraying his father in a biographical documentary. There are a few too many travelogue shots of the Israeli countryside—pacing is not Zsigmond's forte—but the performances are good and the narrative is involving.

The presentation is letterboxed with an aspect ratio of about 1.66:1 and no 16:9 enhancement. The picture looks quite aged, with sullen colors, bland fleshtones and a constant grain. The music is mildly stereophonic and is effective now and then, but most of the time the audio is flat and bland. The film runs 90 minutes, is not captioned, and is accompanied by partial filmographies of York and Ullman.

The Look X-rated (Vivid, UPC#0073214595)

Vampires prey upon libertines. The story isn't all that involved, but the filmmakers spend an extra effort to establish an intriguing mood and milieu, while the possibilities of violence bring spice to the erotic sequences. The picture is quite grainy and the colors are a little dull. The monophonic sound is flat, but the musical score and sound effects have been given above average attention and contribute effectively to the show's atmosphere. Sunny, Alyssa Love, and Laura Palmer are featured in the 71 minute program.

The DVD also contains alternate angle sequences and elaborate hardcore interactive promotional features.

The Look 2000 X-rated (Vivid, UPC#0073214585)

An all-black X-rated program, the narrative, about a photographer who is trying to capture images that will define the coming millennium, gives the show an adequate momentum. The performers are refreshing and the erotic sequences are effective. The picture looks good, with decent fleshtones, reasonably strong hues and a sharp focus. The monophonic sound is adequate. The 70 minute program features Heather Hunter, Miranda Deleon, Janet Jacme, Metty Tigore and Monique. The DVD also contains alternate angle sequences and elaborate hardcore interactive promotional features.

Look Who's Talking (Columbia TriStar, 70109)

John Travolta and Kirstie Alley star in the 1989 romantic comedy about a taxi driver who falls for a single mother. The film's humor is enhanced by the addition of an interior monologue for the child, both before and after it is born, but the gimmick wouldn't work if the basic narrative and the stars weren't so charming.

The picture is presented in letterboxed format on one side, with an aspect ratio of about1.85:1 and an accommodation for enhanced 16:9 playback, and is in full screen format on the other side. The color transfer looks fine and the stereo surround sound is okay. The 90 minute program also has French and Spanish audio tracks in mono, and optional English, French or Spanish subtitles.

And, as a final note, although the movie was directed by a female, Amy Heckerling, old sexual stereotypes apparently die hard. In the beginning there is a well-executed depiction of sperm rushing to inseminate an egg. Setting the theme for the comedy, the sperms are chattering like crazy as they make their way up the canal. The egg, however, remains silent and inanimate.

Lord of Illusions (MGM, 906294)

The film is over 10 minutes longer than the theatrical release and according to writer-director Clive Barker, who speaks on a commentary track, what got left out of the theatrical release was primarily narrative enhancement, sacrificed for the sake of the horror thrills. That 1995 horror thriller does have a real plot is one of its attractions. Scott Bakula is a private detective who specializes in the occult. He becomes involved with a wealthy stage magician who buried a rather demonic cult leader several years earlier and now fears that the cult members are attempting a resurrection. The bar has been pushed so high, however, by Barker and by others, that the usual horror effects don't hold as much of a thrill as they used to. Because the film does have a story (though it develops a few holes toward the end—Barker tends to be too close to his work), it is reasonably enjoyable, but it doesn't break new ground. Barker speaks constantly throughout his commentary. He doesn't go into much detail on the logistics of the shoot and sometimes, talking about the plot, he falls into the trap of telling what is readily viewable onscreen. Still, he clears up a few points and shares some interesting anecdotes about making the film.

The letterboxing has an aspect ratio of about 1.85:1 and an accommodation for enhanced 16:9 playback. The colors are bright, fleshtones are true and the image is sharp. The stereo surround sound and Dolby Digital sound are highly effective, with many decent separation effects and plenty of power. The film's musical score is isolated in Dolby Digital. The 121 minute film can be supported by English or French subtitles. There is also a collection of deleted scenes—supported by Barker's commentary as well—and a red tag theatrical trailer,

Lord of the Dance (see Michael Flatley: Lord of the Dance)

The Lost Boys (Warner, 11748)

Most vampire movies serve as a metaphor to swooning passion, but **The Lost Boys** aligns its horror with teenage drug abuse, and the parallels match very neatly. It helps that the film is stylishly made and cleverly executed, because there would be no message if it were inept. The film is also humorous, an aspect that improves on multiple viewings.

The presentation is letterboxed on one side, with an aspect ratio of about 2.35:1and an accommodation for 16:9 enhanced playback, and in cropped format on the other side. Hues are bright and fleshtones are accurate. The stereo surround sound is good, and the Dolby Digital track is even more powerful, with crisper tones and a stronger flourish. The 1987 film, one of the first to tap the lucrative teenage vampire genre, can be supported by English, French or Spanish subtitles ("Mets-toi, un T-shirt à l'ail—sinon, t'es cuit") and comes with a theatrical trailer, a cast & crew profile and some production notes.

Lost in Space (New Line, N4667)

Much of the film is the dream remake of the TV series you hope it will be. In the place of the saccharinely happy family on the old TV show there is a dysfunctional group of geniuses who can barely get along, headed by William Hurt, whose low key performance is generally wasted in a part that calls for intermittent grandstanding. Mimi Rogers, Matt LeBlanc and Heather Graham are also featured, with Gary Oldman, also underplaying a touch, as the rascally villain. For two-thirds of the film, the script is wonderful, carrying the viewer along in the same space serial format the TV show (which was adapted from a comic book that was adapted from *Swiss Family Robinson*) attempted to invoke. For the last act, however, the narrative gets overly complicated, and while it continues to evoke the TV show in an accurate manner, the convolutions of time travel and other contrivances contradict the modern realism that color the adventures leading up to it. The concluding half hour will not seem as jarring on multiple viewings, and viewers who truly appreciate the inanities of the old show should enjoy the way it has been updated. Casual viewers are likely to be more impatient with the production, but there are tons of special effects to compensate.

The first major studio release to be loaded with DVD-ROM supplements, the movie itself is presented in letterboxed format with an aspect ratio of about 2.3:1 and an accommodation for enhanced 16:9 playback. The colors are solid and fleshtones are accurate in all lighting conditions. The stereo surround sound is wimpy, but the Dolby Digital track has plenty of power and many enjoyable separation effects. The 130 minute film can be supported by English subtitles. Additionally, there is a cast & crew profile section, a complete listing of the TV episodes (each containing a plot synopsis), a music video that works better than it deserves to, and a few production drawings.

There is a documentary about the film's scientific basis, a documentary about the special effects, interviews with the members of the TV show's cast, and a collection of deleted scenes. One deleted sequence arc, involving a large creature, is of particular interest because it is very close in spirit to the old TV show and gives purpose to a character, the younger daughter, who is otherwise consigned to the background for the film's second half. We're very sorry they didn't keep the footage in, even if it didn't mix well with the rough-and-tumble atmosphere that remains.

On a commentary track, the film's director, Steven Hopkins, and screenwriter, Akiva Goldsman, talk about the production. They discuss the usual things, such as working with the actors, staging the key sequences and the problems they encountered while shooting (they could have used more preparation time), but they also go quite a bit into why the film's second half fails, as well as providing a fairly good capsule synopsis of a proposed sequel.

On a second commentary channel producer Carla Fry, cinematographer Peter Levy, editor Ray Lovejoy, and visual effects supervisors Angus Bickerton and Lauren Ritchie speak about the film. This group (recorded individually and intercut) is able to get into a

lot more technical detail on the film's many special effects than Hopkins could cover, and the track will be a must for film students or anybody interested in the technical aspects of pulling off a modern sci-fi blockbuster. Among the most interesting explanations are how the 'super slow motion' light speed effects were achieved (with computer processing) and how the crash of the Jupiter II was staged (they pulled it with a Range Rover).

For those who have a DVD-ROM, the DVD also offers the complete shooting script (with instant access to the identified scene within the film), an elaborate 3-D game and a simpler 'shoot the Robinsons' game, a text expansion of the younger daughter's video diary, a chance to fiddle with some electronic music, a planet-building simulator, a manipulatable robot icon and more background material on the film. Many of the options, such as the diary, have extensive Web links, too, expanding the DVD's capabilities well beyond its source code. We really have to take a moment to remark upon the irony of all this. Here is a property that throughout its entire history has been the laughing stock of science fiction and now, with New Line's release on DVD, it is suddenly at the very forefront of technological entertainment, not only for its mix of DVD and DVD-ROM functions, but in the way the latter is fully integrated with the Internet. That most certainly does compute, so to speak.

The Lost World (Lumivision, DVD0897); (SlingShot, 9819)

Using primitive but charming movie tricks to resurrect the thunder lizards of old, the 1925 silent classic, based on Arthur Conan Doyle's fantasy, is marvelous, with a plot that is noticeably similar to Steven Spielberg's remake. A group of adventurers encounter dinosaurs in a remote part of the jungle and bring one back with them, only to have it get loose in London. The 60 minute running time is little more than half the original theatrical presentation, because it was suppressed in favor of a remake on sound film, and viewers are lucky that any version survives at all.

The source material varies in quality, with some passages appearing fairly damaged and others looking relatively clean. Some sequences are also heavily tinted, and artifacting is fairly noticeable in places. The default musical score is stereophonic and is supplemented by generalized sound effects, but we prefer the option that presents just the music. The option is not presented on the DVD's menu, however, and you have to toggle the player's audio command to shift between the two soundtracks. Also included are an original theatrical trailer—believe it or not, advertising has toned down over the years—and a promotional teaser promoting a "Lost World Puzzle." Willis O'Brien, the animator of *King Kong*, was also the principal animator for **The Lost World**, so excerpts from three of his earlier animated shorts are also presented, along with a short from 1923 that specifically featured animated dinosaurs, a collection of still frame material that describes the footage still missing from the feature, a history of the film and its restoration, and other materials.

The artifacting is less noticeable on SlingShot's reissue, which is otherwise a replication of the earlier transfer, except that still photos, a Web access and SlingShot's logos have been added, and the still frame text materials have been removed (though they are listed on the jacket chapter guide).

Lotus X-rated (Vivid, UPC#0073214159)

The cast members are all made up in Oriental garb, which is good for a few laughs. The narrative is a reasonably efficient *Arabian Nights* concoction, in which a young woman tells her lord several racy stories to pass the time, while the stories are acted out for the viewer. The erotic sequences are fairly standard. The picture is reasonably good, with strong colors (and colorful costumes) and a fairly sharp focus. The sound is also strong. The 75 minute program contains alternate angle sequences and elaborate hardcore interactive promotional features.

Lou Reed: Rock & Roll Heart (Fox Lorber, WHE73011)

No complete numbers are performed, but there is still plenty of music in the 75 minute program. The documentary looks at Reed's varied and uncompromising career, from his childhood and his earliest appearances in New York to his days with the Velvet Underground and his continuing forays into the avant garde. There are a number of wonderful where-are-they-now interviews (you get to see, for example, the individuals who were the basis for *Walk on the Wild Side* and what they think about the lyrics referring to them), rare performance clips and other interesting pieces of social history. More importantly, the program brings an organization to Reed's canon and a perceptive overview to his body of work.

The picture comes from a variety of sources, but contemporary interviews are crisp and the stereo quality is adequate. There is no captioning. Included in the supplement are biographies of many of the interviewees, an incomplete but workable discography (it leaves out his haunting rendition of *September Song*) with links to the song performances in the documentary, a 2 minute clip of a Velvet Underground performance, and fascinating voiceless minute-long video portraits of some of the people in Reed's life.

Love and Anarchy (Fox Lorber, FLV5044)

Although it runs 120 minutes and not the 129 listed on the jacket cover, it still appears that it is Lina Wertmüller's original cut and not the shortened 108 minute cut that was released theatrically in the U.S. We loved the shorter version, with its frantic energy (it was shuffled up a bit, also), but Wertmüller's original version is also highly satisfying. The story is simple—a would-be assassin, played by Giancarlo Giannini, visits his contact, a prostitute, played by Mariangela Melato, who has been weaseling government security secrets out of her clients. While he's at her brothel, however, he falls for another prostitute, played by Lina Polito, and begins to have second thoughts about his mission to murder Mussolini. The film revels in its depiction of the brothel and in Giannini's wild-eyed earthiness. The music is a glorious combination of old Italian pop and folk tunes and a Nino Rota background score, and the cinematography, by Giuseppe Rotunno, is superbly executed. It's our favorite Wertmüller film—for that matter, it's one of the few of hers that we really like—because it doesn't get sidetracked by grotesque indulgences. Wertmüller's cut is somewhat calmer and more methodical than the American cut, but the characters are clearly stated. There is still great humor in their actions and a compelling sadness in their fates.

The picture is letterboxed with an aspect ratio of about 1.72:1 and no 16:9 enhancement, though it still looks a little tight on the sides. The film's opening and footage near the reel-change points are somewhat worn and battered, but other passages within the movie have moderately strong colors and looks reasonably sharp. Strong hues still blur, and we're sure a much better picture could be produced if the original source material could be obtained, but the presentation is workable and we're plain happy to finally have the film. The monophonic sound is okay—the music isn't too badly distorted—and the film is Italian with optional English subtitles.

Love Exchange X-rated (DaViD, D8012)

The picture quality is outstanding. Shot on videotape, the image is consistently well lit and accurately transferred, delivering perfect fleshtones, bright, super crisp colors and a window-like clarity in every shot. The 83 minute program conforms to a standard erotic format, but in sort of a definitive way. The restless female leads seduce a pool maintenance man, an auto repairman, gardeners and a husband's best friend, with an underlying moral that kind of says people are more attracted to what they don't have than what the do. It's basic, but the dramatic interludes flow smoothly and with the image quality looking so exceptional, it works. The sound is fine.

The Love Goddesses (Image, ID4546JFDVD)

A 1965 documentary about famous movie actresses and sex in films is presented with everybody's big sister, Ingrid Bergman, rather incongruously placed upon the jacket cover. Covering stars from the silent days to the early Sixties, the 90 minute program advances in a generally chronological order, with many great film clips, and generalized insight on the reasons behind the popularity of certain actresses or styles. The documentary is letterboxed, with an aspect ratio of about 1.75:1, often trimming the clips on the top and bottom. The quality of the clips also varies, but most look pretty nice, and almost all of them are in black and white. The monophonic sound is adequate. There is no captioning.

Love Jones (New Line, N4786)

A black yuppie romance with a great make-out musical score, Nia Long and Larenz Tate star as an artistically inclined couple (he's a poet, she's a photographer) who have a great time together but are kept apart for most of the movie by contrivances. There is a lot of conversation about relationships and responsibilities, and it is given an African-American slant, turning it into kind of a black **My Night at Maude's**. The performers are attractive and the dialogue is intelligent, so the 110 minute film is reasonably satisfying, provided the viewer is predisposed toward talky romances.

As we mentioned, however, the musical score is wonderful, filled with smooth jazz and penetrating love ballads, and the stereo surround sound is terrific. What's more, there is a Dolby Digital track that is even better, with sharper, better defined separations and more detail. A music video for one of the singles, Lauryn Hill's *The Sweetest Thing*, is also included.

The single-sided dual-layer presentation is letterboxed on one layer, with an aspect ratio of about 1.85:1 and an accommodation for enhanced 16:9 playback, and is in full screen format on the other layer. The letterboxed image masks picture information off top and bottom in comparison to the full screen image and adds very little to the sides, but we preferred the balances within the letterbox framing. The picture quality looks okay, with accurate hues, even in darker sequences. There are also optional English subtitles, a good cast-and-director profile section and a trailer.

Lovesick (Warner, 20011)

Dudley Moore does his usual comedy-of-embarrassment thing as a psychiatrist who falls in love with a patient. Elizabeth McGovern co-stars, with Alec Guinness as an imaginary version of Freud who talks to the hero. The film has its charming and humorous moments, but the premise is a little awkward and Moore's masochism can be tiresome. Marshall Brickman directed the 1983 feature.

The picture is presented in full screen and the source material has some speckling in places. The picture is both sharp and hazy—in other words, the haze, which may be part of the cinematography, looks very crisp. Fleshtones are a little dullish, but basic colors look bright enough. The monophonic sound has some distortion on the upper end during the louder dialogue sequences. The 98 minute program is adequately closed captioned.

Lucky Luke (Simitar, 7361)

Directed by Terence Hill, who also stars, it may not be a great work of art, but it is a fun little comedy-western. It is presented in full screen, but cropping appears to be minimal. The 1990 feature, adapted from the European comic book about the Old West, loses a bit of steam in the second half because of an episodic narrative, and it contains the sort of politically incorrect racial gags one is unlikely to see in American films these days, but it captures the spirit of the comic fairly well. The hero, 'faster than his own shadow,' helps clean up a town, only to find that he's eliminated so much vice the town's economy is threatened. There are lots of slapstick gags, some fairly good stunts, a few clever shoot-outs, and a talking horse. We thought it was cute.

The color transfer looks fine. The source material is regularly visited by minor speckling, but you have to squint to see it. Fleshtones seem reasonably fresh, other hues are bright and the image is fairly sharp. Some of the music sounds a little strained and lip movements do not always match the English dialogue (though they do sometimes), but the monophonic sound is tolerable. The film runs 90 minutes and is not captioned.

Lucky Texan (see The John Wayne Collection)

The Lucy Show (Madacy, DVD99099)

Four half-hour episodes from Lucille Ball's sitcom, which played in the Sixties and early Seventies, are presented, though oddly, they placed two episodes on each side of the platter when four could very easily have been fit onto one side. The opening credit sequence has been messed with a little, but the end credits are in tact, with the original theme song. The episodes are not time encoded and are accompanied by some minor trivia. Neither the picture nor the sound is any good, but at least the shows are in color. The monophonic sound on all the episodes is harsh, with a very limited range and numerous dropouts. There's also an overindulgent laugh track, and the episodes are not captioned. The show's premise has Ball portraying a widow who works as a secretary for a bank VP, played by Gale Gordon.

The worst looking episode is also the most precious. Jack Benny guest stars as himself, and Ball's character takes him on a tour of the bank's vault (replete with gorillas, quicksand and piranhas) to show him how safe his money will be if he deposits it. The situation is farfetched, but the timing between Benny and Ball is wonderful. Too bad the source material has such lousy contrasts. Details are totally obscured by the washed out image and colors are weak. There are also plenty of speckles.

Ball's character has to pretend to be an elderly woman to keep a wealthy elder depositor happy in the companion episode. It is a typical effort (the old guy starts to put the moves on her) and reasonably amusing. Colors are a bit faded, though stronger than the Benny episode, and contrasts are fairly normal. There is a splice, however, that cuts into a joke, and other damage scattered throughout the program, which even slips out of frame at one point.

The two episodes on side two are both so badly out-of-synch the show plays like a dubbed Italian comedy. The source material also has a number of splices, but the colors, though still aged, are fresher and richer than those on side one. In the first episode, Ball's character sneaks away from her job to attend a department store sale and ends up winning a prize and getting her picture in the paper. The funniest sequence, however, is when she accidentally but methodically destroys a china and refrigerator display. In the second episode she baby-sits three chimpanzees, who pretty much steal the show from her.

Lumière & Company (Fox Lorber, FLV5013)

Forty movie directors from around the world were given the opportunity to use the original Lumière Bros. camera and shoot a 50 second reel of film. The 1995 compilation, celebrating the hundredth anniversary of the first Lumière film, combines these 40 segments with shots of the directors at work. Each director is also asked the same generic questions.

Some of the directors work hard to evoke the spirit of the Lumière works, while others use narratives that are far more sophisticated or advanced than was conceived on the older pieces. One director cheats, explaining his movie and providing a context to enhance one's understanding of it, before it unspools. Another seems like a perfect combination of the present and the past, depicting a helicopter landing and taking off again in an ideal evocation of how the older films explored transportation and other technologies. Others do well by imitating the more lighthearted Lumière efforts, including an adept hand-painted depiction of an Indian dancer, Spike Lee's look at a baby's face, an African film—

one of the few to try a straight gag—about a man who scares some fishermen with a crocodile mask, and a shot of some kids placing a hat on a statue. Among the stranger efforts is a Merchant/Ivory bit that looks like a MacDonalds commercial, but the weirdest of all is from Arthur Penn, of all people, involving a man lying beneath a naked pregnant woman.

The three best ones (the only three we wanted to go back and watch a second time) tend to bend the rules to fit their own devices, but leave a viewer with a strong impression of something having been accomplished that exceeds the simple recording of life outside the camera. Andre Konchalovsky starts with a haunting landscape (it is probably the best piece of cinematography in the collection), dollies in on the corpse of a dead dog being feasted upon by flies and then rises again to return to the landscape. David Lynch turns his 50 seconds into a genuine 50 second David Lynch movie, using in-camera cuts to create one of his eerie, dream-like progressions of odd incidents. The best film in the group, however, comes from perhaps the world's most under-rated active director, Claude Lelouch, who captures the entire history of the cinema by showing a man and woman kissing while they spin around, as a chronological succession of camera units stands behind, filming them.

Much of the documentary dialogue is in French, with English subtitles. The image quality of the interviews is passable, and the film's soundtrack is a modest stereo. The program runs 88 minutes. You can access the directors from the chapter guide, but we wish the films themselves had been isolated with chapter encoding.

The Lumière Brothers' First Films (Kino, K106)

Among the very first of the world's filmmakers, the Lumière Brothers, working in France around the Turn of the Century, created hundreds of 50 second film clips, most of them having staged documentary settings but some exploring the parameters of comedy, stunt performances and other budding genres. 85 of those sub-minute films have been collected on the hour-long collection. Kino has chosen not to chapter the individual films, which is a drag. Instead they are bunched into nine generalized categories, although there is a listing of the films on the jacket cover (there is none on the DVD itself).

The movies are old, but have been well preserved and look very sharp, with well-defined contrasts. There are three audio channels. On one audio track there is an original piano score to accompany the films and on another, there is a lecture, in French, by Thierry Fremaux. On the third, with the music playing in the background, Bertrand Tavernier gives a lecture about the films in English and seems to follow the gist of what Fremaux has to say fairly closely. There is no captioning. The films themselves are fascinating, not just because of their age, but because the choices the brothers made served as a foundation for all documentary films that followed.

The films are outstanding, offering time machine-like glimpses on life a hundred years ago as well as revealing the first building blocks in the development of a language of film (the management of perspective was a significant step). The films were shot throughout the world by Lumière stringers and include glimpses of London, New York, Venice, Chicago (a parade of policemen, and every last one of them has a bush mustache), Berlin, Jerusalem, Egypt, Japan, Indochina (a spellbinding shot of children running after the cart holding the camera, including a little naked girl that immediately evokes the famous napalm photograph taken, perhaps of her granddaughter, seven decades later), and elsewhere. There are amusement park rides, acrobats, comedians re-creating stage routines, manufacturers, parades, babies and many other divertissements. The DVD shows what cinema brought to the world—living history.

Luminous Visions (see **Odyssey: The Mind's Eye Presents Luminous Visions**)

Lupin III: The Mystery of Mamo (Image, ID4653SEDVD)

Shot in a different style than most of the Japanese cartoons appearing in America, the artwork has a very comic book look to it, with thin, almost stick-figure characters and marvelously exaggerated facial expressions. The first three quarters of the 102 minute program are super. Lupin is 'the world's best thief' and, in this episode, he is hired by an enigmatic figure to lift a rare jewel from the center of a large pyramid. The last act, however, has a somewhat different tone, as the story becomes more science fiction based, more complicated and less inclined toward quick gags. Still, the overall entertainment is enjoyable, and there is also some appealingly gratuitous nudity as well as a few evocations of paintings by Salvador Dali and others worked into the show's design. The picture is letterboxed with an aspect ratio of about 1.66:1 and no 16:9 enhancement. Colors are a little aged on the 1978 program, but the image is reasonably sharp and stable. The stereo sound is okay. The program is dubbed in English and is not captioned.

Luther Vandross: Always and Forever—An Evening of Songs at Royal Albert Hall (Sony, EVD50119)

The regular stereo soundtrack provides what sounds like a typical concert mix. All the noises are there, but it is a bit generalized and certainly not as good as a CD playback. The Dolby Digital track, however, has a greater range and an airier presence, and when activated your whole viewing room suddenly seems to bristle with a you-are-there ambiance. The music is much stronger, and even though most of the back channel playback is a duplicate of what is coming from the front, the delivery seems livelier and more invigorating. The 88 minute concert is also pretty good, though an interview with Vandross is inserted between each of the numbers, breaking up the flow of the music a little. Vandross performs a dozen well-known numbers from *Ain't No Stoppin' Us Now* to *The Impossible Dream* (he sings *Killing Me Softly* and, refreshingly, does not alter gender in the lyrics), backed up by a large symphony orchestra. The audience seems unusually polite and quiet, but that does not appear to hamper the energy he exerts. The picture is a little soft at times, depending upon the intensity of the stage lighting, but colors and fleshtones look accurate. During some numbers Vandross sways as he sings and when he sways from screen right to screen left the image is smooth, but when he moves in the other direction, the image stutters slightly. The program is supported by English subtitles.

Lynch, David (see **Pretty as a Picture: The Art of David Lynch**)

M

M (Criterion, MMM020)

The classic 1931 Fritz Lang film is about the hunt for a child murderer. The presentation looks its age, but the picture is sharp, contrasts are crisp, and the image is much smooth. The source material has noticeable wear throughout, but the flaws never become intrusive. The monophonic sound is a little muted but, if anything, this helps cut down on the background noise and the presentation is acceptable. The film is in German, with optional English subtitles. This is the 110 minute version of the film, which has had a number of different running times.

Peter Lorre stars as the murderer, who gradually gains a thread of sympathy as he is trapped and captured by members of the underworld and then condemned in a feverish lynching trial held by the criminals. Moral ambiguity aside, the film is a superb procedural and a definitive innovation of crime movie styles.

Mad City (Warner, 15433)

Dustin Hoffman stars as a TV reporter who becomes personally involved in a hostage crisis at a museum, brought on by a laid off museum employee played by John Travolta. Costa Gavras directed. The movie begins badly, rises in quality like a bell curve to a point where it is both enjoyable and stimulating, and then tries for too much and becomes ridiculous again. Because the stars are involved and it is a big budget production, the filmmakers apparently thought they had to bring things to a satirical and emotional crescendo. The film's basic premise, however, is valid (the movie fails at first because the actors have difficulty getting into their parts—after they start working with each other, they both improve) and we can't help thinking that if the drama had been kept at a lower key and the screenwriters had worked from character logic instead of from the desire to dump on news organizations, it could have been a terrific film. As it stands, it is interesting, but ultimately unsettling and a disappointment.

The 115 minute film is presented in letterboxed format on one side, with an aspect ratio of about 2.35:1 and an accommodation for enhanced 16:9 playback, and in full screen format on the other side. The letterboxing adds picture information to the sides of the image and masks off quite a bit from the bottom in comparison to the full screen release. The framing on the widescreen image is more effective, but the full screen image is workable. The colors are rich and look very nice, but the stereo surround sound is weak and even the Dolby Digital track lacks detail, though since most of the movie is talk it doesn't matter too much. The film is also available in French in standard stereo and can be accompanied by English, French or Spanish subtitles. There is a good cast & crew profile section and a short essay about the history of TV news, along with a trailer that has contrived critic quotes.

Mad Dog and Glory (Image, ID4278USDVD)

In an inspired piece of reverse casting, Bill Murray is a mobster and Robert De Niro is an average schmo he befriends. Uma Thurman and David Caruso are also featured in the 1993 production.

The image looks terrific. Colors are bright, sharp and accurate, with solid fleshtones. The picture is letterboxed with an aspect ratio of about 1.85:1 and no 16:9 enhancement. The stereo surround sound is okay, though it doesn't have much energy. The 97 minute program is adequately closed captioned.

Mad Max (Image, ID40820RDVD)

Mad Max has spawned many imitations, all of which have interpreted the film as being about cops fighting punk-garbed bad guys, but not one has recognized that the film's story was secondary to its exhilarating sense of style. It isn't just that the action scenes whip by—a welcome change from the standard three camera and slow motion depiction of every car crash that most other movies employ—but that the widescreen cinematography is reinforcing both the film's setting and its nihilistic themes even during the heat of the chase. The old cropped version made the 1979 film look mangled and slapped together, as if it had scored its success through a couple of well-staged stunts and the appeal of its star, Mel Gibson. Letterboxed, the film, despite its low budget, is both elegant and determined, presenting a bleak view of a possible near future (the film actually contains a motif about crippling), but one in which a moral individual can still succeed within his society, provided he knows his way around a car engine.

The colors are reasonably strong and grain is held to a minimum. Fleshtones are adequate. The letterboxing has an aspect ratio of about 2.4:1 and no 16:9 enhancement. The monophonic sound is functional, with dubbed dialogue and blandly recorded music. There is no captioning.

Mad Max: Beyond Thunderdome (Warner, 11519)

The 1985 film had two directors, George Miller and George Ogilvie, and the movie grinds to a halt during Ogilvie's middle third. Miller, who did the previous two Max films, has a prodigious film style and his sequences, which open and close this movie, are grand. You can go fix yourself a sandwich during the film's middle section though, without bothering to put it on Pause. Mel Gibson and Tina Turner star in the post-Apocalypse action feature.

The film is in letterboxed format on one side, with an aspect ratio of about 2.35:1 and an accommodation for enhanced 16:9 playback, and in cropped format on the other, but the cropping is a waste of time, obscuring too much of the action. The Dolby Digital track is much better than the standard surround track. The mix is in keeping with the energy and clutter of the film's action scenes. While it may not have quite as much rear channel activity as a contemporary release, it still has quite a bit, and the overall blend of sounds and music is grand. The 107 minute film is accompanied by a theatrical trailer, mildly letterboxed on the letterbox side and in full screen on the cropped side. There is a modest cast profile and a reasonably interesting collection of production notes. The film is also available in French, without Dolby Digital, and comes with English, French or Spanish subtitles ("Dos hombres entran, sólo uno sale").

Made in America (Warner, 12652)

Whoopi Goldberg and Ted Danson star in the labored romantic comedy about the fallout, two decades later, from a sperm bank mix-up. Danson is amusing as a boorish used car dealer but Goldberg is too sophisticated an actress for the material and seems as much in place trying to be funny on the bicycle her character rides as a goldfish might. Once in a while the film, which was directed by Richard Benjamin, achieves its goals, but just as often its efforts are too contrived, lacking wit or reason.

The picture is presented in full screen, losing a smidgen on the sides and opening up the top and bottom of the image in comparison to a letterboxed version. The colors are bright and crisp, and fleshtones looks accurate. The stereo surround sound is okay and the 111 minute program is closed captioned with minor paraphrasing.

Madigan (Universal, 20525)

The 1968 Don Siegel police thriller, shot on location in Manhattan and starring the eternally sour Richard Widmark, is an uncommercial, pessimistic work that often leaves a viewer feeling dissatisfied. Henry Fonda is also feature, and the movie basically has two unrelated plots. Fonda is a police commissioner confronting an apparent case of corruption involving one of his oldest associates, played by James Whitmore. Widmark is a detective searching for a murder suspect, with the job pushing his marriage to a near breaking point. The film's realistic setting and anti-heroic drama are certainly interesting, and one of the reasons **Madigan** can leave such a bad feeling is that it is so effectively directed a viewer stays hooked to it and ends up drowning in hopelessness right along with the heroes.

The picture is letterboxed with an aspect ratio of about 2.35:1 and no 16:9 enhancement. The movie was shot on location and the film's colors have a drab realism, but the image is smooth, hues are well defined and the picture is sharp. The monophonic sound has age-related limitations but sounds okay. The 101 minute program can be presented in French and can be supported by English or Spanish subtitles. There is a very good production essay that talks straight about the film's two separate dramas and the problems Siegel had with his producer, Frank Rosenberg. There is also a good-sized cast-and-director profile section and a trailer with some brief nudity.

Madonna: The Girlie Show ~ Live Down Under (Warner, 238391)

The neo-Ziegfeld stage show Madonna puts on is less guided by music than it is by spectacle. Madonna wears a headpiece microphone most of the time, so she must be singing, but it is a wonder that she bothers since she is doing so many other things while blurting out her lyrics. She must have at least a dozen costume changes, every number is elaborately and precisely choreographed, and she is running all over the place. It is quite a production, probably very impressive when seen live and fascinating even on video, with bare-breasted chorus girls (the program is R-rated), constantly shifting scenery and circus-like acrobatics. A few of the songs fit the format fairly well—*Vogue* is especially appropriate—but others are simply background music for the frolicking, and ultimately there are only about sixteen numbers performed in the two hour concert.

The Dolby Digital track is super. The standard stereo surround soundtrack is somewhat dull, emphasizing the secondary nature of Madonna's vocals and the haphazard recording environment of a huge outdoor concert. The Dolby Digital track, however, gives the music an increased dimensionality that frees it from the sounds of the crowd. Instead of a single wall of sound, the music is given space and topography. It doesn't help Madonna's vocals—nothing can help Madonna's vocals—but it does help the band substantially, almost forcing you to get up and dance to their beat. The picture also looks super, though the concert lighting creates subdued fleshtones and limited stage detail. The image is crisp and colors are solid. The optional English subtitling is great, though when Madonna starts jumping around with her whip we're not sure we want to know exactly what it is she is saying.

Madonna: Truth or Dare (Artisan, 60448)

According to the production notes, the shift between black-and-white and color is 'allegorical' in the gossipy Madonna concert-and-more documentary. "Color is used to symbolize the world of light, artifice and theatricality that Madonna lives in public view, while black-and-white conveys the more gritty reality of her private life." The black-and-white backstage sequences look fine and the color concert sequences are superb, with crisp, accurate hues that remain unaffected by the stage lights. The program is presented in letterboxed format on one side, with an aspect ratio of about 1.85:1 and an accommodation for 16:9 enhanced playback, and in full screen format on the other. Cropping appears to be minimal. The stereo surround sound is subdued, but there is a much livelier Dolby Digital track that appears to have basically the same mix, but delivers it with heightened detail and extra power. In addition to the brief production notes, there are profiles of Madonna and of the director, Alek Keshishian, and two entertaining theatrical trailers. The 1991 120 minute program can also be supported by English, French or Spanish subtitles ("Montre-nous comment tu suces, avec cette bouteille").

Mafia! (Buena Vista, 16320)

A spoof on **Casino** and the first two *Godfather* films, with plenty of other lampoons and wild gags thrown in, the humor is constant and some of it is hysterical—at least it was to a young friend who was watching the movie with us and spent much of the time clutching his stomach and rolling on the floor in uncontrolled laughter. He's nine, but adults will likely be amused as well. Jay Mohr stars, with Lloyd Bridges, Christina Applegate and others.

Even the picture quality is a gas—for the 'I believe in America' scene, the image is deliberately grainy, with weak contrasts, to imitate the way *The Godfather* looks on most video releases. When it isn't imitating some other film's look, the colors are strong and the image is sharp. The presentation is letterboxed, with an aspect ratio of about 1.85:1 and no 16:9 enhancement. The stereo surround sound and Dolby Digital sound have some sharply defined directional effects and are worth turning up, but the audio mix doesn't go overboard. The Dolby Digital track is slightly better defined than the standard track. The 87 minute film can be supported by English subtitles and is accompanied by a trailer that contains a number of amusing interviews with the cast and crew.

The Magical Mystery Tour (see The Beatles: The Magical Mystery Tour)

Mahler (Image, ID4328JFDVD)

"I don't want to imitate nature. I want to capture its very essence, so that, if all the birds and the beasts died tomorrow and the world became a desert, when people heard my music they would still know—feel—what nature was." Ken Russell's outstanding biographical drama tells of Gustav Mahler's life in flashbacks and flashbacks-within-flashbacks as he has a reconciliation with his wife during a train ride shortly before his death. **Mahler** is no more a biography of Mahler, however, than **Amadeus** was a biography of Mozart. The 1974 film is about Mahler's music, and it has been storyboarded to his songs and symphonies, continually coaxing the viewer into approaching the most well known passages in his works from different points of view, to show the environment, the emotion, and the spirit which went into the music. Mahler is tough. His symphonies are not the kind of patter one puts on the hi-fi, low, during dinner parties. The movie works as an introduction or as an enlightenment, and it works because Russell has the guts to really takes risks with the images, to push them so far that you understand he is not providing the last word on the subject, he is only celebrating the majesty the music can inspire. The soul of the film, however, is in the almost continual connections it provides between music and images or ideas. Walks in the woods, brass bands, the voice of a loved one or the death of a child all become as clear in the language of the music as they do in the language of images. After watching the film or the DVD, you carry that language with you, increasing your understanding not only of Mahler's works, but of any music you might hear.

The picture, in full screen format, looks a bit bedraggled, with bland colors, speckles, minor grain and other wear. The stereo sound has a limited dimensionality but is a little more flowery than the standard monophonic audio tracks from the mid-Seventies. The 111 minute program is not captioned.

Major Payne (Universal, 20513)

Damon Wayans is a former Marine Special Forces commando turned surplus commodity in peace time, who finds employment as the commander of a junior ROTC unit at a boarding school. Wayans' comical exaggerations of his character's irrepressible killer instincts are basically funny, but the joke wears thin after a while.

The picture is letterboxed with an aspect ratio of about 1.85:1 and an accommodation for enhanced 16:9 playback. The colors look terrific, with bright, detailed hues and true fleshtones. The stereo surround sound is okay, and there is a Dolby Digital track that is more boisterous and has more separations. The film's audio mix is sporadically aggressive, but at its best moments, the DVD delivers the goods. The 98 minute program is also available in French and can be supported by English or Spanish subtitles ("¡Tengo 8 semanas para transformalos de gusanos a cadetes con disciplina!"). There are some good production notes, which explain that the 1995 film is a remake of *The Private War of Major Benson*, as well as a small cast-and-director profile section and a theatrical trailer that boils down to the film's funniest moments.

The Making of A Hard Day's Night (see The Beatles: The Making of A Hard Day's Night)

The Making of Portrait of a Lady (see Short Cinema Journal 1:2 Issue: Dreams)

Malice (PolyGram, 8006336452)

Alec Baldwin, Nicole Kidman and Bill Pullman star in the 1993 film, which manipulates the viewer's emotions every step of the way and never falters in providing satisfying and stimulating entertainment. Set on a college campus, Baldwin is a surgeon, Pullman is a school administrator and Kidder is the administrator's wife. They all live in the same house. Anne Bancroft and George C. Scott

have cameo appearances, but to say any more about the film would spoil the pleasures of discovery that it so adeptly delivers.

The picture is presented in full screen format only. The colors are consistently accurate throughout the presentation and the image is always sharply focused. Whether a scene is set in bright daylight or shadowy darkness, the quality of the image does almost as much to pull the viewer close to the characters as the narrative does. The stereo surround sound is also in excellent shape, though the musical score is not delivered with the intensity one finds on the most elaborate audio transfers. The 106 minute program has optional French subtitles, English captioning, a cast profile section and a trailer.

Mallrats (Universal, 20019)

Kevin Smith's 1995 film, about two young men at a shopping mall who are trying to win back the hearts of their estranged girlfriends, has moments of inspired comedy, but the humor does not flow naturally from the characters. Instead, you can see the filmmakers trying to be funny, using scatology, eccentricity and other contrived devices to squeeze gags out of the narrative. Even when there is a funny line or a crude but humorous moment, the humor is lessened because its context is more artificial than it is pretending to be.

As is evidenced on the DVD, which includes a good hour of deleted scenes, the 96 minute film does not flow naturally. The jokes often seem forced and the timing is uneven. Because it is part of a larger whole, and because there is some humor to it, home video has redeemed some of its reputation, and it can be enjoyable if you like the characters and know what to expect. It just earns the fewest votes for being Smith's best film. Shannen Doherty stars with Jason Lee and, though he isn't listed on the jacket, Ben Affleck also appears.

Fleshtones on the LD are little warmer, but other colors are yellowish and it is clear that hues on the DVD are more accurate. The image is also sharper. The presentation is letterboxed, with an aspect ratio of about 1.85:1 and an accommodation for enhanced 16:9 playback. The stereo surround sound is okay, and there is a 5.1 Dolby Digital channel that enhances the musical score effectively. There is also a French audio track in standard stereo and optional English subtitles.

There is a commentary channel featuring Smith, Lee, Affleck, Jason Mewes (who appears, with Smith, in each of Smith's films), producer Scott Mosier, and Smith collaborator or historian or something, Vincent Pereira. With the DVD's most innovative feature, you can use the alternate angle function to see them all talking in one section of the screen, while the movie is playing (if an annoying logo comes on whenever the alternate angle is available, it can be suppressed—check your DVD player's user manual). There is also a 20 minute retrospective documentary, a collection of publicity stills and the usual production notes, cast profile section and trailer, as well as the elaborate 'deleted scenes' collection.

The film failed in part because the film company started mucking with Smith's vision, but it also failed because Smith's sense of timing was not appropriate for the 'R-teen' comedy genre, which otherwise dumbed down the intellectual gags that make his **Clerks** so engaging. This is especially true of the film's original 20 minute opening, which is the centerpiece of the deleted scenes. It painfully lacks a comic focus and it is a good thing they dropped the sequence, regardless of how much added character information it supplied.

The commentary and documentary provide a fairly complete picture of how the film came together and then fell apart. Each is also very entertaining itself, using the movie as a foil for amusing comments about the filmmaking industry and the stigmas of success (they all rank on Affleck—even Affleck ranks on Affleck). But, as Smith points out, the mere presence of extra features enhances the respectability of **Mallrats**. "By doing this DVD, it makes it seem like this film is this unappreciated piece of genius," Smith says, chuckling.

Mama, Do You Love Me? (Sony, LVD49507)

The Sony Wonder *Doors of Wonder* series takes well known children's picture books and turns them into short animated features, though in order to do so, the stories are padded and songs have been added. **Mama, Do You Love Me?** runs 30 minutes and is set in an Alaskan Inuit village, where a young girl gets into a little bit of trouble—but not too much—when her puppy runs off and she has to chase it. The part from the book, in which the girl's mother compares the depth of her love to various animal activities, appears in the middle of the story.

The animation is simplified in comparison to the book's stylized illustrations. The color quality is passable. The sound is not elaborate, and the program tends to function like a standard, cheap cartoon, despite its exceptional source. There is also a sing-along segment for the show's one song, a multiple choice 'game' that includes live footage of arctic fauna and culture, and a profile of the story's author, Barbara M. Joose. There are optional English subtitles.

Man from Utah (see **The John Wayne Collection**)

The Man in the Iron Mask (MGM, 906203)

An enjoyable superstar cast enlivens an otherwise uninspired adaptation of the swashbuckling classic. Leonardo DiCaprio stars in a dual role, supported by Jeremy Irons, John Malkovich, Gerard Depardieu and Gabriel Byrne. All bring an alertness and competent professionalism to their parts and are dependably appealing, so they are able to muddle through the rather dull script about duplicity and intrigue in the court of Louis XIV. The film works hard to explore the relationships between the characters, but not hard enough to give viewers the kind of excitement or sympathy required to care about those relationships. There are a couple moments in the film where everything comes together quite well—particularly the scene where the king is substituted—but such thrills are never sustained.

The DVD is presented on one side in letterboxed format, with an aspect ratio of about 1.85:1 and an accommodation for enhanced 16:9 playback, and in full screen format on the other side. Either framing seems satisfying. The color transfer looks okay, with stability in the darker sequences and decent fleshtones. The stereo surround sound is adequate and the Dolby Digital track is better, with more power and more pronounced separations. The 132 minute film is also available in French in standard stereo and can be supported by English, French or Spanish subtitles. There is a trailer, which sells the film well and uses a few alternate takes (such as with the Depardieu bird dropping scene), a look at the different design concepts the mask underwent and a few production drawings.

The film's director, Randall Wallace, provides a commentary track, talking mostly about working with the actors but occasionally getting into the technical aspects of a scene or a shot. Wallace says that he disapproves of camera shots and movements that call attention to themselves, but that is precisely what the movie needs to match the stature of its cast—more flamboyance. He also speaks enthusiastically about one sequence where Malkovich's performance brought those around him to tears—which is fantastic, except Wallace didn't get the shot, so viewers have only the briefest glimpse of that passion and may not notice it at all.

A Man in Uniform (Simitar, 7340)

A young actor who lands a role as a cop on a TV episode starts taking his part to heart and walking around the city after hours in his costume. The idea is interesting and parts of the drama are compelling, but not too much comes of it.

The colors are a little greenish and fleshtones are pale, but the image is reasonably sharp. The source material also has a few speckles and other wear marks. The Ultra-Stereo sound is very flat and scratchy. The film runs 99 minutes and is not captioned.

Man of a Thousand Faces (Image, ID4290USDVD)

James Cagney portrays the senior Lon Chaney in the biographical drama. The picture is letterboxed with an aspect ratio of about 2.35:1 and no 16:9 enhancement (shouldn't movies about silent screen stars be shot in a silent screen aspect ratio?). The black-and-white image is spotless, crisp, and maintains accurate contrast levels from beginning to end. The monophonic sound and Dolby Digital mono sound are okay, too. The 122 minute program is closed captioned with very minor abridgments.

Except that he was too old to portray Chaney as a young man (they keep him in clown makeup a lot for the early scenes), Cagney does a superb job recreating Chaney's screen performances and revealing the actor's nobilities and his flaws. The 1957 film conveys the pains of life all too well at times, but it is well rounded and consistently interesting. The moviemaking scenes are great fun, the conflicts are fairly real and reasonably free of euphemism, and Cagney's own energy keeps the movie's momentum rolling.

Man Wanted (Tai Seng, 40054)

A turgid and overly sentimental Hong Kong gangster film, the plot is about an undercover cop who befriends a mob boss and then betrays him. The mob boss returns after a while to extract his revenge. The narrative is highly derivative of John Woo's films, but the movie, directed by Benny Chan, has none of Woo's style. There is plenty of action, but it is rarely invigorating and the emotional sequences are often very drawn out. Simon Yam and Yu Rong Guang star in the 1995 film.

The 92 minute film is letterboxed with an aspect ratio of about 1.85:1 and no 16:9 enhancement. Colors are a little drab and the image is a bit soft, but it looks much nicer than the LD, which is a lot more yellow and a lot hazier. The music has a very slight dimensionality and, otherwise, all of the film's sounds are centered, and there is a subdued high end. The film has tracks in English, Mandarin and Cantonese, and can be supported by optional English subtitles. There are also trailers and filmographies.

The Man Who Fell to Earth (Fox Lorber, FLV5039)

The DVD presents the 140 minute 'European cut' of the 1976 Nicolas Roeg film. It is letterboxed with an aspect ratio of about 2.35:1 and no 16:9 enhancement. The picture is much too dark, losing many details in the shadows, but otherwise colors are very accurate. Fleshtones are deep and skies are blue. When things are brightly lit, the details are also stronger and crisper. The monophonic sound is adequate. The program is not closed captioned and is accompanied by thorough filmographies for the cast and director.

David Bowie portrays an enigmatic and reclusive industrialist, apparently from another planet, who is prevented from capitalizing upon his initial successes, apparently by the government, and falls into an alcohol-fueled entrapment partly of his own making. The added footage contains a lot of frontal nudity and some minor artistic details that were deemed superfluous by the film's distributor.

The Man Who Knew Too Little (Warner, 15626)

Bill Murray stars in what in essence is a mirror opposite of **The Game**. The hero's brother treats the hero to what he believes to be an elaborate improvised street theater performance but what, due to a phone mix-up, turns out to be a genuine spy intrigue. The film could easily have dropped out of the Sixties, and the plot has as many holes as **The Game** has, but if you relax and just let the story flow by you get a classic comedy of the sort Bob Hope used to appear in or Blake Edwards used to make—flawed and silly, but still plenty funny, particularly with Murray's comedy skills leading the way.

The 94 minute film is presented in letterboxed format on one side, with an aspect ratio of about 1.85:1 and an accommodation for enhanced 16:9 playback, and in full screen format on the other side. The letterboxed image trims a little off the top and more off the bottom in comparison to the full screen image and adds a little to the sides. Either framing seems workable. The colors are crisp and fleshtones look accurate. The stereo surround sound is okay, but the Dolby Digital track is much better. It gives the musical score a strong dimensional presence that enhances one's involvement with the film, and provides crisp directional details that tend to hang in the center on the standard stereo track. The film can also be accessed in French or Spanish in Dolby Digital and comes with English, French or Spanish subtitles. There are some production notes, a cast & crew profile, a theatrical trailer and three TV spots, including one that uses footage not seen in the film.

On a commentary track, the director, Jon Amiel, reacts to the scenes as they advance, speaking a bit about how some sequences were staged, about Murray's improvisations, and about what got left out and what was put in after test marketing. He found, for example, that when he took out passages explaining the plot, the audience was able to follow the story better. There are minor gaps in his talk where the movie plays through, but he is able to share a little about what the atmosphere was like during the production and what his conceptions were before it started.

The Man Who Knew Too Much (see **Alfred Hitchcock Collection**)

The Man Who Would Be King (Warner, 858)

A wonderful, spellbinding adventure film clear up to the ending, but even on multiple viewings the inevitability that the heroes will fail is hard to take. Perhaps their fate is difficult to accept because up until that point the movie has been so perfectly plotted that you expect the storytellers to pull one last, well-planted surprise. They don't, but for those who love British India soldiering stories, and for those who get a kick out of Sean Connery and Michael Caine, the movie is still a crown jewel.

The colors look crisp, fleshtones are accurate and the film's dusty hues are carefully detailed and shaded. The film is letterboxed, with an aspect ratio of about 2.35:1 and accommodation for enhanced 16:9 playback. The monophonic sound is strong, and there is a monophonic Dolby Digital track with even more forcefulness and clarity. The 129 minute film is spread to two sides and can be accompanied by English, French or Spanish subtitles. There is a decent cast and crew listing, extensive production notes, trailers for eight of director John Huston's films—including a beautiful looking and marvelously campy one for *Reflections in a Golden Eye*—and an excellent 'making of' featurette, which includes a lot of footage of Huston at work. The featurette also implies, without showing for sure, that Connery did a difficult stunt.

Man with the Movie Camera (Image, ID4589DSDVD)

The intricately planned and executed film attempts to tell everything there is to know about modern civilization in 68 minutes while being its own 'making of' movie at the same time, and it succeeds on all counts. It's like a visualization of the Dewey Decimal system racing across the screen in front of you. Structured to show life in a city from sun up to sun down, the film used editing, special effects, staged sequences, genuine documentary sequences and every other 1929 movie trick or convention imaginable to explore commerce, leisure, physical fitness, nutrition, human relations, health, transportation, and you-name-it. Like *Koyaanisqatsi*, the images pulse and flow, matching your internal body rhythms and shaking you into a frenzy of admiration for the Soviet system or, at least, contemporary urban life.

Although the film was silent, Vertov intended it to be accompanied by live sound, so the stereo surround soundtrack, based on Vertov's concepts, is a dazzling mix of melody and avant garde sounds that sweep you even further into the dynamism of the im-

ages. The picture quality is likely as good as one will find, though contrasts are weak in places, the black-and-white image is grainy at times and the source material has its share of speckles. An error on the jacket cover identifies the DVD's soundtrack as being in Dolby Mono. In fact it is in stereo surround sound, with pure, smooth tones and lots of dimensional energy. On some silent films, such a rambunctious audio track would be distracting, but here it has just the opposite effect, pulling you further into the film's excitements. There is no dialogue, but signs and other Russian text appearing within the film are supported by permanent yellow English subtitles. There is also an excellent commentary channel, by Yuri Tsivian, which uses the film as a jumping off point for discussions on all matters of cinema and critical thinking. The film's masterful blend of images and ideas is ideal for repeat viewings, and it is also ideal for audio commentary, since a fully researched lecture, such as the one given by Tsivian, coordinated to a shot-by-shot unspooling of the film, contains reams of insights, such as explanations for the purposes behind specific combinations of shots. Tsivian also speaks about how the film was produced, and points out that one of the reasons it is so remarkable is that it "works on us as a documentary and a magic show at the same time."

The Man with Two Brains (Warner, 16375)

Steve Martin stars as a scientist who loves the conscience of one woman and the body of another in the 1983 Carl Reiner feature. Reiner chose to play it in a very clownish manner, so that nothing can be taken with even the veneer of seriousness, but that gives the film a tiresome and distancing tone, wholly dependent upon gags that are not consistently funny. Fans will be intermittently amused, but others may become impatient with the program rather quickly. Kathleen Turner, seeming at times to do a Bernadette Peters imitation, co-stars.

The picture is presented in full screen format. The image is soft, but colors look reasonably fresh and fleshtones are viable. The monophonic sound is passable. The 90 minute program is adequately captioned.

The Manchurian Candidate (MGM, 907013)

Only John Frankenheimer would be silly enough to accept as a plot device that a group of soldiers have been brainwashed in three days (with 'drugs and hypnosis'), and have a disaster prevented because some of the soldiers 'remember' the incident. Yet that one piece of science fiction allows the story to exist, with its many layers of political and dramatic explorations. Based upon a political thriller by Richard Condon, which, like many Condon stories, verges on satire, it brilliantly straddles a fine line between absurdity and drama. Its most exaggerated moments successfully raise the film's emotional impact instead of distancing the viewer from the characters, largely because Frankenheimer is consistent in his feel for how far he can push an idea. There is much to the movie that worth analyzing, such as the relationship between Frank Sinatra's character and Laurence Harvey on the crisscrossed levels of class and rank, the use of images of Abraham Lincoln as more than just a prefiguring of the concluding violence. The film even contains a joke that is already on the point of becoming completely obscure, about Heinz Ketchup.

The 1963 black-and-white film is presented in letterboxed format on one side and in cropped format on the other. The letterboxing has an aspect ratio of about 1.85:1 and no 16:9 enhancement. The black-and-white picture transfer is exquisite, with carefully detailed contrasts. The image is crisp and spotless. The monophonic sound, though a little softer than the LD, is fine. The 129 minute political thriller is also available in French and Spanish and comes with English, French or Spanish subtitles ("Raymond, pourquoi ne feriez-vous pas une petite réussite?"). There is an interview with Sinatra, Frankenheimer, and screenwriter George Axelrod, which is more valuable for its assemblage of personalities than it is for any academic measure.

Frankenheimer also provides a commentary. It is a bit sporadic, but he does have some interesting stories about the production (including a valid explanation as to why Sinatra prefers single takes) and some of the choices he made. The film was instantly recognized as a brilliant work, but the story, about a left-wing slap face right-wing slap face left-wing plot to take over the U.S., included the assassination of a political candidate with a rifle, and eighteen months after it was released, the horror of the Kennedy assassination caused the critics, the public, and the film's producers to suppress the movie and its namesake assassin from their memory. It was only after a lengthy passage of time and the pressure of the home video market that the movie has been returned to the public consciousness.

Manhattan Murder Mystery (Columbia TriStar, 71399)

The picture transfer is terrific, from the gorgeous opening shot of the Manhattan skyline at night to the spectacular storeroom-of-mirrors shoot-out at the end. The colors are consistently accurate and are vividly illuminated. The presentation is letterboxed on one side, with an aspect ratio of about 1.85:1 and an accommodation for enhanced 16:9 playback, and is in full screen format on the other side. Like most of Woody Allen's films, the stereo surround sound has a monaural soul but is effectively presented. The 107 minute program has a French language track, optional English or French subtitles, and a trailer.

Allen, who directed, also stars, with Diane Keaton, Alan Alda and others in the story of a nosy couple who come to think their apartment neighbor has murdered his wife. Although the film is frightfully funny in places, it is a very serious work, as close to John Cassavetes as it is to Bob Hope or Alfred Hitchcock. The narrative, in fact, takes a very long time to reach the momentum one is expecting, and some viewers may lack the patience to stay with it. What Allen accomplishes, however, is brilliant, spending as much time exploring relationships and marriages as he does developing the mystery. The portrait of a marriage under strain is basically the same he has painted in several of his other respected films, but the context here is a great deal more fun and so the viewer is more accepting of the foibles and flaws of the heroes.

Maniac (Elite, EE1981)

The 1980 feature is primarily designed for genre fans and has a couple of good screams. It follows around the killer, played by Joe Spinell, cutting away only long enough so the viewer can become familiar with and care about the killer's victims before they are eviscerated. Although he kills both men and women, there is a deliberate eroticism in the murders of the female victims, lending credence to the argument that the film is sadistically misogynist. Nevertheless, there are plenty of viewers who embrace such fantasies so long as the fantasies stay on the screen.

The picture is letterboxed with an aspect ratio of about 1.85:1 with no 16:9 enhancement. The image cannot lose its low budget origins, sporting dulled colors, weak contrasts and lots of grain at times, though we're sure this is the best the 1980 film has ever looked. The stereo surround sound (it is mostly the music that has been enhanced with stereo re-processing) is okay, and the Dolby Digital track is even stronger, bringing more flourish to the proceedings.

The film runs 85 minutes, having been trimmed of a scene present in its original 87 minute running time by the director William Lustig, though that scene is included in a supplement, along with a weird 5 minute promotional clip for a sequel that was never shot. There are more than a half dozen trailers and TV spots, including trailers in Italian, French and German (the cultural differences in how they are constructed are fascinating—the Italian clip emphasizes the killer's Catholic background, the German clip is darker and more direct). In one of the more creative applications of DVD menu technology, blood drips from the killer's knife as you decide which option you want. Unlike the movie itself, it is a subtle but effective touch. Lustig, Tom Savini, editor Lorenzo Marinelli and an associate of Spinell who was present during the shooting, Luke Walter, reminisce on a commentary track about the good old days, when they could make a film for a few thousand dollars and not have to answer to market-oriented producers. Their talk is informative and Lustig provides a number of technical insights that students of film would be well advised to master (pay attention to the actors when they have ideas), but the best part of the talk is the spirit with which it is delivered. They have so much fun remembering what it was like to make a totally naughty movie that it is impossible to condemn them for having done so.

Maniac Cop (Elite, EE3426)

The film, about a large, zombie-like policeman who wanders around killing people, is competently produced for its budget and delivers a satisfying touch here and there, but most of it is fairly routine. The picture has been letterboxed, with an aspect ratio of about 1.85:1 and no 16:9 enhancement, and although it is clear that the image is matted, the framing looks fine. The image is surprisingly soft, and it looks dark, losing details in shadows. The Ultra-Stereo sound is strong when the recording allows it. The mix is a somewhat low budget affair, with a limited dynamic range, but it does have a little energy. There is no captioning.

Additionally, there is an appealing commentary track, featuring director William Lustig, producer Larry Cohen, star Bruce Campbell and composer Bruce Chattaway. Their get-together has a jovial atmosphere and their comments are often quite humorous, though there are also many tips on producing low budget movies. There is also a collection of trailers, including one in French, and footage that was shot two years after production on the 1987 film was completed for insertion in Japanese TV broadcasts. Among the additions is an entirely new ending.

Manic Behavior X-rated (Vivid, UPC#0073215547)

When she discovers her boyfriend was unfaithful, a young woman becomes mentally and emotionally unbalanced. The star, Raylene, is no threat to Meryl Streep, but her performance brings a little variety to what is otherwise a fairly mundane effort, with bland erotic sequences. The picture, from a videotape source, is reasonably sharp and colors are strong, with accurate, detailed fleshtones, but contrasts are a little weak. The sound seems to take on some interference at a couple points, but it may just be a poor application of party noises. Teri Starr, India, and Candy Hill co-star in the 71 minute program. The DVD also contains alternate angle sequences and elaborate hardcore interactive promotional features.

Marat Sade (Image, ID4523WBDVD)

The value of Peter Brooks' filmed record of the still unique play-within-a-play is derived from its significance as a stage work. The narrative depicts the inmates of an asylum, under the guidance of the Marquis de Sade, acting out the death of Jean-Paul Marat a few years after the assassination took place. There are constant asides to add commentary on the French Revolution and on the politics of poverty. The film takes the viewer where the members of the audience could not go, behind the bars. Even though the many close-ups and angled shots of the film lose that aspect of the staging, the movie seeks to formulate the essence of the text and in this it succeeds. It is a record of an important play, and its value is greater than the sum of its cinematic attributes.

The film is deliberately claustrophobic, but the presentation does seem to be slightly cropped. The source material has a few stray marks and the image is a little soft, but the colors on the 1967 production look fresh and the picture looks good if the movie's budget is taken into account. The stereo sound lacks clarity and forcefulness, though it is still coherent. Separation effects are limited. The 114 minute program is not closed captioned. Glenda Jackson, Patrick Magee and Ian Richardson are featured in the cast.

Mariah Carey: Around the World (Sony, CVD50184)

Mariah Carey is so bloody good looking it often seems like an offhand bonus that she happens to sing quite well, too. She performs in many outfits and venues across the globe. The arenas she lands are a little big to do her voice justice, but she hits most of her notes and puts on a simple but energetic stage show. The 45 minute concert program also contains lengthy backstage interviews between some of the songs. The DVD has four music videos as well, *Butterfly*, *Breakdown*, *The Roof* and *My All*, which are accessed separately, along with a profile and discography. The standard stereo surround sound is rather dull, but the Dolby Digital track is very good, with clear separations, a strong bass and well-defined tones. The concert can be supported by optional English, French or Spanish subtitles.

Mario Puzo's The Last Don (Trimark, VM6907D)
Mario Puzo's The Last Don II (Trimark, VM7073D)

Mario Puzo could do little more than shuffle and re-shuffle his one great work, but fans never tire of the wise guy milieu and the Machiavellian plotting, both of which are available in abundance in the miniseries and its sequel.

The original **Last Don**, based upon Puzo's novel, runs 262 minutes and is split to two sides. Danny Aiello stars as the family patriarch and chief mobster, but most of the show belongs to Joe Mantegna, who portrays Aiello's nephew and primary hitman. Jason Gedrick is Mantegna's son. Penelope Ann Miller, Robert Wuhl, Daryl Hannah, k. d. lang (as a movie director!), and Rory Cochrane also appear, with Kirstie Alley giving the best performance in both shows, as Aiello's daughter. Beset with mental instability by the violence that surrounds her, her reactions are often spine-tingling.

If only the rest of the show were that good. Puzo has a great time taking pot shots at Hollywood and its makes-the-Mafia-look-like-the-Girl-Scouts accounting practices, and the rivalry that eventually develops between Gedrick's character and the son of Alley's character is effective as the central narrative, but even though it runs over four hours, the first show is too short. It tries to cram in as much of the novel as it can, and it tends to just go boom, boom, boom from one plot advancement to the next, without taking time to smell the characters. The dialogue is reduced to summaries and simplicities (which might play better when interrupted by commercials) and its pleasures, though viable, are sporadic.

Although it is shorter, running only 178 minutes (it is still spread to two sides—unlike its predecessor, each side has complete opening and closing credits for the two-part program), **Last Don II** is more satisfying because it settles into a single time and story. Patsy Kensit, who also gives a compelling performance, joins the cast and several others drop out—we don't want to spoil things, but Mantegna only appears in dream sequences. Gedrick is the star of **II**, attempting to fortify his power and avoid betrayals on several fronts. The two programs work best, however, as a single day's viewing, giving the viewer an opportunity to bask in Puzo's world and cheer, while they last, for villains.

The color transfer looks okay on the first film, with bright hues and adequate fleshtones, but there is some displacement artifacting and smearing in darker sequences, particularly during the second half. The stereo sound has a basic dimensionality and is functional. Angelo Badalamenti's score deliberately evokes **The Godfather** at one point and often verges on resurrecting it. The picture on **Last Don II** is solid and has no artifacting flaws. The cinematography, however, is less accomplished, and the film has a slightly blander look. The stereo sound is fine. **Last Don** can be supported by optional French or Spanish subtitles ("Tu veux qu'il devienne une tapette? Un liseur de livres?") and also contains English captioning. **Last Don II**, which is not time encoded, has optional English, French and Spanish subtitles. **Last Don** is also accompanied by a promotional featurette that includes an interview with Puzo. Both films are identified as containing footage that did not appear in the broadcast versions, but while **Last Don II** has a couple scenes with nudity (to their advantage—we can't imagine how the scenes worked without it), neither the violence nor the sex seems all that explicit in the first film.

Mark of the Devil (Anchor Bay, DV10601)

The 1969 film is about Reformation witch hunts—similar to the Vincent Price movie, *Conqueror Worm*—and stars Herbert Lom and Udo Kier. The violence is quite graphic, so much so that many viewers will feel the film goes too far to be entertaining, but the narrative also seems right on in its exploration of the hypocrisies and self-serving schemes used by the inquisitors in the name of the Church, and the torture paraphernalia is clearly copied from genuine items used in the day. Hence, to those who can stomach or thrive upon the gross effects, the story will be rewarding and will likely justify the horrors—it may be exploitative, but it is real history.

The presentation is letterboxed with an aspect ratio of about 1.66:1 and no 16:9 enhancement. The image is somewhat worn in appearance, with aged colors and pale fleshtones. Outright damage to the source material, however, seems minimal. The monophonic sound is dubbed and mildly alienating, with a limited range, and the music a bit distorted. The 96 minute program is not captioned or time encoded.

The Mark of Zorro (Image, ID4727DSDVD)

The 1920 silent film, starring Douglas Fairbanks, was the very first of all the Zorro pictures and is one of the few non-comedy silents that can hold the attention of casual contemporary viewers. A rousing collection of stunts and fights cemented by the ever-dependable Zorro business, the 96 minute film is almost impossible to resist.

The windowboxed picture is tinted in orange and yellow, which takes away some detail from the image, though the picture is still fairly sharp and the source material is reasonably clean. There is a Gaylord Carter organ score in moderately dimensional stereo.

Marked for Death (Fox, 4109067)

One of Steven Seagal's better action films, the picture is letterboxed with an aspect ratio of about 2.35:1 and no 16:9 enhancement. The letterboxing adds only a little to the sides and trims quite a bit off the bottom of the image in comparison to the full screen picture, but the framing seems more dynamic and better suited for the action sequences, of which the film has plenty. The colors look deep and bright. The image is crisp and darker scenes are stable. The source material has a couple stray speckles, but on the whole, it looks terrific.

The standard stereo surround sound is good, and the Dolby Digital track has better defined separations and more energy. The 93 minute feature is also available in French in standard stereo and can be supported by English or Spanish subtitles ("Levanta las manos o te vuelo la cabeza"). The jacket chapter guide bears no relation to the encoding.

Seagal is a retired DEA agent who finds he just can't get away from the job when he returns to his hometown. The image of small town America being overrun by Rastafarian gangsters is a bit on the giggle side, but the narrative is brisk and the fight scenes have plenty of crunch.

Marley Magic (Image, ID4708LYDVD)

The relatives of Bob Marley put on an afternoon concert in Central Park. Included are Ziggy Marley and the Melody Makers, Rita Marley, Julian Marley, Damian Marley and Yvad. None have the clarity of expression that made Bob Marley's music so exceptional, and a video record of the event is nowhere near as pleasurable as a relaxed afternoon's attendance at the actual concert would have been, but the 115 minute program conveys the concert's spirit and an appealing variety of styles and approaches to Marley's legacy. The stereo recording is a bit diffuse, but imparts the tone of an outdoor concert accurately. Colors are not intense, but the picture is sharp and hues are adequate.

Mars Attacks! (Warner, 14480)

Tim Burton's delightful alien invasion spoof is an ideal film for the crisp colors a DVD has to offer. Jack Nicholson is miscast in a dual role (as the president and as a hotel developer) that called for someone with stronger comedic skills, but otherwise the film is marvelous fun. The action focuses on two cities, Washington DC and Las Vegas, and the symbolic oppositions—and similarities— these cities evoke are the core of the film. Based perhaps too loosely on a series of bubblegum cards, the movie revels in the exaggerated, overly accessible styles of commercialized art, making fun of movies like *Independence Day* but at the same time suggesting, with the absurdity of Vegas designs and media-fueled politics, that something very Martian is already here. The 106 minute film is presented on one side in letterboxed format and on the other side in cropped format. The letterboxing, which has an aspect ratio of about 2.35:1 and an accommodation for enhanced 16:9 playback, is definitely superior to the cropped image, which loses a good portion of the screen. The image is crisp, the bauble-like colors are shiny and distinct, and fleshtones are rich. The stereo surround sound and Dolby Digital sound are less impressive, with subdued separation effects and hollow tones. Danny Elfman's musical score, however, has been isolated on one of the audio tracks in Dolby Digital. The isolation of the music brings its wit and dexterity into focus, and it also allows the viewer to explore the amusing images without being distracted by the dialogue. The 1996 film is also presented French in Dolby Digital and in Spanish in standard surround, with English, French or Spanish subtitles. Two trailers have been included, along with an elaborate cast list (though the filmographies are abbreviated) and a brief production essay.

Marvin's Room (Buena Vista, 16325)

Adapted from a stageplay, the 1996 feature is loaded with normally over-praised actors who give surprisingly engaging performances. The film has a stageplay ending, which is not as resolute or satisfying as a movie ending, but otherwise it is quite entertaining. Diane Keaton (who earned an Oscar nomination for her performance) and Meryl Streep portray sisters who haven't seen one another in twenty years but are reunited by an illness and other complications. Leonardo DiCaprio plays Streep's troubled son, and Robert De Niro is on hand in an amusing secondary role as a realistic doctor. Both Streep and Keaton draw their personalities and histories beautifully, and when they interact the emotional discharges are glorious.

The picture is letterboxed with an aspect ratio of about 1.85:1 and no 16:9 enhancement. The image is sharp, but the picture does look a little pinkish, with slightly weak contrasts. The film's stereo mix is not elaborate and is adequately presented. The 98 minute program is adequately closed captioned.

Mary Chapin Carpenter Jubilee Live at Wolf Trap (Sony, CVD50126)

The pop folk rock singer Mary Chapin Carpenter is depicted in concert, with the numbers separated by brief interview segments with her, her husband and a couple others. The 86 minute program is presented on two sides. Carpenter's music has a kind of canned, uninteresting structure, but her lyrics are intelligent, forcing a listener to concentrate and penetrate the music more deeply than usual, which results in a generally satisfying experience. Carpenter also shares a couple numbers with Shawn Colvin and Joan Baez. The stereo surround sound is okay, but there is a menu-activated Dolby Digital track that is a lot better, bringing in more surround effects and widening the concert atmosphere. The picture looks terrific and there are lots of scrumptious, well-lit close-ups. The DVD also contains a list of Carpenter's music releases and awards. There is no captioning.

Mary Poppins (Buena Vista, 13854)

The 1964 Walt Disney musical starring Julie Andrews and Dick Van Dyke is lovely, with a gloriously crisp, brightly colored picture and a solid stereo surround soundtrack. The picture has been letterboxed with an aspect ratio of about 1.85:1 and no 16:9 enhancement. The standard soundtrack has a stronger bass than the Dolby Digital track, though the Dolby Digital track has a better defined upper end. Either audio presentation, however, is fully satisfying. The 139 minute film can be supported by optional English subtitles.

It is worth noting the similarity, particularly in the design and emotional impact of the final scene, between **Mary Poppins** and **The Searchers**. In both films the hero is an outsider who returns the children and then leaves, unnoticed, as the family regroups. The philosopher Friedrich Hegel envisioned God as a spiritual catalyst, and while it is unwise to read too much into a movie that has dancing chimney sweeps and talking umbrella handles, there is a power in the deliberate lingering of the final shot, in which Mary Poppins rises above London and into the heavens. There are many people who think of Walt Disney in the same way, and now that his home video company has begun treating its product with the affection and attention it deserves, this would tend to lend credence to the concept.

Mary Shelley's Frankenstein (Columbia TriStar, 78719)

The best sound effect in the 1994 Kenneth Branagh film is the crackling electricity that surrounds you when the monster is getting zapped into life. Your whole viewing room is charged.

The film was generally considered to be a failure, and watching it we longed for stars who would have been less consumed by their parts, but the show is still fun. It has some engaging moments, particularly when Dr. Frankenstein cuts off the head of his deceased bride in order to restore her on another body. Branagh stars as the doctor, with Robert De Niro as the monster and Helena Bonham Carter as Elisabeth. On a detail level, the film has many flaws in its own logic but, as a modern costume adaptation of a horror classic, it gets most of the emotions right and has enough memorable sequences to seem worthwhile.

The picture is presented on one side in letterboxed format, with an aspect ratio of about 1.85:1 and an accommodation for enhanced 16:9 playback, and in full screen format on the other side. The image quality is not as nice as the sound, often looking a bit soft and grainy in darker scenes, though much of that is due to the pre-technological setting. Both the standard stereo surround soundtrack and the Dolby Digital track are great. The film runs 123 minutes and also has French and Spanish language tracks in standard stereo, along with English, French and Spanish subtitles, and a trailer.

Mask (Image, ID4293USDVD)

A depiction of the final year in the life of a young man suffering from a rare deformative disease, **Mask** is an acceptable pop entertainment gamble, but nothing happens in the story that can't be anticipated from its opening minutes. The director, Peter Bogdanovich, hurt his career in the past by taking risks with the material he filmed. In **Mask**, however, Bogdanovich plays it so safe that he never steps off first base. The movie has emotions, but not emotional surprises and, for all its vaunted realism, very little insight.

Eric Stoltz and Cher star in the 1985 production, which is letterboxed with an aspect ratio of about 1.85:1 and no 16:9 enhancement. The cinematography is bland and the picture is a bit dull, although colors look accurate and the image is reasonably sharp. The monophonic sound is fine and the Dolby Digital mono track is even a little stronger. The 120 minute program is closed captioned with substantial paraphrasing, and the program is accompanied by filmographies for Bogdanovich and some of the cast members.

The Mask (New Line, N4011)

Jim Carrey stars in the terrific special effects comedy, about a sheepish bank clerk who takes on the attributes of a cartoon character when he places an enchanted mask over his face. The film is a delight, and while it is the Tex Avery-inspired special effects that initiate its appeal, it is Carrey's performance that sustains the entertainment through multiple viewings. His timing and wildly inventive expressions get funnier the more you are exposed to them.

Despite the many special effects, the film was made on a fairly trim budget and the stereo surround does not have quite the punch movies with extra zeroes in their budgets achieve. Nevertheless, the picture and sound transfers are excellent. The 101 minute film is presented in letterboxed format on one side and in full screen format on the other. The letterboxing has an aspect ratio of about 1.85:1and no 16:9 enhancement, adding some picture information to the sides and masking off picture information from the top and bottom—and adding more picture information on the sides and a little on the top, but masking picture information off the bottom in the special effects sequences. You got all that? Because the special effects are still cut off on the bottom, it is good to have both versions. When the hero catches sight of Cameron Diaz and his tongue rolls down the table, for example, you only get to see the complete tongue on the full screen version. When he pulls out all of his guns, however, and flags come out of them that say, "Bang!," the cropping removes most of the flags and spoils the joke.

The colors are deep and crisp, contributing greatly to the film's exhilarations. The stereo surround sound is weaker than the Dolby Digital track, which has a lot more bass and a lot more energy. There is a French audio track in standard stereo and English, French and Spanish subtitling. There is a theatrical trailer that is letterboxed on the letterboxed side and presented in full screen on the other side.

Also included on the DVD are two deleted scenes, which are very interesting and enjoyable, though neither belonged in the film. The first is an elaborate and amusing sequence, meant to appear at the start of the film, in which Lief Eriksson is shown coming to America for the sole purpose of disposing of the mask. In the second, a major character, who simply disappears from view in the completed film, is killed by the villain in an elaborate and creative manner.

There is a nice commentary track by the director, Charles Russell. He doesn't go into detail about the computer graphics, but he covers every other component of the film quite effectively, explaining what it was like working with the dog (and what he wanted to accomplish—he was more interested in getting the dog to give good sight lines than to do 'tricks'), talking about the contributions of each performer, discussing how he had to fight with the producers to make the film as joyfully silly as it is, describing the low budget shooting logistics and pointing out the scenes or moments that meant the most to him and what inspired them. He describes how, after the first rough cut was assembled, his disappointment when the next-to-the-last scene appears, because he knew that the movie was over and he himself wanted to keep on watching it. You cannot toggle on the commentary track the way you can toggle on the French audio track, incidentally. When you select it, you have to start at the beginning of the film and then chapter search to the point you wish to access.

The Mask of Zorro Columbia TriStar, 21699)

The camera angles are often wrong on the stunts, the identity of Zorro is rarely a secret from the bad guys, the story's basis in history is totally convoluted, the tone shifts between drama and comedy without care and there are all sorts of other shortcomings to the 1998 movie, directed by Martin Campbell, but none of that matters because it is so much fun. Antonio Banderas and Anthony Hopkins are the good guys, slashing zeds in the countryside and in the flesh of the villains. Even when you're not seeing them from the

best angle, the stunts are wonderful, and besides, we're tired of movies where history makes sense. The film is a dashing, energetic frivolity. Like the hero it leaps recklessly from one precarious position to the next but, like the hero, it succeeds on its own bravura.

The stereo surround sound and Dolby Digital sound are terrific. The clangs of the swords and all the other noises during the action sequences have a glorious precision and immediacy, and James Horner's musical score hovers over it all with a terrific dimensionality. There are explosions, too, that bang, shake and rumble. The film is in letterboxed format only, with an aspect ratio of about 2.35:1 and an accommodation for enhanced 16:9 playback. Many scenes are lit by firelight of some sort, giving flesh an overly yellowish tone at times but, on the whole, the colors are accurate and the image is sharp. The 137 minute program has optional English subtitles and comes with a trailer, a 'making of' featurette and a small collection of publicity photos.

Masseuse #3 X-rated (Vivid, UPC#0073214543)

Once in a while an adult program achieves enough narrative and emotional structure to approach the qualities of a legitimate movie and such is the case with **Masseuse #3**. Shot in New York City on 35mm film, the story concerns a naive (but rather maturelooking) college student whose affections are torn between a snotty co-ed and a caring hooker. The erotic scenes often defy the normal conventions for the sake of realism, the drama has a complete beginning, middle and end, and the program does a decent job mixing the emotions of the characters with the erotic activities. There are even some quotable lines of dialogue ("What do you mean you're not gay? Everybody's gay!") and other situations that could make the program popular at parties. The image is fairly grainy and colors are dull, with pale fleshtones. The monophonic sound is workable. The program runs 70 minutes. The DVD contains alternate angle sequences and elaborate hardcore interactive promotional features.

Master P MP: Da Last Don—The Movie (No Limit, P253426)

Although it was produced by music video people and runs 45 minutes, it is a straight movie (there is plenty of music on the soundtrack, but it never dominates the proceedings) in which the hero, played by hip-hop artist Master P, portrays the son of a gangster who inherits the top position when his father is rubbed out, and then has to hold onto it in the face of challenges and betrayals. There is lots of nudity and squib work, and because the film isn't a full-length feature, the boring stuff that is used to pad out such dramas is eliminated. Yet there is still plenty of emotional interaction between the characters and, like we said, if you're in a hurry, then the film provides a convenient fix.

The picture and sound are excellent. The image is very sharp, with bright hues. The stereo surround sound has a terrific bass and plenty of engaging directional effects. The program is not captioned and is accompanied by two music videos, *Live at the Summit* and *Thinkin' Bout You*.

The Matchmaker (PolyGram, 44004)

Janeane Garofalo stars as a workaholic political aide who is sent to Ireland to research her boss' roots. The town she travels to, however, is in the midst of a matchmaking festival, and she gets caught up in it despite herself. It is only after the film gets over its cute Irish intros and starts up the romance, however, that it becomes a tolerable and unpredictable entertainment. Milo O'Shea and David O'Hara co-star.

Fleshtones are flush and lively, and other colors are uniformly bright. The picture is letterboxed on one side, with an aspect ratio of about 2.35:1 with no 16:9 enhancement, and is in full screen format on the other side. The letterboxing masks off picture information on the bottom of the screen in comparison to the full screen release, but adds picture information to the sides and, generally, we liked the framing on the letterboxed version better. The stereo surround sound is dull, but the Dolby Digital track gives the audio a little more dimensionality in places. The 97 minute program is also available in French or Spanish and comes with an elaborate theatrical trailer and a brief cast profile section.

Matchmaking Mama (see **Nothing Sacred**)

Matilda (Columbia TriStar, 86865/9)

Danny DeVito directed the 1996 adaptation of the Roald Dahl story. Set in America but retaining a slightly British feel, the film is about a bright young girl who develops psychokinetic powers to cope with the cruelty around her. The special effects are fairly subdued, however, as the story's emphasis is on comical characters and the young heroine's perseverance. Dahl's plotting is gratifying in comparison to the usual over-manufactured children's film, and the movie sustains just the right amount of humor, action and fantasy to please adults as well as kids.

The movie is presented in full screen format only. The picture transfer looks terrific and the film has a pleasing, child-like color scheme. The stereo surround sound and Dolby Digital sound are okay, though there aren't too many big audio moments. The 98 minute program also has French and Spanish audio tracks in standard stereo, optional Spanish subtitles and English closed captioning.

Matinee (Image, ID4288USDVD)

Set during the Cuban missile crisis in 1962, the film is about a preview showing of a schlock horror film at a theater in Key West. John Goodman plays the film's producer, Cathy Moriarty is his girlfriend, and Simon Fenton is the young teenage hero whose life is improved by the producer's visit. Directed by Joe Dante, fans have been quite enamored by the humorous evocation the schlock horror film, *Mant!*, creates in imitating genre classics from the past, but *Mant!* isn't screened until the end and much of the rest of the movie plays like a weakly conceived episode of **The Wonder Years**.

The picture is letterboxed with an aspect ratio of about 1.7:1 and no 16:9 enhancement. The color transfer is okay, though contrasts look a little light in places, and the stereo surround sound is passable. The 99 minute program is closed captioned with some paraphrasing. There are filmographies for Dante and a few of the cast members

The Matinee Idol (Columbia TriStar, 03303)

Casual viewers, if they have seen any of Frank Capra's silent films at all, are likely most familiar with *The Strongman*, the film he made with Harry Langdon. It is a charming comedy but it is also very typical of how people today think of silent films, the child-like manner of the star rubbing off on the movie itself. Capra's **Matinee Idol**, however, a 1928 silent that was lost and then rediscovered, is a more mature work that is satisfying not only for its historical value but for the sophistication of its entertainment.

Johnnie Walker portrays a Jolson-type stage star, on vacation, who is recruited to fill a bit part in a struggling theatrical troupe and falls for the leading lady, played by Bessie Love. He arranges to have the troupe become part of his Broadway revue without revealing his true identity, using their unintentional ineptness as comic relief. When the heroine finally realizes what is going on, there is an inevitable rift before the reconciliation—and ah, the reconciliation. The film is witty, with a clear-spoken narrative and a brisk pace, and at the end, there is an amazing, dynamically staged shot where the heroine works through a queue of men auditioning for a one-line part ("I love you") before reaching the hero, who is patiently waiting his turn. It would work in a movie today, even with intertitles.

The film is in fabulously good condition. Produced at the very end of the silent era, the image is sharp and almost totally free of damage, with smooth, crisp contrasts and deep blacks. There is an

unobtrusive period stereo musical score and fresh intertitles. The film runs 56 minutes.

Columbia TriStar has also included, on the other side of the platter, a 109 minute documentary, *Frank Capra's American Dream*. The program looks over Capra's career chronologically, supplying a superb analysis of many of his best films and decent, quicker summaries of the others. You come to realize that **It's a Wonderful Life** was the end of Capra's artistic peak—or, actually, it was an epilogue to his output at Columbia that concluded right before the onset of World War II. Interviews with film critics, filmmakers and Capra historians are expertly blended to explore both the obvious aspects of his craft and the less obvious, darker undercurrent. Because the analysis is so adept, it is easy to sit through the segments on films you may have seen dozens of times—such as **Life**, or *Mr. Smith Goes to Washington*—and appreciate them anew. The picture quality on the interviews is excellent, with vivid colors, and most of the film clips are in decent condition. The monophonic sound is fine and the program includes optional English or Spanish subtitles. Ron Howard narrates.

Maui Heat (Image, TSM5131DVD)

A softcore erotic drama about a magazine swimsuit shoot in Hawaii, there is about an equal amount of narrative (the models have flings and fall in love with the various guys working on the shoot, or with each other) and the usual erotic sequences (the most amusing—a couple pretending to be wrapped in passion on an isolated beach while they sit on what is obviously very sharp volcanic rock).

The picture has slightly over-saturated colors and mildly erratic contrasts, though generally the image is workable and the tropical views are appealing. There is a nondescript stereo soundtrack, and the program is not captioned. The program is not time encoded, either, but appears to run about 90 minutes. Additionally, however, there is an extensive 'making of' featurette (the second assistant director, Traci Bugard, shares her filmmaking savvy: "These are camera reports. Okay, these, when the director says, 'Print that one,' then they circle it and then we know which ones to have the lab print"), and a combination of video and still profiles for several of the cast members. Kimberly Dawson, Kimberly Rowe and Kim Yates are featured.

Maverick (Warner, 13374)

Not everyone is charmed by the 1994 feature, but we have found the comedic western to be utterly delightful, even on multiple viewings. The film is letterboxed on one side and in cropped format on the other. The letterboxing, which has an aspect ratio of about 2.35:1and an accommodation for enhanced 16:9 playback, is necessary to take in Vilmos Zsigmond's lovely cinematography, but the cropped version is also quite engaging, with huge, beguiling close-ups of the film's three stars, Mel Gibson, Jodie Foster and James Garner. The color transfer on both sides is beautiful. The image is rich and fleshtones are deep. Even the blown up picture on the cropped side looks very crisp and smooth. The stereo surround sound presents a lighthearted mix with few significant separation effects. The 127 minute film does not have 5.1 Dolby Digital encoding and can be accessed in French as well as English, with English, French or Spanish subtitles. There is a passable cast profile and a reasonably big collection of production notes.

Everybody else is on their own, but those who remember and enjoy the old TV series will be thrilled by the film. As the title character, Gibson has all the mannerisms down, from the way he wears his hat to the inflated fullness in his cheeks, and the mildly episodic but fully engaging narrative justifies everything he does. Garner, who played the character in the series, is also in the film to provide a counter-point of sorts to Gibson's presence, and working between the two of them is Foster, who demonstrates that great acting can also mean executing a formula role with a seductive finesse. The cast is marvelous, the stunts are super, and the whole film captures the spirit of its source so well it is a joy.

Max Fleischer's Superman (see The Superman Cartoons of Max & Dave Fleischer)

McCarthy, Jenny (see Playboy: The Best of Jenny McCarthy)

McKay, Winsor (see Animation Legend: Winsor McKay)

McLintock! (GoodTimes, 0581003)

Although the colors are fairly strong, the film is presented in cropped format and the image is very unstable, shifting from sharp to blurry on almost a shot-by-shot basis. The source material is also littered with speckles and other damage marks, some of which do very strange things—there is this little spiral scratch that travels upwards through the image on several occasions. The monophonic sound seems adequate, though it is best left at a modest amplification. The 125 minute film is also supported by optional English subtitles.

John Wayne and Maureen O'Hara star in the 1963 domestic comedy, which has been given a western setting, although there is almost no action outside of the comedy brawls. He is a wealthy rancher and she is his estranged wife and in the celebrated finale he turns her over his knee and spanks her in front of the entire town. Only because it is Wayne and O'Hara do they get away with it.

Mean Streets (Warner, 15240)

Remember those bar scenes that are bathed in red light? On the LD, which has a fairly decent transfer, the red lights make everything soft and fuzzy looking. Well, on the DVD, not only are the shades of red more easily discernible, but the pinstripes on Harvey Keitel's suit are as sharp as they are in the bright daylight. All of the film's colors are greatly improved on the DVD, to the point where they look so crisp and glossy the movie no longer seems like a low budget feature.

The picture is presented on one side in letterboxed format, with an aspect ratio of about 1.82:1 and no 16:9 enhancement, and in full screen format on the other side. The letterboxing adds nothing to the sides of the image and masks picture information off the top and bottom in comparison to the full screen version, but the framing is more satisfying. The monophonic soundtrack is okay, but the Dolby Digital mono track has more precisely defined tones and a more satisfying range. The 112 minute film can be supported by English or French subtitles and comes with production notes, a cast & crew profile section and a catch-all theatrical trailer.

Martin Scorsese's landmark 1973 film, starring Keitel and Robert De Niro, depicts young men trying to work their way into the mob. The story does not make a very positive portrayal of the values of friendship or family responsibility, but it set the tone for Scorsese's later work, exploring the negative aspects of humanity with artistry and power.

The Meanest Men in the West (GoodTimes, 0581017)

Film and TV enthusiasts may find their curiosity intrigued by the program, credited as having been co-written and co-directed by Sam Fuller. Lee Marvin and Charles Bronson star in the 93 minute program, which also features James Drury and Lee J. Cobb and seems to be some kind of spin-off of the TV series, The Virginian. The Universal production has a 1962 copyright, but Bronson and Marvin look older than that and the show actually appears to have been compiled in the early Seventies.

Whatever its provenance, it is a patchwork mess, with pieces of narrative just barely taped together through voiceover dialogue. Bronson and Marvin play half-brothers, both outlaws, although Bronson is a good guy. Bronson kidnaps Drury and Marvin kidnaps Cobb. Taken at face value, it doesn't amount to much, though there are a couple gunfights and some other passable (though often confused) action sequences. Because of the cast and Fuller's input (in the opening scene, a young boy shoots his step-father), there was enough in the movie to hold our attention, though others may have less tolerance. The picture is workable. Fleshtones are

always a little pale and the image quality shifts at times, but for the most part hues are accurate and the focus is fairly sharp, although the source material does have a number of scratches and speckles. The monophonic sound is okay and the program can be supported by English, French or Spanish subtitles.

The Meaning of Life (see Monty Python's The Meaning of Life)

Meantime (Fox Lorber, FLV5056)

For those of you who are new to movies, Mike Leigh is a British film director who gathers actors together, gives them situations with only a vague outline of a plot, and then sees what happens. When other directors do this sort of thing it can be a meandering disaster, but Leigh has vision and his films are often entertaining, creating characters who are so real you don't mind spending time with them even when not much seems to be happening.

Leigh's 1983 telefilm had the good fortune to include both Gary Oldman and Tim Roth in its cast, as well as Alfred Molina. Vaguely comical, it is about an entire unemployed family living in a small apartment in a drab London housing project. They're all losers, and it almost seems like the point of the film's narrative arc that you begin the movie by looking down on them and generally disliking them, but warm up to the little bits of humanity they almost inadvertently display and, by the end, like them much better, even though almost nothing has changed (Roth's mentally challenged character gets a haircut). How we longed for captions that Fox Lorber has not provided! Parts of the movie are incomprehensible to American ears. Other parts are so much like any dysfunctional family as to be too much like life to entertain, but Leigh always seems to know when to move on, when to adjust the tone, and what he wants from his milieu, so the 103 minute film can be dense and intriguing if you're prepared for its conceptual inertia.

The stereo surround sound is outright bizarre. The dialogue track is muted and drab (and appears to be confined to the right channel), but the music and effects track is remarkably vivid and dimensional. The latter would be terrific, except that it is incongruous with the dialogue track and the film's dull image. The picture is acceptable, since one expects it to have subdued colors and bland fleshtones. It looks a bit aged, and there are some scratches and other wear marks, but it is reasonably sharp and certainly fits with the film's tone. A trailer and cast profile section is also included, but there is no time encoding.

Meet Joe Black (Universal, 20531)

Martin Brest's first feature film, Hot Tomorrows, was so obsessed with death you really wondered if the prodigious director would make it to middle age, and it was a relief when he let go of the subject to turn out a sparse but consistent string of box office bonanzas, the most notable, of course, being Beverly Hills Cop. His magnum opus, Meet Joe Black, has not fared as well, but it is clearly a project from the heart and it cannot be discounted simply because it failed to pull in the big bucks.

At 180 minutes, the film is excessive, but it is not the sort of excess one would expect from the creator of Hot Tomorrows. It is an intensely urbane and dry work of drama, basking in pleasantries instead of comedy and romantic ideals instead of romance. The narrative is fueled by a standard plot about a corporate takeover, and while the movie may have had viewers squirming in the theaters, there is more than enough story to hold one's attention in the comfort of home.

The premise, markedly similar to that of City of Angels, is about a spirit, identified as Death, who takes possession of a human body (naturally choosing Brad Pitt—who wouldn't want to walk around for a while as Brad Pitt?) to find out about why all this living stuff is so important to us humans. Anthony Hopkins, a super-rich financier, becomes his guide, putting the film in Sabrina territory, which mass audiences apparently have a tough time relating to—something about wearing tuxedos to dinner all the time.

Had Meg Ryan played his daughter maybe the movie would have done better, but Claire Forlani is cast as the romantic interest, and her moderately intelligent, restrained performance exemplifies why the film failed in the outside world, as well as why it succeeds on its own terms. The movie's metaphysics are nonsensical, but its emotional wash is refreshing. In contrast to the high camp of *Death Takes a Holiday*, upon which the film is directly based, there is nothing brooding or tango-like about the relationships among the characters. There are, instead, calm but determined searches for affirmations of life and, across the three hours, Brest creates an emotional momentum that supersedes the story's magic—the moral being that just because Death has stopped doesn't mean Life should be called to a halt.

The set designs are lavish and the picture looks gorgeous, with glossy, finely detailed hues and rich fleshtones. The picture is letterboxed, with an aspect ratio of about 1.85:1 and an accommodation for enhanced 16:9 playback. The stereo surround sound is okay and the Dolby Digital sound is very good, with elegant separation effects and a strong dimensionality. The film is also available in French in standard stereo and can be supported by English or Spanish subtitles. There is a cast-and-director profile section, some production notes, a trailer and a brief featurette (Hopkins complains, obliquely, about the number of takes Brest demands).

Meet John Doe (Madacy, DVD99019)

Frank Capra's somewhat dark comedy about a homeless man conned into participating in a newspaper series about despair stars Gary Cooper and Barbara Stanwyck. The 1941 feature evokes the Depression, even though it was made after the worst of times were pretty much over. The performances are super (Edward Arnold is the villain), and the narrative has a systematic energy that is captivating.

The black-and-white picture is trimmed a bit on the sides. The image is soft and mildly grainy, with some speckling and other wear, but it is workable. The monophonic sound is a little noisy and has a somewhat weak presence. There is no captioning, and the 122 minute film is accompanied by some minor text supplements.

Meeting People Is Easy: A Film By Grant Gee About Radiohead (Capitol, C9RH724347786099)

The 95 minute documentary depicts a world tour by the group in a deliberately hip, obscure manner that matches the group's music. There is plenty of behind-the-scenes footage, no matter how incoherent it may seem, and the whole production has a satisfying, modernist tone. The group's music is fascinating, with MOR melodies rising from chaos momentarily and then subsiding again, like a bubble out of lava.

They sound terrific. There are three audio channels, a standard stereo surround soundtrack, a Dolby Digital 5.1 channel and a DTS 5.1 channel. Both the Dolby Digital and the DTS tracks have more force than the standard track, and the DTS track is a little bit better than the Dolby Digital track. Toggling between them, there were times when we couldn't tell them apart, but there were other times where the music on the DTS track seemed to have more substance, and when the music is played during an interview—one of the director's favorite tricks is to make sure you can't understand anything—the conversations are clearer.

Who can tell if the picture is good or not? Some of it is in black and white and some is in color. Much of it was shot grainy, but it seems that the presentation is valid. There is no captioning.

Méliès, George (see **Landmarks of Early Film Volume 2: The Magic of Méliès**)

Melvin Van Peebles' Classified X (Fox Lorber, WHE73013)

A fascinating documentary about the role African-Americans have played in the American motion picture industry, an objective observer might find that not all of Van Peebles' arguments are just.

He does a certain amount of Monday morning quarterbacking, but the thrust of his thesis is wholly valid—Hollywood has, since its inception, relegated African-Americans to a subsidiary position in relation to Americans of European heritage, and because of the nature of motion pictures, that policy has had a disturbing, negative effect upon the American social conscience. As Van Peebles points out in reference to films from the supposedly enlightened Fifties and Sixties, "The actual behavior of a Negro character in any given film might seem predicated on the dramatic needs of that film. But through the accumulation of images from a zillion such films, the same behavior appeared in film after film, shot after shot."

The 52 minute program contains a terrific number of clips. Van Peebles forgoes the utilization of an experienced narrator and presents the material himself, reinforcing his arguments with testimony of his own movie-going experiences. The picture is letterboxed, with an aspect ratio of about 1.85:1 and no 16:9 enhancement. 1.33:1 clips are windowboxed in the middle of the screen. The shots of Van Peebles are sharp and colors are accurate. The source material on the clips is often worn-looking and multi-generational. The stereo sound is fine and the program is not captioned. Few of the clips are identified during the show, but the DVD contains an alphabetical listing of the excerpted films, as well as a Van Peebles profile and filmography.

Memphis Belle (Warner, 12040)

Sort of a **Das Boot** in the air, depicting a single bombing mission over Germany in 1943. The first half hour is a waste of time and can be scanned rapidly without remorse, but once the planes take off, most viewers will become glued to their seats. The special effects are superb, and the tension is almost unbearable. There is even a cutaway interlude, meant, we suppose, to relieve that tension, about the responsibilities of the commander back at the air base, which is so moving that it can bring tears to your eyes and make you long for the simplicity of the drama in the cockpit.

The DVD is presented in letterboxed format on one side, with an aspect ratio of about 1.85:1 and no 16:9 enhancement, and in cropped format on the other side. The letterboxing adds picture information to the sides of the image and loses nothing off the top and bottom compared to the cropped picture. The picture is very sharper, with decent fleshtones and accurate, but military-bland hues. The Dolby Digital track has more directional effects and more dimensionality than the standard track, but some of the dialogue has an awkward, artificial ambiance. The 107 minute film, which stars Matthew Modine and Eric Stoltz, is also available in French in standard stereo and in Spanish in mono and comes with English, French or Spanish subtitles. There is an extensive cast & crew profile, some production notes, a profile of the B-17 and crew functions, and a theatrical trailer, along with trailers for several other Warner aviation titles.

Menace II Society (New Line, N4165)

One of the original 'hood films, the picture is too dark and you lose too many interesting details in the shadows. The blue-black fleshtones do not seem accurate, either. The film is presented in letterboxed format on one side, with an aspect ratio of about 1.85:1 and no 16:9 enhancement, and in full screen format on the other. The letterboxing masks off more than it adds on, but the framing is preferable. The stereo surround sound is not crisp, but there is a Dolby Digital stereo track that has much stronger rear channel activity, a heightened presence and crisper tones. The film is also available in French in standard stereo and can be accompanied by English, French or Spanish subtitles. The 104 minute presentation is the standard 'R' release, not the director's cut.

In addition to the film, about young men growing up amid the violence of Watts in Los Angeles, there is a good theatrical trailer, along with clips from five other New Line films. There is a cast profile section and an informative 11 minute interview with the 1993 film's directors, The Hughes Brothers.

Men in War (Master Movies, DVD5504)

If you're looking for a serious, brisk and very entertaining war movie, you could do a lot worse than Anthony Mann's excellent black-and-white drama. Robert Ryan stars in the 1957 feature, set in Korea, about a platoon stuck behind enemy lines after a retreat, spending the day trying to make it to safety. The film is refreshingly free of stereotypes (for example, everybody in the squad is sympathetic to the scared soldier and shares in picking up his slack) and always keeps moving, as the men tramp across hostile countryside, their number continually dwindling from isolated engagements. In addition to its efficiency, there are several of good fight sequences, where the strategies of both sides are made clear to the viewer. Aldo Ray co-stars and a young Vic Morrow also appears. There is a terrific Elmer Bernstein score, as well.

Perhaps one of the reasons we enjoyed the film so much is that the transfer looks so nice. The image is consistently crisp and clean, with well-defined contrasts. There is some minor smearing at times, but if you sit far enough back from the screen, you probably won't see it. The monophonic sound is fine. The 102 minute feature is not captioned and is accompanied by some minor text supplements.

Mercury Rising (Universal, 20333); collector's (Universal, 20449); DTS (Universal, 20641)

A thriller that exceeds its allotment of unlikelihoods rather early on, Bruce Willis stars as an FBI agent guarding a young autistic boy, who has decoded a top secret cipher that was published in a crossword puzzle magazine, while dodging government assassins—is any of this making sense? The young actor who plays the boy gives a valid performance and Willis does his appealing tough guy bit, giving the film a pleasant emotional atmosphere as the two warm up to each other, but the story is so unrepentantly illogical that the efforts of the performers are wasted. Alec Baldwin is the villain.

The image is letterboxed with an aspect ratio of about 2.35:1 and an accommodation for enhanced 16:9 playback. The colors are fine and the image is sharp, with accurate fleshtones. The stereo surround sound is a little weak, but the Dolby Digital track is good and has the sort of directional activities one expects in an action feature. The 112 minute feature is also available in French and Spanish in standard stereo and can be accompanied by English or Spanish subtitles. There are some production notes about how the most difficult scenes were shot, a cast-and-director profile section and a trailer.

We have no desire to insult the 1998 film's director, Harold Becker. He sounds like a very pleasant man and would probably be terrific company on a fishing trip or something like that. But we are not complimenting him when we say that his commentary on the collector's edition is equal to the quality of the film. Unlike the worst commentaries, he does keep talking through the whole movie, and viewers will probably find his talk quite informative, especially if they are in the sixth or seventh grade. He keeps his comments to the very basics of filmmaking, explaining why they have to hire extras for scenes in public places, why the young boy who plays the autistic child in the film has to stay 'in character' on screen and other simplicities. He does explain how the major special effect sequences were accomplished, such as the final battle on the top of the skyscraper (they're only eight feet off the ground), but more often he explains aspects of the film most viewers will already have assumed.

The collector edition's best feature is a 40 minute documentary about the movie, which discusses almost all aspects of the production and features interviews with much of the cast and crew. The expert who advised the filmmakers about autism, for example, looks at the whole project through the eyes of a civilian, pleasantly glamour struck by his toe dip into Hollywood, while, on the other hand, the young boy who plays the child is learning the art of publicity speak at an all too early age. They do a good job showing how

several interesting special effects were staged, and they focus on what is good about the movie—the relationships between the characters—while ignoring what is bad—the plot, the pacing, the logic, etc. In addition to the documentary, there are several deleted scenes—some of which needed to go, but some of which should have been left in—and a still photo section.

In addition to the picture and sound transfers, and the language options, the essay, cast-and-director profile section and trailer from the standard DVD are also repeated. The supplement can be supported by English subtitles.

The DTS version has no special features, no captioning and is letterboxed with an accommodation for enhanced 16:9 playback. The separation effects and surround effects are a bit more pronounced on the DTS track, but the differences are minimal.

Merle Haggard In Concert (Brentwood, BDVD936)

Three separate concerts have been combined on the single-sided dual-layer DVD, *Merle Haggard: Live in Concert*, which runs 38 minutes, *The Best of Merle Haggard*, which runs 44 minutes and *Poet of the Common Man*, which runs 33 minutes. There is very little repetition of material between the three concerts, and combined, they present an excellent overview of Haggard and his music, which is mostly an efficient and pleasingly rough-edged working class country idiom, with vague forays into jazz structures, particularly during the looser moments of the concerts.

Best of Merle Haggard is the strongest program. Performed before an unseen audience in a small concert hall in Concord, California, the image under the controlled lighting is smooth and bright, with clear details, and the stereo sound is very immediate and full. *Poet of the Common Man* includes some interview sequences that don't flatter Haggard as much as he may think they do (he tends to oversell his humble roots). The Nashville concert is brightly lit, but the image is older than *Best of* and is a bit grainy, with blander fleshtones. The sound is more concert-like and less distinctive, though there is nothing really wrong with that. *Live in Concert* was shot in some sort of outdoor stadium where even the closest seats were so far away from the stage Haggard must have looked like a dot to the concert-goers. The picture is much blurrier and fleshtones are dull, though the cameras are up on the stage with Haggard (the audience probably couldn't tell the cameramen from the musicians) and capture the atmosphere on the stage effectively. The sound is the least dimensional of the three, though tones are still fairly distinctive and it is, technically, stereo.

The programs are not captioned. There is also a Haggard biography (he really did live in an abandoned railroad car when he was a kid) and a couple outtake clips from the interviews in *Common Man*.

Merlin (Artisan, 96531)

The first part of the miniseries is the interesting part, because it deals with everything that takes place before the beginning of movies such as *Excalibur*. The development of CGI effects have made programs like this possible, and the adventure is a captivating journey through the time of legends and magic. The second part, however, is something of a letdown. The show's title and format dictate that the story of King Arthur and Guinevere function as a subplot but, in the legend itself, Merlin is the supporting character and there is no inspired piece of storytelling to reconcile this conflict. The film plods through the action in an uninteresting manner, with no hope of building to a crescendo of special effects that can out-do the first half, since the story does not call for them. But what the heck, you don't even have to watch the second half if you don't want to.

Sam Neill gives a functionally competent performance as the title character, with Rutger Hauer, Miranda Richardson, Helena Bonham Carter, Isabella Rossellini and a particularly effective Martin Short filling substantial roles. The likes of John Gielgud, James Earl Jones and others also appear high in the billing but are on screen for so little time you could show their entire performances in a commercial.

The 182 minute miniseries is presented in single-sided dual-layer format with no break between the first part and the second part, except a brief fade-to-black, and no credits until the program's end. The picture is sharp, with decent fleshtones, accurate hues and nice looking special effects. The stereo surround sound is a bit weak. The quality of the audio is sufficient for communicating the entertainment, but touches of dimensional magic are limited. The film can be supported by Spanish subtitles or English closed captioning and is accompanied by a cast & crew profile, some awkwardly written paragraphs about the historical character, Merlin, and a few production notes. There is also an 18 minute 'making of' featurette that shares some interesting background information on the production (they started making the movie six months before it was broadcast—no wonder the second half seems vague), but doesn't delve too deeply into the show's excellent special effects.

Merry Christmas from Vienna: Plácido Domingo / Ying Huang / Michael Bolton (Sony, SVD62971)

We only cringed once while watching the 72 minute program. That was when Bolton tried to sing Handel's *Joy to the World* and his voice cracked. Most of the time, however, he is less daring and doesn't embarrass himself. The three are supported by the Vienna Symphony Orchestra and conducted by Steven Mercurio. The concert makes a point of drawing on traditional Christmas songs from all over the world. Few are spine tingling, even when Domingo is singing, but the show is suitable highbrow holiday entertainment. The picture quality is very good and the stereo surround sound is fine, with a Dolby Digital surround soundtrack that has more detail and energy.

A Merry War (DVD International, DVDI0720)

Based upon a romantic comedy written by George Orwell and starring Richard E. Grant and Helena Bonham Carter, it is the first film to be based upon an Orwell story other than his two most famous works, and it is much different from either of them, being grounded in reality and free of political allegory. The title—Orwell's story was more sensibly called *Keep the Aspidistra Flying*—refers to the conflicts between men and women. The 1997 feature was directed by Robert Bierman and written by Alan Plater, but they have tried to make it commercial, removing Orwell's darker colorings and his polemics. What is left is a surprisingly cliched and bland story about a would-be poet and his half-hearted attempt to rebel against society. He quits his job so he can concentrate on writing and he moves to a dilapidated neighborhood. His on-again-off-again girlfriend eventually lures him back. If Orwell's name were not on the project, it would seem like a failed effort to cash in on the popularity of understated British romantic comedies, such as **Four Weddings and a Funeral**. Its charm is intermittent, its character motivation is elusive, its romance is dry, its humor is vague, and there is nothing stygian lurking beneath it to compensate—no screen behind the painting, as it were.

The picture is letterboxed with an aspect ratio of about 1.85:1 and no 16:9 enhancement. The color transfer looks fine, with sharp hues and accurate fleshtones. It is mostly the music that is stereophonic, but the audio is fine, and there is also a track containing nothing but the isolated musical score. The 102 minute program is not captioned, and is accompanied by two trailers and a cast & crew profile section.

Bierman and Plater appear on one commentary channel speaking extensively about the filmmaking process, composer Mike Batt spends a half hour on another channel providing an excellent talk on the art of scoring films, and there is a good text biography of Orwell that draws links between his life and the film's narrative. Bierman and Plater talk about the trims and modifications they made to Orwell's story, about staging the scenes on a limited budget, about the cast and crew, and about making movies. It is an informative talk, not only in deconstructing why **A Merry War**

doesn't work (though they're convinced that it does) but in offering practical advice (they couldn't afford to make rain, so Plater changed a line or two of dialogue to say that it was 'about' to rain, still obligating the hero and heroine to find shelter) and sharing worthwhile anecdotes. Batt breaks down his thought process for developing the film's score, and also speaks about how he orchestrates and times the pieces he has composed.

The Message (Anchor Bay, DV10482)

Back in the late Seventies during the 'oil crisis,' Middle Eastern financiers suddenly found themselves flush with cash and prey to the same kind of predatory film producers that have been fleecing people with money since the movies began. From this begat the 220 minute 'epic' shot simultaneously in English and in Arabic with western and Islamic stars. **The Message** told the 'story of Islam' without showing the founder of Islam, Mohammed, since that is an Islamic no-no (a sensible extrapolation of banning icon idolatry). The purpose of the western version seems two-fold, to attempt a Biblical-style desert epic that intercuts battles with moral arguments and historical logistics, and to sell Islamic Public Relations to the west, which, at the time, was in dire need of any positive press it could muster. Of course, the bomb threats that accompanied the movie's theatrical premiers didn't help…

Anyway, hardcore epic junkies will appreciate the desert cinematography, the sets & costumes, the pre-CGI cast of hundreds and the film's running time, but others will balk at the lack of a viable central character, the camera point-of-view shots representing Mohammed, and the dull, seemingly endless political posturing that separate the battles. Anthony Quinn, Irene Papas and Michael Ansara star.

The film is letterboxed with an aspect ratio of about 2.35:1 and no 16:9 enhancement. The source material looks like it hasn't received much of a workout. The colors are bright and fleshtones are decent. The image is a little soft and there are a few scattered markings, but on the whole the transfer looks fine. The program did seem a little more susceptible to digital artifacting than usual, particularly during the film's first half. The stereo surround sound is reasonably strong, with some dimensionality. There is an extensive and competent musical score by Maurice Jarre. There is no captioning. The film is split to two sides and is accompanied by a good 'making of' documentary that runs about an hour (the DVD is not time encoded), a still photo montage, a Mohammed time line, and trailers for both the western and Arabic versions of the film. The actress playing Papas' part in the Arabic version, incidentally, blows her away.

Message to Love: The Isle of Wight Festival—The Movie (Sony, LVD49335)

25 years after the fact, they finally got around to piecing together a filmed record of the Isle of Wight rock music festival. The film is sort of a cynic's **Woodstock**, cutting between performances and the struggles the festival management has to pay the artists to perform and to keep fans without tickets from tearing down the dividers and crashing the concerts. At 121 minutes, it seems a little more rushed than **Woodstock**. You don't get a complete feel for the artists (the camera angles are often haphazard, too), though the atmosphere of the event is sufficiently conveyed. Featured among the performers are The Who, The Doors, Leonard Cohen, Miles Davis (!), Jethro Tull, Ten Years After, Free, The Moody Blues, Emerson Lake & Palmer, Jimi Hendrix, Joni Mitchell (who gets interrupted by a stage intruder and breaks down, telling a delightfully incoherent story about Hopi Indians and tourists as she tries to regain her concentration), Joan Baez (who argues about why she should get paid), Tiny Tim, Donovan and Kris Kristofferson. Where **Woodstock** presented an idealized vision of the-rock-festival-as-love-in, **Isle of Wight** gives a more realistic image of the confusion, apathy and commercialism inherent in the gathering (though it wasn't commercial enough—had the promoters wanted to earn back their investment, they should have worried less about the gate and

more about concessions). Where the music from **Woodstock** became *the* cultural core sample of its era, the music of **Isle of Wight**, though nostalgically exciting and often performed with enthusiasm, shows undeniably that the climate was changing. The music was becoming a job for the performers and a product for the fans instead of a collaborative avant garde tool for smashing the status quo.

The program is split to two sides. Blacks are pure, fleshtones are pink, other colors are bright and the image is fairly sharp. The documentary is still grainy or soft looking much of the time, but viewers are likely to tolerate such compromises for the film's historical value. The stereo sound rarely has much dimensionality, but the music has enough energy to overcome any drawbacks. A text interview with the film's director is also included.

Metheny, Pat (see **Chick Corea Pat Metheny Lee Konitz: Woodstock Jazz Festival**)

Metro (Buena Vista, 13853)

Eddie Murphy stars as, nominally, a San Francisco hostage negotiator. You never see him doing much negotiating. The simplistic plot has three almost unrelated parts, but is basically about the hero's efforts to track down the man who murdered his colleague. The ending even has the villain tying the heroine to a modern day circular saw. If he had a mustache he'd be twisting it. The film doesn't deliver what it promises—fast talking Eddie charming the pants off criminals—and is basically a chase movie with a few confrontation scenes. That said, however, it is mindlessly entertaining for those who require no more than a few Eddie Murphy gags and some gunplay to stay happy.

The 1998 film is letterboxed with an aspect ratio of about 2.35:1, with no 16:9 enhancement. The colors are bright and crisp, but fleshtones tend to look a bit purplish. The audio track is adequate for the Eddie Murphy action film, with the Dolby Digital track delivering more separation effects and better detail than the standard stereo track. The 117 minute feature is also available in French and comes with English or Spanish subtitles, along with a theatrical trailer.

Metropolis (Madacy, DVD99007)

The 115 minute program presents the original 1926 theatrical cut of the Fritz Lang classic and not the modified version that was created in the Eighties as an epic music video. The score, a mix of orchestral pieces, is workable, although the stereophonic sound is rather noisy, has a limited range and a total rear channel bleed. The black-and-white picture is very soft, with limited detail and contrasts. Faces are sometimes so blanched that expressions are impossible to make out, and the image is so tightly trimmed that letters on the intertitles are at times dropped. Students will be able to get the gist of the film from the DVD, but those who want to revel at the brilliance of its design may feel frustrated. Some background notes are also included.

The Metropolitan Opera: Centennial Gala (Pioneer, PA94046D)

When it was first produced in 1983, the 231 minute program was an all-star event of epic proportions, and was certainly a marvelous kind of Met 'greatest hits live' production, but now it is even more compelling because a number of the stars have either retired or passed away. The picture is a bit soft—there never seem to be any hard edges, but colors are adequate and fleshtones are acceptable. The stereo sound does not have a forceful or elaborate mix, but there is an adequate dimensionality and a decent clarity of tone. The vocal recitals can be supported by optional English subtitles. The jacket chapter guide is fine, but the menu chapter guide misidentifies some of the conductors. There is also a lengthy essay about the history of the Met.

We won't bother to list all of the performers or numbers, but among the stellar artists appearing are Leonard Bernstein, Joan Sutherland, Birgit Nilsson, Marilyn Horne, Kathleen Battle, Kiri Te Kanawa, Plácido Domingo, José Carreras and, for those of you who have no interest in opera, the scantily clad Metropolitan Opera Ballet doing the licentious *Bacchanale* from *Samson et Dalila*. There is a real sense during almost all of the performances that the singers are giving more of themselves than usual for the special night, so the program is essentially 231 minutes of encore-style spectacle and excitement.

The Metropolitan Opera: Francesca da Rimini (Pioneer, PA87180D)

Riccardo Zandonai's haunting **Francesca da Rimini** is a Twentieth Century opera with a Nineteenth Century style supported by a mature complexity of themes and passions. The excellent production of the opera was recorded in April, 1984 and stars Plácido Domingo, Renata Scotto and Cornell MacNeil. Scotto is riveting, and while Domingo seems less thorough than he does in later works, his best moments are still quite exciting. MacNeil, the villain (married to Scotto's character, who loves Domingo's character, the villain's brother, all while war rages about them), however, brings such a wonderful vigor to the baritone role that he almost steals the show. The staging is also elaborate and stimulating, and the video direction is competent.

The picture looks reasonably good for a fifteen-year-old video recording. Colors are not intense, but are not distorted or significantly faded, either, and fleshtones are passable. The stereo recording is decent. Playback has a reasonable dimensionality and very clear tones. The 155 minute production is presented on a single-sided dual-layer platter and is in Italian with optional English subtitles.

The Metropolitan Opera: La Bohème (Pioneer, PC95085D)

The January 1982 performance of Giacomo Puccini's **La Bohème** by the Metropolitan Opera is perhaps the best known of all the home video opera programs. It was sort of a matter of timing (1982 was the beginning of home video), combined with the stellar level of the cast and Franco Zeffirelli's seemingly definitive staging that has led to the program's ubiquity, but viewers who want just one opera or want to start out with one opera could do a lot worse. Our only complaint is that the video coverage is not equal to Zeffirelli's vision. The camera angles crop off too much—you can tell from the real long shots that the close-ups are missing more than they should. Teresa Stratas, Renata Scotto and José Carreras star (the presence of only one of the three would be enough to justify the recording), with Richard Stilwell, Allan Monk and James Morris, and James Levine conducting.

The 141 minute program is presented in single-sided dual-layer format. The picture is a little soft, but colors are nicely detailed and fleshtones are rich. The stereo sound is a little reserved, with a bland mix. The opera is in Italian and is supported by permanent white English subtitles.

The Metropolitan Opera: Tosca (Pioneer, PC94025D)

The excellent 1985 Metropolitan Opera recording of **Tosca**, stars Hildegard Behrens (who gives an exceptional performance) and Plácido Domingo (who is his usual competent self), and is directed by Franco Zeffirelli. Compared to a more recent videotape recording, the image looks a little soft at times and is a bit light in places, but generally it is in acceptable condition and sometimes it looks quite good. Colors are reasonably deep and blacks are pure. The stereo sound is fairly strong for a live recording. The 127 minute opera, about a woman who mistakenly betrays her lover and then murders to protect him is essentially a four-character composition. It is in Italian and is supported by permanent white English subtitles.

Michael (Warner, T6306)

A totally charming road movie about three reporters who are trying to drive an angel back to Chicago so they can take pictures of him. John Travolta is terrific as the angel, an individual given to the indulgences of wine, women, song, cigarettes and sugar, but not above bringing peace to a few hearts here and there. William Hurt and Andie MacDowell play two of the reporters, but if you really want to see first class comic acting, check out Bob Hoskins, who plays the reporters' editor with a highly amusing, ever so slightly off kilter British accent. The film is wonderful, a fresh and funny romance delivered by a top notch cast.

The presentation has not been letterboxed, losing a small piece of picture information from the sides of the image and adding quite a bit more to the top and the bottom. The framing is workable. The picture is dark, but we assume the shadows were there for a reason. The colors are strong and, although the image is a little soft in place, the film relies on personalities, not cinematography, to convey its entertainment. There are some nice pop music tunes in the musical score that sound great on the stereo surround soundtrack and the sound effects are delivered effectively. Overall, the stereo surround soundtrack and Dolby Digital tracks are competently designed but unexceptional. The film is also available in French and Spanish without Dolby Digital and has English, French or Spanish subtitles. A somewhat ragged theatrical trailer has also been included, along with a few production notes, background on the Archangel Michael and some cast profiles.

Michael Collins (Warner, 14205)

It is somewhat disturbing that history's most successful terrorists are those who went on to become great statesmen. It gives the act of terrorism an 'end justifies the means' legitimacy, perpetuating the failing horror of mass murder as well as the occasional successful revolution. There is another argument that says the government in power practices terrorism under another name, but the whole point is that it is another name and a different kind of evil, an evil the evils of terrorism inflame instead of negate. Neil Jordan's **Michael Collins**, about the terrorist who spearheaded the final drive for Irish independence, explores this moral dilemma unapologetically. As an entertainment, some viewers may find the movie a little too much of a history lesson, but it is the kind of history lesson movies are really good at. Jordan does not hide the crimes that his hero, who is played by Liam Neeson, commits, and so he tosses the whole argument of whether Collins was justified in his actions or not right into the viewer's lap, which is where it belongs. For those who aren't looking for intellectual edification, the movie has a few good action scenes, a tired but functional triangular love story—Julia Roberts somehow wound up in the film—and a well paced, forward-moving narrative, in which the hero identifies his goals and then succeeds in achieving them. Viewers who focus only on the entertainment aspects of the movie, however, are likely to be disappointed by the film's structure, but viewers who embrace the entire feature as an exploration of the legitimacy or illegitimacy of terrorism should find it highly stimulating.

The picture is vivid and crisp, and there was only one minor artifact in one shot that we noticed, an instance where lamps appeared to momentarily disengage from their posts. Chris Menges' cinematography often utilizes complex shadings and reduced colors to give the film an antique look, and the DVD delivers each lighting shift with perfection. The presentation is letterboxed with an aspect ratio of about 1.85:1 and no 16:9 enhancement, and the framing is consistently well balanced. The Dolby Digital sound has a stronger bass than the standard stereo soundtrack, though neither has much activity on the back channel outside of the battle scenes. A French dialogue track is also offered, along with English, French and Spanish subtitling. The film runs 133 minutes and is split to two sides. On the second side, along with the conclusion of the film, there is a dialog-less theatrical trailer and an excellent 52 minute BBC documentary about the production of the film and the historical events and people upon which it is based.

Michael Crawford in Concert (Warner, 36420)

It is only when he stops between numbers to talk to the audience that Crawford sounds like the scrawny Michael Crawford you used to know, and it's a good thing, too, because otherwise he seems in danger of falling into a Steve Lawrence imitation. The 65 minute concert, set on a formal stage (the Cerritos Center in Los Angeles) and backed by a large orchestra, concentrates on Andrew Lloyd Webber tunes, though he does slip in *Tonight*, *Before the Parade Passes By* and a couple traditional tunes. The music is okay—we've seen much worse Andrew Lloyd Webber concerts released on video—but it is his patter between the numbers that we found surprisingly enjoyable. Even though he has slipped into darker roles these days, he still has a full grasp of the art of comical timing that started his career. His anecdotes are not only amusing, they show a relaxed side that is obscured when he sings, making him more personable and creating a closer connection to the viewer.

Shot in Los Angeles, the picture on the 65 minute concert is super sharp, with vivid colors. The stereo surround sound is okay, although the recording has a fairly bland mix. The program is closed captioned, and is accompanied by an enjoyable but abrupt 5 minute interview with Crawford in which he talks about the songs he sings. There is also a complete Crawford film-and-discography.

Michael Flatley: Lord of the Dance (PolyGram, 4400431892)

The 92 minute program, a spectacular piece of choreography set to Irish folk motifs, is exciting not only for what the dancers accomplish on the stage, but for how it has been received by the general public. Kids, even adolescent and pre-adolescent boys who couldn't care less about dancing, respond to the narrative—a folk legend involving mischievous spirits and challenges of power among leaders—and to the athleticism of the performers. Adults respond to the costumes, which are sexy as all get out (well, that's probably attracting the adolescent boys, too), to the grace and energy of the dancers, to the variety and complexity of the dances and to the beauty of Ronan Hardiman's music, which stays so close to its roots that amplification cannot harm it in the least. The show is so effectively staged that the wild colored lighting and grandiose abstract scenery contribute to the excitement instead of diminishing it. When Flatley ventures beyond his killer tapping ability and masterful folk dancing skills to attempt real ballet moves and leaps, his limitations are revealed, but the spirit of the program is such that one is more inclined to give him points for trying than to take away points for failing. It doesn't detract from Paul Taylor, Mark Morris and the many other modern dance choreographers who have kept the artform alive during the past generation to have Flatley steamroll his way through their turf. In the long run everyone benefits, because Flatley is pulling in new audiences and new enthusiasts, and, unlike some popular artists (Jose Carreras comes to mind), he's teaching them the right way to appreciate his craft by not compromising its basic components. **Lord of the Dance** is a showy production, but its heart is dancing and that heart never stops beating.

The colored lights and foggy stage effects are at odds with the picture quality through most of the program. It is more the fault of the original video recording than of the transfer, but the image is often soft or even blurry, and hues get a bit too hazy at times. The distortion is not enough to dampen the basic excitement. The stereo surround sound has a terrific bass, pleasing dimensionality and plenty of power. In addition to the 92 minute concert, there is an eight minute featurette about Flatley and the production. There are also still frame biographical profiles of Flatley, composer Ronan Hardiman and the two female leads, Gillian Norris and Bernadette Flynn.

Michael Jackson: HIStory on Film Volume II (Sony, EVD50138)

Although Michael Jackson's *Childhood* comes from *Free Willy 2*, the song has strong biographical overtones and the music video, which has nothing to do with the film, is outstanding, a Chris Van Allsberg-style vision of children in airborne sailboats crossing a forest at night. The clip is the highlight of the generally weak follow-up to the first *HIStory* video collection. Also included on the 106 minute anthology is the shorter version of *Thriller*, *Beat It*, the *Motown 25* performance of *Billie Jean*. Fresher material includes another rare live clip, from the *1995 MTV Video Music Awards*, *Scream*, a black-and-white space station thing with Janet Jackson, the ecological-themed *Earth Song*, Spike Lee's somewhat obnoxious *They Don't Care About Us*, shot in Brazilian slums, *Liberian Girl*, *Smooth Criminal*, *You Are Not Alone*, *Stranger in Moscow*, *Blood on the Dance Floor* and *Brace Yourself*. The picture quality is generally good on all the clips, though the older ones are a bit weaker than the newer ones. The stereo surround sound is strong, and there is also a Dolby Digital track with clearer definitions and more energy. The song lyrics can also be toggled on, in case you've ever wondered what it was Jackson was saying. and the stereo surround sound is strong.

Mickey Hart: Planet Drum / Indoscrub (Rykodisc, RDVD51059)

A 'DVD Single' program, the two music videos it contains, *Indoscrub*, which runs 5 minutes and *Endless River*, which runs 3 minutes, both have recognizable imagery. *Indoscrub* is a collection of time-lapse images depicting construction sites and other urban locales. *Endless River* features natural images of water, nature and the moon, though it is edited more energetically than the usual nature image clip. Both numbers emphasize percussion, but are highly appealing, and *Indoscrub* even has a vocal track.

The picture quality looks fine, and the sound is super. The audio is available in both Dolby Digital and DTS (which seems a bit crisper), and has a full dimensionality and strong tonal definitions. There is also a good 9 minute interview with Hart, in which he talks about his background and his music (the image on the interview, however, is somewhat jerky, like a computer video playback). There is no captioning.

Midnight Cowboy (MGM, 906038)

Dustin Hoffman's performance in **Midnight Cowboy** is perhaps even more amazing than his performance in **Rain Man**. In **Rain Man** he expertly follows a certain set of psychological quirks and confinements, but in **Cowboy** his whole appearance changes, as if his face were two inches longer. (And the last shot seems to be a deliberately dark variation of **The Graduate**.) The movie is locked into a sixties stylistic approach that can feel dated, but Hoffman's performance can prevent one from ever tiring of the film. That will surely be the case with **Rain Man** as well, as Hoffman's voice seems to have a subliminally comic rhythm no matter what manner of character he embodies. Jon Voight co-stars in the story of two homeless men who form a bond while eking out a existence in New York City.

The picture is very sharp and delivers details in the creases of the faces and elsewhere superbly. Fleshtones are accurate and other hues look fine. The source material has a few scratches, which are also distinctive on the DVD, but the presentation looks reasonably fresh. The accurate coloring increases the balances in the film's design, which rock between an atmosphere of destitution and ever-present whiffs of hope. The 113 minute film is presented on one side in letterboxed format, with an aspect ratio of about 1.85:1 and no 16:9 enhancement, and on the other side in full screen format. The letterboxing adds no more than a sliver to the sides and masks off a lot of picture information from the bottom of the screen. The film's music was remastered in stereo, although it is pretty much just the music that is given any dimensionality. The audio is strong and never sounds distorted. The program is also encoded with a French monophonic soundtrack. Subtitles are available in English, French and Spanish ("¡Eh, estoy caminando!"), and a theatrical trailer, for the *25th Anniversary* theatrical reissue, is included. For the record, we compared the TV channel surfing scene, which flips through images at a rate of one per frame at one point, to a frame-by-frame LD release, and every still frame was there on the DVD.

Midnight Express (Columbia TriStar, 00549)

An anti-milestone in Turkish-American relations, the film offers a pointed lesson that when one is a guest in a foreign country one should make every attempt to obey that country's laws, or else. It is a xenophobic, macho drama that succeeds by finding the right balance between violence, victimization and the despairs of youth. Brad Davis, Randy Quaid and John Hurt star in the 1978 production, which was directed by Alan Parker from an Oscar-winning Oliver Stone script.

The film is presented in letterboxed format on one side, with an aspect ratio of about 1.85:1 and an accommodation for enhanced 16:9 playback, and in full screen format on the other side. The letterboxing masks picture information off the top and bottom and adds some to the sides in comparison to the full screen version. Fleshtones are subdued in some sequences, but most of the time the image is accurately transferred and complex lighting situations always look stable. The monophonic sound is so strong and mixed with such sophistication it gives off the illusion of stereo. The 121 minute feature also has a French audio track, optional English or French subtitles, a trailer and an interesting 'making of' featurette that includes an interview with the individual upon who's life the story is based.

Midnight in the Garden of Good and Evil (Warner, 14776)

A reporter is in the right place at the right time to cover a murder trial, helping the defense investigate the case as he gathers information for a book about the crime. John Cusack is the reporter. Kevin Spacey, who is top billed, burst onto the scene a couple years earlier, earning an Oscar and working great magic in a number of memorable parts, but he's stiff as a board here as the suspect and there's nothing to his performance that is any fun at all. Some of the supporting roles are more entertaining, including Jack Thompson who convincingly looses his Australian accent to portray the defense attorney, and The Lady Chablis, apparently playing herself or something but doing it with flair. Alison Eastwood, daughter of the film's director, Clint Eastwood, does a passable Cybill Shepherd imitation as the reporter's love interest. There is also what one might believe to be a severely stereotyped portrayal of an effeminate hairdresser if one did not know the part was being played by the real hairdresser himself. The film runs 155 minutes and makes a tolerable courtroom drama, with many passages that seem intentionally comical.

Although it would be better served by a straightforward documentary, Warner has included interviews and portraits of the real people interpreted as characters on the DVD. To access the interviews, you have to negotiate a map of Savannah Georgia and click on specific locations, but for those who are interested in learning more about the film's background, it is worth the effort. The DVD is also accompanied by production and background notes, an extensive cast & crew profile section and a trailer. The film is presented in dual-layer format and is letterboxed, with an aspect ratio of about 1.85:1 and an accommodation for enhanced 16:9 playback. The color transfer generally looks quite impressive. The stereo surround sound and Dolby Digital sound have an unimaginative but serviceable audio mix. The program is also available in French and can be supported by English, French or Spanish subtitles.

Midnight Run (Image, ID4271USDVD)

Robert De Niro and Charles Grodin star in the 1988 road comedy directed by Martin Brest. De Niro is a bounty hunter trying to transport Grodin's character from New York to L.A. with the FBI, the mob and a bounty hunter rival all on his trail. The dialogue is heavy with four-letter words, but otherwise the film is a harmless and amusing effort with strong characterizations and a few witty plot turns.

The presentation is letterboxed with an aspect ratio of about 1.85:1 and no 16:9 enhancement. Darker sequences are a little grainy but overall the picture looks reasonably good, with passable fleshtones and mild, but accurate colors. The stereo surround soundtrack is rather passive, with limited dimensionality. The 127 minute program has no captioning.

Midway (Universal, ID4292USDVD)

The 1976 131 minute film is a satisfying depiction of the Japanese and American logistics that led to the decisive WWII Pacific naval battle, mixed with a very annoying fictional drama about tensions between a naval officer, played by Charlton Heston, and his junior officer son. There is a marvelous cast, including more than just walk on parts by Henry Fonda, Glenn Ford, Toshiro Mifune, Hal Holbrook and others. The history isn't perfect, but it is good enough to give the viewer a sense of how the battle occurred, and the drama is sparse enough to stay out of the way once things really get moving. The presentation is letterboxed with an aspect ratio of about 2.35:1. The color transfer looks okay, with reasonably accurate hues, and except when archive footage is incorporated the image is fairly crisp. The Dolby Digital mono track packs more punch than the standard mono track, and the gunshots seem to vibrate a bit more deeply, though no extra effort has apparently been made to include the film's 'Sensurround' channel. The program is supported by optional English subtitles, but the Japanese cast speaks English, often with rather embarrassing dubbing.

Mighty Aphrodite (Buena Vista, 16451)

Woody Allen's amusing tale is about a father who wants to meet the biological mother of his adopted son. Allen has twiddled with the script, adding a funny Greek chorus to bridge the narrative and punch up the humor, but the story is strong and every choice he makes seems to be the right one. Mira Sorvino's unique performance as the earnest, bubbly prostitute who turns out to be the child's mother is a perfect example. At first she seems awkward, talking and moving to a different rhythm than everyone around her, but as the film unfolds and it becomes more and more her story, everything around her seems to adjust and to blend better with her. As one learns more about her, as she becomes less of an object and more of a person, the whole movie seems to embrace her. Allen stars as the father, with Helena Bonham Carter as his wife and F. Murray Abraham as the leader of the chorus.

The picture is letterboxed with an aspect ratio of about 1.85:1 and no 16:9 enhancement. The cinematography has many subtle lighting effects, often creating a mildly yellowish tone. It is difficult to tell how accurate the image transfer is, but if one assumes that it is consistent, then the brightly colored scenes look sharp and presumably the other sequences appear as they were intended. Like all of Allen's movies, the stereo sound is essentially monophonic and a bit flat. The 1995 feature runs 95 minutes and can be accompanied by optional English subtitles.

Mighty Joe Young (Buena Vista, 16538)

The colors are a little light, the image is soft in places and the standard stereo surround soundtrack is bland, but the Dolby Digital track is super-duper. Joe gets those woofers a' shakin', and there are lots of enjoyable rear channel activity and left-right separations to keep you wondering where he's going to jump next. The picture is letterboxed with an aspect ratio of about 1.85:1 and no 16:9 enhancement. The sequences with Joe look fine, but the film's budget has clearly been held in check, with bland lighting and other compromises outside of the special effects scenes.

The film plays the same way. It is a very entertaining movie, but the acting is awful, the editing cheats like crazy and the script is a patchwork of contrivances. It doesn't matter. The story works, the special effects work and the sound is worth turning up to the max. The 114 minute feature can be supported by English subtitles and is accompanied by a trailer and a featurette that is really just a trailer with a couple interviews thrown in.

The Mikado (Image, ID4529JFDVD)

An utterly joyful, classic musical comedy, the 1938 British soundstage production was cast with the D'Oyly Carte Opera Company, which had a monopoly on the property and had honed its performances for several generations. The result of this, however, is not a tired, rote rendition of the work but instead a practiced, finely detailed explosion of melody and humor. Drawing more from the British music hall tradition than from anything remotely connected to 'opera,' the show itself is a marvelously complicated blend of gags lampooning everything from Far Eastern culture (you can go crazy trying to figure out what decorations or manners are taken from the Chinese, what are taken from the Japanese and what are completely made up with no source at all as an inspiration) to British politics. The stars bring to their film roles every little bit of stage business they and their predecessors discovered audiences responding to, and it is often difficult to focus on one part of the screen because so many talented performers are doing so many funny things all over the place. Foremost, however, is Martyn Green, as Koko, who, when not the center of attention, is constantly doing jigs and otherwise working as if he still were the only one in front of the camera. And yet equally marvelous is Kenny Baker, in what one might call the Dick Powell role, keeping a straight face but still making fun of his part, while never missing his character's true emotional center. One major song is dropped (I've Got a Little List), but otherwise the show is complete, and the pace is so brisk the movie is done before you're anywhere near finished laughing at the gags or swooning over the music. The film only runs 87 minutes but you'd better allow yourself several hours—we ended up starting it all over again as soon as it was finished.

The film is in color and generally looks delightful. Colors are a bit washed out, whites are a bit pinkish, and there is some haze around the strongest hues, but the advantages of how well the program has been preserved outweigh the acknowledgement than an elaborate restoration could probably make it look even better. The monophonic sound is as scratchy in places as the film's 78 RPM soundtrack, but if you keep the volume to a modest level it is fine and the music is no more distorted than one would expect for a film of its age. The show is not captioned. The chapter encoding and jacket guide are lousy ('DVD producers who chapter encode musicals without marking all the songs—they never would be missed, no, they never would be missed.').

Mikhail Baryshnikov's Stories from My Childhood (see **Stories from My Childhood**)

Millie (see **Pre-Code Hollywood: The Risqué Years #1**)

Milton Berle's Buick Hour: Volume One (Image, ID4806BFDVD)
Milton Berle's Buick Hour: Volume Two (Image, ID5467BFDVD)
Milton Berle's Buick Hour: Volume Three (Image, ID5468BFDVD)

The conventional memory is of Milton Berle running around in drag doing warmed over burlesque routines, but **Milton Berle's Buick Hour** (the show is really titled *The Buick Berle Show*) is actually much more intelligent. For one thing, although the program, from 1954–55, has a variety format, it also has a narrative, a sort of show-within-a-show in which Berle frets and struggles to put together his next broadcast, meeting his guest stars, rehearsing, and that sort of thing. The premise is both clever and flexible, letting Berle explore all comic parameters with a sense of purpose that keeps the viewer wondering what will happen next. During the course of the episode, there are also several musical sequences, often featuring classics by Cole Porter, Irving Berlin and such (Herbert Ross did some of the choreography).

Each DVD contains two 50 minute episodes, with full opening and closing credits and sponsor plugs. The black-and-white kinescope source material is in an expectably variable condition, with splices, smears, grain and unreliable contrasts, though more often than not it looks sharp and reasonably clear. The monophonic sound is also inconsistent, usually improving a bit after a weak opening. The dialogue is coherent and most of the music has no significant distortion. The programs are not captioned.

Anybody with an even passing interest in the stars of the bygone era will not want to miss **Volume One** and its opening episode (the premiere of Buick's sponsorship), featuring Tallulah Bankhead and Frank Sinatra. Bankhead spent most of her career on the stage and made very few films, so any footage of her strutting her stuff is precious, but the scenes the three of them share go well beyond that. Their timing and by-play are exquisite, and they even do a 'serious' dramatic skit that is totally captivating. Martha Raye guest stars in the companion episode, and the more often she and Berle flub their lines, the funnier it becomes.

Vic Damone and Jackie Cooper show up in the first episode on **Volume Two**, and they all get some good burlesque material out of Dagmar and Denise Darcel (think Charo). It is more of an ordinary episode than the two in the first volume, but the music is good and the comical mix-ups are enjoyable. The sound is especially weak on the second episode. Not only is the volume low, but the audio is exceptionally noisy. What's more, the show's motif is 'culture,' and, along with actor Paul Douglas, opera singer Marguerite Piazza guest stars. The flaws do not interfere too badly, however, with Piazza's arias.

Berle is ready to unveil the newest Buick, when it is apparently stolen from the set on one of the episodes in **Volume Three**. He calls on famous detectives to help him find it, including Mickey Spillane (plugging his 'latest' bestseller, *Kiss Me Deadly*) and Sherlock Holmes, as played by Basil Rathbone. They get away with jokes they could never use today ("Watson's been giving you too much of that needle. It sounds like 'Drugnet.'") and Rathbone is hysterical ("Is this a Dagmar that I see before me?"). It's a gas. The companion episode features Peter Lawford and a very young Carol Channing.

Mimic (Buena Vista, 14251)

Even though a horror movie is fantasy it has to be true to its own logic and maintain a basis in reality in order to succeed. The special effects in **Mimic**, about human-sized cockroaches getting ready to take over New York City, are pretty good and the action scenes are effectively staged, but the story is so pathetic and uncaring of details that the movie almost isn't worthwhile. One gets the impression that the filmmakers thought they didn't have to try, that they could say or do anything and, so long as they pulled out some bugs, viewers would go along with it. We could fill pages itemizing the mistakes the movie makes, but we will just mention a couple. There are zones in narratives where you can kill children and get away with it, but the filmmakers kill two outside the zone, a third of the way through the movie and after establishing that the kids are cute, bright and innocent. Characters must be resourceful and intelligent to survive adversity, but in the climax of **Mimic** a transit cop supposedly has total knowledge not only of operating an antique train but, without observation, of fixing the long broken wiring that brings electricity to the tracks. There are dozens of moments, big and small, like those throughout the film, and the culmination of flaws makes the movie seem so ridiculous that enjoying it is difficult. Mira Sorvino stars. The 1997 feature is letterboxed with an aspect ratio of about 1.85:1 with no 16:9 enhancement. The film is deliberately darkish, but the subdued hues are accurate, fleshtones look decent and the image is sharp. Some of the poorer special effects look a bit smeary, with inconsistent contrasts, but such moments are fleeting. The upper range is more distinctive on the Dolby Digital track, but the lower range, though present on the Dolby Digital track, is more satisfying on the standard track. The 106 minute film is accompanied by a busy theatrical trailer and can be supported by English subtitles.

Miracles (import, MSDVD04398)

Jackie Chan's 1989 feature is a direct adaptation of *Pocketful of Miracles*, which Chan took on in answer to critics that fretted about the emphasis of action over content in his previous efforts. Chan uses a wonderful period setting and even includes a couple marvelous musical numbers. There are plenty of inventive fight and stunt sequences, but he also delivers the classic story (about a gangster who helps a old woman pretend to be rich to impress the family of her daughter's fiancé), pulling on the heartstrings as adeptly as Frank Capra ever could. It is a wonderful effort and it is a shame that the lower ratio of fights to plot has prevented it from receiving the attention in America that it deserves.

The picture quality is very good. The image is letterboxed with an aspect ratio of about 2.35:1 and no 16:9 enhancement. Fleshtones are not as rich or as detailed as in a Hollywood film, but colors are bright and effectively defined. The source material is free of all but very minor speckling and digital artifacting is minimal. The film's stereo surround mix is not overly elaborate, but there is both a standard track and a Dolby Digital track, which are of equal quality and are adequately delivered. The 122 minute film can be played in either Cantonese or Mandarin and can be supported by optional English, Spanish traditional Chinese, simplified Chinese, Japanese, Vietnamese, Bahasa Malaysian and Thai subtitles, with the subtitles appearing beneath the letterboxed image.

The Mirror Has Two Faces Columbia TriStar, 82525/9)

A film that is so out-of-date it creaks, many people have gotten on the case of the film's director and star, Barbra Streisand, suggesting that she was too vain to execute the 1997 film (about a chaste marriage between two college professors) properly, but in reality she is just out of touch, making a movie that is funny enough (one of the things Streisand still knows how to do, besides sing, is deliver a string of oneliners) and loaded with enough stars that it might just have worked, twenty years ago. It is interesting that the plot has some superficial similarities to **Jerry Maguire**—both are about people who marry first and fall in love afterwards—because, when you see the films in any proximity, the hip confidence and breezy realism of **Maguire** puts the mannered manipulations and tiresome emotional obviousness of **Mirror** to shame.

The film is presented on one side in letterboxed format, with an aspect ratio of about 1.85:1 and an accommodation for enhanced 16:9 playback, and in full screen format on the other side. Because of all the wrinkle-sensitive actresses in the film, the camera lens is constantly dripping with gauze and so sharpness is rarely an attribute of the image. Fleshtones are somewhat pinkish. The picture transfer appears to be accurate, however, so do not try to adjust your set. The stereo surround sound is adequately executed, and the music is reasonably strong, particularly on the Dolby Digital track. The 126 minute film also has French and Spanish audio tracks in standard stereo, optional Spanish and Korean subtitles, and English closed captioning.

Of all the performers in the movie, by the way, we must mention Jeff Bridges, who stands out as the husband of Streisand's character, delivering what has to be one of the worst performances ever by a major actor. His phony line readings and ineptly posed befuddlement make his Boston accent in **Blown Away** seem positively Shakespearean. The riotous giggles he induces when he claims that he is no longer interested in sex is one of the few genuine selling points the movie has.

The Misadventures of James Spawn (Dream Theater, UPC#8763300065)

The fairly elaborate program offers somewhere around 100 different story branches, all of which are on the level of a bad burlesque skit. Don't get us wrong, the show can be somewhat appealing and even addictive in a guilty pleasure sort of way, and there are quite a few amusing video effects scattered throughout it, but the show uses embarrassing ethnic stereotypes, teasing sex jokes (mostly fully clothed, though some of the dialogue contains four-letter words) and other juvenile gags for the bulk of its content. Although the initial decision choice has defined options, the subsequent choices are random (when the player reaches a dead end, the program will return to the last decision point), so there isn't much of an intellectual challenge to 'the game.' There is usually just one choice in each group that actually moves the narrative forward. There are four basic premises, one in which the hero visits a remote motel where the owners like to cannibalize their guests, one in which the hero is a photographer hired to take pictures of a mobster's girlfriend, one in which the hero is stuck in a mostly empty military school with a blonde teacher, and one in which the hero is on the road, coping with a highway patrolwoman and her troublesome younger sister.

The lighting is inconsistent but colors are usually bright. The stereo surround sound and Dolby Digital sound do not have detailed separation effects but the musical score has a strong dimensionality. Although the jacket cover claims that there is also DVD-ROM programming on the disc, we could not locate it. The DVD also contains an essay on the production, describing an elaborate though very low budget effort.

Mischievous (Image, ID4761DRDVD)
Badly acted and rather silly at times, the softcore erotic thriller still manages to deliver what is expected of it, with several welcome plot twists and plenty of effectively staged erotic sequences. The hero meets an old girlfriend at a high school reunion, and her renewed flirtations soon destroy his life, until he plans his revenge.

The picture is quite blurry and grainy, with bland colors. The stereo sound is unremarkable. The 95 minute program is not captioned.

Mission Erotica X-rated (Vivid, UPC0073214609)
Using **Point of No Return** as a narrative template (though not strictly), it has more plot than most of its genre and is a reasonably satisfying program. The filmmakers at least try to tell a bit of story, and the erotic sequences are energetic. The picture looks fairly good, with glossy hues and a sharp focus, and even the sound is reasonably strong. The 71 minute program features Kobe Tai, Asia Carrera, Heather Hunter, Missy, Chloe, Stephanie Swift and Sindee Coxx. The DVD also contains alternate angle sequences and elaborate hardcore interactive promotional features.

Mission: Impossible (Paramount, 154977)
We sympathize with poor Peter Graves, star of the old TV show, who was gnashing his teeth over what the 1996 Brian De Palma film has done to his character. In some ways, the TV show was a deliberate answer to John Le Carré, accepting the premise that cold warfare was twisted but refusing to grant that heroes were not always heroes. The movie's plot is an insult to anyone who has fond memories of more than just the opening theme song. Not only is one of the heroes turned, but the old show's entire concept of teamwork and trust is abandoned after the opening section.

But for those who couldn't care less about the old TV show, the film is terrific. The special effects, which looked so awful on the big screen, are almost seamless, making it easier to accept and enjoy the final action sequence. Except for the scenes that he shares with Vanessa Redgrave and is left looking like a grinning idiot, Tom Cruise is every bit the heroic icon Graves was, and is more physically adept at selling the stunts and sleights of hand. De Palma's sense of style is also continuing to mature. He digests the gimmicky camera angles he used in his earlier films and blends them with more traditional setups to obtain the best of both styles and an atmosphere that remains highly stimulating even when the narrative slows down to catch its breath.

The presentation is in single-sided dual-layer format, letterboxed on one layer with an aspect ratio of about 2.35:1 and no 16:9 enhancement, and hopelessly cropped on the other layer, unless you like those gooey close-ups of Cruise to be as big as possible. The picture is very sharp, with accurate hues. The stereo surround

sound is weak, but the menu-activated Dolby Digital track sounds super, with many high-powered separation effects. No matter how loud it gets—and it gets loud—every noise is precisely defined and delivered, and the quiet room sequence is just as stunning for its absence of noise. The 110 minute film is also available in French in standard stereo and can be accompanied by English or Spanish subtitles ("Como siempre, se algún miembro de su equipo muero o es capturado, el Secretario negrará toda relación a sus actividades. Esta cinta se autodestruirá en 5 segundos"). The film's inspired, high-powered theatrical trailer has also been included.

Mississippi Burning (Image, ID40810RDVD)
"If it opened up a debate to discuss racism in America, and if they used the inadequacy of my film in order to point that out, I'm still proud." So states director Alan Parker at the conclusion of his audio commentary to **Mississippi Burning**. The stimulating procedural, about two FBI agents in 1964, investigating the murder of white and black civil rights workers in the Deep South, is letterboxed with an aspect ratio of about 1.85:1 and no 16:9 enhancement. The picture has a smooth, well-defined image, but fleshtones are a little bland and hues remain somewhat subdued. Blacks are purer, adding to the crispness of the image. The stereo surround sound is workable, though the bass is weak. The 127 minute program is closed captioned with substantial paraphrasing and comes with a theatrical trailer. Gene Hackman and Willem Dafoe star in the 1988 feature.

Parker only addresses the negative reactions to the film that one time and, as an outsider unfamiliar with the subtleties of American politics, he remains slightly naive about what it were critics were complaining about. By emphasizing white characters at the center of a black struggle, and using images of the black struggle to set the atmosphere and historical context, he creates the implication that the white characters were leading the crusade instead of hovering in the periphery. For those who are not offended by this perpetuated and well-meaning distortion, the film is generally quite involving, with Hackman and Dafoe presenting well-rounded, gritty characters whose conflicts with one another alternately spur and impede the investigation. There are times when it seems like it could use some trimming—maybe as much as a half hour—to eliminate the historical context stuff and just get on with the characters at hand and the story but, for the most part, the film works well enough.

Parker generally talks about his experiences on the shoot, including the logistics of reaching the many locations they needed to sustain the film's period look, working with Hackman and the other performers, tidbits about his research into the actual incident upon which the fictional film is based, and how specific lighting and image effects were achieved. He does a good job explaining why certain shots were chosen and even expands to discuss how a director goes about choosing camera angles (most are dictated by circumstances). He also offers one other healthy piece of advice for future filmmakers: Never shoot more than eight takes. If you don't get the performances you want in eight, change the camera angle before trying again.

Mister Roberts (Warner, 16692)
Henry Fonda, James Cagney, William Powell and Jack Lemmon star in the delightful story of frustrated officers and crewman aboard a Navy merchant ship in the waning days of World War II. Based upon a stageplay, the film's comedic rhythms have a universal appeal and the performances of the stars are timeless. Mervyn LeRoy took over direction after John Ford became ill, and only those who were there can tell you who did what, unless it was LeRoy who, thankfully, put a lid on the drinking scenes.

The picture is letterboxed with an aspect ratio of about 2.4:1 and an accommodation for enhanced 16:9 playback. The color transfer is gorgeous and the image is exquisite. Fleshtones are rich, the skies are a deep blue, the focus is sharp and the source material is spotless. The film's soundtrack has been remastered for 5-channel Dolby Digital encoding. Franz Waxman's musical score has been given a strong dimensional presence that for the most part remains integrated with the rest of the film (there are a couple moments of 'surprise' that blurt out a little too strongly). A few sound effects have also been directionalized, which will please some viewers and annoy others. The sound doesn't quite have the freshness of a contemporary recording, but it is in terrific shape and contributes quite a bit to the film's vitality. The film is also available in French in mono and can be supported by English or French subtitles ("C'est moi, enseigne Pulver! Je viens de balancer votre sale palmier à la mer. Qui a dit 'pas de cinema ce soir?'").

The 122 minute program is presented on one side. On the other side there is a super 15 minute clip from an old black-and-white Ed Sullivan program in which Fonda, Cagney and Lemmon re-enact a couple of scenes from the film. There is also a brief clip from a Kennedy Center award ceremony in which Fonda is visibly moved by references to his performance in **Roberts**, and an original theatrical trailer that plays up the film's non-existent sexual content. Additionally, Lemmon provides about an hour's worth commentary, spread through the film with easy-to-follow chapter skip prompts. He has some wonderful stories about working with Cagney, Fonda and Ford, as well as some choice anecdotes about his early days in Hollywood and some solid insights on the craft of acting.

Mistress (Pioneer, DVD9864)

Venting the frustrations almost all would-be filmmakers are likely to experience, the film is about an aging producer attempting to arrange financing for a young filmmaker's script and the compromises they must endure to get backing. The title refers to the female friends of the backers they agree to cast in the film, but it is also about the passions they themselves have for the movies. Robert Wuhl and Martin Landau star in the 1991 feature, with Robert De Niro, Danny Aiello and others. There are some amusing moments and some knowing moments, but the movie is about losers and that's where the story ends up.

The picture is presented in full screen format and the colors are a little bland, with dull fleshtones, though the image is reasonably sharp and generally the presentation is workable. The stereo surround sound has an adequate dimensionality and the 112 minute program is not captioned.

Mitsubishi A6M5 Zero (Program Power, UPC#4017898022)

Also identified as *Roaring Glory Vol. 2*, a pilot/narrator provides a thorough tour of the Japanese WWII fighter plane during the first half-hour, and there is a reenactment of a young pilot's memoirs during the second half hour. There are multiple angle segments and other supplementary features, including an interview with a Japanese Zero pilot—though it is difficult to follow—and kind of home movies of a Japanese air show. There are also stills, which include artistic drawings of the planes in action. The picture quality is passable and the sound is fine. The program is not captioned.

Mob War (Simitar, 7392)

The hero is a public relations man who is hired to improve the image of an alleged mobster. The movie is a surprisingly adept and entertaining portrait of 'organized' crime. To hide its limited budget, much of it is filmed in a cinema vérité style. Hence, the picture can be heavily grainy in places and it doesn't harm the drama. The colors are also limited in range, though again the 'look' of the film usually accommodates the bland hues. The stereo sound is passable, although dialogue loops are easy to catch. The sound boom is visible at times. Except for Jake La Motta, who is quite good as a 'godfather' boss, the cast is made up of unknowns, but each is very effective in his part, and most bring an admirable measure of wit to their roles. The 96 minute film was directed by J. Christian Ingvordsen, who demonstrates both resourcefulness and a mastery of fundamentals, and the 1989 movie is as good at rub outs and car chases as it is at board meetings and Mafia double talk. There is no captioning.

The Mobster's Wife X-rated (Vivid, UPC#0073214586)

The dialogue is creative, the narrative is inspired and the erotic sequences are accomplished. To top things off, Vivid has included two charming half hour 'making of' programs on side two. A mobster gets into trouble with the bride of a big crime boss the night before the wedding, while the mobster's wife and the mobster's mistress both have adventures of their own. The plot is complete, the show makes fun of many Mafia movie conventions, the performances are earnestly comical and the erotic sequences aren't bad. The colors are bright but some sequences are fairly grainy. The dialogue is out of synch in places, but otherwise the sound is acceptable. The 84 minute program stars Lexus, Alexandra Silk, Katie Solo and Derrie Lane, all of whom let their guards down for the roving camera on the 'making of' programs.

Moby Dick (Artisan, 96536)

Amid what can seem like a sea of cultural confection, the cable miniseries adaptation of **Moby Dick** was a remarkable and spellbinding piece of entertainment. Although the film is about grownups, grownups who talk archaically most of the time no less, it manages to hold the attention of children as well as adults. Patrick Stewart, who seems to have been practicing this role for years, stars as Ahab, the one-legged ship captain with a one-whale obsession, and Ted Levine is his frustrated first mate. With a 180 minute running time, the film could play out the narrative without rushing things, so that almost every sailor on the ship has a distinct personality and a contribution to the drama. What the film reminded us of most, however, was our father reading sailing novels to us when we were young, the film using CGI effects to bridge the glory of great storytelling between the past and the present. It is classic literature brought to life, in all its metaphysical glory, psychological complexity and very real excitement.

The program is in a single-sided dual-layer format with a single set of opening and closing credits (the layer switch, however, does not come at the break between the two episodes and seems arbitrarily assigned). With the commercials removed, some of the scene transitions can seem a bit jumpy, but the program is best viewed in one adventurous sitting. The color transfer looks good and the picture is reasonably sharp, though the ship interiors aren't always perfectly detailed. There is a mild stereo surround soundtrack, but separation effects are limited. The film can be supported by Spanish subtitles ("¡Ballena a la vista!") or English closed captioning, and is accompanied by a cast & crew profile section, production notes and a good 20 minute 'making of' featurette.

Mocean Worker: Detonator / Diagnosis (Rykodisc, PPDVD70032)

A 'DVD Single' program, the two cuts on are set to abstract and semi-abstract imagery, and the music is, by design, rather cluttered. *Diagnosis*, which runs 3 minutes, contains footage from the backstage of a concert, from a storm, from Red China and a couple other things, manipulated with colorful lights and drawings. *Detonator*, which runs 4 minutes, uses an extensively manipulated image of people commuting, a circuit board, crash dummies at work, and the musician, Adam Dorn, wandering around Wall Street. The music is fast paced and deliberately repetitious.

There is another 8 minute interview as well, with Dorn. The picture looks okay. The audio is in Dolby Digital only and has the same intensely dimensional playback as **Indoscrub**, though because of its style, the tones are not as elegant. There is no captioning.

Moll Flanders (Anchor Bay, DV10332)

A genuine *Mobil Masterpiece Theatre* production, with Russell Baker's intros and everything, the two-part episode is presented one part to a side, with each part running about 101 minutes. Alex Kingston stars in the colorful Daniel Defoe tale of a woman who descends to crime and destitution because she can't settle down. The script attempts to be a little truer to Defoe than the motion picture adaptations have been though, as Baker dryly points out at the end, she's actually in her sixties instead of the strapping thirty-year old she appears to be by the conclusion of the story. Being designed for television, the show is overloaded with closeups but, bless *Masterpiece Theatre*, it is also abundant with nudity and other Seventeenth Century earthiness. Having plenty of running time to work with, the script can move through each of Moll's adventures without feeling rushed, and the result is an engrossing episodic story of what women can and cannot get away with. Diana Rigg appears as—not to spoil things—the mother figure.

The picture varies a bit in quality. Colors are reasonably strong but there is an artifact-related graininess in darker sequences and weak contrasts at times. Fleshtones are a little pale, but workable. The stereo sound is not elaborate but brings some color and atmosphere to the proceedings. The program can be supported by English subtitles.

The Moment X-rated (Vivid, UPC#0073214524)

Hanging out on the beach walk in Venice CA, a guy has trouble meeting girls until he discovers a trick that no woman can resist. We're not telling what the trick is. The narrative is functional and the erotic sequences are standard. The picture is fairly grainy and fleshtones are often orange. The sound on the 71 minute program is okay. The DVD contains alternate angle sequences and elaborate hardcore interactive promotional features.

Money Kings (Sterling, 7215)

Peter Falk is a bookie whose failing operation is disturbed when his boss makes him take on the boss's nephew as a partner. The characters are believable, and Tyne Daly turns in an enchanting performance as Falk's wife, but after a while it becomes clear that the narrative, like the characters, is trapped with no way out of its poverty, and the movie has one of those let's-just-kill-everybody-and-be-done-with-it endings that solves nothing but finding a way to get to the closing credit scroll.

The picture is letterboxed, with an aspect ratio of about 1.85:1 and no 16:9 enhancement. Colors are bland and the picture often looks dark. The setting is supposed to be grungy, but there are times when the image presentation takes things a little too far. The stereo surround sound has a fairly dimensional, Irish musical score, but everything else stays pretty close to the center. The 96 minute program has optional Spanish subtitles but no English captioning. There is a cast profile section and a trailer.

Money Talks (New Line, N4634)

Chris Tucker and Charlie Sheen star in a functionally entertaining action film. Tucker is unknowingly handcuffed to a foreign arms merchant while being transported to a jail. When the merchant's henchman set them free, he picks up some valuable information and is blamed by the police for the break. He goes to Sheen's character, a TV reporter (Sheen may not be convincing as an astrophysicist or presidential advisor, but as a TV reporter he has no trouble), for help. If you begin analyzing almost any aspect of the story it doesn't make much sense, but the film is a breezy romp through the usual collection of car crashes, explosions and death-defying stunts, and there is enough plot and amusing dialogue to support the pyrotechnics.

The film is in letterboxed format on one side, with an aspect ratio of about 2.35:1 and an accommodation for 16:9 enhanced playback, and in full screen format on the other side. The letterboxing adds a bit to the sides but masks off a lot of picture information from the top and the bottom in comparison to the full screen presentation. Interestingly, in video camera POV shots, the squaring irises have been adjusted to accommodate the corners of the frame on each version. The color quality is nice and details are well defined. The stereo surround sound is a little drab, but the Dolby Digital track is good, delivering the standard sort of action movie sounds. The 95 minute film is also available in French in Dolby Digital and can be accompanied by English, French or Spanish subtitles. Also included are a theatrical trailer (full screen on the full screen side and letterboxed on the letterbox side), cast profiles and clips from a couple other Tucker and Sheen films.

The Money Train (Columbia TriStar, 11079)

We didn't think **The Money Train** looked all that promising when we first saw the theatrical trailer, which has been included on the DVD, but once we saw the film, we realize we were mistaken in our assessment of the film's quality. It is much, much worse.

The filmmakers have the ending mastered, though it is no big deal, but the rest of the film is dull and pointless. By the time the film's halfway point comes along, virtually nothing has happened, and what does finally materialize as the plot—one of the heroes, a cop, in debt and fired, plans and executes a heist of a New York subway train carrying the receipts of the day—is morally reprehensible. In executing the heist, regular subway riders are placed in danger, and the reason the hero is robbing the train in the first place is that he has foolishly been playing cards with mobsters. But, as we said, the film's worst sin is simply that it is boring as all get out, until the last twenty minutes or so. Wesley Snipes and Woody Harrelson, considered a 'team' because they fit their roles well in the strongly scripted *White Men Can't Jump*, star, though their relationship is confusing. It appears that their exact living arrangements and history have been fiddled with in the editing room, and they display a total lack of charisma towards one another when they share the screen.

The film is presented in letterboxed format on one side, with an aspect ratio of about 2.45:1 and an accommodation for enhanced 16:9 playback, and in cropped format on the other side. The cropped image usually looks too cramped. The picture is consistently sharp, with bright, glossy colors and accurate fleshtones. The stereo surround sound and Dolby Digital sound have some punch but their best attribute is their accuracy—for those who have never been there, that is exactly what a New York subway sounds like. The 110 minute program also has a French track and a Spanish track in standard stereo and can be supported by optional English, French and Spanish subtitles. There is a trailer, too.

Monkey Business (Image, ID4284USDVD)

The 1931 black-and-white Paramount production has apparently undergone a fresh picture transfer. The picture is sharp, with crisp contrasts. The source material has plenty of age-related wear, but there do seem to be fewer scratches in places than on past releases, giving the film a chance to run a bit more smoothly. The monophonic sound is workable, again with age-related limitations. There is no closed captioning.

The first half of the amusing 77 minute Four Marx Brothers romp is set on an ocean liner, where the heroes are stowaways. The second half is set at a society party the heroes crash, eventually rescuing an heiress from kidnappers, though the story isn't actually as coherent as that.

Montenegro (Fox Lorber, FLV5017)

A Swedish production with a Yugoslav director, Dusan Makavejev, the 1981 film, a droll comedy about murder and eroticism, was shot in English with an American actress, Susan Anspach, in the central role, as a frustrated Stockholm housewife who abandons her family and moves in with a group of Yugoslav immigrants running a raunchy strip joint. The film is forever taking the sort of unexpected turns one is more likely to encounter in life than in the movies. The humor also comes from these absurd turns of events, such as when the heroine pours her pet dog a bowl of poison and then dares him to drink it, and when she sets her husband's blanket on fire. There is some frontal nudity and erotic situations that were a lot more risqué in 1981 than they are now, but more importantly, Makavejev uses the entertainment and the sensuality to present thoughtful arguments on the politics and value of monogamy.

The cinematography uses spare, cool, modern tones for the heroine's home life and messy, warm, uneven lighting for the world of the immigrants, so the image lacks the gloss of a Hollywood production, but it is clear that the transfer is accurate. The picture is letterboxed with an aspect ratio of about 1.66:1 and no 16:9 enhancement. The monophonic sound is fine when one takes the nature of the production into account. The film runs 97 minutes and is accompanied by a trailer and filmographies for Anspach, co-star Erland Josephson and Makavejev.

Monty Python's Life of Brian Anchor Bay, DV10674)

The harmlessly irreverent 1979 Monty Python comedy set during biblical times isn't a perfect comedy—the movie has some slow and unfocused passages—but it is an excellent blend of humor and philosophy, providing a piercingly witty and instinctively accurate lampoon of sectarian religion at the point where its instigation was perhaps the greatest factor of influence in the subsequent two thousand years of Western history.

Set as it is in the Mideast during the good old days, the film has a sort of dusty look and darker sequences are a little murky, but overall, the presentation is very good. The inherent crispness and subdued saturation of the DVD format add significantly to the stability of the image. The picture is letterboxed, with an aspect ratio of about 1.85:1 and no 16:9 enhancement, adding a little bit of picture information to the sides and trimming picture information off the top and bottom in comparison to full screen presentations. The stereo surround sound is fine. The musical score and a few effects are mildly stereophonic, but separations are limited. There is no captioning. The program is accompanied by a trailer and cast profile section.

Monty Python's The Meaning of Life (Image, ID4226USDVD)

A collection of skits that are often drawn out and fairly pointless, the film generally represented an exhaustion of creativity within the Monty Python format and marked the need for the performers to move on to other things, which they did with great success.

The letterboxing has an aspect ratio of about 1.85:1 and no 16:9 enhancement, and the framing is well balanced, but there is probably some masking involved and certain scenes would likely work better in full frame. There are times when the bottom of the frame feels very tight. The color transfer is very good, with fresh hues and accurate fleshtones. The stereo surround sound is set fairly low and separation effects in the 1983 feature, though pronounced, are rationed to a handful of instances. The 107 minute film is captioned.

Monument Ave. (Buena Vista, 17093)

A tiresome and unlikely tale about Irish hoods and good for nothing lowlifes in South Boston, Denis Leary stars as a smalltime car thief in hock to a gangster, played by Colm Meaney. The milieu is identical to Good Will Hunting, except that the heroes have fewer goals and less sense of responsibility. That the film plays exactly like a dozen other Mean Streets imitators is one thing, but the manner in which the characters get away with their crimes—including murder—is totally unconvincing, and the way their 'hip' small talk centers around the movies belies the validity of their working class culture.

The picture is letterboxed with an aspect ratio of about 1.85:1 and no 16:9 enhancement. The settings are deliberately drab, but the picture looks fine, with sharp contrasts and accurate fleshtones. The stereo surround sound and Dolby Digital sound are good, with the Dolby Digital sound, in particular, delivering a strong dimensionality and smooth tones. The 94 minute program can be supported by optional English subtitles.

Moodtapes: Ocean Reflections (Image, ID4404MTDVD)

Shots of sea life and sea mammals cavorting in the surf are intercut with shots of Pacific beaches and waves. The picture is not as vivid as it is in the best Moodtapes programs. The underwater material has a natural grain, but even the easy shots of the shorelines are a bit off-color (they look overly blue) and contrasts are not finely detailed. There is a pleasantly bland stereo music score, combined with occasional surges of location sounds. The program runs 43 minutes.

Moodtapes: Serenity (Image, ID4403MTDVD)

A program that lives up its title, the cuts chosen usually involve water and are particularly peaceful, with a gentle musical score and unhurried environmental images. The picture on the 56 minute program looks okay and the stereo sound is fine, adeptly combining the music with appropriate natural sound effects.

Moodtapes: Whispering Waters (Image, ID4405MTDVD)

Not recommended if you've had a lot of beer and there are no bathrooms around, the 44 minute collection of images of natural running water—springs, waterfalls, etc.—are set to a mild piano score and water sounds. The picture, from a pristine video tape source, is almost too sharp and the colors are vivid. The stereo surround sound is fine. The program is deliberately not chapter encoded, and accessing the Menu function brings up an essay explaining why.

Moonraker (MGM, 906996)

Whites are pure, fleshtones are accurate and the image is smooth. The picture looks glossy and slick. The dual layer DVD presents the 126 minute film in cropped format on one layer and in letterboxed format on the other. The letterboxing has an aspect ratio of about 2.35:1 and an accommodation for enhances 16:9 playback. The cropped image is fairly useless and tends to look a little grainy in darker sequences. The stereo sound has a strong bass and upper range tones are clearly defined. The DVD also has a Dolby Digital track with primitive separation effects that can be enjoyable if you recognize their limitations. The film is available in French in standard stereo and comes with English, French or Spanish subtitles ("M. Bond…vous déjouez toutes mes tentatives de vous tuer de façon amusante"). There is an enjoyable featurette that focuses primarily on the film's Brazil sequence and a theatrical trailer, along with a brief essay about the space shuttle.

We have always found Moonraker to possess a lasting freshness as a home video title. The fight in the precious glass exhibit, the concluding space battle, the opening free-fall fight and the many other elaborate location stunts are gags on a grand scale. The balance between imagination and humor is just right to keep the viewer attentive and in good temper. The narrative has no plot, but it doesn't need one. The itinerary works well enough as a linking device. Roger Moore is James Bond in the 1979 feature. This is the one where they go up in space and battle with laser guns.

Moonstruck (MGM, 906265)

Cher, director Norman Jewison, writer John Patrick Shanley deliver an excellent commentary track. All three give very thoughtful and educational talks on how the movie was made—the process they went through to arrive at their final decisions and how various problems of craft were overcome (to achieve the right comic timing in the film's glorious climactic kitchen scene, Jewison halted filming and spent a day rehearsing the sequence as if it were a play). Jewison has many interesting things to say, not only about how he came to specific decisions on Moonstruck, but about his other work and the meanings of the film's themes. Shanley focuses mostly on the meanings of the story, its inspirations and how it relates to the real world (he suggests that men color their hair to deny death, while women color theirs to embrace life), but he also discusses the shooting process and interacting with the crew. Cher holds her own with the other two, deconstructing her acting process in different scenes and offering her version on how Jewison and Shanley operated. She also takes the time to thank everybody she forgot to thank when she won her 1987 Oscar.

Oddly, the film is presented in full screen format only, losing a little off the sides and adding picture information that was masked from the top and bottom on letterboxed versions. The framing on the letterboxed image is consistently more satisfying than the open full screen image and it is curious that the filmmakers would let themselves be associated with such an artistic indiscretion. The color transfer, however, is a strong. Fleshtones are viable and the image is sharp. The stereo sound is okay, since the stereo mix isn't all that elaborate, the Dolby Digital doesn't have that much more to offer, though its range and solidity are a bit stronger. Accompanied by a theatrical trailer, the 102 minute film is also available in French in standard stereo and comes with English, French or Spanish subtitles ("Cuando la luna ilumina tus ojos/Como una gran pizza/Es amore").

More! Animation Greats (SlingShot, DVD219)

An entertaining collection of ten National Film Board of Canada cartoons, some of the cartoons have appeared before on other DVD anthologies, but others have not. The important thing is that the cartoons fit together quite well, expanding upon or advancing certain themes from one short to the next. The picture quality is consistently good, with bright, appealing colors and a sharp focus. The sound varies between mono and stereo from cartoon to cartoon, but the quality is fine throughout.

Included are *Cactus Song* (a humorous look at the sounds and music of the desert night), *La Salla* (a very weird piece with an operatic score), *64 Million Years Ago* (a terrific look at dinosaurs), *Evolution* (an amusing look at genetic advancement), *Hot Stuff* (an amusing history of fire), *Every Dog's Guide to Home Safety* (a new pet tries to make his master's house safe, to no avail), *The Family That Dwelt Apart* (the best piece, based upon an E.B. White story, about a family living on a remote island in New England), *The Dingles* (about an old woman and her three cats), *The Old Lady's Camping Trip* (about fire safety on camp outings, but done in a style reminiscent of late Thirties cartoons), and *Every Child* (about an abandoned baby being passed from one owner to the next, utilizing creative human voice sound effects).

More Tales of the City (see Armistead Maupin's More Tales of the City)

More Treasures of The Twilight Zone (see Treasures of The Twilight Zone)

The Mormon Tabernacle Choir: Songs of America (Image, ID5573BVDVD)

Classic standards, such as *My Country 'Tis of Thee* and *The Battle Hymn of the Republic*, are intercut with a soft sell for the Mormon Church. Past Choir videos have stuck to singing and have been fairly pleasing, but the interruptions between the songs, no matter how bland or patriotic, are irksome.

It would be nice to hear the choir recorded with a souped-up sound mix, but even the basic PCM stereo track, which is all the DVD has, conveys incredible scope of the choir's voices. The upper end gets scratchy at times and there doesn't seem to be any lower end at all, but the audio is reasonably articulate if the volume isn't raised too high. The picture is soft, although inserts of American landmarks and icons are sharper. Colors look fine and the 41 minute program is not captioned.

Mortal Kombat (New Line, N4310)

Using a narrative that keeps its forward movement but still tries to be true to the arena-style format of the game, the 1995 film scores most of its points with its terrific special effects, particularly those used to enhance the fight sequences. Robin Shou and Christopher Lambert are featured.

Instead of providing background information on the cast, New Line's keeps in the spirit of the movie and provides background information on the fighting contestants. The film is presented in full screen on one side and letterboxed format on the other. The letterboxing has an aspect ratio of about 1.85:1 and no 16:9 enhancement, adding a bit of picture information to the sides and masking off a bit more from the bottom of the image. Viewers may want to sample both, since there are significant aspects to the movie's otherworldly production design that get lost in each format. A trailer accompanies the film and it is also letterboxed on the letterbox side and in full screen on the full screen side. The image transfer is excellent, always maintaining a crisp picture despite the numerous special effects, darkened settings and relatively low budget production values. The Dolby Digital track is quite boisterous, but the standard track is duller. The 101 minute film is in English or French (the Dolby Digital is in English only) and has English, French or Spanish subtitles.

Mortal Kombat: Annihilation (New Line, N4652)

Robin Shou reprises his role from the first film, with James Remar substituting, awkwardly, the role originally filled by Christopher Lambert. Foregoing the tournament premise of the first movie, **Annihilation** is about a group of scheming demons who are plotting to destroy the Earth. To stop them, the heroes function as they might in a video game, visiting interesting locations, facing challenges, and then learning important clues after the challenges have been overcome. The fight scenes are not staged as well as they were in the first movie and are not as exhilarating, but there are plenty of special effects and lots of action to keep undemanding viewers fully attentive.

The image is sharp and colors are bright. The program is presented in letterboxed format on one side, with an aspect ratio of about 1.85:1 and an accommodation for enhanced 16:9 playback, and in full screen format on the other side. The letterboxing adds a bit to the sides and takes a little off the top and more off the bottom in comparison to the full screen framing, and from a compositional viewpoint we tend to prefer the full screen presentation. The stereo surround sound and Dolby Digital sound are energetic, with the Dolby Digital track having greater detail and more thrust. The 98 minute film is also available in French in Dolby Digital and comes with English, French or Spanish subtitles. There is a theatrical trailer, as well, along with as a couple dozen character and set sketches, a few shots of the models used for the more elaborately designed characters and a profile of each character. There is also a direct access to each fight.

Mortal Thoughts (Columbia TriStar, 50749)

Alan Rudolph's film is a basic tale of blue collar murder, superbly directed and acted, and makes for some terrific entertainment. Demi Moore and Glenne Headly star as longtime friends who try to cover up a murder committed in self-defense. The film is told in flashback during a police interrogation and there really isn't much of a story, but Rudolph demonstrates such a masterful command of the medium and the drama that he makes you care very much about each little revelation and plot development. Bruce Willis also appears, giving an outstanding and utterly convincing performance as the deserving victim. The movie was shot in Bayonne, New Jersey.

The color transfer is very good, and the cinematography, by Elliot Davis, is excellent. Our favorite was a shot of the heroine in a car window as she wrestles with her conscience. It is Christmas, and lights are also reflected on the window, creating a parabolic graph in an apt representation of the path her fortunes have taken. The presentation is letterboxed on one side, with an aspect ratio of about 1.85:1 and an accommodation for enhanced 16:9 playback, and is in full screen format on the other side. The stereo surround sound is also admirable, with an above average surround mix on Mark Isham's musical score and an effectively tense atmosphere.

The 104 minute program also has French and Spanish audio tracks, optional English, French and Spanish subtitles and a trailer.

The Most Dangerous Game (Criterion, MOS020)

The 1932 film, which was sort of the **Speed** of its day, was also the original 'rich guy hunts people for fun' story, with Joel McCrea as the dashing, youthful hero, Fay Wray as the spunky heroine and Leslie Banks, in a marvelous performance, as the wicked and self-obsessed villain. The film, produced by Merian C. Cooper and directed by Ernest B. Schoedsack (at the same time the two were making *King Kong*) with Irving Pichel, runs 63 minutes, yet it is brisk without feeling rushed, leaving a viewer fully satisfied and exceptionally entertained by the end.

The black-and-white picture transfer is somewhat worn in spots and has a number of scratches, speckles and blotches. The inconsistency of the source material also promotes some displacement artifacting. The image is fairly sharp most of the time, however, and when it is free of damage it looks quite nice, with finely detailed contrasts and pure blacks. The presentation is also slightly windowboxed. The monophonic sound is a bit tinny and lacks detail at times. The dialogue is clear, but ambience is limited. The program can be supported by optional English subtitles.

There is also a very good commentary track by commentary track veteran Bruce Eder, who is very adept at drawing the listener through the film and its illustrious personnel.

Most Wanted (New Line, N4635)

Keenen Ivory Wayans wrote and stars in the entertaining action film with a reasonably complicated plot. Wayans is a former commando who is set up as the patsy in an assassination. He escapes, beats every attempt to eliminate him, and stays a step ahead of the bad guys as he tries to figure out what has happened and clear his name. It is consistently enjoyable, with the right mix of narrative and stunts, and Wayans has designed his character to fit his skills effectively, while the other performers, including Jon Voight, Paul Sorvino, Eric Roberts and Robert Culp, are big enough stars to coast on their personalities. Jill Hennessy is also featured.

The film is in letterboxed format on one side, with an aspect ratio of about 2.35:1 and an accommodation for enhanced 16:9 playback, and in full screen format on the other side. The letterboxing adds some picture information to the sides and takes some off the top and bottom in comparison to the full screen presentation, but we prefer the letterbox framing, which seems to deliver both the action and the drama more effectively. The picture is sharp with well-defined hues. The stereo surround sound is fine and the Dolby Digital track has lots of great action movie-type effects. The 99 minute film comes with an overbearing theatrical trailer. It is also available in French in standard stereo and comes with English, French or Spanish subtitles ("Je suis un marine. Je ne pense pas. J'improvise"). The film's musical score has also been isolated on one of the channels, in standard stereo. There is a cast profile and filmography section.

Motel Blue X-rated (Vivid, UPC#0073214581)

A motel worker sees the darker side of life during the course of her day. The narrative is simple but effective and the erotic sequences are well staged. Colors are light and fleshtones are bland, with washy contrasts and mild grain in places. The sound is adequate. The 72 minute program features Kobe Tai, Jamie Lee, Timbee, Lexi Leigh, Jacklyn Lick and Deva Station. The DVD contains alternate angle sequences and elaborate hardcore interactive promotional features.

Mother (Image, ID4579CODVD)

Indulgently melodramatic and turgid, the narrative is about a working woman who becomes politicized when her son is arrested. Directed by Vsevolod Pudovkin, the 1926 film could almost play as a parody of Sergei Eisenstein's work if it were not so constantly dour. Others, however, find the familial and communal emotions and the undeniably superb editing to be sufficient for the film's canonization.

The windowboxed picture appears to be slightly improved over the LD, with a slightly sharper focus and deeper blacks, though the wear marks appear to be the same. The stereo sound and Dolby Digital sound both have background noise that does not occur on the LD's audio track. The white Russian intertitles sometimes obscure the white English subtitles offered as translation.

Mother's Boys (Buena Vista, 16450)

A distasteful thriller that feels like some writer's revenge against an ex-wife, it is a cross between *Kramer vs. Kramer* and *Fatal Attraction*. Jamie Lee Curtis stars as a psychopathic absentee mother who returns to the scene just as her husband, Peter Gallagher, is about to divorce and remarry. The plot has a number of dangling turns and sort of lurches from one contrived tension to the next until it is all wrapped up with a convenient cliff-dropping conclusion. The picture is in letterboxed format only, with an aspect ratio of about 1.85:1 and no 16:9 enhancement. The color transfer looks okay, with reasonably bright hues and accurate fleshtones, though darker sequences are a little soft. The stereo surround sound is passable and the 96 minute program has optional English subtitles.

Mouse Hunt (DreamWorks, 84159)

Nathan Lane and Lee Evans star as two brothers who become obsessed with exterminating a single mouse while they try to restore a mansion in preparation for its sale. Not only does the movie evoke the classic slapstick premises of Laurel and Hardy and the Three Stooges, it also draws from cartoons such as Tom and Jerry, bringing just enough surrealism to the proceedings to maintain an 'anything goes' atmosphere. It is a wonderfully imaginative effort. The camera dives in and out of the building's recesses in an often startling manner, moving effortlessly from the mouse's world to the human world. Lane and Evans are terrific, generating plenty of humor in their pratfalls while playing up the shortcomings (and ever so tiny hints of goodness) in their characters. The production design is exceptional, at times invoking **Brazil**, and through the whole movie, in scene after scene, shot after shot and gag after gag, the mouse looks utterly real.

The film is presented on one side in letterboxed format, with an aspect ratio of about 1.85:1 and an accommodation for enhanced 16:9 playback, and in full screen format on the other side (we found the framing on the letterboxed image to be preferable). The picture looks super, with crisp, vivid hues and intricately detailed contrasts. The stereo surround sound, and, especially, the Dolby Digital sound are outstanding, full of playful directional effects and a solid range of dimensional noise and music. The 98 minute film is also available in Spanish and French, and can be supported by English or Spanish subtitles. There is a cute theatrical teaser, a less effective trailer, a cast & crew profile section (the director, Gore Verbinski, did the first Budweiser frog commercials), and some production notes, along with 12 minutes of deleted scenes. The deleted sequences (scored with temp music from **Amarcord**) would have slowed the pace of the film and deserved to have been removed, but there are still a number of amusing gags that make the scenes worth having.

Moving Target Simitar, 7462)

Michael Dudikoff is a bounty hunter for a bail bondsman who gets caught in a power struggle between Russian mobsters. The script is reasonably good and Dudikoff is a dependable presence, but the film's budget is a bit too low and the action scenes aren't thoroughly covered, giving the movie's most important sequences a ragged and somewhat inept feel. Billy Dee Williams has a supporting part in the 1996 program.

Presented in full screen format only, fleshtones are bland and colors are dull. The Ultra-Stereo surround sound is adequate. The 89 minute program is not captioned.

Mozart / Rossini (Image, ID5087GCDVD)

After rather generic performances of Wolfgang Mozart's *Concerto No. 3*, *Symphony No. 29* and *Symphony No. 40* by the Picardy Sinfonietta Orchestra under Patrick Fournillier, there is a surprisingly engaging conclusion with Gioacchino Rossini's *Il Signor Bruschino Overture*. Staged in the St. Michel De Cuxa Abbey, the 71 minute program seems somewhat run-of-the-mill until it is enlivened by the Rossini piece.

The picture looks okay, though it is not as vivid as other concerts of this nature have been. Fleshtones are bland and contrasts are a bit underdeveloped. The PCM stereo sound is reasonably strong, though dimensionality is limited. There are essays about the Mozart pieces and some of the performers on the jacket, but they are printed in a black-on-dark-purple that is almost impossible to read.

Mozart: The Requiem from Sarajevo (Image, ID4191ANDVD)

A 52 minute concert performance of Wolfgang Mozart's *Requiem* is held in the crumbled remains of a Sarajevo church. Zubin Mehta conducts the Sarajevo Philharmonic and a local choir, joined by José Carreras and Ruggero Raimondi. As the performance unfolds, the images cut away from the performers for archival inserts of the surreal-looking warfare taking place in and around the city. The video coverage of the concert is no better than fair, often cutting to the wrong angle at the wrong time, and the shots of the rubble surrounding the performers is distracting, but the juxtaposition of the concert and the newsreel footage works extremely well and gets its message across loud and clear.

The hall's acoustics tend to dissipate sound and the performance is not on par with recordings from better known and more accomplished musical groups. Raimondi is excellent, but Carreras is stiff and tentative. Nevertheless, the program derives its strength from its ideas and the musical presentation is of sufficient quality to support the concept. The quality of the recording aside, the stereo delivery seems fully adequate and the image quality is fine.

Mozart's Così Fan Tutti: Teatro Alla Scala (Image, ID4358PUDVD)

Daniela Dessi, Delores Ziegler, Jozef Kundlak, Alessandro Corbelli, Adelina Scarabelli and Claudio Desderi are featured in what is essentially a six-character opera, with the La Scala sets striking an ideal proportional balance and stimulating decor. The singing never stops the show, but it is consistently competent, and the cast is at their best when they are performing in unison.

The video direction is okay, though once in a while there is a close up where we'd have preferred seeing more characters. The picture is a little soft but workable and the colors look fine. The stereo sound has a limited range and ambiance, but the balance between the orchestra and the singing is well handled. The program, in dual-layer format, runs 185 minutes and is in Italian with English subtitles.

Mozart's Don Giovanni: Teatro Alla Scala (Image, ID4356PUDVD)

Well, all you old fogies out there may remember how many 78 RPM record platters it took to hold Wolfgang Mozart's **Don Giovanni**? Now, not just the music, but the opera itself is available on a single-sided dual-layer DVD. You have to admit, because of the work's legacy, that there is something impressive about holding the platter in the palm of your hand.

The 1989 La Scala production is fairly workman-like. The sets are a little austere but functional. The video direction follows the drama effectively. The singing is good, but the stereo sound is very center-oriented and somewhat dull, making the production seem a little blander than it probably is. Riccardo Muti conducts with Thomas Allen, Edita Gruberova, Ann Murray and Francisco Araiza. The mildly aged picture is a little soft and bright hues are a bit subdued, but fleshtones are accurate and the presentation is workable.

The 176 minute program is in Italian with permanent English subtitles.

Mr. Ace (Image, ID5373FWDVD)

George Raft portrays a political boss who falls in love with a female gubernatorial candidate, played by Sylvia Sydney, even though she's promising to clean up his machine. It is doubtful any actor could bring the material across with believability, but Raft often seems uncomfortable and distracted. The film is weird enough that some may find it interesting (sexism is rampant, though in character; and the politics are so simplified that a candidate drops out of the race, goes to Nevada for a divorce, comes back to run as an "Independent," and wins), but its deficiencies are readily apparent.

The black-and-white source material has a number of worn sections, but the image is sharp and contrasts look nice, with deep blacks and bright whites. The monophonic sound is adequate and the 83 minute program is not captioned. There are filmographies for Raft and Sidney, as well.

Mr. Baseball (GoodTimes, 0581036)

The basic contrivance is embarrassing, but there are enough funny one liners to make the film, starring Tom Selleck as a slumping major leaguer who is signed up on a Japanese pro team, a tolerable sports comedy. The film's second half is stronger than the first, when Selleck's character finally lets go of his stupidity and begins to pay attention to those around him, and there is enough baseball to please fans of the genre.

The picture is letterboxed with an aspect ratio of about 2.35:1 and no 16:9 enhancement. The image is crisp and hues are accurate. The stereo surround sound is fine. The 108 minute program also has French and Spanish audio tracks, and optional English, French and Spanish subtitles.

Mr. Bean (see The Best Bits of Mr. Bean)

Mr. Magoo (Buena Vista, 14255)

Saddled with a pathetically low jokes-to-footage ratio, the 1997 comedy is a sad disappointment. The potential for a witty slapstick is present, with Leslie Nielsen embodying the elderly myopic cartoon character in a basic but normally serviceable jewel heist narrative. Yet almost nothing funny happens. There are more gags in a seven minute Magoo cartoon than in all the movie, and you sit there waiting patiently for each joke to occur. Additionally, the story's twists and turns rarely make sense, so an intense sense of embarrassed inadequacy soon envelops the production.

The image is letterboxed with an aspect ratio of about 1.85:1 and no 16:9 enhancement. The stereo surround sound and Dolby Digital sound have sharp tones and a few energetic separation effects. The 88 minute film can be supported by English or Spanish subtitles and is accompanied by a theatrical trailer.

Mr. Mumble (import, CPDVD701001)

An engaging comedy action thriller, the hero, played by Michael Chow, is a randy ex-cop, reminiscent of a Japanese cartoon hero. He is incompetent and a dolt when it comes to women, but when bad guys appear he is suddenly agile and unstoppable. The humor is juvenile and a little tiresome, but the action scenes are great and the story, in which he protects a gangster's daughter from a rival gang, is satisfying. The menu commands are all in Chinese, but the film spins up and starts playing without a hassle and is presented in Mandarin or Cantonese with Chinese and English subtitles that appear on the image and cannot be removed. The presentation is letterboxed with an aspect ratio of about 1.85:1 and no 16:9 enhancement. The color transfer looks very nice. Once in a while a shot looks a little soft, but when the cinematography is sharp, which is most of the time, the picture looks super. Colors are bright and glossy, and fleshtones look accurate. The stereo surround sound is also very good—much better than the average

Hong Kong production—and the quality of the image and sound add much to the entertainment. The program runs 96 minutes.

Mr. Nice Guy (New Line, N4662)

One great chase, fight or stunt sequence follows another in the enjoyable 1996 Jackie Chan romp. Directed by Samo Hung, there is just enough plot, about bad guys after a videotape Chan's character has accidentally acquired, to keep things moving (it may have a few extra trims here and there). The action scenes are consistently inventive, cleverly integrating the props in different settings, such as a construction site and a shopping mall, with the logic of the fight or the chase. Richard Norton is well cast as the bad guy, making a decent competitor for Chan in the final showdown.

You can see how much cropping harms the action scene, since the film is presented in both formats, letterboxed on one side with an aspect ratio of about 2.35:1 and an accommodation for enhanced 16:9 playback, and in cropped format on the other side. Because of the film's comic book action, the cropped version is not entirely a waste, and its bam-bam-bam closeups can be enjoyable, but in the heat of the action, things get confusing and you miss some great stunts and reaction shots, left out because there isn't room on the screen to include them.

The picture quality looks terrific, with bright, crisp hues and accurate fleshtones. Unlike some of the Chan films, it doesn't seem that the stereo surround sound has been re-mixed. There are a lot of basic, action movie noises, particularly on the better detailed Dolby Digital track, but even the audio effects are secondary to the surprises of imagination and design in the stunts. The 87 minute film is also available in French in Dolby Digital and can be supported by English, French or Spanish subtitles. There is a trailer and a profile of Chan, with trailers for several of his New Line films.

Mr. Saturday Night (PolyGram, 4400582092)

Billy Crystal spends most of the 1992 movie in old age makeup, and it isn't very convincing old age makeup so there is little wonder that the film, a kind of warmed over variation on *The Sunshine Boys*, was not successful. Crystal is an aging comedian with a propensity for self-destruction at key moments in his career. Here and there he scores a funny joke, but the film can be taxing unless a viewer is fully prepared for its frustrations.

The picture is presented in full screen format only and is somewhat bland. The stereo surround sound is effective, particularly when the comic is backed by a stage band. The 119 minute program has optional English and French subtitles, and a trailer.

Mr. Wong, Detective (see **Mr. Wong Collection**)

Mr. Wong in Chinatown (see **Mr. Wong Collection**)

Mr. Wong Collection (Roan, AED2008)

Boris Karloff portrays the very tall oriental detective, Mr. Wong, in the six Monogram films, *Mr. Wong, Detective* from 1938, *The Mystery of Mr. Wong* from 1939, *Mr. Wong in Chinatown* from 1939, *The Fatal Hour* from 1940, *Doomed to Die* from 1940 and *Phantom of Chinatown* from 1940, the latter actually starring Keye Luke and not Karloff. The mysteries are all impeccably logical and move briskly. Karloff seems utterly incongruous with those around him, but his voice is soothing and the narratives are strong enough to accommodate his almost whimsical presence. If you are a murder mystery aficionado, then you should have no more than a little trouble spotting the least likely suspect in each film, but the stories are suitably complicated and the atmosphere is often highly engaging.

On all the films, there are good looking reels and weaker reels. At their best, the black-and-white images are reasonably clean and relatively sharp. At other times, speckles, grain or softness are more prevalent, but the condition of the source material rarely detracts from the entertainment. We detected a mild displacement artifacting only rarely. The monophonic sound is a little scratchy, but coherent, though we usually had to raise the volume on each movie. The collection is not captioned. Each platter in the two-platter set holds three films.

Two significant character help Wong and bicker with one another in most of the films, Marjorie Reynolds, who plays a gung ho reporter, and Grant Withers, as an earnest but unimaginative detective. In essence, the films play like a good TV series. In the 69 minute *Mr. Wong, Detective*, the victims are murdered in locked rooms with the police often right outside the door. In the 68 minute *Mystery of Mr. Wong*, the victim is murdered for real while performing a skit in which another person 'pretends' to shoot him. In the 68 minute *Mr. Wong in Chinatown*, the victim is murdered in Wong's own parlor, via a poison dart. In the 68 minute *Fatal Hour*, the murderer goes so far out of his way to avoid suspicion that you spot him immediately. A police detective investigating a smuggling operation is murdered, and the cops call in Wong to help them find the killer. A shipping magnate is murdered in *Doomed to Die* while the son of a rival, who wants to marry his daughter, is in the office with him (he's refusing the request) and two more witnesses are outside, yet the son is a nice guy and can't possibly be the one who pulled the trigger. Wong helps to clear him.

Following the series format, the villain in the 62 minute *Phantom of Chinatown* is the least likely suspect, but since there are no other suspects, he is a lot easier to spot. The film is a bit sloppier than the Karloff efforts (and, curiously, Luke's character and Withers' character don't know one another at the start), but there are enough moments of arched eyebrow excitement to satisfy fans.

Mrs. Brown (Buena Vista, 17251)

The 1997 feature is a fascinating but modest look at the latter half of the reign of Queen Victoria, and in particular an exploration of her relationship with the servant who pulled her out of her grief after her husband died. The manners and protocols of the court, as well as the intrigues, are consistently interesting, and the performances, by Judi Dench and Billy Connolly (and Antony Sher as Disraeli), are thorough and often inspired. The narrative, however, is constrained by historical events and is relatively dry, particularly in the film's second half when the two no longer interact as much.

The picture is letterboxed, with an aspect ratio of about 1.85:1 and no 16:9 enhancement. The picture has an unusual number of stray speckles and the image is soft in places, but the colors look fine. The stereo surround sound is lively at first, but then relaxes and becomes less involving. The 105 minute program can be supported by optional English subtitles. There is also a trailer.

MTV Party to Go: Volume 1 (Pioneer, PA98581D)

A 50 minute collection of dance-oriented music videos, the eleven cuts include numbers by Hammer, Paula Abdul, Vanilla Ice, Depeche Mode, Tony! Toni! Tone!, Suzanne Vega and others. The videos often contain abstract images, but are non-narrative and tend to focus on the performer acting either as a dj/rapper or a dancer. The image quality varies slightly from one cut to the next, but colors are always bright and the image is reasonably sharp except during passages of conceptual softness or grain. The stereo surround sound has plenty of bass and the Dolby Digital track has even more energy and separation detail. There is no captioning.

MTV Party to Go: Volume 2 (Pioneer, PA98583D)

We like the selection of songs better than **Volume 1**. It is more consistent in tone, and the music videos accompanying the numbers are generally more stimulating. Included in the collection are Endgame's *Sadness Part 1*, P.M Dawn's *Set Adrift on Memory Bliss*, Jazzy Jeff & The Fresh Prince (read: Will Smith) doing *Summertime*, Naughty by Nature's *O.P.P.*, Another Bad Creation's *Playground*, Boyz II Men's *Motownphilly*, Color Me Badd's *All 4 Love*, Salt-N-Pepa's *Let's Talk about Sex*, C+C Music Factory's *Here We Go Let's Rock & Roll*, Heavy D. & The Boyz's *Now That We Found*

Love, Marky Mark's *Good Vibrations* (hey, we didn't say the collection was perfect), and The KLF's *3 AM Eternal*. The picture quality looks decent on all the clips. The stereo surround sound is okay, and the Dolby Digital track is terrific, with crisper tones, a stronger bass and more distinctive separations. The collection runs 48 minutes and is not captioned.

MTV's Beavis and Butt-Head: The Final Judgement
(Sony, LVD49658)

The collection of seven cartoons and runs 42 minutes, not 50 as is claimed on the jacket cover. The cartoons do not follow a general narrative arc, but they are among the most amusing in the series, including *Scared Straight*, in which the pair visit a penitentiary and find they have a lot in common with the criminals staying there, *No Laughing*, in which the pair are forbidden to laugh during a sex education class and *Manners Suck*, in which the pair flabbergast a guest speaker talking about manners at their school. Other episodes include *The Final Judgement*, in which Beavis apparently dies and goes to heaven, *Liar! Liar!* in which the pair have to take a polygraph test, *The Great Cornholio* in which Beavis wanders around the school crazy after eating too much sugar, and *They're Coming to Take Me Away, Huh, Huh, Huh*, in which the two give the school's new psychologist a real challenge to her skills. The picture quality is fine, with bright sharp colors, and the animation is so limited that video artifacting is unlikely. The stereo surround sound is also energetic and reasonably pumped. There is no captioning.

Much Ado About Nothing (Columbia TriStar, 71759)

Kenneth Branagh's delightful 1993 William Shakespeare adaptation is presented in cropped format on one side and fully letterboxed on the other side. The cropped version is a waste of time, because the rhythm of the images is spoiled by the cramped picture. The letterboxing has an aspect ratio of about 1.85:1 with an accommodation for enhanced 16:9 playback, adding picture information to the sides of the image and losing nothing from the top and bottom. The color transfer has deep, bright hues and very little grain in the shadows. The stereo surround sound is reasonably nice. The jacket chapter guide is a drag, however, consisting of generic one and two-word identifiers in the place of quotations. The 111 minute film is also available in Spanish (a somewhat muted track) and French, and comes with English, French or Spanish subtitles ("Si son haleine était aussi terrible que ses mots, on la fuirait sans cesse!"). There is also a playful theatrical trailer.

Branagh, Emma Thompson, Denzel Washington, Keanu Reeves, Michael Keaton (who is terrific) and others star in the romantic comedy, which was shot in Tuscany. Branagh is able to encapsulate the entire 400 year decline of the King's English in four words, by having Reeves say, "The most exquisite Claudio." Nevertheless, Branagh uses the language of film to make every line of dialogue a joyful treat.

Muddy Waters Live at the Chicago Blues Festival
(Pioneer, PA98589D)

Waters mostly sits on a stool and plays about a dozen similar-sounding numbers in the hour-long concert, but you can't stop your foot from tapping along with him from the beginning to the end. The color changes radically during the course of the program, slipping during one sequence into black and white for a few minutes and going overly yellow elsewhere, but when the camera is adjusted correctly the hues look accurate. The picture is slightly soft, but tolerable. Vocals are a little crisper on the Dolby Digital track, but the Dolby Digital and the standard stereo track sound basically the same and are rather soft overall, with limited separation effects.

Multiplicity (Columbia TriStar, 82449)

A lackluster science fiction comedy about a man who quadruples himself, the letterboxing, which has an aspect ratio of about 2.35:1 and an accommodation for enhanced 16:9 playback, is es-

sential, because the duplication effects that allow the star, Michael Keaton, to appear four times in one shot use up the entire rectangular screen. The color transfer is excellent, and the effects are seamless. There is also a cropped version, on the other side, but has less to offer.

The 1996 film, unfortunately, takes little advantage of its technical accomplishments. It is never more than mildly humorous and often just marks time working itself through the situations created by the premise. Keaton gives each of his bodies a different personality, with the plot presenting him as a harried father, who uses the duplication to spend more time with both his job and his family.

The stereo surround sound is adequate, though the film's sound mix isn't all that interesting. The 117 minute program also has French and Spanish language tracks, optional English, Spanish and French subtitles, and a trailer.

The Munsters' Revenge (GoodTimes, 0581025)

Not the feature film from the late Sixties but a Universal made-for-TV movie from 1981, it stars Fred Gwynne, Al Lewis and Yvonne DeCarlo, with Sid Caesar as the 'villain,' who creates wax museum robot look-alikes of the heroes to commit robberies. The 96 minute movie has the bland, watchable efficiency that hallmark factory TV productions, though the robots also make a pleasing homage to other Universal horror characters.

The picture looks fine. The cinematography is dull but the transfer is adequate. Darker sequences are a bit soft and there is a mild grain here and there, but the colors are generally well defined. The monophonic sound is okay and the film can be supported by English, French or Spanish subtitles.

Murder (see Alfred Hitchcock Collection)

Murder at 1600 (Warner, 14915)

Wesley Snipes is a homicide detective being manipulated by White House advisors and Diane Lane is a Secret Service agent who assists him. Alan Alda and Dennis Miller are also featured. The 1996 film can be fun if you just kind of go with it, but if you start asking too many questions you'll spoil things. The pacing is good and the ending, believable or not, is exciting. The death of one of the aforementioned stars at the end, incidentally, is highly satisfying—a marvelous payback not only for this movie but for a few others he's been in as well.

The image is smooth, even in the darker scenes. The colors are also strong and fleshtones are deep. The movie is presented in letterboxed format on one side of the DVD and in full screen format on the other side. The letterboxing has an aspect ratio of about 1.85:1 and an accommodation for enhanced 16:9 playback, masking picture information off the top and bottom, and adding a little to the sides in comparison to the full screen picture. The standard stereo surround soundtrack is uninspiring. The Dolby Digital track, however, provides a satisfying delivery of the film's sound effects and music. The 108 minute program is also available in French and comes with English, French or Spanish subtitles. There is a passable cast profile section, a few production notes and an interesting theatrical trailer that contains footage which appears to have been shot specifically for it.

Music for Montserrat (Image, ID4559ERDVD)

It helps when you're devastated by an exploding volcano if you are a vacation resort frequented by rock stars, because then they'll be more likely to do a benefit concert for you. At least, that is the motivation behind the 112 minute all-star concert program staged and emceed by George Martin and featuring Phil Collins, Jimmy Buffett, Mark Knopfler, Sting, Elton John, Eric Clapton, Paul McCartney and Carl Perkins. Shot in September 1997 at the Royal Albert Hall in London, the stage performances aren't flashy—even John is dressed conservatively—but the music sounds super. The performers are miked clearly and their vocals are distinctive. Mc-

Cartney plays several Beatles numbers, and everybody fawns over Perkins.

It also helps that the program was expertly recorded. The Dolby Digital channel that has substantially more power than the analog channel. The singing is well defined and the instruments have plenty of energy, while in comparison, the standard stereo track sounds rather reserved, although vocals are still clear. The stage is well lit and the picture looks fine.

The Music Man (Warner, 16768)

Robert Preston portrays a con artist who sells musical instruments and uniforms, but not lessons, to gullible communities. The score contains many memorable numbers, the setting is idyllic Americana and the cast is irretrievably wonderful. The picture is letterboxed with an aspect ratio of about 2.38:1, although there is a bit of picture information on the sides that is still missing. Fleshtones are a little pale, but other hues are reasonably bright, contrasts are sharp and the detail on the image is exhilarating, magnifying decorations and textures to the point where it takes longer to mentally absorb every cut. The Dolby Digital track has a wide dimensionality and brings a rousing sweep to almost all of the film's musical numbers. Some of the ambiance is a little muted, and the standard stereo track is more subdued, but the energy in the grandest moments is exhilarating. With the sound and the picture in such good condition, it is difficult not to be as swept up by the film as the townspeople are by the hero's enthusiasm.

The 151 minute feature can be supported by English or French subtitles ("Vous avez un problème/Ici à River City/Avec un P majuscul/Rimant avec B pour Billard…"). The volume on the music cue over the Main Menu is set too high and is rather annoying. There is a modest cast & crew profile section and some production notes. A half hour retrospective documentary about the film has also been included. It tells the full history of the Broadway musical and the movie, with reminiscences from Shirley Jones (who became pregnant while shooting the 1962 feature), Buddy Hackett, choreographer Onna White and others. The piece is an enjoyable overview of the film's production, with rare behind-the-scenes and newsreel footage, poignant memories and valuable insights.

MusikLaden (see The Best of MusikLaden Live: America; The Best of MusikLaden Live: Volume 1; The Best of MusikLaden: T-Rex / Roxy Music)

My Best Friend's Wedding (Columbia TriStar, 82729)

What an utterly perfect movie **My Best Friend's Wedding** is! It is almost like a benign *Richard III*, with Julia Roberts' character—supposedly the heroine and the center of the story—serving as a walking metaphor of the tensions and doubts that would normally inhabit what otherwise looks like a flawless engagement between the characters of Dermot Mulroney and Cameron Diaz. The film is remarkably fresh in its angle and approach to heroism—or heroine-ism, rather—and it is a freshness that will endure because of the wonderful performances by the three leads and the brilliant direction by P.J. Hogan. When directors succumb to using the widescreen format in a comedy or romance it is often an error, a delusion of artistry that sacrifices a genuine emotional point-of-view for the sake of grandiose self-importance. The widescreen angles in **My Best Friend's Wedding**, however, are consistent in working the dynamics of the characters and placing especially Roberts' character in uncertain surroundings. The picture is letterboxed on one side, with an aspect ratio of about 2.35:1 and an accommodation for enhanced 16:9 playback, and in cropped format on the other side, although the only thing the cropping is good for is gooey close-ups of the stars. The color transfer is excellent, with consistently accurate fleshtones and a crisp focus. There isn't much to a stereo surround audio mix in a film such as this and the standard track and Dolby Digital track are competent but unremarkable. The film is also available in Spanish and French in standard

stereo and can be supported by English or Spanish subtitles. The 105 minute program is effectively closed captioned.

My Blue Heaven (Warner, 12003)

Directed by Herbert Ross, the 1990 film is awkwardly staged and mostly unsatisfying. Martin portrays an Italian mobster in a witness protection program who retains his wiseguy dress and manners despite his incongruous surroundings. It sounds funny on paper, but in practice Martin's exaggerated performance just doesn't click, and while there is a trailer's worth of humor in the premise, there is not a feature's worth.

The picture is presented in full screen format. Conceptually, the film's color scheme has many bright, basic colors, and these look quite nice. The picture is sharp, but fleshtones are overly pinkish in places. The stereo surround sound is quite nice. The 96 minute program has an alternate French audio track and English closed captioning.

My Dinner with Andre (Fox Lorber, FLV5043)

Louis Malle's delightful 1962 exercise, in which Wallace Shawn and Andre Gregory sit in a restaurant and talk for 110 minutes or so about all sorts of slightly crazy things, was shot in 16mm and is very grainy, with slightly yellowish colors. Even with the inherent crispness of the DVD format, the image is somewhat fuzzy in places and hues are inconsistent, though that tends to be how the film has looked since its inception. The monophonic sound is adequate and there are filmographies for the director and the two stars. The chapter guide is keyed to the food being served instead of to the conversation. The film is a clever and innovative sketch of two people whose careers have caused them to over-examine life and become trapped in an endless number of mental paradoxes.

My Fair Lady (Warner, 16668)

The colors are stunning. The Ascot scene looks like 3-D television, and the details of Higgins' study are so clear you can see every little decorative squiggle. Whether it is soft pastel flowers, grimy ditches or the Embassy Ball and all those fancy gowns, the colors remain vivid and exact in shot after shot, gripping your eyes and holding them to the screen so completely you wouldn't mind if every song went on for a dozen extra choruses. The image is glorious.

The 173 minute feature is presented in single-sided dual-layer format, with the layer shift occurring at the Intermission point. The DVD is letterboxed, with an aspect ratio of about 2.4:1 and an accommodation for enhanced 16:9 playback, adding a touch of picture information to the sides in comparison to the LD. We can't get as excited about the stereo surround sound and Dolby Digital sound as we are about the picture. The sound has been remixed, retaining some separation effects, although it is nothing like today's audio mixes. There is an occasional flaw that sends dialogue haphazardly to the rear channel as well as the front, and if you have any sort of delay set on your rear channel, a momentary echo is created. The distortion doesn't spoil the presentation, it just ruffles your attention for a few moments before a colorful costume or object grabs it again. The problem is not as pronounced on the standard stereo surround soundtrack. Although there are passages where the enhanced definition of the Dolby Digital track is a distinct improvement, much of the time the differences between the Dolby Digital track and the standard track are limited. The film is also available in French in mono and can be supported by English or French subtitling ("Massacre et tison d'enfer! Je suis accoutumé à sa frimousse").

The DVD has several supplemental features. There is an original 8 minute 'making of' featurette, produced in 1964 when the film was made, that contains terrific behind-the-scenes footage of the extras getting makeup and costumes. Two songs that were recorded by Audrey Hepburn, before her vocals were replaced by Marni Nixon's, are included, *Wouldn't It Be Lovely* and *Show Me*. In the same way that Broadway cast recordings of well-known musicals are inevitably better than their motion picture counterparts, so too is Hepburn's singing better than Nixon's dubbing, at least on *Wouldn't It Be Lovely*. Hepburn's singing isn't as slick, but she brings more performance and life to the number than the over-produced and homogenized voicing that Nixon provides. Hepburn's rendition of *Show Me*—one of the best songs in the score—is a disaster, but who is to say that with a little more coaching she couldn't have improved upon it?

Robert Harris and James Katz, who organized the film's restoration, provide a commentary track with art director Gene Allen and inserted reminiscences by Nixon. Nixon's comments are intelligent and insightful, as she speaks of Hepburn's gracious friendship, of how much her uncredited role in making the film has helped her career, and of how she approached her task (she had to match Hepburn's acting intentions). She also has a great story about the creation of *I Could Have Danced All Night*.

The Harris, Katz and Allen talk is full of anecdotes and terrific technical detail. They don't try to be comprehensive in their discussion of the film's creation and execution, but what they do have to say is fascinating, about how the sets were designed, about George Cukor and Jack Warner's working methods, about the lighting and the cinematography and what it took to retrieve the picture from a battered, poorly stored negative. They discuss the politics of restoration (with some unacknowledged irony) and share a few intriguing anecdotes (a minor actor died halfway through his role), though at least one story gets censored. Mostly, they are as excited about the picture quality as a first-time viewer might be ("The color of the port is perfect," proclaims Harris enthusiastically as Rex Harrison raises a glass) and the pride they feel at having rescued an important motion picture is obviously secondary to the plain joy they feel soaking up its images.

One final word about Rex Harrison's performance. There are many different types of acting. Harrison had the advantage of playing his role extensively on stage and then bringing it to the screen in a production that attempted to be as faithful to the stage version as possible. The result is outstanding. Every syllable he utters is deliberately and carefully enunciated for the greatest effect. The creators of the stage musical essentially doubled the age of George Bernard Shaw's original Henry Higgins, and the romantic dynamic could have been disastrously embarrassing. Harrison's delivery, however, goes beyond the 'speak/sing' of his musical numbers. His every word and his every movement is a song, and he radiates such a comical harmony that you accept his character's presumptions, no matter how irritating they might be to those around him.

My Favorite Brunette (Madacy, DVD99024)

The 1947 black-and-white Bob Hope comedy has light contrasts and mildly blurry details. Overall, the DVD is watchable if you don't mind some wear. The two-channel monophonic sound is strong but noisy. Hope stars with Dorothy Lamour and Peter Lorre in the 89 minute comedy, about a baby photographer mistakenly hired as a private detective. The plot is coherent but irrelevant, providing just enough of a path for Hope to deliver his comedy, which he does with great finesse.

My Fellow Americans (Warner, 14535)

Jack Lemmon and James Garner portray two ex-presidents on the lam together after being targeted for an assassination by a government agency. The film is a comedy about celebrity, but it takes a few shots at politics and also attempts to capitalize on the **Grumpy Old Men** formula. The casting seems ideal, but the film is just a little too farfetched to work, even for its genre. Parts of it are funny and a couple parts are quite funny, but there are blatant gaps in the narrative and a lot of fooling around that some viewers may not have the patience for.

The stereo surround sound and Dolby Digital sound are passable. The 101 minute program is not letterboxed, losing a bit on the sides of the image compared to the LD, but adding more to the top and bottom. It is the sort of movie where the framing is not all

that critical, however. The colors are strong and the image is sharp. There is a bit more video artifacting than normal, particularly in the film's second half. Along with the cast profile and brief production notes, a theatrical trailer and a four minute blooper reel are included. The 1997 film also comes in French and Spanish (the French is in standard stereo and the Spanish is monophonic) and has English, French or Spanish subtitles.

My Giant (Warner, C2535)

Billy Crystal stars as a talent agent who tries to cash in on an extra-tall Eastern European he meets during a film shoot. The movie has limited humor, a flattened pace and a contrived dramatic structure, but it does have a predictable pathos that some viewers will find comforting.

The 1998 feature is in letterboxed format on one side, with an aspect ratio of about 1.85:1 and an accommodation for enhanced 16:9 playback, and in full screen format on the other side. The letterboxing masks picture information off the top and bottom of the screen in comparison to the full screen image and adds nothing to the sides. Hues are bright and fleshtones are accurate. The stereo surround sound has an uninteresting mix and is not all that different from the Dolby Digital track. The film can be supported by English or French subtitles and is accompanied by some production notes (explaining how Crystal recruited NBA star Gheorghe Muresan—there isn't a single mention in the production notes of the once promising director, Michael Lehmann, though he is included in the cast & crew profile) and a theatrical trailer that extracts every humorous line of dialogue the film has.

My Girl (Columbia TriStar, 50999)

A lot of psychological babble was written about Macaulay Culkin's character dying in the 1991 feature, but not one commentator mentioned what is probably the most disturbing sequence in the film, the bee attack that causes his death. The film is about a pre-adolescent girl living with her father in his funeral parlor. It is played as a light romance (the father gets a girlfriend) set against Serious Lessons About Life. The film retains enough humor to carry a viewer through the dramatics, but it lacks a constituency. Culkin's role is actually a supporting one (cut down further, it seems, by the brevity of the shots in which he is included). The film stars Dan Aykroyd and Jamie Lee Curtis, with Anna Chlumsky giving a relaxed and confident performance as the heroine.

The picture is presented in full screen format and the color transfer is acceptable. The stereo surround soundtrack is also adequate, although the hit-oriented music score is not delivered with much intensity. The 102 minute feature also has a French audio track in stereo, a Spanish track in mono, optional English, French or Spanish subtitles and a trailer.

My Left Foot (HBO, 90373)

Daniel Day-Lewis won an Oscar for his convincing portrayal of an Irish artist who had to overcome poverty and severe cerebral palsy. Based upon a true story, it is told in flashback, conveniently skipping over transitions, but it remains fascinating throughout.

The picture is presented in full screen format only. The color quality is reasonably good, though much of the film is by design dank and cluttered. The monophonic sound is adequate, although the LD was in stereo. The 103 minute feature has optional English, French and Spanish subtitles, which can help viewers "cheat," since the subtitling spells out dialogue that is often (deliberately, for dramatic purposes) incomprehensible when voiced by the speech-impaired hero.

My Life to Live (Vivre sa vie) (Fox Lorber, FLV5035)

Like *Irma La Douce*, Jean-Luc Godard's 1962 **Vivre Sa Vie** had more of an impact when the world of prostitution was still an exotic and mostly unexplored cinematic territory. There are intellectual discussions about love and other stimulating dialogue, there is Michel Legrand's carefully applied balm of a musical score, and there are the images and the editorial rhythm, an experiment in technique that will never age or spoil. The foundation for all this, however, has crumbled a little. The narrative, about a record store clerk played by Anna Karina, backed into prostitution by economic necessity, is approached with a bit too much of a wide-eyed adolescent lust, and portions of the film are an outright tease. Godard was once seen as depicting free-spirited, independent-minded heroines who were forthright with their sexuality and willful in their search for selfhood, even when circumstance held them back. Because of the many cinematic tricks he employed, however, 'Godard the author' is a virtual character in every film he made, and from this perspective his heroines remain totally dominated by his own will and his whims, exploited to act out his male fantasies. It is in **Vivre Sa Vie** that this aspect of Godard's work is especially clear because of its subject matter and the relative simplicity of the narrative compared to his later works.

The black-and-white picture is a little worn in places, but generally looks good, with clear contrasts, smooth blacks, crisp lines and source material that is free of significant damage. The monophonic sound is a bit soft, but is in reasonably good condition. The 85 minute program is in French with optional English subtitles and filmographies for Godard and Karina.

My Man Godfrey (Madacy, DVD99022)

William Powell and Carole Lombard star in the wonderful 1936 screwball comedy about an unemployed bum who is hired by an heiress to be her butler. The last act is awkwardly structured, but the narrative is witty and the dialogue delivery is stunningly quick, making today's features—even today's fast-talking features—seem like they're being performed in molasses.

One or two reels in the 96 minute film have weak contrasts, losing texture details on faces and objects, but for the most part the source material is comparable to the prints we used to see in revival houses. The image is soft and there is evidence of wear, but the presentation is viable and the flaws are rarely distracting. The dialogue seems a little out of synch in places, but the monophonic sound is adequate for the film's age. The film is accompanied by some minor textual supplementary features.

My Night at Maud's (Fox Lorber, FLV5007)

Eric Rohmer's 1969 feature is one of his best. Jean-Louis Trintignant portrays a young engineer who spends an evening and night in chaste conversation with a divorcée, and meets the girl of his dreams, a student, the next day. By the end of the film the viewer recognizes that the girl and the divorcée know one another. The bulk of the film is taken up by one dinner party, and the conversation is achingly intelligent (how come when we go to dinner parties we end up talking about movies and kids—nobody ever brings up Pascal) and yet very real (the characters repeat themselves when they have somebody new to talk to). **My Night at Maud's** is delicately atmospheric (most of the action takes place during a snowbound Christmas holiday) and is subversively pro-Catholic (the two heroes, who are Catholic, are happy and secure at the end; everyone else isn't), but it is, ultimately, about the characters themselves, not their morals or beliefs, and the film's own moral—good conversation and polite behavior can win you the love of your life—is heartening.

The film is presented in full screen format (cropping is minimal or non-existent). It is in black and white and is mildly grainy, with soft contrasts and some minor damage around the reel-change points. The monophonic sound is workable. The film is in French and is supported by white English subtitles, which can dominate the screen during the heaviest conversations. Although the jacket cover lists the running time as 110 minutes, it actually clocks in at 105, which is the running time listed in reference books. There is a Rohmer filmography and a Trintignant filmography.

My Science Project (Buena Vista, DV10824)

A convoluted and pandering 1985 teen sci-fi adventure, many of the actors are clearly older than the high school kids they are playing. A few rejects uncover an alien device and set it off. The device eats up the local electricity and then creates a kind of time/space warp where figures from the past intermingle with the present. They shoot a dinosaur and have a few other fights, but it all looks like it is taking place on a soundstage and none of it makes much sense.

The 1985 feature is presented in letterboxed format on one side, with an aspect ratio of about 2.35:1 and no 16:9 enhancement, and in cropped format on the other side. Cropping tends to make things even more confusing. Colors are a little bland, but fleshtones are okay. The blown-up cropped image, however, looks much softer. There is a modest stereo surround soundtrack, and the 95 minute program is not captioned.

My Secret Life X-rated (Vivid, UPC#0073215599)

A wealthy woman laments the things she's sacrificed for her security and acts promiscuously to soothe her ennui. The picture is sharp, with strong colors and accurate fleshtones, and the erotic sequences are energetic. The sound is okay. The 68 minute program features Jenteal, Mila, Sindee Coxx, and Roxanne Hall.

My Sergei (Panasonic, PDV0024)

A cross between a documentary and a TV movie of the week, the film tells the story of Russian figure skaters Sergei Grinkov and Ekaterina Gordeeva, who danced together since childhood and got married after they became old enough to discover sex. They had a child, but Grinkov died of a heart condition at 28. The film features extensive clips from the pair's competition routines, giving the viewer an opportunity not only to enjoy their skating, which eventually earned an Olympic Gold Medal, but to watch them improve over time. There are no 'dramatic' sequences, but the story of their romance is told in voiceover, with home movies, interviews, photos and some discreet visual re-enactments. The story is touching, and the skating footage is appealing.

The picture quality varies but the contemporary interview sequences are sharp and colors are strong. The skating clips are all reasonably sharp. The clips are monophonic, but some of the narration's background music has a slight dimensionality. The program is not time encoded but appears to run about 90 minutes.

My Stepmother Is An Alien (Columbia TriStar, 61029)

Dan Aykroyd portrays a SETI scientist who attracts the ministrations of a bumbling but svelte alien, somewhat daringly portrayed by Kim Basinger. Much of the comedy falls flat and none of the special effects are interesting.

The picture is presented on one side in letterboxed format, with an aspect ratio of about 1.85:1 and an accommodation for enhanced 16:9 playback, and in full screen format on the other side. The picture quality on the disc varies, but the colors often look a little washed out and a number of scenes appear grainy. The sound is in stereo, but the separations are limited and unimaginative. The 108 minute program also has Spanish and French audio tracks, optional English, French and Spanish subtitles, and a trailer.

My Teacher's Wife (Trimark, VM6911D)

Tia Carrere is top-billed in the well-made romantic comedy about a high school senior who has an affair with the wife of his math instructor. An example of the film's refined sensibilities: The hero likes to draw cartoons for a hobby, and there are brief sequences in the film where the cartoons become animated to reflect the hero's emotional state—and the animation was done by Bill Plympton. The humor is character driven and although many of the characters are teenagers, the film tends to avoid juvenile antics. There are some clichés, particularly in the hero's relationship with his parents, but the film is consistently refreshing and pleasantly amusing, as concerned with the dynamics of friendship as it is with the dynamics of love.

The image is presented in full screen format, but the framing usually seems well balanced. Colors are bright and the image is smooth, with accurate fleshtones. The stereo surround soundtrack has an uninteresting mix and is functional but unremarkable. The 89 minute program has optional English, French and Spanish subtitles. There is also a red tag theatrical trailer, although neither the movie nor the trailer displays or suggests any activity that could be considered exceptionally risqué.

Mysteries of Egypt (SlingShot, DVD9839)

The National Geographic IMAX program begins with an Egyptian grandfather telling his granddaughter about the glories of Egypt's past. It seems like a lame start, until the camera reveals that the grandfather is being played by none other than Omar Sharif, bringing the entire film a sudden air of glamour. The show looks at Egyptian ruins, speculates upon ancient Egyptian life and includes reenactments of the building of the pyramids and of the discovery of King Tut's tomb. There is also the more typical IMAX sequence, flying across the source of the Nile. The 40 minute program jumps around a lot, but it provides a decent sampling of Egypt's past glories and their remains.

The picture looks fine. The show's musical score tries very hard to evoke mystery and grandeur of its subject, but it never quite seems to break free. The stereo surround sound and Dolby Digital sound have plenty of flourish but no really involving directional effects. There are alternate French, Spanish and German language tracks, all in Dolby Digital, and optional English subtitles. A good 18 minute 'making of' featurette, which concentrates on the sequences depicting ancient Egypt, is also included.

Mystery of the Maya (SlingShot, DVD9803)

There is one terrific aerial view of Mayan ruins in the middle of the jungle (didn't they use that shot in *Star Wars*?) but much of the 40 minute IMAX program is uninteresting, visually, and there is about ten minutes of worthwhile information concerning the Mayan civilization (their arithmetic skills are given good coverage) mixed in with a much blander overview of the research being conducted upon the civilization's remains. The picture looks fine, but balances on the Dolby Digital soundtrack seem a little off—the narration is sometimes overwhelmed by the music, and environmental effects are so pronounced they sometimes seem parodistic—so we preferred the standard stereo surround soundtrack. The film is also available in French, Spanish and Mandarin in Dolby Digital, and has not been closed captioned or time encoded.

The Mystery of Mr. Wong (see **Mr. Wong Collection**)

Mystery Science Theater 3000: The Movie (see **This Island Earth**)

N

Naked City (Image, ID5746MKDVD)

As in "There are eight million stories in the naked city. This has been one of them." Jules Dassin directed the engaging 1947 film, which was the first to be shot entirely on location in New York City, establishing a subgenre that has flourished to this day both in theatrical films and on TV. The movie was produced by Mark Hellinger who, in an unusual format, also provides an extensive voiceover narration. Barry Fitzgerald, in a marvelous, earthy performance, stars with Don Taylor as detectives investigating the murder of a young model. Howard Duff is the principal suspect.

The film is a pure procedural, sipping its drama from vignettes in the lives of the people the cops meet during the course of their investigation. Like most groundbreaking films, it establishes what

are now a great many clichés, but like most groundbreaking films, it also does them better. In the final chase, for instance, the villain is getting away when he makes a very stupid mistake that allows the cops to zero in on him. It is something that had to be done for the sake of the story, and in most movies it is a painfully obvious device, but in this one, Hellinger, in the narration, anticipates the villain's error and warns him not to do it. The dumb villain, unable to hear the voice of the cinema god, does it anyway, and the viewer recognizes that, if he hadn't made a mistake here, the villain would have made a different one soon enough.

The black-and-white source material is in reasonably good condition. There is some heavy speckling around a few reel change points and less obtrusive scratches and speckles elsewhere, more often present than not. The contrasts are adequately detailed. The monophonic sound is okay and the 96 minute program is not captioned.

Naked Desert X-rated (Vivid, UPC#0073214545)

A mysterious woman in a light blue negligee wanders around the desert appearing when people are in need or distracted in other ways and then disappearing after a sensual interlude. The plot never amounts to much and the erotic sequences are fairly standard, but the performers are attractive and the genuine, somewhere-to-the-east-of-Lancaster locations create a fresh ambiance. Since most of it is shot in the bright, unhindered sun, the image is sharp and colors are fresh. The stereo sound is passable. Anna Malle, Kylie Ireland and Sandi Beach are featured in the 72 minute program. The DVD contains alternate angle sequences and elaborate hardcore interactive promotional features.

Naked Kiss (Criterion, NAK020)

Samuel Fuller's gnarly drama is about a nurse's aide who tries to overcome her sordid past, but finds that the men she meets in upper crust society are just as perverse, if not more so, than the men she knew before. In the same way that some people chuckle when they are confronted by a life-threatening situation, Fuller combines comedy and drama in his thrillers. It isn't there for relief, it is there to intensify a viewer's nervousness. Part of the film's dialogue uses some unrealistically exaggerated euphemisms, but the plot concerns some very real and base adult emotions. Fuller forces a viewer to surrender to his films by removing all the outside reference points. In other words, you give up criticizing or resisting the entertainment and just start going along for the ride, very early on.

The black-and-white image is super crisp, with vivid contrasts and deep blacks, and the source material is free of damage. The film is letterboxed with an aspect ratio of about 1.75:1 and no 16:9 enhancement. The monophonic sound is cleaner but bland. There is a Dolby Digital mono track, however, that bring a little more color to the dulled tones on the standard track, but there is still a tradeoff on the high end to get rid of the noise. The 1964 program is not captioned and comes with a theatrical trailer. The more one has been exposed to standard cinematic narrative, the more one will appreciate and enjoy Fuller's sometimes radical approach. Hence, the more DVDs you have in your collection, the more this one belongs with them.

Naked on the Beach (Simitar, 7333)

The same ten models appear in two video programs that have been combined on one DVD. In one video program, they cavort upon the beach in skimpy bathing suits, and in the other, the suits are gone. Both, however, contain the same interview sequences, which alternate with the modeling poses. Each segment has a multiple angle function, usually with one shot set a little closer than the other. Additionally, there is a brief 'behind the scenes' segment for the nude program, which essentially shows another camera angle over the shoulder of the primary cameraman, and a 'bloopers' segment for the bathing suit program that isn't all that funny but is the only instance in the 145 minute collection where the models let their guard down and act like real people. The picture quality is passable, with reasonably bright colors and accurate fleshtones. The stereo sound is adequate.

Nanook of the North (Criterion, CC15490)

Robert Flaherty's classic silent 1922 documentary feature was a breakthrough work that brought the concept of non-fiction narrative film reporting into the public consciousness, substantially expanding the recognized potential and capabilities the motion picture medium had for recording aspects of man's existence and other scientific topics. It was so well made that it still works today. While some of the shots are redundant and the pacing is a little slow, the sequences depicting the construction of the igloo or the hunting of the walruses are not just fascinating, they remain fascinating in multiple viewings.

The black-and-white picture is in very nice condition. None of the shots are obscured by age and details are always fairly clear. The image is somewhat soft and looks a little erratic, but it is well preserved and overt damage is minimal. The picture is windowboxed and the program is accompanied by a workable stereophonic chamber music score that is best kept at a modest volume. The film runs 79 minutes and is accompanied by an interesting 8 minute interview with Flaherty's widow, shot in the Fifties, and a still photo section that contains National Geographic-style pictures from Flaherty's northern excursions, as well as photos from the **Nanook** shoot. The portraits are particularly fascinating, as one tends to look at their antiquity and suppose that they represent ethnic characteristics less interfered with by European influences than more recent photos would convey.

Narrow Margin (Artisan, 60484)

Gene Hackman portrays a cop transporting a witness, played by Anne Archer, cross country to testify, with the bad guys hot on their trail in Peter Hyams' highly entertaining thriller. Much of the 1990 film is set on a train. The story has some terrific twists—which the trailer included on the DVD deftly avoids revealing—and lots of hold-your-breath action sequences.

The letterboxing has an aspect ratio of about 2.25:1, with an accommodation for enhanced 16:9 playback, but the LD has a full 2.35:1 aspect ratio and a little more picture information on the sides. The color transfer on the DVD, however, is greatly improved. The image remains a little soft, but hues and fleshtones are much more accurate and the image is a lot less hazy. The stereo surround sound is a little softer than the LD, but is adequate, with atmospheric surround effects and a decent amount of energy during the action sequences. The 99 minute feature is also available in French and can be supported by English closed captioning or Spanish subtitles. There are some good production notes and a cast & crew profile section.

NASA / 25 Years: Triumph and Tragedies (DVD9900
NASA / 25 Years: Volume 1 (Madacy, DVD990011)
NASA / 25 Years : Volume 2 (Madacy, DVD990012)
NASA / 25 Years: Volume 3 (Madacy, DVD990013)
NASA / 25 Years: Volume 4 (Madacy, DVD990014)
NASA / 25 Years: Volume 5 (Madacy, DVD990015)

A number of original NASA documentaries have been compiled on the box set release and are also available as individual volumes. The older the documentaries, the more faded and hazy they are, and the sound is a bit fuzzy, too, particularly when it involves radio transmissions of astronaut voices. Since the documentaries were produced by NASA they have particular limitations and strengths. They are, for the most part, 'selling' America's space program and are, in a way, extended government commercials. But the footage is often fascinating and, as time recedes, the arcane information and images included with the details that contemporary documentaries cannot be bothered with are fascinating. All of the programs are accompanied by brief 'mission summaries,' astronaut biographies and space vehicle profiles. Only **Volume 1** is time encoded,

and the chapter guide function on the programs is pretty useless. There is no captioning.

Volume 1 opens with a hoot, a very badly scripted documentary about Alan Shepard's initial pop fly flight into space, *Freedom 7*. It is written in the second person, a format that works for a moment or two but becomes rather ridiculous by the end of the show. The other three documentaries have a more standard construction. *Voyage of Friendship 7* is about John Glenn's flight, *Four Days in Gemini* is about the first American 'walk' in space during the Gemini 4 mission and *This Is Houston Flight* is about the first docking test, conducted by Gemini 8. Each of the films run about 25 minutes. The DVD also features brief clips of *Things to Come* and *Trip to the Moon*.

Volume 2 covers the moon landings. *The Eagle Has Landed* is a familiar piece, going over the first moon landing by Apollo 11. Until Ron Howard made the hit film, the story of Apollo 13 was not as well known, but *Houston, We've Got a Problem* is an effectively constructed program that takes the viewer through the tense hours of makeshift fixes and manipulations that brought the crew home. The last two documentaries cover the less well remembered moon landings, *Apollo 15 (In the Mountains of the Moon)* and *Apollo 16 - Nothing So Hidden*. A clip of John F. Kennedy's speech about America's commitment to space exploration is also included.

The final moon mission is covered in *On the Shoulders of Giants - Apollo 17*, on **Volume 3**, followed by the less well known and hence fairly interesting *Mission of Apollo-Soyuz* (which is so drained of color it appears black and white), and two programs about the Skylab, *Skylab The First 40 Days* and *Four Rooms, Earth View*. A 'launch montage' film clip is also included.

Four Space Shuttle missions from the early Eighties are detailed on the four documentaries in **Volume 4**. The first two, *Opening New Frontiers* and *We Deliver*, have generalized narration, while the second two, *Launch and Retrieval of Satellites*, and *Satellite Repairs*, fall into a common pattern, using press conference narration by the astronauts to accompany and explain the images. The launch and retrieval of satellites was a primary goal in each of the missions, but other zero-gravity experiments are also discussed, as are some occasional off duty hijinks. The colors, finally, improve. A film clip of an Apollo launch reaching space (and not, as the jacket claims, a montage of Soviet space flights) is also included.

Everything you could want to know about the Challenger disaster is contained in *Challenger - Disaster and Investigation* on **Volume 5**. While some viewers may look upon the material as being a bit morbid, its unflinching thoroughness is gratifying. The section has two parts. The first is a largely unedited half hour depiction of the events leading up to the liftoff and the subsequent explosion. The second part, which also runs a half hour, is an analysis of why the craft's fuel tank exploded, with the evidence carefully but briskly detailed. The companion documentary, *NASA, The 25th Year*, is compiled in part from excerpts of the other documentaries, but provides a fairly decent overview of the space race and NASA's accomplishments (including a segment on NASA's non-space aeronautical developments). At least the colors are stronger. Contrary to a jacket notation, the short film clip is not of the Challenger, but is instead a flying saucer montage from *Plan 9 from Outer Space*.

National Lampoon's Animal House (Universal, 20158)
National Lampoon's Animal House: Collector's Edition (Universal, 20396)

Fleshtones are overly pinkish or even purplish at times on the standard release, and the image is somewhat dark, losing details in mild shadows. The 1978 film is presented in full screen format. The picture is sharp and colors look solid, but the presentation is not as nice as other releases have been. The monophonic sound is adequate and the 109 minute film can be supported by English, French or Spanish subtitles. There are some decent production notes, a cast profile section and an enjoyable trailer that features an alternate (clothed) shot of the Peeping Tom scene.

Where the standard version was presented in full screen format, the **Collector's Edition** is letterboxed with an aspect ratio of about 1.85:1 and an accommodation for enhanced 16:9 playback. The letterboxing, however, masks picture information not only off the top and bottom of the image, but a smidgen off the side as well in comparison to the full screen version. The color transfer on the **Collector's Edition** is a significant improvement over the earlier version, though it still has a way to go to reach the standards set by the best looking DVD presentations. Whites are purer, fleshtones are much more accurate and other hues are better defined. The image is also somewhat sharper, but the picture on the **Collector's Edition** is very dark, and there is a lot more detail on the brightly lit older version, even if it is improperly colored.

The monophonic sound is equal in quality to the monophonic sound on the standard release. The 109 minute feature is accompanied by a very good 45 minute retrospective documentary that discusses the film's conception (a happy accident), the many diverse talents who were brought together to shoot the film and the life-imitates-art experiences of the cast during the shoot. The high-point is an incredible (and unfortunately edited, it should have been allowed to play straight through) sequence of goofing around footage where director John Landis throws out emotional states and John Belushi achieves them with his facial expressions, one after another after another. There is a trailer, some production notes and a cast-and-director profile section. The film is also available in French and Spanish, and can be supported by English, French or Spanish subtitles ("'Les légumes peuvent être très sensuels, vous ne croyez pas?' 'Non, ce ne sont pas les légumes. Ce sont les gens qui sont sensuels'").

The movie remains a masterpiece of frantic, comical inspiration. It captured a generic phenomena which no movie had ever truly grasped before—macho comedy. Belushi is more the film's mascot than its star, and it is the slick repartee between Tim Matheson and Peter Reigert that enables the gross antics of Belushi and the many other comics to slide past your defenses.

National Lampoon's Christmas Vacation (Warner, 11889)

The holiday comedy is presented in full screen format only, though it is doubtful that much, or anything, is lost without letter-boxing. Fleshtones are a little pinkish, but generally the color transfer looks fine, with deep hues and sharp detail. The stereo surround sound is not elaborate, but adequate. The 97 minute film is also available in French and Spanish and comes with English, French or Spanish subtitles ("Un poco de aqua de árbol no le hara mal"). There is a healthy cast and crew profile section, some minor but mildly amusing production notes, and trailers for the four **Vacation** films. The 1989 production, directed by Jeremiah Chechik (this is the one where Juliette Lewis is one of the kids), can be relied upon to generate sufficient laughs if it is put up once every holiday season or so.

National Lampoon's Vacation (Warner, 11315)

The 1983 road comedy is reasonably amusing, with inspired supporting performances by Randy Quaid, Imogene Coca, Beverly D'Angelo and others, and a dependable if stilted lead performance by Chevy Chase. Not everyone will find the film's anxiety or slap-stick to their liking, however. The whole movie goes downhill after a wonderful opening credit montage of old travel postcards, but it goes slowly enough that hopping on for the ride can be tempting if one is in a dumb sort of mood. The picture is presented in full screen format. The image looks a little aged in places, but is usually bright, with accurate fleshtones and solid backgrounds. The monophonic sound is a bit weak and can be supported by English, French or Spanish subtitles ("Le chien a pissé dessus"). The 99 minute film is accompanied by an extensive cast profile section, some production notes and a brief theatrical trailer.

The National Parks (Simitar, 7220)

The 1989 production plays like a film made 30 to 40 years earlier. A good old fashioned travelogue, the 75 minute program visits 14 of the best known parks, sharing arcane information—the piece on Arcadia is dominated by a segment on lobster fishing—and trying its best to be scenic and lighthearted. There is no concentrated effort to describe the parks. There are no maps, no summaries of interest points and no histories, just anecdotal commentary and a look at whatever the filmmaker, Doug Jones, got a good shot of. As a reference tool, it is a bit useless, but if you've just been to one of the parks or are a travelogue junkie, the program will be pleasing. The monophonic sound has what seems like a 40 year old musical score, but the audio is tolerable. The picture quality varies from shot to shot and the source material has a few speckles, but generally the colors are passable. There is more pronounced digital arti-facting than usual, particularly during a river rafting sequence where the image freezes on a systematic basis.

National Velvet (MGM, 906618)

Elizabeth Taylor and Mickey Rooney star in the 1944 feature, about a girl who disguises herself as a male jockey to run her horse in a big race, with an equal amount of dramatic time given over to the quaint Irish town where she and her family live. Although the movie, which is always fun, belongs to Taylor and Rooney, it was Anne Revere, as Taylor's mother, who was justly awarded with an Oscar for her role. Her performance, as a former swimming star who has settled into the quiet life of a small town, is amazingly thorough and touching. Those with a sense of humor, however, might want to watch the film in tandem with **Who's Afraid of Virginia Woolf?** to see how the dreams of childhood can turn into the nightmares of adulthood.

The colors are deep and crisp, fleshtones are accurate and textures are vivid. The monophonic sound is okay and the Dolby Digital mono track is stronger and more detailed. The 125 minute film is also available in French and comes with English, French or Spanish subtitling.

Naturescapes (Simitar, 7223)

Cute little animals scamper about scenic vistas for 45 minutes as peaceful piano music plays in stereo. Although we thought we saw the same shot of a beaver swimming across a pond more than a couple times, the footage does present a nice variety of nature views, most, apparently, from the Rocky Mountains. The picture quality is passable, with accurate colors and a fairly sharp focus. The sound is fine except one moment where, on the copy we viewed at least, there was a really bad blast of audio noise. We'd like to tell you the location, but the DVD is not time encoded.

Navy SEALs (Image, ID40790RDVD)

The commando movie has a decent collection of action scenes and is reasonably entertaining. Charlie Sheen and Michael Biehn star. The film's budget allowed the producers to assist in the urban renewal of a couple Spanish cities (subbing for the Middle East), and the high-tech weaponry is cool (the heroes have a 'heat scope' that can see through concrete).

The letterboxing, which looks cramped on the top and bottom, has an aspect ratio of about 1.9:1 and no 16:9 enhancement. The picture is crisp and smooth, with viable colors, pure blacks and decent fleshtones. The stereo surround sound offers a few choice explosions, though it is not a first class mix. The 113 minute program is captioned.

The Negotiator (Warner, 16750)

A terrific movie, with a fine, meaty role for Samuel L. Jackson, playing a cop who holds several people hostage in an investigator's office while he tries to figure out why he's being framed. Kevin Spacey, as the cop brought in to talk him down, has the sort of role he usually shines in, appearing well into the film in a position of snappy authority, but he doesn't seem to be giving it his all. He's okay, and the movie is consistently entertaining, but someone with a more dynamic presence in his role could have energized the drama even more.

The picture is letterboxed with an aspect ratio of about 2.35:1 and an accommodation for enhanced 16:9 playback. Set in Chicago, the film has a kind of cluttered, urban look to it and the cinematography tends to be functional, but the image transfer looks fine, with accurate fleshtones, solid hues and a sharp focus. The stereo surround sound is okay and the Dolby Digital soundtrack is highly satisfying, with many separation effects contributing to the excitement. The 140 minute film is also available in French in Dolby Digital and can be supported by English or French subtitles. Along with the standard cast & crew profiles, production essays and trailers, there are two featurettes, one 7 minute piece featuring an interview with a genuine LAPD negotiator and one 16 minute segment about utilizing the film's locations.

Neil Diamond: Greatest Hits Live (Sony, CVD49014)

Shot in the moderate sized Aquarius Theatre in Los Angeles that seems to have more stage than audience, the production is well lit, so Diamond is always in sharp focus and fleshtones are rich. He performs more than a dozen numbers—his best known hits, plus the *Carry That Weight* Beatles medley—and while it may be rote for him, he acts energetically and the crowd that is squeezed into the hall responds enthusiastically (well, at least the women do—there are some shots of male audience members standing, pretending to clap their hands and looking rather perplexed).

The menu-activated Dolby Digital track is interesting. It definitely has more power and a stronger sense of presence than the standard stereo surround soundtrack, but Diamond's vocals are routed to the rear channel with a determination that goes well beyond the mild bleed on the regular stereo surround soundtrack. Unless you are sitting up close, you have to raise your center channel substantially or dampen the surround channels to prevent it from sounding like he's singing behind you. The recording is fairly vivid, however, so it is worth the effort. The hour long program, which includes a music video, *This Time*, after the concert is concluded, can be supported by English subtitles.

Neil Simon's The Odd Couple II (Paramount, 335787)

Most of the film has the two heroes, played by Walter Matthau and Jack Lemmon, continually delayed and re-routed as they attempt to get from an airport to a wedding. Simon's writing and his ability to pump out one-liners are amazing, and infectious—as we underwent interruptions while watching the movie, we found ourselves trying to answer innocent questions with the same sort of snappy returns Simon gives his characters. The structure of the narrative will drive many viewers batty, since it is predicated on the heroes not going anywhere, and the basic old age jokes can also be tiresome, but there are so many gags about so many things that it is hard not to laugh or chuckle at least a few times during the course of the movie, and for some viewers that will be enough to justify the entertainment.

The picture is letterboxed with an aspect ratio of about 2.35:1 and no 16:9 enhancement. The image is sharp, with deep colors, and overall, the picture looks terrific. The standard stereo surround soundtrack is weak, but the Dolby Digital track is stronger, with better dimensionality. The film's audio track isn't elaborate, but there is better detail to the Dolby track and a slightly richer atmosphere. The 97 minute film is also available in French in standard stereo and comes with English or Spanish subtitles ("¿Siempre que tienese que meter un cadáver en un auto?"), as well as a joke-filled trailer.

Neil, Vince (see Janine & Vince Neil: Hardcore & Uncensored)

Nemesis (Sterling, 4000)

An action film that pays attention to the superficial trappings of the cyberpunk milieu, the futuristic narrative is composed mostly of chase sequences, but there is enough plot to give the film more class than most of its ilk. Oliver Gruner is the hero, at first searching for rebels who are bent on sabotaging the establishment, and then joining the rebels when the establishment is overtaken by human machines. Tim Thomerson is also entertaining, as the principal villain. The 95 minute program has a number of spectacular stunt sequences, fast moving cyber dialogue, and many explosions. It is also just philosophical enough to make the action intellectually valid.

The presentation is in full screen format. Fleshtones are a little bland and pinkish, but the picture transfer is generally commendable. The stereo surround sound lacks subtlety, but is reasonably energetic. The 92 minute program also has French and Spanish audio tracks, captioning, production notes, a trailer, TV commercials and a 'making of' featurette, containing interviews with many of the filmmakers as well as looks at several major stunts.

The Net (Columbia TriStar, 11619)

Sandra Bullock rather unbelievably portrays a freelance computer troubleshooter who has no friends or acquaintances she can turn to in the real world when she stumbles into a deadly, billion-dollar on-line extortion scheme. The 1995 film is farfetched and rarely convincing, but it is exciting and fun, and you have to concentrate to follow all of the computer stuff, which is also gratifying to some degree. The privacy issues it explores are also worth contemplating.

The picture is presented on one side in letterboxed format, with an aspect ratio of about 1.85:1 and an accommodation for enhanced 16:9 playback, and in full screen format on the other side. The letterbox framing looks fine, never interfering with the computer screen displays. The picture transfer is good and colors are accurate, though once in a while a shot looks a bit soft. The stereo surround sound is okay and the Dolby Digital sound is sharper. The 114 minute feature also has French and Spanish language soundtracks in standard stereo, along with optional Spanish and Korean subtitles, and English closed captioning.

Network (MGM, 906720)

The first hour or so is a perfect pitch replication of a corporation in action, and afterwards, as the satire gets heavier and heavier, the film has that foundation to support it. It also helps that the cast is so rich, including Oscar winners Peter Finch, Faye Dunaway and Beatrice Straight (who won with just two scenes), along with one of William Holden's final and most memorable appearances. The film's advertising said that television would never be the same and that has turned out to be true as the 1976 Sidney Lumet movie firmly implanted itself in the public consciousness.

Fleshtones look pale, other colors are faded and darker scenes look murky. The 121 minute film is presented in letterboxed format on one side, with an aspect ratio of about 1.85:1 and an accommodation for 16:9 enhanced playback, and in full screen format on the other. The letterboxing adds no picture information to the sides of the image and masks off picture information from the top and the bottom in comparison to the full screen image. Since the film is about TV, the full screen framing works a little better. The monophonic sound is bland. The film is accompanied by a theatrical trailer and comes with English, French or Spanish subtitles ("'Je suis fou de rage et j'en ai marre de tout ça!'").

New Fist of Fury (Simitar, 7260)

Jackie Chan stars in the 1976 feature directed by Lo Wei. Set during the Japanese occupation of Taiwan, the good guys' kung fu school is taken over, and a pretty girl teaches the hero how to fight, so he can win it back. The cropped image is reasonably sharp and colors are fair, with bland fleshtones. The monophonic sound has a fairly high volume, which is best kept to a low amplification, and is often shrill or otherwise mildly distorted. The 118 minute film is awkwardly dubbed in English on one channel and presented in the original Cantonese on another, without subtitles. It is accompanied by a brief interview with Chan, as well as a Chan profile and filmography.

New Jack City (Warner, 12073)

The engrossing, nuevo-styled depiction of dedicated cops breaking up a drug empire is super, as thick in character and activity as a crowded disco. It has such a fresh point-of-view that the clichés—the drug kingpin becoming sloppy after he makes it to the top, the cops stretching the law to pin him down, the women not doing much of anything—are well-camouflaged and not damaging. Even the film's more simplistic pronouncements, particularly the blame it lays on Republicans for somehow having caused the drug problem, are presented so zestfully they do not upset the film's pulsating rhythm. Wesley Snipes portrays a drug lord and Ice T is the undercover cop out to bring him down. Mario Van Peebles, Chris Rock and Judd Nelson are also featured.

The 1991 feature is letterboxed on one side, with an aspect ratio of about 1.8:1 and an accommodation for enhanced 16:9 playback, and in full screen format on the other side. The letterboxing adds a bit of picture information to the side of the image and masks off picture information from the bottom and the top in comparison to the full screen release. The picture is sharp, with bright, glossy hues and accurate fleshtones. The stereo surround sound is so aggressive that the remastered Dolby Digital track doesn't really add much. The 101 minute film is also available in French in standard stereo and comes with optional English or French subtitles. There is a cast & crew profile section, some decent production notes and a theatrical trailer.

New Year's Concert Vienna 1987: Johann Strauss (Father and Son) Josef Strauss (Sony, SVD45985)

The 98-minute *Herbert von Karajan His Legacy for Home Video* concert, of music by the Strauss family, contains one highlight after another, and Karajan, though he is weak and has to support himself at times, becomes so relaxed and enthusiastic that by the end he is conducting the audience, which is clapping in rhythm to the *Radetzky March*. Karajan achieves an admirable precision on most of the numbers, and even casual viewers will be able to discern the superiority of the orchestra's performance to the standard generic recordings of the best known waltzes. During the concert, video presentations of the Spanish Riding School in Vienna and the Ballet of the Vienna State Opera were projected in the hall and replace the view of the musicians as the orchestra accompanies the images. The ballet choreography, by Gerlinde Dill, is unremarkable, but it is designed for video and is thus quite effective. The highpoint of the concert, however, is the appearance of Kathleen Battle, who sings *Voices of Spring*. Her performance is outstanding and sobers one's appreciation of the undeniably festive endeavor.

Hues are accurate, and although there is a mild softness in some shots, the picture quality is generally nice. The stereo sound is bright and nicely detailed, and there is a Dolby Digital track with even better detail and energy. The program is accompanied by background notes and the Karajan profile.

Next of Kin (Warner, 670)

It's always interesting to come across an older film in which all the supporting performers have since superseded the star in fame and fortune. Patrick Swayze stars as a hillbilly Chicago cop investigating the mobsters who shot his brother, and the cast includes Bill Paxton, Helen Hunt, Liam Neeson, Ben Stiller, Adam Baldwin, and Ted Levine. The only performer whose star appears to be permanently eclipsed by Swayze is Michael J. Pollard. Anyway, the film is

a typical action crime concoction, competently directed by John Irvin, and the cast has given it an unexpected lease on mortality.

The color transfer looks fine in the bright sunlight and no more than mildly subdued in darker sequences, though fleshtones are a bit bland. The full screen image is crisp and the framing is workable. The 109 minute program is closed captioned with minor paraphrasing.

Niagara: Miracles, Myths and Magic (SlingShot, DVD9840)

A history of human interaction with the Falls is told in the IMAX documentary, presenting reenactments of various incidents where people have fallen over the falls and that sort of thing. The producers do a good job in maintaining the period settings and still including the Falls in their shots. There is also enough variety to sustain the 41 minute running time and plenty of long pans over the churning and dropping water.

The picture is terrifically crisp and detailed. The Dolby Digital 5.1 sound is also fun, with strong surround effects and clear, forceful tones. There are additional audio tracks in French (Canadian), German, Japanese, Mandarin and Korean, as well as English subtitles. A music and effects track is included, and there is a 19 minute 'making of' documentary. The documentary uses a lot of footage from the program, but there are a few interesting 'behind the scenes' sequences, including a shot of a cameraman on a crane way, way, way out over the falls—that's for those of you who thought you wanted to become cinematographers.

The Nice, The Naughty & The Bad X-rated (Vivid, UPC#0073215549)

You gotta give points to whoever came up with the title. The narrative is also inspired, a viable adaptation of *Captain's Paradise*, about an advertising executive who has two wives, each ending up desiring the sort of life the other has. There are a couple other interesting subplots, as well, with a good twist at the end. Colors look drained and fleshtones are light. Some of the dialogue is distorted and difficult to make out, and the stereo sound is generally bland. The 75 minute program stars Jeanna Fine, Chassey Lain and Jill Kelly. The DVD contains alternate angle sequences and elaborate hardcore interactive promotional features.

Nico Icon (Fox Lorber, FLV5012)

A fascinating and highly enjoyable documentary about the German fashion model, Christa Paffgen, who became a pre-New Wave pop singer and led a classic Eurotrash life (she was in *La Dolce Vita*, she had Alain Delon's baby, she hung out with Andy Warhol and Jim Morrison). Her music was ahead of its time—kind of a Nina Hagen in molasses—and she had a severe lack of respect for herself, which guarantees the 67 minute documentary a tabloid conclusion. The show combines terrific interviews with fascinating film clips and great music cuts, and it is also, in its own way, intensely nostalgic for the free-spirited Sixties. The transfer is accurate. Much of the archive footage is naturally rough, but when an interview is properly focused and lit, the DVD conveys it accurately. The sound, though monophonic, is reasonably strong. The DVD also includes handy where-they-are-now profiles of the interviewees and a good home video trailer.

Night and Fog (see **Short Cinema Journal 1:3 Issue: Authority**)

Night Caller From Outer Space (Image, ID5374FWDVD)

A spaceman comes to Earth to collect some women so he can freshen up his civilization, but the guys here take exception to his actions. The title on the print Image has used for the 1965 British production is simply *The Night Caller*. John Saxon stars in the black-and-white feature, which has a number of striking camera angles and only enough special effects to keep the plot moving. The premise may be silly, but the film is executed with a straight face and a serious air, and it is generally an entertaining effort.

The black-and-white picture quality is excellent, with crisp contrasts and rich blacks. The image is smooth and wear is minimal. The monophonic sound is adequate and the 84 minute program is not captioned. There are extensive filmographies for the director, John Gilling, and for Saxon. The chapter encoding and jacket guide are workable.

Night Falls in Manhattan (Paramount, 062927)

Sidney Lumet's1997 film, based upon a novel by Robert Daley, is wonderful storytelling that hits you with one emotional surprise after another. The less one knows about the plot—about a District Attorney investigating police corruption—the better, and the ending is a bit flaccid (a dramatic confrontation happens over the telephone, which works just fine on the printed page but in the movies you have to have the characters in the same room to get the pay-off), but overall the film is a wonderful, engaging experience. Like many crime stories, it's not where you're going but how you get there. Andy Garcia stars, with Richard Dreyfuss in a minor but key role and super supporting performances by Ron Leibman and Ian Holm.

The image is letterboxed with an aspect ratio of about 1.85:1 and no 16:9 enhancement. The picture is sharp and colors are well detailed. Even darker sequences are crisp and smooth. The standard stereo surround soundtrack is fine, and the Dolby Digital track is even better. The film is mostly dialogue and the movie's sound mix is not elaborate, but the Dolby Digital encoding still brings a more distinctive definition to the movie's audio track. The 113 minute feature can be supported by English or Spanish subtitles and is accompanied by a theatrical trailer (which emphasizes Lumet's accomplishments) and two commentary tracks. Lumet speaks on one track, providing a lot of fascinating background information about what he has learned over the years concerning the New York Police Department and about working with the actors. On the second channel, Garcia is joined by Leibman and producers Josh Kramer and Thom Mount to talk about Lumet's working methods and their experiences during the shoot.

The Night Flier (see Stephen King's The Night Flier)

Night Hunger X-rated (Vivid, UPC#0073214567)

There is a reasonably strong narrative and good punchline to **Night Hunger**. Two couples arrive to celebrate the anniversary of another couple at a remote cabin. They discover the woman there, but she claims they've got the date wrong and her husband is nowhere to be found. Just a bloody shoe, a letter about divorce and a few other clues. Oh, and there's some good meat in the refrigerator. The erotic sequences are mostly run-of-the-mill, but the picture looks reasonably good, with bright hues and decent fleshtones. The sound is fine. The 71 minute program features Lené, Chloe, Reylene and Magi. The DVD also contains alternate angle sequences and elaborate hardcore interactive promotional features.

The Night of the Hunted (Image, ID5419SADVD)

Jean Rollin directed the 1980 French film, an excellent low-budget non-effect science fiction feature reminiscent of David Cronenberg's early work, which uses some porn actors and has a lot of nudity and a bit of gratuitous gore. Brigitte Lahaie stars as an amnesiac hitchhiker who can hold onto her memories for only a half-hour or so, constantly forgetting who she is or where she has just come from. It turns out she has been held with a group of other people suffering from a similar condition, and the young man who gives her a ride falls for her before she is retrieved by her doctors. Much of the film was shot in a modern apartment complex, and the symbolic links between the people not knowing who they are and their identity-suppressing surroundings are thematically potent, as are the evocations of anonymous sex. The film's premise is simple, but it is wonderfully executed and gives you something really intelligent to ponder as you ogle at the stars wandering about aimlessly in the nude.

The picture is letterboxed with an aspect ratio of about 1.57:1 and no 16:9 enhancement. The source material has some markings and other evidence of wear, but the colors are reasonably strong and you can make out perfectly the differences between the three principal heroines, one of whom is blonde, one brunette and one a redhead. The image is sharp in well lit sequences, and reasonably stable in darker scenes. The monophonic sound is adequate, though the volume is best held to a modest level, and the film is in French with optional English subtitles. The 93 minute program is accompanied by a trailer and a nice montage of production stills.

Night of the Living Dead (Elite, EE1116); (UAV, 40081); (Madacy, DVD99010); (Master Movies, DVD5516)

There is a joke that comes at the opening. The first few frames present the 96 minute movie as it is commonly seen, looking all scratchy and blurry and everything, with warped sound, and then the Elite logo crashes through the image and the real presentation begins, with a stable soundtrack and a picture that is startling in its clarity and crispness. The restoration Elite performed on the 1968 cult horror classic turned the movie from a curiosity into a legitimate work of art. The film's director, George Romero, and his collaborator John Russo, were experienced professionals who had been making commercials in the Pittsburgh area for several years when they decided to try their hand at a feature length film. Working independently, the distribution deal they cut after the movie was completed is what led to the cheap replication and public domain morass that most viewers are familiar with. Elite's presentation, taken from the filmmakers' own source materials, is almost pristine and comes across as an entirely different movie. With the crisp focus, accurate contrasts and undamaged continuity, the disc unveils for the first time the competence and power of Romero's technique, a technique so accomplished within the restraints of his budget that the movie has entertained fans under viewing conditions that would make it difficult to enjoy even *Star Wars*. Thanks to Elite, the film's poignant look at the relationship between those living and those departed, its intense and systematic thrills and its inspired satire, all implied previously, are exquisitely brought to the fore. It is still nervously funny and horrific, but it is a joke no longer.

Except for one splice, the picture transfer looks gorgeous and the monophonic sound, which is not captioned, is equally admirable. Free of obvious noise and superbly detailed, the disc reveals the movie's soundtrack to be a remarkable low budget accomplishment, with atmospheric and even narrative touches that are usually lost on the bargain basement transfers. The audio still has some natural limitations and shouldn't be amplified too loudly, but it is thrilling.

There are two commentary channels featuring group talks by different members of the production's cast and crew. Since making the movie was a significant event in the lives of most of them, their reminiscences and anecdotes are highly enjoyable. We would recommend, however, not listening to the two channels back to back, since they cover some of the same ground (on one channel, for example, the group will be unable to remember how an effect was accomplished, while on the other channel, they do) and are more rewarding when a little time clouds over a listener's immediate memory. Although there are no text or still frame segments (and virtually no documentation on the jacket), the movie is accompanied by a trailer and a TV ad; an amusing 1990 short film by Kevin S. O'Brien called *Night of the Living Bread*—watch out, it has one great scream; and a selection of the commercials Romero and Russo created during their heyday, including an elaborate and amusing take off on *Fantastic Voyage* (for a laundry detergent) and a shockingly chauvinistic beer commercial about a man relaxing while his wife mows the lawn.

We have understandable difficulty giving blanket approval to movies with a strong content of horror or gore. Even the pleasures of such spectacular DVDs as the **Thing** remake or **Terminator 2** are not accessible to every viewer because of the violence that generates the thrills. We first learned of **Night of the Living Dead**, we are ashamed to say, in an article in the Reader's Digest—though its effect on us was probably the opposite of what the author intended—complaining about the raw and unrestrained images of ghoulry depicted in the movie, particularly the sequence where the little girl gorges on her mother and father (we've heard of children eating you out of house and home, but this is ridiculous…).

It is true that **Night of the Living Dead** is not for everyone, but listening to the commentary can make it a great deal more accessible if one has reservations. The filmmakers were almost all friends and business colleagues, and more than one couple working on the production eventually married. Romero's talent has accelerated his career meteorically, but most of the cast and crew have seen their professional lives advance in a more common pattern of gradual success. Many stayed in Pittsburgh or its equivalent and are, in experience and emotional makeup, more like one's neighbors than like Hollywood filmmakers (even Romero has avoided the scene to a great extent). When you hear how much fun they all had working their hearts out (the movie was made in their spare time), it becomes much easier to accept the film as an elaborate Halloween story and not some kind of alienating concoction meant to undermine the values of our society. Next to producing such a smashing transfer of the film, the DVD's greatest accomplishment is probably its ability to convey the atmosphere and sentiment with which the movie was created. It still may not be for everyone, but it is genuine work of art and entertainment, and there is not a single person involved with the production of the movie, or the DVD, for that matter, who cannot be proud of what was achieved.

Anyway, like we said, Elite's DVD opens with a gag about how bad the movie usually looks, and the UAV, Madacy and Master Movies releases fall right into it, because all three presentations look and sound just like those opening frames on Elite's program.

The monophonic sound is horribly warped on the UAV version. Throughout the presentation, the picture looks too dark, too fuzzy and the framing seems cramped on all four sides. There is no captioning.

The framing is shifted to the left on the Madacy *Hollywood Classics* release, but it still looks cramped. The picture is lighter than UAV's version and there is a little more detail in the shadows, but it also looks foggier, and the sound is much lighter. There are some minor text supplements and a poster. There is no captioning.

Of the three also-rans, the Master Movies *Silver Screen Collector's Edition* is the nicest. It has more detail in the darker areas of the screen than the UAV version, but it doesn't look as hazy as the Madacy version. It still is quite soft and battered compared to Elite's rendition, but it would be passable if you didn't hold it to that higher standard. The framing is about the same as Madacy's version, and the sound, though stronger than Madacy's muted track, is not as bright as the warped UAV track. There is a modest text supplement, optional Japanese subtitles and no English captioning.

A Night to Remember (Criterion, CC1517D)

The other great Titanic movie is a 1958 British film that took a kind of docudrama approach to the story. Along with presenting the captivating film, the DVD is designed to enhance a viewer's knowledge about the actual event, exploring how meticulously and brilliantly the movie restaged what had actually taken place the evening the ship went down.

There is a 1993 documentary about the making of the movie, drawing upon extensive interviews with the film's producer, William MacQuitty, and the author, Walter Lord, who wrote the bestseller upon which the film was based. Additionally, there is alternate audio commentary during the film by Don Lynch and Ken Marshall, the author and the illustrator of a non-fiction book about the ship. The movie's pristine black-and-white picture transfer is letterboxed with an aspect ratio of about 1.66:1 and no 16:9 enhancement, and does full justice to Geoffrey Unsworth's cinematography. The monophonic sound is a bit weak, but the Dolby Digital mono track is good. There is no captioning. The film runs 123 minutes and is the original 'British' version, which is apparently missing a bit of footage that has been included in non-British theatrical presentations.

It is revealed somewhat obliquely in the documentary that **A Night to Remember** was a sleeper hit in America, opening poorly at the box office but then gradually building as word-of-mouth spread. As is pointed out in many different parts of the DVD, the film has no real stars and only the most token of a central character. Although a number of characters are 'composites,' seen having experiences that actually occurred to several different people in real life, the film strove for as great a verisimilitude as a dramatic work could achieve. As the disc commentators often remark, many of the objects replicated within the film were later found by Dr. Robert Ballard when he located the remains of the ship. It is this sense of accuracy that makes the movie so gripping, the sense that for the most part, what the viewer is seeing is how things really happened.

The film is a worthwhile entertainment by itself, but the two principal supplementary features are also highly rewarding. The documentary unearths a lot of behind-the-scenes footage and shows how many of the movie's special effects and major action scenes were achieved. Despite a disconcerting tendency on the part of the commentators to refer to the film's characters as real people, mentioning the actors portraying them only in passing, the alternate audio track not only reinforces an understanding of the film's accuracy, it also enhances the viewer's knowledge about what happened and about how the film was put together.

The film naturally emphasizes the event's emotions, and so the commentary gives a greater emphasis upon the reality of those emotions—the nature of the screams as passengers were forced to leap into the water, the grief felt by the survivors, and even the responses some survivors had while sitting through the film. The disc binds the film even more tightly to its subject, and demonstrates why **A Night to Remember**, in its exploration of men and women coping under critical conditions, is more important than simply serving a macabre fascination for a banner headline tragedy.

A Night With Lou Reed (Image, 4787LYDVD)

Lou Reed plays for about an hour in a New York nightclub with Andy Warhol, among others, looking on. The picture on the 1983 program is quite good. Reed is well lit and the cameras are close. The image is a touch soft, but still nicely detailed. The stereo sound is totally at the mercy of the live recording and is limited in scope. The set sounds pretty much like something recorded in a garage, and Reed's vocals lack the resonance or timbre of his studio work. Even his band has a kind of makeshift sound to it. Reed's fans should still be quite pleased with the show, which includes fourteen numbers, but casual viewers will find it somewhat unvaried and unpolished.

The Night Stalker / The Night Strangler (Anchor Bay, DV10501)

The two pilot films for the *Kolchak* TV series have been released as a double bill. Darren McGavin stars as a reporter investigating mysteries of the occult in a Dan Curtis production that served as one of the main inspirations for *The X-Files*. Richard Matheson wrote the scripts for both films, which have virtually identical narratives, with the hero investigating the deaths of young women, who have been drained of blood, and then having difficulty convincing the authorities that the murderer is supernatural. Shot on location, *Stalker*, from 1971, is set in Las Vegas, while *Strangler*, from 1972, is set in Seattle. Some of the acting is simplified for TV

(McGavin and Simon Oakland, as his boss, scream at each other too much), but both films are still fairly exciting and, despite their similarities. they work well as a double bill.

Colors on *Stalker* are bright and details are vivid, with perfect fleshtones. The quality of *Strangler* is almost as good, although the image is a bit softer in places and darker sequences are a little grainier (most of it due to the cinematography). The monophonic sound is fine and the shows are not closed captioned or time encoded. Each appears on a separate side, with *Stalker* apparently running 72 minutes and *Strangler* running 90 minutes.

The Nightmare Before Christmas (Buena Vista, 13080)

The very special 1993 stop-motion animation film by Tim Burton and Henry Selick is presented with both an English and a French Dolby Digital soundtrack, and the many songs are also in French. The film's transfer is lovely, with not a flaw to be found in the picture or the sound. The picture is letterboxed with an aspect ratio of about 1.66:1. Optional English and Spanish captions are also included ("Y en una noche oscura a y fría/En que la luna brilla/Vuela en la niebla/Como un buitre en el cielo./Y'lo llaman San Atroz"), along with a trailer.

The film is a wonderful experience and its pleasures increase on multiple viewings. About Halloween creatures who attempt to co-opt Christmas, it is not afraid to be a bit ghoulish, though its success comes from the rich characterizations the animators achieved with their often striking figures and beautiful, imaginative settings. The film is also a musical, with a good ten songs (often evocative of Kurt Weill) created by Danny Elfman and much of the regular dialogue approaching verse. Every frame is a work of art, the music is a joy and the mise-en-scene is pure imagination, rendered in solid form.

Nikki Loves Rocco X-rated (Vivid, UPC#0073214532)

After engaging in an erotic interlude on a genuine freeway overpass, a couple attends a dinner party that they mistakenly believe is a swingers' get together. Their enthusiasm, however, is contagious. The story then cuts to a year later, where the other adults who were at the party have indeed embraced the swingers' lifestyle, as a new couple visits for the first time, expecting just a simple dinner party. Anyway, although there isn't much plot, the interludes between the erotic sequences are emotionally believable and create a sufficient premise for the other activities, which are fairly energetic.

Shot on film, the colors are light and the image is grainy at times. The monophonic sound recording is also of limited quality and dialogue is at times difficult to hear without an exaggerated increase in volume. The program runs 74 minutes and stars Nikky Tyler, Melissa Hill, Tabitha Stevens, Kitty Monroe, Davia Ardell and Taboo. The DVD contains alternate angle sequences and elaborate hardcore interactive promotional features.

Nikki Tyler P.I. X-rated (Vivid, UPC#0073214525)

The narrative and dramatic performances are somewhat better than normal as the heroine, a private detective, goes on two cases, following a woman who is cheating on her husband and searching for a girl who has left home and fallen in with a bad crowd. The erotic sequences, however, are fairly tame, even with the reasonably strong emotional performances supporting them.

Shot on videotape, the picture is consistently overlit, with slightly washed out colors and pale fleshtones, though the image is crisp. The sound is okay, though you can hear the filmmakers shouting instructions to the performers in places. The program runs 75 minutes, featuring Tyler and Stacy Valentine. The DVD contains alternate angle sequences and elaborate hardcore interactive promotional features.

Nils Lofgren Live (Image, ID4399CADVD)

After an opening music video, the remainder of the 88 minute program is a straightforward concert. Backed by his band, Lofgren stands in center stage singing and playing his guitar. This lack of

variation will limit the appeal of the show to fans. Lofgren performs many of his own compositions, along with the Beatles' *Anytime at All* and Bill Withers' *Lean on Me*. Lofgren is competent, but lacks the dynamism and charisma the best rock musicians bring to their live appearances, and his music is generally unimaginative. For the most part, the audience is lit in yellow and Lofgren is lit in blue. The picture looks fine and is reasonably sharp, though the image is usually dominated by those two hues. The stereo sound is bland and center-oriented.

9 1/2 Weeks (MGM, 907028)

Colors are accurate and the image is clearly detailed on the ridiculous 1986 we-never-go-anywhere love story. Passages look a bit grainy, but the quality of the image does not create a distraction. The picture is letterboxed with an aspect ratio of about 1.77:1 and no 16:9 enhancement. The stereo surround sound has a limited mix, with dull tones. The 117 minute film, the 'Unrated' cut, is also available in French and comes with English, French or Spanish subtitles ("Je veux regarder le contour de ton corps"), as well as a theatrical trailer. Kim Basinger portrays an art dealer drawn into a lustful relationship with a demanding but attentive broker, played by Mickey Rourke. Directed by Adrian Lyne, whose string of career successes has legitimized his indulgent explorations of romantic sexuality, the added 'unrated' footage makes the commitment of Basinger's character more convincing.

1941 (Universal, 20550)

We continue to read negative comments about Steven Spielberg's wonderful 1979 comedy. Even Spielberg himself, trying to be cool or something, puts it down, but it is a terrific exercise in frantic comical excess and is amenable to multiple, multiple viewings, as we can attest. About the panic that sets in when a Japanese submarine is sighted off the coast of Los Angeles, the gloriously frantic film has a huge cast and multiple plot lines. John Belushi, Tim Matheson and Bobby DiCicco receive the most screen time among those in the extensive, all-star cast.

Universal has released the 145 minute version of the film, with substantial additions to its original theatrical running time of 118 minutes. The additions include some marvelous comedy sequences (two shoplifters run an air raid siren in a department store to create a distracting panic) and a fleshing out of the characters (John Candy's character is more of a racist). The best scene of all—missing from the theatrical version, but surely the film's highpoint now that it has been restored—features Slim Pickens as an inebriated Christmas tree dealer confronting a group of Japanese sailors disguised as trees and trying to chop them down with his ax. As the saying goes, this sequence alone is worth the price of the DVD.

The picture is letterboxed with an aspect ratio of about 2.35:1 and no 16:9 enhancement. Although there are shots where the picture does look reasonably crisp, in many sequences, fog or haze surround the characters and make bright hues fuzzy. The film was apparently shot in a haze (they used smoke in practically every scene, according to the cinematographer, William Fraker), to emphasize the nostalgia of the setting, but the result is a picture that almost never looks like it is in focus. There are also more severe flaws, such as a hazy horizontal band running across the bottom of the image in one scene (an original sequence, not part of the new footage). If you peer beyond the haze, the colors look fresh.

Even with Dolby Digital encoding, the dialogue track is a bit weak and the sound is a little harsh, with limited separation effects. John Williams' energetic musical score has also been isolated on one track, in standard stereo. The film can be supported by English, French or Spanish subtitles ("Oh, regarde. Un louveteau"), and the documentary can also be supported by English subtitles.

Included with the movie is a super, 101 minute retrospective documentary. The filmmakers explain how the movie was originally conceived, how the major effects sequences were executed and what reactions were like after the film was completed. Although they skirt a bit around talking about how the budget ballooned as production commenced, they are forthright in discussing the film's negative reception and profitable-but-not-profitable-enough box office success. Along with behind-the-scenes footage, the documentary includes a few more deleted scenes (including one very funny one where the dummy drinks buttermilk), home movie footage of John Belushi on the set, and other treats.

Along with the documentary, there are additional outtakes (there is a cute one of Belushi and Dan Aykroyd, who never meet in the film, passing each other in the water), a terrific teaser directed by John Milius that features Belushi giving a pep talk to the audience, a regular theatrical trailer and an extensive still frame section of production sketches, publicity and production photos, promotional artwork and a synopsis of the major negative reviews. At one point during the documentary, Spielberg says of the film, "It was written and directed as one would perform in a demolition derby." The movie's constant screaming and atmosphere of destruction did not meet audience expectations when **1941** was first released, but if the film is taken on its own terms it can be a highly enjoyable experience. Spielberg's essential skills as a director prevent the film from falling apart on multiple viewings, and the broad exuberance with which the cast and the special effects technicians tackled their roles can become harder and harder to resist as the action and character interplay become more familiar.

1998 Olympic Winter Games: Hockey Highlights
(Panasonic, SLPDV0003)
1998 Olympic Winter Games: Figure Skating Competition Highlights (Panasonic, SLPDV0001)
1998 Olympic Winter Games : Figure Skating Exhibition Highlights (Panasonic, SLPDV0002)
1998 Olympic Winter Games: Overall Highlights
(Panasonic, SLPDV0004)

The popularity of professional sports in the Twentieth Century is symbiotically tied to radio (the simpler baseball) and television (the more complicated football). In sports, a viewer sees more events of historical importance (well, cultural historical importance) occurring live, on television, than in any other category. Thanks to TV, the entire world has become a Coliseum for the quadrennial Olympic games, and thanks to TV, many professional athletes are now allowed to compete in what was once an 'amateur' event. Indeed, thanks to TV, there aren't even major documentary films any more about the Olympic Games. Instead, there are home video highlight programs.

The programs are drawn from CBS broadcasts of the Games and feature an hour or more of highlights and profiles, with extensive text supplements on all the events and other specific additional features. The picture quality is consistently good, with bright, vivid colors and a very sharp focus, and the stereo sound is probably better than it was in broadcast. The audio usually features the original broadcast narration, with additional explanatory comments. The programs are not time encoded or captioned, and because of their alternate angle features, some standard DVD manipulations, such as Scan or Still, may be suppressed.

The 64 minute **Hockey Highlights** is divided evenly between Men's and Women's Hockey. In case you don't remember, the U.S. Women's team ruled, while the Men's didn't even place. You get less of some games than you would on the sports segment of a local news broadcast, but the medal games are given a little more time and, by the end, you do have a decent sense of how at least a few of the major players handled themselves on the ice. The Women's segment focuses entirely on the competitions involving the U.S. team, while the Men's segment follows both the U.S. and Canadian teams, as well as the Gold medal round that neither was involved in.

One sport that has proven ideal for TV attention spans is figure skating. The sequences last only a few minutes and are fraught with a raw emotion that separates them from recitals or other non-competitive skating displays. **Figure Skating Competition** is a thrilling program, with many spellbinding emotional climaxes and incredible dancing. The 80 minute program (with about 17 additional minutes of alternate angle footage that is free of commentary) gives pretty much equal time to the Women's Free Skating, Men's Free Skating and Pairs competition, with a briefer overview of the controversially judged Ice Dancing competition. One of the narrators, Scott Hamilton, speaks with a puppy dog excitement about routines, and it is easy to get wrapped up in his enthusiasm, particularly when Tara Lipinski, skating after Michelle Kwan, bests Kwan's near-perfect score, and when French skater Philippe Candelero does everything the other skaters have done, but in costume and as a 'character' (with sound effects, too), it is the ultimate blending of sport and entertainment. And in addition to all that skating, the music sounds terrific.

Figure Skating Exhibition Highlights runs about 80 minutes and features the relaxed exhibition performances of Aleksei Yagudin, Yelena Bereshnaya & Anton Sikharulidze, Michelle Kwan, Shae-Lynn Bourne & Victor Kraatz, Todd Eldredge, Anjelika Krylova & Oleg Ovsyannikov, Kyoko Ina & Jason Dungjen, Ilia Kulik, Maria Butyrskaya, Tara Lipinski, Oksana Kazakova & Artur Dmitriev, and Philippe Candeloro, with broadcast narration by Verne Lundquist, Scott Hamilton and Tracy Wilson (the CBS logo remains in the bottom right corner throughout the program). Additionally, there is a 20 minute collection without narration featuring Kulik, Kasakova & Dimitriev, Elvis Stojko, Pasha Grishuk & Evgeny Platov, and Kyoko Ina & Jason Dungjen. This segment has a multiple angle function and, in an innovative programming feature, the alternate angles are shown in the bottom left of the screen.

An 80 minute overview of many of the events, very little on **Overall Highlights** lasts long enough to make much of an impression. The competitions go by so quickly there's no competition within them. You do get plenty of the opening and closing ceremonies and a sampling of luge, ski jumping, downhill racing, speed skating, and snowboarding, as well as the figure skating and hockey competitions again, but it basically just makes you wish you could see a lot more of each event, which, we suppose, is its purpose.

Nixon (Buena Vista, 17246)

Oliver Stone's 1995 feature has a mesmerizing style, mixing film stocks and challenging camera angles, but it was a financial flop and the reason must be that a majority of the populace does not want to face up to the subject, a flaw that often trips up topical films. We're not sure that enough clear information is provided to make the movie fully accessible to future generations—the China sequence is confusing and the Watergate scandal builds mostly off screen—but the movie is an impressive work and, had it been about almost any other subject, it is so well made it would have attracted more viewers just by default. Everyone has always known that Richard Nixon is a great, Shakespearean-styled character—a wildly imperfect but self-aware individual whose efforts had a significant effect upon history, and Stone managed to capture the essence of that, thus making the film as entertaining as it is historically informative.

It is a fun movie, all 191 minutes of it, a jumbled set of flashbacks and flash forwards that follow Nixon's life from his childhood to the day of his resignation, with an emphasis on his years as president. There are loads of famous actors popping up in cameo appearances as news figures of Nixon's era, and there is Stone's slightly paranoid, deep background conspiracy theories that bubble up into the dialogue here and there, but the movie is a coherent, searching exploration of the influences, both outside and within his heart, that guided Nixon's decisions and actions. Anthony Hopkins gives a valid and thorough performance in the title role, one that avoids impersonation but still strives so hard for an accuracy of spirit that when, at the end, Stone includes footage of the real Nixon, you don't at first recognize that it isn't Hopkins.

The picture is letterboxed with an aspect ratio of about 2.35:1 and no 16:9 enhancement. The color transfer looks very good, with precisely defined hues and accurate fleshtones. The stereo surround sound is fine and the Dolby Digital sound has a very strong bass that adds to the film's ominous atmosphere. The program can be supported by optional English subtitles.

No Escape (HBO, 91562)

In an intriguing casting choice, Ray Liotta stars as the enigmatic loner with unsurpassed survival skills whose actions are inevitably heroic. The 1994 film is set in the future, but most of it takes place on an 'escape-proof prison island,' where there is a small enclave of 'good' prisoners (they have windmills) and larger but less organized bands of 'bad' prisoners (they eat rats). The filmmakers have done their homework well and keep the action and stunts in high gear from beginning to end. They also manage the delicate balance of creating sympathetic characters out of hardened criminals without a single female in the cast, which may not be unusual for a prison film but is out of the ordinary for a revved up action picture.

The letterboxing has an aspect ratio of about 2.35:1 and no 16:9 enhancement. The color transfer looks fine, with sharp details and accurate fleshtones. The surround sound is highly enjoyable, full of aggressive noises designed to place the viewer in the middle of the action, and the Dolby Digital track is brighter. Initial copies of the title had directional flaws on the Dolby Digital track that were corrected in subsequent pressing runs. The 118 minute program also has French and Spanish language tracks in standard stereo, optional English, French or Spanish subtitles, a cast profile section, a trailer, TV commercials and a good 'making of' featurette.

No Mercy (Columbia TriStar, 83759)

Richard Gere and Kim Basinger are on the run in the Louisiana swamps. Gere is a police detective and Basinger is a witness, the mistress of the principal villain. The plot is quite basic and its elaborations on character and atmosphere don't amount to much. The 1986 movie thrives on star appeal, however, and there is enough forward movement to keep a viewer hooked.

The picture is presented in letterboxed format on one side, with an aspect ratio of about 1.85:1 and an accommodation for enhanced 16:9 playback, and is in full screen format on the other side. Although the image is a little dark, colors are reasonably accurate and fleshtones look good. The stereo surround sound is a bit dull, but functional. The 108 minute program also has French and Spanish language audio tracks, optional English, French or Spanish subtitles, and a theatrical trailer that works well as an appetizer for the film.

The North Avenue Irregulars (Anchor Bay, DV10829)

A collection of Seventies TV stars are gathered in the formula 1977 Walt Disney comedy, including Barbara Harris, Cloris Leachman, Karen Valentine, Michael Constantine and Ruth Buzzi. Edward Herrmann stars as a church minister who recruits his parishioners to stake out and tail a gambling ring that is upsetting the moral fabric of his community. Even though they are better than the material, the stars are amusing, and there is a typical (but enjoyable) Disney demolition derby finale.

The picture is vivid. The image is crisp, hues are bright and fleshtones are accurate. The presentation is in letterboxed format on one side, with an aspect ratio of about 1.66:1 and no 16:9 enhancement, and is in cropped format on the other side, though the cropped framing is workable. The monophonic sound is fine and the 100 minute program is not captioned.

Nosferatu (Image, ID4098DSDVD)

Keeping in mind that shortly after F.W. Murnau's classic vampire film was produced, in the early twenties, a copyright battle resulted in having nearly all prints of the film destroyed, the presentation is in fine condition. Some sequences are damaged and

all have a rough, aged look, but the picture is reasonably sharp and never alienating. The 81 minute film has fresh intertitles, which are mildly disorienting at first but tolerable afterward, and a slight atmospheric tinting. Character movement and other activities have been meticulously set at their intended speeds, though damage to the film disrupts its evenness from time to time. There is a booming pipe organ score that is presented in stereo on the disc with no significant distortion.

There is also a commentary track by film scholar Lokke Heiss. Heiss gives a generalized but informative talk on the film, providing some production details, some biographical information on the filmmakers and, in a reaction to what is on view at the time, speaking at more length about the film's elaborate symbolic levels. Murnau's artistry is so complex that even those who have studied the film extensively will find some of Heiss' commentary to be informative, such as the suggestion that the ineffectuality of the film's nominal 'hero' was a reflection of Germany's impotence under the Weimar Republic. On the other hand, Heiss also comes up with an occasional comment such as, "The novel, Dracula, can be read as an economic warning of the dangers of foreign ownership of real estate and businesses," that seem to drift a bit from the immediate subject. A small but interesting supplementary still photo archive, featuring conceptual paintings, photographs and other memorabilia, is included as well.

Nosferatu: The Vampyre (Anchor Bay, DV10677)

Two versions of Werner Herzog's have been released on the dual-sided DVD, the 106 minute 56 second English language version and the 106 minute 45 second German version, which is actually known as *Nosferatu: Phantom Der Nacht*.

Herzog's 1979 production has held up quite well. Although his style is deliberately somnambulistic, the film does an excellent job at evoking and updating the F.W. Murnau's silent classic. With a limited budget, it is not intensely stylistic, and the pointlessness of some of Herzog's longer takes can be trying, but it is a unique approach that sustains the work's atmosphere, its psychological and spiritual symbolism, and its moral adventure. Unlike most versions, the male heroes in the film are all losers, and it is the heroine, Lucy, who acts and saves the day. Klaus Kinski, Isabelle Adjani and Bruno Ganz star. Some of the dialogue in the English version is halting and awkward, even by the lax standards of dubbing. Some scenes are identical between the two versions, but others are quite different, with the English version often having a more energetic or interesting staging than the German version.

The film's color scheme is highly appealing. It is often deliberately monochromatic, and these sequences look great. There are also scenes of full color, however, and these look a little grainy, with some over-saturation. On the whole, the presentation is about what one would expect of a low budget European program and is passable. The picture is letterboxed with an aspect ratio of about 1.85:1 and no 16:9 enhancement.

Both versions are in stereo, and the German version also has a 5-channel Dolby Digital track. There doesn't seem to be much of a difference between the 5-channel track and the standard track, however. The film's audio track doesn't really seem to be designed for stereo playback anyway. The music and some of the atmospheric effects are dimensional, but most of the audio is centered, and increasing the volume, even on the 5-channel playback, leads to a fuzzy distortion fairly quickly. One of the nicest effects—the totally creaking door when Kinski sneaks behind Adjani while she sits at a mirror, though the sound comes from the front and not from behind.

The English version is presented with no extra features. Accompanying the German version are optional English subtitles, an interesting 15 minute 'making of' featurette that shows (among other things) Kinski getting his makeup applied, three trailers including a Spanish trailer that uses a montage of publicity stills, and a commentary track featuring Herzog, prompted by Norman Hill.

Where American directors are often reserved speaking about their workmates, Herzog is forthright in talking about Adjani's severe lack of self-confidence and Kinski's wild temper tantrums. He also talks informatively about shooting the movie on a low budget (he claims that the jiggly hand-held shots are a viable substitute for a locked-down camera), about some of his artistic intentions (the long journey to Dracula's castle is a journey through the human soul—and to think Fox, which originally released the film theatrically, wanted him to shorten the sequence; they must not think much of the human soul) and about corralling and organizing 11,000 lab rats (which were painted grey, and look it) for a location sequence.

Nostalghia (Fox Lorber, FLV5041)

Russian director Andrei Tarkovsky made the 1983 film in Italy, and it depicts a Russian scholar in Italy, researching a small town that was visited by an Eighteenth Century Russian composer two centuries earlier. He is accompanied by a Botticelli-esque translator and the two are unable to consummate an affair. The film's sluggish but deliberate pacing, its transfixing images and its dense symbolism (the movie seems to be about the stagnation of Russian communism during the end of the Brezhnev era, at least in spirit, while more specifically it is about the scholar being unable to get much done) can be highly compelling if one has the patience for such things. The clash between the geometric rigidity of Tarkovsky's style and the fluidity of the Italian environment is mesmerizing. On a practical level, even if it puts you to sleep, you may find yourself wanting to replay it often for its dream-like transitions, or you can put it on at parties as background stimulation and a unique conversation starter. The image is sharp, revealing a compelling detail in the textures, and variations of shade and color. The film has many static shots with very little movement, however, so there is a tendency for your eyes to be drawn to the image's flaws. The DVD's transfer rate is quite high—it rarely dips below 7.5—yet you can still notice an occasional artifacting flaw, simply because it is the only thing on the screen that moves. The image is letterboxed with an aspect ratio of about 1.7:1. The monophonic sound seems on par with the LD and is fine. The film is in Italian and there are optional yellow English subtitles, though they are a bit more obtrusive than the white subtitles on the LD. The 120 minute feature is accompanied by a promotional video trailer and filmographies for Tarkovsky and the cast. The DVD is not time encoded and Fox Lorber's chapter encoding is skimpy.

Nothing But Trouble (Warner, 16376)

Dan Aykroyd (under heavy makeup), Chevy Chase, Demi Moore and John Candy (in a dual role) co-star in the generically titled 1991 production, which was also directed by Aykroyd. The film has an outstanding art and production design and was short-changed in the long run by its immediately forgettable title, after being shot under the more intriguing appellation, 'Valkenvania.' Chase and Moore are fancy Wall Street types on their way to Atlantic City when they go off the main highway and end up in a bizarre town from which there is no apparent escape. Yes, the comedy can be annoying or excruciating, but the passage of time has made the presence of the comedians more valuable (it no longer seems like they are just doing their standard routines for the umpteenth iteration, because these days they don't anymore), while the film's imaginative design and satirical excess remain intriguing.

The 93 minute movie is presented in full screen format. The picture is crisp and colors are a strong. Here and there, a shot looks a little washed out or a dark sequence is a little grainy, but on the whole the image detail is rich, giving the viewer a real opportunity to bask in the overabundant set decorations. There is an erratically aggressive stereo surround soundtrack that is fairly pleasing during its more elaborate passages. The program is closed captioned.

Nothing Sacred (SlingShot, DVD1497

The colors are super, but the sharpness of the DVD image enhances the source material's many other flaws and could drive casual viewers to distraction. Essentially, there are passages in the 1937 film where the three strips in the three-strip Technicolor image cannot line up, creating ghosts and double edges. Additionally, each strip appears to have its own share of scratches and other flaws. Fans, however, will not want to miss it, because when everything does line up, and even when most of it lines up, the picture is riveting—almost too brilliantly colored for the dark comical story it is supporting. The film's monophonic sound also has an age-related roughness, but never to the point of distortion.

Frederic March portrays a New York newspaperman who pushes the story of a young woman, played by Carole Lombard, who is facing a terminal illness. The reporter is unaware that the malady was misdiagnosed and, in typical thirties fashion, the two fall in love in spite of themselves after a healthy dose of social satire and screwball hijinks. Directed by William Wellman, the film does not fall into the category of productions that were typically shot in color or at the time, but Lombard's presence has an eerie modernity due to the vivid naturalness of her image, something the disc enhances effectively. The late thirties New York skyline is also breathtaking.

Included with the 73 minute film are an extended promotional color trailer, two Mack Sennett shorts from the late twenties in which Lombard appeared, and 'home movies,' mostly of Lombard and Clark Gable on a hunting trip with friends. The Sennett silents, supported by a Lee Erwin organ score, each contain color sequences and a satisfying level of physical comedy that is consistent with the sophistication of the era. In both, *Campus Vamp* from 1928 and *Matchmaking Mama* from 1929, Lombard has a secondary role as the wrong woman. *Mama* is also notable for a brief glimpse of a see-thru brassiere. The footage of Lombard and Gable at leisure begins mundanely but concludes with some amusing cavorting for the camera with the catch of the day, though it creates a sad poignancy by reminding the viewer that Lombard was unable to escape the fate her character in **Nothing Sacred** managed to circumvent.

Nothing to Lose (Buena Vista, 14254)

Tim Robbins and Martin Lawrence star in the comedy about a man down in the dumps who goes on a joy ride with a carjacker. The narrative is a contrivance, but there is enough of a story to give Robbins and Lawrence room to maneuver. Robbins does it laconically, deriving humor from delayed reactions and slow burns, but Lawrence is quick and precise, his voice smoothed to a perfect pitch for every punchline. Each guy's style feeds the other.

The picture is letterboxed with an aspect ratio of about 1.85:1 and no 16:9 enhancement. Hues are solid and fleshtones are deep. The stereo surround sound is a little dull, but the Dolby Digital track is workable, with engaging separations and a reasonable liveliness. The 98 minute program is also available in French and comes with English or Spanish subtitles ("Escogiste a la vítima equivocada en el día equivocado"), as well as an engaging theatrical trailer.

Nowhere to Run (Columbia TriStar, 52379)

Jean-Claude Van Damme stars as an escaped convict who helps a farm family fight off developers. The plot has a number of unlikelihoods, but the fight scenes are great and the premise, though common, is an ideal action vehicle. Rosanna Arquette co-stars in the 1993 production.

The presentation is letterboxed on one side, with an aspect ratio of about 1.85:1 and an accommodation for enhanced 16:9 playback, and is in full screen format on the other side. The picture quality is adequate. The stereo surround sound is okay, although the mix has no exceptional moments. The 95 minute program also has a French audio track in mono, optional English and French captions and a trailer.

Nude Lap Dancer Championship (Vivid, UPC#0073215540)

Although you do find out who 'wins' at the end, there is no narration or a coherent contest in the blatantly pornographic 67 minute program, just a progression of sequences in which dancers do 'everything but' to select male and female partners, who sit on stage in a chair looking pleasantly amused.

The colors are very rich, fleshtones are deep and the image is reasonably sharp. Set in a nightclub, the pulsating music and ambient crowd sounds are stereophonic. There is no captioning and the DVD contains extensive interactive softcore promotional features.

Number 17 (see Alfred Hitchcock Collection)

Nunsense (Image, ID4587DLDVD)

The video taped recording of a popular comedic stage revue with a six-character cast is presented in the guise of a constantly interrupted convent benefit show. There is a minor narrative floating through the piece, about various things that are happening off stage, to keep the program moving. There are lots of relatively clean jokes, a few 'acts' (such as a ventriloquist sequence), some singing and dancing, and general irreverent fun. There isn't the spontaneity you would feel in an audience, but you do get glimpses of the cast's improvisations and close-ups of their humorous expressions, provided that is where the camera is pointing. Rue McClanahan stars as the Mother Superior. The picture is very sharp and the colors look fine. The stereo sound is adequate. The program runs 112 minutes and is not captioned.

The Nutcracker (see George Balanchine's the Nutcracker)

The Nutt House (Image, ID5613FMDVD)

Quite possibly the worst comedy we have ever seen, it is about an insane identical twin makes life hell for a presidential candidate. The filmmakers are so ashamed of their work that the screenplay credits list both an Alan Smithee, Jr. and an Alan Smithee, Sr. The film opens, for example, with scenes from its climactic pie fight—to get you anticipating such revelry, we suppose—and then tells its tale in flashback. Any idea for a joke is thrown in. At the insane asylum, for example, a Spanish film is playing on the TV. A patient picks up a remote with three buttons that say, "Spanish Channel, French Channel, English Channel." The patient presses "English Channel" and water pours all over him. That's the movie's best gag, unless you count the time the candidate falls off a ledge, naked, and grabs a cactus to hide his manhood from the reporters gathered in front of him. The insane brother imagines he is wearing costumes depending upon which personality has taken control of his head, and those around him react to the imaginary costumes sometimes, but not other times. The film is such monumentally and truly bad cinema that some viewers may wish to add it to their collection, simply as an example of how low the movies can sometimes stoop. Stephen Kearney stars, unable to play even identical twins convincingly. The character's name in the film, incidentally, is spelled with one 't,' not the two used in the title.

The picture is sharp in some sequences and fuzzy in others. Colors, however, are very bright and fresh-looking. The stereo sound has a limited mix. The 88 minute program is not captioned.

The Nutty Professor (Universal, 20148); DTS (Universal, 20459)

A spin-off of the old Jerry Lewis movie that itself was spun off of *Dr. Jekyll and Mr. Hyde*, Eddie Murphy portrays a portly college professor who develops a serum that makes him thin for short periods of time but changes his personality in the process. The movie, directed by Tom Shadyac, starts out with a terrific gag, about a mass of hamsters running loose on the college campus, and proceeds to come up with confident pieces of amusement that are steadily interspersed with competent plot advancements. A lot of the humor is base, but the jokes about bodily functions and such have a heartiness to them that is easy to embrace. The film also has some substantial special effects, and Murphy has several side roles, portraying various members of the professor's family.

The film is presented in letterboxed format, with an aspect ratio of about 1.85:1 and an accommodation for enhanced 16:9 playback. The colors are strong, blacks are pure and the image is sharp. The Dolby Digital track having a bit more presence and stronger dimensionality than the standard stereo surround soundtrack. The 96 minute film is also available in French in standard stereo and comes with English or Spanish subtitles ("¿Y cómo crees que lo lavan? ¿En un autolavado?"). There is a decent collection of presskit production notes and a modest cast-and-crew profile section, and the very successful trailer (it cheats in one spot, pretending that a dream sequence is real).

The sound on the DTS DVD has more ambiance, and tones on the standard DVD sound flat in comparison. The frame transfer rate on the 96 minute program appears to be identical to the previous release.

Nymphomercial (DaViD, D8022)

A collection of weak skits involving items supposedly sold over the TV, the erotic sequences are tolerable, but there isn't much to the script except for a final gag. Colors are a little greenish, contrasts are a bit weak in places and the image is somewhat fuzzy. The sound is fairly strong, or too strong, blasting out at times. The program runs 83 minutes and features Jordan St. James, Brooke Waters, Louise Sherry, and April Diamond.

O

Oasis ...There and Then (Sony, EVD50151)

An 85 minute concert program, there are brief interview sequences between some of the numbers, but it is not enough to disrupt the flow of the music. The program combines footage from a concert staged in 1995 and one staged in 1996 in England and is presented in a fairly straightforward manner. The musicians seem a bit caught up in themselves, but their music is energetic and the crowd seems pleased. Included among the numbers is *I Am the Walrus*. Even under severely tinted stage lighting, the image remains crisp and the colors look confident. The stereo surround sound is okay. There is also a Dolby Digital track that is set a lot louder and brings in more detail to the recording, but the vocals also tend to bleed more to the rear channel, whereas on the standard track they pretty much stay up front. There is no closed captioning.

Object of Obsession (Image, ID4660APDVD)

The LD release ran 97 minutes, while the DVD runs just 91 minutes and is probably the R-rated version rather than the unrated version the jacket claims it is. Directed by Gregory Hippolyte, Erika Anderson is a divorcée who answers a wrong number one night and is soon conned into visiting the loft of the caller, where she is temporarily imprisoned. Scott Valentine co-stars. Sort of a **9 1/2 Weeks** without the rough stuff, the film consciously plays to traditional female erotic fantasies rather than male erotic fantasies, and while there is plenty of nudity, it rarely seems gratuitous, even during several daydream sequences. The narrative also has a couple clever twists in the final act that give the film a sense of cohesion and purpose. The film does not break out of its softcore genre, but it fulfills the basic requirements adeptly. The LD was also in stereo, while the DVD is blandly monophonic. The picture is fuzzy in darker scenes and is generally soft. Colors are reasonably accurate but fleshtones are dull.

Ocean Reflections (see **Moodtapes: Ocean Reflections**)

Oceanscapes (Simitar, 7204)

A 40 minute or so (there is no time encoding) montage of video tape shots of waves and animal life underwater, the program just kind of lurches from one set of images to the next without any real sense of organization or discovery. Many shots have a mild ghosting around brightly lit figures, which we would tend to blame on the source material, but other shots look blurry during movement, and this seems to be more of a problem with the compression, unless the cinematographer was having trouble with his focus. There is also noticeable tiling and some streaking. The stereo soundtrack is adequate, though the relaxed jazz musical score never amounts to much.

October (Image, ID4576CODVD)

There has never been another film like Sergei Eisenstein's **October**. It is a cinematic restaging of a historic event (the Bolshevik revolution), presented like a news documentary. No one character appears for more than a few minutes but, because of Eisenstein's masterful style, the viewer is captured by the flow and drama of the events. The 1927 film is exciting, and even if it were not aspiring to accurately render real occurrences it would still provide valuable lessons in the steps and half steps which lead to revolution. The most important component, however, is the cast. Although characters are seen only briefly, the emotional manipulations are constant. The cliché that the film's hero is the proletariat is true in the most incredible way. Each actor and actress contributes a small but valuable part of his or her self, and when the film is ended it is the general events and not the individuals which the viewer remembers. The movie is more successfully communist than Communism itself.

The original Russian intertitles, which had illegible translations on earlier video releases, have been replaced by new English intertitles, changing the running time and the pace of the editing slightly. The introduction has been eliminated. The sound—incidental noises and a Dimitri Shostakovich musical score—is not smooth, even on the Dolby Digital mono track, and its roughness is a little disappointing. The windowboxed black-and-white picture is in adequate condition. The presentation runs 103 minutes.

October Sky (Universal, 20557)

The small but very pleasing movie is about young boys growing up in a West Virginia coal town and eventually winning a national science contest. The first half of the film is fairly run-of-the-mill, but the second half has many emotional payoffs that make the entire movie a memorable and very special experience.

The film is presented on two layers, in letterboxed format on one layer, with an aspect ratio of about 2.35:1 and an accommodation for enhanced 16:9 playback, and in cropped format on the other layer, although cropping harms the film's atmosphere significantly. The picture transfer looks great, with bright, crisp hues and accurate fleshtones.

We didn't care much for the Dolby Digital 5.1 channel mix, preferring the standard stereo mix instead. There is very little rear channel activity on the Dolby Digital mix, except for occasional surges in the musical score, while the standard mix has a comfortable collection of appropriate rear channel sound effects in addition to the music. Even the front sound on the Dolby Digital track seems more centered than it is on the standard track. There is an alternate French audio track in standard stereo, optional English subtitles, a cast-and-director profile section and a trailer. Contrary to a jacket notation, there is no commentary channel, although there is a very good 20 minute or so 'making of' featurette. It includes an interview with NASA official, Homer Hickman, Jr., whose autobiography served as the basis for the film.

The Occult History of the Third Reich (Madacy, DVD99050)
The Occult History of the Third Reich: The Enigma of the Swastika (Madacy, DVD990501)
The Occult History of the Third Reich: The SS Blood and Soil (Madacy, DVD990502)
The Occult History of the Third Reich : Adolf Hitler (Madacy, DVD990503)

Far more interesting than we expected it to be, the documentaries, released as a box set and as three individual programs, present a fascinating overview of the influences alternative belief systems had upon the Nazis. There is less distinction among the three documentaries than their titles imply. All use black-and-white archival footage (as well as a few faded archival color sequences) and photos in illustration, as a single narrator chronicles the various points each documentary has to make. The footage is often old looking and on the soft, fuzzy, speckled side, but artifacting seems under control. The monophonic sound is also a little fuzzy, but workable. Each documentary is different, but all tell the same tale and reiterate the basic facts, and the titles are only a vague help in differentiating them.

Enigma of the Swastika runs 47 minutes and does focus on the development and use of the Swastika symbol a little more than the others. **The SS Blood and Soil** runs 51 minutes and spends a bit more time tracking the founding, expansion and fascinating independence of the SS than the others do, and **Adolf Hitler**, which runs 54 minutes, gives a few more details to Hitler's biography than the others. They are best taken, however, as one complete program, examining the popularity of late Nineteenth Century mystics and the resurgence of interest in Germanic mythology (such as Richard Wagner's epics) that coincided with the rise of nationalism. It is largely forgotten today how extensive these interests became, but it went to the point that the Nazis essentially discarded Christianity for a more pagan system of beliefs, while at the same time embracing eugenics and other genetically exclusionary ideals. The point that one gathers from the details in all three documentaries is that these ideas had gone beyond the stage of simple abstract concepts and were being put into working practice on many levels in the German government and society as Hitler rose to power. The extent and absurdity of these beliefs appear to have had a direct influence upon the atrocities that followed.

The Odd Couple II (see **Neil Simon's The Odd Couple II**)

Odd Man Out (Image, ID4539JFDVD)

James Mason stars in the 1947 black-and-white drama, directed by Carol Reed, about an IRA terrorist on the run from the police. Not only are blacks pure, but the image is sharp and contrasts are effectively. In shot after shot, there are details in the costumes, the set decorations and the delicate lighting that enhance a viewer's involvement in the drama. The source material still has a number of errant speckles, but presentation looks great. The monophonic sound is okay, though there is some background noise. The story has an inevitability that not everyone will find appealing, but Reed's sense of style is highly attractive and so the DVD magnifies the film's assets considerably.

Odyssey: The Mind's Eye Presents Ancient Alien (Sony, LVD49927)

The mostly abstract 45 minute computer animation program provides a kind of impressionistic view of evolution, shifting between vague shapes or forms and images that parallel more closely the various stages life and specie development. There is also a bonus program, a more appealing and easier to follow piece called *Virtual World*, about a boy who looks at Africa through special goggles. The picture quality is fine on both programs and the pulsating stereophonic electronic musical score is adequate.

Odyssey: The Mind's Eye Presents Computer Animation Showcase (Sony, LVD49926)
Odyssey: The Mind's Eye Presents Computer Animation Classics (Sony, LVD49921)

Showcase runs 46 minutes, **Classics** runs 55 minutes, and each contains about two dozen shorts. Both programs have rich colors and pure blacks, and both are accompanied by an extra 'bonus' short. The stereo sound mix varies from short to short but is adequately presented.

Most of the shorts on **Showcase** have the semblance of a narrative, or at least a premise that holds the viewer's attention for the length of the piece. Among the highlights are a penguin water-skiing behind a killer whale, a Luxo Jr. *Sesame Street* installment, two cuckoo clock figurines who carry on a romance, the disastrous experience of an amateur matador, a super piece about a man walking along a sidewalk as various things happen to him, some jovial bugs, the disastrous experience of a marshmallow at a campout, and many more.

A mix of often-anthologized pieces, new commercials, a few other exercises and a Rolling Stones music video, **Classics** is varied enough to remain interesting, but real computer animation fans will have seen most of it before. The bonus piece on **Showcase** is a comical black-and-white sequence about a dog trying to get a cup of coffee, while the bonus clip on **Classics** is just a disjointed series of shape mutations.

Odyssey: The Mind's Eye Presents Computer Animation Celebration (Sony, LVD49464)

The 50 minute collection of computer animated films contains 21 shorts, many of them amusing and all of them exceptionally creative. Some have appeared on *Sesame Street* or similar venues, but others are independently produced exercises that test the limits of man's imagination and computer processing power. Among the highlights: A photo-realistic sequel to the Oscar-winning *Luxo, Jr.* in which the small desk lamp learns the difference between up and down; several amusing adventures involving a scheming Russian monkey cosmonaut and his victims; an elaborate trip down a desert highway with a group of motorcyclists (their roadkill ranges from sheep to UFOs); living lava lamps; an elaborate roller coaster ride; and much more. The picture looks terrific, with bright, sharp, glossy colors, and the stereo sound is fine. A less interesting German short is included as a 'bonus' and the program is accompanied by promos for other **Mind's Eye** productions.

Odyssey: The Mind's Eye Presents Luminous Visions (Sony, LVD49484)

You not only get a DVD, you also get a 45 minute audio CD of the show's Tangerine Dream score. The DVD also runs 45 minutes and is made up of abstract images flowing and pulsating to the music. The colors and textures are interesting but, as a video art program, the presentation's appeal is limited. The designs are relatively simple compared to a lot of today's computer animation, and movement rarely exceeds predictable patterns. The show is colorful, however. The transfer looks fine, with solid, sharp hues. The stereo surround sound is solid (the CD sounds a little better, though). There are also minute-long excerpts from other **Mind's Eye** programs, a brief interview with the Tangerine Dream and a profile of other works by the video artist, Yoichiro Kawaguchi.

Of Human Bondage (see **Pre-Code Hollywood: The Risqué Years #1**)

Of Mice and Men (Image, ID4571CODVD)

Lewis Milestone's 1939 adaptation of John Steinbeck's novel has scattered markings and a mild haze in places, but the source material is generally clean, sharp looking and thoroughly detailed. The monophonic sound is scratchy but coherent. The 106 minute film is not closed captioned. We have always found Steinbeck's original work to play a bit too literally and a film adaptation, even a good one, can't help but to seem like an instant cliché. The two central characters became popular cartoon lampoons almost instantly. Still, Milestone's effort, taken as much from an intermediate stage-play adaptation as from Steinbeck's novel, is an impressively mature effort that manages to maintain an adult tone and attitude throughout the story. Lon Chaney, Jr., in his best non-genre performance as the big dumb migrant farm worker, and Burgess Meredith, as the little and somewhat smarter migrant farm worker, star, with music by Aaron Copland.

The Official Story (Fox Lorber, FLV5048)

The 1985 Oscar-winner is about a woman who realizes her adopted daughter was the child of political prisoners murdered by the desperate Argentine junta in the mid seventies. The film is tightly constructed, so that the woman and her family can easily be seen as representing the Argentine state, just as the classroom in which the woman teaches can be seen as the state's conscience. There is also a pointed view of a magician at a children's birthday party, pretending to torture a dove, and the real horror his act instills upon his young audience. It is a fairly wrenching film, with strong symbolic overtones. By design, the viewer stays a couple steps ahead of the heroine, and the pacing will seem overly deliberate to some.

The picture is very hazy, with weak colors, and it is also slightly cropped, creating tight, uneven frames, but it still looks much better than the LD. The LD is badly drained of color and looks even blurrier, so when you come to the DVD from having watched a contemporary, decently transferred movie, it looks murky and almost unwatchable, but if you come to it after sampling the LD, it looks refreshing. Some hues are bright, fleshtones are manageable, and the image is reasonably sharp despite the haze. The source material has scattered speckles and a minor scratch or two. The movie's monophonic sound recording has budgetary limitations and the DVD's mono playback is flat, but adequate. The 110 minute program is in Spanish with permanent English subtitles.

Oklahoma! (Fox, 4110865)

The 1955 film was shot in Todd-AO and in Cinemascope, but while it is the Cinemascope version that is the most commonly played—and the one used for cropped TV presentations—the director, Fred Zinnemann, always shot his Todd-AO takes first and that is the version that has been used for the DVD. Although the general staging is the same, camera angles are sometimes different, the lighting is different, the framing is different, and background details are different. In the opening shot, for example, the horse is farther away on the Todd-AO version, and during the opening of *People Will Say We're in Love*, there are extras standing by a bridge on the Todd-AO presentation who are nowhere to be seen on the Cinemascope version.

Two principle factors make the Todd-AO version more entertaining. One is the incredible point-of-view camera angles that were designed to take advantage of the process and put the viewer in the middle of the excitement. Because of the vivid, steady image, the shot underneath the carriage during the *Surrey with the Fringe on Top* has a giddy, you-are-there feeling that the Cinemascope version can't communicate. There is an absolutely incredible shot on the Todd-AO version that shows the train approaching on the left and a man with a pair of horses approaching on the right, coming together in a 'V.' On the Cinemascope rendition, a pan is used to move from the horses to the train, losing the sense of location and drama that the shot achieves. Finally, the performances are better, which is understandable since the performers were more fresh for their Todd-AO takes than for their Cinemascope takes. When you compare the two versions side by side you can see Shirley Jones and Gordon MacRae using twice as many muscles in their faces to deliver their expressions. There is no gross negligence or laziness, just subtle things that they really had no control over as the day wore on but, when taken in total, affect quite strongly how the viewer responds to the characters. This freshness also extends to the dancers, who leap higher and have a more precise coordination on the Todd-AO presentation.

The film is presented in letterboxed format only, with an aspect ratio of about 2.2:1 and no 16:9 enhancement. The brightest hues are mildly over-saturated and fleshtones are a bit indistinct, but generally, the colors look super. There is a Dolby Digital track that has a little stronger presence than the standard track, but the two are fairly similar. Separation effects are limited, and the music is not much more than mildly dimensional, but tones are smooth. The 145 minute program has optional English and Spanish subtitles ("Soy una chica que no puede decir que no…"), a cast & crew profile section, production notes and a trailer.

The Old Dark House (Kino, K113DVD)

James Whale's amusingly eccentric thriller is about travelers waylaid in a house full of oddballs during a storm. Melvyn Douglas, Gloria Stuart and Raymond Massey star as three travelers whose car stalls in front of a sinister-looking mansion during a severely inclement evening. Among the house's inhabitants are Boris Karloff, Eva Moore and Ernest Thesiger. Charles Laughton and Lillian Bond also show up. The inhabitants of the house have their secrets and a little alcohol stirs things up. The general nervousness of the younger female characters doesn't appear to help matters.

The plot is little more than a gathering of contrived incidents and doesn't really go anywhere, but under Whale's direction the film is great fun. Characters holding knives leer at the camera in threatening closeups, other characters are shown reflected in distorted mirrors, an arm appears behind the heroine when she stands in a doorway, and menacing shadows are cast upon blank walls. These and other such effects create a marvelous atmosphere. So long as the characters can interact and advance emotionally, you don't really care about much else, because the mood carries the tension effectively.

The 1932 film was thought to have been lost for some time—the man who rescued it, Curtis Harrington, tells of his efforts in a 7 minute interview that appears after the film is over—and inevitably looks a little rough in spots. The black-and-white image is consistently soft, and is a bit marked up here and there. Contrasts, however, are relatively smooth and, in general, the film looks no different than most 1932 productions that have survived on disc. The source material is generally free of scratches and speckles. The monophonic sound has the expected amount of noise and distortion, but is workable. In addition to the Harrington interview, there is a 9 minute montage of production and publicity photos, set to music, and a still frame segment on Whale featuring photos from each of his movies. There is no captioning.

There are also two commentary tracks, and it is this feature that adds considerably to the value of the package. On one track, James Curtis gives a standard background talk about the filmmakers and the production, with a few insights on the film's artistic components. The other track contains the disc's gem, Stuart, in her mideighties, telling about her experiences making the movie and about her career in Hollywood. Now, we have difficulty remembering what movies we watched yesterday, but Stuart's memory for the details of the shoot is impeccable. It is clear from her statements that she hasn't seen the movie for a while, yet it is equally clear that she is very familiar with its contents. Her stories about making the movie are wonderful (all the British cast members would go off and have tea at 11 and at 4, leaving her and Douglas to sit around and talk about creating an actor's guild) and she also provides her own artistic interpretation of some of the film's best moments. She discusses Whale's directing techniques at length and seems capable of recalling her own state of mind during every shot. It is said that it was James Cameron's exposure to Stuart on the **Old Dark House** LD commentary track (which is what has been replicated on LD) that led to her being cast in *Titanic*, and it's quite possible, for she delivers an outstanding audio performance, recalling details and moods from 60 years earlier as if it were yesterday and speaking

with great lucidity about the production, its meanings and her experiences. It is really no different, in some respects, from the kind of tale her character weaves in Cameron's film.

Oliver! (Columbia TriStar, 02137)

The LD version of the 1968 Oscar-winning musical sounded pretty good but didn't look so hot. The DVD on the other hand, looks terrific, though the sound is a little wanting. The DVD's picture is cool and exact. The image looks so precise and crisp that the choreography becomes more enthralling, the musical numbers more exciting, and the whole movie becomes more of a pleasure to watch. The presentation is in letterboxed format only, with an aspect ratio of about 2.38:1 and an accommodation for enhanced 16:9 playback, adding picture information to all four sides in comparison to the LD.

The standard stereo surround soundtrack has a weaker presence than the LD's standard track. The DVD has been given a Dolby Digital track, which has more strongly defined separation effects and is cleaner than the LD's standard track. In cleaning things up, though, a bit of edge has been taken off the upper end, and so the LD's musical sequences, despite the noise, sound fresher and crisper.

The 146 minute program has been split to two sides, with the break occurring at the Intermission point and side two opening with the Entr'acte. The film also has a French language track (including the songs) in standard stereo, optional English and French subtitles ("Faut piquer dans une poche ou deux…"), a trailer, a good 'making of' featurette from when the film was produced and a nice collection of production stills and ad materials. The chapter encoding and jacket guide are miserly.

Directed by Carol Reed, the musical adaptation of *Oliver Twist*, starring Ron Moody and Oliver Reed, has many dull passages that seem poorly staged or dramatically redundant. The songs, however, are super.

Oliver Twist (Criterion, OLI040)

David Lean's 1948 adaptation is still the best filmed version there is. Dickens's story has one howling coincidence that cheapens an otherwise rich and complex tale about a young orphan who takes up with a band of equally young pickpockets led by an aging deviant. The farfetched plot turn which deposits Oliver in the house of his maternal grandfather is a lazy embarrassment that can cause one to take the story less seriously. The boy playing Oliver, John Howard Davies, is toothy and beset by melancholy, just as one would imagine. Alec Guinness overcomes his poor makeup to give Fagin an air of false grace, zeroing in on the contrast to Oliver's bland and well-meaning guardian. Anthony Newley turns up in an early role as the Artful Dodger. There is clearly more to the relationship between Nancy and Bill and Fagin than was ever written down.

The image is sharp and blacks are shiny. The picture is vivid from beginning to end. The monaural sound is adequate, though it is not as crisp as the picture and a little prone to mild volume fluctuations. The 116 minute program can be supported by optional English subtitles and is accompanied by original theatrical trailers.

Olivier Messiaen: Quartet for the End of Time / Improvisations (Image, ID5085GCDVD)

An organ recital improvisation is followed by a modern quartet, both of which make use of the acoustics in an ancient church's acoustics. Performed in the Paris-Trinity Church, Messiaen himself sits at the keyboard of the church organ for *Improvisations*, exploring the depth of the instrument. It is the *Quartet*, however, featuring Alain Moglia, Michel Arrignon, Sonia Wieder-Atherton and Jean-Claude Henriot, that is the more ethereal and satisfying of the two works. Composed while Messiaen was a German POW, it evokes the songs of birds, the promise of the Apocalypse and the despair of modern existence.

The stereo recording is basic but very satisfying, with pure tones and clear reverberations. The camera alternates between shots of the musicians and examinations of the church's design and decor. The picture is sharp and colors are accurate. The program runs 82 minutes.

On Approval (Image, ID5663DSDVD)

The marvelous four-character 1943 British comedy, based upon a stageplay, was written and directed by Clive Brook, who also stars. The film features Beatrice Lillie, Googie Withers and Roland Culver, as well, as two Victorian era couples who decide to try out being married before they tie the knot. The film runs just 78 minutes and is not as smoothly constructed as Hollywood comedies in the Forties were, but the characters are gloriously conceived—they're all hopelessly spoiled upper class types, even though the men are broke—and the plot is a lot saucier than Hollywood was allowed at the time.

The black-and-white source material is well worn, with scratches, speckles, and other blips, though the image is reasonably sharp most of the time. The monophonic sound is noisy but workable. The 77 minute program is not captioned.

On Deadly Ground (Warner, 13227)

Steven Seagal directed and starred in the 1994 film, about a Nazi-like oil company that has to go 'on line' by a certain day or it will forfeit its mineral rights, and so is murdering everyone in sight—Eskimos, kind-hearted employees, inept stooges—to meet the deadline. Michael Caine co-stars. The film runs 102 minutes and follows the pattern of a typical heroic action thriller. There are some great special effects, including some terrific model work (the huge refinery) and plenty of fights, gunshots and explosions. To this end, the DVD is super, providing a crisp, perfectly colored image that enhances the beauty of the film's design. The picture is presented on one side in letterboxed format, with an aspect ratio of about 2.35:1 and an accommodation for enhanced 16:9 playback, and in uselessly cropped format on the other side.

The standard stereo track is weak, but the Dolby Digital track has crisper separation effects and more oomph, and is lively, at least in spots. The 101 minute program also has a French audio track, in standard stereo, as well as optional English and French subtitles.

On Golden Pond (Artisan, 60749)

The film is letterboxed with an aspect ratio of about 1.85:1 and no 16:9 enhancement. Fleshtones are rich, other colors are very bright and crisp, and the image is clear. The stereo sound is passable and the film can be supported by Spanish subtitling or English closed captioning. The 105 minute program is accompanied by a few production notes, a cast & director profile section and an original theatrical trailer that tells the entire story in two minutes. There is also an excellent 45 minute retrospective documentary that cynics might suggest is more emotionally uplifting and better expressive of the film's themes than the movie itself. The 1981 film's director, Mark Rydell, provides a running commentary, telling anecdotes about the production (the best are repeated in the documentary) and talking about working with the stellar cast, which included Henry Fonda, Katharine Hepburn and Jane Fonda. The documentary is superb, selling the film's strengths (about coming to terms with family and aging, and about the stars) to the point where the film's weaknesses (a simplicity characterized by the trailer) no longer seem relevant.

On Her Back X-rated (Vivid, UPC#0073215524)

A half-hearted ribald take on Renaissance painters, there are some amusing one-liners and funny Italian accents, but the premise tends to get sidetracked by the erotic sequences, which are rarely inspired. Shot on film, colors are a little light and the image is a bit soft, but in relation to most film transfers (as opposed to videotape transfers) of adult programs, it looks okay. The sound is adequate (lots of Mozart, which for them is hardly an anachronism). The 71 minute program features Dyanna Lauren, Anna Malle and Nikki Randall.

Once a Thief (Simitar, 7360)

Our favorite John Woo film is his free-spirited homage to Sixties caper movies, **Once a Thief,** and Woo himself apparently had a soft spot for it, because he remade the movie with a more occidental cast as a pilot for a Canadian TV series. The 101 minute pilot, however, also called **Once a Thief,** is an invigorating concoction with a number of terrific action sequences. The plot is a little different from the feature film but has several of the same elements, with two heroes and a villain all in love with the same woman and all trying to disrupt one another's business. The pilot essentially establishes the heroes as working for a mysterious crime-stopping organization that requires their special skills, often involving heists and similar caper-type black ops. The presentation has an 'R' rating and apparently a few more squibs than the broadcast presentation, which is just fine by us. Among the best stunt sequences is a motorcycle-and-car chase in which the hero, on the cycle, ends up leaping with the cycle onto the top of the car he is following and then grabbing onto the roof for dear life as the cycle goes flying on its way; and an amusing acrobatic heist where the two heroes precariously and awkwardly hang from chandelier to grab a painting protected by an electrical floor. The show doesn't have as much class as the feature film, but it is a fun concoctions.

The picture has bright, clear hues, deep blacks and a crisp image. The stereo surround sound is also strong and reasonably engaging. Contrary to a mistaken listing on the jacket cover, the running time is 101 minutes.

Once Upon a Time in China (import, MSDVD02898)
Once Upon a Time in China II (import, MSDVD02998)
Once Upon a Time in China III (import, MSDVD03098)

Tsui Hark's fabulous martial arts trilogy stars Jet Li. Each of the three films, the original from 1991, **II** from 1992 and **III** from 1993, can be viewed separately, and there is precious little character development across any of them (the hero does gradually fall in love), but the acrobatic stunts and fight scenes are incredibly imaginative and there is always enough narrative to keep things interesting.

Li portrays the legendary Nineteenth Century Chinese martial arts figure Wong Fei Hung, and each DVD contains extensive information about Hung and terrific clips from previous Hung movies, including some marvelously stodgy black-and-white kung fu movies from the Forties and Fifties. The DVDs also have cast profiles and trailers.

The picture on each movie is letterboxed with an aspect ratio of about 2.35:1 and no 16:9 enhancement. Both the color transfer and the stereo sound improve with each episode. By and large, the picture on all three movies looks great for a Hong Kong production. Fleshtones are distinctive, other hues are bright and the image is reasonably sharp. On the first film there is more of a tendency for the image to appear slightly washed out and for colors to take on a slightly yellow tone, but the picture remains quite sharp and, by **III**, the image is as chromatic as a Hollywood musical.

The DVDs are in Dolby Digital, but dimensionality is erratic. The catchy—though very Chinese—musical score has some flourish, but the audio tracks tend to be conservative, with occasional surges of directional effects. Separations are the most pronounced in the third film. The films are available in Cantonese and Mandarin, and can be supported by optional English, traditional Chinese, simplified Chinese, Japanese, Korean, Bahasa Malaysian and Spanish subtitles. The subtitles appear beneath or on the cusp of the letterboxed image.

In the first film, which runs 128 minutes, Li's character is the head of a kung fu school. His town is overrun by gangsters and corrupt foreigners, and he takes it upon himself to clean the place up. The production design is enchanting, with many elaborate sets dressed in period, and the fight scenes are wonderfully inventive. The finale includes an amazing warehouse battle in which Li and the villain leap up and down bales and ladders.

II, which runs 108 minutes, is set in Canton, where Li's character runs afoul of an anti-European cult and is trapped in a siege at an embassy. There is an amazing fight upon stacked and balanced tables, and another up and down and back and forth across bamboo scaffolding. There are no special effect compositions in the film that match the shots of Nineteenth Century warships in the first movie, but the film carries the same spirit and is a worthy follow-up.

As is **III**, which runs 107 minutes and is set in Beijing. Here Li's character comes into conflict with a group of gangsters who are stacking the deck to win a dragon competition. The finale is a spellbinding battle featuring scores of competitors attempting to take their dragons to the top of a rickety tower. The film has a strong blend of humor, action and drama (one character begins as one of the most evil bad guys, but turns into a good guy about halfway through), and is perhaps the most appealing of the three, though they are all invigorating adventures.

One Flew Over the Cuckoo's Nest (Warner, 36222)

Jack Nicholson stars in the 1975 Oscar winner, directed by Milos Forman, as an inmate in a psychiatric hospital who enriches the lives of his fellow inmates before being squashed by the administration.

The picture has deep colors and looks quite sharp. The stereo surround sound is muted. The program is presented in letterboxed format on one side, with an aspect ratio of about 1.85:1 and an accommodation for 16:9 playback, and in cropped format on the other side. The 133 minute film is also available in French in mono and comes with English, French or Spanish subtitles. There is a good cast and crew profile and a decent set of production notes.

100 Girls by Bunny Yeager (Cult Epics, DVD0003)

A female professional photographer who specialized in racy photos of topless and semi-topless women in the late Fifties and Sixties, Bunny Yeager, collected her best photos in a picture book, which was replicated on the DVD. Yeager worked out of the Miami area and did everything from local fashion photography to centerfold spreads for Playboy. The format is fairly simple, but engagingly nostalgic. As the camera pans across each page of the book, Yeager speaks in voiceover about each of her subjects—she seems to remember them all quite vividly—sharing their personality quirks, explaining how well they photographed and even telling what happened to them afterward. Here and there, 16mm footage of one of the subjects has also been included in the 45 minute program. In addition to Yeager's voiceover, there is an unobtrusive, Fifties-style instrumental musical score. The photographs are all black and white, and most of the live color footage is very faded. The program is not closed captioned.

100 Years of Horror (Passport, DV D2226)

Using trailers and 'making of' featurettes, the moderately entertaining genre overview is narrated by Christopher Lee. Although one could easily do a whole documentary on vampire movies alone, **Horror** works its way through the various sub-genres with insightful comments, entertaining footage and an approach that will seem as informative to fans as it is to newcomers. Going beyond just trailers, there are interviews with the offspring of many famous horror stars, color footage of Boris Karloff in his original Frankenstein makeup (joking around on the set), a blooper reel from *Abbot & Costello Meet Frankenstein*, and screen tests from *Dracula*. There is also a segment about William Castle and we took note that while the documentary claims Castle's style has become a lost art, it is actually alive and well in the thrill rides and 3-D films running in the major amusement parks.

The picture quality in the clips varies but they are often overly soft and faded. The monophonic sound is a bit scratchy and there is a lack of crispness in the tone. The 100 minute program is not captioned.

101 Dalmatians (Buena Vista, 14253)

Lost in the concentration on its adaptation from the cartoon is that **101 Dalmatians** is quite similar to **Babe**, though not nearly as classy. The live action film makes extensive use of mechanical animals, with some computer generated ones as well, endowing them with substantially more intelligence than the animals we are intimate with. In some ways the film seems constrained by its partial adherence to the cartoon, particularly when it comes to Glenn Close, who is so intent on being a caricature that she has little time for genuine comical invention.

The presentation is fully letterboxed, with an aspect ratio of about 2.35:1 and no 16:9 enhancement. The picture is crisper, with bright glossy colors and accurate flesh and fur tones. The stereo surround sound is weak, but the Dolby Digital track sports a decent bass, a much crisper tone than the standard track and plenty of engaging directional effects. The 103 minute program is also available in French or Spanish, and comes with optional English subtitling and a theatrical trailer.

One Night Stand (New Line, N4655)

"The use of coincidence in film is a minefield," says Mike Figgis about the central conceit of **One Night Stand**, sadly unaware that there are bits of him scattered all over the place as a result of that minefield. In the past, Figgis has directed some fairly good films and some that were, charitably, more difficult to enjoy. With the superbly crafted **Leaving Las Vegas**, however, he raised the bar, and with **One Night Stand** he comes crashing back down, having failed to reach anywhere near it. The film began as one of those over-priced scripts Joe Eszterhas cons movie companies into buying (he apparently writes them to sell to film executives, not to actually become movies). When it was given to Figgis it was completely re-written and Eszterhas' name does not appear in the credits, which was probably for the best, but the spirit of Eszterhas remains. The characters are superficial, the plot is generated by a whopping coincidence (the married hero, played by Wesley Snipes, has a one night stand with a friend's wife, unaware of who she is; Nastassja Kinski is also featured), and concludes with what can best be described as a punchline. There is no resonance, no penetrating exploration of modern life, no hard edged satirical counterpoint, and no characters that the viewer can give a whit about. Robert Downey, Jr. portrays a friend of the hero who is dying of AIDS, and his sequences are well staged but structurally amount to little more than an elaborate sideshow, failing even to underscore the apparent risks the hero is taking with unprotected sex.

In addition to the Figgis' director's commentary, Figgis' jazz score—one of the few admirable aspects of the film—is isolated on another audio channel. The film is presented in letterboxed format on one side, with an aspect ratio of about 1.85:1 and an accommodation for enhanced 16:9 playback, and in full screen format on the other. The full screen presentation adds picture information to the top and bottom and loses nothing from the sides in comparison to the letterboxed version. The image looks fine, with crisp, glossy colors and accurate fleshtones. The stereo surround sound and Dolby Digital surround are adequate, though the film's sound mix is rarely elaborate. The musical score is not in Dolby Digital. The 104 minute film is available in French in Dolby Digital and comes with English, French or Spanish subtitles, as well as a theatrical trailer.

Figgis defends coincidences in films, pointing out how often they occur in real life, but what he fails to acknowledge is that there are elegant coincidences in films and there are inelegant coincidences. He acknowledges that the film received "catastrophically bad reviews," but focuses in his talk on the few reviewers who went overboard and picked on what were valid aspects of the film, remaining in denial about what must have been voluminous complaints about the movie's weaker attributes. For those who are interested, however, the commentary track is otherwise fairly rewarding. He discusses his working methods, describes in satisfying detail a number of scenes that didn't make it to the final cut, explores the technical requirements for shooting many of the key scenes, talks about what it is like to make a commercial (as he did in the movie) without a client hanging over his shoulder, and provides other informative background tidbits.

One True Thing (Universal, 20440)

A family of intellectuals starts to crack a bit around the seams when the mother is stricken with terminal cancer. Meryl Streep, who earned an Oscar nomination for her effort, Renee Zellweger and William Hurt star in the somewhat uncommercial tale. The filmmakers do a very good job at gradually peeling away the presumptions the characters have about one another (the daughter comes to realize that her respected and demanding father is a failure), and on a technical level the film is earnest and involving. However, the 1998 film is also quite a dry work, and it is doubtful that too many viewers will care about the subtleties the drama has to offer in spiritual nourishment.

The film is letterboxed, with an aspect ratio of about 1.85:1 and an accommodation for enhanced 16:9 playback. The color transfer is very good, with sharp, accurate hues and viable fleshtones. The stereo surround sound is not elaborately mixed, but it is adequately presented, and there is a Dolby Digital track with surprisingly more detail and clarity. The 128 minute film is also available in French in standard stereo and can be supported by English or Spanish subtitles. There is a good 'making of' featurette, a decent production essay, a small cast-and-director profile section and a trailer.

Only You (Columbia TriStar, 73269)

We don't know why people aren't lining up around the block every time a new Marisa Tomei film comes out, but it's their loss. Tomei is marvelous in the pleasant 1994 travelogue romantic comedy directed by Norman Jewison, co-starring Robert Downey, Jr. Tomei's character is chasing after the man she believes to be her true love, though she has never met him. As her moods change and her predicaments advance, the expressions that cross her face, often in no more than brief flickers, allow the viewer to keep a constant monitor upon what is happening to her heart. Her slapstick timing is also delightful. The film is Jewison's attempt to recapture the success he had with **Moonstruck**. It lacks **Moonstruck**'s sense of epic destiny, has a few too many loose ends and spends a bit too much time sightseeing in Italy, where most of it is set, but on the whole it is an appealing and satisfying work.

The color transfer is exquisite and the image is solid, except for a few scattered night shots that appear to have been filmed with an unusual level of grain. The film is presented on one side in letterboxed format, with an aspect ratio of about 1.85:1 and an accommodation for enhanced 16:9 playback, and is in full screen format on the other side. The stereo surround sound is also very good, with many adept surround effects. The 109 minute program also has French and Spanish language tracks, optional English, French and Spanish subtitles, and a trailer.

Open City (Image, ID4102DSDVD)

Made in 1945 just about the day the Germans left Rome and is about life during the German occupation. The tense Roberto Rossellini film draws a specific comparison to the experiences of a communist resistance leader and a priest (who is sympathetic to the resistance), using the drama of betrayal and capture, as well as the humor generated by those trying to live a normal life under adversity, to make the film as entertaining and moving as it is artistically brilliant.

The black-and-white image is full of scratches and other evidence of wear, but that is a traditional flaw in the film's production

and is an acceptable part of the viewing experience. The image is in reasonably good condition, as is the monaural audio track. If one takes the film's production history into account, then the presentation is acceptable, though not pristine. The monophonic sound seems muted, but there is a Dolby Digital mono track that is somewhat stronger, compensating in smoothness what it loses by trying to dampen the background noise. The film runs 105 minutes and is in Italian with white English subtitles.

Open Wide X-rated (Vivid)

Vaudeville-type humor infests the comedy about a dental office, though the narrative has a punchline that excuses the show's silliest gags. The erotic sequences are passable but rarely elaborate and the monophonic sound is okay. The picture is workable. The 71 minute program features Jenteal, Felecia, Ruby, and Julie Rage. The DVD contains alternate angle sequences and elaborate hardcore interactive promotional features.

Operation Shark Attack (Madacy, DVD99037)
Operation Shark Attack: Operation Shark Attack (Madacy, DVD990371)
Operation Shark Attack: Legends of the Killer Shark (Madacy, DVD990373)
Operation Shark Attack: Tales of the Tiger Shark (Madacy, DVD990374)
Operation Shark Attack: Shark Attack Files (Madacy, DVD990372)
Operation Shark Attack: Shark Attack Files 2 (Madacy, DVD990374)

The documentaries, titled *The Shark Files* within the films themselves, are about the relationship between sharks and people, and forego an extensive scientific profile of sharks, but the shows draw upon material taken from all around the world that is consistently fascinating, and there are plenty of shark facts and shark lore slipped into the narration. Additionally, each DVD contains a brief 'shark facts' and shark trivia section.

The two **Shark Attack Files** programs have the most in common, although none of the incidents in the first volume are repeated in the second. The first volume, which runs 45 minutes, profiles the great white shark and its feeding habits, the tiger shark and its feeding habits, and takes a look at several attack incidents (most involving surfers), using genuine news footage and retrospective interviews. There is an extensive section on how Hawaii is combating sharks (including controversy over liberal fishing policies designed to lower the shark population); the efforts taken in South Africa to eliminate sharks from beaches, including the effective use of shark nets; a look at attack stories from a hundred years ago; and, given equal time, the 'Shark Protection and Preservation Association,' who insist that sharks are our friends. **2**, which runs 52 minutes, contains more attack reminiscences, with a greater emphasis upon the injuries incurred; a look at a sea otter rehabilitation clinic in California for animal shark victims; a look at what the real feeding habits of sharks are and why, most of the time, humans aren't all that appetizing; a look at elicit shark fishing; and a pair of scientists who study tiny hammerheads that may hold a key to preventing melanoma.

Operation Shark Attack, which runs 45 minutes, is about the development of a 'shark proof' diving suit. The suit allows the divers to play tug-of-war with the sharks (and deadly sea snakes) using their own arms and legs. The make important discoveries (the jaws of the smaller sharks don't have much pressure—they tear their prey by shaking it) and spend more time amid feeding frenzies than humans ever had before. They also troll for a great white using a human dummy in one of their suits and, sure enough, the suit isn't ripped, though watching the dummy's head disappear into the shark's gaping mouth reinforces the warning that these are activities you should not try at home.

Tales of the Tiger Shark, which runs 52 minutes, looks specifically at the tiger shark, with an emphasis upon attack incidents, research (how sharks are tagged and implanted with monitors), attack prevention, how the tiger shark reacts to captivity, the role the tiger shark plays in Hawaiian legends and a fascinating sequence in which a tiger shark is transported by boat, truck and plane to an aquarium. **Legends of the Killer Sharks**, which runs 52 minutes, looks into the most publicized attacks during the first half of the century, including a fascinating a tale about a shark that attacked bathers in a New Jersey river near Matawan, many miles from the ocean, and the famous Margate Beach attacks in South Africa that still hold the record for most swimmers used as a smorgasbord, or something. There is also a tantalizing shark autopsy (no license plates, but plenty of other stuff) and a look at tour groups that deliberately visit shark-infested waters. No word on the insurance rates.

Underwater shots are often monochromatic blues, but most of the non-archive footage looks very good, with bright, crisp colors. The stereo soundtrack has some separation effects (the narrator on one side and background sounds on the other), although the dialogue is a bit fuzzy on the upper end. The programs are not captioned.

The Opposite of Sex (Columbia TriStar, 01839)

The comedy is about a sixteen-year old girl who upturns the sedate domestic life of her older gay brother when she moves in with him. Christina Ricci and Martin Donovan star, with Lisa Kudrow turning in an amusing performance as one of the brother's friends. The film has a fresh attitude, including a tart voiceover narration by Ricci, and gets away with jokes about homosexuality in the same way that Mel Brooks gets away with jokes about Jews. The characters are generally unique and funny, and once the story's convolutions pick up speed, the film is reasonably entertaining.

The picture is presented in letterboxed format on one side, with an aspect ratio of about 1.85:1 and an accommodation for enhanced 16:9 playback, and in full screen format on the other. Either framing seems to work okay. The color transfer is fine and fleshtones are accurate. The stereo surround sound gives the music a nice dimensionality but has few other notable attributes. The 100 minute film is also in French and can be supported by English or French subtitles.

The film is accompanied by a trailer, by several deleted scenes that would have slowed things down, and by a commentary track featuring the film's writer-director, Don Roos, editor David Codron and producer Michael Besman. This was Roos' first effort as a director and he talks a lot about what he learned as he went along, as well as pointing out the many technical mistakes he made but had no time to rectify. It is reasonably informative, both about the film and about being a filmmaker.

Opus 1 (see **Berlin, Symphony of a Great City/Opus 1**)

Orchestra Rehearsal (Fox Lorber, FL5004)

Federico Fellini's final collaboration with composer Nino Rota (who could be said to have contributed the soul to Fellini's films), the make-believe documentary begins as a comedy about musicians who have the personalities of their instruments and about the irascibility of labor unions, shifts through the documentary 'interviews' into a long series of thoughtful and stimulating metaphors about the meaning of music and the function of the various instruments, and then turns back again to a comedy of anarchy that is redeemed, in the finale, by the sublimity of the music. It is a delightful film—and, for that matter, a good introduction to Fellini—with so much comedy amid the catchy music that repeat viewings are almost essential.

The 1979 film, which is in Italian, runs 72 minutes. We wish the picture transfer could have been a bit better. The presentation is slightly letterboxed, but colors are somewhat pale and sharp edges often have a distinct ghosting, giving the film a slightly smeary, video look. The monophonic sound is a little harsh at times, but that is probably a limitation of the original recording. The DVD has optional yellow English subtitles that are discreet but fully legible, as well as filmographies for Fellini and Rota, and a video trailer.

Organized Crime & Triad Bureau (Tai Seng, 51364)

Danny Lee stars as a dedicated police detective hampered by jurisdictional infighting as he chases after the leader of a jewelry store robbery gang, played by Anthony Wong. Fast-paced and creative, even after the heroes capture the bad guy they have difficulty holding onto him. Having traced him to a crowded resort town, the police use cash, confiscated from the criminals, to pay shopkeepers to close down for the day so they can have an easier time spotting the villain. In another sequence Wong's character is cornered in a hospital operating room and holds a scalpel to the patient's neck when the police barge in. Realizing the patient is a sick child, however, he laments and surrenders, only to get away again later on. The characters, including those in the smaller roles, are effectively drawn, and the film is an ideal mix of procedural action and moral drama (Lee's character does break a few rules to catch his man).

The more we see the 1993 movie, a procedural about the police chasing a mobster—he gets captured a couple times and escapes, but gradually gains partial sympathy with the viewer—the more we enjoy it. It doesn't have the spectacular stunts one associates with the most energetic Hong Kong features, but it is an efficient and entertaining program. The picture is letterboxed with an aspect ratio of about 1.85:1 and no 16:9 enhancement. The colors have the usual diminished luster one associates with low budget Hong Kong productions and contrasts are weak at times, but on the whole the transfer looks okay. The monophonic program can be presented in English, Cantonese or Mandarin with optional English subtitles. Like the picture, the sound has production-related limitations, but remains acceptable when one takes its history into account. The 100 minute film is accompanied by some trailers, and profiles of the cast and of Wong.

Additionally, the director, Kirk Wong, provides a commentary track. The talk is a bit sparse, with Wong chiming in periodically to speak about his career, about Lee's obsession with playing policemen and about staging the film's major scenes. He is articulate and has some interesting stories about the guerrilla-style filmmaking low budget Hong Kong features often have to utilize (like not getting permission to shoot action scenes on public streets), but there are long gaps between anecdotes, particularly in the film's second half.

The Original Fleetwood Mac: The Early Years (Image ID5504CADVD)

Before they became the bland MOR hit generator that everybody knows and loves, Fleetwood Mac was a blues band, and it is as a blues band that they are captured on various films in the 54 minute program. Some of the footage is in black and white, and some is in color. It opens with the summary of the band's formation and early activities, but the rest of the program is a collection of live performances (and a couple montage sequences) as they can be seen gradually edging away from raw, generic blues to a sound that is blander but more of their own creation. The highlight is probably a clip from *Playboy after Dark*, just because of the disparate mix of images the show attempted to achieve. Another revelation to us was the group's instrumental hit, *Albatross*, which appears to have been a turning point in the maturation of the musicians and is placed in the center of the chronologically ordered program.

Although old and somewhat secondhand, the footage looks reasonably good, and there are many nice close-ups. The sound is passable, particularly if you don't really mind the rougher nature of some of the recordings. It is in stereo, but dimensionality is limited.

The Original Three Tenors Concert (PolyGram, 4400712232)

Popularly known as *Three Tenors*, the concert has proved to be a highly popular program. Conducted by Zubin Mehta at a benefit at the Terme di Caraculla in Rome and supported by the combined orchestras of Florence and Rome, Jose Carreras, Plácido Domingo and Luciano Pavarotti take turns singing traditional songs and arias for about an hour, and then join together for 20 minutes of harmonic collaboration. Exchanging high fives as they tramp back and forth from the podium, they clearly appreciate the uniqueness of the event, and their teamwork creates an atmosphere of excitement and free-flowing adrenaline. We don't for a minute believe that Jose Carreras sings *Memory* because he likes the song, but not even the event's commercialism can dampen the basic significance of what the group is accomplishing by appearing together. It not only humanizes the singers and creates some very unique music, it sets a clear precedent that opera superstars long into the future will be forced to live by, to the benefit of fans.

The image on the 86 minute 1990 concert is very crisp and the colors are super. The Dolby Digital track is airier and better detailed than the standard stereo soundtrack. It still didn't stop us from cringing when Carreras breaks into *Maria*, but most of the concert sounds fantastic, with a wide bass, a strong dimensionality (there is a distinct association with the location of the vocals and the position of the three singers on the stage), and brighter tones than the regular stereo track. The chapter listing on the jacket is off by one compared to the program's chapter encoding and, in a related complaint, the *Final Medley* is represented by a single chapter marker.

Orphans of the Storm (Image, ID4676DSDVD)

Our favorite D.W. Griffith film, and perhaps his most accessible epic, Lillian and Dorothy Gish portray peasant sisters, one of whom is blind, who are separated during the French Revolution. In the end, Danton himself saves one of them from the guillotine. Griffith does a superb job recreating the costumes and architecture of the era, and he is as comfortable with the big crowd scenes and evoking social unrest as he is coaxing affecting performances during more intimate moments. A perfect blend of history and pathos, the plot is wonderful and the spectacle is grand, but what really sells the film is Lillian Gish's nothing-held-back performance as the sister who can see. She seems to scream with every inch of her body, embracing the style of acting that was necessary in silent films, yet her emotional states are also conveyed quite subtly and she never succumbs to the backhand-on-the-forehead method to express her feelings.

The program runs 150 minutes—longer than most versions—and movement is natural looking. The presentation is moderately windowboxed and rarely jiggles. The image is lightly tinted, without obscuring too many details. The source material has only slight wear most of the time. There is an unobtrusive stereo musical score, combining an organ with an orchestra.

Otis Redding: Remembering Otis (Pioneer, PA98587D)

A 48 minute collection of concerts from 1966 and 1967 featuring Redding, he first two segments, from a Hammersmith Odeon concert and from a Stax-Volt Tour (the latter featuring cuts from Booker T and the MGs and Sam & Dave as well) are in black and white, while the finale, Redding's set from the Monterey Pop Festival, is in color. All three have been remastered for stereo and given Dolby Digital encoding, with the Dolby Digital track providing markedly better defined tones than the standard stereo track, which sounds soft and almost fuzzy in comparison. The source material varies in quality (the Stax-Volt footage is the clearest) but is often a bit smeary. Nevertheless, fans will embrace the material and even casual viewers will appreciate Redding's unbridled talent and unique vocal energy. Since *Sitting on the Dock of the Bay* wasn't part of any of the concerts, by the way, the studio recording has been included to a montage of Redding stills.

Ottmar Liebert + Luna Negra: Wide-Eyed + Dreaming (Sony, EVD50145)

A barefoot acoustical guitarist with an apparent distaste for ampersands, surrounded, without irony, by lava lamps and accompanied by an electric bass and esoteric percussion instruments, performs a Hispanic-flavored jazz before a live audience. The hour-long program is mostly music, but does include interview sequences with Liebert between some of the numbers, in which he explains that he doesn't like to interrupt his concert performances with talk, although that is precisely what he is doing on the video, forcing you to get his CD if you just want to hear the music and not him. The music sounds terrific and the mix has a fresh immediacy. The image gets a little fuzzy here and there, depending upon the stage lighting, but is generally presentable.

Out for Justice (Warner, 12219)

Steven Seagal portrays a detective hunting down the man who killed his friend. The killer, in the meantime, is off on a drug-crazed murder spree, and even the Mafia wants to rub him out. It is a reasonably busy, if illogical, action feature.

The 1991 film seems out-of-focus in spots, but the transfer looks okay, with accurate fleshtones and stable hues. The program is presented in letterboxed format on one side, with an aspect ratio of about 2.35:1 and an accommodation for enhanced 16:9 playback, and in cropped/full screen format on the other side. Why do we say 'cropped/full screen?' Well, it appears the film was shot in Super-35, but the full screen version is mostly a cropped presentation of the widescreen version, except where the shot requires that you see more picture information on the sides, such as during the opening credit sequence, which is then a replication of the widescreen image with more picture information on the top and bottom.

The film has been remastered for 5-channel Dolby Digital, though we could detect almost no difference between the Dolby Digital track and the standard track. Separation effects aren't all that elaborate. The 91 minute film also has a French audio track in standard stereo and optional English and French subtitles.

Out of Ireland (Shanachie, 948)

An excellent Ken Burns-style documentary written and directed by Paul Wagner, the 112 minute program tells the story of Irish immigration to the United States, giving a kind of parallel history of Ireland and urban America over the past two centuries. The narrative is supplemented by extensive readings from correspondence of earlier eras and commentary by historians, while the images include old photographs, drawings, newsreels, and contemporary shots of the largely unchanged Irish countryside (there were more people living in Ireland 150 years ago than live there today). The film takes the time to explain Irish politics and the causes behind the landlord system that sent so many individuals off to find a better life. There are insightful discussions about the potato famine, the Catholic Church, Irish folk beliefs, the reasons why the Irish gravitated to politics when they arrived in America, and the gradual rise of the Irish from the lowliest minority (dangerous jobs were given to Irish employees instead of 'valuable' slaves) to JFK's triumphant visit to Dublin. The music and the lyrical voices of Ireland (a couple dozen celebrities share in the voiceover chores, including Liam Neeson and Aidan Quinn) seep into one's consciousness throughout the program, and it is an ideal blend of educational content and artistic beauty. The picture quality is very good and the stereo surround sound is fine. There are some minor artifacting effects—primarily during pans across black-and-white photos and, especially, ink drawings, that cause parts of the image to detach from their surroundings—but it is a minor anomaly and not enough to create a distraction.

Out of Sight (Universal, 20340); DTS (Universal, 20589)

A slightly comical Elmore Leonard crime story turned into an inconsequential but charming motion picture by director Steven

Soderbergh. George Clooney is a bank robber who has escaped from a penitentiary and Jennifer Lopez is a U.S. Marshall who meets him and kind of falls for him, even though she is aware of his criminal record. Their probationary romance is complicated by a job the hero wants to pull off before he splits the country. Like other Leonard adaptations, the supporting characters are distinctively written and performed, and the flashback-laden narrative takes many unexpected turns. We found some of the characters to be a bit arch in the finale, and in other spots the performances are very casual. Additionally, some of Soderbergh's stylistic choices don't blend well, but the premise and the Leonard formula are fun, and that sort of rubs off on everything.

The picture is letterboxed with an aspect ratio of about 1.85:1 and an accommodation for enhanced 16:9 playback. The color transfer looks very good, with sharp, accurate hues and nicely detailed fleshtones. There are moments when the image appears to freeze, but that turns out to be Soderbergh somewhat arbitrarily trying to evoke *Breathless* or something. The stereo surround sound and Dolby Digital sound have an efficient mix, with some distinctive separation effects, but the film is a character-oriented drama and the quality of the audio is not critical to the entertainment. There is little difference between the standard stereo track and the Dolby Digital track, though definitions on the Dolby track are a bit crisper. The 123 minute film is also available in French and Spanish, and comes with English or Spanish subtitles.

In addition to the film and a theatrical trailer, there is a 25 minute documentary about the movie, featuring interviews with the cast and crew, and with Leonard. The cast jokes around a bit, but they also talk about working with one another and about their characters. Soderbergh discusses some of the problems he encountered getting the film to work for audiences and his reasoning behind some of the artistic choices he made. There are also 22 minutes of deleted scenes, most of which explain what, within the film, are somewhat jarring shifts in narrative or location. In the documentary, Soderbergh talks about shooting a number of uninterrupted takes for the trunk scene, and the 6 minute take he printed is included (he ultimately chose to break it up with editing, because the shift in tone from the rest of the film was too suffocating for viewers). In typical Universal fashion, the trailer, production notes, and cast & crew profile are sort of hidden in the menu. The trailer is a bit lackluster. Soderbergh and screenwriter Scott Frank provide a running commentary as well, speaking informatively about the production, about how they wrestled with the story and screenplay, and about working with the performers. Again, there is some joking around, but you get a good idea of why the major scenes ended up the way they did, for better or worse.

Directional effects are crisper and more independent, the bass is stronger and the high end is purer and clearer on the DTS version. While the film is more laid back than the standard crime thriller, it does fall into that category and its pleasures are enhanced by the improved sound. Unlike the standard DVD, the program has no extra features and no captioning. The picture is identical to the standard release.

Out of Time (Simitar, 7300)

Jeff Fahey is an archeologist searching for baubles that will lead him to Alexander's tomb. Bad guys are also after the stuff, though they tend to let the hero do their work for them. The film was shot in Egypt and the location photography is pleasing, but the film is predictable and sometimes just a little too contrived to work as mindless fun.

The picture is light and hazy, with a stronger grain in some dark sequences. The stereo sound is pretty flat, but the musical score emphasizes Middle Eastern motifs and is reasonably satisfying. The film runs 98 minutes, is not captioned, and is accompanied by a Fahey filmography.

Outbreak (Warner, 13632)

In the terribly exciting disease-is-loose movie, Dustin Hoffman, who was smart to take the role but is not quite up to the requirements of a modern action film hero (he looks very funny whenever his character is about to perform a perilous stunt), stars as an army disease expert who has to find a cure for a rapidly spreading virus before his superiors decide to just nuke the general area where the disease has blossomed. Directed by Wolfgang Petersen, who brought the same sort of systematic excitement to **In the Line of Fire**, the film is open to many repeat viewings because it is tense from beginning to end and its climax is not the single key to its entertainment.

The DVD also contributes to the film's thrills. The color quality is outstanding, the image is crisp and there are no artifacts to speak of. The standard stereo surround sound is unremarkable, but the Dolby Digital track is outstanding, full of high-energy directional effects pushing you that much more giddily through the whizbang narrative. The picture is letterboxed on one side, with an aspect ratio of about 1.85:1 and an accommodation for enhanced 16:9 playback, and is in full screen on the other. The letterboxing removes some picture information from the top and bottom of the image and adds an equal amount to the sides. We actually liked the full screen presentation the best, because of the tense close-ups inserted between the action scenes, but either one looks just fine. The film is also available in French, without Dolby Digital, and has English, Spanish and French subtitles. The 128 minute film is accompanied by a brief production essay and a reasonably large cast profile, serving as a reminder that the 1995 medical action thriller went into production with two Oscar winners—Hoffman and Morgan Freeman, Jr.—but now has two more on its boards, with both Kevin Spacey and Cuba Gooding, Jr. filling major secondary roles. We suppose this is a good omen for Rene Russo and Donald Sutherland.

Outland (Warner, 14982)

Peter Hyams' **High Noon**-in-space thriller has been released in letterboxed format on one side, with an aspect ratio of about 2.35:1, and in a cropped format on the other side. Contrary to a notation on the jacket cover, the letterboxing has not been enhanced for 16:9 playback. The cropping gives the viewer an enlarged image of some of the special effects, but cuts other effects off at the same time. The image has deep blacks, bright hues and accurate fleshtones. There are some minor problems with details that become more evident on larger screens. There seems to be more artifacting than usual, perhaps because there is just so much contrasty detail and so much camera movement in many of the sequences. Lines seem jittery at times and solid objects seem disconnected. There are sound effects on the DVD's soundtrack that we have never heard before, and the Dolby Digital track is even better, with a stronger range, more power and clearer separations. The 1981 109 minute film is also available in Spanish in mono and comes with English, French and Spanish subtitles, a cast and crew profile, a trailer and some brief production notes. Sean Connery stars in the story about drug smugglers in a mining complex on the Jovian moon, Io, and a single lawman, who is willing to stand up against them in a sort of 'do not forsake Io, my darling' situation.

The Outlaw Josey Wales (Warner, 12588)

Clint Eastwood's character begins as a farmer who is turned into a lethal gunfighter by the brutality of war. He eventually forms close relationships with several companions and manages to retire after eliminating villains that have been trailing him across the West. The 1976 136 minute film, which Eastwood also directed, is an effective blend of action and good humor, playing upon archetypes to move the narrative but relying upon the strengths of the characterizations, notably that of Chief Dan George, to keep the viewer interested in the proceedings.

Colors are by design subdued, to evoke a kind of western atmosphere, but hues are well defined and are bright, with appealing fleshtones. The Dolby Digital mix provides a little more separation detail and better defined tones, although the standard track has a lot of thrust and maybe even a nicer bass. The picture is in letterboxed format only, with an aspect ratio of about 2.35:1 and an accommodation for enhanced 16:9 playback. There is a French track in mono, optional English and French subtitles, a cast & crew profile section, production notes that are fairly informative until they get to the point where they ought to be talking about Phil Kaufman being dropped from the film but at which point they stop, instead, and a theatrical trailer.

Outrage (Simitar, 7330)

Antonio Banderas stars in a lesser Carlos Saura film that has an awkwardly spliced-in title replacing whatever the original Spanish title was. Banderas is a reporter who falls in love with a circus sharpshooter, played by Francesca Neri. The first half of the film depicts their romance, which is pleasant, but not much happens. Then, in the second half, Neri's character is brutally raped and she goes on a rampage of revenge, which is certainly more active, but is also rather alienating. Banderas has nothing to do but worry, and the film is one long emotional dive, with no respite.

The image on the DVD is cropped. The LD ran 108 minutes and the stated running time (there is no time encoding) on the DVD is 100 minutes. The DVD appears to be time compressed, because we could never get it and the LD to synch up for more than a few seconds. The colors are pale, the image is a little hazy, and there is some minor smearing. The film is dubbed in English and is not captioned.

Over the Wire (Image, ID5614FMDVD)

A clever premise saves the erotic thriller from being a total waste of time. The hero is a telephone repairman who happens to be eavesdropping on some lines when he overhears a woman arranging with a hitman to have her sister killed. Obtaining the address of the victim, he goes to her house, meets both sisters and must figure out who is good and who is evil. The film's budget isn't large enough to do the plot justice, the acting is bad (the actress playing the heroine cannot cry convincingly, so for a while you assume her character is faking tears), the direction is weak, and extended softcore erotic sequences periodically stop the film dead, but the basic story is fresh enough to make the program entertaining.

The picture is very soft. Hues are reasonably bright and fleshtones are workable. The stereo sound hasn't much to offer beyond an occasionally pleasant musical score. The 87 minute program is not captioned.

Overboard (MGM, 906566)

A character-motivated comedy from 1987 that gets more and more popular as time passes, Goldie Hawn stars as a spoiled heiress who loses her memory and Kurt Russell is the down-to-earth carpenter who claims her as his wife in revenge for being stiffed on a job. The performers are perfectly cast and the script puts them through their paces in a manner that just gets funnier and funnier the more you can anticipate what will happen to them next.

The picture is letterboxed with an aspect ratio of about 1.85:1 and no 16:9 enhancement. The image is very soft and somewhat hazy. Colors are a little light and fleshtones are very bland. There is a rudimentary stereo surround soundtrack, and the 112 minute film is also available in French and Spanish in stereo, supported by English or French subtitles. A theatrical trailer is included as well.

Oz Encounters (Fox Lorber, WHE73012)

The documentary features interviews with people from Australia who have seen 'broit loits' racing across the sky or have otherwise come into contact with UFOs. The 45 minute program has a few unconvincing photos and videos, but is mostly a collection of talking heads. The people talk about being abducted, having their children abducted, or just seeing something weird, and 'experts' are brought in to verify the possibility that the people are telling the truth. Our favorite was a fellow who had photos, but had trimmed the negatives so that only his favorite shots still existed and not the critical 'before' and 'after' sequencing shots. The expert bemoans this, but still says the guy has genuine evidence. Everybody maintains a straight face for the camera. The program is so short that it is over before it becomes redundant or boring, and one gets the impression that Australia has as many UFOs as it has rabbits. Hanging Rock, here we come. The picture is soft but tolerable and the sound is adequate. There is no captioning.

Ozzy Osbourne Live & Loud (Sony, DVD49151)

The 111 minute program has been split to two sides. Otherwise, the concert program, which includes a lot of backstage inserts and similar decoration by montage, is good. The picture has a natural graininess, but even the strongest colored stage lights do not deteriorate into blurred images. The picture remains sharp and colors are okay. The stereo surround sound isn't bad, and there is a terrific Dolby Digital track with an enhanced bass and a more dimensional mix. Shot during a 1992 U.S. tour, Osbourne plays many of his biggest hits and puts on a very energetic show.

P

Pale Rider (Warner, 11475)

In the dopey but enjoyable **Pale Rider**, Clint Eastwood is a near-omnipresent gunfighter arriving at the time of need to save a group of gold farmers from the greedy terrorism of a wealthy mining operator. The film has skewed religious overtones, particularly skewed since even the innocent are scraping for gold, an unlikely social dynamic, since most of the prospectors have families, and Eastwood's character is never really threatened as he meanders about and wastes the villains. Due to the contrivances, Eastwood is able to stage the final gun battles with a concern only for entertainment and not story logic, while in the casting of Carrie Snodgress as the heroine, Eastwood found an actress who epitomizes the images of pioneers instead of movie stars, in essence giving the film enough grit so that its entertainments are not completely absurd.

The 1985 film is in letterboxed format on one side, with an aspect ratio of about 2.35:1 and an accommodation for 16:9 enhanced playback, and in cropped format on the other side. The sky on the DVD may be a deep blue, but so are fleshtones, horses and everything else. The colors have a kind of pinkish-purplish haze in places, and the image is a little soft. The stereo surround sound, however, is fairly strong with sharp, elaborate tones. The Dolby Digital track is substantially louder and more separated, but also somewhat more garish than the standard stereo track, which we preferred. The 116 minute film also comes with English, French or Spanish subtitles, trailers for **Pale Rider** and **Unforgiven**, a decent sized cast and crew profile and a few quotations from Eastwood on film directing.

Palmetto (Warner, C2533)

Woody Harrelson plays a real dummy in **Palmetto** and seems perfectly cast. The film should please fans of erotic Sun Belt thrillers, though viewers may have difficulty at first adjusting to a hero who is so dense and ethically challenged. Elisabeth Shue, Gina Gershon and Chloë Sevigny co-star in the tale, set in Florida, of a former newspaper reporter who is sucked into a phony kidnapping scheme that has set-up written all over it. Directed by Volker Schlöndorff, the film is very tight and invites multiple viewings, where you no longer have to see the action through the hero's eyes. There is something about the way Sevigny dresses and has her hair, for example, that doesn't seem right, but makes perfect sense once the story is over. In effect, the film is so good and so well made it turned a lot of people off, because it is about characters who are irredeemably sloppy and immoral.

The 1998 film is presented on one side in letterboxed format, with an aspect ratio of about 2.35:1 and an accommodation for enhanced 16:9 playback, and in full screen format on the other side. The letterboxing masks a lot of picture information off the bottom in comparison to the full screen framing and adds a little to the sides, but generally the widescreen image composition is more satisfying and more appropriate to Schlöndorff's intentions. Colors are strong and sharp. The stereo surround sound and Dolby Digital sound are very similar to each other. Both have crisp details, entertaining separation effects and plenty of laid back power. The 119 minute film can be supported by English or French subtitles and comes with a cast & crew profile section, some brief production notes, and a trailer, plus a trailer for the similar **Body Heat**.

Pam & Tommy Lee: Hardcore & Uncensored X-rated (Vivid, UPC#0073214513)

They're young, they're rich, they're in love, and one of them always has to be holding the camera. The program is a collection of home movies that includes the couple's wedding and honeymoon, the latter a boat cruise on Lake Mead (that's how they spell it). The wedding part is boring, but the rest of it should titillate star-struck viewers who think that famous people, like parents, never have sex.

The program runs 76 minutes and all things considered, the picture quality is reasonably good—almost too good at times, making one suspicious as to how spontaneous some of it is. Colors are always somewhat faded and fleshtones are bland, but the image is usually sharp and well lit—they're an outdoorsy couple—and viewers will eventually see what they are expecting to see. The monophonic sound is often muffled, but the volume levels are reasonably consistent, so amplification is effective. The DVD also has a brief collection of still photos taken from the program but, contrary to a claim on the jacket cover, there appears to be no 'extra footage.'

Pancho Villa (Master Movies, DVD5530)

The 1972 production stars the unlikely Telly ("Shaddup!") Savalas in the title role. In fact, one of the film's few assets is its quadrangle cast of TV notables. Along with Savalas, there is Clint Walker (as an American arms smuggler working with Villa), Chuck Connors and Anne Francis. Savalas—gag—also sings the theme song. The film often tries for comedy and fails badly, and only Walker delivers a performance perverse enough to overcome the material consistently, but the picture is so sharp and the colors are so bright and shiny that the plot and other stupidities do not matter in the least. There are plenty of action scenes, the stars chew up the material like crazy, and there is the whole horses-and-trains period thing to hold a fan's attention, while the vivid DVD picture works its movie magic, making silk, or at least some nice rayon, out of a sow's ear.

The picture has been letterboxed with an aspect ratio of about 1.85:1 with no 16:9 enhancement. The monophonic sound is less pristine, with some background noise, scratchy dialogue and a weak upper end (which doesn't help Savalas' singing much), and the film is accompanied by optional Japanese subtitles (but no English captioning) and copious cast and director profiles.

The Paper (Universal, 20011)

We wish all of Ron Howard's 1994 feature was as much fun as its final act. Most of the movie is competent but dull, and it isn't until all of the characters are completely in place and the narrative can really start to bounce them off each other that the performers perk up and the film becomes alive. The movie stars Michael Keaton, Glenn Close, Marisa Tomei and Randy Quaid, and is about a day in the life of a big city newspaper. The highpoint is a fistfight between Keaton and Close that is both marvelous slapstick and a perfect momentary relief from dramatic tension.

The picture is presented in full screen format only, and the color transfer has no severe flaws. The stereo surround sound is okay and the Dolby Digital sound is quite good. The film's sound is well mixed, and whether it is the rumble of the presses or the realistically-toned radio news reports, the audio has a pleasing crispness. The 112 minute program also has a French language track in Dolby Digital, optional English and Spanish subtitles, production notes and a cast-and-director profile section.

Paranoia (Sterling, 7155)

A woman is justly concerned because the man who murdered her family when she was a child is getting out on parole. The story has a couple twists and the film would be reasonably entertaining if the frame transfer rate weren't so low. The cinematography is fairly good—the heroine lives in a nearly black-and-white apartment—and the color transfer is nice, with bright hues and a sharp focus. The artifacting is so heavy, however, that the film is plagued by tiling, smearing and other needless interferences, completely distracting one from the pleasures of the drama.

The stereo surround sound is adequate and the 87 minute program can be supported by Spanish subtitles. There is no English captioning. Brigitte Bako stars, with Larry Drake as the killer.

The Parent Trap (Buena Vista, 15888)

We watched the entire movie thinking that the young actresses playing the twins within the film were twins themselves, not realizing that it was just one clever actress, Lindsay Lohan, and a lot of special effects. Dennis Quaid, doing an impeccable Harrison Ford turn, and Natasha Richardson star as the parents, who divorced, each taking a twin shortly after their children's birth. The twins meet a decade later and plot to bring their parents back together. The film is outstanding, with one spine-tingling discovery after another, and plenty of jovial humor in between. It is a shame, really, that it was sold as a children's film, because it is an excellent romantic comedy for grownups, and deserved many more Oscars than it received.

The picture is letterboxed with an aspect ratio of about 1.85:1 and no 16:9 enhancement. The image is sharp and colors are exact. The stereo surround sound is a little duller than the Dolby Digital sound, but the Dolby Digital track has a nice dimensional atmosphere. The 128 minute program also has a French language track and can be supported by English subtitles. A trailer, containing scenes not included in the film, is also featured.

Parenthood (Universal, 20174)

Ron Howard's on-the-mark comedy about raising families is in full screen format only, though we can't imagine that letterboxing would improve the presentation much. The picture is somewhat grainy, with reasonably accurate colors. The stereo surround sound is in passable condition, with some effectively dimensional sequences. The 124 minute film is also available in French and can be supported by English or Spanish subtitles. There is a well-made theatrical trailer, some good production notes about how Howard developed the script and an extensive cast profile section. Steve Martin, Mary Steenburgen, Rick Moranis, Diane Wiest and Keanu Reeves are featured in the amusing 1989 film. Randy Newman, incidentally, wrote and performs the Oscar-nominated song that plays over the opening credits and sounds about two notes away from being *You've Got a Friend in Me*.

Parents (Pioneer, DVD5278)

That sweet, good natured character actor, Bob Balaban, has directed one of the most grotesque films ever made. Seen mostly through the eyes of a child whose parents (played by Randy Quaid and Mary Beth Hurt) appear to be saving on their butcher bills, the movie is an intense comedy about psychological abuse that will repulse as many viewers as it pleases. The only reaction it will likely not instill is nonchalance. The 1988 film is either subversively attractive or blatantly repellent depending upon your orientation, though it does feature Sandy Dennis in one of her final appearances, an adept turn as a psychologist social worker with limited skills.

The full screen presentation looks a little soft in places, but colors are fine. The stereo surround sound has a limited mix and little except the music is dimensional. The 81 minute program is not captioned and is accompanied by a trailer and a cast-and-director profile section.

The Paris Concert For Amnesty International: The Struggle Continues... (Image, ID5636AMDVD)

An all-star rock 'n' roll extravaganza, the 171 minute program features two or three numbers by Youssou N'Dour, Kassav', Peter Gabriel, Asian Dub Foundation, Radiohead, Tracy Chapman, Shania Twain, Alanis Morissette, an acoustical Bruce Springsteen, and Robert Plant & Jimmy Page. The Dalai Lama also says a few words, and each set is separated by an Amnesty International promotion/commercial created by a well-known animator.

Shot in December 1998, the performances are not exceptional and a video cannot really convey the pleasures to be had in the concert hall as one star followed another, but it is a good record of the event and fans are sure to be pleased with the material. Background musicians and shots of the audience bathed in colored lights are often soft, but the stars are usually well illuminated and that part of the image looks very crisp, with accurate fleshtones and pleasing textural details. The stereo sound is passable, but the Dolby Digital sound is super, with substantially more elaborate directional effects and a more aggressive sense of immediacy. There is no captioning, and the program is accompanied by discographies for all the artists.

Parsifal (Image, ID4580CODVD)

The films of Hans-Jürgen Syberberg are monstrously indulgent epics that often go on for hours, full of unusual visual effects and vague, repetitive, false-literate narratives. What a fabulous inspiration, then, to have Syberberg film Richard Wagner's **Parsifal**. At four hours and fifteen minutes, the piece is a quickie by Syberbergian standards, and with the opera forced upon him as his text, his creativity can be concentrated on the one thing he does well—inventing dynamic images. From the other angle, the deal is also a good one. Musically, **Parsifal** is one of Wagner's most profound and satisfying works. Dramatically, however, it is notoriously slow going. The second act can be summarized in a couple of sentences, and yet takes more than an hour to execute. The work has always been popular as an audio entertainment, but requires the same sort of attendance commitment that a Syberberg film requires when presented live. The joining of Syberberg's visuals and Wagner's music, then, combines the best both artists have to offer.

Throughout the entire film, Syberberg uses an optical collage to decorate his soundstage sets. The viewer is never completely sure what or who is a real component of the shot and what has been added afterward. Puppets appear in the sky, rocks metamorphose before your eyes and characters pass through walls. The sets maintain semblances of how a normal 'Parsifal' stage might be configured, but symbolic statues and other odd objects inevitably loom from the corners. Nor is Syberberg content to simply mess with the backgrounds. Since the cast is lip-synching the singing anyway, two performers alternate appearances as Parsifal, one male and one female.

The 255 minute feature has been issued on two platters, the first running 181 minutes and holding Acts 1 and 2, and the second running 74 minutes with Act 3. The picture is presented in full screen format and appears to be very slightly windowboxed. The image quality has its limitations. It is somewhat soft looking and a bit worn, but colors are viable and the presentation seems quite nice.

The sound is stereo surround, with the surround effects being limited to the more elaborate orchestral passages. There is a periodic flutter on the soundtrack, and a few channel dropouts scattered through the presentation. On the other hand, if your speakers are sophisticated enough, you can hear the singers shuffling on their stools as they record the vocals. The music presentation is quite nice and, when free of the minor errors, quite satisfying. Reiner Goldberg sings Parsifal, Yvonne Minton sings Kundry, and Wolfgang Schone is Amfortas. With the luxury of working in the studio, they all give strong renderings to their parts. The Monte Carlo Philharmonic Orchestra and Prague Philharmonic Choir are also commendable. Actors usually appear completely lost in a Syberberg film, and some do here, though others bring enough of a sense of purpose to their part that they manage to transcend the artifice.

Passenger 57 (Warner, 12569)

Running a brisk 84 minutes and starring Wesley Snipes, the action thriller, about a security officer who upsets an airplane hijacking, is perfect in its concept and brevity. Snipes' martial art moves are mildly amusing, but he is a refreshing presence and the script gives him an opportunity to show off his star power. The good guy drives the bad guys to distraction, gets the girl and saves the day. What more can one want from a movie?

The picture is presented in letterboxed format on one side, with an aspect ratio of about 2.35:1 and an accommodation for enhanced 16:9 playback, and in cropped format on the other side, although cropping seems pretty useless. The colors are true and the image is sharp. Overall, the picture looks fine, with accurate fleshtones and bright hues. The stereo surround sound is bland, but the Dolby Digital track packs a decent punch and is better detailed. The 1992 feature is also available in French in standard stereo and comes with English, French or Spanish subtitles. There are some production notes, an overview of airplane movies and airplane hijackers, a cast and crew profile, and theatrical trailers for nine movies.

Passion Fish (Columbia TriStar, 53289)

John Sayles' 1992 film is about a woman putting her life back together after an accident leaves her paralyzed. Sayles' ability to spin a yarn makes the 135 minute drama a rewarding experience, relying on the rich personalities of the characters instead of on their disabilities to kindle the narrative. Mary McDonnell stars, with Alfre Woodard as the nurse who rescues her from despair while undergoing a rehabilitation of a different sort herself.

The picture is presented on one side in letterboxed format, with an aspect ratio of about 1.85:1 and an accommodation for enhanced 16:9 playback, and in full screen format on the other side. The letterboxing adds a little bit to the sides in comparison to the full screen image, and trims a little off the top and bottom, but the framing is much more satisfying. The colors are accurate and the image is free of distortion no matter how hazy the Louisiana locations become. The stereo surround sound is fine. The 135 minute program has alternate French and Spanish audio tracks and optional English, French and Spanish subtitles.

Patch Adams (Universal, 20586); collector's (Universal, 20546); DTS (Universal, 20629)

Vilified by the critics and embraced by the general public, the film stars Robin Williams as a doctor in training who intuitively understands that the practice of medicine requires skills in human inter-relations—it is the theme of practically every medical drama ever made. We find it utterly bizarre that most critics reacted to the film precisely in the manner that the medical establishment within the movie reacts to the hero. You'd think that the camera setups were wrong, the sound was mis-recorded and the acting was faulty, none of which is true. Directed by Tom Shadyac, it is a competently made film with enormous good humor and many touching moments. The hero himself is flawed—he's something of a genius and unfairly expects his colleagues to be on his level without prompting—but that just demonstrates that the movie has a little more depth than anyone has given it credit for. All we can really say is, 'Critics: Heal thy selves.'

The standard release is in cropped format only and the *Collector's Edition* is in letterboxed format only, with an aspect ratio of about 2.35:1 and an accommodation for enhanced 16:9 playback, adding picture information to the sides and losing nothing from the top and bottom in comparison to the cropped version. As Shadyac explains on the *Collector's Edition* commentary channel, since much of the film is set in cramped hospital rooms and corridors, he used widescreen formatting to open it up a little, so you're basically not getting what the director wanted you to get if you watch the cropped version.

The picture on both presentations looks super, with bright hues and accurate fleshtones (the compact letterbox image makes the colors look a touch sharper). The film does not have a critical stereo surround mix. Some of the pop songs on the music track sound great, but the stereo surround sound and more dimensional Dolby Digital sound are mostly functional and not exotic. The film runs 116 minutes. On both versions, there is also a French audio track in Dolby Digital, optional English subtitles, a cast-and-director profile section and a trailer.

On the *Collector's Edition*, there is a 21 minute documentary about the film, in which you get to see the 'real' Patch Adams (he's quite a character). The documentary can be supported by optional English subtitles, and there is a playback, during the documentary, that offers a 20 minute selection of Marc Shaiman's musical score. There are also some outtakes and bloopers, but they aren't as super as you hope they will be.

The enormously successful Shadyac freely discusses on the commentary channel the mistakes he made that had to be fixed in the editing room—including errors in judgment that he didn't recognize until he got back the results of the previews. He discusses the performances, of course, describing all the different tangents Williams experimented upon (he could have made a whole two hour movie simply of Williams trying out improvisations for one scene), and he talks about the carefully measured shift the film undergoes from comedy to drama. An apparent flaw causes his talk to get drowned out at times during some of the louder scenes, but much of what he has to say is insightful (paraphrasing the real Patch Adams—"The mantra of the mentally ill is 'me me me me me'") or just plain funny ("We did not have to have anybody from the ASPCA on the set during this scene because the squirrels are imaginary").

The DTS version has no special features and no captioning, but presents the film in the same letterboxed format as the *Collector's Edition*, with an accommodation for enhanced 16:9 playback. The picture transfer and frame transfer rates are also identical. The DTS audio track is a little stronger than the Dolby Digital audio track on the other two releases, bringing out more detail in the separation effects and giving the film a little more punch.

Paths of Glory (MGM, 907674)

Stanley Kubrick's riveting study of motivation in war has been given a super transfer. The black-and-white picture is flawless and the monophonic sound is so clear that you can hear the drummers putting down their sticks when the music finishes at the end of the film. The 87 minute feature appears to be slightly windowboxed, and has an alternate French audio track, optional English and French subtitles and a trailer.

Kirk Douglas stars in the immensely repeatable entertainment. It takes place during the First World War and concerns the consequences of a failed assault. There is action and a basic trial and firing squad drama, but the moralities are fleeting and subtle. As a viewer ages, the villains in the 1957 film will change (there are no unblemished heroes), but a compelling fascination with the sequence of events and the emotions of the participants remains steadfast. **Paths of Glory** is also gloriously cinematic, making the transfer all the more valuable. There are long, dizzying tracking shots through the trenches and tipsy camera angles which follow

characters up staircases. The confusion of battle and the ordered world of the high command are both presented on a scale to show the characters overwhelmed by their surroundings.

The Patriot (Buena Vista, 17095)

The first fight doesn't occur until the film's half-way point, and although there are a couple other bloody encounters, the body count is a bit lower than usual on the 1998 Steven Seagal feature. Seagal is a Montana doctor who just happens to also be the world's greatest bacterial warfare expert (he can also rope a steer), which is fortunate when some militant fanatics decide to release some really heavy sniffles in his home town (there is a vague logic to this, because a super-secret bacteria center is located nearby, the hero used to work there, and its where the bad guys got the stuff). It's ludicrous, but reasonably systematic, and if you enjoy Seagal's manner, you probably won't mind his impersonation of Roy Rogers crossed with Jonas Salk and Bruce Lee.

The picture is presented in letterboxed format only, with an aspect ratio of about 2.35:1 and no 16:9 enhancement. The image transfer is good, with sharp hues and accurate fleshtones. The stereo surround sound and Dolby Digital sound are not elaborately mixed, but there are some separation effects, with the Dolby Digital track offering slightly purer definitions. The 90 minute program is adequately closed captioned.

Patriot Games (Paramount, 325307)

Harrison Ford is a CIA official whose family is threatened by terrorists after he interrupts an assassination attempt. There are no submarine miniatures to play against the tech-talk (there are some fancy hardware sequences, but they are brief and are not central to the story) and it is probable that the 1992 film's key sequences could have been more effectively staged than they are but the movie is competently executed and certainly entertaining, even on multiple viewings.

The presentation is letterboxed, with an aspect ratio of about 2.35:1 and no 16:9 enhancement. The image quality is very good, with sharp colors and accurate fleshtones. Although we had difficulty at first with some of Harrison Ford's mumbling, the stereo surround soundtrack is impressive and the Dolby Digital track is even better, with more dimensionality and more active separations. The 116 minute program also has a French audio track in standard stereo, optional English or Spanish subtitles and a trailer.

Patriots (Simitar, 7305)

A tense drama about an American woman who joins the IRA in Northern Ireland and immediately gets herself into big trouble, some of the performances are very good and the film's best scenes are fairly nerve-wracking, so the more mundane aspects of the narrative, which seem like reiterations of a dozen other IRA movies, can be excused. The picture is fairly blurry, with weak colors and tiling in darker portions of the screen. The sound is passable and the film runs 83 minutes. There is no captioning.

Paul Simon: Graceland—The African Concert (Warner, 238136)

Although the 90 minute concert was shot in daylight, it often looks fuzzy, and colors are bland. The concert took place in an outdoor stadium in Zimbabwe. The picture generally depicts the performers—Simon, plus kind of an all-star line up of crossover African pop—but also cuts to the audience and to life on the Zimbabwean roadsides.

The stereo surround sound is quite effective for a live event, and even though the show is set outdoors, neither the upper nor the lower dynamic ranges are lost to the fresh air. By entitling his work *Graceland*, Simon manages to compact the entire history of rock and roll into a simple three step process, from Africa to Elvis to elevator music, but he means well. Optional English subtitles are also available.

Paulie (DreamWorks, 84163)

An episodic tale of an intelligent talking bird's adventures as he travels across America, most of the episodes have something to do with speech and communication, though that is about the only linking device the stories have besides the bird himself. The 1998 film is a low key production but it is humorous—the bird is full of wisecracks—and the effects are clever.

The film is presented on one side in letterboxed format, with an aspect ratio of about 1.85:1 and an accommodation for enhanced 16:9 playback, and in full screen format on the other side. The color transfer looks fine and the image is sharp, though the cinematography is rarely striking. The stereo surround sound and Dolby Digital sound mix are also functional but not elaborate, and there is little difference between them. The 92 minute program also has French and Spanish language tracks in standard stereo, optional English and Spanish subtitles, production notes, a cast-and-director profile section, and a trailer.

Pavarotti: The Event (Image, ID4396CADVD)

One of the best Luciano Pavarotti recitals on video, the 87 minute program was recorded in Milan as part of the World Cup soccer celebrations. Pavarotti sings arias and Italian songs, separated by lengthy but engaging orchestral interludes performed by the Bologna Orchestra and conducted by Leone Magiera. Pavarotti is in top voice and the audience is highly enthusiastic. The picture looks fine, with a crisp focus and accurate, well-lit colors and fleshtones. The stereo recording is fairly basic, with little dimensionality, but the dynamic range is sufficient for delivering the music and vocals without distortion.

Payback (Paramount, 336327)

Mel Gibson is a crook who suffers all sorts of indignities to retrieve the money that is owed him. The 1999 film is a bit on the bloody side and there is an annoying voiceover by Gibson, but the narrative is as systematic as the hero's determination and there is a steady stream of guest stars to keep things interesting as he works his way up the mob's org chart. There are touches of humor as he goes along, as well, though not enough to stop you from wincing when he gets his toes smashed. Next to the violence, the film's main appeal is in the way the hero stays smarter than his adversaries, clear up to the end.

The picture is presented in letterboxed format only, with an aspect ratio of about 2.35:1 and an accommodation for enhanced 16:9 playback. The 101 minute film does not have a distinctive visual style, wavering between looking hard & direct, looking stylish, and looking Sixties retro. The musical score has the same quandaries, but it is better blended. The stereo surround sound is wimpier than the Dolby Digital sound, but the Dolby Digital sound is crisp and has plenty of satisfying directional effects. A well edited teaser, a standard trailer, and a brief featurette that includes a couple behind-the-scenes shots of stunts and some interviews with the cast are also included, as is English subtitling.

The Peacemaker (DreamWorks, 84160)

Nicole Kidman's acting talents are fairly sparse in the action film directed by Mimi Leder. Kidman supposedly portrays an atomic energy scientist who is thrust into a leadership role as the head of a task force tracking down a dozen or so stolen Russian nuclear warheads. This, however, you cannot see in her eyes. George Clooney isn't all that much better as her military liaison, but once the two stop talking and start doing things the film becomes reasonably entertaining. It manages to cover a lot of ground in 124 minutes as the pair go on several adventures while always staying a leap ahead of the inevitable explosions they encounter. Maybe that's why Kidman's so unconvincing. She doesn't know how to delegate.

The DVD is great. The film has an energized audio mix that sounds terrific on the standard stereo surround soundtrack and even better, with more directional detail and greater energy, on the Dolby Digital track. The picture has been letterboxed with an aspect ratio of about 2.35:1 and an accommodation for enhanced 16:9 playback. The color quality is fine, with decent fleshtones and solid hues. The film is also available in Spanish and French in standard stereo and comes with English or Spanish subtitles. Additionally, there is a five minute breakdown of a stunt driving sequence, three minutes of bloopers, a very good teaser trailer, a decent standard theatrical trailer, a small cast-and-director section, and some production notes.

Pearl Jam: Single Video Theory (Sony, EVD50161)

The picture looks fine and the Dolby Digital stereo is okay (it is somewhat crisper than the standard stereo track), but the 45 minute program, about the group recording an album, is rather stodgy. The group is young, and what they have to say about what they've learned is not exactly a revelation, while their performances seem overly controlled and studious. Sure, it's great to see them working, but we'd rather see what the audience of a live concert could draw out of them.

The Pebble and the Penguin (MGM, 905403)

One of the better Don Bluth animation efforts, it would be unfair to compare the film to a top grade Walt Disney effort, but on the level of films such as Quest for Camelot it holds up fairly well. The plot concerns an abducted penguin who has to make a long journey back to his home in time to save his girlfriend from the bad guy. The long backgrounds are dull, but the immediate settings have interesting and stimulating designs. The heroes are penguins, so cuteness comes naturally to them, and the other wildlife of the sea are rendered more realistically, creating an effective contrast. Some of the songs, by Barry Manilow, are actually good, and although the story is woefully predictable, humor and action scenes keep the narrative moving effectively.

The LD was letterboxed, but the DVD is presented in full screen format, losing a little picture information on the sides, but gaining more of the artwork on the top and the bottom of the image. The colors are solid and exact. The stereo surround sound is good, and the DVD has a Dolby Digital track with a bit more energy, though on the whole the film's sound mix is not all that elaborate. The 74 minute feature is also available in French and can be supported by English or French subtitles.

Pecker (New Line, N4731)

Like many of his previous films, John Waters' 1998 feature dwells on juvenile humor and off-color word play with pre-adolescent glee. Yet his timing has become more assured and his moments of comedy more selective, so you do laugh in places, even if you feel embarrassed for having done so. Edward Furlong, who gives just about the only non-artificial-seeming performance in the film (Lili Taylor is also good), stars as a young photographer whose random pictures of his family and friends make him a celebrity in the art world. Most of the characters have forced, unnatural personalities, and their actions and dialogue will seem pointlessly silly if one is not already a dedicated Waters fan. The narrative is slight, however, and the film has a relaxed atmosphere. Christina Ricci, Bess Armstrong and Mary Kay Place co-star, with Waters' usual collection of derelict-looking supporting players.

The picture is letterboxed, with an aspect ratio of about 1.85:1 and an accommodation for enhanced 16:9 playback. The film's colors are often fairly basic and unshadowed, and the transfer renders them with clarity. The stereo surround sound and Dolby Digital sound do not have an elaborate mix, but are competently executed, with the Dolby Digital track providing a bit more dimensionality and enhanced separations. The 86 minute feature can be supported by English subtitles. There is a trailer that spells out the entire plot, a cast-and-director profile, and a nice 10 minute featurette on the professional photographer who took the photos used in the movie. He was working in a camera store, but thanks to the film, his career is finally getting on track.

Waters also provides a commentary, explaining why he chose the various pranks and jokes depicted in the movie—usually because they are among his favorite. He also talks knowledgeably about modern art photography and its apparent lack of design. He speaks about Baltimore, where the movie is set (unlike most movies, he kept the entire film geographically accurate), about his career, and he has nice things to say about the ratings board, which is a rarity for a professed guerrilla filmmaker. He also tries to justify the film's title, citing other movie titles with double entendres as his excuse, but it seems that where those other titles, such as *Shaft* and **In & Out**, have playful secondary meanings, the most common definition of his title (it is supposed to be the name of the hero) is also the most off-color. It is well chosen, though, because it exemplifies the film's level of intelligence and decorum.

Peggy Sue Got Married (Columbia TriStar, 81849)

Kathleen Turner stars Francis Ford Coppola's 1986 time travel fantasy, as a woman, estranged from her husband, who collapses at her high school reunion and reawakens 25 years earlier, a few weeks before graduation. Nicolas Cage, his voice as nasally as ever, co-stars, and Jim Carrey has a significant role—and is up to his usual tricks—as Cage's best friend. Superficially, the film is a comedy about expectations and anachronisms, but it also speaks to the incredible emotional power a high school reunion can have. Not only is one overwhelmed by the presence of long lost friends, one is also faced with resurgent memories of one's earliest sexual experiences and forced to accept the compromises that have come to one's life goals and dreams. The film communicates these emotions cleverly by literally placing the heroine into her past so she can make her choices all over again. Of course it may all be just a dream, but that is irrelevant, since the images and scenes in the movie are real enough to tell a coherent story. The film is seen by some as a formula work by a director on retreat after several financial disasters, but such views shortchange the film's genuine emotional power and the feelings it can pass on to the viewer.

The picture is presented on one side in letterboxed format, with an aspect ratio of about 1.85:1 and an accommodation for enhanced 16:9 playback, and is in full screen format on the other side. The color transfer looks great, with warm, accurate fleshtones and bright, deep hues. The stereo sound is fine. The 104 minute program also has French and Spanish audio tracks and optional English, French and Spanish subtitles.

The Pelican Brief (Warner, 12989)

Julia Roberts and Denzel Washington star in the 1993 political thriller, as they track down the fairly stupid conspirators responsible for murdering two Supreme Court Justices on the same day. Director Alan J. Pakula's fascinating, adept style and the appeal of the two stars are sufficient for keeping the viewer engaged for the movie's full 141 minutes, although multiple viewings are questionable.

The color transfer is excellent, providing crisp hues and an undistorted image no matter how complex the film's lighting becomes. The picture is letterboxed, with an aspect ratio of about 2.35:1 and an accommodation for enhanced 16:9 playback, and it is an absolute necessity for evoking the movie's drama and tensions. James Horner's musical score, as it is presented on the stereo surround soundtrack, is outstanding. Horner uses a typical thriller motif in some segments, carrying one somewhat dull line of music as a constant and then tossing out wild bits of near-noise to represent the dangers that lurk in the seemingly calm urban landscape. The stereo surround sound is good, and the Dolby Digital track is even better. Whether it is the extended rectangularity of the image or the purity of the separation effects, those instrumental pulses have an incredible dimensionality that enhance the film's emotional realism. The film is also presented in French and Spanish without Dolby Digital and comes with English, French or Spanish subtitles. There is a decent cast profile and some production notes, as well as trailers for all four of Pakula's Warner films.

Peking Opera Blues (import, MSDVD03998)

Tsui Hark's inspired 1986 action comedy is set during China's gangster era. The plot is primarily an intrigue, with various characters, some involved with a theater troupe, attempting to steal a few damaging papers from a general. The stars, Brigitte Lin, Sally Yeh and Cherie Chung, bring an adept mix of humor, athleticism and glamour to their roles, and the colorful film would be thoroughly entertaining even if it didn't have so many energetic and witty stunt sequences.

The picture is letterboxed with an aspect ratio of about 1.85:1 and no 16:9 enhancement. The image is grainy in places and colors are a bit light, with mildly pale fleshtones but, on the whole, the picture is pleasing. The source material is in good shape and hues are reasonably detailed. Although erratic, the stereo surround sound and particularly the Dolby Digital sound are quite enjoyable, with distinctive separation effects. Dialog is often muted or a little fuzzy, but when one takes the nature of the production into account, the added joys brought on by the directional effects make it worthwhile. The 102 minute film can be accessed in Cantonese or Mandarin and can be supported by optional English, traditional Chinese, simplified Chinese, Japanese, Korean, Bhassa Malaysian, Thai, Vietnamese and Spanish subtitles. The English subtitles contain a fair share of mistranslations. The program is also accompanied by several trailers (the trailer for **Peking Opera** plays like a music video) and some background notes.

Penny Serenade (Madacy, DVD99015)

Cary Grant and Irene Dunne star as a married couple who undergo several tragedies involving children. The film is told in flashback, keyed to Dunne's character playing records on her record player, and so the first half of the film, at least, is dominated by what would have been considered 'oldies' in 1941. Although the gimmick subsides after the plot really gets into gear, the film is almost a musical, and really grabs your attention the way a musical would.

The black-and-white source material is in fairly battered condition and the image is soft, with plenty of artifacting. However, compared to some of the other Madacy public domain titles we've seen, this one isn't so bad—particularly when viewed on a smaller screen. Those who are sensitive to quality will be too distracted to enjoy the 117 minute film, but those who can tolerate a few imperfections should be able to absorb most of what the program has to offer. The monophonic sound is adequate and the DVD contains a few minor supporting text features.

The People Vs. Larry Flynt (Columbia TriStar, 82459)

Milos Forman's 1996 film, which was understandably made by an immigrant who has a great respect for America's freedoms, underwent a backlash after its initial release, under the mistaken impression that it was glorifying its ultra-sleazy protagonist. It wasn't, it was glorifying the First Amendment, and it says basically everything that everybody in the movie says—the guy's a jerk, but he has his rights. The film plays like a well made TV drama. It can't possibly depict the sex in Flynt's life, so it doesn't try beyond some teasing, token sequences. It is not really comical, but the characters are so genuinely absurd that there is a natural humor in their actions and activities, something Forman has historically tended to underplay and something another director might well have sent over the top.

Woody Harrelson, in the central role, is a necessary bore, but Courtney Love, Edward Norton and the other supporting players are captivating—you can't wait for each one to reappear when they're off screen. Parts of the film are legitimately fascinating—how we wish they'd included the opposing lawyer's arguments in the Supreme Court sequence, so the complete conflict could be weighed by the viewer—but the movie is only sporadically entertaining. Unless one has a compelling urge to relive the creation, success and foibles of Hustler Magazine, the movie holds only a few curiosities and a more begrudging than inspiring affirmation that America works.

The film is presented on one side in letterboxed format with an aspect ratio of about 2.35:1 and an accommodation for enhanced 16:9 playback, and in cropped format on the other side. The cropping obscures too much of the image. The color transfer looks fine and the image is crisp. The stereo surround sound and Dolby Digital sound are adequate, with a functional but rarely lavish mix. The 130 minute film also has French and Spanish language tracks, and optional English and Spanish subtitles.

A Perfect Murder (Warner, 16643)

Been thinking about killing your spouse lately? Instead, why not bury the hatchet and put on **A Perfect Murder**? Don't worry that the film is based upon the same stageplay that inspired Alfred Hitchcock's *Dial M for Murder*. Except for the business with the key the plot is fresh, so fresh that even aficionados of Hitchcock's film will enjoy the fresh twists the filmmakers have concocted. But mostly, the movie is just a chance to wallow in wealth and lust and greed and other evils without getting your feet wet. Michael Douglas, Gwyneth Paltrow and Viggo Mortensen star.

The film is presented on one side in letterboxed format, with an aspect ratio of about 1.85:1 and an accommodation for enhanced 16:9 playback, and in full screen format on the other side. The letterboxing has an aspect ratio of about 1.85:1, adding a little bit to the sides of the image and masking off some from the bottom in comparison to the full screen version, though the framing is generally more satisfying. The picture quality is excellent, bringing bright, detailed hues to the already glossy cinematography.

Since the movie is mostly conversation, except for a murder or two, the stereo surround sound isn't all that showy, but when it does have to supply a punch, it delivers. There is also a Dolby Digital track with a slightly heightened dimensionality. The 108 minute program is also available in French in standard stereo and comes with English or French subtitles. An alternate ending has been included, which is a great improvement from a conceptual and dramatic standpoint, but is not quite as gutsy as it could have been and does not have the correct rhythm. The movie's official ending is duller, but more comfortable. There is a decent cast & crew profile section, a few production notes and two excellent commentary tracks, each of which supports the other to create a larger picture of the whole.

On one track, Douglas, director Andrew Davis and screenwriter Patrick Smith Kelly talk about the alternate endings they tried and how they felt the one they used was the most logical for Paltrow's character. Davis and Kelly also speak about working with the actors, using the New York locations, a few of the shooting problems they encountered and their delight with the script. Douglas shares a few anecdotes about the shoot and talks a little about his approach to the craft of acting, particularly what he learned working in television.

The second track features producer Peter Macgregor Scott, cinematographer Dariusz Walski, production designer Philip Rosenberg, costume designer Ellen Mirojnick and set decorator Debra Schutt. Combined, the talks create a very complete profile of how the film was constructed and how movies are made. Mirojnick, for examples, explains in great detail how she studied the script and then chose fabric and designs for the characters while interacting with the cast, and explains at each point why she made the decisions she made. Hence, to a better degree than even most DVD releases, **A Perfect Murder** offers up both an entertaining movie and a full fledged graduate seminar on filmmaking.

Pergolesi's Lo Frate 'nnamorato (Image, ID4364PUDVD)

Riccardo Muti conducts the ensemble cast, which includes Alessandro Corbelli, Nuccia Focile and Amelia Felle. The staging is quite impressive. The turntable set consists of three circular staircases, providing an ideal variation of levels and confusions to accommodate the modestly peopled baroque romantic comedy,

about the mixed up love lives of servants and their masters. The stage is brightly lit and the picture is nicely detailed, with accurate fleshtones and clear textures.

The singing is competent and the recording is effectively balanced, though dimensionality is limited. The 168 minute single-sided dual-layer program is in Italian with white English subtitles.

Permanent Midnight (Artisan, 60489)

The seductively glamorous world of drug addiction is depicted in the true story about a TV comedy writer who allows substance abuse to dominate his life. Ben Stiller stars, with Elizabeth Hurley. There is a sort of macho cockiness to the hero's actions that supersedes the emotional impact of his social failure. You rarely see him working, so it is hard to understand how he is able to sustain his lifestyle for as long as he does, though since the film is told with flashbacks, it is understandable that this would be all he remembers. Meanwhile, until he hits rock bottom, he sleeps with beautiful women, drives cool cars and wears great clothes (albeit with long sleeves), so why can't everybody live like that? The film runs a brisk 88 minutes. Stiller gives a competent performance, and the details of his drug use are certainly interesting, but that only adds to the mystique of his character's lifestyle.

The presentation is letterboxed, with an aspect ratio of about 1.85:1 and an accommodation for enhanced 16:9 playback. The picture transfer looks good, with bright, solid hues that remain stable in all lighting situations. The stereo surround soundtrack is not overly aggressive, but there is a nice dimensionality and some decent separation effects. The Dolby Digital 5.1 sound mix has slightly stronger directional effects, though the two tracks are reasonably similar. The program is adequately closed captioned.

The film's director, David Veloz, provides a commentary track in which he claims the film is supposed to be comical (there are some funny moments, but the general atmosphere is not grounded in humor), speaks with amazement that some viewers believe the drug scenes make shooting up look appealing, and says that he purposely downplayed the hero's vocational activities. He also fills in the basic logistics of the shoot, talks about adapting to the film's schedule and about working with his crew. Everything that seems misguided about **Permanent Midnight**, however, is right there in his talk, and some viewers may find the commentary more interesting for what Veloz inadvertently reveals about the film's failure than for the filmmaking advice he imparts. Also included on the DVD are four deleted scenes, which would have taken the film a bit off track but are still interesting, a red tag trailer that captures the spirit of the movie better than the movie does, some production notes that fill in details Veloz overlooked in his talk, and a cast & crew profile section.

Phantom of Chinatown (see **Mr. Wong Collection**)

The Phantom of the Opera (Image, ID4097DSDVD)

The 1929 re-edit of the 1925 feature, starring Lon Chaney, runs 92 minutes. The picture is much clean, bright, and sharp—a significant improvement over previous transfers of the film, with more sensible tinting, smoother movement and better contrasts. The musical score is brand new, and is in stereo, with the opera passages, including the heroine's screams, sung by Claudine Coté. Although the singing is a bit disorienting, and the music seems a bit too aware of Andrew Lloyd Webber at times, the score is still highly satisfying and adds to a viewer's enjoyment of the film. The DVD also includes some behind-the-scenes and publicity still frame photos and a silent trailer. The last shot of Chaney, by the way, is a blast.

Phantoms (Buena Vista, 14893)

The spooky 1998 feature has a good needle-in-the-butt jump every five minutes or so. Based upon a story and screenplay by Dean Koontz, the film begins with two young women who drive into a small Colorado resort town, only to find that the place is totally empty. Then they find corpses. Then they start to hear noises. Then none of the cars work and they can't leave. Eventually Ben Affleck and Peter O'Toole appear and the four band together (though the women never do much) to fight the demons that have swallowed the town. The narrative continually raises the stakes (the conclusion includes brief yet elaborate CGI monsters) but never loses the pot. When the film is over and you look back on it, it can seem a bit silly or farfetched, but it keeps you spooked while it's going and you can't ask for more.

The presentation is in letterboxed format with an aspect ratio of about 1.85:1 and no 16:9 enhancement. The image looks fine, with bright, smooth colors even in the darker sequences. We tended to prefer the standard stereo surround soundtrack to the Dolby Digital track, since the standard track seemed to be more aggressive and crisper, while maintaining the same level of separation detail the Dolby Digital track offers, though either one will make you jump at the right moments. The 96 minute program can be supported by optional English subtitles.

Phenomena (Anchor Bay, DV10726)

Dario Argento's 1984 thriller is about a young girl who has a strong affinity with all kinds of insects and a serial killer who is running amok in her boarding school. As is usual in Argento's movies, the identity of the killer is a secret until near the end, but the addition of the insects gives the movie a nice supernatural touch. There are many thrillingly executed sequences and interesting themes about the animals and sexuality, but it is not Argento's strongest work. Jennifer Connelly stars, and Donald Pleasance is also featured.

The film, which was shot in Switzerland, was originally released in the U.S. under the title, *Creepers*, with some 20 minutes or so missing, but is presented on DVD in its full 110 minute gory glory. The picture quality is excellent. Colors are solid, contrasts are sharp, fleshtones are accurate, and you can barely tell it is a low budget Italian production. The image is letterboxed with an aspect ratio of about 1.66:1 and no 16:9 enhancement. There is a Dolby Digital audio track that gives the film's music a smoother and more distinctive delivery than the standard stereo surround soundtrack. There is also a French language track, in mono, and there is no captioning.

Argento, composer Claudio Simonetti (the film has a lot of distracting heavy metal tunes mixed in with his score, but he doesn't seem to mind), journalist Loris Curci and makeup effects artist Sergio Stivaletti are featured on a commentary track, although there are still a few lengthy passages between comments. Prompted by Curci, they talk about the production, about the Italian film industry, about working with the cast and other related matters. It is not an overly informative effort, but there is some worthwhile insight on the film and its genesis. The DVD also features an enjoyable 9 minute interview with Argento from 1985 (he was very young) when he was promoting the film's U.S. release, as well as about 5 minutes of good behind-the-scenes footage and two inspired music videos. There is a trailer and a cast & crew profile section.

Phenomenon (Buena Vista, 13081)

John Travolta stars in what seems like an organic science fiction piece. About a rural mechanic who suddenly acquires unnaturally increased brain capacity, the film remains low-key from start to finish, relying successfully on Travolta's charm to sell its fantasy and uplifting contemplation of existence. It is said that the movie's final act turns some viewers off, but we found it to be as satisfying as the filmmakers clearly intended and can't imagine an alternative that would work any better. Besides, the plot of the film isn't really the point. The movie is an opportunity for Travolta to tickle one's brain and move one's heart, and using his grin and his distracted stammer, he accomplishes both with apparent effortlessness.

The color quality is good and the image is crisp. The letterboxing has an aspect ratio of about 2.35:1 and no 16:9 enhancement,

though there is still a bit of picture information missing from the sides. The stereo surround sound is okay, but the Dolby Digital track is stronger. The film's sound mix is not overly elaborate. The film is also available in French (even the opening credits appear in French on the French version) and comes with Spanish subtitles or English closed captioning. The 123 minute program is also accompanied by an original theatrical trailer.

Philadelphia (Columbia TriStar, 52619)

The first 40 minutes is smart, spellbinding moviemaking. It cuts corners—the hero is already HIV-positive and is dealing with it—and advances in whooshes that keep the viewer not only trying to guess what will happen next but, without alienation, trying to figure out what has already happened. Then there is an ill-considered scene with Jason Robards in a hallway where his motivation as the villain is revealed, and it just doesn't work, taking some of the steam out of the movie which, though still affecting, begins to accumulate the clichés it had so adeptly circumvented at first.

Tom Hanks won an Oscar for his performance in the 1993 feature as the PWA, and Denzel Washington is the apprehensive lawyer he hires to bring forward a job discrimination suit after he is let go from his own position as a legal professional. Jonathan Demme directed. Hanks' performance and the film's better staged scenes endow the movie with a potential to endure the passage of time, something topical films have a great difficulty achieving, but it is only a partially daring work and in repeat viewings the safety nets—like the telefilm-ish family reunion scene—designed to remove complications or distraction from the emotional narrative, come clearer and clearer into view.

The picture is presented in letterboxed format only, with an aspect ratio of about 1.85:1 and an accommodation for enhanced 16:9 playback. The letterboxing masks picture information off the top and bottom of the image and adds nothing to the sides in comparison to full screen versions. In general, the framing created by the letterboxing is fine, but once in a while a head will seem too severely trimmed. The film's color scheme is deliberately subdued, but the image looks sharp, with accurate and sometimes unnerving fleshtones. The stereo surround sound is dull, but the Dolby Digital sound is a little livelier, with more energy and better-defined tones. The 128 minute program also has French and Spanish audio tracks in standard stereo, optional Spanish and Korean subtitles and English closed captioning.

The Philadelphia Story (MGM, 906613)

Cary Grant, James Stewart and Katharine Hepburn all star in the classic 1940 comedy. The black-and-white picture has deliciously crisp lines and rich, detailed contrasts. Freezing the frame on any of the stars' close-ups creates an almost framable glamour portrait. The monophonic sound is somewhat aged. The 113 minute film can be accompanied by English, French or Spanish subtitles. An enjoyable Broadway-oriented theatrical trailer is also featured. For those who are unfamiliar with the work, allow us to say that it is based on a very witty play about a man attempting to muck up his ex-wife's wedding, and has an elaborate construction that generates one amusing moment after another. Hepburn has rarely seemed as radiantly romantic and Grant is in top form and Stewart, as a reporter, is a bonus.

Phoenix (Trimark, VM6901D)

Ray Liotta is a cop with a lot of gambling debts who plans to rob a loan shark for some fast cash. Good rarely comes from such endeavors and Liotta's character eventually finds himself on the run from the law. Some of the imitation Tarantino dialogue is stimulating and the characters are well drawn, but the narrative is old and predictable, and only the staunchest crime film enthusiasts will find its take on the genre to be rewarding, or even tolerable.

The picture is letterboxed with an aspect ratio of about 2.35:1 and no 16:9 enhancement. Contrasts are a little weak in darker sequences, but generally the image is sharp and fleshtones are fine.

The stereo surround sound has little dimensionality or energy. The program has optional French or Spanish subtitles, and English closed captioning. There is also a full screen trailer that tries to sell the 107 minute film as a murder mystery, something it isn't. (Artisan, 60494)

Several people have pointed out that is reminiscent of *Eraserhead*, and there are a number of similarities, with both films being in black-and-white and both depicting men living in isolation. is more of a beginning film, but it has its share of enigmas, icky images and paranoid emotions as the hero strives to separate mathematics from numerology in the world around him. Living in an apartment that he has apparently turned into one large computer, he makes small forays into the outer world to eat and to visit a retired mentor, but when other people begin to intrude on his space—a stock broker dangling a new computer chip for him to use; a student of the Kaballah who recognizes the insight the hero could provide—his fragile emotional stability starts to crumble. Shot in a super-contrast black-and-white film stock that purposefully removes detail and adds grain, and with a deliberately obscure, hip-hop editing style necessitated by the limited budget, the movie has its share of physical and intellectual stimulation. It doesn't really hold any answers, but it toys with you for a while to make you think that it does. Even in the film's opening title sequence, the real value of pi is presented only to the first nine digits and the rest is gibberish.

The film is letterboxed with an aspect ratio of about 1.66:1. We assume that the image is accurately transferred, and the grain never activates any noticeable artifacting. For a super low (five figure) budget, the stereo surround sound is very good, with a strong sense of presence and an involving dimensionality. The 85 minute program is adequately closed captioned.

The DVD also has a number of supplementary features, though they tend to rob the film of its mystique. There are four deleted scenes that clearly fell out of the film's focused mood, though one, involving a slinky, is rather nice. There are a couple edgy trailers, 8 minutes of color behind-the-scenes and Sundance footage, a music video derived from the film's electronic theme music (no lyrics) with color images of ants mixed into black-and-white clips from the film, all too brief excerpts from a 'graphic novel,' a cast & crew profile, a production essay, and some worthwhile background notes about pi. The film also has two commentary tracks, one by director Darren Aronofsky and one by the star, Sean Gullette. Aronofsky sort of explains the movie as it goes along, though he also talks about how it was shot and some of the experiences the crew had during the shoot. Gullette has less to say, but he does provide a lot of interesting material about his character's back-story and discusses the tension of shooting a scene with a gun. He starts to talk about the film stock that was used, but that segment is mysteriously interrupted. Aronofsky also provides commentary over the deleted scenes and both narrate the behind-the-scenes segment.

The Piano (Artisan, 60462)

Set in the wilds of New Zealand some time in the last century, Holly Hunter, Harvey Keitel and Sam Neill star in a Jane Campion's 1992 tale of moral adultery that is heaped in interpretative images, so that the objects and environments under observation by the camera reinforce the viewer's emotional understanding of the characters to a far greater level than in most films. Reminiscent in many ways of Georgia O'Keefe's flower paintings, the symbolism is at once obvious and ambiguous, presenting an interpretative trap that is easy and even inviting to enter but then almost impossible to withdraw.

Grain seems to be an inherent part of the cinematography, so there is no getting around it in image transfers, and it does have a refined, pointillist effect. The colors are strong and the image is appropriately dark, with pure blacks. The dual-layer single-sided platter contains both a full screen version and a letterboxed version, which has an aspect ratio of about 1.85:1 and no 16:9 enhancement. The stereo surround sound is a little soft and does not create an effective atmosphere. The 121 minute film is accompanied by a theatrical trailer and cast profiles with abridged filmographies, and is closed captioned.

Picnic at Hanging Rock (Criterion, PIC100)

The opening title card claims that **Picnic at Hanging Rock** is based upon a true story and is set on "Saturday 14th February 1900," but, as anyone over 110 can tell you, Valentine's Day was a Wednesday that year. Director Peter Weir went back and re-edited the 1975 film, taking out several minutes of footage to 'tighten' it, removing much of the romance between the young man and the girl he rescues. About several Australian school girls who disappear during a day trip, the movie is a cinematic masterpiece of the first order, a miasma of history, poetry, spirituality, nature and sexual awakening.

The 107 minute program (earlier home video releases ran 116 minutes) is in letterboxed format with an aspect ratio of about 1.66:1 and no 16:9 enhancement. The presentation is also helped by the gorgeous, crisp picture transfer and a new Dolby Digital stereo sound mix that gives Zamphir's panflutes an added airiness and throws in a subliminal low register burn at the most unnerving moments. The film is supported by optional English subtitles and is accompanied by a trailer. There was one left-to-right pan across some ferns that seemed to take on a slight artifact instability, but that was the closest the presentation came to having a flaw.

Weir uses many quotations from literature during the film, but they succeed because the atmosphere he creates is mysterious enough to accommodate putting on airs. One of the teenaged schoolgirls, in the sleepy aftermath of a picnic lunch, reads from a book, "Shall I compare thee to a summer's day…" while visually, her innocence and beauty have no equal. Weir opens the film with lines from Edgar Allan Poe in voiceover, "Is all we see or seem, but a dream within a dream?" It is immensely clear that, probably from the day he was old enough to read, Weir's favorite poem is likely another offering from Poe, *Ulalume*.

Pierrot le Fou (Fox Lorber, FLV5046)

Typical of Jean-Luc Godard's work in the Sixties, the 1965 feature is playful and irreverent, as the actors, Jean-Paul Belmondo and Anna Karina, pretend, on and off, to be gangsters, while the world around them generally pays no attention. There are constant digressions, in which the pair read literary quotations or comment philosophically on modern life, and there is also running commentary on the U.S. involvement in Vietnam. The gangster playacting, which sometimes includes a corpse or two, is parodistic enough that the humor generated from it provides the film with its cohesion. The quotations and philosophical treatises are so well chosen that the passages retain their relevancy as time passes, providing a stronger counterbalance to the humor than the sophomoric gags used to fill the gaps in most parodies.

The picture is letterboxed with an aspect ratio of about 2.1:1 and no 16:9 enhancement. Colors are bright and the image is moderately sharp, though some sequences are have weaker contrasts and a bit of grain. The source material does have some scratches and speckles, as well. The monophonic sound is okay. The 110 minute film is in French and there are permanent white English subtitles that appear on the image and are difficult to read in places. For those unfamiliar with the movie, the volume dropouts are deliberate.

Pillow Talk (Universal, 20532)

Rock Hudson and Doris Day star in the marvelously funny 1959 romantic comedy. For those of you who weren't around then, in the old days some telephone systems had 'party lines,' in which several customers shared one phone line. Although each had their own phone (and unique 'ring'), they had to take turns using the line, and could listen in on the other's conversations. In classic bickering lovers style, Hudson's character and Day's character spar over the use of one such line, but then Hudson meets her in person, hiding his identity, and uses his conversations with her on the phone to manipulate her romance with his alter-ego. Hudson's comic abilities have rarely been as fine-tuned, and Day's instinctive talents enable her to respond with an uncanny sympathy to Hudson's cues. The script is very witty (it won an Oscar) and the performers play it to perfection.

The picture is letterboxed, with an aspect ratio of about 2.35:1 and no 16:9 enhancement, and the letterboxing is an absolute necessity because of the film's use of split screen to depict the phone conversations. The color transfer looks great, with very bright hues and accurate fleshtones. The source material does have some speckling in a number of places, though it is never too obvious, and the image is so sharp at times that it can appear slightly distorted, though on the whole, the presentation is quite satisfying. The monophonic sound is okay and the 103 minute feature also comes with optional English and French subtitles, a production essay, a cast-and-director profile and a trailer.

The Pink Panther (MGM, 907041)

The 115 minute film has a different pace than today's comedies, or even the later Clouseau films, and some viewers may get a little antsy with parts of it. On the other hand, the picture looks so nice that you may well savor every scene no matter how drawn out it becomes. David Niven, Robert Wagner, Capucine and Claudia Cardinale co-star. Niven is a jewel thief that Sellers' detective is trying to catch. Our favorite moment could easily be excised from the film without hurting it in the slightest—an entire musical number, exquisitely choreographed for camp and sung in Italian, that occurs at the film's midpoint. Is there a movie executive alive who would ever let such a scene remain today?

The picture looks fabulous. Whites are sparkling pure, fleshtones are accurate and other hues are crisp and precise. In addition to being a very funny film, the 1963 movie is also a showcase of early Sixties fashion and style, and with the film's vivid imagery, it is like you can reach out and touch the past. The film is presented in letterboxed format on one side and in cropped format on the other side, though the cropping obscures gags and adds nothing to the entertainment. The letterboxing has an aspect ratio of about 2.3:1 and no 16:9 enhancement, although even on it, a little picture information is trimmed off the sides. The monophonic sound is aged and somewhat muted, but workable. The film is accompanied by a theatrical trailer and optional English or French subtitles.

The Pink Panther Cartoon Collection: Jet Pink (MGM, 907435)

There is one very funny and, for the series, classic cartoon in the collection, *Little Beaux Pink*, in which Panther and a whiny sheep are at odds with a cattle rancher. A couple of the cartoons have laugh tracks, but most are at least mildly inventive. *In the Pink of the Night* is fairly amusing, about a cuckoo clock working extra hard to wake Panther up, as is *Pet Pink Pebble*, in which Panther gets a rock for a pet. The other shorts include *Jet Pink*, in which he accidentally starts a jet plane, *Pink Blueprint*, in which he tries to get a builder to build a house his way, *The Pink Phink*, in which he and a rival painter do battle with their preferred colors, *Think before You Pink*, in which he tries to cross a street, and *Toro Pink*, in which he becomes a bullfighter.

Most of the cartoons were produced in the late Sixties and early Seventies. A couple of the older ones have soft lines, but most look fine, with bright, solid hues. The monophonic sound is okay. There are optional French subtitles for the cartoon headings ("Une panthère qui doit réfléchir à deux fois") and incidental text (the cartoons are without dialog), and English subtitles to indicate when Henry Mancini's theme kicks in and to identify the scattered sound effects.

The Pink Panther Strikes Again (MGM, 907503)

Not the best in the Peter Sellers series, the 1976 movie still contains enough funny sequences to be well worth obtaining. The first half hour or so is hysterical and the finale isn't bad. Herbert Lom's character kidnaps a scientist and forces him to build a 'doomsday' ray gun, while, once again, assassins attempt to dispatch the hero. The funniest disguises include a hunchback with an inflatable hump and a myopic Swiss dentist. Lesley-Anne Down is featured.

Fleshtones look accurate and other hues are bright The image is sharper and cleaner. The picture is in cropped format on one side and letterboxed format on the other. The letterboxing has an aspect ratio of about 2.35:1 and no 16:9 enhancement, and it is absolutely necessary for the more elaborate gags and gags where there is a lot of lateral movement (in one of the film's highpoints, Sellers' character visits an Oktoberfest where dozens of assassins end up killing one another while trying to dispatch him). The monophonic sound is okay. The 103 minute feature also has a French soundtrack, optional English or French subtitles and a trailer.

Pioneer Karaoke Library Vol. 1 (see Karaoke — The Ladies of Country)

Plan Nine from Outer Space (Passport, DVD700)

Before World War II, there was a group of poets who called themselves 'Surrealists.' They would write down words, drop them into a hat, pull them out randomly, write them down in the order the words came out, and call the works 'poems.' And yet, some of the works, and the way the words fell out with one another, are poems. Thus it is with the random pieces of film which were spliced together to make Edward D. Wood Jr.'s **Plan Nine from Outer Space**, the best awful, the grandest worst, or the most marvelously stupid movie ever made.

Although Passport's transparent logo appears in the bottom right corner throughout the presentation, the picture quality doesn't look bad. The film is slightly windowboxed and is generally free of damage. It is, in fact, nearly identical to the slightly windowboxed LD. The speckles are in the same places, and weaknesses in the edges of well-lit contrasts are also identical. The image on the DVD has slightly deeper blacks, losing some detail in shadows compared to LD, but sharpening greys that look a little washed out on the LD version. On the whole, however, with the exception of the annoying logo, they look identical. Artifacting appears to be kept under reasonable control, although the foggier dark backgrounds get a little smeary at times. The monophonic sound is fully acceptable. There is no captioning.

The back of the jacket implies that the 79 minute film is accompanied by another program. It isn't, but there are about 40 minutes of interview clips and trailers. The interviews, with former members of Wood's, ensemble, and with Martin Landau and Johnny Depp, are terrific. There is even unnerving footage of Bela Lugosi being badgered by a snotty reporter as he leaves a hospital. The trailers are also a gas, reinforcing the spirit of the film as being more than simply another bad movie.

Constructed from brief footage of Lugosi stalking about in a vampire outfit, made right before he died, and a confused flying saucer zombie story, which was filmed several years afterward, the show lurches from one ineptly staged moment to the next, acquiring, as it moves along, the elegance of an inebriated soul who, for a brief moment, can be mistaken for a dancer. The actor playing a grave digger, for example, drops his shovel the first time he grabs for it, and never seems to be able to hold it properly. When he finally manages to get a little dirt on it, he tosses the few pebbles away from the open grave, rather than on top of the coffin. Incompetence? Perhaps, but does not this inability to bury the dead foreshadow the zombie aspect of the plot as well as Lugosi's contrived presence? **Plan Nine from Outer Space** is a necessary addition to anyone's movie collection, because, in comparison, all the other movies collected will seem like masterpieces.

Planetary Traveler (Fox Lorber, WHE73001)

The 40 minute computer graphics program is probably the least interesting aspect of the entire DVD. Created at the home computers of several animators and then shipped to the producer through the Internet, the show supposedly depicts the explorations of various planets by an alien race and amounts to 40 minutes of imaginary landscape designs. Some of it is stimulating, but much of it is redundant or simplistic. There is an elaborate supplementary section, however, that is loaded with sci-fi explanations of what the planets are like, who the aliens doing the exploring are, and what (unseen) civilizations they encountered. There is also an extensive section on how the program was put together and profiles of the artists. All of this is much more stimulating than the actual animation. Anyway, the picture looks very good, with vibrant colors and smooth movement. The stereo surround sound, an electronic score by a former Tangerine Dream alumnus, sounds great, and there is a Dolby Digital track that is even better, with a lot more detail, separation and energy. The program can be subtitled in Japanese, French, Spanish, German or Korean, but there is no English captioning.

The Planets (Image, ID4076DBDVD)

Isao Tomita provides a 55 minute interpretation of Gustav Holst's composition that is set to somewhat worn-looking NASA images. Brief subtitles provide facts about the planets and moons on view. The stereo surround sound is quite good, with lots of directional effects, but Tomita's keyboard orchestration will not be to everyone's liking. The program provides close enough visits to the various orbs (a lot of the computer topographical imaging is utilized) to stimulate the imagination.

Platoon (60454)

Oliver Stone's searing Vietnam War adventure becomes even more tense and exciting when it can be savored with the picture qualities inherent in DVD playback. As is pointed out in several places, the film cost only $6 million to make. Hence, the cinematographer, Robert Richardson, often had to cut corners, which is one reason why previous home video releases have looked so grainy and blandly colored. For the transfer used on the DVD, Richardson was able to tweak the hues in the ways he could only dream about before, and the results are outstanding. Twilight scenes have an eerie, half-lit atmosphere. Night scenes are precise in their darkness and locally lit objects are free of distortion. Colors are bright, fleshtones are accurate and lines are crisp. The picture is letterboxed with an aspect ratio of about 1.9:1 and no 16:9 enhancement. The stereo surround sound is somewhat weak and lacks detail. The Dolby Digital track is stronger, but the surround channels are oddly empty and only activate on rare occasions. The film runs 120 minutes and is accompanied by an hour-long retrospective documentary on the dual layer DVD. The film and the documentary are closed captioned. There is also an interesting theatrical trailer emphasizing Stone's background, and there are two commentary tracks.

Stone's stream-of-consciousness audio commentary is fascinating as a portrait of himself as well as a portrait of the film. He shifts while identifying the figures on the screen as 1) the actors, 2) the characters and 3) the real people upon whom the characters are based, in an almost random manner as if, at times, he believed he was watching the members of his own platoon while viewing parts of the film. Commentary by the movie's technical advisor, Captain Dale Dye, who supervised the 'boot camp' rehearsal and worked closely with Stone throughout the shooting, appears on the other channel. Stone mentions film technique once in a while, and how he worked with the cast a little more often, but most of the time he speaks about what is happening on the screen and why it is happening, not reiterating the story but explaining its sources in his own experiences. It is Dye who provides a sober view of how scenes were set up and shots were achieved, though he also spends time pointing out the movie's many authentic details and the few

times when it was necessary to fudge on reality for the sake of drama. The talks, which last for four hours altogether, create an exhaustive foundation in support of the film's legitimacy and significance.

In the documentary many of the stars and a few of the production personnel reminisce about the making of the movie and what they had to go through. **Platoon** was popular because it was well made (the preparations forced upon the actors were effective, and for many the experience remains an important part of their memories), dramatically powerful and because it conveyed, after a comfortable period of time had elapsed, a realistic portrait of what it had been like to serve in Vietnam.

Playboy: College Girls (Image, ID4131PLDVD)

Eleven models are profiled on the 55 minute program. They talk about their lives and their majors, and each participates in a couple video modeling sessions or erotic skits, usually themed to a career goal or some other topic that was covered in the talk. The colors are bright and the image is reasonably sharp. The stereo sound is okay and the program is not captioned.

Playboy: Farrah Fawcett: All of Me (Image, ID4039PLDVD)

The first 15 minutes of the 71 minute program is the best part, telling how the actress rose like a rocket to stardom on the strength of her looks, becoming, in the late Seventies and early Eighties, the most significant female cultural icon of her day. Except in cases where the reverse was true, every woman wanted her hair and every man wanted her nipples. Then, somewhat daringly, the second segment of the program attempts to explore her fall. Using video footage from Playboy's modeling shoots with her, the actress is depicted being vulnerable and insecure, fretting over her appearance as if she wasn't drop-dead gorgeous even when her makeup is smeared and her hair is ratty. It could have been daring filmmaking, but they reach a point and they pull back, not really exploring her arguments with the magazine, or the nature of her emotional problems and how she overcame them. The program is still superior to the standard Playmate puff piece, and even the nude modeling sequences have a context that keeps them interesting but, if it had been produced independently of those involved, it might have been a significant exploration of fame and ennui.

The picture quality is generally good, with a reasonably sharp image and rich colors. There is an uninteresting but reasonably strong stereo soundtrack and no captioning.

Playboy: Hot Latin Ladies (Image, ID5394PLDVD)

The music accompanying the 54 minute program, which contains only modeling sequences, has a strong and appealing Latin flavor. The picture looks good and is grainy only when, apparently, it is grainy on purpose. The stereo music score is mildly aggressive and is not captioned. The program is accompanied by additional still photos as a secondary menu option and promos for other Playboy programs.

Playboy: Strip (Image, ID5391PLDVD)

One would think that Playboy was being lazy putting out **Strip**, like a fisherman buying fish in the store, but the program includes spirited interviews with the strippers and the dance sequences (most appear staged) that take up the bulk of the program are less monotonous than other strip videos.

The picture is a little soft and some sequences are deliberately hazy, but hues are bright. There is an uninteresting but reasonably strong stereo soundtrack and no captioning. The 50 minute program is accompanied by a still portrait section and other Playboy promotional features.

Playboy: The Best of Jenny McCarthy (Image, ID3974PLDVD)

The full-length profile runs 57 minutes and provides a biographical outline, a few TV clips, photo montages and modeling sequences, but with an emphasis on erotic skits. The colors are good and the image is reasonably sharp, though a few of the skits are a little softer looking. The stereo sound is okay and the program is not captioned.

Playboy: The Best of Pamela Anderson (Image, ID3975PLDVD)

The 55 minute profile includes a superficial biographical sketch, spoken answers to the usual soul-searching unspoken interview questions ('What's your favorite part of a man's anatomy?'), extremely brief TV & film clips, still photo montages and video modeling sequences. The modeling sequences vary in quality, but for the most part the picture is very sharp and colors are vivid. The stereo sound is okay and the program is not captioned.

Playboy: 21 Playmates Centerfold Collection (Image, ID4126PLDVD)

Each segment on the 76 minute program includes a still photo montage, a couple brief voiceover answers to an unspoken interview, and two video modeling sequences. The colors are strong, but most of the segments are soft looking or even blurry. The stereo sound is fine and since the program is not captioned, we have provided 21 precisely transcribed quotations:

"I like the role of woman. And I like the role of her being very feminine, also. I think it's neat."

"I have to admit constraint is not necessarily my strong suit. When I see a door open for a new experience I usually just dive right in."

"Rebecca Ferratti. Not Ferrari, that's the car. I'm Ferratti, the person."

"Being accepted as a Playmate, just one of twelve, was enough to make me happy at the time, but now I'm so much more grateful for being chosen Playmate of the Year because it's just given me a whole lot more to work with. It's given me career opportunities and, of course, financial help, and, uh, help from Playboy employees, themselves."

"It was a personal challenge to me to shoot the pictures in a style of our own."

"I have new experiences almost every day."

"To me, love and sex has to be fantasy-like. That's what it's all about. Sex has to be a fantasy."

"I just did not think of myself as anything that Playboy would be interested in. Mind you, I dreamed. I looked at my dad's Playboys when I was ten. I was like, wow, I would love to be in the magazine."

"I love to sing and I love to perform. I was with the Singing Playmates for almost two years."

"I didn't have any outstanding body parts."

"You don't have to be nervous or anything like that."

"When I was a baby I used to sleep in my mom's bass drum."

"I have this goal for effortless perfection, and that's something that is not easy, and it takes a lot of time and a lot of consideration, and that's something that I work on a lot when I'm by myself."

"Being a California girl means lots of things to different people."

"I think being unpredictable is very romantic."

"When we were kids my mom just slapped a hat on us and put a pair of sneakers on and then off we went in the nude."

"I like going to spots in nature where are real hard to be."

"It's strange to look at a picture of myself that I know millions of people have looked at."

"Playboy has a way of making you feel very comfortable. It's almost like having a mother around."

"When I look at a man, the first thing I notice about him is his eyes. If he has sweet, gentle eyes, I notice the rest of him."

"I, mean, you know, I get compliments, lots of compliments from people, all this, 'You're so pretty,' and this and that. You know, it's nice to be pretty, but don't you like me, too?"

Playboy: 21 Playmates Centerfold Collection: Volume II (Image, ID4132PLDVD)

The following 21 quotations are meticulously transcribed. Most of the clips are from the Eighties and look a bit grainy, though colors are reasonably bright and the stereo sound is adequate. The 84 minute program has not been captioned.

"Shooting for Playboy helped me come out of my shyness."

"Being involved with Playboy has been a great experience for me, but learning is still one of my top priorities. I like to be creative, whether that means modeling, drawing or even making a movie."

"I was sent to Nicaragua when I was twelve to study for two years. I went to the American-Nicaraguan School. That's probably where my interest in visiting other Latin countries began."

"You know what it is about the South that makes me feel like a woman? It's just the basic-ness, the simplicity just of everyday life. There's nothing demanded of you but yet I just try to give it all."

"I met Playboy through the 30th Anniversary hunt."

"Jamaica is the most beautiful island in the world. The people are so happy, so content."

"A lot of people think I'm from Chicago. I'm not. I'm from North Dakota."

"The Playmate phenomena is that, all these women—the twelve women a year—we've all participated, we've all done the same thing. It's a feeling, boy, that I wish every woman could have a chance to feel, but only a chosen few are, and that's what makes it even more special."

"Sometimes when I'm alone I like to envision a faraway place where it's peaceful and serene, unlike the common hustle and bustle I'm seeing every day. It's a place of peace and serenity."

"What is sexy? Music makes me feel sexy, if it's, if it's soft and, and sexy music. There's just, there's sexy music and then there's other music, and, um, I love water. Water makes me feel sexy."

"I think my Playboy pictures are exquisite."

"I like being underwater. Kind of a different world sometimes for me."

"Shooting my layout was a very wonderful experience and I felt like I had a creative hand in the entire process."

"There's been times when people view me as more of a sex object instead of a person, and, whatever I do, whether I'm a Playmate or a doctor or anything, I'm still going to be the same basic person."

"When I found out I was going to be Miss December, um, I couldn't believe it because that's the holiday issue."

"When I'm cooking it gives me a lot of time to fantasize about the things I enjoy."

"The only time I really feel beautiful is when I look at my Playboy pictures."

"Muscular and soft. That's Julie."

"Sometimes when I look at my pictorial I think, 'Is that really me?'"

"After a workout I have to relax. I have to have time to myself to get my mind clear and let my body relax and if certain muscles need to be massaged, I can do it all myself."

"I love to send and receive love letters."

Playboy Video Centerfold: Victoria Silvstedt (Image, ID3973PLDVD)

The usual Playboy centerfold profile runs about 20 minutes, but sometimes they make a big production about it and have it run longer, which is what happens here. The DVD runs an hour, with 'Playmate of the Year' Silvstedt's piece running 40 minutes and a filler piece on Shauna Sand that runs 20. Although the profile is extended, there is no organization to it and the end of each segment within the profile feels like the conclusion of the piece. The profiles combine minor interview sequences with video modeling, vague dialog-less erotic skits and a montage of magazine spreads.

The picture is fairly good, with bright, fresh colors and a crisp image. The stereo sound is okay. A brief menu selection provides a duplication of the magazine centerfold 'fact sheet.' Silvstedt is from Sweden.

Playboy Wet & Wild: The Locker Room (Image, ID5387PLDVD)

The theme is more vague than the title suggests, as the modeling sequences and erotic quasi-skits are linked only by the predisposition of the models to forsake apparel and embrace dampness.

The picture is a bit soft and some sequences are a bit blurrier than others, but on the whole, the image is passable. The program runs 55 minutes and has an uninteresting but reasonably strong stereo soundtrack. There is no captioning, but the presentation is accompanied by a still portrait section and other Playboy promotional features.

Playboy's Asian Exotica (Image, ID4466PLDVD)

A mix of erotic modeling sequences and erotic semi-skits, there is no more than a line or two of narration. The editing is energetic and the picture quality is excellent, with crisp, vivid colors. The audio volume is set exceptionally high, but the stereo is adequate. The 52 minute program is not captioned and is accompanied by additional still photos as a secondary menu option and promos for other Playboy programs.

Playboy's Babes of Baywatch (Image, ID4479PLDVD)

Since they draw from the same gene pool, it is less surprising than the narration makes it out to be that the same models would appear in both Playboy and *Baywatch*. The program opens with a disclaimer that suggests the TV show's producers wanted nothing to do with the Playboy video, which contains no clips, although the 16 models featured are often seen in a beach setting. The 57 minute program contains a segment on each model, plus a 'making of' segment. The picture quality varies from one segment to the next, some looking blurrier than others, though overall the colors are bright and the image is solid. The stereo sound is the usual generic Playboy rock and is reasonably strong, and there is no captioning.

Playboy's Bedtime Stories (Image, ID5412PLDVD)

Although the premise is promising, the execution is not. Supposedly a reenactment of five classic erotic tales (with an annoying framing device about a couple reading to one another), the episodes are more concerned with the posing and nude modeling of the performers than with the pace or execution of the story.

The picture is often blurry or hazy, but colors are usually fairly bright. The 58 minute program has an uninteresting but reasonably strong stereo soundtrack and is not captioned. It is accompanied by a still portrait section and other Playboy promotional features.

Playboy's Biker Babes: Hot Wheels and High Heels (Image, ID4040PLDVD)

Each segment has a motorcycle in it someplace. There are a couple quasi-documentary segments about biker gatherings at Daytona Beach and the like, and a couple that include people actually using a motorcycle, but most of the sequences are just erotic skits that start off with a motorcycle prop and then go elsewhere. The skits have more dialogue than usual, but talk is still limited. The colors are bright and the picture looks fine. The program runs 55 minutes and is not captioned.

Playboy's Complete Massage (Image, ID4049PLDVD)

Everything you could possibly want to know about massaging somebody is included. The 62 minute program has segments on Swedish, Chinese, French and other massage styles. Couples who aren't wearing much clothing demonstrate, while voiceover narration details exactly how their physical contact is executed. In runs by fairly quickly, though, so if someone intends to use it as an in-

structional—as opposed to just ogling the demonstrators—then some reverse scanning will be required. The picture looks sharp, with strong colors, and the stereo sound is fine. There is no captioning.

Playboy's Freshman Class (Image, ID4786PLDVD)

A collection of college-oriented erotic skits are featured on the 59 minute program. There is even a linking device, of three women, who are supposedly about to graduate, reminiscing about being freshmen, or fresh women, as it were. The picture quality is fine. There is a mildly aggressive stereo music score and no captioning. The program is accompanied by additional still photos as a secondary menu option and promos for other Playboy programs.

Playboy's Gen-X Girls (Image, ID4481PLDVD)

Two women briefly discuss various modern lifestyles in the program, as these segments introduce extended erotic modeling sequences that are based upon the discussions. It tries hard to be hip, but like the model on the jacket cover, it fools no one. The picture on the erotic sequences (one, a skit about two women who pester a draftsman in a neighboring apartment, has appeared elsewhere) is fairly soft and a bit erratic, although colors are strong. The program runs 57 minute. There is a mildly aggressive stereo music score and no captioning.

Playboy's Girlfriends (Image, ID5103PLDVD)

Each of the seven erotic skits are introduced with a brief dialogue sequence, but are otherwise enacted to a blandly energetic musical score, as the models frolic with one another in various venues.

The picture is often soft and fleshtones tend to look orangey. The 61 minute program has an uninteresting but reasonably strong stereo soundtrack and is not captioned. It is accompanied by a still portrait section and other Playboy promotional features.

Playboy's Girls in Uniform (Image, ID4038PLDVD)

Not just about the military, it covers everything from Everglades park rangers to theater ushers. The ten segments are a mixture of erotic skits and supposed profiles ("A lot of men don't take me seriously," says the topless 'corporate executive.'), including a sequence where female firefighters get hosed down by their male compatriots. The colors are bright, but the picture is soft and fairly grainy at times. The program runs 57 minutes and is not captioned.

Playboy's Girls Next Door: Naughty and Nice (Image, ID4044PLDVD)

A voiceover narrator provides elaborate introductions for the erotic skits and, if anyone cares, there are a series of epilogs at the end of the program presenting the fate of each character. Nevertheless, the bulk of the show is the standard frolic au natural, and except for two or three of the skits (in the best one, two rock musicians tease an uptight neighbor), the 'plot' is irrelevant.

The picture is fresh-looking, from a video tape source, with accurate fleshtones and a crisp image, except for shots that are deliberately softer. The accompanying energetic musical score is stereophonic and is not as generic sounding as Playboy's musical scores in the past have seemed. The program is not closed captioned and runs just under an hour.

Playboy's Girls of South Beach (Image, ID5396PLDVD)

The program is a mixture of studio modeling sessions (too many, in our opinion), outdoor modeling sessions, a couple of erotic skits and a model interview, though, on the whole, dialogue is minimal. The source material wavers wildly from one shot to the next and much of the 55 minute program is extremely fuzzy. The stereo music score is mildly aggressive and is not captioned. The program is accompanied by additional still photos as a secondary menu option and promos for other Playboy programs.

Playboy's Girls of the Internet (Image, ID5392PLDVD)

Meeting through e-mail is a common fantasy depicted on the 52 minute mix of erotic skits and posing sequences. The image on the sequences is of mixed quality, with some looking reasonably sharp and others looking rather blurry. The colors are fine. The programs has a mildly aggressive stereo music score and is not captioned. There are additional still photos on a secondary menu option and promos for other Playboy programs.

Playboy's Hard Bodies (Image, ID5395PLDVD)

The modeling sessions on the 57 minute program have various workout and sports motifs, and there is some voiceover where the models talk about how much they like their exercises. The picture quality varies, but it is usually on the blurry side, and colors are adequate. The program has a mildly aggressive stereo music score and is not captioned. The show is accompanied by additional still photos as a secondary menu option and promos for other Playboy programs.

Playboy's Rising Stars and Sexy Starlets (Image, ID5393PLDVD)

None of the 'rising stars' are in danger of suffering from nose bleeds. In fact, the only one whose name we recognize is Julie Strain, and that's only because of the other topless videos she's been featured in. The 63 minute program takes a look at a number of actress/models appearing in adult cable programs and the like. Most are interviewed, and the collection combines film clips, erotic skits based upon the interviews (one actress wanted to be a dancer, so in the skit she's a dancer, etc.) and the usual still photo montages. The image is okay, though the interview sequences have poor contrasts. The program has a mildly aggressive stereo music score and is not captioned. It is accompanied by additional still photos as a secondary menu option and promos for other Playboy programs.

Playboy's Sex on the Beach (Image, ID4311PLDVD)

The 51 minute program is a collection of modeling and very loosely plotted erotic skits, most having a beach or at least a water motif. The picture quality is a bit weaker than the others, but workable, with generally bright colors and accurate fleshtones.

The picture is fresh-looking, from a video tape source, with accurate fleshtones and a crisp image, except for shots that are deliberately softer. The accompanying energetic musical score is stereophonic and is not as generic sounding as Playboy's musical scores in the past have seemed. The program is not closed captioned.

Playboy's Sorority Girls (Image, ID4043PLDVD)

The skits have an academic motif. The models introduce each skit. The picture is fuzzy most of the time. The accompanying energetic musical score is stereophonic. The program is not closed captioned and runs just under an hour.

Playboy's Voluptuous Vixens II (Image, ID4046PLDVD)

The 56 minute program contains a number of erotic skits involving exceptionally endowed models, interspersed by with comments by the legendary film director, Russ Meyer, though he has less to say than in the first **Voluptuous Vixens**. He appears briefly between the dialog-less skits, surrounded by women and talking about how nice it is to be in such a situation. The skits feature women who are anatomically designed to Meyer's liking. The picture quality is fine, with bright hues and accurate fleshtones, and the stereo surround sound is reasonably forceful.

Playboy's Women Behaving Badly (Image, ID4047PLDVD)

There is no narration, but few viewers will have difficulty understanding what is going on. The skits are supposed to depict women acting outside of accepted social decorum, but mostly it just shows them having a good time.

The picture is fresh-looking, from a video tape source, with accurate fleshtones and a crisp image, except for shots that are deliberately softer. The accompanying energetic musical score is stereophonic and is not as generic sounding as Playboy's musical scores in the past have seemed. The program is not closed captioned and runs just under an hour.

The Player (New Line, N4032)

Tim Robbins stars as a movie company executive under so much pressure that in a fit of rage he kills someone, an action that in a very odd way humanizes him for the viewer. The 1992 Robert Altman movie is wonderful, salted with cameos and peppered with acerbic glimpses of the motion picture business in action. From the film's opening marathon tracking shot (catching, among many other things, characters talking about famous marathon tracking shots—an early example of the movie's many instances of wry self-examination) through its marvelous ensemble gatherings and beyond, **The Player** is a superbly styled work, sliding through different types of comedy as effortlessly as a rope through the coils of a noose.

The 124 minute film is presented on one side of the DVD and the supplement, including deleted scenes (unnecessary to the film but featuring more choice cameo appearances and other peripheral delights), an Altman interview, behind-the-scenes footage, a trailer and a promotional featurette, are presented on the other. There is also a commentary track featuring Altman and screenwriter Michael Tolkin (though the two were apparently recorded separately), and an enormous cast profile section that includes complete filmographies not only for the principal cast members, but for all the performers making cameo appearances.

The presentation is letterboxed with an aspect ratio of about 1.85:1 and an accommodation for enhanced 16:9 playback. The picture has crisp, deep colors and smooth fleshtones. The image is stable under all lighting conditions and details are clear. The dialogue sounds unusually harsh and separation effects are modest. Although the sound does have a little more flourish on the Dolby Digital track, we found ourselves preferring the standard stereo track, which does a better job at smoothing over the rough edges. The film is also presented in French without Dolby Digital and has English, French or Spanish subtitles. The supplement has no language options or captioning.

Altman talks about details in the film, but draws larger meanings from the things that grab his attention. At one point he says he can't remember who is responsible for the various creative decisions in the film, since moviemaking is a collaborative process, yet he always able to justify the important choices and approaches that were utilized. He explains that many of the choices a director makes in a film come not so much from an artistic vision but from a pragmatic necessity of circumstances, and he also allows as to how substantially different any of his films would look or feel if different production personnel, such as different cinematographers, had worked on them. Tolkin's speaks with a hint of wistfulness about the necessity of giving characters over to actors in a film, and how each performer is more likely than anybody else, even the writer or the director, to look out for a character's best interests. He is fully pleased with the job Altman did, but he is not above identifying what he feels were Altman's shortcomings (the film could have had more paranoia), as well as his own.

Playing God (Buena Vista, 14371)

David Duchovny has an effortless way about him, and an existential, self-depreciating humor that lets him move from serious drama to archetypal heroics without breaking the spell. When a performer has that kind of star power, the material doesn't have to be perfect to succeed. **Playing God** is about a disgraced doctor who becomes friends with a mobster (portrayed with fresh energy by Timothy Hutton) and soon finds himself in the middle of a mob war and an FBI sting. Duchovny has to deliver some obnoxious voiceover narration and pretend to go through drug withdrawals, but he handles both so efficiently that neither is a detriment to the entertainment. The film is consistently enjoyable and involving, with touches of humor, several gunfights and even a lengthy automobile chase. It is a star vehicle, and as Duchovny's star rises, more viewers will likely flock to it.

The picture is letterboxed with an aspect ratio of about 1.85:1, with no 16:9 enhancement. The color transfer is very good, with bright, crisp hues and accurate fleshtones. The standard stereo surround soundtrack is sloppy, with too much bleeding of the dialogue to the rear channels, but the Dolby Digital track is fine, with active separations and lots of punch. The 94 minute film is accompanied by an accurate theatrical trailer and can be supported by English subtitles.

Playmates in Paradise (Image, ID5411PLDVD)

The 58 minute travelogue-style program combines models-as-tourists footage with behind-the-scenes shots of bathing suit models at work (the least guarded and most pleasing aspect of the program) and typical locale nude modeling sessions. The picture varies between sharp looking sequences and hazier sequences. The stereo music score is mildly aggressive and is not captioned. The program is accompanied by additional still photos as a secondary menu option and promos for other Playboy programs.

Pleasantville (New Line, N4728)

People say it is a comedy, but that is according it too many expectations. There are humorous moments and a general sense of satire, but the fable, about two modern teenagers who are transported into the black-and-white, squeaky-perfect world of an old TV sitcom, is more of an entertaining essay on the conflict between conformity and non-conformity. Television is designed to deliver consumers to advertisers and, in the beginning, it often did so with the promise or dream of a happy, predictable utopia. Like a rat that has to keep gnawing, however, advertisers over the years had to increase the emotional realism and irrationality of their entertainment to maintain viewer interest. Taking away the interim steps, the contrast between the old and the new is severe enough to generate humor almost automatically, and it is admirable that **Pleasantville** shows some restraint in mining the subsequent social anachronisms.

The cast includes Jeff Daniels, William H. Macy and J.T. Walsh, with Joan Allen standing out as the TV housewife who starts to realize there is more to life than baking. Tobey Maguire and Reese Witherspoon star, as the teenagers. The film's premise incorporates a number of explorations, into racial conflicts (people gradually become 'colored'), the Garden of Eden (pointedly), the value of literature, sex, gender stereotyping, fascism, and creativity. Each exploration, however, subsides to make way for the next. It is a thoughtful and stimulating fantasy, but it often seems like the filmmakers are groping for something profound and never find it.

The gradual intrusions by color into the black-and-white world make up the film's most impressive visual effects, and these have been rendered with perfection. Because the objects and people who are in color are set off against the black and white around them, the hues seem exceptionally precise and vivid. The effects are often breathtaking. The presentation is in letterboxed format only, with an aspect ratio of about 1.85:1 and an accommodation for enhanced 16:9 playback. The program opens with a 'color adjustment test' that really doesn't make too much sense.

The stereo surround sound and Dolby Digital sound are fine, though the audio mix has nothing that is equivalent to the color effects. The 124 minute film can be supported by (and defaults to) optional English subtitles. There is a very good 32 minute documentary about how the film was made, a small collection of storyboard art, a disappointingly cheap music video with Fiona Apple that combines her lovely version of the Beatles' *Across the Universe* with black-and-white images of rioters trashing a diner, a trailer and a cast & crew profile section. A DVD-ROM option includes the shooting script with incorporated storyboards, and elaborate Web links.

There are also two commentary tracks. On one, the musical score is isolated, with inserted comments by composer Randy Newman between the cues. Newman talks about the score and how it reflects the film's emotions. He also speaks substantially about the other scores he has composed, about his uncle, the composer, Alfred Newman, and generally about the art of composing (and borrowing from the classics). On the other track, the director, Gary Ross, explains how the effects were accomplished, why they were applied in specific places, and talks about what he wanted to achieve with the film. He discusses the film's internal logic (a 'week' in TV land is equal to a half-hour in our time). He also talks about the performers, about the film's cultural references, and about his own political and cultural upbringing. Interestingly, he sees it as 'different' from the norm, because his father was a screenwriter.

Point Blank (Sterling, 7105)

Some arms dealers take hostages in a shopping mall and Mickey Rourke has the 'Bruce Willis role,' picking them off. The plot is hardly logical, but there are plenty of slo-mo gunfights and squibs. The film's lighting has some low budget limitations, but the picture transfer looks okay, at least for those who don't find large, adequately focused close-ups of Rourke to be unsettling. The stereo surround sound is poorly balanced, with gunfire and music coming in much louder than dialogue and everything sounding like it has been pasted together, but there are plenty of separation effects and it is best one not pay too close attention to the dialogue anyway. Although there is no English captioning, the 90 minute program can be supported by Spanish subtitles. There is also a decent cast profile section and a trailer.

Point of No Return (Warner, 12819)

The film's heroine is a cold blooded cop killer who is reformed to become a government assassin, earning the viewer's sympathy as she begins to dislike her murder assignments. Directed by John Badham, it is an action thriller, with a number of brisk gun fights and similarly engaging mayhem. Bridget Fonda and Gabriel Byrne star in the **La Femme Nikita** remake.

The presentation is in letterboxed format on one side, with an aspect ratio of about 2.35:1 and an accommodation for enhanced 16:9 playback, and in cropped format on the other side. The color transfer looks bland, with soft fleshtones and slightly subdued hues. The cropped version enhances some of the close-ups, but makes the action scenes more confusing. The stereo surround sound is weak, but the Dolby Digital track has better disciplined separation effects and a stronger dimensionality. The 1993 feature is also available in French in stereo and in Spanish in mono. There is a cast & crew profile section and some lightweight production notes, including a couple paragraphs that link the film to 'The Pygmalion Legend.'

Police Academy (Warner, 20016)

Trailers for all seven installments have been included, and it is the funniest part of the DVD because no matter how stupid the movies are, they at least have a minute and thirty seconds of viable gags. The premier film, from 1984, runs 96 minutes and is presented in full screen format only, though the framing never looks awkward. The color transfer is okay, but the film's low budget cinematography creates bland fleshtones and uninteresting colors. The monophonic sound is fairly weak, but there is a Dolby Digital mono track that works somewhat better. The film can be supported by English, French or Spanish subtitles and is accompanied by a small cast and crew profile section (the director, Hugh Wilson, went on to make **First Wives Club**), along with very brief but informative production notes. Steve Guttenberg stars in the erratic formula comedy.

Poltergeist (MGM, 906039)

Tobe Hooper and Steven Spielberg's energetic 1982 ghost story looks crisp and glossy, though the source material does have mild speckles and at least one larger scratch. The 115 minute film is presented in cropped format on one side and in letterboxed format, with an aspect ratio of about 2.35:1, on the other. The letterboxed version is much better, but there are sequences, such as the house imploding at the end, that are worth sampling with the enlarged cropped image. Separation effects are well detailed and there is a strong bass, but the dialogue channel on both the regular stereo surround soundtrack and the Dolby Digital track are markedly weak. The film is available in French or Spanish in standard stereo and comes with English, French or Spanish subtitles ("Están aquí").

Popeye (Digital Disc Entertainment, 519)

The 45 minute collection features two cartoons that were created by the Fleischers at Paramount, *Popeye the Sailor Meets Sinbad the Sailor* and *Popeye the Sailor Meets Ali Baba's Forty Thieves*, and two that were produced in the Fifties, *Ancient Fistory* (Popeye as a Cinderella character) and *Cookin' with Gags* (Olive Oyl goes on a picnic with Popeye and Bluto on April Fool's Day). The two Fleischer cartoons, which make use of impressive multi-plane animation, have somewhat pale hues. The two cartoons from the Fifties have a bit more color. On all, the source material looks worn, with soft edges and regular visitations of scratches. On all, as well, the monophonic sound is noisy—with a noticeable hum in a couple places—but coherent. There is no captioning.

Pork Chop Hill (MGM, 907669)

Like its meaty successor, **Hamburger Hill**, **Pork Chop Hill** is a rewarding depiction of a futile battle. Set in the final days of the Korean War and decorated with only minimal patriotic justification, the film depicts a Pyrrhic effort on the part of an American army company to seize and hold a useless hill in support of a negotiations bluff. Practically the whole film is the battle and it has a constant ring of authenticity. Written by the commander who led the charge, the narrative makes clear that battle strategies are fuzzy wish lists, that in the heat of it no one has even the faintest idea of what is going on, and that the winner is usually the side lucky enough to have made the fewest rampant mistakes. However haphazard the efforts of the armies which clash may be, the script is meticulous in capturing the events within the battle which led to victory, so that even though the soldiers have no idea what is occurring, the viewer is never left in a similar quandary. Although restricted by a fifties depiction of violence, the horror and randomness of the slaughter are effectively communicated. Gregory Peck stars in the film with a number of supporting players including Harry Guardino, Rip Torn and George Peppard.

The 1959 feature was directed by Lewis Milestone. Sam Leavitt's stunning black-and-white cinematography has been transferred without a single imposed blemish. The elaborate night photography is undistorted and pitch black remains pitch black. The presentation is letterboxed on one side, with an aspect ratio of about 1.85:1 and no 16:9 enhancement, and is in full screen format on the other side. The letterboxing adds very little to the sides and trims picture information off the top and bottom of the screen in comparison to the full screen version. We prefer the full screen presentation, which doesn't look as cramped. The monophonic sound is reasonably strong. There is an alternate French audio track, optional English and French subtitles, and a trailer. The film runs 98 minutes.

Porky's (Fox, 4109069)

Like **The Crying Game**, this is one of those movies that works much differently on a large theatrical screen than it does on a smaller TV screen. We won't get into why. The 1981 Bob Clark comedy is in letterboxed format with an aspect ratio of about 1.85:1 and no 16:9 enhancement. The image is rather soft and a bit grainy in darker sequences, but hues are reasonably strong and fleshtones look okay. There is a mildly stereophonic audio track. The 99 minute program is also available in French and Spanish in mono and can be supported by English subtitles. There is an amusing trailer. The sex-obsessed comedy, about Florida teenagers in the Fifties playing pranks on each other and taking revenge on a roadhouse that wouldn't serve them, is funniest on the first viewing, but there is enough nudity and enough humor to encourage repeat viewings with some fans.

Porter, Cole (see **You're The Top: The Cole Porter Story**)

The Portrait of a Lady (PolyGram, 4400437972)

Nicole Kidman, John Malkovich and Barbara Hershey star in Jane Campion's difficult adaptation of Henry James' novel—what we have decided is three-quarters of a great film and one-quarter unfinished, the story's emotional resolutions failing to translate as well cinematically as its initial explorations of ambition and desire. Campion has been most successful when she has explored, with a knowing confidence, the erotic yearnings of women, and with James, she can only slip things in around the edges. Kidman, often marching around in a positively frightening coiffure, stars as a wealthy American heiress in the late Nineteenth Century who doesn't marry well. Malkovich is the heavy, with John Gielgud, Shelley Winters and others filling up the costumes. Gielgud proves he's still got what it takes by giving what has to be one of cinema's greatest death yawns. Winters looks fantastic in her part, but as soon as she opens her mouth she spoils it. Her character is supposed to be a bit awkward and out of place, but Winters just sounds too uncomfortable with her dialogue and the effect is disorienting. Malkovich and Hershey act a bit too much like they're in **Dangerous Liaisons** instead of **Portrait of a Lady**, but their characters have to externalize something. Campion tries very hard to enliven the proceedings with abstract images, anachronisms and other pinpricks, but she also avoids getting into the details of the period setting. Where other directors have used the educational aspect of history to reinforce their dramas, Campion seems to glide past it, teasing the viewer with knowledge instead of sharing it. Some viewers will appreciate the dense narrative and the lovely sets and costumes—some may even like Kidman's hair—but others will be lost or apathetic. We're always so happy when a genuinely intelligent movie comes along, however, that we didn't mind its shortcomings.

The color transfer is rich, with accurate fleshtones and bright hues, bringing the fullest beauty to Stuart Dryburgh's outstanding cinematography. The Super-35 film is presented on one side in letterboxed format, with an as aspect ratio of about 2.35:1 and no 16:9 enhancement, and in full screen format on the other side, cropping some picture information off the sides in comparison to the letterboxed image, but adding a bit to the top and a lot to the bottom. The cinematography is so good that either version becomes valid (the letterboxed framing is preferable as the intended framing, but only as a matter of taste) and makes the film worth watching twice (at the least). Letterboxed, the film becomes a modernist view of the Victorian Era, but in full screen the film feels like a more organic representation of its period.

The stereo surround sound is adequate and the Dolby Digital sound is excellent. Not only is the clarity of definition improved and detailed by the Dolby Digital, but independent rear channel separation effects, which are conservatively but pointedly applied, add greatly to the film's richness. The 144 minute film is also accessible in French and can be supported by Spanish subtitles, and English closed captioning.

The Poseidon Adventure (Fox, 4110422)

The director who was hired by producer Irwin Allen for the 1972 cruise ship disaster film, Ronald Neame, was known for dramatic works rather than for action pictures. Neame was a good choice, because the action—the ship is turned upside down by a tidal wave—is so intricately plotted that it would be difficult to botch. One cringes, on the other hand, at the specter of Shelley Winters, Ernest Borgnine and some of the others performing for a director who had less control of the dramatics.

The picture is letterboxed with an aspect ratio of about 2.35:1 and no 16:9 enhancement. The image is crisp and colors look good. The sound is monophonic, while the LD was stereo, and yet, despite the mono, the audio has a fresher ambiance, a stronger bass and is more satisfying, particularly since even the most rudimentary amplifier-stereoizations provide as much separation effects and dimensionality as the LD's stereo track. The 117 minute film is also available in French, can be supported by English or Spanish subtitles, and is accompanied by a trailer and a cast profile section.

The Postman (Warner, 15519)

The first time we saw the trailer for **The Postman** it sent goosebumps up our arms, so you can well imagine our surprise when a friend who lives in a somewhat more sophisticated part of the world informed us that when he'd seen the trailer, the theater exploded in derisive guffaws. Critics tend to gang up on big blockbuster films, complaining that there is nothing original about them, that they pander to a nervous formula of pre-tested success—but look what happens when something comes along that tries to be a bit different. Everybody laughs at it. Unfortunately, the film was directed by Kevin Costner, who tends to underline the obvious, thereby encouraging the search and discovery of unintended punchlines, particularly with viewers who resent his past successes.

The Postman takes a common movie setting—the fragmented, technologically hindered world of the post-apocalypse—and does something legitimately thoughtful about it, exploring the bonds, the fears and the habits that hold a society together. The film is so much about America that, unlike **Waterworld**, it didn't even do well overseas. At its best, it gets to the heart of what makes people proud about the American spirit. At its worst, you look at the action scenes and almost wish they had been directed by Kevin Reynolds. It also runs 178 minutes, so those who haven't bought the premise or the ideal are going to get awful itchy by the time the third act rolls around. That's where home video comes in. It may well have been torture trying to watch the movie in a theater, but in the comfort of one's home you can give **The Postman** its due, taking all the imagination, character interaction and inspiration it has to offer, while overlooking its weaknesses. The hero within the story isn't asking for anything more than that form those around him.

The presentation is in single-sided dual-layer format, letterboxed with an aspect ratio of about 2.35:1 and an accommodation for enhanced 16:9 playback. The picture quality is excellent, with crisp, detailed hues and accurate fleshtones. The stereo surround sound is okay and the Dolby Digital soundtrack is super, with many dimensional separation effects and a strong bass. The film is also available in French in Dolby Digital and can be supported by English, French or Spanish subtitles ("Ni la neige, ni la pluie, ni la choler, ni la nuit n'empêchent ces messengers d'accomlir leur course"). There is a cast & crew profile section, brief and uninteresting essays on the production and on post-apocalyptic films, an informative 10 minute segment about the movie's special effect sequences (such as the pointless cable car ride) narrated by the effects supervisors, and the legendary trailer ("There used to be a postman for every street in a America. They wore uniforms and hats, just like this one").

The Postman Always Rings Twice (Warner, 673)

Warner has included a letterboxed theatrical trailer of the 1981 feature, but the film itself is presented in full screen. The picture is less grainy than on previous home video releases, and fleshtones are rich, doing reasonably justice to the film's challenging cinematography. The Dolby Digital monaural track has more power and clarity than the standard mono track. The 121 minute film can be supported by English, French or Spanish subtitles and is accompa-

nied by a cast profile section and a few production notes about the creation of the script. The trailer is accompanied by trailers for the older version of the film and for **Mildred Pierce**. Jack Nicholson and Jessica Lange star in the heated tale of adultery and murder, directed by Bob Rafelson.

Pot O' Gold (Madacy, DVD99030)

James Stewart and Paulette Goddard break into song as they walk down the street and solve all their problems by getting a big break on a radio show. The 1941 film makes a good showcase for Stewart's amenable and energetic personality, and Goddard brings a solid presence to the non-musical sequences and the romance.

The black-and-white source material is a little worn in places and looks soft. The edges of the picture are dark, but contrasts are reasonably clear in the center. The backgrounds have a pulsating grain, but if you don't stare at them too closely the presentation is tolerable. The monophonic sound is scratchy and the high end is clipped. The 85 minute program is not captioned.

The Power of One (Warner, 12411)

It is almost axiomatic that movies about the white experience in South Africa are beside the point, but John G. Avildsen's surprising 1992 effort turns out to be a significant exception to this rule. The film is about mythmaking and the characters say as much. When the hero, a young boxer and songwriter, is cheered by the black characters for his saint-like actions, it is not the least bit offensive. Avildsen avoids the trap of "bearing witness" because he uses the inhuman cruelties condoned by the South African government during the Forties and Fifties as an intricate part of the landscape—not something to be 'discovered,' but something that is constantly present. He then uses that setting to explore the various ways that heroism can be manifested, both by those who are oppressed and those who are not a target of oppression. Morgan Freeman, Armin Mueller-Stahl and John Gielgud have supporting roles. Stephen Dorff stars.

The picture is presented in letterboxed format only (actually, it is windowboxed), with an aspect ratio of about 1.85:1 and no 16:9 enhancement. The image is very sharp and colors are bright, but some sequences have a little background grain, made unstable by artifacting and there is an occasional speckle, though such flaws are fleeting. For the most part, the image is striking. The stereo surround sound is also highly appealing, with a deep range and nice atmospheric effects. The 127 minute program has English captioning.

Practical Magic (Warner, 16322)

Based upon a novel by Alice Hoffman, the 1998 effort is free of the usual Hollywood claptrap and is a special little film about magic, female bonding and romance. It has a cast that can only make the movie more famous as time advances, with Sandra Bullock and Nicole Kidman portraying sisters who are knowledgeable in the art of witchcraft but unable to control what fate has in store for them. The narrative is quite elaborate (Bullock's character loses a husband, murders another man and falls in love with a third), yet it unfolds easily and with great charm. The performances are super, particularly during the scenes Bullock and Kidman share, and the film has rewards of both a supernatural nature and something entirely more earthbound. The presentation is in letterboxed format only, with an aspect ratio of about 2.35:1 and an accommodation for enhanced 16:9 playback. The picture looks fine, with sharp, nicely detailed colors and accurate fleshtones. The stereo surround sound and Dolby Digital sound have some basic separation effects and are reasonably satisfying, with the Dolby Digital track providing a slightly sharper playback. The 104 film is also available in French in Dolby Digital and can be supported by English or French subtitles. On the other side of the platter, there is a collection of TV spots, a trailer that plays exactly like a TV spot, and two documentaries about the film with enjoyable behind-the-scenes footage, such as a shot of director Griffin Dunne tickling Bullock in the armpit. Unfortunately, to access the documentaries, you have to play an annoying game (select rosemary, mint, grapes and lavender).

During the film, there is a commentary track featuring Dunne, Bullock with producer Denise Di Novi, and composer Alan Silvestri. Each speak in extended segments. Silvestri supplies the most focused analysis of the film, explaining the emotional context for his musical choices. The others tend to talk a lot about how everybody got along on the set, as well as a bit about the logistics of the shoot (Washington's San Juan Islands standing in for New England) and a general description of the production.

Pre-Code Hollywood: The Risqué Years #1—Of Human Bondage / Kept Husbands / Millie (Roan, AED2004)

The brief jacket copy accompanying the interesting triple bill of mature dramas from the early days of sound films talks about the implementation of the Code, but what is suggested by the three films is that while the code was used to suppress saucy subject matter, what it was really doing was reining in female independence. Although there are token 'happy' endings in which the heroine comes back into the fold, all three are about women who are in control of their lives, maintaining a leg up on the men around them.

Bette Davis stars in the 1934 *Of Human Bondage*, as a waitress who dominates her relationship with a weak-willed doctor, played in typical limp noodle fashion by Leslie Howard. Davis has a Cockney accent and takes charge of every scene she's in. The film runs 82 minutes.

In Lloyd Bacon's 1931 *Millie*, starring Helen Twelvetrees, the heroine divorces her husband when she discovers his infidelity, but refuses alimony or custody of her child, and gets a job to support herself. When the new men in her life attempt to supplement her finances, she turns them down as well, wishing to avoid all obligations. It is only when her own daughter matures that she starts to make choices based upon someone else's needs, and soon she is standing trial for murder. The 84 minute film is an entertaining look at the flapper era, with barely veiled references to prostitution, homosexuality and other matters, and it advances briskly.

Joel McCrea is a steel mill worker and Dorothy Mackaill is the mill owner's daughter, who takes a fancy to him in the 1931 *Kept Husbands*. At first they're in love and have a good time, but she wants to continue living in the lifestyle to which she is accustomed, and he wants to be more responsible for their livelihood. Although the heroine learns her lesson at the end, she spends almost the entire 76 minute film enjoying not having learned it. (Tom Hanks is commonly compared to Jimmy Stewart, but there is a lot of Joel McCrea in what he does, as well.)

All three films are in black and white. *Millie* is in very nice condition. There is isolated wear, but the images are fairly sharp and contrasts are nicely detailed. *Kept Husbands* is grainy, with fairly constant vertical scratches and a softer focus. *Of Human Bondage* also looks softer, and damage to the source material is a bit more prevalent, but we've seen versions that look a lot worse. There is grain in a lot of places and a number of scratches in some segments, but the image is crisp and the presentation is workable. On all three, the monophonic sound is noisy but adequate for the age of the programs, though the audio on *Kept Husbands* is a little extra scratchy. There is no captioning, no menus and no chapter guide.

Predator (Fox, 4109068)

The picture is letterboxed with an aspect ratio of about 1.85:1 and no 16:9 enhancement. The presentation is substantially better than the letterboxed LD, which looks washed out in comparison. Some of the darker jungle shots are grainy (as are a few close-ups, as if they were constructed optically from wider angle shots), but for the most part the image is solid and hues are accurate (the interior helicopter sequence, lit in a strong red, is on the money). The

stereo surround sound is as good or perhaps a little better than the LD's stereo, and the DVD has a menu-activated Dolby Digital track with even stronger definitions and more separation detail. The 107 minute film is also available in French in standard stereo and comes with English or Spanish subtitles ("Si revelas nuestra posición una vez màs, te desangro en silencio y te dejo aquí") and an interesting though not wholly satisfying theatrical trailer.

We have found the film to be tremendously effective home video entertainment, the sort of stimulating action picture with fantastic production values which is just smart enough and plenty exciting enough to provide a totally involving collection of thrills. You could make a case that the creature that massacres the U.S. reconnaissance commandos in **Predator** represents the evils of war or covert activity, but the movie is too much fun to bother. You can also make a case that the filmmakers fudged the ending, which by all rights ought to have been an atomic explosion. Otherwise, the script is a marvelously witty bait and switch, which will be especially enjoyable to future generations less aware from publicity campaigns and word of mouth as to what the story is actually about. Arnold Schwarzenegger stars as the leader of a commando group who comes across something unexpected while on a mission in the jungle. Violent and exciting, the movie is great home video, something which will keep you tense and thrilled for at least the first three or four dozen viewings, and it makes a wonderful, exciting disc for Saturday afternoons while Mom is out shopping.

Prehistoric Women (Anchor Bay, DV10679)

A safari guy chasing after a wounded leopard touches the horn of a rhinoceros statue and is transported to a world where brunette women rule and blondes are slaves. The 1966 film, also known as *Slave Girls*, is daffy, but it somehow manages to stay true to its internal logic, and the scenes of all the dark haired women bossing around all the light haired women has a certain appeal that in all likelihood transcends gender orientation.

The transfer is terrific. The film is letterboxed with an aspect ratio of about 2.35:1 and no 16:9 enhancement. The color transfer is very nice, with deep fleshtones, bright hues and sharp details. Even the darker sequences are stable and clear. The monophonic sound is fine. The 90 minute program is not captioned. The other side contains a trailer, two TV commercials, and a 24 minute *World of Hammer* episode, focusing on movies about 'lost worlds' and such.

Presenting Felix the Cat (Image, ID5532BKDVD)

A two-hour compilation of silent Felix the Cat cartoons, another combination of two hour-long video cassette collections, the source material is heavily windowboxed, though less seems to be trimmed from the edges. Some of the black-and-white cartoons are worn and contrasts are weak, but even then, the basic ink drawings are clear enough to make out what is going on. One cartoon is tinted, which is not all that appealing, and there is a stereophonic organ score that is best kept at a subdued volume.

The opening cartoon, *Paramount Magazine* (Felix's debut), comes from 1919, but the remaining cartoons, *Felix Saves the Day*, *Felix in the Swim*, *Felix Turns the Tide*, *Felix Lends a Hand*, *Felix Minds the Kid*, *Felix in the Bone Age*, *Felix the Ghost Breaker*, *Felix Wins Out*, *Felix Revolts*, *Felix Gets Broadcasted*, *Felix in Hollywood*, *Felix in Fairyland*, *Felix out of Luck*, *Felix Goes A-Hunting* and *Felix Finds 'Em Fickle*, come from 1922, 1923 and 1924. The cartoons become progressively more sophisticated, but even the most complicated ones are not too far way from what somebody could accomplish drawing on the sheets of a scratch pad and then flipping the corner.

The best cartoon is probably *Felix Revolts*, in which the town Felix is living in attempts to ban cats, until he makes arrangements with the town's mice. Also intriguing is *Felix Saves the Day*, about a very bloody war between cat and mice. What we found most interesting about the collection, however, was the development of cartoon gags—which ones went on to be used again and again and which fell by the wayside. There is a gag in *Felix Minds the Kid* that seems quite imaginative and kind of a breakthrough in the way cartoons can be utilized. The child Felix is watching loosens a balloon in his mouth, gets blown up himself, and floats out the window. It seems like a standard gag now, but back in 1922 it really took some innovative thinking to conceptualize.

President Clinton's Grand Jury Video: August 17, 1998 (Media Galleries)

Taken off a satellite feed and placed into the hands of consumers three weeks later, the release was still stale news by the time it made it to DVD. The colors are pale and the image is soft, with Clinton's skin looking somewhat pasty. There are occasional hiccups and rolling bars, but such diversions are isolated. The monophonic sound is scratchy and regularly buffeted by the recording environment. Clinton is miked, while the voices of the lawyers off camera are weak and distanced. The single-sided dual-layer program runs a few seconds over four hours and features one camera angle. Clinton never becomes angry but he does get a little petulant at times when the questioners refuse to play his definition game. His stalling techniques are for the most part successful, never allowing the grand jury members, who are naturally more eager to cut through the legal mumbo-jumbo than the lawyers, to ask more than a handful of sensible questions. Except for the classic sound bite in which Clinton questions the meaning of the word 'is' (he was, with some validity, asking if it referred to the present or the past tense) and a few discussions of R-rated activities, there is little within the four hours to entertain or educate, though the material can serve as a reminder that not only are leaders people like everybody else, but when they screw up, they screw up big.

Presumed Innocent (Warner, 12034)

There is nothing like a good, serious courtroom drama to while away a couple of hours. The film has some mildly critical problems that prevent it from being as successful as it could have been—the one which comes immediately to mind is that Harrison Ford could have played the movie more appealingly using his cheery, flippant personality instead of his serious, world-weary personality—but it also has many pleasingly subtle touches and the standard emotional barrages one associates with a decent murder mystery. Viewers who become too upset over minor inconsistencies to appreciate the entertainment shouldn't be watching such programs to begin with. The film was directed by Alan J. Pakula.

The picture is solid and bright, with deep, rich blacks, though fleshtones are a little bland. The picture is letterboxed on one side, with an aspect ratio of about 1.85:1 and no 16:9 enhancement, and is in full screen format on the other. The full screen image loses a little picture information on the side but adds more to the top and bottom. Either version is workable, but the framing on the letterboxed image is preferable. The stereo surround sound is passable, particularly since the film is mostly conversation. The film is also available in French and Spanish, and comes with English, French or Spanish subtitles. There is a decent cast-and-crew profile, some good production notes and a theatrical trailer.

Pret-à-Porter (see Ready to Wear)

Pretty as a Picture: The Art of David Lynch (Image, ID4810TKDVD)

Superficially, it is a promotional film for Lost Highway, but the 81 minute documentary is much more than that. There are clips of Lynch's earliest experimental films, an Eraserhead reunion with Lynch and the film's stars as they stroll around the location of the shoot, a detailed look at Lynch's bizarre paintings and behind-the-scenes reminiscences about many of Lynch's films. There is a substantial participation by Lynch and his friends, and terrific footage from both sides of the camera. The DVD also contains an additional 14 minutes of interviews and some snapshots of Lynch growing up. The film imparts a very strong sense of his working

methods, his personality, and the themes that attract him. It's the next best thing to another Lynch movie or TV show.

The picture looks fine. The clips are all in great shape and are letterboxed where appropriate (the Eraserhead footage looks terrific). The music is mildly stereophonic and the program is not captioned.

Pretty Woman (Buena Vista, 14260)

We loved **Pretty Woman** and we don't even wear dresses. The movie is a pure romance. Normally, a film such as this would have some sort of thriller subplot—danger imposed upon the hero or heroine to increase a viewer's stake in their fate. Instead, the subplot is about financial maneuvering and is quite subsidiary to the love story, about a very rich man who has taken a wrong turn and buys directions from a prostitute, ending up hiring her as a date for the week. From that point on, it is star power, with Julia Roberts and Richard Gere filling every imaginable fantasy a viewer could manifest while watching the film. It is so much fun that a more involved plot distraction would just drag things down.

The 125 minute 'Director's Cut' is presented on the DVD. The extra six minutes or so of footage do not amount to much. The added sequences are mostly trims that were taken out to tighten up the running time, though there is one oddball scene where Richard Gere's character is threatened by street toughs and he gets out of the fix by motioning to his chauffeur, who has a gun. The longer running time doesn't harm the film any, especially for those who are already enamored with it, but there are no great revelations or hot sex scenes, just more dreamy pictures of Gere and Julia Roberts getting to know each other and a few other minor embellishments.

The picture is letterboxed with an aspect ratio of about 1.85:1, with no 16:9 enhancement. The letterboxing adds no more than a smidgen to the sides of the image and masks off picture information from the top and the bottom in comparison to full screen versions, but the framing on the letterboxed version looks good, and helps focus a viewer's attention on the characters. The colors are sharp and fleshtones are accurate. The stereo surround sound is sufficient for the conversation-oriented film. The program can be supported by optional English subtitles. You have to know the movie to find the title song sequence, because the chapter guide is no help.

The film's director, Garry Marshall, provides commentary on the analog track. Marshall comes from the Bronx and has a deceptively folksy voice, imparting a pleasant humor and easygoing attitude. His insights on the filmmaking process, however, are consistently informative, whether it is his secret for shooting movies on Hollywood Boulevard (have a lot of cash handy) or how he got Gere and Roberts to do the movie together (just introduce them, then get out of the way). His talk is quite entertaining, mixing an apparently natural gift for comedy (it must run in the family, Penny Marshall is his sister) with the kind of knowledge that only an experienced filmmaker can share.

Pride and Prejudice (Image, ID4354ANDVD)

The excellent six-part miniseries adaptation of the Jane Austen story has been released as a two-platter set. The first platter is in dual-layer format and contains four 53 minute episodes. The second platter is in single-layer format and contains the final two episodes. Each episode is presented with full opening and closing credits. The picture looks quite blurry at times and a bit grainy even when the blur is under control. Colors are reasonably fresh, however, and fleshtones are workable. The stereo sound is adequate for this type of program and is reasonably strong, adding a touch of dimensionality to the proceedings.

Colin Firth and Jennifer Ehle star in the 1996 production. If we were to nit-pick, we would say that a number of the performers have been encouraged to overplay their parts a bit and, unlike the classic MGM film, the marriage between the heroine's mother and father lacks a believable emotional bond. There are, however, a great many things to admire about the program. There is a dance sequence in the climax of the second episode that is brilliantly executed, bringing together several plot strands and whipping up loads of tension while putting the characters through an elaborate and exhausting choreography. The advantage of the miniseries format is its ability to convey lapses of time realistically. The feelings of the characters grow and shift naturally and believably, allowing the viewer to savor not only the story's romantic resolution, but every incidence of frustration or delight leading up to it.

Primal Fear (Paramount, 328327)

Courtroom drama enthusiasts and those who swoon over Richard Gere's every grin will probably like the film. Gere portrays a hotshot Chicago lawyer defending a young man accused of murdering a prominent Catholic church official. There is virtually no action and, except for a couple of isolated incidents, there is no sex or violence. The film is all talk, and it isn't that much of a mystery, intent more upon exploring characters than in being elegantly clever. Like we said, for those who take delight in dramatic explorations of the judicial process, it is valid entertainment (the courtroom sequences are superbly edited), but those who are expecting more than that may be disappointed. It is also worth noting, in these days of raised consciousness, that although the female characters are in positions of power, Gere's character runs circles around them.

The picture is letterboxed with an aspect ratio of about 1.85:1 and an accommodation for enhanced 16:9 playback. The image is incredibly crisp, bringing details to the colors and a vivid immediacy to well lit objects. The stereo surround sound is a little weak, and even the Dolby Digital track doesn't have quite enough dimensional immediacy, but the film's audio mix is not elaborate and the sound is fully acceptable. The 130 minute film is available in French in standard stereo and can be supported by English or Spanish subtitles. An effective theatrical trailer is also included.

Primary Colors (Universal, 20283); DTS (Universal, 20469)

Mike Nichols directed the 144 minute feature—which seems to reach at least one conclusion at what turns out to be its halfway point—based upon Bill Clinton's experiences in the 1992 presidential primaries with, what one assumes, are at least some fanciful exaggerations. Unlike **Wag the Dog**, which really wasn't about specific people, **Primary Colors** lives and dies by its association with real individuals, which is something a lot of viewers just don't want to deal with. Remember how nothing happened with Ronald Reagan's films when he was elected? John Travolta's performance as the Clinton figure is wonderfully humorous, with more texture and substance than an actor could achieve in a *Saturday Night Live* impersonation, but with that same sense of devilish parody. The best parts of the movie are the parts that seem the least far-fetched—you really believe that as soon as the cameras are switched off after the televised confessional, the candidate's wife pulled away from her husband like he was the plague. There are many funny, little things throughout the film—knowing amusements about politicking and character interaction that would be funny in any context. But, that's all there is. The story is the story of the primary, and even with suicides and scandals it doesn't seem to go anywhere or be about anything important, except selling out. It is more like a comical soap opera that one has caught only a part of—though perhaps that is a badge of how true to life it really is.

The presentation is letterboxed, with an aspect ratio of about 2.35:1 and an accommodation for enhanced 16:9 playback. The colors are very bright and sharp. The stereo surround sound and Dolby Digital sound are fine, though the film's audio mix is not all that elaborate. The Dolby Digital track is crisper than the standard track. The film is also available in French in Dolby Digital and can be supported by English or Spanish subtitles. There is a somewhat cluttered theatrical trailer, a few production notes, and a decent cast profile section. The 144 minute program is presented in single-sided dual-layer format.

The DTS audio is sharper and a little more lively on the audio on the standard DVD, and the improvements may help kindle the humor a bit in your subconscious, though the advantages are limited. The frame transfer rate on the 144 minute program is actually a little lower than the rate on the standard release, though for the most part the two are so close that differences are irrelevant. The letterboxing is identical and there are not other features, or captioning.

Prime Suspect (Simitar, 7584)

An executive is detained in the murder of a young girl and his reputation is severely harmed by the subsequent media coverage, although it is eventually proven that he didn't do it. The 1981 telefilm, starring Mike Farrell and Veronica Cartwright, with Teri Garr, contains some interesting similarities to what would later happen in the Atlanta Olympics bombing case, but there really isn't much to the drama, which is about the hero and his troubles, not solving the mystery. The source material has some scratches on it, the image is a little grainy, and the colors are a little bland, but workable. The monophonic sound is adequate and the 93 minute program is not captioned.

Prime Suspect 1 (Anchor Bay, DV10334)
Prime Suspect 2 (Anchor Bay, DV10335)

Each program runs about 200 minutes (not the 230 listed on the jacket) and is presented on two sides, necessitating a break halfway through the show. There are no other interruptions, however, as the closing credits for the individual episodes that make up each drama have been held for an extended scroll at the end. The image quality leaves much to be desired. Darker sequences are a little smeary, colors are a bit faded and fleshtones are somewhat yellowish. The picture is often mildly grainy as well, but since the programs are police procedurals, the presentation has a documentary feel and we never really felt its shortcomings hampered our entertainment. The sound is set a little low, but amplification does not generate excess distortion. Both programs can be supported by optional English subtitles.

Helen Mirren stars as a chief homicide inspector in a country that can have a queen and a female prime minister but still gets bent out of shape over a female detective. In **1**, she achieves her post after a popular male detective has a heart attack, and then has to clean up the mess he was making of a serial murder investigation. In **2**, which is set a year later, a decomposed body is dug up in the garden of a house in a black neighborhood right as tensions between the authorities and the residents are at a boiling point. In both stories, the bad guys make some very convenient mistakes right when they should be keeping their cool, but that's bad guys for you. Both narratives twist and twist so that every time you think you understand how the murder was committed, something unexpected is revealed. The performances are impeccably realistic and the cast is super (Ralph Fiennes even shows up in **1** for a small role, as a punk). The running times allow the stories to embellish psychological detail, extend moral arguments and give the plots the opportunity to run a complete course. It used to be that you could get lost in a mystery for an afternoon by reading one, but now you can watch one (make that two) to the same effect.

Prince of Darkness (see **John Carpenter's Prince of Darkness**)

The Princess and the Pirate (HBO, 90666)

The glorious Technicolor hues on the 1944 feature look fantastic. The image is consistently crisp and the colors are carefully delineated. The costumes and the sets are gorgeous, and they look super when replicated with the sharpness of DVD playback. The volume on the sound is set a little low, but raising it does not bring on too much distortion. The audio is available in its original mono and in a remastered stereo that brings a little more dimensionality to the background noises and music. The 94 minute program also has French, Spanish and Italian audio tracks, optional English, Spanish and French subtitles, a cast profile section and a trailer.

Bob Hope portrays a traveling performer who is kidnapped by a pirate ('The Hook'), escapes with a Princess, and connives his way through numerous misadventures. At one point Hope hangs his hat and jacket on Hook's hook and then escapes when the hook gets caught in a bulkhead. Walter Brennan also appears for an amusing turn. Many of Hope's topical one-liners will be beyond today's viewers, but his delivery is timeless. There is a surprise cameo at the end that ties the film up nicely, but you may have to explain to your kids why it is so funny.

The Princess and the Pirate (Simitar, 7218)

The *Good Housekeeping Kids* title card reads, "*Sandokan The TV Movie.*" The 75 minute cartoon has no time encoding. The anthropomorphized tiger hero is a prince who has been forced out of his kingdom. He becomes a pirate and has a number of run-ins with the new rulers before unmasking the true villain and returning to his proper throne. He also has to rescue the heroine a number of times. The animation is so stilted it is difficult to say if the jerky movements, inconsistent focus and smeared lines are a problem with the DVD or the original source material. The colors are quite bright and stationary drawings look sharp, but any significant movement becomes irritating to look at after a while. The sound seems to be in stereo and is adequately delivered.

Princess Warrior (Simitar, 7308)

The fun-dopey film starts out on another planet, as a swords and breasts thing, and then transports to contemporary Earth. The other planet is ruled by women, and the villain is chasing the heroine in order to eliminate her and seize the throne. The chase takes them here, where they have trouble dealing with dominant males, but not too much trouble. The film is witty, but two-thirds of it is an extended chase, so it gets a little drawn out in the second half. The colors often look a bit drained and the image is slightly grainy at times. The stereo sound is a bit flat. The film runs 84 minutes and is not captioned.

Prison on Fire (import, 5062)

Chow Yun-Fat stars with Tony Leung in the 1987 Ringo Lam drama. Leung is a nerd who is sent to prison on an involuntary manslaughter charge and Fat is the more savvy convict who befriends him. They try to serve their time and weather the rough and tumble prison politics. The other convicts are mean, though they're a lot nicer than convicts in American films these days and everybody keeps their buttons buttoned. The violence is realistic rather than stylized (the final fight is so Tyson-esquely real it will make you cringe), but it is of secondary importance to the drama, which centers on whether or not Leung's character will smarten up enough not to get himself killed.

The picture is letterboxed with an aspect ratio of about 1.7:1 and no 16:9 enhancement. Colors look reasonably strong and fleshtones are accurate. Contrasts are a bit weak and the image is a little soft, but for a Hong Kong production the picture looks pretty good. The 101 minute stereo program is in Cantonese and Mandarin and is supported by optional subtitling in English, traditional Chinese, simplified Chinese, Japanese, Indonesian, Malaysian, Thai, Korean and Vietnamese. There are some mild separation effects and an occasional dimensionality. Star profiles are available in most of the languages, and there are trailers.

Private Benjamin (Warner, 11075)

Goldie Hawn portrays a sheltered young woman who finds her independence by joining the Army. The 1980 service comedy has a fairly standard format—boot camp, success in war games, and then something critical—but it was a breakthrough role for Hawn and that works both ways—her performance is definitive. The image is not cropped, but there is a lot of superfluous picture information on the top and bottom of the full screen presentation that

masking would have prettied up. The color transfer looks crisp and hues are bright, but fleshtones are a touch pinkish. The monophonic sound is bland, but there is a Dolby Digital mono track that is stronger and more effective. The 110 minute film is also available in French and can be accompanied by English, French or Spanish subtitles ("Ça n'existe qu'en vert?"). There is a decent cast and crew profile section and an enjoyable theatrical trailer.

Private Obsession (Image, ID5616FMDVD)

We don't mind watching all the cruddy movies that are released on DVD, because every once in a while one comes along that is so exquisitely bad it leaves us floating in giggles for days afterward. Shannon Whirry stars as a fashion model and feminist proponent ("Let me tell you a little about men, ladies," she says during a speech she gives for having been named 'Woman of the Year' by the 'Women's Press Club,' "They'd tell you anything they want you to hear."). She is kidnapped by a wealthy stalker, played by Michael Christian, who comes across as a second rate Adam West. She then has to use her psychological wiles to get free. Full of unrated softcore sex (when she tries to escape through the slot where Christian's character passes her food, she gets stuck, and Christian has to rub butter on her breasts to pull her back in), gloriously bad acting (Whirry, throat parched, struggles to draw a cup of water from the back of a toilet, unsure of what to do with the ballast; the worst acting, however, belongs to Christian, who plays each scene as if he had no idea what his emotions were in any of the others), and all sorts of strange little details that help to make the film a camp classic (Rip Taylor has one bizarre scene as a gay travel agent). The film also veers from comedy to serious drama and back several times, though the more intense the drama the more humorous it is. A sure-fire winner at parties, and boy, does it get funnier on multiple viewings.

The picture is tolerable. Fleshtones lack intensity, contrasts are weak and there is a mild grain, but that is pretty much run-of-the-mill for this sort of film and hues are reasonably bright. The stereo sound is flat, but the mix is marvelous, with separation effects popping up at several ideally inopportune moments. The 101 minute program is not captioned.

Private Parts (Paramount, 332517)

The genuinely funny story of a radio disc jockey who defies his manager and achieves top ratings at the same time, Howard Stern stars as a slightly nicer version of himself in the biographical tale, and several of the people who work with him on his radio show co-star as themselves, as well. The 1997 film is full of sex and is rated 'R,' but there is something oddly harmless about the nude scenes, with the editing carefully cutting away before most viewers will start to feel uncomfortable in mixed company. The film is very smart. It tackles some of Stern's darker material, particularly a sequence where he jokes on the radio about his wife's miscarriage, but it avoids a lot of Stern's meanness and his taunting of visitors and call-ins, twisting things around so that his only negativity is directed at those who want to suppress his spirit. Drawing from the best of Stern's years on the air, some of the radio skits are hysterical. The mixture of comedy and anti-establishment rebellion is marvelous, and in including the story of Stern's marriage, there is enough normalcy and romance to anchor the film in the heart of almost any viewer.

The picture is presented in letterboxed format only, with an aspect ratio of about 1.85:1 and no 16:9 enhancement. The framing often looks a bit cramped on the top and bottom (Stern has lots of hair and what looks like a very big head, so the top of the screen is forever cutting into it). The color transfer is okay, but fleshtones are bland or indistinct at times and the image is a little soft here and there. The stereo surround sound is good, particularly when classic rock 'n' roll songs kick in, and the Dolby Digital track has more power and greater dimensionality. The 108 minute program also has a French soundtrack and optional English and Spanish subtitles.

Private SNAFU (see The Complete Uncensored Private SNAFU: Cartoons from World War II)

Prizzi's Honor (Anchor Bay, DV10833)

John Huston's delightful 1985 tale is about the problematic romantic life of a hitman. Jack Nicholson stars, with Kathleen Turner, and Anjelica Huston won an Oscar for her supporting performance as one of Nicholson's flames. The ending takes some getting used to, but the script maintains a nice balance between Machiavellian plot twists, laid-back characterizations, and war of the sexes humor.

The picture is presented on one side in letterboxed format, with an aspect ratio of about 1.85:1 and no 16:9 enhancement, and is in cropped format on the other side. The letterboxing provides a more satisfying presentation than the lopsided cropped version. The color transfer is about the same as the LD, with slight richer fleshtones, but the image is much crisper. The film has always had rather bland colors, but the added crispness makes the presentation less distracting. There is a mildly stereophonic audio track, beneficial primarily to Alex North's enjoyable musical score. The 129 minute program is not captioned.

Procol Harum (Pioneer, PA99614D)

The band does not play its two best known hits on the *Best of MusikLaden* offering, but there is a very nice and representative selection of their output, including *A Salty Dog*, *Simple Sister*, *Magdalene My Regal Zonophone*, *Pilgrim's Progress*, *Shine On Brightly* and others, and you also get one of the most gloriously bad rock songs ever recorded, *Grand Hotel*. Contrary to the stated 45 minute running time on the jacket cover, bonus tracks after the end credit scroll stretch the running time to 52 minutes. The bonus tracks are from a live staging, but the others appear to be studio efforts in which the band is superimposed upon video effects. Although the borders between the people and the backgrounds are loose and smeary, the picture quality is quite good. The colors are strong and the musicians are clear, with realistic fleshtones. The Dolby Digital sound is fairly sharp, though the standard track is duller, particularly on the upper end. The program is not captioned.

The Professional (Columbia TriStar, 74749)

The French Russell Mulcahy, Luc Besson, crossed the Atlantic to direct the 1994 feature in New York City. Jean Reno and Natalie Portman star, with Gary Oldman in an amusingly wired performance as the main bad guy. The narrative is gobbledygook about a hitman and an adolescent girl who become chums, pitting them against a group of villainous policemen. The film's style, however, is rapturous, as is the case with most of Besson's otherwise nonsensical work, and the movie makes a terrific action DVD.

The color transfer looks super and the stereo surround sound is a knockout. The letterboxing has an aspect ratio of about 2.35:1 and no 16:9 enhancement. The image is flawless, no matter how awkward the lighting conditions become. The audio mix is exceptionally sharp and the gunshots are super, especially on the Dolby Digital track. The 110 minute program also has French and Spanish audio tracks in mono, optional English, French or Spanish subtitles, and a trailer.

Progeny (Sterling, 7185)

A good, grotesque thriller, Arnold Vosloo stars as a surgeon whose wife becomes pregnant shortly after the couple has a lost-time/abduction experience. Then the baby starts kicking a little earlier than normal. Two things we admire quite a bit about the film: There is an ambiguity all the way to the end about whether the aliens are real or the surgeon, who ends up cutting his wife open to try and grab the monster, is just imagining things; and every character action after the established premise is logical—the characters all say or do exactly what you would say or do if you

were in their situation. There are a number of unnerving special effects and model sequences, and a general atmosphere if icky uncertainty. One of the creators of **Re-Animator**, Brian Yuzna, directed.

The picture is letterboxed with an aspect ratio of about 1.85:1 and no 16:9 enhancement. The color transfer looks fine, with sharp hues and accurate fleshtones. The stereo surround sound is fairly strong, with smooth tones, lots of dimensional activity and a nice bass. There are optional Spanish subtitles, but no English captioning.

Accompanying the film are a trailer, a collection of production photos, a cast & crew profile section, storyboards for three scenes, with an optional toggle alternate angle view of the appropriate moment within the film, some good interviews with the cast and crew, a 'trivia game,' and three fascinating interviews with people who claim to have been alien abductees (one suggests the aliens are coming from another dimension rather than outer space). There are also two commentary channels, one featuring Yuzna and producers Jack F. Murphy and Henry Seggerman, and one (the better of the two) with the writers, Stuart Gordon and Aubrey Solomon. On the Yuzna track, they talk in general terms about how the production was staged and about working with the cast, while the writers discuss how each scene was conceived and developed, and what its purpose is. Both also talk about their research into alien abductions and the unusual uniformity to most abductee stories (calling Carl Jung, calling Carl Jung).

Prom Night (Anchor Bay, DV10327)

Perhaps the most typical of the original teen slasher films, **Prom Night** has a 'who's doin' it?' plot instead of a supernatural plot, stars the acknowledged slasher queen, Jamie Lee Curtis, and takes place mostly in a high school, where the killer skulks about and opens the arteries of several kids who once witnessed an accidental death. The 1980 film has touches of macabre humor, and Leslie Nielson, whose straight roles now all look like parodies, co-stars. What the film doesn't have is any good screams. Directed by Paul Lynch, there are no decent shock cuts and only a few suitably gruesome inserts; but as compensation, there is this terrific extended dance number where Curtis struts her stuff as the Queen of the Prom.

Fleshtones look reasonably accurate and other colors, though not vivid, are workable. The image is sharper, though it still retains a little haze in places. The picture is letterboxed with an aspect ratio of about 1.85:1 and no 16:9 enhancement. The monophonic sound is a little adequate. A theatrical trailer has also been included. The 91 minute program is not captioned.

The Prophecy (Buena Vista, 16454)

Several terrific actors—Elias Koteas, Eric Stoltz, and Christopher Walken (Amanda Plummer also has a marvelous bit part)—give dizzyingly wonderful performances in what eventually becomes a tale about rival factions of angels battling on Earth, with Satan of all people stepping in to assist the good guys. Koteas is a cop investigating a strange murder that leads him to a small Southwestern town where a young girl has become possessed. The film's theological banter is stimulating and the performances are good enough to carry what otherwise might seem like pretentious or improbable dialogue (even Satan has some great one-liners). The filmmakers have difficulty getting all the pieces of the narrative together, but once the parts are in place, the entertainment is stimulating and the film's themes are thoughtful.

The image is letterboxed with an aspect ratio of about 2.35:1 and no 16:9 enhancement. Hues are a bit drab and contrasts lack detail in the darker sequences but, generally, the image is acceptable. The Ultra-Stereo surround sound has some functional rear channel effects and a viable dimensionality. The 97 minute program can be supported by English subtitles.

Protector (Sterling, 7125)

Mario Van Peebles is a cop investigating mob murders. You'll spot the secret bad guy in practically the first frame, but the story has plenty of forward motion and psychological color, the action scenes have plenty of energy, the sex scenes are hot and Van Peebles does a good job anchoring it. Randy Quaid (with a bald head), Rae Dawn Chong, Ben Gazzara and Zerha Leverman co-star in the 94 minute program, which was shot in Buffalo.

Presented in full screen, the picture looks okay and colors are bright, although some intense hues are a little soft. The stereo surround sound is not elaborate, but passable. The film can be supported by Spanish subtitles, but there is no English captioning. There is also a cast profile section and a trailer.

Protocol (Warner, 11434)

Goldie Hawn is a Washington DC cocktail waitress who becomes involved in a political intrigue after she prevents the assassination of an Arabian emir. Her character has no downside, and the 1984 film is as cheerful as it is farfetched.

The picture is presented in full screen format and the framing looks okay. The colors are bright and the image is sharp. The film's stereo surround sound mix has limited dimensional effects but is passable. The 96 minute program is closed captioned with some paraphrasing.

Psycho (Universal, 20251)

Alfred Hitchcock's classic, definitive 1960 murder thriller has been issued on a single-sided dual-layer platter with a wealth of supplementary materials. The 109 minute film is accompanied by a 100 minute retrospective documentary, the famous theatrical trailer (Hitchcock giving a tour of the house and motel), several shorter re-release trailers, an interesting 'press kit on film,' footage from the movie's premier, the shower scene (though it ends when the victim collapses, not with the pan away from the eyeball) presented with and without the film's musical score (why they couldn't just offer it once with two alternate tracks is beyond us), the storyboards for the shower scene, production photos, a production essay, a cast-and-director profile section and advertising materials.

The documentary is terrific. Janet Leigh and Hitchcock's daughter, Pat Hitchcock O'Connell, who had a part in the film, give extensive interviews, as do the movie's assistant director, Hilton Green, the screenwriter, Joseph Stefano (who was in analysis at the time and brought a substantial psychoanalytical subtext to the film), and other production personnel. Clive Barker also shows up for a few brief words. The documentary works its way methodically through the film, discussing the inspiration for each major sequence and how each sequence was shot. There are many anecdotes about the filming (Leigh is utterly charming as she talks with a twinkle in her eye about her nude scenes and about kissing John Gavin) and a good overview of the film's most important artistic components. The running time gives it a chance to go into details thoroughly and compensates for the lack of a commentary track. The documentary also includes a brief shot of Leigh beginning to remove her bra that was suppressed by the film's censors. Interestingly, the re-release trailers promote the film as being rated 'M' although the DVD now carries an 'R' rating.

The film is presented in letterboxed format with an aspect ratio of about 1.85:1 and no 16:9 enhancement. We have a little problem with the letterboxing. It adds picture information to the sides of the image in comparison to full screen versions, and this we applaud, but it masks picture information off the top of the image and especially off the bottom, and this we don't like as much. The movie was shot with a TV crew and the letterboxing makes the image composition look cramped. Additionally, there are shots for the shower scene where Hitchcock used a hard matte, and with the letterboxing these shots cannot be identified. Still, it is a minor quibble.

The black-and-white image is sharp and spotless, with excellent contrasts, and at its best moments it is so vivid it almost appears three dimensional. The monophonic sound is bright and smooth. The film has an alternate French audio track and can be supported by optional English or Spanish subtitles ("Elmejor amigo de un chico es su madre"). The documentary, which is in English only, can be supported by optional English, French or Spanish titles.

Psycho (Universal, 20538)

Like Norman dressing up in his mother's clothing, Gus Van Sant filmed a color version of **Psycho**. The skeleton of Alfred Hitchcock's 1960 classic is still visible beneath Van Sant's taxidermy, but the replication sits imperfectly upon its frame. Some consumers will have no use at all for the *Collector's Edition* DVD, but those with open minds, an interest in the art of filmmaking and really good sound systems will not want to pass the program by. Especially those with really good sound systems.

The stereo surround sound and Dolby Digital sound are outstanding. The film's audio mix is superb, with constant, playful separation effects that are rendered with utter purity by the DVD's audio delivery. In addition to Bernard Herrmann's classic score, which fills one's viewing area, Van Sant has taken the flat monophonic sound design of the original movie and turned it into total three-dimensional audio, with voices, environmental noises and specific effects given equal measure on all five channels. It is different from a standard audio mix, which is designed to give you a sort of atmospheric involvement; instead, it uses more clearly defined noises. It is as if Van Sant has brought color to the original film's soundtrack, as well as to its images.

What was Van Sant up to remaking **Psycho**, anyway, and why on earth would he do it? Well, for one thing, it's never been done before, really. There have been some TV movies that have basically replicated classic movies in a kind of updated setting, but Van Sant went for a nearly shot-by-shot copy of the original. In fact, he carried the DVD of the original film to the set every day and referred to it for lighting, blocking and even performance questions.

For another thing, as he explains on the DVD's commentary channel, there is a great body of public out there that refuses to watch black-and-white movies, and are therefore missing a terrific (though, as it turns out, somewhat talky) thriller. Finally, and this he makes no mention of, so we are guessing, Van Sant is a vanguard independent filmmaker who, with a couple successes under his belt, was finding himself being dragged deeper and deeper into the morass of Hollywood commercialization. While his **Psycho** is unabashedly a studio film, it is also, by its very concept, a grand, thumb-your-nose-at-pretensions satire on what Hollywood does.

While Van Sant could replicate camera angles and sets, and find the same locations Hitchcock used thirty or so years earlier, he had to use new actors to play the characters. The film proves, to all film theorists paying attention, that the human factor is integral to the artistic value of a motion picture. Some of the performances are terrific—especially Julianne Moore, who has the Vera Miles role, and William H. Macy, in the Martin Balsam part. Viggo Mortensen is also amiably goofy in the John Gavin part and some of the marvelously inspired cameos Van Sant used for the incidental parts, such as James Remar (as the cop), Philip Baker Hall (as the elderly sheriff) and Robert Forster (as the psychiatrist), had us cheering with pleasure as each appeared. But Vince Vaughn can't cut it as Norman Bates. Whether it is because Van Sant has urged too many of Anthony Perkins' mannerisms on him, or whether it is just his limitations as a performer, he is miscast and fails to sell an emotional believability in the movie's central role. In the Janet Leigh part, Anne Heche is also somewhat erratic and seemingly distracted. Perhaps, because these two parts are so central of the film, nobody could play them well, but, as is evidenced by Moore's performance (which is very unlike Miles), the more the performers brought their own concepts to their parts, the better they made the movie, even if it became less like its source.

The commentary starts off very badly. Van Sant is joined by Heche and Vaughn, but they're all giggling and speaking haltingly as they search for a conversational format. Vaughn teases Heche terribly about her love scenes with Mortensen, and they sound as if they had no concept whatsoever of how they were messing with a classic. But, once they get warmed up and work out a speaking protocol, the talk improves considerably. Van Sant includes a lot of technical information about what he drew from Hitchcock, what he changed and how various shots and scenes were accomplished. Heche and Mortensen speak very informatively about the art of screen acting, and all three talk about the thematic differences between the original and the remake, the flaws in the original, and other related subjects.

The film is presented in letterboxed format only, with an aspect ratio of about 1.85:1 and an accommodation for enhanced 16:9 playback. The picture looks super, with bright, crisp hues and accurate fleshtones. Van Sant didn't just shoot the movie in color. He and his production designer and costume designer applied colors to the film with great wit. The 104 minute program has a French audio track in standard stereo, optional English subtitles, production notes, a cast-and-director profile section, a wild, wonderful trailer (though it is very different from the film) and DVD-ROM screen savers. There is also a 30 minute documentary, which gives the other production personnel an opportunity to vent their opinions about the project. The documentary has many terrific behind-the-scenes sequences (yes, even of the shower sequence, including more direct views of Heche) and a head-on examination of the project's validity.

Psycho II (GoodTimes, 0581034)

The picture is presented in full screen format, but the framing works very well and we're sure almost nothing is missing from the sides. Fleshtones are a little bland, but colors are fairly well detailed and the image is very crisp. The stereo surround soundtrack tends to have isolated separation effects and a weaker general dimensionality, but for a 1983 mix, it's pretty decent. The 103 minute program can be supported by English, French or Spanish subtitles ("Mère! Oh, mon Dieu! Mère. Du sang! Du sang!"), and there are some brief production notes.

Tony Perkins reprises his role as Norman Bates, being pestered by Vera Miles and Meg Tilly. The narrative has lots of what's-going-on-here turns and Perkins' gives an engaging, if-you-can't-beat-'em-join-'em performance. People who worship the original may be offended, but if there must be exploitational sequels to classic movies, let them have fun the way this does.

Puccini's La Fanciulla del West (Image, ID4359PUDVD)

The world's first spaghetti western, the opera is superbly staged. The cluttered Forty-Niner mining camp set is jammed with cast members and creates a claustrophobic atmosphere that is enhanced further by the video's tight camera angles. The cast is super, headed by Plácido Domingo, Juan Pons and Mara Zamieri.

The presentation is also well lit, with a sharp, crisp image and very detailed colors. The stereo sound hasn't much dimensionality, but is sufficiently clear to convey the quality of the singing and its effectively balanced orchestral accompaniment. The 142 minute production, conducted by Lorin Maazel, is presented on a single-sided dual-layer platter in Italian with white English subtitles. The jacket plot synopsis contains a couple typos.

Pulp Fiction (Buena Vista, 13850)

The very funny, very violent and very adult 1995 film revitalized the use of language in action movies and presents an inspired cross-section of seedy characters, played with wonderful panache by John Travolta, Samuel L. Jackson, Bruce Willis, Uma Thurman and others. The film's humor may be less forthrightly amusing outside of a crowded theater, but the depth of its ironies and wit remains; you just take it more seriously. A lot has been written about **Pulp Fiction** and we don't wish to repeat things, though it is

worth noting, as has been pointed out elsewhere, that the general narrative takes three common gangster film themes—an affair with the mobster's wife, the boxer not throwing the fight, and the gunman going straight—and approaches each one with a fresh angle.

The 154 minute feature is presented on a single-sided dual-layer platter in letterboxed format, with an aspect ratio of about 2.35:1 and no 16:9 enhancement. The film's widescreen cinematography often takes full advantage of the rectangular image composition, making the letterboxing essential. The picture is reasonably sharp, with bright hues, though fleshtones are a little bland. The Dolby Digital track has more pronounced separation effects than the standard stereo track and has a reasonably strong presence. The sound has a marvelous separation mix, with highly memorable and very serious-sounding gunshots and smooth, rich tones that deliver the pop musical score with class. A Spanish language track is also available and the film can be supported by optional English subtitles.

Pure Country (Warner, 12593)

It is a tradition as old as film with sound that popular music stars occasionally appear in movies portraying only slightly modified versions of themselves, suffering from the hardships and anxieties of being popular music stars. Usually, these movies are awful, and the star goes back to being a popular music star, leaving the movies to performers who can act. One such indiscretion, **Pure Country**, headlines the popular country western singer, George Strait. Oscar-bound, he is not.

The picture is presented on one side in letterboxed format, with an aspect ratio of about 1.85:1 and an accommodation for enhanced 16:9 playback, and in full screen format on the other side. The color transfer looks fine, with crisp, bright hues and accurate fleshtones. The standard stereo surround soundtrack is poorly mixed and alienating, but the Dolby Digital track is much better. The sound effects are sensibly distributed, and even though the audio track is louder, it pulls you into the movie instead of distancing you from the action. The film is also available in French and Spanish (Strait singing and somebody else talking), and can be accompanied by English, French or Spanish subtitles ("Il n'y a pas de chanson sans paroles"). There is a theatrical trailer, a decent cast & crew profile section, and a Strait discography (a filmography would be rather short).

The 113 minute film is about a popular country western singer who gets tired of his over-choreographed stage show and decides to play hooky, an act that allows him to meet the love of his life, played by Isabel Glasser, and reformulate his performance concepts. The badness of the genre is epitomized by the huge close-ups of Glasser at the end, as she cries tears of ecstasy while watching Strait sing. Sure, it is in character, but the editorial weight of the visual commentary on Strait's abilities is impossible to ignore, just as it is impossible to take seriously. But then there is Granny's advice, when a friend of the star comes looking for him, "Sometimes a tree grows too fast and the roots don't develop. And sometimes you have to chop off the top of that tree to let the roots catch up." In summary, the film does for country western music what it does for horticulture.

Purple Rain (Warner, 11398)

A lot of bass has been added to the Dolby Digital track, but the songs sound super and the extra rumble helps them penetrate every part of you. The regular stereo surround sound is good, but the Dolby Digital track is terrific. Not only does the picture have accurate colors, it is free of grain and looks as slick as the film deserves. The presentation is not letterboxed, and the movie is so stylish that it might have benefited from masking, though the framing still looks well balanced. The 111 minute 1984 musical, about rock club singers in Minneapolis, is accompanied by a theatrical trailer that introduces the movie's star in the days when he still had a name. There is also a cast profile section and a decent production essay.

English, French or Spanish subtitles are also available. The chapter encoding is not up to Warner's usual standards and rarely marks the beginnings of the songs.

Pushing Hands (Image, ID5618FMDVD)

One of Ang Lee's earlier films (it appears older than its 1995 copyright), it is about an elderly man who has recently immigrated to America, living with his son's family and trying to cope with retirement. The film begins too slowly, with long silent passages that show the man and his daughter-in-law in their daily routines, as they uncomfortably trip over one another. The portrait of domesticity, as it is presented, also fails to ring completely true because there just aren't enough minor details in the scenes where the family interacts. Lee's narrative magic starts to work, however, as the film progresses and the characters become more familiar. There is even an enjoyable martial arts sequence.

The picture is presented in full screen, but it probably should have been matted. The sound boom is visible in one sequence and generally the framing seems too open on the top and bottom. Hues are reasonably strong, but the image looks worn, with minor speckles and a general softness. The monophonic sound is adequate. Most of the film is in English, but there is some Chinese, supported by permanent English subtitles. The 107 minute program is not otherwise captioned.

Q

Q: The Winged Serpent (Anchor Bay, DV10485)

Larry Cohen's 1982 feature is more amenable to home video than it was to theatrical presentation. On the one hand, it is a very cheap, badly paced monster movie, about a creature that terrorizes New York City but hides from detection by 'flying in front of the sun,' and can seem stupid as all get out when one is sitting on hard seats and forced to take it in without breaks. But in a more relaxed environment, it is easier to see why the film is such a darling with some critics and fans. The special effects, though sparse, are creative and work better without magnified projection. The performances, though wacky and a bit aimless (Michael Moriarty, Candy Clark, David Carradine and Richard Roundtree are featured), have a wit that puts them on a different level from the acting in the usual cheap monster movie. The film remains an acquired taste, but it is somewhat more accessible on the small screen.

The picture is letterboxed with an aspect ratio of about 1.85:1 and no 16:9 enhancement. The colors are solid and exact, with decent looking fleshtones. The monophonic sound has a dulled ambiance but is workable. The 93 minute program is not time encoded or captioned.

Quantum Leap: The Pilot Episode (Image, ID4301USDVD)

The episode title is a play on words—the episode is mostly about test pilots, although there is an extended secondary segment in which the hero becomes a baseball player. Scott Bakula stars in the entertaining fantasy series, as a man who keeps jumping from one body to another, ending up almost anywhere in the past, with Dean Stockwell as the controller who tries to help him get through each new identity crisis. In such instances, we would much more prefer to have an entire series instead of just a single episode, but it is still better than nothing at all. The writing is fairly intelligent and witty, and the performers are adept. Most of the episodes fit an hour slot, but this one is longer, running 93 minutes. The picture is soft and is grainy in places, with slightly aged colors. The sound has a mild stereo mix, giving the music some dimensionality. There is no closed captioning.

Quartet for the End of Time (see Olivier Messiaen: Quartet for the End of Time/Improvisations)

Quatermass and the Pit (Anchor Bay, DV10505)

Modern special effects have compromised the impact the 1967 Hammer film can have on a viewer, but for genre fans it remains an admirable production with an intelligent script and a few legitimate excitements. We recall seeing the movie around the time of its original release and finding it to be quite unnerving. Andrew Keir (as Quatermass, the rocket scientist), James Donald and Barbara Shelley star in the story about a discovery of an ancient spaceship, during the digging of a subway tunnel in London, that leads to revelations about man's origins and the existence of demons (apparently by chance, the story echoes both Arthur C. Clarke's *2001* and *Childhood's End*).

The presentation is letterboxed with an aspect ratio of about 1.66:1 and no 16:9 enhancement. Hues are solid but dull and fleshtones are a little bland, though on the whole the image is reasonably appealing. The sound has been remastered for Dolby Digital, which is a little silly, but fun, and the DVD's stereo surround and Dolby Digital soundtracks are enjoyable. The surround effects are primarily bleeds of generalized sounds from the front channel and the dimensionality brought to the audio cannot disguise its aged construction, but the enhanced bass that has been added to the key action sequences is marvelous, creating kind of a Sensurround effect that takes one small step, at least, to making the film unnerving again.

The movie runs 98 minutes and is accompanied by several trailers and TV commercials, and a 25 minute *World of Hammer* episode that focuses on Hammer sci-fi features, with lengthy clips from a number of older black-and-white films. There is no captioning.

The film's screenwriter, Nigel Kneale, and director, Roy Ward Baker, by voice both elderly British gentlemen, provide a modest commentary track. There are gaps in their talk and they don't say too much about what is happening on the screen, but they do talk plenty about how the film was developed and they do breakdown one sequence on a shot-by-shot basis to explain the filmmaking process. They also reminisce about Hammer, providing an overview of the company's history, badmouth Brian Donlevy, who had played Quatermass in an earlier film, and explain how some of the movie's less-than-ground-breaking anti-gravity special effects were accomplished (a guy with a fishing rod). Kneale, by the way, got the name, 'Quatermass,' out of the phone book.

Queen: "We Will Rock You" (Pioneer, PA96568D)

The group's icy pure vocals are compromised by the live recording on the classic 90 minute concert program, but some listeners may feel it is for the better. The regular stereo surround soundtrack is drab, but the Dolby Digital track is fairly good, with active rear channel separations and a significant clarity of detail that the standard track lacks. The picture looks sharp and fleshtones are accurate. There is no captioning.

The Quest (Universal, 20258)

Jean-Claude Van Damme's pleasurable directoral debut is no work of art, but something seems to happen every five minutes or so. Roger Moore and James Remar co-star with Van Damme to spruce up the cast, and the story is simple and coherent. The second half, in fact, is pretty much taken over by an extended tournament sequence, which offers one fight after another. It is set in the Twenties and was shot in Southeast Asia, and if you don't watch it now you're likely to come across it on TV some Saturday afternoon in the future.

The letterboxing has an aspect ratio of about 2.35:1 and no 16:9 enhancement. Much of the film is on the dark side, but fleshtones are decent and there is a reasonable stability in dim, torch-lit sequences. The stereo surround sound is somewhat weak, but the Dolby Digital track brings the audio more dimensionality and brighter tones. The 95 minute feature is also available in French without Dolby Digital and can be accompanied by English or Spanish subtitles. There are some interesting production notes, a brief cast profile section and a theatrical trailer.

Quest for Camelot (Warner, 16607)

The animation and artwork are fantastic, some of the characters are cute and there are several very well staged scenes, but the Holy Grail of a good cartoon, narrative, is beyond the film's grasp. It takes forever to get started, there are put-'em-to-sleep songs in the middle of action sequences, the film's mood does a complete reversal from one sequence to the next, and the plot (a young girl and a blind guy have to retrieve Excalibur from a haunted forest before the bad guys get it) is mostly a contrived amalgam of chases and fights. It is like the filmmakers had many of the pieces, but they didn't know how to fit them together right.

The 86 minute cartoon (77 minutes before the end credits) has been issued on a dual-sided DVD, with the film appearing on one side and special features included on the other. The DVD does show off the animation very well. There are breathtaking perspectives, effective and even exciting blends of CGI and traditional artwork, and rich, carefully detailed colors, all of which are presented on the disc crisply and accurately. The film is letterboxed with an aspect ratio of about 1.85:1 and an accommodation for enhanced 16:9 playback. The stereo surround sound is a bit more pedestrian, revving up to accelerated separation effects at predictable moments and then coasting on a fairly center-oriented mix the rest of the time. To this end, the standard stereo surround soundtrack is a little more even than the Dolby Digital track, though most viewers will prefer what the Dolby Digital encoding can deliver during the film's showiest scenes. The film is also available in French in Dolby Digital and can be supported by English or French subtitles. There is a music-only track, in Dolby Digital.

After the film is over, there are interviews with the stars who voiced the film, a 'work in progress' look at one of the song numbers, and a three-step breakdown of one of the film's best CGI sequences. Additionally, there is a Steve Perry music video, trailers for Warner's children's and Arthurian films, and brief essays on animation and Warner's cartoon tradition.

The Quick and the Dead (Columbia TriStar, 73519)

How many ways are there to shoot a showdown? Sam Raimi comes up with quite a few in the 1995 tournament western feature starring Sharon Stone and Gene Hackman and Leonard DiCaprio. About a gunfighting contest in which sixteen entrants shoot themselves down to a final two, there is just enough of a back story, concerning three or four of the characters, to hold the film together, at least superficially. The situation is absurd, but Raimi's sense of style and his wry humor are ideal for repeat viewings, and the show is as fun as it is silly.

The presentation is letterboxed on one side, with an aspect ratio of about 1.85:1 and no 16:9 enhancement, and is in full screen format on the other side. The picture transfer is very good, with a number of complicated lighting situations presented with complete accuracy. The stereo surround sound is also well produced, though it doesn't have quite the same energy that the images do, but there is a rousing Dolby Digital track that is more engaging. The 105 minute program also has a French audio track in mono, optional English and French subtitles and a trailer.

The film has no sex, but the violence is marvelous. In one sequence, for example, a character is shot in the forehead. Rather than just slumping downwards, he does a backward somersault before plopping dead to the ground some ten feet from where he had been standing.

The Quiet Man (Artisan, 53361)

John Ford's playful, joyous romantic comedy is about a boxer who returns to his hometown in Ireland. As with so many of Ford's films, the 1952 feature succeeds in evoking the emotions of its era while maintaining a dignity that has allowed it to age gracefully. The tomboyish romance between the John Wayne and Maureen O'Hara's characters, for example, is so full of positive spirit and unmasked desire that it is impossible to become upset with the disrespect given to the financial rights of the heroine. The same is true of the sentimentalized portrait the film creates of a somewhat imaginary Ireland. Wayne's character, who finds the town is exactly as he remembers it, becomes a stand-in for every viewer in search of the unfettered world that is locked in the memories of childhood.

The picture transfer is imperfect. At its best, the Technicolor image is gorgeous and, throughout the presentation, the fields and trees are never not an emerald green. The source material, however, is clearly a couple steps away from its origins, bringing a softness to the edges of the colors, halos at times around bright objects and inconsistent hair colors and fleshtones. Some reels are weaker than others, and in the weakest, the image is fuzzy, with bland hues and indistinct complexions. The larger the screen, the worse it looks, as well. The overall impression we take away from it, however, after drying our eyes, is of its best moments, where the colors are pot o' gold vivid, fleshtones are rich and the film's look feeds the drama like dried peat feeding a fire.

The monophonic sound is a little soft and has some noise in places, but it is workable. The 129 minute feature is closed captioned with minor paraphrasing. The film is accompanied by an informative 25 minute retrospective documentary hosted by Leonard Maltin, featuring interviews with some of the younger production personnel and intelligent background information on Ford, Wayne, and the production's logistics. The documentary is not captioned.

R

R.E.M.: Road Movie (Warner, 238443)

A 90 minute concert and light show, although it is a straightforward stage performance, the rock group has a lot of energy and good music, and the program is highly appealing. The picture looks outstanding, with crisp, smooth colors and a spotless, glossy image. The stereo surround sound is okay, and there is a Dolby Digital track of equal power, with slightly better separation effects and less bleeding to the rear channels. There is optional English subtitling, so a viewer can quickly assess the intelligence of the lyrics and how well they are integrated with the energetic music.

Rabid Dogs (import, LMDVD001)

Mario Bava shot the crime-and-hostage thriller, (*Cani Arrabiati*) in 1974, but the man who was putting up the financing died and ownership of the film fell into limbo before the post-production could be completed. Bava passed away as well, but his followers and fans endured, and they completed the post-production work—including the shooting of a little footage to fill out the film's opening sequence. After premiering the film in a couple festivals, it was issued to the world on DVD exclusively.

The film is terrific. Three men commit an armed robbery, but their getaway car breaks down, so they hijack another car, taking the driver and a couple other hostages with them. The bulk of the 96 minute film is spent inside the car as they drive around the outskirts of Rome, trying to avoid the authorities and reach a safe house. Then, at the end, there is a wonderful, jaw-dropping plot turn (the film is based upon a quintessential story from the Ellery Queen Magazine) that will make you want to go and watch the entire movie a second time. This is Bava, so some of the violence is a little gruesome and there are a few frank sexual situations, but the exploitation components add significantly to the film's tension (as does Stelvio Cipriani's pulsating score) and give the film a raw, 'life's underbelly' atmosphere. **Rabid Dogs** is also the only Bava film set in contemporary times that does not have a fantasy element.

The movie is in Italian with optional yellow English or German subtitles that are a bit small, so as not to interfere with the images. The film's components were sitting around shelves unattended, so the image is not in a pristine condition. Colors are often faded and the picture looks a little grimy at times—but the film was not shot to look immaculate to begin with and the condition of the source material, which has been meticulously labored upon, can also be seen to add to the film's atmosphere. The image is never distorted enough to undercut the film's hold on a viewer's attention. The audio is presented in Dolby Digital mono and the same caveats apply—it is a little rough, but not unduly so. In addition to the movie there is a trailer that contains a lot of gore, elaborate profiles and comprehensive filmographies of Bava and the cast (including a few posters and stills from their other works), and an excellent essay, by Tim Lucas of Video Watchdog fame, about the reconstruction of the film and Bava's career. The DVD also contains a profile of Lucas.

Rachel's Man (Simitar, 7249)

The Israeli production of an *Old Testament Bible* story from 1977 stars Mickey Rooney, Leonard Whiting and Rita Tushingham (now there's a combination). The 92 minute narrative relies a bit too much on voiceover narration and remains fairly superficial as it ticks off the events in the life of the hero, Jacob, who leaves his own family under stressful circumstances and hooks up with a shepherd and his daughters. The picture is terribly hazy at times and colors are somewhat faded, adding to the impression that the low budget production is just a bunch of people in some loose fitting costumes, practicing a Christmas pageant. The monophonic sound is bland but adequate, and there is no captioning.

Radiohead (see **Meeting People Is Easy: A Film By Grant Gee About Radiohead.**)

Radioland Murders (Image, ID4224USDVD)

A long-standing project that percolated in the mind of George Lucas for a couple of decades, most of the juice apparently evaporated. The narrative concerns the premiere evening of a fledging radio network, whose staff is being systematically knocked off by an unknown assassin. The hokey programs performed live and being broadcast by the network are used to underscore what is happening to the hero and heroine as they try to solve the crimes. We admit to laughing once in a while, since the film, directed by Mel Smith, does manage to achieve the quality of a decent TV movie, but it has no zingers and certainly never has enough sequential laughs to build up any sort of hysterical momentum. Mary Stuart Masterson stars with Brian Benben, while the actor who might have made the material work, Christopher Lloyd, is buried in an extended cameo as a sound effects man. He's not even the killer.

The letterboxing has an aspect ratio of about 2.35:1 and no 16:9 enhancement. The film uses very bright, playful hues, and the colors are consistently pleasing, but there is a mild haze at times, which may be a conceptual thing with the cinematography. The stereo surround mix is quite fun, and the DVD's delivery is not a drawback. The 108 minute 1994 film is closed captioned.

Rage Against the Machine (Sony, SVD50160)

The hard rocking, politically aware group's concert sequences are presented with deliberate wear there is no telling what the picture is supposed to look like, but it appears to be sharp and correctly colored. The standard audio track is kind of a mesh of loud instruments and unclear vocals, so the separations brought by the Dolby Digital are invigorating, letting the viewer merge the film's stereo separations inside the mind instead of outside. The addition of optional lyrics is also welcome, because the songs are intelligent but you can't always hear what the singer is saying. The 70 minute program combines a concert sequence with a half dozen music videos, including *Killing in the Name*, *Bullet in the Head*, *Freedom*, *Bulls on Parade*, *Memory of the Dead*, and *People of the Sun*. The DVD also contains a political activist reading list and a listing of organizations to contact.

Raging Bull (MGM, 906040)

Both the letterboxed version and the full screen version of the 129 minute are on one side of the DVD, using dual-layer playback. The letterboxing has an aspect ratio of about 1.85:1 and no 16:9 enhancement, adding a sliver to the sides but masking off a lot more from the top and bottom of the image in comparison to the full screen presentation. Both have the same crisp black-and-white picture, which is an incredible improvement in detail over what we had thought had been a fairly good looking LD. The blacks are truer, but the most noticeable improvement is in the image sharpness, which adds a whole new level of texture to practically every object and image in the film.

The improved picture heightens the intensity and realism of Martin Scorsese's highly respected 1980 boxing drama, starring Robert De Niro. The film's stereo mix has always been subdued, with little in the way of separation effects or even dimensional ambiance. French and Spanish audio tracks are also offered, in mono. The Spanish is fine, but the French track is muffled in places, with some of the dialogue difficult to hear without amplification. English, French and Spanish subtitles are also available, and there is a theatrical trailer.

Raid on Rommel (GoodTimes, 0581012)

Richard Burton, with blond hair, stars in the 1971 production, directed by Henry Hathaway, about commandos who team with medical POWs to sabotage German installations near Tobruk in Africa.

The 98 minute program has been letterboxed with an aspect ratio of about 2.35:1 with no 16:9 enhancement. The source material is in great shape, with no more than a few scattered speckles, and the colors look fine on the dusty WWII desert action film, with decent fleshtones and nice blue skies. The monophonic sound is okay (though, among other things, the movie has a very strange sound mix—as if footage from another movie had been included with its soundtrack still affixed) and the film can be supported by English, French or Spanish subtitles, none of which translate the lengthy sections of German dialogue.

Except for the hair, Burton's presence is subdued, and there are shots in the film where it looks like he is supposed to deliver dialogue, but forgets. There are several extended action scenes, but most of the film is about how the heroes trick the unwitting Nazis into believing they are a legitimate German medical convoy. Normally, such goings on would try a viewer's patience, particularly since Burton is so out of it, but the letterboxing and the decent-looking picture are enough to hold a fan's attention. The desert vistas may serve as an unintentional metaphor for the film's artistry, but in widescreen they are captivating, turning filler into escapism right before your eyes.

Rain Man (MGM, 906041)

Dustin Hoffman portrays an autistic adult spirited away from his nursing home by an eager younger brother, played by Tom Cruise, who wants to use his enigmatic number crunching abilities at the gaming tables in Las Vegas. Except for the two stars in the cast, the 1988 Oscar-winner has the feel of a good TV pilot—an involving establishment of character with no forthright conclusion.

Both the letterboxed version and the full screen version of the 133 minute are presented on a single side in dual-layer format. The letterboxing has an aspect ratio of about 1.85:1 and an accommodation for enhanced 16:9 playback. The picture is sharp and colors are rich. The stereo surround sound is somewhat weak, but the Dolby Digital track is workable. The presentation also features a lengthy theatrical teaser and comes in French, in standard stereo, and in Spanish, in mono. There are also English, French or Spanish subtitles.

The Rainbow Fish (Sony, LVD49944)

The Sony Wonder *Doors of Wonder* series takes well known children's picture books and turns them into short animated features, though in order to do so, the stories are padded and songs have been added. **Rainbow Fish** features two stories by Marcus Pfister, the title story and *Dazzle the Dinosaur*. In book form, both use special shiny material in parts of the illustrations The animators do their best to make the shiny spots shiny, too, and they have used the material in the jacket art. **Rainbow Fish** is about a stuck-up fish who doesn't have any friends because he's so vain. We hate the book, but kids like it because of the shiny stuff and the underwater illustrations, and they will probably respond to the 15 minute cartoon in the same way.

The *Dinosaur* story is a 15 minute retread of any number of **Land Before Time** videos, but kids eat those up, too. The picture quality looks fine, though the animation is fairly basic, beyond the evocation of the artwork. The stereo surround sound has a strong dimensional presence though specific directional effects are limited. We actually tend to use the DVD as a test for hooking up surround speakers, just because the rear channels come on like gangbusters at the start without losing an inherent pleasantness. There is no captioning.

The Rainmaker (see **John Grisham's The Rainmaker**)

Raising Cain (Universal, 20386)

Brian De Palma's split-personality thriller featuring a showy performance by John Lithgow as the multi-faced villain is letterboxed, with an aspect ratio of about 1.85:1 and an accommodation for enhanced 16:9 playback. The picture is sharp, colors are fine and fleshtones look good. The stereo surround sound is fresh and adds to the film's frights. The 91 minute program is also available in French and Spanish in stereo and can be supported by English or Spanish subtitles. There are some production notes, a cast-and-director profile section and a theatrical trailer. Derivative of De Palma's *Sisters*, the 1992 feature can seem a bit contrived and confusing at first, but once everything is in place the narrative is involving and the performances are fun. Constructed in a cinematic style worthy of its schizophrenic protagonist, the movie is one long, satisfying tease that invites repetition

Rambling Rose (Artisan, DVD69000WS)

Benefiting from what is clearly a labor of love by the movie's director, Martha Coolidge, the DVD not only presents an excellent transfer of the film, it provides an unusually rich collection of supplementary materials that increase a viewer's understanding of the movie and of the filmmaking process. It is this latter aspect which those who do not anticipate an interest in the release should take under consideration. We have heard many film directors speak about their work on alternate audio tracks and few have been as lucid as Coolidge in describing the essential factors that brought each scene of the movie to the screen. Students who are looking for a career in filmmaking should commit Coolidge's talk to memory, but even those with only a passing interest in the process will find her comments enlightening.

A combination of sleepy Southern nostalgia and implied sexuality, **Rambling Rose** is both comical and touching, capturing the dreamlike comfort of a period drama with a liveliness often missing from such endeavors. Set in the thirties in the Deep South, Laura Dern stars as an abused teenager who comes to live with a family which soon discovers they must display a great deal of tolerance to help her put her life together. Robert Duvall is wonderful as the father and Diane Ladd is fascinating as the mother, but it is Dern's show and she projects a titillating innocence that is not quickly forgotten.

The picture is letterboxed with an aspect ratio of about 1.7:1 and no 16:9 enhancement. The deliberately yellowed colors are rich and the image, though bathed in a softening nostalgic haze, is somewhat sharper. The stereo surround sound is fine, providing a dimensionality to the music and the ever-present crickets (the film is set in the South, during the Depression). The 122 minute film is not captioned.

Coolidge reacts to each scene at hand, explaining what she was after, what she had to do to get it, how she got around last minute problems, and pointing out unusual or interesting facets that might otherwise escape casual notice. Somehow, she also manages to describe the film's development history, characterize the major cast and crew members, and speak at length about Calder Willingham's script (from his novel) and the meanings she derived from it. There is a curiosity that makes her talk all the more intriguing. Apparently, during the timeframe of the film's production, one of the cast members suffered an injury that severely hurt her back. Coolidge never explains how it happened (if it was off the set or on) nor describes the production-related panic that we would imagine must have occurred when the accident took place, but she often describes the logistical problems that the injury created in specific scenes where the actress appeared and the solutions to those problems.

The film has an alternate ending and you can call that ending up separately through the menu or you can, if you choose, watch the entire movie and have it route automatically to the alternate ending. There are outtakes, also covered by Coolidge's commentary (as is the alternate ending), behind-the-scenes footage narrated by Coolidge (identified as a 'featurette'), complete profiles of the cast and crew, selections of changes that occurred during the development of the script, an extensive look at the costumes, locations and set designs, and a look at some storyboards. Film schools should be buying the DVD in bulk and passing it out in every class, but even casual viewers will find **Rambling Rose** to be infinitely rewarding, as an entertainment and as a revelation of how entertainment is created.

Rambo: First Blood Part II (Artisan, 60466)

The director of the Sylvester Stallone action feature, George P. Cosmatos, delivers a commentary track for the 95 minute feature, reminiscing about the production and how he approached the principal scenes. He explains how the entire film was shot in Mexico (they did a good job—we would never have guessed), the reasoning behind some sequences (although it makes you wince, the torture scene is necessary so Rambo can then waste the camp without remorse), and how specific effect sequences were achieved. He also falls a little bit into play-by-play and allows some lengthy gaps in his talk, but fans are sure to find most of what he reports to be informative. There is also a featurette that runs a half hour and focuses on author David Morrell, who wrote **First Blood**, and also discusses in detail the Joseph Campbell myth structure of all three films.

The picture is letterboxed, with an aspect ratio of about 2.4:1 and an accommodation for enhanced 16:9 playback. Colors are reasonably strong and the image is sharp. There are some directional effects, but the stereo surround sound is not elaborate and there is no Dolby Digital track. The film can be supported by English closed captioning or Spanish subtitles ("'Señor, ¿ganaremos esta vez?' 'Esta ves tú lo decidirás'") and is accompanied by a trailers, 'spoken' production notes supported by text, an extensive cast & crew profile section, and a multiple choice 'trivia' game.

Rambo III (Artisan, 60467)

The third installment in the Sylvester Stallone guerrilla action series, with its cut-out villains and unswerving plot about a rescue mission at an Afghan fortress, is letterboxed with an aspect ratio of about 2.4:1 and an accommodation for enhanced 16:9 playback. The colors are bright and the image is sharp. The stereo surround sound has some lively separation effects, but there is no Dolby Digital track.

The director of the 1988 feature, Peter Macdonald, provides a sporadic commentary track. Macdonald was an assistant director on the production, taking over when Russell Mulcahy was dropped. He talks a little bit about the staging of various scenes and about Stallone, but his comments are limited. There is also a featurette, which is more of a music video without a rock song than it is anything else. It runs 6 minutes. The 102 minute film can be supported by English closed captioning or Spanish subtitles, and is accompanied by a trailer, 'spoken' production notes supported by text, an extensive cast & crew profile section, and a multiple choice 'trivia' game.

Ran (Fox Lorber, FLV5034)

Akira Kurosawa's take on *King Lear*, the image is letterboxed with an aspect ratio of about 1.85:1 and no 16:9 enhancement. It is set high on the screen, with permanent white English subtitles appearing beneath the letterboxed image in support of the Japanese dialogue. The colors are bright and fleshtones are passable. The stereo sound is reasonably nice, with a steady dimensionality and some good directional effects. The 160 minute 1988 feature is presented in dual-layer format and comes with a home video trailer.

When you hear crickets on a movie soundtrack, it is usually meant to invoke the feeling of a hot summer's day. Akira Kurosawa uses the constant chirping of crickets in **Ran** as mocking laughter to belittle the foolishness of the aging lord who has misjudged the loyalties and affections of his three sons. Kurosawa uses every blade of grass and every breath of wind to tell his story. As the drama darkens, so do the clouds. Even though every word of dialogue is different, the sexes of many of the characters have been changed, the settings, costumes, and social etiquette are foreign, and details of the plot are changed or switched around, **Ran** is unmistakably *King Lear*. This says much about the power of Shakespeare's writing, that the drama can be changed so extensively without losing the central themes; and it says much about the power of Kurosawa's direction, that he could change so much and still produce the most cogent and engaging interpretation of *Lear* yet put to film.

Randy Rides Alone (see **The John Wayne Collection**)

Ransom (Buena Vista, 13075)

The 121 minute version released on DVD was the one that earned all the money in the theaters, but it is inferior to the 18 minute longer *Director's Cut* that is available on LD. The DVD is letterboxed with an aspect ratio of about 1.85:1 and no 16:9 enhancement. The picture is a bit dark, but sharp, bringing out more detail in well-lit scenes and losing a bit of detail when the lighting is subdued. The film's sound mix is functional rather than showy, and the stereo surround sound and Dolby Digital tracks deliver it effectively. There is also a French language Dolby Digital track and English or Spanish subtitles, along with a theatrical trailer that gives away one of the principal plot turns—but it worked, it sold the movie very well. The kidnapping thriller stars Mel Gibson, Rene Russo and Gary Sinise.

The Rat Pack (HBO, 91551)

The title of the TV movie is a bit misleading, because it is primarily about Frank Sinatra's relationship with John F. Kennedy and not about the making of *Robin and the Seven Hoods* and that sort of thing. The 120 minute film does a superb job at sketching rich, believable behind-the-scenes portraits of a half dozen very famous personalities, and it adeptly explores many political realities of the early Sixties. The performances are very good, particularly Joe Mantegna as Dean Martin, Don Cheadle as Sammy Davis, Jr. (as an example of the film's unexpected strengths, there is a dream sequence in which Davis performs *I've Got You Under My Skin* in front of protesting Nazis) and Ray Liotta as Sinatra, and the film is

quite entertaining. Not only does it explore Sinatra's popularity and artistry, but it delves rather deeply into the underside of American politics.

Intense colors are quite blurry and the image is grainy in places. Hues are reasonably strong, but the focus is soft at times. The stereo surround sound is okay. The show is also available in Spanish, and can be supported by English, French or Spanish subtitles ("Il est trois heures moins le quart, Il n'y a plus personne ici, A part toi et moi. Alors prépare-les, Joe, J'ai un petite histoire, Que je pense, tu devrais connaître. On boit, mon ami, A la fin d'un bref épisode, Sers-en up pour ma chérie, Et un autre pour la route"). There is a cast & crew profile section and a 4 minute featurette.

Raven (Image, ID4263LIDVD)

A reasonably clever plot turn at the end allows the Burt Reynolds film to conclude on an upswing, but it is not enough to rescue the whole film, which is generally pretty dumb. Reynolds is a former special forces operative, believed dead, who returns and begins assassinating his old bosses. The film's hero is his former partner, who also seems to be an assassination target. The story is fairly ridiculous, the action scenes are not well staged and the performances are drab, leaving very little for a viewer to hang onto. Except stupidity. Our favorite moment: Reynolds' character pages one of the bad guys. The bad guy receives the page, tells his secretary to 'trace the call' and then dials the number. Reynolds picks up the phone and tells the bad guy not to bother tracing the call, because he's not going to stay on the phone that long. So why didn't the bad guy wait and look up the location of the phone number before dialing? It seems that, even though technology marches on, with low budget screenwriters, old habits are hard to break.

The picture, presented in full screen, has fairly richer colors and a slightly weak stereo surround soundtrack. The colors are bright and crisp. The stereo is loud but not elaborate. The 97 minute program is closed captioned.

Raw Deal (Anchor Bay, DV10337)

The hero, played by Arnold Schwarzenegger, doesn't accomplish much. He goes undercover to join a Chicago mob operation, hangs out for a while, and then kills everybody, not that this isn't an ideal subject for a relaxing, rainy afternoon. The picture is sharp. Contrary to a jacket notation that lists the wrong aspect ratio, the 1986 film has been letterboxed at about 2.35:1 with no 16:9 enhancement. Hues are bright but yellowish, making hues generally appealing—forests look greener, for example—except for pure whites or other overly distorted swatches of color. The stereo sound is dullish, with limited separation effects or dimensionality. The 97 minute program has not been closed captioned.

Ray Davies: Return to Waterloo / Come Dancing with The Kinks (Image, ID4705LYDVD)

Two over-the-hill video programs, from the British rock band, The Kinks, and vocalist Ray Davies, have been issued as a double bill. Conceived and directed by Davies, who also stars, the 59 minute *Return to Waterloo* is a kind of extended narrative music video, combining about nine numbers into a typical, commuter's 'middle age crisis' and daughter-leaving-home tale. The title refers to a round-trip commuter ticket and the narrative involves the daydreams and nightmares of a middle-aged businessman going to work on the train one morning. Tim Roth shows up as a young punk.

The 36 minute *Come Dancing* is a separate collection of videos from the Kinks' later years, including what seem like rote live versions of *Lola* and *You've Really Got Me*. The stereo sound has a limited range. The picture on *Waterloo* looks soft, grainy and a little worn, with dull hues. There is also a ratcheting artifact effect during some camera movements. The image on the individual music videos varies, but none is all that strong.

Ready to Wear (Buena Vista, 17100)

Opening on a bottle of Christian Dior's Poison (to which, we have always thought, there ought to be added another 's'), Robert Altman's comedy proceeds to interweave more than two dozen characters in a satire of the hoopla surrounding the big fashion shows in Paris. The film isn't very good—many of the characters just disappear as the end approaches, without a resolution to their stories—but it is often quite enjoyable, with its huge ensemble cast, numerous activities and plenty of easy targets for humor. Although we are in no position to judge how accurately it lambastes the pretensions of the fashion industry and press, much of the satire rings true and there are many clever subtleties in the quality of both the clothing designs and the theatrics of the individual shows. There is also a satisfying air to the style Altman creates by mixing everything together, and it holds up long enough that one is less concerned when it starts to fall apart. True, there is also a dumb motif running through the movie of people accidentally stepping in dog manure but, as a character says at one point, "There will be great lapses in taste, but there will also be dazzling moments."

The picture is letterboxed with an aspect ratio of about 2.1:1 and no 16:9 enhancement. The image is sharp and colors are bright most of the time, but there are shots at times that look softer, with weaker contrasts. We preferred the standard stereo surround soundtrack to the 5.1 Dolby Digital track. The 5.1 track has a slightly stronger presence, but the standard track has more appropriate rear channel effects, while the rear channels on the 5.1 track less often employed. The 133 minute program has optional English subtitles, and standard subtitles that appear during the brief foreign language passages. The movie itself was called *Pret-A-Porter*, with the inane Americanized title added at the last minute before the film's theatrical release. On the DVD, the movie's real title appears on the image and the translated title appears in the subtitles. There is also a trailer.

Re-Animator (Elite, EE4324)

The wild, witty and wonderfully gory black comedy about bringing the dead back to life is letterboxed with an aspect ratio of about 1.85:1 and no 16:9 enhancement, providing a tiny bit more picture information on the sides of the image but masking off quite a bit more from the top compared to full screen home video versions. Nevertheless, the framing is well balanced and draws the viewer into the action better than the older versions did. The color transfer is an immense improvement over the earlier releases—it is the first time the filmmakers were actually involved in transferring the movie to video—and enables a viewer to become more involved with the narrative and less distracted by grain and haze. The film still has a low budget look to it, but image details and the rather sophisticated lighting employed by the filmmakers are replicated superbly. Fleshtones are consistently accurate. The monophonic sound is fairly free of distortion and the Dolby Digital mono track is provides a near-stereo like presence during much of the musical score. The program is not captioned. The 86 minute 'Official Director's Cut' is accompanied by two red tag trailers, some TV spots, scenes that have appeared in other home video versions of the film, and a few outtakes that have never been seen before.

There are also two alternate audio tracks, presenting commentary during the screening of the film. On one, the director, Stuart Gordon, provides details on how the film was made, going into its history, the research that he did (the people who work in morgues are so lonely they were glad to talk to him), his technical approach (it was his first film, and he learned as he worked), and other little fun details ("The scene of the head being cut off from the body with the shovel, um, was really inspired by growing up in Chicago and having to shovel snow and break ice."). He starts to wear out in the second half, but on the whole his talk is highly informative and insightful, both in terms of the film's dramatic content and as a guide to low budget filmmaking.

On the other track, which extends over the trailers, the producer, Brian Yuzna, and cast members Jeffrey Combs, Robert Sampson, Barbara Crampton and Bruce Abbott have sort of a reunion screening where they reminisce about making the picture and laugh at each other's onscreen foibles. This is somewhat less informative than Gordon's talk, but it certainly conveys the atmosphere that must have existed when the film was being made and its humor is contagious. Nowhere in the supplement, we would like to point out, does anyone comment on Richard Band's music being a carbon copy of Bernard Herrmann's score for **Psycho**, though it is revealed that the hero of **Re-Animator** is named after **Psycho**'s author, Robert Bloch. At one point, Crampton, who can be excused for her ignorance, mentions how great the music sounds in a certain scene and everyone else suddenly goes quiet.

The Real McCoy (Universal, 20397)

Kim Basinger plays a talented bank robber who specializes in after hour withdrawals. On parole and trying to go straight, she is forced to plan and participate in one last heist, which she pulls off while managing to turn the tables on her tormentors. The plot cheats again and again, fiddling with time, incorporating character actions that make no sense whatsoever and otherwise defying logic so wantonly that only the most gung ho or dense viewers will accept its sequence of events. Val Kilmer and Terence Stamp costar, and Russell Mulcahy directed. Like any Mulcahy production, the 1993 film tends to look even better than it plays.

The presentation is letterboxed with an aspect ratio of about 1.85:1 and no 16:9 enhancement. The picture is sharp and colors are bright, with no significant drawbacks. Generally, the film's audio mix is adequate and aggressive, but not exceptional. And although the separations on the Dolby Digital track are a little different from the standard track, the two are fairly similar overall. The film is also available in French and Spanish without Dolby Digital and can be supported by English or Spanish subtitles. There are some mildly embarrassing presskit production notes ("'In many societies, even here in America, women are still regarded as ornaments to a man's success,' added [producer Martin] Bregman, 'I wanted to make a film that celebrated the spirit of a strong woman in an unconventional, and hopefully, entertaining manner'"), a brief cast-and-director profile section, and a briskly paced theatrical trailer that hides all too well the film's lethargy.

Reality Bites (Universal, 20234)

A meandering look at the X-generation that is less hip than it pretends to be (it uses *My Sharona* for a theme song for godsake), **Reality Bites** is sporadically entertaining but rarely insightful. Essentially a romantic triangle about a woman, fresh out of college, trying to start a career in video and torn in love between a slick successful type and a grungy layabout, Winona Ryder, Ethan Hawke, Janeane Garofalo and Ben Stiller (who also directed) star, and their performances rescue what charm the film has.

The picture is letterboxed with an aspect ratio of about 1.85:1 and an accommodation for enhanced 16:9 playback. The picture quality is very good. The image is sharp and colors are fresh. The stereo surround sound is a bit weak, but the Dolby Digital track has clearer, deeper tones and more specific separation effects. The 1994 film has a fairly standard audio mix, however. The program is also available in French and can be supported by English or Spanish subtitles. Some production notes, a cast profile section and a theatrical trailer accompany the 99 minute film.

Reap the Wild Wind (Universal, 20437)

John Wayne, Ray Milland and Paulette Goddard star in the 1942 Cecil B. DeMille Paramount production, about salvage captains and deliberate boat wrecks in Key West in the 1840's. It's a terrific movie, until the plot takes a very stupid turn at about the three-quarter mark. A young Susan Hayward and equally fresh Robert Preston also appear. For those who aren't up on their movie trivia, Goddard had the second best screen test for Scarlett O'Hara, and she gets to use that aspect of her talent, playing a slightly tomboyish Southern belle who becomes the center of a conflict between the two men. This is one of the few movies in which John Wayne's character dies, however, and his character deserves it, which is what is wrong with the film.

The film also contains worse than usual negative African-American stereotyping. The Technicolor picture is scrumptious. The film won an Oscar for special effects (in those days they handed them out for making boats look cool) and there are many crisp, breathtaking shots of seascapes, Antebellum interiors and Hollywood wardrobes. Fleshtones have glorious Technicolor tans, and every shot is so vivid your video monitor becomes a diorama. Our one complaint would be over the frame transfer rate. The source material is super, but it is not perfect, so there are occasional instabilities in the image, along with a few scattered speckles. If you stay focused on the foreground, you don't notice anything wrong, but if your eyes start to wander to the backgrounds, the image displays the unnatural shifts and blurs associated with digital artifacting. The monophonic sound is fine. The 124 minute program is also available in Spanish and can be supported by English, French or Spanish subtitles. There is a terrific re-release trailer, hosted by DeMille, a well-researched production essay and a cast-and-director profile section.

Rebecca's Secret (Digital Versatile, DVD133)

Neither the first nor the last dopey, unacknowledged softcore adaptation of **Diabolique**, the filmmakers come up with a couple fresh variations on the idea, but the farther away they get from the original story, the less sense it makes. It's all just an excuse to show naked people, anyway, and there are quite a few, though the primary male performer has a sock covering his you-know-what. You probably aren't supposed to see the sock, so when you do get a glimpse of it, it is rather amusing. The picture is grainy as all get out, with flat colors and bland fleshtones. The monophonic sound is wobbly and noisy. There is no captioning, no menu and precisely one chapter marker, placed at about the 83 minute program's halfway point.

Record of Lodoss War (Image, ID4411CTDVD)

Each episode in the thirteen-episode Japanese sword-and-sorcery animated adventure runs about 22 minutes. The episodes are bunched into collections of three (from a previous home video release), so closing credits and a single trailer for the single next episode occur every three episodes. There is, however, a common intro and a 'commercial break' on every episode. The color quality on the 1991 production is adequate, and lines are reasonably sharp. The music is mildly stereophonic, but otherwise things remain fairly centered. The program can be accessed in Japanese or in English and can be supported by optional English subtitles.

We wish that we could get as excited about the show as the fans crowding the theater in the 5 minute promo featurette that appears at the end, but there isn't much to recommend. The narrative is rarely compelling, the characters are typical archetypes and are not particularly witty or inspiring, and the artwork is rarely imaginative. The hero is a young warrior who, with a group of companions, is trying to protect his land from evil invaders, evil magicians and other strife. There isn't much blood, and even less sex. The show manages to go through the motions, so genre fans will find it watchable, but there's no real magic to any of its components.

Red Arrows Rolling in the Sky (Pioneer, PSID97004)

An ideal demonstration program for those who like to treat their guests to flyovers (it helps if your rear speakers have good woofers) and other zippy sound effects. The 50 minute program depicts the synchronized British flying team from every angle, including ground preparations, aerobatic flying set to music, flying accompanied only to real sounds, cameras in the ground, cameras on the planes and cameras on other planes nearby. The picture is outstanding, with crisp, ultra-vivid colors, doing particular justice to the b right red planes themselves. There is a terrific stereo surround soundtrack and a really terrific Dolby Digital track, which has much stronger directional energy and greater detail.

Red Corner (MGM, 907023)

Courtroom dramas set in other countries are fun, because you not only get the courtroom drama and accompanying mystery, you also get a crash course on alternate justice systems. Richard Gere stars as a businessman who is framed for murder in China and discovers that he is guilty until proven innocent. The film attracted attention as being some sort of podium Gere could use to razz the Chinese, but that isn't really how the movie plays, since there are good Chinese characters and bad Chinese characters. Besides, the characters who run the American embassy are all jerks. Although there isn't much of a mystery, there is plenty of suspense and the film is a satisfying piece of exotic escapism, one that lets you learn a little bit along the way.

Fleshtones are overly pink on the image is dark, losing some details in the shadows. The presentation is letterboxed with an aspect ratio of about 1.85:1, with an accommodation for enhanced 16:9 playback. The stereo surround sound is bland, but the Dolby Digital track has a reasonably strong atmosphere. The 122 minute film is also available in French in Dolby Digital and comes with English, French or Spanish subtitles.

The film's director, Jon Avnet, provides a running commentary. He doesn't go into too many details about choosing shots, except to point out the lighting and cinematography from time to time. Nor does he have much to say about the performances, except to describe Gere's physical capabilities and the difficulty of directing actors in a foreign language. He does have a lot to say, however, about the research he did on China (did you know that the military owns most of the discos?), the elaborate computer effects used to sell the location (the film was shot mostly in L.A.—you could have fooled us), and the stereotypes he confronted during the course of the production. Toward the end he kind of falls back on describing the action, but he has enough anecdotes and cultural insights to make the talk worthwhile.

Red Dawn (MGM, 906998)

Red Dawn is an antidisestablishmentarianistic fantasy about a Russian/Cuban invasion of the Midwestern United States. A group of high school kids, who seem to have been the only ones who hightailed it to the mountains when the Russians landed, spend close to two hours of movie time cleverly disrupting the invasion with guerrilla tactics. Then, because no other ending could be found for the story, they stop playing hide and seek to stand and shoot it out with their enemy.

The 1984 feature is in full screen format on one side and in letterboxed format on the other side. The letterboxing has an aspect ratio of about 1.85:1 with no 16:9 enhancement, and adds nothing to the sides of the image, masking off picture information from the top and bottom in comparison to the full screen version. The picture has somewhat pale but workable colors and an occasional errant speckle. The stereo surround sound is not as elaborate as one of today's features, but it is workable. The film is also available in French and comes with optional English, French or Spanish subtitles. A theatrical trailer is included with the 114 minute film and a jacket insert features production and 'trivia' info.

Red Heat (Artisan, 60445)

The 1988 Walter Hill film stars Arnold Schwarzenegger as a Soviet police detective who travels to America to bring back a drug dealer, and ends up teaming with a Chicago cop, played by James Belushi, when the bad guy escapes.

The colors are very rich and textures are clear. The presentation is letterboxed on one side, with an aspect ratio of about 1.85:1 and no 16:9 enhancement, and in full screen format on the other. The letterboxing masks off picture information from the top and bottom of the screen in comparison to the full screen presentation. We prefer the full screen framing, but either one is workable. The stereo surround sound and Dolby Digital sound have that sheer, jamming punch of an audio track that knocks you out of your seat in scene after scene. Fueled primarily by James Horner's hard edged musical score, the audio track thunders in every dramatic scene and blasts away in every action sequence. The 106 minute film is accompanied by a very dark-looking theatrical trailer, a cast & crew profile section and a few production notes. The film is also available in French without Dolby Digital and in Spanish in mono, and can be accompanied by English, French or Spanish subtitles.

Red Line (Image, ID5619FMDVD

Like cars and car chase movies? Then we've got a nifty one for you. Chad McQueen stars—and, in a shot-for-shot homage to **Bullitt** at one point, he even drives his father's green Mustang—as a small time thief and race driver who is hired by a mobster, played by Jan-Michael Vincent, to steal a couple of cars. The plot is a little contrived, the acting isn't so great and the budget is tight, but many scenes are expertly conceived and directed, and the film is full of memorable moments (the hero is about to steal a car when the wife of one of the villains and her lover sneak into the garage to have a fling). The filmmakers do a lot of nail-biting, camera-on-the-hood shots as they go racing around the streets of L.A., and at one point there is a chase through a graveyard, with tombstones bursting left and right. Additionally, Vincent's presence is one of the most bizarre, geek-like efforts we've ever seen. Apparently shot shortly after his accident—his hospital tags are still on his wrist—his face is heavily bruised and, while the script makes references to it as something that happened to the character, every closeup is an excruciating reminder of how desperate his career has become, though at the same time you have to give the guy credit—due to the circumstances, he delivers the best and most strenuous performance he has given in a very long time.

Fleshtones suffer now and then from the limited lighting budget (they spent a lot of money on cars, though, smashing up Porches and Corvettes every which way). The colors are a little yellowish as well, but overall the picture is workable, and the cars look cool. The image is reasonably sharp. The stereo sound is pretty good, with a lot of nice sound effects. The 98 minute program is not captioned.

Red River (MGM, 906042)

Filmed with more cattle than anyone could ever hope to assemble today, Howard Hawks' classic 1948 cattle drive adventure is a perfect mixture of huge, exciting action sequences and entertaining characterizations. John Wayne and Montgomery Clift play Captain Bligh and Fletcher Christian-type roles on a 1000-mile cattle drive in the old west. Wayne's performance is so good as he gradually shifts from a resourceful leader to a vengeful paranoid that you are disappointed when he snaps out of it at the end. There are gun fights and storms and fist fights and rescues and the greatest stampede ever. There are even girls and kissing, and since the movie was directed by Hawks, you can bet the heroine doesn't blink when an arrow goes through her shoulder.

The black-and-white image has clean contrasts and deep blacks. The source material has some wear here and there, but the crisp and smooth image adds to the movie's thrills. The monophonic sound is subdued, holding down age-related noise, but cramping the film's ambiance as well. Contrary to a jacket notation, there is no Dolby Digital mono track. The DVD can also be supported by English, French or Spanish subtitles ("Tu ferais bien d'épouser cette fille, Matt").

The Red Shoes (Criterion, RED070)

Michael Powell and Emeric Pressburger's outstanding dramatic primer to the passion and artistry of ballet has been given a meticulous and comprehensive transfer. The film's colors are spellbinding, and are replicated with a clarity one might think was impossible for any technology to achieve. The source material for the 1948 British production has some minor speckling, especially around the reel-change points, and is a little soft, but the film's imagery is so captivating such age-related shortcomings are easily overlooked, particularly when its chromatic range is so exhaustive. The same goes for the monophonic sound, which is actually in fairly strong condition with very little distortion. The 134 minute feature can be supported by optional English subtitles.

The plot is about a young ballerina and a young composer who join a ballet company and eventually fall in love. Ballet, however, is a physical and emotional interpretation of music set to the human form, and it is in the spirit of that interpretation that Powell and Pressburger use their cinematic skills, to expand and resonate not just upon the beauty of ballet, but upon the sweat and pain of artistic achievement that are behind it. The film culminates in the breathtaking original ballet sequence identified by the title, which resonates on the characters and their relationships. Incredibly well directed, there are so many small, purposeful details present in every scene, and even every frame, that a viewer can watch the film scores of times and still discover new angles of meaning and feeling.

The film and the ballet resonate even more in the superb supplementary materials accompanying the film. There is a commentary channel, splicing together remarks by film scholar Ian Christie, stars Marius Goring and Moira Shearer, cinematographer Jack Cardiff, composer Brian Easdale and fan Martin Scorsese, that is so tightly produced it sounds like a radio documentary. An ideal mixture of production history, reminiscences and relevant interpretations, the commentary provides many fascinating background details and an enhancement to the film's meanings. There is also another channel, on which Jeremy Irons reads excerpts from a novelization Powell and Pressburger created several decades after the film was released. The narration is carefully juxtaposed with every scene, as if Irons were telling us the story and showing us its illustrations, and the writing adds a lovely blanket of detail to much of the film. Both the commentary and the novelization have been given their own chapter menus. There is also a trailer, a still photo section, photos of memorabilia Scorsese has collected and an elaborate Powell and Pressburger filmography, replete with film clips.

Finally, there is a montage of sketches for the big ballet sequence that can be shown in full screen or played, as an alternate angle, in split screen with the sequence from the completed film. The music to the ballet plays on the soundtrack, but on another audio option, the original Hans Christian Anderson story ('parable' would be more accurate—it has angels and priests and is essentially about vanity in the face of God) upon which the ballet and, in a more sophisticated manner, the film are based, is also read by Irons. Since the ballet interpretation of the Anderson tale is expressionistic, it helps to hear the original story to understand the ending of the movie itself, in which the heroine is flung off an escarpment in an act of apparent martyrdom that seems at odds, emotionally, with the film's engine of individualism. (The key to the ending—follow the shoes, not the characters.)

A final word is appropriate concerning the ballet, which illustrates Powell's talents. Viewers may find the ballet to be misleading, since they are expecting, dramatically, to see the heroine give it her all in front of the audience. Instead, the dance expands from the confines of the stage in the manner of a Busby Berkeley effort. In Berkeley musicals, this effect was utilized to demonstrate that movies could go where stage shows could not. In **Red Shoes** clues are placed so that one realizes, perhaps on subsequent viewings, that the impressionistic ballet is actually a representation of the ballerina's concentration as she performs. This is brought to a crescendo by the final image of the piece, an ocean surf that appears to be breaking against the edge of the stage. It is, in fact, applause.

Red Sun (UAV, 40082)

The 1972 western, starring Charles Bronson, Toshiro Mifune and Alain Delon, was not a widescreen production, so cropping is minimal and the framing looks okay. By and large, the image does, too. The presentation is nowhere near as nice as a transfer working off original source material would be, but fleshtones are tolerable, other colors are reasonably strong, and the focus is generally sharp. Damage seems modest or, at the most, isolated. The monophonic sound is weaker, particularly during the more orchestral moments of the Maurice Jarre's musical score, but the voices are not distorted and, for most of the 113 minute movie, the soundtrack is not busy enough to call attention to itself. Terence Young directed the western, in which Bronson and Mifune are paired, attempting to retrieve a rare sword from Delon. The stars are terrific—Capucine and Ursula Andress also appear—and the action scenes are great.

Red Vibe Diaries: Object of Desire X-rated (Metro, UPC#5135312290)

Yet another of the many direct steals from *Belle de Jour*, it is about the wife of a doctor who gets a day job when her husband becomes too busy at work to give her the attention she desires. Designed, apparently, for couples, the cinematography is extra artistic and the erotic sequences are stretched out and somewhat uninteresting. The picture is a little blurry at times and fleshtones look overly pinkish in places. There is an occasionally stereophonic musical score, though all other sounds remain centered. The program runs 103 minutes and features Stacy Valentine and Misty Rain.

Reed, Lou (see **A Night with Lou Reed**)

Reefer Madness (Madacy, DVD99026)

The 67 minute movie, about a high school student who gets 'hooked' on marijuana and then blamed for a murder that occurred while he was stoned, is a hysterical over-reaction that makes the drug much more attractive (give a girl a couple of puffs and she'll go all the way) than it could ever really hope to be.

Madacy's black-and-white source material is badly battered, with many scratches and splices. The image is smeary, contrasts are so weak that details are obscured, and grain is rampant. Sure the film is old and was never intended for the immortality it has achieved, but there's got to be some copy floating around in better condition than this. The monophonic sound is harsh and noisy, too. The film is accompanied by a few background notes.

The Reggae Movie (Pioneer, PA98586D)

A terrific collection of performance sequences from several all-star concerts held in different places on the globe, the 100 minute program features 21 cuts from about a half dozen festivals, each performed by a different artist, including Dean Fraser, Garnett Silk, Inner Circle (the only group to have two cuts), Steel Pulse, Shinehead, Mystic Revealers, Burning Spear, Beres Hammond, Ziggy Marley, Dennis Brown, Maxi Priest and others. The lighting conditions vary slightly from one set to the next, but the image remains very crisp and colors are vivid, with rich fleshtones. There is no captioning. The stereo surround sound is good, but there is a Dolby Digital soundtrack that is excellent, with a strong dimensionality and well-balanced separation effects that are unhindered by the live environment. You feel like you're there with the audience.

Regina (Digital Versatile, DVD108)

A really bad single-set, four-character drama with a beguiling cast, Ava Garner, Anthony Quinn and Ray Sharkey star in the 1982 international production directed by Jean-Yves Prate. Anna Karina also appears, although she doesn't say anything until near the end. Unfolding like an awkwardly written stageplay, the story is about a reunion between a son who has been gone for a couple months and his over-protective parents. When he brings home his fiancée, they flip. Secrets from the past are also revealed. The dialogue is so arch and so embarrassing that if lesser personages were appearing

it would be a waste of time. Well, it's still a waste of time, but both Garner and Quinn have a commanding presence, and while you expect it from Quinn, it is a surprise to see Garner so lucid. We wish she'd done more primetime soaps and stuff.

The presentation is also awful. The source material is full of video flaws that throw passages of the program out-of-synch with the dialogue and otherwise distract one's attention—although by about the halfway point, one's attention is in dire need of distraction. Colors are bland, there are lots of speckles and edges have a double ghosting in places. The monophonic sound has no high end and a lot of noise. The 86 minute program is not captioned.

The Reincarnation of Isabel (Image, ID4610SADVD)

There are lots of bare breasts and a few hokey gore effects in the 1972 feature directed by Renato Polselli under the title *Riti, Magie Nere e Segreto Orge nel Trecento* (literally, according to the subtitles: *Rites, Black Magic and Secret Orgies in the 14th* [13th?] *Century*). The film is set in modern day, with numerous flashbacks to the 'previous lives' of the characters, who have gathered at a castle unaware that their past life links spell doom, particularly for the unusual number of virgins in the group. The film is incoherent and campy, but with the right number of rowdy guests watching it, you could have a fun time.

The film is letterboxed with an aspect ratio of about 1.7:1 and no 16:9 enhancement. Colors are a little light, but workable, and there is sporadic wear. The image is sharp. The monophonic sound is adequate. The film is in Italian and is supported by optional white English subtitles. The *Redemption* title is accompanied by an engaging trailer and a ridiculous, lengthy made-for-video prologue.

The Relic (Paramount, 331547)

A good old-fashioned monster movie, Peter Hyams directed the rip-roaring 1997 horror thriller, about a mutating beast that is loose in a natural history museum the night of a big gala. Penelope Ann Miller and Tom Sizemore star, with James Whitmore and Linda Hunt in rare but engaging supporting roles. The film would be easy enough to pick apart and criticize, and the narrative is fairly predictable, but the important components are in place—the special effects look good, there are plenty of decent shocks, some fairly witty dialogue and the heroes save the day despite the stupidity of their superiors. It is great fun and a worthy contribution to a much maligned genre.

The picture is letterboxed with an aspect ratio of about 2.35:1 and an accommodation for enhanced 16:9 playback. For the most part, the colors are smooth and glossy, and fleshtones look great, even in darker sequences. The stereo surround sound and Dolby Digital sound have high-powered surround effects and plenty of energy during the film's big thrill sequences. The Dolby Digital track has a better defined and more active mix than the standard track. The 109 minute program also has a French soundtrack in standard stereo, English closed captioning and a trailer.

The Replacement Killers (Columbia TriStar, 21629)

A no-nonsense action film designed to introduce Chow Yun-Fat to American audiences, the narrative has a few gaps in logic, but the action scenes are fairly constant, so you rarely have time to stop and think about it. Yun-Fat is an assassin who balks at killing a child, thereby placing himself at the top of his employer's hit list. Mira Sorvino is a documents forger who ends up helping him after the bad guys waste her office. Those who require substance with their action had best look elsewhere, but those who like their gunfights in slow motion and their characters stoically nonchalant (even Sorvino) will find plenty of satisfactions. The 1998 film was directed by a music video director making his feature film debut, Antoine Fuqua.

The film is presented on one side in letterboxed format, with an aspect ratio of about 2.35:1 and an accommodation for enhanced 16:9 playback, and in full screen format on the other side. The letterboxing adds a bit to the sides, but masks off quite a lot more from the top and the bottom in comparison to the full screen image. The film's style is better served by the letterboxed image, but the action scenes are often more pleasing with the full screen image. The picture is very sharp and the color transfer is accurate, even in tough lighting situations. The stereo surround sound is passable and the Dolby Digital track is a little stronger, with better defined separations and a more energetic dimensionality. The 88 minute film also has French and Spanish audio tracks in standard stereo, optional English, French and Spanish subtitles, a trailer and a short 'making of' featurette.

The Requiem from Sarajevo (see Mozart: The Requiem from Sarajevo)

Reservoir Dogs (Artisan, 60442)

Quentin Tarantino's 1991 film is about a robbery gone sour and the desperation of the few participants who escape. Much of it is set in a warehouse meeting place, with carefully measured flashbacks filling in details as they are needed for the advancement of the story. The film is violent, sullen, and has the atmosphere of a slaughterhouse, but its bluntness and technical fortissimo are magnetic. When the 100 minute program is concluded, viewers will tend to sit a while in silence, recovering from its impact. Harvey Keitel stars.

The film is presented in letterboxed format on one side and cropped format on the other. The letterboxing has an aspect ratio of about 2.35:1 and no 16:9 enhancement, masking a little off the bottom and top compared to the full screen version but adding substantially to the sides for a more comfortably framed image. Colors are strong and the image is solid. The stereo surround sound is good, and the Dolby Digital encoding adds some nice separation effects at key moments. The film's soundtrack makes greatly humorous and ironic use out of some bad seventies pop songs, which, frankly, never sounded better. The film is accompanied by a theatrical trailer (cropped on the cropped side and slightly letterboxed on the letterboxed side) and comes with English, French or Spanish subtitles. There is a reasonably large cast and crew profile section and some good production notes, though the notes claim that the film was inspired by **The Killing**, never mentioning **City on Fire**.

Restoration (Buena Vista, 17316)

It is Samuel Pepys country—London in the late Seventeenth Century—and Robert Downey, Jr., in a superbly nuanced performance, portrays a doctor who rises to prominence as the king's physician, falls out of grace and eventually redeems himself (he marries the king's mistress as a beard, and then falls for her). The movie runs 118 minutes, but it seems much bigger than that, as if it were a full-fledged historical epic. There are few terrific matte shots of a rancid London—the Thames is a solid green—and other carefully placed touches of scope or opulence that give the film a contrived but effective sense of scale. The supporting players are all outstanding, each one overcoming the drawbacks one usually associates with his or her performances to deliver the characters with absolute feeling and wit, including Sam Neill as Charles II, David Thewlis as a fellow physician, Meg Ryan as a patient, and Hugh Grant as a devious portrait painter. What we cannot emphasize enough, however, is that, unlike some exercises in lavish period decoration, the story is strong enough to support every indulgence.

The 1995 feature is letterboxed with an aspect ratio of about 1.85:1 and no 16:9 enhancement. Fleshtones are accurate and hues are bright. The cinematography has a faint softness, but it is a deliberate style and the transfer carries it without causing any distortion. The stereo surround sound is also good, though it is usually just the musical score that receives much in the way of surround effects. The 118 minute feature has English captioning. There is a theatrical trailer and a brief but decent featurette.

Return of the Blind Dead (see Tombs of the Blind Dead & Return of the Blind Dead)

Return of the Boogeyman (Simitar, 7213)

The 1994 movie, originally called *Boogeyman III*, is a badly acted, meandering thriller about a woman, being treated by a psychiatrist, who has dreams of a masked killer. There is some nudity and a few gruesome murders, but the production is so inept you can't get much enjoyment from it. The cinematography is awful and most of the film is a blurry mess. The sound is generally monophonic and weakly recorded, but there are modest surges in the musical score from time to time that may have minor stereophonic elements. The DVD is not time encoded and runs about 75 minutes.

Revenge (Columbia TriStar, 50219)

The film got bad reviews and put-downs all over the place, and there is absolutely nothing original about it, but Tony Scott's 1989 feature has such a languid atmosphere, succulent imagery and grand star appeal that we find most of it to be totally captivating. So Sun Belt that it's actually South of the Border, Kevin Costner stars as a former jet pilot who visits the estate of a Mexican gangster, played by Anthony Quinn, and soon enough starts dabbling with the gangster's main squeeze, played by Madeleine Stowe. Obviously, one cannot equate being a jet pilot with being a rocket scientist.

The film's final act is flaccid. Based upon a Jim Harrison story, the logic of the conclusion is valid, and it is satisfying that the filmmakers do not succumb to the cliché of a bloodbath, but the rhythm and the mood of the film collapses, and up to that point the movie was living off its rhythm and its mood. Still, most of it is highly inviting escapism, particularly when DVD playback can deliver Scott's images and sounds with such vivid intensity.

The film is presented in letterboxed format on one side, with an aspect ratio of about 2.35:1 and an accommodation for enhanced 16:9 playback, and in cropped format on the other side. The letterboxed image is more appealing. Colors are wonderfully exact and immediate, and the picture has a striking freshness. The stereo surround sound is also super, with lots of good sub-woofer effects and plenty of dimensional touches. The 123 minute program is also available in Spanish and French, and comes with English, French or Spanish subtitles. A trailer is also included.

Revenge of the Pink Panther (MGM, 907502)

Our favorite part of the 1978 feature is Peter Sellers' Swedish sailor disguise, with an inflatable rubber parrot on his shoulder (which keeps losing air) and a phony wooden leg that gets caught in open knotholes on the dock where he is sleuthing. **Revenge** (the one with Dyan Cannon and Robert Webber, in which the French mafia attempt to assassinate the poor inspector) may not be quite as tight as the films which preceded it, but it has enough choice comical sequences to be worth a viewer's while and some, like the sailor get-up, which can leave one chuckling for weeks afterward.

The picture is very soft, almost fuzzy looking. Fleshtones are okay, wood tones are strong, and whites are pure. Despite the soft image, the picture looks sharp and smooth. The presentation is letterboxed on one side and is in cropped format on the other side. The letterboxing has an aspect ratio of about 2.35:1 and an accommodation for enhanced 16:9 playback, though a little on the sides are still trimmed. The monophonic sound is adequate. The 99 minute feature also has a French soundtrack, optional English or French subtitles and a trailer.

Richard Pryor Live! In Concert (MPI, DVD7084)

The picture may look like it has bad artifacting problems, but rest assured, previous home video releases didn't look any better. The ratcheting halos that follow Pryor's head movement may be a little distracting, but through the grain and the weak colors you can still see his facial expressions, which are critical to his performance, and his performance is worth the trouble of tolerating the lousy picture.

The stand up routine runs 78 minutes—which is impressive in itself—and Pryor talks about his childhood, his heart attack, dogs, hunting deer, sex, the differences between white people and black people, and lots of other topics. The sound is adequate and the program can be supported by English, French or Spanish subtitles, for the expansion of your foreign language four-letter vocabulary. There is also a biography of Pryor and an extensive filmography and discography.

Riders of Destiny (see **The John Wayne Collection**)

Riefenstahl, Leni (see **The Wonderful, Horrible Life of Leni Riefenstahl**)

The Right Stuff (Warner, 20027)

The audio track has been mixed for Dolby Digital and it is super. The sound mix on the 1983 film doesn't push the envelope on the bass and is not as sophisticated as the sound on later jet pilot movies would become, but there are still a lot of fun swooshing and directional effects, and the Dolby Digital mix also enhances Bill Conti's Oscar-winning score. The 193 minute film is spread to two sides in letterboxed format. The letterboxing has an aspect ratio of about 1.85:1 and an accommodation for enhanced 16:9 playback. The picture is very crisp and detailed, and the colors are rich. The standard stereo surround sound is a little tinny. The DVD also comes with a French soundtrack, without Dolby Digital, and has subtitling in English, French or Spanish. A theatrical trailer has been included and there is a decent cast profile section, along with profiles of the real Mercury astronauts, a glossary for all the lingo used in the film and a few production notes.

Except for the touches of mysticism and comedy that some viewers may think are overdone, the film is practically a definitive interpretation of the beginnings of America's space program. It is because it is so comprehensive that its inclusion of the wives of the astronauts is so gratifying. On multiple viewings the performances of the actresses loom large, perhaps because the wives are so powerless and yet so integral to the project. More so than their idealized husbands, they represent the real America.

Rick Wakeman Live (Image, ID4401CADVD)

For those who first learned about the wives of Henry VIII with the help of a rock album, the live concert, which includes a couple selections from Wakeman's *Wives of Henry VIII* opus, is little more than a depiction of Wakeman crouched in front of his keyboards, tinkling away, backed up in percussion and vocals by Ashley Holt and Tony Fernandez. Those who fail to find Wakeman's music stimulating will discover that a visual depiction of his musicianship is hardly more arresting. At least Keith Palmer does it upside down and with knives.

The stage lighting is not always accommodating, occasionally casting Wakeman in a red-orange blur, but when the lights are brighter, which is most of the time, the image is very crisp and colors look accurate. The stereo sound is also unexpectedly strong, though the mix is not elaborate.

Ricochet (HBO, 90638)

Russell Mulcahy directed the 1991 film, about a psychotic criminal, played by John Lithgow, who takes revenge upon an up-and-coming assistant district attorney, played by Denzel Washington. For the most part, the movie is a standard urban action picture and Mulcahy gives it a sleek, sophisticated look. The performances, including a nice turn by Ice T as a drug lord, are entertaining and the film is watchable, but Mulcahy allows a few too many improbabilities to slip into the script and the finale is somewhat less convincing than the movie needs it to be.

The surround sound and Dolby Digital sound are good, with a pounding beat and clear definitions. The picture is letterboxed, with an aspect ratio of about 1.85:1 and an accommodation for en-

hanced 16:9 playback, and the framing is very appealing. The color transfer is adequate. The 108 minute program also has a French soundtrack in stereo, a Spanish soundtrack in mono, optional English, French or Spanish subtitles, a cast profile section, production notes and a trailer.

Ring of Fire (SlingShot, DVD1097)

The sort of film IMAX does extremely well, it is a 40 minute documentary that travels around the Pacific Rim presenting mini-documentaries and spectacular images coordinated to the theme of the Earth's instability. Mt. St. Helens, the recent San Francisco earthquake, Japanese monkeys hanging out in hot springs and Hawaiian lava flows are just a few of the memorable sequences the program contains. The IMAX image quality is super, with strong colors and a sharp focus. The stereo surround sound has a lively bass and bright tones. There is no 5.1 Dolby Digital track.

Ringmaster (Artisan, 60736)

Where do all the people on *The Jerry Springer Show* come from? That is the question that **Ringmaster** attempts to answer. The top-billed Springer basically has a supporting role, playing himself, as the bulk of the 95 minute film is about a trailer park mother and daughter who land a spot on the show with the lovers they have shared. The film humanizes them with romantic comedy complications, which begin to accelerate in the hours leading up to the taping. Springer's own scenes are pandering and self-consciously apologetic, but the other performers are fresh and their adventures can sustain a viewer's interest if personal prejudice toward the subject is not overpowering.

The picture is presented in letterboxed format only, with an aspect ratio of about 1.85:1 and no 16:9 enhancement. The cinematography is workmanlike and the image transfer looks fine, with bright hues and serviceable fleshtones. There is a 5.1 Dolby Digital track, though the mix is not elaborate and the audio, like the imagery, is blandly competent (there are, however, comical sound effects during the sex scenes). There is English captioning, a cast profile section, some production notes, a trailer, a music video, and a commentary track by the director, Neil Abramson. Abramson makes a few guarded comments about the aspects of Springer's life that couldn't be included in the film, and he talks a little bit about the logistics of the production (it was shot and cut very quickly). He also talks about working with the performers, about the camera setups the TV show uses, and about some of the script modifications, but on the whole, he doesn't have all that much to say.

Rio Grande (Artisan, 43456)

The action in the 1950 John Ford film concerns a band of renegade Indians who cause trouble in the U.S. and then run into Mexico for safety. The drama, however, concerns the conflict created when the son of an Army commander is assigned to the commander's fort, and the boy's mother, played by Maureen O'Hara, arrives to have the assignment rescinded. John Wayne portrays the commander. The representation through military procedure of the normally silent emotional stresses within a family is an effective device, and it is astutely combined with the action sequences to create a classic work, compromised only by the folksy comic and musical relief that some viewers may feel has been applied a bit too thickly.

The black-and-white image has a few scattered speckles, but it looks very sharp most of the time, and the contrasts are beautifully detailed. The image is gorgeous, and its vivid intensity adds to the entertainment. The monophonic sound is passable and the 105 minute program also has optional French and Spanish audio tracks, as well as optional English, French and Spanish subtitles. There is a trailer, and an excellent 20 minute retrospective documentary. Among other things, there are lengthy interviews with Ben Johnson and Harry Carey, Jr. in which they reminisce about working with Ford.

Risky Business (Warner, 11323)

Along with a reasonable sized cast profile section, there are some interesting production notes, telling about filming on location in Highland Park, Illinois and about using Tangerine Dream for the musical score, which was a fairly radical idea if you think about it and probably one of the reasons why the film rose above the standard teen hijinks comedy. The 1983 feature stars Tom Cruise and Rebecca DeMornay and is about a high school kid who sets his house up as a bordello when his parents leave on a summer vacation.

The 99 minute film is presented in letterboxed format on one side, with an aspect ratio of about 1.85:1 and an accommodation for enhanced 16:9 playback, and in full screen format on the other side. The letterboxing masks some picture information off the top and bottom and adds some to the sides. Generally, the letterbox framing works better, but either version is functional. The colors look moderately fresh, and the image is sharp. The stereo sound is okay, but the mix is a little dated. The film is also available in French in stereo and in Spanish in mono, and comes with English, French or Spanish subtitles. There is a brief theatrical trailer that is letterboxed on the letterboxed side and in full screen on the full screen side.

Riti, Magie Nere e Segreto Orge nel Trecento (see The Reincarnation of Isabel)

The River (Universal, 20427)

Mel Gibson and Sissy Spacek are farmers in financial trouble after a flood, with Scott Glenn practically twisting his mustache and calling in the mortgage. There is one disorienting but satisfying segment in the film's middle, where Gibson's character goes off to work as a scab in a factory and Spacek's character tries to farm alone, but otherwise the film is rather mundane, and its upbeat ending is unconvincing. The 1984 drama gets by on star appeal, but it looks like it was shooting for an Oscar and ended up not hitting the side of the barn.

The picture is letterboxed with an aspect ratio of about 1.85:1 and an accommodation for enhanced 16:9 playback. The picture quality is excellent, with bright, sharp hues and accurate fleshtones. The stereo surround sound is okay, and the 124 minute film has been given a Dolby Digital track that has slightly better definitions, but neither track has much surround activity. There is also a French audio track, in standard stereo, optional English and Spanish subtitles, production notes, a cast-and-director profile section and a trailer.

The River Wild (Universal, 20043)

Following the standard artistic river metaphor, the 1994 white water rafting thriller begins slowly, a drip at a time, gradually building in momentum and flourish until it reaches a splashy and frantic climax. Meryl Streep and David Strathairn are a married couple held hostage during a vacation outing by a desperate criminal, played by Kevin Bacon. First their chances for happiness and then their very lives seem to be rushing past them, and it is only when they dare to navigate the river's most dangerous chasms, where several tributaries meet in swirling confusion, that they can dump the bad guy and repair their union.

The picture is in letterboxed format only, with an aspect ratio of about 2.35:1 and an accommodation for enhanced 16:9 playback. Fleshtones are consistently accurate and the image is crisp in all lighting conditions. The stereo surround sound is super, immersing the viewer in the trickles and roars of rushing water. It also packs a strong punch at appropriate moments. Jerry Goldsmith's score, though not exceptional, is efficient in its suspense-building tasks and it, too, is amplified by the clarity and energy of the disc's audio track. The 112 minute program also has French and Spanish audio tracks, optional English and Spanish subtitles, production notes and a cast-and-director profile section.

Road to Morocco (Image, ID4281USDVD)

The Bob Hope and Bing Crosby desert classic has the usual mix of tomfoolery and songs, made enduring by the impeccable comic timing of the leads and the general vaudevillian atmosphere of the production. Dorothy Lamour co-stars in the 1942 feature, playing a princess who wants to marry and then murder one of the heroes, so she can then marry a nasty sheik, played by Anthony Quinn.

The black-and-white source material has some instances of wear and the image is a little soft in places but, for the most part, the presentation is fine. The monophonic sound has some age-related limitations, but is workable. The 82 minute program has been closed captioned with minor paraphrasing.

Road to Utopia (Image, ID4291USDVD)

Bob Hope and Bing Crosby sing and pratfall through Alaska with a map to a gold mine. Contrasts are still a bit soft in places, there is a little grain in some scenes and there is some minor speckling. On the whole, however, the 1946 feature is in pretty good shape, the image is reasonably sharp and the source material is free of major damage. The monophonic sound is fine, though some age-related noise is inevitable. The 89 minute feature, which co-stars Dorothy Lamour of course, is closed captioned with minor paraphrasing. It is not the strongest of the Road films, but it contains plenty of amusements.

The Road Warrior (Warner, 11181)

The Dolby Digital stereo track is quite interesting. The major audio components are distinctly separated, so that the music seems slightly removed from the sound effects and the dialogue. The audio track on the 1981 film is not as slick as a Hollywood production these days and has some basic flaws, including distorted dialogue in places and erratic volume levels on some effects. The standard stereo surround soundtrack sounds muted at times, and the sounds are blended together. By keeping everything separate, the Dolby Digital track gives the film a greater sense of being an 'event' and increases its theatricality. It may be flawed, but the car engines sound super, the bass washes over everything when it should, and the mix is great fun.

The 95 minute film is presented on one side in letterboxed format with an aspect ratio of about 2.35:1 and no 16:9 enhancement, and in cropped format on the other. In the theatrical presentation of The Road Warrior, the film opens with a squarish, monochrome image depicting a montage from the first Mad Max and, to explain the setting, a brief summary of World War III. The sound is subdued and pensive. Then, the sides of the image thrust out to the left and right. First, there is then a quick cut to the intake valves of Max's souped up engine and then to a headlight POV of a desert highway rushing across the bottom of the screen from seemingly all angles. The sound explodes, too, with the roar of the engine and an intensification of Brain May's Holstian musical score. On the cropped version of the movie, the emotional effect of the sequence—a revved up version of This Is Cinerama—is lost. The letterboxed version, however, keeps the opening sequence boxed in the middle of the screen until it lets loose, and although the effect isn't quite the same on one's monitor as it would be on a 30-foot screen, it is still thrilling.

The image transfer has a few oddities, including a couple of grainy night sequences, an occasional squeezed look, and an experimental, shifted outline effect, but it is clear from the well lit sequences that the fleshtones are accurate, the picture is sharp and smooth, and the colors are precise. There are some motion artifacts during a couple of the chases, but they do not linger and most viewers won't even see them. A trailer, which calls the film 'Mad Max 2,' is included on both sides, as are production notes and biographical sketches of Mel Gibson and George Miller. There is also a French soundtrack in standard stereo, and subtitling in English and Spanish. Mel Gibson stars as a loner who reluctantly helps a group of white-tunic-garbed good guys protect their gasoline from a band of post-apocalyptic, punk-and-hockey-garbed bad guys.

Roaring Glory Vol.1 (see **Grumman F6F Hellcat**)

Roaring Glory Vol.2 (see **Mitsubishi A6M5 Zero**)

Rob Roy (MGM, 906260)

Liam Neeson stars in the early Eighteenth Century tale, set in Scotland, about a clansman who must go on the run from the authorities because of a wicked deception on the part of the villainous nobility. The narrative is worth analyzing for the manner in which it depicts the hero, who is entirely without faults himself, but is undone by the flaws and shortcomings of those around him—but don't worry, the film has a happy ending. Neeson cuts a terrifically earthy figure as the hero, Jessica Lange, with her accent down pat (though all involved speak a 'light Scottish' that probably has nothing to do with the way those characters would actually have spoken in those days), is excellent in the critical role as the hero's wife, and Tim Roth is equally rousing as the absolutely evil bad guy. The film concludes with an outstanding sword fight that is as exciting as it is instinctively realistic.

The film is letterboxed with an aspect ratio of about 2.35:1 and an accommodation for enhanced 16:9 playback. The images are highly appealing, particularly in the outdoor sequences. The picture is nicely detailed and the colors are nice. The stereo surround sound is very good, with nice separation effects and a smooth clarity in high volume sequences. The Dolby mix is much nicer than the standard mix, with a deeper bass and more separation detail. The program also has English, French or Spanish subtitling.

Robin Hood (Kino, K116DVD)

The 1924 Douglas Fairbanks spectacle is rather surprising, forsaking the standard set pieces—there is no 'first encounter' between Hood and Friar Tuck or Little John, and no archery contest—to concentrate instead on the hero's relationship with his king. Initially a nobleman, he doesn't even appear as Robin Hood until the film's halfway point. Nevertheless, the 120 minute movie has terrific action sequences and is as fun as any Robin Hood film.

The presentation is heavily tinted and its appeal is hampered in this regard (tinting tends to hide image detail), though the picture is workable. It is also slightly windowboxed. There is a sort of deliberately tinny and mildly stereophonic score performed by Eric Boheim and the Elton Thomas Salon Orchestra.

Robin Hood: Prince of Thieves (Warner, 14000)

Kevin Costner stars in the grand 1991 production, which has plenty of action scenes, along with romance, humor, and a worthy social conscience. The 144 minute program is in a slightly letterboxed format, with an aspect ratio of about 1.75:1 and no 16:9 playback, and is split to two sides. The picture is a little soft, with dark, rich colors and decent contrasts. The stereo surround sound is reasonably boisterous, though there is no Dolby Digital track. The film is also available in French and comes with English, French or Spanish subtitles. There is a decent cast and crew profile and a very good production notes section that includes a history of Robin Hood and a survey of the movies about him. There is also a teaser trailer and a regular trailer that do a good job at selling the 1991 film's sense of adventure and action.

RoboCop (Criterion, CC1543D); (Image, ID40710RDVD)

Paul Verhoeven's 1987 film is about a policeman who is killed in the line of duty and then brought back as a bio-mechanical robot, retaining a glimmer of his former memories. Although the narrative is serious, the setting is a satirical representation of the near-future, exaggerating the effects of corporate greed and social bankruptcy.

Criterion's presentation contains a few brief clips of graphic violence that had to be removed from the standard version of the film to avoid ratings purgatory. Some of them change the tone of the 103 minute movie a bit, but there was so much violence retained in the standard version of the film that viewers will likely take the new images of spraying flesh and gushing blood in their stride.

The picture on the Criterion presentation is letterboxed with an aspect ratio of about 1.7:1 and no 16:9 enhancement. The stereo surround sound has some flashy moments, but the dialogue is a little raspy and the bass is a bit light. Criterion's supplement includes an elaborate essay combined with motion sequences, by Paul M. Sammon, that explores how various visual effects in the film were achieved. In addition, there is a segment on storyboards, showing one sequence in tandem with the scene from the finished film, and then a selection of other scenes on storyboards, including several, such as RoboCop standing over the grave of his alter-ego, that did not make the final cut, a teaser and a trailer.

In addition to the supplemental features, there is audio commentary Verhoeven, scriptwriter Ed Neumeier, producer Jon Davison and Sammon. Davison gives a clear view of the production logistics and Neumeier explains how the film evolved. Verhoeven relates the violence depicted in **RoboCop** directly to the violence and horror he saw as a child while living in occupied Holland. He also details the allusions he included of Christ's crucifixion and resurrection, and while such an interpretation of the film may be artistically dubious, it is strong evidence that the filmmakers approached the project in a correct frame of mind.

The stereo surround sound on Image's release seems about comparable or a little weaker than Criterion's stereo, though for a movie like this, even subdued the sound on the science fiction action film is fairly boisterous and engaging. The picture transfer is a noticeable improvement over Criterion's DVD, with much clearer, sharper and more accurate colors. The 103 minute presentation, which has no extra features, is the standard version of the film. It has been letterboxed, with an aspect ratio of about 1.85:1 and no 16:9 enhancement, and is captioned.

Robocop 2 (Image, ID40720RDVD)
Robocop 3 (Image, ID40730RDVD)

The programs are letterboxed, with an aspect ratio of about 1.85:1 and no 16:9 enhancement, adding a bit to the sides of the image while taking picture information off the top and bottom in comparison to full screen versions. The letterboxing is nicely composed and preferable to the full screen framing. Both have color transfers that are substantial improvements over previous home video releases. Hues are sharp and glossy, and fleshtones are accurate. The stereo surround sound is less invigorating, though functional, the programs do not have Dolby Digital tracks. Both are closed captioned.

2, from 1990, runs 116 minutes and was a marketing error, repeating the heavy level of violence from the first film and missing out on the children's market, which had become enamored with the character thanks to a plastic toy line and a cartoon series. For adults, it isn't as hard edged as the first film, but the action scenes are great. Peter Weller and Nancy Allen repeat their roles from the first film. Allen returns in **3**, from 1994, with Robert John Burke filling in for Weller. The 105 minute film committed an opposite marketing error by being designed for kids, long after the Robocop fad had subsided. The character becomes something of a superhero—he even flies—and the action scenes and dramatic narrative are more comic book-like. It can still be fun, but its intelligence is limited.

The Rock (Buena Vista, 13077)

Nicolas Cage is terrific in the summer action blockbuster, holding his own with Sean Connery and enlivening every scene he is in. The plot, about bad guys taking over Alcatraz and threatening to gas San Francisco, is pretty farfetched and the title, in fact, turns out to be a misnomer, since the island is presented as being hollowed out with elaborate mining tunnels, sewers and unattended but functioning machinery. The film is also over-edited, making many sequences difficult to follow on an initial viewing. Still, it can seem witty, intelligent and vital if you don't take it too seriously.

The picture is letterboxed, with an aspect ratio of about 2.35:1 and no 16:9 enhancement, and has a glossy, slick color transfer. The stereo surround sound is super, and there is a Dolby Digital track with better separations and more thrust. The 136 minute film is presented on one side and comes with a theatrical trailer, a French language soundtrack and English or Spanish subtitles.

Rock 'N' Roll High School (SlingShot, LDVD0797)

The irreverent 1979 trashing of pop music movies, produced on a stranglehold-tight budget by Roger Corman, combines typical high school movie parody gags with a typical anti-establishment narrative. The film's claim to immortality, however, rests upon the brilliant casting of the punk band The Ramones, in the part usually reserved for groups like Herman's Hermits. Not only is the band funny in a bargain basement Beatles sort of way, but their music is legitimately anarchic. The inclusion of the band essentially gave the filmmakers carte blanche, for no matter how juvenile the gags are and how makeshift the drama, the music excuses it all.

The picture transfer looks super, with bright colors, great looking fleshtones and a reasonably sharp image. The letterboxing has an aspect ratio of about 1.85:1 and no 16:9 enhancement, and the framing looks well balanced. The monophonic sound is a little hiss, but is workable, and the 93 minute program is not captioned. The release was subject to some scattered manufacturing flaws and the DVD's chapter guide is one number off the actual chapter encoding.

There is an audio commentary track featuring the film's director, Allan Arkush, the producer, Michael Finnell, and the screenwriter, Richard Whitley, accessed by toggling on the audio command rather than going through the menu. They discuss all aspects of the production, from how they bagged the Ramones and then convinced Corman that punk was in and disco was out, to why Joe Dante had to come in and direct some key scenes on the last couple days of the shooting. There isn't too much technical information, but the general background information and gossip about the film's creation and legacy are sure to please fans and will also be of interest to most casual viewers. There is also a trailer, a brief interview with Corman, a couple of radio ads and 20 minutes of live Ramones numbers, the latter two items played over a montage of publicity stills.

Rocky (MGM, 906043)

The film has a kind of low budget urban look to it, and fleshtones will never be pure, but the color transfer looks very nice. Although there are still minor scratches and speckles on the source material, fleshtones have some pinkness missing from earlier home video versions, and where there are strong, well-lit colors, such as during the final fight, when the sweat glistens on the backs of the fighters and the rope surrounding the ring is a pure red, the DVD looks super.

The 119 minute film is presented on one side letterboxed, with an aspect ratio of about 1.85:1 and no 16:9 enhancement, and in full screen on the other side. The letterboxing masks off picture information from the top and bottom of the image and adds nothing to the sides. The stereo surround sound and Dolby Digital surround have more detailed separations than the LD's stereo soundtrack. We did notice one curiosity, however. At the end of the 14th round in the final fight, the commentator's dialogue ceases abruptly. It sounded strange until we put on the LD and realized that, in the film's original sound mix, the commentator's voice was supposed to be so buried by the other noises that you wouldn't notice when it stopped. With the enhanced mix, it becomes obvious. The 1976 film is also presented in French and Spanish, but those soundtracks are monophonic. English, French and Spanish subtitles are also available, and there is an interesting original theatrical trailer. Sylvester Stallone stars in the 1976 boxing drama, which re-

mains a bright inspiration, genuinely romantic and genuinely thrilling.

Rocky II (MGM, 9006731)
Rocky IV (MGM, 906732)

The colors on both films are vivid and crisp. Both DVDs are in full screen format on one side and are letterboxed on the other side, with an aspect ratio of about 1.85:1 no 16:9 enhancement, adding almost nothing to the sides and masking off picture information from the top and bottom. Either framing seems workable on either movie. **II** runs 119 minutes and **IV** runs 91 minutes. The stereo sound is bland on both films, but **IV** has a Dolby Digital track that is somewhat livelier. Rear channel effects remain limited. The films are accompanied by their respective trailers, French and Spanish soundtracks, and English, French or Spanish subtitling. **II**, from 1979, is about Rocky's rematch with his opponent from the first film and **IV**, from 1985, is the somewhat sillier effort where he fights a Russian. Watching the two films in order, by the way, gave us one revelation. Rocky is the first fighter in the world who became more intelligent and articulate the more he fought.

Rod Serling: Submitted for Your Approval (Panasonic, PDV0023)

An 86 minute *American Masters* biography of Serling, the 1998 program is in black and white and uses a wealth of old TV clips, not only from **Twilight Zone**, but from the many live TV productions that first established Serling's reputation as one of the preeminent dramatists of the new medium. The best time to watch the documentary is after you've spent the day gorging yourself on old **Twilight Zone** episodes, because by then the themes that were central to Serling's passion—the desire to retrieve one's childhood, the sometimes impotent rage against authority, and the release of atonement—are vividly enmeshed in your own emotions.

The program interviews a number of people who worked with Serling, as well as his family, and there are many insightful comments by Serling himself, who, in potentially paradoxical fashion, was always very aware of his own creative process and his position in the intersection between art and commerce. The program generalizes, going for a kind of artistic impression of Serling (the black and white is not just to accommodate the clips, but to evoke Serling's palette) that it does not entirely succeed at conveying, but it is still a worthwhile program for those who are interested in television's beginnings, Serling, or the potential of human imagination. The picture quality is very good, and there is a strong stereophonic musical score backing up the interviews.

Rodgers & Hammerstein: The Sound of Movies (Image, ID4512ANDVD)

For those who can't get enough of *Getting to Know You*, the 97 minute program is a movie lover's documentary. From a scholarly point-of-view, it has the air of a cart drawing the horse, as it is about movies that have been based upon works by Rodgers & Hammerstein, and uses clips from the films for a good portion of its content, though there are also interviews with those who worked on the films, pertinent digressions (such as a split screen look at the Todd-AO and CinemaScope renditions of **Oklahoma**), and—and this is what makes the disc really worthwhile—extra footage of some sort from almost every movie, be it audition reels from *The Sound of Music* or a number that got dropped from **State Fair**. The documentary does put the films in a correct perspective (the three different versions of **State Fair** always confused us in the past, but no longer), and has informative things to say about each movie, but it is ultimately of value for what it provides as entertainment.

The picture has crisp hues and a sharp focus. The stereo sound could use a little embellishment but is adequate for the documentary format. The program has not been closed captioned.

Roll on Texas Moon (see **Roy Rogers Collection 1**)

Rollerball (MGM, 907015)

James Caan stars as a successful athlete living in a futuristic world where individualism is frowned upon. Participating in a high-tech version of roller derby where death among the contestants is commonplace, he tells his employers that he doesn't want to retire and he gets away with it. The film is so wrongheaded that it will never be mistaken for a true vision of the future (women are commodities again, and guests at formal wear cocktail parties shoot trees for fun) and its lesson—the guy who can bust the most heads is the hero—flies in the face of the film's nobility-of-the-individual theme. The movie's three action sequences are elaborate enough to make the title popular among disc owners, but even there the characters just go around in circles. The 1975 film's worst sin, however, is simply that it exists. There are so few intelligent science fiction movies that is disheartening to see such expense and energy wasted on such a dumb one.

The 125 minute film is presented on one side in letterboxed format, with an aspect ratio of about 1.85:1 and no 16:9 enhancement, and in cropped format on the other side. The letterboxing adds picture information to the sides and loses nothing from the top or bottom in comparison to the cropped image. The image is reasonably sharp, but colors are a little pale, fleshtones are bland and some scenes have a bit more grain. The stereo sound comes from an older effort with a limited dynamic range, though the Dolby Digital track with somewhat more pronounced rear channel effects. The film is also available in French in standard stereo and comes with English, French or Spanish subtitles, along with a 'game' that tests how well you paid attention to the film. There is an amusing 'making of' featurette in which the director, Norman Jewison, suggests that this is what life will be like twenty years hence—i.e., 1995.

Jewison provides a commentary track, as well. He laughs a bit about the assumptions that didn't come true, or that came true slightly differently (he's a bit hard on himself for showing a TV separated to four different screens, but it is actually a pretty good imitation of a PIP function) and discusses what messages he was trying to convey (about the pattern of increased violence in sports—he's Canadian, and laments the disgusting way that fights increased in hockey games after the league scored their TV contract). He didn't change our opinion of the film (he's actually proud of the scene where the decadent rich people shoot trees for fun), and he doesn't have too much to say, but he does provide some background information about the production (he cast Caan because of *Brian's Song* and never mentions *The Godfather*) and how the complicated game sequences were shot. One other note: At one point he professes to be shocked that, after the film came out, people approached him about franchising the sport, but in fact we recall an article in Sports Illustrated before the film was released where the movie's producers, hoping for a hit, were rubbing their hands over just the same idea.

Rollercoaster (Universal, 20439)

Timothy Bottoms is an extortion bomber picking on amusement parks and George Segal is the 'rollercoaster inspector' who foils his plans. The 1975 film was originally released in Universal's sub-woofer thrill format, 'Sensurround,' and has given a 'Dolby 1.1' mix, a standard monophonic track with an enhanced bass. The effects, however, are not elaborate.

The picture is letterboxed with an aspect ratio of about 2.35:1 and no 16:9 enhancement. The picture quality is excellent, with bright, sharp colors and accurate fleshtones. Bass aside, the monophonic sound is adequate, with smooth tones. The 119 minute film is also available in French and can be supported by English or Spanish subtitles. There are some production notes, a cast-and-director profile section and a trailer. Richard Widmark and Henry Fonda are also featured in the blandly executed thriller.

Rolling in the Sky: Asas de Portugal (Pioneer, PSI99212D)

Pioneer's **Rolling in the Sky** series has pretty much the same format from one program to the next, but they are treasures from the heavens for airplane enthusiasts, looking at precision flying teams from every angle imaginable.

We'll bet you didn't even know Portugal had an air force, or can explain, in 25 words or less, why they need one. The Portuguese countryside, however, provides a fresh landscape as a backdrop for the jets, which are shown flying in formation every which way, from the ground, from the air, and from the cockpits of the planes themselves. The cameras also explore them on the ground, poking into every orifice and lingering over every dial. And if that's not enough, many of the acrobatic maneuvers are very impressive. The flights are depicted both against a stereophonic musical score and with 'natural sounds' only. The stereo surround is great, with lots of separation and direction effects. The picture is immaculate and hues are bright. The 48 minute program has no menu function.

The Rolling Stones: Bridges to Babylon Tour '97–'98 (Warner, 36440)

Although it is not as vivid as **Live at the Max**—which is the best of the post-Seventies Stones concert programs—the picture looks good. The stage is brightly lit, so all those thousands of people at the concert sitting so far away that the musicians look like rolling pebbles can watch the gigantic stage screens to make out what is going on. There are often angles where the lights shine into the camera, washing things out, but generally, colors are bright and the image is solid.

The Dolby Digital mix holds the vocals to the front and keeps the crowd sounds in the back most of the time, while on the standard stereo surround soundtrack, the vocals bleed to the back. The Dolby Digital track brings order to the live recording, but both tracks are substantially softer than the audio tracks on the LD. Although there are a few exceptions, the performances of many of the songs are musically inert and fans will be more responsive to what they are seeing than to what they are hearing. The 120 minute program has not been subtitled, but is closed captioned. Oh, and although the concerts spliced together to create the video are all set in large arenas, we didn't see a single youngster in any of the audiences.

Rolling Stones: Live at the Max (Image, ID4380ERDVD)

The best of the modern Rolling Stones concerts was shot in the IMAX format. The 85 minute program gives the viewer an unusually immediate perspective of the performing stage. Taken from the 'Steel Wheels' tour, in which the stage looks like it was left over from an arena production of *Starlight Express*, the image is so crisp that you have what seems like a close-up of one of the musicians and get the rest of the band in the same shot. The audio is also exceptionally good, capturing the raw flaws of a live concert but with a vivid immediacy that even the best studio recordings are unable to convey.

Rolling Stones: Voodoo Lounge (Image, ID4379ERDVD)

Almost none of the concert is new material—only Keith Richards' *The Worst* has not been played to death already—and the stadium environment is so over-amplified that all semblance of melody or anything but beat completely disappears. Mick Jagger no longer sings. He yells the words with at best slight changes of pitch. As an event, the show is a rather grand production and makes for satisfying theater—though the video editing often isolates the action and hides much of what is happening at a given moment—but the program is a definite step down from and earlier Stones concerts. The 94 minute program is often bathed in smoke, creating a haze around the performers, but the picture quality is passable. The stereo sound is loud, but separations are limited. The chapter guide is off by one.

Romeo + Juliet (see William Shakespeare's Romeo + Juliet)

Ronin (MGM, 907439)

John Frankenheimer directed the old fashioned, pre-MTV-style action film, shot on location all over France. The story is about a group of hired thugs chasing after a suitcase, and it is full of *French Connection*-type car chases and unmanipulated gunfights. Robert De Niro and Jean Reno star, and there is a modest plot twist at the end that brings everything to a satisfying conclusion, even though you never find out what was in the suitcase.

If the film's basic premise and dramatic execution don't thrill you, the DVD's Dolby Digital track could very well make all the difference in the world. Not even the standard stereo surround soundtrack is as much fun as the Dolby Digital track, which has almost as many left-right rear channel separation effects as it has left-right front channel separation effects, and it has lots and lots of those. You got chickens behind you on one side, cars on the other, voices in front on one side, gun shots on the other and music everywhere, needling your excitement. In addition to the wonderfully detailed matrix, the audio has an impressive purity and smoothness of tone that delivers each effect or line of dialogue with such clarity your attention is riveted by every noise for the film's entire 121 minutes.

The film is presented in letterboxed format on one side, with an aspect ratio of about 2.35:1 and an accommodation for enhanced 16:9 playback, and in full screen format on the other side. Shot in Super-35, the letterboxed image masks off picture information from the bottom of the screen while adding a little to the sides. The letterboxed framing is sexier, but either presentation is valid and the full screen version gives some of the more frantic action sequences a rewarding alternate perspective.

Frankenheimer went so far as to cover up objects in his locations that had bright colors to maintain a kind of somber, rainy autumn look that again evokes thrillers from another era (today, everything has a high gloss). Nevertheless, the picture quality is highly compelling, with perfectly delineated hues and richly detailed contrasts.

The film is also available in French in Dolby Digital and can be supported by English or French subtitles. An alternate ending that is more satisfying from an artistic standpoint, but one that test audiences did not like as much, has been included. For some reason, the sound for the sequence is routed to the left channel only. Frankenheimer provides a running commentary, talking about how he approached various scenes, about filming the harrowing car chases, about working with the cast and crew, about what he was trying to accomplish in the film's major sequences, and about filmmaking in general. He also points out a number of minor details, such as identifying when he was using the actual cast members in shots where doubles might have sufficed.

Rooster Cogburn (...and the Lady) (Universal, 20170)

John Wayne maintained essentially the same personality through most of his films in the Sixties and Seventies, so something like **Rooster Cogburn**, where he has put on an eye patch and combed his hair weird, is a real treat, because he is acting. He hams it up and it is a joy to watch him not because of any great command of craft, but because he is someone very familiar with is letting loose a little. The movie, which also stars Katharine Hepburn, is quite captivating. If you do obtain the DVD, you should spend one viewing making a conscious effort to watch whoever is not at the center of attention, because both Hepburn (who is not as awkward as Wayne, but is still clearly enjoying herself) and Wayne are performing for the camera even when it isn't pointing straight at them. And if that weren't enough, the movie has a wonderful second-rate TV ham, Anthony Zerbe, chewing up scenery with bits of business of his own as the bad guy. The scenery itself is captivating and is also a bit overplayed. Most of the 1975 movie was shot in Oregon and has a National Forest look to it.

The letterboxing has an aspect ratio of about 2.35:1 and no 16:9 enhancement. Colors are strong, but fleshtones are overly pinkish. The source material is in reasonably good condition. The monophonic sound is acceptable. The 108 minute film is also available in French and Spanish and can be accompanied by English or Spanish subtitles ("Me dormí y soñé que la vida era una fascinación. Desperaté para enterarme que es una obligación"). There is a brief collection of production notes, a small cast profile segment and an enjoyable theatrical trailer.

Rosewood (Warner, 14536)

A tough film, based on true events, about a holocaust-type mass murder of the residents of a predominantly black Florida town in the Twenties, John Singleton directed the 1997 feature, which stars Ving Rhames, Jon Voight, Esther Rolle and others. The first half of the film depicts the events leading up to the massacre and the second half depicts the two-day slaughter, with the narrative gradually settling on efforts to save a group of children. The exciting last act, where the children are smuggled past a carousing, anarchic lynch mob, is superbly staged, evoking the great action scenes of the silent era, and rescues what had been, up to that point, an honorable but extremely depressing work. Singleton is meticulous in making the characters fully rounded and morally complex human beings, and the film can be compared favorably to *Schindler's List*, not in terms of scale, but in its exploration of genuine day-to-day evil. Few viewers want to face up to these sort of horrors happening so close to home, however, particularly when they are just looking for a little entertainment.

The picture has rich hues and clear details that bring the viewer close to the film's textures and atmosphere. The stereo surround sound is a little bland, though the Dolby Digital track is livelier. The 148 minute film is split to two sides and is presented in letterboxed format, with an aspect ratio of about 2.35:1 and an accommodation for enhanced 16:9 playback. The film is also available in Spanish without Dolby Digital and has English, French or Spanish subtitles. There is a theatrical trailer, a cast profile and some production notes. The DVD also has an exclusive commentary track by Singleton, though it is something of a disappointment. Singleton spends most of the time describing the events on the screen. He shares a few anecdotes about the shoot, a few tidbits of extra historical information, a little bit on the films that influenced his approach to the production (such as *The Ox-Bow Incident*), and a couple technical details, but he never strays too far from his play-by-play commentary on the characters and the action.

Rossini (see Mozart/Rossini)

Rossini's La Donna del Lago (Image, ID4363PUDVD)

Not one of the strongest *Teatro Alla Scala* offerings, the sets are huge, but dark—except during the last act—and the staging, by Werner Herzog, seems overly ponderous and static. Like most all La Scala productions, the singing is more than adequate, with June Anderson, Rockwell Blake, Chris Merritt and Martine Dupuy, but there are several arias where the singers appear to choose the safe vocal path over the daring one (and one wonders if they would have made the same choices if the program weren't being recorded). The narrative, inspired by Walter Scott, is about romance and deception among warring nobles in the Scottish highlands. The picture quality is okay, although, because of the stage lighting, colors are a bit indistinct and some darker sequences look a little murky. The stereo sound is passable, though the recording tends to favor the singing over the orchestra. The single-platter dual-layer program runs 164 minutes.

Rossini's William Tell: Teatro Alla Scala (Image, ID4357PUDVD)

It takes two platters to hold the 237 minute opera. Act I, running 77 minutes, appears on the first platter and the remaining three acts appear on the single-sided dual-layer second platter, running 160 minutes. The set design is outstanding, using large projection screens that display various Alpine images—mountains, running water, trees—to establish a scene. The mildly aged picture is somewhat soft, but fleshtones are adequate and other hues are workable. The stereo sound has a subdued but workable mix. The singing, from Giorgio Zancanaro, Cheryl Studer, Chris Merritt and Giorgio Surjan, conducted by Riccardo Muti, is very strong and the basic drama of the music is thoroughly conveyed. The opera is in Italian with permanent English subtitles.

Roswell - The Roswell Report: Case Closed (Image, ID4372DODVD)

Narration is minimal on the 30 minute program, which spends most of its time running a generic musical score to military archive footage of test balloons and the objects they carry into the sky. The program does make a token effort to debunk the government's explanation of the Roswell incident, but it mostly looks like it is trying to be a music video, perhaps for The Weather Channel. The picture quality varies depending upon the clip, but it usually looks fairly worn. The monophonic sound has a reasonably decent range.

Roujin Z (Image, ID4409CTDVD)

The first half of the Japanese cartoon is excellent. Set a bit in the future, the story is about a nurse in training who is providing in-home care to an elderly patient when the patient is selected to be placed in an advanced automated care unit. Concerned about his well being, she uncovers flaws in the automation, only to be reprimanded by her superiors for her efforts. The animation is outstanding, and the show's focus on realistic settings, characters and situations is captivating. In the second half, however, the care unit goes crazy and turns into a giant, rampaging robot. The cartoon remains competently executed, but its shift to what is basically an action picture with a one-gag punchline ending is disappointing after the opening acts promised so much more.

The picture is letterboxed with an aspect ratio of about 1.7:1 and no 16:9 enhancement. The color transfer looks fine and the image is sharp. The source material is free of significant damage. The film is available in English or in Japanese, with optional English subtitles that provide an alternate translation to the English dubbing. There are also a few permanent English subtitles for signs and other Japanese texts within the show.

Rounders (Buena Vista, 16449)

A toothless **Mean Streets** with a poker theme, the normally transfixing John Dahl directed the 1998 film, which stars Matt Damon and Edward Norton, with a terrific supporting turn by John Malkovich. The performances are all entertaining, but the characters act predictably and the film is enjoyable only if one does not have high expectations for it. Curiously, there is no concluding scene for Norton's character, either.

The presentation is letterboxed with an aspect ratio of about 2.35:1 and no 16:9 enhancement. The film's cinematography is interesting, switching from a generally colored scene to scenes of near monochromatic shadings. Assuming this isn't just a fault of the transfer, the presentation looks quite good, although strongly illuminated reds are somewhat blurry. The stereo surround sound and Dolby Digital sound are okay, with the Dolby Digital mix providing a particularly strong dimensionality when the musical score activates. The 121 minute feature can be supported by English subtitles, and it is accompanied by a full screen trailer that has footage not included in the film.

Route 9 (Sterling, 7195)

Two small town cops come across a drug deal massacre and decide to steal some of the money before calling it in, but as they attempt to cover up their crime they start getting deeper and deeper into trouble. Kyle MacLachlan, Peter Coyote and Wade Andrew Williams star in the enjoyable drama, which you know can't possibly end well for the heroes. The performers are appealing and the narrative pulls you right along, down the road to ruin.

The picture looks okay, although hues come off a bit light at times. The stereo surround sound is fine, and there is a Dolby Digital track with more sounds and better detail. The 102 minute feature can be supported by Spanish subtitles, but there is no English captioning. There is a trailer, an extensive cast & crew profile section, and a commentary track by MacLachlan and director David MacKay. MacLachlan and MacKay talk about the production, the characters and working with the other members of the crew. There are scattered tidbits about filmmaking that are worthwhile, and a few interesting anecdotes.

Roxy Music (see **The Best of MusikLaden T-Rex/Roxy Music**)

Roy Rogers Collection 1 (Roan, AED2005)

If the movies contained on the single-sided, dual-layer platter, *Days of Jesse James*, *King of the Cowboys* and *Roll on Texas Moon*, are not rediscovered by some future generation as the ultimate in hip, then our society and culture do not deserve to survive. The films are too idealized and too precious to disappear from America's collective heart, and if we can no longer look upon them with innocent pleasure, we can still admire them for the efficiency of their mise-en-scene and the purity of their ideals. Produced by Republic Pictures in the early Forties, the three films—representative of a larger series—are basically well-made 'B' pictures built around the talents of Rogers, who looks and acts like a young William Shatner, but can sing better.

In *Days of Jesse James*, from 1939, Rogers is teamed with Gabby Hayes, as the two pose as ex-cons to infiltrate the James gang, only to discover that somebody else has really been doing the worst robbing and murdering (they actually let James go—was the Production Code paying attention?). Both *King of the Cowboys*, produced in 1943 and *Roll On Texas Moon*, produced in 1946, take place in 'modern' times, where cars and telephones are as ubiquitous as horses. In *Cowboys*, which co-stars Smiley Burnette, Rogers goes undercover with a traveling vaudeville act to catch a group of saboteurs who are using the act as a cover. In *Texas Moon*, which has Hayes and Dale Evans, he investigates rising tensions between sheep ranchers and cattle ranchers when the former accuse the latter of murder. There is a running gag involving Hayes and a sheep who insists on sleeping with him. All three films have musical sequences, but the most wonderfully surreal are in *Texas Moon*. All three have dependable stunts and action sequences as well, with Republic's special effects shop turning in some good car crashes and that sort of thing. Rogers seems to move through all three without getting a speck on him—even when he gets shot, he doesn't bleed—but he is the epitome of America's youthful optimism and able leadership, and even today you feel 'safe' when he shows up to take on the villains.

All three features are in black and white, and are in reasonably decent shape, with most wear confined to the reel-change points. The day-for-night sequences tend to be so dark you can't make out details in the shadows, but that beats having them overlit and trying to imagine it is dark. The monophonic sound on all three is aged but workable and the DVD is not captioned. The layer break is set in the middle of *King of the Cowboys*. *Days of Jesse James* runs 53 minutes, *Cowboys* runs 70 minutes and *Roll on Texas Moon* runs 67 minutes. *Cowboys* is said to have been combined from an Armed Services print and a standard theatrical print to create the most complete version of the film in existence. There are also 2 minutes of alternate footage for *Cowboys* (with stronger references to the War), as well as a *Cowboys* trailer and an amusing color theatrical promo for the Roy Rogers Riding Club, in which Rogers, bless his heart, recites the 'Cowboy Prayer.'

The Royal Hunt of the Sun (Simitar, 7229)

The jacket lists the film's running time at 88 minutes, the DVD's 'Film Facts' section lists it at 128 minutes, one reliable reference book lists it at 118 minutes, another at 121 minutes, and the DVD actually runs 97 minutes. The source material is a rather battered print, with plenty of speckles, scratches and even some splices, but the color quality is reasonably strong. The presentation is letterboxed, with an aspect ratio of about 2.2:1 and no 16:9 enhancement, and it still looks a little tight on the sides, though it is certainly a major improvement over the cropped version one sees on broadcast TV. The letterbox bands are blue instead of black, which we found somewhat distracting. The image also loses its vertical control at around the 33 minute mark for a little bit and drops to the bottom of the screen before being re-adjusted. The monophonic sound is quite weak and has to be amplified substantially, though otherwise it has no really big problems and the music usually seem to be at the correct pitch.

Robert Shaw portrays the explorer, Francesco Pisarro, and Christopher Plummer is the Inca king he holds for ransom in the adaptation of Peter Shaffer's play. Plummer is terrific as the very bizarre, alien-like Inca, but Shaw is less convincing—not as a Spanish soldier, he plays that just fine, but in the emotional transformation his character undergoes while in the Inca's presence. The film is a stimulating spectacle and, while it doesn't have enough blood and guts for the action crowd (there is only one battle), those who enjoy historical adventures—particularly intellectually stimulating ones—should be pleased. Whether they will like the DVD or not is another matter, for the presentation is not pristinely more than has been available in the past.

Royal Wedding (UAV, 40082); (Madacy, DVD99025)

The source material UAV has used for the 1951 public domain MGM musical varies in quality from reel to reel, and even from scene to scene. Some segments look very drained and have a bad double ghosting and smears around moving figures, while other segments are reasonably colorful and less distorted. There is some damage and a few splices, particularly around the reel-change marks. At its best, however, the sharpness on the DVD, when it isn't distorted, makes the somewhat more consistent LD, which isn't all that fresh, look overly soft. We actually prefer the monophonic sound on the DVD. It is in much rougher condition, but it is more immediate, as well. In comparison, the sound on the LD has gone through so much noise reduction it sometimes sounds like the characters are singing in another room.

The Madacy Hollywood Classics version, however, is even worse. Although the image is smoother, colors and fleshtones are less accurate and there are massive audio and video dropouts scattered throughout the program. The audio seems on par with the UAV version.

Stanley Donen directed the 93 minute film about American stage performers in London. Fred Astaire and Jane Powell star. The narrative is a weak effort, but the movie remains memorable for its inventive dance sequences, notably a scene where Astaire dances with a hat rack and some gym equipment, a scene where Astaire and Powell dance on the floor of a tilting ship, and, most famously, the scene where Astaire dances on the ceiling and walls of a hotel room.

Rude (Simitar, 7294)

A small but ambitious film about urban life, there are essentially three unconnected narratives that are intermingled and linked by a voiceover spiel from a pirate radio deejay. In the primary narrative, the husband of a young policewoman shows up on her doorstep after being released from prison and tries to start a fresh life with her. In the two secondary narratives, a young artist's memories and imagination intrude on her solitude after her boyfriend moves out, taking most of her furniture and appliances with him, and a

young boxer starts to recognize that his own sexuality may differ from that of his macho boxing buddies.

Some sequences have a music video look to them, but generally the film's experiments in style are invigorating. The cinematography has a limited budget and details still get lost in shadows, but the colors are deep, bright and sharp. The stereo surround sound is well detailed and lively, making the 89 minute film seem a bit classier. Some sequences are presented in a highly stylized fashion, but it never becomes confusing or overly obscure. Some of the experimentation and dramatics comes across as sophomoric but, just as often, the filmmakers succeed in their dares, and there is a tendency to admire what works in the film and to tolerate what doesn't.

Rudolf Nureyev / Margot Fonteyn in Tchaikovsky's Swan Lake (PolyGram, 4400702012)

One of the best recorded versions of the classic ballet, Fonteyn's performance is a remarkable blend of outstanding pantomime and superb, flawless dancing, and Nureyev's incredibly precise and fluid performance is almost equally astonishing. Even the cygnets are in unison, which has not been the case on a number of renditions we've seen. The 1966 film was shot on a stage, but without an audience, allowing the camera to be in good position and edits to remain invisible most of the time (there is even one cut in the middle one of Nureyev's leaps, yet it works just fine). Unlike some ballet videos, the choreography is rarely obscured by the editing choices. The color transfer is excellent. There is a mild aging effect around the edges and in some of the darker corners, but colors are generally bright, fleshtones look good and the image is solid. The stereo surround sound is very good when one takes the age of the recording into account (the mix is not elaborate) and the Dolby Digital track has smoother, deeper tones, though separation effects on the two tracks are pretty much identical.

The Rugrats Movie (Paramount, 333997)

The popular film spin-off of a popular children's cartoon—something that is harder to pull off than it looks—is told largely from a child's point of view, but with enough grown-up humor slipped into the mix to keep adults attentive, the 81 minute feature is a smart blend of realistic antics and exaggerated cartoon action.

The single-sided dual-layer DVD presents a letterboxed version on one layer and a full screen version on another. The letterboxing has an aspect ratio of about 1.77:1 and no 16:9 enhancement, masking a lot of picture information off the top and bottom and adding just a little to the sides. Because it comes from a TV show, or because the framing just looks better, we preferred the full screen image. The color transfer is fine. The animation falls into a sort of halfway point between a well-made television cartoon and a fancy animated feature film, but the colors are rich and the focus is sharp. The stereo surround sound and Dolby Digital sound are great fun. There are many simple but energetic separation effects, and the audio has a lot of energy. There is also a French language track, English closed captioning, a trailer and a 4 minute *Catdog* promotional short.

Rumble Fish (Universal, 20389)

Based upon one of S.E. Hinton's realistic juvenile novels, the narrative covers several days during which important changes occur in the hero's life. He loses his girlfriend, drops out of school, is involved in a couple of fights, and witnesses a tragedy caused by his brother's return. Francis Ford Coppola's directoral pizzazz makes the film highly repeatable and stimulating, and he pays close attention to the greater social transitions Hinton was exploring with her characters, but the melodrama becomes a bit thick at the end and, conversely, what happens to the characters—even at the climax—never seems all that important. Matt Dillon and Mickey Rourke star, with youthful appearances by Nicolas Cage, Samuel L. Jackson and others.

The strikingly stylized black-and-white cinematography looks terrific, with effectively detailed contrasts. The picture is letterboxed, with an aspect ratio of about 1.85:1 and no 16:9 enhancement, adding significant picture information in comparison to full screen versions. The stereo surround sound is also great, with a strong bass, pure tones and distinctive separation effects. The film is also available in French and can be supported by English, French or Spanish subtitles. There are some production notes, a cast profile section and a theatrical trailer that includes a color shot not used in the film.

Rumble in the Bronx (New Line, N4410)

True, **Rumble in the Bronx** isn't a very good film, and it doesn't help that the American distributor has snipped about 15 minutes of narrative out of it, but it has plenty of Jackie Chan's wild stunts and action scenes. Chan portrays a visitor to the States (as has been pointed out elsewhere, the film, though set in New York, was shot in Vancouver and looks it) who runs afoul of a motorcycle gang and comes into the possession of some stolen diamonds a crime syndicate would like to obtain. The story is fairly silly, and the cuts make parts of it difficult to follow. The action scenes are really nowhere near as good as in the best Chan films, but they do hold up well in comparison to, say, the typical James Bond picture. There is one leap between buildings that makes your heart jump out of your mouth and a chase on a hovercraft through downtown Vancouver—whoops, New York—that is as much fun as the tank chase in **GoldenEye**.

The stereo surround sound is substantially softer than the surround sound on the LD. They almost seem like different mixes. Voices on the DVD are much lighter and the sound effects seem suppressed or distanced. Fortunately, the DVD has a Dolby Digital track that is about on par with the LD (which didn't have Dolby Digital). The specific Dolby Digital effects are stronger than the stereo effects on the LD, but the dialogue on the LD still seems to carry a bit more weight than the dialogue track on the Dolby Digital mix. The 91 minute film is presented in letterboxed format on one side, with an aspect ratio of about 2.35:1 and an accommodation for enhanced 16:9 playback, and in cropped format on the other. Cropping hurts some of the action sequences but doesn't seem to do much other damage, and the close-ups it creates can be appealing as an alternate view of the film. The picture looks super, and details are sharp. The cropped image looks good, too. A theatrical trailer for the American release appears in letterboxed format on the letterboxed side and in cropped format on the cropped side. There is also a brief biography and reasonably lengthy filmography for Chan. The film is available in French without Dolby Digital (even the French dialogue sounds more forceful than the English dialogue on the standard stereo track) and comes with English, French or Spanish subtitles.

Run Silent, Run Deep (MGM, 907500)

The classic submarine adventure, with Clark Gable as the Ahab-like captain and Burt Lancaster as his no-nonsense exec, is in letterboxed format on one side, with an aspect ratio of about 1.66:1 and no 16:9 enhancement, and in cropped format on the other side. Directed by Robert Wise, the 1958 feature, set during World War II, has several effective plot turns and a number of exciting—though now somewhat commonplace—submarine action sequences. The cast, which also includes Jack Warden and Don Rickles, is great fun, and the film delivers everything one wants from a submarine movie.

The black-and-white picture quality is excellent. Contrasts are carefully defined and the image is crisply detailed and effectively textured. Damage to the source material is minimal and most sequences are spotless. The monophonic sound is fine. The 93 minute feature has optional English and French subtitles, and a trailer.

Runaway Train (MGM, 907018)

A film that we disliked at first but that has grown on us over time, John Voight and Eric Roberts star in the macho 1985 action film, about two escaped convicts stuck on an out-of-control locomotive barreling through the wilderness. The Andrei Konchalovsky feature, from a story by Akira Kurosawa, is in letterboxed format on one side, with an aspect ratio of about 1.66:1 and no 16:9 enhancement, and in cropped format on the other side. Fleshtones are a bit pinkish, but never severely so, and contrasts are a little dark, but manageable (the LD looks nicer). The stereo sound is okay. Dimensional effects are limited and the dialogue has a subdued dynamic range, but the audio is a little zestier than a monophonic track would be. The 112 minute film is also available in French and comes with English, French or Spanish subtitles, along with a theatrical trailer.

The Running Man (Artisan, 60455)

Arnold Schwarzenegger stars in the silly but fast-paced and satirical futuristic action film, in which he has to get from one place to another in a life-or-death TV game show. The picture is a little too dark and fleshtones are a bit too purplish. The image is in letterboxed format, with an aspect ratio of about 1.85:1 and no 16:9 enhancement, and is in full screen format on the other side. The letterboxing adds nothing to the sides of the image and masks off screen information from the top and bottom in comparison to the full screen image, which is the version we prefer. The stereo surround sound mix on the 1987 feature is not all that elaborate. The sound is a little harsh, but reasonably energetic. The 101 minute film is apparently accompanied by English closed captions. There is also an effective theatrical trailer.

Running on Empty (Warner, 11843)

River Phoenix stars with Martha Plimpton in the 1988 teen romance directed by Sidney Lumet. Phoenix portrays a high school student who is forever changing schools because his parents are wanted by the law, and the dilemma that develops when he falls in love.

The picture is presented in full screen format. Fleshtones and wood tones are accurate, other hues are sharp and well detailed, and the image is crisp. The monophonic sound is somewhat weak, but there is a Dolby Digital mono track that is a bit brighter. The 116 minute film also has a French mono track and is adequately closed captioned.

The movie strains credibility, but never ceases to be thoroughly involving. It asks viewers to believe that a pair of socially maladjusted criminals would be in every other way the model of harmonious domesticity, but uses that premise to create an intriguing dilemma for the boy. The script writers even had the audacity to stir rich grandparents into the plot convolutions. Everything in **Running on Empty** is false, but it is the sort of falsity that makes people fall in love with the movies and helps them run away, at least for a while, from the problems that are dogging them.

Rush Hour (New Line, N4717)

Jackie Chan pairs with Chris Tucker in the 1998 action comedy about two cops from opposite sides of the Pacific who team to find a kidnapped girl. Parts of the story may be illogical and there is more grandstanding than there is character development, but the performances are very funny, the stunts are outstanding and the film is effectively paced, preventing the viewer from questioning too much about what is going on. Elizabeth Peña and Philip Baker Hall are also on hand, and there is a consummate Lalo Schifrin musical score.

The program is letterboxed with an aspect ratio of about 2.35:1 and an accommodation for enhanced 16:9 playback. The picture is glossy, with bright, crisp colors. The stereo surround sound and Dolby Digital sound are fine, and the gunshots and music are distributed with zest. The 97 minute program can be supported by English subtitles.

The director, Rob Ratner, provides a fairly informative commentary. He's in his twenties, and **Rush Hour** was his second feature film, so he talks a lot about what he's learned so far about making movies, explaining, as well, why Chan, who has probably had scores of offers to make films in the U.S., chose his project. He talks about integrating improvisations with the script and about how the two actors worked together ("The same way that Jackie adlibs physically when he'll grab a prop and use it in a fight, Chris will use a person to work off of"). He explains the reasoning behind his most significant choices and offers a little background on the logistics of the shoot.

Movie fans, however, may be even more enamored by an excellent second commentary track from Schifrin, who speaks between the cues of his isolated score. (It is also a kick to watch the comical body movements of Chan and Tucker in the action scenes without the dialogue or sound effects.) Schifrin talks about his entire career, sharing many anecdotes and insights, and is also adept at breaking down his thought process for scoring the film at hand, offering tidbits that only dedicated students of music would know (in Chinese music, notes such as A sharp and B flat are differentiated, which is why it sounds off key to western listeners) and citing examples from his past work to explain why he approached each theme in the manner that he did. It all comes together at the end, when he shares a lengthy reminiscence about growing up around opera, states that he felt the score should be operatic for the big final shootout, and then gives way as the music swells with an energetic grandeur. It sent chills down our spine.

We never thought we'd get tired of 'making of' movies but, at 40 minutes, the 'making of' featurette included on the DVD has just about everything but the crew doing dishes in a kitchen sink. The good stuff is great—Chan goofing off on the set (he can make a circle with one hand and a square with the other at the same time), Tucker adlibbing, outtakes, etc.—but there are shots of takes being rewound on video monitors and other redundant sequences that even the most dedicated fans will feel impatient with.

Also included on the DVD are Ratner's student film, *What Ever Happened to Mason Reese*, in which the former advertising star is assassinated by the altitude-challenged Michael J. Anderson from *Twin Peaks*; a brief collection of deleted scenes that explain where the heroes got their tuxedos but otherwise have little to offer; two music videos, one incredibly colorful effort by Heavy D (including a commentary by Ratner, who explains how the colors were achieved, with a new Fuji film stock) and one set in Hong Kong by Dru Hill (also with commentary); a good cast & crew profile section; and the very successful trailer. There is also DVD-ROM material, featuring the script and a couple games.

Rush Week (Simitar, 7295)

The kind of movie that **Scream** was making fun of, it is a typical slasher feature, fairly low in the gore department but with a little topless nudity and some very amusing 'threat' sequences as the masked killer stalks his victims with a double bladed axe (it looks great as a shadow). The 1989 film is set, obviously, in a college fraternity milieu, and the heroine is a young journalism major who apparently isn't taking any classes as she tracks down the story of several missing coeds. The picture is somewhat bland with dull fleshtones. There are smears, tiling and other artifact distortions in the darker shots. The stereo sound is reasonably loud but the mix is bland. The film runs 94 minutes. Roy Thinnes stars as the college dean and Greg Allman is also bopping around. The DVD includes a Thinnes filmography and is not captioned.

S

Sabotage (see **Alfred Hitchcock Collection**)
The Sadist (Allday, 97080001)

A full fledged *Deluxe Widescreen Collector's Edition* of a lurid low budget 1963 thriller, Arch Hall, Jr. (his father ran the company

and tried to turn him into a rock star through the movies) portrays a merciless delinquent killer, who takes three teachers hostage at a remote rest stop. This poses an interesting marketing point, because although the teachers are the nominal heroes of the film, the movie's target audience clearly identifies with the villain. He toys with them and humiliates them as they try to come up with schemes for escaping. There is nothing cheesy about the movie. It is a serious concoction and, although it lacks complexity, it is relatively efficient and unafraid of raw emotions.

The black-and-white image looks terrific, with strong contrasts and a crisp focus. During the middle of the film, small circles appear on the image momentarily in a couple of shots, but overall the source material is in very good condition for an obscure drive-in type film, and the monophonic sound is fine. The picture is letterboxed with an aspect ratio of about 1.66:1. The 91 minute movie is accompanied by trailers for two other Fairway films and some interesting production notes. The DVD's most valuable component, however, is a commentary track by acclaimed cinematographer Vilmos Zsigmond. Prompted by Stuart Galbraith IV, Zsigmond talks about everything from the behind-the-scenes skinny on how **Sadist** was shot to how he got out of Hungary with documentary footage of the 1956 Russian invasion to details on shooting *McCabe and Mrs. Miller* and *Close Encounters*. His talk is a perfect mix of technical insight and general information, as well as providing a portrait of his own personality and aesthetic sense. It is a must for film students, even those who had expected to pass on studying **The Sadist**, and casual viewers as well will find it to be at least as interesting as the film itself.

Sagebrush Trail (see **The John Wayne Collection**; **Young Duke Series: The Fugitive**)
The Saint (Paramount, 154967)

A somewhat cerebral spy film based upon the suave TV series, Val Kilmer stars as an international thief who becomes emotionally involved with one of his victims, played by Elisabeth Shue. We don't know about you, but our eyes roll up to the sky whenever anybody starts talking seriously about cold fusion, yet that is the linchpin of the film's plot, a formula that the Russian Mafia wants to obtain to solve the former socialist republic's energy crunch. Much of the film was shot on location in Moscow.

There are a few modest action scenes and some high tech paraphernalia, but most of the film emphasizes the conflicts of personality between the hero and those he meets, and the hero's ability to baffle his opponents. We liked it, but we doubt many viewers have quite as eccentric a taste for adaptations of arcane TV shows, and that cold fusion stuff does get pretty silly towards the end.

The picture is letterboxed with an aspect ratio of about 2.27:1 and an accommodation for enhanced 16:9 playback. The stereo surround sound is a little light, and the menu-activated Dolby Digital track is good, with lots of separation effects, a strong and busy bass, and a nice clarity of detail. The 118 minute film is also available in French in standard stereo and can be supported by English or Spanish subtitles. There is a theatrical trailer, and the film's director, Phillip Noyce, provides a commentary track.

Noyce reads much of his talk from prepared notes, but he has a clear and forceful voice that is easy to follow. His focus is on the film's background and production. He talks about growing up in Australia and how, because of that country's infamous history, he responded to the criminal hero in the novels that were the basis for the TV show and previous films. He doesn't talk too much about working with the camera, but he covers all other aspects of the shoot thoroughly, speaking at length about how the actors helped form their parts; how the music was conceived and contributes to specific scenes; how filters were applied to achieve certain color schemes; how those color schemes were maintained; how and why the sound effects were applied; how the foreign dubbed releases were prepared (he runs a bit of the soundtrack in French); how the Russian locations were utilized (the rat race in the night club was for real); and what it means to be a director. The film's special effects coordinator, Robert Grasmere, also pops up briefly to explain how some of the key effects were done.

Sally of the Sawdust (Image, ID4739DSDVD)

W.C. Fields stars in D.W. Griffith's 1925 circus film, adding his own brand of entertainment to Griffith's melodramatics. The mix is very effective. The narrative has the typical Griffith pathos and last minute rescue but, thanks to the presence of Fields and the stimulating setting, it is a mature work with an adept blend of comedy and drama.

There is a very slight windowboxing. The black-and-white picture looks quite good for its age and has a very slight mauve tint. The image is very sharp, there are no major instances of damage and minor wear marks are rarely intrusive. The stereo soundtrack features a pleasant piano score, taken from the film's original cue sheets and performed by Philip Carli. The film runs 113 minutes and movement is natural looking.

Salò (Criterion, CC1539D)

Ostensibly about a group of Italian Fascists gathered at a country estate during the War and performing de Sade-style rituals on a collection of young male and female prisoners, Pier Paolo Pasolini's pornographic film is less a political condemnation than a raw demonstration of the invidious power Age exercises over Youth. The film is also anti-erotic—it is pretty much anti-everything—but it has obtained a cult following for the numbing severity of its artistic posturing and for the few scattered moments of legitimate eroticism Pasolini sprinkled through the work like bait for a trap.

The image is letterboxed with an aspect ratio of about 1.85:1 and no 16:9 enhancement. The picture is very soft, but colors are deep and fleshtones are workable. The monophonic sound is fairly scratchy and muted, but seems appropriate. The film is in Italian and is accompanied by optional English subtitles. Voyager identifies their presentation of the 1975 feature as the 'uncut, uncensored version.' The LD jacket listing said the film's running time was 115 minutes, while the DVD's listing is a more accurate 112 minutes (the time encoding clocks in at 111 minutes and 29 seconds). Reference works, however, claim the film runs 117 minutes.

Salomé (see **Clive Barker's Salomé & The Forbidden**)

Salt of the Earth (Pioneer, DVD1005)

The 1954 film was made by blacklisted filmmakers about a strike among Hispanic mine workers in New Mexico. Based upon an inspiring true story, about the wives of miners who join picket lines, the film has a satisfying, upbeat conclusion. It was made under great duress (the cast members were arrested, or had never acted before; none of the processing plants would touch the negatives; even sound studios turned down the filmmakers when they wanted to work on the audio track), and so the movie's rhythm is inconsistent. Visually, it is an impressive film, and the first three-quarters of an hour would probably work better if all the dialogue and narration were replaced with a few well-chosen title cards. Many of the actors were non-professionals, real miners from New Mexico. Their line readings continually bring the pace of the film to a halt, but the black-and-white cinematography always gives the viewer stimulating input, and the whole cast perks up when they stop their contrived suffering and begin to relive the actual year and a half they spent on strike. The politics are elaborate, as the wives of the miners win gains not only from the mining company, but from their husbands. The drama is redeemed in the movie's second half, as the nitty-gritty strategies by both parties in a mine worker strike really start to unfold. The story has also a happy ending, which helps immeasurably in movies like this.

The source material has an inevitable amount of minor wear and the image jiggles slightly, but picture is very crisp and often very clear. The monophonic sound is adequate. The 94 minute film is accompanied by *The Hollywood Ten*, a 15 minute documentary about America's political environment at the time **Salt** was being made (some of the members of the 'Hollywood Ten' contributed their efforts to **Salt**). Additionally, the DVD has many rewarding text supplements, including extensive, original editing notes, an itemization of the movie's shooting schedule, a copious time line about the production, extensive cast & crew profiles, many production photos and essays about the black list, the real mining strike that inspired the film and other related topics. If **Salt of the Earth** is a movie that needs a context to be fully appreciated, then the superb DVD delivers everything a viewer requires to admire the film. Neither film is captioned.

Sam Kinison: Why Did We Laugh? (Fox Lorber, WHE73007)

A documentary about the comedian who shouted a lot, since Kinison died young (in a car crash that was the other guy's fault), there is plenty of room in the 93 minute program to provide a complete biography and still have time for a liberal selection of his best routines. Rare video footage from his earliest gigs are included and there are reminiscences from his family and friends that provide a fairly well-rounded portrait of his hard-driving life. One gets the sense that, artistically, he had already stalled by the time he died and had not found the steps to the next plateau, yet there is also the sense that although his material was strongly misogynist he would not have faded into obscurity the way Andrew Dice Clay has. He wasn't cynical about his act, just wired and, sometimes, over-wired. The picture quality varies depending upon the source material. Some of the clips are very grainy and others look quite fresh. The sound is uneventful and is not captioned.

Samurai I: Musashi Miyamoto (Universal, SAM100)
Samurai II: Duel at Ichijoji Temple (Universal, SAM110)
Samurai III: Duel at Ganryu Island (Universal, SAM120)

We tend to look at Hiroshi Inagaki's **Samurai** trilogy as a single five hour epic. Toshiro Mifune stars as the title character in the first film, who gradually ages and becomes wiser as the films, which were produced in 1954, 1955 and 1956, progress. He is also involved in a protracted triangular romance that earns resonance and power the longer it takes to be resolved. The films are very rewarding (the first has a complete enough narrative that it can be watched separately, if you want to sample just one), painting a detailed picture of the Japanese past with enough drama and action to keep a viewer fully attentive.

The picture on the three movies is presented in full screen format. The colors are somewhat faded but usually workable. The image is also fairly soft looking in places, and has its share of stray markings. The monophonic sound is a bit weak but passable and the films are in Japanese supported by optional English subtitles. **I** runs 93 minutes, **II** runs 103 minutes and **III** runs 104 minutes. Each is accompanied by an enjoyable original Japanese theatrical trailer.

Sanctuary (Sterling, 7055)

The hero is a former commando for a super secret government agency who retires to the priesthood when he becomes disgusted by intra-agency shenanigans, but is then drawn back to the intrigue when his former boss raises the stakes. The stunt work is very good and the story, sometimes told as a flashback within a flashback, is involved enough to keep one concentrating. Mark Dacascos stars.

Because of the film's budget, the picture quality is inconsistent, but the best sequences look sharp, with glossy colors. Bright hues in weaker sequences tend to be blurry and darker scenes are a bit grainy or slightly mis-colored. The stereo surround sound is terrific for the film's budget and genre, with smooth, energetic tones and plenty of aggressive separation effects. The 103 minute film can be supported by Spanish subtitles and is accompanied by an effective trailer and brief profiles of the cast and the director.

Sandokan the TV Movie (see **The Princess and the Pirate**)

The Sands of Iwo Jima (Republic, 45570)

The classic 1949 Allan Dwan feature stars John Wayne as a sergeant who whips his inexperienced squad into shape and takes them into battle.

The black-and-white picture transfer is outstanding. The image is spotless and smooth, with crisp, finely detailed contrasts. The monophonic sound is fine. The 102 minute program also has a Spanish language track, optional English, French or Spanish subtitles ("Nous combattons pour notre pays/Dans les cieux, sur terre et sure les mers…") and a trailer. There is a 16 minute retrospective documentary as well, hosted by Leonard Maltin. Although he says little about the battles upon which the film is based, the story of how the film was made (it was all shot at Camp Pendleton) and its subsequent success is well covered, including interviews with surviving personnel and with Wayne's son.

As a drama, the film has not aged well, and its non-battle scenes can be taxing, but the battle sequences are exciting and the immaculate picture quality can carry a viewer through even the worst cliches.

The Santa Clause (Buena Vista, 14898)

The 1994 film has been so popular that we have noted a significant increase in the instances of people misspelling Kris Kringle's other name, and it is a brisk, imaginative comedy that provides the right mix of humorous one liners, special effects and holiday emotions. Tim Allen stars as a divorced father who becomes the real Santa, much to the delight of his son, who gets to go along in the sleigh. The script is a mess, the characters, even the hero, are wildly inconsistent, and the special effects don't look that great. There is a sense of effortlessness, however, that overrides these other considerations. The film looks like it was thrown together without much attention to the finer details, but it is a workable fantasy. It is funny and it gets to the heart of what Christmas is about—believing in Santa Claus when all logic and reason say you should not.

The picture looks excellent, with sharp, pure and very fresh-looking colors. Fleshtones are accurate and the darker portions of the image are solid. The presentation is letterboxed with an aspect ratio of about 1.85:1 and no 16:9 enhancement. The film's audio track is fairly basic and not all that showy, but the stereo surround sound and Dolby Digital soundtracks are adequate. The 97 minute film is accompanied by a good theatrical trailer. The movie is also available in French in standard stereo and can be supported by English subtitles.

Sappho Sextet X-rated (Lipstik, 31172)

The hardcore effort, which runs 70 minutes, is set in an exercise gym, where the owners convince patrons they will have better workouts if they are nude, and then videotape the exercises for subsequent sale. The program features older-looking images with grain, ghosting, aged colors, and substantial video smearing in places, as well as monophonic sound that is often distorted on the upper end and subject to sporadic dropouts. Narrative development is limited and the erotic staging has a somewhat dated feel.

Sarah McLachlan: Video Collection 1990–1998 (Nettwork, 500019)

An impressive collection of music videos, there is nothing overly original about any of the clips, nor is there anything exceptional about McLachlan's singing, but her vocals have a pleasing clarity and the videos have a very satisfying variety of styles. No two are alike. In one, McLachlan is dressed as Biblical characters in a succession of Old Testament tableaux, in another she's a torch singer in a cabaret, in another she's in the woods, in another she's in the desert, in another she's a mud creature near a stream and in another she's on the floor in the lobby of skyscraper. In some she's dressed to the nines and in others she's naked. We never got tired of the collection, because, like her vocals, the images were always fresh.

The picture on the older videos is somewhat grainy or hazy, with over-saturated hues, but the newer videos are sharper, with more stable colors. The stereo sound is fine, with most of the songs sounding like good studio recordings. The 63 minute program features *Vox, Steaming, Ben's Song, The Path of Thorns, Into the Fire, Drawn to the Rhythm, Possession, Hold On, Good Enough, I Will Remember You, Building a Mystery, Sweet Surrender* and *Adia*.

The Satanic Rites of Dracula (Anchor Bay, DV10503)

The 1973 Hammer feature is set in London in the early Seventies, and it has the atmosphere of a spy movie. Christopher Lee is Dracula, the head of a corporation who is bent on taking over the world, and Peter Cushing is Van Helsing, working for British Intelligence. Joanna Lumley is Van Helsing's daughter. The film is brisk and has plenty to offer, including gore, sex, motorcycle chases, and Sixties decor.

The image is sharp, and hues are bright and pleasing, but fleshtones are indistinct. The monophonic sound seems a bit muted. There is no captioning. The 87 minute film is presented on one side. On the other, there are American and British theatrical trailers, plus a half hour *World of Hammer* episode. Hosted by Oliver Reed, the offering contains extended excerpts from a number of Hammer Dracula films, but the narration is rarely informative.

Savage Garden: The Video Collection (Sony, CVD50170)

The DVD has just five videos and runs 20 minutes, but the videos are brand new and not just dusted off greatest hits being recycled. The group is young and their music has no real edge, but it is energized and moderately complex, so it is easy to get hooked on their act. The videos are cluttered, but appealingly busy and add to the songs without reiterating them visually. The picture looks fine. The stereo surround sound and menu-activated Dolby Digital sound are excellent, with a strong sense of immediacy and a full dimensionality. The DVD also contains a profile of the Australian band and optional English lyrics.

Scared to Death (see **The Bela Lugosi Collection**)

Scarface (Universal, 20175)

Brian De Palma's influential modern gangster film stars Al Pacino as a Cuban drug lord in Miami. We have problems with Pacino's accent and feel that the film's last act goes over the top, but the first half of the film is riveting and others are enthralled by the movie's excesses.

The 1983 film is letterboxed with an aspect ratio of about 2.35:1 and no 16:9 enhancement. Fleshtones are a bit pinkish, the image is a little dark, removing details from the shadows, and image has a slightly worn look in places, but it is generally acceptable. The stereo sound is a little subdued, but the film's dated mix is not very elaborate. The film can be supported by English, French or Spanish subtitles. There is a good retrospective documentary that is also subtitled, an extensive collection of outtakes and several trailers. The 170 minute film is presented on a single-sided dual-layer platter and also comes with a brief cast profile and production note section. We could not locate the production stills section the jacket notes claim are included.

In the documentary, screenwriter Oliver Stone admits to having used cocaine for a while and claims that writing the screenplay was an integral part of his withdrawal therapy. Al Pacino, who stars, admits that he took his accent over the top, in an anticipation of De Palma's usual film style. And De Palma points out that the famous chainsaw scene, like the drill scene in *Body Double*, is all based upon the power of suggestion, with no gore beyond a little splatter of red here and there. The film was initially rated 'X' by the MPAA, but was upgraded without changes after De Palma brought lawyers and experts to a hearing to justify the truthfulness of the film's depiction of the Florida drug business. At least he didn't have to justify Pacino's accent. The documentary covers most of the production and is fairly interesting—except for a few key establishing shots, the outdoor scenes were done in Los Angeles (you could have fooled us)—but some key facets to the film are left unmentioned, including the music, the costumes and the influences of **The Texas Chainsaw Massacre** and *Miami Vice*. The outtakes, which haven't been given individual chapters, don't add much to an understanding of the film (one character, who dies early on, is fleshed out a little better), though they do let the viewer bask a bit longer in the movie's atmosphere. There are about 200 publicity and production photos, including some of Stone's father and De Palma's father.

The Scarlet Pimpernel (Madacy, DVD99023)

The 1934 black-and-white classic about a British aristocrat who rescues members of the French aristocracy from the guillotine has very little action and quite a bit of talk, but it has romantic appeal (the Pimpernel's wife doesn't realize her husband is a dashing hero) and a fair amount of intrigue. Leslie Howard, in whom a heroic demeanor is a near impossibility, nevertheless stars.

The picture is very blurry throughout, with plenty of scratches and other wear beneath the blur. Artifacting is rampant and the monophonic sound is harsh, with a distorted upper end. The 95 minute program is not captioned.

Scent of a Woman (Universal, 20260)

The director, Martin Brest, frames the story of a suicidal blind man, portrayed to widespread honors by Oscar-winner Al Pacino, in a rousingly upbeat tale about a school boy who won't snitch on his classmates. Running 157 minutes, the film is long enough to be two movies because it *is* two movies, or rather one sandwiched between two halves of another, and due to Bo Goldman's relentlessly witty dialogue and Pacino's pleasing performance, Brest can flirt with suicide, despair other weighty subjects and still leave viewers grinning and wiping away a tear or two. Chris O'Donnell co-stars.

The 1992 drama is presented in dual-layer format. The picture is letterboxed with an aspect ratio of about 1.85:1 and an accommodation for enhanced 16:9 playback. The colors are somewhat pale throughout, with bland fleshtones, though the image is sharp. The stereo surround sound, which features a striking musical score by Thomas Newman, has a limited dimensionality compared to more elaborately mixed audio tracks, but is in passable condition. The film is also available in French and can be supported by English or Spanish subtitles ("¿Me escuchas? Son perlas de sabiduría"). There is an informative production notes section that talks about Pacino's preparation for his role, and a brief cast profile section.

Sci-Fighters (Image, ID5620FMDVD)

Roddy Piper stars as a detective in the future investigating the spread of an alien virus. Some of the film seems to have been directly inspired by **Blade Runner**—shot for shot in one sequence—with a bit of **Alien** thrown in. Although it is ultimately concerned with action and not speculation—the villain gets wasted, but a larger threat is left unresolved—the futuristic touches give the viewer more than fistfights and gunplay to savor.

Hues are a somewhat drained and fleshtones are bland, but the image is reasonably sharp and the transfer probably does the cinematography all the justice it can. The stereo sound has a few decent separation effects and is passable. The 94 minute program is not captioned.

The Scope X-rated (Vivid, UPC#0073214588)

A man finds a telescope that lets him see the future, but the images he views interfere with his love life. The narrative is efficient and reasonably clever, and the erotic sequences are adequate. Colors are a little light, some fleshtones are yellowish and the image is mildly grainy. The monophonic sound is weak, with scattered dropouts. The 71 minute program features Madelyn Knight, Sind-

ee Coxx, Nina Hartley, Sharon Kane and Kimberly. The DVD contains alternate angle sequences and elaborate hardcore interactive promotional features.

Scream (Buena Vista, 13070); Collector's (Buena Vista, 15638)

The regular R-rated 111 minute version of the self-consciously definitive 1996 slasher thriller is presented on the standard version, even though the commentary channel it contains comes from an unspooling of the longer director's cut version, featuring director Wes Craven and screenwriter Kevin Williamson, including the references to the footage of blood-curdling gore that is no longer there. There is also an enjoyable red tag theatrical trailer.

The DVD producers have gone through a lot of trouble to release a *Collector's Series Widescreen* edition, too, and the supplement includes some nice behind-the-scenes materials that haven't appeared anywhere before, but the producers still used the standard theatrical cut of the film instead of the gorier and more unnerving director's cut. Since the audio commentary track appears on the standard DVD as well, what you get for the premium price of the *Collector's Series* edition is a 'making of' featurette, some production sketches, extra interviews with the cast and crew where they talk about their favorite horror movies, additional behind-the-scenes footage of Drew Barrymore's shoot, and lots of trailers and TV spots.

On both, the picture has been letterboxed, with an aspect ratio of about 2.35:1 and no 16:9 enhancement. Fleshtones are deep but contrasts are a little too dark and some details get lost in the shadows. Colors are crisp and the picture is generally acceptable. The stereo surround sound is adequate, and the Dolby Digital track has a powerfully manipulative dimensionality, with lots of thrust. Both have English subtitling.

Scream 2 (Buena Vista, 14377)

There is no moment in the sequel equal in emotional resonance to the scene in the first film where the heroine overhears two other girls talking about her in the bathroom, but the sequel does pay superior attention to character development and story in comparison to the average slasher sequel, along with providing the requisite more murders and more frights. The 1997 film is set on a college campus and stars the gang left standing at the end of the first movie, including Neve Campbell, Courteney Cox and David Arquette.

The film is letterboxed with an aspect ratio of about 2.35:1 and no 16:9 enhancement. The picture has bright, sharp colors and decent fleshtones. The stereo surround sound and Dolby Digital sound toss up crisp little surprises at appropriate moments. The 120 minute film can be supported by English subtitles, and there is a marvelous theatrical trailer.

Screamers (Columbia TriStar, 11869)

A genuine science fiction movie and a good one, two warring factions on a mining planet must combine forces when a self-generating weapon released by one of the sides achieves evolution. Directed by Christian Duguay, the 1995 film was written by Dan O'Bannon and Miguel Tejada-Flores and based upon a story by Phillip K. Dick. Peter Weller stars. The narrative has logical flaws and other shortcomings, but it conveys the big ideas very nicely—indeed, it is the ultimate logical conclusion to the contemporary arguments about the banning of land mines. It also has an effective, other-worldly atmosphere and there are some exciting action sequences.

The presentation is letterboxed on one side, with an aspect ratio of about 1.85:1 and an accommodation for enhanced 16:9 playback, and is in full screen format on the other. Colors are reasonably sharp and fleshtones remain consistent in difficult lighting situations. The stereo surround sound and Dolby Digital sound are okay, though the film's audio mix hasn't got the power of the big budget sci-fi productions. The 108 minute program also has

French and Spanish audio tracks, optional English, French or Spanish subtitles, and a trailer.

Sea of Love (Universal, 20226)

Al Pacino and John Goodman give engaging performances as detectives investigating a murderer preying upon those who search for romance in personal ads. Ellen Barkin is the main suspect. The mystery is fairly simple, but the film's exploration of vulnerability has an enduring appeal.

The picture is presented in full screen format only. Fleshtones are slightly purplish, but the image is very sharp and the presentation is workable. The stereo surround sound has a limited mix and details are not carefully defined, but the audio is not distorted. The 113 minute 1988 production is also available in French and comes with English or Spanish subtitles ("Yo creo en la atracción animal"). There is a very interesting trailer that has shots and scenes that didn't make it to the film's final cut, as well as a production notes section and a small cast profile section.

Search for the Great Sharks (SlingShot, DVD9836)

Any program about sharks has a basic appeal, but the IMAX presentation doesn't offer much more than that. Most of the program depicts shark scientists trying out a new shark repellent (it doesn't work) and a Plexiglas-type shark cage (since the sharks can't smell through it, they aren't as attracted to the people inside). The film uses some cheap editing effects to enhance the excitement, and if you can't get enough of sharks, then the program certainly delivers, but its value is limited.

The picture quality is fine, though there are some minor artifacting effects that create faint ratcheting and smears as the brighter sharks pass by through the dimly lit water. The Dolby Digital sound is not elaborately dimensional, but seems adequate. There are alternate French, Spanish, Castilian, German, Japanese and Chinese language tracks, as well as a music-and-effects track, all in Dolby Digital, and optional English subtitles. The program runs 38 minutes and is accompanied by an 8 minute 'making of' featurette.

The Searchers (Warner, 14651)

Many consider John Ford's **The Searchers** to be John Wayne's best movie. It is certainly one of his best performances. He laughs and cries and has genuine changes of heart. The story is more problematic. Wayne portrays a Confederate war vet who returns to his brother's homestead, which, after a moment's grace, is burned to the ground by an Indian raiding party. His niece is kidnapped and most of the story covers the years he spends trying to locate her. And the first time they find her, he tries to shoot her, for she is grown, nubile, and clearly knows her way around a teepee. **The Searchers** is controversial because of the attitudes expressed by the characters, in all likelihood quite natural for their time and setting. Indian men are usually referred to as 'bucks.' Women who have been retrieved from their clutches are insane or catatonic. Yet it is this attitude, far more than director Ford's penchant for loving details of the Old West, that gives the film its edgy power. The hero, personified by Wayne, is no better than the Native American terrorists he is chasing, and everyone in the film knows this.

The 1956 film is presented on one side in letterboxed format, with an aspect ratio of about 1.85:1 and an accommodation for 16:9 enhancement, and in full screen format on the other. The letterboxing adds picture information to the sides of the image and takes a bit off the bottom in comparison to the full screen presentation. The letterbox framing is superb.

The outstanding color transfer even makes the white snow look whiter. Tricky lighting sequences, such as scenes taking place at sunset, remain accurate no matter how complex the shadows and shadings become. The fleshtones are rich, and the occasional glob of bright color slipped in here and there is stunning. Most of the film has earthy, Old West tones, which obtain an almost varnished veneer with the Technicolor restoration. The monaural sound retains a mild scratchiness one would associate with the film's age, but it is acceptable. The 119 minute film is accompanied by wonderful excerpts from two episodes of a promotional black-and-white *Warner Bros. Presents* television series, hosted by Gig Young, from the Fifties, showing behind-the-scenes footage and interviews with some of the cast. There is also a small cast and crew profile section, a few minor production notes and a trailer. The film can also be accessed in French or Spanish and can be accompanied by English, French and Spanish subtitles ("Ne comptez pa là-dessus.").

Seasons: A Journey Through Vivaldi—Cyberlin (Platinum, 2310)

Some good-looking African wildlife footage accompanies the classical music program. Cyberlin, conducted by Lee Johnson, is a mix of strings, woodwinds, piano and percussion, but it makes for a somewhat bland interpretation of Vivaldi's *Four Seasons*, essentially filling in and suppressing the tensions of Vivaldi's original composition by overloading the orchestration with instruments. The piece runs 32 minutes and the program concludes with a much stronger 23 minute work, *The Colors of a Soul*, written by Johnson and better adapted to Cyberlin's format. The Dolby Digital track is airier and better separated than the standard track.

Seberg, Jean (see **From the Journals of Jean Seberg**)

The Secret Adventures of Tom Thumb (PolyGram, 8006355872WR01)

A superb but very bizarre 57 minute stop-motion animated feature combines what appears to be stop motion live action using human actors with clay figures and other manipulated objects. The narrative follows the experiences of the thumb-high hero, who is born to human parents, but is taken away to a science lab, where he escapes with the help of some strange creatures and eventually meets more of his own kind, all of whom are being terrorized by humans. Then, the small ones go on the attack. The animation is outstanding, providing not only foreground action, but enough background action (insects wandering around the characters, for example) and shifts in setting to support many extra viewings. The images are consistently fascinating and a little bit disturbing. Fans of the medium, however, will find it to be 57 minutes of sheer brilliance.

Colors are a little light, but generally the picture quality looks good, with reasonably sharp details. Darker sequences are stable. The picture is presented in full screen format, and it is difficult to say whether a smidgen is missing from the sides or not, though there would be no more than that. The stereo sound is okay, and has a modest dimensionality. There is virtually no dialogue (only a few scattered words in the mumblings of the characters are discernible) and so there is no captioning. Included with the film is a 10 minute short by the same filmmakers entitled *The Saint Inspector*, which is basically an imaginative, single-gag featurette, about a very fat man living on top of a large pole. There is also a biography of the filmmakers and a listing of the awards **Tom Thumb** has received.

Secret Agent (see **Alfred Hitchcock Collection**)
Secret Games 3 (Simitar, 7364)

Clearly inspired by *Belle de Jour*, the Gregory Hippolyte film morphs into a psycho thriller, but in the beginning parallels to *Belle de Jour* are blatant and much of the movie is given over to softcore erotic sequences. This is the R-rated version, and the running time, which has no similarity to the time listed on the jacket cover, logs in at 80 minutes. The image is a little hazy in places, but the colors are strong and the picture is workable. The stereo sound has limited separation effects but, it seems unusually amplified and comes across with a crisp immediacy. There is no captioning.

The Secret Garden (Warner, 19000)

The classic story, about an orphaned girl who helps teach her bedridden cousin to walk and appreciate life, is given a modern and more generalized approach in the 1993 feature, directed by Agnieszka Holland, so that its emotional payoffs are more subdued and, in theory, more far-reaching. Maggie Smith portrays the wicked housekeeper.

The film is letterboxed on one side, with an aspect ratio of about 1.85:1 and an accommodation for enhanced 16:9 playback, and in full screen format on the other side, with more picture information added to the top and the bottom of the image and some taken away from the sides. The cinematography is outstanding and the letterboxed framing is preferred, but the full screen images pose no real problems. The colors are a little dark and somewhat pink, but overall they look terrific. The image is crisp and smooth. The stereo surround sound is quite satisfying, with plenty of energy and separation effects. The 102 minute film is supported by English, French or Spanish subtitles, and is accompanied by cast and crew profiles, extensive production notes and a couple trailers.

The Secret Life of Walter Mitty (HBO, 90654)

Danny Kaye portrays a chronic daydreamer who becomes involved in real intrigue. The movie shows the daydreams, and some are clever because of the subtle ways they include details from the outside. Boris Karloff co-stars.

The Technicolor hues look fabulous. Each color is solid and glossy, and the enhanced detail created by the crisp DVD playback gives every gorgeous chromatic display an eye-popping vividness. The colors are so grand that, rather like the hero, you tend to let your mind wander across them and forget to pay attention to the story. The transfer rate rarely rises above midlevel, but we could detect no significant artifacting. The 110 minute film is presented in English in either monophonic or stereo playback, with the stereo bringing a mild dimensionality to the musical score, and is also available in French or Italian in mono, with optional English, French or Spanish subtitles. The DVD's chapter encoding offers a cute alternate chapter selection that takes the viewer directly to the daydream sequences. There is an introduction/interview with co-star Virginia Mayo, an original trailer, and a cast & crew profile section.

The Secret of Anastasia (UAV, 40089)

A made-for-video animated program that tells the tale of a Russian princess who tries to prove her heritage to a group of exiled aristocrats while secret police lurk about intending to abduct her. The program runs an hour and is combined with a half-hour cartoon, *Snow White and the Magic Mirror*, another obvious feature film derivation. Both efforts, however, are reasonably entertaining. *Snow White* has quite a bit of humor (the mirror does celebrity imitations), while **Anastasia** is a decent mix of action and narrative, with a strong ending. The animation on both efforts is equal to a typical TV show and works just fine. The colors are solid and bright, and the sound is adequate. The program is not captioned.

The Secret of My Success (Universal, 20412)

Michael J. Fox stars in the farcical comedy in which his MBA character works his way up from the mailroom in a short period of time. His character has no dark side, but the 1987 film is very appealing. Helen Slater and Margaret Whitton co-star as his amorous interests.

The picture is letterboxed with an aspect ratio of about 1.85:1 and no 16:9 enhancement, masking picture information off the top and bottom in comparison to a full screen version and adding a little to the sides. The framing looks fine. The color transfer is good, the image is sharp and fleshtones are accurate. The stereo surround sound is workable, but the audio is a little muted. The 101 minute film is also available in French and Spanish, and can be supported by English or Spanish subtitles. There is a decent production essay, a brief cast and director profile section and two very similar theatrical trailers.

The Secret of NIMH (MGM, 907037)

Don Bluth's meticulously animated feature is in full screen format. An informal survey tells us that young children have difficulty following the 1982 film's narrative, about extra-intelligent mice trying to establish a new home, but the artwork is so captivating that it really hardly matters. The mice move from one dilemma to the next, and your attention follows because the images are so imaginative and the colors are so compelling.

There are a few minor speckles here and there, and the deepest reds are mildly blurry, but the color transfer looks beautiful and hues are effectively delineated. Despite the occasional blurs, the details are exquisite. There is a kind of generalized stereo mix and some tones are a bit clipped, though the sound presentation is passable. The 82 minute program can be supported by English or French subtitles and is accompanied by an original and somewhat stodgy trailer.

Secrets X-rated (DaViD, D0190)

The only dialogue is presented in voiceover. The heroine is a call girl visiting several clients, with the semblance of a narrative pretending to explore corruption and immorality among the wealthy in L.A. Without the characters talking to one another, however, there is only so much that can be accomplished. Some of the erotic sequences are energetically staged, but the premise is bland. Shot on film, the image is erratic, shifting in quality from one sequence to the next. In general, colors are a bit light and the picture is somewhat blurry. The monophonic sound is tolerable. Ashlyn Gere, Zara Whites, Jeanna Fine, Samantha Strong, Sunny McKay, Danielle Rodgers, Valerie Stone, Nicole Wild and Krystina King are featured in the 85 minute program.

The Seduction of Mimi (Fox Lorber, FLV5020)

Although the jacket cover lists running time of Lina Wertmüller's film as 89 minutes, as do several reference books, the movie actually runs 105. Many of Wertmüller's early films were trimmed and rearranged by the distributor and, covering a lot of narrative ground, the 1972 movie deliberately jumps ahead in time without much warning in places, but the presentation appears to be fairly complete. The film is letterboxed with an aspect ratio of about 1.75:1 and the color transfer looks quite good, with bright hues and accurate fleshtones. The source material does have a few noticeable damage marks early on, but on the whole the presentation is admirable. The monophonic sound is fine and the program is in Italian with optional yellow English subtitles (which identify the film's real title, "Mimi the Metalworker Wounded in Honor").

Giancarlo Giannini, made up to look like Charlie Chaplin, stars as a Sicilian blue collar worker who takes in a mistress during a job in the north and brings her back with him when he is transferred home. Wertmüller's sense of comedy is based on a kind of grimy realism that does not seem as severe today as it did when the film first appeared, and the film's topical political comments (essentially concerning the interests of the communists and the interests of the Mafia) turn out to have enduring pragmatic insights. There are extensive filmographies for Wertmüller, Giannini and co-star Mariangela Melato, and sharp-eyed film enthusiasts will be amused by the typographical error in Giannini's listing.

Selena (Warner, 14909)

Jennifer Lopez stars as the Mexican-American singing star (she spoke no Spanish as a child) who was shot by a deranged employee just as her career was about to leap into the American mainstream. Edward James Olmos co-stars as Selena's father, and adeptly carries the dramatic weight of the movie, including some of the best speeches but also some of the most contrived conflicts, on his shoulders. The movie undoubtedly simplifies and glosses over the truth—and until her tragic end (which is downplayed in the film) there really wasn't much in her life for Hollywood to sink its fangs into—but it also crystallizes and preserves the essence of what Selena accomplished in her brief meteoric career. Unlike an album or a book, **Selena** gives the viewer an opportunity to recognize the links between the artist and her art, and to better appreciate both because of the dimensions those links create.

Shot in Super-35, the 129 minute feature is presented on one side in letterboxed format, with an aspect ratio of about 2.35:1, and in full screen format on the other. The full screen image crops a bit off the sides but adds substantially to the top and bottom of the picture in comparison to the letterboxed image. Most of what it adds, though, is filler, and the film has a tighter, more dynamic feel when presented in the letterboxed format. The color transfer looks good, with sharp, glossy hues and accurate fleshtones. The stereo surround sound is dull and even the Dolby Digital track seems a little soft and under detailed. The film is also presented in French and Spanish in Dolby Digital and can be accompanied by English, French or Spanish subtitles. There is a decent sized cast profile section and production notes that explain how some, but not all, of the film's most interesting sequences were achieved.

Serenity (see **Moodtapes: Serenity**)

The Serpent and the Rainbow (Image, ID4625USDVD)

Wes Craven's breakthrough 1987 film is about a scientist investigating voodooism. Bill Pullman stars in the film, which seems in a number of ways similar to—and would make a good double bill with—**Altered States**. The film remains grounded in reality for most of its 98 minute running time, and it is only at the end that it cops out by delving more completely into fantasy. It is still an enjoyable film, particularly after a viewer is aware of where it is headed, but our feeling has always been that folks went overboard for it because they were just happy to see Craven moving beyond things like **Shocker**.

Anyway, the picture on the DVD looks terrific. It is letterboxed with an aspect ratio of about 1.85:1 and an accommodation for enhanced 16:9 playback. Colors are bright, fleshtones are accurate, the image is sharp and even darker sequences look solid, with detailed contrasts. The stereo surround sound has some energy and plenty of dimensionality. The program is accompanied by a fairly compete Craven filmography and is not captioned.

Sesame Street's 25th Birthday: A Musical Celebration (Sony, LVD51319)

The 60 minute collection features highlights from the *Sesame Street* TV program, including *Rubber Duckie, Alligator King #7, "C" Is for Cookie, Count It Higher* and many more. It is not focused intensely on learning, but there are a few songs about counting and other educational subjects. The regular puppet characters and a few guest stars are seen, but none of the regular human performers who appear on the show are included. Because of the emphasis upon the puppets and the animation, most children will find the DVD fairly entertaining and a strong candidate for automatic replay. Some of the clips are monophonic, but most of the program is in stereo. Colors are so bright that there is a mild haze around yellows and reds, but otherwise the image is very sharp and even the oldest clips look fresh. There is no captioning.

Seven (New Line, N4381)

Brad Pitt and Morgan Freeman are detectives (with a rebellious student/patient teacher relationship) investigating murders staged by a serial killer with a strong creative bent in the superbly moody thriller. Although set in a generic city in the present day, the movie has an atmosphere reminiscent of **Blade Runner**—it's constantly raining—and the crime scenes look like something out of **Brazil**.

The director, David Fincher, was meticulous about maintaining the 1995 film's dark tone. He even used a special printing process on a few of the theatrical prints but, outside of major metropolitan venues, viewers were left with a film that looked so dark they could

barely see what was going on. The picture transfer on the DVD is true to Fincher's original vision. The colors are consistently accurate and the image is shiny and crisp, no matter how dark and murky the film's environment becomes. For some reason, the 127 minute film is split to two sides. Although they've found an appropriate place for the side break, the interruption is still bothersome. The film is letterboxed with an aspect ratio of about 2.35:1 and no 16:9 enhancement. The standard stereo surround sound is not as bright as the Dolby Digital track, but the Dolby Digital track is excellent, with carefully measured variances in volume—when the movie wants to knock you over, it does—and elaborate separation details. The program is also available in French in standard stereo and can be supported by English, French or Spanish subtitles. There is an elaborate cast profile section, as well.

Seven Beauties (Fox Lorber, FLV5040)

Considered by some to be Lina Wertmüller's masterpiece, Giancarlo Giannini stars as an Italian soldier during WWII who does what he must to survive in a concentration camp, while flashbacks depict how he ended up in the army, after murdering his sister's pimp. It is an audacious work, and we tend to find it somewhat superficially grotesque, but there is no denying the power and mordant humor of its best sequences.

The picture is letterboxed with an 1.7:1 and no 16:9 enhancement. The picture is sharp and is free of noticeable wear. Colors are reasonably strong, fleshtones are workable and, on the whole, the presentation looks very good. The monophonic sound is also in reasonably good condition. The 1972 film is available in either Italian or English and can be supported by optional English subtitles.

Seven Brides for Seven Brothers (MGM, 906567)

Howard Keel and Jane Powell star in the 1954 classic, about pioneers who kidnap a group of women to be their brides. The musical is brilliantly conceived, with wonderful, straightforward songs, fantastically athletic dancing, superbly integrated choreography and enjoyable romantic conflicts. It is hard to resist in any format.

The film is presented in letterboxed format only, with an aspect ratio of about 2.55:1 and no 16:9 enhancement. The bright, solid hues and accurate fleshtones are so precise that every shot is captivating and every musical number is transcendent. The film has been given a Dolby Digital track, but we could not tell any difference between that track and the standard track. Both have a limited dimensionality and separation effects, but provide a better Hi-Fi tone than a mono track could muster. The 102 minute feature has optional English and French subtitles ("Je suis un homme solitaire/Je traîne mes tristes jours/Où est la femme qui aura pitié de moi/Et que m'aimera en retour/Je ne peux tout de même pas…"), a trailer, and a 35 minute retrospective documentary, hosted by Keel. The documentary is wonderful, gathering many of the original cast members as well as director Stanley Donen and choreographer Michael Kidd. They explain how the film was conceived, how it was produced under adverse conditions (a change in regimes caused its budget to get sliced), and how it succeeded in the end (it got booked into Radio City Music Hall instead of the film MGM had shifted its money into, **Brigadoon**). Kidd also talks about how he worked out the dances and several cast members speak about the perils of performing the liveliest leaps.

The 7 Brothers Meet Dracula (see **The Legend of the 7 Golden Vampires**)

The Seven-Per-cent Solution (Image, ID4269USDVD)

If you have any friends who enjoy life and literature but, because of some sort of cultural isolation, are not familiar with **The Seven-Per-Cent Solution**, you can delight them by putting on the disc and scanning directly to the point where Sherlock Holmes and Dr. Watson arrive in Austria. From there you can let the film play out for about ten minutes and they will see everything through the eyes of Holmes instead of the eyes of Watson, who has tricked

Holmes into traveling to Vienna to cure the detective of a drug addiction. As Holmes reaches the final destination, charges up the stairs to grapple with the evil Dr. Moriarty, and is confronted, instead, by Dr. Sigmund Freud, the effect is marvelous even when you know everything which is going to happen and is totally magical for those who were unprepared for the surprise.

The movie works so well at this point because of the quality of the acting. Nicol Williamson, while he might not embody a traditional image of Holmes, is an excellent choice to embody Holmes beset by cocaine. He is rude. The reaction of many people when they learn that Robert Duvall is playing Dr. Watson—"but why?"—is answered in the seriousness of his portrayal. Duvall presents a Watson who is more believable than most others have been, one who is Holmes' equal, perhaps even his superior in emotional stability, but one who recognizes the supremacy of the detective's intellectual abilities and willingly accommodates Holmes' need of an assistant. Finally, there is Alan Arkin as Freud. His performance is the rare sort which increases one's appreciation of the craft of acting. He penetrates no inner psyche. Instead, in the best tradition of performers who give pleasure to their audiences, he puts on the beard and the accent, lifts his eyebrow every time Holmes drops a clue about the source of his addiction, and generally shows with his hands and his body that he is a young but serious man who thinks. His cooperative sparring with Williamson is all that a movie needs to make a viewer happy.

The presentation is in full screen format only, but it is likely the image composition would benefit from letterboxing. The image is very grainy, fleshtones are light and other hues are a bit pale. The monophonic sound is subdued and requires amplification, but there is a mono Dolby Digital track that is stronger. The 1976 film runs 114 minutes.

The Seven Samurai (Criterion, SEV040)

Presented on one single-sided dual-layer platter, Akira Kurosawa's 203 minute action adventure film looks terrific. The black-and-white source material is clearly the same that was used for previous home video releases, but blacks are purer, the image is crisper and minor scratches and speckles have been cleaned up. The 1954 classic still looks somewhat aged, but skin textures are more vivid and the improved contrasts accentuate the compositional designs of each shot. The monophonic sound is okay, and the Dolby Digital mono track is a bit cleaner, toning down the wobble that intrudes once in a while on the musical score. The film is in Japanese and can be supported by optional English subtitles.

There is also a commentary track, by Michael Jeck, who has plenty of time to tell a history of the movie's production and also get into its artistic meaning. His knowledge is thorough and he is as at ease discussing Kurosawa's camera technique as he is discussing the economics of the Japanese film industry. If Jeck is remiss at anything, it is perhaps in the concentration on the mechanical elements of the narrative, particularly when the environment is involved. He points out that Kurosawa's use of wind and rain is deliberate, and tells how these occurrences affect the rhythm of the story, but he fails to note that these and other components have specific spiritual meanings that remain consistent throughout Kurosawa's films (e.g., rain is the cleansing of the soul).

Seven Years in Tibet (Columbia TriStar, 21819)

Brad Pitt stars as an Austrian mountaineer caught in Tibet at the start of World War II and the relationship he develops with the young Dalai Lama until the Chinese invade. The scenic vistas, scattered action scenes and cultural/historical explorations provide plenty of stimulating input. The film falls short of achieving higher goals because many of the changes that happen to Pitt's character occur offscreen and the narrative's memoir format retains a self-serving tone, but such drawbacks are really only worth considering when one is handing out awards and such. As a competent piece of entertainment it works fine. If you are an enthusiastic subscriber to the National Geographic you will enjoy the movie very much, and it contains enough legitimate history to give you an informed overview of Tibetan society and make you very angry at the Red Chinese. Jean-Jacques Annaud directed.

The 136 minute 1997 feature is presented on one side in letterboxed format, with an aspect ratio of about 2.35:1 and an accommodation for enhanced 16:9 playback, and in cropped on the other side. The cropped image, however, loses much of the film's exotic atmosphere. The picture transfer looks very nice, with crisp, accurate hues that make the mountain vistas all the more compelling. We were less impressed with the sound. The volume level on both the stereo surround soundtrack and the Dolby Digital track seems a bit subdued, but even when raised the separation effects and dimensionality feel somewhat limited. The film's musical score has a moderate ambiance, and then there are those sub-woofer-friendly Tibetan horns or whatever they are, but the audio track never seems to rise to its potential. The Dolby Digital track is a little better separated, but differences between the two tracks remain limited. The program also has a French language track in standard stereo, and optional English, French and Spanish subtitles.

The Seventh Floor (Simitar, 7319)

A passable psychological thriller, Brooke Shields stars as the widow of a partner in an advertising firm, who is getting squeezed out by the other partners. At the same time, however, she is oblivious to another threat against her that is far more dangerous. The Australian production has several interesting plot turns and even ends on a kind of science fiction or supernatural note. Provided one isn't expecting too much reality from it, the film is intriguing and Shields is an engaging heroine.

The picture looks fairly good. Colors are little bland but sharp, and fleshtones look fine. The sound is apparently monophonic, or stereo with a very limited mix, but is adequately delivered. The program runs 99 minutes and is accompanied by a Shields filmography. There is no captioning.

The Seventh Seal (Criterion, SEV100)

The image is sharp, with vivid contrasts, deep blacks and hardly a speckle of wear. Benefiting from a fresh transfer, even the full screen framing is improved, with more picture information on the sides of the image. The 1957 Ingmar Bergman classic is so famous, many of its images and ideas seem cliched, but the transfer brings new life to the film and cheats Death a bit longer. The monophonic sound is fine. The film is in Swedish with optional white English subtitles, and can also be accessed in English, though the dubbing seems incongruous with the medieval setting. There is a commentary channel by Peter Cowie. The talk is a bit heavy on the interpretation side, but it provides a decent primer on the film for students of the cinema or anybody so inclined. There is also a summary of Bergman's work, and there is a terrific Swedish theatrical trailer (which gives away the ending). Max Von Sydow and Bibi Andersson star in the allegorical tale of a knight and a traveling theatrical troupe who are dogged by a black-caped figure as they wander the countryside in the era of pestilence and straw pillows.

The Seventh Sign (Columbia TriStar, 70079)

The 1988 feature is presented in letterboxed format on one side, with an aspect ratio of about 2.35:1 and an accommodation for enhanced 16:9 playback, and is in cropped format on the other side. This in one of those films, however, where the cropping is worth a peek, because you can never tell when a character was going to pop up and startle the heroine. The letterboxing provides a more proper and involving presentation of the film, but it does remove a little of the nervousness enhanced by the trimming on the cropped presentation.

The movie is easier to take on multiple viewings, anyway, after the nature of its allegorical narrative is no longer a surprise. Demi Moore stars as an expectant mother whose unborn baby is apparently the linchpin of the Apocalypse. **Seventh Sign** may not be completely logical, but the story is different than most supernatural thrillers (it is reminiscent of Peter Weir's *The Last Wave*) and the performers are entertaining.

The picture transfer looks good. Hues are stable in all lighting conditions and fleshtones are consistently accurate. The stereo surround sound is adequate and the mix is reasonably good. The 97 minute program also has a French soundtrack and optional English and French subtitles.

Sex and the Other Man Simitar, 7456)

A second-rate three-character stageplay was turned into a 1995 film of equal stature with a hopelessly inept title. The story's stageplay structure is still painfully evident as a couple kidnap another man, leave him tied up while they make love, and then take turns leaving the room so the conversation can gradually reveal secrets about each of the characters. Kari Wuhrer is reasonably compelling and Stanley Tucci, the best known of the three, gives a competent performance—Ron Eldard is also featured—but the dramatic manipulations are never well enough disguised to let one be entertained or intrigued by the characters for more than brief moments at a time. At its worst, it is arch, illogical and tiresome, and its better moments are not insightful enough to compensate.

The full screen picture has weak contrasts, soft colors and pale fleshtones. The stereophonic sound is mostly not stereophonic, though the dialogue is clear enough to serve its purpose. The 89 minute program is not captioned.

Sex Censored X-rated (Vivid, UPC#0073214508)

A woman is trying to meet a deadline for an article about sex in literature, when the figures she is writing about suddenly pop up in her study to adjust her attitude. There are fewer erotic sequences than usual, and those that are included are rarely creative, but some of the dialogue is actually spent on valid discussions of literature, which has to count for something.

The colors are adequate, though darker portions of the screen are a bit smeary, and fleshtones are passable. The sound is a somewhat muted and requires amplification for clarity. The program runs 70 minutes. The DVD contains alternate angle sequences and elaborate hardcore interactive promotional features.

Sex Crimes (Simitar, 7210)

The only nudity occurs in the very first scene and there are only a couple other scenes of erotic content in the 88 minute program. The opening scene also involves saran wrap and whipped cream, but not with any logical sort of application. Most of the film is about a private detective tracking down the murderers of a financier. Some of the performances are tolerable (others are hopeless) and the plot keeps moving, but the movie, on the whole, is pathetically bad, and the DVD is no help. We have no idea if the fuzzy images and jerky background movements are part of the film's inept cinematography or artifact flaws in the DVD, but either way they are not pleasant to watch. The colors look drained and fleshtones are pale. There are several instances where the image jerks forward in the digital equivalent of a bad splice. The sound, which we suppose is stereophonic, is also quite alienating. It has zilch ambiance and seems disconnected from the images. There is no captioning.

sex, lies, and videotape (Columbia TriStar, 90489)

Steven Soderbergh's amusing tale of sibling rivalry and voyeurism is about two sisters with opposing personalities, the husband of one having an affair with the other, and a stranger whose video camera hobby upsets the domestic balance in the lives of both sisters. The film is a romance, but its addictive appeal is partially due to the camera setups and cinematography. There is one scene in one of the sisters' apartments where one character—the earthy one—is in a wood brown room and is dressed in warm tones, while the other—the prissy one—is dressed in white and is in a white outer room. The camera frames them so that the brown

room is in the center of the image, with the white room enveloping it, and the composition shows not only the dichotomy between the two women, but the 'inner' drive and 'outer' veneer that the characters must cope with. James Spader, Andie MacDowell, Peter Gallagher and Laura San Giacomo are featured.

The 1989 film is presented on one side in letterboxed format with an aspect ratio of about 1.85:1 and an accommodation for enhanced 16:9 playback, and in full screen format on the other side. The letterboxing masks off picture information from the bottom and top of the image, and adds an equal amount to the sides, but either framing seems workable. The image is richly colored and finely detailed.

There is both a stereo surround soundtrack and a 4-channel Dolby Digital soundtrack, but we really couldn't tell the difference between the two since most of the film is just conversation. The 99 minute film is also available in French and Spanish in standard stereo and comes with English, French or Spanish subtitles ("Faisons une vidéo") as well as an enjoyably saucy trailer. Soderbergh provides a commentary track with Neil LaBute (director of **In the Company of Men**). Recorded several years and jobs after the film was made, the talk is fresh and allows Soderbergh to view the work from a wider and more experienced perspective. The track is highly informative, as the two directors discuss in detail how to work with actors and some of the more technical aspects of the shoot.

Sex Machine X-rated (Vivid, UPC#0073214529)

A **Crying Game**-style twist provides a rousing finale. The narrative is about a widow listening to a tape her late husband has left her, with flashbacks to the husband's infidelities. Shot on videotape, the colors are strong, fleshtones are accurate and the image is crisp. The dialogue has an erratic volume, but the monophonic sound is passable. The program runs 72 minutes and features Sindee Coxx, Micki Sinn, Melissa Hill and Jill Kelly. The DVD contains alternate angle sequences and elaborate hardcore interactive promotional features.

Sex Show X-rated (Vivid)

A fairly humorous 79 minute program about the tribulations of a host for a *Tonight Show*-type adult entertainment program, the action switches between his 'on air' performance and the problems backstage, where guests are delayed by erotic distractions and he himself is being stalked by an unhappy lover. The erotic sequences are fairly standard, but the premise and its elaborations are reasonably creative. The picture appears to be from a film source, but is in very good condition, with accurate colors and a crisp focus. The dialogue is badly recorded, fading in and out of volume depending upon where the characters are positioned. With that exception, the monophonic soundtrack is workable. The DVD contains alternate angle sequences and elaborate hardcore interactive promotional features.

Sex Zone X-rated (Vivid, UPC#0073214499)

The narrative begins promisingly, about a woman and a man on the run from drug dealers, and the performances make a decent stab at depicting addiction, but the conclusion to the 75 minute program is rushed, which is a disappointment. Some of the erotic sequences are freshly staged. The picture is rather grainy when the characters are not in direct outdoor light, and colors are a little bland. The sound is adequate. The DVD contains alternate angle sequences and elaborate hardcore interactive promotional features.

Sexual Malice (Simitar, 7269)

A woman who has become bored with her marriage begins an affair with a male stripper that ends in murder. The 96 minute 1993 film is heavily padded with softcore erotic sequences, but the story has some nice, logical twists, so fans of the genre should be pleased. The picture is reasonably sharp and colors are reasonably good, though the quality of the cinematography is inconsistent, with some sequences appearing more hazy or paler. The stereo sound is reasonably strong but a bit distorted on the high end and has not been captioned. Diana Barton is featured.

Sgt. Bilko (Universal, 20279)

Based upon the old Phil Silvers TV show (which, people seem to forget, was originally spun off of *You'll Never Get Rich*), Steve Martin stars as a conniving motor pool sergeant whose income schemes are threatened when an old commander visits his base. Dan Aykroyd does a very nice turn in the Paul Ford role, but every time we looked at Martin our brain longed to see Silvers in the part, hustling away. Still, the film is an enjoyable romp, with a number of humorous moments and a coherent narrative.

The presentation is letterboxed with an aspect ratio of about 2.35:1 and an accommodation for enhanced 16:9 playback. Colors are bright and fleshtones are passable. The audio mix is not elaborate but adequate. The stereo surround sound is a little weak, but the Dolby Digital track is okay. The 95 minute program is also available in French and Spanish in Dolby Digital and comes with English or Spanish subtitles ("¡Hagan eso de agarrar el rifle por abajo!"). There are some production notes, a cast profile section and a funny theatrical trailer.

Sgt. Kabukiman N.Y.P.D. (Troma, DVD9600)

Sporting an eye-catching holographic cover, the irreverent Troma film is accompanied by elaborate supplementary materials. Even the co-director, Lloyd Kaufman, speaking on a very well conceived commentary track, admits that the 1991 film was not one of his better efforts. About a New York cop who is given super powers by a dying Japanese mystic, the film straddles the dividing line between being a typical jokey Troma gross-out exercise and being a humorous comic book-style action film without committing to either genre. This is especially true of the DVD, which features the 105 minute 'Unrated Director's Cut,' with extensive gore sequences and an excruciatingly long car chase where the hero is dressed in a clown suit. Still, the film has its charms, particularly for those who enjoy the Troma brand, and the supplement, which appears on the other side of the DVD, is worthwhile.

It has been our experience that low budget film directors tend to be more involved in all aspects of their production, unlike the highly protected and somewhat isolated big budget film directors, and so they often have more interesting and practical things to say on their commentary tracks. Kaufman's track on **Kabukiman** is even better than his excellent commentary track on **Class of Nuke 'Em High**. He talks about how the film was financed (Japanese investors who, he admits, were disappointed with the end result), how and where it was shot, who contributed in front and behind the camera, and how he had trouble selling it after it was finished. He has an amusing story about how the monkey in the film was almost eaten by a lion it had been teasing, another story about how he almost got caught in the middle of a car crash he was staging, and an insightful tale about an attempt by an affirmative action group to close down his set to promote minority hiring, until they discovered that he hires more minorities than anybody in the film business (they come cheaper—what the group should have done was taken a hard look at the racial stereotypes within his films, which are unflattering at best).

The film's star, Rick Gianasi, speaks for about 15 minutes over appropriate clips from the film on side two. Much of side two contains typical Troma promotional burlesques, which some viewers will have the patience for and some will not (a couple sequences are identical to **Nuke 'Em High**, but several more are original), but there is an animated treatment for a proposed Sgt. Kabukiman cartoon that runs for several minutes, as well as a dozen or so movie stills and trailers for all of Troma's DVDs. The picture transfer on the film looks okay, with bright colors and a reasonably sharp image. The stereo sound is a low budget effort with subdued dimensional effects. The program is not captioned.

The Shadow (Universal, 20012)

We would have preferred having the hero's voice routed more exclusively to the surround track, but nevertheless the stereo surround sound and Dolby Digital sound a good deal of fun. Not only does the Shadow's voice beckon from every direction, but there is a strong, well-defined bass and a solid middle range of sounds, all of which add greatly to the film's pleasures.

Based not upon the popular radio program but the pulp magazines that inspired it, Alec Baldwin stars as the title character, battling for Manhattan and the world against a descendant of Genghis Khan, represented in a career-descending sort of way by John Lone. Directed by Russell Mulcahy, the film is great for a viewing or two, but it loses its uniqueness rather quickly and fails to achieve the right balance between fantasy and realism.

The 1994 feature is presented in full screen format only. Mulcahy likes to have things look glossy and that comes through on the disc, though the picture does become a bit grainy in places. Fleshtones look okay. The 108 minute program also has a French Dolby Digital track, and English and Spanish subtitles.

Shadowbuilder (see Bram Stoker's Shadowbuilder)

Shadowlands (HBO, 90968)

A genuine tearjerker of the first order, Richard Attenborough's 1993 film stars Anthony Hopkins as the famous author, C.S. Lewis, and Debra Winger as his wife, who dies just as they are learning the value of loving one another. The film has a relaxed intellectual atmosphere—it is set at Oxford—and is as much about Lewis' attempts to codify and analyze sorrow as it is about their relationship. Winger and Hopkins are delightful and the film delivers heartache without bitterness or schmaltz, a rare accomplishment in or out of Hollywood.

The DVD adds to the 133 minute film's pleasures considerably. There is an thoughtful and very satisfying 5 minute 'making of' featurette, accompanied by about an additional 10 minute of outtakes where the cast members speak further and in more depth about their characters and the film's meanings. Included is a comment that had never dawned on us before, but seems instinctively true—all love relationships end in pain. In other words, if you don't break up, one of you eventually dies. There is also a 7 minute montage of behind-the-scenes footage with live sound, showing a number of sequences in the film being shot, and a trailer and a half dozen TV commercials, along with the usual cast & crew profile section.

The picture is in letterboxed format only, with an aspect ratio of about 2.35:1 and no 16:9 enhancement. The picture quality is very good, with bright, crisp hues and accurate fleshtones. The stereo surround sound is not elaborate but is adequately delivered. There are alternate French and Spanish audio tracks, and English, French and Spanish subtitles.

Shadows of the Invisible Man (see Dose Hermanos: Shadows of the Invisible Man)

Shakedown (GoodTimes, 0581018)

The stunts are so wild the producers had to put an admonishment at the end warning viewers that the stunts were performed by professionals and should not be attempted at home. Darn—we were just going to run out, get into a Porsche, drive to the airport as a jet plane is warming up, identify immediately the plane we want when we spot it on the runway and race to it during takeoff, climb onto the wheels, set off an explosion to destroy the jet in mid air, and escape unscathed. Well, it looks easy enough when you see Sam Elliott doing it.

Elliott's presence is just one of the 1988 film's advantages. Normally his long flowing locks and gruff appearance prevent him from becoming a believable character, but here, as a cop who has probably been undercover for too long, he fits right in. The story is about police corruption and drug lords, and also stars Peter Weller, who portrays that most popular character, a distracted public defense attorney who believes his client in spite of himself. Much of the film is contrived and weakly scripted, but it is still an enjoyable effort.

The picture is presented in full screen format only, but the color transfer is impeccable, with bright, solid hues and accurate fleshtones. The stereo sound is fine and the 96 minute program has optional English, French and Spanish subtitles.

Shalako (Anchor Bay, DV10621)

Nothing on the platter label tells you which side of the 1968 western starring Sean Connery and Brigitte Bardot is letterboxed and which side is cropped, and the opening credits on both sides are letterboxed. The cropping, which is on side one, is fairly useless, though it does give you bigger close-ups of the stars. The letterboxing has an aspect ratio of about 2.35:1 and no 16:9 enhancement. The color transfer looks terrific. Fleshtones are rich and hues are carefully delineated. There is an occasional minor speckle that hints at the film's age, but for the most part, it looks terrific. The sampling rate, however, is unusually low, running at about half of the standard rate, and whenever the camera moves, parts of the background, away from what your eye should be centered on, go soft momentarily. It isn't a major flaw, but some viewers will find it mildly distracting. The monophonic sound is okay and the 113 minute feature is not captioned.

Honor Blackman is also featured, with Stephen Boyd and Jack Hawkins. A group of effete game hunters wander onto a reservation and are threatened by bloodthirsty Apaches. Connery is a scout who tries to save them, in spite of themselves. Blackman's demise is memorable—it's the only thing we could recall from seeing the film when it first came out. Based upon a novel by Louis L'Amour, the Edward Dmytryk film is sustained by its star power. The action scenes aren't all that well handled, but the narrative has plenty of forward movement and it's a kick seeing Connery and Bardot so far out of their element (his hairpiece is a gas).

Shallow Grave (PolyGram, 8006352752)

In movies, money always seems to bring out the worst in people, and that is what happens in Danny Boyle's **Shallow Grave**, about three roommates at odds about what to do with the suitcase full of cash they discover with a fresh corpse in their apartment. The 1995 film, set in Scotland, is a terrific mix of bright dialogue, sharp performances, languid camera angles and violent tension. The Scottish accents also add to the lyricism of the dialogue, and the setting is fresh and different.

The single-sided dual-layer presentation is letterboxed on one layer, with an aspect ratio of about 1.85:1 and an accommodation for enhanced 16:9 playback, and is in full screen format on the other side. The color transfer looks crisp and hues are accurate even in dim light. The stereo surround sound rarely uses much power, but it is nicely detailed and sharply defined. The 92 minute program has optional French subtitles and English captioning.

Shame X-rated (Vivid, UPC#0073215528)

Shot on film, it is an elaborate western with lots of production value, about men who have been dressing up as Indians and abducting women. Led by an enigmatic Indian female, the women band together and fight back. Although there are the obligatory erotic sequences, the film is not shot or edited like a standard hardcore feature, but like a real western, with outdoor vistas, detailed costumes and locations, and a far greater variety of camera angles than is common on X-rated features.

The program is almost monochromatically orange, probably on purpose, though it looks murky and grainy. The monophonic sound is muffled and requires amplification. The 81 minute program features Kaitlyn Ashley, Leena and Isis. The DVD also contains alternate angle sequences and elaborate hardcore interactive promotional features.

Sharky's Machine (Warner, 22024)

The heart of the film is a re-working of *Laura*, but the romance is at odds with the generally violent tone of the film. Based upon a William Diehl story, Burt Reynolds directed the film and stars in the title role, as a vice detective who feels the heat after his investigations uncover corruption at some very high political levels. Despite Reynolds' use of overlapping dialogue in the ensemble scenes and a gritty pugnacity in the action sequence, the film has a slow pace and is of primary interest to fans.

The source material still has some noticeable scratches, and fleshtones are not as fresh as they could be, but for the most part colors are bright and the image is sharp. The picture is in full screen format and the framing seems workable. The jazz musical score on the stereo surround soundtrack tends to overpower everything else, but the presentation is adequate. The 122 minute program is closed captioned with minor paraphrasing.

She (Kino, K114)

Randolph Scott and Nigel Bruce star as explorers in the Arctic who uncover a lost civilization living in a large, cozy, well-illuminated underground nook. Helen Gahagan is their leader, an immortal, and a look-alike ancestor of Scott's character stole her heart several centuries before. The narrative has the format of a cliffhanger serial, but the production is fancier, with elaborate crane shots, lovely matte paintings and a few special effects that defy explanation. The 1935 Merian C. Cooper production directed by Irving Pichel and Lansing Holden.

Although the source material is heavily scratched, with a couple disruptive splices, the image is sharp. In the weakest passages, the black-and-white picture has smeary edges and weak contrasts, but other sequences look reasonably crisp, with smooth and nicely detailed contrasts. The monophonic sound and Dolby Digital mono are weak, eliminating noise, but removing too much ambience at the same time. The 94 minute program is not captioned.

Shine (New Line, N4546)

With the exception of a couple brief sequences placed near the beginning for obvious reasons, Geoffrey Rush, who won the Oscar for his performance, does not appear until the 105 minute film's final 40 minutes. What he does when he finally arrives on the screen, however, is exhausting, and it is a total physical and psychological makeover that conveys the full essence of the pianist David Helfgott and his idiosyncratic, slightly unglued demeanor. The director, Scott Hicks, worked on the film for more than a decade before finally bringing it to the screen, and for the most part it is very effectively designed. There are a few sequences, however, such as Helfgott's initial breakdown, that Hicks seems too close to and appears unwilling to share with viewers less steeped in Helfgott's biography. Such sequences are momentarily disorienting, breaking the spell the movie has over the viewer, but they are also minor annoyances in what is otherwise an admirable and uplifting accomplishment. Tracing Helfgott's life from childhood, the film is intended to create an emotional portrait of the ebbs and flows in his experiences, as opposed to the specifics of his biography, demonstrating the power music has to keep the musician, however tenuously, linked to the rest of the world.

The film is presented in letterboxed format only on one side of the DVD, with the trailer, Rush's witty Golden Globes acceptance speech, and an interview with Hicks presented on the other side. The interview gives the viewer a worthwhile overview of the film's conception and production. These segments do not have subtitling. Hicks also provides a written introduction to the film on the jacket cover that summarizes what he was attempting to accomplish. The letterboxing has an aspect ratio of about 1.85 and an accommodation for enhanced 16:9 playback. The image is sharp and you can see details and textures in well-lit portions of the screen, but the picture is often a bit too dark and fleshtones are a little too pinkish. The stereo surround sound is not forceful, but the Dolby Digital track is reasonably satisfying. The film is featured as well in

French without Dolby Digital and comes with English, French or Spanish subtitles, along with a small cast profile section.

The Shining (Warner, 17369)

In the commentary channel on **Storm of the Century**, Stephen King talks about his dissatisfaction with Stanley Kubrick's **The Shining**, and claims that was his motivation for sponsoring the TV miniseries remake. He also admits that the ratings failure of the miniseries was probably due to the popularity of the original movie. Well, we're glad he went and made it again, but we're also glad Kubrick did his version. The 1980 film is that rare sort of horror movie that gets under your skin and imbedded in your memory, forgoing cheap thrills (there are moments where Kubrick deliberately chooses the least startling camera angle for a shot) to achieve something that is far more disturbing. We know people that feel uncomfortable to this day looking at pictures of Jack Nicholson or watching him act because of his performance as the mountain resort caretaker who goes mad and chases after his family with an axe. The film has many narrow sets, which seem to go in tandem with another popular Kubrick shot, the close-up with the bare forehead and eyes pointing upward, lit from below. Kubrick has often been accused of making 'dry' or non-humanist films, but a look at the performances of Nicholson, Shelley Duvall and others in **The Shining** demonstrates why this is a misconception. Because of his technical mastery, he is able to induce practically raw emotions from his cast, and their reactions to the horror are so believable you forget it is a fiction.

The film is presented in full screen format. There are many shots where it is clear that there is nothing but empty space above or below the characters, not only ruining the balance of the composition, but upsetting the film's claustrophobic atmosphere. There are speckles in the opening shot, and in several other places during the 144 minute film. The color transfer is lackluster. Hues are purposefully light and drab, and fleshtones still look accurate most of the time, but there are sequences where the image looks just a little too washed out or hazy, and fleshtones seem a bit too peachy. The monophonic sound is good and there is an alternate French audio track, optional English and French subtitles, and a trailer. Also included is an excellent 35 minute documentary by Kubrick's daughter, Vivian, that contains some of the only available footage of her father at work. The program explores aspects of a movie shoot most 'making of' featurettes avoid, particularly in its depiction of the actors preparing for their roles (and getting chewed out by the director). The video transfer on the short contains some track patterns and other minor flaws.

Shivers (Image, ID4602AVDVD)

David Cronenberg's first film, (also known as *They Came from Within*, among other things), the 1975 feature, a wonderfully grizzly horror film with an admirable artistic resonance, is about the occupants of a large apartment complex who become infested by a grotesque, mouse-sized parasitic slug that transfers its offspring to a new victim during sex. Blood abounds, as does Cronenberg's disdain for the sterility of modern design and happy endings. The film is a beginning (and low budget) effort, with erratic performances and an inconsistent pace, but it is also a very promising work that is both more thrilling and more rewarding than many of its kind.

Because of its low budget origins, there are limits to how nice the picture can look. Many shots are grainy, with pale colors, light contrasts and anemic fleshtones, though when the lighting is bright, hues are reasonably accurate and sharp. Also, the image jiggles a little in places, facilitating a digital artifacting flaw that causes brightly colored segments of the screen to appear detached from their surroundings. The picture is presented in full screen format, which we assume is how it was intended to be seen. The monophonic sound is okay, though it, too, has limitations one associates with its budget. There is a good, modern-sounding musical score. The 87 minute feature is not captioned and is accompanied by a theatrical trailer, as well as an excellent 10 minute interview with Cronenberg, where he talks about his experiences as a first time feature director and how **Shivers** was in many ways ahead of its time.

Shock X-rated (VCA)

The picture is crisp and the colors are vivid, but movement, especially during the non-erotic sequences, has a ratchety, video-on-computer look. When the distortion is not obvious the picture, which was shot on videotape, looks fine, and the narrative, about a virtual reality journey into a psychotic mind, almost allows the producers to get away with the effect, but it occurs just a little too often and too conveniently to be art. The program runs a full 130 minutes and is quite good for the genre, with a thoughtful plot, excellent special effects and inventive erotic sequences. The sound, which appears to be mildly stereophonic, has no problems. The extensive cast includes Jeanna Fine, Shayla LaVeaux, Juli Ashton, Tyffany Million and a number of others. The DVD includes cast profiles for several of the performers.

Shock Corridor (Criterion, SHO040)

Sam Fuller's **Shock Corridor** is a sober but deeply satirical depiction of a modern asylum, in which the patients are clearly intended to remind one of various American political and social philosophies. The narrative concerns a reporter who has himself committed in order to solve a murder. The closer he comes to the truth, however, the closer he comes to going insane himself. Filmed in Fuller's cigar-in-your-face style, the movie is an intense and memorable experience, and one well worth having even if repeat viewings are best separated by long periods of distraction.

The black-and-white image is super crisp, with vivid contrasts and deep blacks, and the source material is free of damage. The film is letterboxed with an aspect ratio of about 1.9:1 and no 16:9 enhancement. The monophonic sound is cleaner but bland. There is a Dolby Digital mono track, however, that bring a little more color to the dulled tones on the standard track, but there is still a tradeoff on the high end to get rid of the noise. The 1963 program is not captioned and comes with a theatrical trailer.

Shocker (Universal, 20436)

Guess what! It turns out it was Mitch Pileggi who plays the greasy supernatural psycho killer in Wes Craven's 1989 feature. We bet he's glad the movie wasn't a big enough hit to start a franchise. Anyway, the film is in letterboxed format, with an aspect ratio of about 1.85:1 and an accommodation for enhanced 16:9 playback. The color transfer looks very nice, with bright, smooth hues and a sharp focus, making the film's legitimately creepy first act all the more thrilling and its wild, surreal finale all the more spectacular.

Peter Berg stars as a high school football player who develops a psychic link with the killer and then must do battle after the killer is executed and comes back as a sort of electrically charged ghost who leaps from one host to the next. Near the end, Berg and Pileggi chase one another through a series of video screen images, a sequence that is as creative as it is nonsensical.

The stereo surround sound has a limited effects mix, but the hard rock musical score is very dimensional and there is a strong bass. The 110 minute film is also available in French and can be supported by English or Spanish subtitles. There is an informative production essay, a small cast-and-director profile section and a brief trailer.

Shoot Out (GoodTimes, 0581037)

If you're in the mood for a western and you're not too picky, you can do worse than the 1971 Universal feature produced by Hal Wallis, directed by Henry Hathaway and starring Gregory Peck. Peck is a former bank robber recently released from the pen, who is journeying to confront his old partner. The partner hires some young gunslingers to follow him, but being youthful and cocky, they interact with him instead. There is also a child, tagging along with Peck's character, reintroducing him to humanity. The story takes some contrived turns and does a lot of meandering as well, but the atmosphere is right and the performers are enjoyable, so unless you've got to get somewhere yourself, it's easy to sit back and go along for the ride.

The picture is also quite pleasing. The opening credits are windowboxed, so you can see that not an iota is missing from the edges of the full screen presentation. Some sequences are grainy and hues throughout are a little light, but the image is sharp and colors are well defined, so that even though the picture is imperfect, Hathaway has such an eye for his western settings that the image is usually quite pleasing. The monophonic sound is fine and the 94 minute program can be supported by optional English, French or Spanish subtitles.

Shoot the Piano Player (Fox Lorber, FLV5075)

Charles Aznavour stars as the title character, who becomes involved with gangsters. The 1960 François Truffaut film is a deft mix of humor and pessimistic drama, as amusing as it is bitter.

The black-and-white picture is sharp, with well-defined contrasts and very little wear to the source material. Occasionally the image has a little too much grain, but not very often. The letterboxed image is set high on the screen, with permanent English subtitles appearing beneath it to support the French dialogue. The letterboxing has an aspect ratio of about 2.251 and no 16:9 enhancement. The monophonic sound is a little scratchy but acceptable. The program is accompanied by trailers for a number of Truffaut films. Watch for the shadow of the camera, incidentally, at 14:48.

Short Cinema Journal 1:1 Issue: Invention (PolyGram, 4400465652)

A collection of sophisticated short films in a wide range of genres, it opens with a stop-motion animated short from the Will Vinton studios, directed by Mark Gustafson, called *Mr. Resistor*, which uses junk store objects, especially electrical doodads, to construct an amusing story about a wire figure man who covets the arms of a bowling trophy icon. That is followed by another animated sequence, a cartoon entitled *The Big Story*, in which three characters, all variations of Kirk Douglas, argue about a newspaper assignment. The segment that has been given an 'alternate' angle, presenting the original pencil tests, and in using the angle toggle, you can jump back and forth between the tests and the completed work.

The longest segment in the DVD is the 25 minute featurette *Some Folks Call It a Sling Blade*, a warm up to **Sling Blade** that was written and produced by Billy Bob Thornton, who also stars, but was directed by George Hickenlooper. The film is very similar to the opening 18 minutes of **Sling Blade**, and along with Thornton the film also features J.T. Walsh in the role he retained in the feature film. Molly Ringwald, however, is given the part that Thornton eventually hired an unknown Arkansas actress for, as the reporter interviewing Thornton's character. The film is in black-and-white and Hickenlooper's approach to many of the shots is more arty and less effective than the humanistic approach Thornton eventually used.

Among the other shorts on the DVD are a German film by Pepe Danquart, *Black Rider*, about an elderly woman who starts complaining when a black immigrant sits next to her on a bus; *Trouble*, by Carrie Blank, about a young girl who shoplifts to support her reading habits while her mother, played by Tovah Feldshuh, remains oblivious to her vices; an excellent 11 minute interview profile of the film director Michael Apted, that covers the highlights of his career as well as his philosophies on life and filmmaking; excerpts from the film *Baraka*, with the director, Mark Magidson, providing commentary on an alternate audio channel; *This Unfamiliar Place*, a brief documentary by Eva Ilona Brzeski about her father, a Polish immigrant who survived the Nazi invasion; another brief documentary, *Goreville*, about a genuine American town

whose citizens have a strong passion for owning firearms; *John Lee Hooker - Performance & Interview*, a superb 6 minute clip of Hooker talking in closeup and then performing in a music video that features a number of dancers; *Shape without Form*, a traditional abstract short film that has something to do with human suffering—the director, Stephen Berkman, tries to explain it on an alternate audio track; *Henry Rollins - Easter Sunday in NYC* by Albert Watson, a combination interview and performance video that is accompanied by three extra stereo Rollins numbers on three alternate audio tracks; and three very striking commercials, including one for an electric car, one for a video game and one, using the Tacoma Narrows Bridge, for Pioneer car stereos.

With more than 137 minutes of programming on one side, the DVD is not time encoded, though the jacket chapter listing provides exact running times for each sequence. The chapter search function cannot generally be used, because the DVD is designed to be accessed only from its own on-screen menu. Some sequences are Dolby Digital encoded and others are not. Throughout the collection, however, the picture quality is excellent and the sound is rich.

Short Cinema Journal 1:2 Issue: Dreams (PolyGram, 4400553932)

The second volume of the outstanding anthology series contains the half hour film that inspired **12 Monkeys**, Chris Marker's *La Jetée*. Made in the early Sixties, the film is a montage of black-and-white photographs (a 'photo-roman' as it is described in its own credits) accompanied by a voiceover narration (in English) that works sort of like a film treatment, telling a story that was perhaps too abstract to make into a real movie, even in the days of **Alphaville**. Although somewhat more impressionistic and far more poetic, the narrative essentially follows the same path as **12 Monkeys**, acquiring a great deal of resonance as the hero gets bumped between the past, the present and the future in a journey to find himself.

That piece alone would be worth obtaining the DVD for, but the **Journal** has much more to offer. There is a stunning 25 minute black-and-white film shot by Jane Campion before she began her feature work, *A Girl's Own Story*, which explores many of the themes she continues to return to, including the isolation of adolescence and the awkwardness of budding sexuality. A gloriously surreal short, *Eye Like a Strange Balloon*, by Guy Maddin, is open to dozens of viewings as it depicts a fantastic underwater train ride. Fred Savage stars in a dandy student film, *A Guy Walks into a Bar*, by Carmen Elly. Reminiscent of the works by Robert Rodriguez, the film has a terrific narrative, about a young man who picks up the wrong hitchhiker, and is a great deal of fun. A fascinating promotional reel for a film in search of funding, *The Big Brass Ring*, from a story by Orson Welles, was directed by George Hickenlooper and features just one extended sequence, starring Malcolm McDowell as an aging political advisor being queried by a young muckraking reporter. A shocking excerpt from an uncompleted documentary, *Vincent: The Junkie Chronicles*, by Michael Failia, is intended to de-glamorize drug use and features an interview with an articulate junkie, who talks about how the veins throughout his body have gradually failed him, and even shows him shooting up into a huge open sore on his calf. There is also another somewhat surreal short film, *Depth Solitude*, about a man who lives at the bottom of a swimming pool in a diving suit, and two animated shorts, *Cafe Bar*, from the early Seventies that was one of the first to make use of mutating sketches to depict a symbolic flow of emotions during what is, on the surface, a mundane occurrence, and *Bride of Resistor*, a stop-motion animation piece using found materials that is a sequel to a short appearing in the first **Journal**. Although *Bride* lacks the sense of originality the first short conveyed, it has a terrific punchline. And that is all on side one. Side two contains an exceptional, raw 55 minute 'making of' film, *The Making of Portrait of a Lady*. Focusing primarily on Jane Campion's work with the actors, the documentary filmmakers intrude upon the most intimate conversations and essentially capture a portrait of a movie that came close to tanking.

The picture quality is fairly good throughout the collection, although some of the black-and-white pieces are prone to mild tiling, smearing and other artifact flaws, including the *Making of Portrait* film. The sound quality varies from piece to piece but is in good condition over all. There are several listings of the chapters in the DVD packaging and they tend to vary at identifying what is and is not covered by supplementary features. Although it is claimed that there is an alternate video track for *A Guy Walks into a Bar*, we could not access it. *Bar* and *Big Brass Ring* feature filmmaker commentary tracks that discuss how the movies were shot and what went on during the production. *Depth Solitude* features alternate narrative tracks in French and Swedish.

Short Cinema Journal 1:3 Issue: Authority (PolyGram, 4400569612)

Alain Resnais' riveting 1956 documentary film about the Holocaust, *Night and Fog*, is the centerpiece of **3**. The theme of the third issue is 'authority,' a motif reflected not only in the shorts themselves, but in many of the audio commentaries accompanying them. As with past issues, there is also playful connective material between each short that we are not going to bother to get into. The picture transfers are competent and the sound, some of which is in stereo, is fine. The pieces are accompanied by informative production notes that are accessed through the Title function.

It must be remembered that until the mid to late Seventies, the Holocaust had undergone a kind of collective state of partial denial—not a disavowal of its occurrence, but an inhibition on the part of the arts and other media to explore it as a subject. *Night and Fog* was one of the few exceptions to this phenomena, and while it remains stunning even now after *Schindler's List*, *Shoah* and other works have provided a thorough elaboration, one can imagine how devastating it must have been to viewers when it first appeared. There are shots of people huddled, naked, awaiting execution, shots of the heads of victims being placed neatly in a pile, shots of cloth made from human hair and so many other horrifying atrocities. Yet Resnais focuses as much attention on something just as horrifying—the aesthetics of the genocide; that humans would not just kill other members of their species en masse, but that they would be evil enough to try and do it with style. The 30 minute film, which is partially in color, is accompanied by a 10–15 minute alternate commentary track by David Shepard, who describes the film's production history in better detail than the production notes can accommodate.

The collection's animated short, *Dada*, by Piet Kroon, is a clever and thought-provoking film about a world where people balance books on their heads and those with the most books are the most respected. The hero is a father who becomes exasperated when his child is born with too round a head to balance a book. The film is imaginative, and although its messages are fairly clear, it is so thoroughly thought out you are happy to share in the ideas and amusements of the filmmakers. Kroon, speaking on an alternate track during the 4 minute short, talks about shooting the cartoon with a universal language of images rather than dialogue, and how the work landed him a job at Warner Bros., though he doesn't talk about any of the compromises he's been forced to make in his new capacity.

Viewed without any background information, *Flying over Mother*, which is in Russian and is about a Russian cosmonaut remembering his childhood as he apparently plummets to disaster, seems humorous but incomplete—for one thing, you never learn what the cosmonaut's fate is. But then the credits roll by and you realize there are virtually no Russian names in the credit scroll, and if you look really close you learn what is verified in the 10 minute short's two accompanying commentary tracks—the film was made in an Australian film class by people who had no knowledge of

Russian whatsoever, and in that context its accomplishment is somewhat more admirable. The director, Michael James Rowland, gives a thorough talk about why he made the film and what its meanings were for him, while producer Melanie Coombs talks on her track about the actual production and how making a movie is like a non-divorcible marriage. She also says that the most difficult thing about making a film is communication—everything else is just details once you can accurately convey to others what your vision is.

A 15 minute Brazilian film, *Os Camaradas*, directed by Bruno de André, is a Kafka-esque tale about a young man who delivers a package to a house and is subsequently detained for an indefinite length of time. *Joe*, by Sasha Wolf, is pretty much a one-gag piece, about a man in a hospital of some sort whose shoes become smeared and how he fixes them. In Wolf's commentary track she goes into detail about mental illness and the film's resonances, as well as explaining her own fairly interesting background as the child of a producer of TV commercials. The black-and-white film runs 10 minutes.

An amusing black-and-white 8 minute 'experimental' film, *The Whites*, is accompanied by an equally irreverent yet intelligent commentary by the director, Natasha Uppal, in which she answers in a normal voice to questions that are posed in the same, incomprehensibly distorted tones used for the dialogue in the film. The short, which is presented in rapid movement, depicts the activities of a family who drink invisible liquids, eat off bare bones and do other recognizable but still somewhat absurd acts while the characters relate to one another as they would in a real family (the children are played by adults). Some experimental films are self-evident and limited, but others achieve a mix of cerebral inspiration and visual mystery that can be repeatedly compelling, and *The Whites* falls into this latter category.

Also included are a tantalizing 'making of' featurette about a low budget crime film we are unfamiliar with, *Montana*, including extra interviews with four of the cast members; an interview with Ernest Dickerson in promotion of his upcoming feature, *Blind Faith*, which looks like it would make a pretty good stageplay but doesn't seem all that cinematic; a monologue by Michael McKean that tends to overstate the drawbacks of authority; a jokey bookend introduction with an alternate angle providing its storyboards, including panels for shots that proved too expensive to complete; and a trailer for **The Game**.

A Shot in the Dark (MGM, 907501)

The picture is presented on one side in letterboxed format and on the other side in cropped format. The second Peter Sellers Inspector Clouseau movie places the Clouseau character in the middle of a murder farce, which takes a secondary priority to Sellers' clowning. It was **A Shot in the Dark**, and not **The Pink Panther**, that set the tone for the Clouseau series. One advantage of the wider image is the opportunity to watch George Sanders' reaction shots. If you've seen the movie enough times to have it memorized, it might be worthwhile watching it once without taking your eyes off Sanders in the scenes where he appears. His air of bored indifference helps him to keep a straight face, but sometimes his resolve appears to teeter.

The letterboxing has an aspect ratio of about 2.35:1 and an accommodation for enhanced 16:9 playback. The color transfer is good, with accurate fleshtones and fresh hues, and the picture is sharp. The monophonic sound is fine. The 102 minute program also has a French soundtrack, optional English or French subtitles, and a theatrical trailer.

Shout (GoodTimes, 0581021)

A film John Travolta made during his 'dark' period, Travolta fans will not want to miss it. Not only does he dance (briefly, but with Linda Fiorentino!), but he sings and his face is thin. The 1991 feature actually has a lot going for it. A young and vivacious Heather Graham has a significant role, and even Gwyneth Paltrow shows up in a small part. The film is set in the Fifties in Texas, at a home for juvenile delinquents. Travolta is a music teacher who turns the boys on to rock 'n' roll. James Walters stars, as the most rebellious of the delinquents. If it weren't for the cast, the film would be somewhat tiresome and predictable, but both Travolta and Graham have the ability to enthrall a viewer, and the music does the rest.

The picture is presented in full screen format, but the framing seems workable. In some sequences, fleshtones look a little yellowed, the image seems a bit grainy and colors are a bit drained, but other passages are stronger, with fairly glossy hues and, frankly, once we really got into it, we forgot to pay attention to the picture quality at all. The stereo surround soundtrack serves the music well, although directional effects are limited. The 89 minute program can be supported by English, French or Spanish subtitles.

Show Boat (MGM, 906614)

The 1951 musical's brilliant Technicolor images are amazing. The DVD's presentation sent tears running down our cheeks during the spectacular and deftly edited opening segment. The best color sequences, such as the *After the Ball* scene, are riveting for their chromatic pleasures alone. The DVD does have a little artifact trouble with the fog bound *Ol' Man River* sequence—which is also heavily scratched and could use some general cleaning—but otherwise the presentation is super. In shot after shot, the colors alone justify the film, and the success of the transfer improve other aspects of the movie as well. Ava Gardner's performance, for example, is greatly enhanced by the accuracy of the image. It brings out subtleties in her expressions, which add depth to her character, transmitting quiet changes in her emotional responses. Her closeups gain so much power from the quality of the cinematography that the film's themes of tragedy and renewal are directly enhanced.

The regular monophonic sound is a little weaker than the Dolby Digital mono track. The recording is aged and has both some scratchiness and weakness in the high end, but so long as you don't push the volume too much, it works fine. The 108 minute film is supported by English, French or Spanish subtitles ("Los peces nadan, los pájaros vuelan…") and there is a theatrical trailer.

Showdown in Little Tokyo (Warner, 12311)

A silly but busy action film stars Dolph Lundgren and Brandon Lee, as cops who are trying to break up yakuza activity in Los Angeles. They rarely try to arrest people, however, preferring instead to beat them up or kill them. The plot is illogical (the bad guys are going to distribute drugs around the country in beer bottles), but there are more than enough fight sequences and other genre delights to hold viewers in search of an escape from thinking.

Although the full screen framing isn't too awkward, some of the action scenes seem a bit confused in places. The image is often grainy and although the film has a glossy look, fleshtones are a little drab and contrasts in some darker sequences are weak. The stereo surround sound is adequate and the 78 minute program can be supported by English closed captioning.

Sid & Nancy (Criterion, CC15400)

From the jacket essay to the audio commentary, nobody seems gung-ho over **Sid and Nancy**. Although parts of the movie are praised, the various contributors to the disc seem, at best, ambivalent about the film as a whole. The thing is, while for any other film, such a reserved air might be embarrassing, in the spirit of what **Sid and Nancy** depicts—a core legend of the punk rock era—such antipathy enhances the package, evoking the film's achievements better than unabated admiration could ever accomplish. "I don't know that anyone's ever made a rock bio-pic that's so unrelievedly sordid, squalid, sick and repulsive. And it has such a bad ending," says one commentator. "There's nothing really I want to say about the film that I hated," says another, "because it's sort of unfair, you know." "I don't know, I'm not, am I a huge fan of the

movie?" asks still another, the star, in fact, Gary Oldman, "I don't know if I am." If this isn't the urbane intellectual equivalent of throwing beer bottles at the musicians because you like them, it comes reasonably close. The 111 minute film is letterboxed with an aspect ratio of about 1.75:1 and no 16:9 enhancement. Although the film has a moderately grimy look to it, the accuracy and solidity of the DVD's picture are appreciable. The stereo sound is passable and there is no captioning.

There are several very appropriate and compelling clips from the documentary *D.O.A.: A Right of Passage*, which clearly inspired the makers of **Sid & Nancy**, along with an intriguing 'making of' movie, *England's Glory*, that is quite unlike most 'making of' movies. Presenting interviews with the filmmakers at unguarded moments, their negative comments about the production seem only half in jest. Also featured are the band's first uncensored television interview, which happened on a slow news day and sent the British press screaming with free publicity, and an interesting audio segment, which is billed as an interview with Vicious but is in reality a surreptitiously taped phone conversation. It is, nevertheless, fascinating.

Appearing on the audio track that accompanies the film itself are the screenwriter, Abbe Wool, interested bystanders Greil Marcus, Julien Temple and Lech Kowalski, and Oldman and co-star Chloe Webb. The director, Alex Cox, did not participate. Wool explains where the filmmakers were coming from with their approach and discusses some of the movie's production logistics. Marcus, Temple and Kowalski provide more contextual commentary and analyze how well the film fulfills its intentions. The two stars shift between talking about what was required of them for their roles and what they learned about the figures they were representing. Webb, who admits to having taken heroin in the past herself, is particularly intriguing.

One of the big surprises for viewers who have not seen the movie in a couple of years is that Courtney Love has a small but noticeable role, and is part of the film's death iconography. The movie itself, depicting the lives of Vicious and Nancy Spungen from about the point that the TV interview occurred until Spungen's murder about five years later, has held up quite well as the fads it was exploring from the tail end have faded. It is essentially about two teenagers who use fame to get as many drugs as they can before they die, and the joke of the film is that they are devoted to one another wholeheartedly, as, apparently, were the real pair. It is the contrast between this indivisible bond and the absolute deterioration of everything else around them, from music to their own bodies, that gives the film both its wicked humor and its humanity.

The Siege (Fox, 4111053)

It's the FBI versus the Army versus terrorists in the ludicrous 1998 thriller. The film is based upon a novel and so it has some decent plot turns, as well as a good action scene about every 10 minutes or so, but the story just gets more farfetched and more farfetched as it goes along (and preachy, too), undermining whatever chance its positive attributes have to hold your attention. Set in New York City, Denzel Washington and Annette Bening star in what starts out as sort of a *Little Drummer Girl* intrigue and ends up being a kind of *Seven Days in May* fiasco. Bruce Willis is featured in a key but fairly brief supporting role.

The picture is letterboxed with an aspect ratio of about 2.35:1 and no 16:9 enhancement. The image looks fine, with crisp fleshtones and accurate hues. The stereo surround is weaker than the Dolby Digital track, but the Dolby Digital track is fairly energetic, with a strong dimensionality and engaging details. The 115 minute program also has a French audio track in standard stereo, optional English or Spanish subtitling, and a trailer.

The Silence of the Lambs (Criterion, CC1530D); (Image, ID40690RDVD)

Exploring the dangers of life from a safe distance is what movies are all about. The difference between a sane person, who allows the pleasures of violent fantasy to pass through the thought process, and an insane person, who feels compelled to act those fantasies out, may be as thin as the difference between a .200 and a .300 batter, and the best executed entertainments on the subject can leave you wondering just how close you really are to that line.

The Criterion release is loaded with extra features, while Image presents just the movie. Criterion's basic picture transfer, however, is weaker than Image's effort. The colors on Image's presentation are more accurate, better detailed and sharper. Criterion's picture, in comparison, is hazy and pinkish. Both versions are letterboxed with an aspect ratio of about 1.85:1 and no 16:9 enhancement, but Image's version has more picture information on all four sides of the frame. The stereo surround sound is about equal on both versions and is passable. Criterion's version is not captioned, but Image's is. The 1990 Oscar winner runs 118 minutes.

The extras, however, make the Criterion effort worthwhile. There is a commentary channel featuring director Jonathan Demme, Jodie Foster, Anthony Hopkins, screenwriter Ted Tally and FBI advisor John Douglas; about 20 minutes of outtakes; elaborate storyboard details, production drawings and comparisons; elaborate excerpts from an FBI manual that classifies murders (including the titillating case studies); and the even more fascinating verbatim quotations from famous serial killers and mass murderers as they talk about their childhood, their experiences in crime and how they see the world. The most interesting outtake is a complete rendition of a fairly convincing TV preacher sermon that appeared on a monitor in the background of one scene.

Along with audio commentary by Jonathan Demme, Jodie Foster, Anthony Hopkins and screenwriter Ted Tally, the head of the FBI's Behavioral Science Unit, John Douglas, chimes in at appropriate moments to compare the actions of the characters in the film to real crime and criminology. Much of the supplementary section is a simple mundane progression of text essays, but after a few biographical sketches of the filmmakers, the essays focus on the categorization of serial killers and an exploration of their psyches, including extensive quotations from the killers themselves.

Demme, Foster and company provide a well rounded portrait of the film's production. Foster sees a great deal of symbolism in her role, but keeps the secret of how she achieved her remarkably steady and vulnerable performance to herself. Hopkins is more open about his approach to his craft and is understandable enamored with what the film has meant for his career. Demme provides a decent overview of the film's creation and many specific details about what he was after in various scenes.

As a result of Voyager's improvements, we found ourselves responding to the themes in **Silence of the Lambs** more thoroughly and deeply. When we watched Image's disc we enjoyed the narrative, but as we watched Voyager's we enjoyed the characters, not only for their interaction with each other, but for their moods, unspoken thoughts and desires. Ostensibly the film is about a woman who succeeds in a male world, but from the viewpoint of the villain, she is only a pawn to whom he has sacrificed a mildly important piece in order to gain a much greater advantage. The problem is that if you start looking at things from the villain's point of view for too long, you can really get into trouble.

Silent Running (Universal, ID4229USDVD)

The 1971 film was directed by the special effects supervisor of **2001**, Douglas Trumbull, and attempted to revisit the special effects work done on **2001**, though with a story that was light years more primitive. Bruce Dern, whose overwrought performance serves only to remind viewers that Trumbull began by directing small plastic models, stars as the only concerned crew member on a greenhouse spacecraft holding Earth's last vegetation. When the order comes to junk the cargo, he rebels and tries to save a few trees—something else they were doing in Seattle until everybody started moving there. The narrative is ludicrous on several levels and the film is simplistic and ponderous, but the special effects are

impressive and the film's heart is in the right place even if its head is nowhere to be found.

The letterboxing has an aspect ratio of about 1.85:1 and no 16:9 enhancement. The picture is reasonably fresh, though a bit soft at times, and fleshtones look good. Darker sequences pure and sharp. The monophonic sound is a little weak, but there is a Dolby Digital mono track that is stronger. Music on the comes off a little tentative, but generally the audio is acceptable. The 90 minute film is accompanied by English closed captioning.

Silent Steel (SlingShot, DVD9854)

Want to feel totally inadequate? Check out the interactive movie game with multiple choice pathways. Given the camera's point-of-view, the viewer is a submarine commander. Subordinates explain the details of a problem and then turn to you, as captain, for orders. You have three optional answers, but the way they stare at you, and sort of roll their eyes when you answer poorly, is enough to make you think you're incapable of making toast, let alone running a nuclear powered submarine.

Each plot path takes about 20–30 minutes to complete, but the endings on some of the constructed stories are a bit incoherent. We came across one instance where the answer we selected did not elicit a correct response. The submarines themselves are CGI generated, but the interior dramas were shot with real humans. The stereo surround sound and Dolby Digital sound have a generally dimensional presence, although separation effects are limited. The cinematography and picture quality are bland but functional. The program also has a German language track and optional English, French or German subtitles.

Silkwood (Anchor Bay, DV10886)

Meryl Streep is an employee at a plant that makes plutonium rods for nuclear reactors. Her company is so incompetent that the only thing preventing complete public exposure of its errors is the intense fear of mass layoffs, a fear that is soon supplanted by the even more frightening prospect of deadly radiation poisoning. Directed by Mike Nichols, the 1983 film is sporadically compelling, but it can also seem sleepy and meandering. The performances of the three stars, Meryl Streep in one of her best efforts, Kurt Russell and Cher, are what have given the film its popularity and durability. Its realism can only go so far, and the movie never obtains the unifying dramatic tension more fictionalized stories are capable of delivering.

The 131 minute film is presented in letterboxed format on one side, with an aspect ratio of about 1.85:1 and no 16:9 enhancement, and in full screen format on the other side. The letterboxing adds picture information to the sides of the image and masks picture information off the bottom and top in comparison to the full screen version, but the framing is more appealing. The image is very sharp and colors are accurate, although the movie's color scheme is deliberately drab. The monophonic sound is adequate and the program is not captioned.

Silvstedt, Victoria (see **Playboy Video Centerfold: Victoria Silvstedt**)

Simon Birch (Buena Vista, 17241)

The young actor who plays the title role, Ian Michael Smith, does a competent job with the part, but there is nothing else about the film that is particularly unique (except for a very nice surprise cameo at the beginning and end). Smith portrays a diminutive twelve-year old with congenital impairments. He hangs out with his best friend in a small Maine town and has some interaction with the other kids, though he isn't exactly 'one of the gang.' The two of them try to determine who the friend's father is (the friend's mother is unmarried), and they make mischief—the film's funniest sequence involves a botched Christmas play—wrapping up the story with a suitably dramatic and emotional third act. There are minor inconsistencies that lead one to take the film less seriously—

the boys are playing non-playoff little league baseball at the end of October, in Maine; although the film is set in 1964, Smith is using hearing aids that weren't developed until later, when batteries and circuits got smaller; and the story's stated theme, that Simon taught his friend to believe in God, is never demonstrated—but it is a fairly basic and predictable memory play (the inevitable death of Smith's character is announced in the opening scene). Some viewers will respond to the characters and enjoy the film, but others will be too impatient to savor its good will.

The 1998 feature is letterboxed format only, with an aspect ratio of about 1.85:1 and no 16:9 enhancement. The picture is sharp and colors are bright, with adequate fleshtones. The stereo surround sound and Dolby Digital sound are okay, though the mix is not elaborate. The 114 minute program also has a French language track in standard stereo, optional English subtitles, and a trailer that shamelessly includes the cameo, while playing up the film's comical elements.

A Simple Wish (Universal, 20271)

Kathleen Turner is a fairy godmother turned evil and Amanda Plummer is her sidekick, a former dog. Both brighten the film with their performances, but not even they can rescue the whole movie, which is too dumb and unfunny to entertain. Martin Short stars, as an inept fairy godmother on his first assignment. Short's take on the character and the comedy doesn't work, but that's not the film's real problem. The script is a lazy mess that uses wishes to get itself out of predicaments rather than letting the characters fend for themselves, and although the movie has many special effects (too many), there is nothing magical about it.

The picture is letterboxed with an aspect ratio of about 1.85:1 and an accommodation for enhanced 16:9 playback. The color transfer looks fine, with bright, crisp hues and presentable flesh-tones. The stereo surround sound is drab, but the Dolby Digital track has a few engaging separation effects. The film is also available in French and Spanish in standard stereo and comes with English or Spanish subtitles. The 90 minute program is accompanied by some production notes, a cast profile section and a theatrical trailer.

Sin-a-matic 3 X-rated (Vivid, UPC#0073215565)

The 141 minute collection of unrelated interludes doesn't spend too much time on preliminaries. The most inspired sequence is the opener, where two young ladies from 'Beverly Hills' go cruising in an inner city neighborhood to meet men. The lighting varies and some sequences are grainy, but generally the image is sharp and fleshtones look accurate. The sound is fine and the program is accompanied by elaborate hardcore interactive promotional features.

Sinatra, Frank (see **Suddenly**)

Sinatra Gold: Collector's Edition (Triton, DVD9826)

A reasonably thorough five-part biography of Frank Sinatra, the images are compiled from trailers, Sinatra's old TV shows, newsreels and other public domain sources, but there are some terrific interviews (particularly from the actresses who worked with him) and a lot of rarely seen footage. Each episode runs about 46 minutes, apparently designed for an hour TV slot. There is some repetition of material from one episode to the next, but it is always presented from a slightly varied angle so as not to be a direct copy of the previous coverage. The size of the program accommodates a reasonably complete telling of the public aspects of Sinatra's life and still allows for comprehensive coverage of his music career, his film career and his television and performance career. It doesn't dig too deeply, but as an overview of his life, it is a reasonable place to start.

Three episodes are presented on one single-sided platter, and two episodes are on another. Each platter also has two karaoke numbers (Come Fly with Me and Witchcraft) set to a very nice collection of still photos, as well as very complete discographies and

filmographies. The quality of the source material varies from one clip to the next. Most aren't in bad shape and artifacting is rarely evident. The DVD has a 5.1 Dolby Digital channel, but the Dolby Digital track is indistinguishable from the standard track. The narration is stereophonic, as is some of the music, but most of the source material is monophonic and remains centered. Tonal quality is smooth and nicely detailed, however, and while no songs are played from start to finish, there are enough excerpts to satiate even the most demanding fans. The presentation is not captioned.

The Sinful Nuns of Saint Valentine (Image, ID4618SADVD)

A film that is much better than its orgy-oriented jacket copy implies, it is about intrigue and duplicity in a convent during the Spanish Inquisition. Directed by Sergio Grieco in 1974 as Le Scomunicate di S. Valentino, the film has its share of whippings, murders and insane nuns, but it also has heroism, romance, swashbuckling excitement and a happy ending. The erotic violence is spicy without becoming a turn off, and it is of secondary importance to the narrative and its political themes. The image is letterboxed with an aspect ratio of about 2.2:1 and no 16:9 enhancement. The source material is a little battered and colors are pale. The image is also a bit blurry here and there. The monophonic sound is a bit distorted in places but tolerable. The 98 minute program is in Italian with optional white English subtitles that appear beneath the letterboxed image. The Redemption title is accompanied by an engaging trailer and a ridiculous, lengthy made-for-video prologue.

Singin' in the Rain (MGM, 906262)

Like **The Wizard of Oz**, the improvement in picture clarity and color on the **Singin' in the Rain** DVD is absolutely stunning. The film's Technicolor hues and designs are so luxuriant that the slight increase in detail and accuracy created by the DVD playback is magnified in multiples by the original intensity of the image. We can't watch the Broadway Melody segment on DVD without our heartbeat doubling and we only wish there were colors like that in real life.

The monophonic sound is free of distortion and effective. In addition to English, the film is available in French or Spanish, with English, French or Spanish subtitles ("Moïse suppose que ses roses sont écloses…"). MGM's inept original theatrical trailer (The lengthy discussion of the need to put sound into movies is shown almost in its entirety, and then Jean Hagen's hysterical punchline, which would have doubled the audience for the picture, is left out.) is also included. The joyous 1951 musical starring Gene Kelly, Donald O'Connor and Debbie Reynolds runs 103 minutes.

Single White Female (Columbia TriStar, 51439)

Bridget Fonda and Jennifer Jason Leigh star in the popular thriller about a psychotic roommate. Set in Manhattan, the 1992 film is effectively constructed and makes no major errors as it builds up its suspense. Because the narrative has to stretch a bit to get the characters into place, the film does not make a great impression as an artistic accomplishment, even within the confines of the genre. Nevertheless, it is an easy film to relax with, and is sort of a neo-camp classic.

The picture is presented on one side in letterboxed format, with an aspect ratio of about 1.85:1 and an accommodation for enhanced 16:9 playback, and is in full screen format on the other side. The color transfer looks fine. Fleshtones are always accurate, even when the cinematography and lighting give the characters Pierrot complexions. The stereo surround sound is expertly mixed and contains many subtle but satisfying effects. The 107 minute program also has French and Spanish audio tracks in mono, optional English, French and Spanish subtitles, and a trailer.

Singles (Warner, 12410)

People probably look upon Cameron Crowe's 1992 romantic comedy with a twinge of nostalgia now, unless they are so sick and tired of hearing about Seattle that they don't want to deal with the film at all. Kyra Sedgwick, Bridget Fonda and Sheila Kelley star as the title characters, who are trying to cope with love and independence while living in what was then the most exposed vein of America's cultural pulse. The movie has a strong narrative and delightfully conceived characters. Perhaps the most promising aspect to it, however, is an inspired comical performance turned in by Matt Dillon in a supporting role, as a grungy rock musician.

The 95 minute feature is presented in letterboxed format on one side, with an aspect ratio of about 1.85:1 and an accommodation for enhanced 16:9 playback, and in full screen format on the other side. The letterboxing adds just a sliver to the sides and masks off picture information from the top and bottom compared to the full screen version, but the framing is stronger. Fleshtones are a bit orangey, but the color transfer is okay and the image is reasonably sharp. The stereo surround sound is passable and the music, when appropriate, has a strong dimensionality. The presentation also has a French audio track, optional English and French subtitles, and a trailer. As an extra treat, Warner has included two marvelous comical sequences that were judged to be too eccentric to make the theatrical cut. In one, various magazine covers talk to one of the heroes. In the second, a sequence is played out in French, with amusingly hip subtitles. This latter segment is particularly joyful and is guaranteed to leave a viewer smiling when the disc concludes.

Sirens (Buena Vista, 18795)

A minister, traveling to his newest post with his wife, stops to visit an artist to quell an upcoming exhibition of scandalous paintings and quickly becomes confounded by the artist's intransigence and the free spirited behavior of several randy models in the mildly comical erotic drama. Set in Australia, the film stars Hugh Grant, who has a rare ability of being able to portray desperately foolish characters without embarrassing himself. It is the quality of his performance that anchors the film, enabling the viewer to embrace the eccentricities of the other characters and accept what happens to them. Elle Macpherson and Sam Neill are among the co-stars. Sustaining a near mythic atmosphere, the occasionally erotic film is an engaging adult comedy with strong artistic sensibilities.

The picture looks fabulous. The artist lives on sort of the edge of society, with one foot in the wilderness so to speak, and the images of greenery and unspoiled vistas—which are always presented as a thematic reinforcement of what is happening to the characters and never just for the sake of their own beauty—are ideal for the glossy clarity the DVD delivers. The image is extremely crisp and colors are very precisely defined. The presentation is letterboxed with an aspect ratio of about 1.85:1 and no 16:9 enhancement. The stereo surround sound is also luscious, with many enjoyable atmospheric details. The 94 minute program can be supported by optional English subtitles.

Six Days Seven Nights (Buena Vista, 15641)

An insubstantial romance that tries to stay afloat on star power, Harrison Ford and Anne Heche star, spending a little over half the movie bickering and getting to know one another on a deserted island. There's pirates on the island, but fortunately the film doesn't spend too much time with them, and David Schwimmer almost steals the show as Heche's more realistically human fiancé. The locale is exotic, the stars are certainly appealing and periodically believable, and viewers who like them will find the film just as likable, but there isn't much more to it than that.

The picture is letterboxed with an aspect ratio of about 2.35:1 and no 16:9 enhancement. The tropical settings in the tropical sun are all bright and crisp, with luscious colors, but even darker sequences look real good, in an expensive Hollywood movie kind of way. The stereo surround sound and Dolby Digital sound are okay, but there is nothing exceptional about the delivery or the mix. The Dolby Digital track has more body and more distinctive separations than the standard track. The 102 minute program is also

available in French and can be supported by English subtitles. There is a theatrical trailer as well, and it is interesting to examine the clip after watching the film. It tries to make the movie seem more exciting and lively, but in reality, it gives away every thrill there is to be had.

Sixteen Candles (Image, ID4270USDVD)

If you turned off your monitor and just listened to the soundtrack, **Sixteen Candles** would still be funny. The dialogue is letter perfect and delivered with instinctive naturalness. "I just thought that turning sixteen would be so major that I'd wake up with an improved mental state that would show on my face," announces Molly Ringwald's character in the beginning. Instead, her family forgets that it is her birthday and her only suitor is a blond-headed waif with an ego the size of a school bus. **Sixteen Candles** has a few of the crazy-teenagers-coming-of-age elements, but it is more like **Risky Business** in its approach, undercutting the frivolity with a cynical view of the values held by the young. Unlike **Risky Business** though, the cynicism in **Sixteen Candles** is light and natural and disappears in a puff when the right boy comes along.

The letterboxing has an aspect ratio of about 1.85:1 with no 16:9 enhancement. The image is a little soft at times, but the colors are bright and fleshtones look accurate. The monophonic sound is solid. The 93 minute 1984 film is not captioned.

The '60s (Trimark, VM7084D)

A 171 minute TV miniseries about the tumultuous decade that many people still equate with America growing up, most of the film follows the experiences of three young white adults from one Chicago family as they undergo a political and cultural awakening in various parts of the country. In the best spirit of the Sixties, however, there is also a token subplot, about a young black man who undergoes a similar maturation. Although the film has more cliches than there were roach clips in Jerry Garcia's desk drawer, it is still an enjoyable trip down memory lane. Was it really that much like a circus?

One of the show's biggest assets is its pop song musical score and even though many of the songs have been on the radio constantly for the past four decades (some are less often aired, such as cuts by Nico, Lou Reed and Jefferson Airplane), the syzygy of the Sixties music and Sixties images creates a solar burst of nostalgic feelings—you're so busy relating to the memories you don't want a drama more complicated than the one that is offered to interfere with your pleasure.

The picture looks fine and the stereo sound is super. There's a nice, heavy bass, and the songs sound rich and alive. The program is split to two sides at what appears to be the break between the first evening and second evening broadcast, although there is only one set of opening and closing credits. An 8 minute interview with producer Linda Obst is offered, in which she speaks enthusiastically about the project and the era. A collection of quotations from the Sixties and a cast profile section are also included. The program can be supported by optional English, French or Spanish subtitles. The chapter encoding and guides are not nearly as much fun as they could have been.

Skinner (Simitar, 7342)

For those of you who cannot resist a really sick slasher film that features both Traci Lords and Ricki Lake, you will probably have fun with **Skinner**. Ted Raimi portrays a psycho killer who likes to peel off the skin of his victims and walk around wearing their hides as costumes. Lake is his unsuspecting landlady, upon whom he is developing a crush, and Lords is a mysterious something-or-other who is searching for Raimi's character to extract revenge. It is gross and impolite (when Raimi's character puts on the skin of a black co-worker he has murdered, he takes on a Stepin' Fetchit accent), but the performances are just competent enough that the film delivers what is promises, which is likely all that fans require.

The picture is horribly grainy and hazy-looking, with imperfect colors that shift wildly from scene to scene due to lighting inconsistencies. The monophonic sound is noisy and subject to fluctuations in volume. The 81 minute 1993 film is not captioned. Filmographies for Lake and Lords are also included.

Slap Shot (Universal, 20328)

George Roy Hill's 1977 sports comedy that set the precedent for many other sports comedies. Paul Newman stars as the player and eventual coach of a minor league hockey team that boosts attendance by playing up the rough stuff. The 123 minute film is a little long, but the performances are enjoyable and the narrative, if not fresh, at least seems reliable. Michael Ontkean co-stars.

The picture is letterboxed, with an aspect ratio of about 1.85:1 and an accommodation for enhanced 16:9 playback. Fleshtones are a bit pale, other hues are a little light in places, and there is a stray speckle or two, but the image is sharp and the colors are generally well defined and delineated. The monophonic sound is okay. The film is also available in French and Spanish and can be supported by English or Spanish subtitles. There are some production notes, explaining, among other things, how Ontkean prepared himself for his striptease scene, and there is a cast-and-director profile section and a trailer.

Slaughterhouse-Five (Image, ID4227USDVD)

George Roy Hill's 1972 adaptation of Kurt Vonnegut's novel is about an optometrist having a fanciful nervous breakdown with flashbacks to WWII. It disguises a mean-spirited contempt for humanity with the imposition of coy whimsy.

The letterboxing has an aspect ratio of about 1.85:1 without an accommodation for 16:9 playback. Although the hues are light at times, the image quality is reasonably good, with workable fleshtones and no more than a mild grain in darker sequences. The monophonic sound is dull, but the Dolby Digital mono track is fine. The musical score is by Glenn Gould. The 103 minute program is closed captioned.

Sleepers (Warner, 14482)

Every star in Barry Levinson's 1996 feature has a supporting role except maybe Jason Patric. The film has an unusual structure, and while we don't think it works all that well, we still found it refreshing in its attempt to circumvent the norm. In a nutshell, the narrative is about four young boys who are sent to reform school, where they are abused by guards. A couple decades later, two of the boys kill one of the guards on the street, but what should have been a cut-and-dried murder trial becomes complicated when another of the four boys is assigned to prosecute the case.

The film runs 148 minutes, but the first hour is taken up by the kids, with nostalgic images of their antics in New York's Hell's Kitchen just gradually giving way to the real plot. One of the problems with the movie is that you don't get to spend enough time with the stars. The film's best scene, in fact, takes place between Vittorio Gassman and Wendell Pierce, with none of the top-billed performers in attendance. Brad Pitt, Dustin Hoffman, Robert De-Niro and Kevin Bacon all have their moments, but they remain distant and superficial characters, without enough screen time to let you see what is in their hearts. In its attempt to span time and tackle an elaborate sequence of events, Sleepers is admirable, but as an entertainment it is somewhat more taxing.

The film is split in half and presented on two sides. The presentation is letterboxed, with an aspect ratio of about 2.35:1 and an accommodation for enhanced 16:9 playback, and the image composition often makes full use of the rectangular frame. The end credit scroll has been artificially enlarged, and Warner has accidentally left off the elaborate disclaimers appearing between the end of the movie and the beginning of the credits, which explore the claim of a factual basis for the narrative. The picture looks excellent, with a sharp, detailed image. The bass still packs a punch on the standard stereo and Dolby Digital tracks, surround details are subdued and there just isn't much activity in the mix. The film is also available in French in Dolby Digital and can be supported by English, French or Spanish subtitles. A trailer and the production notes appear on both sides.

Sleepless in Seattle (Columbia TriStar, 52415/52419)

Tom Hanks and Meg Ryan star in Nora Ephron's wonderfully felt and highly successful 1993 romantic tease, their characters not meeting until the end of the film and the movie being about how right they are for each other. Tearfully romantic, the film is also immensely witty and had us laughing hysterically on more than one occasion. Although the movie is not one where picture or sound quality are critical to a viewer's entertainment, both components are nevertheless superbly rendered on the DVD.

Colors are crisp, fleshtones are accurate and there is never a hint of distortion in the darkest scenes or the deepest hues. The image has been letterboxed, with an aspect ratio of about 1.85:1 and an accommodation for enhanced 16:9 playback, and the framing is always well balanced. The stereo surround soundtrack delivers the film's popular music score with a fidelity that matches the CD soundtrack. The 105 minute program also has French and Spanish language tracks, with Spanish or Korean subtitles ("Es para mujeres") and English closed captioning.

Sleepover X-rated (Vivid, UPC#0073214517)

Usually adult programs have very little plot, so an adult program that actually has a clever plot is almost too good to be true. Sleepover is about three women on a camping trip. Their car breaks down and three brothers offer to help them, but nothing is what it seems, except the erotic sequences, of course, which are fairly straightforward and efficient.

Fleshtones are overly pinkish in some sequences and more natural looking in others. The image is sharp, but there is some grain in the darker sequences. Dialog is often wind buffeted on the audio track, and even indoor the recording isn't all that strong. The 75 minute program features Kobe Tai, Alexandra Silk, Kelly Jean and Stephanie Swift. The DVD contains alternate angle sequences and elaborate hardcore interactive promotional features.

Sleuth (Anchor Bay, DV10409)

The 139 minute two-character mystery thriller is split to two sides in letterboxed format, with an aspect ratio of about 1.66:1 and no 16:9 enhancement. The image still seems a little tight on the sides, however. Michael Caine and Laurence Olivier star in the 1972 feature, adapted from a three-character play, about two gentlemen attempting to psych each other out. The color transfer looks nice, with decent fleshtones and smooth, solid hues, but fleshtones are still somewhat pale and once in a while the edges of things tend to smear a little. The monophonic sound is passable, although some of the dialogue, particularly Olivier's voice, seems a bit raspy, and the musical score's mid-range bumps into a wall now and then. The sound disappears, too, about a minute before the movie actually ends. The program is not captioned.

Sliding Doors (Paramount, 335767)

The very creative and highly satisfying romantic comedy is about the two paths a woman's life could have taken had she or had she not caught a particular train. The film advances as if each option was actually occurring, and the result is sort of two movies with the same characters, expertly shuffled together. Gwyneth Paltrow stars.

The DVD looks super, with sharp, smooth, accurate hues and on-the-money fleshtones. The picture is letterboxed with an aspect ratio of about 1.85:1 and no 16:9 enhancement. The stereo surround sound and Dolby Digital sound are okay, although the audio mix is not elaborate, and the 99 minute program can be supported by English or Spanish subtitles.

Sling Blade (Buena Vista, 13676)

The plot of **Sling Blade** is a variation on *We're No Angels* and Billy Bob Thornton's performance in the lead role is classic Old School-style acting, but the film, which Thornton also wrote and directed, creates a fresh and vital portrait of small town America. It is an independent production, shot on a very low budget, and like so many independent films it is willing to discard the standard patterns and discover new realities. The hero is a recently discharged mental patient who befriends a young boy and several other Capra-esque characters while searching in a befuddled manner for a substitution to the regimentation and security the hospital had given him. The pacing is as slow as molasses, but it is as sticky, also, and so the viewer is held spellbound as Thornton's character, whose lower jaw seems permanently thrust forward, aimlessly gathers his thoughts to speak or to move.

The film was shot on a low budget, so the image looks a little dreary at times, and the audio track is a bit noisy and is not elaborate, but the DVD presents the 135 minute film in what is probably an accurate representation of the original production. Although the jacket cover and player read-out say that the DVD is in Dolby Digital 5.1, we could not get the Dolby Digital channel to activate. The regular stereo surround channel is okay, giving the musical score an effective dimensionality. The color presentation is fine and the picture is sharp, with pure blacks. The film is letterboxed with an aspect ratio of about 1.85:1 and no 16:9 enhancement. The film is also available in French and comes with English or Spanish subtitles ("Algunos lo llaman el podón, pero yo la llamo cuchilla Kaiser").

Slums of Beverly Hills (Fox, 4110379)

The coming-of-age comedy is about a family ducking landlords by moving from one apartment to another on the fringes of Beverly Hills. The young heroine, played by Natasha Lyonne, tries to cope with her budding sexuality and the craziness around her. Alan Arkin portrays her father and Marisa Tomei is her cousin. The film has some cute moments—notably when the heroine first tries a vibrator—but there isn't much to the narrative and viewers are as likely to be bored as to be charmed.

The picture is letterboxed with an aspect ratio of about 1.85:1 and no 16:9 enhancement. Colors are solid and effectively detailed. The stereo surround sound is not elaborately mixed though it has a basic dimensionality, and while Rolfe Kent's musical score is catchy, it gets redundant after a while. The 91 minute program can be supported by English or Spanish subtitles. Although the jacket cover claims there is a 5.1 English audio track and a French audio track, neither appears to be accessible. There is a trailer and a small cast profile section.

Small Soldiers (DreamWorks, 84161)

Joe Dante's cross between **Gremlins** and *Toy Story* is like much of Dante's work, a little too eccentric to be a big box office hit. Still, the narrative, about toys accidentally installed with computer chips that give them genuine intelligence, is well conceived, the special effects are engaging, and the mix of humor and escalating action creates a momentum that will keep receptive viewers happily attentive to the end.

But perhaps best of all, so far as the DVD is concerned, the Dolby Digital audio track is super. The toy sounds come from everywhere, and the filmmakers have no reservations about deftly shifting between pint-sized noises and blockbuster-sized crashes and explosions when the entertainment calls for it. The incredible dimensionality given to Jerry Goldsmith's musical score is equal to the mixes given to his work on the **Star Trek** films, not only underscoring the humor and excitement, but pulling the viewer far enough into the film's world that the movie's perceived flaws become irrelevant. The stereo surround soundtrack is also fairly good, with plenty of energy and a strong bass, but it lacks the level of separation definition the Dolby Digital track is able to deliver. The 110 minute film is also available in French and Spanish in

standard stereo surround and comes with English, French or Spanish subtitles ("Vous êtes la crème des appelés et peu seront élus!").

The picture is also terrific. Colors are bright and contrasts are finely detailed. The image is letterboxed with an aspect ratio of about 2.25:1 and an accommodation for enhanced 16:9 playback. Contrary to a notation on the back of the jacket, the DVD is not double sided, but is presented on one side in dual-layer format. The layer shift point, however, is arbitrarily chosen and spoils the careful pace of a scare sequence.

The DVD also comes with several rewarding supplementary segments. There is a 10 minute 'making of' documentary that goes into excellent detail on how the special effects were achieved, as well as providing a thorough profile of the cast (including the voice cast—Tommy Lee Jones is the main toy, backed by former **Dirty Dozen** stars Ernest Borgnine, George Kennedy, Jim Brown and Clint Walker) and including quite a few gags designed specifically for the documentary (including 'interviews' with the toys). Additionally, there is a 5 minute blooper reel (in the best one, the lead actress, Kirsten Dunst, accidentally puts on a motorcycle helmet backwards), 6 minutes of deleted scenes (some involving the special effects), a trailer that works much better at selling the film than the **Gremlins**-derivative trailers we saw, a 2 minute sampling of the PlayStation video game inspired by the film, a cast-and-director profile section and some production notes.

Smokey and the Bandit (Universal, 20411)

Let us reflect a moment upon the success of **Smokey and the Bandit**. In retrospect, it was the pinnacle of Burt Reynolds' box office popularity and the debut-slash-pinnacle of Hal Needham's directing career. Shot in 1976 and released in 1977, it rode the wave, in Jimmy Carter's wake, of the New South's the-Civil-War-is-finally-behind-us fashionability. It was also one of the first films to cash in on a fad that presaged the popularity of Internet chat room anonymity, the CB radio craze. By all reports, the stars made up their dialogue as they went along (if Needham's other movies are a reflection of his real talents he should never have let go of **Smokey**'s editor), but Reynolds had been working hard on developing a consistent, winning screen persona and had genuinely tapped into the essence of what made him attractive. Sally Field may not have won any Oscars yet, but she had the energy and talent that said she would, and working with Reynolds appeared to liberate her from her inhibitions. Even singer Jerry Reed contributes to the mix, his dialogue providing a smooth vocal counterpoint to the frenzy of the action. Finally, Jackie Gleason, whose career had been settling into an autumnal quasi-retirement, reawakened not only his popularity but his own talent for comedy with his broad slapstick performance as the primary villain, an egotistical redneck sheriff. Although they seem run-of-the-mill now, at the time, Needham's car stunts were groundbreaking and eye-popping, landing the film second only to **Star Wars** at the box office that year. It is, however, because of these many other factors that the film is still great fun to watch, though the stunts remain good enough to give the film its raison d'être.

The film in letterboxed format, with an aspect ratio of about 1.85:1 and no 16:9 enhancement, adding nothing to the sides of the image and masking off picture information from the top and bottom compared to full screen versions. The framing looks fine, however, and helps the viewer focus on the performers. The picture looks fairly good, with bright hues and passable fleshtones. The image is sharp and details are clear. The monophonic sound is fine. The 96 minute program is also available in French and Spanish, and can be supported by English or Spanish subtitles ("Pisa el acelerator a fondo"). There is a theatrical trailer, some production notes and a cast and director profile section.

Snake & Crane: Arts of Shaolin (Simitar, 7253)

The 1977 film has a tight, well-developed narrative, a mystery in which Jackie Chan's character is investigating the disappearance of a group of monks. The film is relatively free of comedy and the fighting skills of Chan's character are fully developed from the beginning, making him a sort of 'mysterious stranger' quasi-super hero, who walks into a messy situation and cleans things up. The picture is cropped, with bland fleshtones, dull hues and occasional instances of damage on the source material. The 99 minute film presented in English on one track and Cantonese on another. The monophonic sound is always fairly rough, with warped or muffled music, and the Cantonese track doesn't sound all that much better. There is no captioning.

Snake Eyes (Paramount, 335417)

Remember how all the critics raved about the opening '20 minute shot' in **Snake Eyes**? Well, it only runs 13 minutes and there are two or three fairly obvious wipe cuts, though it is still a tour-de-force piece of real-time filmmaking. The whole first two-thirds of the movie, about an assassination during a prizefight, are fantastic. The director, Brian De Palma, dazzles the viewer with one beguiling cinematic trick after another; the stars, Nicolas Cage and Gary Sinise, spin their own powerful magic; and the story is an ideal mix of intrigue and excitement. The final third is not bad, but it is mediocre, and it is hard to believe that better choices couldn't have been made with the premise. A lot of De Palma's movies are like that though, and once you get over the letdown, multiple viewings can be as captivating as the initial screening.

The presentation is in letterboxed format with an aspect ratio of about 2.35:1 and no 16:9 enhancement. The image is incredibly vivid, hues are precise and the film's lighting is so perfectly applied that the picture often looks three dimensional. The Dolby Digital sound mix is highly competent and there are some enjoyable separation effects (during a split-screen sequence, the dialogue gets split along with the images), though the audio is not as elaborate as it is in a busier action thriller. The standard stereo surround soundtrack is almost as strong. The 98 minute feature is also available in French in standard stereo and is closed captioned with minor abridgements. The poorly conceived trailer (it gives away too much) is included as well.

Sneakers (Universal, 20178)

The wholly entertaining film has a wonderful cast, headed by Robert Redford and Sidney Poitier, and is about an amiable group of computer nerds who are hired to steal a decoding device and then discover they are pawns in an elaborate scheme of corruption. The plot has many good twists and turns, as well as some marvelous high tech gadgets and gags.

The 1992 feature is letterboxed, with an aspect ratio of about 1.85:1 and an accommodation for enhanced 16:9 playback. The picture looks good with strong hues and solid shadows. The stereo surround sound is workable, but separation effects are modest and dialogue is a little raspy. The 125 minute film is also available in French and Spanish and can be accompanied by English or Spanish subtitles. An effective theatrical trailer is included, along with an extensive cast profile section and some production notes.

Snow White: A Tale of Terror (PolyGram, 4400469072)

Fairy tales lost their innocence twice. The first time was right at the beginning, because they started out full of violence and sex and it wasn't until later that they got cleaned up. Now, however, people are scrubbing away that cleanliness to get back to the original dirt and, what's worse, they're doing it self-consciously, which is where the real loss of innocence arises. In the 1997 film, an interesting live action interpretation of the famous fairy tale starring Sigourney Weaver (as the witch and her mirror image), the handsome prince falls out of a window and the heroine ends up with one of the dwarfs. The film is a little sleepy and a little too knowing at times, but it is engaging, bloody and suitably magical for those who have the patience. Sam Neill co-stars. We don't know what it is with

him. In some movies he's great, in others he's awful, and this film, unfortunately, is one of the latter.

The single-sided dual-layer presentation is letterboxed on one layer with an aspect ratio of about 1.85:1 and no 16:9 enhancement, and is in full screen format on the other layer. The cinematography uses warm tones and the disc transfer looks pretty good, although the less light on the screen, the more chances are that edges will be a little soft. The stereo surround sound mix rarely has much in the way of separation effects and power is limited. The 100 minute program has English captioning and a trailer.

Snow White and the Magic Mirror (see **The Secret of Anastasia**)

Soldier (Warner, 16958)

Kurt Russell stars in the 1998 science fiction feature as a man, programmed since birth for fighting, who discovers his humanity after he is discarded and makes friends with a group of castaways on a planet-sized garbage dump. The film delivers what it promises—lots of explosions, high-tech battles and sci-fi imagery, integrated with a viable story and characters—and should please fans.

It is presented on one side in letterboxed format with an aspect ratio of about 2.35:1 and an accommodation for enhanced 16:9 playback, and in cropped format on the other side. The cropping is so awkward it is barely watchable. Although the settings are often darkish or illuminated through smoke and that sort of thing, the picture quality looks fine, with sharp hues and stable contrasts. The stereo surround sound and Dolby Digital sound are suitably energetic, with the Dolby Digital track having more specific separation effects. The bass also seems a little stronger and the overall audio a little fuller than the Dolby Digital track on the LD. There is one particularly good effect, during the planet's periodic and ferocious dust squalls, that whooshes across your viewing area, and there is plenty of directional gunfire and that sort of thing. The 99 minute program is also available in French in Dolby Digital and can be supported by English or French subtitles.

There is a trailer, a cast & crew profile section and a commentary track by director Paul Anderson, producer Jeremy Bolt and, showing up a bit after the halfway point, one of Russell's co-stars, Jason Isaacs. They discuss the film's schedule and deconstruct the movie's various components. Russell spent a year and a half working out to prepare for the role, and then broke his ankle during the shoot. The talk is reasonably informative.

Some Folks Call It a Sling Blade (see **Short Cinema Journal 1:1 Issue: Invention**)

Somebody Has to Shoot the Picture (Universal, 0581038)

Death row movies usually fall into two categories—serious dramas in which the condemned is eventually executed, and fanciful thrillers, in which the condemned is saved, often right before the switch is thrown. The 1990 cable film is a mix of both types, but we won't get more specific, for fear of spoiling things. Roy Scheider gives a pleasing performance as a burnt out news photographer who starts doing a David Hemmings with his negatives while covering the execution of a cop killer. Bonnie Bedelia is also quite interesting as the cop's wife, who turns out to have a history of promiscuity. The performances are good enough to sustain multiple viewings, but it is that first viewing that you won't want to interrupt.

The picture is presented in full screen format and the framing looks fine. The image is a little soft and contrasts are not finely detailed, but colors are fresh and fleshtones look good. The stereo surround sound has little rear channel activity, but front channel separations are decent and the audio is about what you can expect from a TV film. The 104 minute program can be supported by English, French or Spanish subtitles.

Sometimes They Come Back/Sometimes They Come Back Again (see Stephen King's Sometimes They Come Back/Sometimes They Come Back Again)

Somewhere in Time (Universal, 20294)

Christopher Reeve stars as a playwright who wills himself back in time to meet the love of his life. Based upon a story by Richard Matheson and directed by Jeannot Szwarc, the 1980 film operates under a logic that seemingly makes no sense whatsoever, but is so awash in romantic longing that its impossibilities are irrelevant— hence the narrative's structure is also its theme, that with love, nothing is impossible. Jane Seymour and Christopher Plummer co-star.

The picture is letterboxed, with an aspect ratio of about 1.85:1 and no 16:9 enhancement, adding very little to the sides of the image and masking picture information off the top and bottom in comparison to full screen versions, but providing a more satisfying framing in the process. The image is often grainy and a little soft, but the color transfer looks very good, with bright hues and accurate fleshtones. The monophonic sound is clean and John Barry's luscious score, though confined by the mono playback, is free of distortion. The 104 minute film is also available in Spanish and French, and comes with English or Spanish subtitles. There are some production notes, a cast and director profile section, and a trailer.

Sophie's Choice (Artisan, 60487)

In addition to the 150 minute 1982 film, there is a 50 minute documentary about the movie and the Holocaust, and an audio commentary by the director, Alan J. Pakula. The documentary and the commentary combined form a complete insight on the film's background and creation. There are also a few production notes, a trailer and a cast-and-director profile section. The film has been letterboxed with an aspect ratio of about 1.85:1 and no 16:9 enhancement. Nestor Almendros' delicately lit cinematography, with its complex levels of saturation and subtle impositions of shadow, has been meticulously replicated. The fleshtones are perfect, the image is solid and the colors, when in full bloom, are exquisitely formed. The 1982 film is 'presented in stereo for the first time,' though separation effects are limited. The audio is fine, and Marvin Hamlisch's score has a mild dimensionality that gives the whole film a greater sense of poignancy. The program can be supported by Spanish subtitles, but contrary to a jacket notation, there appears to be no closed captioning.

Meryl Streep, giving an exceptional performance, stars in the 1982 feature with Kevin Kline and Peter MacNicol, the latter portraying a young writer who meets a Holocaust survivor troubled by the horrors in her past. The retrospective documentary provides an overview of how the film was made, but places a primary focus on the Holocaust and how Sophie's Choice represents the experiences of those who survived. By itself, the documentary would seem a bit off track, but in tandem with Pakula's excellent audio commentary, it provides a very well rounded analysis of the film's accomplishments and importance. Pakula talks quite a bit about working with the performers and, to a lesser extent, the other members of his crew (trails off a little at the end, however). He avoids the trap of telling what is happening on the screen by focusing instead on what he was trying to achieve in each scene, leaving the viewer to decide whether or not he succeeded (the reasons for the double-suicide, for example, are not readily apparent, though they are there if you study the film carefully). He also shares many insights into his own approach to his craft, explaining why he chooses various camera angles (his philosophy is that the more you try to show in a scene, the less you achieve) and other, more idiosyncratic (but justified and enlightening) likes and dislikes, revealing as much about his other films as about the film at hand. (He also lets slip a couple of times an apprehension about portions of Peter MacNicol's performance, though in each case he quickly backtracks.) If you haven't seen the movie in a while, it may come

as a surprise that the film holds up so well in a comparison to *Schindler's List*. Pakula's use of desaturated colors prefigures the black-and-white cinematography of *Schindler's List* almost directly, and his economic but careful depiction of Auschwitz is as horrifying as any sequence in *Schindler*, especially the title sequence, but also the nerve-wracking scene between Sophie and the commandant's daughter.

Sorcerer (Universal, 20420)

William Friedkin's astute (except for the awful title) 1977 remake of **Wages of Fear** is about four men in two dilapidated trucks transporting old dynamite through 200 miles of mountains and jungles. It stars Roy Scheider and several European actors. There is an incredible sequence in which the trucks crawl across a rope bridge in the middle of a downpour that is the ultimate in precarious grandstanding. Not only are there several marvelous action scenes, however, but the film also creates a rich, fatalistic mood. In depicting characters who have escaped from life, **Sorcerer** allows the viewer to do the same, and then goes for an exhilarating ride.

Friedkin is on record stating his disapproval of letterboxing non-widescreen films, so the full screen presentation is viable. We wish that the movie's really cool Tangerine Dream Overture would be restored to the home video presentation, however, and the movie could use a fresh transfer. Although the colors are reasonably bright, the image is still quite grainy and, in some darker sequences, looks almost as unstable as the dynamite. Such instability also leads, here and there, to artifacting effects, though they are generally kept under control. There are also quite a few scratches and speckles on the source material. The film's stereo soundtrack could use a little boost, too. While the recording may have been state-of-the-art for its day, it could probably be sweetened now in a manner that would enhance the film's pleasures considerably. The 122 minute program can be supported by English, French or Spanish subtitles. There are some good production notes, a cast-and-director profile section and a trailer that has no idea how to market the film.

Sorceress (Image, ID5622FMDVD)

The barely coherent, quasi-softcore concoction is about women who control others through spells and compete to see their husbands succeed at the office. Linda Blair, one of the few cast members to keep her clothes on throughout, stars with Edward Albert and Julie Strain. Despite the vamping and fantasy elements, the film is awkwardly constructed and tends to lurch from one plot line to the next, never following any idea long enough to build up much interest. On the whole, it is less fun than the jacket cover implies.

The picture is somewhat grainy, with bland fleshtones, and slightly washed out hues, though the image is reasonably sharp and the presentation is workable. The stereo surround sound is passable and the 89 minute program is not captioned.

SoundStage Series: An Evening With...Harry Chapin (Platinum, 2307)

Sitting in an intimate concert setting with a live audience, Chapin sings nine of his lengthy story songs (most are thicker in meaning and detail than ballads) pausing between them to talk to the audience and, at one point, to thoughtfully answer questions. The Dolby Digital track is much louder than the standard stereo track on the hour-long program, but the standard track has a more legitimate presence, with better rounded tones and purer separations. Unlike some performances, the live environment enhances the quality of Chapin's music and provides an exhilarating alternative to his studio recordings. The picture is a little pasty at times, but workable. Fleshtones are slightly pale and contrasts are subdued, but not to a point of distraction.

Included in Chapin's set is one song that made us swear, the first time we first heard it, we would find an occupation that would allow us to be near our children as much as possible, *Cat's in the Cradle*. And so we write about home video.

South Pacific (Fox, 4110864)

Joshua Logan's 1958 adaptation of the Rodgers & Hammerstein musical about life on a military base in the Pacific during WWII was mastered directly from the original 65mm elements, many of the music scenes were shot with colored filters that looked awful on faded prints and older video presentations but look incredible on the DVD. The most spectacular example of this is the *Bali Hai* number. On older versions, it seems that there are few mild shifts in shading and little else. On the DVD, the colors go through a full kaleidoscope of gorgeous changes in perfect unison with the song's emotions, creating what must be one of the loveliest sequences ever captured on color film. Throughout the presentation, the colors are much fresh, bright and sharp, and while the improvements do not solve the movie's innate dramatic flaws (embarrassing romantic conflicts based upon race), like the music the images go a long way in compensation.

The picture is in letterboxed format only, with an aspect ratio of about 2.2:1 and no 16:9 enhancement. In some sequences, the image appears to freeze briefly between cuts, but this was a flaw on the LD as well and is probably being utilized to cover scratches or splices. The stereo surround sound is very good, but the Dolby Digital track improves on it, bringing better defined tones and more specific bass effects, and creating a grander, more engaging playback. The 157 minute program is accompanied by optional English and Spanish subtitles ("Voy a lavarme a ese hombre de mi cabeza…"), a cast & crew profile section, production notes and an enjoyable Movietone News clip about the première.

South Park Volume 1 (Warner, 36594)
South Park Volume 2 (Warner, 36595)
South Park Volume 3 (Warner, 36596)

Each DVD contains four 25 minute episodes from the vulgar and occasionally funny Comedy Central cable cartoon series, with full opening and closing credits, and jokey introductions by the show's already seen-too-often creators, Trey Parker and Matt Stone. When each episode is over the program returns to the main menu, which we found annoying. The picture quality is passable and the stereo sound is fair. Colors are very bright and the image is usually sharp. The audio is subject to mild dropouts and dialogue is a bit muffled in places, but the show's audio is shrill in concept, so any further distortion is difficult to isolate. Stereo effects are limited. There is no captioning or other special features.

If you want to sample one collection, we would recommend **Volume 2** because it contains the one episode that adequately accommodates the show's foul-mouthed format, the first Halloween episode, *Pinkeye*, in which the town is overrun by zombies until the kids figure out how to counter-act the undead plague. The other episodes are more in keeping with the show's standard format, but they provide a workable variety of gags. The collection's other highpoint is *Damien*, in which Jesus Christ has a wrestling bout with The Devil. In *An Elephant Makes Love to a Pig*, the kids attempt some genetic engineering the old fashioned way. In *Death*, the hooded title figure chases the kids while the town's elders protest a TV show comprised entirely of jokes about passing wind.

Most fans, however, will probably identify **Volume 3** as the one to get, in that it contains the 'classic' Christmas episode about a piece of excrement that talks, *Mr. Hankey, The Christmas Poo*, as well as an inspired sendup of Japanese monster movies, *Mecha-Streisand*, and an amusing Thanksgiving episode, *Starvin' Marvin*. Technically, the Christmas episode might well be the show's best effort, artistically, because it tackles the PC-ification of Christmas head on and also has an interesting psychological subtext—does the hero actually see *Mr. Hankey*, or does he have serious psychological problems (one might ask the same of Parker and Stone). In *Mecha-Streisand*, Barbra Streisand turns into a giant monster and goes on a rampage, and in *Starvin' Marvin*, the kids send away for

a sports watch and get an African orphan instead. In *Tom's Rhinoplasty*, which rounds out the collection, the kids fall in love with their substitute teacher and then try to become lesbians when they learn that is what she is.

The show's first episode, a modern *Miller's Tale*, *Cartman Gets an Anal Probe*, is featured on **Volume 1**. Because it was the show's pilot, the animation is plagued by shadows and other minor flaws, though the rest of the episodes in the collection look fine. The show introduces the relationships between the main characters as one is given implants by aliens and the little brother of another is abducted. The kids go on a hunting trip in *Volcano*, but the excursion is interrupted by an eruption. In *Weight Gain 4000*, the kids' teacher attempts to assassinate Kathie Lee Gifford, and there is a smattering of valuable social commentary in *Big Gay Al's Big Gay Boat Ride*, in which one of the kids discovers his pet dog is gay.

Space Age (Simitar, 7402)

Four fairly good documentary programs about the exploration of outer space have been released on one single-sided dual-layer DVD. Each episode runs 55 minutes and is narrated by Patrick Stewart. Most of the material is fresh. There is one episode about plans for a manned Mars mission (they're working on a nuclear propellant that will get them there in three months instead of fourteen), one about establishing a permanent base on the moon (with a look back on the Apollo program, but from kind of a different perspective), an episode about spy and military satellites and an episode about what we've learned from the Hubble telescope and other satellites pointing outward. The picture quality varies depending upon the archive material employed, but it is generally in good condition and the sound is fine. The DVD also has a profile of Stewart and is not captioned.

Space Jam (Warner, 16400)

Based with great wit upon a true story, **Space Jam** provides a whole new look at basketball player Michael Jordan's foray into professional baseball. No one is calling it a docudrama, however, because it is the Looney Tunes characters who help him snap out of it and recognize his true calling. Both Jordan and the Looney Tunes characters play themselves, and the film is a high energy blending of animation and live action. It lacks the psychological depth or political intensity of *Who Framed Roger Rabbit* (another movie based upon real events), but it has the same kind of zest, some marvelous humor and plenty of splashy effects that look and sound terrific on disc.

The image is presented in a mildly cropped format that seems annoyingly tight at times. Otherwise, the picture is outstanding, both crisp and glossy, and the animation always looks smooth and sharp. The stereo surround sound and Dolby Digital sound are good. The 88 minute film is accompanied by a theatrical trailer, English, French or Spanish subtitles, production notes and a cast & crew profile section that covers both the live actors and the animated performers thoroughly.

Space Truckers (Sterling, 7205)

The jokey and uneven outer space adventure was intended for the theaters but ended up going straight to home video. Dennis Hopper stars as an independent hauler who is given a mysterious cargo to transport to earth. Stephen Dorff and Debi Mazar are his companions. They have to cope with space pirates, the cargo itself, and other problems, but it is rarely all that involving. The film just doesn't feel like a major motion picture, despite its letterboxed image. The tone is often irreverent, although the film only makes a half-hearted attempt at comedy (which isn't Hopper's forte, anyway). The action scenes are repetitious, the special effects are usually second rate, and there isn't much of a narrative, just the heroes coping with situations as they arise.

The letterboxing has an aspect ratio of about 2.35:1 and no 16:9 enhancement. Colors are bright and the image is very sharp, although fleshtones are a little pinkish in places. The stereo surround sound is passable but not elaborate. The 96 minute program has optional Spanish subtitles, but no English captioning. In the DVD's most innovative and satisfying feature, the film's storyboards are offered as a subtitling option that can be toggled on and off at will. There is a 26 minute 'making of' documentary that gets to be a bit embarrassing when everybody starts talking about how great the movie is. There are also production notes, a trailer, a DVD-ROM script option, a simple trivia game, some nice looking conceptual art and production photos (you have to go through the game to get to it), as well as a director commentary channel from Stuart Gordon. Gordon doesn't say much about the production's problems, but he does have interesting things to say about the scientific basis for the various designs and effects, as well as talking about his experiences on the shoot, how the look of the film was developed, and some of the changes the script went through. He also breaks down the effects as they occur and points out other interesting details.

Spandau Ballet (Image, ID4398CADVD)

Their music is a bit too smooth for our taste, but the 96 minute concert program is fairly impressive. The picture is solid and the stage lighting is effective, creating a crisp, accurately colored picture that would make any rock group look exciting. The program's stereo sound is also strong. The separation mix is fairly basic, but the audio has a pleasing immediacy and the recording does not seem hampered by the live environment. The 1990 concert is uninterrupted and the image editing is effectively varied. There is no captioning.

The Spanish Prisoner (Columbia TriStar, 02608)

Written and directed by David Mamet, Campbell Scott stars as an engineer on the verge of developing a hot product who becomes entrapped in a confidence scam. The film relies on having a very intelligent hero act very stupidly to put the plot in place. The ending, however, makes no sense whatsoever if you examine it closely, even though it is such a relief, after seeing the hero get buried so deep, that you're happy it happens. Mamet's dialogue is full of halting, staccato rhythms and interruptions that sound artificial as often as they sound ultra-realistic (an argument in favor of having someone else direct Mamet's writing). The story is entertaining, however, and Mamet is gambling that since he lets the hero off the hook at the end, you'll accept everything else. It's just another confidence game, but one many viewers will be willing to invest in. Steve Martin co-stars.

The film is presented on one side in letterboxed format, with an aspect ratio of about 1.8:1 and an accommodation for enhanced 16:9 playback, and in full screen format on the other. Either framing seems workable. The color transfer looks okay, with decent contrasts and adequate fleshtones. There is a modest stereo soundtrack, though it is mostly the music that has any dimensionality. The 110 minute film is also available in French or Spanish and can be supported by English, French or Spanish subtitles. There is a trailer, as well.

Spartacus (Universal, 20181)

The audio track has been given Dolby Digital encoding, bringing a wonderful sense of detail and precision to the film's restored soundtrack. The standard stereo on the DVD is fine. The Dolby Digital track, however, is more aggressive and dimensional, though it must be recalled that this is a remix for the restored 196 minute (including the Overture) theatrical release and not the original, less complex audio from the 1960 film. Rear channel activity is still somewhat limited. The presentation is letterboxed with an aspect ratio of about 2.35:1 with no 16:9 enhancement. The colors are terrific. Thanks again to the restoration, the picture looks gorgeous, with deep, rich colors and wonderful fleshtones. The film, which is presented in single-sided dual-layer format, can also be accessed in French in standard stereo and can be supported by English or

Spanish subtitles ("'¿Comes ostras?' 'Cuando las tengo, amo.' '¿Comes caracoles?' 'No, amo'"). There is a production essay about the film and the restoration, and a good cast & director profile section.

Stanley Kubrick directed the engaging Roman epic, starring Kirk Douglas. The restored scenes give **Spartacus** a greater feeling of intricacy and completeness, and add even more intelligence to what was already the most intelligent of the pre-Christian era motion picture epics.

Spawn (New Line, N4610)

Don't worry about the mistake in the running time listing on the jacket cover. The movie is the R-rated 98 minute version (the jacket incorrectly says 94 minutes). If you saw **Spawn** in the theater, you didn't see **Spawn**. There are over 200 changes in footage and dialogue between the PG-13 theatrical release and the R-rated DVD. The movie is not overly violent—all things considered—but it isn't the wimpy kit glove version, either, and John Leguizamo's dialogue is a lot more creatively distasteful. The film, an adaptation of the comic book and HBO animated series about an assassin who returns from Hell to fight evil (don't ask, it all makes sense—maybe not the first time, but after you've been exposed to the material for a while), is loaded with nifty computer animation effects and a properly existential attitude. The editing is also creative, with imaginative wipes and other cute transitions. Michael Jai White stars, with Martin Sheen and Leguizamo as the villains.

The few scenes in daylight look great, and dark sequences are pure and crisp, with fleshtones and other hues maintaining an accuracy even in the shadows. The presentation is letterboxed, with an aspect ratio of about 1.85:1 and an accommodation for enhanced 16:9 playback. The surround sound is suitably aggressive with some great directional effects and a strong bass, and the Dolby Digital track is even better, with better defined directional effects and a greater general flourish. The movie is also available in French in standard stereo and comes with English, French or Spanish subtitles, as well as a theatrical trailer.

On an alternate audio track, creator Todd McFarlane, director Mark Dippé, producer Clint Goldman and visual effects supervisor Steve "Spaz" Williams (the hero's dog in the movie is also named 'Spaz') provide an amusing and informative group commentary. Dippé and Williams get off to a great start by telling a funny story about how they used to work at ILM until one night they were goofing off and snuck into George Lucas' office, only to get caught by security guards and summarily fired. They talk about the daunting task of bringing the effects-heavy film in on budget and the compromises they felt they made to achieve that goal. They mix technical explanations on how certain effects were achieved with explanations about what the hell (hey, we're being literal here) the movie is about, details and editorial comments about the changes made to reach the PG-13 marketing goal and anecdotes about the shoot, including some choice (and favorable) descriptions of Sheen and Nicol Williamson. Oh, and yes, Leguizamo did indeed eat worms in one scene, much to the consternation of the animal protection person covering the set.

The whole second side of the DVD platter is given over to additional supplementary materials. There is a very good made-for-cable 22 minute 'making of' featurette; a further 20 minute commentary/interview with McFarlane (he speaks more about the creation of the comic, adapting it to various formats and getting the uninformed to bankroll his projects); character sketches, including comparison live action clips; three original McFarlane drawings including his very first sketch of Spawn, which has apparently never been published before; a good music video (very little of the movie appears) from Filter & The Crystal Method; a wild 'hidden' 'Parental Advisory' music video from Marilyn Manson; a trailer for the HBO animated program; and a passable cast-and-crew profile section.

Spawn (see Todd McFarlane's Spawn)

Spawn 2 (HBO, 91487)

The 140 minute program represents the 'second season' of the HBO animation program and is split evenly to two sides with a single set of opening and closing credits. It is fairly easy to spot the division points between each of the six episodes, and they might actually play a little better if one took some time between them. The episodes follow a complete narrative arc, in which Spawn's former wife and her husband are threatened by villains, who do not want an illegal arms market exposed. There is plenty of gore, drugs and other seamy activities, and the animated show remains an innovative blend of extreme style and penetrating metaphysics, but it also seems a bit redundant after the first set of episodes, as if the animators or the producers were apprehensive about breaking too far away from what worked for them the first time out.

The picture is solid, despite the many darkish sequences, and lines are sharp. The stereo surround sound is good and there is a Dolby Digital track with more power and intensity. The program also has a Spanish soundtrack in regular stereo and optional English, French and Spanish subtitles. There is also a brief interview with Spawn creator Todd McFarlane, a cast-and-crew profile section, and some minor DVD-ROM features.

The Specialist (Warner, 13574)

The script has plenty of inconsistencies, some of the action scenes are not particularly well staged and the stars, Sylvester Stallone and Sharon Stone, are not terribly convincing in their roles, but it is a fun movie and its pleasures are sufficient inspiration for overlooking its shortcomings. You may not find the love scenes convincing, but some of the death scenes are pretty spectacular. The movie has lots of explosions, both little ones and grand ones. Three like actors, James Woods, Eric Roberts and Rod Steiger, have almost as much screen time as Stallone in the movie's first half and do a great job trying to out-evil one another. The plot was at some point a real book and so retains a few more complexities than the typical mindless action concoction. Set in Miami, the story is about an ex-CIA operative hired to rub out some mobsters.

The film is presented on one side in letterboxed format, with an aspect ratio of about 1.85:1 and an accommodation for 16:9 enhanced playback, and in full screen format on the other side. The full screen image adds picture information to the bottom of the screen and takes off picture information from the sides in comparison to the letterboxed version. Although either is workable, we tended to prefer the letterbox framing. With purer blacks and a crisper focus, the image is consistently sharp, colors are glossy and fleshtones are accurate. The stereo surround sound has the sort of energetic mix one comes to expect from a film like this and the Dolby Digital track that is even better, with more detailed separations and a stronger bass. The 110 minute film is also available in French and Spanish in standard stereo and can be accompanied by English, French or Spanish subtitles. There are also a couple of production notes, cast profiles and a theatrical trailer that is letterboxed on the letterbox side and in full screen on the full screen side.

Species (MGM, 906034)

The highly enjoyable sci-fi thriller is about a movie-type team of experts chasing a monster that looks like a beautiful woman around Los Angeles. Unless you have a Ph.D. in molecular biology, the plot is convincing and fairly clever. The special effects are relatively inexpensive for a larger budgeted film, but are competent enough to convey the ideas of the filmmakers. We had to laugh at one invention the script writers came up with, as one of the heroes, effectively portrayed by Forest Whitaker, is an 'empath' who has a slight extra sensory perception. This enables him to tell the other heroes what the monster is up to and in doing so move the plot forward, which he does on several occasions, but there are other times when the heroes aren't suppose to know what the monster is doing, and so Whitaker's character gets sent off screen for some obtuse reason and only reappears when it is time to get moving again. Nevertheless, the concept of the four heroes works terrifically well and the horror film, directed by Roger Donaldson, is thoughtful, witty and exciting.

The dual-layer DVD contains both the letterboxed and the cropped version of the 108 minute film on a single side. The letterboxing on the science fiction thriller, which has an aspect ratio of about 2.35:1 with an accommodation for enhanced 16:9 playback. From an artistic standpoint the rectangular image compositions on the letterboxed version are clearly superior, but except for a bit of added confusion in one or two action sequences, those who don't like letterboxing will find that the cropped version is a viable alternative presentation. To show the woman changing into a monster, for example, the filmmakers sometimes use only a close-up of her eye, and on the cropped version, with the eye filling the entire screen, the effect is particularly thrilling. The color transfer on the letterboxed version looks great, with crisp, consistently accurate hues. There is a bit of grain in some of the darker sequences (the finale takes place in a sewer and a cave), but the picture is never compromised. The grain is somewhat more noticeable on the blown up cropped image. The Dolby Digital track is strong and the audio effects add significantly to the excitement, but the standard stereo surround soundtrack is much weaker. There is also a French audio track with Dolby Digital and Spanish with regular surround sound, along with optional subtitling in English, French or Spanish, and a theatrical trailer.

Species II (MGM, 907036)

Some bad science fiction movies aren't worth watching, but others can be fun, and the fun increases as time advances. In a couple of decades, much of **Species II** will seem as dopey as Fifties sci-fi movies do today. The film's scientific foundation is way, way off base, and if you don't crack up laughing now at its depiction of the first manned Martian landing (among other things), you will soon enough. There are lots of special effects, yet many of them already look a little dated. Additionally, Mykelti Williamson does a shameless Will Smith impersonation in his role as one of the astronauts. But, the narrative keeps moving forward and continuously evolves, so the film never bogs down in its stupidities. It keeps coming up with new ones, instead.

The 93 minute feature is presented in single-sided dual-layer format, letterboxed with an aspect ratio of about 1.85:1 and an accommodation for enhanced 16:9 playback on one layer, and presented in full screen format on the other. The letterboxing loses some picture information on the top and bottom of the image and adds a bit to the sides. Either framing seems workable. The picture looks super, with sharp, accurate colors and intricately detailed contrasts. The stereo surround sound and Dolby Digital sound are fine and deliver the sort of energy and excitement one expects of them. The film is also available in French in standard stereo and comes with English or French subtitles. There is a fairly risqué green tag trailer and a collection of four brief sequences featuring extra bumps and grinds that were trimmed to hold down the movie's rating.

Michael Madsen, Natasha Henstridge and Marg Helgenberger repeat their roles from the first film, chasing down more hybrid aliens with strong sex drives (what more do you need for a movie, right?). The director, Peter Medak, provides a commentary channel, too, talking about the shoot, about being a director, about working with the cast (he compares Henstridge to Jessica Lange), about the problems he encountered and how they were surmounted, and about how he overcame his doubts concerning the material. Well, somebody had to believe in it.

Specimen (Simitar, 7460)

Sort of a Firestarter meets the Terminator, **Specimen** is a pretty good low budget sci-fi action thriller. The hero is a young man of uncertain parentage. Fires ignite around him whenever he is angered. He travels to his mother's home town to investigate his background, unaware that an unstoppable being is leaving a wake of corpses tracking him. The special effects aren't fancy, but the story is good, the performers are pleasant and there are enough fights and fires to keep genre fans satisfied.

Fleshtones are dull and stronger hues are a little fuzzy, but colors are reasonably fresh and the image is workable. The sound is a lot of fun. There is both a standard stereo surround soundtrack and a Dolby Digital track. The Dolby Digital track has wider separations and more rear channel activity, although the dialogue track on the standard stereo channel is more clearly defined. The mix can't match a big Hollywood production, but it is an enjoyable effort nonetheless. The 85 minute program is not captioned.

Speed (Fox, 4109164)

A great DVD movie if there ever was one, **Speed** is a smashing, high velocity piece of entertainment with terrific performances, great stunts and a narrative that never slows down. The picture is in letterboxed format only, with an aspect ratio of about 1.85:1 and no 16:9 enhancement. The film's cinematography tends to be functional and disregards perfection, but the well-lit parts of the image are nicely detailed and fleshtones are accurate.

The audio track is full of effects that had us jumping out of our seat, and delivers a powerhouse punch during each of the film's big smash-ups. Details are always precisely defined, but what the heck, every production, artistic and emotional component of the movie is a thrill. The stereo surround sound is terrific and the Dolby Digital sound is even better. The 115 minute film is also available in French. It comes with English or Spanish subtitles ("Hay una bomba en un autobús") and a theatrical trailer that was so exciting it made us want to watch the whole movie all over again. Keanu Reeves and Sandra Bullock star.

Speed 2 (Fox, 4110400)

The image is in letterboxed format only, with an aspect ratio of about 2.35:1 and no 16:9 enhancement. The colors are sharp and fleshtones look great. The disc's stereo surround sound track is always in high gear, with directional effects, deep bass shudders, boat sounds, water sounds and a whole lot more. The Dolby Digital track is even better, with more clearly defined separations, very active rear channel separations and a deeper more pervasive low end. The 125 minute feature also has a French language track in standard stereo, optional English or Spanish subtitles and a trailer.

The movie is rather ridiculous and not well made, but if you abandon all logic and just go along for the ride, it can be engaging, particularly if you've got your sound turned up. Willem Dafoe is a wacko who commandeers the computer system of a cruise ship and makes life miserable for the passengers remaining on board, including Sandra Bullock and Jason Patric. The opening stunt sequence is so badly edited you can't tell what is happening, and the script defies common sense at every plot turn. No matter, you aren't going to show your friends the whole movie anyway, just the part where the boat crashes into the town.

Sphere (Warner, 15331)

An obnoxious science fiction film with a plot that has been used many times before, Dustin Hoffman, Samuel L. Jackson and Sharon Stone star as three science experts investigating a spacecraft at the bottom of the sea. The narrative is adequately constructed, but it is too obviously a reworking of things like *Galaxy of Terror* to get one much excited over the fate of the characters. Individual sequences also seem poorly staged, so that frights and excitements are diluted.

The picture looks super. The presentation is letterboxed with an aspect ratio of about 2.35:1, with an accommodation for enhanced 16:9 playback. The colors are consistently crisp and precise, and the image is spotless. The stereo surround sound is uninspired, and although the Dolby Digital track is stronger, the film's sound mix is dull. The 1998 film is also available in French in standard

stereo and comes with English, French or Spanish subtitles. The 135 minute program accompanied by three TV commercials and a good, unpolished 15 minute documentary about the film's special effects. Along with explaining how everything was done, the effects supervisor, Jeff Okun, also points out that Hollywood had best not forget how things were done in the past, lest money be wasted doing things in an expensive manner when a perfectly good, inexpensive alternative is available.

Jackson provides a running commentary, accompanied by a few scattered reflections from Hoffman. Jackson is personable and does a reasonably good job at telling the story of the film's production from his point of view, talking about the personnel he interacted with, explaining how he managed his own performance and sharing a number of anecdotes about the shoot. His talk is both humorous and informative, but its scope is limited by his perspective and he does run a bit out of steam in the second half. He is plain laudatory about working with Hoffman, but both actors share more complex insights on working with Sharon Stone. Hoffman also speaks about his experiences on the set, about working with the director, Barry Levinson, and makes several very oblique references to the film's failure.

Spice World: The Spice Girls Movie (Columbia TriStar,

Setting back positive role models for women at least fifty years, the vague, London-set musical has something to do with the pressures of preparing for a concert, but it is mostly a collection of vignettes featuring the five no-two-are-alike singers. Their confectionery music is readily addictive and, for those who don't care a whit about depth of personality, the singers themselves have an equally confectional appeal. None of it amounts to much, but there are scattered efforts to be humorous and fans won't care what happens so long as the girls are around to sing once in a while, which they do.

The movie is in letterboxed format on one side, with an aspect ratio of about 1.85:1 and an accommodation for enhanced 16:9 playback, and in full screen format on the other side. The letterboxing adds a bit to the side in comparison to the full screen image but masks off a little picture information from the top and bottom. We prefer the full screen framing. The color transfer fine, with bright, candy-colored hues and accurate fleshtones. The stereo surround sound is engaging, although the Dolby Digital track, with demure separation effects, is less appealing. The 93 minute film is also available in Spanish and French in standard stereo and comes with English, French or Spanish subtitles ("Mon petit esquimau, Tu fais bondir mon couer, Tu es bon comme du bonbon, Tu es mon dandy de sucre..."). Additionally, there is a concert performance music video (*Mama*), though it lacks the zest of the performance numbers within the film. There is also an enjoyable theatrical trailer that includes some fresh material.

Spies & Lovers X-rated (Vivid, UPC#0073214591)

A man and a woman who are spying on their unfaithful mates eventually hook up with one another. The story and erotic sequences are adequate, but unexceptional. Much of the action is set in an empty TV studio. Colors are reasonably bright and the image is sharp. The sound is strong. There is no time encoding but the program runs about 70 minutes and features Janine, Randi Rage, Toni James and Lysa Reese. The DVD contains alternate angle sequences and elaborate hardcore interactive promotional features.

Spies Like Us (Warner, 16885)

Chevy Chase and Dan Aykroyd star in John Landis' lighthearted 1985 espionage comedy, about two CIA rejects who are used as decoys on a mission to locate a secret missile base in Russia. Although the stars were nearing the end of the popularity phase of the their careers, they still exhibit a reasonable amount of comic energy which, combined with the spy spoof gags, makes for an amusing program. The narrative pacing is a bit off, letting the actors have extra time to milk their routines, and it probably seemed excruciating in a theater unless the rest of the audience was laughing up-roariously, but it works fine on come-and-go-as-you-please home video.

Fleshtones are somewhat bland and other hues are a little light, but the image is clean. The 102 minute program is presented in full screen format but, for Landis movies, that is not a drawback, since they tend to work better on TV than they do as theatrical presentations anyway. The stereo sound is modest and is adequately closed captioned.

Spike & Mike's Sick and Twisted Festival of Animation
(Lumivision, DVD1997); (SlingShot, DVD9814)

The 100 minute collection of grotesque short film features an intro and 34 shorts. Most of the shorts, however, exist to gross out the viewer, and the monotony of severed body parts, exaggerated bowel movements and other unseemly antics can kick in fairly rapidly. Here and there a short shows an artistic flair that allows its form to overcome its content—we particularly liked a piece involving painted finger puppets—but most of the time it just seems like the artists are wasting their talents on juvenile matters. The picture quality is fine, the source material is in decent condition and most of the shorts have modest audio tracks with whiffs of stereo. There is no captioning.

There appears to be no difference between the original release and the reissue.

Spirits of the Dead (Image, ID4420WBDVD)

The letterboxing has an aspect ratio of about 1.75:1. The color transfer is very weak, however, pulling the rug out of the Federico Fellini segment of the three-part Edgar Allan Poe anthology and compromising the Louis Malle and Roger Vadim segments as well. Colors are very pale, the source material has some wear, and the image is often soft. The audio track is available in a French language version and an English language version, with unremovable yellow English subtitles that provide an alternate translation to the English dubbing. Both tracks are somewhat noisy, with a limited range. The 1968 film runs 117 minutes, a combination of three separate segments from the three directors based on premises by Edgar Allan Poe.

The first of the three, directed by Vadim, is so often bad-mouthed by those discussing the movie that we have inevitably acquired a great affection for it, like one would with the runt of a litter. It stars Jane Fonda and Peter Fonda, or, rather, it stars Jane Fonda and has Peter in a couple of scenes before he may or may not turn into a horse who then draws Jane inexorably to her death. Sounds like Poe, right? The events take place in medieval times or in the 1960s. With Vadim there really isn't any difference. Fonda rides the horse naked, takes a bath with a parlor maid, and wears haute couture medieval leather outfits. Revival houses have been known to drop the segment entirely, but they are missing the point. The piece establishes a bemused and irreverent mood, cleansing the palate, as it were, for the quality of the following two efforts.

Malle's *William Wilson* is about a mean-spirited man whose bad deeds are interrupted by a spoilsport Doppelganger. Alain Delon has most of both parts, and Brigitte Bardot shows up with jet black hair. It is a forthright parable, told with such economy that one need not comprehend a word of the dialogue to understand exactly what is happening.

If the silly Vadim episode represents cinema at its lowest capability and the tight storytelling of the Malle episode represents cinema at its most efficient narrative execution, then Fellini's *Toby Dammit* represents cinema at its most transcendent. The piece opens with an airplane landing at an airport near Rome which, with a simple, grotesque red wash on the film, equates the descent into Rome with a descent into Hell. Terence Stamp portrays the title character, an inebriated movie star who, after milling with the demons and lost souls of Rome's café society, goes on a sports car joyride which ends with his decapitation.

Spiritual Kung Fu (Simitar, 7261)

Jackie Chan stars in the 1978 feature directed by Lo Wei. The cropping makes no effort to scan and action slips in and out of view randomly. The colors are passable but the image is often very blurry, to a point of creating eye strain, and damage to the source material is rampant.

The narrative is also weak, delving into a strained comedy involving ghosts that will try the patience of all but the most undemanding viewers. The plot is what we have come to surmise as the most typical of all the kung fu plots, in which the supremacy of the good guys' kung fu school is taken by the bad guys in an underhanded manner, and it is up to the novice hero to improve his skills sufficiently and retrieve the honor of his clan/school/temple. The film's second half, is stronger, but the antics with the ghosts, who teach the hero how to fight, are reminiscent of the antics of a particularly bad birthday party clown.

The film runs 94 minutes and has passages that feel a bit truncated. The audio also disappears for the film's final minute. The film is awkwardly dubbed in English on one channel and presented in the original Cantonese on another, without subtitles. It is accompanied by a brief interview with Chan, as well as a Chan profile and filmography.

The Sports Bloopers Encyclopedia (Simitar, 7205)

A badly executed DVD, the 90 minute program has no time encoding but is chapter encoded to mark its alphabetically organized segments. Each segment contains clips of varying quality depicting a specific sport or theme. Few of them are really bloopers. Some are good defensive plays, minor missteps (high school gymnasts blowing their dismounts) or crashes in sports, such as mountain bike racing, where crashes are expected. The problem is that the program does not play linearly from beginning to end. When it reaches the end of one chapter it skips over several before settling on another. The on-screen menu search is no help, because it is crossed-referenced (choose 'Boxing' and you get sent to 'Knock-Outs') instead of identifying the specific chapters available. We did find that manual chapter skipping from beginning to end could get us, eventually, to each sequence in order, but it was an ordeal few viewers are going to want to bother with. A narrator introduces each segment, but a bland musical score accompanies most of the footage. Some clips are repeated, a few are repeated several times. The 90 minutes does allow for a decent variety of subjects, but little of the footage is spectacular, funny or in any way exciting, and even less is worth viewing more than once.

The Spy Who Loved Me (MGM, 907016)

The 1977 Roger Moore James Bond feature, though it breathed new life into the franchise, still has a polyester feel to it, with some jokes, as well as the whole Giza sequence, seeming quite dated. The elimination of the villain is also uncomfortably cold-blooded. With the DVD, however, the film is definitely a pleasure to view, as the transfer captures the full spirit of original theatrical presentation. The dual-layer single-sided presentation presents the 125 minute film in letterboxed format, with an aspect ratio of about 2.35:1 and an accommodation for 16:9 enhancement on one layer, and in cropped format on the other layer. The cropping is rather pointless, however, and not worth viewing. The colors look very accurate and most of the grain from earlier transfers has been eliminated. The stereo surround sound is greatly improved over the older versions, and the Dolby Digital track has an even better disciplined bass and better defined separations. The film is available in French as well, and comes with English, French or Spanish subtitles ("Donde hay un océano, un biólogo marino jamás está de vacaciones"). There is also a bland theatrical trailer that pretty much takes one through the plot of the film, an outstanding three-and-a-half minute 'making of' featurette about production designer Ken Adams and the construction of the huge Pinewood Studios set, and a brief essay about Richard Kiel.

Stagecoach (Warner, 35078)

From the makeup on Claire Trevor to the plateau-spotted horizons, John Ford's 1939 feature is a perfectly realized work of entertainment, one that is appealing on every level. It depicts a precarious stagecoach journey running parallel to a group of marauding Indians. The passengers cross social strata in a pre-cliché manner, and unlike later iterations of the formula, their interactions, besides forwarding the drama, have workable symbolic overtones, with much to say about the America of yesteryear and the America of today. John Wayne stars, and he's wonderful, too—youthful, heroic, able, and just a touch innocent. Tim Holt appears briefly, but the contrast between the two stars and their later successes is aptly delineated. Perhaps most contemporary young stars follow the Holt model (an idiot grin and a puppy dog-like enthusiasm for action) because Wayne was truly incomparable.

The black-and-white picture has few errant markings, a slightly crisp image, and deep contrasts. The 91 minute presentation still looks a little aged, but there are no severe drawbacks. The monophonic sound is okay, and there is a monophonic Dolby Digital track that is even a bit stronger. The film can be supported by English, French or Spanish subtitles. There are some minor production notes, a very extensive cast and crew list, and theatrical trailers for six Ford and Wayne films.

Stalingrad (Fox Lorber, FLV5036)

Before *Saving Private Ryan* raised the ante, the 1992 German production was considered to be pretty much state-of-the-art for its depiction of the horrors of World War II. Directed by Joseph Vilsmaier, the 150 minute epic follows a squad of German soldiers sent to participate in the siege of Stalingrad. There are several effectively staged battles and lots of horrific gore, yet the film manages to maintain its dramatic balance and hold the viewer's attention as the squad, and the whole German army, for that matter, dwindles to a near-barbaric state.

The single-sided dual-layer release is letterboxed with an aspect ratio of about 1.7:1 and no 16:9 enhancement. The color transfer looks very good. The film, of course, is deliberately dreary, but hues are accurate and fleshtones look fine. The stereo surround sound is also very good, with strong separation effects and a sporadic but satisfying dimensionality. The film is available in English or German and can be supported by optional English subtitles. Two American trailers are also included, along with a cast & crew profile section.

Stand and Deliver (Warner, 16377)

Calculus never seemed like more fun than it does in the enjoyable 1987 drama about an inner-city math instructor who whips his students into numeric shape, probably saving many of their lives at the same time, and then must battle the experts who think that because the kids are poor, they cheated. Edward James Olmos—giving a spellbinding, Oscar-nominated performance—stars, with Lou Diamond Phillips and Andy Garcia.

The film is presented in full screen format. Fleshtones are a bit indistinct, but the image is reasonably sharp and most hues are fairly bright. The transfer is a bit old, however. There are some dark speckles in places and a little bit of artifacting in the softer backgrounds. The monophonic sound is fairly strong and the 103 minute feature is closed captioned with some paraphrasing.

Stand By Me (Columbia TriStar, 07669)

Most of Rob Reiner's innovative 1986 adaptation of a Stephen King story movie concerns an overnight hike taken by four young boys who are tramping along some railroad tracks, having heard that a dead body can be found a few miles out of town. Set in the late Fifties, the film explores their personalities and their coming-of-age, doing so with a freshness and a realistic tone that is rarely captured with such success. River Phoenix, Wil Wheaton, Corey Feldman and Kiefer Sutherland star, with Richard Dreyfuss in the framing sequence.

The picture is presented in letterboxed format only, with an aspect ratio of about 1.85:1 and an accommodation for enhanced 16:9 playback. The colors look fresh and contrasts appear accurate, but there is a nostalgic haze in many sequences and fleshtones are bland. The monophonic sound is strong, except for the pie-eating sequence, which has an annoying (and again, possibly deliberate) reverb. The 89 minute film also has French and Spanish audio tracks, optional Spanish and Korean subtitles, and English closed captioning.

Star 80 (Warner, 20013)

Mariel Hemingway and Eric Roberts star in Bob Fosse's take on the life of Playboy model Dorothy Stratten, and their performances are quite good. Hemingway, in particular, manages to convey what is going on behind her eyes in every shot. The 1983 film is well made and informative, exploring the jealous frustrations of the model's husband and the contrast of his collapsing world to the widening array of experiences her maturity brings to her, but it isn't all that much fun. Structured with flashbacks and fictional interviews, the inevitability of the conclusion hangs heavily over the drama and the tone is rarely inviting. Fosse's *Lenny*, which used the same structure, worked because it could play off Lenny Bruce's humor as a counterpoint, but there is less substance to Hemingway's nudity, particularly in this day and age, and the film has an academic air that it never shakes, no matter how good or gossipy the performances become.

Colors look fresh, but the image still has a mildly aged appearance. The film is presented in full screen format. Fleshtones are a bit pinkish and some sequences are a little grainy, but most hues look reasonably strong. The monophonic sound and Dolby Digital mono sound are a bit clipped on the high end and the centering of the musical score is surprisingly disorienting, but the film's sound mix was fairly sophisticated for its day and the audio seems in keeping with the rest of the presentation. The 103 minute program is closed captioned with minor paraphrasing.

A Star Is Born (Image, ID42135SZDVD); (Master Movies, DVD5523)

The Image version of William Wellman's 1937 Hollywood drama looks better, with deeper, sharper colors and a cleaner monophonic audio track, but the film is so intensely colorful that even the Master Movies version looks okay. Both presentations have overly dark sequences and a good share of scratches and other markings. Both audio tracks are somewhat noisy and aged, though again, the noise is significantly more pronounced on the Master Movies version. Image presents just the 111 minute film, but the Master Movies program is accompanied by an extensive cast & crew profile and can be supported by optional Japanese subtitles. Janet Gaynor and Frederic March star in the classic tale of rising and falling Hollywood stars.

The Star Packer (see **The John Wayne Collection**)

Star Trek: First Contact (Paramount, 15497)

Although the time travel narrative (the 'Borg' try to mess with the past) has plenty of logical shortcomings (what's to stop the bad guys from inundating the past with their attacks?), the 1998 film is reminiscent of the best TV episodes and gives the regular cast members a great opportunity to stretch their talents. The special effects are also appealing.

The image is consistently crisp and precise, with incredible chromatic detail and consistently perfect hues. The film is letterboxed with an aspect ratio of about 2.35:1 and an accommodation for enhanced 16:9 playback. The stereo surround sound is outstanding. **Star Trek** movies always have great sound, and the mix on **First Contact** is state-of-the-art, with numerous directional effects, crisp definitions and lots of energy. The music is superbly recorded, creating an atmosphere of high entertainment that few films ever communicate. The Dolby Digital track is ideal, taking full advantage of the separations and the bass. The 111 minute film is also available in French in standard stereo and can be supported by English or Spanish subtitles ("Ponga rumbo a la Tierra. Máxima velocidad luz"). The movie's original teaser trailer and standard theatrical trailer have both been included.

Star Trek: Generations (Paramount, 329887)

This is the one where William Shatner meets Patrick Stewart. The image looks terrific, and the special effects are nicely detailed. The presentation is letterboxed with an aspect ratio of about 2.35:1 and no 16:9 enhancement. The stereo surround sound and Dolby Digital sound are good. Generally speaking, the 1994 film's sound mix is wonderful, show-off type stuff, and the DVD delivers it successfully. The 117 minute film is also available in French in standard stereo and can be supported by English or Spanish subtitles ("He salvado galaxias antes de que su abuelo andara en pañales"). It is great to see the **Next Generation** characters doing their thing on the big screen, but the finale lacks the crescendo one expects from a feature film.

Star Trek: Insurrection (Paramount, 335887)

The best odd-numbered **Star Trek** movie ever (the ninth), it plays like a well made TV episode. The crew has to save a small colony from aliens who want to destroy it. There are some gaps in the logic (particularly concerning why the heroes don't know about the plot against the colony, since they appear, at the beginning, to be assisting in its execution) and there are more immediate gaps that apparently come from trimming the pace of the final act, but the show makes good use of all seven stars and has plenty of engaging sequences. Unlike previous films, the episode does not try to advance some greater plot or instigate other elaborations; it simply depicts one skirmish in the efforts of the heroes to protect the galaxy from villainy, which is enough entertainment as far as we're concerned.

The Dolby Digital sound is outstanding, bringing your viewing area right into the center of the action. Jerry Goldsmith's musical score is so effectively mixed it sounds like it is coming from a dozen differently placed speakers, and when the gizmos start shooting at the heroes, you start ducking right along with them. The standard stereo track isn't as interesting. The picture is presented in letterboxed format only, with an aspect ratio of about 2.35:1 and an accommodation for enhanced 16:9 playback. The color transfer is solid and the image is very sharp. The 103 minute program also has a French language track in standard stereo, English closed captioning, a teaser, a trailer and an enjoyable featurette (which is supported by French subtitles and English captioning).

Star Trek VI: The Undiscovered Country (Paramount, 323017)

One of the best offerings in the series, the film has an entertaining mix of action and character. This is the one in which it appears that the heroes are responsible for assassinating a peace envoy from their enemies, the Klingons.

The picture is letterboxed, with an aspect ratio of about 1.95:1 and no 16:9 enhancement. Hues look accurate, with a nice gloss, and the image is much sharp, with pure blacks. The stereo surround sound is super, but the Dolby Digital track is even better, with more separation detail, sharper definitions and a stronger, more varied bass. The 113 minute program, said to contain material not featured in the theatrical release, is also available in French and is adequately closed captioned. There is a standard theatrical trailer and a very nice teaser, narrated by Christopher Plummer, that shows a montage of images from the TV show and the previous films. And can somebody tell us why, with all this fancy, futuristic technology, the pilots of the Enterprise don't have force field seat belts to stop them from getting thrown on the floor at the slightest bump?

Star Trek V: The Final Frontier (Paramount, 320447)

The worst **Star Trek** movie of all, the presentation is letterboxed with an aspect ratio of about 2.35:1 and no 16:9 enhancement. Some of the smokier sequences are a little hazy, but generally, details are very sharp, hues are strong and fleshtones look good. The Dolby Digital encoding provides a few more distinctive separation effects and slightly sharper tones than the standard stereo track, but the two are about the same in quality and impact, even when the directionality varies between them. Both are superb, with a terrific dimensionality. The 106 minute program also has a French language track in standard stereo, English closed captioning, a bad teaser trailer and a somewhat stronger standard trailer. In the 1989 episode, directed by William Shatner, a fanatic shanghais the Enterprise and takes it to the 'center of the Galaxy' for a religious experience.

Stardust 2 X-rated (Vivid, UPC#0073215578)

Technically a sequel, though one need not have seen its predecessor, it is about a Hollywood talent scout in Nebraska. The heroine is a stripper who longs to be in pictures, and the two meet, though they don't get together in this episode. Other characters include the owner of the strip club, the film executives and a talking moose—don't ask.

The erotic sequences are fairly standard and the 68 minute program doesn't amount to much. The picture quality is reasonably good, with bright, solid hues and accurate fleshtones. The filmmakers employ digital effects in places, however, that are indistinguishable from artifacting flaws. The sound is okay and the program is accompanied by elaborate hardcore interactive promotional features.

Stargate (Artisan 60440)

Released before dual-layer DVD capabilities were perfected, the 119 minute film is split to two sides (the 'A' and 'B' identifications on the label are kind of buried in a catalogue number). The picture quality is excellent. The image is incredibly crisp, and the colors are intense and ultra-vivid. Every shot is stunning, and the image quality sells the fantasy from beginning to end.

James Spader and Kurt Russell star, with Jaye Davidson as the villain. By logical means, the two heroes journey to another planet where they discover a civilization very much like that of Ancient Egypt—again for logical reasons—enslaved by an alien being who pretends to be a god. The 1994 film is terrific fun—a grand science fiction adventure with real science and real adventure—and the picture on the DVD increases its appeal all the more. The picture is letterboxed with an aspect ratio of about 2.35:1 and no 16:9 enhancement. The standard stereo surround soundtrack is a little bland, but the Dolby Digital track is very energetic, with an active bass and lots of busy special effects. The film also comes in French, without Dolby Digital, and has English, French or Spanish subtitles. A trailer and a teaser have been included, along with cast profiles but, contrary to the jacket notation, there are no production notes.

Starman (Columbia TriStar, 04129)

One of the few advantages to having the cropped version of the 1984 John Carpenter feature on one side, along with having the letterboxed version on the other side, is that the movie's best moment happens in a long shot, where Jeff Bridges remains in character as the camera pulls away from the back of a truck, and on the letterboxed image he's just too tiny to see, but on the blown up cropped image, you can watch him stay in character even though he's miles away.

Bridges portrays an alien being who has morphed into the deceased husband of a widow, played by Karen Allen, who you get to see twice as much of on the letterboxed version, because in the cropped version the scanning always favors Bridges. Bridges makes his mannerisms look twice removed, as if someone inside his head were pulling switches and levers to make the body function. Like the limits of memory, the alien is not a perfect copy, but again, like memory, the truth of the emotional bond between the two of them supersedes the flaws.

The letterboxing has an aspect ratio of about 2.35:1 and an accommodation for enhanced 16:9 playback. The color transfer looks okay, with accurate fleshtones. The stereo surround sound mix is competent, but rarely interesting. The 115 minute program also has French and Spanish audio tracks, and optional English, French and Spanish subtitling.

Starship Troopers (Columbia TriStar, 71719)

As perfect a movie as there ever could be for DVD, **Starship Troopers** is a smashing production. The picture is letterboxed, with an aspect ratio of about 1.85:1 and an accommodation for enhanced 16:9 playback. The color transfer is excellent, with crisp, solid hues and accurate fleshtones from beginning to end. The stereo surround sound is very good, with plenty of power and a strong dimensionality, and the Dolby Digital track is even better, with very detailed separation effects and a thrilling bass. The program is also available in French in standard stereo and can be accompanied by English, Spanish or French subtitles. The 130 minute film is presented on one side. On the second side, there is an 8 minute 'making of' featurette, a dandy theatrical trailer, several deleted scenes (stretching out the romances), an alternate (slightly more cynical) ending, interesting screen tests for stars Casper Van Dien and Denise Richards that show how their performances were established, and a presentation of two effects-heavy sequences showing the scenes in various stages of development. The collection is not elaborate, but it is worthwhile

The director, Paul Verhoeven, and screenwriter, Ed Neumeier (who apparently was closely involved in all aspects of the production) provide a running commentary on one of the film's audio tracks. They don't say too much about the standard technical details, such as why certain camera angles were chosen or how the performers trained for their roles, they don't give too much background on how the production was developed, and they say nothing about the delays that were encountered at the end, when the film's release was moved from early summer to late fall. They do, however, spend time identifying and breaking down the special effects, talking about what the film's thematic intentions were (the similarity between Neil Patrick Harris and Tom Courtenay in *Dr. Zhivago* was deliberate), and giving some of the back story. They talk about the negative audience responses to Richards' character in previews and how they modified it, and they reflect upon Verhoeven's war experiences as a child and how that affected his art. The talk is not thorough or systematic, but it is informative, and gives the filmmakers a chance to answer the many critics who seemed to completely misinterpret the movie's pleasures.

Starship Troopers is terrific. We hear that only twelve-year old boys really like it, which is why it had a rather low plateau at the box office, but you can count us among the twelve-year olds. Much has been made of the slightly satirical tone the story takes in presenting the semi-fascist world government of the future, but less commented upon is what this does for the plot. In order for the later special effects sequences to have any real meaning, the characters must be established, but establishing characters can be a boring routine. The addition of the political speculation to the other images of the future creates a fresh and stimulating (even debatable) environment, keeping the viewer fully attentive until it is time to start killing the giant bugs. Even then, the film is intelligent enough to throw in a few brief doubts concerning the morality of killing the bugs—not enough to undermine the heroes, who are just doing their jobs, but enough to prevent the film from seeming like a single-minded us vs. them slaughter. Throughout the film, the odd political slant keeps the viewer slightly off-center and attentive to nuances. The action scenes are spectacular, and there are so many that the film's second half is practically one giant demo se-

quence. There is a lot of gore, but Verhoeven never lingers on it, using glimpses of horror to stir the imagination of the viewer.

Starting Over X-rated (Vivid, UPC#0073215522)

A simple but directly told story with a satisfying ending, it is about a woman who moves to Las Vegas after she discovers that her boyfriend has used all her money to buy another woman a ring. The erotic sequences are fairly ordinary and the image is a little dull and grainy. The monophonic sound is okay. The 74 minute program features Jenna Jameson, Anna Malle, Felecia and Dallas. The DVD also contains alternate angle sequences and elaborate hardcore interactive promotional features.

State Fair (Fox, 4110867)

The unblemished, crisp Technicolor picture makes it hard to believe the film was produced in 1945. The image is flawless, and the colors, though they do not glow, look so fresh and solid the characters seem to leap out of the screen. The sound is monophonic and comes across somewhat duller than the artificial stereo on the LD. The 100 minute program has optional English or Spanish subtitles ("Nuestra feria estatal es una gran feria estatal/No te la pierdas, ne siquiera llegues tarde/Desde dólares hasta rosquillas/Nuestra feria estatal/Es la mejor feria del estado"), a trailer, a cast & crew profile section and some production notes.

The film itself, directed by Walter Lang and featuring a Rodgers & Hammerstein score, is too pure and folksy for some contemporary viewers (the plot concerns a pair of romances that bloom at a state fair), but those who enjoy such Americana will appreciate the blue ribbon effort Fox has put into the DVD. Jeanne Crain, Dick Haymes and Dana Andrews star.

Stella Dallas (HBO, 90760)

Barbara Stanwyck stars as a woman of low breeding and poor aesthetic taste who wants the best for her daughter. In the beginning of the 1937 King Vidor classic, Stanwyck looks too alert and you can't believe her character would really become that dumb. After she commits faux pas upon faux pas, Stella's personality finally suppresses Stanwyck's class and the story starts to work. The ending, where she stands outside in the rain to watch, through a window, her daughter's wedding, is one of those grand conceptual moments that make people love the movies.

The black-and-white picture is a touch grainy in places and the image is a little soft, with mild artifacting in the less steady backgrounds. Contrasts are fairly well delineated, however, and wear to the source material is minimal. The monophonic sound is solid, and HBO has also spruced it up with an optional stereo surround mix that gives the music and sound effects a workable dimensionality. Purists will prefer the mono track, but as a variation, the stereo isn't bad. The 106 minute film is also available in French, Spanish and Italian in mono and can be supported by English, French or Spanish subtitles. There is a cast & crew profile section.

The Stepford Wives (Anchor Bay, DV10326)

Both Ira Levin's novel and the subsequent 1975 Bryan Forbes film (from a William Goldman script) have entered the public consciousness as a manifestation of the desires many men have to stifle the independence of their wives. 'Stepford Wife' is even used as an adjective to describe a woman who appears (usually from afar) to have taken on her housecleaning chores with a robotic sense of perfection, or to describe a husband's unreasonable expectations for his wife's behavior. This is an indication of both the film's success and its failure. It is very good at delivering the one clear idea of its premise, but the idea is so self-evident that everyone knows what the movie is about already, and there's nothing more to it. The film, which stars Katherine Ross and Paula Prentiss, is entertaining as a concept, but not as a narrative, and it might have been a lot more satisfying if the creators—all men, by the way—had found a way to let the heroine win in the end.

Fleshtones can get fairly orange at times, but the presentation is tolerable. The picture is letterboxed with an aspect ratio of about 1.75:1. The monophonic sound also has an aged tone with a weak upper end. The 115 minute is not captioned.

Stephen King's Sometimes They Come Back / Sometimes They Come Back Again (Trimark, VM6786D)

The double bill of ghost tales are both inspired by the same Stephen King short story. The second film is more a remake than a sequel. Both films are about a trio of Fifties hoods who come back from the dead to pester the people responsible for sending them there. The original film, from 1991, stars Tim Matheson and Karen Allen, and works best as a star vehicle, putting the actors through their paces as they attempt to cope with murderous ghosts bent upon revenge. The 1996 remake has fewer stars (Michael Gross is top billed) and way more gore effects, making it the more appealing of the two efforts. The same trio return, but from a different death scenario, and this time they're also trying to raise the devil and achieve immortality. Neither story is strong in the logic department, but some viewers will find each to be an adequate genre exercise.

Each film appears on a separate side of the DVD. Both films are presented in full screen format, which doesn't appear to harm either presentation. Although the image is a little soft in places, the picture on *Sometimes They Come Back Again* is fairly good, with bright hues and workable fleshtones. The stereo surround sound is adequate. The image on the first film is a little softer, fleshtones are a little blander and colors are a touch more aged, but again, the presentation is workable. The stereo sound is somewhat duller and rarely adds to the entertainment. The first film runs 96 minutes and the second runs 98 minutes. Both films are closed captioned in English and can accompanied by optional Spanish or French subtitles.

Stephen King's Storm of the Century (Trimark, VM7035D)

The 256 minute miniseries is the perfect DVD to watch during a blizzard. For one thing, it's long, like a blizzard is, and for another, it is set in the middle of a whopper itself, so you can feel cozy watching one while you're experiencing another. The plot has no crescendo twist and the hero doesn't articulate his arguments the way we would have, but it is an involving story that keeps you watching. Set on a small island off the coast of Maine, a mysterious stranger appears just as a humongous storm is getting under way. He murders an elderly woman and is arrested, but he seems to know the innermost secrets of every citizen, and guarding him in jail is not a fun task, particularly when the weather outside is so frightful. The show is nicely paced, so that just as you begin to tire of one set of events, it moves on to the next elaboration.

Split to two sides, the show is presented in full, with a single set of opening and closing credits. The picture looks good, with decent fleshtones and darker scenes (much of the film) that are solid and stable. The surround sound has those directional demonic whispers that get used a bit too often these days but still seem rather creepy. There are optional English and Spanish subtitles, and a cast profile section.

There is also an excellent commentary track by King, intercut with comments by director Craig Baxley. Due to the length of the program, there are also longish gaps between some of the comments. King's track is so good, however, that we wish he'd take a pause from fiction and do a book on the art of writing. Everything he says is fairly basic, but he instinctively finds the essence of every concept, communicating it clearly and succinctly. He gives a historical overview of the miniseries format and explains why, when he suggested that he do an 'original' story instead of one based upon a previous work, the network was receptive—networks, mind you, are rarely receptive to radically new ideas. He also breaks down the process of constructing the miniseries itself (he honestly didn't know how the story would end when he began), likening its nightly divisions and commercial breaks to the major

divisions and chapter subdivisions of a novel. In addition to this, he talks about the story, about the cast and about what works in the movie and what doesn't. He has no compunctions about pointing out where the efforts of an actor or others fall short. Baxley's talk is less interesting, but he does fill in details of how the film was executed (some of it was shot in Toronto, some in Maine; he also points out the different types of fake snow that were utilized) and other background information on the production.

Stephen King's The Night Flier (HBO, 91466)

If you think of the 1998 film as a kind of *Weird Tales* story stretched into a feature, it isn't bad. Miguel Ferrer stars as a reporter investigating the apparent attacks by a Cessna-riding vampire, who lands at small airports after dark and drains the blood from whatever personnel are still hanging around. The story has a couple basic twists and there are plenty of modest but enjoyable gore effects, but the whole thing only works if one's expectations are suitably limited. It has atmosphere and a comic panel-style story to tell, but little else to offer.

The picture is presented in full screen format only. The color transfer looks fine, with bright hues and accurate fleshtones. The stereo surround sound is limited in detail but has a nice dimensionality. The 97 minute program has optional English, French and Spanish subtitles.

Stephen King's Thinner (Artisan, 46296)

The director, Tom Holland, provides an audio commentary track. Although some of his commentary is redundant, describing what is happening on the screen, he is assisted by actor Joe Mantegna in recalling stories from the production and how various shots were accomplished.

Two aspects of his talk are of particular interest. Watching a video of the movie unspool, he complains about the brightness of the film's darker scenes, which is how they are presented on DVD, lacking the shadows and half images he intended these sequences to have. The video technicians have increased the brightness for video playback, compromising what artistry the film has. The second aspect concerns the film's ending, which was arrived at backwards, from test screening results, and has an unsatisfying feel of compromise and incomplete resolution to it. From Holland's descriptions, his original endings might have been better, if harder to accept on the first viewing.

All in all, the film is moderately enjoyable but too imperfect to create a lasting affection. About a man withering away under a gypsy curse, the makeup effects never come close to achieving the level of ghoulishness presented in the advertising art, leaving the viewer with a sense that the movie doesn't deliver on its promises. The presentation is letterboxed with an aspect ratio of about 1.85:1 and no 16:9 enhancement. Darker scenes are a little grainy, but colors are generally accurate and the image is clean. The stereo surround sound and Dolby Digital sound rarely interesting, though there is one gun fight that is pretty good. The 92 minute program also has optional English, French and Spanish subtitles, and an extended featurette that shows how many of the makeup effects were achieved.

Stepmom (Columbia TriStar, 02852)

Even the dopiest movies can become totally watchable if they are filled with movie stars who know what they are doing. The second half isn't bad, but the first half is pretty ridiculous, what with Julia Roberts playing an ace fashion photographer who's all thumbs when it comes to taking care of her boyfriend's kids. Her flaws are contrived and the narrative goes nowhere for a very long time. Yet, even at its worst, with Roberts and Susan Sarandon (as the mother of the children) doing their thing, the movie is difficult to resist, and it is so much fun watching them share the screen that multiple viewings are inevitable. Roberts has all of her little smiles and her aura of self-confidence (even when her character is blowing her babysitting chores), charming the viewer the instant the camera catches her, and then Sarandon enters and lords over the space around her like a queen. Hearts already beating fast, because of the talents of one actress, double in speed when the other appears. By the end, everybody's crying and the viewer will be hardpressed not to join in.

The 1998 Chris Columbus feature is in letterboxed format on one side and in cropped format on the other. The letterboxing has an aspect ratio of about 2.35:1 and an accommodation for enhanced 16:9 playback. The picture transfer looks fine, with sharp lines and accurate fleshtones. The stereo surround sound and Dolby Digital sound are rather uninteresting, and the music tends to surge in places. The 125 minute program has optional English subtitles, a cast-and-director profile section, a trailer and a brief 'making of' featurette that includes interviews with the stars.

Steve Vai: Alien Love Secrets (Image, ID5496SSDVD)

"An interesting thing about the guitar is there's no way that you can play the same note twice. Nobody really can." So says ace rock guitarist Steve Vai on the commentary track. Although he is painted in gold for a couple of them and there are plenty of colored lights, most of the seven instrumental music videos rarely waver from a straight-on observation of Vai fingering his guitar. There is a reason for this—the project was originally meant to document his playing in a manner that sheet music is unable to impart, and only became music videos after one thing led to another.

All seven cuts are terrific, full of energy and complex chord progressions. The stereo surround sound is great, and the Dolby Digital sound is even better, with more strongly defined detail and more kick. The image is a little soft, but workable, and colors are fairly strong. Four of the numbers have an alternate angle option. The video collection runs about 40 minutes (the program is not time encoded), but there is also an interview with Vai, in which he talks about his background and influences. A Vai discography is included, as well, and the menu offers one option that lets you program the order of playback for as many as ten slots. Vai's commentary is excellent, talking about technique, about the task of being a guitarist, and about the specific numbers and what inspired them.

Stevie Nicks: Live at Red Rocks (Image, ID4703LYDVD)

Stevie Nicks only sings nine numbers in the 57 minute concert program, and most of the songs seem to get dragged out with instrumental interludes. She's probably trying to save her voice, which comes across much flatter than it does in her studio recordings. The credits claim that Mick Fleetwood and Peter Frampton are also present, but they don't get in the way, which is just as well. A few optical effects create the impression that lightning is flashing during *Dreams*, but, in general, the material could have used more natural elements and fewer manufactured ones.

The show's audio mix, however, is quite good, and the unique Red Rocks acoustics are effectively captured and delivered—Nicks' voice stays in front, while it is echoes of the music that show up in the rear. The 1987 program is not as well lit as it is recorded. Although faces are clear, the edges are often quite red and fuzzy, and Nicks' Eighties mop of curls becomes a sort of floating, illuminated, unbound bale of cotton following her head. The program has a standard stereo track only and is not captioned.

Stevie Ray Vaughan and Double Trouble: Live from Austin, Texas (Sony, EVD50130)

The 63 minute program is a compilation of performances Vaughan made for a local Austin TV show during the Eighties. The picture is bright and intimate, and the stereo sound is super charged. Colors are brighter and fleshtones are deep. The regular stereo track sounds fresh and lively, and the Dolby Digital track has greater clarity, greater energy and a significantly heightened bass. It's super, and provides an ideal venue for Vaughan's hyper-powered blues guitar. There is also English subtitling.

The Sting (Universal, 20165)

Colors are very accurate and the image is finely detailed. The image on the 129 minute film is presented in full screen format, which is in keeping with its period tone. The monophonic sound has a reasonably strong presence. The 1973 Oscar-winner can also be accessed in French or Spanish and can be accompanied by English or Spanish subtitles ("Luther dijo que podiá aprender de ti. Ya sé beber"). There are a few production notes and a small cast profile section as well. George Roy Hill directed the period caper comedy, which stars Paul Newman, Robert Redford and Robert Shaw. Selling the film was not exactly a tough assignment. All they had to do was prove that Robert Redford and Paul Newman appear in the same shots.

Stories from My Childhood: Volume 1 (Image, ID5521FJDVD)
Stories from My Childhood: Volume 2 (Image, ID5522FJDVD)
Stories from My Childhood: Volume 3 (Image, ID5523FJDVD)
Stories from My Childhood: Volume 4 (Image, ID5524FJDVD)

A very fine collection of Soviet cartoons have been issued in a series entitled *Mikhail Baryshnikov's Stories from My Childhood*. It is unclear when, exactly, the cartoons were originally produced. Most run about an hour each, though there are shorter features, as well. Much of the animation (though varied) is not elaborate and the artwork is rarely striking, but the artistry is efficient and by no means bland. Each cartoon, most of which are based upon folk tales, has a very strong narrative and good character development. The cartoons have been given celebrity voices (including Shirley MacLaine, Kathleen Turner, Cathy Moriarty, Jim Belushi, Mickey Rooney, Harvey Fierstein, Bill Murray, Rob Lowe and many others) and mildly stereophonic musical scores. There are also French and Spanish language tracks, with credits for the primary alternate language voices (such as Catherine Deneuve) listed on the jackets. There is some speckling here and there, and the source material is usually a bit soft, but generally the picture quality looks fine and colors are decent. There is no captioning.

Three cartoons are featured in **Volume 1**, *The Snow Queen*, *The Wild Swans* and *Alice and the Mystery of the Third Planet*. *The Snow Queen* is a fairly straightforward telling of the Hans Christian Anderson tale, about a young girl who braves many hardships (and meets many friends) to save a young boy who has been possessed by the an evil winter spirit. *The Wild Swan* is a variation on *Swan Lake*, about a young woman who must undergo hardships and complete a difficult task to free her brothers, who have been turned into swans. Shifting gears slightly, *Alice and the Mystery of the Third Planet* is a contemporary science fiction tale, about a young girl who has a number of adventures with strange creatures on different, abstract-looking planets. The animation on *Wild Swan* is very much like a picture book, with stylized backgrounds and impressionistic details. The image on *Alice* is very sharp, with bright hues.

Two cartoons are contained in **Volume 2**, *Ivan and His Magic Pony*, about a young man who is sent on a series of increasingly difficult quests by a selfish king, and *Pinocchio and the Golden Key*, a basic telling of the Pinocchio story with minor variations. The narrative on *Pony* is especially pleasing, and the artwork on *Pinocchio* is fairly involving.

A brief telling of *Cinderella* on **Volume 3** runs through the tale too quickly to offer much pleasure, but the other cartoons are more satisfying, *Twelve Months*, in which a spoiled princess, who thinks she can dictate the course of nature, is shown up by a little girl who can, and the amusing *Wishes Come True*, about a good natured lumberjack who saves a fairy and is given, unbeknownst to him, the power to make his wishes come true (Edward James Olmos does the Spanish track). There is also the *Pinocchio*-like fable, *The Snow Girl*, about an elderly couple whose adopted child ought not sit too close to the fire, *The Last Petal*, which has a more modern animated look, about a young girl who has as many wishes granted as there are petals on a flower, and the dialog-free *House on Chicken Legs*, a kind of barnyard naturalists exercise, with nice artwork, set to *Pictures at an Exhibition*.

Perhaps the best of all the cartoons is *Beauty and the Beast* on **Volume 4**. Rivaling the finest efforts of the Fleischer brothers, the artwork is a dazzling blend of realistic human settings and luminescent enchantment. The story is well told, too. The animation is also fairly nice on *The Prince, The Swan and the Czar Saltan*, though it is not quite as meticulous. The narrative, by Alexander Pushkin, is about an exiled prince and a magic swan who helps facilitate his return. The animation is somewhat simpler and more stylized in *The Nutcracker*, while the narrative takes a slightly different perspective (there's more about the mice) upon the classic tale. The animation is equally stylized in *The Golden Rooster*, another Pushkin story, about a King who makes a deal to save his kingdom, but then falls for an enchantress and tries to cancel the agreement.

Storm Of The Century (see Stephen King's Storm Of The Century)

Storm Over Asia (Image, ID4672DSDVD)

In Vsevolod Pudovkin's 1928 Russian silent feature, a young Mongol has a run-in with capitalists at the market place. He escapes, joins the partisans, is captured and is about to be executed when the generals decide, because of some ancient documents he is carrying, to make him a puppet leader. They've chosen the wrong man, however, because he rises to the position and becomes a true leader of his people, leading the charge to overthrow the oppressors. The film is as fiercely anti-Buddhist as it is anti-capitalist, but it is a wholly entertaining work with humor (at the expense of the Buddhists), plenty of action scenes, and a rousing patriotic narrative.

The cinematography is often strikingly composed and there are a number of sequences that provide textbook examples of great filmmaking—one that caught our eye was of an approaching cavalry unit that shifts from single file to being spread across the horizon in a seamless long shot. The source material has its share of wear, but is in workable condition, with the worst damage occurring early on. Movement is smooth, and there are fresh English intertitles.

The stereo surround musical score accompanying the film, composed by Timothy Brock and performed by the Olympia Chamber Orchestra, is outstanding. A fervent mixture of all the appropriate genres and styles evoked by the film itself, the score is so good it is worth listening to with the picture turned off. Normally, we like to keep the audio track subdued to a modest volume on silent films, but this one we kept turning higher and higher, especially for the exciting and inspired finale.

The Story Lady (Image, ID5568BVDVD)

Jessica Tandy stars in a TV film that is generally designed for children, with a drama too simplistic and cliched for adults. Tandy is a widow who starts a cable access story hour that gets picked up for national syndication, only to be overly commercialized in the process. Stephanie Zimbalist co-stars as a workaholic single-mother producer, who has been ignoring her earnest daughter, who becomes Tandy's friend. The 1991 drama is painted in broad strokes and is easily dismissed by adult viewers, until the final and legitimately touching act, in which Charles Durning shows up as a judge who sets everything straight.

The picture is a little grainy and bright hues glow a bit too much, but fleshtones are workable and other colors are fairly accurate. The stereo sound mix is basic but functional. The 93 minute program is not captioned.

The Strange Love of Martha Ivers (Master Movies, DVD5524)

The awkwardly titled 1946 release stars Barbara Stanwyck, Van Heflin and Kirk Douglas in a story about blackmail and guilt in a small town. Heflin is an itinerant who happens to pass through his home town, setting off a panic with the town's power couple, Stanwyck and Douglas (in his first screen role), who believe that he knows their dirty secrets. If it had not been Douglas' first role, he likely would have switched parts with Heflin, but the odd casting doesn't hurt the film's lingering star appeal. Anyone familiar with the Production Code will anticipate what is going to happen to the principal characters after the first ten minutes or so, but the Lewis Milestone film is able to coast on the personalities of the stars, and it really doesn't need more than its collection of confrontations and romantic interludes to captivate the viewer.

The source material is generally free of wear and looks real good. The black-and-white picture is smooth and reasonably sharp. There are still a couple of splices and an occasional quivering artifact, but such intrusions are minor. The monophonic sound is passable, with fairly subdued noise. The 1946 film runs a full 115 minutes, not the 95 listed on the jacket cover. There are optional Japanese subtitles and a decent cast and crew profile.

Strangeland (see Dee Snider's Strangeland)

The Stranger (Master Movies, DVD5525)

That ultimate rarity, an Orson Welles film which made a profit on its original theatrical run, stars Welles, Loretta Young and Edward G. Robinson. The 1946 thriller is about the search for a Nazi war criminal in a small Connecticut town. Stylistically, the film is often as astonishing as every Welles movie proved to be, and while the story lacks the thematic resonance of his most highly respected works, it does clearly explore important themes, about America and Nazism, about living with evil, and about what can and cannot be hidden in a small town. Robinson is marvelous as the hero, and the performances pull the viewer smoothly past what incongruities there are in the plot.

The picture looks soft, washed out and grainy. The source material also has a number of markings and other indications of wear, and the full screen framing seems overly tight. The monophonic sound has plenty of background noise, though the audio is workable. The 95 minute program is accompanied by a decent cast and crew profile, and has optional Japanese subtitles.

Stranger by Night (Simitar, 7349)

A passable murder mystery with an unlikely but creative solution, Steven Bauer and William Katt are police detectives investigating a serial killer, but gradually, more and more clues start pointing to Bauer as the suspect. The picture looks okay and the stereo sound is fine. The program runs 96 minutes and is not captioned.

Strangers on a Train (Warner, 15324)

A 101 minute 'Hollywood Version' and a 103 minute 'British Version' of Alfred Hitchcock's 1951 murder swap thriller appear one to a side. There are three chapters that contain differences between the two versions, and otherwise the picture transfer appears to be the same on both sides. Here and there the 1951 black-and-white feature looks a bit worn and scratched, and it could use some freshening, but the image is incredibly sharp and textures are vivid. The monophonic sound requires some extra amplification but has no severe flaws. The principal differences between the two versions are a truncated ending on the British version and an expansion of the sequence where Robert Walker's character first meets Farley Granger and invites him to his private compartment on the train. There are no great revelations, but any variation on a work as significant as **Train** is fascinating and there are thematic enhancements to the relationship between the hero and the villain in the British cut. The DVD also contains five Hitchcock trailers, for

Train, *Foreign Correspondent*, *I Confess*, *Dial M for Murder* and *North by Northwest*. All are unique, as most of Hitchcock's trailers were, and most try to put the viewer in the hero's shoes ("You had made the mistake of speaking to a stranger on a train…"). In addition to the trailers, there is some silent newsreel footage of Hitchcock on the **Train** set, doing some promotional work, and a brief production essay. The program is also available in French and comes with English, French or Spanish subtitles.

Strauss, Johann (see **New Year's Concert Vienna 1987: Johann Strauss (Father and Son) Josef Strauss**)

Straw Dogs (Anchor Bay, DV10607)

Dustin Hoffman and Susan George are superb in the 1971 Sam Peckinpah film as a bickering couple who move to a remote farmhouse in the British countryside and end up defending it from drunken locals one night. While it is the film's action scenes that justify its entertainment, its biting, satirical portrait of marriage is what gives the drama a lasting resonance.

Contrary to a jacket notation that lists the letterboxing at 1.75:1, the aspect ratio measures approximately 1.85:1, adding more picture information to the sides and the top of the image but masking some from the top in comparison to other letterboxed versions. Although we wish that fleshtones could be warmer, the picture transfer is excellent. Colors, although a bit subdued in some sequences, are crisply defined and hues are solid. The picture is pretty much free of the haze that has dogged past home video releases and the presentation is highly satisfying. The monophonic sound is clear and reasonably strong. The film runs 117 minutes, and is not captioned.

Among other things, **Straw Dogs** is an intense satire on marriage. From the beginning, when two women are shown lugging a 'man trap' to a car, to the end, when Hoffman is driving in the same car, unaware that his passenger is a child murderer, the movie blasts away at the problems of domestic relationships and intimacy. The episodes during which Hoffman and George pick at each other take up more of their time than the moments when they are on good terms. Their ability to make decisions, or to 'act' (which has always been promoted as the film's ostensible purpose, though its real lessons are far more complicated), is hopelessly inept, but somehow they manage to survive, and, more pragmatically than heroically, to endure.

Street Fighter II: The Animated Movie (Sony, LVD49753)

Like the feature film, to which the animated program bears no relation other than their common video game source, the cartoon spends most of its 96 minute running time introducing the characters and just a bit at the end executing the rest of the plot. A Japanese production that is presented in English, it takes the characters from the game and places them in various locales around the world, with the bad guy kidnapping and brainwashing some while the good guys get to the others and try to stop the bad guy's plans. The animation has the Japanese style of mildly jerky movement and wide-eyed faces. The artwork is not as good as the best efforts we've seen, but there are touches of imagination now and then. The action is enjoyable, the plot is understandable and the show is reasonably satisfying, particularly for fans of the game. The fight scenes also have a bit of blood and gore.

The colors are bright, the image is crisp and some of the artwork is decently detailed. The picture is letterboxed with an aspect ratio of about 1.85:1. The stereo surround sound is reasonably strong and the soundtrack includes music by several rock bands including Alice in Chains. There is no captioning.

Street Legal X-rated (Vivid, UPC#0073214594)

A band of female car thieves trick their marks out of their autos until an undercover cop beats them at their own game. The story isn't bad and the erotic sequences are passable. Colors are a little dull—it's difficult to light the interior of a car for so much activity—but the image is sharp. Outdoor sequences are plagued by wind buffeting, but otherwise the sound is okay. The 75 minute program features Nikki Tyler, Anna Malle, Jill Kelly and Melissa Hill. The DVD contains alternate angle sequences and elaborate hardcore interactive promotional features.

A Streetcar Named Desire (Warner, 36041)

You can see the individual hairs on Marlon Brando's arm on the DVD, while on the LD they just kind of blend into the skin. The black-and-white source material looks mildly worn, and the increased sharpness of the DVD image may make the scratches and speckles more noticeable, but the improved contrasts and textures make it worthwhile. The monophonic soundtrack is passable. The *Director's Cut* version of the 1951 film runs 125 minutes and can be supported by English, French or Spanish subtitles ("J'ai toujours dû compter sur la bonté…d'inconnus."). There is a cast profile section and some production notes.

About three minutes of footage spread to about six different places comprise the additions in the *Director's Cut* version. Originally removed to honor the Production Code in 1951, the material is not flagrantly risqué and even viewers who have seen the movie many times may not be able to immediately identify the changes. Yet overall, there is a stronger focus on what the drama is really about, a clarification of the innuendoes that still, because the script was written with the Code in mind, had to remain innuendoes. The rape scene, for example, still ends with the breaking of the mirror before the rape is begun, but there is less ambiguity about what is going to happen and that it will go beyond the physical abuse which, in the past, the cracks in the mirror seemed to represent.

Streetfighter (Universal, 20216)

Jean-Claude Van Damme and Raul Julia star in the film, about a UN commando force out to stop a mad dictator. The action comedy, inspired by a video game, is busy and playful, with an enjoyable production design.

The 102 minute movie is letterboxed with an aspect ratio of about 2.35:1 and no 16:9 enhancement. The picture looks crisp, with bright, glossy colors. The Dolby Digital track is stronger and clearer than the standard stereo surround soundtrack, with better defined separation details. There is also a French language track in standard stereo and optional English, French or Spanish subtitles, as well as a production notes section and a cast profile section.

There is also a commentary track by the film's director, Steven De Souza, a 'making of' documentary, behind-the-scenes footage depicting the shooting of a couple scenes, three deleted scenes (from the film's choppiest sequence), commercials and trailers, a complete run through of the footage presented as a newscast on monitors at the show's opening (impressively, it is done in pretty much a single take), a short storyboard presentation followed by the appropriate clips replayed from the film, examples of the video game, an amusing text segment on the phony language used in the dictator's country, conceptual sketches, production photos, and advertising artwork. The supplements are also captioned.

De Souza tells stories about the production and about his own career on the commentary. He manages to convey a fairly clear idea of how the film was put together and points out, among other things, the clever ways that he spun the film out of the video game components.

Streets of Fire (Universal, 20236)

The 1984 Walter Hill film stars Michael Paré, Amy Madigan, Rick Moranis and Diane Lane. Willem Dafoe and Bill Paxton are also featured. Set in kind of a fantasy megalopolis where automobiles, clothing and other elements of style have a Fifties tone, while firearms, music and attitudes have an Eighties feel, the film is about a loner who is hired to retrieve a music star kidnapped by a biker gang. The movie's atmosphere is reminiscent of a comic book and its abstract locale was a turnoff for the general public, but the action scenes are satisfying, the music, by Ry Cooder, is pleasing. If you can relax, accepting the basic premise, then **Streets of Fire** is reasonably fun and (because it differs from the norm) refreshing.

The image is letterboxed with an aspect ratio of about 1.8:1 and no 16:9 enhancement. The color transfer is sharp and hues are rich, which helps the movie a lot since its glossy design is one of its chief assets. Another asset, the movie's stereo sound, is well served by the Dolby Digital encoding. The standard stereo surround soundtrack is weaker, but the Dolby Digital track has better defined separations and better controlled tones. The 93 minute film can also be presented in French in standard stereo and comes with English or Spanish subtitles ("Cada día compro y vendo personas que valen más que tú"). There are production notes, a cast & crew profile, and a music-oriented theatrical trailer.

Strictly Supernatural: Tarot & Astrology (Fox Lorber, WHE73008)

Two 50 minute documentaries on the occult are combined. Both programs are narrated by Christopher Lee, both have very nice looking pictures, with bright colors and a sharp focus, and both have reasonably strong stereo audio tracks, though little more than the background music has much dimensionality. The 50 minute running time seems sufficient for each subject and the programs are not captioned. The history of each practice is outlined in excellent detail, as is its method of function. Examples are provided and various people who practice the art are interviewed. Both essentially provide excellent primers on their respective subjects. Although skimming over the number cards, *Tarot* goes into extensive detail about the two dozen face cards and what they represent. Interestingly, *Astrology* does not go into details on the personalities and traits associated with each of the sun signs, but there is a lengthy segment discussing statistical studies that have supported aspects of the practice and studies that have shot down other aspects.

Striking Distance (Columbia TriStar, 53689)

Bruce Willis portrays a homicide detective booted down to harbor patrolman, only to find that the corpses have followed him to the river. The identity of the villain, not to mention his residence, is made fairly obvious early on, but the story is reasonably entertaining, the few action sequences are adequately stimulating and the performers are attractive. The 1993 film makes excellent use of its Pittsburgh locations, and the talented Sarah Jessica Parker co-stars.

The picture is presented on one side in letterboxed format with an aspect ratio of about 1.85:1 and an accommodation for enhanced 16:9 playback, and is in full screen format on the other side. The color transfer looks sharp and is consistently accurate. The stereo surround sound is suitably energetic and nicely mixed. The 102 minute program also has French and Spanish language tracks, optional English, French and Spanish subtitles and a trailer.

Stroker Ace (Warner, 11322)

Want some good ol' boy action? How about the 1983 Hal Needham comedy from Burt Reynolds' Loni period? Reynolds is a star NASCAR driver, though he never seems to win a race, and Loni Anderson is his sponsor's rep. Jim Nabors, who has appeared in motion pictures all too rarely, co-stars. There are some stunts, but not the go-for-broke kind that mark Needham's best work, and while the in-jokes may have cracked up the filmmakers, comedy aimed at the general public is limited. What the film reminded us most of was the Elvis Presley vehicle *Speedway*, without the songs.

The picture is presented in full screen format, though the framing looks fine. The color transfer is good and the image is sharp, though that doesn't necessarily help Anderson, whose ceramic complexion must have been a wonder to behold on the big screen. Colors are bright and blacks are pure. The monophonic sound is

fine and the 95 minute program is closed captioned with minor paraphrasing.

Stupid Little Golf Program (see **Leslie Nielsen's Stupid Little Golf Program**)

The Substitute (Artisan, 60449)

Tom Berenger stars as a former mercenary who poses as a substitute teacher at an inner city high school to crack an elaborate drug ring. The film has quite a few sequences set at night and in shadows, and the cinematography is not all that glossy, but the image is extremely crisp and the colors always look dead on. The program is letterboxed on one side, with an aspect ratio of about 1.85:1 and no 16:9 enhancement, and is presented in full screen format on the other. The letterboxing adds very little to the sides of the image and masks a lot more off the top and bottom in comparison to the full screen image, but either one works. The Dolby Digital track is more energetic and splashy than the regular stereo surround soundtrack, but both seem a bit hollow, as if the audio punches have no follow through. The 114 minute program is also available in French without Dolby Digital and comes with English, French or Spanish subtitles. There is a modest cast profile section and a theatrical trailer that is letterboxed on the letterbox side and in full screen on the full screen side.

The Substitute 2: School's Out (Artisan, 60481)

Identified as a sequel only because it has the same sort of plot, there is no direct relationship to the first **Substitute** film. Treat Williams stars as a former commando who takes his brother's teaching position in a high school after the brother is murdered. The plot has a couple red herrings but never really settles on a believable story, and its unlikelihoods—the bad guy is running a chop shop in auto maintenance class—make the first **Substitute** film seem like a beacon of verisimilitude. Nor is Williams exactly in the Jet Li category when it comes to martial arts, though he is a competent enough actor to pull off most of the action scenes. What is most disappointing, however, is the ending. Ideally, Williams' character ought to be moved enough by his experiences to take over his brother's position on a permanent basis, but instead it seems like he can't wait to get out of there, as if teaching the kids—he was doing a good job holding their attention—was beneath him.

The single-sided dual-layer presentation is letterboxed on one layer, with an aspect ratio of about 1.85:1 and no 16:9 enhancement, and is in full screen format on the other layer. The letterboxing adds nothing to the sides of the image and masks off picture information from the top and bottom in comparison to the full screen version. Colors are bright and the image is sharp most of the time, though it still looks a bit soft in places. The stereo surround sound is okay, but the dialogue is out-of-synch in places, and the Dolby Digital track, which delivers a stronger and better detailed separation mix, is in synch. The 90 minute program can be supported by Spanish subtitles or English closed captioning. There is a trailer (implying that it is set in the same school as the first film), some production notes (though an overview is apparently missing) and a cast & crew profile section.

Subway (UAV, 40097)

Luc Besson's silly 1985 feature is presented in cropped format and is dubbed in English, although Christopher Lampert does his own dubbing. Most of the dubbing, however, is disorienting, as is the severe cropping. Colors are pale, lines are indistinct and artifacting smears are constant. The audio is stereophonic, but the music sounds like it was recorded underwater. The 104 minute program is not captioned.

In typical French fashion, **Subway** is a chic film about the homeless. They live in garrets throughout the Paris Metro and continually outwit the security forces attempting to impose society upon them. If it sounds like fun, you're out of luck, because it is not. The characters speak in symbols that make less sense than most subway maps. They are rude and unsympathetic, yet the film approaches them as if they were the cutest group of misfits ever to panhandle a public thruway. Characters perform major actions on impulse because the filmmakers can't think of any other reason or motivation for their activity and it ends when everyone runs out of steam.

Succubus (Anchor Bay, DV10562)

A film that was rated 'X' in 1969, though it is rather tame by today's standards, has been issued in cropped format. Janine Reynaud, one of the groovy sisters in **Kiss Me Monster**, stars as a performance artist who falls under the influence of a hypnotist and then apparently, after having lots of hallucinations about past lives, kills a couple people. The convoluted story is tedious and nonsensical, although anything from the Sixties that has blood and breasts, not to mention lesbianism, is bound to appeal to some viewers. The European locations are also an asset. On the other hand, the filmmakers try very hard to evoke Jean-Luc Godard and *La Dolce Vita*, but they are nowhere near in the same league.

The cropping is often a noticeable annoyance. The source material is a bit worn and many sequences look overly pale. The hallucinations are purposefully hazy, but that, too, can be annoying after a while. The program is dubbed in English, but the camera is rarely pointing at the person talking, so it works okay. The monophonic sound has a weak range, but is tolerable. The 78 minute program is not captioned and is accompanied by a trailer that includes quite a few naughty bits.

Sudden Fear (Kino, K115DVD)

Joan Crawford is a wealthy heiress who discovers that her husband and his lover (Jack Palance and Gloria Grahame) are plotting her murder. She tries to turn the tables on them but things don't work out as planned. Crawford, who was nominated for an Oscar, gives an excellent performance in the 1952 film, without a hint of the campiness that usually crept into her roles during that era. Palance and Grahame are also terrific, and the film is a good combination of clever plotting, solid characterization and plain old-fashioned suspense.

The black-and-white source material is tolerable. Some reels look fairly sharp and others look somewhat warn and grainy. There is some displacement artifacting and a few other odd jiggles, but the flaws are not extensive enough to become distracting. The image presentation is adequate when one understands that this is not a lavishly preserved studio film. The monophonic sound is somewhat weak, but there is a Dolby Digital mono track that is stronger. There is little background noise and a nice sounding Elmer Bernstein musical score. The 110 minute feature is not captioned.

Suddenly (Master Movies, DVD5529); (Brentwood, BDVD921); (Madacy, DVD99040)

Sterling Hayden and James Gleason are the heroes in the 1954 feature, caught in a *Desperate Hours* situation when Frank Sinatra, as a contract hit man accompanied by a pair of cronies, takes over a house with a view of a train station where the U.S. president is scheduled to pull in. It is a tense and enjoyable thriller, and Sinatra gives a very believable performance as the frustrated villain.

The 75 minute film runs just 72 minutes on the Master Movies presentation, which appears to be time compressed, because we could never get it to synch up with the Brentwood version. Brentwood's presentation is letterboxed, with an aspect ratio of about 1.68:1 and no 16:9 enhancement, and the Master Movies version is presented in full screen format, losing nothing on the sides and unmasking the top and bottom compared to the Brentwood version. The black-and-white image on the Master Movies presentation, however, looks gorgeous. Brentwood's presentation is typical of what one usually sees of the public domain title. Although

watchable, the reel-change points are battered, there are other stray scratches and speckles, contrasts are weak, losing details in shadows and overlit portions of the screen, and the image is soft. On the Master Movies presentation, the source material is spotless, the picture is crisp and contrasts are finely detailed. The monophonic sound is louder on the Brentwood version and you pick up more atmosphere, but it is also somewhat nosier than the Master Movie's audio, which is thinner, but cleaner. The Master Movies presentation is not captioned and is accompanied by a few text supplements.

The Brentwood presentation is accompanied by a half hour look at Sinatra's career, using movie trailers that are in very poor condition. The quality of the clips is alienating (facilitating noticeable artifacting) and the narrative, which focuses on his film career, is superficial. The monophonic sound is tentative and a little noisy in places. The DVD is not captioned and comes with a Sinatra trivia quiz.

The Madacy version of **Suddenly** is substantially blurrier than even Brentwood's version, and the monophonic sound is more muffled. The full screen presentation runs 75 minutes and is not captioned.

Suicide Kings (Artisan, 60472)

Four young men (later joined by a fifth) kidnap a mobster, hoping to use the ransom to pay the ransom on another kidnap victim. The story jumps all over the place and eventually the viewer discovers that all is not what it seems, so that while the bulk of the movie appears to be about the by-play between Christopher Walken, who plays the mobster, and the five boys—including Henry Thomas and Sean Patrick Flanery—a deeper corruption is gradually revealed. The film is tough and humorous (they slice off the mobster's pinkie—fortunately not on camera), reveling in the nervous immaturity of the heroes and the determined confidence of their victim. When it comes time to wrap up the plot, however, there are several sudden contrivances, and the final, final twist seems to come up a bit short (surely, the protagonists were prepared for this eventuality). Because of the film's modern, complex structure, the entertainment is intriguing as it goes along. You have to concentrate to follow what is happening, and you are rewarded with a dry, earthy humor and a wide range of carefully measured and challenging moral quandaries (if you were each of the characters, what would you do?). While the ending may be a bit of a letdown, it is a sufficient validation for the mystery behind it.

The 103 minute 1998 film is letterboxed with an aspect ratio of about 1.85:1 and an accommodation for enhanced 16:9 playback. The cinematography is a little inconsistent in the low budget feature, but colors are stable and the image is reasonably sharp. The stereo surround sound is weak, but the Dolby Digital track is better, though again, the film's budget prevents a really grand effort. The film can be supported by English closed captioning or Spanish subtitles and is accompanied by production notes and a large cast & crew profile section. There are trailers (the earliest one tried to sell the movie as a comedy), posters and a brief storyboard sequence, as well as an interesting 'alternate angle' segment that allows the viewer to switch between a scene from the movie and a behind-the-scenes shot of the sequence being filmed. There is also a 3 minute clip from the film that can be played back with various audio components, such as the music or the sound effects, allowing the viewer to analyze the contribution each component makes to the play of the scene. The film's director, Peter O'Fallon, provides a commentary, too, over the film and the alternate endings (for the alternate endings, the commentary is on the first audio track and the film's sound is on the second track), accompanied on the film by producer Wayne Rice. O'Fallon shares many anecdotes about the shoot and does a little play-by-play, as well as providing some general thoughts on what he wanted to achieve and how well he thinks he succeeded.

A Summer to Remember (Simitar, 7277)

The TV movie is about two children who befriend an orangutan. One of the kids is deaf and both know sign language, so they are able to communicate with the ape, who was also trained in the language and escaped from his keepers in an automobile accident. Tess Harper and James Farantino portray the kids' parents (who don't know what is happening) and Louise Fletcher is also featured. The ape is real and the film is a passable family feature.

The picture transfer looks fairly good. There are a few speckles around the reel change points but colors are reasonably fresh and fleshtones are accurate. The image is solid and blacks are smooth. The monophonic sound is fine. The 1984 film runs 94 minutes, is not captioned, and is accompanied by partial filmographies of Harper and Farantino.

Summertime (Criterion, SUM060)

It is symptomatic of the weak material that no one has ever come up with a decent title for the Arthur Laurents play *The Time of the Cuckoo*. Adapted as a stage musical, it was called *Do I Hear A Waltz?* and for David Lean's film version of the play, it was given the generic title **Summertime**. The story is about a spinsterish administrative assistant who finally finds romance in the labyrinthine alleys and piazzas of Venice. The moral—that girls should not wait so long to fall in love—is embarrassing, but at least the film retains some dignity through the combined talents of Lean and Katharine Hepburn.

Hepburn's performance has moments of great strength, but the context drains her appeal, and were it not for the picture transfer the program would have little to offer. The 1955 feature looks fabulous. Every piazza, every church fresco, and the multitude of toy-like facades that make the city so inviting are reproduced with an accuracy which would be impossible to duplicate without a plane ticket. Even the reflections in the canals are gorgeous. Even the garbage is gorgeous. The monophonic sound and Dolby mono track are presentable. The 100 minute program is not closed captioned and is accompanied by a theatrical trailer.

Sundance (see **Film-Fest DV. Issue 1: Sundance**)

Sunday in the Park with George (Image, ID4586MBDVD)

Stephen Sondheim, James Lapine, Mandy Patinkin and Bernadette Peters gather on a commentary track to talk about the creation of the outstanding stage production. It is not a well-organized talk—at one point Sondheim begins to speak about how the show originated, but he gets interrupted and never comes back to it—and there are occasional embarrassing silences where they get distracted by watching the show or something and nobody speaks. Fans and even casual viewers, however, will thrive on every word when the artists do engage in conversation and humorous reminiscences. There are oodles of gossipy, behind-the-scenes stories about how the show was put together, lots of terrific technical stage talk and insight, more insight on stage acting, lots of trivia about the painter, George Seurat, and plenty of other information somebody who had just finished watching the show would want to know. At its best, the commentary does for making musical plays what most DVD commentaries do for making films.

The musical itself is a spine-tingling creation, about Seurat's painting of 'A Sunday Afternoon on the Island of La Grande Jatte' and the experiences of one of his descendents, also an artist, in contemporary times. The video was produced in 1986 and does a fair but not a great job at isolating important business while maintaining the full tableau. The picture is a little hazy, with slightly bland colors, and there are some errors, apparently on the source material, generating minor roll bar appearances in a couple spots, among other things, and even an audio dropout or two. The stereo sound is adequate, but a little confined. The 146 minute program is not captioned.

Super Bowl 1998 (see **The Best One Ever**)

Super Slide (Image, TE1001DVD)

The ultimate surfing DVD, it has three parts. There is a basic surfing documentary, which runs 60 minutes and talks about the transition of popularity from short boards back to the traditional—although refined—long boards, with an extensive history of the hundred year sport and lots of great surfing footage. The picture is sharp and colors are accurate. The stereo sound is fine.

There is also a 27 minute collection of interviews, with the director and with some of the experts who appear in the film (one of the film's joys is seeing the archival footage of the young, hot surfers and then seeing them now, as old guys). The most interesting segments are about the surfers who are hounding long time board makers, having them dig into their closets and pull out old templates from the early Sixties, so they can make boards by following the older designs, but with sensible updates. Another board maker talks about how lousy wood became when aircraft manufacturers started grabbing the best lumber, and how that segued into boards made of inorganic materials. Finally, there is a 29 minute collection of nine music videos—set mostly to the images from the documentary—featuring Sly & Robbie, Birth Through Knowledge, Purple Bosco, Fantastic Planet, Solid Foundation, The Cat Mary and others.

Super Speedway (Image, ID46220WDVD)

The IMAX picture has a window-like clarity (without the dead bugs and oil splatters one would normally get driving over 200 MPH on a racetrack) and the sound is as pure and crisp as it is loud and directional. Imagine your viewing room turning into the Indianapolis 500. Now, imagine how much trouble you'll get into, with people who just don't understand, when you raise the volume on your amplifier.

The 50 minute program follows the creation of an Indianapolis 500 race car, from its first designs to its first win, at the same time profiling the life of former champion Mario Andretti and his equally successful son, Michael. It is very interesting, particularly as the car undergoes various design tests and adjustments, and the Andretti family angle gives the show a human face.

The show is IMAX at its best, with an incredibly sharp, vivid, smooth picture, even when the camera is barreling down the straightway at 220 MPH. And the stereo surround sound is fantastic, only it's dull as dishwater compared to the multi-directional Dolby Digital track. VROOM! The DVD puts you right on top of the engine, right in the middle of the track and everywhere the action is, with noises zipping, zapping and open throttle roaring every which way, a veritable encyclopedia of Doppler effects.

There is also a companion 'making of' feature that basically runs as long as the program itself, though it could stand to lose about half its footage. The material depicting the staging of the race at the end is interesting, but there is a lot of superfluous footage and no more than moderate narration. Not to mention that although the program shows how the cameras were set up in every scene, there is never even a hint as to how the audio was recorded.

The programs are also available in French Canadian, Mandarin, and American Spanish, all in Dolby Digital, and come with a director profile. There is no captioning.

Supercop (Buena Vista, 13852)

Jackie Chan portrays an undercover cop in the 1992 Hong Kong production who helps a drug lord escape from a Red Chinese prison in order to break up his organization. The stunt sequences are fabulous, particularly the grand finale, which involves a helicopter, a moving train and a motorcycle, and the narrative is a little stronger than many of Chan's efforts. Michelle Yeog co-stars.

The image is slick-looking, fleshtones are accurate and other colors are crisp. The picture is letterboxed with an aspect ratio of about 2.35:1 and no 16:9 enhancement. The film has been dubbed in English, and the audio mix has also been sweetened in comparison to the original, slightly longer Cantonese version. The stereo surround sound is aggressive, and there is a Dolby Digital track with more distinctive separation effects and a stronger bass. The 91 minute program can be accompanied by English or Spanish subtitles.

The Superman Cartoons of Max & Dave Fleischer (Image, ID4388BRDVD)

Max Fleischer's Superman (Fox Lorber, WHE73010)

There is nothing comparable to the cycle of Superman shorts created by Max & Dave Fleischer for Paramount in the early Forties. The cartoons depict grownups instead of animals or children, and they represent possibilities in imaginative entertainment that have barely been tapped to this day. Created with quasi-rotoscoping, they combine pleasing imaginative fantasies with a serious, detective-film atmosphere and a futuristic/art deco setting. In some, Superman battles prehistoric monsters and in others he just subdues Nazi thugs (the cartoons were made during the war years and a couple have strongly negative stereotyping of Asians). There is a distinct lack of characterization, but this is compensated by the dark emotional mood and by the consistently unique images.

The 147 minute Image program is presented on a single-sided dual-layer platter and includes all 17 cartoons produced by the Fleischers, plus the Private SNAFU short *SNAFUperman*. The picture quality looks super, too. Although there are some minor speckles and scratches, hues are solid, lines are crisp, and the colors are accurate. The monophonic sound is strong and clearer. There is no captioning.

A subset of the cartoons has been released by Fox Lorber. The picture transfers are nowhere near as nice as Image's DVD, but the Fox Lorber release does have one advantage—the soundtracks have been remastered in stereo, which is great fun, particularly on the Dolby Digital track, which has well-defined rear channel effects and a terrific boom of a bass. There is no captioning. Nine cartoons are featured in the 100 minute collection, the original short, *The Mechanical Monsters, Electronic Earthquake, Billion Dollar Limited, Arctic Giant, The Bulleteers, Magnetic Telescope, Volcano* and *Terror on the Midway*, plus a bonus Fleischer featurette, *Play Safe*, about a dog saving a boy on a train.

Superthruster Sly and Robbie (Palm Pictures, PPDVD70022)

The 'DVD single,' contains one music number in Dolby Digital, *Zen Concrete*, set to images from *Ghost in the Shell*, one music number in standard stereo, *Superthruster*, set to images of the musicians obscured by artistically applied video interference, an alternate mix of *Superthruster* with a different vocalist and sax player, set to the same images, and a 6 minute interview with the musicians (which could use subtitles). Each video runs about 4 minutes. The music is a habit-forming, hyped-up Jamaican electronic funk, and the Dolby Digital track is substantially stronger than the standard track. Additionally, there is a DVD-ROM section containing a lot more music (basically, a CD's worth), essays about the musicians and a number of still photos. The DVD also contains a lot of promos for other programming.

The Surgeon (Simitar, 7343)

A psycho doctor has developed an adrenaline serum (he needs bodies to do it) that keeps him alive after bad accidents and other things, so even when the heroes locate him and eliminate him, their job is not completely over. Isabel Glasser and James Remar star, with Malcolm McDowell and Peter Boyle making guest appearances. The 100 minute film has some good gore effects but isn't very intriguing. Fleshtones are a little pale and the image is slightly grainy, but workable. The Ultra-Stereo surround sound is erratic but reasonably energetic in places. There is no captioning.

Swan Lake (see Rudolf Nureyev / Margot Fonteyn in Tchaikovsky's Swan Lake)

Swashbuckler (Universal, 20514)

A pirate film from the mid-seventies that stars Robert Shaw—like many Universal films in that era, the movie has a manufactured feel to it, with extras always looking like extras and backlot sets always looking like backlot sets. Adding to the problem, the director, James Goldstone, never finds the right balance between comedy and action, and each tends to undercut the other. Shaw is engaging and the final act is the most pleasing, but many viewers have difficulty making it that far. James Earl Jones, Genevieve Bujold, Beau Bridges and Peter Boyle co-star.

The 1976 feature is presented in letterboxed format, with an aspect ratio of about 2.35:1 and an accommodation for enhanced 16:9 playback. The picture is sharp, colors are bright and hues are well defined, with accurate fleshtones. The monophonic sound is adequate. The 102 minute feature is also available in French and can be supported by English or Spanish subtitles. There is a theatrical trailer that sounds like a throwback from the early Sixties, a cast-and-director profile section and a few production notes.

Sweet As The Come X-rated (Vivid, UPC#0073215503)

The erotic sequences are nicely staged and the narrative, about an older couple and a younger couple who swap partners, isn't bad. The picture is a little murky, though colors are reasonably strong when the lighting is good. The sound is adequate, although you can hear the crew shouting instructions to the performers in a couple spots. The DVD is not time encoded but appears to run a little over an hour. Raylene, Alexandra Silk and Inari Vachs are featured. The DVD also contains alternate angle sequences and elaborate hardcore interactive promotional features.

The Sweet Hereafter (New Line, N4654)

"Hey, let's invite a bunch of people over, make a big bowl of popcorn and watch that movie about all the children being killed in a school bus accident!" or "Hey, let's turn down the lights, pour some drinks, stretch out on the couch and watch that movie about all the children being killed in a school bus accident…" No matter how you approach it, the 25-cent summary of **The Sweet Hereafter** is its own worst enemy. The 1997 film, directed by Atom Egoyan, is a penetrating entertainment, with an ending that resonates long after the film's conclusion, but getting people to pay attention after they learn what it is about is a challenge. The film uses the accident as a tease, structured with flashbacks so that it is not even shown until the halfway point, and then only in a long shot. Like that long shot, the movie is emotionally distanced—very distanced—and it has to be, because it is not its intention to be a handkerchief movie—it would drown as quickly as the children on the bus if its purpose was to generate tears. Yet it does treat the accident and the victims with respect as it explores, through the eyes of the nicest, sincerest ambulance-chasing lawyer you could ever meet, the lingering grief and frustration of the town that lost most of its children because of one icy patch on a hilly road. The film explores the psychology of the characters rather than the emotions, and its achievement is that it holds the emotions at bay so you can see the psychology clearly and learn about yourself and those around you through its lessons. Egoyan's mastery of style and the story's little surprise twists are so magnetic that the movie is not only worth viewing, but worth viewing many times. So forgive us for the smarmy opening to this review, but if it kept you reading it did its job. Besides, while **Sweet Hereafter** may not be a popcorn movie, it is perfectly appropriate for the drinks/lights down/couch viewing experience.

The picture is letterboxed with an aspect ratio of about 2.35:1 and an accommodation for enhanced 16:9 playback, and represents the intended framing of the image as Egoyan designed it. Colors are crisp and vivid, fleshtones are accurate, whites are white and the image quality throughout is captivating. The stereo surround sound has slightly weaker tonal definitions than the Dolby Digital track. Mychael Danna's musical score has been isolated on another track, again in Dolby Digital. Watching the film's images with just the musical score can also be a haunting experience. The 116 minute film is available in French in Dolby Digital as well and comes with English, French or Spanish subtitles.

In addition to an audio commentary from Egoyan and novelist Russell Banks, the single-sided dual-layer DVD presents a half hour reading-and-discussion seminar, with Banks reading excerpts from the novel for comparison to specific parts of the film and discussing the transition of the book into the film with Egoyan. There is also a half hour interview with Egoyan conducted by Charlie Rose from Rose's PBS program. Both sequences are mildly redundant when compared to the commentary track, but they do offer some fresh perspectives as well as a chance to look the film's creators in the eye. There are U.S. and Canadian theatrical trailers (the Canadian trailer sells the film much better, though pretends the movie is a courtroom drama). Additionally, in the cast profile section, there are video interview clips with each of the principal cast members as they talk about their roles and about working with Egoyan. Finally, the film includes extensive allusions to Robert Browning's *The Pied Piper of Hamelin*, and the DVD presents the complete poem and artwork from a book that is used by the characters.

Sweet Talker (Pioneer, DVD68918)

Brian Brown is a con artist who attempts to scam a defunct seaside town with a phony treasure scheme, but ends up falling in love and helping the town's economy in spite of himself. The story is so predictable you wonder when Brown is going to break into 'Seventy-Six Doubloons,' but the South Australia location is appealing, and the 1990 film is pleasantly humorous. Karen Allen co-stars.

It also helps that the picture and sound are in good shape. The image looks super, with bright, vivid colors and crisp details. The stereo surround sound is also strong and although the mix is not elaborate, tones are well defined. The 91 minute program is not captioned.

Swept Away (Fox Lorber, FLV5001)

Lina Wertmüller's 1974 film would in all probability be reviled had it been directed by a man. Giancarlo Giannini and Mariangela Melato star in what is a fairly basic movie situation, a working class guy and a rich woman abandoned on a desert island. Their romance is spiced up with what might best be called the Ayn Rand School of Interpersonal Relationships, but it is also deliberately cast in political terms, with the 'poor' character and the 'rich' character swapping positions of power when they must fend for themselves on the island. The humorist in us has always wanted to see Lea Massari stroll in from behind a rock at the height of the drama, but Wertmüller's confident visual style and the film's basic psychological outrageousness (not to mention the to-die-for attractiveness of both performers) has enabled **Swept Away** to endure as a legitimate classic, carrying just enough satire to fend off those who would condemn or censor its sexual fantasies.

The letterboxing has an aspect ratio of about 1.85:1 and no 16:9 enhancement. The image looks very nice, particularly since much of the film is set in the summer sun. Colors are rich and fleshtones are nicely detailed. The monophonic sound is acceptable. The 116 minute film is in Italian with optional English subtitling.

Swimsuit (Simitar, 7271)

A 1984 95 minute TV film that feels a bit like a pilot, William Katt stars as the head of an advertising agency who takes six 'beginners' as models for a summer-long bathing suit shoot with the understanding that a couple of them will win a long term contract. The narrative, which has comical overtones, focuses on the characters and how the gig changes their lives. We've mentioned this before with other films, but it applies again here—because the movie was designed for TV there is something compulsively watchable

about it, even though on a cognitive level it is pretty dopey. Catherine Oxenberg is also featured, with Cyd Charisse in a kind of guest star role, as the client. The picture quality looks fairly good. Colors are bright, the tan, taut bodies of the stars look delectable, and the image is reasonably sharp. The monophonic sound is fine and the program is accompanied by partial filmographies for Katt and Charisse. The program is not captioned.

Swing Craze (Simitar, 7577)
Swing Craze & Next Generation Swing (Simitar, 7578)

We could do the one-two and the three-four, but it took the longest time to figure out the five-six. No matter, Simitar has released the enjoyable program of instruction separately and in a bundle with a CD of swing music. **Swing Craze** actually contains three programs, the title program, also identified as *Get into the Swing of Things*, which is a half hour overview of the revitalized swing craze and its roots, *Club Swinging*, also called *Swing Craze Six Count Basic Swing*, which is a 50 minute instructional of the basic steps and arm movements, and *Advanced Swinging*, a more complex 16 minute instructional of 'East Coast Swing.' The longer instructional has fresh colors and a solid picture. The other two are a little a bit grainy but acceptable. The stereo sound is not elaborate, but is functional, and the programs are not captioned.

The documentary is not well organized, but gives the viewer a decent taste of what all the excitement is about. The longer instructional is the best part of the collection. A methodical effort takes the viewer from putting one foot in front of the other to doing everything but those wild somersaults, and you can always use a repeat loop if you're having trouble getting something down. The longer instructional has one instructor who speaks and demonstrates with his partner, as several other pairs also demonstrate the moves. In the shorter instructional, it is just a single pair of instructors, but both speak.

The CD opens with a Louis Prima number and then goes on to 13 contemporary recordings of swing classics, which have blander orchestrations than the original recordings but better, smoother stereo.

Swingers (Buena Vista, 14378)

Jan Favreau stars as a frustrated young man between relationships and Vince Vaughn is his fast-talking buddy. The over-praised 1997 comedy ends correctly but is generally too male-oriented and smug to have a broad appeal. The females are all caricatures and the males, who dominate the show's point-of-view, are boorish, making the film work more like the screenwriter's wish fulfillment than an entertainment. There is some humor in the foolishness of the heroes' impulses, but the sentiment of those impulses is not as easy to laugh at.

The picture is sharp, with reasonably bright hues and accurate fleshtones. The image is letterboxed with an aspect ratio of about 1.85:1 and no 16:9 enhancement. The stereo surround sound is okay. Separation effects are modest, but there is a nice musical score (swing music) that is effectively presented. The 96 minute film can be supported by English or Spanish subtitles and comes with a theatrical trailer.

The Swinging Cheerleaders (Anchor Bay, DV10826)

There was, as film historian Johnny Legend and director Jack Hill point out so succinctly on the commentary track, a brief flowering genre known as 'the cheerleader film,' of which this is a pantheon title. Jo Johnston, Colleen Camp, Rainbeaux Smith and Rosanne Katon are featured in the 1974 production (begun in January, in theaters by May), which actually has a limited amount of nudity and enough of a narrative (a reporter joins the squad and uncovers a point-shaving scam) to keep you from leaving the drive-in. Today the film endures for its quaint simplicity, its post-hippie pre-disco production design, and what nudity it does have.

The picture is letterboxed with an aspect ratio of about 1.66:1 and no 16:9 enhancement. The color transfer looks great and wear is minimal. Hues are bright and fleshtones are passable. The monophonic sound is fine and there is no captioning. The 91 minute program is accompanied by a couple TV commercials and a profile of Hill. On the commentary track, Hill, prompted by Legend, tells you everything you could ever want to know about the movie and its personnel (including who slept with whom), as well as a lot about Hill's brand of filmmaking and what it was like being in the center of the swinging Sixties and Seventies.

The Swiss Conspiracy (Simitar, 7251)

The 1975 feature stars David Janssen, with Ray Milland, Senta Berger, Elke Sommer, John Saxon and others. The film's official running time is 88 minutes, but the jacket lists the running time at 85 minutes and it actually clocks in at 82. It appears to be a TV print, with four letter words blanked out, so it wouldn't be surprising if a bedroom scene or two were missing as well. The picture quality is very weak. It has a sort of second hand look, with faded colors and soft edges, as well as a number of scratches and splices. The monophonic sound is extremely muted and is not captioned. Directed by Jack Arnold, the movie itself isn't bad and we must admit we had a good time watching it. Janssen is a private investigator hired by a Swiss banker to investigate the blackmailing of several important clients. The solution to the mystery is clever (the film's title is a big clue) and the stars are enjoyable. The disco scene is also a gas.

SwitchBack (Paramount, 331207)

A rather convoluted tale about an FBI agent chasing after his son's kidnapper and what one assumes is a related subplot about a young man who is hitchhiking through the Rocky Mountains, Dennis Quaid, Danny Glover and Jared Leto star, with R. Lee Ermy delivering a fine supporting performance as a sheriff attempting to balance the pressures of his investigation into a local murder by the kidnapper with the politics of an election. The first half of the film is stuffed with red herrings, but everything is laid out in the second half, turning the film into a straightforward chase thriller. Except for the performances, there's no art to it, but it is mindlessly watchable.

The presentation is letterboxed with an aspect ratio of about 2.35:1 and no 16:9 enhancement. The color transfer looks super, with vivid, crisp hues, and the stereo surround sound and Dolby Digital sound are fine. The audio track has a number of well-applied separation effects and plenty of punch when the drama calls for it. The 118 minute program is also available in French in standard stereo and can be supported by English or Spanish subtitles. A theatrical trailer that deftly avoids giving away spoilers is also included.

T

Taboo 17 X-rated (Metro, UPC#5135312682)

A female cat burglar takes advantage of distracted couples to go about her business, although sometimes she just can't help but get in on the distractions. The narrative is not elegantly executed, but the erotic sequences are imaginative.

The 90 minute film is split to two sides, running a little over 50 minutes on one side and a bit over 30 minutes on the other. The picture quality is outstanding, with bright, vivid hues and fleshtones, and the stereo sound is fine.

The program is also accompanied by about 20 minutes of behind-the-scenes footage, which lets you see the performers with their guards down, and a jokey commentary track by the director and a couple other members of the crew. There is some valid production information within the commentary about the camera setups, the length of the working day, and other such details, but

there is also a lot of fooling around, so it is difficult to tell when they are being serious and when they are not. The program also has a multiple angle option and other hardcore promotional materials. Misty Rain, Roxanne Hall, Syndee Steele, Inari Vachs and Caressa Savage are featured.

Take the Money and Run (Anchor Bay, DV10835)

Woody Allen's first original feature, the 1969 crime film spoof has a badly paced narrative, but its scattershot humor has endured, while its structure has actually become more common and easier to tolerate as the years have passed. Allen portrays a nebbish bank robber, who tries to raise a family while in and out of prison. Everybody has one gag sequence from the film that they really enjoy (we have always been amused when the hero is sent into 'the hole' with an insurance salesman) and, in multiple viewings, it is easy to overlook the failed one-liners and focus on the humor Allen is able to generate from the material and the performances.

The picture is presented on one side in full screen format and on the other side in letterboxed format, with an aspect ratio of about 1.66:1 and no 16:9 enhancement. The letterboxing masks picture information off the top and bottom of the image and doesn't appear to add anything to the sides. The color transfer looks very nice. Fleshtones are accurate, the black-and-white sequences are pure and other hues are bright. The image is sharp, and the source material is in decent shape. Although there are a couple unintentional scratches, they seem to fit right in with the intentional ones. The monophonic sound is reasonably strong and the 85 minute program is not captioned.

Tai Chi II (Tai Seng, 46114)

The breezy kung-fu movie has plenty of gravity-defying fights and no overt fantasy components. Directed by Yuen Woo Ping, who also did the similarly engaging **Wing Chun**, Jacky Wu stars as the son of a martial arts expert just coming into his own, who meets a nice young woman and helps her and her friends spoil the plans of several evil opium merchants. The narrative has a few loose ends—one major character disappears for a long period of time and then reappears without explanation—but the film is brisk and enjoyable, matching the inventive fight choreography with appealing characters and pleasant humor.

The letterboxed image is set a little high on the screen, and the aspect ratio is about 1.66:1 with no 16:9 enhancement. The picture is much sharper than the LD, which looks hazy in comparison, and colors are better detailed. The image retains some mild imperfections associated with Hong Kong productions, including softness, periodic grain, scattered speckles, a blurriness in the most intense hues and somewhat bland fleshtones, but overall the presentation is passable. The monophonic sound is available in English, Mandarin and Cantonese, with optional English subtitles. Music tends to sound a bit wobbly on the English track. There are also trailers and profiles of the cast and the director.

A Tale of Two Kitties (Simitar, 7201)

Recommended for ages two to seven—though seven would be pushing it—it is a blandly animated program about two cats living in a farmhouse. A Polish production that has been adequately dubbed into English, the cartoon runs about an hour and has several songs to bridge the minor narrative advances. The story is primarily about anticipating the arrival of a third cat, who is coming with a human to visit from the city. There are digressions, and the animals imagine what the cat will be like. The story is flaccid and the artwork is free of complexity. The animation is so simplistic that a viewer need not worry about video artifacts. Colors are bright. Some reds are a little fuzzy but otherwise the image is sharp. Don't hold us to it, but the soundtrack appears to be mildly stereophonic. It is adequately delivered. There is no time encoding or captioning.

Tales from the Crypt Presents Bordello of Blood (Image, ID4225USDVD)

Tales from the Crypt Presents Demon Knight (Image, ID4233USDVD)

Both of the enjoyable horror exercises are letterboxed, with an aspect ratio of about 1.85:1 and an accommodation for enhanced 16:9 playback. The colors on **Bordello of Blood** have deep hues and grain is minimal. The color quality on **Demon Knight** looks fine, with solid hues and accurate fleshtones, though there is some wear-related speckling in evidence here and there. The stereo sound on **Demon Knight** is okay, with a decent bass and some good separation effects. The stereo sound on **Bordello of Blood** is quite energetic, and there is a Dolby Digital track with better-defined separations and a sharper bass. Both programs are closed captioned.

Demon Knight, from 1995, runs 92 minute. The story is fairly simple and so the padding offered by the **Tales from the Crypt** introduction is helpful, but the primary narrative is also fairly entertaining and the film, with its exaggerated gore and steady thrills, lives up to its promise. Basically about a group of people trapped in a boarding house and fending off demons for a night, it may seem comic book-like, but it is efficiently constructed, briskly executed and devilishly amusing. Billy Zane, portraying the main villain, gives a fun, relaxed performance that contrasts nicely with the serious and fairly desperate heroes.

"I feel like I'm in a bad **Tales from the Crypt** episode," says Dennis Miller all too accurately, a little over halfway through **Bordello of Blood**, a 1996 feature running 87 minutes. The vampire-themed film has some replayable gore sequences and a little humor here and there, but it is nowhere as energetic or involving as **Demon Knight**. Miller stars as a private detective investigating disappearances tied to a whorehouse where customers seem to go in but never come out. You'd think somebody would have noticed before Miller, but that is just one of the script's many internal inconsistencies. If you do put on the film, stick with it, because the best effect sequences come near the climax, where Miller rocks with a pump squirtgun full of Holy Water, but getting there can generate a bit of impatience.

Tales from the Hood (HBO, 91217)

Each of the five stories in the minority-themed 1995 horror anthology has supernatural elements, but each is also tied closely to the real horrors of inner city life, including police brutality, child abuse, racist politicians, prisons and gang violence. There are a couple of good screams and several other exciting moments, though on the whole the film will play much better in a crowded city theater on a Saturday night than in the confines of one's video room, where the limitations to the film's wit are more in evidence. Only one story, a bizarre piece about a convict undergoing a special rehabilitation program, escapes from the confines of its initial concept. The other 'tales' are fun, but predictable.

The picture is presented in full screen format only. The color transfer is okay. The image is sharp and hues are effectively defined. Once in a while a darker scene will take on some grain, but other dark sequences are clear. The stereo surround sound is reasonably strong. The 98 minute program also has a Spanish audio track in mono and optional English, French and Spanish subtitles.

Tales of Ordinary Madness (Image, ID4782SIDVD)

Why is it that serious movies about sex sometimes seem so ridiculous? Directed by Marco Ferreri, an Italian, **Tales of Ordinary Madness** is, at times, worse than **9 1/2 Weeks**, though at other times it approaches a more literate and rewarding level of quality. Ben Gazzara portrays an alcoholic poet, based on the writings of Charles Bukowski, who spends his time pawing women and getting wasted. Since he's a poet, however, he talks about his actions with an elevated sense of importance, and since the 1981 movie's writers have poetry on the brain, the other characters talk about it that way, too. It doesn't help the movie, which is set mostly in Los Angeles, that the English dialogue has an awkward cadence at times, increasing the imposed artificiality of the hero's relationships ("I want to be ****ed until I have nothing left for the others," a prostitute tells him, and, after they get ready, "Now give it to me. Take my soul with your…." Well, you get the picture.). You could make the argument that the whole film is seen through the poet's imagination, but it doesn't make it any less giggle-inducing. There are some genuinely erotic sequences, and there are some sequences, such as when he fondles an underage runaway, that would be banned if the movie weren't so closely associated with poetry. Most of the 102 minute film, however, is about his gradual descent into homelessness and despair, though that doesn't seem to stop him from picking up girls. Their nasals must be clogged.

The picture is letterboxed with an aspect ratio of about 1.8:1 and no 16:9 enhancement. The colors are bright and fleshtones are fine, but the image is a little soft, with some speckling and a couple scratches. The monophonic sound is adequate and the program is not captioned.

Talk Dirty to Me: Part Ten X-rated (DaViD, D8043)

"At this point in my career, after doing about 700 videos and films over 14 years, I still enjoy having sex with the girls on camera and making these movies." So declares adult film actor/producer Steve Drake on the commentary track. Drake stars as a drifter who breezes into town to look up an old flame. He also connects with a female radio talk show host, and that earns him a few more acquaintances. The narrative is limited but functional and the erotic scenes are standard but reasonably energetic. The picture, from a videotape source, is a little inconsistent. Most of the time, the image is reasonably sharp and colors are acceptable, but in some sequences the focus is a little soft and hues are a bit light. The monophonic sound is fine. The 85 minute program also features Kylie Ireland, Missy, Nici Sterling and Tracy Love. "Very rarely are these scenes choreographed in advance. You let the performers just kind of go at it and the cameraman just kind of follows along and tries to capture it all." Drake does fall into a play-by-play commentary at times, but he has a number of interesting and pragmatic insights on the adult filmmaking business, as well as a professional's viewpoint on the art of lovemaking. He also reassuringly claims, with some foundation of logic, that the actresses prefer smaller, rather than larger, partners, because there is less wear and tear.

The Taming of the Shrew (Direct, 21392)

The production stars Franklin Seales, Karen Austin, Larry Drake and Bruce Davison. Although it would never qualify for a slot in a season with the Royal Shakespeare Company, the show is staged with a broad humor (e.g., every time the town of Pisa is mentioned, everyone on the stage pauses to lean sideways) that not only makes each scene a great deal of fun, but takes the edge off the play's hardball sexual politics. Seales and Austin are terrific. Their by-play is exceptionally physical, making their emotional changes credible. The presentation leaves out the play's oft-dropped prologue. The picture has rich colors, although it is rather soft and even a little blurry in places. The sound is fully coherent. Contrary to a notation on the jacket cover, the program runs 116 minutes.

Tangerine Dream: The Video Dream Mixes (Image, ID5500CADVD)

A collection of travel footage modified with artificial solarization effects and other manipulations provide the visual accompaniment to most of the 60 minute program. There are a few shots of the group, mixed in as well. We would have respect for the disc if they'd taken all the footage themselves, but as the end credits indicate, a lot of it is stock, so what's the point? The group's music is a seemingly unending collection of electronic chord progressions more suited to the background than the foreground of one's attention. Although the stereo mix is strong, with plenty of dimensionality, it is not playful or as involving. The video effects on the images seem more annoying than artistic. The color transfer appears accurate and the stereo sound is okay.

Tango and Cash (Warner, 11951)

Sylvester Stallone and Kurt Russell are teamed in the farfetched but energetic feature. The film's comical elements help to excuse the exaggerated action sequences and crazy plot, about two cops who are framed and sent to prison, and their war against a drug cartel. Teri Hatcher and Jack Palance are also featured in the 1989 film, which was directed by Andrei Konchalovsky. It is presented in letterboxed format on one side, with an aspect ratio of about 2.35:1 and no 16:9 enhancement, and in cropped format on the other side, though the cropping is awkward. The picture is crisp and colors are accurate. The many darkly lit scenes also look very sharp. The Dolby Digital track sounds terrific, with lots of separation effects and plenty of punch. The regular stereo surround soundtrack is somewhat duller and less involving. The 97 minute film is also available in French without Dolby Digital and comes with English, French or Spanish subtitles ("Rambo, c'est une lopette"). There is a small cast profile section, some brief production notes about the stunt sequences (Russell's hair got singed) and a trailer that hides the film's weaknesses effectively.

Tarzan in Manhattan (Simitar, 7273)

An enjoyable 1989 TV movie, the hero has to rescue his chimp from a rich villain running an illegal animal experiments lab. The film plays it all with a straight face, even the humor, and demonstrates what a reliable entertainment concept the Tarzan character can be. Joe Lara stars as the title character, with Kim Crosby as his Jane, a taxi driver, Tony Curtis as Jane's father and Jan-Michael Vincent as the bad guy. The colors are a little light at times and the image is a bit grainy, but fleshtones are adequate and the presentation is workable. The sound, which appears to be stereophonic, is reasonably strong. The film runs 94 minutes, is not captioned, and a partial filmography of Curtis is included.

Taxi Driver (Columbia TriStar, 02269)
Taxi Driver: Collector's Edition (Columbia TriStar, 03481)

The landmark film tapped into the culture of modern alienation and loneliness so intuitively that it is said to have inspired a would-be presidential assassin in his attempt to change history. The film style is so powerful, the psychology so fascinating, and the narrative so involving that the movie is a highly intelligent and intense form of entertainment. Robert De Niro stars in the 1976 production, written by Paul Schrader and directed by Martin Scorsese. Released originally as a standard DVD, the program was later reissued as a Collector's Edition.

The picture transfer and even the data transfer rate appear to be the same on both presentations. The image is letterboxed, with an aspect ratio of about 1.78:1 and an accommodation for enhanced 16:9 playback. Although the presentation is billed as having been 'remastered,' the source material still has a number of minor speckles, colors in places seem to teeter on the edge of spoiling, and very bright hues tend to take on a mild blur. On the whole, however, the presentation is satisfying. The pale fleshtones and slightly murky night sequences are really in keeping with the film's thematic intentions and do not distance a viewer from the entertainment.

The stereo surround sound on the two DVDs is also identical. There are no significant separation effects, but Bernard Herrmann's engrossing jazz score has a satisfying dimensionality and a steady purity of tone. The 114 minute film also had a French audio track on the older DVD, with optional Spanish subtitles ("¿Hablas conmigo? Entonces, ¿con quién diablos hablas? ¿Hablas conmigo?") and English closed captioning.

The Collector's Edition is in English only, but can be accompanied by optional English, Spanish, Portuguese, Chinese, Korean and Thai subtitles. There is a trailer, a collection of advertising artwork, filmographies for the cast and director, and a storyboard-and-still photo breakdown of the climactic shootout. A 70 minute retrospective documentary is also included, featuring insightful comments by the cast and the filmmakers. They describe the efforts made to get the film produced (Scorsese had to get some feature experience under his belt first), the working methods of the actors (Foster recalls how De Niro prepared her for working with him, by encouraging her to become bored with his presence) and details from individuals such as makeup expert Dick Smith on how the bloody finale was achieved. There is then an additional 10 minute photo montage of production stills, over which the director of the documentary, Laurent Bouzereau, shares a few anecdotes that didn't make the documentary's final cut.

The Collector's Edition DVD also has an elaborate non-DVD-ROM screenplay link. You can read through the original screenplay, or you can jump between the screenplay and the film. At any time during the playing of the film, you can also jump to the screenplay, a function we could activate on newer players, but not on older ones. Much of the film's atmosphere and tone, which has been credited to Scorsese, is actually spelled out in Schrader's script, though as they point out in the documentary, the screenplay touched a nerve in the two of them and in De Niro, and all were of essentially the same mind in conceiving the film.

A Taxing Woman (Fox Lorber, FLV5042)

The Japanese film, about a demure tax investigator who is always a step ahead of the cheats she is auditing, is a delight, depicting the step by step process government agents use to snare unreported income, in a way which makes bookkeeping look as fun as searching for treasure. The film also has a superbly executed matter-of-fact style, capturing, for example, the multiple introductions and confusion which can happen during a first day on the job, and the messy hygiene which follows lovemaking. Following a normal dramatic pattern, the film opens with a number of short scores and then settles into depicting the big one, but at 127 minutes it ends much too quickly and leaves one wishing for more.

Contrary to a notation on the jacket cover, the image is presented in full screen. Bright hues are strong and fleshtones are workable, but the picture does have a slightly worn, soft, low budget, foreign look to it. The sound is a bit flat and there is a little background noise, but it is functional. The 127 minute film is in Japanese and is supported by permanent white English subtitles. The 1987 production is accompanied by filmographies for the stars, Nobuko Miyamoto and Tsutomu Yamazaki, and an American theatrical release trailer. The program is not time encoded.

Teatro Alla Scala (see Cilea's Adriana Lecovreur: Teatro Alla Scala; Mozart's Così Fan Tutti: Teatro Alla Scala; Mozart's Don Giovanni: Teatro Alla Scala; Rossini's La Donna del Lago; Rossini's William Tell: Teatro Alla Scala)

Teddy Edwards Sextet (see Jazz Scene USA: Cannonball Adderley Sextet / Teddy Edwards Sextet)

Teenage Mutant Ninja Turtles (New Line, N4121)

The enjoyable and now almost nostalgic 1990 live action hit has been given a fresh picture transfer. The picture is much less grainy than the LD. Blacks are solid, colors are bright, and the image looks very nice, though some sequences retain a faint grain (the film was shot on a modest budget). The film is presented in letterboxed format, with an aspect ratio of about 1.85:1 and an accommodation for 16:9 playback on one side, and in full screen format on the other side. The letterboxing takes some picture information off the top and bottom and adds a little to the side, but either framing is workable. The stereo surround sound is okay, but there is a super Dolby Digital track with a stronger bass, more rear channel effects, more separation detail and more energy. The 95 minute film is also available in monophonic French and comes with English, French or Spanish subtitles ("Las Adolescentes Tortugas Ninja"). There is a theatrical trailer as well as trailers for other New Line family films, profiles of the Turtles and other characters, and a well designed and engaging interactive 'maze' game.

The four heroes are human-sized turtles who enjoy eating pizza and practicing martial arts. Teaming with several others, they battle villains who attempt to organize the youngsters of the city into a burglary ring. The film remains witty and the special effects are cute.

TeleVoid (Simitar, 7320)

The 50 minute program (plus about 10 minutes of end credits) is a collection of excerpts from mostly computer-generated or video-manipulated animation shorts (there is one significant claymation sequence) set to a mostly instrumental rock music score. Some of the images look like leftover footage from a video game, but much of it is stimulating and adeptly varied. Nevertheless, there is no narrative to the program, just the steady flow of images, but from the DVD's menu, the viewer can also access seven of the original animated shorts (out of about two dozen) that were used in the program. Seen as they were originally intended, several of the shorts, *Monster Party* by Valérie Hullier (a superb exploration of texture and the human body), *Free-Quent Objects* by Kazuma Morino, *Exmemoriam* and *Limbes* by Beriou, and *Mistaken Identity* by Timothy S. Keon, are excellent, and communicate an emotional and symbolic dynamic that is completely lacking when the sequences from them are just part of the larger anthology. *Mad Doctors of Borneo* by Webster Colcord (the claymation work) and *Ju Ju Shampoo* are shorter, single-gag pieces, but still worth having in their entirety. The picture quality is very good, with stable, crisp colors, and the stereo surround sound is fine.

The Temple of Poon X-rated (DaViD, D0578)

An amusing satire on the practice of archeology, it is about an explorer who is cursed with erotic dreams after he opens an ancient tomb. Shot on videotape, the image quality and transfer are excellent, with crisp, precise hues and accurate, well-lit fleshtones. The monophonic sound isn't bad, either. The 87 minute program stars Tyffany Million, Kaitlyn Ashley, Jill Kelly, Heather Lee, Kimberly Kyle, Nancy Vee and Bridgette Monroe.

Temptation of a Monk (Fox Lorber, FLV5014)

The Chinese epic is about a general who quits the military, after his leaders are killed in a coup, and becomes a monk, gradually learning to embrace the monk ideals. Wu Hsin-Kuo and Joan Chen star in the film, which was directed by Clara Law. Although it is a formal drama and not an exploitation film, the gore and sex are terrific, and the action scenes are exciting.

The cinematography is also quite lovely and the color transfer is reasonably faithful. The image is a little cropped, but the framing never leaves out anything important. The colors are a bit flat, but acceptable, and the image is crisp. The source material has a number of minor wear marks. The stereo sound has a modest separation mix and some noise at times, but seems workable. The 118 minute film is in Mandarin with white English subtitles that cannot be toggled off and are a little intrusive at times. The DVD also has filmographies for a couple of the cast members and a theatrical trailer.

The Temptations (Artisan, 99032)

Contrary to a time notation on the jacket cover that suggests abridgement, the miniseries runs a full 173 minutes. The colors look solid and bright, and fleshtones are nicely detailed. The stereo surround sound is great.

You need a miniseries length to cover the history of the pop group, which managed to sustain its popularity, albeit with some ups and downs, through several periods of musical fads, gaining and losing members along the way. Although they appeared to be in total unison on the stage, the group had many conflicts among themselves, success breeding the character flaws that are deftly suggested by the second meaning of the show's title. The film explores the development of the group's music and harmonies, and the their experiences in the glamorous world of musical stardom. Inevitably it skims past some developments and changes, and the lows seem slower than the highs, but it is an entertaining program with terrific music that enables a viewer to understand the dynamics of an important phase in American music. There is also the thrill, in the early scenes, of imagining how all those famous Detroit musical stars interacted and tripped over one another before they became famous. The program is adequately closed captioned and is accompanied by a Temptations discography, a large cast profile section and some production notes.

10 (Warner, 2002)

There is a bad artifact jump at the beginning of the *Bolero* scene and other, less obvious flaws throughout. The 123 minute film is presented in letterboxed format on one side and cropped on the other. The letterboxed side, has an aspect ratio of about 2.35:1 and an accommodation for enhanced 16:9 playback, The cropped version gives you a chance to take in a few choice close-ups, but the cropping often destroys the pacing of the comedy and isn't good for much. The presentation is tolerable, but there are times when the picture is a bit too dark or soft. The monophonic sound is flat. The film is available in French as well, and comes with English, French or Spanish subtitles. There is a small cast profile, a theatrical trailer and a more elaborate 'making of' featurette. Dudley Moore stars as a middle aged man who makes a fool of himself stalking a newlywed. The 1979 Blake Edwards film emphasizes the many pratfalls endured by the hero as he stumbles through his life. Some people think it is funny, but most just like to gaga at Derek, and in this regard the letterboxed version is the only video presentation in which she is properly displayed.

The Ten Commandments (Paramount, 155087)

Charlton Heston stars as Moses, with Yul Brynner, Edward G. Robinson, Anne Baxter, Yvonne De Carlo and others in the two-platter 220 minute Cecil B. DeMille Biblical epic. The film is terrifically entertaining and time has not cheapened its special effects. The narrative is elaborate, there are many spectacular action scenes, and the art direction is super. The film had several scriptwriters and is not necessarily admired for its screenplay, but check out how beautifully executed the scene is where Heston's character first learns of his birthright. There are two characters, each with different goals that would be better served if they did not interact, and yet their personalities compel them to keep probing and to spill the beans. You would be hard-pressed to find a scene in contemporary film that is so firmly psychological in its execution. Love that Red Sea split also—it makes a fabulous demo sequence.

The picture looks gorgeous. The Technicolor hues are splendid and the film's color design is glorious. Fleshtones are rich, and the 1956 film's splendid costumes and set decorations are vivid. The picture is letterboxed, with an aspect ratio of about 1.75:1 and an accommodation for enhanced 16:9 playback. The Dolby Digital sound is much more enjoyable than the standard stereo surround soundtrack. The film does not have constant separation effects, but there are a number of enjoyable directional moments, and the whole soundtrack has substantially more flourish on the Dolby Digital track than on the standard track. The film also has a French standard stereo soundtrack and is closed captioned. The platter break is set at the Intermission, and the film is accompanied by trailers for three different theatrical runs.

Tender Loving Care (DVD International, DVDI0719)

The single-sided platter contains a legitimate erotic thriller that has been broken up into sixteen segments, separated by computer game-type sequences (in which one navigates through a house, examining clues) and pieces of a lengthy 'personality' test that governs which footage from the movie you will view. The test itself takes two hours, the film runs close to 90 minutes, and you can spend who knows how long wandering through the house; but, since the responses to the test alter not only the movie, but the test itself, the temptation to 're-take' the test and re-run the film using different personalities (you do have more than one personality, don't you?) is quite compelling.

The film features John Hurt (who gives a nice, crisp performance), Michael Esposito, Beth Tegarden and Marie Caldare. Esposito and Caldare portray a married couple who have recently experienced a tragedy and Tegarden is a live-in nurse/therapist playing psychological games to help them through their grief. Hurt is the doctor in charge of the case, and the show's narrator. The program is very erotic—at last, a video game you can play with a date!—not only within the film (if you say, during the 'test,' that you don't like sex, though, the nude scenes are truncated), but within the house tour, which contains extensive texts about eroticism in art, the psychology of sexual deviants, and Eastern sexual literature. These digressions add to the depth of the program's themes, and also heighten anticipation for the film's erotic sequences. So, on the other hand, this is probably not a DVD for the whole family to play together.

You can stop the program at any time and acquire an 18-digit code that will let you start up where you left off. When the cinematography is good, the picture quality is as well, but there are many instances where the film is over lit or out of focus, and you can even catch the film crew in reflections in several places (or is that part of the game?). The program is letterboxed with an aspect ratio of about 1.9:1 and no 16:9 enhancement. The stereo surround sound is passable and the program is not captioned.

The changes activated by alternate answers in the test often don't amount to much, though we were able, eventually, to activate a different ending. Response times to movement through the house or answering the test can be exhaustingly slow, which is probably the DVD's biggest drawback. It's taxing enough to be locked into the thing as dinner and bedtime slip by unnoticed, but to be sitting there tapping your foot while each new screen gradually arrives is frustrating. Within the house tour, there are a number of film clips from public domain materials, such as a Betty Page striptease, and other amusements.

The test has questions about the story, about art and about one's beliefs and one's personality. You can access a personal 'analysis,' based upon your answers, in each section, but it is rarely penetrating.

Tender Times (see Wacky Babies & Tender Times)

Tenebre (Anchor Bay, DV10727)

Like most of Dario Argento's films, it is a psycho slasher thriller and a whodunit, and as wildly as the narrative twists, it makes sense down to the smallest detail when you go back over it. Two factors make the film—our favorite Argento movie—exceptional. The first is Argento's mastery of style, which seemed to have reached a height with the 1982 production. The locations and sets are compelling, the music and sound are precisely applied, and there is one incredible crane shot that pulls a viewer across the outside of a house and into a murder, like levitating in a dream. The editing is terrific and there are several good scares. The second is the casting of Anthony Franciosa in the lead, as a thriller writer whose works the killer is claiming as inspiration. Franciosa was a secondary film star in the Sixties and Seventies who achieved greater recognition on the TV. There is both a warmth and a slickness to his manner that is ideal for the role, and his charisma validates the narrative. The film is also unabashedly gory—Anchor Bay's presentation is unrated, running 101 minutes—and the blood provides a wonderfully giddy release to the drama's tensions. Because the hero writes the same sort of thriller that **Tenebre** is, Argento includes token apologies or justifications for the movie's misogynistic bent by having the writer defend his novels, but the film is executed so brilliantly that there is also something else at work within it. A sort of raw bestiality is unleashed whenever the

camera is in the presence of a beautiful woman, and whether it is a wild dog or one of the murderers (whoops—spoiler) reacting to her presence, the atmosphere becomes so primitive and unrestrained it seems to expose and objectify the relentless energy of sexual aggression.

The picture transfer is outstanding. The image is sharp, the source material is completely free of wear, and the colors are fresh and exact. The presentation is letterboxed with an aspect ratio of about 1.9:1 and no 16:9 enhancement. The film has been re-mixed for stereo and has Dolby Digital encoding. While some of the directionalized effects seem unnecessary, the dimensionality created by the mix is wonderfully involving, and the scares we mentioned are given a definite boost by the intensity of the audio playback. The film's original Italian soundtrack is also presented, in mono. There is a trailer, a cast & crew profile section, and a brief look at the film's visual and sound effects. Apparently, the end credits to the American release contained a pop song Argento knew nothing about, so the original end credit music appears on the film, but the credits with the pop song are presented in the supplement.

Argento, composer Claudio Simonetti and journalist Loris Curci also provide a commentary track. Curci prompts the two with questions, some of which are answered and some of which are brushed off (Argento 'can't remember' what it was like working with Franciosa). Argento reveals that it was Theresa Russell who dubbed one of the heroines for the English version. They talk about what they can remember about the production and about the film's meanings. Fans will be pleased, but others may be impatient.

Tequila Sunrise (Warner, 11821)

Mel Gibson stars as a former drug dealer trying to go straight, with Kurt Russell as the cop who continues to dog him and Michelle Pfeiffer as their shared romantic interest in the 1988 production, which was written and directed by Robert Towne. The film's cinematography gives fleshtones a slightly tentative solidity, but the image is crisp and hues are clearly differentiated. The picture is letterboxed on one side, with an aspect ratio of about 1.85:1 and an accommodation for enhanced 16:9 playback, and is in full screen format on the other side. The letterboxing adds a bit to the sides and masks off the bottom, but either framing seems to work well. The mildly stereophonic sound is reasonably strong. The 115 minute film is also available in French and Spanish and can be accompanied by English, French or Spanish subtitles. There is a good cast and crew profile section, a couple brief production notes and a theatrical trailer.

Additionally, the film's producer, Thom Mount, provides audio commentary. Mount starts out strongly, but runs out of steam after a half hour or so. While he still has some interesting things to say during the remainder of the film, he tends to take longer pauses and is more apt to indulge in play-by-play descriptions of what is happening on the screen. His producer's view of the production is interesting. He goes much further into how the project was developed than directors usually do, and talks more generally about the production as opposed to the day-to-day shooting, though for key sequences, such as the sunset shot and Pfeiffer's love scene, he appears to be familiar with all the details. He tells about how the restaurant set used in the film was then sold to a restaurant company and turned into a real restaurant on Hollywood Boulevard. He also talks about Towne's troubled relationship with Warner, about how the company was very enthusiastic about the script but then seemed taken aback by the plot after the movie was made, and about how Russell patterned his performance after the basketball coach, Pat Riley. We knew that slicked-back hair had to have come from somewhere.

Terminal Velocity (Buena Vista, 16319)

A formula thriller with a skydiving theme, Charlie Sheen stars as an expert parachutist who is roped into an intrigue involving Russian hoodlums by Nastassja Kinski. There is not a single plot turn that can hold up under close examination, but if you let the movie breeze by, untethered by common sense or logic, it can be an enjoyable experience. The grand finale, in which the hero must rescue the heroine from the locked trunk of an automobile, in free-fall, will have even the most jaded action film fans gnawing at their fingernails.

The Dolby Digital track has more energy, better defined separations and more dimensionality than the standard track, and it brings more energy to the action scenes. The image is crisp, with bright hues, and fleshtones are accurate. The picture is letterboxed with an aspect ratio of about 2.35:1 and no 16:9 enhancement. The 102 minute film is also available in French in Dolby Digital and can be supported by English subtitles. The film is accompanied by a theatrical trailer that gives away many of the story's twists.

The Terminator (Image, ID3949NSBDVD)

James Cameron's 1984 sci-fi thriller is as strong a romance as it is an action film and special effects showcase. The picture is letterboxed with an aspect ratio of about 1.9:1 and no 16:9 enhancement, adding nothing to the sides of the image and masking off picture information from the top and bottom in comparison to the full screen trailer that accompanies the film. We don't care all that much for the letterboxing, finding it a bit too tight at times, particularly on the top of the image. The color transfer is terrific, however, and the modestly budgeted cinematography is as free of grain as it is probably going to get. The image is sharp, fleshtones are workable, and when the lighting allows, the colors are bright. The sound is presented in mono, without the artificial stereo that other home video releases have featured, but it is so strong it is almost as good as stereo anyway. Arnold Schwarzenegger, Michael Biehn and Linda Hamilton star in the film, which runs 107 minutes. There is no captioning.

Terminator 2: Judgment Day (Artisan, 60441)

James Cameron's inspired follow-up to his original sci-fi action feature is grand entertainment that makes ideal home video viewing. The Dolby Digital track is a blast, with huge, gloriously directional sounds crashing through from all over the place and making the title a primary choice when it comes to demonstrating one's DVD system. Compared to the Dolby Digital track, the regular stereo surround soundtrack is boring. The picture looks fantastic, with super crisp hues and accurate fleshtones, even in difficult, darkly lit sequences. The image is letterboxed, with an aspect ratio of about 2.35:1 and an accommodation for enhanced 16:9 playback. The 136 minute film (not the 152 minute director's cut; nor is it 139 minutes, as the jacket cover mistakenly lists) is presented on one side in dual-layer format. The DVD also has French and Spanish audio tracks in standard stereo, along with a 'DVS' descriptive track featuring voiceover narration that describes the action—like a child's cassette tape program—between the dialogue. It may be the ideal way to play DVDs in your car. There is also the movie's marvelous teaser trailer, along with the standard, over-abundant theatrical trailer, cast and crew profiles and a few production notes.

Terrified (Image, ID4659APDVD)

The talented Heather Graham stars in the decent stalker thriller. Graham brings a wry sense of irony to her role, and an emotional charge to the erotic sequences, while the suspense scenes work the genre's format effectively, with an interesting, though not totally unexpected twist at the end. The heroine's reaction to her attacks, however, will seem absurd to most viewers, and the film is basically a one-idea movie that goes on much too long before its payoff. The picture is grainy in places and very yellowish, with bland fleshtones. The stereo surround sound is passable. The 87 minute film is not captioned.

The Terror (UAV, 40092); (D-Vision, DVD1004)

Although Boris Karloff gets top billing, Jack Nicholson stars in the 1963 Roger Corman feature that was shot because Corman wrapped up The Raven early and still had everybody under contract. Nevertheless, it is a reasonably engaging film, in which Nicholson is a Nineteenth Century French officer who happens upon a castle where a mysterious woman appears and disappears. Karloff is the castle's owner, with a secret past. There is a lot of wandering down halls, waiting for something hoary to jump out, but Corman does that sort of thing very well.

Neither DVD looks all that hot. The film was shot in Vistascope and is presented in cropped format, though the cropping isn't too bad. The two presentations are nearly identical and both are a strain, with such a numbingly fuzzy and badly colored picture that the movie is almost unwatchable. The image is quite murky, and although colors are bright, contrasts are weak and smearing is common. The monophonic sound is also fairly noisy and mildly distorted. D-Vision's release has no extra features. UAV has included a theatrical trailer and an interesting documentary about Nicholson's career that appears to have been produced specifically for the DVD. The image quality is very weak and they get some of their facts wrong (they forget Goin' South), but there are intriguing clips from Nicholson's early black-and-white films, from trailers of his later movies, and still photos to provide an overview of his work.

Terror of Mechagodzilla (Simitar, 7476)

The incomprehensible 1978 feature has been issued in cropped format only. Hues are reasonably bright, but the image is often grainy and looks a little battered in places. Fleshtones also vary in quality. Basically, the story is about aliens who re-build the evil mechanical Godzilla and also employ an ancient dinosaur monster to defeat Godzilla and conquer the world. With the help of Godzilla and a few pesky humans, however, their plan is foiled.

The cropping is an annoyance and the 79 minute program is rarely engaging, though the Dolby Digital mix helps it considerably. The film is dubbed in English. The standard track presents the standard monophonic sound, while the menu-activated Dolby Digital track provides occasional rear channel enhancements, periodic bursts of dimensionality, and wonderful sub-woofer thumps whenever the big guy lumbers through. There is no captioning. The film is accompanied by five home video trailers for five Godzilla films, a text-based 'trivia' game about each feature, and a general 2 minute montage of photos and artwork. There are also DVD-ROM features, such as screen savers.

Tetsuo: The Iron Man (Image, ID4266FLDVD)

The 67 minute 1992 black-and-white Japanese film is a surrealistic comedy for viewers who savor the grotesque. It depicts several characters whose body parts are gradually being changed into junk metal, like Nipsey Russell in The Wiz, and the apparent anxiety this causes them. At one point, for example, the hero's penis turns into a two foot long, rotating drill, which grinds through doors and tables as he chases his girlfriend around their apartment. The film is frantic and abstract, using stop motion animation, gross special effects and obscure camera angles to deliver a high pitched, hypnotic, cyber-metallurgical nightmare. It is also so fragmented that some viewers may feel it becomes tedious after a half hour or so, but others will feel compelled to avoid blinking from beginning to end.

The full screen image is deliberately blurry, grainy or otherwise distorted in places, but it is also very crisp and smooth most of the time, so one assumes that the DVD is an acceptable rendition of the original work. The monophonic sound is a bit muted, but there is a mono Dolby Digital track that has a slightly more pleasing range. The film has a scattering of Japanese dialogue that is supported by permanent white English subtitles.

The Texas Chainsaw Massacre (Pioneer, DVD0123)

"This raw, silent footage you are about to see [of a dead dog] was discarded and re-shot with the armadillo after Tobe Hooper realized how repulsive the footage was. 'It was just too gross for me,' Tobe said." So states one of the introductory title cards to one of many segments of extra footage. As Hooper admits on the film's commentary track, however, he was seriously trying to land a 'PG' rating for the 1974 film, and even though it ended up with an 'R,' most of its violence is, intentionally, implied. The film achieved its well-earned reputation as a masterpiece of giddy terror by withholding more gore than it shows, and letting the viewer's imagination create the horror. Hence, those who open the DVD thinking they are going to get a smorgasbord of blood that was deemed too heavy for the censors are going to be a bit disappointed—even the shot of the dead dog that unnerves Hooper isn't that big of a deal.

The 84 minute film is presented in letterboxed format, with an aspect ratio of about 1.85:1 and no 16:9 enhancement, masking some picture information off the bottom and adding a little to the sides in comparison to full screen versions of the film. Keeping the film's extreme low budget origins in mind, the color transfer is workable. Fleshtones are bland and other hues are subdued, but grain seems under control and the image is reasonably crisp. There is a Chace-enhanced stereo soundtrack that gives the film a modest dimensionality, and the film's original mono track is also included. There is no captioning.

The filmmakers seem to have all their dailies still sitting around, and so the extent of what was filmed for several key scenes is presented in the supplement, along with a handful of brief shots that were removed from the final cut, more for artistic reasons than censorious ones. The value in the collection of this footage is not only its view of how the film was staged, but of how it was edited. There is also a collection of bloopers and a group of shots that allow the viewer to study the set decorations in detail. Trailers for all the **Texas Chainsaw Massacre** movies are presented. There is also a montage of international film posters, other advertising artwork, and production photos.

Hooper, cinematographer Daniel Pearl and actor Gunnar Hansen sit together during an unspooling of the film on the commentary track and reminisce about the production. The talk isn't well organized, but contains enough information to be of value. Among the highlights is a confession that at one point the actress playing the heroine was actually slashed by an actor getting into his part, but there was such a frenzy during the scene that everyone assumed her reaction was just part of the act. The filmmakers also admit that the movie is not in fact based upon a true story, and even profess bewilderment that fans believe it is, just because the film's opening scroll says that it is (you can't trust anything, these days). We had always assumed that the attendant at the gas station was supposed to be Leatherface without his mask, but the filmmakers never explain who he is, and state elsewhere that the villain is purposefully never seen without his head gear, so we were mistaken.

An energetic, ground-breaking film in its day, repeat viewings of the movie play to the original experience of seeing it for the first time. (The story is about a group of young people who park their van in the wrong backwoods area and are terrorized by a family of literally bloodthirsty weirdos.) Since other horror and slasher movies have surpassed it or imitated it (even **Silence of the Lambs** falls into this latter category), new viewers may be somewhat bewildered at what all the excitement was about, but there is still enough frantic action and emotional anarchy to hold one's attention, particularly during the last act, where the heroine is pretty much screaming without stop. As Hooper points out on the commentary channel, it even took a half dozen years or so before viewers started to realize how comical the film really is.

That Old Feeling (Universal, 20259)

From the guaranteed laugh-inducing opening sequence to the pleasantly conceived conclusion, the 1997 film is a marvelous romantic comedy with plenty of humor and brisk, screwball-style plot turns (about a divorced couple who reunite at their daughter's wedding). The ever reliable Carl Reiner directed the movie, which stars Bette Midler, Dennis Farina and Paula Marshall. Some have questioned the casting of Farina, who usually plays in cops and robbers movies, but he makes a believable partner for Midler and has always exhibited a talent for humor when the material allows him to go in that direction. Midler is a gas, and can turn even innocuous moments into hysterical center pieces.

The picture is in letterboxed format, with an aspect ratio of about 1.85:1 and an accommodation for enhanced 16:9 playback. The image has bright, crisp hues and accurate fleshtones. The audio mix is fairly basic but engaging. The stereo surround sound is a little weak, but the Dolby Digital track has better definitions and a stronger presence. Except for a few golden oldie pop songs, the stereo surround sound hasn't much to offer, anyway. The 106 minute feature is available in French and Spanish in standard stereo and comes with English or Spanish subtitles ("¡Rechacé a uno de los Beatles!"). There are some minor production notes, a decent cast profile section and an amusing theatrical trailer.

Thelma & Louise (MGM, 906727)

Susan Sarandon and Geena Davis star in the 1991 feature, about two women who go off for a weekend outing and, through a series of events, become outlaws. It is a terrific movie with enjoyable performances, a great sound mix and beautiful cinematography, and the DVD delivers it all and then some. The film is presented in letterboxed format on one side, with an aspect ratio of about 2.35:1 and no 16:9 enhancement, and in cropped format on the other side. The colors are bright and fresh, with decent fleshtones. The cropped version looks much grainier, however. The Dolby Digital track has better center channel-side channel separations, but much less rear channel activity than the standard stereo track, and the standard stereo track also seems to have more detail up, though it lacks energy. The film is also accompanied by a commentary track from director Ridley Scott, a theatrical trailer and an 'alternate ending' where the two women live, sort of. The 129 minute film is also available in French in stereo and in Spanish in mono and comes with English, French and Spanish subtitles.

Scott's commentary is excellent, talking not only about the film on a micro and macro level, but about his entire career in an informative and insightful manner. It is certainly a talk we would recommend to all budding filmmakers, and even casual viewers will have their consciousness, so to speak, about what movies are supposed to do, raised by Scott's comments. At one point early on, when he is talking about the options he had in approaching the movie, he cites *Silkwood*, acknowledging its quality, as a path he didn't want to take, giving the movie a documentary feel as the scriptwriter had envisioned. He felt, instead, that both he, the performers and, ultimately, the viewers, could have 'fun' with the film and still absorb its more serious messages. He talks about how he shot the film (usually with two cameras running at once), the importance of casting (something we often hear on commentary tracks, though it is still probably the best kept secret of good filmmaking), and the factors that dictated many of the choices he made.

They Came from Within (see **Shivers**)

They Got Me Covered (HBO, 01255)

Bob Hope portrays a newspaperman who chases down a Nazi spy ring in D.C., despite his chickenhearted instincts in the 1942 feature. There is enough plot to support the 93 minute running time and enough humor to make it worth one's while.

The black-and-white picture looks sharp and smooth, with minimal speckling. The monophonic sound is fine and there is also a stereo track with a slightly more atmospheric musical score. There are also French, Spanish and Italian audio tracks, optional English, French and Spanish subtitles, a cast profile section and a trailer.

They Live (Universal, ID4234USDVD)

The letterboxing has an aspect ratio of about 2.35:1, with an accommodation for enhanced 16:9 playback and with much more detail on the edges of the image than the cropped version could allow. The colors are excellent. The image is crisp, with bright hues and accurate fleshtones. Separation effects are minimal, but the stereo surround sound maintains a fairly effective presence. The 94 minute program is closed captioned.

Designed as an alternative to Carpenter's big budget efforts, Roddy Piper fills a role that seems more suited for Kurt Russell and the film has several extended sequences that could use trimming, but the concept—aliens who look like humans live among us and can only be identified with special glasses—is marvelous. Once you get used to the ending, multiple viewings are engaging.

They Were Expendable (MGM, 907661)

John Ford's 1945 tribute to the PT boats in World War II is an impressively composed and executed work that is very entertaining (at least after the first excruciating ten minutes are over). Robert Montgomery and John Wayne star, providing enough characterization in their personalities to give the 'human' side of the war an emphasis over an underlying fascination with the logistics and tactics of the PT boats. The film has many memorable scenes, with Ford, the war fresh in his mind, working to capture the atmosphere and realistic drama that was inherent in the conflict.

The black-and-white picture is fairly sharp most of the time, with effective contrasts and pure whites, although some outdoor and night sequences are a little softer. Wear to the source material is minor, and the monophonic sound is adequate. The 135 minute feature has optional English or French subtitles, and a trailer.

Thief (MGM, 907024)

Michael Mann's revised 124 minute cut of his 1981 feature is actually a little shorter than the original theatrical release, but new scenes have been added and others tightened to make the film stronger and better paced. The picture is letterboxed with an aspect ratio of about 1.85:1 and no 16:9 enhancement. Some sequences look sharp and others are very grainy, but the image is slightly crisper than the LD and helps to stabilize the weakest sequences, creating less of a distraction. The stereo surround sound is a little weak, but the Dolby Digital track has better defined separations and better detail. The film can be supported by English, French or Spanish subtitles and is accompanied by a theatrical trailer. There is also a commentary track by Mann and star James Caan, but it is not very satisfying. It would have been nice if Mann had talked the revisions, but he never says a peep. Instead, he and Caan, with little preparation, react to the film as it is unspooling, sharing some anecdotes about how the film was made but more often describing what is happening on the screen or simply not talking at all. It is nice to hear Caan speak about a work of which he is justly proud, but on the whole, the dialogue has little to offer

Caan stars as a professional thief whose vocational independence is compromised after he realizes his dream of settling down and starting a family. Shot in Mann's unique, languid style, the film is best not analyzed too closely, not only for questionable plot turns, but for the whiffs of macho symbolism Mann has failed to suppress in his script. Tuesday Weld and Jim Belushi co-star. The film also marked the first screen appearance of Dennis Farina, who was a Chicago cop before Mann selected him for the film. The movie is peopled with genuine detectives and thieves (often playing each other), and is notable for the realism with which it presents the heist sequences.

The Thief of Bagdad (Image, ID4235DSDVD)

The Douglas Fairbanks classic runs 139 minutes and would have been better if it had been trimmed a little before its initial release. The plot, about a thief who falls in love with a princess and then faces numerous challenges to beat rivals in retrieving a treasure that will earn her hand, takes a long time to get revved up. The 1924 silent film is spectacular, but the filmmakers apparently felt that they had to justify the expense by stretching out the narrative. The movie was directed by Raoul Walsh but was conceived and produced by Fairbanks. There are many terrific special effects, including an underwater sequence that we can't imagine how they pulled off, and some appropriately huge crowd scenes. The movie requires patience and commitment to be enjoyed, but the rewards are plenty.

Although the film certainly shows its age, tinting is subdued, the picture is sharp and overt damage is minimal. The film is accompanied by a monophonic Gaylord Carter musical score that sounds okay on both the standard track and the Dolby Digital mono track.

The Thin Red Line (Simitar, 7231)

Andrew Marton's 1964 film adaptation of James Jones' novel is no gung-ho patriotic war movie. Although it gets sentimental during its final minute and a half, it is otherwise a searing, raw look at how men's souls collapse under battle. Jack Warden and Keir Dullea star. Warden is comfortable in his role as the hard driving sergeant, but Dullea unexpectedly shines as the private who teeters on the edge of madness amid the slaughter of battle.

The black-and-white presentation is unappealing. Contrasts look good, but the video transfer is very soft and there are skips, scratches and other distractions. The Cinemascope production is also cropped, so we were actually judging only about half the film. The monophonic sound is adequate and the 99 minute program is not captioned.

The Thing (Universal, 20329)

John Carpenter's film, with its bleak-as-an-Antarctic-night ending, did not burn up the box office when it first came out, but over time, and particularly with the more flexible viewing environment of home video, it has become a classic. The 109 minute film is letterboxed with an aspect ratio of about 2.35:1 and no 16:9 enhancement. Although some of the color tones are questionably the transfer looks fine, and the image is sharp. There is some sporadic noise on the standard stereo surround soundtrack, but for a 1982 feature the mix is pretty good. The Dolby Digital track, however, is even better. The noise is cleaned up, directional effects are more distinctive and the range is better detailed. The film is available in French in standard stereo and can be accompanied by English or Spanish subtitles ("¿Eres el único que logró salir?"). There is a production essay and individual profiles of Carpenter and Kurt Russell.

There is an excellent 84 minute retrospective documentary, some interesting deleted footage and a number of other fascinating supplements (the exterior set, for example, was constructed in the summer, so that winter snows would give it a natural coating, and there are snapshots of how the place looked before the snow engulfed it). Carpenter and Russell also provide a jovial commentary track. Most of the hard information they share is reiterated in the documentary, but it is fun to spend the 109 minutes reminiscing with them (at one point during their talk there is the very distinctive 'cling' of a beverage glass of some sort). Carpenter has done a number of commentary channels and he always seems to do better when he has somebody else to bounce off of, a function Russell, as a professional entertainer, can perform with great flair.

The documentary goes into every aspect of the film with great detail, discussing the concept of the all-male cast (particularly as they were stuck in the middle of nowhere while shooting the exteriors—and it was an all-male crew, as well), how to approach a scene where a dozen people just sit around and talk (analyzing how Carpenter does this can be an excellent lesson for film students), how the wild special effects were accomplished in the days before computers (including special effect designer Rob Bottin's work-induced physical collapse), and how the script was developed and modified as the shooting progressed. The only aspect of the film that is not given extensive treatment is Ennio Morricone's musical score. Carpenter talks about it a bit on the commentary track, but never mentions how derivative or evocative it is of Carpenter's own film score compositions, and why this was so. There is also decent collection of production drawings, a breakdown of several special effect sequences, a look at Albert Whitlock's matte paintings, storyboards, behind-the-scenes photos and an exciting original trailer. Both the documentary and the film are adequately captioned.

Let's talk about the movie's ending a moment. Everybody, on the commentary track and in the documentary, says again and again that the ending is deliberately ambiguous, that they, as filmmakers, had no idea if either of the two characters still alive in the final shot were possessed by the alien. But if you watch the movie oodles of times, and particularly if you see the outtakes that have been included on the disc, you realize that when a character is taken over, his personality changes. We believe—and, since an artist no longer owns a finished product (it is up to others to interpret the artist's subconscious), our word is as good as any—that neither man has been taken over, that both have a steely aura of self-possession that can't allow them to trust the other guy, but that proves, to us at least, they are still in full control of their souls.

Things To Do in Denver when You're Dead (Buena Vista, 17094)

The overly written and mostly uninteresting, vaguely comical tale is about a hood who runs afoul of an important mobster and wanders around town waiting to get knocked off. Andy Garcia stars, with Christopher Lloyd and Treat Williams in amusing supporting roles as eccentric henchmen and Christopher Walken, William Forsythe and Gabrielle Anwar in more standardized parts. The filmmakers try very, very hard to be unusual and risqué, and some viewers will be happy enough with what they've accomplished, but the story doesn't really seem to go anywhere, the script's quirks seem too deliberate, and the characters aren't the sort one can sympathize with in any kind of depth.

The picture is in very good condition. Many of the film's scenes are shot in dark or near-dark settings and were it not for the precision of the image you would have no idea what was going on. The presentation is letterboxed with an aspect ratio of about 1.85:1 and no 16:9 enhancement. The stereo surround sound is excellent and the Dolby Digital 5.1 channel is even better, with lots of punch and a strongly dimensional atmosphere. The 115 minute program has optional English subtitles, a trailer and a brief 'making of' featurette.

Thinking Big (Simitar, 7215)

The children's film about a magical talking teddy bear runs 60 minutes. The bear takes the hero, a young boy, into social situations where he would normally not be welcome, disguising him for those around him but not for the viewer. The boy learns to see the world from a different set of perspectives and matures. The talking teddy bear thing—mostly a hand puppet—works okay and, in consideration of the film's genre and budget, the show is reasonably effective. The colors are light, fleshtones are pale and the image is slightly grainy. The monophonic sound is passable and the program is not captioned.

Thinner (see Stephen King's Thinner)

30th Anniversary of Rock 'N' Roll: All-Star Jam with Bo Diddley (Pioneer, PA92434D)

Accompanying Diddley in the 45 minute 1985 concert are Ron Wood, Carl Wilson, Mick Fleetwood, John Mayall, and Chuck Negron, to name just a few. There are about a half dozen numbers,

accompanied by several backstage sequences. The stereo surround sound is typical for a jam-type concert, with most of the music blending together, losing the purity a studio recording would have but gaining a gritty naturalism that is appropriate for the genre. The DVD has a Dolby Digital track, however, that does provide some significant separations, at least getting the vocals to the center and the audience to the back, and adding extra punch to the bass as well, giving the entire concert a sense of spectacle that the standard stereo track cannot quite achieve. The picture is somewhat grainy but colors are identifiable and the presentation is workable.

This Is Spinal Tap (Criterion, CC1529D)

The first cut of the 82 minute rock music comedy ran over four hours, so there is a wealth of material to draw from for a supplement, and the DVD bulges with extras. Rob Reiner's precious 1984 make-believe documentary is letterboxed with an aspect ratio of about 1.7:1 and no 16:9 enhancement. The picture is reasonably free of grain, the colors are fairly sharp. Since the film imitates a rock documentary intentionally, the transfer can accommodate flaws without seeming flawed itself. The stereo sound is adequate and there is no captioning. There are two commentary channels that run during the film, featuring most of the cast and principal crew. A number of the preliminary drawings and completed designs used in the film are presented on the menu montage.

There are oodles of outtakes, the highpoint probably being a gut-wrenchingly funny sequence in which Bruno Kirby, who played the chauffeur, gets stoned, strips down to his underwear, and sings a full rendition of All of Me before passing out. Many of the outtakes track subplots that were ultimately dropped from the film or, like the Kirby sequence, feature very funny scenes that just ate up too much time reaching their punchline.

There is a twenty minute demonstration reel, which the filmmakers shot to obtain financing, that is like an abbreviated and less hysterical version of the completed film, and a clip from a 1979 skit that marked the first appearance of the group, with Reiner appearing as an imitation Wolfman Jack. There are some very funny trailers that do little to promote the film but instead feature a make-believe documentary about a cheese festival. There is a 'music video' and a put-on of a TV commercial for a collection of the group's hits.

Contrary to the fears of director Rob Reiner, who speaks on one of the two alternate audio tracks that run over the film itself, the thorough documenting of how the film was put together (we were surprised to learn that the entire movie was shot in L.A.) does nothing to harm its charm or magic. Reiner dutifully points out the errors in continuity, but in that the film has the format of a documentary, viewers readily accept that the editing will compress conversations and otherwise alter the location of the individuals on the screen from shot to shot. Speaking with Reiner, producer Karen Murphy and editors Robert Leighton and Kent Beyda explain how the film was conceived and executed, while on the other track, the stars who play the three principal band members, Christopher Guest, Michael McKean and Harry Shearer, contribute their insights and reflections.

As the filmmakers explain, the movie gradually became a cult favorite and, since the performers loved their parts and loved the music, the urge to continue the gag became impossible to resist, and pretty soon they started playing real gigs, beginning on a double bill with Iron Butterfly, which must have been positively surreal, and eventually headlining a 1992 tour.

This Island Earth (Image, ID4268USDVD)
Mystery Science Theater 3000: The Movie (Image, ID4282USDVD)

For the uninitiated, **Mystery Science Theater**, based upon a popular cable program, takes an old science fiction movie—the 1955 Technicolor **This Island Earth**—and unspools parts of it while characters, sitting in silhouette in the bottom of the screen, make fun of the action. The characters are supposedly watching the show for the first time, but they talk about it as if they'd seen it many times before. The concept is great for junk TV, but as a film it doesn't work too well. There are no budding Woody Allens among the screenwriters and only about 10 percent of the comments are even remotely humorous. Oddly, they even let a number of potent dialogue lines ("The jerking around must have caused a flameout") pass without a word. Another problem is that **This Island Earth** is actually one of the better Fifties sci-fi features—about scientists invited to visit another planet—so, while parts of it are certainly dated enough to stand as fodder for such lampooning, it is also intelligent enough that long sections are immune to ridicule. Fans of the cable program may be tickled (the 74 minute film works best if, like the TV show, you sample bits of it at a time rather than trying to sit through the whole thing at once), but most viewers will find the effort a waste of time.

Mystery Science Theater is letterboxed with an aspect ratio of about 1.85:1 and no 16:9 enhancement. The non-**Earth** passages have bright, crisp colors. The clips from **This Island Earth** look a bit washed out. The stereo surround sound is reasonably strong. **This Island Earth** itself runs 86 minutes and has an improved color transfer. The image is very crisp and colors are accurate, though hues are a little subdued. The source material still has a few scratches and things, as well. The standard monophonic sound is weak, but there is a Dolby Digital mono track that is reasonably strong. Both DVDs are adequately closed captioned.

This Metal Mind (Simitar, 7200)

A collection of second-rate computer animation images set to an energetic but bland music score, it runs about 40 minutes (there is no time encoding). Amid the abstract images and pulsating colors, there are occasional formations of rocket ships, buildings, dragons, fish and other recognizable objects. The animation is so hollow that grade school children will probably be producing such images in a few years, but at least the picture is reasonably free of artifacts or other compromises. The colors are bright and the image is sharp. The stereo surround sound is also reasonably strong.

This Sporting Life (Image, ID4538JFDVD)

Richard Harris stars as a young rugby player who tries to romance his reclusive, widowed landlady, portrayed by Rachel Roberts. Much of the film, directed by Lindsay Anderson, is told in flashback as Harris' character recovers from a field injury. The 1963 black-and-white British production, set in a northern industrial city, is deliberately pessimistic and dreary, though edited in a confusing, piecemeal style, the movie is superior to its narrative. As the plot advances and emotional turns become more unlikely, the flow of the film becomes more disjointed and abstract, disguising the story's weaknesses, particularly the rather arbitrary fate of Roberts' character. Harris' character, a coal miner trying to raise his lot in life through his athletic prowess, is excited about playing at first, but by the end he is disillusioned and exhausted. The rugby sequences are fairly impressive—Harris appears to be playing in front of a very large crowd, and this in the days before digital effects—and overall the film is an interesting if somewhat depressing tale, more valuable perhaps to those exploring Anderson's enigmatic film career than to those looking for an existential sporting drama.

The image is sharp on the black-and-white picture, and textures are clear. The picture is letterboxed with an aspect ratio of about 1.66:1 and no 16:9 enhancement. The monophonic sound is adequate. The 134 minute program is not captioned.

The Thomas Crown Affair (MGM, 907442)

Steve McQueen and Faye Dunaway star in the morally ambiguous tale about an insurance agent investigating the mastermind of a bank heist. The film defies the conventional notions of star-fueled caper films, and the more often you watch it the more you start to realize what an utterly evil character McQueen portrays. Dunaway is actually the hero, and what happens to her at the end is akin, in some respects, to what happens to the hero at the end of **Seven**. In any case, although the film has the look of a formula effort (with classy Sixties graphics and split screens) it has a subtle emotional complexity that has allowed it to endure.

The presentation is letterboxed on one side, with an aspect ratio of about 1.81:1 and no 16:9 enhancement, and is in full screen format on the other side. The full screen picture loses only a smidgen of information on the sides and adds picture information to the top and bottom, but the split-screen sequences are essentially letterboxed, indicating that the rectangular framing was the framing the filmmakers intended. Fleshtones are very pale, other hues are drab and whites are yellowish. The monophonic sound is adequate, though the music recording loses a little on the upper end in places because of age. The 102 minute program can be supported by English or French subtitles ("Rond, comme un cercle dans une spirale, Comme une roue dans une roue, Sans fin ni commencement sur un dévidoir perpétuel, Une boule de neige sur une pente ou un ballon de carnaval…") and is accompanied by a trailer.

The movie's director, Norman Jewison, provides a commentary track. He has a bit of fun talking about the good old days of movies, before the suits came in and wrecked everything. Of course, he doesn't mention that the reason that happened is because too many filmmakers nearly busted the movie companies they were making films for, but anyway…**The Thomas Crown Affair** was written by a Boston lawyer who'd never done a screenplay before and it was a skinny little script, so Jewison, who had Haskell Wexler as a cinematographer and Hal Ashby as an editor, stretched things out with the polo games and gliders and that sort of thing. He talks about the dynamics of using multiple split screens and recalls that some images are probably in the movie because the editors were smoking too much marijuana while they were working on the film. They came up with the idea for the multiple screens at the last minute and just sort of put it together as they went along. He also talks about the acting styles of McQueen, Dunaway and some of the supporting players, and how he worked with them. In digression, he has a couple interesting things to say about Alfred Hitchcock and about McQueen's final days. It is not a dense talk, but it is a pleasant, chatty look at how movies were made in the late Sixties and why **The Thomas Crown Affair** works as a film even though it shouldn't.

A Thousand Acres (Buena Vista, 14252)

Based upon a prize-winning novel that brought a humanist face and a feminist perspective to a contemporization of *King Lear*, the film, with its stellar cast of Jessica Lange, Michelle Pfeiffer, Jason Robards and Jennifer Jason Leigh, has a lot going for it and it is watchable in an involving sort of way, but it is readily apparent that the film could be a lot better than it is—as if a movie company bought the rights to it because of its reputation but didn't know where to go from there. The screenplay leaves too much happening off screen and rushes through several of the key scenes it does bother to include, so that the performers are left with the unhappy task of announcing rather than showing events and changes to the viewer. Lange and Pfeiffer portray sisters who have acquired their father's farm. When the story slows down, the performances take over and there are plenty of juicy emotions, but the narrative never works up a momentum. The ideal medium for the film is probably television, where commercial interruptions would disguise the transitional breaks.

The picture is smooth and sharp, with accurate fleshtones. The image is letterboxed with an aspect ratio of about 1.85:1 and no 16:9 enhancement. The Dolby Digital track has plenty of power, but the standard track is weak. The 106 minute program can be accompanied by English subtitles. A promising theatrical trailer is also included.

The Three Musketeers (Kino, K117DVD)

Douglas Fairbanks portrays D'Artagnan and the plot is very similar to Richard Lester's remake, in which the heroes upset a plan to steal some diamonds and embarrass the French queen. The 1921 production is good fun, with large sets and many elaborate action sequences

The picture is in black-and-white and has plenty of wear marks, though it is certainly watchable. It is slightly windowboxed. There is mildly stereophonic score, emphasizing the organ, performed by Eric Boheim and the Elton Thomas Salon Orchestra. The film runs 118 minutes.

The Three Musketeers (Fox Lorber, FLV5029)
The Four Musketeers (Fox Lorber, FLV5030)

We do not subscribe to the concept, as others do, that the two Richard Lester films are of equal quality. **The Three Musketeers** is a happy accident that is free of the sour ending originally planned by Lester and screenwriter George MacDonald Fraser, both of whom can be oppressively cynical if given half a chance. Because Lester shot too much footage, the original film was split in two, and so the delightful first movie ends on an upbeat, with everybody, including the villains, still alive and scheming. The film's comedy and action have not fallen out of style, and Raquel Welch delivers what was probably the pinnacle role of her career as Michael York's accident-prone paramour. Richard Chamberlain, Oliver Reed, Geraldine Chaplin and Charlton Heston also appear. Although, to its credit, **The Four Musketeers** has a more complicated plot, its incompleteness is not entirely disguised. Characters leap from one locale to the next without explanation, or are dropped from view and never heard from again. So much footage has been included to make a legitimate film out of it that the comedy and action are thinned out, and a few characters do finally die at the end, which isn't very much fun at all. **The Three Musketeers** is like Christmas Eve, all excitement and anticipation, and **The Four Musketeers** is like Christmas Day, without presents.

Although more segments of **Four Musketeers** have slightly fresher colors, the image presentation on the two programs is essentially the same. Both have been letterboxed with an aspect ratio of about 1.63:1 and no 16:9 enhancement, a framing we occasionally found questionable, such as in the scene where Christopher Lee's one-eyed character fails to notice York hiding in a closet. So little of York's hand can be seen that it is easy to miss the gag.

In general, the color transfer looks good, though it is a bit aged. Darker scenes are a little grainy, some sequences seem a bit washed out, and there are times when the fleshtones look yellowish, though at other times the fleshtones look good and other hues are crisp. The essential colors of the films are conveyed and details are adequate. We are not as satisfied by the DVD transfer rate, which almost never rises above mid-range. In darker sequences, the image is smeary, and throughout both movies there are times when ratcheting, tiling and other digital artifacts are clearly visible, much more so than in other major DVD releases. The monophonic sound is fairly strong and free of distortion. There is no closed captioning. **The Three Musketeers**, from 1974, runs 106 minutes and **The Four Musketeers**, from 1975, also runs 106 minutes, contrary to the notations on the jacket covers. Oddly, the print used for **Four Musketeers** has French language credits at both the beginning and the end. The names of Alexander Salkind, Frank Finlay and Faye Dunaway are misspelled on both jackets, but if you really want some amusement, check out what they've done to 'Louis XIII' in the jacket credits on **Three Musketeers**.

The Three Musketeers (Simitar, 7216)

The 70 minute animated program follows the standard narrative about retrieving the Queen's diamonds, adding a few touches of cartoon humor (there is an owl who helps out) but failing to play up the friendship among the four swordsmen. The animation is very jerky and the artwork is bland, making the program diffi-

cult to watch. There also appears to be digital artifacts, including a number of image freezes, and the source material is damaged at several points. The colors are somewhat dull and sloppy, but that appears to be part of the cartoon. The monophonic sound also has variances in tone and volume, but not enough to cause any significant problems. The music is bad enough anyway, even without the limited dynamic range.

The Three Stooges: Curly Classics (Columbia TriStar, 02856)
The Three Stooges (Madacy, DVD99096)
The Three Stooges : Sing a Song of 6 Pants / Brideless Groom (Madacy, DVD99011)
The Three Stooges (Digital Disc, 566)

Six rather classic Three Stooges shorts are gathered on the 108 minute Columbia TriStar release. The black-and-white images are reasonably sharp, but contrasts are not always finely detailed and the source material seems a little worn around the edges. The monophonic sound is adequate. The shorts also have Spanish and Portuguese audio tracks, as well as optional English, French, Spanish and Portuguese subtitles. Chapter encoding identifies the beginnings of the shorts only.

Included are the 1940 *A Plumbing We Will Go* (escaping from the police, they pretend to be plumbers and go to work in a mansion, eventually messing things up so badly that the water comes out of the electrical circuits), the 1934 *Men in Black* (they are new doctors in a hospital, generally making a mess of things 'for duty and humanity'), the 1945 *Micro-Phonies* (they are radio station janitors trying to fix a radiator and eventually start fooling around with the radio equipment, when one is mistaken for an opera singer after lip-synching; they then cause a ruckus at a society party), the 1934 *Punch Drunks* (one becomes a super boxer whenever he hears *Pop Goes the Weasel*; it's one of the few shots where the three characters are strangers to one another at the beginning), the 1934 *Three Little Pigskins* (with Lucille Ball in a small part; the three are mistaken for college football players and are hired by a desperate professional team), and *Woman Haters* from 1934 (performed in verse; the three join a 'Woman Haters' club, one gets married and then tries to hide his indiscretion during the honeymoon train ride). While we would prefer a larger anthology, the DVD collection offers an excellent introduction to the anarchic comedy team.

Some Stooges shorts have also found their way into public domain collections. Madacy's **The Three Stooges** contains four shorts, *Disorder in the Court* (the three are witnesses in a murder trial, and proceed to wreak havoc in the courtroom), *Malice in the Palace* (a Shemp Howard episode, the three are Mideastern waiters who obtain a map to find a diamond), *Sing a Song of Six Pants* (another Shemp episode, the three are dry cleaners, who discover the combination to a safe in a gangster's pants) and *Brideless Groom* (a variation on *Seven Chances*, also with Shemp, who has to marry before a certain time to earn an inheritance). The latter two have also been released separately by Madacy as a *Hollywood Classics* title, **The Three Stooges Sing a Song of 6 Pants / Brideless Groom**, with Curly on the cover although Shemp appears in both. The source material (identical on the two releases) is a little more battered than what Columbia TriStar offers, particularly on *Sing a Song of 6 Pants*. All four are softer, less detailed, and have more scratches and speckles, but all four are watchable. The monophonic sound is somewhat scratchy, and goes out of synch in spots (particularly on *Sing a Song of Six Pants*), but it is usually tolerable, and the collections are not captioned.

The four shorts available in Madacy's **The Three Stooges** are also available on Digital Disc's **The Three Stooges**, but the picture is blurrier and contrasts are weaker. Parts of the image look washed out in places, as well. The sound is on par with Madacy's release (and is better synchronized) and, unlike Madacy's effort, all four shorts appear on one side for easy access. The collection is not captioned.

Three Tenors (see The Original Three Tenors Concert)

Throttle Junkies (Simitar, 7346)

Junkies is a compilation of three half hour video programs, the title piece, Sick Air and What's Up!. Most of the footage in all three programs depicts dirt bikes flying through the air in large empty lots or national wildlife areas or something, often looking like grasshoppers. There is also a decent amount of footage, however, of leaping water-skiers, leaping skateboarders, leaping bicyclists, leaping surfers and other such thrill seekers. Most of the time they land on their feet, but not always. There is some tiresome extraneous footage showing the bikers in more relaxed moments and unintentionally suggesting that biking activities are scrambling the maturation areas of their brains; and there are music videos, compiled to hard rock interpretations of tunes such as Time Warp and All My Love, that recycle a lot of the footage seen elsewhere on the programs. Although the quality of the source material varies, the best footage looks excellent, with crisp, vivid colors, and even the camcorder stuff looks pretty decent. The stereo sound is also fairly strong.

Tieta of Agreste (Fox Lorber, FLV5038)

Sonia Braga stars in the marvelous Jorge Amado tale. She portrays a cosmopolitan woman who returns to her remote, provincial hometown after leaving several decades earlier in shame. She's apparently rich, and she's able to make a call to a senator and get the town electrified within a week of arriving. Her stepdaughter accompanies her, and falls in love with a local man who is likely to become the town's next mayor. Meanwhile, she herself sets her sights on her nephew, a buff Adonis being wrangled into the priesthood by her pious sister, who caused all the trouble in the first place so many years ago. The 1996 feature, directed by Carlos Diegues, is very charming, and thanks to Amado's craftsmanship, it avoids dramatic simplifications. Every character has good and bad in them, and it becomes one of the film's lessons to make you see that such is the case in the world around you as well. Amado himself appears in the opening shot, reading the story to the viewer.

There is no indication of it on the jacket cover, but the film is letterboxed, with an aspect ratio of about 1.66:1 and no 16:9 enhancement. The image transfer looks very nice. The source material is totally free of damage, colors are bright, contrasts are manageable (a little weak in darkly lit sequences) and the image is reasonably sharp. There is also an incredible, unspoiled beach in the movie—perhaps the only thing in the film more lovely than Braga—and in the bright sun the image is so crisp you'll want to leap through your monitor to splash in the waves.

The monophonic sound is okay—the soundtrack has a pleasing mix of Brazilian musical styles—and the film is in Brazilian Portuguese with optional, unobtrusively yellow English subtitles. The 115 minute film is not time encoded and is accompanied by cast-and-director filmographies and an interesting 7 minute promotional featurette that appears to have been designed for investors or perhaps foreign distributors. It contains a lot of interesting behind-the-scenes footage as well as an awkward stab at the film's marketing spin, "A feel-good comedy of incest, greed and corruption."

Tiger Bay (Image, ID4536JFDVD)

Hayley Mills gives a captivating performance as a child who witnesses a murder and then becomes friends with the murderer in the 1959 feature. Directed by J. Lee Thompson, the film is beautifully constructed, tugging the viewer along with a strong plot, richly drawn characters and compelling dilemmas. Set in Cardiff, the film is also part of the post-War British neo-realist tradition, using the grit of the working class port town as if it were another character. Horst Buchholz and John Mills, who beams every time he shares a scene with Hayley, co-star.

Although the source material has a number of scratches and speckles, the black-and-white picture looks super. The image is so crisp and contrasts are so detailed that textures are as clear as the objects they emboss. The 1.33:1 image is presented with a slight windowboxing that varies from one shot to the next, particularly on the lower part of the screen. The monophonic sound is fine and the 102 minute program is not captioned.

Till the Clouds Roll By (Master Movies, DVD557); (Madacy, DVD99008)

The Jerome Kern bio-musical that MGM let slip into the public domain has been drawn from that domain by Master Movies. Contrary to the mistaken time listing on the jacket cover, the program runs a full 135 minutes, on one side of the DVD, and appears to be reasonably intact. The Technicolor colors are bright, but the image is very soft and contrasts are weak. The monophonic sound is soft, with no bass, but the music is not severely distorted. The film is accompanied by a small cast and crew profile section but, contrary to another jacket notation, there are no Japanese subtitles.

The Madacy Hollywood Classics presentation is sharper and whites are purer, but the colors are much blander. What should be green comes out as blue, and fleshtones, which looks fairly accurate on the Master Movies version, are pale or yellowed on the Madacy version. Madacy's sound is much louder and a little crisper. While the Master Movies audio track comes across as cleaner, we found ourselves responding more to the brightness of the Madacy audio track. There is a very minor text supplement and no captioning.

Robert Walker's relaxed performance of Jerome Kern helps to cue the viewer that one's concentration should be on the music instead of the person. The 1946 movie has several other things going for it as well. It opens with a twenty minute synopsis of Showboat, giving Lena Horne a chance to at least sample the role which should have been hers. Later on, Judy Garland has two elaborate production numbers that Vincente Minnelli stepped in to direct. Finally, there is the movie's grand finale, a medley of Kern tunes performed by different artists and concluding with Frank Sinatra, in a white tuxedo, singing Old Man River. Now, some folks are understandably put off by this spectacle, but we think the Sinatra piece is terrific and a wonderful way to end the movie. It was the only method the filmmakers could use to present the song stripped of its literalness, to convey the message to the viewer that Old Man River, which has many meanings, is also about music itself.

Tim Burton's The Nightmare Before Christmas (see The Nightmare Before Christmas)

Time Bandits (Criterion, CC1551D); (Anchor Bay, DV10685)

Terry Gilliam's delightful 1981 fantasy is about a young boy who travels through time with six midgets. The delightfully peripatetic narrative jumps from one era to the next, eventually landing in a place of fantasy peopled by strange creatures and controlled by the Devil. It is the wonderful ensemble performances of the midgets, David Rappaport, Kenny Baker, Jack Purvis, Mike Edmonds and Malcolm Dixon, that enables the film to endure a great many multiple viewings, encouraging laughter through anticipation long after the jokes and fantasy surprises have been memorized.

The picture and sound transfers are identical on the two DVDs and is letterboxed, with an aspect ratio of about 1.85:1 and no 16:9 enhancement. Shot on a modest budget, the colors are dullish in places and darker sequences are a little murky, but the presentation is workable, and when the lighting is strong, the hues are bright and crisp. Full screen versions add picture information to the top and bottom and are more pleasing, however, because of the film's imaginative production design, but the framing on the letterboxed DVDs is workable. The data transfer rate on the Anchor Bay version stays in the midrange, while the Criterion transfer rate is in the upper midrange. The stereo sound has limited separation effects and a mild, periodic dimensionality. Both DVDs are accompanied by a trailer. The Anchor Bay presentation is not captioned.

The Criterion presentation, which has optional English subtitles, contains a 3 minute 'Scrapbook' montage that provides an effective look at many aspects of the production. They are able to squeeze in quite a bit of interesting material, often using multiple screens, into the three minutes, giving the viewer at least a taste of how some of the special effects were accomplished, how the designs were developed and other behind-the-scenes glimpses. There is also a commentary track featuring Gilliam with inserts from Michael Palin, John Cleese, David Warner and former child actor Craig Warnock. Warner laments not having won an Oscar for his performance so he could rise to the podium and literally 'thank the little people.' Warnock, who played the boy in the film and is now all grown up, is particularly interesting, as he describes his experience from the perspective of his childhood memories. Gilliam explains how the special effect sequences were accomplished, talks about working with the cast (including his awkward interaction with Ralph Richardson), and speaks a bit about what the film was meant to accomplish, which was specifically to provide an alternative to syrupy, 'safe' family films. We can't agree completely with his condemnation of material values and what he sees as anti-aesthetic lifestyles (regardless of their unseemly appearance, clear vinyl slip covers preserve expensive couches, which not all families can afford to replace, from the damage young children cause), but we do concur with his basic desire to create an original fantasy that both children and adults can identify with, and time has proven that he achieved his goal.

A Time To Kill (Warner, 14317)

We were watching this bland, by-the-numbers courtroom drama when all of a sudden Kevin Spacey shows up as the prosecuting attorney and energized the entire film, like lightning hitting a house. The film is about a white lawyer defending a black client in Mississippi who has been accused of shooting his daughter's rapists. It is loaded with big name talent, and a few other stars also enliven the proceedings, including Patrick McGoohan, as the judge, and Ashley Judd. More often, however, they function as Samuel L. Jackson, who plays the defendant, functions, giving extremely competent performances that never rise above the material. Based upon a John Grisham novel, the plot holds almost no surprises and just meanders its way through a racially charged incident as if that were enough to validate a viewer's time. Spacey, however, brings real movie star magic to his role, and his every arched eyebrow is riveting. Since the rest of the film is competent, his presence is sufficient to make the whole endeavor worthwhile. The movie may be predictable, and his character may be predictable, but within those confines you never know which way he's going to jump or where he's going to land. The film's primary stars, by the way, are Sandra Bullock and Matthew McConaughey. Bullock has what amounts to a supporting role and the most embarrassing part, involving a token assault in which the life and virtue of her character are spared solely because she is a star.

The 150 minute 1996 feature is presented on two sides in letterboxed format, with an aspect ratio of about 2.35:1 and an accommodation for enhanced 16:9 playback. The color transfer looks good (the contrasts handle both the black and white faces effectively, even in the same shot) and the stereo surround sound has a number of forceful passages. The program also comes in French in Dolby Digital, and can be supported by English, French or Spanish subtitles. There is a theatrical trailer and backgrounds on more than a dozen cast and crew members.

Timecop (Universal, 20147/20047)

The widescreen 1994 sci-fi action film has been issued in cropped format only, even though the director, Peter Hyams, doubles as his own cinematographer and works exclusively in the widescreen format. For those who can tolerate the truncated image and subsequently confused fight scenes, the picture is sharp and

colors are nice, though there are instances where the image looks a little grainy. The stereo surround soundtracks is adequate and the Dolby Digital track is reasonably forceful and involving. The film is also available in French in standard stereo and comes with English or Spanish subtitles. There is a decent presskit production essay and a modest cast-and-crew profile segment, along with the 99 minute film's creative and enticing theatrical trailer. Jean-Claude Van Damme stars as the title character.

Timeless... (Image, ID4214CRDVD)

Although the 43 minute program follows the standard format of mixing people-less video images of the natural environment—in this case, most were shot in the Pacific Northwest and in the Southwest—with unassertive instrumental music, the mix is a little more varied than most. There is never a sense that one is seeing the same shot or even the same topic twice (everything from beach surf to high timber forests is included), and the extensive use of time-lapse photography gives many of the visuals a fresh and revealing angle. The music, too, is better varied in style than most, and has a little more personality as well. As is common, and for that matter, necessary, with such programs, the picture and stereo surround sound quality is excellent.

The Tin Cup (Warner, 14318)

Kevin Costner stars in Ron Shelton's engaging romantic comedy about professional golf, portraying the manager of a broken down driving range who decides to enter the U.S. Open after he meets a woman who has a little more class than the sort he is used to associating with. Renee Russo, Cheech Marin and Don Johnson costar. The film runs 135 minutes and the golf competition segment doesn't begin until the mid-way point. The characters are thoroughly molded, the romance is pleasant and the golf stuff is unobnoxiously poetic. Like the game, the film is relaxed and somewhat inconsequential, enjoyable more for the experience of its viewing than for what it finally achieves.

The film is presented in letterboxed format on one side, with an aspect ratio of about 2.35:1 and an accommodation for enhanced 16:9 playback, and in cropped format on the other side, with the letterboxing adding substantially more to the sides of the image and losing nothing on the top and bottom in comparison to the cropped image. The letterboxed version is preferable, but the way the film has been composed, the cropping isn't all that awkward, except now and then. The cropped image, however, is a little blurrier than the letterboxed image, and one is more apt to see an occasional artifact. Colors are reasonably bright. The stereo surround sound is bland, but the Dolby Digital track has more enhanced detail. The film is also available in French in standard stereo and has English, French or Spanish subtitles.

The Tin Drum (Kino, K104)

Volker Schlöndorff directed the 1979 adaptation of the Günter Grass novel, set mostly in Danzig, about a young boy who refuses to grow older as, in the world around him, the Nazis rise to power. The film won many awards, including the Best Foreign Film Oscar, and is dense with meanings and possible interpretations. Sometimes humorous and sometimes grotesque, the movie also contains images of sexuality involving the young boy, that were strong enough to get the film kicked out of Blockbuster. Taken at face value, the narrative is intriguing and provides a worthy history lesson, but its calculated absurdities and bizarre emotional turns will not appeal to all viewers. The picture is letterboxed with an aspect ratio of about 1.68:1 and no 16:9 enhancement. The color transfer (the movie has 'tin toy colors') looks flawless and the image is free of damage. The monophonic sound is strong. The 142 minute film is in German, with unmutable yellow English subtitles. Maurice Jarre's almost abstract musical score has been isolated on one of the analog channels during the film, and listening to it without the dialogue or sound effects is particularly eerie. There is a 14 minute supplement that actually appears at the end of the movie, offering a montage of production sketches, costume sketches, production photos and storyboards with comparative passages from the film.

Schlöndorff also provides a rewarding commentary track. He talks extensively about the production, from the initiation of the screenplay to trimming out scenes to reach the final running time. He has plenty to say about all the major cast and crew members, his own autobiography and insights on the directors he apprenticed with (his profile of the way Louis Malle would 'seduce' his whole crew is particularly fascinating). He explains how specific scenes were accomplished, how he cast the key role (and how he worked with the boy to get the performance he wanted), and discusses the various meanings of certain scenes. He also says what happened to all the drums, in case, by the end of the film, you wish you had one (sorry, most of them were destroyed).

Tina Turner Live in Amsterdam: Wildest Dreams Tour
(Image, ID4024ERDVD); DTS (Image, ID4637ERDVD)

Turner's uninterrupted 113 minute stage show is energetic and snazzy. She's backed by a gigantic screen and surrounded by billowing smoke, flashing lights, and sexy dancers. She sings a mix of newer and older hits, and she has the kind of act where the compromises brought to her studio recordings by the live environment do not matter in the least. The first part of *Proud Mary* isn't as languid as it should be, but the second part is frantic to the max. Interestingly, the addition of *GoldenEye* to her lineup gave her a tentpole production number that improved her entire set over earlier concerts, even though few of the other numbers changed.

The stage lights are so bright they sometimes obscure Turner, particularly when she wears her sequin dress, but on the whole the picture is terrifically crisp and the colors are excellent. The depth-of-field is amazing, and even when the lighting isn't hitting them directly, every member of the audience in the huge arena is in perfect focus. If you have a big screen and you stand close, on some of the top-of-the-hall shots it looks so realistic you feel like you're going to fall in. The stereo surround sound is substantially weaker than the Dolby Digital soundtrack. On the Dolby track, the concert recording is loud yet sufficiently detailed to bring melody to the noise and delivers an adequate rendition of the high-energy concert recording. There is no captioning.

The DTS release is definitely louder than the standard release, but whether within that loudness there is improved detail is more difficult to say. What we can say is that the DVD's sound doesn't hold a candle to the DTS LD, which has a more detailed bass, better defined separation effects and less distortion all up and down the sonic line. The frame transfer rate on the DTS DVD is about twice the frame transfer rate on the standard DVD.

Titanic (Image, ID4511ANDVD

We've seen many programs about the Titanic in our day, but the one that taught us the most about what happened to the ship and what it meant to the world was the four-part A&E documentary presented on the dual-layer DVD. The 192 minute program is divided in two parts but actually represents a four-part TV broadcast, exploring everything from the building of the ship, to what details are known about its last moments, to the effect the sinking had on the media and to Robert Ballard's discovery of its remains. The picture and stereo sound transfers are very good, and the program is not captioned.

The Titanic (Simitar, 7208)

Two minutes into the documentary there is a sequence depicting an attempt to contact Titanic survivors through a seance, so you know this isn't a National Geographic thing. The 62 minute program appears to be a pastiche of footage from other documentaries, and there is even a clip from **A Night to Remember**. We did learn some pieces of trivia we hadn't known before—the Titanic was the first ocean liner to have a swimming pool, which is as good a demarcation between the past and modern times as any—and, as a brief overview of the incident, it gives you a fairly well rounded

introduction. The show's construction, however, creates about a dozen endings, as visits to the ship by Dr. Robert Ballard and subsequent plunderers are each depicted in 'present' time (apparently, each sequence is drawn from a documentary that was current when it was produced—a failure to note the date when survivors are being interviewed is one of the show's biggest frustrations) and there is no sense of drama or thematic focus to the material. Colors are consistently faded and the image is a bit blurry most of the time. There is a brief disruption in the presentation around the 27 minute mark that appears to be a flaw in the transfer. The sound is either monophonic or a very subdued stereo, but it is coherent, despite the frail British accents of some of the elderly survivors.

The Titanic Expedition (Madacy, DVD99056)
The Titanic Expedition: The Search (Madacy, DVD990561)
The Titanic Expedition: The Discovery (Madacy, DVD990562)
The Titanic Expedition: Titanic Remembered (Madacy, DVD990563)

Sick of documentaries about the Titanic? So are we, but we never get tired of laughing and therefore enjoyed the two awful, awful documentaries about a group of earnest, dollar-signs-in-their-eyes scientists who didn't find the ship, **The Titanic Expedition: The Search** and **The Titanic Expedition: The Discovery**. The 46 minute programs are also part of a box set, **The Titanic Expedition** that Madacy has bundled with **The Titanic Expedition: Titanic Remembered**, a re-packaged 60 minute documentary Madacy also released as **The Titanic / The Mystery & The Legacy: Titanic Remembered**.

Dr. Robert Ballard these guys aren't. They've got one machine, that can send up sonar or video images, but not both at the same time, and that's when it's working properly. The expedition is a comedy of errors, enhanced by the fact that while they think they've got a chance of being the first to find the boat you know that since Ballard isn't there, they ain't going to find squat. But it isn't just that these guys are the scientists who couldn't record their data straight. The narration on the documentaries, particularly on **The Discovery**, is hysterical ("Mike Harris, expedition leader. Dreamer with a dream. A man with the patience of Job and the guts to find the way to make the dream come true"). **Search** is a flat out failed mission that occurred before Ballard found the ship. They barely get the equipment working when a storm comes up and shuts them down before they have a chance to find the boat, let alone (as one expeditioner is heard planning) the safe in the purser's office. **The Discovery** is more ambiguous. If you will recall, Ballard did not publicize the coordinates of his find, and it looks like this was one of the groups that went out with a good guess of where Ballard had been. Footage of the Titanic from later expeditions is inserted during some descriptive sequences about its sinking, but the only thing they get, at the end of the show, are some very blurry video pictures of a propeller (the purser's safe will have to wait) that may or may not be the Titanic's.

Titanic Remembered is a fairly interesting documentary about Titanic memorabilia that includes interviews with survivors and the descendants of survivors. The picture on the two expedition documentaries is fairly fuzzy and grainy, with faded colors and occasional video glitches. The picture on **Titanic Remembered** is a little stronger, though there is still some grain and hues are light. The monophonic sound on the programs is of limited quality. There is no captioning and the programs are accompanied by minor text supplements.

Titanic / The Mystery & The Legacy (Madacy, DVD99034)
Titanic / The Mystery & The Legacy: Echoes of the Titanic (Madacy, DVD99034)
Titanic / The Mystery & The Legacy: Titanic Remembered (Madacy, DVD990342)
Titanic / The Mystery & The Legacy: Edward J. Smith,

The Captain of the Titanic (Madacy, DVD990343)
Titanic / The Mystery & The Legacy Titanic: End of an Era (Madacy, DVD9900344)
Titanic / The Mystery & The Legacy: The Mystery & The Legacy (Madacy, DVD9900345)

Four episodes from a 1992 British documentary plus a slightly stronger American documentary have been collected in the series, which is available as a box set and as individual releases.

Although the running time of each episode is listed on the jacket as 55 minutes, the times actually vary. The picture quality is generally acceptable. The monophonic sound has a weak upper end and the interviews on the British documentaries are sometimes difficult to understand. Even the narration sounds raspy or distorted in places. The programs are not captioned and are accompanied by text profiles of a couple well-known figures involved in the disaster, along with a few other facts that differ in subject on each volume.

Echoes of the Titanic runs 51 minutes and mostly explores the aftermath of the event, focusing on newspaper headlines, silent films (one that included substantial footage of the captain when he was in charge of a sister ship) and later follow-ups, including interviews with elderly survivors and extended clips from **A Night to Remember**. **Titanic Remembered** runs 60 minutes and contains the same sort of material, with more survivor interviews and interviews with people who knew survivors. The first part of the 56 minute **Captain of the Titanic** presents a thorough profile of Edward J. Smith, but the second half slips into the same sort of generalized reminiscences that fill the first two episodes. **End of an Era**, which runs 60 minutes, goes into more detail about the voyage, but also includes many highlights from the other three episodes, as well as a lot more footage from **Night to Remember**.

The American documentary, **The Mystery & The Legacy**, is a more satisfying program. It starts out by explaining how boats float and then explores the Titanic's design innovations and the various factors that led to its chance destruction. It also looks at a novel that seemed to predict the disaster, and other aspects of superstition surrounding the ship and the voyage. None of the documentaries offer the sort of comprehensive or lucid narrative available in the A&E **Titanic** documentary, but fans desperate for every last word on the subject will find a few fresh insights and information scattered about the various programs.

Titanica (Buena Vista, 14892)

The 67 minute IMAX program (edited and revised from a longer and duller IMAX film) depicts a Russian excursion to the resting spot of the Titanic, interwoven with archival footage and survivor interviews, with the revisions. The show's audio doesn't contribute much to an understanding of its subject, but the added dimensionality and power provided by the Dolby Digital track are sure to please some viewers. The picture quality is terrific. The program can be supported by optional English subtitles.

To Cross the Rubicon (Simitar, 7262)

An interesting film about relationships, Patricia Royce and Lorraine Devon star as thirtysomething roommates who still can't get over the vague hope that every guy they date will be 'the one.' There are natural seeming ebbs and flows to the emotions of the characters, and the dialogue is often intriguingly practical.

The 105 minute film, ultimately, is not about much, but the characters seem so real that you can get caught up in their problems fairly easily. The colors are somewhat bland and the image is soft, with darker sequences looking a bit smeary. The stereo sound has a limited dimensionality and is not captioned.

To Die For (Columbia TriStar, 73439)

Gus Van Sant's 1995 comedy, from a screenplay by Buck Henry, is about a starstruck young woman who wangles her way onto a cable program in a small New Hampshire town as a weather woman, and then arranges her husband's murder when she thinks their relationship is holding back her career. Nicole Kidman gives a wonderful performance in what could easily have been an over-the-top role as the heroine and Matt Dillon is effective as her unsuspecting and baffled spouse.

The picture is presented on one side in letterboxed format with an aspect ratio of about 1.85:1 and no 16:9 enhancement, and is in full screen format on the other side. We tend to prefer the full screen presentation, which accommodates the video monitor sequences better. The picture transfer is very satisfying, with accurate colors and a crisp focus. The stereo surround soundtrack has a hot pop music score and adeptly shifts in volume levels for emotional effect, with the Dolby Digital track providing a bit more solidity and clarity of definition. The 106 minute program also has a French language track in standard stereo, optional English or French subtitles and a trailer.

To Kill a Mockingbird (Universal, 20252)

The retrospective documentary accompanying the film on the *Collector's Edition* release is so good it gave us goosebumps. More than just a promotional overview of the film, the 90 minute program, *Fearful Symmetry*, by Charles Kisleyak, is a work of art itself. Shot in black-and-white, the documentary provides a retrospective of the film's production and its relationship with the Pulitzer Prize-winning Harper Lee novel (a number of excerpts are read in voiceover). It also is an enchanting portrait of what the South was like in the late Thirties. The director of **Mockingbird**, Robert Mulligan, and the producer, Alan Pakula, are both featured, but they do not dominate the program, since they are also given a chance to vent their memories on the DVD's audio commentary track. Instead, there are interviews with the surviving cast members (including the kids, now middle-aged grownups), screenwriter Horton Foote, composer Elmer Bernstein, residents of the town where Lee grew up—the novel was based upon her memories—and comments from a prominent black Alabama lawyer, Cleophus Thomas, who credits the film with inspiring him toward a career in law and easily squelches any effort there might be to create a backlash over the film's racial conflicts. Sure, the white lawyer is seen as the savior of the black community, but because the film's point-of-view is so carefully oriented toward its youthful protagonists and because the lawyer, ultimately, fails to win, the film isn't selling a paternalistic message, it is just offering several conflicting perspectives of which this is simply one of the more prominent. It is the complexity behind that viewpoint that has allowed the film to endure.

The documentary is beautifully composed, working off the movie and a knowledge of Lee's background to explore a wealth of themes and nostalgias. Among the many revelations: one of the child characters is based upon Truman Capote. Kisleyak gets the performers to open up (the man who played the young boy tells how he despised the girl playing his sister and tried to injure her; Gregory Peck, and several others, have some very amusing stories about the personality of the actor playing the villain, James Anderson, who was apparently perfectly cast) and manages to place both Lee's novel and the film in a larger social perspective. The documentary doesn't dwell on the negative social aspects of the South, but instead celebrates what was good about the old days and what more has been gained through the changes that, to at least a minor degree, Lee helped inspire.

The most important points brought up in the commentary track are covered in the documentary, to which the commentary works as sort of an addendum, but Pakula and Mulligan also share a few more anecdotes about working with the cast, composing the film and other related details about the production. It is a fairly laid back talk that seems in keeping with the film's atmosphere.

The picture is letterboxed, with an aspect ratio of about 1.85:1 and no 16:9 enhancement, losing nothing on the top and bottom of the image and adding picture information to the sides compared to previous home video releases, creating a much more satisfying frame composition. The black-and-white image is crisp, clean and smooth, with deeper blacks and bright whites. The monophonic sound is strong and free of noise. The 129 minute film is also available in French and can be supported by English or Spanish subtitles. There is also a theatrical trailer (introduced by Peck), some production notes and a cast & crew profile section.

To Kill with Intrigue (Simitar, 7239)

The 1976 Jackie Chan feature is almost worth viewing if you can accept the cropped image. The cropping does not blatantly interfere with the flow of the action and you are rarely aware of its presence. The colors are faded and fleshtones are pale, but there is a consistency and crispness to the hues that makes the color scheme fairly attractive, and as the film progresses, the fading subsides, so that some shots near the end look very nice. Damage to the source material is also manageable.

The story is entertaining, about a young champion who sends his girlfriend away to protect her and then spends most of the movie trying to get her back, meeting characters and solving political conflicts along the way. He also undergoes a substantial spiritual maturation, which is effectively conveyed. It is interesting that Chan, wearing a long wig in a more traditional-styled heroic role than the bumpkin characters he usually plays, uses an entirely different fighting style to match the sophistication of his character. Contrary to the running time listed on the jacket cover, the program runs 99 minutes. The film is awkwardly dubbed in English on one channel and presented in the original Cantonese on another, without subtitles, and is accompanied by a brief interview with Chan, as well as a Chan profile and filmography.

Todd McFarlane's Spawn (HBO, 91425)

A compilation of six episodes from the animated cable series, the 140 minute program is split to two sides. There is a single running narrative, sort of an introduction to the character (the bad guys kidnap the child of the hero's former wife) that is wrapped up by the show's conclusion. Because the episodes have been blended, the narrative can seem a bit erratic and repetitious, but such drawbacks are slight. The program on a whole is marvelously violent and an effective animation of McFarlane's comic that will be highly appealing to fans. It has the sort of dark atmosphere and a complex narrative that one longs for in an animated program.

The picture quality looks terrific, with bright, sharp, solid colors. The stereo surround sound has an effective rear channel presence and some nice separation effects, but there isn't much power to it, as it ultimately is a TV mix and not a movie mix. There is also a Spanish language track in mono and optional English, French and Spanish subtitles.

McFarlane also provides a rewarding running commentary across the entire program. How was he able to lure animators who could have earned more money working elsewhere? "We could only sell them the dark and the black and the coolness of it, because we couldn't match them, basically, in terms of paycheck. You will find that there are a lot of creative people in the animation business that are getting sick and tired of drawing unicorns and little frogs." He talks about what is happening on the screen, but only as a reference to delve into the show's background and its production. He discusses the show's moral complexities, its focused market (McFarlane calls anyone who understand his work 'Mom'), and how he achieved its distinctive look while marshaling the forces of animation (including coping with the work shipped off to Korea). He explains the numbers appearing periodically on the screen (they depict how much longer the hero has to exist) and other obscure plot points. McFarland also provides practical advice, such as the reasoning behind placing the characters in different locales for their meetings instead of using the same locale over and over.

On both sides, there is a look at the storyboards, the trailer for the **Spawn** movie, an introductory interview with McFarlane, profiles of the characters and a profile of McFarlane.

Tokyo Drifter (Criterion, TOK050)

Imagine a whole, serious movie like the *Girl Hunt* sequence from *The Bandwagon*, mixed, perhaps, with **The Naked Kiss**, and you can begin to approach the joys to be had in Suzuki Seijun's incoherent but shagadelic **Tokyo Drifter**. The 1966 film is a colorful and quirky gem. Seijun was a director of Japanese 'B' movies, the sort that never made it to prestigious international festivals or onto the Godzilla/Zato Ichi circuit but served to fill up the lower half of theatrical double bills in Japan just as 'B' movies did here. And, just like in America, while a majority of the 'B' movies were formula efforts of no lasting value made by assembly line directors, the limited budgets allowed some cinematic artists to experiment wildly so long as they met certain basic requirements, something that Seijun did, just barely.

The fact that you can hardly understand the plot of **Tokyo Drifter** won't matter on multiple viewings, and by then you may even start to understand most of it. What will matter are the gorgeous Pop Art sets, the bizarre musical sequences, the confusing but balletic action scenes and the film's gunbutt attitude. The hero, played by Watari Tetsuya (playing a character also named 'Tetsuya'), is a lieutenant for a retired crime boss who isn't being allowed to go straight. After a while the hero goes on the run, but wherever he is, goons show up and try to eliminate him. Even though there is a Hollywood-style saloon brawl and Tetsuya at times appears to break into song, the gangster atmosphere is maintained. Because of budget limitations, action scenes are often missing key insert shots that would make them understandable, but they are imaginatively staged and you get the gist of it most of the time.

The picture is letterboxed, with an aspect ratio of about 2.1:1 and no 16:9 enhancement, and has a slightly squeezed look at times. The colors look great and the image sharp. The monophonic sound is a little noisy but workable. The 83 minute film is in Japanese with optional English subtitles and includes an extended and informative interview with the elderly and dapper Seijun, in which he talks about his filmmaking methods (getting the performers into costume early helps them find their characters), his career and the movies at hand.

Tol'able David (Image, ID4729DSDVD)

A melodrama directed by Henry King, the 1921 film was shot on location in the mountains of western Virginia, and is about a young boy who comes of age when tragedy strikes his family and three villainous backwoodsmen move in next door. The film is old fashioned in the best sense, depicting attitudes and manners that are no longer relevant, but depicting them with sincerity, so that contemporary audiences can understand, free of ridicule, the moral values of the past. The film's climax is well-paced and very exciting, while the rest of the film is fascinating, not only depicting an idyllic locale, but seeming to exist in one as well.

The windowboxed black-and-white image is vaguely greenish— not enough to qualify as tinting, but enough to set it apart from true blacks and greys. The picture is sharp and effectively detailed, however, and wear is minimal. There is a nice musical score performed by a small orchestra and presented in stereo without making a nuisance of itself. After the 94 minute film is concluded, there is a 16 minute interview sequence with the elderly King, recorded in the Eighties, where he talks about his career and about the film.

The Toll Gate / His Bitter Pill (Image, ID4728DSDVD)

The presentation on *The Toll Gate*, a wonderful 1920 silent western starring William S. Hart, is watchable, but the image is very battered, and a moderately heavy tinting obscures details even more. Some sequences look solarized and others are substantially littered with scratches and other wear, but there are plenty of closeups of Hart that look clear and other sequences that are reasonably sharp and free of overt damage. The 73 minute feature has its original intertitles and an appropriately overbearing stereo music score that combines organ and orchestra. Hart is a bandit who is betrayed by his partner. He eventually escapes and seeks revenge, but his quest is tempered when he meets a woman and her child living alone on a ranch. Character interactions are strong and the stunts are lively. The film is filled with marvelous western iconography and it is a joy to watch Hart, one of the first great cowboy stars, do his thing. It is also unusual to see him play such an amoral figure, which gives the film a lasting sense of maturity.

The 20 minute companion piece, *His Bitter Pill*, is identified on the jacket cover as a parody (of Hart), and was produced in 1916. Mack Swain is a calorie-challenged sheriff who must rescue his gal from a slicker but less virtuous rival. A Mack Sennett comedy, the pratfalls are fairly standard, but the setting is a little different from the usual Sennett effort. The source material is in better condition than *Toll Gate*. The black-and-white image is soft, but speckling isn't bad and wear marks are limited.

Tom Jones (HBO, 90664)

This is Tony Richardson's ill considered 1991 'director's cut' of the 1964 Oscar-winner. Before he passed away, Richardson trimmed about 8 minutes from the film for a restoration release, claiming that the older cut wouldn't suit the breakneck speed today's audiences demand from their comedies. Nothing could be further from the truth, however, and all the 121 minute version presented on the DVD does is lose some choice comical moments and worthwhile character development. The real shame is because the cut had Richardson's approval, the original version may never see the light of day again.

There is no indication of it on the jacket, but the picture is letterboxed, with an aspect ratio of about 1.7:1 and no 16:9 enhancement. Although the film underwent a 'color restoration,' the source material is in very weak condition and darker scenes are often quite grainy. There are also a number of scratches and other markings, and fleshtones are a bit purplish. The sound was remastered for stereo, giving the music a slightly wider presence, though the mix remains essentially monophonic. The DVD is also presented in French and Spanish in mono and comes with English, French or Spanish subtitles ("Les femmes sont gagnées par la raison, et non par la force"). There is also a modest cast profile section and an interesting pre-Oscar theatrical trailer.

Tombs of the Blind Dead & Return of the Blind Dead (Anchor Bay, DV10561)

Two classic Spanish zombie movies directed by Amando de Ossorio have been issued as a double bill.

The splatter effects provide a payoff, but the essential appeal of *Tombs*, shot in Portugal in 1971, is in the atmosphere that it creates, careening from one character to another and following narrative vectors at odd angles, the way a dream changes course as it develops. This atmosphere also makes the program a strong candidate for repeat viewing. The central premise concerns a band of skeletal knights who rise from the grave after midnight and start eating anybody who happens to be camped out in the ruins of their castle.

Billed as the sequel to *Tombs*, *Return* uses the same zombie knights and their backstory, but otherwise has no relationship to the previous film, so you don't get to find out what happened after the *Tombs*' end. The zombies rise from their graves, apparently for the first time in 500 years, and wreak vengeance upon the small town responsible for their internment. In the second half, a handful of characters are trapped in a church. The 1972 film has almost none of the sex the first movie had and even the gore is toned down some. The zombies (who ride zombie horses) are cool looking and the narrative is tolerable, but fans who found the first film to be a worthy indulgence will be disappointed.

Blacks are pure and the image is sharp, but both films retain an aged look, with bland fleshtones, dullish hues and weak contrasts. Both movies are letterboxed with an aspect ratio of about 1.66:1 and no 16:9 enhancement. *Tombs*, which runs 102 minutes (and contains gore closeups and some minor nudity previously missing

from a U.S. theatrical release that was about 15 minutes shorter), is in Spanish with permanent English subtitles and *Return*, which is dubbed in English, runs 90 minutes. On both, the monophonic sound is aged but functional.

Tombstone (Buena Vista, 13078)

Kurt Russell stars as Wyatt Earp, along with Val Kilmer, Sam Elliott, Michael Biehn and many other talented, engaging performers. They fit so well into the western landscape that the story bursts forth from their interaction, like lightening from intersecting clouds. (Russell's moment of recognition, right before the gunfight at the OK Corral, that the shooting is really going to occur, will be branded in your film memories forever.) There is so much story, in fact, that some minor characters disappear without acknowledgment and other plot turns pop up without explanation.

The color transfer is imperfect, but the pink-orange shadings often look nice, particularly during indoor scenes, scenes near sunset or other situations where there is no reference to indicate that the hues are incorrect. The presentation is letterboxed with an aspect ratio of about 2.35:1 and no 16:9 enhancement. The stereo surround sound is terrific, with a punchy bass and an energetic ambiance. The 130 minute film is available in French and Spanish, and comes with English or Spanish subtitles ("Diles que voy para allá y que voy con el infierno, ¿me oyes?").

Tommy and the Computoys: Sing Along (Image, ID5560M3DVD)
Tommy and the Computoys: The Story (Image, ID5561MBDVD)

The children's program has a deathly pace and uninteresting characters. Running 86 minutes, the computer animated **Story** is a collection of brief vignettes accompanied by voiceover narration. A few segments in the show's second half are complex enough to be moderately interesting, but for the most part the animation is so basic and the narratives are so lacking that the program amounts to little more than bobbing shapes and colors. Still, one cannot discount the attention spans of youngsters being held by anything colorful that moves and makes noises, and the show does serve that function. The colors are solid and the monophonic sound is adequate.

A 59 minute program with more simplistic computer animation is also available. There are no lyrics appearing on the screen, so it isn't a true 'sing along,' but at least some of the songs are familiar, giving the program more of a handle for kids to latch onto. Again, a couple of the segments are complex enough to be interesting, but most are too basic to stimulate the imagination. Like the first, the colors look fine, and the show's stereo sound is pretty much identical to the mono sound on the other program. There is no captioning on either program.

The Tommyknockers (Trimark, VM68420)

Jimmy Smits, Marg Helgenberger, Joanna Cassidy, Traci Lords, E.G. Marshall and others star in the entertaining 181 minute 1993 Stephen King miniseries, about a town slowly becoming possessed by something evil. While the program is certainly one of King's more fantastic tales, the miniseries format gives the narrative an opportunity to build a more thorough foundation than a shorter feature film can manage. Although a few too many sympathetic characters bite the dust, the show is a satisfying extravaganza, with plenty of creepy moments and a resolute conclusion.

Although there are a couple instances where one can see vertical lines running through the image, the picture looks good, with solid, crisp colors and accurate fleshtones. Technically, the program is stereophonic, but except for a few of the strongest passages in the musical score, there are no separation effects and very little dimensionality. The program is closed captioned with minor paraphrasing and can be supported by French or Spanish subtitles. There's also a home video trailer.

Tomorrow Never Dies (MGM, 907025)
Tomorrow Never Dies: Special Edition (MGM, 906756)

GoldenEye was a breakthrough in the James Bond film series, but not every movie can or should have such a distinction. **Tomorrow Never Dies** is a worthy follow-up feature, not quite as elaborate or as creative, but filled with a sufficient number of pleasures and a couple of good surprises (including an amusing allusion to **Citizen Kane**). Pierce Brosnan reprises his role as the gentleman agent, and Michelle Yeoh does such a good job as the female lead that she gets to mess up some bad guys without Brosnan's assistance. Jonathan Pryce, acting a little too broadly, is the villain.

The 118 minute film is presented on the standard edition on a dual-layer single-sided platter in letterboxed format on one layer, with an aspect ratio of about 2.35:1 and an accommodation for enhanced 16:9 playback, and in a pointless cropped format on the other. The picture quality looks fine, with crisp, solid and accurate hues. The stereo surround sound and Dolby Digital sound are a little less impressive. The film's sound mix is suitably active and the DVD reflects those efforts, but the mix feels at times like it is improperly balanced. In particular, the music seems unusually subdued during fight sequences. The film also comes in French in standard stereo and can be accompanied by English, French or Spanish subtitles ("Dit-moi, James, dors-tu toujours avec un revolver sous l'oreiller?"). A fully loaded theatrical trailer is also featured.

The **Special Edition** is presented in letterboxed format only, with a picture and sound transfer that is identical to the standard edition (including the language options), and comes with an extensive number of supplementary features. The most interesting is an optional angle function that superimposes the storyboards as black outlines on a corner of the image during many of the action sequences. There is a music-only track in standard stereo (one of the more inherently entertaining because of the way the composer, David Arnold, keeps slipping the 007 theme into the mix) and two commentary tracks, one from director Roger Spottiswoode, who is prompted by Dan Petrie, Jr., and one by effects supervisors Vic Armstrong and Michael G. Wilson. Spottiswoode provides a basic but informative background about the shoot as well as some anecdotes and a few insights. Perhaps the most interesting aspect to his talk are his oblique references to how a James Bond movie is constructed—the challenges to come up with things that are new but not outside the format. Armstrong and Wilson's talk is less interesting, primarily because the major action and effects sequences were already aptly deconstructed by Spottiswoode, and because outside of those sequences Armstrong and Wilson are no better than any two well-informed film patrons sitting in front of you at a movie theater and talking loudly.

There is also a 45 minute James Bond documentary entitled *The Secrets of 007* that covers not just **Tomorrow** but the whole Bond series, with a fresh Sean Connery interview, an interesting retrospective look at *On Her Majesty's Secret Service* and many other delights; a Sheryl Crow music video (apparently, several music stars 'competed' for the chance to do the title song); a brief interview with Arnold about the score; a four-minute look at how the various elements are brought together in the special effects shots including how the 'menacing helicopter' shot was achieved; a quick but well-designed summary of the gadgets used in the movie; and a couple trailers, including a well-made teaser.

Finally, let us take note of Judi Dench's role as 'M' and the celebrated differences between men and women. We tried to picture the previous M, Bernard Lee, playing the key dramatic scenes Dench performs, where she is sticking up for Bond after her superiors have dismissed his efforts, and it was just impossible to imagine a male boss doing that kind of thing. He'd still support 007, but quietly, never arguing or insulting the wrong-headed ministers he was working for. This isn't a judgment evaluation, just an interesting look at the subtleties gender can bring to a role.

Tony Bennett: MTV Unplugged—The Video (Sony, CVD49193)

Very little of it is really unplugged, but Bennett performs for an hour with a small band in the intimate live *MTV Unplugged*. The whole program runs 72 minutes, with the concert followed by some brief but informative interviews and a music video for *Steppin' Out with My Baby*. Bathed in blue and red lights, the image is crisp and accurately detailed, but fleshtones are obscured by the lighting and Bennett sometimes takes on a Kabuki complexion. The sound is presented in regular stereo and Dolby Digital stereo. The Dolby Digital track is much more aggressive, as if everybody were standing closer to the microphones, but the bass is a little heavy and the regular stereo track—if you turn it up—has a less elaborate yet smoother mix.

Bennett opens the **Unplugged** concert with flat, grating renditions of two very special songs, *Old Devil Moon* and *Speak Low*. When he moves on to the brassier numbers, such as *Fly Me to the Moon* and *Steppin' Out with My Baby*, he can't do as much damage, but even then it is what he represents—a singer of songs from the days when lyricists and melodists had class—that excites listeners, not the weak, empty vocals and over-familiar phrasings that are actually coming through his microphone.

Top Gun (Paramount, 016297)

We have never completely understood why **Top Gun** has attracted such attention—we don't even want to go into what a silly movie (in which Tom Cruise portrays a Navy jet pilot) we think it is except for the half dozen action sequences—but there is no denying that is well suited for delivering an organized mass of loud noises and zippy visuals that can easily leave video cassettes in the dust. The DVD's standard stereo surround soundtrack is less aggressive, but the Dolby Digital track is super, with solid details from all angles, a killer bass, and the front channels packing even more blasting power as the jets seem to crisscross right above your head.

The film is encoded in dual-layer format and the picture is presented on one layer letterboxed, with an aspect ratio of about 2:1 and no 16:9 enhancement, and in full screen format on the other layer. The letterboxed version adds nothing to the sides of the image and is masked off on the top and bottom in comparison to the full screen version. In cockpit close-ups, the masking tends to cut off the lips of the characters, and in general the extra hardware on view in the full screen presentation is more satisfying than the artistic framing on the letterboxed presentation. The color transfer is consistently accurate, with stability in the most difficult lighting situations. The 109 minute film is also available in French in standard stereo and can be accompanied by English or Spanish subtitles ("Tu ego intenta hacer lo que tu cuerpo no puede").

Tornado! (see **Killer Twisters! and Lethal Lightning Super Storms**)

Tornado Run (Simitar, 7206)

One genre that it would seem difficult to produce on a small budget is the contemporary military aviation action movie, and the makers **Tornado Run** don't really try. They use mostly stock footage for the flight sequences and, with the bare minimum of exceptions, keep the action on the ground. This is the kind of movie where ruthless arms dealers have movie memorabilia in their offices. The plot, in which an advanced military strike force is sabotaged so nuclear arms can be smuggled to terrorists, is pretty much phoned in, while the characters on the screen pose and act like they know what they're talking about. If you're really, really bored and love planes it beats sitting in your back yard and watching jet trails, but not by much.

The footage is in a wide variety of conditions, but the transfer appears to be accurate. It delivers a crisp image on the rare occasions where the cinematography is that accommodating, and does its best to deliver accurate colors and a solid image otherwise. The sound appears to be monophonic and is bland, with some disorienting shifts in ambiance. The 1995 program has not been time encoded and runs about 90 minutes. There are two instances where the picture freezes for a moment and the program searches before continuing, but otherwise the presentation is free of obvious glitches.

Tosca (see The Metropolitan Opera: Tosca)

Total Recall (Artisan, 60439)

Arnold Schwarzenegger and Sharon Stone star in the clever 1990 science fiction thriller, which runs 113 minutes, about a construction worker who may or may not be on a secret mission to Mars.

Both the full screen and the letterboxed versions are presented, one to a side. The letterboxing has an aspect ratio of about 1.85:1 and no 16:9 enhancement, adding a little to the sides and trimming a little off the top and bottom. The framing on the letterboxed version is generally more satisfying, but there are production designs that get masked off and are better displayed in the full screen image. The picture is smooth, with rich colors and clear detail. Here and there a shot looks grainy, but for the most part the image looks slick and is so sharp that the minutiae in the special effects can be fully appreciated. The standard stereo surround sound is strong, but the Dolby Digital track is even better. Not only do all the explosions and other action noises take on a greater livelihood, but Jerry Goldsmith's score is given an outstanding dimensionality that draws the viewer into the middle of the excitement. The DVD also has a French language track in standard stereo, and has English, French or Spanish subtitles. There is an interesting and arty theatrical teaser, along with a standard action-oriented theatrical trailer. There is a modest cast and crew profile with incomplete filmographies.

The Towering Inferno (Fox, 4110429)

The more often we watch the 1974 disaster epic, about a burning skyscraper, the more we appreciate Steve McQueen's performance. At first, only the corniest aspects stand out, such as his grin when a group of firemen volunteer for a dangerous assignment, but in multiple viewing, the terse, seemingly emotionless manner with which his character, a fire chief, goes about his business, takes on a subtle excitement, that of a seasoned professional applying his skills to a difficult task. The real test of an actor or actress is not whether they can do *Hamlet*, but whether they can step into a part such as those offered in **The Towering Inferno** and make an audience care for them (or despise them, in the case of Richard Chamberlain's engagingly spineless villain). The scenes with McQueen and Paul Newman are all too brief, but they are as thrilling as any of the explosions, because the two are true movie stars who need only a high concept to get them started. Thank goodness for the letterboxing, which lets the viewer verify that they were both really on the set at the same time.

Irwin Allen produced the film and directed some of the action scenes, with the dramatic sequences guided by the director of record, John Guillermin. The movie's flaws, however, are the flaws one associates with Allen's work, particularly the illogical physics of the building and the fire, and the limited character advancement (the film had a great many stars, but very little emotional development). The grandness of the film's vision is enough to provide an engaging level of mindless entertainment, but the story's arbitrary and sometimes pointless turns prevent it from delivering more.

The picture has fresh, solid colors and a crisp image, even in the problematic fire and smoke sequences. The presentation is letterboxed with an aspect ratio of about 2.35:1 and no 16:9 enhancement. The stereo surround sound is good, and there is a Dolby Digital track with an enhanced dimensionality, though the sound mix on the 1974 feature is not elaborate. The 165 minute program can be supported by English or Spanish subtitles ("Es un incendio.

Todos los incendios son graves"), and is accompanied by a trailer and a cast profile section.

The Toxic Avenger (Troma, 9000)

The 1985 gross-out comedy is presented in full screen format, losing nothing on the sides and unmasking the top and bottom for a less cinematic image in comparison to letterboxed versions. The 82 minute film looks cheap and a bit worn, but hues are reasonably fresh. The image is sharp and colors are bright. The monophonic sound is adequate and there is no captioning. A collection of deleted scenes and scenes that have appeared in alternate cuts of the film are included. There is also a nice collection of production stills and a large collection of promotional trailers, supplements and gags. The director and part-owner of Troma, Lloyd Kaufman, provides a commentary track, an enjoyable mix of irreverent comments, off-color remarks and legitimate reports on how the film was shot and what happened during the shooting. Kaufman is totally pragmatic when it comes to the quality of the films, and readily conveys the fun he had making it, in an informative manner. The DVD also comes with a numbered slip of paper signed by Kaufman.

Trail Beyond (see The John Wayne Collection)

The Train (MGM, 907539)

A group of wily French railroad employees stop the Germans from looting a cache of Impressionist paintings during the waning days of the Occupation. Burt Lancaster stars, with Paul Scofield as the bad guy, in the 1964 John Frankenheimer film that was, as Frankenheimer points out on an alternate audio commentary, probably the last action film ever shot in black-and-white. The picture looks gorgeous. Frankenheimer used black-and-white so he could take advantage of the depth of field focus, especially during the many elaborate train sequences, and the image is so sharp and so free of impediments you can see every detail on every boxcar from one end of the train to the other. The image is glossy and often thrilling. The presentation is letterboxed with an aspect ratio of about 1.66:1 and no 16:9 enhancement. The monophonic sound is a bit subdued, eliminating audio noise without harming the ambience. The 133 minute feature can be supported by English or French subtitles, and there is a trailer.

There are often steady gaps between Frankenheimer's comments, though when he does speak he is so informative the only reason the gaps are frustrating is that you wish he was saying twice as much. His talk isn't all that organized, but as he goes along he seems to manage to cover most aspects of the production, including the logistics involved, his strategy for approaching certain scenes, and last minute adjustments—Lancaster's character gets shot in the leg by a German, for example, because Lancaster injured himself on his day off.

The film is terrific. Based upon a real event but enhanced for the sake of entertainment, the movie was shot in France and much of Frankenheimer's supporting crew was French. Most of the train engines were real and there are at least a half dozen crashes and derailments during the course of the film, many happening inches away from the camera. As Frankenheimer instinctively understood, there is something about steam engines and black-and-white filmmaking that goes together gloriously well, and the DVD takes full advantage of it.

Trainspotting (Buena Vista, 13851)

We don't care what anybody says, the 1997 film definitely glamorizes drug use, for it makes shooting up heroin a seductive experience, despite all the awful side effects, social ostracism and other nasty things that happen to the characters. The film is reminiscent of *A Clockwork Orange* (deliberately, according to the director, Danny Boyle) and follows the adventures of one young man and his mates as he bounces between addiction and detox, and between making something of himself and flushing everything quite literally down the toilet. It is an artistic inspiration to approach the subject with an optimistic sense of humor, and there is a scene where a baby dies that will really separate the hardcore believers in black comedy from the posers. The film doesn't necessarily cross over a line of bad taste, but it does seem to define the border and it is just a little too indulgent to be the breakthrough work of art everybody initially thought it was. If you have an open mind it is a fun movie, but if you are at all squeamish, it can be a turn-off.

The picture is letterboxed with an aspect ratio of about 1.85:1 and no 16:9 enhancement. Fleshtones are a little pinkish, but other colors are bright and crisp. The stereo surround soundtrack and Dolby Digital soundtrack are okay. The Dolby Digital track is preferable, with better separation effects and clearer details. The 94 minute film can be accompanied by English subtitles, which can help a viewer substantially in translating the dense Scottish accents of the performers.

Trapped X-rated (Vivid, UPC#0073215548)

The narrative is nonsensical, something about a married couple coming home and finding strangers in their house having fun; then they hire a new maid. The erotic sequences are rarely creative and the picture is soft, with noticeable artifacting flaws. Colors are reasonably fresh. The sound is bland. Kobi Tai, Tasha, Julia Rage and Gina Rome are featured in the 70 minute productions. The DVD contains alternate angle sequences and elaborate hardcore interactive promotional features.

Trapper County War (Simitar, 7291)

A couple of kids from New Jersey, on their way to California, run into trouble when they pass through the proverbial hick town. Robert Estes stars, with Bo Hopkins as the good sheriff and Don Swayze as the evil deputy, whose scuzzy parents 'own' the town. The film's set piece comes at the conclusion, where the hero teams up with a Vietnam vet, played by Ernie Hudson, and uses the vet's large collection of war memorabilia to hold off the town until Hopkins can arrive. On the whole, however, the 1989 movie is rather predictable and not too interesting until Hudson shows up.

Dark sequences are a little murky, but the picture is acceptable, with reasonably accurate colors and workable fleshtones. The monophonic sound is bland but passable. The 97 minute program is accompanied by a filmography for Estes.

Trash (Image, ID4732PYDVD)

Although some performers reappear as different characters, **Trash** is essentially a direct sequel to **Flesh**, with Joe Dallesandro's character a couple years older, a couple years more strung out and a couple years more broke. The 1970 film may be Paul Morrissey's best effort, for it retains the feel of a documentary—Dallesandro shoots up on camera—giving the movie a political resonance, while adding humor. Morrissey lets the characters come alive and speak with enthusiasm about sexual practices, collecting usable garbage, cheating on welfare and other subjects that rarely come up in civil conversations. It is the enthusiasm that drives the humor, and its look at the underside of the Sixties is perhaps even funnier now than it was then.

The 110 minutes film is presented in full screen format. The source material on has incidental damage and other evidence of wear, but colors are surprisingly rich and there is no more grain or fuzzy blurring than what the original cinematography brought to the source. The monophonic sound is passable. There is no captioning.

Travel the World By Train I: Europe 1 (Pioneer, PSI99201D)
Travel the World By Train IV: North America (Pioneer, PSI99206D)
Travel the World By Train VII: Central America (Pioneer, PSI99207D)

Each program tries to cover so much ground in an hour that there is almost no chance to savor the rides. The programs depict rides and various rail lines in various continents. A narrator talks about the train only in superficial terms and makes equally generalized statements about the train's major stops. There are shots inside and outside and from a helicopter and stuff, but just as you start getting settled on one, the show jumps to the next one. When the program reaches a remote enough spot, then it becomes a bit more interesting, but even then the pleasures do not last long.

On all the programs, the video quality looks terrific (it is a Japanese series), with bright, solid hues. We spotted one instance of artifact ratcheting, during a circular helicopter pass, but otherwise the presentation is immaculate. There is a stereophonic music score and the steady drone of the train on the rails, but there is nothing special about the audio mix. The programs are in English on one track and Japanese on another. There is no captioning.

Europe 1 begins in London and travels to Italy, Austria and on to the Swiss Alps. It is only when it reaches the smaller Alpine excursions that it ceases to be a generic travel program and becomes a little more intriguing, as the engine chugs its way up to Europe's highest train station.

The only interesting part of **North America** is the beginning, which takes a look at some small Alaskan rail lines, including one that is served by a single engine/car. The rest is overly familiar, and while they do dredge up trivia about each city they visit, they don't linger.

By the standards established in these critiques, **Central America** is a more intriguing program, because the train lines are smaller and more obscure. The program visits routes in Mexico, Guatemala, Costa Rica, Jamaica and Cuba, traveling up steep hillsides and crossing rickety bridges that have no railings and very old-looking wood. Good thing we're just watching it on the TV. Throughout the series, attention is paid to the food served in the cars, and this leads to a rather amusing punchline in Cuba, where they offer just one menu item—an orange drink and a ham sandwich—and you're only allowed one per person. Oh, and for entertainment in the rail stations while you're waiting for the train, they play Fidel Castro speeches on the video monitors. Makes us glad we live in a democracy.

Tread / ReTread (Simitar, 7357)

A compilation of two good mountain bike videos, the filmmakers travel across the planet to show bikers tackling everything from the Himalayas to the streets of New York City. The many varied terrains are fascinating, and the programs also present profiles of bikers, races, crashes, controlled flips and other aspects of the recreation. The one thing they don't show much of, however, is how they shot the films, which make filming mountain climbing or surfing look like a breeze. Apparently, it can only be done with a stationary camera, taking in very brief clips of the bikes passing by, except when long helicopter or telescopic lens shots can be employed. The terrain is usually too rough to carry the camera on some other moving vehicle and the ride is too bouncy for a steadicam to follow. The picture quality varies according to the source, but the transfer looks fine. The stereo musical score is fairly energetic. The combined running times of the two shows is 162 minutes.

Treasures of The Twilight Zone (Panasonic, PDV0006)
More Treasures of The Twilight Zone (Panasonic, PDV0014)

Two of the three episode on the initial **Treasures** collection have a similar theme, though we won't say which two, in order not to spoil things. The show's pilot episode, *Where Is Everybody?*, from 1959, stars Earl Holliman as an amnesiac who wanders into an apparently deserted town, although cigars are still burning in the ashtrays and pots of coffee are percolating on the stoves. George Takei shows up in what is identified as a 'lost' episode from 1964, *The Encounter*, a very weird piece about a WWII vet and a young Japanese gardener who are locked in an attic and start replaying the war. The ending is unintentionally funny and the drama does not shy away from ethnic confrontation. While the premise may be a bit lame compared to the standard **Twilight Zone** effort, the episode is consistently fascinating. The third episode was a budget-saving pick-up, also from 1964, the highly admired French short film based upon a famous American short story, *An Occurrence at Owl Creek Bridge*, about a soldier who escapes a hanging.

On **More Treasures**, *The Eye of the Beholder* from 1960, is classic episode about a woman who undergoes plastic surgery to unusual results, and *The Howling Man* from 1960, starring John Carradine, is about monks who keep a very special prisoner and a passerby who feels compelled to release him. The third episode, *The Masks*, from 1964, was directed by Ida Lupino and is about a wealthy dying man who has one last surprise for his sniveling heirs.

The episodes, which are all in black-and-white, look terrific. There are no noticeable scratches or speckles, and contrasts are smooth and finely detailed. The picture has pure blacks, sharp lines and pronounced textures. The monophonic sound is very good for an old TV show. The menu selections on the DVDs are good fun—there is giant eyeball that looks at the choice you make. You can watch the episodes individually or choose to play all three straight through.

The two DVDs have the same supplementary material: An excellent half hour interview with Mike Wallace and Rod Serling that was conducted just before the series got under way (along with the many insights Serling provides about writing for television in its formative years, the interview itself is fascinating as being representative of promotional journalism in the late Fifties, and it is far less slick than such interviews are today, even on the local news); a wonderful 7 minute 'pitch' Serling shot to convince potential sponsors that the show would be worth supporting; and background essays on the show and on Serling. Additionally, there are essays and filmographies for each featured episode. The DVDs are not captioned.

Trees Lounge (Pioneer, DVD60291W)

The kind of movie you'd expect Steve Buscemi to make, his directoral debut is sort of an anti-*Cheers*, about the listless lives of several individuals who spend most of their time hanging out in a Long Island bar. Buscemi also stars, and he has collected an amiable cast to back him up, including Anthony Lapaglia, Elizabeth Bracco, Carol Kane, Daniel Baldwin and others. As for the specific narrative, Buscemi's character develops a relationship with a seventeen-year old girl, winningly played by Chloë Sevigny, which enrages her father. There are other plot strands, as well. The film is laid back and the characters are all a little miserable, but some viewers will enjoy their company. The movie is well made, it just has low aspirations.

The picture is letterboxed with an aspect ratio of about 1.85:1 and no 16:9 enhancement. The image is a little hazy, particularly in the smoke-filled bar, and fleshtones are pale, but the colors look solid. The stereo surround sound is not forceful, but the mix is reasonably atmospheric and worth amplifying. The 94 minute feature is not captioned.

There is a music video that showcases the film's fairly catchy title tune, and a trailer. On one of the analog channels, Buscemi provides a running commentary. It is not a very intense or elaborate talk, but he does explain what he was trying to achieve and discusses the challenges he encountered during the filming. He admits to having used drugs in the past, talks about how he met each of his co-stars, and essentially provides a pleasant, rambling monologue that seems appropriate for the film.

Tremors (Universal, 20218)

Kevin Bacon and Fred Ward star with Michael Gross, Finn Carter and Reba McEntire in the thrilling tale of a group of people who are trapped in a dinky desert town by huge, carnivorous worms. The film never takes itself too seriously, but never breaks its spell, either. It is nearly a perfect blend of humor, thrills and pleasing special effects. The film is letterboxed with an aspect ratio of about

1.85:1 and no 16:9 enhancement. In comparison to the full screen film clips presented in the supplement, the top and bottom of the letterboxed image have been masked off, and only a sliver has been added to the sides. The image may seem a bit tight here and there, but generally the framing looks well balanced. The color transfer is super, with consistently accurate hues and a sharp focus. The same is true of the stereo surround sound. It has a fairly basic mix, but adds to the fun at the right moments. The 95 minute film is also available in French and Spanish and comes with English or Spanish subtitles.

There is a 50 minute 'making of' feature. Unlike most 'making of' programs, this one seems less likely to serve a dual purpose in a broadcast medium, since the final quarter of it is free of dialogue, showing silent footage of the monsters being constructed and tested while a suite from the musical score plays on the soundtrack. Most of the film's big effect sequences are explained in clear detail, as is the film's somewhat unusual casting and the story of the script's genesis. The film's original ending, which was replaced by an ending that was urged on the filmmakers by a rowdy preview audience, is shown, and it is clearly better—the filmmakers should have trusted their initial instincts. In addition to the documentary, there are a few outtakes, a couple of theatrical trailers and several more involved 'featurette' trailers, including three that profile Bacon, Gross and McEntire respectively. Many make use of the Jerry Lee Lewis, song, *Whole Lotta Shakin'*, though the song doesn't appear in the movie itself. A modest group of still photos and a trailer for the sequel are also included.

Tremors 2: Aftershocks (Universal, 20296)

It would be a mistake to watch **Tremors 2** immediately after viewing the first film. **2** is an enjoyable monster movie that can hold its own against the typical Full Moon production, but it has nowhere near the quality or originality of the earlier feature. Fred Ward and Michael Gross re-create their roles, hunting for more worms in Mexico. The movie's budget is clearly smaller, and while the filmmakers are clever, the limitations of their resources put a damper on the film's thrills. Then, in the second half, the script modifies the monsters, changing them into small, walking creatures to take advantage of computerized digital effects. The narrative shift is at complete odds with the logic of the first film, and of the first half of the second film, but it enables the movie to generate some excitement and bring some variety to the concept.

The image is letterboxed with an aspect ratio of about 1.85:1 and no 16:9 enhancement. The picture is bright and vivid, with accurate hues. The stereo surround sound is a little light, but adequate. The 100 minute program can also be presented in French and Spanish and can be supported by English or Spanish subtitles. The made-for-home-video feature is accompanied by a 'theatrical' trailer, a production essay and a cast & crew profile.

Trespass (GoodTimes, 0581006)

Two white guys fight off a bunch of black guys in an abandoned factory. Whether it is because nobody in the movie has appealing morals or because the action scenes are too frantic and undefined, Walter Hill's 1992 film is not as satisfying as his best movies. Some viewers won't care and will be quite happy with the film's gritty conflicts, but except for Ice T, who gives one of his typically lyrical screen performances, it is difficult to sustain an interest in the characters or their goals.

The picture is in letterboxed format only, with an aspect ratio of about 1.8:1 and an accommodation for enhanced 16:9 playback, though we tend to prefer the framing on full screen presentations of the film. The image is a little grainy in darker sequences, but fleshtones are rich. The stereo surround sound lacks the high powered delivery one would normally expect from the subject matter. The 104 minute program also has optional French or Spanish subtitles, English captioning, and some production notes.

T-Rex (see **The Best of MusikLaden T-Rex/Roxy Music**)

The Trial (Image, ID4265FLDVD)

Kyle MacLachlan stars in a worthwhile adaptation of Franz Kafka's abstract bureaucratic nightmare. The film is calm and dreamlike, building on a precisely honed Harold Pinter script to create a constantly ambiguous but always fascinating drama. Jason Robards and Anthony Hopkins are featured in supporting roles. Shot in Prague, the film deftly turns the ordinary into the surreal, staging the hero's interactions with his tormentors in tenements and abandoned lots.

Colors are somewhat pale and the image is a little unstable in places. Details, however, are clear and crisp. The stereo surround sound is identical to the LD—there is a fairly good Carl Davis score—but contrary to a notation on the jacket cover there is no Dolby Digital 5.1 encoding. The 1992 BBC production runs 120 minutes.

A Tribute to Stevie Ray Vaughan (Sony, EVD50144)

Of all the top, world class guitarists performing in the memorial concert, B.B. King's performance is the best, eliciting an incredible dimension of sounds and emotions from his instrument. Several artists, including Bonnie Raitt, Eric Clapton, Dr. John and Vaughan's backup band, Double Trouble, perform numbers that evoke Vaughan's electric blues genre, and followed by an all-star jam session. Each number is preceded by an interview sequence where the performer talks about Vaughan's influence.

The picture is brightly lit and crisp, with accurate hues. The stereo sound is okay, and the Dolby Digital track is highly energized and carefully detailed. The program can be supported by English subtitles and comes with a Vaughan discography.

The Trigger Effect (Universal, 20061)

David Koepp's 1996 abstract disaster film is about the near-total breakdown in civilization when the power goes out over a widespread area. The film is unusual and will spur the imaginations of some viewers, but others will find it contrived and tiresome. Kyle MacLachlan and Elisabeth Shue star as a young married couple who watch their neighborhood collapse into anarchy. Although the movie is cinematic, the dialogue has a staccato staginess that is meant to imitate real conversation but, in film, ends up sounding artificial. The drama is in much the same condition. It is obvious what the filmmakers are up to, exploring how close we urbane humans are to being animals and how much infrastructure we take for granted, but they are unable to go beyond the central theme of their thesis. At first, the situation is interesting, but it remains predictable and really isn't all that different from a nuclear disaster drama or something. Curiously, the film's climax is defeated by its medium. It won't spoil things to tell you that in the end the hero makes a conscious decision not to shoot another man in order to take his car. For the hero, it's a big choice, but for a movie viewer inundated with scores of people shooting one another all the time on film, it's a 'who cares' moment.

The presentation is in letterboxed format only, with an aspect ratio of about 1.85:1 and an accommodation for enhanced 16:9 playback. The color transfer is outstanding, with crisp, accurate hues, even in the darkest scenes. The stereo surround sound is good, and the Dolby Digital track has sharper, more energetic separation effects. The 95 minute program also has a French audio track, optional English subtitles, production notes, a cast-and-director profile section and a trailer.

A Trip to the Moon (see **Landmarks of Early Film**)

Tron (Buena Vista, 14256)

Anyone who has ever worked in data processing will appreciate the 1982 Disney film, which combines live action and computer animation to depict an anthropomorphic journey through the logic circuits of a computer. Since the basic suspense adventure plot is successful, the film is both entertaining and thought provoking.

Jeff Bridges stars as a computer hacker who is transformed into an electronic being and journeys through a computer—an early virus.

The picture quality is outstanding. The colors are exceptionally crisp and superbly detailed. The animation is super, but even the live action sequences are enlivened by the accuracy of the hues. The presentation is letterboxed with an aspect ratio of about 2.2:1 and no 16:9 enhancement. Rear channel effects on the Dolby Digital track are better defined than on the standard track, though in general the audio quality on the two channels is similar. The audio mix may be a bit primitive, but it works quite well within the context of the film and is effectively delivered on the DVD. The 96 minute film can also be presented in French or Spanish and is accompanied by an enjoyable original theatrical trailer, which includes footage not used in the film.

The film's visual metaphors are beautifully executed—shots of the 'real world' are made to look like silicon chip patterns, and the world inside the computer, depicted with computer animation, is visualized using the descriptive metaphors that programmers and technicians often employ when speaking about hardware or software components. The easiest way to describe the interaction of computer programs is to use the terms of human interaction. The filmmakers take this a step further and depict the programs as humans, adding metaphysics by having the programs speak of their users as 'gods.' (In the real world, however, a much lower opinion of users is the norm.)

Tropical Rainforest (Lumivision, DVD0197); (SlingShot, 9811)

One of the first three commercially released DVDs, the 40 minute IMAX program looks at the ecology of a rainforest, how scientists study rainforests, and how rainforests are being destroyed. You can see the digital smears when the airborne cameras go zipping across the treetops, but the colors are accurate and blacks are solid. The picture is also sharp, and the video artifacts never accumulate enough to create a problem. The stereo sound is bright and contains many satisfying separation effects

What shocked us the most about SlingShot's reissue was how much more elaborate the surround separations are on the Dolby Digital track in comparison to the original release. Sounds that seem to circle in front of you on the old DVD go all around you on the new one, and other tones have a greater detail and dynamic range. The digital artifacting flaws that dogged the original release has been cleaned up. Artifacting aside, the picture looks identical to the older release, if not a touch softer. The images vary in quality. The best passages are vivid and gripping, while other segments have less distinctive colors. The program is also available in Dolby Digital in French, Spanish, German, Dutch, Japanese, Korean and Mandarin, and can be supported by English subtitles. Although the logo on the jacket suggests that the DVD contains PC-ROM functions, it offers nothing more than a promotional Web link.

Troublemakers (Image, ID5628FMDVD)

Terence Hill and Bud Spencer team up for the 1994 comedy western. The 103 minute film is horribly cropped. Colors are a little light, with dull fleshtones and some grain. The stereo sound is dubbed in English, with no captioning, and has a mild dimensionality. The music is by Pino Donaggio.

The film, which was directed by Hill, is like most Hill & Spencer features, a combination of extremely low humor and fancy gunplay where few characters ever really get hurt. Hill and Spencer portray estranged brothers who team up as bounty hunters. Ruth Buzzi plays their mother, if that tells you something. The narrative tends to run in circles and the whole thing is fairly silly, but for fans of the Hill & Spencer films, it delivers all that is expected and is reasonably enjoyable. Dumb, but enjoyable.

Trucks (Trimark, VM6876D)

The film is apparently a remake of *Maximum Overdrive*. Now, *Maximum Overdrive* is hardly the film that stands atop our 'wish they would remake' list, and **Trucks** has a number of loose ends that, like the picture quality, appear to have been dictated by the budget, but overall the film is less silly than *Overdrive* and more consistently engaging. The movie, which is officially based upon the Stephen King short story, has no significant stars and is about a group of people in a remote diner surrounded by menacing trucks that have acquired some kind of intelligence. The trucks don't let the people leave, but they need some of them for gas, so they don't kill them all, either. The character types are basic but adequate and the action is moderately creative.

Colors are bland and fleshtones are dull, though the image is reasonably sharp. The picture is letterboxed with an aspect ratio of about 1.85:1 and no 16:9 enhancement. The stereo surround sound is pretty good, conveying a fairly bright ambiance and active dimensionality. The 99 minute film is accompanied by a trailer and has optional Spanish subtitles.

True Lies (Fox, 4111054)

Opening just like a James Bond film, the first sequence builds up to a spectacular opening stunt, except that there is no spectacular opening stunt. Instead, the movie just cuts to the next scene. James Cameron's 1994 film does have spectacular stunts later on, but the movie, an awkward marital farce bookended by an exciting but depthless terrorist chase, can leave one dissatisfied.

The picture is in letterboxed format only, with an aspect ratio of about 2.35:1 and no 16:9 enhancement. The image quality is outstanding, crisp and detailed in even the darkest sequences, with precise colors and accurate fleshtones. The stereo surround sound is a little reserved, but the Dolby Digital track is very energetic, with precise separation effects and lots of energy. The 141 minute program also has a French language track in standard stereo, optional English and Spanish subtitles and a trailer.

Arnold Schwarzenegger stars as an intelligence operative whose wife, played by Jamie Lee Curtis, is unaware of his real profession. Tom Arnold received a lot of positive press for his co-starring role as Schwarzenegger's partner, but there are dozens of character actors in Hollywood who could have done a better job with the part. The film's elaborate finale is rousing, but the DVD will generally be more useful as material to show off one's home video system than as entertainment.

True North (Simitar, 7329)

Images of Alaska are set to the electronic music of Paul Speer, Jonn Serrie, James Reynolds and Tangerine Dream on the 45 minute program. The picture looks sharp throughout and the color is fine although the blues seem a bit strong. Footage holds to a specific theme for each of the program's nine numbers and ranges from views of the northern lights and of icebergs, to eagles catching fish and a seacoast being massaged by waves. The music is a bit aggressive but well integrated with the rhythm of the images. The stereo sound is fine.

True Romance (Warner, 13158)

In retrospect, Quentin Tarantino's script looms as a larger influence on the 1993 film than Tony Scott's direction. The film is filled with Tarantino-isms, and Scott's patented commercial-slick direction only seems to get in their way. Christian Slater and Patricia Arquette star (the pair fall in love and steal a suitcase full of dope from the mob), with all sorts of soon-to-be-famous people popping up in supporting roles, including Brad Pitt, Gary Oldman, Samuel L. Jackson and Val Kilmer.

The film runs 121 minutes and includes some footage that did not appear in the movie's theatrical release. It is in letterboxed format on one side, with an aspect ratio of about 2.35:1 and no 16:9 enhancement, and in cropped format on the other. The cropping is manageable, but the letterboxed image is much better designed. The picture is crisp, with strong colors. Even though separation effects are very limited, the audio design is engaging and the sound is enjoyable. There is a decent cast and crew profile section, some mi-

nor production notes, a nice theatrical trailer and English, French or Spanish subtitles.

True Stories (Warner, 11654)

John Goodman is featured prominently in David Byrne's quirky look at life in a small Texas town, which gets off to a great start but sort of runs out of steam about halfway through. The 1986 film is kind of a musical—Byrne was the leader of The Talking Heads—and the song interludes sustain its momentum, but there is no narrative really (some characters, such as Goodman's, are seen following through on plans, but that is about the only forward movement the plot has), just ironic observations on the economics and culture of the town and the idiosyncrasies of its inhabitants. Byrne, who directed, also appears in the film, as a sort of host and tour guide. All the really original ideas seem to be jammed into the first part of the movie, so that the second half becomes more repetitious and less insightful, but it is a different kind of entertainment, and its uniqueness is one of its primary strengths.

The picture has been slightly cropped, as is evidenced by the letterboxing in the end credit sequence. Since much of the movie feels like a music video, the cropping really doesn't upset things. The color transfer looks great. Hues are deep and bright, and fleshtones look fine. The image is sharp, and damage to the source material is minimal. The stereo surround sound has an occasional dimensionality, but separation effects are limited. The 89 minute program is closed captioned with substantial paraphrasing.

The Truman Show (Paramount, 331127)

The beauty of **The Truman Show** is that if they gave you any more of the story or the details than they do (about a man's entire life is being surreptitiously broadcast as a TV show), it probably wouldn't work. We were dying to know the backstory of the actress playing Truman's wife, and probably everybody wants to see what happens after the closing credits start rolling, but the film is perfectly executed, tantalizing you with this wild, crazy idea, using it to explore some intriguing emotional and epistemological concepts, and then ducking out before it has to pay for its audacity. It is in this context that Jim Carrey is perfect for the lead, because anybody less inherently entertaining would give you more time to pick the premise apart instead of just rolling with it.

The picture is crisp, blacks are pure, hues are vivid, fleshtones are accurate and details are precise. The image is letterboxed with an aspect ratio of about 1.66:1 and no 16:9 enhancement. The stereo surround sound is okay, and the Dolby Digital soundtrack is even better, with a strong dimensionality and crisper details. The film has a number of inspired separation effects and is worth amplifying. The 103 minute program is also available in French in standard stereo and is supported by English closed captioning. There is a teaser and a standard trailer, and it is rather interesting that they both spell out the film's premise, but with very different structures.

Truth or Consequences N.M. (Columbia TriStar, 82699

Kiefer Sutherland's directorial debut reeks of Quentin Tarantino worship and the drama is sophomoric, but the show is watchable. Sutherland also stars, with Vincent Gallo and Mykelti Williamson. A gang kills a drug dealer and steals a suitcase of drugs, only to find that both the cops and the mob are on their trail. They travel across the Southwest, jumping from one stolen vehicle to the next and picking up a couple hostages along the way. They also talk about esoteric things such as Yogi Bear, but it all manages to sound like a cliché anyway. There are a few energetic gunfights and other action movie requirements, and the film can be entertaining provided one is not expecting something even remotely profound.

The picture is presented on one side in letterboxed format, with an aspect ratio of about 1.85:1 and an accommodation for enhanced 16:9 processing, and in full screen format on the other side. The cinematography lacks intensity and some shots seem a bit washed out, but for the most part the picture is passable. There is a fairly hip selection of pop tunes in the musical score that sound good on the stereo surround sound and Dolby Digital soundtracks. The Dolby Digital track is a little better detailed than the standard track, but both are workable. The 107 minute film is also available in Spanish and French in standard stereo and can be supported by English, French or Spanish subtitles. There are trailers for the movie and for two other films starring Sutherland.

Truth or Dare (see Madonna: Truth or Dare)

The Tune (Image, ID3358PCDVD)

Best known for his animated shorts that depict sketched faces going through elaborate changes or distortions, Bill Plympton's work has appeared in several DVD anthologies. The 69 minute animated feature—which is really sort of a collection of shorts bridged together—is about a young songwriter suffering from anxiety over a deadline. The narrative takes the hero through what in essence are dream sequences where he witnesses the wild image shifting and displacement common to Plympton's work. At its best, Plympton's animation spurs the imagination with its breathless mutations. At its worst, it gets kind of grotesque at times. Because of the show's subject however, each sequence is accompanied by a musical number and, secondary to the animation, the program presents sort of a study of popular song styles. The picture looks fine, with bright, sharp colors, and the stereo sound is a little hissy but passable. There is no captioning.

Turandot (BMG, 74321609172)

Giacomo Puccini's opera was based upon a Chinese folk tale, so it is not a total clash of cultures that the sweepingly lyrical masterpiece should be staged by the Chinese in Beijing's Forbidden City complex. Zubin Mehta conducts an opera company from Florence, while Zhang Yimou directs the spectacular production with Peking Opera manners and costumes. Giovanna Casolla, Barbara Frittoli and Sergei Larin star. Both Frittoli and Casolla are super, with sustained vocal manipulations. Larin is competent but not as daring (he drops off in *Nessun Dorma* before the orchestra kicks in). More so than most productions, however, the singing is just one component of the entertainment—the dancing, the costumes and the sheer scale of the production are all captivating.

Despite the huge outdoor setting, the voices are effectively miked and the orchestra is immediate. The stereo surround sound is super, with pure, forceful tones and an encompassing dimensionality. The picture is fantastic. Shot on videotape, the image is sharp and exquisitely colored, with the stunningly hued silk costumes replicated to the minutest detail. The image is letterboxed with an aspect ratio of about 1.8:1 and an accommodation for enhanced 16:9 playback.

The DVD has a number of ambitious features and a few ancillary drawbacks. The program itself is not time encoded, so there is no way to determine what chapter you are watching. Navigating the menu requires both the Menu button and the Title button, the latter usually ignored by most DVD producers. There is no jacket chapter listing for the program itself, though there is a menu chapter guide.

The opera is in Italian and can be supported by optional English, French, German, Italian, Japanese and Chinese subtitles. A number of program segments have alternate angles, so you can chose between a close-up of the costumes and central characters, a long shot of the whole, grand stage, or toggle between the two, without losing the subtitles.

In addition to the program described above, which is in 2-channel Dolby stereo, the entire opera can be replayed to a collection of production and publicity photos in PCM stereo (it could be our imagination, but it seems like the PCM track comes from an alternate recording). The PCM track has more energy but less delicate coloring than the Dolby track. This playback is time encoded, run-

ning 110 minutes, and is accompanied by a jacket chapter guide, but no menu chapter guide.

There is also a 7 minute synopsis of the film, spoken in narration to another collection of stills, and a 28 minute 'making of' featurette (which can be supported by French, Italian, Japanese and Chinese subtitles) that shows how effectively Mehta and Yimou achieved a blending of cultures in a grand, once-in-a-lifetime venue.

Turbulence (Sony, LVD49922)

A 25 minute abstract video images program, there are brief visions of flower-like and spider-like forms interacting, but most of the program consists of mutating geometric shapes and textures, the sort of thing they'll be doing in Fifth Grade computer art in a couple of years. Nevertheless, the pictures are pretty and the colors are mesmerizing. The stereo surround sound, an electronic musical score, takes good advantage of the surround capabilities to bubble all over the place. The picture is sharp looking and colors are stable.

Turner, Tina (see Ike & Tina Turner)

12 Monkeys (Universal, 20186); DTS (Universal, 20462)

Bruce Willis stars as a mental patient who believes he has been sent from the future to track down the source of a civilization-destroying virus. It should be noted that the Terry Gilliam film made gobs of money at the box office and that this implies most viewers found the ending to be satisfying. Brad Pitt received a let's-encourage-these-kinds-of-career-choices Oscar nomination for his role as a fellow inmate in the institution where Willis' character is incarcerated during the first quarter or so of the film. Madeleine Stowe is their doctor. The movie is imbued with Gilliam's unique sense of design, as well as his fascination with the clutter of urban decay. From the title on down, the film is also filled with red herrings, but in a world of literal-minded action thrillers **12 Monkeys** is actually a breath of fresh air, a popular film that is intelligent enough to keep the viewer emotionally off-balance and guessing which way the story will turn.

The letterboxing, which has an aspect ratio of about 1.85:1 and an accommodation for enhanced 16:9 playback, is tight on the top and bottom. The colors are richer and better defined than on all previous home video releases. The image is also a little darker, but details in the shadows are still clear. The film has a deliberately cluttered look and color accuracy really isn't an important factor in its entertainment so long as it remains within certain parameters, but the presentation is quite satisfying. The stereo surround sound is a little weak, but the Dolby Digital track provides a crisp, energetic delivery of the film's sound mix. The 130 minute movie is also available in French in Dolby Digital and comes with English, French and Spanish subtitles. There is a brief production essay, a small cast profile section, and a good collection of still frame material, including production drawings, behind-the-scenes photos, marketing concepts and storyboards. The still frame section features production photos, a few conceptual drawings and promotional materials.

There is also a commentary by Gilliam and a documentary. The documentary was originally commissioned by Gilliam, in part, to use as 'evidence' if he ran into the same problems with Universal that he ran into when he made **Brazil**. The documentary was therefore able to capture a few arguments, show why one of the performers, a child who had great eyes but couldn't act, was fired, and include other types of situations one normally doesn't see in publicity-minded 'making of' features. The program lacks the sense of analysis that Universal's retrospective documentaries have, however, and while the story of how **12 Monkeys** was conceived is told reasonably well, there are still many details, which would be of interest to fans, that did not make it into the show. Very little is said about the computer graphic effects used to create the runaway zoo animals, for example, and while there are worthwhile glimpses of the cast members working on their parts, there are no direct interviews with them. A lot of footage is spent on the film's disastrous first preview and a devastating focus group inquiry conducted at its conclusion. The filmmakers then fret about these results but do very little and the next thing you know, the film is a miraculous hit. After the documentary is over, a theatrical trailer is included that proves the final marketing plan had a handle on how to sell the film properly.

The most valuable and worthwhile component of the DVD, however, is a running commentary by Gilliam and producer Charles Roven. In fact, it is best to use the documentary as sort of an introduction to the commentary, so you can picture what Gilliam and Roven are talking about. In addition to discussing how specific scenes were conceived and staged (and how Gilliam was feeling—he seems to have a great recollection for his emotional state at every point during the shoot), they contemplate details on the production that the documentary misses, provide an analysis of the completed work, and share instructive insights to the filmmaking process in general. Gilliam is able to step back and say why things worked or where he came up short. He is helped along, as apparently he was during the film's production, by Roven, who keeps him focused and gives him someone he can bounce his ideas off.

The DTS release has no special features and is not even captioned, though the picture transfer and letterboxing is identical to the standard release. The DTS track is a bit more energetic than the Dolby Digital track on the standard release, but most of the time we couldn't tell the difference between the two, while the DTS LD not only has even more energy, but stronger definitions and clearer separation effects. The frame transfer rate on the standard release stays consistently in the midrange, while the transfer rate on the DTS release stays consistently in the mid-upper range.

20,000 Leagues under the Sea (Image, ID4666DSDVD)

Featuring some of the world's first underwater cinematography, including images of divers cavorting about on the ocean floor, the 1916 silent film version combines Jules Verne's *20,000 Leagues* with *Mysterious Island*, and it advances in a choppy fashion that is unlike the most accomplished movie storytelling of its era. Also, underwater images being so new, the movie stops dead at times just to gawk at what for today's viewers will be mundane images of the deep. Nevertheless, fans will revel in the film's spectacle and even casual viewers may find the production to be an intriguing curiosity.

Despite some mild damage here and there the picture is in fairly good condition for its age. The image is tinted, but the effect is never distracting. There is an overblown stereophonic music score, by Alexander Rannie and Brian Benison, which a viewer may choose to play up or tone down depending upon how much that viewer gets into the spirit of the show. The 101 minute film even has an Intermission.

Twilight (Paramount, 3344957)

It takes a half hour or so to stop looking at the stars in Robert Benton's 1998 feature as stars and to accept them as characters. Paul Newman is top-billed as a retired detective who becomes involved in a series of murders when he tries to make a blackmail payment for a friend. Gene Hackman, Susan Sarandon, James Garner (who gives the second best performance in the film, after Margo Martindale) and Stockard Channing are among the co-stars, and it doesn't help that some of them are playing movie stars in the story, because that just reinforces their own stellar presences. Once the plot really gets underway the film becomes entertaining for something other than the pleasure of its cast, but the mystery is fairly straightforward—even the twists are straightforward—and the film's primary appeal will rest on how much satisfaction the viewer receives from seeing such famous screen personalities interacting and showing off their advanced maturity.

The presentation is in letterboxed format with an aspect ratio of about 1.85:1 and no 16:9 enhancement. The picture is incredibly sharp and precise, with perfect hues and consistently accurate fleshtones. The stereo surround sound and menu-activated Dolby Digital sound are great, though the mix is fairly laid back. The 96 minute film is also available in French in standard stereo and can be supported by English or Spanish subtitles. There is a theatrical trailer, too.

The Twilight Zone (see Treasures of The Twilight Zone)

The Twilight Zone Vol. 1 (Panasonic, PDV0007)
The Twilight Zone Vol. 2 (Panasonic, PDV0008)
The Twilight Zone Vol. 3 (Panasonic, PDV0009)
The Twilight Zone Vol. 4 (Panasonic, PDV0010)
The Twilight Zone Vol. 5 (Panasonic, PDV0011)
The Twilight Zone Vol. 6 (Panasonic, PDV0012)
The Twilight Zone Vol. 7 (Panasonic, PDV0016)
The Twilight Zone Vol. 8 (Panasonic, PDV0017)
The Twilight Zone Vol. 9 (Panasonic, PDV0018)
The Twilight Zone Vol. 10 (Panasonic, PDV0019)
The Twilight Zone Vol. 11 (Panasonic, PDV0020)
The Twilight Zone Vol. 12 (Panasonic, PDV0021)
The Twilight Zone Vol. 13 (Panasonic, PDV0022)

The episodes look terrific. The black-and-white images are crisp and precise, and when the source material is a little worn, the image is still very smooth and sharp. The monophonic sound is fine and the episodes are not captioned. Each DVD holds three or four episodes and is accompanied by a general (and well written) background on the show and on Rod Serling, plus specific comments about each episode featured on that volume. The episodes run a bit under a half hour each.

Vol. 1 includes *Night of the Meek* (Episode 47 from 1960), *The Invaders* (Episode 51 from 1961) and *Nothing in the Dark* (Episode 81 from 1962). *Meek* was shot on videotape and has a slightly rougher appearance than the other two, though there is also a sense of immediacy to the tape recording that film cannot duplicate. Art Carney stars as a department store Santa Claus who becomes the real thing one Christmas Eve. *Invaders* is the classic Agnes Moorehead episode in which she portrays, without dialogue, a woman living in a cabin who is threatened by a tiny spacecraft. Similar in spirit, Gladys Cooper and Robert Redford star in *Nothing in the Dark*, about an elderly woman living alone in a tenement who receives a mysterious visitor. The picture on both episodes looks super.

Everybody's two favorite commercial airline **Twilight Zone** tales, *Nightmare at 20,000 Feet* (Episode 123 from 1963) in which William Shatner sees a boogeyman on the airplane's wing, and *The Odyssey of Flight 33* (Episode 54 from 1961), in which a passenger plane slips through a time warp and sees dinosaurs, are included on **Vol. 2**. Also featured are *Time Enough to Last* (Episode 8 from 1959) with Burgess Meredith as the sole survivor of a nuclear holocaust who overcomes despair when he realizes that the written word has endured, only to have fate play one final trick upon him, and *The Monsters Are Due on Maple Street* (Episode 22 from 1960) about a neighborhood that panics when the power goes out. The two plane episodes are in excellent condition. *Time Enough to Last* is a bit washed out and *Maple Street* is a little soft, with less detailed contrasts, but the image on both is still fully acceptable.

Vol. 3 opens with the Fountain-of-Youth tale, *Kick the Can* (Episode 86 from 1962), followed by *Steel* (Episode 122 from 1963) in which Lee Marvin is the manager of a broken down android boxer who chooses to take the boxer's place in a big match, *A Game of Pool* (Episode 70 from 1961) in which Jonathan Winters and Jack Klugman have a metaphysical contest where it is best not to win, and *Walking Distance* (Episode 5 from 1959) in which Gig Young portrays a businessman who has a brief opportunity to revisit his childhood. *Pool* looks super, *Walking Distance* and *Steel* are good, and *Kick the Can* is okay.

Meredith stars again in *Mr. Dingle, the Strong (Episode 55* from 1961) **Vol. 4**, as a weakling who is given super-human strength by some aliens, but just uses his new-found powers to show off. Most of the action takes place in a bar, and Don Rickles co-stars. The episode has some amusing moments, though it also seems a bit drawn out. *Two (Episode 66* from 1961) stars a very youthful Elizabeth Montgomery and Charles Bronson as, once again, the only survivors of an atomic war. A man who can change his face at will uses his power to bilk people out of cash until his games catch up with him in *The Four of Us Are Dying (Episode 13* from 1960). Klugman portrays a down-on-his-luck trumpeter in *A Passage for Trumpet (Episode 32* from 1960). His attitude changes after he meets a divine figure who also knows how to play the horn. *Two* looks super, *Dingle* and *Trumpet* look good and *The Four of Us Are Dying* is okay.

Ray Bradbury's superb *I Sing the Body Electric (Episode 100* from 1962), on **Vol. 5**, is about children adjusting to an android nanny after their mother passes away. What is exceptional about the script is that it concludes the essential narrative about five minutes before the end, so that it can explore some highly metaphysical themes is a brief epilogue. The eerie *Long Distance Call (Episode 58* from 1961) has a common plot, about a little boy who talks to his dead grandmother on a toy phone, but it is executed exceptionally well and Billy Mumy, as the boy, is terrific. Richard Basehart is an astronaut stranded on a planet apparently inhabited by only one other creature—a female—while his home world is destroyed in a war in *Probe 7 – Over and Out (Episode 129* from 1963). Tying together the themes of a couple of those episodes, *The Lonely (Episode 7* from 1959), is about a convict on an extraterrestrial world who is given a female android as a companion, and then finds it hard to leave her when his sentence is commuted. Jack Warden stars. *Long Distance Call* is another videotape episode, though it looks very nice. The other three are in good condition.

All four episodes on **Vol. 6** have a common theme of life after death. *Deaths-Head Revisited (Episode 74* from 1961) is about a former Nazi general who becomes trapped in a haunted concentration camp. The program was exceptional in its time for addressing the subject of the Holocaust, and is still very moving and unnerving. Lee Marvin, Lee Van Cleef and Strother Martin are featured in the cast of *The Grave (Episode 72* from 1961), about a gunfighter who is apprehensive about visiting the cemetery where his rival is buried. It has a terrific atmosphere and you can't beat the all-star cast (Marvin has some nice moves with a gun). A man may or may not have come back from the dead in *The Last Rites of Jeff Myrtlebank (Episode 88* from 1962). It is an amusing little tale, deriving a lot of humor from its hillbilly setting. Dub Taylor and Edgar Buchanan have supporting parts. An interesting allegorical piece, *The Passerby (Episode 69* from 1961), is about soldiers returning home from the Civil War on a long and weary road. One, played by James Gregory, stops to help a widow. It is by no means a classic episode, but it does demonstrate how stimulating, eerie and just plain different an average episode could be in comparison to most of what was on television in those days. That is why it is appearing on DVD and the other stuff is not.

The classic Inger Stevens episode about a woman driving cross-country and being followed by a mysterious figure, *The Hitch-Hiker (Episode 16* from 1960), is on **Vol. 7**, as is *Perchance to Dream (Episode 9* from 1959), another episode with a 'dream' theme, which has vague similarities with *Nightmare on Elm Street*. Richard Conte portrays a patient trying to convince his psychiatrist that a beautiful woman is trying to kill him within his dreams. In *Shadow Play (Episode 62* from 1961), Dennis Weaver is trapped in a sort of **Groundhog Day** cycle, in which he is repeatedly sentenced to death and sent to the electric chair. Everybody has a **Twilight Zone** episode that scared the beejeezus out of them as a child, and with us it was *King Nine Will Not Return (Episode 37* from 1960), in which Robert Cummings portrays a downed bomber pilot having hallucinations. It still gives us the willies.

Stories about aliens and UFOs inhabit **Vol. 8**, including the classic tale about unusually hospitable visitors to Earth, *To Serve Man (Episode 89* from 1962), and *Third from the Sun (Episode 14* from 1960) with Fritz Weaver as an armaments worker who attempts to take his family away in a spaceship before a war begins. Edward Andrews co-stars. A variation on a common tale, *The Shelter (Episode 68* from 1961) is about the sudden panic among friends and neighbors when it looks like the country is under attack and only one family is prepared. A little girl has an unusual friend with magic powers in *The Fugitive (Episode 90* from 1962), but two mysterious men are looking for the friend. The conclusion is somewhat unexpected. A couple of the episodes have some minor speckling.

William Shatner stars in *Nick of Time (Episode 43* from 1960) on **Vol. 9**, about a man who becomes addicted to a fortune telling machine. *It's a Good Life (Episode 73* from 1961), another 'mind control' episode, was the episode that inspired the Joe Dante segment in the feature film. Billy Mumy portrays a domineering child who exerts an unusual influence over his family. Shelly Berman stars in *The Mind and the Matter (Episode 63* from 1961), about a man who is able to define the world around him, but never without glitches. Buddy Ebsen stars in the fourth episode, *The Prime Mover (Episode 57* from 1961). Sort of a cross between **Phenomenon** and **Rain Man**, Ebsen plays a cafe owner with psychokinetic abilities who gets dragged to Las Vegas by his best friend.

Buster Keaton stars in the most memorable of the four episodes on **Vol. 10**, all of which deal with time travel. Keaton is a janitor in the 1890's in *Once upon a Time (Episode 78* from 1961), who is transported to the Sixties (he's shocked to see that steak is selling for $1.49/lb.). The 1890 sequences are executed in the style of a silent film, and Keaton gets to do many wonderful routines during the course of the show. Jesse White is also featured. A World War I pilot lands at a modern airbase in *The Last Flight (Episode 18* from 1960), and the experience shows him his destiny. Cliff Robertson is a pioneer in *A Hundred Yards over the Rim (Episode 59* from 1961), who needs medicine for his child and is able to get it, in the Twilight Zone. An aging actor with a bad marriage is given a chance to relive his past, but he finds that it really wasn't all that much better than the present in *The Trouble with Templeton (Episode 45* from 1960). Brian Ahern stars.

Robertson is back again as a ventriloquist whose dummy apparently has a mind of its own in *The Dummy (Episode 98* from 1962) on **Vol. 11**, a collection of animate inanimates episodes. Usually in such stories, it is the ventriloquist who is mad, but when you enter the Twilight Zone, it's the dummy who's flipped. A famous episode, *The After Hours (Episode 34* from 1960) stars Anne Francis as a shopper who gets the ultimate run around in a department store. Telly Savalas is a step-father being hounded by his step-daughter's toy in *The Living Doll (Episode 126* from 1963), though the DVD presentation includes a spoken trailer by Serling. Everett Sloane is a tourist in Las Vegas who becomes obsessed with playing a slot machine in the fairly simple psychological drama, *The Fever (Episode 17* from 1960).

'Second chances' is the binding theme of **Vol. 12**. One episode, *The Trade-Ins (Episode 96* from 1962), is about an elderly couple who want to move their minds into youthful bodies. *Mr. Denton on Doomsday (Episode 3* from 1959) is another western, with Dan Duryea, Martin Landau and Doug McClure, about a washed up gunfighter who receives a potion that allows him to once again hit his mark, for a limited time, at least. Ida Lupino is a former screen star past her prime who wishes she could perform a reverse Purple Rose of Cairo in *Sixteen Millimeter Shrine (Episode 4* from 1959). Martin Balsam co-stars, as her agent. The cinematic qualities of the episode are exceptional and the image is often striking. Shot on videotape, the picture on *The Lateness of the Hour (Episode 44* from 1960) is incredibly immediate and vivid. There is some smearing in the quicker camera pans, but otherwise the presentation is gorgeous. Inger Stevens is featured again, as the restless daughter of a doctor who has a number of android servants. The denouement is guessable, but the execution is still intriguing.

The episode that inspired the John Landis segment of the feature film, *A Quality of Mercy* (*Episode 80* from 1961), has been included on **Vol. 13**. Dean Stockwell stars as a lieutenant in the South Pacific who suddenly finds himself literally in his enemy's shoes. Leonard Nimoy appears, briefly, and Albert Salmi gives one of his reliable performances (he was a terrific actor who never broke out of television the way his contemporaries did). Or maybe it was *Judgment Night* (*Episode 10* from 1959) that inspired the Landis sequence, since it is about the same thing, a German U-Boat commander who suddenly finds himself on a British ship in the Atlantic that has broken off from its convoy (Patrick Macnee has a small part). Both episodes are entertaining, not so much for how they end but for the drama along the way. *The Purple Testament* (*Episode 19* from 1960) is about a lieutenant who can see which of his men is going to die. *The Obsolete Man* (*Episode 65* from 1961), with Burgess Meredith and Fritz Weaver, is a Kafkaesque tale about a librarian who turns the tables on his executioner after being sentenced to death because society no longer needs him.

Twins (Universal, 20266)

Arnold Schwarzenegger and Danny DeVito are the title characters, sidestepping some crooked goings-on to search for their mother. The comedy can be enjoyable, but not when looking at the picture is a strain.

The picture is in soft focus throughout, and is often excessively blurry. The colors are strong, but at times the grain is so intense it brings an unnatural texture to solid backgrounds. The 107 minute film is presented in full frame format and has a passable stereo surround soundtrack. The 1988 film is also available in French and Spanish and can be supported by English or Spanish subtitles ("Nada más sentarme creí que estaba delante de un espejo"). There are some production notes, a cast profile section and an effective theatrical trailer.

Twister (Warner, 20100)

Remember the Greek legend about Odysseus and the Sirens, and how he had himself tied to a mast so he could listen to their song without drowning himself? Yeah, the legend is supposed to represent sex or something, but it also is an apt description for the thrill movies like **Twister** can give you. If you stand close to your speakers your hair might get ruffled a bit, but in principle you can sit through the whole movie and feel each thrill as the hero and heroine drive again and again into the maelstrom without the least physical danger to your person or belongings. The thrill is so strong that it also carries you past the rather silly story, about cyclone scientists who want to increase the warning time for twister touchdowns and also get a divorce. Some of the dialogue is laughable, but once the nasty winds start throwing cows and trucks around, concerns about such matters disappear in a puff. The director, Jan De Bont, has done a superb job on what is really a fairly silly script. Recognizing that the human side of the tale has limited potential, he emphasizes close-ups of the two stars, Helen Hunt and Bill Paxton, and just lets the domination of their faces on the screen provide the human presence the dialogue and written characterizations were unable to achieve. It is enough to get you through the low parts, or even through the rousing finale, where the heroes are being hit by debris flying at more than 100 MPH and come out of it with nary a scratch.

The 1996 hit is presented on one side in letterboxed format, with an aspect ratio of about 2.35:1and an accommodation for enhanced 16:9 playback, and in cropped format on the other side. The action scenes are better with the letterboxing, but the cropping is passable. An early DVD release, there is some digital artifacting, but the picture is sharp and the colors are excellent. The stereo surround sound and Dolby Digital sound are aggressive, and contribute significantly to the thrills. The 113 minute film is also in French in Dolby Digital and can be supported by English,

French or Spanish subtitles. The thrilling teaser trailer is included, as well.

Two English Girls (Fox Lorber, FLV5076)

François Truffaut's 1971 film plays like motion picture illustrations to a novel. Based upon a story by Henri-Pierre Roché, it is set near the Turn of the Century and explores the romances a young man experiences over the course of several years with two sisters. Jean-Pierre Léaud stars. Truffaut's masterful depiction of the intricate fluidity of emotion passing between the heroes and his celebration of the period setting fully compensate for the narrative's teases—something always prevents the characters from forming a permanent bond. While the extensive voiceover narration confines the film's aspirations, it succeeds beautifully within its limitations.

The film used to run 108 minutes, but the disc has a running time of 130 minutes, including footage Truffaut reinstated in the film shortly before he passed away. The extensions reinforce the film's format and add a wealth of detail to its atmosphere. The cinematography, by Nestor Almendros, has an incredibly complex color scheme, reinforced by the film's art direction and costumes. Each scene has a dominant hue, employed so extensively that flesh-tones often change in pallor from one sequence to the next. The transfer never achieves the clarity or smoothness that is evident in the projection of a film, but the image always manages the subtle differences in shading within each color sequence that the film-makers intended. The source material looks like it has been handled a bit, but is free of severe wear. The image also looks soft and hazy in darker sequences. The presentation is letterboxed, with an aspect ratio of about 1.6:1 and no 16:9 enhancement. The monophonic sound is okay, and the French dialogue is supported by permanent English subtitles. The chapter encoding is paltry. The program is accompanied by trailers for a number of Truffaut films.

Two Lost Worlds (Image, ID5377FWDVD)

A very bizarre hour-long film, it starts out as a pirate movie, turns into a western (in Australia) and a romance, and then becomes a dinosaur (or big lizards with things taped on their backs) film. James Arness stars in the enjoyably bad and blissfully brief 1950 adventure, which has a marvelously dopey voiceover narration to keep things moving. We had some trouble keeping track of the secondary characters (we swear that one appears in a shot after he's supposed to be dead), but that just means we need to watch the movie more times to get everything straight. We look forward to it.

The black-and-white picture looks super. There is damage at the reel-change points, but otherwise the image is crisp, contrasts are nicely detailed and blacks are deep. The monophonic sound is adequate (there is a wonderfully over-indulgent symphonic score) and the program is not captioned. A very thorough Arness filmography is also included.

Two-Minute Warning (Universal, 20425)

Made during one of the pendulum swings in the disaster movie genre, the Universal production is about a faceless sniper who (during the film's last act) shoots people randomly at the Super Bowl. Most of the film's 115 minute running time (not 126 as is listed on the jacket cover) is taken up by the insipidly written mini-dramas involving the eventual victims and the gradual recognition by the police that a situation is brewing. The 1976 film has one of those 'stars in squares at the bottom of the poster' casts, including Charlton Heston, John Cassavetes, Gena Rowlands, Martin Balsam, David Janssen, Beau Bridges and several others. Except for the pre-ratings-crackdown gore shots, however, the film is a lame concoction that doesn't amount to much.

The picture is letterboxed with an aspect ratio of about 2.35:1 and no 16:9 enhancement. The colors are reasonably bright and the image is sharp, though the film has the bland factory-style cinematography Universal often employed for such features. The monophonic sound is dullish and the music has a slightly muted upper end. The film is also available in French and Spanish, and can be supported by English or Spanish subtitles. There is a decent production essay, a large cast profile section and a trailer.

2001: A Space Odyssey (MGM, 906309); (Warner, 65000)

The sort of program that will make DVD converts of the non-believers, MGM has done a magnificent job putting Stanley Kubrick's 1968 science fiction masterpiece onto DVD. The DVD uses the same transfer of 65mm source materials that was used for the best LD releases, but the advantages in DVD image delivery are remarkable. The 148 minute program is presented in single-sided dual-layer format. The picture is incredibly sharp. You can see the individual threads of the fishnet stockings on the Russian female scientist that are only general blurs on the LD and you can see the shadow of a helicopter on the landscape during the 'Beyond the Infinite' sequence, at 130:29.

In addition to the crispness of the image, the colors are also a little more stable and a little truer, though these differences with the LD are less distinctive. The source material has a stray marking here and there, and one rather large scratch. The image is letterboxed with an aspect ratio of about 2.2:1, sadly without 16:9 enhancement.

Dolby Digital encoding doesn't really bring much to the soundtrack, which remains fairly noisy and centered. None of the audio flaws are overly distracting and the quality is sufficient for maintaining the film's spell. The film is also available in French in mono and can be supported by English, French or Spanish subtitles ("D'accord pour procédure d'urgence et remplacement unité AE-35"). An excellent 20 minute talk by Arthur C. Clarke, from 1968 when the film was released, is included as well, as are trailers.

Warner's presentation is identical to the MGM release. In fact, although the jacket has a new catalogue number, the platter retains MGM's catalogue number.

2001 is an examination of the true maturity of contemporary mankind, observed against a scale that ranges from the beginning of human beings to their potential evolutionary manifestations. With every passing year, the film becomes a more remarkable achievement, since, by and large, science fiction movies still haven't caught up to it in terms of intelligence or even special effects.

2010: The Year We Make Contact (MGM, 907046)

Many people wanted to know what happened at the end of **2001** and for a long time, one theory was as valid as the next. What was left open in the film and in Clarke's novelization is the fate of the Earth and mankind when the astronaut/Ulysses returns from his voyage. To cash in a sequel, Clarke chose out of many possible scenarios, but even though the rendition is his and the film adaptation follows Clarke's novel closely, it can't be the definitive follow-up to **2001**. He had to step on his paint to get out of his corner.

There is plenty of tension to serve the drama, even on multiple viewings, as the American and Russian crew travel in the Russian ship to investigate the American craft abandoned at the end of **2001**. The mystery of HAL's nervous breakdown is given a pat explanation, but HAL's heroics at the end are to be cheered. The Earth scenes that begin **2010** are often belittled, but they are not totally without merit. The most powerful moment comes when Dr. Heywood Floyd (Roy Scheider) returns to Hawaii from Washington DC, a trip which in another era took many months. His wife (Madolyn Smith) is blasé about it ("How was Washington?") but is stunned when he announces a few moments later that he is going to Jupiter and will be away for more than two years. The world that had gotten so small has become large again and sailors are once more leaving their families to voyage far from home.

The colors look bright, and the picture is crisp and effectively detailed. The presentation is letterboxed with an aspect ratio of about 2.35:1 and no 16:9 enhancement. The stereo surround sound is a bit weak, but the Dolby Digital delivers a reasonably good separation mix and plenty of nice bass effects. The 114 minute 1984 feature is also available in French in standard stereo

and can be supported by English, French or Spanish subtitles ("Mon Dieu! C'est plein d'étoiles!"). The film is accompanied by an excellent 8-minute 'making of' featurette (it includes a blooper reel of attempts to fake zero gravity). Roy Scheider, John Lithgow, Helen Mirren and Bob Balaban star in the 1984 production, directed by Peter Hyams.

Two Undercover Angels (Anchor Bay, DV10822)

Those wild, shagadelic heroines from the marvelous Sixties Italian spy movie, **Kiss Me Monster**, appear as well in another terrific, totally incoherent thriller. Janine Reynault and Rossana Yanni star as two beautiful models or something who investigate the mysterious disappearances of several other beautiful women. It seems a mad artist is having his werewolf friend kill them while he paints the murders. Although the film is not quite as exhilarating as **Kiss Me Monster**, it still takes a couple viewings to figure out what is going on, and uses many of the same sets that **Monster** did, making an ideal companion on a double bill.

The picture is presented in full screen format and appears to be at least a little bit cropped. The source material is worn in a number of places, and has stray speckles here and there even in the best passages. The color transfer, however, looks reasonably good. There is some grain, and really strong oranges and reds are blurry, but other hues are bright and nicely detailed, and fleshtones aren't bad if the lighting is decent. The sound is stereophonic, but don't get your hopes up. The film is badly dubbed—that's one of its many charms—but tones are muted and the audio track is a bit noisy. The 75 minute feature is accompanied by an entertaining trailer and is not captioned.

Two Women (Madacy, DVD99020)

The 1960 Vittorio De Sica feature is a very fine movie, about a mother and her daughter who leave Rome during World War II to escape the air raids only to discover that the horrors of war have followed them to the countryside. Sophia Loren won an Oscar for her performance, even though the film is in Italian, and Jean-Paul Belmondo is also featured in an early role.

Unfortunately, the DVD is horrible and cannot be used for anything but a reference to the film's narrative. The black-and-white picture has the constant artifacting one associates with a multigenerational video copy, where every straight line and shift in contrast is turned into a cluster of small squares. The image is smeary and details are obscured in every shot. The monophonic sound is also noisy and distorted, and the white English subtitles are fairly blurry. The program runs 93 minutes and is accompanied by some minor production information.

U

Under the Gun (Image, ID5629FMDVD)

Richard Norton stars as a nightclub owner trying to embezzle a load of money and skip town during one evening. Norton is the hero, because everybody else in the film is even more corrupt and despicable, including the cops. The 1995 Australian production, supposedly set in Canada, has one setting and is a jumble of fight scenes, betrayals and vague stabs at humor. We found it tiresome, but dedicated Norton fans may have some use for it.

Much of the film is set at night or in the partial darkness, but the picture is reasonably sharp. Fleshtones are dull, but other hues are adequate. The stereo sound is a little harsh, with modest dimensionality. The 91 minute program is not captioned.

U. S. Marshals (Warner, 15625)

It doesn't have the humanism or the class of **The Fugitive**, but **U.S. Marshals**, which features Tommy Lee Jones in a continuation of the role he instigated in **The Fugitive**, is an entertaining action feature. Wesley Snipes co-stars as the escapee, involved in some kind of government agency double-cross. Jones isn't given the whitewater rhythm he had in the first movie, but he is still an engaging presence. The stunt and special effect sequences are elaborate and the plot keeps the film moving along, which is all you really need when you've already got the popcorn.

The presentation is letterboxed, with an aspect ratio of about 1.85:1 and an accommodation for enhanced 16:9 playback. The picture quality is excellent, with crisp hues and accurate fleshtones, and the stereo surround sound and Dolby Digital sound are enjoyable, with the Dolby Digital track delivering more detailed separation effects. The 131 minute feature can also be accessed in French in standard stereo and comes with English, French or Spanish subtitles.

Along with the trailer for the film, there is a fairly interesting breakdown of the plane crash sequence, though, as with other Warner interactive features, it is presented in a pointlessly annoying manner, forcing the viewer to select each of its segments separately. Additionally, there is a 10 minute documentary about what, exactly, U.S. Marshals are and how long they've been around, followed by trailers for two other Marshal movies from Warner, *Wyatt Earp* and *Cahill*, and three TV commercials. The director, Stuart Baird, has about 40 minutes of commentary scattered through the 131 minute film, though fortunately the viewer is guided through the largest gaps in his talk with chapter advance instructions. He talks a bit about how the plane crash sequence and the escape onto the train were achieved and points out a few sequences where he improvised an improvement upon the script. He spends much of his time doing a play-by-play, with some added background information. He also talks a little about technique, about learning while working and about making sure there is enough coverage for the editing, but on the whole his talk is not elaborate or vital.

U-Turn (Columbia TriStar, 32529)

The narrative isn't new, but the performances are wonderful and the premise is nearly always reliable when you have the right actors trying to do one another in. Sean Penn stars as a man on his way to pay off some gambling debts, who pulls into a remote Arizona town with car trouble and becomes embroiled in plots and counterplots by a husband and wife intent upon ceasing their union with extreme prejudice. Featuring an intensely manipulated visual style (and accompanying audio mix), director Oliver Stone uses jump cuts, oddball wipes, extreme close ups, tipped camera angles and other eccentric filmmaking devices, but they are never randomly applied and they never, ever do not work. The rush of intriguing images is so captivating, especially with quality DVD playback, that the film totally becomes the sort of cerebral escapist entertainment Stone intends it to be.

Nick Nolte, evoking John Huston at times, does some of his best work as the film's villain. Jennifer Lopez is suitably steamy as the femme fatale. Powers Boothe, Jon Voight, Billy Bob Thornton, Claire Danes and Joaquin Phoenix are also on hand and most are fairly amusing (Boothe's role, as the local sheriff, is a bit more serious, but he is better than he has been in a long time). Even Liv Tyler shows up, as an extra. The music, by Ennio Morricone, is also super.

The presentation is in letterboxed format on one side, with an aspect ratio of about 1.85:1 and an accommodation for enhanced 16:9 playback, and is in full screen format on the other side. Stone and his cinematographer, Robert Richardson, experimented with what can best be described as an industrial film stock, creating somewhat heightened colors that the DVD glorifies in every frame. The stereo surround sound and Dolby Digital soundtracks are equally splashy, with detailed separations effects and plenty of punch. The 125 minute program also has French and Spanish audio tracks in standard stereo, optional English, French and Spanish subtitles, and a trailer.

UFO and Paranormal Phenomena (Madacy, DVD990006)
UFO and Paranormal Phenomena: Message from Another Dimension (Madacy, DVD990061)
UFO and Paranormal Phenomena: Encounters of the Fifth Kind Part 1 (Madacy, DVD990062)
UFO and Paranormal Phenomena: Encounters of the Fifth Kind Part 2 (Madacy, DVD9900063)
UFO and Paranormal Phenomena: The Mystery of Life and Death Part 1 (Madacy, DVD9900064)
UFO and Paranormal Phenomena: The Mystery of Life and Death Part 2 (Madacy, DVD9900065)

Five rather monotonous UFO documentaries are available in a boxed set and as individual releases. The hour-long programs have a lot of footage relating to Finland and may have originated there in another form. The narration is in English, but there are lengthy interviews with abductees and the like from all over the world, which are supported by English subtitles.

The programs are primarily of people talking, and there are occasional surges of humor when a particularly loony witness starts describing an encounter, but most of the material is just sort of vague and unconvincing. All of the programs discuss various UFO incidents from around the world. In addition, **Message from Another Dimension** deals specifically with channeling to UFOs, **Encounters of the Fifth Kind Part 1** is about government cover-ups and includes some very graphic footage of a human corpse that has supposedly been gutted by aliens, and **Part 2** focuses on abductions and alien impregnations (they always take the babies afterwards, of course). The two **Mystery of Life and Death** episodes touch on UFOs peripherally, concentrating instead on mediums, channelling and other psychic phenomena. The highpoint of **Part 1** comes at the end, where we meet a woman who claims to be in contact with famous dead singers, such as Louis Armstrong, Elvis Presley and Mario Lanza. They even show her 'singing' Armstrong's rendition of *What a Wonderful World*, but the entire sequence, both the singing and the interview, are out of synch, so instead of lip-synching the song, it looks like she's playing catch up. **Part 2** covers dreams, reincarnation and miracle healing. The picture is a little soft on all the programs, but colors are generally bright and presentable, and the sound is reasonably strong. Each DVD has both shared and unshared supplementary features. Most are extremely brief, but there is one feature that we enjoyed, an 'incident' map, where you can select on a site and then read about the specific incident.

UFO: They Are Here (Simitar, 7222)

There's nothing like a good UFO documentary to stimulate the imagination and this gives you two in one. The program is a combination of two 43 minute 'hour' episodes of a documentary show entitled *From Beyond*, hosted by Joey Travolta. The programs combine talking head interviews with 'experts' and contactees, along with lots of contact video footage, photos and other illustrations. The people and their earnest tales are great fun, as is listening to some of the 'experts' turn verbal somersaults in order to debunk the stories and at the same time debunk their own debunking to keep in the spirit of the program. The various paper plates, cigars, hubcaps and other objects being tossed in the air and photographed are also highly enjoyable. The picture quality varies from one sequence to the next. Some of the interviews look sharp and are well colored, while others are hazy or dusty looking. Although the reality programs cropping up like mushrooms on Fox these days demonstrate that people can capture almost any accident or unusual event on camcorder video, no one has yet to record a real alien hopping out of his space ship and picking a daisy. The motion footage is mostly blurry and is inevitably presented without any semblance of context. The monophonic sound is passable.

The Ultimate Space Experience (Image, DVD99045)

The 48 minute image music program uses NASA footage. The material is somewhat worn looking, with weak colors, but it is adequately varied, drawing from the moon flights, the shuttle flights and other sources. The show ends with the Challenger explosion. The gung-ho but inartistic musical score is in stereo, with a modest dimensionality. A few essays about the space program are included with the menu.

Ultraman II (Digital Multimedia, 00143)

Four 20 minute episodes from the animated TV series are compiled on the program. The initial episode introduces the hero, who turns into the title character when he puts a star thing on his chest. In the first episode, he battles dinosaur monsters in the Arctic. In the others he battles a tornado monster, a red cloud monster and giant crocodile monsters. There are references in each episode to the previous or the next episode, but the narratives are essentially free-standing. The plots are rather weak (he defeats the crocodile monsters by throwing them into the sea) and do not vary much from one episode to the next. The animation is stilted, and the source material is a little dirty here and there. Colors are somewhat bland, but workable, and the monophonic sound is tolerable. The program is not captioned.

Ulysses' Gaze (Fox Lorber, FLV5067)

We predict that in the far future there will be but one major demarcation in history—before film and after film. With the inevitable rounding off, the beginning of history recorded on film will be seen as the beginning of the Second Millennium. Everything that happened before that time, though recorded on paper and in drawings, will be considered sketchy and unreliable, while everything after that point, recorded in motion picture images, will be perceived as being truth, regardless of the uncertainties that truth represents. So the search for lost film is a big thing, a mythologically-sized big thing, and that is the primary justification for Theo Angelopoulos' **Ulysses' Gaze**.

If you looked up in a reference book why most people hate foreign films you would probably see pictures of **Ulysses' Gaze** staring back at you. It runs 173 minutes and stars Harvey Keitel, as a film archivist who takes a meandering journey across the Balkans and back again in search of 'three reels of undeveloped film' by Greece's earliest filmmakers. Much of the film is in Greek, supported by permanent English subtitles, but Keitel speaks English a lot, as well. During the journey he witnesses the terror and anarchy that has destroyed civilization in Yugoslavia, and the inanities of political repression and Communism. He meets women that seem to be symbolic of something or rather and he is intimate with a couple of them. He often just sort of stares at the countryside in achingly long, slow takes, though he does interact with characters and view minor occurrences. Either the film will make total sense—with Keitel's character witnessing history, environment, humankind and cinema in a stream-of-consciousness blend of discovery and experience—or it will seem like a totally incoherent, pointless mess, or you'll be sleeping soundly about 20 minutes into it.

The stereo surround mix is excellent, with detailed separations, a nice dimensionality and lots of power. It can't match up to a bit Hollywood effort, but for its budget and situation, the audio is quite impressive. The picture is letterboxed with an aspect ratio of about 1.58:1 and no 16:9 enhancement. Most of the time the picture looks good. The cinematography tends toward natural or unassertive light, creating blanched fleshtones and a mild grain in darker sequences. Some sequences also have a vague warp or a few scattered blips that we would associate with a momentary disruption in the transfer process, and there is some minor speckling. With the grain and the archive footage, there is also some minor artifacting, though it isn't obtrusive. There is also a trailer and some filmographies.

Ulzana's Raid (GoodTimes, 0581035)

Robert Aldrich's enjoyable, violent 1972 western depicts a cavalry unit that is trying to out-smart a group of renegade Apaches.

Burt Lancaster stars as a cavalry scout who has to teach the narrow minded army officers how to think like Indians. Bruce Davison co-stars. Lancaster gives a rewarding performance, and the chess-like strategies each side employs to outfox the other are as entertaining as the energetic action sequences.

The picture is presented in moderately cropped format. Darker sequences can get fairly grainy, and the film has a kind of dusty look to it, but colors and fleshtones are reasonably strong, and in the bright sun the image is smooth. The frame transfer rate swings wildly from high to low, but any artifacting flaws are momentary and rarely noticeable. The monophonic sound has a nice, solid range and clear tones. The 103 minute feature can be supported by English, French or Spanish subtitles.

The Umbrellas of Cherbourg (Fox Lorber, FLV5003)

The presentation is letterboxed with a screwy 1.45:1 aspect ratio, cropping a substantial amount of the image from each side of the original film. The movie's colors are rich, deep, and glorious. The image is so crisp and so glossy it almost seems three dimensional, and such qualities are essential to sell the 1964 film's all-singing dialogue and archetypal romance (based upon Marcel Pagnol's *Fanny* trilogy, about young lovers who are separated). The sound was remastered for stereo during a restoration effort. The age and nature of the recording are sometimes strained under the pressures of Dolbyization, but the overall effect is an added grandeur despite occasional lapses of raspiness. The DVD is not time encoded. We did not set a stopwatch to it, but it does seem to be slightly time compressed. The stated running time is 91 minutes. The film is in French and comes with yellow English subtitles that can be toggled off for those who don't care about having the dialogue translated or just want to enjoy the art design. The chapter encoding is weak, identifying only the film's title card segment separators and none of the songs. There is also a very poorly conceived theatrical trailer for the restoration reissue, filmographies for director Jacques Demy, composer Michel Legrand and Catherine Deneuve, and a brief notation concerning the restoration.

Uncle Buck (Universal, 20317)

Macaulay Culkin turns out to have a major role in the film, as one of the youngsters John Candy's character is babysitting, and it is likely that it was his performance in that 1989 film, under John Hughes' direction, that enabled him to land the *Home Alone* spot. Candy is a bachelor uncle, asked to watch the kids for a week in an emergency and inevitably providing them with a different and better rounded outlook on life by the time his stay is ended. The bad guys—school administrators, randy boyfriends—are easy targets for Buck's wrath, and there are no really bright or unanticipated sequences to liven up the plot.

The film is letterboxed with an aspect ratio of about 1.85:1 and an accommodation for enhanced 16:9 playback. The picture has bright, sharp hues and accurate fleshtones. The stereo surround sound is okay and the film has a reasonably creative sound mix for its genre. The 100 minute feature is also available in French and Spanish and can be supported by English or Spanish subtitles. There are a few production notes and cast profiles for Candy and co-star Amy Madigan.

Uncle Sam (Elite, EE7262)

There have already been psycho Santa Clauses, pumpkins, leprechauns, and who knows what else, so now it is time for the Fourth of July killer. Written by Larry Cohen and directed by William Lustig, the film seems to work backwards from its title and is about a serviceman killed in action, whose corpse awakens and takes to punishing those in a small American town that have been disrespectful to their country. It is an uninspired effort, however, with very few thrills or decent applications of gore—and even less sex. The narrative has little logic and minimal forward movement, and the ending has all the excitement of a wet firecracker.

The presentation is letterboxed with an aspect ratio of about 2.35:1 and no 16:9 enhancement. The picture looks fine, with accurate colors and a sharp focus. The stereo surround sound has been given a conscientious mix, with many distinctive separation effects and a strong bass. The Dolby Digital track is even better, with clearer separations and a better defined low end. The 90 minute program is not captioned and is accompanied by a theatrical trailer. Lustig and one of the stars, Isaac Hayes, provide a jovial commentary. Lustig talks about the production, provides some insights on low budget filmmaking and shares a number of anecdotes about the cast, while Hayes provides an Ed McMahon-ish support.

Under Seige (Warner, 12420)

The picture has very bright colors and crisp details. The image is letterboxed on one side, with an aspect ratio of about 1.85:1 and an accommodation for enhanced 16:9 playback, and in full screen on the other side. The full screen version loses a tiny bit on the side but adds more to the bottom and fills your screen with the movie, so unless you are a letterbox fanatic, you will probably prefer it. The regular stereo surround soundtrack is good, but the Dolby Digital track has bigger, more directional noises and is grandly entertaining. We could watch the 1992 Andrew Davis movie, about the hijacking of a Navy battleship, in mono and have a great time, but the audio pleasures are substantial and are highly pleasing. The 103 minute film is also available in French and Spanish without Dolby Digital and can be accompanied by English, French or Spanish subtitling ("Un cuistot n'a pas fait ça"). There is a cast profile section and some interesting production notes about shooting the film without leaving Alabama's Mobile Bay. There is also an efficient theatrical trailer that is presented in full screen on the full screen side and letterboxed on the letterboxed side. Steven Seagal is the hero and Tommy Lee Jones and Gary Busey are the bad guys.

Under Siege 2: Dark Territory (Warner, 13665)

What made the original Under Siege an exceptional piece of entertainment was the script's tight logic. The hero was where he was for a reason, the bad guys were doing what they were doing for a reason, and the two just got into each other's way. The 1995 sequel lacks that logic, and so it isn't as much fun or as compellingly repeatable. Steven Seagal reprises his role as the former Navy SEAL who happens to be in the wrong place at the right time, but this time it is a train, and there isn't really any good reason as to why he is there. Additionally the bad guys, led by a nerdish Eric Bogosian, have this plan to make money by destroying Washington DC with a death ray satellite, but how they are going to earn that money makes no sense whatsoever. It does not seem necessary, or wise, that they hijack a train to set up their control station, either. What Under Siege 2 does have, however, is a large budget for stunts and special effects, so it isn't a complete waste of time. If you can get over the ridiculous plot, the execution is enjoyable in a cliffhanger serial sort of way and much of the spectacle is well suited for DVD.

The program is presented in full screen on one side and in letterboxed format on the other, with an aspect ratio of about 1.85:1 and an accommodation for enhanced 16:9 playback. The letterboxing adds a little picture information to the sides of the image and takes off some from the top and bottom, though either version is workable. The colors are accurate and fleshtones are rich. The stereo surround sound is passable, but the Dolby Digital track is a lot more energized. The 100 minute film is also available in French and can be accompanied by English, French or Spanish subtitles. There is a decent cast-and-crew profile and some interesting production notes on the special effects, along with the eight trailers again.

Under the Gun (Image, ID5629FMDVD)

Richard Norton stars as a nightclub owner trying to embezzle a load of money and skip town during one evening. Norton is the hero, because everybody else in the film is even more corrupt and despicable, including the cops. The 1995 Australian production, supposedly set in Canada, has one setting and is a jumble of fight scenes, betrayals and vague stabs at humor. We found it tiresome, but dedicated Norton fans may have some use for it.

Much of the film is set at night or in the partial darkness, but the picture is reasonably sharp. Fleshtones are dull, but other hues are adequate. The stereo sound is a little harsh, with modest dimensionality. The 91 minute program is not captioned.

Undercover (Simitar, 7363)

A female cop starts enjoying her job too much when she pretends to be a prostitute. Athena Massey stars in the Gregory Hippolyte film, which contains a number of softcore erotic sequences, but enough of a plot to stitch them together if you like that sort of thing. This is the R-rated version, which runs 82 minutes. The picture quality is very good, with smooth, solid hues and a crisp focus. The stereo sound lacks subtlety, but is relatively loud and seemingly energetic. There is no captioning.

Underground (Simitar, 7310)

An extremely murky, pointless film, the acting is so horrible it is funny, but that is about the film's only asset. The oft-used plot, which is printed in its entirety on Simitar's jacket, is about a strip club that is a front for a white slavery operation. Every few minutes of story, however, are separated by lengthy, half-hearted topless dancing sequences. This would probably appeal to fans, except that the picture is so dark and so fuzzy you can't see enough to get excited about. The monophonic sound is flat and listless. The program runs 87 minutes and is not captioned.

The Underneath (Universal, 20445)

Steven Soderbergh directed the fairly common tale of robbery, lust and murder in his unique, elliptical style. Unfolding through flashbacks within flashbacks, Peter Gallagher and Elisabeth Shue star in the film, set in Austin, about an ex-gambler who talks his ex-wife's gangster boyfriend into staging an armored car robbery. Soderbergh's choices keep the viewer concentrating upon the characters and what they are up to, making it much more entertaining than it would have been if the story had been told in a straightforward manner. Soderbergh's methods could be considered overly artistic, but the drama is not important enough to spoil in that manner, so it comes across as fun, instead.

The picture is letterboxed with an aspect ratio of about 2.35:1 and no 16:9 enhancement. Hues are bright and nicely detailed, and fleshtones are accurate. The stereo surround sound is subtly but intricately mixed, with satisfying separation effects, and only the Dolby Digital track has slightly crisper definitions. The 100 minute program can be supported by English, French or Spanish subtitles, and is accompanied by a production essay, a cast-and-director profile section, a demonstration of how much is missing when the film is scanned and cropped, and a theatrical trailer.

Unforgiven (Warner, 12531)

Telling the story of a retired gunfighter tempted by a bounty offered for the murder of a man who harmed a prostitute, Clint Eastwood, who directed and stars, anchors the film firmly in reality and draws his entertainment from the characters. Supported by Gene Hackman, Morgan Freeman, and in a small but key role, Richard Harris, Eastwood has the latitude to explore the fabric of his story in a comprehensive manner, allowing him to teach the viewer about history, about people and about morality through the talents of his cast. And unlike some of his previous movies, the film's action scenes are never stylized or superhuman, yet they still provide enough release of tension to justify the viewer's investment in the characters.

Eastwood loves setting scenes in the darkness or semi-darkness, and the DVD is able to stay close to the original intentions and still convey the action within the scene. The picture is soft, but colors look accurate. The 127 minute movie is presented in letterboxed format on one side, with an aspect ratio of about 2.35:1 and an accommodation for enhanced 16:9 playback, and in cropped format on the other, with the letterboxed image looking a bit sharper than the cropped image. The stereo surround sound is bland, but the Dolby Digital track has greater power and clearer details. The film is also presented in French in standard stereo, and can be supported by English, French or Spanish subtitles. There is background information on three of the cast members and a list of the film's awards.

Union City (Fox Lorber, FLV5047)

Not even the stunt casting of Deborah Harry is enough to rescue the lame 1981 feature. Loosely based on a crime short story from the thirties by Cornell Woolrich, it is set mostly in an apartment building and concerns the lives of several tenants. There is a murder, some infidelity and a lot of aimless talking, but the film is an amalgam of half-formed ideas masquerading as art.

Although hues are deep, the image is dark, and whites look greenish. Other colors are also imperfect, and a bit flat. The transfer rate is decent, but the source material is so murky that artifacting, particularly tiling and the disconnection of objects, is often evident. The picture is presented in full screen format and the framing looks okay. The monophonic sound has a limited range and some background noise, though the music is not significantly distorted. The 87 minute program is not time encoded or captioned, and is accompanied by a good still photo section (the photos have captions) and some filmographies.

Universal Soldier (Artisan, 60474)

Jean-Claude Van Damme and Dolph Lundgren star as Vietnam vets turned cyborgs who are chasing one another across the Southwest. Director Roland Emmerich's talents are in strong evidence, saving on expensive special effects by using models and regular stunts, but maintaining a grand vision of action and destruction. The 1992 film is witty and enjoyably paced, with a great many inventive action sequences and enough of a human plot to justify the carnage.

Hues are just a bit too purplish, and while it makes the flesh-tones look a little pink, other colors are slightly distorted. Whites also look whiter on the LD. The stereo surround sound is bland, though the Dolby Digital track better detailed. The film is presented in letterboxed format only with an aspect ratio of about 2.35:1 and no 16:9 enhancement. The 102 minute feature is closed captioned and is accompanied by optional Spanish subtitles, a production essay, a cast profile, a teaser, a trailer and a good 7 minute 'making of' featurette (Ally Walker makes a stronger impression in the featurette than she does in the film).

Unknown Island (Image, ID5378FWDVD)

The special effects are ridiculous, but the 1948 film, shot in yellow-less Cinecolor, is a gas. Richard Denning and Virginia Grey star as adventurers who journey to an island inhabited by dinosaurs (or large bobbing puppets, depending upon whether you believe your ears or your eyes) and barely escape, some 72 minutes later, with their lives. The tensions among the adventurers provide plenty of drama, and the special effects are so outlandishly archaic they are spellbinding.

Despite the inherent softness and chromatic limitations of the Cinecolor image, it looks terrific, and artifacting is minimal. Overt damage is confined to the reel-change points, though there are some other scattered speckles and scratches but, on the whole, the presentation is satisfying. The monophonic sound is fine and the program is not captioned.

Unsolved Mysteries of World War II (Madacy, DVD99032)
Unsolved Mysteries of World War II: The Riddle of Rudolf Hess / The Strange Death of Celi Raubal / Drugs and the Fuhrer (Madacy, DVD990321)
Unsolved Mysteries of World War II: Hitler's Secret

War / Kill Hitler (Madacy, DVD990322)
Unsolved Mysteries of World War II: Decision at Dunkirk / Stalin's Secret Armies (Madacy, DVD990323)
Unsolved Mysteries of World War II: Hitler's Secret Weapon / Enigma of the Swastika / Himmler's Castle (Madacy, DVD990324)
Unsolved Mysteries of World War II: The Eagle & the Swastika / The Last Days of Hitler (Madacy, DVD990325)

A bunch of bite-sized documentaries have been gathered for the series (the on-screen title is *Unsolved Mysteries of the Second World War*), which is available as a boxed set or as five individual collections. The documentaries, which run 20 to 30 minutes, are fairly entertaining, going into detail on arcane aspects of the European war. The visuals consist entirely of archival footage (there are no interviews with scholars or that sort of thing), which varies in quality but is usually watchable. The programs are narrated and the monophonic sound is adequate. There is no captioning. Each DVD is accompanied by brief text supplements.

The programs tend to pose questions more often than they answer them. *The Riddle of Rudolf Hess* explores Hess' career in the Third Reich and his baffling 1941 plane trip to England (it's pretty clear the authorities knew he was coming), but it remains a fairly superficial account. The murder of a niece who might have been Hitler's main squeeze before Eva Braun is examined in *The Strange Death of Celi Raubal*. Did Adolf himself pull the trigger? Anybody who could have told us is now dead. Hitler's physician and his erratic medical care is discussed in *Drugs and the Fuhrer*, which speculates on the various diseases (gonorrhea? Parkinson's?) he may have had.

A half hour program malappropriately identified on the jacket cover as *Hitler's Secret War*, the film is actually titled just *The Secret War* and provides an excellent overview of the Allied efforts at breaking German codes. While more details of the actual process would have been most welcome, the episode is thorough and enlightening. *Kill Hitler*, which runs 20 minutes, chronicles the numerous assassination attempts on the Fuhrer's life, creating a generalized view of the political climate in Germany and in the German military as it goes along.

Decision at Dunkirk asks why Hitler let the British slip away at Dunkirk and surmises that it had something to do with Hitler's admiration/fear of the British. The 25 minute program gives fairly good coverage of the Blitzkreig and the British retreat, though without maps it can only do so much. *Stalin's Secret Armies* looks at Stalin's habit of lying about his troop strength, something that served him well not only with his enemy, but with his gullible allies as well, getting them to send him more aid than he probably needed.

Although most of *Hitler's Secret Weapon* is about rockets, there are tantalizing snippets about the development of jet planes and about a plan to put something other than explosives in the rockets. It was Madam Blatavansky who was the first to tie together a common symbol for the sun among a number of cultures with a representation of the 'Aryan Race' according to *The Enigma of the Swastika*. The episode looks at the early party maneuvering in pre-War Germany and the popularization of the cult ideas Blatavansky initiated and Hitler adopted. There is also some interesting, early color film of Nazi parades. Each episode runs 25 minutes. A brief but fascinating 13 minute piece concludes the collection, *Himmler's Castle*, about Heinrich Himmler's dreams of establishing the SS as independent nationals, along the lines of the Vatican or something.

On December 11, 1941, Adolf Hitler had it made. He hadn't blown it in Russia yet. Except for that pesky Britain, he had Europe at his feet. And America was distracted by the Japanese. He also had a policy of never declaring war against anybody. He'd just attack them instead. So why, on December 11, did he declare war against America? It was the only time he ever did such a thing, and it brought the focus of American intentions back to the European theater. Everybody knows Hitler was a stupid man, but this was really stupid, like the dog who won't stop barking at the big bear. *The Eagle & The Swastika* examines the fallout from Hitler's declaration and looks at the political shift within America that occurred because of his actions. The 24 minute program never answers the questions it has posed, but it is still fascinating, exploring attitudes and nuances that were forgotten in the rush to get on with the war. The 13 minute *Last Days of Hitler* goes over fairly familiar ground—what actually happened, where the bodies are, etc. It also suggests that Mussolini's fate hung heavily over Hitler as a demonstration of what others would do if he didn't take care of it himself.

The Untold Story (Tai Seng, 45254)

The 95 minute film is a crime procedural set in Macao, about a restaurant owner who murders people he doesn't like and uses their flesh for his pork buns. The police are lazy and take a terribly long time in following up on the clues that lead to his arrest. Apparently, the program is based upon a real incident. There is a lot of humor, not just in the antics of the police officers but in the exaggerated grotesqueness of the crimes. The film turns darker in the end, when a flashback shows the villain murdering small children, but those who thrive on meat grinder-style violence will find that **Untold Story** has a whole banquet of severed flesh and gore to munch on. The film was directed by Danny Lee, who also stars as the leader of the police investigation, with Anthony Wong in an award-winning performance as the killer.

The picture is letterboxed with an aspect ratio of about 1.85:1 and no 16:9 enhancement. Whites look white and fleshtones, though soft, look true. The image is sharp and details are well defined. The film still has a low budget, Hong Kong look to it, but the presentation is workable. The mono sound is fairly weak. The program is available in Cantonese and Mandarin, with optional English subtitles. There are trailers, a cast profile, and two commentary tracks, one by Wong and one by the film's director, Herman Yau, both prompted by Miles Wood. Yau's track has many longish gaps between comments. Wong's track is better at first, but the second half also has longish gaps. Yau talks a bit about the production, the film's background, and how he got Hong Kong to look like Macao. Wong talks about his experiences during the shoot and his acting career, and both contemplate the film's level of violence and its odd shift in sympathies when the killer himself is tortured by the police.

Urban Legend (Columbia TriStar, 03091)

We love murder mysteries, and although movies such as **Scream** and **Urban Legend** are sold as horror films, they're essentially whodunits, on adrenaline. Set on a college campus, the killer (or killers) is using contemporary folklore as a motif for the murders, with good reason, and nobody believes the heroine when she starts to piece together what is happening. On the downside, the film utilizes the same urban legends every other movie about urban legends uses, and we're sure if you really picked apart the plot you'd find a number of illogical occurrences, but the film keeps you guessing, stops you from blinking, and exercises the screaming portion of your vocal chords on several occasions. Who cares if there are a few loose ends along the way?

The film is presented in letterboxed format on one side, with an aspect ratio of about 2.35:1 and an accommodation for enhanced 16:9 playback, and in cropped format on the other side. The color transfer looks fine, with bright, crisp colors and effective details in the shadows, although fleshtones are a little bland. The stereo surround sound and Dolby Digital sound have some enjoyable separation effects, with the Dolby Digital track conveying a bit more dimensionality. The 100 minute program is also available in French in standard stereo and can be supported by English or French subtitles.

In addition to a smart trailer and an extensive cast profile section, there is an excellent collection of behind-the-scenes footage, narrated by the director, Jamie Blanks, including a deleted scene

that would undoubtedly have ended up being almost everyone's favorite moment if it had been left in, even though it diverts slightly from the narrative path. The movie is also accompanied by a commentary track featuring Blanks, screenwriter Silvio Horta, and supporting star Michael Rosenbaum (Jared Leto is top-billed). For Blanks and Horta, it was their first feature film and they have fun talking about the experience. They never get too technical, but they have plenty of stories about the production to relate and they convey a general sense of how they set things up.

The Usual Suspects (PolyGram, 8006302272)

The wonderfully dense crime thriller is accompanied by commentary by director Bryan Singer and screenwriter Christopher McQuarrie on the analog audio track. Singer and McQuarrie provide a standard sort of talk about the movie, discussing what was involved with shooting various sequences and why they were emphasizing the things they emphasized. There is a surprise at the end credit scroll, however, and we assume it is not simply an error—the pair's voices rise in multiple layers to explain the film's secrets, simultaneously drowning out the explanation with a cacophony of other comments. If it is on purpose, it is a nice touch.

The film has many nice touches as well. The attention that has been paid to its cast, which includes Gabriel Byrne, Oscar winner Kevin Spacey and Chazz Palminteri, has sort of spoiled its twists a bit, but the lying flashbacks and other feints can keep a viewer doubting logical intuition on the first run through. The important thing is how well the movie works on its third or fourth viewings, where the bigger curiosities in the plot (there is a very large sum of money in the back of a van for no apparent reason) become harder to wave off. It is at that point that the viewer will really begin to appreciate the flair of the dialogue, the delightful eccentricities in the performances and the gorgeous style with which everything has been put together.

The 1995 production is presented in letterboxed format on one side, with an aspect ratio of about 2.35:1 and no 16:9 enhancement, and in full screen format on the other. The letterboxing crops picture information off the bottom of the screen in comparison to the full screen image, but adds a lot to the sides as well and is generally the preferred framing. The colors are accurate and the image is crisp, enhancing a viewer's concentration. The stereo surround sound is super, with many engaging separation effects. The 108 minute program is accompanied by Spanish subtitles and English closed captioning. There is a theatrical trailer, as well as trailers for a couple other PolyGram releases and a 'promo reel.' There is also a cast profile section.

#

Vacation (see National Lampoon's Vacation)

Vampire Journals (Full Moon, 8001)

Shot in the cavernous Old World buildings of Eastern Europe, it is a fairly talky horror feature, though there are a few good gore sequences. The hero is a member of the undead himself, but he bides his time trying to eliminate others of his kind, and spends most of the movie trying to save a beautiful concert pianist from the main vampire villain. The movie does not rise above the ordinary, but dedicated vampire fans will probably find it engaging.

The picture has a natural grain and is heavy on the shadows, but the image quality is good, with a sharp focus and accurate, though moodily lit and conceptually anemic, fleshtones. The stereo sound is reasonably energetic although the mix is not very sophisticated. Contrary to a misleading jacket notation, the film itself runs 81 minutes. It is accompanied by one of Full Moon's laudable *Video-Zone* 'making of' segments, as well as the usual collection of trailers and merchandise promotions.

Vampires (see John Carpenter's Vampires)

Vampyr (Image, ID4308DSDVD)

Carl Theodor Dreiser's 1932 classic is aged, of course, and so its hazy black-and-white picture and fuzzy monophonic audio track are to be expected—and with the film's mesmerizing, dream-like narrative, a little blur doesn't really hurt—but the German audio track is supported by grotesque, Gothic typescript English subtitles, which are presented in white on huge black bands, leaving the impression that someone had slapped electrical tape across the bottom of the image. Fortunately, dialogue in the 72 minute film is incidental, so the distraction is not constant, but it is annoying. The film, a gloriously dream-like rumination on vampires, was made under strained financial conditions and looks like it has spent a couple hundred years in a coffin. The monophonic sound on the 1932 production was used more for atmosphere than for specific effects, and the dialogue is deliberately (and dreamily) near the point of inaudibility. There is also some digital artifacting in the darker backgrounds.

Upping the ante, or perhaps in apology for the subtitling, Image has rounded out the program with a delightful 26 minute 1934 stop-motion animation short, *The Mascot*, by Ladislas Starewicz. The incredibly complex and meticulous piece depicts a toy puppy who ventures into the city to obtain an orange for his mistress and must hold onto it at a Devil's Ball before he can get it home. The source material is stronger than **Vampyr**. While it is more light-hearted, the short does share some thematic points with Dreyer's film and they make a worthwhile double bill.

Van Beuren Studio (see Cartoons That Time Forgot: From the Van Beuren Studio)

The Vanishing (Image, ID4264FLDVD)

The converging story of a young man haunted by the mysterious disappearance of his girlfriend and the guardedly obsessive behavior of the psychopath who abducted her is set mostly in France and has a jumpy, intercut narrative that works only because the film has a low-budget "artistic" look to support the mood it is trying to create. The ending is obnoxious, but in creating a striking psychological portrait of the two principal characters and depicting some rather unnerving events, the 1988 film overcomes its drawbacks.

The picture is presented in full screen. Fleshtones are fairly accurate coloring, and other hues are somewhat rich and well detailed. The monophonic sound weak, but there is a Dolby Digital mono track that is reasonably strong. The 102 minute film is in French and Dutch, supported by permanent English subtitles that fail to translate several important images of text.

Vaughan, Stevie Ray (see A Tribute to Stevie Ray Vaughan)

Vegas Vacation (Warner, 14906)

We can well imagine that theatrical audiences sat through **Vegas Vacation** stone faced, but the film is the kind of stupid comedy that can seem funnier in the confines of one's home, even in the company of a limited number of viewers who are not feeding laughter to one another. Chevy Chase and Beverly D'Angelo reprise their roles from the other films in the **Vacation** series, as a married couple suffering through adventures of ineptitude. In this installment, Chase's character becomes addicted to gambling while the rest of his family make out somewhat better. We've seen plenty of comedies that aren't funny at all and this is not one of them. It is predictable and does not strive for much, but the humor is steady and the characters have heart. The movie didn't do all that great at the box office, but it probably made a profit on product place-

ments alone. It is littered with them, everything from Marlboro ads to what is essentially a promotional clip for Siegfried and Roy.

The 95 minute program is presented in full screen only, adding more picture information to the bottom but losing some from the sides in comparison to a letterboxed image. The picture looks fine. The stereo surround sound is passable and the Dolby Digital sound is reasonably bright. The 1987 feature also has a French Dolby Digital track and comes with English, French or Spanish subtitles. There is a theatrical trailer, a few cast profiles and some production notes.

Velvet Goldmine (Buena Vista, 17096)

Independent filmmaker Todd Haynes avoids selling out with his exploration of the lives of glam-rock musicians in the early Seventies. Although the film was nominated for an Oscar (for costumes), it never settles into a standard format—even the costumes are somewhat subdued, looking more realistic than what one might expect if it was an over-the-top Hollywood production. The film's structure is fairly similar to *Eddie and the Cruisers*, about a reporter interviewing people (and telling the story in flashback) while trying to locate a former glam-rocker who has dropped out of sight. Specific plot points are sometimes vague and Haynes seems strained at times to just maintain the period atmosphere and dramatic momentum. There are a lot of gay-oriented emotions and gay sex sequences, which will limit the film's appeal with a general viewership, but its elaborate roman à clef is a nice tease and the fact that it never goes Hollywood (though it celebrates certain aspects of Hollywood to no end) is gratifying. A title card at the beginning recommends that you turn the volume to its maximum setting (did the message appear that way in the theaters, too?), but cynics might suggest it is just to compensate for the lack of energy in the music, which is an on-the-money imitation of what many of the actual glam-rock tunes sounded like. One might say that is why the music itself failed so quickly, because the musicians were more interested in posing than in playing.

The presentation is letterboxed with an aspect ratio of about 1.85:1 and no 16:9 enhancement. When bereft of makeup, fleshtones are rather pale, but that seems to be integral to the film's style, and when the movie becomes flamboyant, the color transfer is there to support it. The standard stereo surround sound is fairly similar to the Dolby Digital sound, though there is more detail and a wider tonality on the rear channels of the Dolby Digital track. Music aside, the film's sound mix is not an elaborate effort. The 119 minute program can be supported by optional English subtitles and comes with a green tag trailer that tries very hard to make it look like the normal movie it isn't.

The Vengeance of She (Anchor Bay, DV10687)

A nice looking blonde in a sort of amnesiac trance wanders aboard a yacht on the Riviera where a bunch of Eurotrash characters are having a party. One thing leads to another and eventually they land in Africa, where the heroine starts wandering again, followed by a guy who has become smitten with her even though she doesn't talk much. She is kidnapped and eventually brought to this secret ceremonial place where some other guy needs her to become immortal or something. The plot of the 1967 Hammer Production is rather incoherent, but it does shift gears a number of times, so even though it never amounts to much, it changes just often enough to prevent one's attention from wandering. Much of it was actually shot in the African desert, as well.

The film is nicely letterboxed, with an aspect ratio of about 1.66:1 and no 16:9 enhancement. The color transfer looks fine, with reasonably bright hues, accurate fleshtones, and minimal wear to the source material. The monophonic sound is okay and there is an enjoyable Sixties musical score. The 101 minute program is not captioned. The other side contains a trailer, two TV commercials, and a 24 minute *World of Hammer* episode, focusing on movies about 'lost worlds' and such.

Verdi's Attila (Image, ID4360PUDVD)

Conducted by Ricardo Muti, the opera features Samuel Ramey, Giorgio Zancanaro, Cheryl Studer and Kaludi Kaludov. Musically, it is not one of Verdi's stronger efforts, but the narrative, with everybody trying to kill the barbarian conqueror, makes an appealing video program, and without intermissions the 1991 show runs a brisk 115 minutes. The La Scala sets are impressive and the singing, particularly by Ramey and Zancanaro, is quite good. The picture is a little soft in places, but colors are strong and fleshtones are acceptable. The stereo sound mix is one of the better efforts in the series, with a bit more dimensionality than normal. The program is in Italian with permanent white English subtitles.

Verdi's I Vespri Siciliani (Image, ID4361PUDVD)

A dance interlude that runs more than a half hour is one of the most elaborate to appear in an opera on video, essentially giving the viewer a two-for-one deal in the 211 minute production. Riccardo Muti conducts the elaborate and impressive La Scala production, which features Cheryl Studer, Chris Merritt (who shows particular stamina) and Ferruccio Furlanetto. The singing is very competent and the staging is quite grand, with breathtaking sets and a huge cast. The video direction is fine for the opera, though, as usual, the ballet choreography is massacred by the isolating camera angles.

The picture quality is not the best in the La Scala series. Fleshtones are okay, but the image is soft and there is a mild and sometimes greenish haze around the hair and faces of the cast. The stereo sound is quite strong and the recording is very good, achieving an ideal balance for a live production between the vocals and the orchestra. The single-sided dual-layer program is sung in Italian with permanent white English subtitles.

Vertigo (Universal, 20183)

Purists might quibble in principle with what has been done to the 1958 film's audio track or its transfer from VistaVision to 65mm on the 'restored' presentation of Alfred Hitchcock's masterpiece, but the rich unblemished colors and the glorious stereo surround sound bring greater clarity and feeling to the film's complex but powerful emotions. Indeed, the restoration team of Robert Harris and James Katz can be seen as acting just as the hero in the film acts, trying to dress up and change the movie to turn it into what it used to be. Only they've succeeded, so their tale has a happy ending—the DVD.

The picture is letterboxed, with an aspect ratio of about 1.85:1 and no 16:9 enhancement, adding picture information to the sides of the image and losing nothing on the top or bottom compared to standard home video releases. The 'restored' colors look completely different at times. Grass that was brown on the old versions is green on the new, and grey suits become blue suits. With everything else that was going on in the film, the movie was also an elaborate experiment in color, in which Hitchcock employed ideas about the use of color in films that he had been talking about for years beforehand. Seen accurately, the film's colors are mesmerizing, not only heightening the details of the story and the environment, but playing upon the viewer's psychological response to the characters. A couple reels could not undergo the level of restoration that the rest of the film was given, so there are a few grainier sequences where the colors aren't as strong, but for the most part the film looks wonderful.

The most elaborate sprucing up, however, has been saved for the audio track, which is, technically, very different from the monophonic track that originally accompanied the film. The restoration team recovered the original stereo recordings of Bernard Herrmann's musical score—the movie sometimes goes on for five or ten minutes at a stretch without dialogue, so it uses a lot of music—and in order to use the recordings, they had to duplicate all the film's sound effects anew. Working from Hitchcock's extensive notes and, of course, the original soundtrack, they generally avoided adding sounds that weren't there before, going through instead

to recreate the sounds where the sounds belong. So, the movie has an elaborate stereo surround soundtrack that can engulf one's viewing room, and while its design may or may not be what Hitchcock intended, it gives the movie an operatic aura. The standard stereo surround soundtrack is a little bland, but the Dolby Digital track is lively.

The 128 minute film can be accompanied by English, French or Spanish subtitles ("Si tu me perds, tu sauras que je voulais continuer de t'aimer"). There is also a production essay about the restoration and a cast & crew profile (with a couple of curiosities or errors in Hitchcock's filmography). Along with a commentary track by Harris, Katz and one of the producers of **Vertigo**, Herbert Coleman, there is an excellent retrospective documentary about the film and the restoration, an alternate ending used in some foreign theatrical releases, a couple of trailers and a still archive featuring production designs, storyboards, behind-the-scenes photos and ad artwork.

The still frame archive section is sort of a sampler, and many of the items also appear in the documentary. There are storyboards for a couple sequences, a few set design drawings, and some production stills and advertising materials. The documentary contains some nice behind-the-scenes footage, interviews with several of the artists who worked on the film, including Kim Novak and Barbara Bel Geddes, and provides the viewer with a decent overview of the film's production and its artistry. The film's original theatrical trailer and the trailer for the restoration are also included.

Harris and Katz provide reams of interesting technical information about the condition of the source material and what they had to do to repair it, and then coax equally interesting tales from Coleman about how the film was created and what it was like working with Hitchcock and the other artists involved in the production. The commentary track also features occasional inserts from other speakers, who talk specifically about an aspect of the film they are most familiar with. Here and there the talk gets sidetracked or redundant, but overall it is informative and justifies, on a scene-by-scene basis, the effort Harris and Katz went through to restore the film. One other interesting revelation—Coleman confirms that very shortly before the film's premiere, Hitchcock tried to take out Novak's flashback sequence. Although it did no harm to James Stewart's character, it was a foolish move because it robbed Novak's character of a justification for her emotions, but fortunately Hitchcock backed down and the sequence was reinserted—though according to Harris and Katz, it is a couple generations more removed from the source than the rest of the footage.

The plot of **Vertigo** is so tentative and so in contrast to the typical romantic mystery that had any movie director less talented than Hitchcock tried to make it, it would have crumbled immediately. Most of the movie is a ghost story, though there is nothing in it that is unreal. What makes the film stand out from Hitchcock's other works—or from the other works of almost all other movie directors, for that matter—is how palpable the desires of Novak's character and Stewart's character become. As you follow the logic of Stewart's actions, you are drawn into his perversion. It is a clear mapping not of one emotional state, but of an entire emotional process, and there is just enough bait of a crime thriller to guide the viewer into the trap.

The Very Best of the Bee Gees: Live! One for All (MPI, DVD9802)

The three Bee Gees reunite for a 1990 concert in Australia. During the course of the 102 minute performance they sing most (27) of their greatest hits. Oddly, they stand rather far apart from one another and only share a single microphone on a couple numbers, but the concert is a basic, exciting production by one of the world's most popular bands, and the video presentation is energetic and involving. The live recording is not as pure as their studio recordings and their voices are a little older (they aren't as pretty as they used to be, either), but the gist of the songs are the same. The stage lighting contains many strongly colored shadings, but even when the colors are so strong they create a haze around the singers, the image is crisp and solid. The colors are accurate and the picture is smooth. The stereo surround sound is fine, with detailed separations and plenty of power but, contrary to the jacket logo, there is no Dolby Digital track. An album discography and a generalized but informative 'timeline' have also been included. There is no captioning.

VH1: Divas Live (Sony, EVD50175)

Can you imagine Celine Dion being anti-climactic? She is when she comes on after Aretha Franklin and Mariah Carey perform a duet of *Chain of Fools*. Such are the pleasures of the marvelous 80 minute concert program, and that's only the half of it. Gloria Estefan, Shania Twain and Carole King are also on hand, and they all join together at the end for *Natural Woman*, which makes even *Chain of Fools* seem like an intro. Each singer does a number or two solo, but it is the duets and multi-star performances that make the show so unique and unblinkably exciting. It's not just that they're there, doing it. Their performances are outstanding, with each giving her all in the company of the others.

The DVD's picture and sound comply with the performances. The image is sharp and colors are vivid. The stereo surround sound and Dolby Digital sound have an immediate and encompassing resonance, and crisp tones. The program can be supported by English, French or Spanish subtitles ("Renverse le rythme. J'adore la percussion").

Victory (Warner, 708)

John Huston's 1981 tale about Allied POWs facing Germans in a soccer match stars Sylvester Stallone and Michael Caine, along with Pelé. The narrative is structured to build toward an escape that doesn't occur and the ending, where the heroes blend into a crowd of Parisians, is somewhat dissatisfying and farfetched, but if you know what to expect then the film is a reasonably entertaining exercise combining two genres (POW films and sports) that aren't often blended.

The picture is letterboxed on one side, with an aspect ratio of about 2.35:1 and an accommodation for enhanced 16:9 playback, and is in cropped format on the other side, though the cropping tends to look off-balance and awkward. The picture transfer is very good, with crisp hues and accurate fleshtones. The stereo soundtrack is fine, though it is only Bill Conti's exceptional musical score that is given much dimensionality, and even that is limited. The 116 minute film is also available in French in mono and comes with English, French or Spanish subtitles, along with some production notes (including backgrounds on a number of the soccer players in the film), a cast profile section and an original theatrical trailer.

Video Essentials (Image, ID3944ISFDVD)

A guide for fine-tuning your audio-video system, the less interested you are in the DVD, the more likely you will have something to gain from using it. If you've never touched the controls for your TV's 'picture,' 'hue,' 'brightness,' etc., then following the step-by-step voiceover instructions to the proper adjustments will make you think you have purchased a new TV. Even if you have fiddled with the controls in the past, there is no way, unless you do it professionally or have used **Video Standard**, that you could have gotten it right, and however decent your picture looks now, it is going to look even better. Is that important? Of course it is! As DVDs prove on a daily basis, the better a movie looks the more enjoyable it becomes, no matter what the movie is.

The process for adjusting one's monitor involves a lot of going back and forth because every time one setting is changed, it affects the others, but the program is methodical and patient, and provides images from the real world at its conclusion so you can see if your adjustments are valid. At the end there are a number of patterns that are presented without explanation. Also included in the

pattern section is a still frame, diagrammed explanation of how a color television works and definitive patterns for determining 1.66:1, 1.78:1 and 1.85:1 aspect ratios in both standard playback and 16:9 enhanced playback. The audio section does not provide tests for determining the dynamic range of one's speakers or anything like that, but it is useful for making sure that the basic hook up and balances are correct, whether one has a simple stereo system, a Dolby surround system or Dolby Digital. The 'pink noise' used for the tests is held to a sensible volume and is not annoying.

If you follow the program the way they have designed it, then the DVD works fine, but if you try to set out on your own, you'll find the dictatorial chapter controls of the DVD system highly frustrating. It has layers of chapters for the different sections and timed sequences or title segments for the still frames. If you follow the program along, it's easy, but God forbid you should try to go back a chapter to check on something once you've passed it. You practically have to start the whole thing over. The program works, though, and it is worth the effort. The DVD comes with Dolby Digital surround sound, Spanish standard surround sound, Japanese standard surround sound and English or Spanish subtitles.

Videodrome (Universal, 20387)

James Woods stars as the operator of a small cable channel who gets hooked on bizarre videos that cause hallucinations. Partially allegorical, though about what we're still not sure, the 1983 film will be too weird for some viewers and pointless for others, but it seems to strike a careful balance between emotion and philosophy, and is to be celebrated for asking questions instead of answering them.

The picture is letterboxed with an aspect ratio of about 1.85:1 and no 16:9 enhancement. The colors look good, fleshtones are fine and the image is sharp. The source material has one or two stray markings, but on the whole the image is quite pleasing. The monophonic sound is also fairly strong, though details on the upper end aren't very crisp. The 89 minute film is also available in French and comes with English or Spanish subtitles ("La pantalla de T.V. es la retina del ojo de la mente"). There is a wonderful, animated punk-style theatrical trailer (Deborah Harry co-stars), some good production notes and a cast profile section.

Vigilante (Anchor Bay, DV10493)

It is instructive post-*Jackie Brown* to return to **Vigilante** and see Robert Forster in a typical career role. He seems to sleepwalk through the standard stuff—but then, the 1982 movie does, too—and when he's called upon to deliver a more complicated set of emotions, such as in the courtroom scene after the judge has given the punk who killed his character's child a suspended sentence, he nails it every time.

The image is letterboxed with an aspect ratio of about 2.35:1 and no 16:9 enhancement. The picture is radically grainy but effectively detailed. Colors are also bright and accurate. The standard stereo track is a bit weak, but the Dolby Digital track has added strength and better defined separations. A French language track has been included, in standard stereo. There is also a commentary track, a jovial reminiscence from director William Lustig, Forster, Fred Williamson and Frank Pesce—and again, Forster's new found stardom makes the talk all the more precious. There is an extensive collection of domestic and foreign trailers, and a still photo montage. There is no captioning.

An inelegant and generally unappealing *Death Wish* variation, the fragmented narrative has two entwined plots. In one, Forster is sent to jail for a courtroom outburst when the man who murdered his child and assaulted his wife is let off with a suspended sentence. In the other, Williamson runs a vigilante group that is working its way up the org chart of a drug ring. Shot in New York, the film has a dank, urban look. The editing lacks the kind of rhythm that would energize a viewer's adrenaline, and so the violence seems crude, the chase scenes seem stretched out and the dramatic sequences seem dull or, in the case of the prison scenes, silly.

The commentary track offers proof that even the dopiest films have somebody who believes in them. Williamson, of course, is an established junk film director himself, and so his reflections on Lustig's filmmaking skills are worthwhile. The group has a lot of fun joking about the production, but they also provide a substantial number of tips and stories about making inexpensive action movies.

The Viking Queen (Anchor Bay, DV10688)

Don Murray is a Roman Governor in the 1967 Hammer production who falls in love with a local princess while trying to quell a rebellion among the Druids in Britain. Somebody named Carita co-stars, and if you can believe that she's a charismatic ruler capable of making those hard administrative choices, then you're probably wondering why Don Murray didn't play Roman Governors more often. Anyway, the battle sequences are legitimately engaging, the drama has decent momentum and, for those of you uninterested in dramatic momentum, there's a lot of kind of naked women running around.

The picture is letterboxed with an aspect ratio of about 1.85:1 and no 16:9 enhancement. The color transfer looks great, with accurate, crisp fleshtones and bright hues. Damage seems minimal and artifacting flaws are limited, though some sequences look a little jerky. The monophonic sound is okay, but there is some distortion on the upper end and the audio is best kept at a modest volume. There is no captioning.

The 91 minute film is presented on one side of the platter. The other side contains a trailer and a 24 minute *World of Hammer* episode, focusing on movies about 'lost worlds' and such.

Village of the Damned (Universal, 20444)

We continue to enjoy the John Carpenter feature every time we put it on. We think it is because of the film's multiple-part structure—it is actually kind of different stories put back-to-back, about the conception of the kids, the pregnancies, the birth and then the power struggle with them. The film keeps mutating, coming up with one set of fascinating ideas and then going on to another before you can pin it down. Christopher Reeve stars with Kirstie Alley as doctors investigating a phenomenon involving multiple simultaneous births in a small California town. The story is set across a decade and would be easy to pick apart, but such activity would divert attention from the film's chief asset, its general mood and atmosphere, which improves on multiple viewings.

The picture is letterboxed with an aspect ratio of about 2.35:1 and an accommodation for enhanced 16:9 playback. Colors are crisply defined. Fleshtones look a little pinkish on the LD and a little pale on the DVD, with the ideal point seemingly somewhere between the two, but for the most part the DVD's hues are satisfying and the image is sharp. The stereo surround sound and Dolby Digital sound have some good surround effects and an eerie atmosphere. The film is also available in French in standard stereo and can be supported by English or Spanish subtitles. There are some very good production notes, a cast-and-director profile section and a trailer.

Vincent: The Junkie Chronicles (see Short Cinema Journal 1:2 Issue: Dreams)

Virtual Desire (Image, ID5630FMDVD)

The softcore erotic film pretends to be a mystery, but is so unmysterious it fools nobody. When the wife of a retired baseball player is murdered, it is discovered that the man had been having extra-marital affairs—gobs of them—with gorgeous anonymous women he meets through a few minutes' typing on the Internet. As if. The film tries to pretend that one of these women is the murderess, but it also presents the killer in so obvious a manner that the later red herrings are a waste of time. Anyway, the film is really an excuse to present the extramarital affairs in elongated flashbacks,

with the erotic sequences taking up the bulk of the movie's 94 minute running time. The acting is terrible.

The picture is often quite grainy and even well lit scenes are a little soft, with bland fleshtones. The stereo sound is uneventful and the 94 minute program is not captioned.

Virtual Encounters (Full Moon, 8003)

The 84 minute film is a softcore erotic exercise with barely a token plot, about an uptight woman who relaxes her inhibitions after visiting a futuristic virtual reality service. The elaborate, dialog-free erotic interludes, presented as the virtual reality sequences but staged like any other erotic video program with maybe a bit more pantomime, take up most of the show. The picture is often hazy or grainy. Colors are light but workable and the stereo sound is reasonably strong. Trailers for the film and four other Full Moon titles are also included.

Virus (Universal, 20431); DTS (Universal, 20642)

There are bad movies and then there are very stupid but enjoyable movies and this 1999 feature falls comfortably into the second category. Jamie Lee Curtis, Donald Sutherland and William Baldwin star in the monster thriller, about an alien intelligence that penetrates the computers of a ship and starts using the machine shop to build doodads that are part stray components and part human. It wants to conquer the world, and the heroes just want to get off the boat without becoming talking toaster ovens. There is almost nothing that is original about it (for redundancy, see **Deep Rising** or contact your local Borg recruiting office), but the special effects are elaborate, the stars, even when they over act, are appealing, and the required excitements keep grinding away for 99 minutes (actually 90 minutes, there is a very long end credit scroll). This is what movies were meant to do.

The entertainment is enhanced by the nice picture and sound transfer. The Dolby Digital track has many well-defined separation effects and keeps pulling you back to the action when your attention starts to wander. Even the standard stereo surround soundtrack is lively. The picture is in letterboxed format only, with an aspect ratio of about 2.35:1 and an accommodation for enhanced 16:9 playback. The color transfer looks fine, with crisp hues and accurate fleshtones. The program has an alternate French audio track, in standard stereo, optional English subtitles, production notes, a cast-and-director profile section, and a trailer.

There is no indication of it on the jacket cover, but there is also a good, decent-sized documentary about creating the special effects, a standard 'making of' featurette (which repeats a lot of the material from the other documentary), and a commentary channel by the director, John Bruno, secondary cast members, Marshall Bell and Sherman Augustus, and composer Joel McNeely (who has to be prompted, but has many insightful things to say about music when he's asked the right questions). They talk about the logistics of the shoot (a lot of it was done on a real boat in Virginia, with backgrounds hidden by CGI fog), about the special effects, and jovial anecdotes about the production (apparently practically everyone lost his or her temper at one point or another). It is not a comprehensive talk, but it avoids addressing the script's weaknesses—all of the best dialogue lines, incidentally, were adlibs—and explores the complex experience of making an elaborate special effects feature with enthusiasm. We recommend watching the documentaries first, so you are familiar with the behind-the-scenes personnel the commentators are referencing.

The DTS version has no special features and no captioning, though the DTS audio does not seem significantly stronger than the Dolby Digital track on the standard release. There may be some stronger separation definitions, but the differences are very minor. The frame transfer rate is more likely to stay in the upper range, while on the standard release it swings between the upper and mid range, but otherwise the picture transfer is identical, as well.

Vision Quest (Warner, 11459)

Matthew Modine stars in a serious drama about a high school wrestler trying to reach his weight class to take on a tough opponent. The film has had a fanatical following on home video because Madonna appears in it for about two minutes, singing a song in a tavern. Basically, though, if you can relate to high school wrestling, you'll probably like it, and if you can't, you won't. Linda Fiorentino co-stars in the 1985 feature, which was shot in Spokane, WA.

The picture is presented in full screen format, but the framing seems workable. Fleshtones are a little bland, but, on the whole, the image looks decent, with solid, crisp and reasonably fresh-looking hues. There is a stereo surround soundtrack, but little more than the music and a few atmospheric effects have much dimensionality. The 107 minute program is adequately closed captioned.

Viva Las Vegas (MGM, 906615)

Elvis Presley movies comprise some of the most frustrating attempts at entertainment in existence. You want to like them, but most are so poorly written and edited that nothing happens between the songs. You wear yourself out, emotionally, chasing what scraps of narrative there are. **Viva Las Vegas** is presented on one side in letterboxed format, with an aspect ratio of about 2.35:1 and an accommodation for enhanced 16:9 playback, and in cropped format on the other side, but it is the letterboxing that preserves the only two assets that make the film worthwhile, the car race during the last fifteen minutes that saves the movie, and the Ann-Margret dance numbers, which make it worth saving. When you see the car race cropped, it is no different than any gratuitous cut-and-paste effort, with barely discernible continuity and confused suspense. With the full widescreen image, however, the sequence is terrific, especially on a larger monitor. The track rises and dips and your stomach goes right with it. The placement of the cars is easy to keep track of, and the scene, unlike most of the film, is completely involving. The dance scenes are not as harmed when the picture is cropped, but the numbers are still much more satisfying when all the chorus dancers can be viewed moving in unison behind the stars. The colors are vivid, the image is crisp and the picture is intoxicating. The blown up cropped image is a little softer and the cropping is disorienting. The monophonic sound seems to be missing its high end and is somewhat bland. The 1963 film runs 86 minutes and is also available with French dialogue (the singing is in English), can be supported by English, French or Spanish subtitles and is accompanied by a theatrical trailer.

Vivaldi: The Four Seasons (Sony, SVD46380)

Herbert von Karajan himself sits down for one of the keyboards on the *Herbert von Karajan His Legacy for Home Video Series* program from October, 1987, with the Berlin Philharmonic and Anne-Sophie Mutter. Mutter brings a distinctive tone to her solo passages, which are the highlight of the program and are accompanied by beautifully framed close-ups of her and her violin, but on the whole the 45 minute work lacks the precision of the best renditions of the piece, as if Karajan was stretching himself a little too thin by playing and conducting at the same time, compromising his control over the flow of the music.

The picture looks as good at times, but is more prone to a softer image and is less intensely lit. The program uses telephoto lenses with small focus ranges, so the backgrounds are sometimes blurry or grainy, and even though the transfer rates is consistently high, once in a while there is a bit of a quiver. The Dolby Digital 5.1 audio track is significantly better than the standard stereo track, with a sweeter, better-detailed sound.

Vive L'Amour (Fox Lorber, FLV5016)

A Chinese film that has been given a French title, the 1996 feature, directed by Tsai Ming-Liang, has very little dialog—in fact it runs for 20 minutes before the first conversational subtitle appears—and tells its story with images, often images in which very little occurs.

The narrative is basically about three people who have access to an empty apartment. Two of them, a real estate agent and a street vendor, use one of the bedrooms for a couple of one night stands. The third, another young man, sneaks in and out, spying on the couple and using the place to crash when the others aren't around. The film has some fine erotic sequences and works as sort of an intriguing, anti-*Jules and Jim*, but there is also quite a bit of footage that seems pedestrian—literally, since it consists of inartistic shots showing the characters walking here or there to no specific purpose—and it often feels like a half hour's worth of narrative has been stretched to a 118 minutes for no apparent purpose.

The picture quality is passable, though the source material has the limited contrasts and slightly yellowed fleshtones one associates with low budget overseas productions. The picture is letterboxed with an aspect ratio of about 1.75:1 with no 16:9 enhancement. The monophonic sound is passable and the film is in Mandarin with permanent English subtitles. Filmographies for the director and cast are also included.

Vivre Sa Vie (see **My Life to Live (Vivre Sa Vie)**)

Volcano (Fox, 4110402)

Eschewing such bothersome details as character and drama, the disaster film in which Los Angeles gets a very nasty geological zit, jumps pretty much right into the special effects stuff and never lets up. It is a horrendously expensive looking film and a pretty silly one, but for DVD playback one can accommodate, and indeed embrace, such indiscretions.

The 1997 feature is in letterboxed format only, with an aspect ratio of about 2.35:1 and an accommodation for enhanced 16:9 playback. The picture is sharp, fleshtones are rich and the image is very strong, even in the many difficult night shots illuminated by the molten cityscape. The stereo surround sound is super and there is a Dolby Digital track that is even better, with tones that are so much sharper and better detailed that the standard track is sleepy in comparison. There are many surround effects whenever things start dropping or hissing, and on the Dolby Digital track there is a nice detachment to Alan Silvestri's essential musical score. The 103 minute program also has a French audio track in standard stereo, optional English or Spanish subtitles, a trailer and a cast profile section. The menu, appearing as a seismograph display, is also amusing.

Tommy Lee Jones stars as the emergency services guy who saves the day and Anne Heche co-stars as a lava expert who helps.

Voluptuous Vixens (Image, ID3991PLDVD)

The 54 minute Playboy program features Russ Meyer, who talks about his career and preferences in the female form, between modeling sequences and skits that feature women who conform to Meyer's ideal. The quality of the picture varies from sequence to sequence. In some, bright colors are slightly fuzzy or there is a mild haze that goes beyond the intended mood-setting gauze, while others look fairly sharp. The colors are generally strong and fleshtones are accurate. The usual generic jazz scoring has a forceful presence on the stereo soundtrack.

Voodoo (Simitar, 7327)

Corey Feldman and Jack Nance star in an entertaining thriller about a voodoo cult disguised as a college fraternity. Feldman is the new transfer student who needs a place to stay, just as the leader needs one more victim to turn himself immortal. The show is reasonably exciting and the performances are enjoyable.

The picture looks fine, with as accurate colors as the cinematography will allow and a sharp focus. The Ultra-Stereo surround sound is very good, with crisp, vivid tones and some nice separation effects. The film runs 91 minutes and is not captioned.

W

Wacky Babies & Tender Times (Simitar, 7528)

The two hour-long wildlife documentaries by Marty Stouffer, whose own formative years were the subject of **Wild America**, are compilation programs of baby animal footage, but they are dissimilar in format. *Tender Times*, the better of the two, is a straightforward documentary about how young animals acquire the skills they will need as adults, and how, with the help of their parents, they survive (or fail to survive) the dangers of the wilderness. *Wacky Babies* gives lip service to these points with a straight narration, but also has lame, **Homeward Bound**-style 'voices' for the animals as they get into fixes (a young fox's nose is grabbed by a snapping turtle, in one of the film's most memorable sequences) and otherwise display uncertain judgment toward the world around them.

The picture quality is okay. Colors are not vivid, but they are functional and the source material seems to be in reasonably good shape. The monophonic sound is fine and the films are not captioned.

Wag the Dog (New Line, N4658)

Made on the fly while they were waiting to do **Sphere**, Barry Levinson's political satire, **Wag the Dog**, starring Dustin Hoffman, ended up doing better business than either **Sphere** or the film that was supposed to be a blockbuster political satire, **Primary Colors**. As Levinson mentions on the audio commentary, it is easy to find fault with political satire because such satire has to exaggerate things, but it cannot exaggerate things too much. Shot in 29 days (as it proudly claims in the credit scroll), the film is a good example of an entertainment that should be enjoyed for what it has to offer instead of being criticized for what it doesn't achieve. Although there are strong and apparently purely coincidental similarities to Bill Clinton's infidelity problems (the fictional president in the film is viewed in a photo embracing a young woman wearing a beret whom he has seduced in a private room next to the Oval Office), the real target seems to be the Ronald Reagan administration and its talent for tackling a crisis with a symbolic distraction. Robert De Niro co-stars but fails to deliver a performance that comes even close to the joy Hoffman extracts from his part. Nor can the film hold a candle to *Tanner '88* when it comes to humor, audacity or an understanding of the American political process. None of that matters. It is still a daring piece of work, particularly for major filmmakers to have concocted and executed, and its narrative rides a careful edge of absurdity, which exposes genuine discrepancies created by the conflict between democracy and media, without alienating the viewer. It is a fun movie that takes a devilish delight in cutting those in power down to size.

Levinson provides a running commentary with extended inserts from Hoffman. It is a measure of the film's quality that Hoffman's contribution is more thoughtful and informative than his talk on **Sphere**. He seems to take the task very seriously and really tries to teach or share his knowledge about acting and about the film's meanings. Levinson's talk is worthwhile, too. He covers all aspects of the production and also has a lot to say about what the film was trying to accomplish.

There is also an interesting five minute interview with William H. Macy, who has a small part in the film and talks about the longstanding friendship he has had with the film's screenwriter, David Mamet. A half-hour documentary about political films is presented, as well. It includes interviews with filmmakers who have been involved with political films in the past, such as Budd Schulberg and John Frankenheimer, as well as Tom Brokaw, Dee Dee Myers and others. The documentary is an earnest survey of how Ameri-can politics are interpreted in both fiction and non-fiction films, but it is rarely insightful and Macy's little talk about Mamet is far more eye-opening. There is also an even weaker text essay about political films, a trailer, and cast & crew profiles.

The film is presented in letterboxed format on one side, with an aspect ratio of about 1.85:1 and an accommodation for enhanced 16:9 playback, and in full screen format on the other side. We prefer the full screen image, which delivers the movie's many video sequences without masking off the top and bottom of the image, and even has a little more picture information on the side. The color transfer looks fine and the picture is sharp. The stereo surround sound and Dolby Digital sound are adequate, though there isn't much of a difference between the two. The 96 minute film does not have an elaborate sound mix. The movies is also available in French in Dolby Digital and can be supported by English or French subtitles ("Vous allez incorporer le chaton plus tard?").

Wages of Fear (Criterion, WAG050)

Henri-Georges Clouzot's compelling adventure film is about transporting a cargo of prickly dynamite through a jungle on bad roads in a broken down truck (we're surprised nobody gets the hiccups). The ending is a little too existential for us Americans, but otherwise the story is highly accessible and captivating. Yves Montand stars in the 1953 feature.

The presentation runs 148 minutes and contains scenes that were not in the original American theatrical presentation. The black-and-white source material is not pristine, but there are no severe flaws. The image is reasonably sharp, and contrasts are pure. The monophonic sound is a little subdued but clean. The film is in French and can be accompanied by optional English subtitles, although these do not support the brief English language sequences.

Waking Ned Devine (Fox, 4110385)

A dead person is discovered holding a winning lottery ticket in the charming 1998 feature. Set in a small and remote Irish town, the emphasis is upon the personalities of the villagers, but the narrative careens forward with utmost logic and so while you take delight in the company of the characters, you also can't wait to see what will happen to them next. The one criticism that could be leveled against it is that the whole movie is too calculated and sweet, but that is a common complaint about many classics. Ian Bannen is top-billed.

The film is in letterboxed format only, with an aspect ratio of about 2.35:1 and no 16:9 enhancement. The image is crisp and the lovely green hills are deeply and accurately hued. The stereo surround sound carries a nice dimensionality for the pleasingly Irish musical score and the dialogue is usually easy for American ears to follow. The 91 minute program has optional English and Spanish subtitles, a cast-and-director profile section and a trailer.

A Walk in the Sun (Madacy, DVD99029)

We'd like to report that Lewis Milestone's superb portrait of World War II is highly satisfying, but the transfer is so erratic we could not bring ourselves to recommend it for more than a reference to the film's narrative. The copy we viewed locked in several sequences, dropped the audio track, and displayed other flaws suggesting some sort of contaminants in the pressing. When it played clearly, the monophonic sound is relatively strong, although it has a clipped reverberation that some viewers may find distracting. The opening night scenes are very murky. The subsequent daylight scenes have well-defined contrasts, but the image wobbles in and out of focus. The source material is littered with minor scratches and speckles, and there are a few bigger splices, as well. Dana Andrews, Richard Conte, Lloyd Bridges and others star in the 1946 film, about an American platoon in Italy, crossing the countryside and then taking a farmhouse from some Germans. The 117 minute feature is not captioned.

Walkabout (Criterion, WAL120)

The picture transfer is outstanding on Nicolas Roeg's unforgettable adventure classic. Although the film was made in 1971, the image is spotless and the colors are incredibly fresh. The film's cinematography is exceptional and the disc upholds the purity and beauty of the images in shot after shot. The picture is letterboxed with an aspect ratio of about 1.77:1 without 16:9 enhancement. The monophonic sound has a bit more background noise than one is accustomed to on a Hollywood feature, but is in fine shape. The film runs 100 minutes and is the unedited 'director's cut,' accompanied by two trailers and optional English subtitling. There is also a commentary track, mixing reminiscences from Roeg and from the film's star, Jenny Agutter.

A teenage girl (Agutter) and her much younger brother (who turns out to have been played by Roeg's son) are abandoned in the Australian outback. They are saved by a young Aborigine, played by David Gumpilil, and wander back to civilization, as the relationship between the girl and the Aborigine leads to a tragedy. Many of the motifs and ideas that were developed in Roeg's later films are hinted at or experimented with in **Walkabout**, particularly those dealing with the questionable value of civilization, the uncertainty of time and speculation about uneasy links between memory and prophecy. The film's design is so compelling that the movie can get away with long passages of no or insignificant dialogue (the child talking to himself). The cinematography has a hand in bringing viewers back for multiple viewings, but beyond the story and the scenery, it is Roeg's choices in staging the scenes and in blending emotional revelations with his observations of the environment that gives the movie its depth. The characters are so isolated and so real you feel as if you are with them, and so the slightest mummers of emotional conflict, or of understanding, are instantly communicated.

Roeg and Agutter speak—separately—on one of the analog channels. Roeg uses a frustrating verbal shorthand, as if you'd been hanging out with him for so long that you were supposed to immediately understand his references and follow his train of thought. When something he says is understandable it is usually fairly interesting, and even when he's being incoherent, there are sudden flashes of insight that lead you to believe he's worth listening to. He talks about the production logistics, about some of the things he wanted to capture in the film and some more general ideas about what movies are supposed to accomplish. The movie has many subjects but one is how thin the layer of modern life is that shelters us from a subsistence lifestyle. Roeg has a particularly confused story about Gumpilil at Cannes, but the point he makes at its conclusion is clear and concise (Roeg often edits his films the same way, seeming to present random ideas, but somehow coalescing into an important concept). Gumpilil instinctively knew which utensils to use at a fancy dinner, simply by following the logic of the arrangement, something a French reporter would have substantially more difficulty in doing, trying to follow the logic of natural signs to find food in the wild.

Agutter also speaks about the story's meanings, but spends most of her time providing a more detailed and personal reminiscence of the shoot, including what it was like working with Roeg and with Gumpilil. She was young, and in many ways her experiences on the shoot mirrored her character's formative experiences in the film. Thus, listening to her talk is, emotionally, almost like listening to the film's heroine, now 25 years older, remember the adventure.

The Wall That Heals (Simitar, 7243)

The 50 minute documentary is about the Vietnam Veterans Memorial. Narrated by Lou Gossett, Jr., the program includes interviews with many government officials, including the former president, George Bush, and presents a thumbnail sketch of the war and the 'mood at home,' along with a history of the memorial's creation and a look at how it is utilized today. There is nothing very dynamic about the program's construction, but the reminiscences of those whose loved ones are named on the Wall are often moving. The picture and sound are okay, and the program is accompanied by a biographical sketch of Gossett that is riddled with typos. The DVD contains DVD-ROM programming as well, including a searchable listing of the names on the memorial.

Waltz of the Toreadors (Image, ID4535JFDVD)

Peter Sellers stars as a retired general, living in a mansion, who is still chasing after every available woman he meets, much to the consternation of his bed-ridden wife. Based upon a play by Jean Anouilh, the narrative has a number of structural similarities to *Smiles of a Summer Night* and holds the same sort of moral. The 1962 film, directed by John Guillermin, is at times a farce and at times a melancholy portrait of aging's irreversibility. Sellers often acts like he is some other character in costume, however, and the repetitiveness of the conflicts is tiresome. Except to fans who like anything that came out of Britain in the Sixties, the film's appeal will be limited.

Some reels are more colorful than others, but even at its most chromatic, hues on the DVD look somewhat dull. The image is sharp, but fleshtones are pale. The picture is letterboxed with an aspect ratio of about 1.75:1 and no 16:9 enhancement. The monophonic sound is adequate. There is no captioning.

Wanted X-rated (DaViD, D0559)

Several amusing erotic skits tied to mix-ups in a singles advertising service provide a cohesive narrative. Shot on film, the image is somewhat grainy and hues are a little bland. The monophonic sound is passable. The program runs 87 minutes and features Misty Rain, Olivia, Shelby Stevens, Tera Hart, Vanessa Chase and Debi Diamond.

The War (Universal, 20533)

A nostalgic depiction of life in rural Mississippi in the early Seventies, Jon Avnet directed the 1994 feature, which stars Kevin Costner, though Elijah Wood is top billed. Costner is a Vietnam vet trying to fit back into civilian life, but the emphasis of the movie is on his kids, who are coping with a group of bullies and generally trying to entertain themselves without money. The film is not bad, but it never really amounts to much and is, at best, a collection of a few well-staged nostalgic and dramatic incidents. It has a few memorable sequences (particularly a climactic rescue in a water tower), but its orientation toward the kids limits the scope of its drama.

The presentation is letterboxed, with an aspect ratio of about 1.85:1 and an accommodation for enhanced 16:9 playback. The letterboxing on the DVD adds a bit more picture information on the sides in comparison to the letterboxed LD. The LD tends to have a slightly pinker image, with slightly brighter colors. In some scenes, the image on the LD is preferable and fleshtones on the DVD are a bit drained, while in others, the fleshtones on the LD look too pink and the DVD looks better. The image on the DVD is sharp and free of haze. The stereo surround sound is okay, and there is a Dolby Digital track that is brighter and more dimensional. The 126 minute feature also has a French Dolby Digital track, optional English captioning, a trailer, production notes and a cast-and-director profile section.

The War of the Worlds (Paramount, 053037)

Gene Barry, who has never been much of an actor but has always known how to be a star, plays the dashing scientist/witness in producer George Pal's 1952 adaptation of H.G. Wells' classic. Set in the Fifties, but before television, the narrative is true to its source and is very effective at building up tension while stripping away the assumptions of civilization. The 85 minute film's pace is super, never bogging down in the talk that padded many other Fifties science fiction adventures, and there are a couple sequences that remain frightening to this day. Pal's special effects work is also very pleasing.

The picture is presented in full screen format. Fleshtones are rich, the Martian spaceships are glossy, and the backgrounds are vivid. The colors are smooth and the image is sharp. The DVD retains the film's original mono track (not the remastered stereo track that was on the LD), which is adequately presented. There is also a French mono track, English closed captioning and an engaging Fifties trailer.

The War Room (Trimark, VM6916D)

We were dying to see the documentary, but when Trimark Home Video finally released it on DVD we were so sick of the whole subject we wanted nothing to do with it. But now, with whiffs of Iowa and New Hampshire in the air again, we started to get interested, and so we finally put on the feature.

Although the 1993 D.A. Pennebaker documentary about the 1992 election campaign (George Bush vs. Bill Clinton) received an Oscar nomination, it did not deserve it. It follows a tradition that began with Theodore White's groundbreaking book of reporting, *The Making of the President 1960*, in which he was allowed to hover behind the scenes during the campaign and then write, after everything was over, about the strategies each side employed to best the other side. Such stories are so common now after elections are done that one pictures small, smoke filled rooms in which one corner is jammed from floor to ceiling with people holding notepads and tape recorders. Pennebaker was allowed, in 1992, to bring in his camera to watch the Clinton campaign in action. In theory, he recorded their lightning responses to media fires and their daily manipulation of the 'lead' story of the campaign, but in practice, he only caught these things glancingly. Without the context of print reporting, the documentary would be mystifyingly oblique, and that is how it will seem in the future, when viewers are no longer familiar with the saga of Gennifer Flowers and what Ross Perot thought he was doing. What it does offer is a sampling of the atmosphere in Clinton's campaign headquarters (the film covers ten months in 96 minutes, so it never stays too long on anything) and a visual record that supports (but does not illuminate) what print journalists had written, about the clarity of purpose with which the campaign staff saw and approached each issue and dilemma.

The documentary's footage changes in quality from one shot to the next. Most of the time colors are quite bright and fleshtones are manageable. The picture is often quite grainy as well, however, and from this grain there are occasional eruptions of digital artifacting. The presentation is in full screen format. The stereo sound has a workable dimensionality and allows you, if you concentrate, to hear background conversations as well as foreground conversations. The foreground conversations can be supported by English closed captioning.

The War Wagon (Universal, 20298)

John Wayne teams with Kirk Douglas in the entertaining 1967 western caper. The picture is letterboxed with an aspect ratio of about 2.35:1 and no 16:9 enhancement. Generally, the color transfer looks very nice, though some scenes do seem to be a bit too dusty. The image is sharp and nicely detailed. Bright hues are a little subdued, but fleshtones are workable. Dialog is a little scratchy on the monophonic audio track. The 101 minute film is also presented in French and Spanish, and comes with English or Spanish subtitles ("¿Siempre llevas una pistola encima de los calzoncillos?"). There is a theatrical trailer, a few production notes and a cast profile section.

The plot goes through some convolutions so that Wayne and Douglas can rob thousands of dollars in gold without offending Western-hero standards and practices laws. The 1967 film was made at a time when the counter-culture was beginning to make inroads in the motion picture business. That it remains engaging when so many movies from that era have become dated and diffi-

cult to tolerate is proof that the Establishment could do some things very right.

WarGames (MGM, 907056)

The 1983 film, about a boy who hacks into a Defense Department computer and almost starts a global thermonuclear war, has been issued in letterboxed format only, with an aspect ratio of about 1.85:1 and no 16:9 enhancement. The picture looks fairly grainy, with light colors. The stereo surround sound is a little soft, but provides an adequate presentation of the film's antiquated audio track. The DVD has a Dolby Digital track as well, but it isn't as good as the standard track. Rear channel activity is minimal and the ambiance is less dimensional. The film is also available in French in mono and can be supported by English, French or Spanish subtitles. There is a trailer, too, and An audio commentary from director John Badham and writers Lawrence Lasker and Walter F. Parkes.

Badham identifies the two scenes (one was the scene with the two computer nerds) that were directed by Martin Brest before he was removed from the film, but he doesn't go into details as to why Brest was dropped and he doesn't say much about what it was like to step into a project that was already running at full speed. The writers have some informative points to share about the writing process—if characters have to say the obvious, have them do it in an argument—and talk extensively about the conflicts they had over the logic of various plot points (everybody concedes that the smoke coming out of the computers at the end was a bit much, but that the other fudges worked fairly well). Their talk is mainly reactive to what is happening on the screen, as each scene triggers memories about the filming. The commentary is selective, but much of it is worthwhile, about the movie and about the process of moviemaking.

Watch Me (Image, ID5631FMDVD)

A woman in her underwear is peering through a telescope with a perplexed expression on her face and her hands in a 'Goodness, me!' position across her chest on the gloriously tacky jacket cover. The 1995 movie itself is a spatially confusing tale about a photographer, his unfaithful wife and their dancer tenant, who watches the wife cheat on the photographer while the photographer, unaware of his wife's hanky-panky, watches the dancer getting aroused by what she is watching. Got it? The thing is, it seems to all be taking place in one vertical building, so how they can be looking into one another's windows is beyond us. The erotic sequences are elaborate and are designed to appeal to both genders, but we prefer the jacket cover, which at least has a sense of humor to it.

Colors are a bit pale, fleshtones are bland and the image is grainy in places. The stereo sound is passable and the 87 minute 1995 program is not captioned.

Warriors of Virtue (MGM, 907434)

Ronny Yu's first American feature, which seems Asian in spirit, was shot partially in Beijing and partially in Vancouver. The nonsensical plot is about a young boy who falls into a draining sewage tank and wakes up in a mystical land, where he helps the forces of good, including five kangaroo creatures who make up the title characters, defeat the forces of evil. He then comes to, not having yet fallen into the drain. Go figure. It takes about 20 minutes for the fantasy part to kick in, which may make some youngsters restless, and the actual narrative, once the kid gets to the fantasy part, is sort of limp, which is going to make older viewers especially restless. There are Chinese-style fights, with lots of leaping and mid-air activities, which could seem fresh and unique to viewers not steeped in Hong Kong action films, but it isn't enough to keep one interested in the fate of the characters.

The film has many creative special effects, but you won't be able to see a few of them on the DVD because the widescreen movie has been issued in cropped format only, with the sides of the picture lopped off. The image is sharp, with mildly subdued hues and accurate fleshtones. The stereo surround sound is terrific, with lots of separation effects and power, and the Dolby Digital track is even more fun, with isolated rear channel effects and clearer details. The 103 minute program is also available in French in standard stereo and can be supported by English or French subtitles. There is a trailer, as well.

The Waterboy (Buena Vista, 16540)

Adam Sandler portrays a late bloomer who channels his anger into playing effectively at defensive positions on a college football team. We have to admire that the screenwriters made the hero a defensive player instead of an offensive player, though sure enough, by the end, they couldn't resist putting him on offense. The film is a comedy, with a broad humor that scores plenty of laughs, and the narrative is playfully uplifting. It's a formula star vehicle, but it demonstrates why there are successful formulas and stars.

The picture is letterboxed with an aspect ratio of about 1.85:1 and no 16:9 enhancement. The picture is sharp and colors are bright. The stereo surround sound and Dolby Digital sound are okay, delivering an adequate audio mix that enhances most of the scenes without calling too much attention to itself. The 90 minute program is also available in French in standard stereo and can be supported by English subtitles. There is a trailer that methodically spells out the film's premise and a featurette that pretty much does the same thing, but with a few behind-the-scenes shots and a couple quick interviews.

Way Down East (Image, ID4677DSDVD)

Lillian Gish stars as a compromised woman who finds sanctuary working as a maid at a large farm until her past again confronts her in D.W. Griffith's 1920 silent feature. The finale, the 'ice flow rescue,' is an amazing piece of filmmaking that involved shooting in both summer and winter, smoothly integrating realistic close-ups with daring stuntwork. The film's tone may seem antiquated to some, but Gish's performance is timeless, the narrative is always involving, and Griffith's technique is constantly impressive. He took a Nineteenth Century pop hit and turned it into a Twentieth Century work of art.

The black-and-white source material, which has a mild tinting, is in rough condition, with many spots, watermarks and scratches. The image is also rather fuzzy in places, but one assumes that it is probably in the best possible condition for its age and history. The picture is slightly windowboxed, but as can be seen during the intertitles, the lower edge of the frame is masked. The movie runs 146 minutes and movement always looks natural. The monophonic audio track has been taken from Vitaphone discs that were produced just eight years after the film itself, and while it, too, is a bit rough in places, it is less disorienting than many of the full-scale stereophonic scores other silent films have been given.

We Remember Marilyn (Passport, DVD2223)

An actress reads Marilyn Monroe's words in voiceover, which alternates with a standard narration, to clips culled from movie trailers and elsewhere. There are many rare clips, scenes from Monroe's very first walk-on appearances, an interview with Edward R. Murrow, a very funny bit with Jack Benny, scenes from her aborted final film and a lot of newsreel footage. The 95 minute program may not provide a definitive take on Monroe's career, but it is interesting and informative, tracking her battles with 20th Century Fox over the kinds of roles they kept handing her, and the ups and downs of her marriages. The picture quality varies with the source material of the clips but is never overly sharp or colorful. The weaker the source, the more tiling and other artifacting there is. The monophonic sound is adequate and is not captioned.

Webb Pierce and Chet Atkins (Shanachie, 601)

Here's a DVD for all your friends with eyebrow rings and navel studs. We're kidding, of course, but the program is so dated it is appealingly campy, and it seems right in tune with today's avant garde sensibilities. Taken from gorgeous 35mm footage of Grand Ole Opry concerts during the mid Fifties, the more than two dozen clips alternate between Pierce, who sings, and Atkins, who plays instrumentals on his guitar. The sets and costumes are vintage Opry, and the only disadvantage to the 51 minute program is that the composition and staging never changes. Neither musician moves around much, and the static repetitiveness of the numbers can deflate their charm after a while. Nevertheless, the program is valuable as a historical document, and as an introduction to some classic Country-Western music that is not heard much any more, even on Country-Western channels. The source material has a steady stream of scratches and speckles, but they never get in the way of the drop-dead hues and perfect fleshtones. The monophonic sound is super and is rarely compromised by the age of the recording.

The Wedding Singer (New Line, N4660)

The very smart and charming romantic comedy seems to appeal as much to young boys—who are normally dismissive of anything involving kissing—as it does to all other age and gender groups. Adam Sandler smoothly expands his range and capabilities portraying the title character, who has a deft talent for enhancing the romance of others but is having a harder time with his own love life. The film's jokes have a nice range to them, from character humor, jokes about the Eighties (the film is one of the first to explore 'Eighties nostalgia') and slapstick, to lovey-dovey gags and witty one liners but, most importantly, from Sandler's smile on down, the film has a warmth and sense of good feeling that makes even the hero's lowest moments seem sweet. Drew Barrymore co-stars, with a deliberately bad hair-do that makes all good hair-dos seem evil.

The presentation is in letterboxed format on one side with an aspect ratio of about 1.85:1 and an accommodation for enhanced 16:9 playback, and in full screen format on the other side. The letterboxing adds a little to the sides of the image and trims a lot off the bottom in comparison to the full screen version, but it seems less cramped. The image is sharp, with accurate fleshtones and crisp hues. The color transfer looks great, with precise, crisp hues and accurate fleshtones. The stereo surround sound is bland and even the Dolby Digital sound is modest. Although the movie has an extensive Eighties-themed soundtrack, however, the quality of the audio is not critical to the entertainment and the presentation is fully acceptable. The film is also available in French in Dolby Digital and comes with English, French or Spanish subtitles ("Oh tout ce que je veux/C'est viellir avec toi…").

In addition to an extensive cast & crew profile section, there is a full-fledged karaoke segment (with or without 'in the style of' vocals, set to stills from the film) offered for five of the established Eighties hits from the movie but, sadly, not for the film's more entertaining original songs. There is also a regular still photo section, though the images take up less than half the screen space, and a trivia game.

Weekend at Bernie's (Artisan, 60488)

A film we never tire of watching, Andrew McCarthy and Jonathan Silverman star as two junior executives invited to a beach house for a weekend after they uncover an embezzlement scheme at their firm. The embezzler is murdered and, because of a series of events, they feel they have to maintain the illusion that he is still alive in order to protect themselves, doing so by driving about town with the corpse, which is wired to wave at passers by. The slapstick is marvelous, the premise is delightfully fresh and the cast is enjoyable.

Colors are pale and fleshtones are pinkish, particularly during the indoor sequences. The picture is letterboxed with an aspect ratio of about 1.85:1 and no 16:9 enhancement. The stereo surround sound is rather confined and unassertive, but is adequately delivered. The 101 minute program also has a French soundtrack and can be supported by Spanish subtitles or English closed captioning. There is an uproariously funny trailer, a small cast-and-director profile section and some decent production notes that spell out the logistics of the shoot.

"Weird Al" Yankovic: The Videos (Image, ID4105AADVD)

A little of Al Yankovic can go a long way, so some viewers may find the 74 minute compilation to be a bit much for one sitting. The collection contains 21 Yankovic music video parodies, from the decade-old *Ricky*, *Eat It* and *Like a Surgeon* up to the more recent *Gump* and *Amish Paradise*. Some are highly inspired, particularly a claymation piece called *Jurassic Park* that is sung to *MacArthur Park*, but many are one-joke gags that don't promise much in the way of repeat play and are best sampled independently of the other cuts. The older videos are somewhat blurry while the latest ones are crisper. Colors are generally bright and the stereo surround sound is adequate.

Weird Science (Image, ID4232USDVD)

There is a certain point in a young man's life—roughly the six months between being 14-and-a-half and being 15—when he will appreciate **Weird Science**. Directed by John Hughes, the 1985 movie is about a pair of fifteen-year-old boys who, through a bit of magic, create a cover girl who will perform their every wish, the joke being that they don't know what to do with her once they create her.

The film is letterboxed with an aspect ratio of about 1.85:1 and no 16:9 enhancement. The framing looks fine and the color transfer is very nice, with bright, crisp hues and accurate fleshtones. The stereo surround sound is also reasonably strong, though the mix is limited. The 93 minute program is identified as a 'Home Video Version' apparently because of song rights, and is captioned.

Werewolf (Simitar, 7293)

Most bad films are simply mediocre, but every once in a while we come across a movie so horrendously inept that it is worthwhile entertainment, and the ridiculous **Werewolf** is such a film. The director makes the actors stand still when they speak, and the actors are already so bad that the bad direction and bad editing amplify their inexperience. The heroine is so untalented that not only can she not deliver her lines convincingly, she can't even look around a room without appearing self-conscious and unnatural. The film is set in the Southwest (the copyright on the end credit scroll calls the movie 'Arizona Werewolf'), but most of the main performers have Eastern European accents, which they try desperately to suppress. The story is really dopey—this guy hires this other guy to infect people with werewolf blood so he can catch one, or something— but the film's ineptness doesn't end there. Scenes that begin in the daytime suddenly turn into night. There is not a single fistfight in the entire film where it looks like one person landed a punch on another, and the sound effects are inevitably mis-synched. The music is awful, drawing attention to itself instead of to the film's supposed thrills. And then there's the werewolf makeup, which looks different in every shot. Needless to say, we had a great time watching the DVD and giggled plenty from beginning to end. It's even funnier on multiple viewings. The picture is sharp, with smooth, deep and crisp colors, and the Ultra-Stereo surround soundtrack is energetic. The movie runs 95 minutes and is not captioned.

West of the Divide (see Young Duke Series: The Fugitive)

West Side Story (MGM, 906733)

Everybody, when they're walking down the street, has, at one time or another, lifted an arm or a leg to pirouette instead of trudge. The film is popular for many reasons but it is perhaps most popular because it encourages feelings of grace inside the viewer. Most street punks are rude, belligerent and selfish, but you don't walk down the street wishing they could dance, you walk down the street wishing you could. For three hours or four hours (you can't watch the DVD without going back and replaying sections) **West Side Story** lets you feel what it would be like to float past the grime.

In its day, the LD's picture was terrific, but it looks awful compared to the DVD. Fleshtones look totally pink, and other colors are over-saturated and quite blurry on the LD, while the DVD looks crisp, with accurate fleshtones and solid, effectively detailed hues. The picture is letterboxed with an aspect ratio of about 2.25:1 and an accommodation for enhanced 16:9 playback.

The stereo surround sound has been freshened up, but there is still age-related noise when the volume is raised, and separation effects are minimal. Additionally, there isn't much of a difference between the standard track and the Dolby Digital track (the LD's Dolby Digital track is substantially better). We couldn't tell one from the other. The 152 minute 1961 film can be supported by English or French subtitles ("Ce garçon-là il a tué ton frère. Oublie ce garçon. Trouve un autre partenaire") and is accompanied by a terrific older reissue trailer (technically not an 'original' as is claimed on the jacket cover).

West Side Story (see Dave Grusin Presents West Side Story)

The Westerner (HBO, 90665)

Directed by William Wyler, the 1940 production uses the Judge Roy Bean stories as a basis for an engaging drama that explores the farmers vs. cattlemen conflict and the moral ambiguities of frontier justice. Walter Brennan won an Oscar playing the scurrilous Bean. Gary Cooper basically plays his straightman, though with just enough twinkle to let the viewer know he isn't buying it for a moment. The movie has some terrific action sequences, a mature and satisfying romance, and a narrative that always manages to turn in unexpected directions.

There is some scattered speckling, but for the most part the black-and-white picture looks very nice, with finely detailed contrasts and a sharp focus. The monophonic sound is passable, and there is a remastered stereo soundtrack that has more flourish and a workable dimensionality. The 100 minute program has alternate French, Spanish and Italian audio tracks in mono, optional English, French and Spanish subtitles, and a cast & crew profile section.

Westworld (MGM, 907014)

The 1973 film is 83 minutes long and basically puts forward its premise—a vacation resort where androids cater to the fantasies of the guests—twists the plot—the androids get sick and start killing the guests—and then ends before the concepts become exhausted. Plagued in the past by deteriorated film stock that we had been led to believe would never look decent, colors are bright, fleshtones are rich, the image is sharp. Sequences that looked like a pointillist painting on the letterboxed LD release are solid and clear on the DVD. The entire film is enlivened by the quality of the image, and the already repeatable sci-fi thriller becomes all the more engaging.

The picture is letterboxed with an aspect ratio of about 2.35:1 and an accommodation for enhanced 16:9 playback. The stereo sound does not have an elaborate mix and is not as crisp as the LD's stereo, but it is workable. The film is also available in French in mono and can be supported by English or French subtitles. A trailer is included, too.

Wet Shorts: The Best of Liquid Television (Sony, LVD48435)

Not every MTV animated short gets spun off into its own series, so a bunch that didn't, along with a few of the short **Aeon Flux** pieces that also appear on **Aeon Flux**, are featured on the 90 minute collection. There are more than 30 shorts, including several *Stick Figure Theatre* works (our favorite—they match recorded sounds from things like **Night of the Living Dead** and the Hindenberg crash to simple drawings), Bobby & Billy pieces (what looks like drawings from old beginning reader books, but with grosser narratives), Crazy Daisy Ed (a hip talking flower), and plenty of other pieces, utilizing everything from computer animation (a metallic ant attacks a city) to puppets (a *Jack and the Beanstalk* takeoff with a car and a Chia pet) to every type of art medium imaginable. Some of the sketches make no sense, some are very funny and some are simply admirable efforts that don't go anywhere, but as an anthology they are an impressive reminder that the art of the short film is thriving and is still at the forefront of innovative cinema. The picture transfer looks fine and the stereo sound is good. There is no captioning.

Whales (SlingShot, DVD9805)

With the low register calls of the humpback whales testing the limits of your subwoofer and the clarity of the IMAX cinematography bringing a near three-dimensional image to your monitor, the IMAX program is an outstanding DVD. Patrick Stewart narrates the 60 minute (or so—the program is not time encoded) documentary, which bounces around the world to look at several different species of whales in a variety of locations. There is nothing comprehensive about the documentary, but it is rich in trivia and generalities, looking at how some whales eat and live, and how they interact with man.

The IMAX cinematography is stunningly crisp and the picture transfer never fails it. Even the underwater sequences are beautifully detailed. The stereo surround sound is super, but it is the five channel Dolby Digital soundtrack that best replicates the IMAX experience, with eerie whale calls recreated so purely don't be surprised if you find a 50 ton behemoth on your doorstep the following morning. The program is also available in German, Japanese and Mandarin in Dolby Digital, can be supported by optional English subtitles and is accompanied by a trailer and an interesting 17 minute 'making of' documentary.

What Dreams May Come (PolyGram, 4400582752)

Its metaphysics will tick off some people and its emotionalism will tick off others, but almost everybody will be transfixed by the special effects, particularly on the DVD, which has an exquisite picture transfer that captures every hue and detail with stunning perfection. Everyone in the movie is dead, wandering around in what he or she pictures Heaven and the Other Place to be, and many of the conceptualizations relate to paint and paintings, requiring a myriad of colors. The film's focus, however, is more upon the nature of love and coping with grief. There is a lot of conversation that requires concentration to follow. On one level, the film is relentlessly sad, which is why its spectacular interpretation of the afterlife is so essential to its success, as a balm for the exposed sorrows. Robin Williams and Annabella Sciorra star, with Cuba Gooding, Jr. as Williams' guide.

The film is presented in letterboxed format, with an aspect ratio of about 2.35:1 and an accommodation for enhanced 16:9 playback (watch for the shadow of the camera on the left when the hero first runs into the highway tunnel). Its palette is incredibly rich, and the DVD provides such a crisp, vivid picture that each splotch of color is both transcendent and utterly real. There are some displacement effects, but they also appear on the LD and are not an artifacting flaw. Although not as detailed as its imagery, the film's audio is fairly elaborate, with an atmospheric dimensionality and separation effects that transport the viewer deeper into the picture. The bass is also quite strong. The Dolby Digital track has more flourish and crisper separations than the standard track.

The 113 minute program has optional French or Spanish subtitles, English closed captioning, 2 trailers, a 'making of' featurette, a breakdown of how some of the special effects were accomplished, a still photo collection of the film's elaborate artwork, a cast-and-director profile section, 'wallpaper' of the movie's images from DVD-ROM, and an alternate ending. Amusingly, the menu has you choose between Heaven and Hell before going forward, though each appears to bring you to the same location (Hell is

cooler). On a commentary track, the film's director, Vincent Ward, reads from prepared statements, talking some about how the film was made, and focusing mostly on his interpretation of the story and the characters.

The alternate ending is more sophisticated and technically stronger than the actual ending, but it stretches things out a little more and touches on the politically volatile concept of when a soul enters an unborn child. The featurette has interviews with many of the cast and crew, lots of behind-the-scenes material, including footage of how the special effects were generated, and a brief clip of Richard Matheson, whose novel was the foundation for the film. In a separate segment, effects expert Joel Hynek and art director Josh Rosen explain with examples how the effects were conceived and applied (they had a whole database of just brushstrokes, for one thing). Rosen also talks about the challenge of creating a 'painting' landscape, something that is 'halfway' between 2D and 3D, requiring illumination that is closer, with offhand religious overtones, to stained glass.

Whatever Happened to Baby Jane? (Warner, 11051)

What marvelous casting against type it was to have Joan Crawford as the good sister and Bette Davis as the bad sister! By necessity, Crawford virtually disappears for the final third of the film, but while she is around she looks so angelic it almost becomes hard to believe all those nasty things people say about her.

The picture is sharp, with very crisp lines and finely detailed contrasts. The presentation is letterboxed with an aspect ratio of about 1.85:1 on one side and cropped on the other side, but the cinematography's framing is often critical to the pace and mood of the drama, so the cropped version is a waste of time. Contrary to the jacket notation, there is no accommodation for enhanced 16:9 playback. The film has been remastered in Dolby Digital surround, which provides a bit of dimension to the musical score, though it remains fairly centered. The regular stereo surround soundtrack is very muted, weaker than both the Dolby Digital track. There is a wobble on the audio track around the 63 minute mark, but it is present on the LD, too. The film is also available in French and comes with English, French or Spanish subtitles ("Hay ratas en el sótano"). There is a cast & crew profile section and some production notes about the macabre 1962 thriller, directed by Robert Aldrich.

Wheels, Heels and Hot Licks (Simitar, 7331)

The documentary program is first and foremost a collection of interviews with heavy metal rock musicians, but you wouldn't be able to tell that from the cover, since the program is being sold for its segments that feature topless models gyrating on motorcycles. There are several lengthy topless segments in the 60 minute program, but these sequences are filler. The meat of the program is the interviews, where the rockers, including Don Dokken of Dokken, Sammy Hagar, Chuck Billy of Testament, one of the Doobie Brothers and others, talk about their love of motorcycles (the topless models are also all professed cycle enthusiasts) and their tattoos—oh, yes, some of the program is also about tattooing. Anyway, there's more to the show than is implied by the jacket art.

The picture is a bit murky at times, depending upon the source material, with bland colors, though the topless modeling sequences are a little crisper. The stereo sound is loud, but separation effects are limited and the program is not captioned.

When a Stranger Calls Back (GoodTimes, 0581026)

The 1993 sequel to the more unnerving *When a Stranger Calls* was written and directed by the creator of the first film, Fred Walton. Both Carol Kane and Charles Durning resurrect their roles, though in a more matured capacity. Like the first effort, the film has a distinctive three-part structure, including a harrowing opening half hour when a babysitter is placed in peril by a shapeless voice. Indeed, the film's first hour is chilling but, finally, Walton paints himself into a corner and has to come up with an explanation for what has been going on. The one he produces is barely feasible and is not in keeping with the verisimilitude of the original film. Nevertheless, the sequel does have its strong points, not only in the screams that are generated and in the way that Kane ages her character, but also as a deliberate fable about female vulnerability in contemporary society (Kane's character is now the manager of a women's crisis center) which was, after all, the essence of the folktale to begin with.

The picture is presented in full screen format only. Colors are somewhat bland, but the presentation is passable. The stereo surround sound mix has a direct bearing on the plot—we won't say why—and contributes significantly to the disc's thrills. The 94 minute program has optional English, French and Spanish subtitles.

When Trumpets Fade (Warner, 91480)

John Irvin's superb and fairly expensive-looking cable film is a portrait of fear on the battlefield—not cowardice, exactly, but the instincts soldiers follow to protect themselves, and how their leaders learn to infuse those instincts with aggression. Set during a costly WWII battle that was subsequently negated by the Battle of the Bulge, the hero is a private who is rapidly field-promoted to an officer, despite his cynical distaste for authority. The fighting scenes are exciting and quite elaborate (with carnage that would have been unthinkable a couple decades ago), and the dramatic tension does not lessen when the gunfire subsides. Unlike so many WWII movies of the past, the soldiers by and large have no idea what they are doing and little desire to accomplish anything more than avoid getting shot or blown up. And yet, they somehow manage to overcome their motivational constraints and defeat their enemy when the right leader is guiding them.

The cinematography is a little hazy—fog is a major obstacle on the battlefield—but the picture is sharp, with carefully delineated shades of grey, brown and weary green. Fleshtones are good. The stereo surround sound has a decent separation mix for a cable production and is satisfying. The 92 minute film is also available in Spanish and can be supported by English, French or Spanish subtitles. There is a cast & crew profile section, as well.

When We Were Kings (PolyGram, 4400458472)

The Oscar-winning documentary is about the prizefight between George Foreman and Muhammad Ali in 1974 in Zaire. The film is very enjoyable, exploring the circus-like atmosphere surrounding the event and the personalities of many of the individuals involved with the fight. The two central characters are thoroughly and memorably profiled, and when the fight is finally staged, you're ready for it. The filmmakers assume a little too much knowledge on the part of the viewer and as time recedes that knowledge—such as why Ali didn't already have the title—will be less easy to come by (the jacket cover essay is brief, but helps to fill in several gaps). Nevertheless, the story has a stranger-than-fiction fascination and the people in it are larger than life.

The 87 minute film is accompanied by a brief reminiscence about making it by the director, Leon Gast, though he doesn't explain exactly why it took 20 years for the movie to get put together. Since it is a documentary, the quality of the source material varies from one sequence to the next, but generally the presentation has sharp, reasonably accurate hues. The film is presented on one side in letterboxed format, with an aspect ratio of about 1.85:1 and no 16:9 enhancement, and in full screen format on the other side. Because the film is a documentary, however, the full screen image is preferable to the letterboxed image, which trims picture information off the top and bottom of the screen and adds nothing to the sides. There is stereo surround soundtrack, and the filmmakers use a concert that was held in coordination with the fight, featuring B.B. King, James Brown and others, to insert music at appropriate moments. Stereo effects are minimal and the 94 minute film can be accompanied by English, French or Spanish subtitles.

Where the Boys Aren't 7 X-rated (Vivid, UPC#0073215536)

One of the weaker entries in the series, **Where the Boys Aren't 7** has a nominal narrative about infidelity among female couples in an all-female bar, but nobody seems too sincere about it and the set dressings are spare. After the opening sequence, in which one of the actresses sings a nightclub number, it's all downhill. The erotic sequences are reasonably energetic, however.

The show runs 63 minutes, followed by a 10 minute 'making of' sequence that is the most appealing part of the program. The picture, from a video tape source, is very good, with bright, crisp hues and accurate fleshtones. The sound is reasonably strong and the program features Christy Canyon, Janine, Asia Carrera and Jenna Jameson. The DVD also contains alternate angle sequences and elaborate hardcore interactive promotional features.

Where the Boys Aren't 10 X-rated (Vivid, UPC#0073215505)

An all-female **West Side Stor**y with a happy ending is the best way to describe **Where the Boys Aren't 10**. The story is amusing, as are the cast's performances as members of rival female street gangs. The erotic sequences are fairly busy, even though they are limited to a single gender. The picture is a little washed out and overly orange in places and fleshtones are a bit drab. The sound is okay and the 71 minute program features Janine, Leslie Glass, Tia Bella, Dyanna Lauren, Kobe Tai and Heather. The DVD also contains alternate angle sequences and elaborate hardcore interactive promotional features.

Where the Red Fern Grows (UAV, 40083)

The 1974 film is a competently produced family feature about a young boy in the Oklahoma Ozarks and his two raccoon dogs. The plot is basically about him raising his dogs and growing up a bit himself in the process, but the 98 minute film's pacing is effective, the scenery is nice and the animals are enjoyable. James Whitmore portrays the boy's grandfather.

The picture looks okay. The image wobbles a bit in the beginning and there is a stray mark or two later on, but for the most part the image is sharp and the colors are accurate. The monophonic sound has a little trouble with music, warping some of the higher notes, and there is some background noise, but the dialogue is unhindered and the sound effects are okay. The program is not captioned.

Where the Red Fern Grows II: The Classic Continues (UAV, 40093)

The sequel to the family-oriented **Where the Red Fern Grows** doesn't introduce a juvenile character until the 40 minute mark and is about a young man who returns from WWII with an artificial leg and an uncertainty about his future. Wilford Brimley repeats his role as the young man's grandfather, with Doug McKeon as the hero and Chad McQueen. The 90 minute film is mostly talk, with a few incidents to keep the story moving, but not much really happens and the emotional crises are fairly superficial.

The picture is very grainy, especially during the first half, and colors are substantially drained throughout, with red remaining stronger than the other elements. Fleshtones are anemic. The monophonic sound is adequate and has not been captioned.

While You Were Sleeping (Buena Vista, 13680)

The delightful 1995 romantic comedy stars Sandra Bullock, Bill Pullman and a purposely comatose Peter Gallagher. Capsule summaries of the clever plot do not do it full justice, since the film's appeal lies not only in its romantic complications—caused when the heroine is mistaken for the fiancée of a man in a coma—but in the contrasts it depicts of family life and loneliness, for it is those contrasts that lock the heroine into her innocent deceptions. The film also has a number of inspired throwaway gags, such as a hysterical moment that has nothing to do with the plot, when a paper boy slips on some ice.

The picture is letterboxed with an aspect ratio of about 1.85:1, and no 16:9 enhancement. Fleshtones are a little purplish, but the picture is sharp and most hues are quite bright. The stereo surround sound is fine. The 103 minute program is also available in French and can be accompanied by English or Spanish subtitles. The movie comes with an efficient theatrical trailer and we noticed that one particular shot, where the landlord's son bends over, was substituted from the shot in the film to show a little less flesh.

Whispering Waters (see **Moodtapes: Whispering Waters**)

White Man's Burden (HBO,91289)

With so many movies that are so much alike, it is always refreshing to see something that is genuinely different. **White Man's Burden**, in which the standard roles for Negroes and Caucasians have been switched, fails one crucial test—if the story had been cast along normal racial lines, it would seem dull and predictable—but the concept is fresh enough that the film remains interesting despite the banality of its narrative. Harry Belafonte stars as a wealthy businessman kidnapped by a worker, played by John Travolta, who has been dismissed from one of his plants. Unable to get the money he feels owed him, Travolta's character drags Belafonte around for the weekend, while in the background we witness the effects of poverty upon an oppressed populace. Once in a while there is something startling and disorienting, such as when a child surfs through TV channels on a remote and sees blacks on all the programs except a crime news report, and it can also be fascinating to see how often you forget that the roles of the background characters are reversed. For us, this was all the intellectual stimulation the film required to remain entertaining—the two stars give low key, unassuming performances—but others will understandably desire something more substantive than the 1995 movie is capable of delivering.

The presentation is letterboxed with an aspect ratio of about 1.85:1 and no 16:9 enhancement. The film had a fairly low budget and so the picture disintegrates a little in tough lighting situations, but the image transfer looks fairly accurate and fleshtones are okay. The stereo surround sound and Dolby Digital sound are also limited in effect, but seem adequately transferred. The 89 minute program also has a Spanish language track in mono, optional English, French and Spanish subtitles, a trailer and a 'making of' featurette.

White Squall (Buena Vista, 17247)

A really terrible movie, Ridley Scott's 1996 feature is one long string of boys-become-men clichés. The film is so thematically bland and so unremarkable it is near torturous to sit through. Based on a true incident, Jeff Bridges stars as the captain of a schooner crewed by a group of teenage boys who are combining sailing lessons and regular school work. The film's big set piece—a sudden storm that knocks the boat over and kills a couple of the students—isn't depicted until near the end and really isn't all that exciting, just noisy and relievedly more busy than the action that has come before it.

There is a souped-up stereo surround soundtrack and better detailed Dolby Digital encoding, but the film is so monotonous neither the audio nor the pretty and accurately transferred images can help to make it worthwhile. The picture is presented in letterboxed format, with an aspect ratio of about 2.35:1 and no 16:9 enhancement. The 129 minute program is accompanied by is an alternate French audio track, optional English subtitles, a trailer and a 5 minute featurette.

White Zombie (Roan, AED2001)

Uneven both in tone and drama, the 1932 horror feature ends quite well, essentially excusing the flaws building up to it and leaving the viewer with lingering memories of its better moments. Bela Lugosi portrays a mysterious Haitian landowner who saves on contributing to his employees' health plans by using the undead to

tend and process his sugar cane. When he meets a young, fetching newlywed, he decides to acquire her services for his household, a choice that inevitably leads to his undoing. In addition to its innovative sound effects, the film has many haunting images—the workers plodding in silhouette to the fields and endlessly turning a cane grinder; the heroine appearing at the window of the villain's mansion, situated on a high, seaside cliff. It loses its momentum, however, whenever there is an expository dialogue scene. Such scenes are generally staged in a poor manner and not conceived with a strong clarity of purpose.

The feature was shot on a very small budget and cannot be expected to appear in perfect condition. There are plenty of scratches and speckles, though there are many scenes where the damage is barely noticeable. Contrasts are reasonably sharp and blacks are pure, an improvement over the somewhat more battered LD. While displacement artifacting cannot be completely eliminated, it is rarely noticeable. The image is substantially windowboxed. The monophonic sound, though ancient, is coherent and is not supported by captioning. The film runs 66 minutes.

There is an audio commentary track, by Lugosi expert Gary Don Rhodes, in which he provides an overview of the film's production and background (it was, officially, the first 'zombie' movie), as well as a more academic interpretation of its imagery. One of his more interesting insights—audiences in 1932 would have been very aware of Haiti, where the film is set, because America had just finished one of its periodic military forays into the republic and political opinion would have been assuaged by the depiction of the locals as a mindless peasantry in need of outside assistance. There are also two terrific interviews with Lugosi, one a 6 minute staged interview from 1932 with Dorothy West and another, running 3 minutes, from 1951, about work he had just done in London. There is also a trailer.

The Who: Live at the Isle of Wight Festival 1970 (Image, ID4698ERDVD)

The Who released a concert album in the late Sixties, *Live at Leeds*, that was considered at the time to be a definitive example of its genre and is still looked upon as a minor classic, so it is understandable that some fans should be extremely excited about the concert video, which was not only recorded in the same era, but runs more than twice as long as the LP and, of course, is accompanied by moving pictures. The concert is broken into two parts, actually, with the first part representing much of the material that appeared on *Live at Leeds* and the second part being the group's standard abridgment of *Tommy*. The concert began at 2:00 a.m., which is a time when many young people just start getting their energy, and musically and culturally the program is marvelous, a cross between the grandiose potential of rock in its still formative stages and the kinetic precision of the musicians who played every note as if they could not imagine a tomorrow.

The picture on the 85 minute program is grainy and colors are faded, but the image is reasonably clear and consistent. The show's editing is very good, avoiding cliché cuts and always matching the excitement generated by the performances. The stereo sound is a little dull, but for the most part the rough, makeshift ambiance of the live environment is conveyed, and the instruments and vocals are reasonably clear. The program is not captioned.

Who Am I? (see **Jackie Chan's Who Am I?**)

Who's Afraid of Virginia Woolf? (Warner, 12414)

Cinematographer Haskell Wexler speaks for the first 100 minutes on an alternate audio track in the 131 minute feature. He begins his talk by stating that he worked on the 1966 film a long time ago and cannot remember too much, and then proceeds to supply a highly informative and detailed discourse on the production of the film, with pertinent digressions to his other experiences in motion pictures. He explains how and why the lighting in specific scenes was achieved, what it was like working with all that primitive equipment way back when, describes first hand how Richard Burton would drink like a fish during lunch and still nail his part—and hit his marks—in the afternoon, and talks about the tensions brought by the studio on first-time director Mike Nichols. Film students will find his technical insights to be highly rewarding, but even casual viewers will find their appreciation of the film enriched by his descriptions of what went on behind the scenes. **Who's Afraid of Virginia Woolf** can be very silly material—about adults playing odd psychological games when they are far too drunk to actually have their wits about them—if it is not presented with the exact amount of distractions, but Nichols does just that, as Wexler details. Dirty laundry has rarely seemed so appealing.

The black-and-white cinematography looks terrific, with incredibly sharp details and textures. The presentation is letterboxed on one side, with an aspect ratio of about 1.85:1 and no 16:9 playback, and presented in full screen on the other side. The letterboxing masks off a lot more picture information on the top and bottom of the image than it adds to the sides, but the framing is significantly stronger and pulls you deeper into the drama. The monophonic sound is much weaker than the Dolby Digital mono track. The film can also be supported by English, French or Spanish subtitles ("¿Alcohol de 90 parati, Martha?" "Si. 'Nunca mezclo, nunca me preocupo'") and there is a decent cast and crew profile section, along with a small collection of production notes.

As for the film itself, we find ourselves responding more and more to Richard Burton's performance with each viewing, particularly during the show's first half, before the necessities of drama start driving the characters a little too hard. It is his youth which we find most striking and it is probably the key to why his character has failed in life, if not to the work's title as well. He has dressed himself in the trappings of middle age and performs its functions, but in the twinkle of Burton's eye there is a child who won't let go, and it is the kind of psychological subtext that only the most talented actor could accomplish without spoiling his other illusions.

Why Do Fools Fall in Love (Warner, 16916)

The cute but longish biographical drama is about the 'first black teen idol,' Frankie Lymon. Although Lymon's career was mostly a downhill spiral after a brief stay at the top, and although he died a drug addict, the film manages to maintain a charming and humorous atmosphere by casting the story as testimony in a trial where three women claiming to be his widows bicker over his estate. Larenz Tate is Lymon, with Halle Berry, Vivica Fox and Lela Rochon as the wives and, in an inspired piece of casting, Little Richard playing himself for the trial sequences. When the plot is forced to work its way to a conclusion, the film starts to slow down a bit, but the performances are enjoyable and the music sounds terrific.

The film is presented on one side in letterboxed format, with an aspect ratio of about 1.85:1 and an accommodation for enhanced 16:9 playback, and in full screen format on the other side. The full screen image adds more picture information to the bottom of the screen and takes very little off the side, but we found the framing on the letterboxed version to be more consistently satisfying. The color transfer looks fine, with bright, solid hues and accurate fleshtones. The stereo surround sound and Dolby Digital sound deliver the musical sequences with aplomb and generally have a nice dimensionality, with the Dolby Digital track displaying a little more body than the standard track. The 116 minute film is also available in French and can be supported by English or French subtitles ("L'amour, c'est pour les idiots"). There is a cast & crew profile section and a small production essay, as well as a trailer, which includes a clip from a scene that didn't make it to the final cut of the film.

There is also a commentary track, featuring the director, Gregory Nava, the screenwriter, Tina Andrews and, piping up only once in a while, a producer (there were several), Paul Hall. The commentary is very enlightening and increased our affection for the film considerably, something that rarely happens even with the

best talks. Andrews researched Lymon's life for years before the script went into production, and readily identifies the links between the film's dramatizations and the real events (much of the courtroom dialogue was taken from actual transcripts). Nava is able to articulate his reasons for choosing certain camera movements and other artistic decisions—something not all directors are able to verbalize—and leads the viewer through a comprehensive tour of how the film was made while pointing out many of the film's subliminal intentions. Their talk is deceptively casual, but loaded with insight both on the film and on the process of filmmaking.

Why We Fight (see **World War II**)

Wild America (Warner, 15580)

The story of the teenage years of three wildlife documentary filmmakers, the 1997 film has great potential, but it never lives up to it. Jonathan Taylor Thomas stars as the youngest of the three brothers, with Devon Sawa and Scott Bairstow. The film is cheaply put together (the kids are better actors than the adults), the animal effects are often so obviously fake they break one's concentration, and the editing is jumbled at times, spoiling the dramatic buildup of specific scenes. The film's TV commercials played it up as a wildlife adventure movie, but that is only its middle act, where the boys set out to film endangered species, with the first and last sections being about the home life of the boys on the wrong side of the tracks in Arkansas. It is too inept to accomplish much, however, and remains unbelievable even after you find out it was a true story.

The 107 minute film is presented on one side in letterboxed format, with an aspect ratio of about 2.35:1 and an accommodation for enhanced 16:9 playback, and in cropped format on the other side. The cropping is workable from a framing standpoint, but you lose a lot of the movie. The colors are fine, the blacks are pure and the image is solid. The stereo surround sound is bland and even the Dolby Digital track has a weak bass. The film is also available in French and comes with English, French or Spanish subtitles. There is a decent cast-and-crew profile, a few production notes and a theatrical trailer that sells the movie much better than the TV commercials did.

Wicked City (Image, ID4664FLDVD)

A lively Hong Kong fantasy action film that is sure to please fans, Tsui Hark produced the 1992 feature, which was directed by Peter Mak. The film suggests that monsters, called 'reptoids' on the dubbed track, who have taken human form, live in human society but seek to destroy mankind. Some monsters, however, are friendly to humans, and there is the sort of intramural fighting common to organized crime. The heroes are two cops, one of whom is secretly half a monster, who are sent to take down a wealthy industrialist monster, only to discover that the industrialist is really pro-human and it is his renegade son the cops should be worried about. The appeal of the film is its wild-and-woolly action sequences. Of course, with the film's limited budget, there is a lot of editing and patchwork special effects, but there is always enough visual information to get the point across, and if things are confusing now and then, so much the better—this is not the kind of premise you want to analyze too closely. No two monsters are alike, and since shooting doesn't seem to do too much good, the cops usually have to behead them to make sure they're down, and even that doesn't work, sometimes. Based upon a comic book, Jacky Cheung and Michelle Li star. The film moves quickly, there are plenty of fantasy and action sequences, and the story is coherent enough to tie everything together. You can't really ask for more.

The picture is letterboxed with an aspect ratio of about 1.75:1 and no 16:9 enhancement. The color transfer looks very nice, with bright hues and decent fleshtones. The image is a little soft in places and there are a few scattered speckles, but the presentation looks great for a Hong Kong production. The monophonic sound is available in both Cantonese and in English, with optional English subtitles that provide a different translation than the English dubbing. The film runs 87 minutes. The chapter encoding and jacket guide are limited.

The Wild Bunch (Warner, 14034)

Sam Peckinpah's 1969 masterpiece about bank robbers on the run in the Old West is greatly enhanced by the precision of the DVD transfer. The flashback sequences, for example, blend seamlessly with the rest of the movie and add to the emotional resonance without distracting from the immediate narrative. The scenes bridging the action sequences are so perfectly composed and edited that the rhythm of the film flows beautifully as the characters are developed and the background political conflicts are laid out. The heroes are all nasty killers with limited morals, and yet you care about what happens to them and are genuinely interested in seeing them succeed (it helps that many of the people they meet are just as nasty). William Holden's rare performance is free of many of the personality ticks typifying his other screen appearances, and he gains tremendous depth while remaining stoic and dignified. The film is a magnificent action and adventure drama with a moral resonance that seeps in from around the edges while the characters are gradually forced to become self-aware and spiritually responsible.

The Oscar-nominated, 32 minute featurette, *The Wild Bunch: An Album in Montage*, accompanies the 145 minute *Original Director's Cut*. The movie is presented in letterboxed format on two sides, with the featurette and a standard theatrical trailer available only on the second side. The featurette is outstanding. Drawn from extensive black-and-white footage showing Peckinpah, not just at work, but in the act of creating, *Album in Montage* focuses on the shooting of about a half dozen scenes, with voiceover reminiscences explaining how Peckinpah conceived each scene and what it was like to be with him.

The film itself has a dusty, Western coloring, but fleshtones are consistently accurate and every image looks crisp and precise. The letterboxing has an aspect ratio of about 2.35:1 and no 16:9 enhancement. The stereo surround sound and Dolby Digital surround sound are about equal in quality. Although the film's original soundtrack was enhanced for the *Director's Cut*, the audio still has an older ambiance and is best held to a modest volume to prevent distortion. The sound effects have a dullness to them and the music—which is terrific—is often centered with its components seeming to be too bunched together. English, French and Spanish subtitles are available. There is an extensive cast profile and a detailed itemization of the footage restored to the *Director's Cut*.

The Wild One Columbia TriStar, 06239)

The black-and-white image looks gorgeous from beginning to end. The picture is crisp, with highly detailed contrasts and smooth blacks. The film is presented in full screen format only and the framing looks fine. The monophonic sound is fine, and there is also a French soundtrack, as well as optional English or French subtitles ("'Johnny, contre quoi tu te rebelles?' 'Qu'est-ce que tu as?'"), and a classic theatrical trailer.

A young Marlon Brando stars as the leader of a motorcycle gang who somewhat inadvertently cause a great deal of trouble in a small town. Despite the out-of-date slang and an amusingly phallic second-place trophy, it is still possible to take the 1954 movie seriously because of Brando's steady swagger. The brief 79 minute running time and basic dramatics make the program highly repeatable entertainment.

Wild Things (Columbia TriStar, 02411)

The plot twists in **Wild Things** have a sort of exponential advancement. The first significant one doesn't occur until the film's halfway point, right after the side change, but then the next occurs at the next point halfway to the end, and the next at the next half-

way mark and so on, until you reach the end credit scroll, which has about a half dozen more twists jammed into it as all the names of the people who made the movie are rolling by. The plot turns are great fun, but the necessity of their presence forces the first half of the narrative to remain oblique and unsatisfying. Even as a whole, you don't really get to peer into the hearts of the characters, basking in their flaws, until that final credit scroll. The movie is still good fun—the sex is hot and the stars are enjoyable—but because of the way it is designed it sacrifices what the best crime dramas are the richest for—the opportunity given viewers to identify with the poor slobs caught up in their moral disasters. To this end, Matt Dillon, as the central protagonist, a high school guidance counselor accused of rape, probably gives the weakest performance—he's too armored. Kevin Bacon is more engaging, as the police detective investigating the case. Neve Campbell, Denise Richards, Bill Murray and the all too rarely seen Carrie Snodgress also appear.

The film is presented on one side in letterboxed format, with an aspect ratio of about 2.35:1 and an accommodation for enhanced 16:9 playback, and in cropped format on the other side. The picture looks super, with bright, crisp hues, complete stability in the darker sequences and accurate fleshtones. The stereo surround sound and Dolby Digital sound have a few pleasing separation effects and a reasonably strong presence, with the Dolby Digital track providing a fuller dimensionality and better defined separations than the standard track. The film is also available in French in standard stereo and can be supported by English or French subtitles.

There is a group commentary track on the DVD that includes director John McNaughton, editor Elena Maganini, producers Rodney Liber and Steven Jones, composer George Clinton and cinematographer Jeffrey Kimball. They are all gathered together for the talk, but the format does not work too well, since each is afraid of interrupting the other and so they often remain silent (except, alas, at one point, where somebody is telling a fascinating story about a grip who discovered a dead body floating down a river during the shoot—the story gets cut off and they never return to it). Only Clinton has the wherewithal to consistently pop in at appropriate moments to explain his contributions. When they do speak, they talk a lot about the logistics of the shoot, about battling Florida mosquitoes (even on the ocean), about working with the actors (Bill Murray kept everyone in good spirits) and about the lighting tricks they had to use to compensate for Florida's dynamic weather. There is also a trailer and three brief deleted sequences, mostly showing more of Murray's improvisational prowess, including what is actually a reel of witty rejoinders he provides in response to a single line of dialogue by another character.

William Shakespeare's Romeo + Juliet (Fox, 4110421)

The 1996 film isn't perfect, but it scores so many points on concept that it is utterly thrilling and satisfying despite its flaws. Set in southern Florida (most of the movie was shot in Mexico) in modern day, but using Shakespeare's dialogue, the film achieves a best of both worlds synergy, combining action-in-the-'hood-type gunfights and MTV visuals with some of the most beautiful poetry ever written. Sure, the film goes overboard on style, but it's Shakespeare, so you can't say that it skimps on content. Leonardo DiCaprio and Claire Danes star. Not all the line readings are perfect and some performers are miscast. They drop the poignant 'nightingale/morning lark' bit and Paris, once again, does not die at the end. None of that matters (well, we really did miss the 'nightingale/morning lark' part). On top of presenting a classic love story (the final death sequence is brilliantly handled, so that the lovers make one final tragic but conscious connection before passing on) and a hip, street-smart action movie (with loads of intriguing designer guns—one even has a key dangling from the handle), the film is an important artistic accomplishment, proving—or at least reminding those who need reminding—that Shakespeare's writing is as relevant and mesmerizing today as it was 400 years ago.

The picture is letterboxed with an aspect ratio of about 2.35:1 and no 16:9 enhancement. The color transfer is flawless and the image is consistently crisp, even in shots where the cinematography is deliberately grainy. The stereo surround sound is outstanding and the Dolby Digital track is a total knock-out. On the Dolby Digital track, each level of sound is clearly separated and defined, and each has a power that fires straight through you. Even the regular stereo soundtrack, however, is revved up and marvelously detailed. The 120 minute program also has a French audio track in standard stereo, optional English and Spanish subtitles ("Mis labios, como dos ruborosos peregrinos, están pronto/A suavizar con un tierno beso tan rudo contacto") and a trailer. (Fox identifies the program as just *Romeo & Juliet* on the jacket spine, although the film's proper title appears on the front and on the platter.)

William Tell (see Rossini's William Tell: Teatro Alla Scala)

Willy Wonka & the Chocolate Factory (Warner, 14546)

The intensely colorful 1971 feature is an ideal showcase for the ability of DVDs to deliver deep, rich and spectacular hues. The colors look fabulous, not just in the candy factory scenes, but throughout the film. The film is presented in letterboxed format on one side, with an aspect ratio of about 1.85:1 and an accommodation for enhanced 16:9 playback, and in full screen format on the other side. Since both are available, one need no longer worry about losing a particular chromatic bon-bon because of cropping or masking. Remastered for stereo, the film's soundtrack is cleaner and more forceful than its old monophonic mix and has a greater dimensionality, particularly on the Dolby Digital track. The 100 minute film is accompanied by an extensive cast profile section, some modest production notes and two trailers, one for the original release and one for the *25th Anniversary* reissue. The 1971 film is also available in French in standard stereo and in Spanish in mono, and can be supported by English, French or Spanish subtitles ("El Caramelero puede…").

The film, burdened with an anti-box office title, is an enduring cult favorite. It isn't pushy, which is why it can take several viewings to really settle into the imagination. Like any clever confection it may seem light, but it becomes addicting quickly enough. The story divides fairly evenly into two separate narrative sections, the first being the introduction of the children who "win" golden tickets to tour the candy factory, and the second being that tour. The story includes some mild lessons on over-indulgence and behaving oneself, but in an equal amount it says that a little indulgence and harmless misbehaving is quite all right. It is a fantasy that at times seems to have landed right in Munchkin Land, but it is never that far removed from a child's image of reality, the image that is still locked inside of us all.

Winds of the Wasteland (see The John Wayne Collection)

Wing Chun (Tai Seng, 34984)

Set in pre-technological China, Michelle Yeoh stars as the owner of a tofu store, whose beautiful and highly popular salesclerk is kidnapped by bandits. Yeoh's character also has a sister, and the three women are competing for the heart of a young stranger, who helps the two sisters retrieve the clerk. The stranger's martial arts skills are good, but Yeoh is the star and her powers are greatest of all. The fights are super, and would alone make the film worthwhile for fans, but the interplay between the characters is also highly entertaining, and the narrative adeptly ties everything together.

The picture is letterboxed, with an aspect ratio of about 1.75:1 and no 16:9 enhancement. The colors are okay. The image is a little soft now and then, some sequences are a bit washed out, and once in a while a scratch pops up, but fleshtones are usually crisp and

other hues are bright most of the time. The film has three audio tracks, Mandarin, Cantonese and English, and is accompanied by optional English subtitles. The dubbing reminded us of the many martial arts films we used to see on the TV on Saturday afternoon. There are times when a specific subtitle sentence will have a translation that is opposite of the translation in the dubbing, but the general meaning of the conversation remains consistent. The monophonic sound is bland, but the Dolby Digital track is a little stronger. The 93 minute film is accompanied by trailers and cast profiles.

Wing Commander (Fox, 4112171)

We tried to get some young friends to watch the 1999 sci-fi action feature with us, but they wondered off after the first half hour or so. Like World War II naval movies, the film has no clearly defined villains, just 'an enemy' that is cruising a quadrant of the galaxy in large battleships. The heroes have to secure an important navigational device and then get home before the enemy attacks. Based upon a popular computer game, the film is at times reminiscent of a western, at times reminiscent of a submarine movie and at times reminiscent of an aircraft-carrier-and-navy-pilots movie, but the character interactions are simplistic and uninteresting—there is no finesse to the emotional manipulations, the special effects are plentiful but tacky, and the narrative just grinds away, attempting one formula turn after another without generating any sense of involvement. If you can't fool kids, who can you fool?

The DVD looks and sounds terrific, however. All that computer graphic imagery, though fake-looking, comes across as incredibly sharp and incredibly vivid. The picture is in letterboxed format only, with an aspect ratio of about 2.35:1 and no 16:9 enhancement. The stereo surround sound is super, with many separation effects, and the Dolby Digital track is even better, with more elaborate separations and a stronger punch. The 100 minute program can be supported by optional English subtitles and is accompanied by photos of several cast members, a deceptively exciting trailer and a couple TV commercials.

Wings of JSDF: Japan Self-Defense Forces Hunters (Pioneer, PSI99216D)

No dialogue accompanies the 55 minute program that looks at the various planes in Japan's quasi-air force. The cameras look at all aspects of the planes, on the ground and in the air, and you get to see some of them shooting guns and missiles, which is cool. Some of the in-flight camera angles from outside the aircraft are also very impressive. The picture quality looks fine throughout the program. A musical score runs through the entire show, so there is no opportunity to jack up the jet sounds, and separation effects are modest but competent. In addition to fighters, there are AWACs and what is apparently identified as the 747 used by Japan's leader (i.e., their 'Air Force One').

Winning (Universal, 20526)

Paul Newman, Joanne Woodward and Robert Wagner star in the story of a race car driver who loses his touch for a while when he discovers that his wife has been unfaithful. The film runs 123 minutes, yet its narrative content is slight, and there are as many shots of Newman and Woodward gazing dreamily into one another's eyes as there are of Newman, helmeted and oil-streaked, gripping the wheel of a vibrating auto. The film goes nowhere except in circles, but fans of the stars will hardly mind. The performances are competent and the 1969 film, though it takes its time, tells a complete story.

The presentation is letterboxed with an aspect ratio of about 2.35:1 and no 16:9 enhancement. The romantic parts were shot in a let's-lose-a-decade-off-the-cheeks haze and as a result, the picture is often on the blurry side. The fleshtones are a little pale, but otherwise the colors look accurate enough and the presentation is workable. The music is presented in a moderately stereophonic format and some car sounds zip from one side to the other, but the stereo mix is usually subdued and the audio is passable. The 123 minute film can be supported by English, French or Spanish subtitles and is accompanied by a pretty good production essay, a short cast-and-director profile section and a fairly dishonest trailer.

Wishmaster (Artisan, 60456)

The enjoyable Wes Craven-produced evil genie movie directed by Robert Kurtzman, has a number of special features. Tammy Lauren, styled to evoke Linda Hamilton, stars as the woman who accidentally releases the demonic being from entrapment within a special gem. Although a little effort might have made the script even more clever and engaging (the genie traps people by turning their wishes against them), the film is reasonably entertaining and has quite a few well-staged special effects. Accompanying the 90 minute film is a good 24-minute 'making of' featurette that shows how many of the effects were achieved. There is also a commentary track featuring Kurtzman and screenwriter Peter Atkins, who tell how the project was developed (everyone's initial reaction to the idea of an 'evil genie' movie was negative), how the effects were accomplished (some of their comments overlap with the featurette, but give more details) and share a few anecdotes about the shoot (their van got stolen).

The 1997 film is presented in full screen format on one side and in letterboxed format on the other side, with an aspect ratio of about 1.85:1 and an accommodation for enhanced 16:9 playback. The letterboxing adds nothing to the sides of the image while taking away from the top and bottom, but even though we could see more of the special effects, we tended to prefer the letterbox framing. The picture quality is excellent. The colors are good and the image is crisp, creating distinctive edges among the hues and making objects seem vivid and immediate. The stereo surround sound is workable and the Dolby Digital track has a strong bass and engaging separation effects. The program is closed captioned.

Witchcraft (Simitar, 7263)
Witchcraft Part II (Simitar, 7265)

The occult thriller and its offspring are not very good, even within the constraints of the genre. Identical in style, both appear to have been shot with film, but include some sequences that involve video effects. Both have fairly fuzzy pictures with dullish, grainy colors and both have jacked up stereo surround soundtracks that aren't elegant but get the job done. Neither film is captioned.

Witchcraft is a variation on Rosemary's Baby. A young mother comes to stay at her mother-in-law's house after the birth of her son, and soon discovers that strange things are going on. There is some gore, but no fright and neither the acting nor the film's style is all that accomplished.

The legitimacy of the sequel, which makes effective use of clips from the earlier movie, is the one aspect of the films which is praiseworthy. Witchcraft II is about the son, grown and about to come of age. He is unaware of his past and is subject to a battle between the forces of good and evil. Although the cast is new, the acting still stinks and the cinematic qualities are not any stronger than the first film, but there is more sex, and the story does come to a satisfying conclusion. Since there are many flashbacks to the first film in II, you can follow the story well enough without viewing its predecessor.

The Witches of Eastwick (Warner, 11741)

Three suburban women manifest the Devil and proceed to give him Hell. The witty script, based upon a novel by John Updike, leans heavily on the ironies and tensions of suburban living. The film is presented in letterboxed format on one side, with an aspect ratio of about 2.35:1 and an accommodation for enhanced 16:9 playback, and in cropped format on the other side. The letterboxing is consistently more satisfying, giving you three of the film's female stars, Cher, Susan Sarandon and Michelle Pfeiffer, in a shot where the cropped version can only give you two. The picture is

crisp and colors are vivid, giving the film a fresh, immediate look that adds to its vitality. The stereo surround sound is totally wimpy compared to the DVD's super-charged Dolby Digital track. Rear channel activity serves primarily as an echo to what is going on in front, but the sounds are significantly enhanced, with greater detail and power. John William's musical score has also been isolated on one of the audio tracks in Dolby Digital and the 118 minute film is presented in French as well, without Dolby Digital. There are English, French and Spanish subtitles, cast and crew profiles, including a biography of John Updike, and some production notes, including a brief history of witches. An enjoyable theatrical trailer is presented in full screen format on the cropped side and slightly letterboxed on the letterboxed side.

The 1987 horror comedy, which also stars Jack Nicholson, has held up very well and remains highly entertaining, particularly when the presentation is as lovely and energized as it is on the DVD. Part of its popularity probably rests in the cloudiness of its message; each viewer gazing upon it will have a singular interpretation of good and bad in the actions of the characters. It must have been a very dynamic date movie, since it starts out being kind of anti-male, but then ends up being kind of anti-female. Everyone who watches it will squirm at some point. Despite all the special effects, however, the story is basically true to life. Whenever men and women get together, there will always be sorcery and witchcraft, in abundance.

With Honors (Warner, 13079)

Brendan Fraser and Joe Pesci star in the comedy about a homeless man and a college student. Pesci's character comes across Fraser's misplaced senior thesis, and divvies it back to him a page at a time in exchange for food and lodging. Although sporadically insightful, the dramatic situations and college talk often ring false, and the narrative is fairly predictable. It is only Pesci's convincing presence that keeps the viewer, like the hero, fascinated with the proceedings. Patrick Dempsey and Moira Kelly are also featured, with Gore Vidal as a professor.

The picture is presented in full screen format, adding a bit to the bottom and losing some from the sides in comparison to letterboxed versions. The color transfer is reasonably accurate and sharp, with adequate fleshtones. The stereo surround sound has a nice amount of power in places and is satisfying. There is also a French language track in stereo, and English closed captioning. The 1994 feature runs 101 minutes.

Without Limits (Warner, 14905)

Highly respected, having receiving widespread praise among film critics, the story of Steve Prefontaine as told by Robert Towne, turns out to be as boring as jogging. Although it was much sloppier in its execution, the television movie that dealt with the same subject, Prefontaine, had a more interesting story and created a more affecting portrait of the runner. Towne stays on the surface and has no clear goal for his film or his hero, just some platitudes about racing and life. The performances are achingly dull, or worse—before the Oscar nominations were announced, Donald Sutherland was highly touted for his supporting role as the coach, yet more than once we had to lower our eyes in embarrassment over the lines he is given (such as when he questions the security at the Munich Olympics)—and it is only Towne's technical competency at guiding the sound, the cinematography and editing that makes the movie at all watchable.

The 1998 film is in letterboxed format on one side, with an aspect ratio of about 2.35:1 and an accommodation for enhanced 16:9 playback, and in full screen format on the other side. The full screen image adds a lot of picture information to the bottom in comparison to the letterboxed image and loses enough on the side to drop significant characters here and there. The color transfer is excellent. Hues have a subtle but carefully delineated softness, with each slight variation of shade as distinctive as the next.

The film's love scenes thrive on Jefferson Airplane tunes and, throughout the movie, pop music and incidental sound effects are deftly applied with a full dimensionality that does all it can to draw the viewer into each scene. It just is a shame that there's nothing going on once you get there. The Dolby Digital track is even better, with stronger, crisper definitions and more energy. The 118 minute feature is also available in French in Dolby Digital and can be supported by English or French subtitles. There is a trailer that tries its best, a modest cast & crew profile section and a brief essay about Prefontaine's accomplishments off the racetrack.

The Wiz (Universal, 20534)

An urban-oriented adaptation of **The Wizard of Oz** directed by Sidney Lumet, Diana Ross, who is too old and just not plucky enough for the part, and Michael Jackson star in the somewhat bloated but sporadically enlivening musical. The 1978 film has a highly stylized, though mostly vacant, New York setting. The viewer is treated to an elaborate art design, a rousing musical score, and many engaging moments by the supporting performers, particularly Nipsey Russell as the Tin Man, but the movie is ultimately so empty it might as well be set in Kansas.

The picture is in letterboxed format only, with an aspect ratio of about 1.85:1 and no 16:9 enhancement. The picture is reasonably colorful and the hues are stable, but the source material does have a little damage in places and it could probably be a little crisper. The stereo surround sound has an older mix, with limited rear channel effects, and there is a four-channel Dolby Digital track that seems indistinguishable from the standard track. The 135 minute feature can be supported by English or French subtitles ("Ne me faites pas part des mauvaises nouvelles/Car je me réveille déjà de méchante humeur/Alors, ne me dites pas des horreurs") and is accompanied by an excellent 'making of' featurette that shows how real New York locations were utilized for the fantasy, as well as a how the show came into being and how the musical numbers were shot. There is also a standard trailer, production notes, and a cast-and-director profile section.

The Wizard of Oz (MGM, 906044)

For three decades American families gathered around their television sets every year to watch a tale of a young girl who journeys into a fantasy land and, from her experiences, realizes there's no place like home. **The Wizard of Oz** was, in a way, one of the first and most significantly re-watchable home video hits, and is probably more effective as family entertainment on television, where its threatening, 'camp' imagery is held in check, than it is on a big screen.

The black-and-white sequence is crisp, and when Dorothy lands in Oz, the colors are richer and sharper than ever before. Fleshtones are accurate and finely detailed. Even Billie Burke's hair, for example, looks much more detailed and realistic than in the past, changing from a general golden blond on LD to a feathered auburn blond. The monophonic sound is offered up in English, Spanish or French, can be supported by English, French or Spanish subtitles ("Nous représentons la Confrérie des Sucreries…"), and the 102 minute film is accompanied by a theatrical trailer.

Wolf (Columbia TriStar, 71755)

Let other movies do the fancy special effects, because Mike Nichols' 1994 intellectual werewolf movie this movie is fine for what it is—the cast is enjoyable and the plot is fully entertaining. Jack Nicholson portrays a book editor who becomes more skilled at office politics after he is bitten by a wolf, eventually running off into the woods with the daughter (Michelle Pfeiffer) of the publishing house's owner. There are a few surprises and many nice touches along the way. Nichols stages the film competently and never lets the story's cerebral aspects get in the way of the entertainment.

The picture is letterboxed on one side, with an aspect ratio of about 1.85:1 and an accommodation for enhanced 16:9 playback,

and is in full screen format on the other side. The image is crisp and nicely detailed throughout the film, and the many darker sequences create no problems whatsoever. The stereo surround sound and Dolby Digital sound are not showy, but have a number of good separation effects (a whistling tea pot had us running to make sure we'd turned off our stove). The125 minute program also has French and Spanish audio tracks in standard stereo, optional Spanish and Korean subtitles, and English closed captioning.

Woman of the Year (MGM, 906646)

Spencer Tracy and Katharine Hepburn star in the 1942 feature, directed by George Stevens. This is the one where she is a political reporter and he is a sportswriter. The black-and-white image is very crisp, with deep blacks and detailed contrasts. The monophonic sound is okay and the are also French and Spanish language tracks. The 114 minute film can be supported by English, French or Spanish subtitles, and is accompanied by an original theatrical trailers.

The film is about the adjustments a couple must make to be married and to maintain the affections which brought them together to begin with. Like most of the Tracy/Hepburn films, it avoids the normal male/female stereotypes while embracing the genders of the two stars. If you want to know how movies could be sexy back when they weren't allowed to be, or if you just want an enjoyable two hours of romantic comedy, **Woman of the Year** is an excellent choice.

A Woman Under the Influence (Pioneer, PSE98161)

Gena Rowlands stars as a the wife of a construction foreman, played by Peter Falk. She has a nervous breakdown and then comes back, a little calmer but not very cured. The improvisational style deadens the pace of every scene, while the characters act with erratic behavior far more common in real life than in the movies. All this would be tolerable if Rowlands was believable in the central role, but she isn't, perhaps because John Cassavetes' 1974 film is just too ambitious. She can hit the emotions, but she is not a screenwriter and she, like the other performers, often can't find dialogue that would come naturally from her character. As a mother to the couple's kids she is utterly unconvincing, talking to them like a distracted school teacher who has just begun the term. Interacting with the adults she is on firmer ground but there is a lot of self-conscious stalling while she and the other performers try to find their way through a scene.

The 147 minute has been released on a two-sided DVD. The colors look quite nice, with reasonably accurate fleshtones and bright hues. The picture is a little soft and grainy, however, and there is some minor evidence of wear. The film is presented in full screen format and on some monitors the sound boom will be visible in a number of scenes. The monophonic sound is a little dull. There is no captioning.

Women in Revolt (Image, ID4733PYDVD)

The film is a failure, and will be of interest only to fans who just can't get enough of director Paul Morrissey's milieu. Morrissey utilized transvestite performers quite effectively in **Flesh** and especially **Trash**, but in **Women** he gives them free reign without enough narrative to work through. Ostensibly about a group of radical feminists who want to eliminate men, the performers thrash about and just plain try too hard to be funny. Even when there are glimmers of genuine humor, it usually turns out to be at the end of a scene, so the situation changes and things go back to not being funny. We were reminded of Valerie Solanas, the radical feminist played by Lili Tyler in *I Shot Andy Warhol*, and the film could very well have been inspired by her writing, but it is an amalgam of half-formed ideas played out as an unpracticed burlesque.

The 99 minutes film is presented in full screen format. The source material on has incidental damage and other evidence of wear, but colors are surprisingly rich and there is no more grain or fuzzy blurring than what the original cinematography brought to the source. John Cale did the music, and the monophonic sound is passable. There is no captioning.

Women of Valor (Simitar, 7276)

Susan Sarandon and Kristy McNichol star in the 1986 TV film, about Army nurses captured and incarcerated by the Japanese in the Philippines. Although the movie stays within broadcast standards, it doesn't pull any punches and presents a fairly brutal portrait of life in the POW camps. The emotional conflicts are somewhat simplified and, despite some token backpedaling, its negative representation of the Japanese is rather intense, but for those who find the basic parameters of the POW genre to be engaging, the film is enjoyable and its genre variations—such as giving birth in captivity—are intriguing.

The colors are a little aged, dark sequences are bit unstable and the set decoration is intentionally grimy, but the presentation is workable. The monophonic sound is adequate. The 95 minute program is accompanied by partial filmographies for Sarandon and McNichol, and is not captioned.

The Wonder Years (see The Best of The Wonder Years)

Wonders of the Deep (Madacy, DVD99054)
Wonders of the Deep: Costa Rica / Cocos Islands, The Galapagos (Madacy, DVD990541)
Wonders of the Deep: Emerald Sea / British Columbia / Shipwrecks (Madacy, DVD990542)
Wonders of the Deep: Australia, Queensland (Madacy, DVD990543)

Six episodes from a very good 22 minute ('half hour') travel program have been collected in the box set and are also available in groups of two on the three individual releases. The picture looks terrific on all the episodes and the monophonic sound is strong. The underwater photography is usually well lit and very colorful, with a crisp, solid image. The shows are not captioned and are accompanied by brief essays reiterating and expanding upon some of the information contained in each episode. The shows function as true travel programs and spend almost as much time above water as below, but it is a nice mix. They visit a particular locale and look at the sights, hook up with a local diving tour service who gets some terrific promotion from the visit, and then examine with clarity and fascination many of the unusual plants and animals found beneath the waves in that area.

The episodes have been paired for geographic similarities. Both shows in **Costa Rica / Cocos Islands, Galapagos** look at the waters off islands in the Eastern Pacific. Among the more interesting sights are a huge school of hammerheads (the program does better than any other we've watched in explaining what a hammerhead's unusually shaped head is for), huge manta rays, tortoises (are there any still around that knew Charlie Darwin?), sea lions, penguins and many others.

Perhaps the most interesting programs, however, are **Emerald Sea / British Columbia / Shipwrecks**, since they look at an area outside of the tropics and not usually covered in scuba programs, northern Vancouver Island. There are lots of octopus, a very interesting eel, dolphins, jelly fish, sea cucumbers, sea pens and other interesting anemones, as well as a look at the deliberate sinking of a destroyer to create an artificial reef and other ships that now play host to underwater life.

Australia, Queensland visits the continent's more remote shores, looking at giant clams (not as dangerous as legend would have it), sharks (now they're dangerous), gigantic cod that feed out of the diver's hands, some friendly eels, crocodiles, flatworms and many more. All three programs are filled with creatures of chromatic splendor, and the DVDs are so accurate you may see water dripping out the side of your monitor.

The Wonderful, Horrible Life of Leni Riefenstahl (Kino, K107DVD)

The 188 minute 1993 documentary provides a general biography of Riefenstahl's life, using a liberal number of clips from her films, archival materials (including extensive footage that she shot privately over the years), and interviews, in which the filmmakers take her to the locations where she made her movies and ask her to talk about her experiences. She is quite a talker.

Riefenstahl's two greatest works, *Triumph of the Will* and *Olympia*, were both essentially financed by Adolf Hitler, and although Riefenstahl never joined the Nazi party, she certainly schmoozed with them as any ambitious German citizen might have, given the opportunity. The film spells out the conflicts superbly, and Riefenstahl makes a fairly convincing argument that she was oblivious to much of what was going on, being wrapped up in the productions of her films instead (it can be argued that both *Triumph of the Will* and *Olympia* have endured because they are oblivious to the deeper concepts of Nazism). She also apologizes profusely and consistently—saying she hates *Triumph of the Will* and wishes she'd never made it—and can't understand why so many people refuse to consider that she's repented.

What the film also shows, however, is how brilliant a filmmaker Riefenstahl was, particularly in her instinct for black-and-white cinematography and her feel for the rhythm of editing. By sharing clips of all her films, the documentary brings out aspects of her talent that are less clear when the works are viewed individually. To give one example—an editing trick she learned from another director while working on her first film, advancing the action subtly during a montage, is then seen applied in the later films with further sophistication, particularly in the Olympic Games movie, *Olympia*, where many contestants in a sequence are blended by the editing into a single athlete. Riefenstahl's insights on the filmmaking process are often highly valuable and, in the spirit of artistic accomplishment, they transcend petty political consideration.

The picture quality, a mix of color footage and black and white, is fine. The sound is primarily monophonic and is adequately presented. The narration and some of the dialogue are in English, without closed captioning, and most of the film clips and conversations with Riefenstahl are in German with permanent English subtitles.

Woodstock: The Director's Cut (Warner, 135439)

Wow! **Woodstock** in Dolby Digital! Warner has released the 225 minute **Director's Cut**, splitting the movie to two sides of the DVD. Since the widescreen documentary film is often quite grainy or soft-looking, the faint improvements to the sharpness of the image and accuracy of the colors do not account for much. Warner has provided a varying letterboxing to imitate the film's shifts between multiple image widescreen and single image standard screen compositions. The regular stereo surround sound is not as good as the LD. It has less power and less detail. But the DVD's Dolby Digital track is the best of all, with a monster bass and an acute clarity of tone all up and down the scale. Listening to it is like standing underneath the speakers at the concert itself. The program has English, Spanish and French subtitles ("En nous concentrant, nous pourrons peut-être arrêter la pluie?"), but no other special features.

Opening with the movie's MPAA rating bursting into flames, carrying an Intermission title card that features the film's favorite four letter word, and adding footage that widens the breadth of the documentary, the **Director's Cut** is a surprisingly moving and effective program, and a significant improvement over the traditional 185 minute feature film. The additional music sequences are of very high quality, though none were showy enough to survive the movie's final cut the first time out, including excellent and superbly photographed performances of Canned Heat doing *A Change Is Going to Come*, Jefferson Airplane doing *Won't You Try/Saturday Afternoon*, and Jimi Hendrix performing *Voodoo Chile*. In addition to the music sequences, director Michael Wadleigh has also expanded the interview and added a substantial amount of crowd-and-environs footage. Perhaps the movie might have been more daunting to first time viewers at this length, but in retrospect the entire documentary content is improved by the additions, giving the viewer a better feeling for the quality and intelligence of the music, a sense of how the mood and weather advanced during each day of the festival, and a more detailed portrait of the varying philosophies ascribed to by the attendees.

Woodstock Jazz Festival (see **Chick Corea Pat Metheny Lee Konitz: Woodstock Jazz Festival**)

Working With Orson Welles (Image, ID5668GADVD)

A collection of reminiscences by the actors and technicians who worked on his films, particularly *Othello*, *F for Fake* and the uncompleted *The Other Side of the Wind*, is combined with a few clips and trailers in the 94 minute 1993 program. Some of the stories are quite funny and taken together a portrait of Welles' professional persona begins to emerge. There is an emphasis on the interviews, so repeat potential is a bit limited, but it is still a fun program, and now that time has passed, it is as valuable for its footage of departed personages such as Susan Strasberg as it is for the profiles of Welles himself. The color interviews are very sharp and the black-and-white footage looks fine. The monophonic sound is also bright and solid, and the program is not captioned. An extensive Welles filmography is also included.

The World of Volcanoes (see **Killer Volcanoes and Deadly Peaks**)

World War II (Madacy, DVD99000)
World War II: Prelude to War / The Nazis Strike (Madacy, DVD990001)
World War II: Divide and Conquer / The Battle of Britain (Madacy, DVD990002)
World War II: The Battle of Russia / The Battle of China (Madacy, DVD990003)
World War II: War Comes to America / D-Day: The Normandy Invasion (Madacy, DVD990004)
World War II: The World at War / Appointment in Tokyo (Madacy, DVD990005)

A number of the superbly conceived World War II *Why We Fight* films, many directed by Frank Capra and narrated by Walter Huston, have been issued in a box set and as individual releases. The D-Day film and **World at War – Appointment in Tokyo** are not *Why We Fight* features, but are on the same level of cinematic and narrative quality.

The black-and-white source material is consistently shaky, but not overly distorted. Since the documentaries were largely drawn from footage shot under adverse conditions, scratches and other wear are inevitable, but it is also likely that, somewhere, better source material exists than what has been used. The films are in black and white, and some artifacting accompanies the grainiest and most jittery segments, though such flaws are rarely distracting. There are also a few frame skips and a few severe splices scattered throughout the films. The monophonic sound has its share of noise and distortion, but the narration is coherent and the music is bearable. None of the programs are time encoded. Each platter contains, in addition to the two 30–40 minute films, a brief film clip (such as an excerpt from *Triumph of the Will*), still photos of a couple propaganda posters, and several brief biographical profiles of wartime figures. The programs are not captioned.

In addition to the efficiency of the editing and the power of adept storytelling, the films also look at the war from a different perspective than one has today, particularly in the documentation of events, such as the invasion of Norway, that no longer receive much attention. *Prelude to War* is an overview of what America stands for and how dastardly the leaders of the Axis powers are, but it does so in elegant and compelling terms. *The Nazis Strike* and *Divide and Conquer* look at Germany's step-by-step encroachments on the rest of Europe in great detail, breaking down such events as the takeover of Czechoslovakia and the conquering of Poland that today are looked upon as no more than preliminary skirmishes.

The Battle of Britain is a better story when the true behind-the-scenes facts are known, but the film emphasizes British resolve and is exhilarating as an emotional turning point in the tale of the War. There are many facts in both **The Battle of Russia** and *The Battle of China* that rarely get much of an airing today, particularly the lengthy posturing that went on in China as Japan edged its way across the mainland. *War Comes to America* was the final *Why We Fight* feature and is another rousing examination of American spirit and moral imperative. The D-Day film looks at the elaborate preparations that went into the invasion. *World at War* seems to draw footage from all the other films to give an overview of the War's political conflicts and major turning points. It is narrated by Paul Stewart. *Appointment in Tokyo*, which has a fuzzier, copy-of-a-copy picture, looks at the loss of The Philippines and the gradual Allied efforts to re-take the islands.

The World's Greatest Animation (Image, ID4530JFDVD)

A cartoon anthology that lives up to its title, the DVD contains sixteen cartoons, most of which would fall onto anybody's list of the best non-Hollywood animated short films. There is, for example, *Balance*, a thrilling stop motion piece about human figures teetering on a suspended platform, and *Creature Comforts*, a very amusing claymation piece, ostensibly interviewing animals in a zoo. There is the claymation *Sundae in New York*; the utterly addictive *The Cat Came Back*; a typical Bill Plympton effort, *Your Face*; an early computer animation piece inspired by Tex Avery, *Technological Threat*; *Tango*, in which a number of live action activities are combined to appear in as if they are happening repetitiously in a room; Will Vinton's claymation effort, *The Great Cognito*, in which a figure changes into WWII personages; the narrative cartoons, *Crac!* (about a rocking chair), *Special Delivery* (about a dead mailman), *Every Child* (about an abandoned baby being passed from one house to the next), *A Greek Tragedy* (about three female statues who start goofing off), and *The Big Snit* (about a couple playing a game while a war is going on); *The Fly*, from his point-of-view; *Charade*, in which animated figures act out movie titles; and *Anna & Bella*, a poignant piece about the romantic lives of two sisters.

The picture and audio quality are comparable to the LD and the pieces are all in good condition, with solid, stable colors and fairly clean source material (there is some incidental wear). The cartoons are all presented in mono although some, such as *The Cat Came Back*, have appeared in stereo elsewhere. The collection runs 105 minutes.

World's Greatest Roller Coaster Thrills (Image, ID4384GHDVD)

The 3-D effects are a haphazard by-product of the program's cinematography and have nothing to do with the show itself, capitalizing instead upon the optical illusion created when one watches left-right camera movement (or right-left object movement) with one's right eye darkened. Nevertheless, even without the sporadic 3-D effects, fans will surely appreciate the show.

The program visits Marineland in Niagara Falls Ontario, Blackpool Pleasure Beach, Drayton Manor, and Alton Towers in England, Buffalo Bill's Resort in Las Vegas, La Feria Chapultepec Magico in Mexico, Luna Park in Sydney Australia, Dreamworld and Sea World on the coast of Brisbane in Australia, Ocean Park in Hong Kong, and a huge but portable German coaster. After a profile of the park, each ride is shown twice, once from multiple, edited angles and once unedited from the front seat. The front seat shots are then replayed at the end without interruption. The program runs 82 minutes. The picture is fine. The stereo sound is too realistic to provide much in the way of thrills.

The World's Luckiest Black Man X-rated (Vivid, UPC#0073215526)

With almost no dialogue and 101 actresses in sort of a harem setting, the program is a 118 minutes of solid, well, you know. It is relentless, but the variations are sufficient to keep fans intrigued. The picture looks good, with bright, sharp hues and effectively detailed fleshtones. The sound is adequate.

The World's Luckiest Man X-rated (Vivid, UPC#073214160)

There is no narrative, but the premise is engaging, with 101 actresses gathered in the backyard of a mansion to service a single male porno star. As each takes her turn, the others play volleyball with inflatable dolls and engage in other witty activities. The picture quality is good, with decent fleshtones and a sharp focus. The monophonic sound captures ambient dialogue, but there really isn't much conversation going on at the center of the action. The 74 minute program is accompanied by an additional 20 minute sequence in which the women who aren't busy amuse themselves in a large swimming pool, and an enjoyable 10 minute 'making of' sequence that breaks down some of the barriers to present the actresses in genuinely unguarded moments.

Wrongfully Accused (Warner, 16129)

There's at least one gag every ten seconds, even during the end credits. Leslie Nielson stars in the thriller film parody, a take-off on **The Fugitive** and several dozen other movies. Because there are so many funny things in the film, it can be as much fun to just jump into it anywhere and sample a bit. Indeed, the movie may work better if you take breaks from it every so often, before humor satiation sets in. The narrative is a little convoluted, but it seems to serve the material well enough, and if one gag doesn't seem funny, the next or the next after that will.

The film is presented in full screen format, but that is probably to its advantage, enabling the viewer to take in more of the gags that might have been masked off a letterboxed version. The colors are bright, the image is sharp and fleshtones look fine. The stereo surround sound is okay and the Dolby Digital sound has some enjoyable separation effects. The 86 minute film is also available in French in Dolby Digital and can be supported by English, French or Spanish subtitles ("J'aimerais brosser votre tableau un jour." "Etes-vous femme de ménage?" "Non, portraitiste").

Also featured on the DVD are a wonderful and all-too-brief mix of serious and comical interviews with the cast and crew, an excellent (serious) 8 minute breakdown of the film's special effects, 'live' production notes that discuss how several major sequences were shot (with a pun-heavy voiceover narration), a nice collection of publicity stills (though it has no end marking, it just loops around to the beginning again), a standard cast profile section, a reliably amusing trailer and TV commercial, and a Web-linked trivia game that we could never get to work right.

Wuthering Heights (HBO, 90729)

The black-and-white transfer is a stunningly and rapturous recreation of Gregg Toland's outstanding cinematography. The presentation looks so good that even the slightest artifacting is noticeable, although such discrepancies are minimal. Due to its precision and smoothness, you become aware of Toland's incredible design, of how, in almost every shot, the whitest or brightest object always appears in the center of the picture, and how, then, variations on the design are utilized at key moments (when Kathy proclaims "I am Heathcliff," she is surrounded by light).

And what emotions the drama has! The 1934 film, directed by William Wyler and starring Merle Oberon, Laurence Olivier and David Niven (whose performance in a rather thankless role becomes particularly admirable on multiple viewings), is a whirling vane that spins upon the loves of its two protagonists, who let their mood swings get the best of them at critical moments in their lives. It once was easy for viewers to step away and view their actions as capricious, but with the DVD's transfer and Toland's cinematogra-phy constantly drawing you toward their hearts, it is easier to understand that the passion bringing them together is just too untame to hold them.

The monophonic sound is in very good condition and free of most age-related noise. There are also tracks in French, Spanish and Italian, along with optional English, French or Spanish subtitles. There is a 10 minute interview with Geraldine Fitzgerald, who portrayed Niven's sister, along with a trailer for the 103 minute film.

X

The X-Files: Fight the Future (Fox, 4110394)

David Duchovny and Gillian Anderson star in what is essentially another episode of the TV series, and not a very good one. Those who like the film are responding legitimately to the quality of the TV series upon which it is based, and its strengths are those of the TV show—the witty by-play between the characters, the overriding atmosphere of mystery and paranoia, and a few functional action sequences. There are some exciting sequences, some interesting images, and many pleasures endemic to the show itself. But it is kind of a lame movie. More so than normal, the heroes are handed every lead and explicate themselves from trouble without logic, while the special effects sequences are just bigger versions of the special effects already used on the TV series.

Producer Chris Carter and director Rob Bowman provide a commentary track, talking about the differences between the big screen and the little screen, and their philosophies on designing the TV show as well as the film. Speaking separately, they both talk about being awe-inspired over the presence of Martin Landau, about dividing the responsibilities (Carter is in charge of the concept and was apparently always around to kibitz, but Bowman was in charge of the film) and about how the big show sequences were shot. One speaks with some surprise about discovering how different a feature film is from a TV episode, both in what the audience expects (you have to keep moving forward, with very little time to stop and smell the roses) and why costs are so high (everything has to 'look big'; and if you work weekends to meet a deadline, the dollars burn fast). At times they fall into providing a play-by-play about what is happening on the screen and, like the movie, the talk seems designed for fans and non-fans alike, but there are interesting details and insights. Much of the film's plot is explained, and while it is still illogical, at least it becomes less incomprehensible.

There is also a 'half hour' promotional 'making of' program that makes the movie look a lot more exciting than it really is, two engaging theatrical teasers and a decent theatrical trailer. The 'making of' piece goes into detail about the explosion sequence and the bee sequence, while providing a brief overview of the series and its transition to film.

The picture is letterboxed with an aspect ratio of about 2.35:1 and no 16:9 enhancement. The presentation is blissfully free of Carter's intro, which plagued all other home video renditions of the film. Colors are precise and sharp. The many darker sequences are stable and effectively detailed. The stereo surround sound and Dolby Digital sound have a modest number of flamboyant effects, with the Dolby Digital track providing more dimensionality and energy. The film runs 122 minutes, adding one brief conversational sequence not in the theatrical film that relates more to the series than to the movie at hand. The film also has a French soundtrack in standard stereo, and both the movie and the documentary can be supported by optional English or Spanish subtitling.

Xtreme Janine X-rated (Vivid, UPC#0073215574)

The first 13 minutes are repeated, extending the program's complete running time to 86 minutes. Otherwise, the program is competently produced. The actress, Janine, is seen interviewing fellow actresses for parts in a pair of elaborate all-female erotic sequences, which are then followed by the completed sequences. The show opens with a title card that claims that the interview footage is genuine, though it seems a little more polished than the interview sequences in some of the other **Xtreme** programs. Nevertheless, it is an energetic and engaging show. The picture looks good, with bright hues and crisp fleshtones. The sound is adequate. There are multiple angle sequences and elaborate hardcore interactive promotional features.

Xtro: Watch the Skies (Image, ID5632FMDVD)

Unlike its two predecessors, to which it is related in name only (the film's end credit title card is just *Watch the Skies*), the 1995 program is relatively original and creative, about a group of marines sent to defuse bombs on a remote island that has been used as a military practice target. When they get there, however, they discover that their superiors had ulterior motives and there is an alien on the loose with a bad attitude. For the film's very limited budget, the special effects are excellent and the movie is expertly directed, by Harry Bromley Davenport. The camera angles are consistently efficient, yet artistic, and the cast members give performances that clearly tax the upper limits of their talents. The film is no great masterpiece, but it is certainly entertaining and continually exceeds expectations as it progresses.

The picture quality is erratic depending upon the lighting, but in its best sequences the image is sharp and colors are bright, with viable fleshtones. Darker sequences are grainier and murkier. The stereo sound is inconsistent and a little distorted in places. The 97 minute program is not captioned.

XXX X-rated (DaViD, D8023)

Two detectives investigate a murder that leads them to uncover a blackmail plot. The narrative is coherent and the erotic sequences are passable. The picture quality looks fine, with sharp hues and adequate fleshtones. The monophonic sound is okay. The 80 minute program features Melissa Hill, Sindee Cox and Kim Katraine.

Y

The Year of Living Dangerously (MGM, 906638)

The 1982 film, directed by Peter Weir, doesn't so much have an ending as a sweeping up of loose pieces, and had the filmmakers developed a more gripping dramatic conclusion, it might have been much more successful. The movie's atmosphere, however, makes it a compelling DVD. The romantic angle between Mel Gibson and Sigourney Weaver may be concluded at a distance, but while it is close up the viewer is likely to become as smitten as the characters. The Indonesian setting (the movie takes place near the end of Sukarno's reign, using the country's political turmoil as a backdrop for the story of a rookie correspondent, played by Gibson, and his relationship with an enigmatic photographer, played by Linda Hunt, who steers him toward Weaver's character, an intelligence attaché) and the eccentricity of the characters is sufficient for creating a mood of adventure and exotic romance. Sometimes with home video, mood is all a viewer is looking for.

The film is presented in letterboxed format, with an aspect ratio of about 2.35:1 and an accommodation for enhanced 16:9 playback. Colors are accurate and finely detailed, and fleshtones look solid. The stereo sound does not have elaborate separation effects, but there is a viable dimensionality. The 115 minute film is also presented in French and Spanish in mono, and can be accompanied by English, French or Spanish subtitles. There is a theatrical trailer as well, which has very nice graphics.

Yellowstone (SlingShot, DVD9808)

The IMAX travel program looks at the history of the park (including re-enacted depictions of early visitors) and explores the most interesting landforms and wildlife. It is not time encoded, but apparently runs 60 minutes. The image composition is designed for big, big screens and includes many precision-detailed vistas that make an effective transition from IMAX to DVD. Highlights include a peek down the innards of a geyser and the woozy, almost three-dimensional views of canyons and steep escarpments. The picture is sharp and colors are accurate. The stereo surround sound and Dolby Digital sound have a deliberate dimensionality, but there are not many sequences where it is worth much, as it is mostly the flourishing musical scores and a few incidental location noises that show up on the surround channels. The audio is also available in German and Mandarin.

Yes (see **Anderson Bruford Wakeman Howe: An Evening of Yes Music Plus**)

Yes: Live in Philadelphia 1979 (Image, ID5501CADVD

The poorly lit, 51 minute, six-song concert, the picture is a hazy blur much of the time, though Image has done a good job keeping artifacting to a minimum. The bottom of the screen will display a constant video interference on some monitors, and at one point a video roll bar passes through the image. The sound has none of the purity found in the group's studio recordings and is too flat to provide the kind of raw edge those studio recordings could use. Any tone outside the middle range tends to go fuzzy.

Yessongs (Image, ID4209CLDVD)

It is hard to say how relevant the 1973 world tour of the rock group Yes will be for today's video audiences. The concert film has a grainy, blue picture. Yes was known for their precise, electronic compositions and while their work was attractive when it came from a studio session, it is utter cacophony in cavernous auditoriums. There are a few, short inserts of biological/nature footage that help the pace. The filmmakers err, however, when they include the sound of frantic whistles and clapping on a shot of a bored and immobile audience hardly moving in their seats. The most popular portion of the concert is a Rick Wakeman medley of Christmas tunes (we're not kidding) that today's listeners will probably find a bit schmaltzy. Well, what can you expect from such an old-fashioned group? The stereo sound is subdued by the live recording and only die hard fans are really going to be interested in the 72 minute 1974 program.

Ying Huang (see **Merry Christmas from Vienna: Plácido Domingo Ying Huang Michael Bolton**)

Yosemite Watersongs (Image, PDL5756DVD)

Set to the music of Windham Hill artist Douglas Spotted Eagle, the deftly edited and very lovely 35 minute program depicts different aspects of Yosemite during different seasons with a captivating combination of water, light and nature. In one sequence, there is a rainbow formed in a waterfall by horizontal light that sets it against a dark background—quite a rarity.

The image is presented in full screen format and is exceedingly crisp, with precise colors and shadings in every shot. The standard stereo surround sound is sharper and more encompassing than many 5-channel Dolby Digital tracks. On an alternate track, there is a commentary by the video artist, Sterling Johnson, who talks about Yosemite, about how he captured the various shots, and about what he wanted to achieve. He explains that he likes to use dissolves but he once had to work for a guy who hated dissolves, so, as a result, every dissolve he employs is thoroughly justified, drawing the viewer through the images as effectively as Spotted Eagle's music does. There is also a chapter link from a map of Yosemite to sequences from the program, a couple of promo clips, and DVD-ROM materials, including screen savers, greeting cards and wallpaper.

You've Got Mail (Warner, 16954)

We looked at the opening scenes of Nora Ephron's 1998 effort as sort of the Barnes & Noble of romantic comedies. It seemed to lack the charm or the precision of its inspiration, Ernst Lubitsch's *The Shop Around the Corner*, and was getting by only on the size of its stars and reliability of the general concept. But then, about halfway through, we arrived at a scene that is taken directly from the earlier film, where Tom Hanks' character, a chain bookstore executive, first realizes that Meg Ryan's character, a small bookshop owner, is his anonymous Internet pen pal, and pesters her while she tries to shoo him away. Here the talents of the two stars take command of the film, and they deliver the material with such joyful competence that we were won over for the rest of the movie. It is still a weakly conceived and poorly directed film, but it is a highly enjoyable and satisfying, weakly conceived and poorly directed film.

Adding to the fun, the DVD is an inspired creation that begins with the movie and then expands upon its use of the Internet, its use of New York City and its use of children's literature to enhance one's appreciation of the film and the passions of the filmmakers. As Ephron points out on a commentary track, New York City itself is like the Internet—big and foreboding at first, it turns out to be a collection of small, almost isolated communities, and the DVD is ideal for exploring both the City and the Web.

The DVD has regular film-related features, and it also has a collection of DVD-ROM materials. The DVD-ROM can send you directly to Warner's own chat site, where you can work up a relationship with your own anonymous soul mate, though we'll bet big bucks your correspondent will not spell or punctuate as accurately as the heroes do in the film. Other DVD-ROM materials include the aforementioned, grammatically accurate cyber correspondence from the movie, which has been replicated in full, along with comparative scenes from **You've Got Mail**, *The Shop Around the Corner*, and another weak remake, *In the Good Old Summertime* (Nov. '91), a tour of the locations used in the film, a juke box-style playback option of the songs used in the film, 'sounds' from New York City, a bibliography of the books mentioned in the movie, and the typical collection of screen savers and other cyber-paraphernalia.

The film is presented in letterboxed format only, with an aspect ratio of about 1.85:1 and an accommodation for enhanced 16:9 playback. The picture looks fine, with crisp, accurate colors, and the stereo surround sound and Dolby Digital sound are okay, with the film's budget bringing an enhanced immediacy and smoothness to the pop songs on the musical score. There is also a 'music only' track, including the pop songs, in standard stereo.

Included with the 120 minute film for standard DVD playback is a 15 minute promotional featurette, much of which is conducted as an interview with Ephron, who talks more about writing than about other elements of the film; a less flexible than the DVD-ROM but still rewarding 'tour' of the movie's locations (these are accompanied by behind-the-scenes shots of the location shoots, plus enlightening commentary by Ephron on everything from the practical functions of certain New York establishments to the reason why Starbucks has lowered the crime rates in America's cities); a terrific 4-minute promotional trailer for *Shop Around the Corner*, in beautiful condition, that includes a brief word from Lubitsch, as well as a standard trailer for *Good Old Summertime* and two trailers for **You've Got Mail**; and a cast & crew profile section.

Additionally, there is the commentary channel featuring Ephron and producer Lauren Shuler Donner. They cover lots of details about the production, the players, how their own backgrounds (in publishing) related to the film and what they were after in the story. Ephron's shortcomings are readily apparent—she is repeatedly proud of having hidden what ought to be a major gag (where Hanks' chat handle comes from), obscuring it so well that probably nobody sees it—but her passion is also apparent, for the story concept and for the New York neighborhood she used as its location. As she and Donner share these passions with the listener, an affection and respect for the film grows and grows.

Young Duke Series: The Fugitive (UAV, 40079)

John Wayne's 'B' westerns are always floating around, and UAV has released a package of three of them where the films have been edited down to 22 minutes each, probably to fit them into half hour TV slots. The films, originally produced in the early Thirties, have also been re-named, colorized, and given stereo musical scores. The DVD features the title film, which is actually *Sagebrush Trail*, along with *On the Run*, which is actually *Desert Trail*, and *Next of Kin*, which is actually *West of the Divide*. Trimming the films down to 22 minutes creates some minor confusions. It comes as a surprise, for example, when the heroine picks up a flashlight in **Fugitive**, because you think it is taking place in the old west, but in the real *Sagebrush Trail*, you see the hero escape from a contemporary prison and you understand he's just high tailed it to a place where they still use horses. Nevertheless, the plots remain coherent and many of the best stunts have been retained, so the films can be enjoyable.

In **Fugitive**/*Sagebrush Trail*, Wayne, blamed for a murder he didn't commit, pretends to join an outlaw gang in their hideaway, so he can uncover the real murderer. In *On the Run*/*Desert Trail* he is blamed for a rodeo robbery and several other crimes, and has to duck the law while he identifies the real criminals. In *Next of Kin*/*West of the Divide*, he pretends to join a gang that is harassing a rancher, but actually helps the rancher defend the place.

The colorization on the three films is quite good, with the colors staying in the lines, fleshtones looking realistic and incidental colors providing a cheerful enhancement to the setting. There are other problems with the transfers, however. *Next of Kin* is in the worst condition, often looking dark and fuzzy, and *On the Run* looks best, appearing bright and reasonably crisp, with **Fugitive** falling somewhere in between. On all three, however, there are moments where the image starts to warp, as if one were looking at it underwater. The stereo sound is tolerable but mildly anachronistic. Each movie is interrupted twice by forced pauses during its first half.

Young Frankenstein (Fox, 4109070)

Mel Brooks and Gene Wilder's black-and-white horror spoof has been given a beautiful transfer, with crisp, finely detailed contrasts and rich blacks. The presentation increases the joys of watching the film substantially, because the essence of the film is its recreation of the atmosphere of James Whale's 1931 **Frankenstein** and its sequels, and the better the picture looks, the better that atmosphere is communicated. The image is letterboxed with an aspect ratio of about 1.85:1, adding a bit of picture information to the sides of the image and masking off more from the top and bottom in comparison to full screen versions. The full screen version is a better conceptual match to the Whale film, but the framing on the letterboxed version is more artfully composed and focuses a viewer's attention better on the comedy. The monophonic sound is okay, though there is some scratchiness in the background during the quieter moments. The 105 minute film is also available in French and Spanish, and can be supported by optional English subtitles. The supplement is not captioned. There is a 40 minute documentary about the film that features many of the primary filmmakers, except Brooks. The 1974 movie was Wilder's idea, though he began collaborating with Brooks very early in the process, while the two were working on **Blazing Saddles**. The documentary, called *Making FrankenSense of Young Frankenstein*, is reasonably informative, moving systematically through the various aspects of the film's production, as most documentaries of this sort do. The comments by the cinematographer, Gerald Hirschfeld, are especially interesting, as he describes the formula he had to find for mixing the classic styles inspired by the Whale film with the more practical lighting styles required of slapstick comedy, and how he almost got fired before he figured it out. The absence of Brooks appears intended to give the piece a more balanced view of the film's creation.

A collection of trailers and TV spots are included, which are a step above most trailers and TV spots in that they are narrated by Brooks and are comical masterworks in and of themselves. In fact, it is interesting to compare them to the one trailer that isn't narrated by Brooks, because the gag lines in the narration fall flat without him. There a couple of interesting interviews with Wilder, Cloris Leachman and Marty Feldman that were conducted by a Mexican TV crew during the filming, and there are a number of deleted scenes. As is often the case, the deleted scenes would have slowed the pace of the film and do not belong in it, but they are a wonderful addition to the DVD. Among the more notable are a lengthy opening sequence involving the reading of Baron Frankenstein's will, which contains a number of amusing character actors; several scenes elaborating upon the romance between Wilder's character and Teri Garr; and a shot, intended for the closing credits, in which the entire cast descends a staircase and waltzes past the camera. There is a collection of bloopers (mostly involving the actors getting the giggles) and a presentation of a scene (the introduction of Feldman's character) in French, Spanish and Japanese. Additionally, there is a collection of about 500 production photos, broken into chapters for easier access. The photos are terrific, but we were disappointed none of them were in color.

Brooks' primary contribution to the DVD is a running commentary. It is hopelessly disorganized, as he is continually distracted by the action on the screen and flits from one subject to another, often interrupting himself. We admire the fact that he spends a lot of time acknowledging the contributions of his crew, but listeners are apt to find these passages uninteresting unless they know the people he is talking about. There is a natural sense of comedy in the way he speaks (see the trailers), so his commentary is entertaining to a certain extent, and once in a while he comes up with something interesting, such as when he suggests, more than once, that Wilder and Garr had a fling, but his talk is far less informative than the standard film director commentary, getting by more on charm than substance.

As for the film, we have never found it to be the comedy classic others claim it is, though it is certainly amusing and holds up well on repeat viewings. It is best seen in a crowded theater, however, where laughter at the slightest gags ("Pardon me, boy, is this the Transylvania Station?") can make the comedy appear funnier. Otherwise, there can seem to be longish passages of misfires between moments of truly inspired humor, something the art direction and cinematography can cover for a while, but not indefinitely.

Young Guns (Artisan, 60473)

Loaded with a full barrel of young 'brat pack' actors—Charlie Sheen, Emilio Estevez, Keifer Sutherland, Lou Diamond Phillips—the film blazes away with action and simple dramatics. Ostensibly concerned with the early escapades of Billy the Kid, the movie mixes gunfights with just enough personality interludes to justify its existence. It is by no means a great film, but it is such a welcome and legitimate rejuvenation that it deserves a round of rowdy cheers.

It makes only one attempt to explore the already fully-mapped genre, by maintaining a burnt color scheme that often makes the images look like tinted daguerreotypes. Throughout the entire movie, no color escapes subjugation, and long stretches of footage are completely brown and white. The effect works nicely, and is replicated on the DVD without difficulty. The picture transfer is acceptable. The picture is letterboxed on one side, with an aspect ratio of about 1.85:1 and no 16:9 enhancement, and is in full screen format on the other side. The letterboxing adds nothing to the sides of the image and masks picture information off the top and bottom in comparison to the full screen image. The audio mix on the 1988 feature is workable but not elaborate. The 102 minute film can be supported by Spanish subtitles and is apparently ac-

companied by English closed captioning. There is a cast profile section, an informative but poorly written production notes segment, a good theatrical trailer and an enjoyable 7 minute 'making of' featurette ("A movie that combines the considerable talents of Hollywood's hottest half-dozen…").

Young Hercules (Universal, 20163)

The 1997 TV movie is totally consistent with the series format of Sam Raimi's **Hercules** TV series and holds the same pleasures. The narrative squeezes a lot of events into the 93 minute running time, as Hercules first enters training with other young warriors and then travels with fellow student Jason and a few others to retrieve the Golden Fleece, learning humility and the limitations of his power along the way. There is a terrific CGI sequence involving a giant snake, a less expensive but still enjoyable battle against a giant, and lots of fancy footwork and swordplay. The film is good fun and never slows down. The picture quality is excellent, with crisp, solid colors and accurate fleshtones. The stereo sound is also good for a TV production and the show can be accompanied by English, French or Spanish subtitles.

Young Pocahontas (see **The Amazing Feats of Young Hercules**)

You're the Top: The Cole Porter Story (Fox Lorber, WHE73005)

The hour-long documentary contains many reminiscences, footage of Porter himself and clips from films where his songs have been used, as well as rare clips of performances, by famous personalities, of his songs on the stage and on TV. The documentary provides a reasonable biography of Porter, explaining the logic behind his marriage and painting a portrait of his social life. Without seeming gossipy, the interviews touch on his homosexuality, the horrendous accident that left him paraplegic, and the mistakes that were made during decisions concerning his recovery treatments. It is difficult for the program to adhere to its chronological structure and keep an upbeat mood, but the songs are always there in support, and Porter did produce several great works after the accident. The program is narrated by Bobby Short. The monophonic sound is passable and the picture is okay. The DVD also features a brief biographical essay about Porter's start in life and a partial listing of shows and songs. There is no captioning.

Y2K: Practical Solutions for Home Preparedness (Simitar, 7624)

The documentary tries to detail practically everything that could go wrong when the clock strikes twelve on December 31, 1999. As one expert explains, "I mean if worst case scenario happens, there's nobody that's going to able to, you know, take care of everybody." Like there is now? But let this not suggest that the only thing not working on January 1 is the practicality of **Y2K: Practical Solutions for Home Preparedness**, because it is actually a comprehensive overview of how to prepare your home for all disasters, not just annoying little software flaws.

There's segments on turning your spacious spare room (double the kids up if you have to) into a virtual grocery store, with instructions on how to eat the oldest stuff first, information on how to communicate without electronics (you're supposed to put colored blankets in your windows for the emergency services people—green if everything is hunky-dory, yellow if things aren't going too well and red if you're seeing the white tunnel and your great-grandmother is motioning you to come forward), keeping your house warm, maintaining a supply of fresh water (mmm, toilet tank beverages—is there enough to go around?) and even taking care of your pets (which can always come in handy if the spare room grocery store runs out and you feel like a snack). The 67 minute program has a dullish stereo mix and an inconsistent picture. Colors are sometimes light or smeary, though usually the presentation is adequate. There is no captioning.

Z

The Zapruder Film (see Image of an Assassination: A New Look at the Zapruder Film)

Zazel X-rated (Metro, UPC#5135312184)

What looks like one long 75 minute perfume ad, it has only scattered erotic activity, and mostly depicts elaborately costumed women in exotic settings, lolling about. There is only voiceover narration—about a woman trying to come up with a perfume advertising campaign—and the program tends to wear out its welcome rather quickly, despite all the costumes. Shot on film, the picture is soft, with fuzzy hues, though the colors are reasonably bright. The monophonic sound is dullish.

Zeram (Image, ID4665FLDVD)

A cartoon-like Japanese science fiction action film, some of the monsters are rubbery, the show is dubbed, and initially it all seems fairly silly, but there are other special effects—some stop motion work and some mechanical—that are very well done and, on the whole, the film is likely to entertain genre fans. A bad alien lands on Earth pursued by a female bounty hunter. She is eventually aided by two bumbling humans who develop a crush on her. The narrative is easy to follow, but is not overly simplistic, and the action scenes are engagingly staged for what must have been a fairly limited budget.

The picture is letterboxed with an aspect ratio of about 1.85:1 and no 16:9 enhancement. The image is a bit dark and often soft looking, with bland fleshtones, though the colors are tolerable. Dubbing aside, the stereo surround sound is fairly strong and has an effective separation mix. The 97 minute program is not captioned.

Zero Effect (Warner, C2534)

A witty contemporary evocation of Sherlock Holmes, Ben Stiller stars as the Watson character, a former lawyer who runs errands and does the grunt work for an emotionally reclusive but brilliant detective, played with great élan by Bill Pullman. Ryan O'Neal is their client. The premise would make an outstanding TV series and is quite delightful as a film, as Pullman's character digs through the mysteries within the mysteries to get to the truth, at the same time driving Stiller's character to distraction with his eccentricities and distracted focus. The ending of the film is almost a direct paraphrasing of the opening lines to Arthur Conan Doyle's *A Scandal in Bohemia*, and throughout the film there are unforced allusions to Holmes and his methods.

The film is presented in letterboxed format on one side, with an aspect ratio of about 1.85:1 and an accommodation for enhanced 16:9 playback, and in full screen format on the other side. The color transfer looks good, with crisp, accurate hues and rich fleshtones, and darker areas of the screen are stable and smooth. The stereo surround sound and Dolby Digital sound are adequate, with a pleasant dimensionality but no elaborate separation effects. The film can be supported by English or French subtitles and is accompanied by a cast & crew profile section, some very brief production notes and a theatrical trailer.

The director, Jake Kasdan, provides a commentary track. Kasdan, who also wrote the script, makes no mention of the film's parallels to the Sherlock Holmes stories (perhaps the similarities were subconscious) and talks in general terms about the production, the story and working with the cast. He rarely gets too specific, saying, for example, that he wishes he could have done a scene differently without explaining what he would change. Here and there he provides some technical details about a camera set-up and the like, but other times he just talks about why he thinks Pullman is so funny.

Ziggy Stardust and the Spiders From Mars: The Motion Picture (Image, ID4704LYDVD)

The early Seventies concert, depicting David Bowie during his first rise to fame, has some historical value, but the stage lighting is limited and the cinematography is reduced to capturing generalized illuminated lines against a dark background, with few facial details even during Bowie's closeups. Those seeking a view of glam-rock during its infancy will have to strain their eyes to catch the glam.

The mildly stereophonic sound is passable. Bowie sings the songs he was promoting at the time, but few have endured—except for a couple singles, we never hear them on FM radio any more—and the 89 minute program is mostly for dedicated fans. There is no captioning.

Zombie (Anchor Bay, DV10500)

True, the Lucio Fulci film, with its overabundant gore effects, still doesn't have much of a sense of humor, but the DVD provides such an enhanced sensory input that it doesn't matter. Yes, the lighting is still bargain basement, but it is clear every last bit of color to be had has been coaxed from it. Some dark sequences remain moderately smeary and the image is grainy in a few scenes, but there is a stability and confidence to the presentation that, like George Romero's early works, makes the inexpensive cinematography work in its favor, conveying a raw atmosphere where all sorts of grimy disgusting things can and do happen. The image is subject to noticeable digital smearing and disconnections, particularly in the film's grainier sequences. The letterboxing, with an aspect ratio of about 2.35:1 and no 16:9 enhancement, is also a revelation. The images are not formally composed the way they are in a Hollywood epic, but there is balance to the shots and much more going on than the cropped disc was capable of covering.

The stereo surround sound is a blast. The loosely post-synchronized dialogue remains raspy and the audio hasn't been glossed over, but there is a more pronounced bass (making for bigger explosions, among other things), a wider musical score and more environmental sounds coming from the rear. There is also a Dolby Digital track, where the sound mix is even better defined and distributed. Like an audience in a crowded theater, the enhanced soundtrack gets the viewer onto the movie's wavelength, making it more difficult to remain aloof from the gory, repulsive fun. There is no captioning.

Tisa Farrow, Richard Johnson and Ian McCulloch star in the 1979 feature, most of which is set on a Caribbean island where flesh-eating, animate corpses have run amok. The film runs 91 minutes and is accompanied by a trailer, TV commercials and radio commercials ("You are what they eat"). There is also an audio commentary track, by McCulloch, prompted by the editor of *Diabolik* Magazine, Jason J. Slater. McCulloch talks about his career, about what shooting the film was like, a little bit about working with Fulci and his fellow actors, and a few other relevant memories that pop into his mind. They both stop talking during the big effect sequences (McCulloch had never seen the movie before). McCulloch is personable and has some interesting stories, but the insight he offers is modest.

Stay Away from Mean Jean!

by
Dinah Good

illustrated by
Raphael De La Rosa

AuthorHouse™
1663 Liberty Drive
Bloomington, IN 47403
www.authorhouse.com
Phone: 1-800-839-8640

Published by AuthorHouse 03/29/2012

ISBN: 978-1-4685-2862-6 (sc)

Library of Congress Control Number: 2012902987

authorHOUSE®